1965	1966	1967	1968	1969	1970	1971	1972	1973	1974	1975	1976	1977	1978	1979
2.6	2.5	2.3	2.1	2.2	2.1	2.1	2.3	3.2	2.8	2.7	2.3	2.0	2.1	2.2
1.1	1.0	1.0	1.0	0.9	1.0	1.0	1.0	1.0	1.4	1.5	1.4	1.6	1.5	1.7
4.5	4.5	4.5	4.5	4.6	4.6	4.7	4.7	4.8	4.7	4.3	4.4	4.4	4.6	4.7
15.3	15.4	14.8	14.8	14.4	12.7	12.4	12.7	13.0	12.3	11.5	12.1	12.5	12.7	12.3
10.3	10.3	10.0	10.0	9.7	9.4	9.1	8.9	8.7	8.8	8.8	8.9	8.8	8.6	8.6
4.0	3.9	3.9	3.9	3.9	4.0	4.0	4.0	3.9	3.8	4.1	4.1	4.1	4.1	3.8
6.5	6.5	6.5	6.5	6.5	6.6	6.5	6.6	6.6	6.9	6.9	6.6	6.5	6.6	6.6
9.0	8.8	8.9	9.1	9.1	9.2	9.2	9.1	9.0	8.7	8.9	9.0	9.0	8.9	8.6
3.5	3.4	3.3	3.2	3.2	3.2	3.2	3.3	3.3	3.3	3.0	3.2	3.2	3.2	3.2
11.7	11.4	11.6	11.6	11.7	11.9	12.1	12.0	11.7	11.8	12.0	11.7	11.8	11.9	11.8
—	—	—	—	—	—	—	—	—	—	—	—	—	—	—
—	—	—	—	—	—	—	—	—	—	—	—	—	—	—
—	—	—	—	—	—	—	—	—	—	—	—	—	—	—
—	—	—	—	—	—	—	—	—	—	—	—	—	—	—
—	—	—	—	—	—	—	—	—	—	—	—	—	—	—
38.6	38.5	37.9	37.7	37.5	37	36.8	36.9	36.9	36.4	36	36.1	35.9	35.8	35.6
7.9	7.2	6.6	6.3	5.9	5.7	5.6	5.3	5.1	5.1	5.0	4.9	4.5	4.1	3.8
0.9	0.8	0.8	0.8	0.8	0.8	0.7	0.7	0.7	0.8	0.8	0.8	0.8	0.9	0.9
4.6	4.6	4.4	4.5	4.7	4.6	4.8	4.8	4.9	4.7	4.2	4.1	4.3	4.5	4.6
23.4	24.3	24.1	24.0	23.8	22.7	21.6	21.5	21.9	21.3	19.7	19.8	19.7	19.7	19.7
56.7	58.0	59.2	60.2	61.1	62.1	62.7	62.7	62.8	63.4	64.9	64.8	64.8	65.2	65.7
6.6	5.1	4.9	4.3	3.7	4.1	4.6	4.9	4.6	4.7	5.3	5.6	5.8	5.6	5.3
2.63	2.73	2.85	3.02	3.22	3.40	3.63	3.90	4.14	4.43	4.73	5.06	5.44	5.87	6.33
11.67	11.78	11.93	12.12	12.31	12.35	12.56	12.93	13.00	12.76	12.45	12.59	12.72	12.83	12.78
911	874	879	906	877	753	885	951	924	759	802	975	895	820	844
4,042	3,769	3,679	3,637	3,353	2,735	3,060	3,152	2,901	2,187	2,112	2,425	2,093	1,793	1,704
4.5	5.1	5.5	6.2	7.0	8.0	7.4	7.2	7.4	8.6	8.8	8.4	8.0	8.7	9.6
2.7	2.3	2.4	1.9	2.1	2.7	2.4	2.9	1.9	–0.5	–0.6	2.7	1.7	1.7	1.3
184	207	222	256	288	292	309	354	397	438	448	513	576	653	736
189	215	243	268	286	313	340	370	400	453	533	573	620	682	760
–5	–8	–21	–12	2	–21	–31	–16	–3	–15	–85	–61	–44	–29	–24
261	264	267	290	278	283	303	322	341	344	395	477	549	607	640

EIGHTH EDITION

MICROECONOMICS

PARKIN

To change the way students see the world—that has been my aim throughout the eight editions of this book.

The cover depicts a landscape viewed through a geometric icon.

The landscape is the economic world. And the icon represents the clarity that economic science brings to our view and understanding of the economic world.

When we view the landscape without the economic lens, we see questions but not answers. The lens provides answers by enabling us to focus on the unseen forces that shape our world. It is a tool that enables us to see the invisible.

This book equips students with the economic lens, shows them how to use it, and enables them to gain their own informed and structured view of the economic world.

EIGHTH EDITION

MICROECONOMICS

MICHAEL PARKIN

University of Western Ontario

Boston San Francisco New York
London Toronto Sydney Tokyo Singapore Madrid
Mexico City Munich Paris Cape Town Hong Kong Montreal

Publisher	Greg Tobin
Editor in Chief	Denise Clinton
Senior Acquisitions Editor	Adrienne D'Ambrosio
Director of Development	Kay Ueno
Project Manager	Cynthia Sheridan
Editorial Assistants	Margaret Beste and Mina Kim
Managing Editor	Nancy Fenton
Senior Designer	Charles Spaulding
Photo Researcher	Beth Anderson
Supplements Editor	Heather McNally
Director of Media	Michelle Neil
Senior Media Producer	Melissa Honig
Senior Marketing Manager	Roxanne Hoch
Rights and Permissions Advisor	Dana Weightman
Senior Manufacturing Buyer	Carol Melville
Copyeditor	Barbara Willette
Cover Design	Leslie Haimes
Technical Illustrator	Richard Parkin
Text Design, Project Management and Page Make-up	Elm Street Publishing Services, Inc.

Photo credits appear on page C-1, which constitutes a continuation of the copyright page.

ISBN: 978-0-321-41661-2; 0-321-41661-9 (ISBN-10)

Library of Congress Cataloging-in-Publication Data

Parkin, Michael, 1939–
Microeconomics/Michael Parkin. — 8th ed.
p. cm.
Includes index.
ISBN 0-321-41661-9; 978-0-321-41661-2 (alk. paper)
1. Microeconomics. I. Title.
HB172.P24 2008
338.5—dc22

1 2 3 4 5 6 7 8 10—CRK—11 10 09 08 07

to Robin

Michael Parkin received his training as an economist at the Universities of Leicester and Essex in England. Currently in the Department of Economics at the University of Western Ontario, Canada, Professor Parkin has held faculty appointments at Brown University, the University of Manchester, the University of Essex, and Bond University. He is a past president of the Canadian Economics Association and has served on the editorial boards of the *American Economic Review* and the *Journal of Monetary Economics* and as managing editor of the *Canadian Journal of Economics*. Professor Parkin's research on macroeconomics, monetary economics, and international economics has resulted in over 160 publications in journals and edited volumes, including the *American Economic Review*, the *Journal of Political Economy*, the *Review of Economic Studies*, the *Journal of Monetary Economics*, and the *Journal of Money, Credit and Banking*. He became most visible to the public with his work on inflation that discredited the use of wage and price controls. Michael Parkin also spearheaded the movement toward European monetary union. Professor Parkin is an experienced and dedicated teacher of introductory economics.

PREFACE

This book presents economics as a serious, lively, and evolving science. Its goal is to open students' eyes to the "economic way of thinking" and to help them gain insights into how the economy works and how it might be made to work better.

I provide a thorough and complete coverage of the subject, using a straightforward, precise, and clear writing style.

Because I am conscious that many students find economics hard, I place the student at center stage and write for the student. I use language that doesn't intimidate and that allows the student to concentrate on the substance.

I open each chapter with a clear statement of learning objectives, a real-world student-friendly vignette to grab attention, and a brief preview. I illustrate principles with examples that are selected to hold the student's interest and to make the subject lively. And I put principles to work by using them to illuminate current real-world problems and issues.

I explain modern topics, such as dynamic comparative advantage, game theory, the principal-agent problem, and the modern theory of the firm, public choice theory, and information and uncertainty using the familiar core ideas and tools.

Today's course springs from today's issues—the information revolution and the new economy, the economic shockwaves after 9/11 that continue to affect our lives, and the expansion of global trade, investment, and offshore outsourcing. But the principles that we use to understand these issues remain the core principles of our science.

Governments and international agencies place emphasis on market-oriented reforms and deregulation as they seek to promote economic welfare. This book helps students to evaluate these policies.

To help promote a rich, active learning experience, I have developed a comprehensive online learning environment featuring a dynamic e-book, interactive tests, study plans, and tutorials, daily news updates, and more.

The Eighth Edition Revision

Microeconomics, eighth edition, retains all of the improvements achieved in its predecessor with its thorough and detailed presentation of modern economics, emphasis on real-world examples and critical thinking skills, diagrams renowned for pedagogy and precision, and path-breaking technology.

Highlights of the Micro Revision

In this edition, I have sought to highlight the central challenge of designing incentive mechanisms to enable choices made in self-interest to be in harmony with the social interest. In addition to being thoroughly updated, these microeconomics chapters feature the following six major changes:

1. **The Economic Problem** (Chapter 2): This chapter has three main changes:
   (1) It now provides an explanation of marginal cost that enables the student to see why economists graph a marginal value midway between the initial and final level.
   (2) It presents a more careful and better illustrated explanation of the gains from specialization and trade, and economic coordination.
   (3) It gives an improved account of how individual choices get coordinated.
2. **Demand and Supply** (Chapter 3): This chapter has a revised explanation and comprehensive illustration of the effects of the combined changes in demand and supply.
3. **Efficiency and Equity** (Chapter 5): The chapter has been extensively revised in four main ways:
   (1) I have deleted the short refresher on efficiency and now refer the reader back to Chapter 2, where this topic is introduced and explained.
   (2) I have added a new section that describes the eight alternative methods that might be used to allocate scarce resources: market price, command, majority rule, contest, first-come-first-served, lottery, personal characteristics, and force. By laying out these alternatives, we are better able to evaluate the ability of the market to achieve an efficient outcome. I return to these alternatives later in the chapter and ask whether there are situations in which one of them might improve on the market allocation.
   (3) I have completely rewritten the sections that show the equivalence of demand and marginal social benefit and supply and marginal social cost to place the emphasis on moving from the individual to society. Consequently, I now derive the market demand and supply curves in this chapter and also explain the connections between individual and economy-wide consumer surplus and producer surplus.
   (4) I have rewritten the case study on a water shortage in a natural disaster to review the fairness and efficiency of the market compared with its alternatives.
4. **Utility and Demand** (Chapter 7) now opens with an explanation of how a change in income and a change in prices changes the budget line. This material parallels the explanation of the consumer's budget in Chapter 8 (the indifference curve chapter) but is less technical and does not use the budget equation. (The section on individual demand and market demand has been removed from this chapter because it is now done in Chapter 5—see above).
5. **Demand and Supply in Factor Markets** (Chapter 17): This chapter now includes an explanation of efficiency wages, compensating differentials, and discrimination. The implications of the distinction between economic rent and opportunity cost are explained. The technical discussion of present value has been moved to an appendix.
6. **Economic Inequality** (Chapter 18): This chapter now includes an explanation of the effects of globalization on the distribution of income both within a country and across countries. By studying this material, the student will see how globalization is contributing to increased inequality in the rich countries while lifting millions of the world's poorest people from extreme poverty.

Features to Enhance Teaching and Learning

Here I describe the chapter features that are designed to enhance the learning process. Each chapter contains the following learning aids.

Chapter Openers

Each chapter opens with a one-page student-friendly, attention-grabbing vignette. The vignette raises questions that both motivate the student and focus the chapter. I carry this story into the main body of the chapter and relate it to the chapter-ending *Reading Between the Lines* feature for a cohesive learning experience.

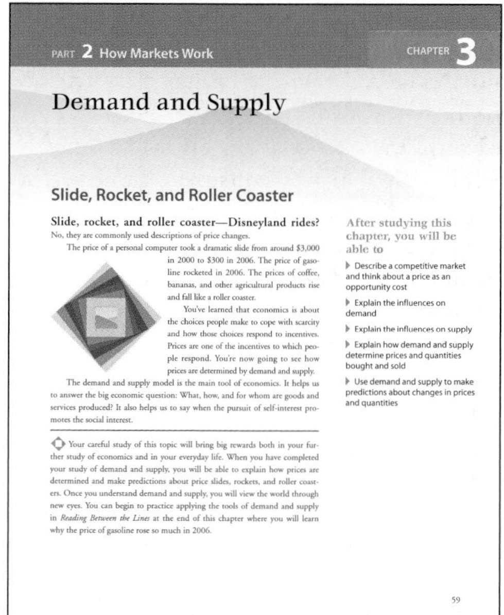

PART 2 How Markets Work CHAPTER 3

Demand and Supply

Slide, Rocket, and Roller Coaster

Slide, rocket, and roller coaster—Disneyland rides? No, they are commonly used descriptions of price changes.

The price of a personal computer took a dramatic slide from around $3,000 in 2000 to $300 in 2006. The price of gasoline rocketed in 2006. The prices of coffee, bananas, and other agricultural products rise and fall like a roller coaster.

You've learned that economics is about the choices people make to cope with scarcity and how those choices respond to incentives. Prices are one of the incentives to which people respond. You're now going to see how prices are determined by demand and supply.

The demand and supply model is the main tool of economics. It helps us to answer the big economic question: What, how, and for whom are goods and services produced? It also helps us to say when the pursuit of self-interest promotes the social interest.

Your careful study of this topic will bring big rewards both in your further study of economics and in your everyday life. When you have completed your study of demand and supply, you will be able to explain how prices are determined and make predictions about price slides, rockets, and roller coasters. Once you understand demand and supply, you will view the world through new eyes. You can begin to practice applying the tools of demand and supply in *Reading Between the Lines* at the end of this chapter where you will learn why the price of gasoline rose so much in 2006.

After studying this chapter, you will be able to

- Describe a competitive market and think about a price as an opportunity cost
- Explain the influences on demand
- Explain the influences on supply
- Explain how demand and supply determine prices and quantities bought and sold
- Use demand and supply to make predictions about changes in prices and quantities

59

After studying this chapter, you will be able to

- Describe a competitive market and think about a price as an opportunity cost
- Explain the influences on demand
- Explain the influences on supply
- Explain how demand and supply determine prices and quantities bought and sold
- Use demand and supply to make predictions about changes in prices and quantities

Chapter Objectives

A list of learning objectives enables students to see exactly where the chapter is going and to set their goals before they begin the chapter. I link these goals directly to the chapter's major headings.

In-Text Review Quizzes

A review quiz at the end of most major sections enables students to determine whether a topic needs further study before moving on. This feature includes a reference to the appropriate MyEconLab study plan to help students further test their understanding.

REVIEW QUIZ

1. What is the distinction between a money price and a relative price?
2. Explain why a relative price is an opportunity cost.
3. Think of examples of goods whose relative price has risen or fallen by a large amount.

myeconlab Study Plan 3.1

Key Terms

Highlighted terms within the text simplify the student's task of learning the vocabulary of economics. Each highlighted term appears in an end-of-chapter list with page numbers, in an end-of-book glossary with page numbers, boldfaced in the index, in the Web glossary, and in the Web Flash Cards.

leads to an increase in the demand for *most* goods, it does not lead to an increase in the demand for *all* goods. A **normal good** is one for which demand increases as income increases. An **inferior good** is one
...reases as income increases.
...rtation has examples of both
...rior goods. As incomes increase,
...vel (a normal good) increases
...ng-distance bus trips (an infe-

Key Terms

Change in demand, 62
Change in supply, 67
Change in the quantity demanded, 65
Change in the quantity supplied, 68
Competitive market, 60
Complement, 63
Demand, 61
Demand curve, 62
Equilibrium price, 70
Equilibrium quantity, 70
Inferior good, 64
Law of demand, 61
Law of supply, 66
Money price, 60
Normal good, 64
Quantity demanded, 61
Quantity supplied, 66

Normal good A good for which demand increases as income increases. (p. 64)

North American Free Trade Agreement An agreement, which became effective on January 1, 1994, to eliminate all barriers to international trade between the United States, Canada, and Mexico after a 15-year phasing-in period. (p. 408)

Diagrams That Show the Action

Through eight editions, this book has set new standards of clarity in its diagrams. My goal has always been to show "where the economic action is." The diagrams in this book continue to generate an enormously positive response, which confirms my view that graphical analysis is the most powerful tool available for teaching and learning economics. But many students find graphs hard to work with. For this reason, I have developed the entire art program with the study and review needs of the student in mind.

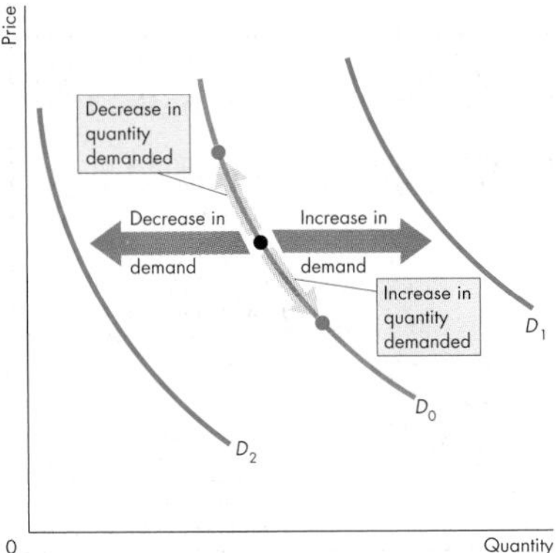

The diagrams feature

- Original curves consistently shown in blue
- Shifted curves, equilibrium points, and other important features highlighted in red
- Color-blended arrows to suggest movement
- Graphs paired with data tables
- Diagrams labeled with boxed notes
- Extended captions that make each diagram and its caption a self-contained object for study and review.

End-of-Chapter Study Material

Each chapter closes with a concise summary organized by major topics, lists of key terms (all with page references), problems, critical thinking questions, and Web Activities.

The end-of-chapter problem section includes news-based and real-world problems that are new to this edition. Solutions to the odd-numbered problems are provided on MyEconLab; the even-numbered problems are left for students to solve on their own. This arrangement offers help to students and flexibility to instructors who want to assign problems for credit.

Reading Between the Lines

In *Reading Between the Lines*, which appears at the end of each chapter, I show the student how to apply the tools they have just learned by analyzing an article from a newspaper or news Web site. The eighth edition features 20 new articles. I have chosen each article so that it sheds additional light on the questions first raised in the Chapter Opener.

Special "You're the Voter" sections in selected chapters invite students to analyze typical campaign topics and to probe their own stances on key public policy issues. Critical Thinking questions about the article appear with the end-of-chapter questions and problems.

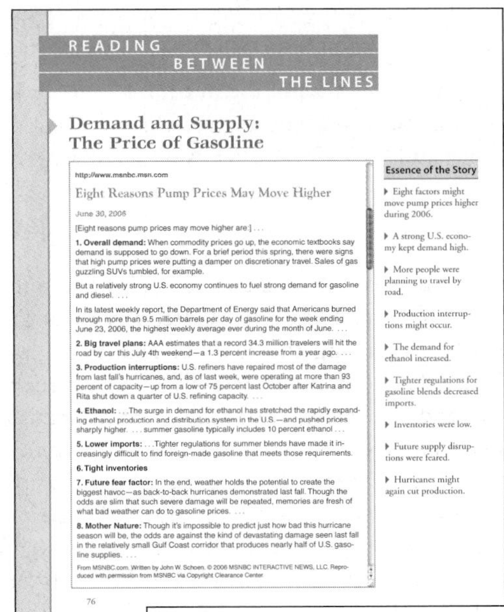

READING BETWEEN THE LINES

Demand and Supply: The Price of Gasoline

http://www.msnbc.msn.com

Eight Reasons Pump Prices May Move Higher

June 30, 2006

[Eight reasons pump prices may move higher are:] . . .

1. Overall demand: When commodity prices go up, the economic textbooks say demand is supposed to go down. For a brief period this spring, there were signs that high pump prices were putting a damper on discretionary travel. Sales of gas guzzling SUVs tumbled, for example.

But a relatively strong U.S. economy continues to fuel strong demand for gasoline and diesel. . . .

In its latest weekly report, the Department of Energy said that Americans burned through more than 9.5 million barrels per day of gasoline for the week ending June 23, 2006, the highest weekly average ever during the month of June. . . .

2. Big travel plans: AAA estimates that a record 34.3 million travelers will hit the road by car this July 4th weekend—a 1.3 percent increase from a year ago. . . .

3. Production interruptions: U.S. refiners have repaired most of the damage from last fall's hurricanes, and, as of last week, were operating at more than 93 percent of capacity—up from a low of 75 percent last October after Katrina and Rita shut down a quarter of U.S. refining capacity. . . .

4. Ethanol: . . . The surge in demand for ethanol has stretched the rapidly expanding ethanol production and distribution system in the U.S.—and pushed prices sharply higher. . . . summer gasoline typically includes 10 percent ethanol . . .

5. Lower imports: . . . Tighter regulations for summer blends have made it increasingly difficult to find foreign-made gasoline that meets those requirements.

6. Tight inventories

7. Future fear factor: In the end, weather holds the potential to create the biggest havoc—as back-to-back hurricanes demonstrated last fall. Though the odds are slim that such severe damage will be repeated, memories are fresh of what bad weather can do to gasoline prices. . . .

8. Mother Nature: Though it's impossible to predict just how bad this hurricane season will be, the odds are against the kind of devastating damage seen last fall in the relatively small Gulf Coast corridor that produces nearly half of U.S. gasoline supplies. . . .

From MSNBC.com. Written by John W. Schoen. © 2006 MSNBC INTERACTIVE NEWS, LLC. Reproduced with permission from MSNBC via Copyright Clearance Center.

Essence of the Story

- Eight factors might move pump prices higher during 2006.
- A strong U.S. economy kept demand high.
- More people were planning to travel by road.
- Production interruptions might occur.
- The demand for ethanol increased.
- Tighter regulations for gasoline blends decreased imports.
- Inventories were low.
- Future supply disruptions were feared.
- Hurricanes might again cut production.

76

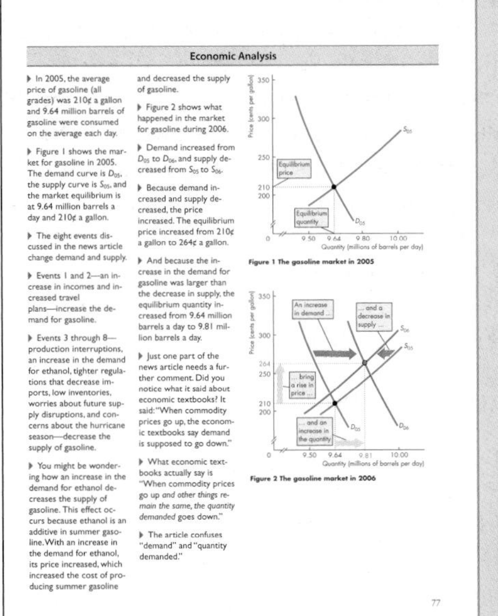

Economic Analysis

- In 2005, the average price of gasoline (all grades) was 210¢ a gallon and 9.64 million barrels of gasoline were consumed on the average each day.
- Figure 1 shows the market for gasoline in 2005. The demand curve is D_{05}, the supply curve is S_{05}, and the market equilibrium is at 9.64 million barrels a day and 210¢ a gallon.
- The eight events discussed in the news article change demand and supply.
- Events 1 and 2—an increase in incomes and increased travel plans—increase the demand for gasoline.
- Events 3 through 8—production interruptions, an increase in the demand for ethanol, tighter regulations that decrease imports, low inventories, worries about future supply disruptions, and concerns about the hurricane season—decrease the supply of gasoline.
- You might be wondering how an increase in the demand for ethanol decreases the supply of gasoline. This effect occurs because ethanol is an additive in summer gasoline. With an increase in the demand for ethanol, its price increased, which increased the cost of producing summer gasoline and decreased the supply of gasoline.
- Figure 2 shows what happened in the market for gasoline during 2006.
- Demand increased from D_{05} to D_{06}, and supply decreased from S_{05} to S_{06}.
- Because demand increased and supply decreased, the price increased. The equilibrium price increased from 210¢ a gallon to 264¢ a gallon.
- And because the increase in the demand for gasoline was larger than the decrease in supply, the equilibrium quantity increased from 9.64 million barrels a day to 9.81 million barrels a day.
- Just one part of the news article needs a further comment. Did you notice what it said about economic textbooks? It said: "When commodity prices go up, the economic textbooks say demand is supposed to go down."
- What economic textbooks actually say is "When commodity prices go up *and other things remain the same, the quantity demanded* goes down."
- The article confuses "demand" and "quantity demanded."

Figure 1 The gasoline market in 2005

Figure 2 The gasoline market in 2006

77

For the Instructor

This book enables you to achieve three objectives in your principles course:

- Focus on the economic way of thinking
- Explain the issues and problems of our time
- Choose your own course structure

Focus on the Economic Way of Thinking

You know how hard it is to encourage a student to think like an economist. But that is your goal. Consistent with this goal, the text focuses on and repeatedly uses the central ideas: choice; tradeoff; opportunity cost; the margin; incentives; the gains from voluntary exchange; the forces of demand, supply, and equilibrium; the pursuit of economic rent; the tension between self-interest and the social interest; and the scope and limitations of government actions.

Explain the Issues and Problems of Our Time

Students must *use* the central ideas and tools if they are to begin to *understand* them. There is no better way to motivate students than by using the tools of economics to explain the issues that confront today's world. Issues such as globalization and the emergence of China and India as major economic forces; the new economy with new near-monopolies such as eBay and Google; the widening income gap between rich and poor; the post-9/11 economy and the reallocation of resources toward counterterrorism and the defense that it entails; HIV/AIDS and the enormous cost of drugs for treating it; the disappearing tropical rain forests and the challenge that this problem of the commons creates; the challenge of managing the world's water resources; the looming debt that arises from our newly emerged federal budget deficit and the even greater fiscal problems that arise from the Social Security obligations to an aging population; our vast and rising international deficit and debt; and the tumbling value of the dollar on the foreign exchange market.

Choose Your Own Course Structure

You want to teach your own course. I have organized this book to enable you to do so. I demonstrate the book's flexibility in the flexibility chart and alternative sequences table that appear on pp. xxv–xxvi. You can use this book to teach a traditional course that blends theory and policy or a current policy issues course. Your micro course can emphasize theory or policy. The choice is yours.

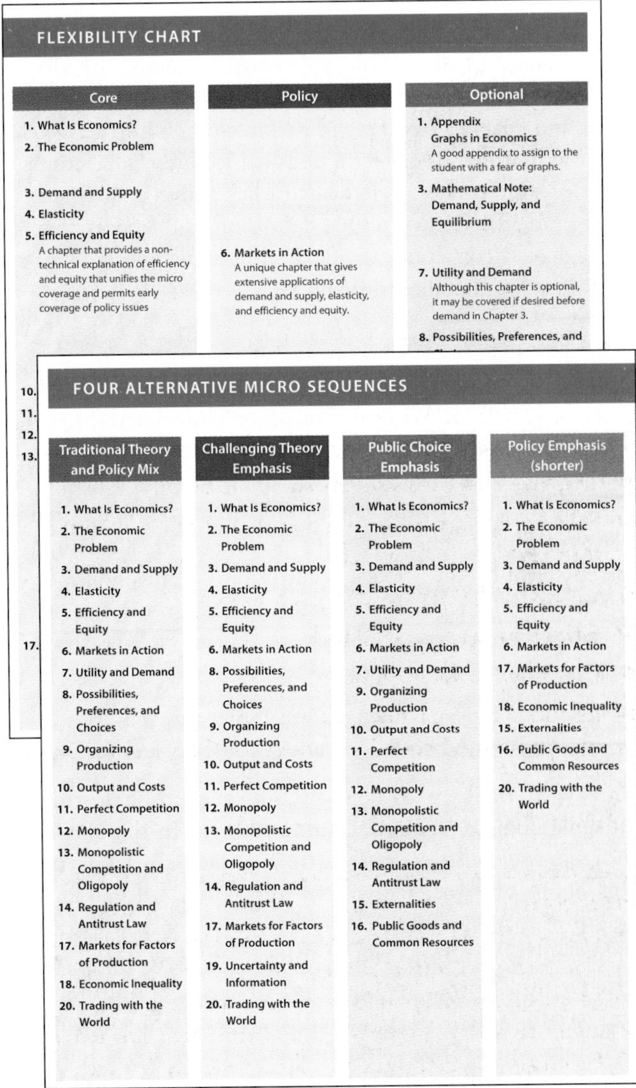

FLEXIBILITY CHART

Core	Policy	Optional
1. What Is Economics?		1. Appendix Graphs in Economics A good appendix to assign to the student with a fear of graphs.
2. The Economic Problem		3. Mathematical Note: Demand, Supply, and Equilibrium
3. Demand and Supply		
4. Elasticity		
5. Efficiency and Equity A chapter that provides a non-technical explanation of efficiency and equity that unifies the micro coverage and permits early coverage of policy issues	6. Markets in Action A unique chapter that gives extensive applications of demand and supply, elasticity, and efficiency and equity.	7. Utility and Demand Although this chapter is optional, it may be covered if desired before demand in Chapter 3.
		8. Possibilities, Preferences, and

FOUR ALTERNATIVE MICRO SEQUENCES

Traditional Theory and Policy Mix	Challenging Theory Emphasis	Public Choice Emphasis	Policy Emphasis (shorter)
1. What Is Economics?	1. What Is Economics?	1. What Is Economics?	1. What Is Economics?
2. The Economic Problem	2. The Economic Problem	2. The Economic Problem	2. The Economic Problem
3. Demand and Supply	3. Demand and Supply	3. Demand and Supply	3. Demand and Supply
4. Elasticity	4. Elasticity	4. Elasticity	4. Elasticity
5. Efficiency and Equity	5. Efficiency and Equity	5. Efficiency and Equity	5. Efficiency and Equity
6. Markets in Action	6. Markets in Action	6. Markets in Action	6. Markets in Action
7. Utility and Demand	8. Possibilities, Preferences, and Choices	7. Utility and Demand	17. Markets for Factors of Production
8. Possibilities, Preferences, and Choices	9. Organizing Production	9. Organizing Production	18. Economic Inequality
9. Organizing Production	10. Output and Costs	10. Output and Costs	15. Externalities
10. Output and Costs	11. Perfect Competition	11. Perfect Competition	16. Public Goods and Common Resources
11. Perfect Competition	12. Monopoly	12. Monopoly	20. Trading with the World
12. Monopoly	13. Monopolistic Competition and Oligopoly	13. Monopolistic Competition and Oligopoly	
13. Monopolistic Competition and Oligopoly	14. Regulation and Antitrust Law	14. Regulation and Antitrust Law	
14. Regulation and Antitrust Law	17. Markets for Factors of Production	15. Externalities	
17. Markets for Factors of Production	19. Uncertainty and Information	16. Public Goods and Common Resources	
18. Economic Inequality	20. Trading with the World		
20. Trading with the World			

Instructor's Manual

The Instructor's Manual integrates the teaching and learning package and serves as a guide to all the supplements. Each chapter contains a chapter outline, what's new in the eighth edition, teaching suggestions, a look at where we have been and where we are going, a list of available overhead transparencies, a description of the electronic supplements, additional discussion questions, answers to the Review Quizzes, solutions to end-of-chapter problems, additional problems, and solutions to the additional problems. The chapter outline and teaching suggestions sections are keyed to the PowerPoint lecture notes.

Lecture Notes Ready to use lecture notes from each chapter are grouped in the second section of the Instructor's Manual. These notes run approximately 3 to 5 pages and enable a new user of Parkin to walk into a classroom well armed to deliver a polished lecture. The lecture notes provide concise statements of key material, alternate tables and figures, key terms, definitions, and boxes that highlight key concepts, provide an interesting anecdote, or suggest how to handle a difficult idea.

Worksheets Another innovative feature of the Instructor's Manual is a set of Worksheets prepared by Patricia Kuzyk of Washington State University. These Worksheets ask students to contemplate real-world problems that illustrate economic principles. Examples include showing the effect of the catastrophic events of 9/11 using a marginal cost/marginal benefit diagram, and calculating the effects of funding Social Security for the huge number of baby-boomer retirees. Instructors can assign these as in-class group projects or as homework. There is a Worksheet for every chapter of the book.

Three Test Banks

Three Test Banks with nearly 6,500 questions, provide multiple-choice, true-false, numerical, fill-in-the-blank, short-answer, and essay questions. Mark Rush of the University of Florida reviewed and edited all existing questions to ensure their clarity and consistency with the eighth edition and incorporated over 300 new questions written by Constantin Ogloblin of Georgia Southern University. All three Test Banks are available in Test Generator Software (TestGen with QuizMaster). Fully networkable, it is available for Windows and Macintosh. TestGen's graphical interface enables instructors to view, edit, and add questions; transfer questions to tests; and print different forms of tests. Tests can be formatted with varying fonts and styles, margins, and headers and footers, as in any word-processing document. Search and sort features let the instructor quickly locate questions and arrange them in a preferred order. QuizMaster, working with your school's computer network, automatically grades the exams, stores the results on disk, and allows the instructor to view or print a variety of reports. These Test Banks are available in hard copy and electronically on the Instructor's Resource Disk and in the instructor's resources section of MyEconLab and the Instructor's Resource Center.

PowerPoint Resources

Robin Bade and I have developed a full-color Microsoft PowerPoint Lecture Presentation for each chapter that includes all the figures from the text, animated graphs, and speaking notes. The slide outlines are based on the chapter outlines in the Instructor's Manual, and the speaking notes are based on the Instructor's Manual teaching suggestions. The presentations can be used electronically in the classroom or can be printed to create hard-copy transparency masters. This item is available for Macintosh and Windows.

Clicker-Ready PowerPoint Resources

This edition features the addition of clicker-ready PowerPoint slides for the Personal Response System you use. Each chapter of the text includes ten multiple-choice questions that test important concepts. Instructors can assign these as in-class assignments or review quizzes.

Overhead Transparencies

Full-color overhead transparencies of over 100 figures from the text will improve the clarity of your lectures. They are available to qualified adopters of the text (contact your Addison-Wesley sales representative).

Instructor's Resource Disk

Fully compatible with Windows and Macintosh computers, this CD-ROM contains electronic files of every instructor supplement for the eighth edition. Files included are: Microsoft® Word and Adobe® PDF files of the Instructor's Manual and Test Bank; complete PowerPoint® slides; and the Computerized TestGen® Test Bank. Add this useful resource to your exam copy bookbag, or locate your local Addison-Wesley sales representative at www.aw-bc.com/replocator to request a copy.

MyEconLab

MyEconLab is an online course management, testing, and tutorial resource. Instructors choose how much, or how little, time to spend setting up and using MyEconLab.

For each chapter, and requiring no instructor set-up, students get two preloaded Sample Tests, a Study Plan, and tutorial help. The online Gradebook records each student's time spent and performance on the Tests and Study Plan and generates reports by student or by chapter.

Instructors can assign Tests, Quizzes, and Homework in MyEconLab using five resources:

- Pre-loaded Sample Test questions
- Study Plan questions
- Test Bank questions
- Self-authored questions using Econ Exercise Builder
- Problems similar to the end-of-chapter problems

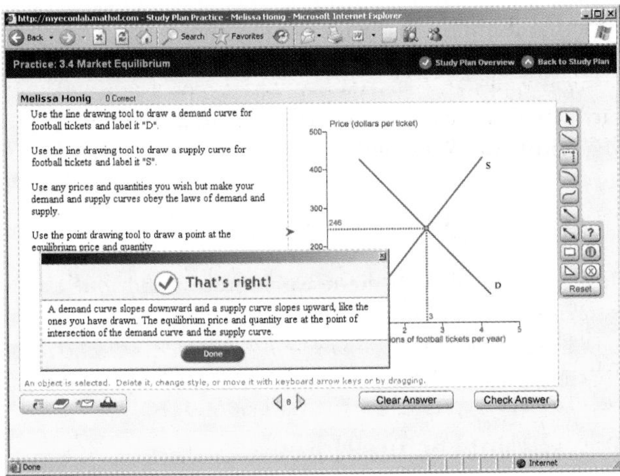

Tests use multiple-choice, graph drawing, and free response questions, many of which are generated algorithmically so that they present differently each time they are worked.

MyEconLab grades every problem, even those with graphs, and, when working a Study Plan, students get immediate feedback with links to additional learning tools.

Customization and Communication MyEconLab in CourseCompass provides additional optional customization and communication tools. Instructors who teach distance-learning courses or very large lecture sections find the CourseCompass format useful because they can upload course documents and assignments, customize the order of chapters, and use communication features such as Digital Dropbox and Discussion Board.

For the Student

Four outstanding support tools for the student are

- Study Guide
- MyEconLab
- Student PowerPoint Lecture Notes
- Econ Tutor Center

Study Guide

The eighth edition Study Guide by Mark Rush of the University of Florida is carefully coordinated with the text, MyEconLab, and the Test Banks. Each chapter of the Study Guide contains

- Key concepts
- Helpful hints
- True/false/uncertain questions
- Multiple-choice questions
- Short-answer questions
- Common questions or misconceptions that the student explains as if he or she were the teacher

Each part allows students to test their cumulative understanding with questions that go across chapters and work a sample midterm examination.

MyEconLab

MyEconLab puts students in control of their own learning through a suite of testing, practice, and study tools tied to the online, interactive version of the textbook and other media resources.

Within MyEconLab's structured environment, students practice what they learn, test their understanding, and pursue a personal Study Plan generated from their performance on Sample Tests and tests set by their instructors.

At the core of MyEconLab are the following features:

- Sample Tests, two per chapter
- Personal Study Plan
- Tutorial Instruction
- Graphing Tool

Sample Tests Two Sample Tests for each chapter are preloaded in MyEconLab, enabling students to practice what they have learned, test their understanding, and identify areas in which they need to do further work. Students can study on their own or they can complete assignments created by their instructor.

Personal Study Plan Based on a student's performance on tests, a personal Study Plan is generated that shows where further study is needed. The Study Plan consists of a series of additional practice exercises with detailed feedback and guided solutions and keyed to other tutorial resources.

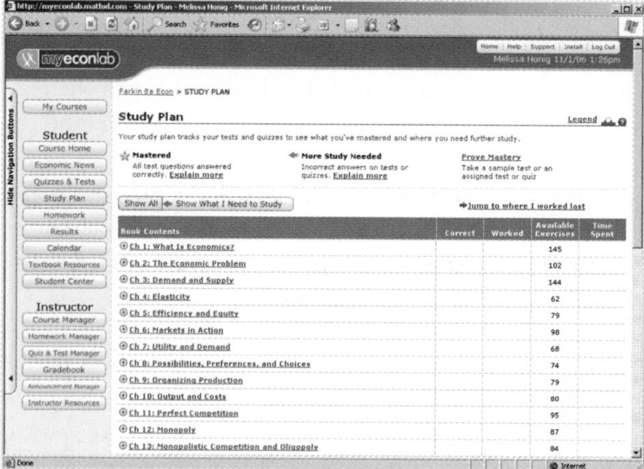

Tutorial Instruction Launched from the exercises in the Study Plan, tutorial instruction is provided in the form of step-by-step solutions and other media-based explanations.

Graphing Tool A graphing tool integrated into the Tests and Study Plan exercises enables students to make and manipulate graphs so that they better understand how concepts, numbers, and graphs connect. Questions that use the graphing tool (like all the other questions) are automatically graded.

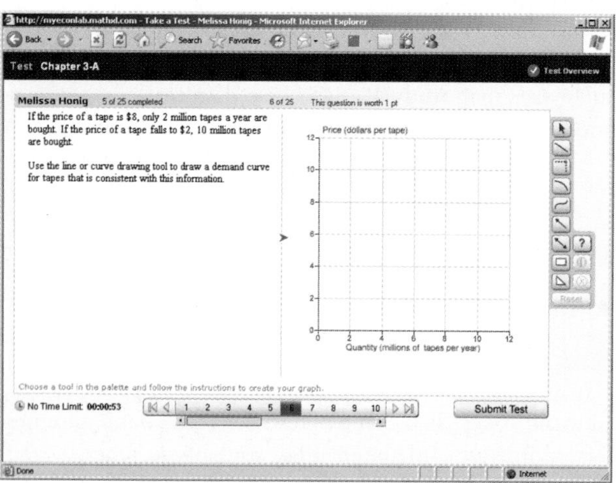

Additional MyEconLab Tools

1. eText
2. Animated figures—every figure from the textbook in step-by-step animations with audio explanations of the action
3. Glossary—a searchable version of the textbook glossary with additional examples and links to related terms
4. Glossary Flashcards—every key term as a flashcard, allowing students to quiz themselves on vocabulary from one or more chapters at a time
5. Ask the Author—email economic-related questions to the author
6. *Economics in the News*—daily updates during the school year of news items with links to sources for further reading and discussion questions
7. Links for Web Activities—all the links needed for the Web Activities in the textbook
8. eThemes of the Times—archived articles from *The New York Times*, correlated to each textbook chapter and paired with Critical Thinking questions
9. Research Navigator (CourseCompass version only)—extensive help on the research process and four exclusive databases of credible and reliable source material including *The New York Times*, the *Financial Times*, and peer-reviewed journals

PowerPoint Lecture Notes

Robin Bade and I have prepared a set of PowerPoint lecture notes especially for students. These notes contain an outline of each chapter with the textbook figures animated. Students can download these lecture notes from MyEconLab, print them, and bring them to class or use them in creating their own set of notes for use when preparing for tests and exams.

Econ Tutor Center

Staffed by qualified, experienced college economics instructors, the Econ Tutor Center is open five days a week, seven hours a day. Tutors can be reached by phone, fax, e-mail or White Board technology. The Econ Tutor Center hours are designed to meet your students' study schedules, with evening hours Sunday through Thursday. Students receive one-on-one tutoring on examples, related exercises, and problems.

Special Editions and Alternative Formats

Three special editions of the eighth edition text are available:

- Economist.com Edition
- The Wall Street Journal Edition
- Financial Times Edition

Economist.com Edition

The premier online source of economic news analysis, Economist.com provides your students with insight and opinion on current economic events. Through an agreement between Addison-Wesley and *The Economist,* your students can receive a low-cost subscription to this premium Web site for 12 weeks, including the complete text of the current issue of *The Economist* and access to *The Economist's* searchable archives. Other features include Web-only weekly articles, news feeds with current world and business news, and stock market and currency data. Professors who adopt this special edition will receive a complimentary one-year subscription to Economist.com.

The Wall Street Journal Edition

Addison-Wesley is also pleased to provide your students with access to *The Wall Street Journal,* the most respected and trusted daily source for information on business and economics. For a small additional charge, Addison-Wesley offers your students a subscription to *The Wall Street Journal* and WSJ.com. Ten-week and 15-week subscriptions are available. Adopting professors will receive a complimentary one-year subscription to *The Wall Street Journal* as well as access to WSJ.com.

Financial Times Edition

Featuring international news and analysis from FT journalists in more than 50 countries, the *Financial Times* will provide your students with insights and perspectives on economic developments around the world. The Financial Times Edition provides your students with a 15-week subscription to one of the world's leading business publications. Adopting professors will receive a complimentary one-year subscription to the *Financial Times* as well as access to FT.com.

Two alternative formats of the eighth edition text are available:

- Books à la Carte Plus Edition
- SafariX Textbooks Online

Books à la Carte Plus Edition

For the student who wants a more flexible portable text, there is a three-hole punched version of *Microeconomics.* Students who use this version can take only what they need to class, incorporate their own notes, and save money. This version is packaged with a laminated study card and comes with access to MyEconLab.

SafariX Textbooks Online

By subscribing to Web books in SafariX Textbooks Online at www.safarix.com, the student can obtain an electronic version of the text at a price up to 50 percent off the suggested list price of a print textbook.

Acknowledgments

I thank my current and former colleagues and friends at the University of Western Ontario who have taught me so much. They are Jim Davies, Jeremy Greenwood, Ig Horstmann, Peter Howitt, Greg Huffman, David Laidler, Phil Reny, Chris Robinson, John Whalley, and Ron Wonnacott. I also thank Doug McTaggart and Christopher Findlay, co-authors of the Australian edition, and Melanie Powell and Kent Matthews, co-authors of the European edition. Suggestions arising from their adaptations of earlier editions have been helpful to me in preparing this edition.

I thank the several thousand students whom I have been privileged to teach. The instant response that comes from the look of puzzlement or enlightenment has taught me how to teach economics.

It is a special joy to thank the many outstanding editors, media specialists, and others at Addison-Wesley who contributed to the concerted publishing effort that brought this edition to completion. Denise Clinton, Editor-in-Chief for Economics and Finance, was a constant source of inspiration and encouragement and provided overall direction to the project. Adrienne D'Ambrosio, Acquisitions Editor for Economics and my sponsoring editor, played a major role in shaping this revision and the many outstanding supplements that accompany it. Adrienne brings intelligence and insight to her work and is the unchallengeably pre-eminent economics editor. Kay Ueno, Director of Development, brought her huge professional experience to managing the development effort. Cynthia Sheridan, Development Editor, worked tirelessly to bring reviews in on time and consolidate and summarize them. Michelle Neil, Director of Media, continued her remarkable work to improve MyEconLab and Melissa Honig, Senior Media Producer and Doug Ruby, Content Lead for MyEconLab, ensured that all our media assets were correctly assembled. Roxanne Hoch, Senior Marketing Manager, provided inspired marketing strategy and direction. Barbara Willette provided a superbly careful and consistent copy edit. Charles Spaulding, Senior Designer, designed the cover and package and yet again surpassed the challenge of ensuring that we meet the highest design standards. Joe Vetere provided endless technical help with the text and art files. And Ingrid Benson with the other members of an outstanding editorial and production team at Elm Street kept the project on track on an impossibly tight schedule. I thank all of these wonderful people. It has been inspiring to work with them and to share in creating what I believe is a truly outstanding educational tool.

I thank our talented eighth edition supplements authors—Sue Bartlett, University of South Florida; Constantin Ogloblin of Georgia Southern University; Pat Kuzyk, Washington State University; and Jeff Reynolds, Northern Illinois University.

I especially thank Mark Rush, who yet again played a crucial role in creating another edition of this text and package. Mark has been a constant source of good advice and good humor.

I thank the many exceptional reviewers who have shared their insights through the various editions of this book. Their contribution has been invaluable. I particularly thank Barry Falk and Kenneth Christianson for their extraordinarily careful accuracy reviews.

I thank the people who work directly with me. Jeannie Gillmore provided outstanding research assistance on many topics, including the *Reading Between the Lines* news articles. Richard Parkin created the electronic art files and offered many ideas that improved the figures in this book. And Laurel Davies managed an ever-growing and ever more complex MyEconLab database.

As with the previous editions, this one owes an enormous debt to Robin Bade. I dedicate this book to her and again thank her for her work. I could not have written this book without the unselfish help she has given me. My thanks to her are unbounded.

Classroom experience will test the value of this book. I would appreciate hearing from instructors and students about how I can continue to improve it in future editions.

Michael Parkin
London, Ontario, Canada
michael.parkin@uwo.ca

Reviewers

Eric Abrams, Hawaii Pacific University
Christopher Adams, Federal Trade Commission
Tajudeen Adenekan, Bronx Community College
Syed Ahmed, Cameron University
Frank Albritton, Seminole Community College
Milton Alderfer, Miami-Dade Community College
William Aldridge, Shelton State Community College
Donald L. Alexander, Western Michigan University
Terence Alexander, Iowa State University
Stuart Allen, University of North Carolina, Greensboro
Sam Allgood, University of Nebraska, Lincoln
Neil Alper, Northeastern University
Alan Anderson, Fordham University
Lisa R. Anderson, College of William and Mary
Jeff Ankrom, Wittenberg University
Fatma Antar, Manchester Community Technical College
Kofi Apraku, University of North Carolina, Asheville
Moshen Bahmani-Oskooee, University of Wisconsin, Milwaukee
Donald Balch, University of South Carolina
Mehmet Balcilar, Wayne State University
Paul Ballantyne, University of Colorado
Sue Bartlett, University of South Florida
Jose Juan Bautista, Xavier University of Louisiana
Valerie R. Bencivenga, University of Texas, Austin
Ben Bernanke, Chairman of Federal Reserve
Margot Biery, Tarrant County Community College South
John Bittorowitz, Ball State University
David Black, University of Toledo
Kelly Blanchard, Purdue University
S. Brock Blomberg, Claremont McKenna College
William T. Bogart, Case Western Reserve University
Giacomo Bonanno, University of California, Davis
Tan Khay Boon, Nanyard Technological University
Sunne Brandmeyer, University of South Florida
Audie Brewton, Northeastern Illinois University
Baird Brock, Central Missouri State University
Byron Brown, Michigan State University
Jeffrey Buser, Columbus State Community College
Alison Butler, Florida International University
Tania Carbiener, Southern Methodist University
Kevin Carey, American University
Kathleen A. Carroll, University of Maryland, Baltimore County
Michael Carter, University of Massachusetts, Lowell
Edward Castronova, California State University, Fullerton
Subir Chakrabarti, Indiana University-Purdue University
Joni Charles, Texas State University
Adhip Chaudhuri, Georgetown University
Gopal Chengalath, Texas Tech University
Daniel Christiansen, Albion College
Kenny Christianson, Binghampton University
John J. Clark, Community College of Allegheny County, Allegheny Campus
Meredith Clement, Dartmouth College
Michael B. Cohn, U. S. Merchant Marine Academy
Robert Collinge, University of Texas, San Antonio
Carol Condon, Kean University
Doug Conway, Mesa Community College
Larry Cook, University of Toledo
Bobby Corcoran, Middle Tennessee State University, retired
Kevin Cotter, Wayne State University
James Peery Cover, University of Alabama, Tuscaloosa
Erik Craft, University of Richmond
Eleanor D. Craig, University of Delaware
Jim Craven, Clark College
Elizabeth Crowell, University of Michigan, Dearborn
Stephen Cullenberg, University of California, Riverside
David Culp, Slippery Rock University
Norman V. Cure, Macomb Community College
Dan Dabney, University of Texas, Austin
Andrew Dane, Angelo State University
Joseph Daniels, Marquette University
Gregory DeFreitas, Hofstra University
David Denslow, University of Florida
Mark Dickie, University of Central Florida
James Dietz, California State University, Fullerton
Carol Dole, State University of West Georgia
Ronald Dorf, Inver Hills Community College
John Dorsey, University of Maryland, College Park
Eric Drabkin, Hawaii Pacific University
Amrik Singh Dua, Mt. San Antonio College
Thomas Duchesneau, University of Maine, Orono
Lucia Dunn, Ohio State University
Donald Dutkowsky, Syracuse University
John Edgren, Eastern Michigan University
David J. Eger, Alpena Community College
Harry Ellis, Jr., University of North Texas
Ibrahim Elsaify, Goldey-Beacom College
Kenneth G. Elzinga, University of Virginia
Antonina Espiritu, Hawaii Pacific University
Gwen Eudey, University of Pennsylvania
Barry Falk, Iowa State University
M. Fazeli, Hofstra University

Philip Fincher, Louisiana Tech University
F. Firoozi, University of Texas, San Antonio
Nancy Folbre, University of Massachusetts at Amherst
Kenneth Fong, Temasek Polytechnic (Singapore)
Steven Francis, Holy Cross College
David Franck, University of North Carolina, Charlotte
Roger Frantz, San Diego State University
Mark Frascatore, Clarkson University
Alwyn Fraser, Atlantic Union College
Marc Fusaro, East Carolina University
James Gale, Michigan Technological University
Susan Gale, New York University
Roy Gardner, Indiana University
Eugene Gentzel, Pensacola Junior College
Scott Gilbert, Southern Illinois University at Carbondale
Andrew Gill, California State University, Fullerton
Robert Giller, Virginia Polytechnic Institute and State University
Robert Gillette, University of Kentucky
James N. Giordano, Villanova University
Maria Giuili, Diablo College
Susan Glanz, St. John's University
Robert Gordon, San Diego State University
Richard Gosselin, Houston Community College
John Graham, Rutgers University
John Griffen, Worcester Polytechnic Institute
Wayne Grove, Syracuse University
Robert Guell, Indiana State University
Jamie Haag, Pacific University, Oregon
Gail Heyne Hafer, Lindenwood University
Rik W. Hafer, Southern Illinois University, Edwardsville
Daniel Hagen, Western Washington University
David R. Hakes, University of Northern Iowa
Craig Hakkio, Federal Reserve Bank, Kansas City
Bridget Gleeson Hanna, Rochester Institute of Technology
Ann Hansen, Westminster College
Seid Hassan, Murray State University
Jonathan Haughton, Suffolk University
Randall Haydon, Wichita State University
Denise Hazlett, Whitman College
Julia Heath, University of Memphis
Jac Heckelman, Wake Forest University
Jolien A. Helsel, Kent State University
James Henderson, Baylor University
Jill Boylston Herndon, University of Florida
Gus Herring, Brookhaven College
John Herrmann, Rutgers University
John M. Hill, Delgado Community College
Jonathan Hill, Florida International University
Lewis Hill, Texas Tech University
Steve Hoagland, University of Akron
Tom Hoerger, Fellow, Research Triangle Institute
Calvin Hoerneman, Delta College
George Hoffer, Virginia Commonwealth University
Dennis L. Hoffman, Arizona State University
Paul Hohenberg, Rensselaer Polytechnic Institute
Jim H. Holcomb, University of Texas, El Paso
Harry Holzer, Georgetown University
Linda Hooks, Washington and Lee University
Jim Horner, Cameron University
Djehane Hosni, University of Central Florida
Harold Hotelling, Jr., Lawrence Technical University
Calvin Hoy, County College of Morris
Ing-Wei Huang, Assumption University, Thailand
Julie Hunsaker, Wayne State University
Beth Ingram, University of Iowa
Jayvanth Ishwaran, Stephen F. Austin State University
Michael Jacobs, Lehman College
S. Hussain Ali Jafri, Tarleton State University
Dennis Jansen, Texas A&M University
Garrett Jones, Southern Florida University
Frederick Jungman, Northwestern Oklahoma State University
Paul Junk, University of Minnesota, Duluth
Leo Kahane, California State University, Hayward
Veronica Kalich, Baldwin-Wallace College
John Kane, State University of New York, Oswego
Eungmin Kang, St. Cloud State University
Arthur Kartman, San Diego State University
Gurmit Kaur, Universiti Teknologi (Malaysia)
Louise Keely, University of Wisconsin at Madison
Manfred W. Keil, Claremont McKenna College
Elizabeth Sawyer Kelly, University of Wisconsin at Madison
Rose Kilburn, Modesto Junior College
Robert Kirk, Indiana University—Purdue University, Indianapolis
Norman Kleinberg, City University of New York, Baruch College
Robert Kleinhenz, California State University, Fullerton
John Krantz, University of Utah
Joseph Kreitzer, University of St. Thomas
Patricia Kuzyk, Washington State University
David Lages, Southwest Missouri State University
W. J. Lane, University of New Orleans
Leonard Lardaro, University of Rhode Island
Kathryn Larson, Elon College
Luther D. Lawson, University of North Carolina, Wilmington
Elroy M. Leach, Chicago State University
Jim Lee, Texas A & M, Corpus Christi
Sang Lee, Southeastern Louisiana University

Robert Lemke, Florida International University
Mary Lesser, Iona College
Jay Levin, Wayne State University
Arik Levinson, University of Wisconsin, Madison
Tony Lima, California State University, Hayward
William Lord, University of Maryland, Baltimore County
Nancy Lutz, Virginia Polytechnic Institute and State University
Murugappa Madhavan, San Diego State University
K. T. Magnusson, Salt Lake Community College
Mark Maier, Glendale Community College
Jean Mangan, Staffordshire University Business School
Michael Marlow, California Polytechnic State University
Akbar Marvasti, University of Houston
Wolfgang Mayer, University of Cincinnati
John McArthur, Wofford College
Amy McCormick, Mary Baldwin College
Russel McCullough, Iowa State University
Gerald McDougall, Wichita State University
Stephen McGary, Brigham Young University-Idaho
Richard D. McGrath, Armstrong Atlantic State University
Richard McIntyre, University of Rhode Island
John McLeod, Georgia Institute of Technology
Mark McLeod, Virginia Tech
B. Starr McMullen, Oregon State University
Mary Ruth McRae, Appalachian State University
Kimberly Merritt, Cameron University
Charles Meyer, Iowa State University
Peter Mieszkowski, Rice University
John Mijares, University of North Carolina, Asheville
Richard A. Miller, Wesleyan University
Judith W. Mills, Southern Connecticut State University
Glen Mitchell, Nassau Community College
Jeannette C. Mitchell, Rochester Institute of Technology
Khan Mohabbat, Northern Illinois University
Bagher Modjtahedi, University of California, Davis
W. Douglas Morgan, University of California, Santa Barbara
William Morgan, University of Wyoming
James Morley, Washington University in St. Louis
William Mosher, Clark University
Joanne Moss, San Francisco State University
Nivedita Mukherji, Oakland University
Francis Mummery, Fullerton College
Edward Murphy, Southwest Texas State University
Kevin J. Murphy, Oakland University
Kathryn Nantz, Fairfield University
William S. Neilson, Texas A&M University
Bart C. Nemmers, University of Nebraska, Lincoln
Melinda Nish, Orange Coast College
Anthony O'Brien, Lehigh University
Norman Obst, Michigan State University
Constantin Ogloblin, Georgia Southern University
Mary Olson, Tulane University
Terry Olson, Truman State University
James B. O'Neill, University of Delaware
Farley Ordovensky, University of the Pacific
Z. Edward O'Relley, North Dakota State University
Donald Oswald, California State University, Bakersfield
Jan Palmer, Ohio University
Michael Palumbo, Chief, Federal Reserve Board
Chris Papageorgiou, Louisiana State University
G. Hossein Parandvash, Western Oregon State College
Randall Parker, East Carolina University
Robert Parks, Washington University
David Pate, St. John Fisher College
James E. Payne, Illinois State University
Donald Pearson, Eastern Michigan University
Steven Peterson, University of Idaho
Mary Anne Pettit, Southern Illinois University, Edwardsville
William A. Phillips, University of Southern Maine
Dennis Placone, Clemson University
Charles Plot, California Institute of Technology, Pasadena
Mannie Poen, Houston Community College
Kathleen Possai, Wayne State University
Ulrika Praski-Stahlgren, University College in Gavle-Sandviken, Sweden
Edward Price, Oklahoma State University
Rula Qalyoubi, University of Wisconsin, Eau Claire
K. A. Quartey, Talladega College
Herman Quirmbach, Iowa State University
Jeffrey R. Racine, University of South Florida
Peter Rangazas, Indiana University-Purdue University, Indianapolis
Vaman Rao, Western Illinois University
Laura Razzolini, University of Mississippi
Rob Rebelein, University of Cincinnati
J. David Reed, Bowling Green State University
Robert H. Renshaw, Northern Illinois University
Javier Reyes, University of Arkansas
Jeff Reynolds, Northern Illinois University
Rupert Rhodd, Florida Atlantic University
W. Gregory Rhodus, Bentley College
Jennifer Rice, Indiana University, Bloomington
John Robertson, Paducah Community College
Malcolm Robinson, University of North Carolina, Greensboro
Richard Roehl, University of Michigan, Dearborn
Carol Rogers, Georgetown University

William Rogers, University of Northern Colorado
Thomas Romans, State University of New York, Buffalo
David R. Ross, Bryn Mawr College
Thomas Ross, Baldwin Wallace College
Robert J. Rossana, Wayne State University
Jeffrey Rous, University of North Texas
Rochelle Ruffer, Youngstown State University
Mark Rush, University of Florida
Allen R. Sanderson, University of Chicago
Gary Santoni, Ball State University
John Saussy, Harrisburg Area Community College
Don Schlagenhauf, Florida State University
David Schlow, Pennsylvania State University
Paul Schmitt, St. Clair County Community College
Jeremy Schwartz, Hampden-Sydney College
Martin Sefton, University of Nottingham
Esther-Mirjam Sent, University of Notre Dame
Rod Shadbegian, University of Massachusetts, Dartmouth
Gerald Shilling, Eastfield College
Dorothy R. Siden, Salem State College
Mark Siegler, California State University at Sacramento
Scott Simkins, North Carolina Agricultural and Technical State University
Chuck Skoro, Boise State University
Phil Smith, DeKalb College
William Doyle Smith, University of Texas, El Paso
Sarah Stafford, College of William and Mary
Frank Steindl, Oklahoma State University
Jeffrey Stewart, New York University
Allan Stone, Southwest Missouri State University
Courtenay Stone, Ball State University
Paul Storer, Western Washington University
Richard W. Stratton, University of Akron
Mark Strazicich, Ohio State University, Newark
Michael Stroup, Stephen F. Austin State University
Robert Stuart, Rutgers University
Della Lee Sue, Marist College
Abdulhamid Sukar, Cameron University
Terry Sutton, Southeast Missouri State University
Gilbert Suzawa, University of Rhode Island
David Swaine, Andrews University
Jason Taylor, Central Michigan University
Mark Thoma, University of Oregon
Janet Thomas, Bentley College
Kiril Tochkov, SUNY at Binghamton
Kay Unger, University of Montana
Anthony Uremovic, Joliet Junior College
David Vaughn, City University, Washington
Don Waldman, Colgate University
Francis Wambalaba, Portland State University
Rob Wassmer, California State University, Sacramento
Paul A. Weinstein, University of Maryland, College Park
Lee Weissert, St. Vincent College
Robert Whaples, Wake Forest University
David Wharton, Washington College
Mark Wheeler, Western Michigan University
Charles H. Whiteman, University of Iowa
Sandra Williamson, University of Pittsburgh
Brenda Wilson, Brookhaven Community College
Larry Wimmer, Brigham Young University
Mark Witte, Northwestern University
Willard E. Witte, Indiana University
Mark Wohar, University of Nebraska, Omaha
Laura Wolff, Southern Illinois University, Edwardsville
Cheonsik Woo, Vice President, Korea Development Institute
Douglas Wooley, Radford University
Arthur G. Woolf, University of Vermont
John T. Young, Riverside Community College
Michael Youngblood, Rock Valley College
Peter Zaleski, Villanova University
Jason Zimmerman, South Dakota State University
David Zucker, Martha Stewart Living Omnimedia

Supplements Authors

Sue Bartlett, University of South Florida
James Cobbe, Florida State University
Carol Dole, State University of West Georgia
John Graham, Rutgers University
Jill Herndon, University of Florida
Sang Lee, Southeastern Louisiana University
Patricia Kuzyk, Washington State University
James Morley, Washington University, St. Louis
William Mosher, Clark University
Constantin Ogloblin, Georgia Southern University
Edward Price, Oklahoma State University
Jeff Reynolds, Northern Illinois University
Mark Rush, University of Florida
Della Lee Sue, Marist College
Michael Stroup, Stephen F. Austin State University

FLEXIBILITY CHART

Core

1. What Is Economics?

2. The Economic Problem

3. Demand and Supply

4. Elasticity

5. Efficiency and Equity
A chapter that provides a non-technical explanation of efficiency and equity that unifies the micro coverage and permits early coverage of policy issues

10. Ouput and Costs

11. Perfect Competition

12. Monopoly

13. Monopolistic Competition and Oligopoly

17. Markets for Factors of Production

Policy

6. Markets in Action
A unique chapter that gives extensive applications of demand and supply, elasticity, and efficiency and equity.

14. Regulation and Antitrust Law
Introduces the public-choice theory of government, sets the scene for the following policy chapters, and explains the positive theory of regulation and antitrust law.

15. Externalities

16. Public Goods and Common Resources

18. Economic Inequality

Optional

1. Appendix Graphs in Economics
A good appendix to assign to the student with a fear of graphs.

3. Mathematical Note: Demand, Supply, and Equilibrium

7. Utility and Demand
Although this chapter is optional, it may be covered if desired before demand in Chapter 3.

8. Possibilities, Preferences, and Choices
A full chapter on this strictly optional topic to ensure that it is covered clearly with intuitive explanations and illustrations. The more common brief treatment of this topic makes it indigestible. The chapter has an appendix that explains the relation between marginal utility and indifference curves.

9. Organizing Production
This chapter may be skipped or assigned as a reading.

19. Uncertainty and Information

20. Trading with the World

FOUR ALTERNATIVE MICRO SEQUENCES

Traditional Theory and Policy Mix	Challenging Theory Emphasis	Public Choice Emphasis	Policy Emphasis (shorter)
1. What Is Economics?	1. What Is Economics?	1. What Is Economics?	1. What Is Economics?
2. The Economic Problem	2. The Economic Problem	2. The Economic Problem	2. The Economic Problem
3. Demand and Supply	3. Demand and Supply	3. Demand and Supply	3. Demand and Supply
4. Elasticity	4. Elasticity	4. Elasticity	4. Elasticity
5. Efficiency and Equity	5. Efficiency and Equity	5. Efficiency and Equity	5. Efficiency and Equity
6. Markets in Action	6. Markets in Action	6. Markets in Action	6. Markets in Action
7. Utility and Demand	8. Possibilities, Preferences, and Choices	7. Utility and Demand	17. Markets for Factors of Production
8. Possibilities, Preferences, and Choices	9. Organizing Production	9. Organizing Production	18. Economic Inequality
9. Organizing Production	10. Output and Costs	10. Output and Costs	15. Externalities
10. Output and Costs	11. Perfect Competition	11. Perfect Competition	16. Public Goods and Common Resources
11. Perfect Competition	12. Monopoly	12. Monopoly	20. Trading with the World
12. Monopoly	13. Monopolistic Competition and Oligopoly	13. Monopolistic Competition and Oligopoly	
13. Monopolistic Competition and Oligopoly	14. Regulation and Antitrust Law	14. Regulation and Antitrust Law	
14. Regulation and Antitrust Law	17. Markets for Factors of Production	15. Externalities	
17. Markets for Factors of Production	19. Uncertainty and Information	16. Public Goods and Common Resources	
18. Economic Inequality	20. Trading with the World		
20. Trading with the World			

BRIEF CONTENTS

CONTENTS

Summary (Key Points, Key Figures and Tables, and Key Terms), Problems, Critical Thinking, and Web Activities appear at the end of each chapter.

CHAPTER 10 Output and Costs 219

CHAPTER 11 Perfect Competition 239

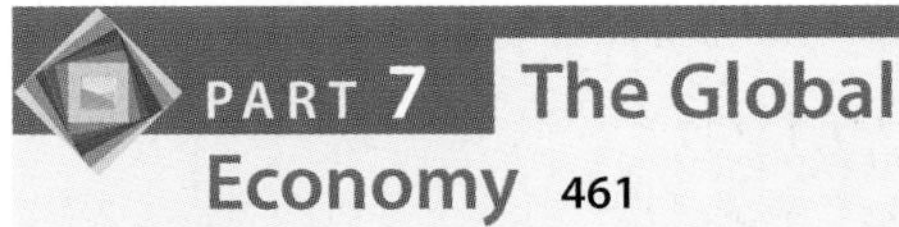

What Is Economics?

Understanding Our Changing World

You are studying economics at a time of enormous change. Much of the change is for the better. The information age with its laptop computers, wireless Internet connections, iPods, DVD movies, cell phones, video games, and a host of other gadgets and toys has transformed the way we work and play. And as we crank up the rate of production of these high-tech goods and services, our incomes and the incomes of people in China, India, and other countries are expanding rapidly.

But some change is for the worse. As the new millennium began, the U.S. economy slipped into recession. Businesses fired hundreds of thousands of workers and cut production. Then, on September 11, 2001, terrorist attacks generated shockwaves that are still reverberating around the global economy and have no visible end. Natural disasters such as Hurricane Katrina and the Indian Ocean tsunami wiped out the homes and devastated the lives of millions. And the onslaught of AIDS has lowered the life expectancy in some African nations to just 33 years.

The events and forces that we've just described are changing today's world. Your course in economics will help you to understand how these powerful forces shape our world. This chapter takes the first step. It describes the questions that economists try to answer, the way they think about those questions, and the methods they use in the search for answers. And an appendix explains the types of graphs that economists use in their search for answers.

After studying this chapter, you will be able to

- Define economics and distinguish between microeconomics and macroeconomics
- Explain the two big questions of economics
- Explain the key ideas that define the economic way of thinking
- Explain how economists go about their work as social scientists

Definition of Economics

All economic questions arise because we want more than we can get. We want a peaceful and secure world. We want clean air, lakes, and rivers. We want long and healthy lives. We want good schools, colleges, and universities. We want spacious and comfortable homes. We want an enormous range of sports and recreational gear from running shoes to jet skis. We want the time to enjoy sports, games, novels, movies, music, travel, and hanging out with our friends.

What each one of us can get is limited by time, by the incomes we earn, and by the prices we must pay. Everyone ends up with some unsatisfied wants. What we can get as a society is limited by our productive resources. These resources include the gifts of nature, human labor and ingenuity, and tools and equipment that we have produced.

Our inability to satisfy all our wants is called **scarcity**. The poor and the rich alike face scarcity. A child wants a $1.00 can of soda and two 50¢ packs of gum but has only $1.00 in his pocket. He faces scarcity. A millionaire wants to spend the weekend playing golf *and* spend the same weekend at the office attending a business strategy meeting. She faces scarcity. A society wants to provide improved health care, install a computer in every classroom, explore space, clean polluted lakes and rivers, and so on. Society faces scarcity. Even parrots face scarcity!

Faced with scarcity, we must *choose* among the available alternatives. The child must *choose* the soda *or* the gum. The millionaire must *choose* the golf game *or* the meeting. As a society, we must *choose* among health care, national defense, and education.

Not only do I want a cracker—we all want a cracker!

The choices that we make depend on the incentives that we face. An **incentive** is a reward that encourages an action or a penalty that discourages one. If the price of soda falls, the child has an *incentive* to choose more soda. If a profit of $10 million is at stake, the millionaire has an *incentive* to skip the golf game. As computer prices tumble, school boards have an *incentive* to connect more classrooms to the Internet.

Economics is the social science that studies the *choices* that individuals, businesses, governments, and entire societies make as they cope with *scarcity* and the *incentives* that influence and reconcile those choices. The subject divides into two main parts

- Microeconomics
- Macroeconomics

Microeconomics

Microeconomics is the study of the choices that individuals and businesses make, the way these choices interact in markets, and the influence of governments. Some examples of microeconomic questions are: Why are people buying more DVDs and fewer movie tickets? How would a tax on e-commerce affect eBay?

Macroeconomics

Macroeconomics is the study of the performance of the national economy and the global economy. Some examples of macroeconomic questions are: Why did incomes in the United States grow rapidly in 2006? Can the Federal Reserve keep incomes growing by cutting interest rates?

REVIEW QUIZ

1. List some examples of scarcity in the United States today.
2. Use the headlines in today's news to provide some examples of scarcity around the world.
3. Use today's news to illustrate the distinction between microeconomics and macroeconomics.

myeconlab **Study Plan 1.1**

Two Big Economic Questions

Two big questions summarize the scope of economics:

- How do choices end up determining *what*, *how*, and *for whom* goods and services get produced?
- When do choices made in the pursuit of *self-interest* also promote the *social interest*?

What, How, and For Whom?

Goods and services are the objects that people value and produce to satisfy human wants. Goods are physical objects such as golf balls. Services are tasks performed for people such as haircuts. By far the largest part of what the United States produces today is services such as retail and wholesale trade, health care, and education. Goods are a small part of total production.

What? What we produce changes over time. Seventy years ago, 25 percent of Americans worked on farms. That number has shrunk to 3 percent today. Over the same period, the number of people who produce goods—in mining, construction, and manufacturing—has shrunk from 31 percent to 17 percent. The decrease in farming and manufacturing is reflected in an increase in services. Seventy years ago, 45 percent of the population produced services. Today, more than 80 percent of working Americans have service jobs. Figure 1.1 shows these trends.

What determines the quantities of corn, DVDs, and haircuts and all the other millions of items that we produce?

How? Goods and services are produced by using productive resources that economists call **factors of production**. Factors of production are grouped into four categories:

- Land
- Labor
- Capital
- Entrepreneurship

Land The "gifts of nature" that we use to produce goods and services are called **land**. In economics, land is what in everyday language we call *natural resources*.

FIGURE 1.1 Trends in What We Produce

myeconlab

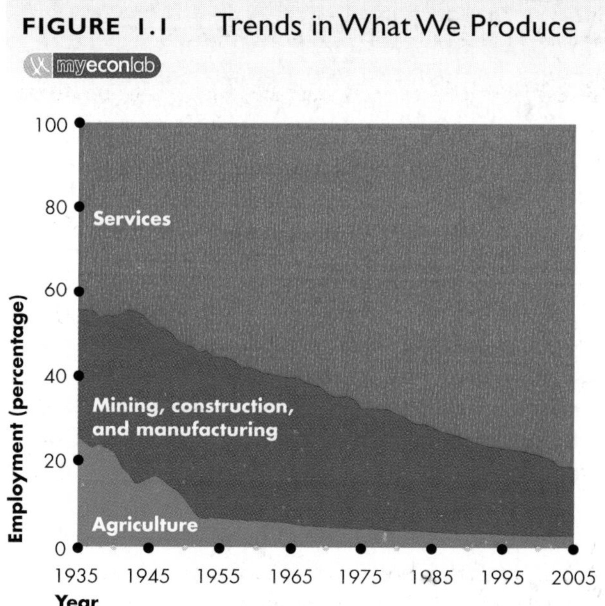

Services have expanded, and agriculture, mining, construction, and manufacturing have shrunk.

Source of data: U.S. Census Bureau, *Statistical Abstract of the United States.*

It includes land in the everyday sense together with metal ores, oil, gas and coal, water, and air.

Our land surface and water resources are renewable and some of our mineral resources can be recycled. But the resources that we use to create energy are nonrenewable—they can be used only once.

Labor The work time and work effort that people devote to producing goods and services is called **labor**. Labor includes the physical and mental efforts of all the people who work on farms and construction sites and in factories, shops, and offices.

The *quality* of labor depends on **human capital**, which is the knowledge and skill that people obtain from education, on-the-job training, and work experience. You are building your own human capital right now as you work on your economics course, and your human capital will continue to grow as you gain work experience.

Human capital expands over time. Today, 86 percent of the population of the United States has completed high school and 28 percent have a college or university degree. Figure 1.2 shows these measures of the growth of human capital in the United States over the past century.

Capital The tools, instruments, machines, buildings, and other constructions that businesses use to produce goods and services are called **capital.**

In everyday language, we talk about money, stocks, and bonds as being capital. These items are *financial* capital. Financial capital plays an important role in enabling businesses to borrow the funds that they use to buy capital. But financial capital is not used to produce goods and services. Because it is not a productive resource, it is not capital.

Entrepreneurship The human resource that organizes labor, land, and capital is called **entrepreneurship.** Entrepreneurs come up with new ideas about what and how to produce, make business decisions, and bear the risks that arise from these decisions.

How do the quantities of factors of production that get used to produce the many different goods and services get determined?

For Whom? Who gets the goods and services that are produced depends on the incomes that people earn. A large income enables a person to buy large quantities of goods and services. A small income leaves a person with few options and small quantities of goods and services.

People earn their incomes by selling the services of the factors of production they own:

- Land earns **rent.**
- Labor earns **wages.**
- Capital earns **interest.**
- Entrepreneurship earns **profit.**

Which factor of production earns the most income? The answer is labor. Wages and fringe benefits are around 70 percent of total income. Land, capital, and entrepreneurship share the rest. These percentages have been remarkably constant over time.

Knowing how income is shared among the factors of production doesn't tell us how it is shared among individuals. You know of lots of people who earn very large incomes. Movie director Steven Spielberg made $332 million in 2005. And Bill Gates' wealth increased by $5 billion in 2005 from the operations of Microsoft.

You know of even more people who earn very small incomes. Servers at McDonald's average around $6.35 an hour; checkout clerks, bartenders, cleaners, and textile and leather workers all earn less than $10 an hour.

FIGURE 1.2 A Measure of Human Capital

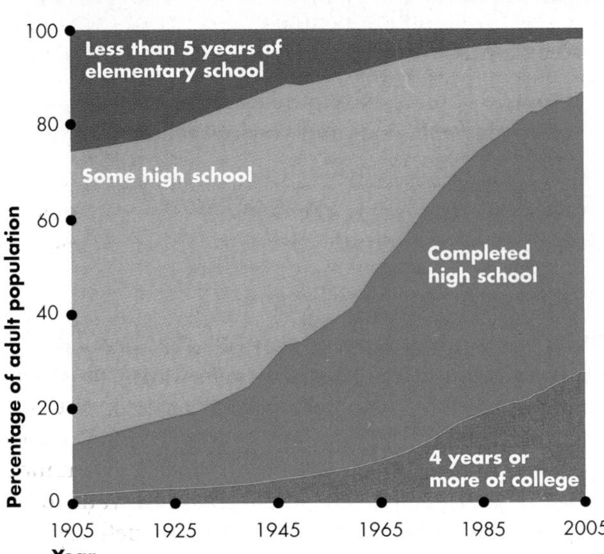

Today, 28 percent of the population has 4 years or more of college, up from 2 percent in 1905. A further 58 percent have completed high school, up from 10 percent in 1905.

Source of data: U.S. Census Bureau, *Statistical Abstract of the United States.*

You probably know about other persistent differences in incomes. Men, on the average, earn more than women; whites earn more than minorities; college graduates earn more than high-school graduates.

We can get a good sense of who consumes the goods and services produced by looking at the percentages of total income earned by different groups of people. The 20 percent of people with the lowest incomes earn about 5 percent of total income, while the richest 20 percent earn close to 50 percent of total income. So on the average, people in the top 20 percent earn more than 10 times the incomes of those in the bottom 20 percent.

Why is the distribution of income so unequal? Why do women and minorities earn less than white males?

Economics provides some answers to these questions about what, how, and for whom goods and services get produced.

The second big question of economics that we'll now examine is a harder question both to appreciate and to answer.

When Is the Pursuit of Self-Interest in the Social Interest?

Every day, you and 300 million other Americans, along with 6.6 billion people in the rest of the world, make economic choices that result in *what*, *how*, and *for whom* goods and services get produced.

Are the goods and services produced, and the quantities in which they are produced, the right ones? Do the factors of production employed get used in the best possible way? And do the goods and services that we produce go to the people who benefit most from them?

You know that your own choices are the best ones for you—or at least you think they're the best at the time that you make them. You use your time and other resources in the way that makes most sense to you. But you don't think much about how your choices affect other people. You order a home delivery pizza because you're hungry and want to eat. You don't order it thinking that the delivery person or the cook needs an income. You make choices that are in your **self-interest**—choices that you think are best for you.

When you act on your economic decisions, you come into contact with thousands of other people who produce and deliver the goods and services that you decide to buy or who buy the things that you sell. These people have made their own decisions—what to produce and how to produce it, who to hire or whom to work for, and so on. Like you, everyone else makes choices that they think are best for them. When the pizza delivery person shows up at your door, he's not doing you a favor. He's earning his income and hoping for a good tip.

Could it be possible that when each one of us makes choices that are in our own best interest, it turns out that these choices are also the best for society as a whole? Choices that are the best for society as a whole are said to be in the **social interest.**

Economists have been trying to find the answer to this question since 1776, the year of American independence and the year in which Adam Smith's monumental book, *The Nature and the Causes of the Wealth of Nations*, was published. The question is a hard one to answer, but a lot of progress has been made. Much of the rest of this book helps you to learn what we know about this question and its answer. To help you start thinking about the question, we're going to illustrate it with ten topics that generate heated discussion in today's world. You're already at least a little bit familiar with each one of them. They are

- Privatization
- Globalization
- The new economy
- Economic response to 9/11
- Corporate scandals
- HIV/AIDS
- Disappearing tropical rainforests
- Water shortages
- Unemployment
- Deficits and debts

Privatization November 9, 1989, is a date that will long be recalled in the world's economic history books. On that day, the Berlin Wall tumbled, and with its destruction, two Germanys embarked on a path toward unity.

West Germany was a nation designed on the model of the United States and Western Europe. In these nations, people own property and operate businesses. Privately owned businesses produce goods and services and trade them freely with customers in shops and markets. All this economic activity is conducted by people who pursue their own self-interest.

East Germany was a nation designed on the model of the Soviet Union—a centrally-planned economy. In such an economy, people are not free to operate businesses and trade freely with each other. The government owns the factories, shops, and offices, and it decides what to produce, how to produce it, and for whom to produce. Economic life is managed in detail by a government economic planning agency, and each individual follows instructions. The entire economy is operated like one giant firm.

The Soviet Union collapsed soon after the fall of the Berlin Wall and splintered into a number of independent states, each of which embarked on a process of privatization. China, another centrally-planned economy, began to encourage private enterprise and move away from sole reliance on public ownership and central economic planning during the 1980s.

Today, only Cuba, North Korea, and Vietnam remain centrally-planned economies.

Do publicly owned businesses coordinated by central economic planning serve the social interest better than private businesses that trade freely in markets as they do in the United States? Or is it possible that our economic system serves the social interest more effectively?

Globalization When world leaders meet, anti-globalization protests accompany them. *Globalization*—the expansion of international trade and investment—has been going on for centuries, but during the 1990s, advances in microchip, satellite, and fiber-optic technologies brought a dramatic fall in the cost of communication and accelerated the process. A phone call or even a video-conference with people who live 10,000 miles apart has become an everyday and easily affordable event. Every day, 20,000 people travel by air between the United States and Asia, and a similar number travel between the United States and Europe.

The explosion of communication has globalized production decisions. When Nike produces more sports shoes, people in China, Indonesia, or Malaysia get more work. When more people use credit cards, people in Barbados key in the data from sales slips. When Sony creates a new game for PlayStation 3, or Steven Spielberg creates an animation sequence in a movie, programmers in India write the code. And when China Airlines buys new airplanes, Americans who work for Boeing build them.

As part of the process of globalization, the United States produces more services and fewer manufactured goods. And China and the small economies in East Asia produce an expanding volume of manufactures.

Some economies of Asia are also growing more rapidly than are those of the United States and Europe. And on current trends, China will be the world's largest economy by 2013. The rapid economic expansion in Asia will bring further changes to the global economy as the wealthier Chinese and other Asians travel and buy more of the goods and services that the United States and other parts of the world produce. Globalization will proceed at an accelerated pace.

But globalization is leaving some behind. The nations of Africa and parts of South America are not sharing in the prosperity that globalization is bringing to other parts of the world.

Is globalization a good thing? Whom does it benefit? Globalization is clearly in the interest of the owners of multinational firms that profit by producing in low-cost regions and selling in high-price regions. But is globalization in *your* interest and the interest of the young worker in Malaysia who sews your new running shoes? Is it in the social interest?

The New Economy The 1980s and 1990s were years of extraordinary economic change that have been called the *Information Revolution*. Economic revolutions don't happen very often. The previous one, the *Industrial Revolution*, occurred between 1760 and 1830 and saw the transformation from rural farm life to urban industrial life for most people. The revolution before that, the *Agrarian Revolution*, occurred around 12,000 years ago and saw the transformation from a life of hunting and gathering to a life of settled farming.

According the events of the last 25 years the status of those two previous revolutions might be a stretch. But the changes that occurred during those 25 years were incredible. And they were based on one major technology: the microprocessor or computer chip. Gordon Moore of Intel predicted in 1965 that the number of transistors that could be placed on one integrated chip would double every 18 months (Moore's law). This prediction turned out to be remarkably accurate. In 1980, a PC chip had 60,000 transistors. By 2000, chips with more than 40 million transistors were in machines like the one you use.

The spinoffs from faster and cheaper computing were widespread. Telecommunications became much faster and cheaper, music and movie recording became more realistic and cheaper, millions of routine tasks that previously required human decision and action were automated. You encounter these automated tasks every day when you check out at the supermarket, call directory assistance, or call a government department or large business.

All the new products and processes and the low-cost computing power that made them possible were produced by people who made choices in the pursuit of self-interest. They did not result from any grand design or government economic plan.

When Gordon Moore set up Intel and started making chips, no one had told him to do so, and he wasn't thinking how much easier it would be for you to turn in your essay on time if you had a faster PC. When Bill Gates quit Harvard to set up Microsoft, he wasn't trying to create an operating system to improve people's computing experience. Moore and Gates and thousands of other entrepreneurs were in hot pursuit of the big payoffs that many of them achieved. Yet their actions did make millions of people better off. They did advance the social interest.

But were resources used in the best possible way during the information revolution? Did Intel make the right quality of chips and sell them in the right quantities for the right prices? Or was the quality too low and the price too high? And what about Microsoft? Did Bill Gates have to be paid $30 billion to produce the successive generations of Windows? Was this program developed in the social interest?

The Economic Response to 9/11 The awful events of September 11, 2001, created economic shockwaves that will last for some years and changed *what, how,* and *for whom.*

The biggest changes in production occurred in travel, accommodation, and security. Much business travel was replaced by teleconferencing. Many vacationers left the air and went onto the highway. Foreign trips were cut back. Airlines lost business and ordered fewer new airplanes. Banks wrote off millions of dollars in losses on loans to airlines.

But sales of SUVs and RVs increased. And airports, although operating at lower capacity, beefed up their security services. Tens of thousands of new security agents were hired, and state-of-the-art scanners were installed.

Thousands of people made choices in pursuit of their self-interest that led to these changes in production. But were these changes also in the social interest?

Corporate Scandals In 2000, the names Enron and WorldCom meant corporate integrity and spectacular success. Today, they are tainted with scandal.

Founded in 1985, Enron expanded to become America's seventh largest business by 2001. But its expansion was built on an elaborate web of lies, deceit, and fraud. In October 2001, after revelations by one of its former executives, Enron's directors acknowledged that by inflating reported income and hiding debts, they had made the firm appear to be worth much more than it actually was. Enron executives Jeffrey Skilling and Kenneth Lay were convicted of fraud that made them millions of dollars but wiped out the stockholders' wealth.

Scott Sullivan, a highly respected financial officer, joined WorldCom in 1992 and helped to turn it into one of the world's telecommunications giants. In his last year with the company, Sullivan's salary was $700,000 and his bonus (in stock options) was $10 million. But just ten years after joining the company, Sullivan was fired and arrested for allegedly falsifying the company's accounts, inflating its book profits by almost $4 billion, and inflating his own bonus in the process. Shortly after these events, WorldCom filed for bankruptcy protection in the largest bankruptcy filing in U.S. history, laid off 17,000 workers, and wiped out its stockholders' wealth.

These cases illustrate the fact that sometimes, in the pursuit of self-interest, people break the law. Such behavior is not in the social interest. Indeed, the law was established precisely to limit such behavior.

But some corporate behavior that is legal is regarded by some as inappropriate. For example, many people think that the salaries of top executives are out of control. In some cases, executives who receive huge incomes bring ruin to the companies that they manage.

The people who hired the executives acted in their own self-interest and appointed the best people they could find. The executives acted in their own self-interest. But what became of the self-interest of the stockholders and the customers of these firms? Didn't they suffer? Aren't these glaring examples of conflict between self-interest and the social interest?

HIV/AIDS The World Health Organization and the United Nations estimate that about 40 million people were suffering from HIV/AIDS in 2005. During that year, 3 million died from the disease and there were 4 million new cases. Most of the HIV/AIDS cases—25 million of them in 2005—were in Africa, where incomes average around $7 a day. The most effective treatment for this disease is an antiretroviral drug made by large multinational drug companies. The cost of this treatment is around $2,700 a year—more than $7 a day. For sales to poor countries, the cost has been lowered to around $1,200 a year—$3.30 a day.

Developing new drugs is a high-cost and high-risk activity, and if it were not in the self-interest of the drug companies, they would stop the effort. But once a drug is developed, the cost of producing it is just a few cents a dose. Would it be in the social interest for drugs to be made available at the low cost of producing them?

Disappearing Tropical Rainforests Tropical rainforests in South America, Africa, and Asia support the lives of 30 million species of plants, animals, and insects—approaching 50 percent of all species on the planet. These rainforests provide us with the ingredients for many goods, including soaps, mouthwashes, shampoos, food preservatives, rubber, nuts, and fruits. The Amazon rainforest alone converts about 1 trillion pounds of carbon dioxide into oxygen each year.

Yet tropical rainforests cover less than 2 percent of the earth's surface and are heading for extinction. Logging, cattle ranching, mining, oil extraction, hydroelectric dams, and subsistence farming are destroying an area the size of two football fields every second, or larger than New York City every day. At the current rate of destruction, almost all the tropical rainforest ecosystems will be gone by 2030.

Each one of us makes economic choices that are in our self-interest to consume products, some of which are destroying this natural resource. Are our choices damaging the social interest? If they are, what can be done to change the incentives we face and change our behavior?

Water Shortages The world is awash with water—it is our most abundant resource. But 97 percent of it is seawater. Another 2 percent is frozen in glaciers and ice. The 1 percent of the earth's water that is available for human consumption would be sufficient if only it were in the right places. Finland, Canada, and a few other places have more water than they can use, but Australia, Africa, and California (and many other places) could use much more water than they can get.

Some people pay less for water than others. California farmers, for example, pay less than California households. Some of the highest prices for water are faced by people in the poorest countries who must either buy from a water dealer's truck or carry water in buckets over many miles.

In the United Kingdom, water is provided by private water companies. In the United States, public enterprises deliver the water.

In India and Bangladesh, plenty of rain falls, but it falls during a short wet season and the rest of the year is dry. Dams could help, but not enough have been built in those countries.

Are the nation's and the world's water resources being managed properly? Are the decisions that we each make in our self-interest to use, conserve, and transport water also in the social interest?

Unemployment During the 1930s, in a period called the *Great Depression*, more than 20 percent of the U.S. labor force was unemployed. Even today, about 30 percent of the African American teenage labor force is unemployed. Why can't everyone who wants a job find one? If economic choices arise from scarcity, how can resources be left unused?

People get jobs because other people expect to make a profit by hiring them. And people accept jobs when they think the pay and other conditions are good enough. So the number of people with jobs is determined by the self-interest of employers and workers. But is the number of jobs also in the social interest?

Deficits and Debts On a typical day since September 30, 2002, the U.S. government has run a budget deficit of $1.71 billion, which means that the government's debt has increased each day by that amount. On July 11, 2006, the day these words were written, your personal share of the outstanding government debt was $28,140.

Also, during 2006, Americans bought goods and services from the rest of the world in excess of what foreigners bought from the United States to the tune of almost $800 billion. To pay for these goods and services, we borrowed from the rest of the world.

These enormous deficits and the debts they create cannot persist indefinitely, and the debt will somehow have to be repaid. And it will most likely be repaid by you, not by your parents.

Are the choices that we vote for and make through our federal government and the choices we make when we buy from and sell to the rest of the world in the social interest?

We've just looked at ten topics that illustrate the big question: Do choices made in the pursuit of self-interest also serve the social interest?

You'll discover, as you work through this book, that much of what we do in the pursuit of our self-interest does indeed further the social interest. But there are areas in which the social interest and self-interest come into conflict. You'll discover the principles that help economists to figure out when the social interest is being served, when it is not, and what might be done when it is not.

REVIEW QUIZ

1 Describe the broad facts about *what*, *how*, and *for whom* goods and services get produced.
2 Use headlines from the recent news to illustrate the potential for conflict between self-interest and the social interest.

myeconlab **Study Plan 1.2**

The Economic Way of Thinking

The questions that economics tries to answer tell us about the *scope of economics.* But they don't tell us how economists *think* about these questions and go about seeking answers to them.

You're now going to begin to see how economists approach economic questions. First, in this section, we'll look at the ideas that define the *economic way of thinking*. This way of thinking needs practice, but it is powerful, and as you become more familiar with it, you'll begin to see the world around you with a new and sharp focus.

Choices and Tradeoffs

Because we face scarcity, we must make choices. And when we make a choice, we select from the available alternatives. For example, you can spend the weekend studying for your next economics test and having fun with your friends, but you can't do both of these activities at the same time. You must choose how much time to devote to each. Whatever choice you make, you could have chosen something else instead.

You can think about your choice as a tradeoff. A **tradeoff** is an exchange—giving up one thing to get something else. When you choose how to spend your weekend, you face a tradeoff between studying and hanging out with your friends.

Guns Versus Butter The classic tradeoff is between guns and butter. "Guns" and "butter" stand for any pair of goods. They might actually be guns and butter. Or they might be broader categories such as national defense and food. Or they might be any pair of specific goods or services such as cola and bottled water, baseball bats and tennis rackets, colleges and hospitals, realtor services and career counseling.

Regardless of the specific objects that guns and butter represent, the guns-versus-butter tradeoff captures a hard fact of life: If we want more of one thing, we must trade something else in exchange for it.

The idea of a tradeoff is central to the whole of economics. We'll look at some examples, beginning with the big questions: What, How, and For Whom? We can view each of these questions about goods and services in terms of tradeoffs.

What, How, and *For Whom* Tradeoffs

The questions what, how, and for whom goods and services are produced all involve tradeoffs that are similar to that between guns and butter.

***What* Tradeoffs** What goods and services get produced depends on choices made by each one of us, by our government, and by the businesses that produce the things we buy.

Each of these choices involves a tradeoff. Each one of us faces a tradeoff when we choose how to spend our income. You go to the movies this week, but you forgo a few cups of coffee to buy the ticket. You trade off coffee for a movie.

The federal government faces a tradeoff when it chooses how to spend our tax dollars. Congress votes for more national defense but cuts back on educational programs. Congress trades off education for national defense.

Businesses face a tradeoff when they decide what to produce. Nike hires Tiger Woods and allocates resources to designing and marketing a new golf ball but cuts back on its development of a new running shoe. Nike trades off running shoes for golf balls.

***How* Tradeoffs** How goods and services get produced depends on choices made by the businesses that produce the things we buy. These choices involve a tradeoff. For example, Krispy Kreme opens a new doughnut store that has an automated production line and closes an older store with a traditional kitchen. Krispy Kreme trades off labor for capital.

***For Whom* Tradeoffs** For whom goods and services are produced depends on the distribution of buying power. Buying power can be redistributed—transferred from one person to another—in three ways: by voluntary payments, by theft, or through taxes and benefits organized by government. Redistribution brings tradeoffs.

Each of us faces a *for whom* tradeoff when we choose how much to contribute to the United Nations' famine relief fund. You donate $50 and cut your spending. You trade off your own spending for a small increase in economic equality.

We face a *for whom* tradeoff when we vote to increase the resources for catching thieves and enforcing the law. We trade off goods and services for an increase in the security of our property.

We also face a *for whom* tradeoff when we vote for taxes and social programs that redistribute buying power from the rich to the poor. These redistribution programs confront society with what has been called the **big tradeoff**—the tradeoff between equality and efficiency. Taxing the rich and making transfers to the poor bring greater economic equality. But taxing productive activities such as running a business, working hard, and saving and investing in capital discourages these activities. So taxing productive activities means producing less. A more equal distribution means there is less to share.

Think of the problem of how to share a pie that everyone contributes to baking. If each person receives a share of the pie that is proportional to her or his effort, everyone will work hard and the pie will be as large as possible. But if the pie is shared equally, regardless of contribution, some talented bakers will slack off and the pie will shrink. The big tradeoff is one between the size of the pie and how equally it is shared. We trade off some pie for increased equality.

Choices Bring Change

What, how, and for whom goods and services are produced changes over time. And choices bring change. The quantity and range of goods and services available today in the United States are much greater than those in Africa. And the economic condition of the United States today is much better than it was a generation ago. But the quality of economic life (and its rate of improvement) doesn't depend purely on nature and on luck. It depends on many of the choices made by each one of us, by governments, and by businesses. And these choices involve tradeoffs.

One choice is that of how much of our income to consume and how much to save. Our saving can be channeled through the financial system to finance businesses and to pay for new capital that increases production. The more we save and invest, the more goods and services we'll be able to produce in the future. When you decide to save an extra $1,000 and forgo a vacation, you trade off the vacation for a higher future income. If everyone saves an extra $1,000 and businesses invest in more equipment that increases production, future consumption per person rises. As a society, we trade off current consumption for economic growth and higher future consumption.

A second choice is how much effort to devote to education and training. By becoming better educated and more highly skilled, we become more productive and are able to produce more goods and services. When you decide to remain in school for another two years to complete a professional degree and forgo a huge chunk of leisure time, you trade off leisure today for a higher future income. If everyone becomes better educated, production increases and income per person rises. As a society, we trade off current consumption and leisure time for economic growth and higher future consumption.

A third choice is how much effort to devote to research and the development of new products and production methods. Ford Motor Company can hire people either to design a new robotic assembly line or to operate the existing plant and produce cars. The robotic plant brings greater productivity in the future but means smaller current production—a tradeoff of current production for greater future production.

Seeing choices as tradeoffs emphasizes the idea that to get something, we must give up something. What we give up is the cost of what we get. Economists call this cost the *opportunity cost.*

Opportunity Cost

"There's no such thing as a free lunch" expresses the central idea of economics: Every choice has a cost. The **opportunity cost** of something is the highest-valued alternative that we give up to get it.

You can quit school, or you can remain in school. If you quit school and take a job at McDonald's, you earn enough to buy some CDs, go to the movies, and spend lots of free time with your friends. If you remain in school, you can't afford these things. You will be able to buy these things when you graduate and get a job, and that is one of the payoffs from being in school. But for now, when you've bought your books, you have nothing left for CDs and movies. And doing assignments leaves no time for hanging around with your friends. The opportunity cost of being in school is the highest-valued alternative that you would have done if you had quit school.

All the *what, how,* and *for whom* tradeoffs that we've just considered involve opportunity cost. The opportunity cost of some guns is the butter forgone; the opportunity cost of a movie ticket is the number of cups of coffee forgone.

And the choices that bring change also involve opportunity cost. The opportunity cost of more goods and services in the future is less consumption today.

Choosing at the Margin

You can allocate the next hour between studying and e-mailing your friends. But the choice is not all or nothing. You must decide how many minutes to allocate to each activity. To make this decision, you compare the benefit of a little bit more study time with its cost—you make your choice at the **margin**.

The benefit that arises from an increase in an activity is called **marginal benefit**. For example, suppose that you're spending four nights a week studying and your grade point average (GPA) is 3.0. You decide that you want a higher GPA and decide to study an extra night each week. Your GPA rises to 3.5. The marginal benefit from studying for one extra night a week is the 0.5 increase in your GPA. It is *not* the 3.5. You already have a 3.0 from studying for four nights a week, so we don't count this benefit as resulting from the decision you are now making.

The cost of an increase in an activity is called **marginal cost**. For you, the marginal cost of increasing your study time by one night a week is the cost of the additional night not spent with your friends (if that is your best alternative use of the time). It does not include the cost of the four nights you are already studying.

To make your decision, you compare the marginal benefit from an extra night of studying with its marginal cost. If the marginal benefit exceeds the marginal cost, you study the extra night. If the marginal cost exceeds the marginal benefit, you do not study the extra night.

By evaluating marginal benefits and marginal costs and choosing only those actions that bring greater benefit than cost, we use our scarce resources in the way that makes us as well off as possible.

Responding to Incentives

Our choices respond to incentives. A change in marginal cost or a change in marginal benefit changes the incentives that we face and leads us to change our choice.

For example, suppose your economics instructor gives you a problem set and tells you that all the problems will be on the next test. The marginal benefit from working these problems is large, so you diligently work them all. In contrast, if your math instructor gives you a problem set and tells you that none of the problems will be on the next test, the marginal benefit from working these problems is lower, so you skip most of them.

The central idea of economics is that we can predict how choices will change by looking at changes in incentives. More of an activity is undertaken when its marginal cost falls or its marginal benefit rises; less of an activity is undertaken when its marginal cost rises or its marginal benefit falls.

Incentives are also the key to reconciling self-interest and social interest. When our choices are *not* in the social interest, it is because of the incentives we face. One of the challenges for economists is to figure out the incentive systems that result in self-interested choices being in the social interest.

Human Nature, Incentives, and Institutions

Economists take human nature as given and view people as acting in their self-interest. All people—consumers, producers, politicians, and public servants—pursue their self-interest.

Self-interested actions are not necessarily *selfish* actions. You might decide to use your resources in ways that bring pleasure to others as well as to yourself. But a self-interested act gets the most value for *you* based on *your* view about value.

If human nature is given and if people act in their self-interest, how can we take care of the social interest? Economists answer this question by emphasizing the crucial role that institutions play in influencing the incentives that people face as they pursue their self-interest.

Private property protected by a system of laws and markets that enable voluntary exchange are the fundamental institutions. You will learn as you progress with your study of economics that where these institutions exist, self-interest can indeed promote the social interest.

REVIEW QUIZ

1. Provide three everyday examples of tradeoffs and describe the opportunity cost involved in each.
2. Provide three everyday examples to illustrate what we mean by choosing at the margin.
3. How do economists predict changes in choices?
4. What do economists say about the role of institutions in promoting the social interest?

myeconlab **Study Plan 1.3**

Economics: A Social Science

Economics is a social science (along with political science, psychology, and sociology). Economists try to discover how the economic world works, and in pursuit of this goal (like all scientists), they distinguish between two types of statements:

- What *is*
- What *ought to be*

Statements about what *is* are called *positive* statements, and they might be right or wrong. We can test a positive statement by checking it against the facts. When a chemist does an experiment in her laboratory, she is attempting to check a positive statement against the facts.

Statements about what *ought to be* are called *normative* statements. These statements depend on values and cannot be tested. When Congress debates a motion, it is ultimately trying to decide what ought to be. It is making a normative statement.

To see the distinction between positive and normative statements, consider the controversy over global warming. Some scientists believe that centuries of the burning of coal and oil are increasing the carbon dioxide content of the earth's atmosphere and leading to higher temperatures that eventually will have devastating consequences for life on this planet. "Our planet is warming because of an increased carbon dioxide buildup in the atmosphere" is a positive statement. It can (in principle and with sufficient data) be tested. "We ought to cut back on our use of carbon-based fuels such as coal and oil" is a normative statement. You can agree or disagree with this statement, but you can't test it. It is based on values.

Health-care reform provides another economic example of the distinction. "Universal health care will cut the amount of work time lost to illness" is a positive statement. "Every American should have equal access to health care" is a normative statement.

The task of economic science is to discover positive statements that are consistent with what we observe and that help us to understand the economic world. This task can be broken into three steps:

- Observation and measurement
- Model building
- Testing models

Observation and Measurement

The first step toward understanding how the economic world works is to observe it. All science needs data. Economists observe and measure data on all aspects of economic behavior, some examples of which are the quantities of resources available, wage rates and work hours, the quantities of goods and services produced and consumed and their prices.

Model Building

The second step toward understanding how the economic world works is to build a model. An **economic model** is a description of some aspect of the economic world that includes only those features of the world that are needed for the purpose at hand. A model is simpler than the reality it describes. What a model includes and ignores result from assumptions about what is essential and what are inessential details.

You can see how ignoring details is useful—even essential—to our understanding by thinking about a model that you probably see every day: the TV weather map. The weather map is a model that helps to predict the temperature, wind speed and direction, and precipitation over a future period. The weather map shows lines called isobars—lines of equal barometric pressure. It doesn't show the interstate highways. The reason is that our theory of the weather tells us that the pattern of air pressure, not the location of the highways, determines the weather.

An economic model is similar to a weather map. For example, an economic model of a cell phone network might tell us the effects of the development of a new low-cost technology on the number of cell phone subscribers and the volume of cell phone use. But the model would ignore such details as the colors of the covers on people's cell phones and the tunes they use for ringtones.

Testing Models

The third step is testing models. A model's predictions might correspond to the facts or be in conflict with them. By comparing the model's predictions with the facts, we can test a model and develop an economic theory. An **economic theory** is a generalization that summarizes what we think we understand about the economic choices that people make and the performance of industries and entire economies. It is a bridge between an economic model and the real economy.

The process of building and testing models creates theories. For example, meteorologists have a theory that if the isobars form a particular pattern at a particular time of the year (a model), then it will snow (reality). They have developed this theory by repeated observation and by carefully recording the weather that follows specific pressure patterns.

Economics is a young science. It was born in 1776 with the publication of Adam Smith's *Wealth of Nations* (see p. 54). Over the years since then, economists have discovered many useful theories. But in many areas, economists are still looking for answers. The gradual accumulation of economic knowledge gives most economists some faith that their methods will, eventually, provide usable answers to the big economic questions.

But progress in economics comes slowly. Let's look at some of the obstacles to progress in economics.

Obstacles and Pitfalls in Economics

We cannot easily do economic experiments. And most economic behavior has many simultaneous causes. For these two reasons, it is difficult in economics to unscramble cause and effect.

Unscrambling Cause and Effect By changing one factor at a time and holding all the other relevant factors constant, we isolate the factor of interest and are able to investigate its effects in the clearest possible way. This logical device, which all scientists use to identify cause and effect, is called *ceteris paribus*. ***Ceteris paribus*** is a Latin term that means "other things being equal" or "if all other relevant things remain the same." Ensuring that other things are equal is crucial in many activities, and all successful attempts to make scientific progress use this device.

Economic models (like the models in all other sciences) enable the influence of one factor at a time to be isolated in the imaginary world of the model. When we use a model, we are able to imagine what would happen if only one factor changed. But *ceteris paribus* can be a problem in economics when we try to test a model.

Laboratory scientists, such as chemists and physicists, perform experiments by actually holding all the relevant factors constant except for the one under investigation. In non-experimental sciences such as economics (and meteorology), we usually observe the outcomes of the simultaneous operation of many factors. Consequently, it is hard to sort out the effects of each individual factor and to compare them with what a model predicts. To cope with this problem, economists take three complementary approaches.

First, they look for pairs of events in which other things were equal (or similar). An example might be to study the effects of unemployment insurance on the unemployment rate by comparing the United States with Canada on the presumption that the people in the two economies are sufficiently similar. Second, economists use statistical tools—called econometrics. Third, when economists can, they perform experiments. This relatively new approach puts real subjects (usually students) in a decision-making situation and varies their incentives in some way to discover how they respond to a change in one factor at a time.

Economists try to avoid fallacies—errors of reasoning that lead to a wrong conclusion. But two fallacies are common, and you need to be on your guard to avoid them. They are the

- Fallacy of composition
- *Post hoc* fallacy

Fallacy of Composition The fallacy of composition is the (false) statement that what is true of the parts is true of the whole or that what is true of the whole is true of the parts. There are many everyday examples of this fallacy. Standing at a ball game to get a better view works for one person but not for all—what is true for a part of a crowd is not true for the whole crowd.

The fallacy of composition arises in many economic situations that stem from the fact that the parts interact with each other to produce an outcome for the whole that might differ from the intent of the parts.

For example, a firm fires some workers to cut costs and improve its profits. If all firms take similar actions, income falls and so does spending. The firm sells less, and its profits don't improve.

Or suppose that a firm thinks it can gain market share by cutting its price and mounting a large advertising campaign. Again, if the one firm takes these actions, they work. But if all firms in an industry take the same actions, the firms end up with the same market share as before and lower profits.

***Post Hoc* Fallacy** Another Latin phrase—*post hoc, ergo propter hoc*—means "after this, therefore because of this." The *post hoc* fallacy is the error of reasoning that a first event *causes* a second event because the first occurred before the second. Suppose you are a visitor from a far-off world. You observe lots of people shopping in early December, and then you see them opening gifts and partying in the holiday season. "Does the shopping cause the holiday season?," you wonder. After a deeper study, you discover that the holiday season causes the shopping. A later event causes an earlier event.

Unraveling cause and effect is difficult in economics. And just looking at the timing of events often doesn't help. For example, the stock market booms, and some months later the economy expands—jobs and incomes grow. Did the stock market boom cause the economy to expand? Possibly, but perhaps businesses started to plan the expansion of production because a new technology that lowered costs had become available. As knowledge of the plans spread, the stock market reacted to *anticipate* the economic expansion. To disentangle cause and effect, economists use economic models and data and, to the extent that they can, perform experiments.

Economics is a challenging science. Does the difficulty of getting answers in economics mean that anything goes and that economists disagree on most questions? Perhaps you've heard the joke "If you laid all the economists in the world end to end, they still wouldn't reach agreement." Surprisingly, perhaps, the joke does not describe reality.

Agreement and Disagreement

Economists agree on a remarkably wide range of questions. And often the agreed-upon view of economists disagrees with the popular and sometimes politically correct view. When Federal Reserve Chairman Ben Bernanke testifies before the Senate Banking Committee, his words are rarely controversial among economists, even if they generate endless debate in the media and Congress.

Here are 12 propositions with which at least 7 out of every 10 economists broadly agree:

- Tariffs and import restrictions make most people worse off.
- A large budget deficit has an adverse effect on the economy.
- A minimum wage increases unemployment among young workers and low-skilled workers.
- Cash payments to welfare recipients make them better off than do transfers-in-kind of equal cash value.
- A tax cut can help to lower unemployment when the unemployment rate is high.
- The distribution of income in the United States should be more equal.
- Inflation is primarily caused by a rapid rate of money creation.
- The government should restructure welfare along the lines of a "negative income tax."
- Rent controls cut the availability of housing.
- Pollution taxes are more effective than pollution limits.
- The redistribution of income is a legitimate role for the U.S. government.
- The federal budget should be balanced on the average over the business cycle but not every year.

Which of these propositions are positive and which are normative? Notice that economists are willing to offer their opinions on normative issues as well as their professional views on positive issues. Be on the lookout for normative propositions dressed up as positive propositions.

REVIEW QUIZ

1. What is the distinction between a positive statement and a normative statement? Provide an example (different from those in the chapter) of each type of statement.
2. What is a model? Can you think of a model that you might use (probably without thinking of it as a model) in your everyday life?
3. What is a theory? Why is the statement "It might work in theory, but it doesn't work in practice" a silly statement?
4. What is the *ceteris paribus* assumption and how is it used?
5. Try to think of some everyday examples of the fallacy of composition and the *post hoc* fallacy.

myeconlab **Study Plan 1.4**

SUMMARY

Key Points

Definition of Economics (p. 2)

- All economic questions arise from scarcity—from the fact that wants exceed the resources available to satisfy them.
- Economics is the social science that studies the choices that people make as they cope with scarcity.
- The subject divides into microeconomics and macroeconomics.

Two Big Economic Questions (pp. 3–8)

- Two big questions summarize the scope of economics:
  1. How do choices end up determining *what, how,* and *for whom* goods and services get produced?
  2. When do choices made in the pursuit of *self-interest* also promote the *social interest*?

The Economic Way of Thinking (pp. 9–11)

- Every choice is a tradeoff—exchanging more of something for less of something else.
- The classic guns-versus-butter tradeoff represents all tradeoffs.
- All economic questions involve tradeoffs.
- The big social tradeoff is that between equality and efficiency.
- The highest-valued alternative forgone is the opportunity cost of what is chosen.
- Choices are made at the margin and respond to incentives.

Economics: A Social Science (pp. 12–14)

- Economists distinguish between positive statements—what is—and normative statements—what ought to be.
- To explain the economic world, economists develop theories by building and testing economic models.
- Economists use the *ceteris paribus* assumption to try to disentangle cause and effect and are careful to avoid the fallacy of composition and the *post hoc* fallacy.
- Economists agree on a wide range of questions about how the economy works.

Key Terms

PROBLEMS

myeconlab **Tests, Study Plan, Solutions***

1. Apple Computer Inc. decides to make iTunes freely available in unlimited quantities.
   a. Does Apple's decision mean that tunes are no longer scarce?
   b. Does Apple's decision change the incentives that people face?
   c. Is Apple's decision an example of a microeconomic or a macroeconomic issue?
   d. How does Apple's decision change the opportunity cost of a tune?
2. Which of the following pairs does not match:
   a. Labor and wages?
   b. Land and rent?
   c. Entreprenuership and profit?
   d. Capital and profit?
3. Explain how the following news headlines concern self-interest and the social interest:
   a. Wal-Mart Expands in Europe
   b. Taco Bell Opens in Canada
   c. McDonald's Moves into Salads
   d. Food Must Be Labeled with Nutrition Information
4. The night before an economics exam, you decide to go to the movies instead of staying home and working your MyEconLab study plan. You get 50 percent on your exam compared with the 70 percent that you normally score.
   a. Did you face a tradeoff?
   b. What was the opportunity cost of your evening at the movies?
5. Which of the following statements is positive, which is normative, and which can be tested?
   a. The U.S. government should cut its imports.
   b. China is the United States' largest trading partner.
   c. If the price of antiretroviral drugs increases, HIV/AIDS sufferers will decrease their consumption of the drug.
6. Which statement illustrates the fallacy of composition and which the *post hoc* fallacy?
   a. You'll see more if you stand on your toes.
   b. Everyone should leave home an hour earlier to avoid the rush hour traffic.
   c. People who smoke cigarettes face an increased risk of lung and heart diseases.

*Solutions to odd-numbered problems are provided.

CRITICAL THINKING

1. As London prepares to host the 2012 Olympic Games, concern about the cost of the event increases. An example:

   Costs Soar for London Olympics—The regeneration of East London is set to add extra £1.5 billion to taxpayers' bill.

   The Times, London, July 6, 2006

   Is the cost of regenerating East London an opportunity cost of hosting the 2012 Olympic Games? Explain why or why not.

WEB ACTIVITIES

myeconlab **Links to Web sites**

1. Visit CNNMoney.com
   a. What is the top economic news story today?
   b. With which of the big questions does it deal? (It must deal with at least one of them and might deal with more than one.)
   c. What tradeoffs does the news item discuss?
   d. Write a brief summary of the news item in a few bulleted points using as much as possible of the economic vocabulary that you have learned in this chapter and that is in the key terms list on p. 15.
2. Visit *Resources for Economists on the Internet.* This Web site is a good place from which to search for economic information on the Internet. Click on "Blogs, Commentaries, and Podcasts."
   a. Click on the Becker-Posner Blog and read the latest blog by these two outstanding economists.
   b. As you read this blog, think about what it is saying about "what," "how," and "for whom" questions.
   c. As you read this blog, think about what it is saying about self-interest and the social interest.
3. Visit the Bureau of Labor Statistics and find information about employment, unemployment, and earnings in your state. Also find information about employment, unemployment, and earnings for the United States and compare your state with the nation as a whole.

Graphs in Economics

After studying this appendix, you will be able to

- Make and interpret a time-series graph, a cross-section graph, and a scatter diagram
- Distinguish between linear and nonlinear relationships and between relationships that have a maximum and a minimum
- Define and calculate the slope of a line
- Graph relationships among more than two variables

Graphing Data

A graph represents a quantity as a distance on a line. In Fig. A1.1, a distance on the horizontal line represents temperature, measured in degrees Fahrenheit. A movement from left to right shows an increase in temperature. The point 0 represents zero degrees Fahrenheit. To the right of 0, the temperature is positive. To the left of 0 (as indicated by the minus sign), the temperature is negative. A distance on the vertical line represents altitude or height, measured in thousands of feet. The point 0 represents sea level. Points above 0 represent feet above sea level. Points below 0 (indicated by a minus sign) represent feet below sea level.

By setting two scales perpendicular to each other, as in Fig. A1.1, we can visualize the relationship between two variables. The scale lines are called *axes*. The vertical line is the y-axis, and the horizontal line is the x-axis. Each axis has a zero point, which is shared by the two axes and called the *origin*.

We need two bits of information to make a two-variable graph: the value of the x variable and the value of the y variable. For example, off the coast of Alaska, the temperature is 32 degrees—the value of x. A fishing boat is located at 0 feet above sea level—the value of y. These two bits of information appear as point A in Fig. A1.1. A climber at the top of Mount McKinley on a cold day is 20,320 feet above sea level in a zero-degree gale. These two pieces of information appear as

FIGURE A1.1 Making a Graph

myeconlab

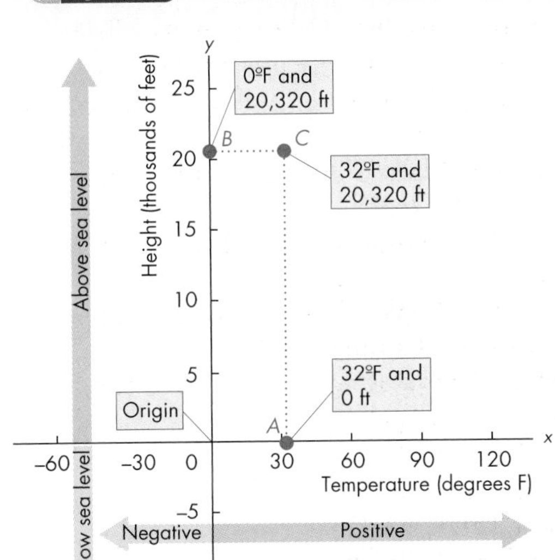

Graphs have axes that measure quantities as distances. Here, the horizontal axis (x-axis) measures temperature, and the vertical axis (y-axis) measures height. Point A represents a fishing boat at sea level (0 on the y-axis) on a day when the temperature is 32°F. Point B represents a climber at the top of Mt. McKinley, 20,320 feet above sea level at a temperature of 0°F. Point C represents a climber at the top of Mt. McKinley, 20,320 feet above sea level at a temperature of 32°F.

point B. On a warmer day, a climber might be at the peak of Mt. McKinley when the temperature is 32 degrees, at point C.

We can draw two lines, called *coordinates*, from point C. One, called the y-coordinate, runs from C to the horizontal axis. Its length is the same as the value marked off on the y-axis. The other, called the x-coordinate, runs from C to the vertical axis. Its length is the same as the value marked off on the x-axis. We describe a point in a graph by the values of its x-coordinate and its y-coordinate.

Graphs like that in Fig. A1.1 can show any type of quantitative data on two variables. Economists use three types of graphs based on the principles in Fig. A1.1 to reveal and describe the relationships among variables. They are

- Time-series graphs
- Cross-section graphs
- Scatter diagrams

Time-Series Graphs

A **time-series graph** measures time (for example, months or years) on the *x*-axis and the variable or variables in which we are interested on the *y*-axis. Figure A1.2 is an example of a time-series graph. It provides some information about the price of gasoline. In this figure, we measure time in years starting in 1973. We measure the price of gasoline (the variable that we are interested in) on the *y*-axis.

The point of a time-series graph is to enable us to visualize how a variable has changed over time and how its value in one period relates to its value in another period.

A time-series graph conveys an enormous amount of information quickly and easily, as this example illustrates. It shows

- The *level* of the price of gasoline—when it is *high* and *low*. When the line is a long way from the *x*-axis, the price is high, as it was, for example, in 1981. When the line is close to the *x*-axis, the price is low, as it was, for example, in 1998.
- How the price *changes*—whether it *rises* or *falls*. When the line slopes upward, as in 1979, the price is rising. When the line slopes downward, as in 1986, the price is falling.
- The *speed* with which the price changes—whether it rises or falls *quickly* or *slowly*. If the line is very steep, then the price rises or falls quickly. If the line is not steep, the price rises or falls slowly. For example, the price rose quickly between 1978 and 1980 and slowly between 1994 and 1996. The price fell quickly between 1985 and 1986 and slowly between 1990 and 1994.

A time-series graph also reveals whether there is a **trend**—a general tendency for a variable to move in one direction. A trend might be upward or downward. In Fig. A1.2, the price of gasoline had a general tendency to fall during the 1980s and 1990s. That is, although the price rose and fell, the general tendency was for it to fall—the price had a downward trend. During the 2000s, the trend has been upward.

A time-series graph also helps us to detect fluctuations in a variable around its trend. You can see some peaks and troughs in the price of gasoline in Fig. A1.2.

Finally, a time-series graph also lets us compare the variable in different periods quickly. Figure A1.2 shows that the 1970s and 1980s were different from the 1990s. The price of gasoline fluctuated more during the 1970s and 1980s than it did in the 1990s.

You can see that a time-series graph conveys a wealth of information. And it does so in much less space than we have used to describe only some of its features. But you do have to "read" the graph to obtain all this information.

FIGURE A1.2 A Time-Series Graph

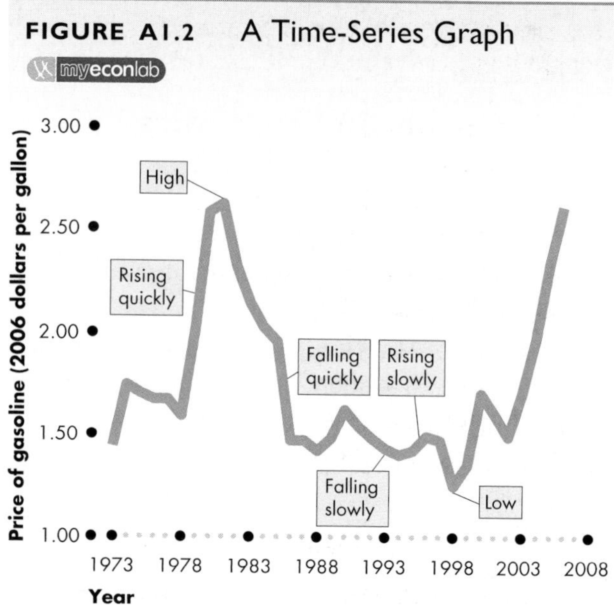

A time-series graph plots the level of a variable on the *y*-axis against time (day, week, month, or year) on the *x*-axis. This graph shows the price of gasoline (in 2006 dollars per gallon) each year from 1973 to 2006. It shows us when the price of gasoline was *high* and when it was *low*, when the price *increased* and when it *decreased*, and when the price changed *quickly* and when it changed *slowly*.

Cross-Section Graphs

A **cross-section graph** shows the values of an economic variable for different groups or categories at a point in time. Figure A1.3, called a *bar chart*, is an example of a cross-section graph.

The bar chart in Fig. A1.3 shows 10 leisure pursuits and the percentage of the U. S. population that participated in them during 2005. The length of each bar indicates the percentage of the population. This figure enables you to compare the popularity of these 10 activities. And you can do so much more quickly and clearly than by looking at a list of numbers.

FIGURE A1.3 A Cross-Section Graph

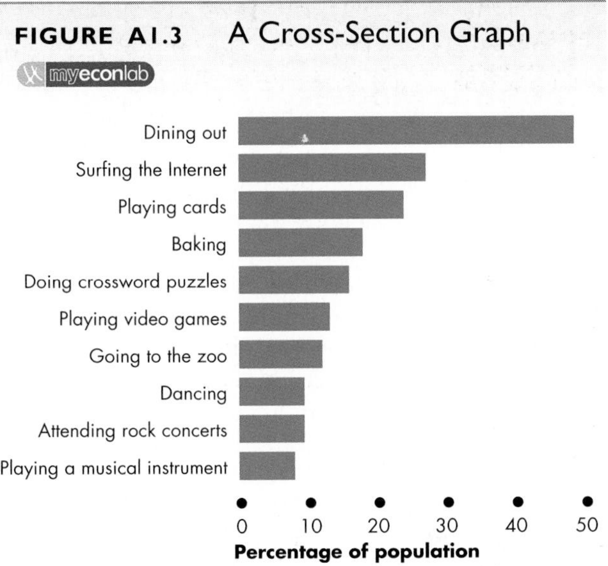

A cross-section graph shows the level of a variable across categories or groups. This bar chart shows 10 popular leisure activities and the percentage of the U.S. population that engages in each of them.

Scatter Diagrams

A **scatter diagram** plots the value of one variable against the value of another variable. Such a graph reveals whether a relationship exists between two variables and describes their relationship. Figure A1.4(a) shows the relationship between expenditure and income. Each point shows expenditure per person and income per person in a given year from 1990 to 2000. The points are "scattered" within the graph. The point labeled *A* tells us that in 1996, income per person was $20,613 and expenditure per person was $18,888. The dots in this graph form a pattern, which reveals that as income increases, expenditure increases.

Figure A1.4(b) shows the relationship between the number of international phone calls and the price of a call. This graph shows that as the price per minute falls, the number of calls increases.

Figure A1.4(c) shows a scatter diagram of inflation and unemployment in the United States. Here, the dots show no clear relationship between these two variables. The dots in this graph reveal that there is no simple relationship between these variables.

FIGURE A1.4 Scatter Diagrams

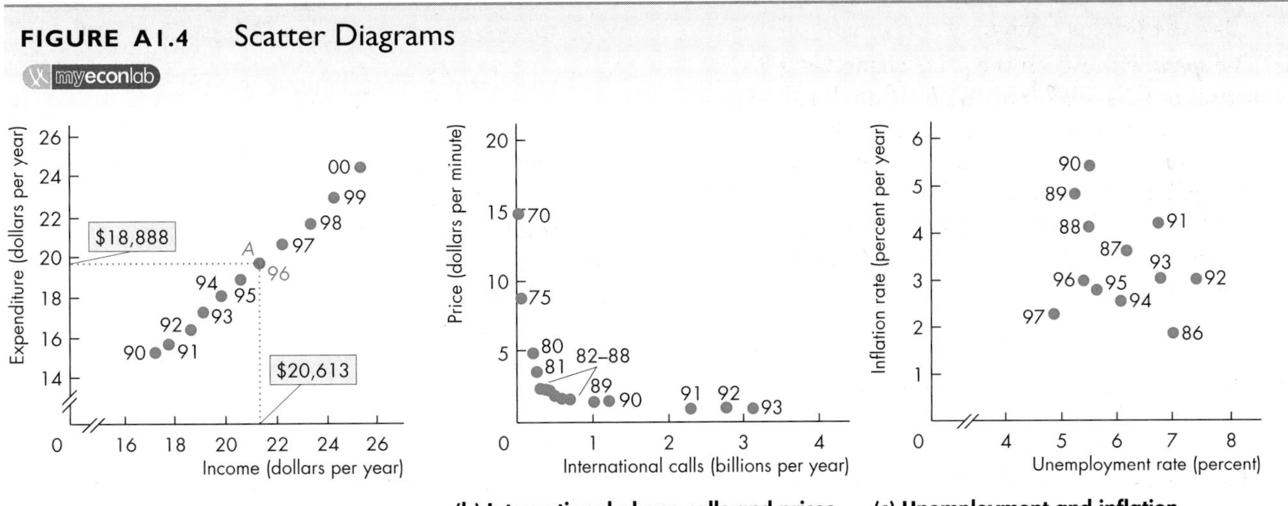

(a) Expenditure and income

(b) International phone calls and prices

(c) Unemployment and inflation

A scatter diagram reveals the relationship between two variables. Part (a) shows the relationship between expenditure and income. Each point shows the values of the two variables in a specific year. For example, point *A* shows that in 1996, average income was $20,613 and average expenditure was $18,888. The pattern formed by the points shows that as income increases, expenditure increases.

Part (b) shows the relationship between the price of an international phone call and the number of calls made. This graph shows that as the price of a phone call falls, the number of calls made increases. Part (c) shows a scatter diagram of the inflation rate and unemployment rate in the United States. This graph shows that inflation and unemployment are not closely related.

Breaks in the Axes Two of the graphs you've just looked at, Fig. A1.4(a) and Fig. A1.4(c), have breaks in their axes, as shown by the small gaps. The breaks indicate that there are jumps from the origin, 0, to the first values recorded.

In Fig. A1.4(a), the breaks are used because the lowest value of expenditure exceeds $14,000 and the lowest value of income exceeds $16,000. With no breaks in the axes, there would be a lot of empty space, all the points would be crowded into the top right corner, and we would not be able to see whether a relationship exists between these two variables. By breaking the axes, we are able to bring the relationship into view.

Putting a break in the axes is like using a zoom lens to bring the relationship into the center of the graph and magnify it so that the relationship fills the graph.

Misleading Graphs Breaks can be used to highlight a relationship. But they can also be used to mislead—to make a graph that lies. The most common way of making a graph lie is to use axis breaks and to either stretch or compress a scale. For example, suppose that in Fig. A1.4(a), the *y*-axis that measures expenditure ran from zero to $45,000 while the *x*-axis was the same as the one shown. The graph would now create the impression that despite a huge increase in income, expenditure had barely changed.

To avoid being misled, it is a good idea to get into the habit of always looking closely at the values and the labels on the axes of a graph before you start to interpret it.

Correlation and Causation A scatter diagram that shows a clear relationship between two variables, such as Fig. A1.4(a) or Fig. A1.4(b), tells us that the two variables have a high correlation. When a high correlation is present, we can predict the value of one variable from the value of the other variable. But correlation does not imply causation.

Sometimes a high correlation is a coincidence, but sometimes it does arise from a causal relationship. It is likely, for example, that rising income causes rising expenditure (Fig. A1.4a) and that the falling price of a phone call causes more calls to be made (Fig. A1.4b).

You've now seen how we can use graphs in economics to show economic data and to reveal relationships. Next, we'll learn how economists use graphs to construct and display economic models.

Graphs Used in Economic Models

The graphs used in economics are not always designed to show real-world data. Often they are used to show general relationships among the variables in an economic model.

An *economic model* is a stripped-down, simplified description of an economy or of a component of an economy such as a business or a household. It consists of statements about economic behavior that can be expressed as equations or as curves in a graph. Economists use models to explore the effects of different policies or other influences on the economy in ways that are similar to the use of model airplanes in wind tunnels and models of the climate.

You will encounter many different kinds of graphs in economic models, but there are some repeating patterns. Once you've learned to recognize these patterns, you will instantly understand the meaning of a graph. Here, we'll look at the different types of curves that are used in economic models, and we'll see some everyday examples of each type of curve. The patterns to look for in graphs are the four cases in which

- Variables move in the same direction.
- Variables move in opposite directions.
- Variables have a maximum or a minimum.
- Variables are unrelated.

Let's look at these four cases.

Variables That Move in the Same Direction

Figure A1.5 shows graphs of the relationships between two variables that move up and down together. A relationship between two variables that move in the same direction is called a **positive relationship** or a **direct relationship.** A line that slopes upward shows such a relationship.

Figure A1.5 shows three types of relationships, one that has a straight line and two that have curved lines. But all the lines in these three graphs are called curves. Any line on a graph—no matter whether it is straight or curved—is called a *curve.*

A relationship shown by a straight line is called a **linear relationship.** Figure A1.5(a) shows a linear

FIGURE A1.5 Positive (Direct) Relationships

myeconlab

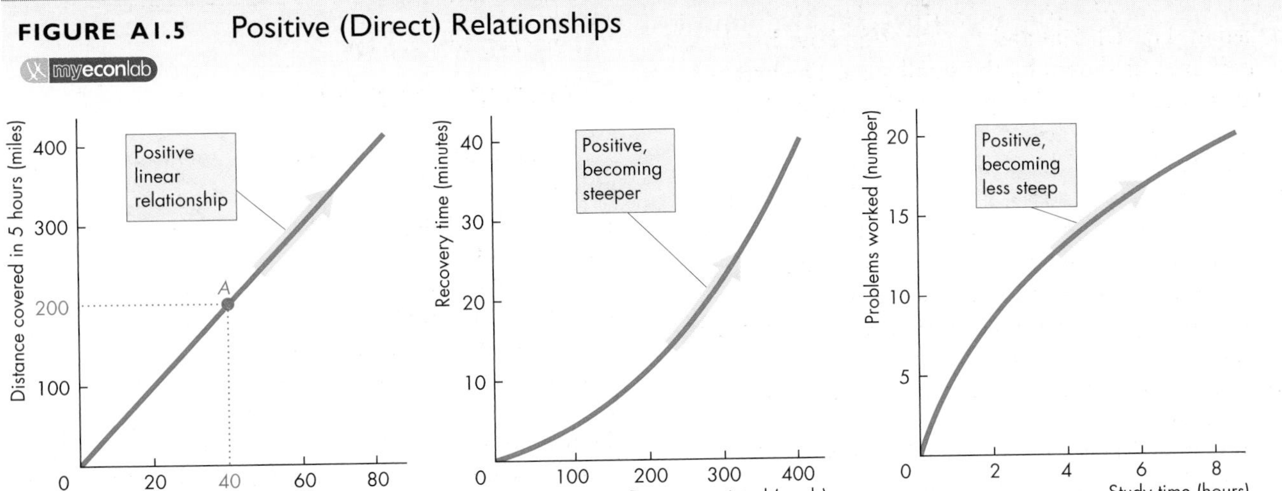

(a) Positive linear relationship **(b) Positive, becoming steeper** **(c) Positive, becoming less steep**

Each part of this figure shows a positive (direct) relationship between two variables. That is, as the value of the variable measured on the *x*-axis increases, so does the value of the variable measured on the *y*-axis. Part (a) shows a linear relationship—as the two variables increase together, we move along a straight line. Part (b) shows a positive relationship such that as the two variables increase together, we move along a curve that becomes steeper. Part (c) shows a positive relationship such that as the two variables increase together, we move along a curve that becomes flatter.

relationship between the number of miles traveled in 5 hours and speed. For example, point *A* shows that we will travel 200 miles in 5 hours if our speed is 40 miles an hour. If we double our speed to 80 miles an hour, we will travel 400 miles in 5 hours.

Figure A1.5(b) shows the relationship between distance sprinted and recovery time (the time it takes the heart rate to return to its normal resting rate). This relationship is an upward-sloping one that starts out quite flat but then becomes steeper as we move along the curve away from the origin. The reason this curve slopes upward and becomes steeper is because the additional recovery time needed from sprinting an additional 100 yards increases. It takes less than 5 minutes to recover from sprinting 100 yards but more than 10 minutes to recover from sprinting 200 yards.

Figure A1.5(c) shows the relationship between the number of problems worked by a student and the amount of study time. This relationship is an upward-sloping one that starts out quite steep and becomes flatter as we move away from the origin. Study time becomes less productive as the student spends more hours studying and becomes more tired.

Variables That Move in Opposite Directions

Figure A1.6 shows relationships between things that move in opposite directions. A relationship between variables that move in opposite directions is called a **negative relationship** or an **inverse relationship**.

Figure A1.6(a) shows the relationship between the number of hours available for playing squash and the number of hours for playing tennis when the total is 5 hours. One extra hour spent playing tennis means one hour less playing squash and vice versa. This relationship is negative and linear.

Figure A1.6(b) shows the relationship between the cost per mile traveled and the length of a journey. The longer the journey, the lower is the cost per mile. But as the journey length increases, even though the cost per mile decreases, the fall in the cost is smaller the longer the journey. This feature of the relationship is shown by the fact that the curve slopes downward, starting out steep at a short journey length and then becoming flatter as the journey length increases. This relationship arises because some of the costs are fixed, such as auto insurance, and the fixed costs are spread over a longer journey.

FIGURE A1.6 Negative (Inverse) Relationships

myeconlab

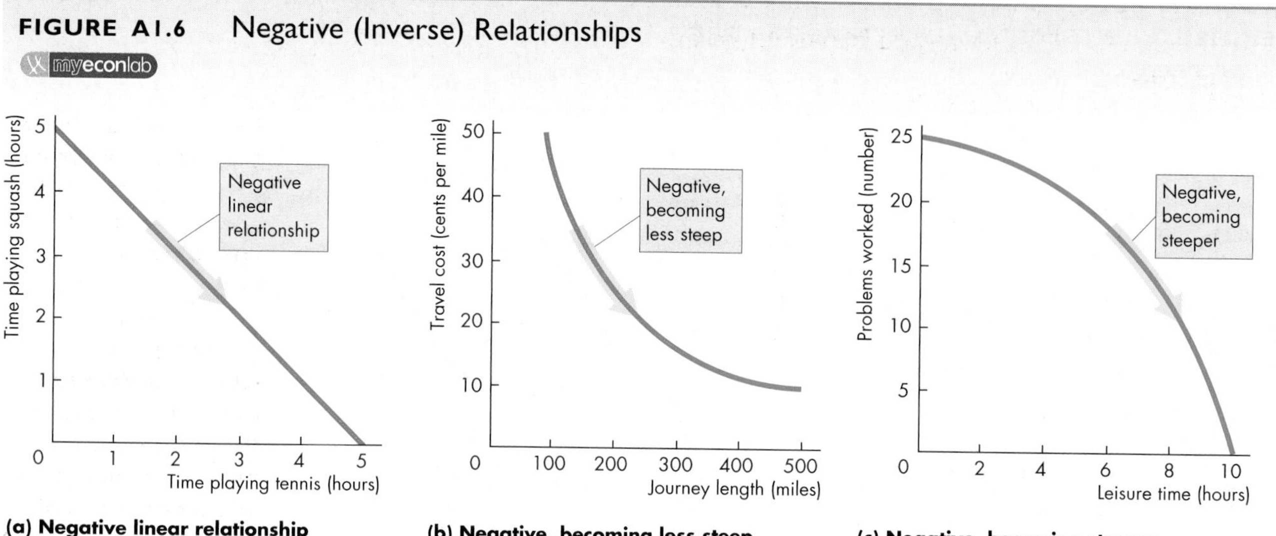

(a) Negative linear relationship

(b) Negative, becoming less steep

(c) Negative, becoming steeper

Each part of this figure shows a negative (inverse) relationship between two variables. That is, as the value of the variable measured on the *x*-axis increases, the value of the variable measured on the *y*-axis decreases. Part (a) shows a linear relationship. The total time spent playing tennis and squash is 5 hours. As the time spent playing tennis increases, the time spent playing squash decreases, and we move along a straight line. Part (b) shows a negative relationship such that as the journey length increases, the travel cost decreases as we move along a curve that becomes less steep. Part (c) shows a negative relationship such that as leisure time increases, the number of problems worked decreases as we move along a curve that becomes steeper.

Figure A1.6(c) shows the relationship between the amount of leisure time and the number of problems worked by a student. Increasing leisure time produces an increasingly large reduction in the number of problems worked. This relationship is a negative one that starts out with a gentle slope at a small number of leisure hours and becomes steeper as the number of leisure hours increases. This relationship is a different view of the idea shown in Fig. A1.5(c).

Variables That Have a Maximum or a Minimum

Many relationships in economic models have a maximum or a minimum. For example, firms try to make the maximum possible profit and to produce at the lowest possible cost. Figure A1.7 shows relationships that have a maximum or a minimum.

Figure A1.7(a) shows the relationship between rainfall and wheat yield. When there is no rainfall, wheat will not grow, so the yield is zero. As the rainfall increases up to 10 days a month, the wheat yield increases. With 10 rainy days each month, the wheat yield reaches its maximum at 40 bushels an acre (point *A*). Rain in excess of 10 days a month starts to lower the yield of wheat. If every day is rainy, the wheat suffers from a lack of sunshine and the yield decreases to zero. This relationship is one that starts out sloping upward, reaches a maximum, and then slopes downward.

Figure A1.7(b) shows the reverse case—a relationship that begins sloping downward, falls to a minimum, and then slopes upward. Most economic costs are like this relationship. An example is the relationship between the cost per mile and speed for a car trip. At low speeds, the car is creeping in a traffic snarl-up. The number of miles per gallon is low, so the cost per mile is high. At high speeds, the car is traveling faster than its efficient speed, using a large quantity of gasoline, and again the number of miles per gallon is low and the cost per mile is high. At a speed of 55 miles an hour, the cost per mile is at its minimum (point *B*). This relationship is one that starts out sloping downward, reaches a minimum, and then slopes upward.

FIGURE A1.7 Maximum and Minimum Points

myeconlab

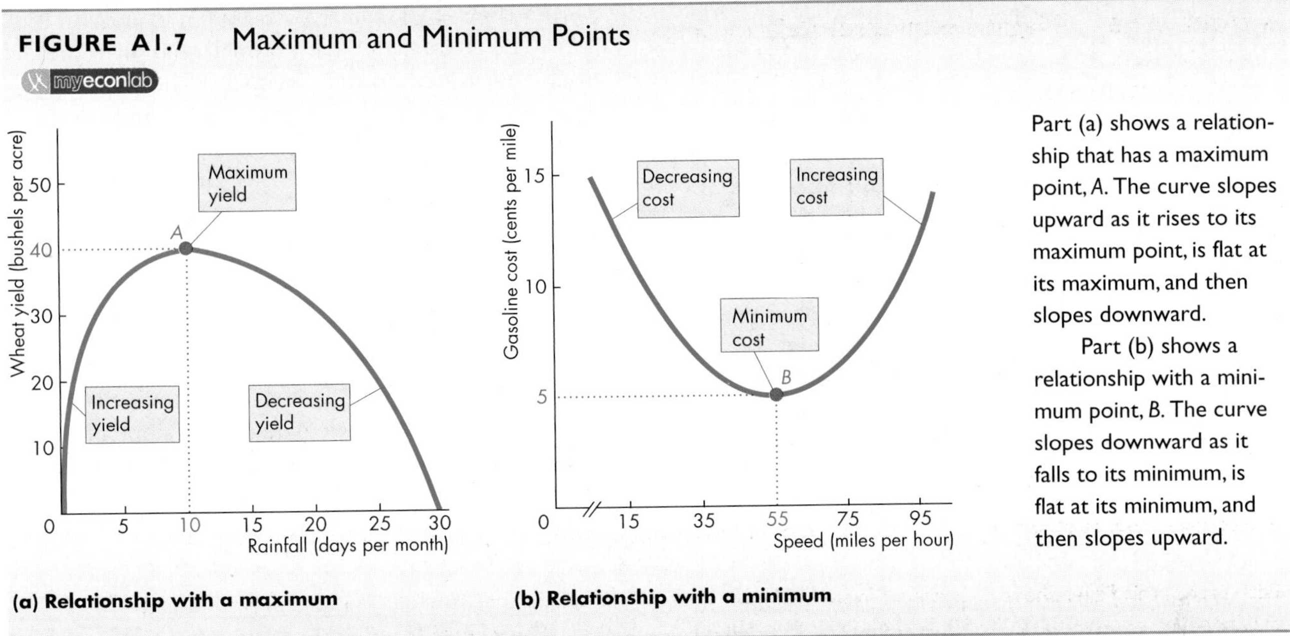

(a) Relationship with a maximum

(b) Relationship with a minimum

Part (a) shows a relationship that has a maximum point, *A*. The curve slopes upward as it rises to its maximum point, is flat at its maximum, and then slopes downward.

Part (b) shows a relationship with a minimum point, *B*. The curve slopes downward as it falls to its minimum, is flat at its minimum, and then slopes upward.

Variables That Are Unrelated

There are many situations in which no matter what happens to the value of one variable, the other variable remains constant. Sometimes we want to show the independence between two variables in a graph, and Fig. A1.8 shows two ways of achieving this.

In describing the graphs in Fig. A1.5 through A1.7, we have talked about curves that slope upward or slope downward, and curves that become less steep or steeper. Let's spend a little time discussing exactly what we mean by slope and how we measure the slope of a curve.

FIGURE A1.8 Variables That Are Unrelated

myeconlab

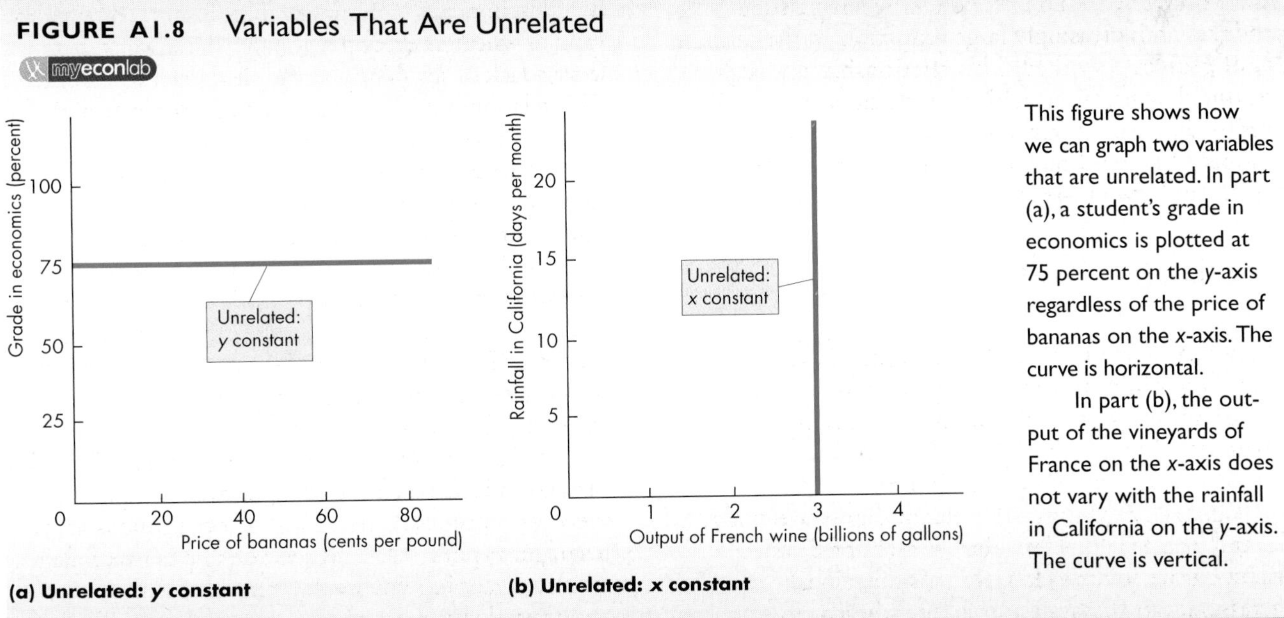

(a) Unrelated: *y* constant

(b) Unrelated: *x* constant

This figure shows how we can graph two variables that are unrelated. In part (a), a student's grade in economics is plotted at 75 percent on the *y*-axis regardless of the price of bananas on the *x*-axis. The curve is horizontal.

In part (b), the output of the vineyards of France on the *x*-axis does not vary with the rainfall in California on the *y*-axis. The curve is vertical.

The Slope of a Relationship

We can measure the influence of one variable on another by the slope of the relationship. The **slope** of a relationship is the change in the value of the variable measured on the *y*-axis divided by the change in the value of the variable measured on the *x*-axis. We use the Greek letter Δ (*delta*) to represent "change in." Thus Δy means the change in the value of the variable measured on the *y*-axis, and Δx means the change in the value of the variable measured on the *x*-axis. Therefore the slope of the relationship is

$$\Delta y / \Delta x.$$

If a large change in the variable measured on the *y*-axis (Δy) is associated with a small change in the variable measured on the *x*-axis (Δx), the slope is large and the curve is steep. If a small change in the variable measured on the *y*-axis (Δy) is associated with a large change in the variable measured on the *x*-axis (Δx), the slope is small and the curve is flat.

We can make the idea of slope clearer by doing some calculations.

The Slope of a Straight Line

The slope of a straight line is the same regardless of where on the line you calculate it. The slope of a straight line is constant. Let's calculate the slopes of the lines in Fig. A1.9. In part (a), when x increases from 2 to 6, y increases from 3 to 6. The change in

FIGURE A1.9 The Slope of a Straight Line

myeconlab

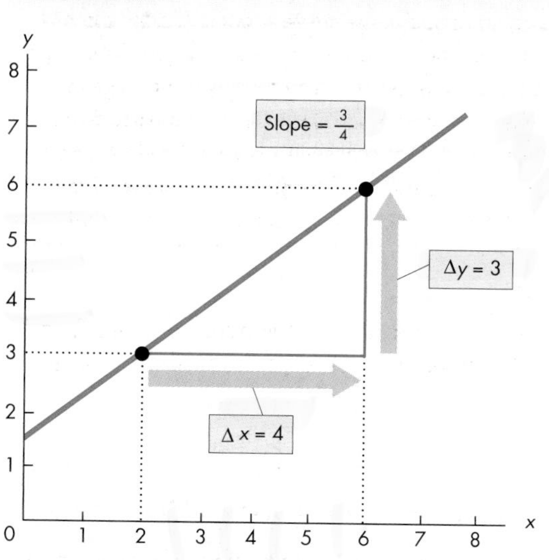

(a) Positive slope

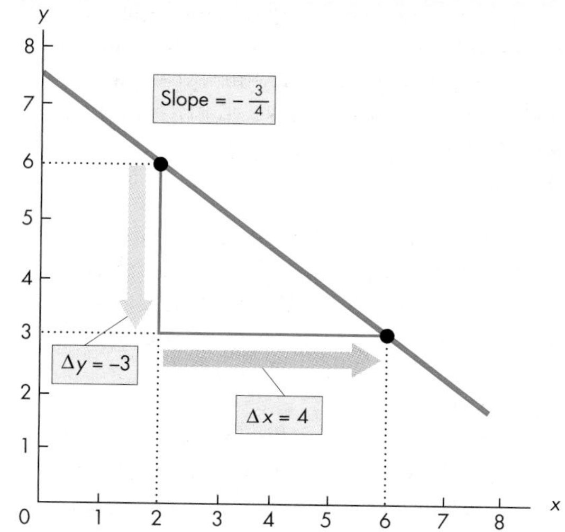

(b) Negative slope

To calculate the slope of a straight line, we divide the change in the value of the variable measured on the *y*-axis (Δy) by the change in the value of the variable measured on the *x*-axis (Δx), as we move along the curve. Part (a) shows the calculation of a positive slope. When x increases from 2 to 6, Δx equals 4. That change in x brings about an increase in y from 3 to 6, so Δy equals 3. The slope ($\Delta y/\Delta x$) equals 3/4. Part (b) shows the calculation of a negative slope. When x increases from 2 to 6, Δx equals 4. That increase in x brings about a decrease in y from 6 to 3, so Δy equals –3. The slope ($\Delta y/\Delta x$) equals –3/4.

x is +4—that is, Δx is 4. The change in y is +3—that is, Δy is 3. The slope of that line is

$$\frac{\Delta y}{\Delta x} = \frac{3}{4}.$$

In part (b), when x increases from 2 to 6, y decreases from 6 to 3. The change in y is *minus* 3—that is, Δy is –3. The change in x is *plus* 4—that is, Δx is 4. The slope of the curve is

$$\frac{\Delta y}{\Delta x} = \frac{-3}{4}.$$

Notice that the two slopes have the same magnitude (3/4) but the slope of the line in part (a) is positive (+3/+4 = 3/4), while that in part (b) is negative (–3/+4 = 3/4). The slope of a positive relationship is positive; the slope of a negative relationship is negative.

The Slope of a Curved Line

The slope of a curved line is trickier. The slope of a curved line is not constant, so the slope depends on where on the curved line we calculate it. There are two ways to calculate the slope of a curved line: You can calculate the slope at a point, or you can calculate the slope across an arc of the curve. Let's look at the two alternatives.

Slope at a Point To calculate the slope at a point on a curve, you need to construct a straight line that has the same slope as the curve at the point in question. Figure A1.10 shows how this is done. Suppose you want to calculate the slope of the curve at point A. Place a ruler on the graph so that it touches point A and no other point on the curve, then draw a straight line along the edge of the ruler. The straight red line is this line, and it is the tangent to the curve at point A. If the ruler touches the curve only at point A, then the slope of the curve at point A must be the same as the slope of the edge of the ruler. If the curve and the ruler do not have the same slope, the line along the edge of the ruler will cut the curve instead of just touching it.

Now that you have found a straight line with the same slope as the curve at point A, you can calculate the slope of the curve at point A by calculating the slope of the straight line. Along the straight line, as x increases from 0 to 4 ($\Delta x = 4$) y increases from 2 to 5 ($\Delta y = 3$). Therefore the slope of the straight line is

FIGURE A1.10 Slope at a Point

myeconlab

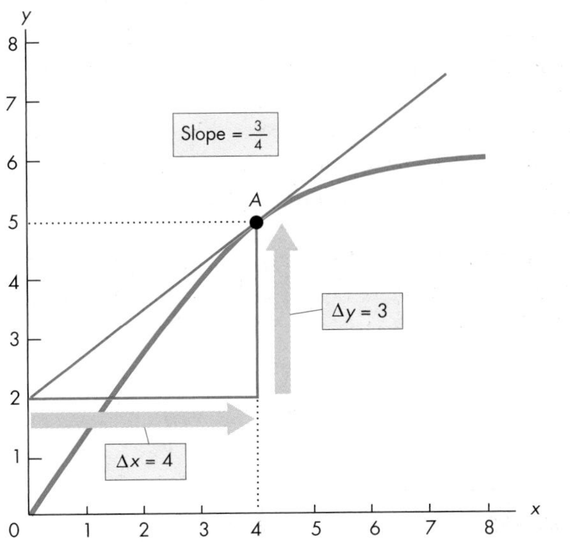

To calculate the slope of the curve at point A, draw the red line that just touches the curve at A—the tangent. The slope of this straight line is calculated by dividing the change in y by the change in x along the line. When x increases from 0 to 4, Δx equals 4. That change in x is associated with an increase in y from 2 to 5, so Δy equals 3. The slope of the red line is 3/4. So the slope of the curve at point A is 3/4.

$$\frac{\Delta y}{\Delta x} = \frac{3}{4}.$$

So the slope of the curve at point A is 3/4.

Slope Across an Arc An arc of a curve is a piece of a curve. In Fig. A1.11, you are looking at the same curve as in Fig. A1.10. But instead of calculating the slope at point A, we are going to calculate the slope across the arc from B to C. You can see that the slope at B is greater than at C. When we calculate the slope across an arc, we are calculating the average slope between two points. As we move along the arc from B to C, x increases from 3 to 5 and y increases from 4 to 5.5. The change in x is 2 ($\Delta x = 2$), and the change

FIGURE A1.11 Slope Across an Arc

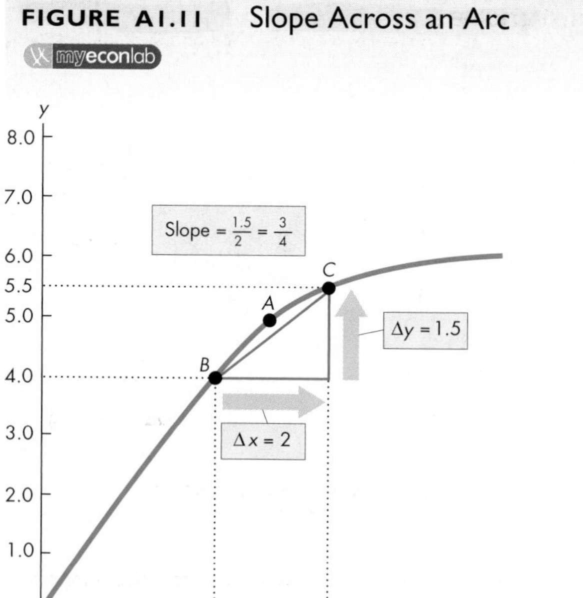

To calculate the average slope of the curve along the arc *BC*, draw a straight line from *B* to *C*. The slope of the line *BC* is calculated by dividing the change in *y* by the change in *x*. In moving from *B* to *C*, Δx equals 2 and Δy equals 1.5. The slope of the line *BC* is 1.5 divided by 2, or 3/4. So the slope of the curve across the arc *BC* is 3/4.

in y is 1.5 ($\Delta y = 1.5$). Therefore the slope is

$$\frac{\Delta y}{\Delta x} = \frac{1.5}{2} = \frac{3}{4}.$$

So the slope of the curve across the arc *BC* is 3/4.

This calculation gives us the slope of the curve between points *B* and *C*. The actual slope calculated is the slope of the straight line from *B* to *C*. This slope approximates the average slope of the curve along the arc *BC*. In this particular example, the slope across the arc *BC* is identical to the slope of the curve at point *A*. But the calculation of the slope of a curve does not always work out so neatly. You might have some fun constructing some more examples and some counterexamples.

You now know how to make and interpret a graph. But so far, we've limited our attention to graphs of two variables. We're now going to learn how to graph more than two variables.

Graphing Relationships Among More Than Two Variables

We have seen that we can graph the relationship between two variables as a point formed by the *x*- and *y*-coordinates in a two-dimensional graph. You might be thinking that although a two-dimensional graph is informative, most of the things in which you are likely to be interested involve relationships among many variables, not just two. For example, the amount of ice cream consumed depends on the price of ice cream and the temperature. If ice cream is expensive and the temperature is low, people eat much less ice cream than when ice cream is inexpensive and the temperature is high. For any given price of ice cream, the quantity consumed varies with the temperature; and for any given temperature, the quantity of ice cream consumed varies with its price.

Figure A1.12 shows a relationship among three variables. The table shows the number of gallons of ice cream consumed each day at various temperatures and ice cream prices. How can we graph these numbers?

To graph a relationship that involves more than two variables, we use the *ceteris paribus* assumption.

Ceteris Paribus We noted in the chapter (see p. 13) that every laboratory experiment is an attempt to create *ceteris paribus* and isolate the relationship of interest. We use the same method to make a graph when more than two variables are involved.

Figure A1.12(a) shows an example. There, you can see what happens to the quantity of ice cream consumed when the price of ice cream varies when the temperature is held constant. The line labeled 70°F shows the relationship between ice cream consumption and the price of ice cream if the temperature remains at 70°F. The numbers used to plot that line are those in the third column of the table in Fig. A1.12. For example, if the temperature is 70°F, 10 gallons are consumed when the price is 60¢ a scoop, and 18 gallons are consumed when the price is 30¢ a scoop. The curve labeled 90°F shows consumption as the price varies if the temperature remains at 90°F.

We can also show the relationship between ice cream consumption and temperature when the price of ice cream remains constant, as shown in

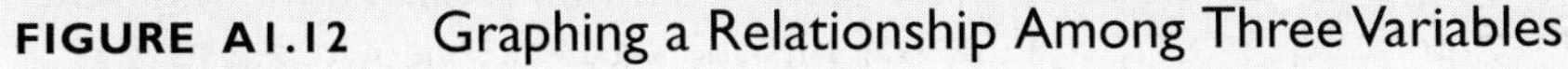

FIGURE A1.12 Graphing a Relationship Among Three Variables

myeconlab

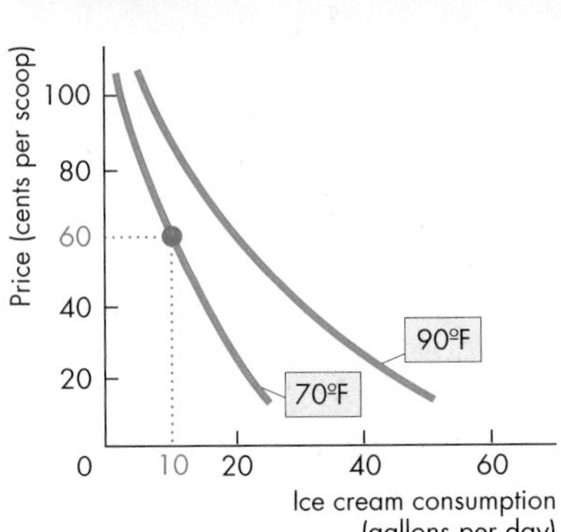

(a) Price and consumption at a given temperature

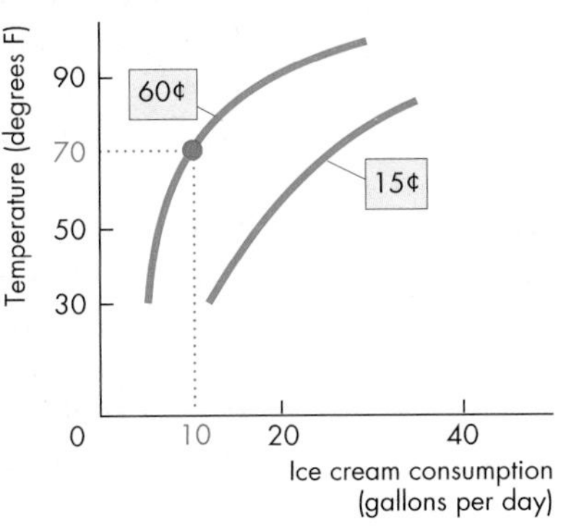

(b) Temperature and consumption at a given price

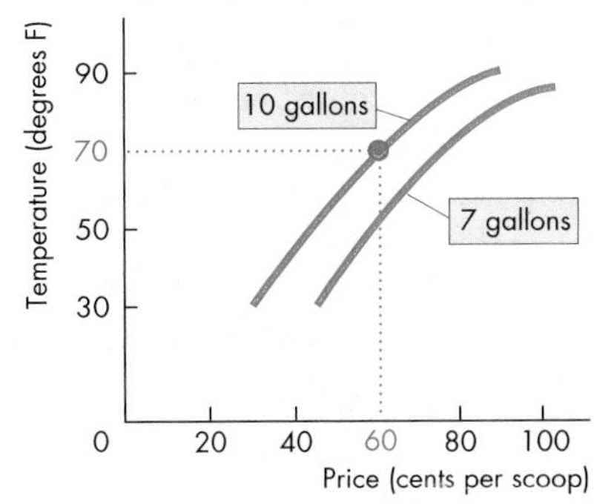

(c) Temperature and price at a given consumption

Price (cents per scoop)	**Ice cream consumption** (gallons per day)			
	30°F	**50°F**	**70°F**	**90°F**
15	12	18	25	50
30	10	12	18	37
45	7	10	13	27
60	5	7	10	20
75	3	5	7	14
90	2	3	5	10
105	1	2	3	6

Ice cream consumption depends on its price and the temperature. The table tell us how many gallons of ice cream are consumed each day at different prices and different temperatures. For example, if the price is 60¢ a scoop and the temperature is 70°F, 10 gallons of ice cream are consumed. This set of values is highlighted in the table and each part of the figure.

To graph a relationship among three variables, the value of one variable is held constant. Part (a) shows the relationship between price and consumption when temperature is held constant. One curve holds temperature at 90°F and the other holds it at 70°F. Part (b) shows the relationship between temperature and consumption when price is held constant. One curve holds the price at 60¢ a scoop and the other holds it at 15¢ a scoop. Part (c) shows the relationship between temperature and price when consumption is held constant. One curve holds consumption at 10 gallons and the other holds it at 7 gallons.

Fig. A1.12(b). The curve labeled 60¢ shows how the consumption of ice cream varies with the temperature when the price of ice cream is 60¢ a scoop, and a second curve shows the relationship when the price is 15¢ a scoop. For example, at 60¢ a scoop, 10 gallons are consumed when the temperature is 70°F and 20 gallons when the temperature is 90°F.

Figure A1.12(c) shows the combinations of temperature and price that result in a constant consumption of ice cream. One curve shows the combinations that result in 10 gallons a day being consumed, and the other shows the combinations that result in 7 gallons a day being consumed. A high price and a high temperature lead to the same consumption as a lower price and a lower temperature. For example, 10 gallons of ice cream are consumed at 70°F and 60¢ a scoop, at 90°F and 90¢ a scoop, and at 50°F and 45¢ a scoop.

◆ With what you have learned about graphs, you can move forward with your study of economics. There are no graphs in this book that are more complicated than those that have been explained in this appendix.

Mathematical Note:
Equations of Straight Lines

If a straight line in a graph describes the relationship between two variables, we call it a linear relationship. Figure 1 shows the *linear relationship* between a person's expenditure and income. This person spends \$100 a week (by borrowing or spending previous savings) when income is zero. And out of each dollar earned, this person spends 50 cents (and saves 50 cents).

All linear relationships are described by the same general equation. We call the quantity that is measured on the horizontal axis (or x-axis) x, and we call the quantity that is measured on the vertical axis (or y-axis) y. In the case of Fig. 1, x is income and y is expenditure.

A Linear Equation

The equation that describes a straight-line relationship between x and y is

$$y = a + bx.$$

In this equation, a and b are fixed numbers and they are called constants. The values of x and y vary so these numbers are called variables. Because the equation describes a straight line, the equation is called a *linear equation.*

The equation tells us that when the value of x is zero, the value of y is a. We call the constant a the y-axis intercept. The reason is that on the graph the straight line hits the y-axis at a value equal to a. Figure 1 illustrates the y-axis intercept.

For positive values of x, the value of y exceeds a. The constant b tells us by how much y increases above a as x increases. The constant b is the slope of the line.

Slope of Line

As we explain in the chapter, the *slope* of a relationship is the change in the value of y divided by the change in the value of x. We use the Greek letter Δ (delta) to represent "change in." So Δy means the change in the value of the variable measured on the y-axis, and Δx means the change in the value of the variable measured on the x-axis. Therefore the slope of the relationship is

$$\Delta y / \Delta x.$$

To see why the slope is b, suppose that initially the value of x is x_1, or \$200 in Fig. 2. The corresponding value of y is y_1, also \$200 in Fig. 2. The equation of the line tells us that

$$y_1 = a + bx_1. \tag{1}$$

Now the value of x increases by Δx to $x_1 + \Delta x$ (or \$400 in Fig. 2). And the value of y increases by Δy to $y_1 + \Delta y$ (or \$300 in Fig. 2).

The equation of the line now tells us that

$$y_1 + \Delta y = a + b(x_1 + \Delta x) \tag{2}$$

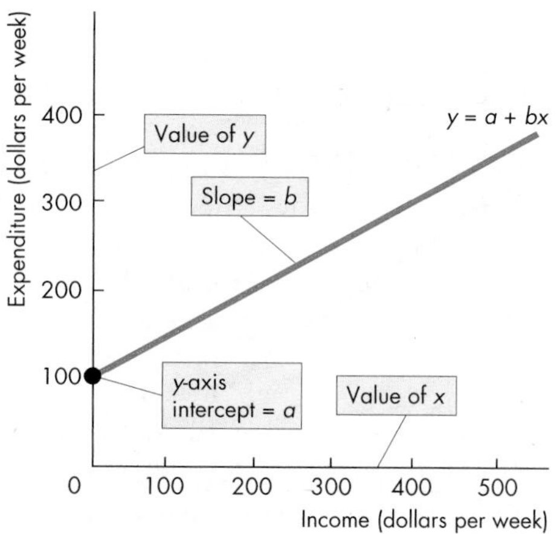

Figure 1 Linear relationship

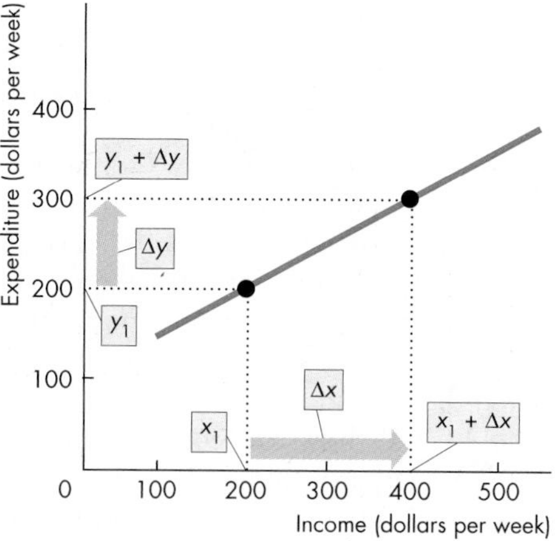

Figure 2 Calculating slope

To calculate the slope of the line, subtract equation (1) from equation (2) to obtain

$$\Delta y = b\Delta x \qquad (3)$$

and now divide equation (3) by Δx to obtain

$$\Delta y/\Delta x = b.$$

So the slope of the line is b.

Position of Line

The y-axis intercept determines the position of the line on the graph. Figure 3 illustrates the relationship between the y-axis intercept and the position of the line on the graph. In this graph, the y-axis measures saving and the x-axis measures income.

When the y-axis intercept, a, is positive, the line hits the y-axis at a positive value of y—as the blue line does. Its y-axis intercept is 100. When the y-axis intercept, a, is zero, the line hits the y-axis at the origin—as the purple line does. Its y-axis intercept is 0. When the y-axis intercept, a, is negative, the line hits the y-axis at a negative value of y—as the red line does. Its y-axis intercept is –100.

As the equations of the three lines show, the value of the y-axis intercept does not influence the slope of the line. All three lines have a slope equal to 0.5.

Positive Relationships

Figure 1 shows a positive relationship—the two variables x and y move in the same direction. All positive relationships have a slope that is positive. In the equation of the line, the constant b is positive. In this example, the y-axis intercept, a, is 100. The slope b equals $\Delta y/\Delta x$, which is 100/200 or 0.5. The equation of the line is

$$y = 100 + 0.5x.$$

Negative Relationships

Figure 4 shows a negative relationship—the two variables x and y move in the opposite direction. All negative relationships have a slope that is negative. In the equation of the line, the constant b is negative. In the example in Fig. 4, the y-axis intercept, a, is 30. The slope, b, equals $\Delta y/\Delta x$, which is –20/2 or –10. The equation of the line is

$$y = 30 + (-10)x$$

or

$$y = 30 - 10x.$$

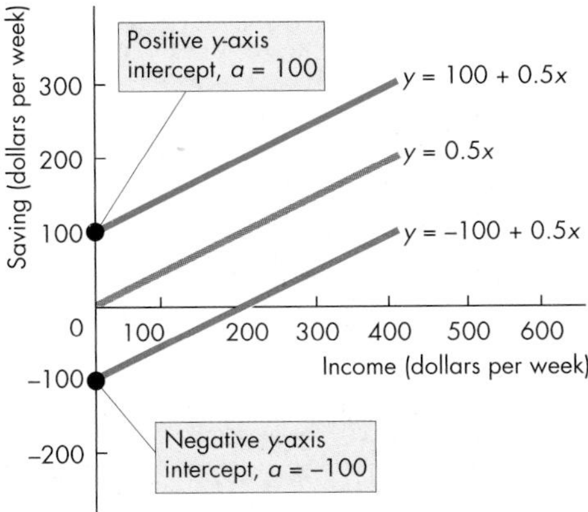

Figure 3 The *y*-axis intercept

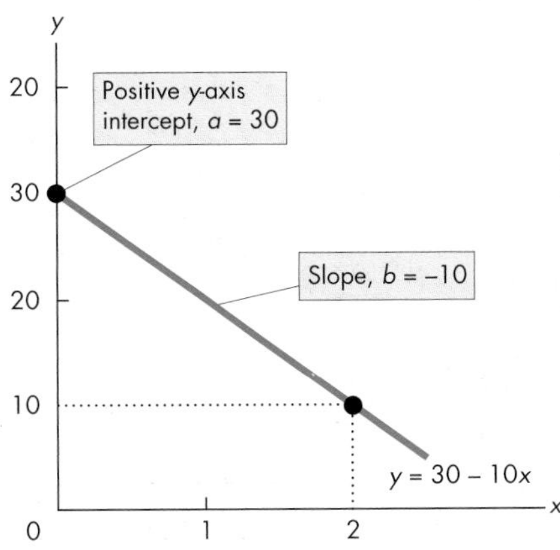

Figure 4 Negative relationship

SUMMARY

Key Points

Graphing Data (pp. 17–20)

- A time-series graph shows the trend and fluctuations in a variable over time.
- A cross-section graph shows how variables change across the members of a population.
- A scatter diagram shows the relationship between two variables. It shows whether two variables are positively related, negatively related, or unrelated.

Graphs Used in Economic Models (pp. 20–23)

- Graphs are used to show relationships among variables in economic models.
- Relationships can be positive (an upward-sloping curve), negative (a downward-sloping curve), positive and then negative (have a maximum point), negative and then positive (have a minimum point), or unrelated (a horizontal or vertical curve).

The Slope of a Relationship (pp. 24–26)

- The slope of a relationship is calculated as the change in the value of the variable measured on the y-axis divided by the change in the value of the variable measured on the x-axis—that is, $\Delta y/\Delta x$.
- A straight line has a constant slope.
- A curved line has a varying slope. To calculate the slope of a curved line, we calculate the slope at a point or across an arc.

Graphing Relationships Among More Than Two Variables (pp. 26–27)

- To graph a relationship among more than two variables, we hold constant the values of all the variables except two.
- We then plot the value of one of the variables against the value of another.

Key Figures

Key Terms

Cross-section graph, 18
Direct relationship, 20
Inverse relationship, 21
Linear relationship, 20
Negative relationship, 21
Positive relationship, 20
Scatter diagram, 19
Slope, 24
Time-series graph, 18
Trend, 18

REVIEW QUIZ

1. What are the three types of graphs used to show economic data?
2. Give an example of a time-series graph.
3. List three things that a time-series graph shows quickly and easily.
4. Give three examples, different from those in the chapter, of scatter diagrams that show a positive relationship, a negative relationship, and no relationship.
5. Draw some graphs to show the relationships between two variables
   a. That move in the same direction.
   b. That move in opposite directions.
   c. That have a maximum.
   d. That have a minimum.
6. Which of the relationships in question 5 is a positive relationship and which a negative relationship?
7. What are the two ways of calculating the slope of a curved line?
8. How do we graph a relationship among more than two variables?

myeconlab **Study Plan 1.A**

PROBLEMS

myeconlab **Tests, Study Plan, Solutions***

The spreadsheet provides data on the U.S. economy: Column A is the year, column B is the inflation rate, column C is the interest rate, column D is the growth rate, and column E is the unemployment rate. Use this spreadsheet to answer problems 1, 2, 3, and 4.

	A	B	C	D	E
1	1995	2.8	7.6	2.5	5.6
2	1996	2.9	7.4	3.7	5.4
3	1997	2.3	7.3	4.5	4.9
4	1998	1.6	6.5	4.2	4.5
5	1999	2.2	7.0	4.4	4.2
6	2000	3.4	7.6	3.7	4.0
7	2001	2.8	7.1	0.8	4.7
8	2002	1.6	6.5	1.6	5.8
9	2003	2.3	5.7	2.7	6.0
10	2004	2.7	5.6	4.2	5.5
11	2005	3.4	5.2	3.5	5.1

1. a. Draw a time-series graph of the inflation rate.
   b. In which year(s) (i) was inflation highest, (ii) was inflation lowest, (iii) did it increase, (iv) did it decrease, (v) did it increase most, and (vi) did it decrease most?
   c. What was the main trend in inflation?
2. a. Draw a time-series graph of the interest rate.
   b. In which year(s) (i) was the interest rate highest, (ii) was the interest rate lowest, (iii) did it increase, (iv) did it decrease, (v) did it increase most, and (vi) did it decrease most.
   c. What was the main trend in the interest rate?
3. Draw a scatter diagram to show the relationship between the inflation rate and the interest rate. Describe the relationship.
4. Draw a scatter diagram to show the relationship between the growth rate and the unemployment rate. Describe the relationship.
5. Draw a graph to show the relationship between the two variables x and y:

x	0	1	2	3	4	5	6	7	8
y	0	1	4	9	16	25	36	49	64

   a. Is the relationship positive or negative?
   b. Does the slope of the relationship increase or decrease as the value of x increases?
   c. Think of some economic relationships that might be similar to this one.
6. Draw a graph that shows the relationship between the two variables x and y:

x	0	1	2	3	4	5
y	25	24	22	16	8	0

   a. Is the relationship positive or negative?
   b. Does the slope of the relationship increase or decrease as the value of x increases?
   c. Think of some economic relationships that might be similar to this one.
7. In problem 5, calculate the slope of the relationship between x and y when x equals 4.
8. In problem 6, calculate the slope of the relationship between x and y when x equals 3.
9. In problem 5, calculate the slope of the relationship across the arc when x increases from 3 to 4.
10. In problem 6, calculate the slope of the relationship across the arc when x increases from 4 to 5.
11. Calculate the slope of the relationship shown at point A in the following figure.

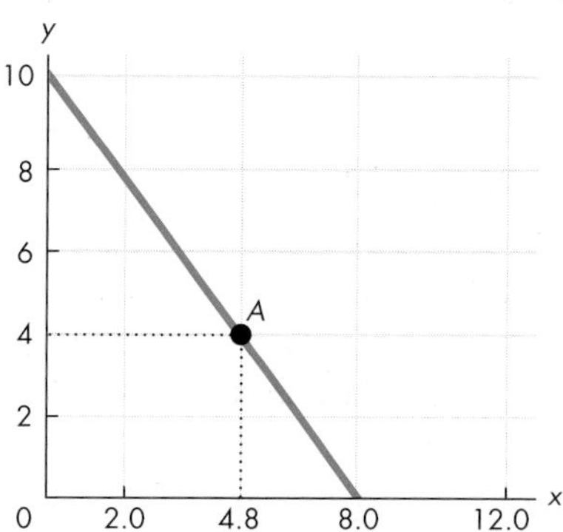

12. Calculate the slope of the relationship shown at point A in the following figure.

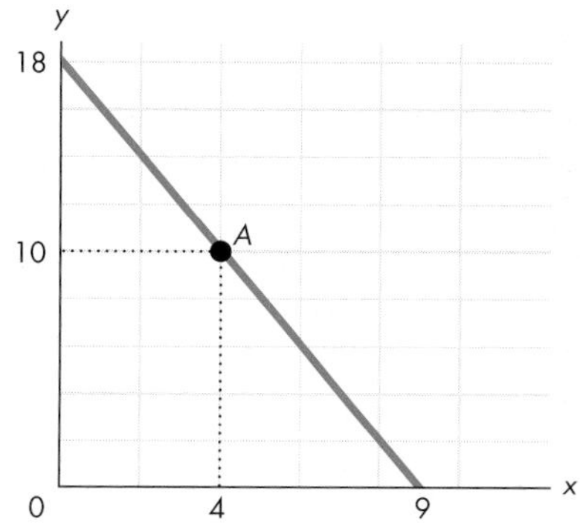

*Solutions to odd-numbered problems are provided.

13. Use the following figure to calculate the slope of the relationship.

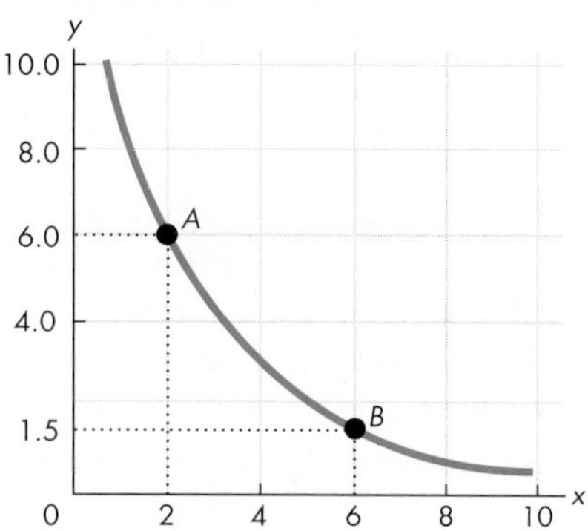

a. At points *A* and *B*.
b. Across the arc *AB*.

14. Use the following figure to calculate the slope of the relationship.

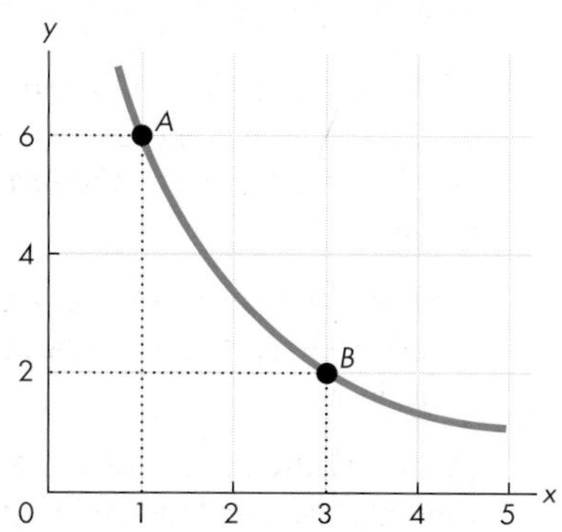

a. At points *A* and *B*.
b. Across the arc *AB*.

15. The table gives the price of a balloon ride, the temperature, and the number of rides a day.

Price (dollars per ride)	Balloon rides (number per day)		
	50°F	70°F	90°F
5.00	32	40	50
10.00	27	32	40
15.00	18	27	32
20.00	10	18	27

Draw graphs to show the relationship between
a. The price and the number of rides, holding the temperature constant.
b. The number of rides and temperature, holding the price constant.
c. The temperature and price, holding the number of rides constant.

16. The table gives the price of an umbrella, the amount of rainfall, and the number of umbrellas purchased.

Price (dollars per umbrella)	Umbrellas (number per day)		
	0	1	2
	(inches of rainfall)		
10	7	8	12
20	4	7	8
30	2	4	7
40	1	2	4

Draw graphs to show the relationship between
a. The price and the number of umbrellas purchased, holding the amount of rainfall constant.
b. The number of umbrellas purchased and the amount of rainfall, holding the price constant.
c. The amount of rainfall and the price, holding the number of umbrellas purchased constant.

WEB ACTIVITIES

myeconlab Links to Web sites

1. Find Consumer Price Index (CPI) for the latest 12 months. Make a graph of the CPI. During the most recent month, was the CPI rising or falling? Was the rate of rise or fall increasing or decreasing?
2. Find the unemployment rate for the latest 12 months. Graph the unemployment rate. During the most recent month, was it rising or falling? Was the rate of rise or fall increasing or decreasing?
3. Use the data that you obtained in questions 1 and 2. Make a graph to show whether the CPI and the unemployment rate are related to each other.
4. Use the data that you obtained in questions 1 and 2. Calculate the percentage change in the CPI each month. Make a graph to show whether the percentage change in the CPI and the unemployment rate are related to each other.

CHAPTER 2

The Economic Problem

Good, Better, Best!

We live in a style that surprises our grandparents and would have astonished our great-grandparents. MP3s, video games, cell phones, gene splicing, and personal computers, which didn't exist even 25 years ago, have transformed our daily lives. For most of us, life is good and getting better. But we still make choices and face costs.

Perhaps the biggest choice that you will make is when to quit school and begin full-time work. When you've completed your current program, will you remain in school and work toward a postgraduate degree or a professional degree? What are the costs and consequences of this choice? We'll return to this question in *Reading Between the Lines* at the end of this chapter.

When we make our choices, we pursue our self-interest. Do our choices also serve the social interest? And what do we mean by the social interest?

We see an incredible amount of specialization and trade in the world. Each one of us specializes in a particular job—as a lawyer, a journalist, a homemaker. Why? How do we benefit from specialization and trade?

Over many centuries, social institutions have evolved that we take for granted. They include firms, markets, and a political and legal system that protects private property. Why have these institutions evolved?

These are the questions that we study in this chapter. We begin with the core economic problem—scarcity and choice—and the concept of the production possibilities frontier. We then learn about the central idea of economics: that the pursuit of the social interest means using resources efficiently. We also discover how we can expand production by accumulating capital, expanding our knowledge, and specializing and trading with each other. What you will learn in this chapter is the foundation on which all economics is built.

After studying this chapter, you will be able to

- Define the production possibilities frontier and calculate opportunity cost
- Distinguish between production possibilities and preferences and describe an efficient allocation of resources
- Explain how current production choices expand future production possibilities
- Explain how specialization and trade expand our production possibilities
- Describe the economic institutions that coordinate decisions

Production Possibilities and Opportunity Cost

Every working day, in mines, factories, shops, and offices and on farms and construction sites across the United States, 138 million people produce a vast variety of goods and services valued at $50 billion. But the quantities of goods and services that we can produce are limited both by our available resources and by technology. And if we want to increase our production of one good, we must decrease our production of something else—we face tradeoffs. You are going to learn about the production possibilities frontier, which describes the limit to what we can produce and provides a neat way of thinking about and illustrating the idea of a tradeoff.

The **production possibilities frontier** (*PPF*) is the boundary between those combinations of goods and services that can be produced and those that cannot. To illustrate the *PPF*, we focus on two goods at a time and hold the quantities produced of all the other goods and services constant. That is, we look at a *model* economy in which everything remains the same (*ceteris paribus*) except for the production of the two goods we are considering.

Let's look at the production possibilities frontier for CDs and pizza, which stand for *any* pair of goods or services.

Production Possibilities Frontier

The *production possibilities frontier* for CDs and pizza shows the limits to the production of these two goods, given the total resources available to produce them. Figure 2.1 shows this production possibilities frontier. The table lists some combinations of the quantities of pizzas and CDs that can be produced in a month given the resources available. The figure graphs these combinations. The *x*-axis shows the quantity of pizzas produced, and the *y*-axis shows the quantity of CDs produced.

The *PPF* illustrates *scarcity* because we cannot attain the points outside the frontier. They are points that describe wants that can't be satisfied. We can produce at any point *inside* the *PPF* and *on* the *PPF*. These points are attainable. Suppose that in a typical month, we produce 4 million pizzas and 5 million CDs. Figure 2.1 shows this combination as point *E* and as possibility *E* in the table. The figure also

FIGURE 2.1 Production Possibilities Frontier

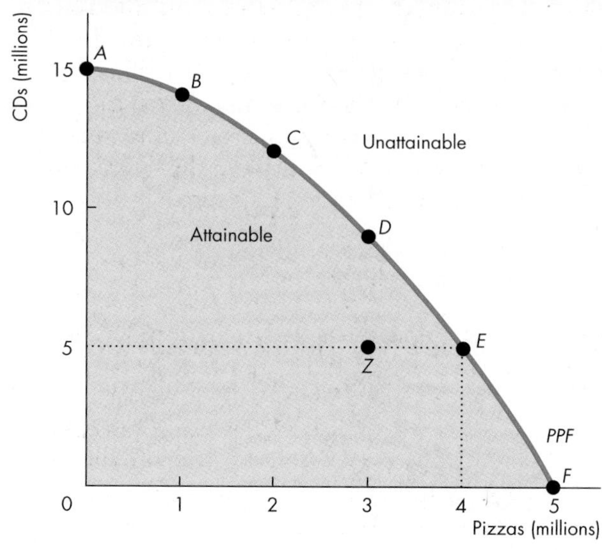

Possibility	Pizzas (millions)		CDs (millions)
A	0	and	15
B	1	and	14
C	2	and	12
D	3	and	9
E	4	and	5
F	5	and	0

The table lists six points on the production possibilities frontier for CDs and pizzas. Row *A* tells us that if we produce no pizza, the maximum quantity of CDs we can produce is 15 million. Points *A, B, C, D, E,* and *F* in the figure represent the rows of the table. The line passing through these points is the production possibilities frontier (*PPF*).

The *PPF* separates the attainable from the unattainable. Production is possible at any point *inside* the orange area or *on* the frontier. Points outside the frontier are unattainable. Points inside the frontier such as point *Z* are inefficient because resources are wasted or misallocated. At such points, it is possible to use the available resources to produce more of either or both goods.

shows other production possibilities. For example, we might stop producing pizza and move all the people who produce it into producing CDs. Point *A* in the figure and possibility *A* in the table show this case. The quantity of CDs produced increases to 15 million, and pizza production dries up. Alternatively, we might close the CD factories and switch all the resources into producing pizza. In this situation, we produce 5 million pizzas. Point *F* in the figure and possibility *F* in the table show this case.

Production Efficiency

We achieve **production efficiency** if we cannot produce more of one good without producing less of some other good. When production is efficient, we are at a point *on* the *PPF*. If we are at a point *inside* the *PPF*, such as point *Z* in Fig. 2.1, production is *inefficient* because we have some *unused* resources or we have some *misallocated* resources or both.

Resources are unused when they are idle but could be working. For example, we might leave some of the factories idle or some workers unemployed.

Resources are *misallocated* when they are assigned to tasks for which they are not the best match. For example, we might assign skilled pizza makers to work in a CD factory and skilled CD makers to work in a pizza shop. We could get more pizzas *and* more CDs from these same workers if we reassigned them to the tasks that more closely match their skills.

If we produce at a point inside the *PPF* such as *Z* in Fig. 2.1, we can use our resources more efficiently to produce more pizzas, more CDs, or more of *both* pizzas and CDs. But if we produce at a point *on* the *PPF*, we are using our resources efficiently. We can produce more of one good only if we produce less of the other. That is, along the *PPF*, we face a *tradeoff.*

Tradeoff Along the *PPF*

Every choice *along* the *PPF* involves a *tradeoff*—we must give up something to get something else. On the *PPF* in Fig. 2.1, we must give up some CDs to get more pizzas or give up some pizzas to get more CDs.

Tradeoffs arise in every imaginable real-world situation, and you reviewed several of them in Chapter 1. At any given point in time, we have a fixed amount of labor, land, capital, and entrepreneurship. By using our available technologies, we can employ these resources to produce goods and services. But we are limited in what we can produce. This limit defines a boundary between what we can attain and what we cannot attain. This boundary is the real-world's production possibilities frontier, and it defines the tradeoffs that we must make. On our real-world *PPF*, we can produce more of any one good or service only if we produce less of some other goods or services.

When doctors say that we must spend more on AIDS and cancer research, they are suggesting a tradeoff: more medical research for less of some other things. When the President says that he wants to spend more on education and health care, he is suggesting a tradeoff: more education and health care for less national defense or less private spending (because of higher taxes). When an environmental group argues for less logging, it is suggesting a tradeoff: greater conservation of endangered wildlife for less paper. When your parents say that you should study more, they are suggesting a tradeoff: more study time for less leisure or sleep.

All tradeoffs involve a cost—an opportunity cost.

Opportunity Cost

The *opportunity cost* of an action is the highest-valued alternative forgone. The *PPF* helps us to make the concept of opportunity cost precise and enables us to calculate it. Along the *PPF*, there are only two goods, so there is only one alternative forgone: some quantity of the other good. Given our current resources and technology, we can produce more pizzas only if we produce fewer CDs. The opportunity cost of producing an additional pizza is the number of CDs we *must* forgo. Similarly, the opportunity cost of producing an additional CD is the quantity of pizzas we *must* forgo.

For example, at point *C* in Fig. 2.1, we produce fewer pizzas and more CDs than at point *D*. If we choose point *D* over point *C*, the additional 1 million pizzas *cost* 3 million CDs. One pizza costs 3 CDs.

We can also work out the opportunity cost of choosing point *C* over point *D* in Fig. 2.1. If we move from point *D* to point *C*, the quantity of CDs produced increases by 3 million and the quantity of pizzas produced decreases by 1 million. So if we choose point *C* over point *D*, the additional 3 million CDs *cost* 1 million pizzas. One CD costs 1/3 of a pizza.

Opportunity Cost Is a Ratio Opportunity cost is a ratio. It is the decrease in the quantity produced of one good divided by the increase in the quantity produced of another good as we move along the production possibilities frontier.

Because opportunity cost is a ratio, the opportunity cost of producing an additional CD is equal to the *inverse* of the opportunity cost of producing an additional pizza. Check this proposition by returning to the calculations we've just worked through. When we move along the *PPF* from *C* to *D*, the opportunity cost of a pizza is 3 CDs. The inverse of 3 is 1/3, so if we decrease the production of pizza and increase the production of CDs by moving from *D* to *C*, the opportunity cost of a CD must be 1/3 of a pizza. You can check that this number is correct. If we move from *D* to *C*, we produce 3 million more CDs and 1 million fewer pizzas. Because 3 million CDs cost 1 million pizzas, the opportunity cost of 1 CD is 1/3 of a pizza.

Increasing Opportunity Cost The opportunity cost of a pizza increases as the quantity of pizzas produced increases. Also, the opportunity cost of a CD increases as the quantity of CDs produced increases. This phenomenon of increasing opportunity cost is reflected in the shape of the *PPF*—it is bowed outward.

When a large quantity of CDs and a small quantity of pizzas are produced—between points *A* and *B* in Fig. 2.1—the frontier has a gentle slope. A given increase in the quantity of pizzas *costs* a small decrease in the quantity of CDs, so the opportunity cost of a pizza is a small quantity of CDs.

When a large quantity of pizzas and a small quantity of CDs are produced—between points *E* and *F* in Fig. 2.1—the frontier is steep. A given increase in the quantity of pizzas *costs* a large decrease in the quantity of CDs, so the opportunity cost of a pizza is a large quantity of CDs.

The *PPF* is bowed outward because resources are not all equally productive in all activities. People with several years of experience working for Sony are good at producing CDs but not very good at making pizzas. So if we move some of these people from Sony to Domino's, we get a small increase in the quantity of pizzas but a large decrease in the quantity of CDs.

Similarly, people who have spent years working at Domino's are good at producing pizzas, but they have no idea how to produce CDs. So if we move some of these people from Domino's to Sony, we get a small increase in the quantity of CDs but a large decrease in the quantity of pizzas. The more of either good we try to produce, the less productive are the additional resources we use to produce that good and the larger is the opportunity cost of a unit of that good.

Increasing Opportunity Costs Are Everywhere Just about every activity that you can think of is one with an increasing opportunity cost. We allocate the most skillful farmers and the most fertile land to the production of food. And we allocate the best doctors and the least fertile land to the production of health-care services. If we shift fertile land and tractors away from farming to hospitals and ambulances and ask farmers to become hospital porters, the production of food drops drastically and the increase in the production of health-care services is small. The opportunity cost of a unit of health-care services rises. Similarly, if we shift our resources away from health care toward farming, we must use more doctors and nurses as farmers and more hospitals as hydroponic tomato factories. The decrease in the production of health-care services is large, but the increase in food production is small. The opportunity cost of a unit of food rises.

This example is extreme and unlikely, but these same considerations apply to any pair of goods that you can imagine.

REVIEW QUIZ

1. How does the production possibilities frontier illustrate scarcity?
2. How does the production possibilities frontier illustrate production efficiency?
3. How does the production possibilities frontier show that every choice involves a tradeoff?
4. How does the production possibilities frontier illustrate opportunity cost?
5. Why is opportunity cost a ratio?
6. Why does the *PPF* for most goods bow outward so that opportunity cost increases as the quantity produced of a good increases?

myeconlab **Study Plan 2.1**

We've seen that what we can produce is limited by the production possibilities frontier. We've also seen that production on the *PPF* is efficient. But we can produce many different quantities on the *PPF*. How do we choose among them? How do we know which point on the *PPF* is the best one?

Using Resources Efficiently

You've seen that we achieve production efficiency at every point on the *PPF*. But which point is best? What quantities of CDs and pizzas best serve the social interest?

This question is an example of real-world questions of enormous consequence such as: How much should we spend on treating AIDS and how much on cancer research? Should we expand education and health-care programs or cut taxes? Should we spend more on the preservation of rainforests and the conservation of endangered wildlife?

To answer these questions, we must find a way of measuring and comparing costs and benefits.

The *PPF* and Marginal Cost

The **marginal cost** of a good is the opportunity cost of producing one more unit of it. We calculate marginal cost from the slope of the *PPF*. As the quantity of pizzas produced increases, the *PPF* gets steeper and marginal cost of a pizza increases. Figure 2.2 illustrates the calculation of the marginal cost of a pizza.

Begin by finding the opportunity cost of pizza in blocks of 1 million pizzas. The first million pizzas cost 1 million CDs, the second million pizzas cost 2 million CDs, the third million pizzas cost 3 million CDs, and so on. The bars in part (a) illustrate these calculations.

The bars in part (b) show the cost of an average pizza in each of the 1 million pizza blocks. Focus on the third million pizzas—the move from *C* to *D* in part (a). Over this range, because the 1 million pizzas cost 3 million CDs, one of these pizzas, on the average, costs 3 CDs—the height of the bar in part (b).

Next, find the opportunity cost of each additional pizza—the marginal cost of a pizza. The marginal cost of a pizza increases as the quantity of pizza produced increases. The marginal cost at point *C* is less than it is at point *D*. On the average over the range from *C* to *D*, the marginal cost of a pizza is 3 CDs. But it exactly equals 3 CDs only in the middle of the range between *C* and *D*.

The red dot in part (b) indicates that the marginal cost of a pizza is 3 CDs when 2.5 million pizzas are produced. Each black dot in part (b) is interpreted in the same way. The red curve that passes through these dots, labeled *MC*, is the marginal cost curve. It shows the marginal cost of a pizza at each quantity of pizza as we move along the *PPF*.

FIGURE 2.2 The *PPF* and Marginal Cost

myeconlab

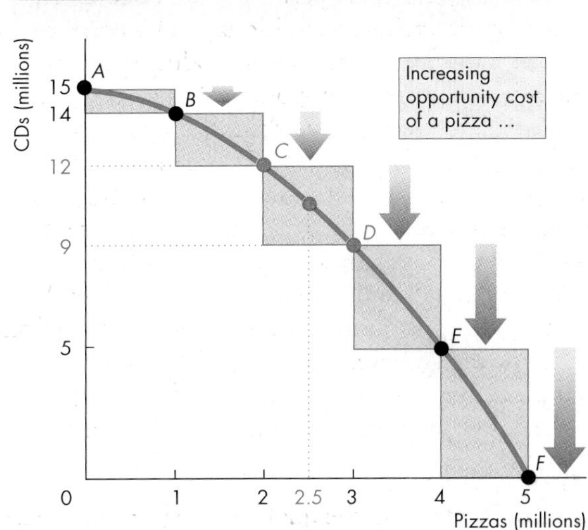

(a) *PPF* and opportunity cost

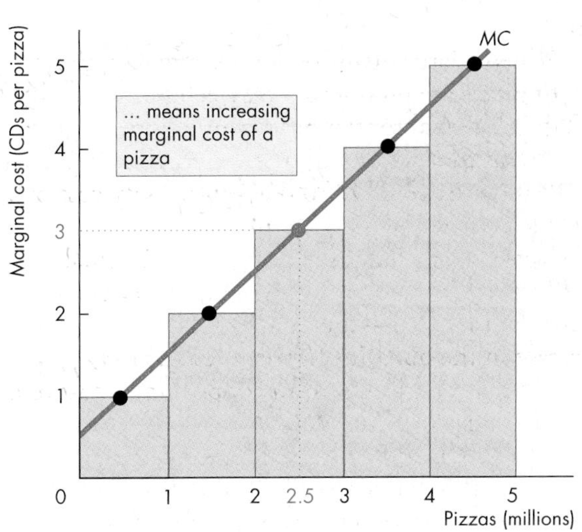

(b) Marginal cost

Marginal cost is calculated from the slope of the *PPF*. As the quantity of pizzas produced increases, the *PPF* gets steeper and the marginal cost of a pizza increases. The bars in part (a) show the opportunity cost of pizza in blocks of 1 million pizzas. The bars in part (b) show the cost of an average pizza in each of these 1 million blocks. The red curve, *MC*, shows the marginal cost of a pizza at each point along the *PPF*. This curve passes through the center of each of the bars in part (b).

Preferences and Marginal Benefit

Look around your classroom and notice the wide variety of shirts, caps, pants, and shoes that you and your fellow students are wearing today. Why is there such a huge variety? Why don't you all wear the same styles and colors? The answer lies in what economists call preferences. **Preferences** are a description of a person's likes and dislikes.

You've seen that we have a concrete way of describing the limits to production: the *PPF*. We need a similarly concrete way of describing preferences. To describe preferences, economists use the concept of marginal benefit. The **marginal benefit** from a good or service is the benefit received from consuming one more unit of it.

We measure the marginal benefit from a good or service by the most that people are *willing to pay* for an additional unit of it. The idea is that you are not willing to pay more for a good than it is worth to you. But you are willing to pay an amount up to what it is worth. So the willingness to pay for something measures its marginal benefit.

Economists use the marginal benefit curve to illustrate preferences. The **marginal benefit curve** shows the relationship between the marginal benefit from a good and the quantity of that good consumed. It is a general principle that the more we have of any good or service, the smaller is its marginal benefit and the less we are willing to pay for an additional unit of it. This tendency is so widespread and strong that we call it a principle—the *principle of decreasing marginal benefit.*

The basic reason why marginal benefit from a good or service decreases as we consume more of it is that we like variety. The more we consume of any one good or service, the more we can see other things that we would like better.

Think about your willingness to pay for pizza (or any other item). If pizza is hard to come by and you can buy only a few slices a year, you might be willing to pay a high price to get an additional slice. But if pizza is all you've eaten for the past few days, you are willing to pay almost nothing for another slice.

In everyday life, we think of what we pay for goods and services as the money that we give up—dollars. But you've learned to think about cost as other goods or services forgone, not a dollar cost. You can think about willingness to pay in the same terms. The price you are willing to pay for something is the quantity of other goods and services that you are willing to forgo. Let's continue with the example of CDs and pizzas and illustrate preferences this way.

FIGURE 2.3 Preferences and the Marginal Benefit Curve

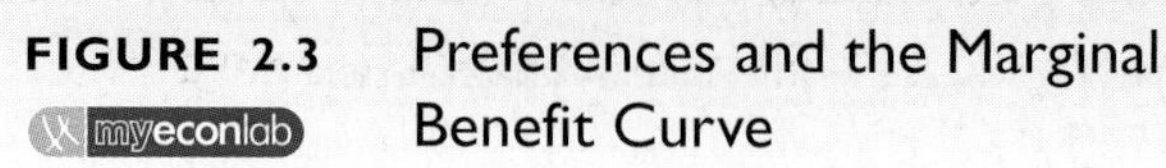

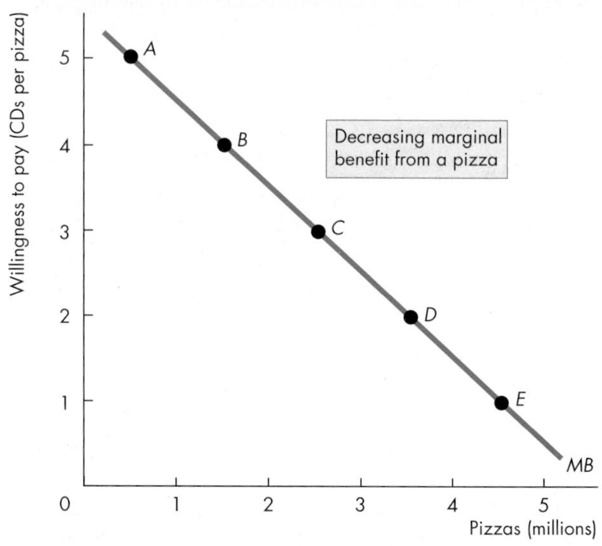

Possibility	Pizzas (millions)	Willingness to pay (CDs per pizza)
A	0.5	5
B	1.5	4
C	2.5	3
D	3.5	2
E	4.5	1

The smaller the quantity of pizzas produced, the more CDs people are willing to give up for an additional pizza. If pizza production is 0.5 million, people are willing to pay 5 CDs per pizza. But if pizza production is 4.5 million, people are willing to pay only 1 CD per pizza. Willingness to pay measures marginal benefit. And decreasing marginal benefit is a universal feature of people's preferences.

Figure 2.3 illustrates preferences as the willingness to pay for pizza in terms of CDs. In row *A*, pizza production is 0.5 million, and at that quantity, people are willing to pay 5 CDs per pizza. As the quantity of pizza produced increases, the amount that people are willing to pay for it falls. When pizza production is 4.5 million, people are willing to pay only 1 CD per pizza.

Let's now use the concepts of marginal cost and marginal benefit to describe the efficient quantity of pizzas to produce.

FIGURE 2.4 Efficient Use of Resources

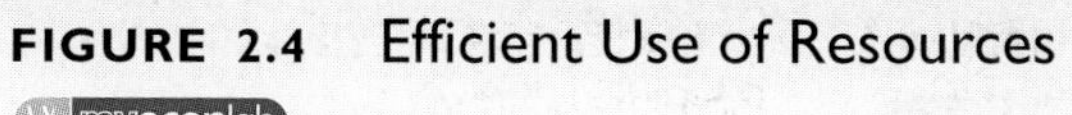

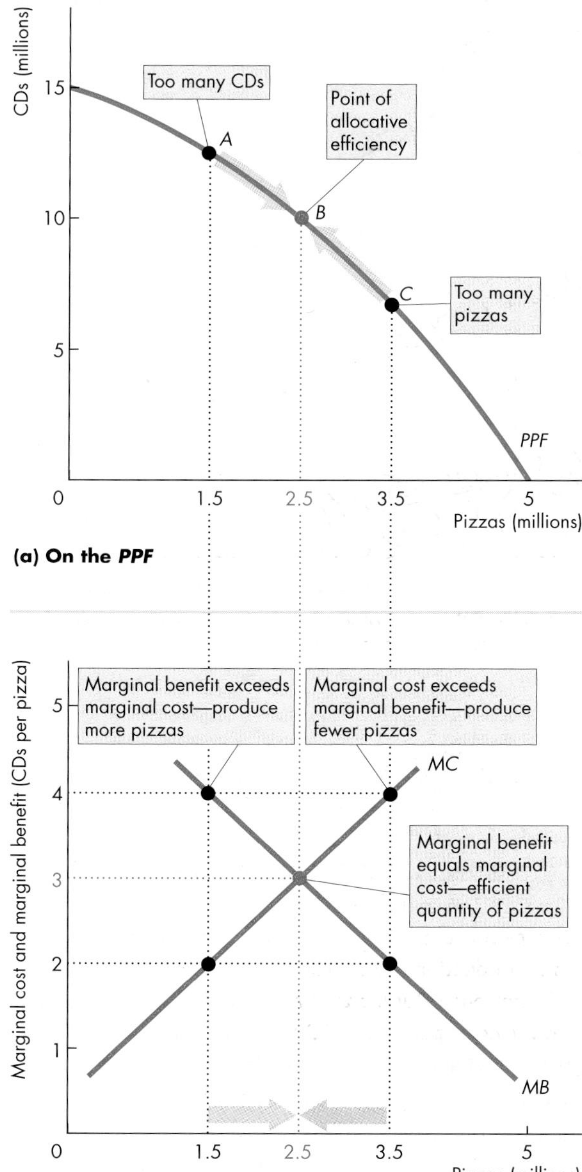

(a) On the PPF

(b) Marginal benefit equals marginal cost

The greater the quantity of pizzas produced, the smaller is the marginal benefit (*MB*) from pizza—the fewer CDs people are willing to give up to get an additional pizza. But the greater the quantity of pizzas produced, the greater is the marginal cost (*MC*) of pizza—the more CDs people must give up to get an additional pizza. When marginal benefit equals marginal cost, resources are being used efficiently.

Efficient Use of Resources

When we cannot produce more of any one good without giving up some other good, we have achieved *production efficiency*, and we're producing at a point on the *PPF*. When we cannot produce more of any good without giving up some other good that we *value more highly*, we have achieved **allocative efficiency** and we are producing at the point on the *PPF* that we prefer above all other points.

Suppose in Fig. 2.4, we produce 1.5 million pizzas. The marginal cost of a pizza is 2 CDs, and the marginal benefit from a pizza is 4 CDs. Because someone values an additional pizza more highly than it costs to produce, we can get more value from our resources by moving some of them out of producing CDs and into producing pizzas.

Now suppose we produce 3.5 million pizzas. The marginal cost of a pizza is now 4 CDs, but the marginal benefit from a pizza is only 2 CDs. Because the additional pizza costs more to produce than anyone thinks it is worth, we can get more value from our resources by moving some of them away from producing pizzas and into producing CDs.

But suppose we produce 2.5 million pizzas. Marginal cost and marginal benefit are now equal at 3 CDs. This allocation of resources between pizzas and CDs is efficient. If more pizzas are produced, the forgone CDs are worth more than the additional pizzas. If fewer pizzas are produced, the forgone pizzas are worth more than the additional CDs.

REVIEW QUIZ

1. What is marginal cost? How is it measured?
2. What is marginal benefit? How is it measured?
3. How does the marginal benefit from a good change as the quantity produced of that good increases?
4. What is allocative efficiency and how does it relate to the production possibilities frontier?
5. What conditions must be satisfied if resources are used efficiently?

myeconlab **Study Plan 2.2**

You now understand the limits to production and the conditions under which resources are used efficiently. Your next task is to study the expansion of production possibilities.

Economic Growth

During the past 30 years, production per person in the United States has doubled. Such an expansion of production is called **economic growth**. Economic growth increases our *standard of living*, but it doesn't overcome scarcity and avoid opportunity cost. To make our economy grow, we face a tradeoff—the faster we make production grow, the greater is the opportunity cost of economic growth.

The Cost of Economic Growth

Economic growth comes from technological change and capital accumulation. **Technological change** is the development of new goods and of better ways of producing goods and services. **Capital accumulation** is the growth of capital resources, including *human capital*.

Because of technological change and capital accumulation, we have an enormous quantity of cars that enable us to produce more transportation than was available when we had only horses and carriages; we have satellites that make global communications possible on a scale that is much larger than that produced by the earlier cable technology. But if we use our resources to develop new technologies and produce capital, we must decrease our production of consumption goods and services. New technologies and new capital have an opportunity cost. Let's look at this opportunity cost.

Instead of studying the *PPF* of pizzas and CDs, we'll hold the quantity of CDs produced constant and examine the *PPF* for pizzas and pizza ovens. Figure 2.5 shows this *PPF* as the blue curve *ABC*. If we devote no resources to producing pizza ovens, we produce at point *A*. If we produce 3 million pizzas, we can produce 6 pizza ovens at point *B*. If we produce no pizza, we can produce 10 ovens at point *C*.

The amount by which our production possibilities expand depends on the resources we devote to technological change and capital accumulation. If we devote no resources to this activity (point *A*), our *PPF* remains at *ABC*—the blue curve in Fig. 2.5. If we cut the current production of pizza and produce 6 ovens (point *B*), then in the future, we'll have more capital and our *PPF* will rotate outward to the position shown by the red curve. The fewer resources we devote to producing pizza and the more resources we devote to producing ovens, the greater is the future expansion of our production possibilities.

FIGURE 2.5 Economic Growth

myeconlab

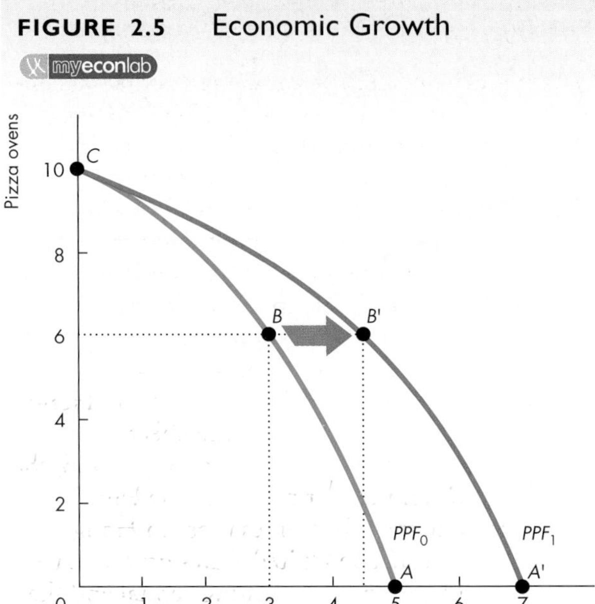

PPF_0 shows the limits to the production of pizza and pizza ovens, with the production of all other goods and services remaining the same. If we devote no resources to producing pizza ovens and produce 5 million pizzas, our production possibilities will remain the same PPF_0. But if we decrease pizza production to 3 million and produce 6 ovens, at point *B*, our production possibilities expand. After one period, the *PPF* rotates outward to PPF_1 and we can produce at point *B*', a point outside the original PPF_0. We can rotate the *PPF* outward, but we cannot avoid opportunity cost. The opportunity cost of producing more pizzas in the future is fewer pizzas today.

Economic growth is not free. To make it happen, we devote resources to producing new ovens and less to producing pizza. In Fig. 2.5, we move from *A* to *B*. There is no free lunch. The opportunity cost of more pizzas in the future is fewer pizzas today. Also, economic growth is no magic formula for abolishing scarcity. On the new production possibilities frontier, we continue to face a tradeoff and opportunity cost.

The ideas about economic growth that we have explored in the setting of the pizza industry also apply to nations. Let's look at two examples.

Economic Growth in the United States and Hong Kong

If a nation devotes all its resources to producing consumption goods and none to advancing technology and accumulating capital, its production possibilities in the future will be the same as they are today. To expand production possibilities in the future, we must devote fewer resources to producing consumption goods and some resources to accumulating capital and developing technologies. The decrease in today's consumption is the opportunity cost of tomorrow's increase in consumption.

The experiences of the United States and Hong Kong make a striking example of the effects of our choices on the rate of economic growth. In 1966, the production possibilities per person in the United States were more than four times those in Hong Kong (see Fig. 2.6). The United States devoted one fifth of its resources to accumulating capital and the other four fifths to consumption. In 1966, the United States was at point *A* on its *PPF*. Hong Kong devoted one third of its resources to accumulating capital and two thirds to consumption. In 1966, Hong Kong was at point *A* on its *PPF*.

Since 1966, both countries have experienced economic growth, but growth in Hong Kong has been more rapid than that in the United States. Because Hong Kong devoted a bigger fraction of its resources to accumulating capital, its production possibilities have expanded more quickly.

By 2006, the production possibilities per person in Hong Kong had reached 80 percent of those in the United States. If Hong Kong continues to devote more resources to accumulating capital than we do (at point *B* on its 2006 *PPF*), it will continue to grow more rapidly than the United States. But if Hong Kong increases consumption and decreases capital accumulation (moving to point *D* on its 2006 *PPF*), then its rate of economic growth will slow.

The United States is typical of the rich industrial countries, which include Western Europe and Japan. Hong Kong is typical of the fast-growing Asian economies, which include Taiwan, Thailand, South Korea, and China. Growth in these countries slowed during the Asia crisis of 1998 but quickly rebounded. Production possibilities expand in these countries by between 5 and almost 10 percent a year. If such high growth rates are maintained, these other Asian countries will eventually close the gap between them and the United States, as Hong Kong has done.

FIGURE 2.6 Economic Growth in the United States and Hong Kong

myeconlab

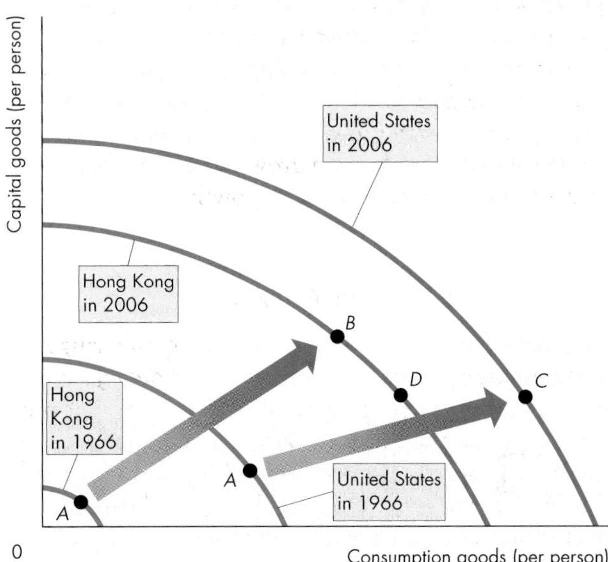

In 1966, the production possibilities per person in the United States were much larger than those in Hong Kong. But Hong Kong devoted more of its resources to accumulating capital than did the United States, so its production possibilities frontier has shifted outward more quickly than has that of the United States. In 2006, Hong Kong's production possibilities per person were 80 percent of those in the United States.

REVIEW QUIZ

1. What generates economic growth?
2. How does economic growth influence the production possibilities frontier?
3. What is the opportunity cost of economic growth?
4. Why has Hong Kong experienced faster economic growth than the United States?

myeconlab **Study Plan 2.3**

Next, we're going to study another way in which we expand our production possibilities—the amazing fact that *both* buyers and sellers gain from specialization and trade.

Gains from Trade

People can produce for themselves all the goods that they consume, or they can concentrate on producing one good (or perhaps a few goods) and then trade with others—exchange some of their own goods for those of others. Concentrating on the production of only one good or a few goods is called *specialization.* We are going to discover how people gain by specializing in the production of the good in which they have a *comparative advantage* and trading with each other.

Comparative Advantage and Absolute Advantage

A person has a **comparative advantage** in an activity if that person can perform the activity at a lower opportunity cost than anyone else. Differences in opportunity costs arise from differences in individual abilities and from differences in the characteristics of other resources.

No one excels at everything. One person is an outstanding pitcher but a poor catcher; another person is a brilliant lawyer but a poor teacher. In almost all human endeavors, what one person does easily, someone else finds difficult. The same applies to land and capital. One plot of land is fertile but has no mineral deposits; another plot of land has outstanding views but is infertile. One machine has great precision but is difficult to operate; another is fast but often breaks down.

Although no one excels at everything, some people excel and can outperform others in a large number of activities—perhaps even in all activities. A person who is more productive than others has an **absolute advantage**.

Absolute advantage involves comparing productivities—production per hour—while comparative advantage involves comparing opportunity cost.

Notice that a person who has an absolute advantage does not have a *comparative* advantage in every activity. John Grisham is a better lawyer and a better author of fast-paced thrillers than most people. He has an absolute advantage in these two activities. But compared to others, he is a better writer than lawyer, so his *comparative* advantage is in writing.

Because people's abilities and the quality of their resources differ, they have different opportunity costs of producing various goods. These differences in opportunity cost are the source of comparative advantage.

Let's explore the idea of comparative advantage by looking at two smoothie bars: one operated by Liz and the other operated by Joe.

Liz's Smoothie Bar Liz produces smoothies and salads. In Liz's high-tech bar, she can turn out either a smoothie or a salad every 90 seconds—see Table 2.1. If Liz spends all her time making smoothies, she can produce 40 an hour. And if she spends all her time making salads, she can also produce 40 an hour. If she splits her time equally between the two, she can produce 20 smoothies and 20 salads an hour. For each additional smoothie Liz produces, she must decrease her production of salads by one, and for each additional salad she produces, she must decrease her production of smoothies by one. So

> Liz's opportunity cost of producing 1 smoothie is 1 salad,

and

> Liz's opportunity cost of producing 1 salad is 1 smoothie.

Liz's customers buy smoothies and salads in equal quantities, so she splits her time equally between the two items and produces 20 smoothies and 20 salads an hour.

Joe's Smoothie Bar Joe also produces both smoothies and salads. But Joe's bar is smaller than Liz's. Also, Joe has only one blender, and it's a slow old machine. Even if Joe uses all his resources to produce smoothies, he can produce only 6 an hour—see Table 2.2. But Joe is good in the salad department, so if he uses all his resources to make salads, he can produce 30 an hour.

TABLE 2.1 Liz's Production Possibilities

Item	Minutes to produce 1	Quantity per hour
Smoothies	1.5	40
Salads	1.5	40

TABLE 2.2 Joe's Production Possibilities

Item	Minutes to produce 1	Quantity per hour
Smoothies	10	6
Salads	2	30

Joe's ability to make smoothies and salads is the same regardless of how he splits an hour between the two tasks. He can make a salad in 2 minutes or a smoothie in 10 minutes. For each additional smoothie Joe produces, he must decrease his production of salads by 5. And for each additional salad he produces, he must decrease his production of smoothies by 1/5 of a smoothie. So

Joe's opportunity cost of producing 1 smoothie is 5 salads,

and

Joe's opportunity cost of producing 1 salad is 1/5 of a smoothie.

Joe's customers, like Liz's, buy smoothies and salads in equal quantities. So Joe spends 50 minutes of each hour making smoothies and 10 minutes of each hour making salads. With this division of his time, Joe produces 5 smoothies and 5 salads an hour.

Liz's Absolute Advantage You can see from the numbers that describe the two smoothie bars that Liz is four times as productive as Joe—her 20 smoothies and salads an hour are four times Joe's 5. Liz has an absolute advantage—she is more productive than Joe in producing both smoothies and salads. But Liz has a comparative advantage in only one of the activities.

Liz's Comparative Advantage In which of the two activities does Liz have a comparative advantage? Recall that comparative advantage is a situation in which one person's opportunity cost of producing a good is lower than another person's opportunity cost of producing that same good. Liz has a comparative advantage in producing smoothies. Her opportunity cost of a smoothie is 1 salad, whereas Joe's opportunity cost of a smoothie is 5 salads.

Joe's Comparative Advantage If Liz has a comparative advantage in producing smoothies, Joe must have a comparative advantage in producing salads. His opportunity cost of a salad is 1/5 of a smoothie, while Liz's opportunity cost of a salad is 1 smoothie.

Achieving the Gains from Trade

Liz and Joe run into each other one evening in a singles bar. After a few minutes of getting acquainted, Liz tells Joe about her amazingly profitable smoothie business that is selling 20 smoothies and 20 salads an hour. Her only problem, she tells Joe, is that she wishes she could produce more because potential customers leave when her lines get too long.

Joe isn't sure whether to risk spoiling his chances by telling Liz about his own struggling business. But he takes the risk. When he explains to Liz that he spends 50 minutes of every hour making 5 smoothies and 10 minutes making 5 salads, Liz's eyes pop. "Have I got a deal for you!" she exclaims.

Here's the deal that Liz sketches on a table napkin. Joe stops making smoothies and allocates all his time to producing salads. And Liz increases her production of smoothies to 35 an hour and cuts her production of salads to 5 an hour—see Table 2.3(a).

TABLE 2.3 Liz and Joe Gain from Trade

(a) Production	**Liz**	**Joe**
Smoothies	35	0
Salads	5	30
(b) Trade	**Liz**	**Joe**
Smoothies	sell 10	buy 10
Salads	buy 20	sell 20
(c) After trade	**Liz**	**Joe**
Smoothies	25	10
Salads	25	10
(d) Gains from trade	**Liz**	**Joe**
Smoothies	+5	+5
Salads	+5	+5

They then trade. Liz sells Joe 10 smoothies and Joe sells Liz 20 salads—the price of a smoothie is 2 salads—see Table 2.3(b).

After the trade, Joe has 10 salads—the 30 he produces minus the 20 he sells to Liz. And he has the 10 smoothies that he buys from Liz. So Joe doubles the quantities of smoothies and salads he can sell—see Table 2.3(c).

Liz has 25 smoothies—the 35 she produces minus the 10 she sells to Joe. And she has 25 salads—the 5 she produces plus the 20 she buys from Joe—see Table 2.3(c). Both Liz and Joe gain 5 smoothies and 5 salads—see Table 2.3(d).

Liz draws a graph (Fig. 2.7) to illustrate her suggestion. The blue *PPF* in part (a) shows Joe's production possibilities. He is producing 5 smoothies and 5 salads an hour at point *A*. The blue *PPF* in part (b) shows Liz's production possibilities. She is producing 20 smoothies and 20 salads an hour at point *A*.

Liz's proposal is that they each produce more of the good in which they have a comparative advantage. Joe produces 30 salads and no smoothies at point *B* on his *PPF*. Liz produces 35 smoothies and 5 salads at point *B* on her *PPF*.

Liz and Joe then trade—exchange—smoothies and salads at a price of 2 salads per smoothie or 1/2 of a smoothie per salad. Joe gets smoothies for 2 salads each, which is less than the 5 salads it costs him to produce them. And Liz gets salads for 1/2 a smoothie each, which is less than the 1 smoothie that it costs her to produce them.

With trade, Joe has 10 smoothies and 10 salads at point *C*—a gain of 5 smoothies and 5 salads. Joe moves to a point *outside* his *PPF*.

FIGURE 2.7 The Gains from Trade

myeconlab

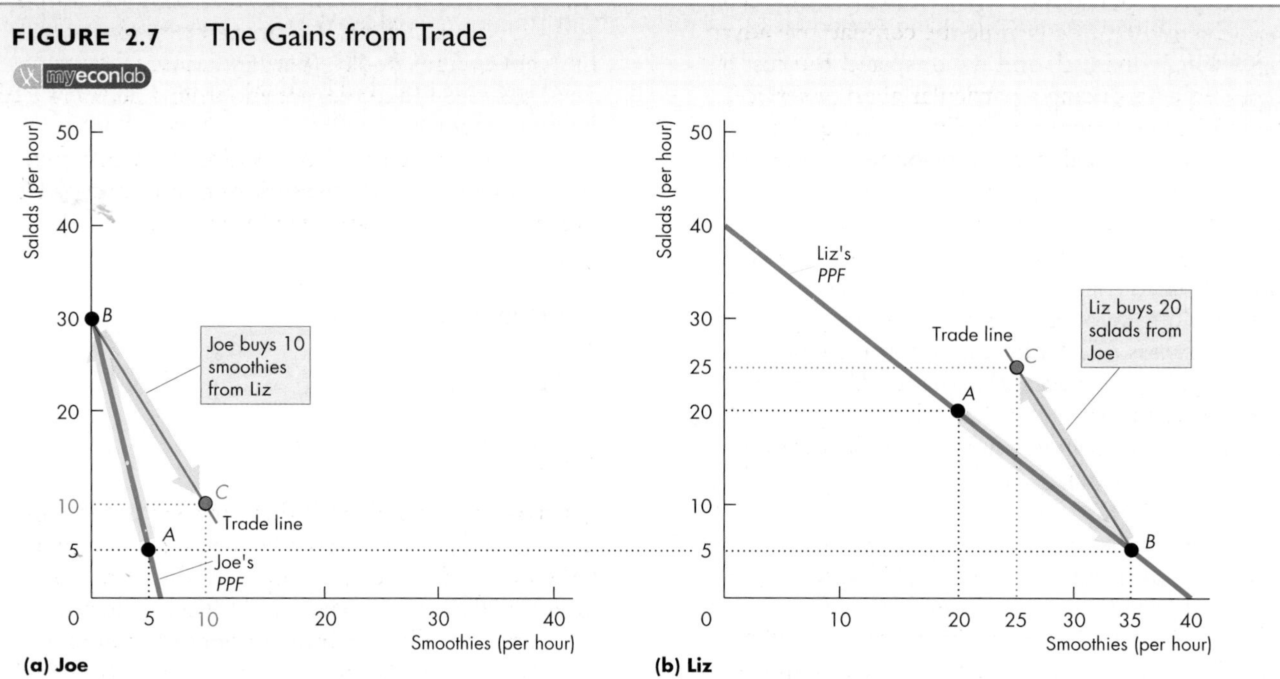

Joe initially produces at point *A* on his *PPF* in part (a), and Liz initially produces at point *A* on her *PPF* in part (b). Joe's opportunity cost of producing a salad is less than Liz's, so Joe has a comparative advantage in producing salads. Liz's opportunity cost of producing a smoothie is less than Joe's, so Liz has a comparative advantage in producing smoothies.

If Joe specializes in salad, he produces 30 salads and no smoothies at point *B* on his *PPF*. If Liz produces 25 smoothies and 5 salads, she produces at point B on her *PPF*.

They exchange salads for smoothies along the red "Trade line." Liz buys salads from Joe for less than her opportunity cost of producing them. And Joe buys smoothies from Liz for less than his opportunity cost of producing them. Each goes to point *C*—a point outside his or her *PPF*. Both Joe and Liz increase production by 5 smoothies and 5 salads with no change in resources.

With trade, Liz has 25 smoothies and 25 salads at point *C*—a gain of 5 smoothies and 5 salads. Liz moves to a point *outside* her *PPF.*

Despite Liz's absolute advantage in producing smoothies and salads, both Liz and Joe gain from producing more of the good in which they have a comparative advantage and trading.

The gains that we achieve from international trade are similar to those achieved by Joe and Liz in this example. When Americans buy T-shirts from China and when China buys Boeing aircraft from the United States, both countries gain. We get our shirts at a lower cost than that at which we can produce them, and China gets its aircraft at a lower cost than that at which it can produce them.

Dynamic Comparative Advantage

At any given point in time, the resources and technologies available determine the comparative advantages that individuals and nations have. But just by repeatedly producing a particular good or service, people become more productive in that activity, a phenomenon called **learning-by-doing**. Learning-by-doing is the basis of *dynamic* comparative advantage. **Dynamic comparative advantage** is a comparative advantage that a person (or country) possesses as a result of having specialized in a particular activity and, as a result of learning-by-doing, having become the producer with the lowest opportunity cost.

Singapore, for example, pursued dynamic comparative advantage when it decided to begin a biotechnology industry in which it initially didn't have a comparative advantage.

REVIEW QUIZ

1. What gives a person a comparative advantage?
2. Distinguish between comparative advantage and absolute advantage.
3. Why do people specialize and trade?
4. What are the gains from specialization and trade?
5. What is the source of the gains from trade?
6. How does dynamic comparative advantage arise?

myeconlab Study Plan 2.4

Economic Coordination

People gain by specializing in the production of those goods and services in which they have a comparative advantage and then trading with each other. Liz and Joe, whose production of salads and smoothies we studied earlier in this chapter, can get together and make a deal that enables them to enjoy the gains from specialization and trade. But for billions of individuals to specialize and produce millions of different goods and services, their choices must somehow be coordinated.

Two competing economic coordination systems have been used: central economic planning and decentralized markets.

Central economic planning might appear to be the best system because it can express national priorities. But when this system was tried, as it was for 60 years in Russia and for 30 years in China, it was a miserable failure. Today, these and most other previously planned economies are adopting a decentralized market system.

To make decentralized coordination work, four complementary social institutions that have evolved over many centuries are needed. They are

- Firms
- Markets
- Property rights
- Money

Firms

A **firm** is an economic unit that hires factors of production and organizes those factors to produce and sell goods and services. Examples of firms are your local gas station, Wal-Mart, and General Electric.

Firms coordinate a huge amount of economic activity. A Starbucks coffee shop, for example, might buy the machines and labor services of Liz and Joe and start to produce salads and smoothies at all its outlets.

But if a firm gets too big, it can't keep track of all the information that is needed to coordinate its activities. For this reason, firms themselves specialize and trade with each other. For example, Wal-Mart could produce all the things that it sells in its stores. And it could produce all the raw materials that are used to produce the things that it sells. But Sam Walton would not have become one of the wealthiest people in the world if he had followed that path. Instead, Wal-Mart buys from other firms that specialize in the production of a narrow range of items. And this trade takes place in markets.

Markets

In ordinary speech, the word *market* means a place where people buy and sell goods such as fish, meat, fruits, and vegetables. In economics, a *market* has a more general meaning. A **market** is any arrangement that enables buyers and sellers to get information and to do business with each other. An example is the market in which oil is bought and sold—the world oil market. The world oil market is not a place. It is the network of oil producers, oil users, wholesalers, and brokers who buy and sell oil. In the world oil market, decision makers do not meet physically. They make deals throughout the world by telephone, fax, and direct computer link.

Markets have evolved because they facilitate trade. Without organized markets, we would miss out on a substantial part of the potential gains from trade. Enterprising individuals and firms, each pursuing their own self-interest, have profited from making markets—standing ready to buy or sell the items in which they specialize. But markets can work only when property rights exist.

Property Rights

The social arrangements that govern the ownership, use, and disposal of anything that people value are called **property rights**. *Real property* includes land and buildings—the things we call property in ordinary speech—and durable goods such as plant and equipment. *Financial property* includes stocks and bonds and money in the bank. *Intellectual property* is the intangible product of creative effort. This type of property includes books, music, computer programs, and inventions of all kinds and is protected by copyrights and patents.

Where property rights are enforced, people have the incentive to specialize and produce the goods in which they have a comparative advantage. Where people can steal the production of others, resources are devoted not to production but to protecting possessions. Without property rights, we would still be hunting and gathering like our Stone Age ancestors.

Money

Money is any commodity or token that is generally acceptable as a means of payment. Liz and Joe didn't use money in the example above. They exchanged salads and smoothies. In principle, trade in markets can exchange any item for any other item. But you can perhaps imagine how complicated life would be if we exchanged goods for other goods. The "invention" of money makes trading in markets much more efficient.

Circular Flows Through Markets

Figure 2.8 shows the flows that result from the choices that households and firms make. Households specialize and choose the quantities of labor, land, capital, and entrepreneurship to sell or rent to firms. Firms choose the quantities of factors of production to hire. These (red) flows go through the *factor markets*. Households choose the quantities of goods and services to buy, and firms choose the quantities to produce. These (red) flows go through the *goods markets*. Households receive incomes and make expenditures on goods and services (the green flows).

How do markets coordinate all these decisions?

Coordinating Decisions

Markets coordinate decisions through price adjustments. To see how, think about your local market for hamburgers. Suppose that some people who want to buy hamburgers are not able to do so. To make the choices of buyers and sellers compatible, buyers must scale down their appetites or more hamburgers must be offered for sale (or both must happen). A rise in the price of a hamburger produces this outcome. A higher price encourages producers to offer more hamburgers for sale. It also encourages some people to change their lunch plans. Fewer people buy hamburgers, and more buy hot dogs. More hamburgers (and more hot dogs) are offered for sale.

Alternatively, suppose that more hamburgers are available than people want to buy. In this case, to make the choices of buyers and sellers compatible, more hamburgers must be bought or fewer hamburgers must be offered for sale (or both). A fall in the price of a hamburger achieves this outcome. A lower price encourages firms to produce a smaller quantity of hamburgers. It also encourages people to buy more hamburgers.

FIGURE 2.8 Circular Flows in the Market Economy

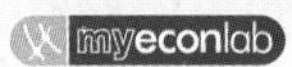

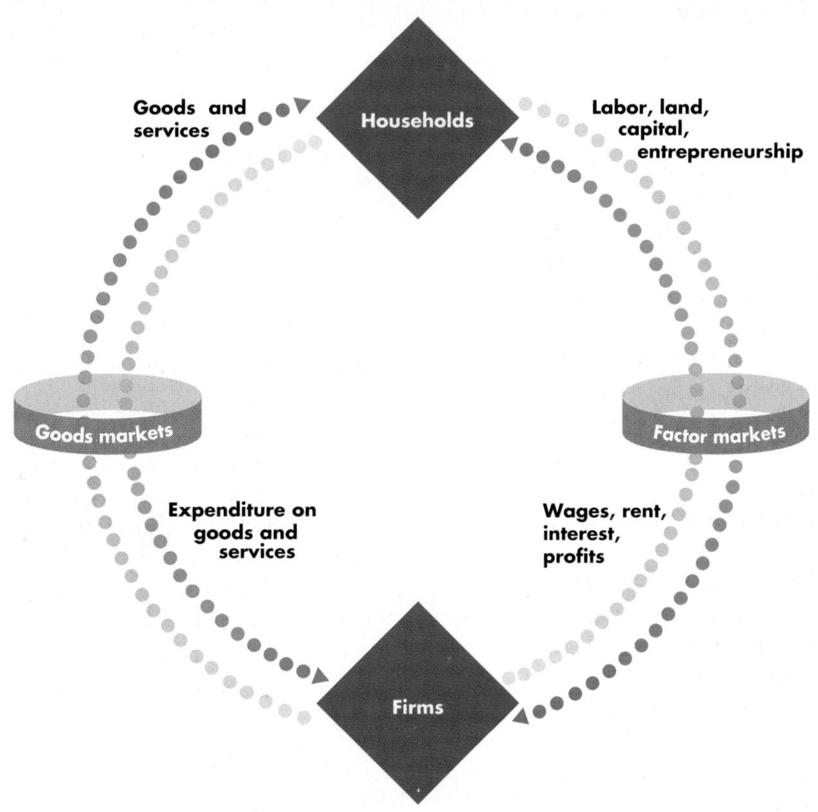

Households and firms make economic choices and markets coordinate these choices.

Households choose the quantities of labor, land, capital, and entrepreneurship to sell or rent to firms in exchange for wages, rent, interest, and profit. Households also choose how to spend their incomes on the various types of goods and services available.

Firms choose the quantities of factors of production to hire and the quantities of goods and services to produce.

Goods markets and factor markets coordinate these choices of households and firms.

The clockwise red flows are real flows—the flow of factors of production from households to firms and the flow of goods and services from firms to households.

The counterclockwise green flows are the payments for the red flows. They are the flow of incomes from firms to households and the flow of expenditure on goods and services from households to firms.

REVIEW QUIZ

1. Why are social institutions such as firms, markets, property rights, and money necessary?
2. What are the main functions of markets?
3. What are the flows in the market economy that go from firms to households and from households to firms?

myeconlab **Study Plan 2.5**

You have now begun to see how economists approach economic questions. Scarcity, choice, and divergent opportunity costs explain why we specialize and trade and why firms, markets, property rights, and money have developed. You can see all around you the lessons you've learned in this chapter. *Reading Between the Lines* on pp. 48–49 gives an example. It explores the *PPF* of a student like you and the choices that students must make that influence their own economic growth—the growth of their incomes.

READING BETWEEN THE LINES

The Cost and Benefit of Education

http://bostonworks.boston.com

MBA Grads May See Higher Compensation

May 29, 2005

Good news, business school graduates: That MBA will likely land you a fat salary.

Those are the findings of Consultants News, a publication of New Hampshire-based Kennedy Information Inc. that serves the consulting industry. It found that graduates of the nation's top business schools are expecting higher pay for their degree and some just might get it.

The newsletter said MBA students from top business schools expect to receive up to 20 percent more in total compensation this year based on their interviews with consulting firms.

"On average, base salary for this year's MBAs is almost $110,000, up about 10 percent over last year," said the newsletter. It noted that some firms, hoping to temper the salary rise, increased signing bonuses by nearly 30 percent.

The newsletter based its findings on information collected from 85 MBA students from a dozen high-ranked business schools, including Yale University, the University of Pennsylvania, the University of Chicago and the University of California at Los Angeles. It found that the average salary this year will be $109,000, up from $98,751 in 2004. The increase is the first since 2002, when salaries rose to $99,082, up from $92,253 in 2000.

Essence of the Story

- Consultants News reports the results of a survey of 85 MBA graduates from 12 top business schools.
- The average compensation of MBA graduates was expected to be 20 percent higher than in the previous year.
- The average base salary for a 2005 MBA was $109,000, up about 10 percent over the previous year.
- Recent average salaries were $92,253 in 2000, $99,082 in 2002, and $98,751 in 2004.

Economic Analysis

- Education increases human capital and expands production possibilities.
- The opportunity cost of a degree is forgone consumption. The payoff is an increase in lifetime production possibilities.
- Figure 1 shows the tradeoff facing a high school graduate between education goods and services and consumption goods and services on the blue *PPF*.
- Working full time, this person is at point *A* on the blue *PPF* in Fig. 1.
- By attending a university, the student moves from point *A* to point *B* along her *PPF*, forgoes current consumption (the opportunity cost of education), and increases the use of educational goods and services.
- On graduating from the university, earnings jump, so production possibilities expand to the red *PPF* in Fig. 1.
- Figure 2 shows a university graduate's tradeoff. The blue curve is the same *PPF* as the red *PPF* in Fig. 1.
- Working full time, this person earns enough to consume at point C on the blue *PPF* in Fig. 2.
- By pursuing an MBA, the student moves from point *C* to point *D* along her *PPF*, forgoes current consumption (the opportunity cost of an MBA), and increases the use of educational goods and services.
- With an MBA, a person's earnings jump again, so production possibilities expand to the red *PPF* in Fig. 2.
- For people who have the required ability, the benefits of postsecondary and postgraduate education are large.

You're the Voter

- With the huge return from postsecondary and postgraduate education, why don't more people remain in school longer?
- Would you vote for higher taxes to provide public scholarships to encourage more people to pursue postgraduate education? Explain why or why not.

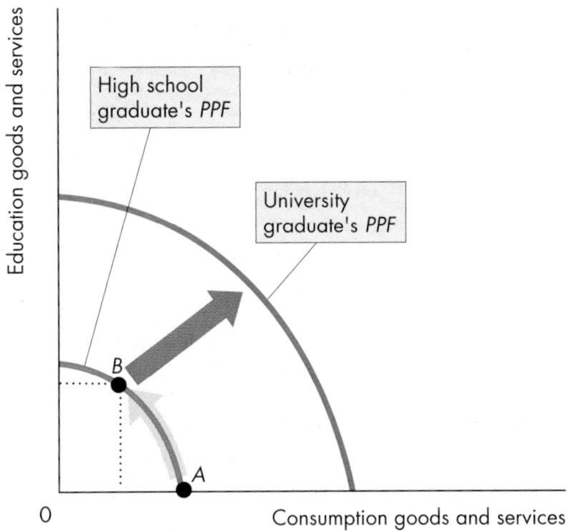

Figure 1 High school graduate's choices

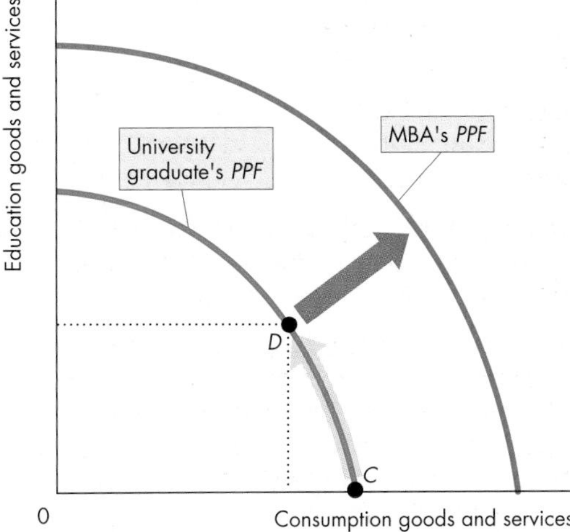

Figure 2 University graduate's choices

SUMMARY

Key Points

Production Possibilities and Opportunity Cost (pp. 34–36)

- The production possibilities frontier, *PPF*, is the boundary between production levels that are attainable and those that are not attainable when all the available resources are used to their limit.
- Production efficiency occurs at points on the *PPF*.
- Along the *PPF*, the opportunity cost of producing more of one good is the amount of the other good that must be given up.
- The opportunity cost of all goods increases as the production of the good increases.

Using Resources Efficiently (pp. 37–39)

- The marginal cost of a good is the opportunity cost of producing one more unit.
- The marginal benefit from a good is the maximum amount of another good that a person is willing to forgo to obtain more of the first good.
- The marginal benefit of a good decreases as the amount of the good available increases.
- Resources are used efficiently when the marginal cost of each good is equal to its marginal benefit.

Economic Growth (pp. 40–41)

- Economic growth, which is the expansion of production possibilities, results from capital accumulation and technological change.
- The opportunity cost of economic growth is forgone current consumption.

Gains from Trade (pp. 42–45)

- A person has a comparative advantage in producing a good if that person can produce the good at a lower opportunity cost than everyone else.
- People gain by specializing in the activity in which they have a comparative advantage and trading with others.
- Dynamic comparative advantage arises from learning-by-doing.

Economic Coordination (pp. 45–47)

- Firms coordinate a large amount of economic activity, but there is a limit to the efficient size of a firm.
- Markets coordinate the economic choices of people and firms.
- Markets can work efficiently only when property rights exist.
- Money makes trading in markets more efficient.

Key Figures

Key Terms

PROBLEMS

myeconlab **Tests, Study Plan, Solutions***

1. Use the figure to calculate Wendell's opportunity cost of one hour of tennis when he increases the time he plays tennis from
   a. 4 to 6 hours a week.
   b. 6 to 8 hours a week.

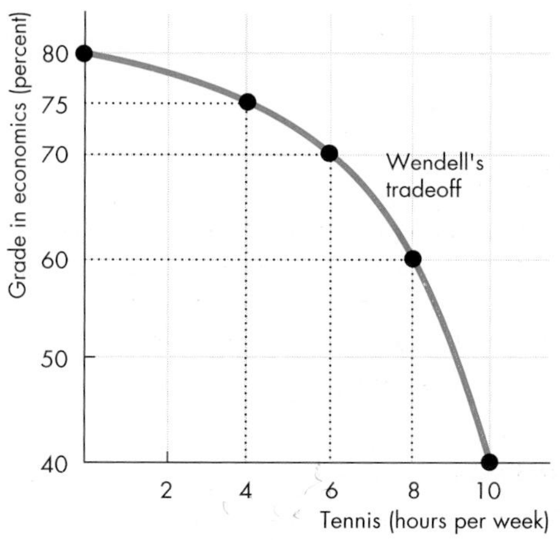

2. Wendell, whose *PPF* is shown in problem 1, has the following marginal benefit curve.

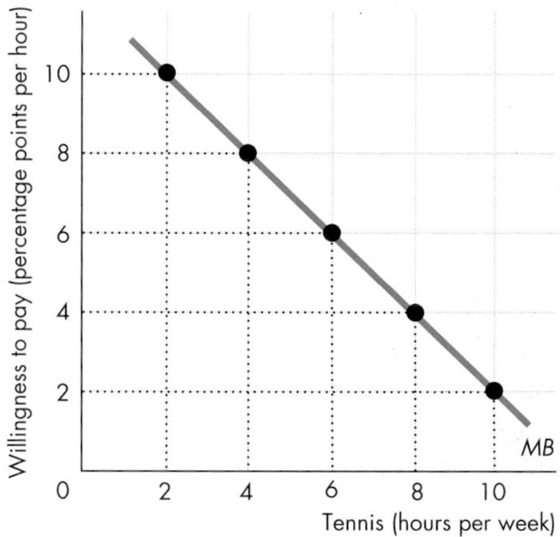

   a. If Wendell uses his time efficiently, what is his grade and how many hours of tennis does he play?
   b. Explain why Wendell would be worse off getting a higher grade.

*Solutions to odd-numbered problems are provided.

3. Sunland's production possibilities are

Food (pounds per month)		Sunscreen (gallons per month)
300	and	0
200	and	50
100	and	100
0	and	150

   a. Draw a graph of Sunland's *PPF*.
   b. What is Sunland's opportunity cost of producing 1 pound of food?
   c. What is Sunland's opportunity cost of producing 1 gallon of sunscreen?

4. In Sunland, which has the production possibilities shown in the table in problem 3, preferences are described by the following table.

Sunscreen (gallons per month)	Willingness to pay (pounds per gallons)
25	3
75	2
125	1

   a. Draw a graph of Sunland's marginal benefit from sunscreen.
   b. What is the quantity of sunscreen produced in Sunland if it achieves allocative efficiency?

5. A farm grows wheat and produces pork. The marginal cost of producing each of these products increases as more of it is produced.
   a. Make a graph that illustrates the farm's *PPF*.
   b. The farm adopts a new technology that allows it to use fewer resources to fatten pigs. Use your graph to illustrate the impact of the new technology on the farm's *PPF*.
   c. With the farm using the new technology described in part b, has the opportunity cost of producing a ton of wheat increased, decreased, or remained the same? Explain and illustrate your answer.
   d. Is the farm more efficient with the new technology than it was with the old one?

6. Tom can produce 40 balls per hour or 4 bats per hour. Tessa can produce 80 balls per hour or 4 bats per hour.
   a. Calculate Tom's opportunity cost of producing a ball.
   b. Calculate Tessa's opportunity cost of producing a ball.
   c. Who has a comparative advantage in producing balls?

d. If Tom and Tessa specialize in producing the good in which each of them has a comparative advantage, and they trade 1 bat for 15 balls, who gains from the specialization and trade?

Suppose Tessa buys a new machine for making bats that enables her to make 20 bats per hour. (She can still make only 80 balls per hour.)

e. Now who has a comparative advantage in producing bats?
f. Can Tom and Tessa still gain from trade?
g. Would Tom and Tessa still be willing to trade 1 bat for 15 balls?

CRITICAL THINKING

1. After you have studied *Reading Between the Lines* on pp. 48–49, answer the following questions:
   a. At what point on the blue *PPF* in Fig. 1 on p. 49 are resources allocated efficiently? Explain and illustrate your answer.
   b. Suppose that tuition rises. How does higher tuition change the opportunity cost of education and how does it change the student's *PPF*s in Fig. 1 and Fig. 2?
   c. Do you think that people obtain an efficient quantity of education? Explain why.
2. Before the Civil War, the South traded with the North and with England. It sold cotton and bought manufactured goods and food. During the war, one of Lincoln's first actions was to blockade the ports, which prevented this trade. The South had to increase its production of munitions and food.
   a. In what did the South have a comparative advantage?
   b. Draw a graph to illustrate production, consumption, and trade in the South before the Civil War. Was the South consuming inside, on, or outside its *PPF*?
   c. Draw a graph to show the effects of the Civil War on consumption and production in the South.
   d. Did the Civil War change any opportunity costs in the South? Did the opportunity cost of everything rise? Or did items cost less? Use graphs to illustrate your answer.
3. Ethanol can be produced from either sugar or corn. A gallon of ethanol costs 90¢ to produce from Brazilian sugarcane and $1 to produce from U.S. corn. The U. S. Department of Agriculture expects 20 percent of the corn harvest to be used to produce ethanol in 2007, an increase of 34 percent from 2006.
   a. Does the United States have a comparative advantage in producing ethanol?
   b. Will the opportunity cost of producing ethanol in the United States increase in 2007?
   c. Could the United States gain by importing ethanol (or sugarcane) from Brazil?
4. "America's baby-boomers are embracing tea for its health benefits," said *The Economist* (July 8, 2005, p. 65). The article went on to say: "Even though the climate is suitable, tea-growing [in the United States] is simply too costly, since the process is labor-intensive and resists automation."

   Using the information provided:
   a. Sketch two *PPF*s for the production of tea and other goods and services: one in the United States and the other in India.
   b. Sketch the marginal benefit curve for tea in the United States before and after the baby-boomers appreciated the health benefits of tea.
   c. Does the United States produce tea or import it?
   d. Does the change in preferences toward tea have any effect on the opportunity cost of producing tea?

WEB ACTIVITIES

myeconlab **Links to Web sites**

1. Obtain data on the tuition and other costs of enrolling in the MBA program at a school that interests you.
   a. Draw a *PPF* that shows the tradeoff that you would face if you decided to enroll in the MBA program.
   b. Do you think the marginal benefit of an MBA exceeds the marginal cost?

Your Economic Revolution

You are making progress in your study of economics. You've already encountered the big questions and big ideas of economics. And you've learned about the key insight of Adam Smith, the founder of economics: Specialization and exchange create economic wealth.

You are studying economics at a time that future historians will call the *information revolution.* We reserve the word "revolution" for big events that influence all future generations.

During the *Agricultural Revolution*, which occurred 10,000 years ago, people learned to domesticate animals and plant crops. They stopped roaming in search of food and settled in villages and eventually towns and cities, where they developed markets in which to exchange their products.

During the *Industrial Revolution*, which began 240 years ago, people used science to create new technologies. This revolution brought extraordinary wealth for some but created conditions in which others were left behind. It brought social and political tensions that we still face today.

During today's *Information Revolution*, people who embraced the new technologies prospered on an unimagined scale. But the incomes and living standards of the less educated are falling behind, and social and political tensions are increasing. Today's revolution has a global dimension. Some of the winners live in previously poor countries in Asia, and some of the losers live here in the United States.

So you are studying economics at an interesting time. Whatever *your* motivation is for studying economics, *my* objective is to help you do well in your course, enjoy it, and develop a deeper understanding of the economic world around you.

There are three reasons why I hope that we both succeed: First, a decent understanding of economics will help you to become a full participant in the information revolution. Second, an understanding of economics will help you to play a more effective role as a citizen and voter and enable you to add your voice to those who are looking for solutions to our social and political problems. Third, you will enjoy the sheer fun of *understanding* the forces at play and how they are shaping our world.

If you are finding economics interesting, think seriously about majoring in the subject. A degree in economics gives the best training available in problem solving, offers lots of opportunities to develop conceptual skills, and opens doors to a wide range of graduate courses, including the MBA, and to a wide range of jobs.

Economics was born during the Industrial Revolution. We'll look at its birth and meet its founder, Adam Smith. Then we'll talk about the progress that economists have made and some of the outstanding policy problems of today with one of today's most distinguished economists, Robert Barro of Harvard University.

PROBING THE IDEAS

The Sources of Economic Wealth

"It is not from the benevolence of the butcher, the brewer, or the baker that we expect our dinner, but from their regard to their own interest."

ADAM SMITH
The Wealth of Nations

The Father of Economics

Adam Smith *was a giant of a scholar who contributed to ethics and jurisprudence as well as economics. Born in 1723 in Kirkcaldy, a small fishing town near Edinburgh, Scotland, Smith was the only child of the town's customs officer (who died before Adam was born).*

His first academic appointment, at age 28, was as Professor of Logic at the University of Glasgow. He subsequently became tutor to a wealthy Scottish duke, whom he accompanied on a two-year grand European tour, following which he received a pension of £300 a year—ten times the average income at that time.

With the financial security of his pension, Smith devoted ten years to writing An Inquiry into the Nature and Causes of the **Wealth of Nations**, *which was published in 1776. Many people had written on economic issues before Adam Smith, but he made economics a science.*

Smith's account was so broad and authoritative that no subsequent writer on economics could advance ideas without tracing their connections to those of Adam Smith.

The Issues

Why are some nations wealthy while others are poor? This question lies at the heart of economics. And it leads directly to a second question: What can poor nations do to become wealthy?

Adam Smith, who is regarded by many scholars as the founder of economics, attempted to answer these questions in his book *The Wealth of Nations*, published in 1776. Smith was pondering these questions at the height of the Industrial Revolution. During these years, new technologies were invented and applied to the manufacture of cotton and wool cloth, iron, transportation, and agriculture.

Smith wanted to understand the sources of economic wealth, and he brought his acute powers of observation and abstraction to bear on the question. His answer:

- The division of labor
- Free markets

The division of labor—breaking tasks down into simple tasks and becoming skilled in those tasks—is the source of "the greatest improvement in the productive powers of labor," said Smith. The division of labor became even more productive when it was applied to creating new technologies. Scientists and engineers, trained in extremely narrow fields, became specialists at inventing. Their powerful skills accelerated the advance of technology, so by the 1820s, machines could make consumer goods faster and more accurately than any craftsman could. And by the 1850s, machines could make other machines that labor alone could never have made.

But, said Smith, the fruits of the division of labor are limited by the extent of the market. To make the market as large as possible, there must be no impediments to free trade both within a country and among countries. Smith argued that when each person makes the best possible economic choice, that choice leads as if by "an invisible hand" to the best outcome for society as a whole. The butcher, the brewer, and the baker each pursue their own interests but, in doing so, also serve the interests of everyone else.

Then

Adam Smith speculated that one person, working hard, using the hand tools available in the 1770s, might possibly make 20 pins a day. Yet, he observed, by using those same hand tools but breaking the process into a number of individually small operations in which people specialize —by the *division of labor*—ten people could make a staggering 48,000 pins a day. One draws out the wire, another straightens it, a third cuts it, a fourth points it, a fifth grinds it. Three specialists make the head, and a fourth attaches it. Finally, the pin is polished and packaged. But a large market is needed to support the division of labor: One factory employing ten workers would need to sell more than 15 million pins a year to stay in business.

Now

If Adam Smith were here today, the computer chip would fascinate him. He would see it as an extraordinary example of the productivity of the division of labor and of the use of machines to make machines that make other machines. From a design of a chip's intricate circuits, cameras transfer an image to glass plates that work like stencils. Workers prepare silicon wafers on which the circuits are printed. Some slice the wafers, others polish them, others bake them, and yet others coat them with a light-sensitive chemical. Machines transfer a copy of the circuit onto the wafer. Chemicals then etch the design onto the wafer. Further processes deposit atom-sized transistors and aluminum connectors. Finally, a laser separates the hundreds of chips on the wafer. Every stage in the process of creating a computer chip uses other computer chips. And like the pin of the 1770s, the computer chip of today benefits from a large market—a global market—to buy chips in the huge quantities in which they are produced efficiently.

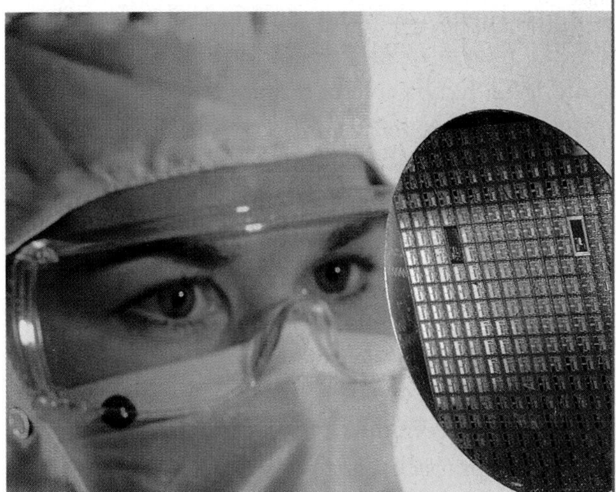

Many economists have worked on the big themes that Adam Smith began. One of these is Robert J. Barro of Harvard University, whom you can meet on the following pages.

TALKING WITH

Robert J. Barro

Robert J. Barro is Paul M. Warburg Professor of Economics at Harvard University and a senior fellow at the Hoover Institution of Stanford University. Born in 1944 in New York City, he was a physics undergraduate at the California Institute of Technology and an economics graduate student at Harvard.

Professor Barro is one of the world's leading economists and has done research on every aspect of macroeconomics, with a focus in recent years on economic growth and the interaction of economics and religion. Currently, he is studying the impact on stock markets and other asset markets of rare disasters—world wars, great depressions, epidemics, natural disasters. In addition to his many scholarly books and articles, his books, Getting it Right: Markets and Choices in a Free Society *(MIT Press, 1996) and* Nothing Is Sacred: Economic Ideas for the New Millennium *(MIT Press, 2002), explain, in nontechnical language, the importance of property rights and free markets for achieving economic growth and a high standard of living. He has just completed a new intermediate macroeconomics book,* Macroeconomics: A Modern Approach, *to be published by Thomson Learning. His articles in* Business Week *and the* Wall Street Journal *provide an accessible analysis of an incredible range of current economic issues.*

Michael Parkin talked with Robert Barro about his work and the progress that economists have made since the pioneering work of Adam Smith.

Professor Barro, your first degree was in physics. Why did you switch to economics when you went to graduate school?

For me, economics provided an ideal combination of technical analysis with applications to social problems and policies. Physics—or really mathematics—provided a strong background for economic theory and econometrics, but it was not until later in graduate school that I thought I acquired good economic insights. Overall, the transition from physics to economics was a relatively easy one for me, and I have never regretted the choice to switch fields. (Perhaps it also helped that, after taking courses from the great Richard Feynman at Caltech, I recognized that I would never be an outstanding theoretical physicist.)

Let's talk first about markets and choices in a free society. What is the central theme and message of your books on these vital issues?

In the long run, the central distinction between successful and unsuccessful economies is the extent to which they foster free markets and provide functioning institutions that support property rights and the rule of law. These points were highlighted by the failure of Communist economies, notably the former Soviet Union and China under Mao, in comparison with the successes of western societies, which relied more on markets and choices. These days China has arguably become the most capitalistic country on earth. For example, on a recent trip there, I saw a statue of Adam Smith on the campus of the South-Western University of Finance and Economics in Chengdu. As far as I know, there is no such statue at any U.S. or Canadian university.

Much of your research has focused on the same question that Adam Smith addressed in his. How do Adam Smith's speculations look today in light of what econo-

mists have discovered over the past two centuries? What are some of the key things we know today that Adam Smith didn't know?

Smith's topic about the source of the wealth of nations is often rephrased in modern research in terms of which factors determine the long-term rate of economic growth. Of course, for an economy to become wealthy, it has to sustain strong economic growth over a long period. A lot of progress has been made since the early 1990s in attaining an empirical understanding of the determinants of economic growth. There are no "silver bullets" for growth, but there are a number of favorable policies, institutions, and national characteristics that have been identified.

There are no 'silver bullets' for growth, but there are a number of favorable policies, institutions, and national characteristics that have been identified.

For example, growth is stimulated by strong rule of law, high levels of human capital in the forms of education and health, low levels of nonproductive government spending (and associated taxes), international openness, low fertility rates, and macroeconomic stability (including low and stable inflation). Given these and other factors, growth tends to be higher if a country starts off poorer. That is, convergence—in the sense of the poor tending to grow faster than the rich—holds in a conditional sense, when one holds constant an array of policies and national characteristics. However, convergence does not apply in an absolute sense because the poorest countries tend to have the worst policies and characteristics (which explains why they are poor).

Is there anything that rich countries can do to help poor countries grow faster? Or does successful economic growth come only from self-help?

Mostly, economic growth has to come from internal improvements in institutions and policies and from domestic accumulations of human and physical capital. There is no evidence that the rich countries can help through welfare programs, such as foreign aid and debt relief. On the contrary, there is some evidence that, because of the low quality of governance in most developing countries, foreign aid goes mainly to increased government spending and corruption. In the bad old days, the rich countries also provided governance (though not aimed especially at the interests of the governed). However, no one wants to return to the era of colonialism.

How does international trade influence economic growth? Could the rich countries do more by opening themselves to free trade with poor countries? Or is it enough for poor countries to just get on with opening their doors to free trade as Hong Kong did?

The rich countries could help to spur economic development by opening themselves more to trade in goods and services, technology, and financial transactions. Protectionist policies, notably in agriculture and textiles, are harmful to developing countries as well as to consumers in rich countries. President Bush's policies have been a mixed bag in this area; negative aspects were protectionism for steel, agriculture, and timber, as well as threats of protectionism against Chinese goods, especially textiles. Of course, on agricultural protectionism, Western Europe is even worse than the United States.

I am optimistic that the monetary authorities of the United States and many other countries have become committed to price stability and have learned that high inflation does not stimulate growth.

Inflation was subdued in the United States for most of the 1990s and early 2000s. Is inflation still a problem of the past or should we start worrying about again?

I am optimistic that the monetary authorities of the United States and many other countries have become committed to price stability and have learned that high inflation does not stimulate growth. Central banks seem also to have learned a lot about the mechanics of achieving price stability. The appointment of

Ben Bernanke as U.S. Federal Reserve chair was an excellent move. I think he will move the United States over time toward a more formal regime of inflation targeting, and this will be a good idea.

Some of your recent work has been on the interaction of religion and economic performance. Does religion influence the economy? Or does economic performance influence religion?

My coauthor (and wife), Rachel McCleary, and I have found that both directions of causation are important. Economic development tends to reduce religious participation and beliefs, though the effect is not strong, and the United States is an exception to the usual pattern. Subsidy to organized religion through establishment of state religion tends to increase participation, but some forms of regulation of the religion market tend to reduce participation. Religious beliefs related to an after-life—notably, beliefs in hell and heaven—tend to foster growth (a result reminiscent of the theorizing by the sociologist Max Weber). However, for given beliefs, greater participation in formal religion seems to reduce growth. We think the last effect involves the time and other resources used up in religious participation.

Economists have found the framework or methodology that makes economics the core social science, and its impact has been felt greatly by other fields, such as political science, law, and history.

What remains in today's macroeconomics of the contribution of Keynes?

Probably, Keynesian economics is most influential today in analyses that stress the real effects of monetary policy—either as sources of business fluctuations or as ways to smooth out the cycle. This situation is ironic because Keynes himself deemphasized monetary shocks as a source of fluctuations. He stressed the excesses of the private economy—including the amplifying effects of multipliers and the sensitivity of investment to shifting expectations—and the potentially beneficial role of offsetting fiscal policies. Empirically, the multiplier seems to have existed only in the mind of Keynes.

What advice do you have for a student who is just starting to study economics? Is it a good subject in which to major? If so, what other subjects would you urge students to study alongside economics? Or is the path that you followed, starting with physics (or perhaps math) and then moving to economics for graduate school, more effective?

Economics is an excellent field for an undergraduate to study whether one chooses to become an economist or—more likely—if one goes into other fields, such as business or law. Economists have found the framework or methodology that makes economics the core social science, and its impact has been felt greatly by other fields, such as political science, law, and history.

These days, economic reasoning is being applied to the study of an array of social topics, including marriage and fertility, crime, democracy, and legal structure. As another example, I am currently participating in a project that involves the interactions between economics and religion (see www.wcfia.harvard.edu/religion for a description). This work is partly about how economic development and government policies affect religiosity and partly about how religious beliefs and participation influence economic and political outcomes. So perhaps in the future, economics will also be important for studies in theology. No doubt, many economists (including me) have imperialistic tendencies, but this is because they have a great product to sell. As for other complementary subjects to study, the most valuable one is probably mathematics, which provides many of the useful tools to carry out theoretical and empirical inquiries.

CHAPTER 3

Demand and Supply

Slide, Rocket, and Roller Coaster

Slide, rocket, and roller coaster—Disneyland rides?

No, they are commonly used descriptions of price changes.

The price of a personal computer took a dramatic slide from around $3,000 in 2000 to $300 in 2006. The price of gasoline rocketed in 2006. The prices of coffee, bananas, and other agricultural products rise and fall like a roller coaster.

You've learned that economics is about the choices people make to cope with scarcity and how those choices respond to incentives. Prices are one of the incentives to which people respond. You're now going to see how prices are determined by demand and supply.

The demand and supply model is the main tool of economics. It helps us to answer the big economic question: What, how, and for whom are goods and services produced? It also helps us to say when the pursuit of self-interest promotes the social interest.

Your careful study of this topic will bring big rewards both in your further study of economics and in your everyday life. When you have completed your study of demand and supply, you will be able to explain how prices are determined and make predictions about price slides, rockets, and roller coasters. Once you understand demand and supply, you will view the world through new eyes. You can begin to practice applying the tools of demand and supply in *Reading Between the Lines* at the end of this chapter where you will learn why the price of gasoline rose so much in 2006.

After studying this chapter, you will be able to

- Describe a competitive market and think about a price as an opportunity cost
- Explain the influences on demand
- Explain the influences on supply
- Explain how demand and supply determine prices and quantities bought and sold
- Use demand and supply to make predictions about changes in prices and quantities

Markets and Prices

When you need a new pair of running shoes, want a bagel and a latte, plan to upgrade your cell phone, or need to fly home for Thanksgiving, you must find a place where people sell those items or offer those services. The place in which you find them is a *market.* You learned in Chapter 2 (p. 46) that a market is any arrangement that enables buyers and sellers to get information and to do business with each other.

A market has two sides: buyers and sellers. There are markets for *goods* such as apples and hiking boots, for *services* such as haircuts and tennis lessons, for *resources* such as computer programmers and earthmovers, and for other manufactured *inputs* such as memory chips and auto parts. There are also markets for money such as Japanese yen and for financial securities such as Yahoo! stock. Only our imagination limits what can be traded in markets.

Some markets are physical places where buyers and sellers meet and where an auctioneer or a broker helps to determine the prices. Examples of this type of market are the New York Stock Exchange and the wholesale fish, meat, and produce markets.

Some markets are groups of people spread around the world who never meet and know little about each other but are connected through the Internet or by telephone and fax. Examples are the e-commerce markets and currency markets.

But most markets are unorganized collections of buyers and sellers. You do most of your trading in this type of market. An example is the market for basketball shoes. The buyers in this $3 billion-a-year market are the 45 million Americans who play basketball (or who want to make a fashion statement). The sellers are the tens of thousands of retail sports equipment and footwear stores. Each buyer can visit several different stores, and each seller knows that the buyer has a choice of stores.

Markets vary in the intensity of competition that buyers and sellers face. In this chapter, we're going to study a **competitive market**—a market that has many buyers and many sellers, so no single buyer or seller can influence the price.

Producers offer items for sale only if the price is high enough to cover their opportunity cost. And consumers respond to changing opportunity cost by seeking cheaper alternatives to expensive items.

We are going to study how people respond to *prices* and the forces that determine prices. But to pursue these tasks, we need to understand the relationship between a price and an opportunity cost.

In everyday life, the *price* of an object is the number of dollars that must be given up in exchange for it. Economists refer to this price as the **money price**.

The *opportunity cost* of an action is the highest-valued alternative forgone. If, when you buy a cup of coffee, the highest-valued thing you forgo is some gum, then the opportunity cost of the coffee is the *quantity* of gum forgone. We can calculate the quantity of gum forgone from the money prices of the coffee and the gum.

If the money price of coffee is $1 a cup and the money price of gum is 50¢ a pack, then the opportunity cost of one cup of coffee is two packs of gum. To calculate this opportunity cost, we divide the price of a cup of coffee by the price of a pack of gum and find the *ratio* of one price to the other. The ratio of one price to another is called a **relative price**, and a *relative price is an opportunity cost.*

We can express the relative price of coffee in terms of gum or any other good. The normal way of expressing a relative price is in terms of a "basket" of all goods and services. To calculate this relative price, we divide the money price of a good by the money price of a "basket" of all goods (called a *price index*). The resulting relative price tells us the opportunity cost of the good in terms of how much of the "basket" we must give up to buy it.

The theory of demand and supply that we are about to study determines *relative prices,* and the word "price" means *relative* price. When we predict that a price will fall, we do not mean that its *money* price will fall—although it might. We mean that its *relative* price will fall. That is, its price will fall *relative* to the average price of other goods and services.

REVIEW QUIZ

1. What is the distinction between a money price and a relative price?
2. Explain why a relative price is an opportunity cost.
3. Think of examples of goods whose relative price has risen or fallen by a large amount.

myeconlab Study Plan 3.1

Let's begin our study of demand and supply, starting with demand.

Demand

If you demand something, then you

1. Want it,
2. Can afford it, and
3. Plan to buy it.

Wants are the unlimited desires or wishes that people have for goods and services. How many times have you thought that you would like something "if only you could afford it" or "if it weren't so expensive"? Scarcity guarantees that many—perhaps most—of our wants will never be satisfied. Demand reflects a decision about which wants to satisfy.

The **quantity demanded** of a good or service is the amount that consumers plan to buy during a given time period at a particular price. The quantity demanded is not necessarily the same as the quantity actually bought. Sometimes the quantity demanded exceeds the amount of goods available, so the quantity bought is less than the quantity demanded.

The quantity demanded is measured as an amount per unit of time. For example, suppose that you buy one cup of coffee a day. The quantity of coffee that you demand can be expressed as 1 cup per day, as 7 cups per week, or as 365 cups per year.

Many factors influence buying plans, and one of them is the price. We look first at the relationship between the quantity demanded of a good and its price. To study this relationship, we keep all other influences on buying plans the same and we ask: How, other things remaining the same, does the quantity demanded of a good change as its price changes?

The law of demand provides the answer.

The Law of Demand

The **law of demand** states

> Other things remaining the same, the higher the price of a good, the smaller is the quantity demanded; and the lower the price of a good, the greater is the quantity demanded.

Why does a higher price reduce the quantity demanded? For two reasons:

- Substitution effect
- Income effect

Substitution Effect When the price of a good rises, other things remaining the same, its *relative* price—its opportunity cost—rises. Although each good is unique, it has *substitutes*—other goods that can be used in its place. As the opportunity cost of a good rises, people buy less of that good and more of its substitutes.

Income Effect When a price rises and all other influences on buying plans remain unchanged, the price rises *relative* to people's incomes. So faced with a higher price and an unchanged income, people cannot afford to buy all the things they previously bought. They must decrease the quantities demanded of at least some goods and services, and normally, the good whose price has increased will be one of the goods that people buy less of.

To see the substitution effect and the income effect at work, think about the effects of a change in the price of an energy bar. Several different goods are substitutes for an energy bar. For example, an energy drink could be consumed instead of an energy bar.

Suppose that an energy bar initially sells for $3 and then its price falls to $1.50. People now substitute energy bars for energy drinks—the substitution effect. And with a budget that now has some slack from the lower price of an energy bar, people buy even more energy bars—the income effect. The quantity of energy bars demanded increases for these two reasons.

Now suppose that an energy bar initially sells for $3 each and then the price doubles to $6. People now buy fewer energy bars and more energy drinks—the substitution effect. And faced with a tighter budget, people buy even fewer energy bars—the income effect. The quantity of energy bars demanded decreases for these two reasons.

Demand Curve and Demand Schedule

You are now about to study one of the two most used curves in economics: the demand curve. And you are going to encounter one of the most critical distinctions: the distinction between *demand* and *quantity demanded.*

The term **demand** refers to the entire relationship between the price of the good and the quantity demanded of the good. Demand is illustrated by the demand curve and the demand schedule. The term *quantity demanded* refers to a point on a demand curve—the quantity demanded at a particular price.

Figure 3.1 shows the demand curve for energy bars. A **demand curve** shows the relationship between the quantity demanded of a good and its price when all other influences on consumers' planned purchases remain the same.

The table in Fig. 3.1 is the demand schedule for energy bars. A *demand schedule* lists the quantities demanded at each price when all the other influences on consumers' planned purchases remain the same. For example, if the price of a bar is 50¢, the quantity demanded is 22 million a week. If the price is $2.50, the quantity demanded is 5 million a week. The other rows of the table show the quantities demanded at prices of $1.00, $1.50, and $2.00.

We graph the demand schedule as a demand curve with the quantity demanded on the *x*-axis and the price on the *y*-axis. The points on the demand curve labeled *A* through *E* correspond to the rows of the demand schedule. For example, point *A* on the graph shows a quantity demanded of 22 million energy bars a week at a price of 50¢ a bar.

Willingness and Ability to Pay Another way of looking at the demand curve is as a willingness-and-ability-to-pay curve. And the willingness and ability to pay is a measure of *marginal benefit.*

If a small quantity is available, the highest price that someone is willing and able to pay for one more unit is high. But as the quantity available increases, the marginal benefit of each additional unit falls and the highest price that someone is willing and able to pay also falls along the demand curve.

In Fig. 3.1, if only 5 million energy bars are available each week, the highest price that someone is willing to pay for the 5 millionth bar is $2.50. But if 22 million energy bars are available each week, someone is willing to pay 50¢ for the last bar bought.

A Change in Demand

When any factor that influences buying plans other than the price of the good changes, there is a **change in demand.** Figure 3.2 illustrates an increase in demand. When demand increases, the demand curve shifts rightward and the quantity demanded at each price is greater. For example, at a price of $2.50, on the original (blue) demand curve, the quantity demanded is 5 million energy bars a week and on the new (red) demand curve, the quantity demanded is 15 million energy bars a week. Look closely at the numbers in the table and check that the quantity demanded at each price is greater.

FIGURE 3.1 The Demand Curve

myeconlab

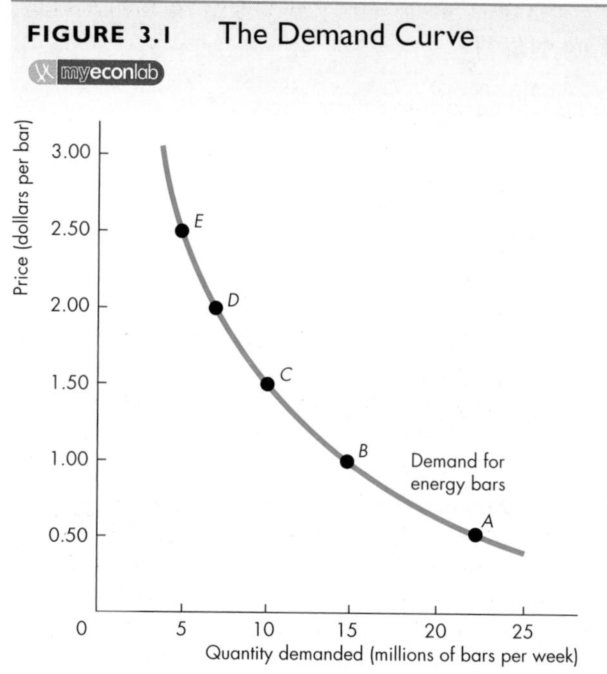

	Price (dollars per bar)	Quantity demanded (millions of bars per week)
A	0.50	22
B	1.00	15
C	1.50	10
D	2.00	7
E	2.50	5

The table shows a demand schedule for energy bars. At a price of 50¢ a bar, 22 million bars a week are demanded; at a price of $1.50 a bar, 10 million bars a week are demanded. The demand curve shows the relationship between quantity demanded and price, other things remaining the same. The demand curve slopes downward: As price decreases, the quantity demanded increases.

The demand curve can be read in two ways. For a given price, the demand curve tells us the quantity that people plan to buy. For example, at a price of $1.50 a bar, people plan to buy 10 million bars a week. For a given quantity, the demand curve tells us the maximum price that consumers are willing and able to pay for the last bar available. For example, the maximum price that consumers will pay for the 15 millionth bar is $1.00.

Six main factors bring changes in demand. They are changes in

- The prices of related goods
- Expected future prices
- Income
- Expected future income
- Population
- Preferences

Prices of Related Goods The quantity of energy bars that consumers plan to buy depends in part on the prices of substitutes for energy bars. A **substitute** is a good that can be used in place of another good. For example, a bus ride is a substitute for a train ride; a hamburger is a substitute for a hot dog; and an energy drink is a substitute for an energy bar. If the price of a substitute for an energy bar rises, people buy less of the substitute and more energy bars. For example, if the price of an energy drink rises, people buy fewer energy drinks and more energy bars. The demand for energy bars increases.

The quantity of energy bars that people plan to buy also depends on the prices of complements with energy bars. A **complement** is a good that is used in conjunction with another good. Hamburgers and fries are complements, and so are energy bars and exercise. If the price of an hour at the gym falls, people buy more gym time *and more* energy bars.

Expected Future Prices If the price of a good is expected to rise in the future and if the good can be stored, the opportunity cost of obtaining the good for future use is lower today than it will be when the price has increased. So people retime their purchases—they substitute over time. They buy more of the good now before its price is expected to rise (and less afterward), so the demand for the good today increases.

For example, suppose that a Florida frost damages the season's orange crop. You expect the price of orange juice to rise, so you fill your freezer with enough frozen juice to get you through the next six months. Your current demand for frozen orange juice has increased, and your future demand has decreased.

Similarly, if the price of a good is expected to fall in the future, the opportunity cost of buying the good today is high relative to what it is expected to be in the future. So again, people retime their purchases. They buy less of the good now before its price

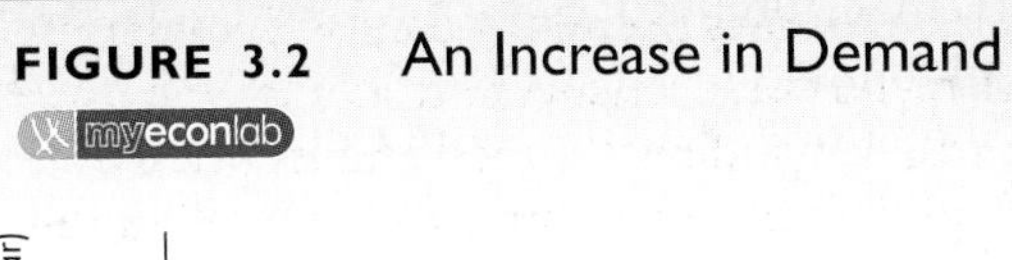

FIGURE 3.2 An Increase in Demand

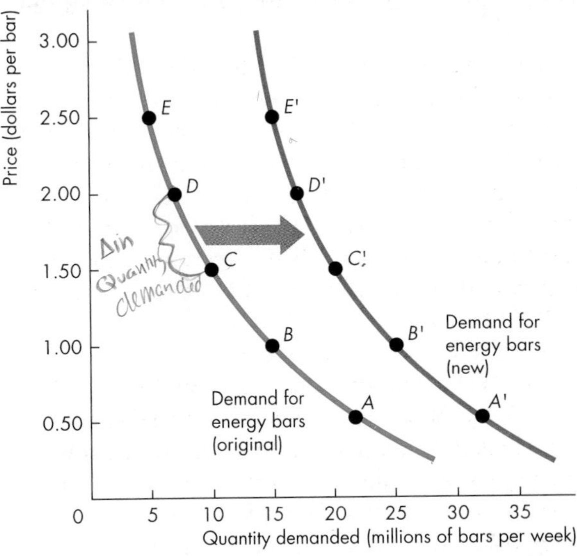

	Original demand schedule			New demand schedule	
	Original income			New higher income	
	Price (dollars per bar)	**Quantity demanded** (millions of bars per week)		**Price** (dollars per bar)	**Quantity demanded** (millions of bars per week)
A	0.50	22	*A'*	0.50	32
B	1.00	15	*B'*	1.00	25
C	1.50	10	*C'*	1.50	20
D	2.00	7	*D'*	2.00	17
E	2.50	5	*E'*	2.50	15

A change in any influence on buyers' plans other than the price of the good itself results in a new demand schedule and a shift of the demand curve. A change in income changes the demand for energy bars. At a price of $1.50 a bar, 10 million bars a week are demanded at the original income (row *C* of the table) and 20 million bars a week are demanded at the new higher income. A rise in income increases the demand for energy bars. The demand curve shifts *rightward*, as shown by the shift arrow and the resulting red curve.

falls, so the demand for the good decreases today and increases in the future.

Computer prices are constantly falling, and this fact poses a dilemma. Will you buy a new computer now, in time for the start of the school year, or will you wait until the price has fallen some more? Because people expect computer prices to keep falling, the current demand for computers is less (the future demand is greater) than it otherwise would be.

Income Consumers' income influences demand. When income increases, consumers buy more of most goods; and when income decreases, consumers buy less of most goods. Although an increase in income leads to an increase in the demand for *most* goods, it does not lead to an increase in the demand for *all* goods. A **normal good** is one for which demand increases as income increases. An **inferior good** is one for which demand decreases as income increases. Long-distance transportation has examples of both normal goods and inferior goods. As incomes increase, the demand for air travel (a normal good) increases and the demand for long-distance bus trips (an inferior good) decreases.

Expected Future Income When income is expected to increase in the future, demand might increase now. For example, a salesperson gets the news that she will receive a big bonus at the end of the year, so she decides to buy a new car right now.

Population Demand also depends on the size and the age structure of the population. The larger the population, the greater is the demand for all goods and services; the smaller the population, the smaller is the demand for all goods and services.

For example, the demand for parking spaces or movies or energy bars or just about anything that you can imagine is much greater in New York City (population 7.5 million) than it is in Boise, Idaho (population 150,000).

Also, the larger the proportion of the population in a given age group, the greater is the demand for the goods and services used by that age group.

For example, during the 1990s, a decrease in the college-age population decreased the demand for college places. During those same years, the number of Americans aged 85 years and over increased by more than 1 million. As a result, the demand for nursing home services increased.

TABLE 3.1 The Demand for Energy Bars

The Law of Demand

The quantity of energy bars demanded

Decreases if:	*Increases if:*
The price of an energy bar rises	The price of an energy bar falls

Changes in Demand

The demand for energy bars

Decreases if:	*Increases if:*
The price of a substitute falls	The price of a substitute rises
The price of a complement rises	The price of a complement falls
The price of an energy bar is expected to fall in the future	The price of an energy bar is expected to rise in the future
Income falls*	Income rises*
Expected future income falls	Expected future income rises
The population decreases	The population increases

*An energy bar is a normal good.

Preferences Demand depends on preferences. *Preferences* determine the value that people place on each good and service. Preferences depend on such things as the weather, information, and fashion. For example, greater health and fitness awareness has shifted preferences in favor of energy bars, so the demand for energy bars has increased.

Table 3.1 summarizes the influences on demand and the direction of those influences.

A Change in the Quantity Demanded Versus a Change in Demand

Changes in the factors that influence buyers' plans cause either a change in the quantity demanded or a change in demand. Equivalently, they cause either a movement along the demand curve or a shift of the demand curve. The distinction between a change in the quantity demanded and a change in demand is the same as that between a movement along the demand curve and a shift of the demand curve.

A point on the demand curve shows the quantity demanded at a given price. So a movement along the demand curve shows a **change in the quantity demanded.** The entire demand curve shows demand. So a shift of the demand curve shows a *change in demand.* Figure 3.3 illustrates these distinctions.

Movement Along the Demand Curve If the price of a good changes but everything else remains the same, there is a movement along the demand curve. Because the demand curve slopes downward, a fall in the price of a good increases the quantity demanded of it and a rise in the price of the good decreases the quantity demanded of it—the law of demand.

In Fig. 3.3, if the price of a good falls when everything else remains the same, the quantity demanded of that good increases and there is a movement down the demand curve D_0. If the price rises when everything else remains the same, the quantity demanded of that good decreases and there is a movement up the demand curve D_0.

A Shift of the Demand Curve If the price of a good remains constant but some other influence on buyers' plans changes, there is a change in demand for that good. We illustrate a change in demand as a shift of the demand curve. For example, if more people work out at the gym, consumers buy more energy bars regardless of the price of a bar. That is what a rightward shift of the demand curve shows—more energy bars are demanded at each price.

In Fig. 3.3, when any influence on buyers' planned purchases changes, other than the price of the good, there is a *change in demand* and the demand curve shifts. Demand *increases* and the demand curve *shifts rightward* (to the red demand curve D_1) if the price of a substitute rises, the price of a complement falls, the expected future price of the good rises, income increases (for a normal good), expected future income increases, or the population increases. Demand *decreases* and the demand curve *shifts leftward* (to the red demand curve D_2) if the price of a substitute falls, the price of a complement rises, the expected future price of the good falls, income decreases (for a normal good), expected future income decreases, or the population decreases. (For an inferior good, the effects of changes in income are in the direction opposite to those described above.)

FIGURE 3.3 A Change in the Quantity Demanded Versus a Change in Demand

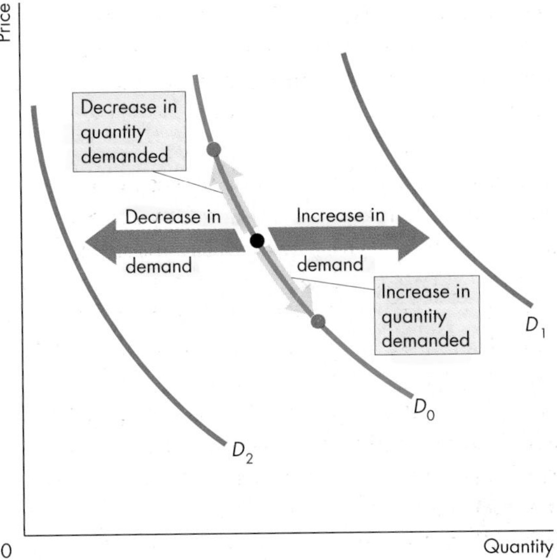

When the price of the good changes, there is a movement along the demand curve and *a change in the quantity demanded,* shown by the blue arrows on demand curve D_0. When any other influence on buyers' plans changes, there is a shift of the demand curve and a *change in demand.* An increase in demand shifts the demand curve rightward (from D_0 to D_1). A decrease in demand shifts the demand curve leftward (from D_0 to D_2).

REVIEW QUIZ

1. Define the quantity demanded of a good or service.
2. What is the law of demand and how do we illustrate it?
3. What does the demand curve tell us about the price that consumers are willing to pay?
4. List all the influences on buying plans that change demand, and for each influence, say whether it increases or decreases demand.
5. Why does demand not change when the price of a good changes with no change in the other influences on buying plans?

myeconlab **Study Plan 3.2**

Supply

If a firm supplies a good or service, the firm

1. Has the resources and technology to produce it,
2. Can profit from producing it, and
3. Plans to produce it and sell it.

A supply is more than just having the *resources* and the *technology* to produce something. *Resources and technology* are the constraints that limit what is possible.

Many useful things can be produced, but they are not produced unless it is profitable to do so. Supply reflects a decision about which technologically feasible items to produce.

The **quantity supplied** of a good or service is the amount that producers plan to sell during a given time period at a particular price. The quantity supplied is not necessarily the same amount as the quantity actually sold. Sometimes the quantity supplied is greater than the quantity demanded, so the quantity bought is less than the quantity supplied.

Like the quantity demanded, the quantity supplied is measured as an amount per unit of time. For example, suppose that GM produces 1,000 cars a day. The quantity of cars supplied by GM can be expressed as 1,000 a day, 7,000 a week, or 365,000 a year. Without the time dimension, we cannot tell whether a particular number is large or small.

Many factors influence selling plans, and again one of them is the price. We look first at the relationship between the quantity supplied of a good and its price. And again, as we did when we studied demand, to isolate this relationship, we keep all other influences on selling plans the same and we ask: How, other things remaining the same, does the quantity supplied of a good change as its price changes?

The law of supply provides the answer.

The Law of Supply

The **law of supply** states:

> Other things remaining the same, the higher the price of a good, the greater is the quantity supplied; and the lower the price of a good, the smaller is the quantity supplied.

Why does a higher price increase the quantity supplied? It is because *marginal cost increases.* As the quantity produced of any good increases, the marginal cost of producing the good increases. (You can refresh your memory of increasing marginal cost in Chapter 2, p. 37.)

It is never worth producing a good if the price received for the good does not at least cover the marginal cost of producing it. So when the price of a good rises, other things remaining the same, producers are willing to incur a higher marginal cost and increase production. The higher price brings forth an increase in the quantity supplied.

Let's now illustrate the law of supply with a supply curve and a supply schedule.

Supply Curve and Supply Schedule

You are now going to study the second of the two most used curves in economics: the supply curve. And you're going to learn about the critical distinction between *supply* and *quantity supplied.*

The term **supply** refers to the entire relationship between the price of a good and the quantity supplied of it. Supply is illustrated by the supply curve and the supply schedule. The term *quantity supplied* refers to a point on a supply curve—the quantity supplied at a particular price.

Figure 3.4 shows the supply curve of energy bars. A **supply curve** shows the relationship between the quantity supplied of a good and its price when all other influences on producers' planned sales remain the same. The supply curve is a graph of a supply schedule.

The table in Fig. 3.4 sets out the supply schedule for energy bars. A *supply schedule* lists the quantities supplied at each price when all the other influences on producers' planned sales remain the same. For example, if the price of a bar is 50¢, the quantity supplied is zero—in row *A* of the table. If the price of a bar is $1.00, the quantity supplied is 6 million energy bars a week—in row *B*. The other rows of the table show the quantities supplied at prices of $1.50, $2.00, and $2.50.

To make a supply curve, we graph the quantity supplied on the *x*-axis and the price on the *y*-axis, just as in the case of the demand curve. The points on the supply curve labeled *A* through *E* correspond to the rows of the supply schedule. For example, point *A* on the graph shows a quantity supplied of zero at a price of 50¢ an energy bar.

FIGURE 3.4 The Supply Curve

myeconlab

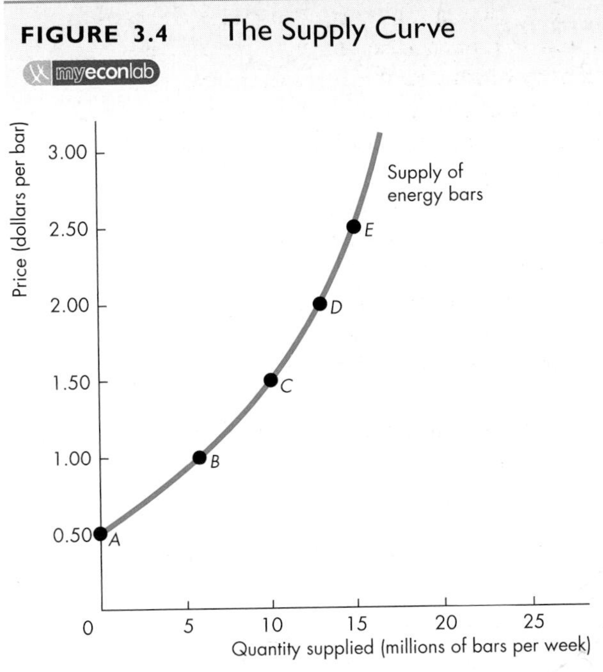

	Price (dollars per bar)	Quantity supplied (millions of bars per week)
A	0.50	0
B	1.00	6
C	1.50	10
D	2.00	13
E	2.50	15

The table shows the supply schedule of energy bars. For example, at a price of $1.00, 6 million bars a week are supplied; at a price of $2.50, 15 million bars a week are supplied. The supply curve shows the relationship between the quantity supplied and price, other things remaining the same. The supply curve slopes upward: As the price of a good increases, the quantity supplied increases.

A supply curve can be read in two ways. For a given price, the supply curve tells us the quantity that producers plan to sell at that price. For example, at a price of $1.50 a bar, producers are willing to supply 10 million bars a week. For a given quantity, the supply curve tells us the minimum price that producers are willing to sell one more bar. For example, if 15 million bars are produced each week, the lowest price at which someone is willing to sell the 15 millionth bar is $2.50.

Minimum Supply Price Just as the demand curve has two interpretations, so too does the supply curve. The demand curve can be interpreted as a willingness-and-ability-to-pay curve. The supply curve can be interpreted as a minimum-supply-price curve—a curve that shows the lowest price at which someone is willing to sell. And this lowest price is *marginal cost.*

If a small quantity is produced, the lowest price at which someone is willing to sell one more unit is low. But as the quantity produced increases, the marginal cost of each additional unit rises and the lowest price at which someone is willing to sell also rises along the supply curve.

In Fig. 3.4, if 15 million bars are produced each week, the lowest price at which someone is willing to sell the 15 millionth bar is $2.50. But if 10 million bars are produced each week, someone is willing to accept $1.50 for the last bar sold.

A Change in Supply

When any factor that influences selling plans other than the price of the good changes, there is a **change in supply**.

Five main factors bring changes in supply. They are changes in

- The prices of productive resources
- The prices of related goods produced
- Expected future prices
- The number of suppliers
- Technology

Prices of Productive Resources The prices of the productive resources used to produce a good influence its supply. The easiest way to see this influence is to think about the supply curve as a minimum-supply-price curve. If the price of a productive resource rises, the lowest price a producer is willing to accept rises, so supply decreases. For example, during 2006, as the price of jet fuel increased, the supply of air transportation decreased. Similarly, a rise in the minimum wage decreases the supply of hamburgers.

Prices of Related Goods Produced The prices of related goods and services that firms produce influence supply. For example, if the price of energy gel rises, the supply of energy bars decreases. Energy bars and energy gel are *substitutes in production*—goods that can be produced by using the same resources. If the price of beef rises, the supply of cowhide increases. Beef and cowhide are *complements in production*—goods that must be produced together.

Expected Future Prices If the price of a good is expected to rise, the return from selling the good in the future is higher than it is today. So supply decreases today and increases in the future.

The Number of Suppliers The larger the number of firms that produce a good, the greater is the supply of the good. And as firms enter an industry, the supply in that industry increases. As firms leave an industry, the supply in that industry decreases.

Technology The term "technology" is used broadly to mean the way that factors of production are used to produce a good. Technology changes both positively and negatively. A positive technology change occurs when a new method is discovered that lowers the cost of producing a good. An example is new methods used in the factories that make computer chips. A negative technology change occurs when an event such as extreme weather or natural disaster increases the cost of producing a good. A positive technology change increases supply, and a negative technology change decreases supply.

Figure 3.5 illustrates an increase in supply. When supply increases, the supply curve shifts rightward and the quantity supplied at each price is larger. For example, at $1.00 per bar, on the original (blue) supply curve, the quantity supplied is 6 million bars a week. On the new (red) supply curve, the quantity supplied is 15 million bars a week. Look closely at the numbers in the table in Fig. 3.5 and check that the quantity supplied is larger at each price.

Table 3.2 summarizes the influences on supply and the directions of those influences.

A Change in the Quantity Supplied Versus a Change in Supply

Changes in the factors that influence producers' planned sales cause either a change in the quantity supplied or a change in supply. Equivalently, they cause either a movement along the supply curve or a shift of the supply curve.

A point on the supply curve shows the quantity supplied at a given price. A movement along the supply curve shows a **change in the quantity supplied**. The entire supply curve shows supply. A shift of the supply curve shows a *change in supply*.

FIGURE 3.5 An Increase in Supply

myeconlab

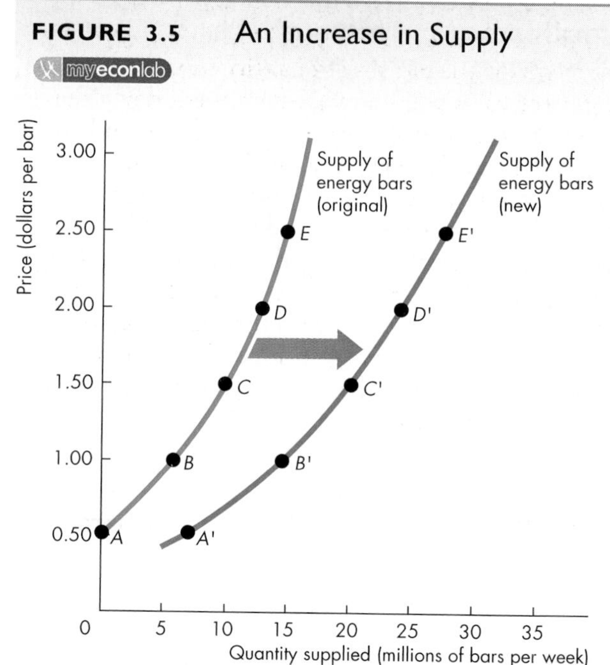

	Original supply schedule Old technology			New supply schedule New technology	
	Price (dollars per bar)	Quantity supplied (millions of bars per week)		Price (dollars per bar)	Quantity supplied (millions of bars per week)
A	0.50	0	A'	0.50	7
B	1.00	6	B'	1.00	15
C	1.50	10	C'	1.50	20
D	2.00	13	D'	2.00	25
E	2.50	15	E'	2.50	30

A change in any influence on sellers' plans other than the price of the good itself results in a new supply schedule and a shift of the supply curve. For example, with a new, cost-saving technology for producing energy bars, the supply of energy bars changes. At a price of $1.50 a bar, 10 million bars a week are supplied when producers use the old technology (row *C* of the table) and 20 million energy bars a week are supplied when producers use the new technology. An advance in technology *increases* the supply of energy bars. The supply curve shifts *rightward*, as shown by the shift arrow and the resulting red curve.

Figure 3.6 illustrates and summarizes these distinctions. If the price of a good falls and everything else remains the same, the quantity supplied of that good decreases and there is a movement down the supply curve S_0. If the price of a good rises and everything else remains the same, the quantity supplied increases and there is a movement up the supply curve S_0. When any other influence on selling plans changes, the supply curve shifts and there is a *change in supply*. If the supply curve is S_0 and if production costs fall, supply increases and the supply curve shifts to the red supply curve S_1. If production costs rise, supply decreases and the supply curve shifts to the red supply curve S_2.

TABLE 3.2 The Supply of Energy Bars

The Law of Supply

The quantity of energy bars supplied

Decreases if:	*Increases if:*
■ The price of an energy bar falls	■ The price of an energy bar rises

Changes in Supply

The supply of energy bars

Decreases if:	*Increases if:*
■ The price of a resource used to produce energy bars rises	■ The price of a resource used to produce energy bars falls
■ The price of a substitute in production rises	■ The price of a substitute in production falls
■ The price of a complement in production falls	■ The price of a complement in production rises
■ The price of an energy bar is expected to rise in the future	■ The price of an energy bar is expected to fall in the future
■ The number of bar producers decreases	■ The number of bar producers increases
■ A negative technology change in energy bar production occurs	■ A positive technology change in energy bar production occurs

FIGURE 3.6 A Change in the Quantity Supplied Versus a Change in Supply

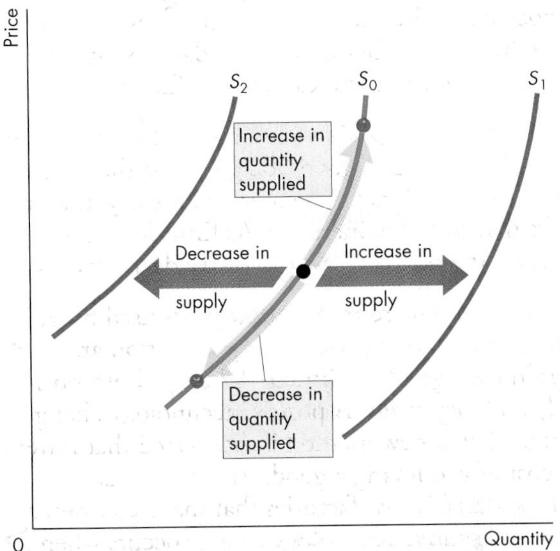

When the price of the good changes, there is a movement along the supply curve and *a change in the quantity supplied,* shown by the blue arrows on supply curve S_0. When any other influence on selling plans changes, there is a shift of the supply curve and a *change in supply*. An increase in supply shifts the supply curve rightward (from S_0 *to* S_1), and a decrease in supply shifts the supply curve leftward (from S_0 *to* S_2).

REVIEW QUIZ

1. Define the quantity supplied of a good or service.
2. What is the law of supply and how do we illustrate it?
3. What does the supply curve tell us about the producer's minimum supply price?
4. List all the influences on selling plans, and for each influence, say whether it changes supply.
5. What happens to the quantity of Palm Pilots supplied and the supply of Palm Pilots if the price of a Palm Pilot falls?

myeconlab **Study Plan 3.3**

Now we're going to combine demand and supply and see how prices and quantities are determined.

Market Equilibrium

We have seen that when the price of a good rises, the quantity demanded *decreases* and the quantity supplied *increases.* We are now going to see how prices coordinate the plans of buyers and sellers and achieve an equilibrium.

An *equilibrium* is a situation in which opposing forces balance each other. Equilibrium in a market occurs when the price balances the plans of buyers and sellers. The **equilibrium price** is the price at which the quantity demanded equals the quantity supplied. The **equilibrium quantity** is the quantity bought and sold at the equilibrium price. A market moves toward its equilibrium because

- Price regulates buying and selling plans.
- Price adjusts when plans don't match.

Price as a Regulator

The price of a good regulates the quantities demanded and supplied. If the price is too high, the quantity supplied exceeds the quantity demanded. If the price is too low, the quantity demanded exceeds the quantity supplied. There is one price at which the quantity demanded equals the quantity supplied. Let's work out what that price is.

Figure 3.7 shows the market for energy bars. The table shows the demand schedule (from Fig. 3.1) and the supply schedule (from Fig. 3.4). If the price of a bar is 50¢, the quantity demanded is 22 million bars a week but no bars are supplied. There is a shortage of 22 million bars a week. This shortage is shown in the final column of the table. At a price of $1.00 a bar, there is still a shortage but only of 9 million bars a week. If the price of a bar is $2.50, the quantity supplied is 15 million bars a week but the quantity demanded is only 5 million. There is a surplus of 10 million bars a week. The one price at which there is neither a shortage nor a surplus is $1.50 a bar. At that price, the quantity demanded is equal to the quantity supplied: 10 million bars a week. The equilibrium price is $1.50 a bar, and the equilibrium quantity is 10 million bars a week.

Figure 3.7 shows that the demand curve and the supply curve intersect at the equilibrium price of $1.50 a bar. At each price *above* $1.50 a bar, there is a surplus of bars. For example, at $2.00 a bar, the surplus is 6

FIGURE 3.7 Equilibrium

myeconlab

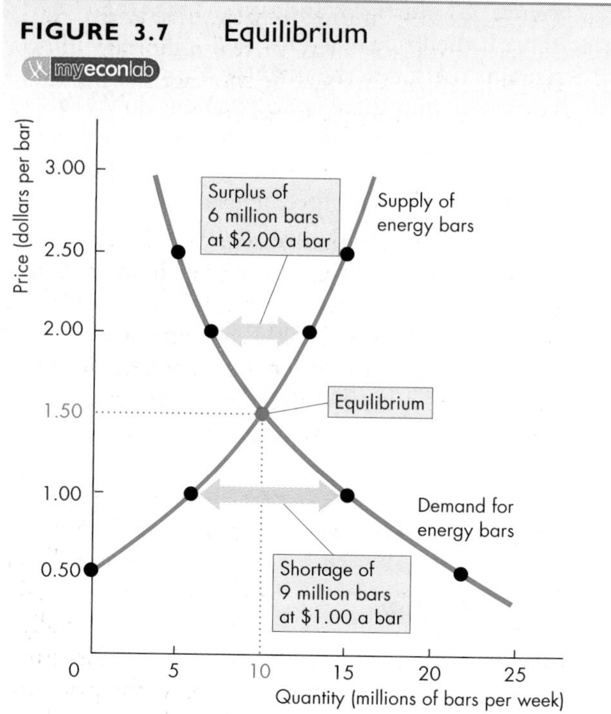

Price (dollars per bar)	Quantity demanded	Quantity supplied	Shortage (–) or surplus (+)
	(millions of bars per week)		
0.50	22	0	–22
1.00	15	6	–9
1.50	10	10	0
2.00	7	13	+6
2.50	5	15	+10

The table lists the quantity demanded and the quantity supplied as well as the shortage or surplus of bars at each price. If the price is $1.00 a bar, 15 million bars a week are demanded and 6 million are supplied. There is a shortage of 9 million bars a week, and the price rises.

If the price is $2.00 a bar, 7 million bars a week are demanded and 13 million are supplied. There is a surplus of 6 million bars a week, and the price falls.

If the price is $1.50 a bar, 10 million bars a week are demanded and 10 million bars are supplied. There is neither a shortage nor a surplus. Neither buyers nor sellers have any incentive to change the price. The price at which the quantity demanded equals the quantity supplied is the equilibrium price. And 10 million bars a week is the equilibrium quantity.

million bars a week, as shown by the blue arrow. At each price *below* $1.50 a bar, there is a shortage of bars. For example, at $1.00 a bar, the shortage is 9 million bars a week, as shown by the red arrow.

Price Adjustments

You've seen that if the price is below equilibrium, there is a shortage and that if the price is above equilibrium, there is a surplus. But can we count on the price to change and eliminate a shortage or surplus? We can, because such price changes are beneficial to both buyers and sellers. Let's see why the price changes when there is a shortage or a surplus.

A Shortage Forces the Price Up Suppose the price of an energy bar is $1. Consumers plan to buy 15 million bars a week, and producers plan to sell 6 million bars a week. Consumers can't force producers to sell more than they plan, so the quantity that is actually offered for sale is 6 million bars a week. In this situation, powerful forces operate to increase the price and move it toward the equilibrium price. Some producers, noticing lines of unsatisfied consumers, raise the price. Some producers increase their output. As producers push the price up, the price rises toward its equilibrium. The rising price reduces the shortage because it decreases the quantity demanded and increases the quantity supplied. When the price has increased to the point at which there is no longer a shortage, the forces moving the price stop operating and the price comes to rest at its equilibrium.

A Surplus Forces the Price Down Suppose the price of a bar is $2. Producers plan to sell 13 million bars a week, and consumers plan to buy 7 million bars a week. Producers cannot force consumers to buy more than they plan, so the quantity that is actually bought is 7 million bars a week. In this situation, powerful forces operate to lower the price and move it toward the equilibrium price. Some producers, unable to sell the quantities of energy bars they planned to sell, cut their prices. In addition, some producers scale back production. As producers cut the price, the price falls toward its equilibrium. The falling price decreases the surplus because it increases the quantity demanded and decreases the quantity supplied. When the price has fallen to the point at which there is no longer a surplus, the forces moving the price stop operating and the price comes to rest at its equilibrium.

The Best Deal Available for Buyers and Sellers When the price is below equilibrium, it is forced upward. Why don't buyers resist the increase and refuse to buy at the higher price? Because they value the good more highly than the current price and they can't satisfy their demand at the current price. In some markets—for example, the markets that operate on eBay—the buyers might even be the ones who force the price up by offering to pay a higher price.

When the price is above equilibrium, it is bid downward. Why don't sellers resist this decrease and refuse to sell at the lower price? Because their minimum supply price is below the current price and they cannot sell all they would like to at the current price. Normally, it is the sellers who force the price down by offering lower prices to gain market share.

At the price at which the quantity demanded and the quantity supplied are equal, neither buyers nor sellers can do business at a better price. Buyers pay the highest price they are willing to pay for the last unit bought, and sellers receive the lowest price at which they are willing to supply the last unit sold.

When people freely make offers to buy and sell and when demanders try to buy at the lowest possible price and suppliers try to sell at the highest possible price, the price at which trade takes place is the equilibrium price—the price at which the quantity demanded equals the quantity supplied. The price coordinates the plans of buyers and sellers, and no one has an incentive to change it.

REVIEW QUIZ

1. What is the equilibrium price of a good or service?
2. Over what range of prices does a shortage arise?
3. Over what range of prices does a surplus arise?
4. What happens to the price when there is a shortage?
5. What happens to the price when there is a surplus?
6. Why is the price at which the quantity demanded equals the quantity supplied the equilibrium price?
7. Why is the equilibrium price the best deal available for both buyers and sellers?

myeconlab **Study Plan 3.4**

Predicting Changes in Price and Quantity

The demand and supply theory that we have just studied provides us with a powerful way of analyzing influences on prices and the quantities bought and sold. According to the theory, a change in price stems from a change in demand, a change in supply, or a change in both demand and supply. Let's look first at the effects of a change in demand.

An Increase in Demand

When more and more people join health clubs, the demand for energy bars increases. The table in Fig. 3.8 shows the original and new demand schedules for energy bars (the same as those in Fig. 3.2) as well as the supply schedule of energy bars.

When demand increases, there is a shortage at the original equilibrium price of $1.50 a bar. To eliminate the shortage, the price must rise. The price that makes the quantity demanded and quantity supplied equal again is $2.50 a bar. At this price, 15 million bars are bought and sold each week. When demand increases, both the price and the quantity increase.

Figure 3.8 shows these changes. The figure shows the original demand for and supply of energy bars. The original equilibrium price is $1.50 an energy bar, and the quantity is 10 million energy bars a week. When demand increases, the demand curve shifts rightward. The equilibrium price rises to $2.50 an energy bar, and the quantity supplied increases to 15 million energy bars a week, as highlighted in the figure. There is an *increase in the quantity supplied* but *no change in supply*—a movement along, but no shift of, the supply curve.

A Decrease in Demand

We can reverse this change in demand. Start at a price of $2.50 a bar with 15 million energy bars a week being bought and sold, and then work out what happens if demand decreases to its original level. Such a decrease in demand might arise if people switch to energy gel (a substitute for energy bars). The decrease in demand shifts the demand curve leftward. The equilibrium price falls to $1.50 a bar, and the equilibrium quantity decreases to 10 million bars a week.

FIGURE 3.8 The Effects of a Change in Demand

myeconlab

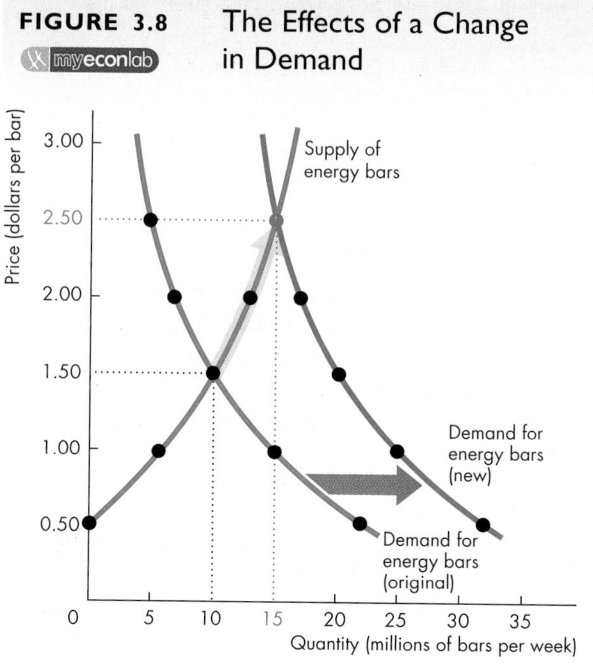

Price (dollars per bar)	Quantity demanded (millions of bars per week) Original	New	Quantity supplied (millions of bars per week)
0.50	22	32	0
1.00	15	25	6
1.50	**10**	20	**10**
2.00	7	17	13
2.50	5	**15**	**15**

Initially, the demand for energy bars is the blue demand curve. The equilibrium price is $1.50 a bar, and the equilibrium quantity is 10 million bars a week. When more health-conscious people do more exercise, the demand for energy bars increases and the demand curve shifts rightward to become the red curve.

At $1.50 a bar, there is now a shortage of 10 million bars a week. The price of a bar rises to a new equilibrium of $2.50. As the price rises to $2.50, the quantity supplied increases—shown by the blue arrow on the supply curve—to the new equilibrium quantity of 15 million bars a week. Following an increase in demand, the quantity supplied increases but supply does not change—the supply curve does not shift.

We can now make our first two predictions:

1. When demand increases, both the price and the quantity increase.
2. When demand decreases, both the price and the quantity decrease.

An Increase in Supply

When Nestlé (the producer of PowerBar) and other energy bar producers switch to a new cost-saving technology, the supply of energy bars increases. Figure 3.9 shows the new supply schedule (the same one that was shown in Fig. 3.5). What are the new equilibrium price and quantity? The price falls to $1.00 a bar, and the quantity increases to 15 million a week. You can see why by looking at the quantities demanded and supplied at the old price of $1.50 a bar. The quantity supplied at that price is 20 million bars a week, and there is a surplus of bars. The price falls. Only when the price is $1.00 a bar does the quantity supplied equal the quantity demanded.

Figure 3.9 illustrates the effect of an increase in supply. It shows the demand curve for energy bars and the original and new supply curves. The initial equilibrium price is $1.50 a bar, and the quantity is 10 million bars a week. When the supply increases, the supply curve shifts rightward. The equilibrium price falls to $1.00 a bar, and the quantity demanded increases to 15 million bars a week, highlighted in the figure. There is an *increase in the quantity demanded* but *no change in demand*—a movement along, but no shift of, the demand curve.

A Decrease in Supply

Start out at a price of $1.00 a bar with 15 million bars a week being bought and sold. Then suppose that the cost of labor or raw materials rises and the supply of energy bars decreases. The decrease in supply shifts the supply curve leftward. The equilibrium price rises to $1.50 a bar, and the equilibrium quantity decreases to 10 million bars a week.

We can now make two more predictions:

1. When supply increases, the quantity increases and the price falls.
2. When supply decreases, the quantity decreases and the price rises.

FIGURE 3.9 The Effects of a Change in Supply

myeconlab

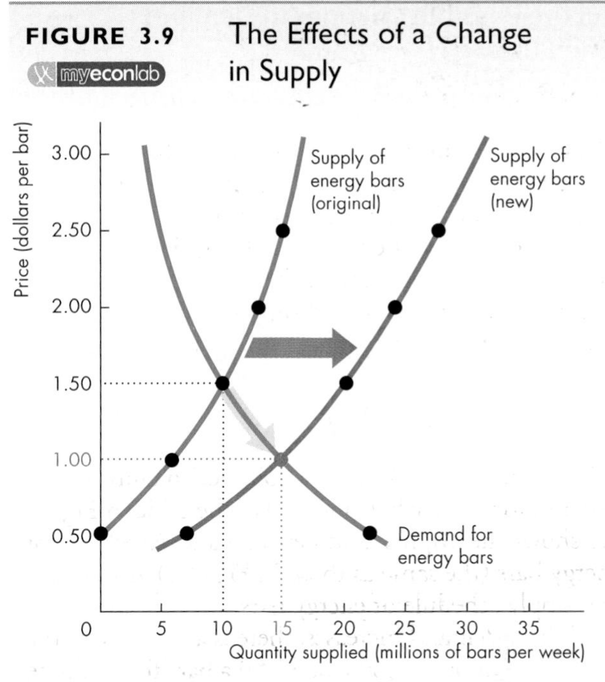

Price (dollars per bar)	Quantity demanded (millions of bars per week)	Quantity supplied (millions of bars per week)	
		Original	New
0.50	22	0	7
1.00	15	6	15
1.50	**10**	**10**	20
2.00	7	13	25
2.50	5	15	30

Initially, the supply of energy bars is shown by the blue supply curve. The equilibrium price is $1.50 a bar, and the equilibrium quantity is 10 million bars a week. When the new cost-saving technology is adopted, the supply of energy bars increases and the supply curve shifts rightward to become the red curve.

At $1.50 a bar, there is now a surplus of 10 million bars a week. The price of an energy bar falls to a new equilibrium of $1.00 a bar. As the price falls to $1.00, the quantity demanded increases—shown by the blue arrow on the demand curve—to the new equilibrium quantity of 15 million bars a week. Following an increase in supply, the quantity demanded increases but demand does not change—the demand curve does not shift.

All the Possible Changes in Demand and Supply

You can now predict the effects of a change in either demand or supply on the price and the quantity. And with what you've learned, you can also predict what happens if *both* demand and supply change together. To see what happens when both demand and supply change, let's summarize what you already know.

Change in Demand with No Change in Supply The first row of Fig. 3.10, parts (a), (b), and (c), summarizes the effects of a change in demand with no change in supply. In part (a), with no change in either demand or supply, neither the price nor the quantity changes. With an *increase* in demand and no change in supply in part (b), both the price and quantity increase. And with a *decrease* in demand and no change in supply in part (c), both the price and the quantity decrease.

Change in Supply with No Change in Demand The first column of Fig. 3.10, parts (a), (d), and (g), summarizes the effects of a change in supply with no change in demand. With an increase in supply and no change in demand in part (d), the price falls and quantity increases. And with a decrease in supply and no change in demand in part (g), the price rises and the quantity decreases.

Increase in Both Demand and Supply You've seen that an increase in demand raises the price and increases the quantity. And you've seen that an increase in supply lowers the price and increases the quantity. Fig. 3.10(e) combines these two changes. Because either an increase in demand or an increase in supply increases the quantity, the quantity also increases when both demand and supply increase. But the effect on the price is uncertain. An increase in demand raises the price and an increase in supply lowers the price, so we can't say whether the price will rise or fall when both demand and supply increase. We need to know the magnitudes of the changes in demand and supply to predict the effects on price. In the example in Fig. 3.10(e), the price does not change. But notice that if demand increases by slightly more than the amount shown in the figure, the price will rise. And if supply increases by slightly more than the amount shown in the figure, the price will fall.

Decrease in Both Demand and Supply Figure 3.10(i) shows the case in which demand and supply *both decrease*. For the same reasons as those we've just reviewed, when both demand and supply decrease, the quantity decreases, and again the direction of the price change is uncertain.

Decrease in Demand and Increase in Supply You've seen that a decrease in demand lowers the price and decreases the quantity. And you've seen that an increase in supply lowers the price and increases the quantity. Fig. 3.10(f) combines these two changes. Both the decrease in demand and the increase in supply lower the price. So the price falls. But a decrease in demand decreases the quantity and an increase in supply increases the quantity, so we can't predict the direction in which the quantity will change unless we know the magnitudes of the changes in demand and supply. In the example in Fig. 3.10(f), the quantity does not change. But notice that if demand decreases by slightly more than the amount shown in the figure, the quantity will decrease. And if supply increases by slightly more than the amount shown in the figure, the quantity will increase.

Increase in Demand and Decrease in Supply Figure 3.10(h) shows the case in which demand increases and supply decreases. Now, the price rises, and again the direction of the quantity change is uncertain.

REVIEW QUIZ

1 What is the effect on the price of an MP3 player (such as the iPod) and the quantity of MP3 players if (a) the price of a PC falls or (b) the price of an MP3 download rises or (c) more firms produce MP3 players or (d) electronics workers' wages rise or (e) any two of these events occur together? (Draw the diagrams!)

myeconlab Study Plan 3.5

Now that you understand the demand and supply model and the predictions that it makes, try to get into the habit of using the model in your everyday life. To see how you might use the model, take a look at *Reading Between the Lines* on pp. 76–77, which uses the tools of demand and supply to explain the rising price of gasoline in 2006.

FIGURE 3.10 The Effects of All the Possible Changes in Demand and Supply

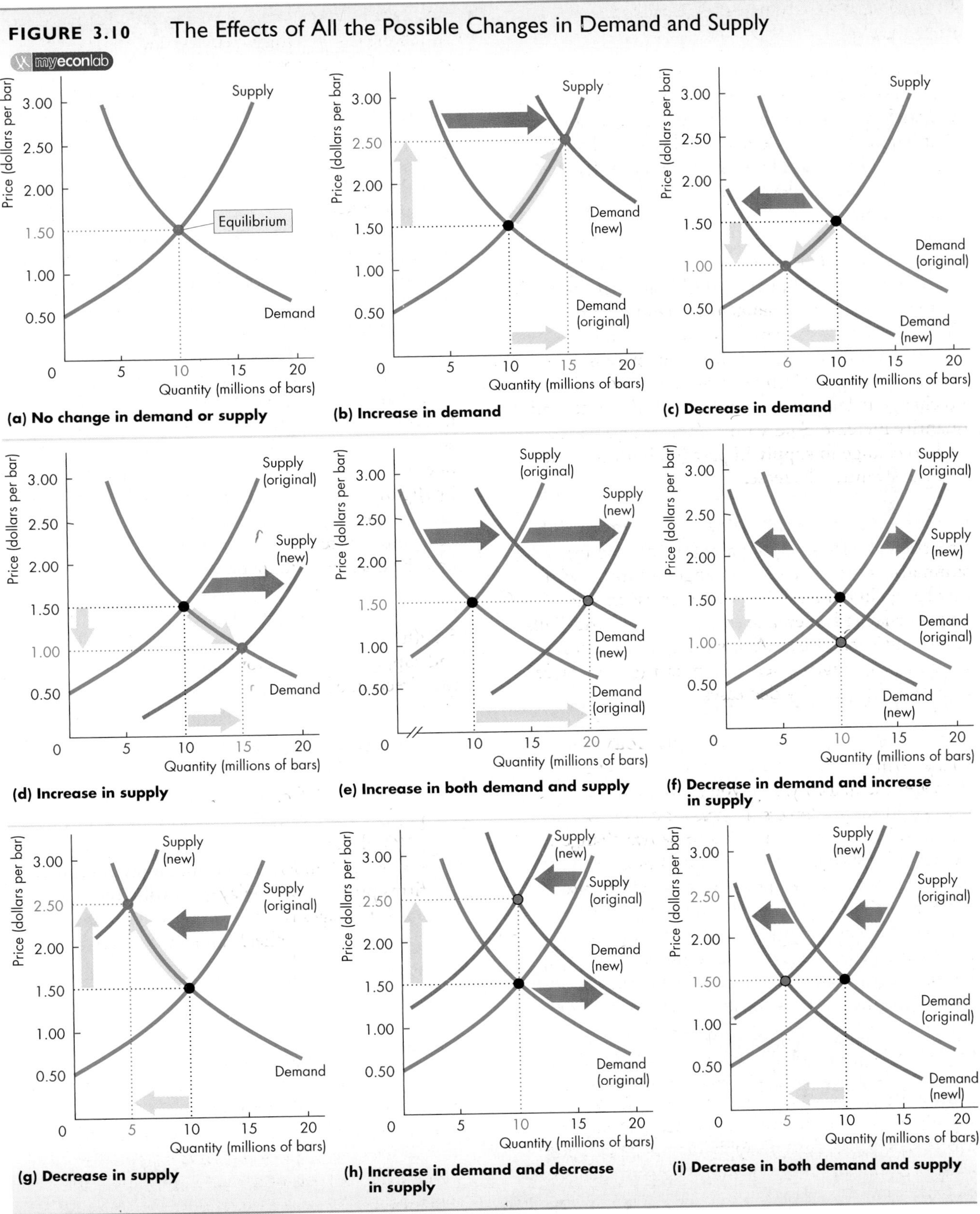

(a) No change in demand or supply

(b) Increase in demand

(c) Decrease in demand

(d) Increase in supply

(e) Increase in both demand and supply

(f) Decrease in demand and increase in supply

(g) Decrease in supply

(h) Increase in demand and decrease in supply

(i) Decrease in both demand and supply

READING BETWEEN THE LINES

Demand and Supply: The Price of Gasoline

http://www.msnbc.msn.com

Eight Reasons Pump Prices May Move Higher

June 30, 2006

[Eight reasons pump prices may move higher are:] . . .

1. Overall demand: When commodity prices go up, the economic textbooks say demand is supposed to go down. For a brief period this spring, there were signs that high pump prices were putting a damper on discretionary travel. Sales of gas guzzling SUVs tumbled, for example.

But a relatively strong U.S. economy continues to fuel strong demand for gasoline and diesel. . . .

In its latest weekly report, the Department of Energy said that Americans burned through more than 9.5 million barrels per day of gasoline for the week ending June 23, 2006, the highest weekly average ever during the month of June. . . .

2. Big travel plans: AAA estimates that a record 34.3 million travelers will hit the road by car this July 4th weekend—a 1.3 percent increase from a year ago. . . .

3. Production interruptions: U.S. refiners have repaired most of the damage from last fall's hurricanes, and, as of last week, were operating at more than 93 percent of capacity—up from a low of 75 percent last October after Katrina and Rita shut down a quarter of U.S. refining capacity. . . .

4. Ethanol: . . .The surge in demand for ethanol has stretched the rapidly expanding ethanol production and distribution system in the U.S.—and pushed prices sharply higher. . . . summer gasoline typically includes 10 percent ethanol . . .

5. Lower imports: . . .Tighter regulations for summer blends have made it increasingly difficult to find foreign-made gasoline that meets those requirements.

6. Tight inventories

7. Future fear factor: In the end, weather holds the potential to create the biggest havoc—as back-to-back hurricanes demonstrated last fall. Though the odds are slim that such severe damage will be repeated, memories are fresh of what bad weather can do to gasoline prices. . . .

8. Mother Nature: Though it's impossible to predict just how bad this hurricane season will be, the odds are against the kind of devastating damage seen last fall in the relatively small Gulf Coast corridor that produces nearly half of U.S. gasoline supplies. . . .

Essence of the Story

- Eight factors might move pump prices higher during 2006.
- A strong U.S. economy kept demand high.
- More people were planning to travel by road.
- Production interruptions might occur.
- The demand for ethanol increased.
- Tighter regulations for gasoline blends decreased imports.
- Inventories were low.
- Future supply disruptions were feared.
- Hurricanes might again cut production.

Economic Analysis

▶ In 2005, the average price of gasoline (all grades) was 210¢ a gallon and 9.64 million barrels of gasoline were consumed on the average each day.

▶ Figure 1 shows the market for gasoline in 2005. The demand curve is D_{05}, the supply curve is S_{05}, and the market equilibrium is at 9.64 million barrels a day and 210¢ a gallon.

▶ The eight events discussed in the news article change demand and supply.

▶ Events 1 and 2—an increase in incomes and increased travel plans—increase the demand for gasoline.

▶ Events 3 through 8—production interruptions, an increase in the demand for ethanol, tighter regulations that decrease imports, low inventories, worries about future supply disruptions, and concerns about the hurricane season—decrease the supply of gasoline.

▶ You might be wondering how an increase in the demand for ethanol decreases the supply of gasoline. This effect occurs because ethanol is an additive in summer gasoline. With an increase in the demand for ethanol, its price increased, which increased the cost of producing summer gasoline and decreased the supply of gasoline.

▶ Figure 2 shows what happened in the market for gasoline during 2006.

▶ Demand increased from D_{05} to D_{06}, and supply decreased from S_{05} to S_{06}.

▶ Because demand increased and supply decreased, the price increased. The equilibrium price increased from 210¢ a gallon to 264¢ a gallon.

▶ And because the increase in the demand for gasoline was larger than the decrease in supply, the equilibrium quantity increased from 9.64 million barrels a day to 9.81 million barrels a day.

▶ Just one part of the news article needs a further comment. Did you notice what it said about economic textbooks? It said: "When commodity prices go up, the economic textbooks say demand is supposed to go down."

▶ What economic textbooks actually say is "When commodity prices go up *and other things remain the same, the quantity demanded* goes down."

▶ The article confuses "demand" and "quantity demanded."

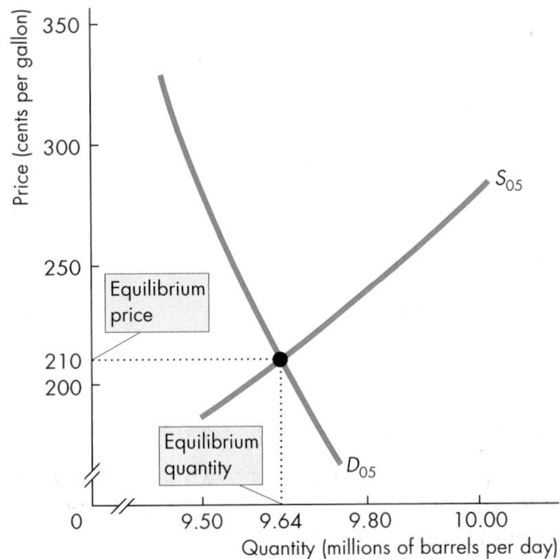

Figure 1 The gasoline market in 2005

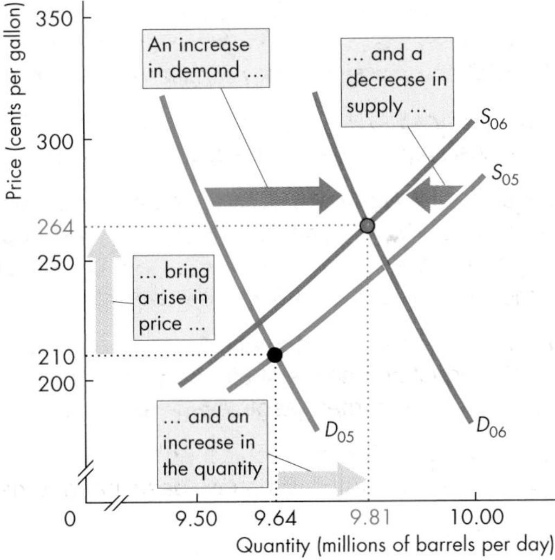

Figure 2 The gasoline market in 2006

Mathematical Note
Demand, Supply, and Equilibrium

Demand Curve

The law of demand says that as the price of a good or service falls, the quantity demanded of that good or service increases. We can illustrate the law of demand by drawing a graph of the demand curve or writing down an equation. When the demand curve is a straight line, the following equation describes it:

$$P = a - bQ_D,$$

where P is the price and Q_D is the quantity demanded. The a and b are positive constants.

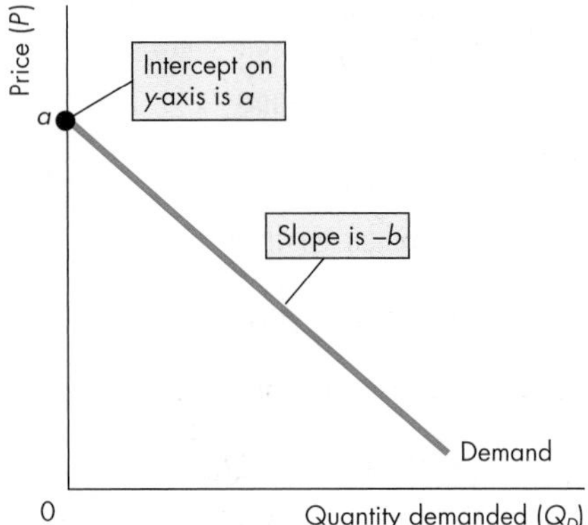

The demand equation tells us three things:

1. The price at which no one is willing to buy the good (Q_D is zero). That is, if the price is a, then the quantity demanded is zero. You can see the price a on the graph. It is the price at which the demand curve hits the y-axis—what we call the demand curve's "intercept on the y-axis."
2. As the price falls, the quantity demanded increases. If Q_D is a positive number, then the price P must be less than a. And as Q_D gets larger, the price P becomes smaller. That is, as the quantity increases, the maximum price that buyers are willing to pay for the last unit of the good falls.
3. The constant b tells us how fast the maximum price that someone is willing to pay for the good falls as the quantity increases. That is, the constant b tells us about the steepness of the demand curve. The equation tells us that the slope of the demand curve is $-b$.

Supply Curve

The law of supply says that as the price of a good or service rises, the quantity supplied of that good or service increases. We can illustrate the law of supply by drawing a graph of the supply curve or writing down an equation. When the supply curve is a straight line, the following equation describes it:

$$P = c + dQ_S,$$

where P is the price and Q_S is the quantity supplied. The c and d are positive constants.

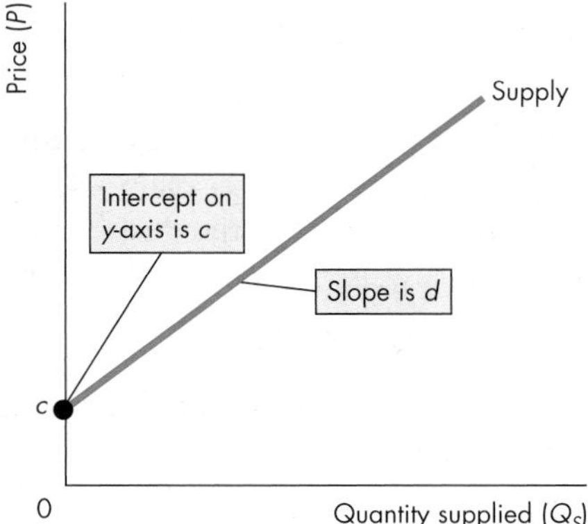

The supply equation tells us three things:

1. The price at which sellers are not willing to supply the good (Q_S is zero). That is, if the price is c, then no one is willing to sell the good. You can see the price c on the graph. It is the price at which the supply curve hits the y-axis—what we call the supply curve's "intercept on the y-axis."
2. As the price rises, the quantity supplied increases. If Q_S is a positive number, then the price P must be greater than c. And as Q_S increases, the price P get larger. That is, as the quantity increases, the minimum price that sellers are willing to accept for the last unit rises.
3. The constant d tells us how fast the minimum price at which someone is willing to sell the good rises as the quantity increases. That is, the constant d tells us about the steepness of the supply curve. The equation tells us that the slope of the supply curve is d.

Market Equilibrium

Demand and supply determine market equilibrium. The figure shows the equilibrium price (P^*) and equilibrium quantity (Q^*) at the intersection of the demand curve and the supply curve.

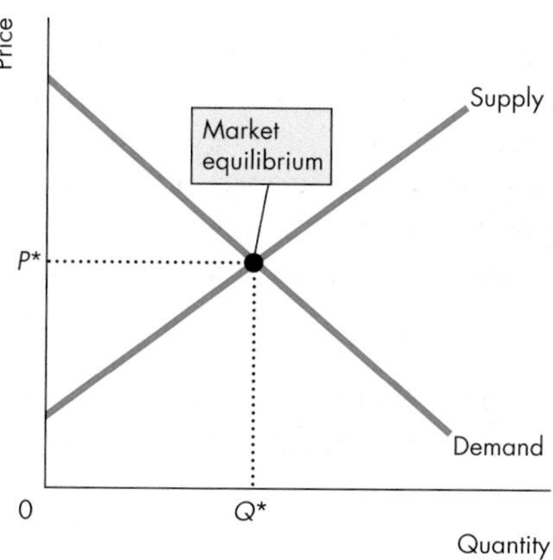

We can use the equations to find the equilibrium price and equilibrium quantity. The price of a good adjusts until the quantity demanded equals the quantity supplied. That is,

$$Q_D = Q_S.$$

So at the equilibrium price (P^*) and equilibrium quantity (Q^*),

$$Q_D = Q_S = Q^*.$$

To find the equilibrium price and equilibrium quantity, substitute Q^* for Q_D in the demand equation and Q^* for Q_S in the supply equation. Then the price is the equilibrium price (P^*), which gives

$$P^* = a - bQ^*$$
$$P^* = c + dQ^*.$$

Notice that

$$a - bQ^* = c + dQ^*.$$

Now solve for Q^*:

$$a - c = bQ^* + dQ^*$$
$$a - c = (b + d)Q^*$$
$$Q^* = \frac{a - c}{b + d}.$$

To find the equilibrium price, (P^*), substitute for Q^* in either the demand equation or the supply equation.

Using the demand equation, we have

$$P^* = a - b\left(\frac{a - c}{b + d}\right)$$
$$P^* = \frac{a(b + d) - b(a - c)}{b + d}$$
$$P^* = \frac{ad + bc}{b + d}.$$

Alternatively, using the supply equation, we have

$$P^* = c + d\left(\frac{a - c}{b + d}\right)$$
$$P^* = \frac{c(b + d) + d(a - c)}{b + d}$$
$$P^* = \frac{ad + bc}{b + d}.$$

An Example

The demand for ice-cream cones is

$$P = 800 - 2Q_D.$$

The supply of ice-cream cones is

$$P = 200 + 1Q_S.$$

The price of a cone is expressed in cents, and the quantities are expressed in cones per day.

To find the equilibrium price (P^*) and equilibrium quantity (Q^*), substitute Q^* for Q_D and Q_S and P^* for P. That is,

$$P^* = 800 - 2Q^*$$
$$P^* = 200 + 1Q^*.$$

Now solve for Q^*:

$$800 - 2Q^* = 200 + 1Q^*$$
$$600 = 3Q^*$$
$$Q^* = 200.$$

And

$$P^* = 800 - 2(200)$$
$$= 400.$$

The equilibrium price is \$4 a cone, and the equilibrium quantity is 200 cones per day.

SUMMARY

Key Points

Markets and Prices (p. 60)

- A competitive market is one that has so many buyers and sellers that no one can influence the price.
- Opportunity cost is a relative price.
- Demand and supply determine relative prices.

Demand (pp. 61–65)

- Demand is the relationship between the quantity demanded of a good and its price when all other influences on buying plans remain the same.
- The higher the price of a good, other things remaining the same, the smaller is the quantity demanded—the law of demand.
- Demand depends on the prices of related goods (substitutes and complements), expected future prices, income, expected future income, population, and preferences.

Supply (pp. 66–69)

- Supply is the relationship between the quantity supplied of a good and its price when all other influences on selling plans remain the same.
- The higher the price of a good, other things remaining the same, the greater is the quantity supplied—the law of supply.
- Supply depends on the prices of resources used to produce a good, the prices of related goods produced, expected future prices, the number of suppliers, and technology.

Market Equilibrium (pp. 70–71)

- At the equilibrium price, the quantity demanded equals the quantity supplied.
- At prices above equilibrium, there is a surplus and the price falls.
- At prices below equilibrium, there is a shortage and the price rises.

Predicting Changes in Price and Quantity (pp. 72–75)

- An increase in demand brings a rise in the price and an increase in the quantity supplied. A decrease in demand brings a fall in the price and a decrease in the quantity supplied.
- An increase in supply brings a fall in the price and an increase in the quantity demanded. A decrease in supply brings a rise in the price and a decrease in the quantity demanded.
- An increase in demand and an increase in supply bring an increased quantity but an uncertain price change. An increase in demand and a decrease in supply bring a higher price but an uncertain change in quantity.

Key Figures

Key Terms

PROBLEMS

myeconlab Tests, Study Plan, Solutions*

1. William Gregg owned a mill in South Carolina. In December 1862, he placed a notice in the *Edgehill Advertiser* announcing his willingness to exchange cloth for food and other items. Here is an extract:

   1 yard of cloth for 1 pound of bacon
   2 yards of cloth for 1 pound of butter
   4 yards of cloth for 1 pound of wool
   8 yards of cloth for 1 bushel of salt

   a. What is the price of butter in terms of wool?
   b. If the price of bacon was 20¢ a pound, what do you predict was the price of butter?
   c. If the price of bacon was 20¢ a pound and the price of salt was $2.00 a bushel, do you think anyone would accept Mr. Gregg's offer of cloth for salt?
2. Classify the following pairs of goods and services as substitutes, complements, substitutes in production, or complements in production.
   a. Bottled water and health club memberships
   b. French fries and baked potatoes
   c. Leather purses and leather shoes
   d. SUVs and pickup trucks
   e. Diet coke and regular coke
   f. Low-fat milk and cream
3. "As more people buy computers, the demand for Internet service increases and the price of Internet service decreases. The fall in the price of Internet service decreases the supply of Internet service." Is this statement true or false? Explain your answer.
4. What is the effect on the price of a recordable CD and the quantity of recordable CDs sold if
   a. The price of an MP3 download rises?
   b. The price of an iPod falls?
   c. The supply of CD players increases?
   d. Consumers' incomes increase?
   e. Workers who make CDs get a pay raise?
   f. The events in (a) and (e) occur together?
5. The following events occur one at a time:
   (i) The price of crude oil rises.
   (ii) The price of a car rises.
   (iii) All speed limits on highways are abolished.
   (iv) Robots cut car production costs.

*Solutions to odd-numbered problems are provided.

   Which of these events will increase or decrease (state which occurs)
   a. The demand for gasoline?
   b. The supply of gasoline?
   c. The quantity of gasoline demanded?
   d. The quantity of gasoline supplied?
6. The figure illustrates the market for pizza.

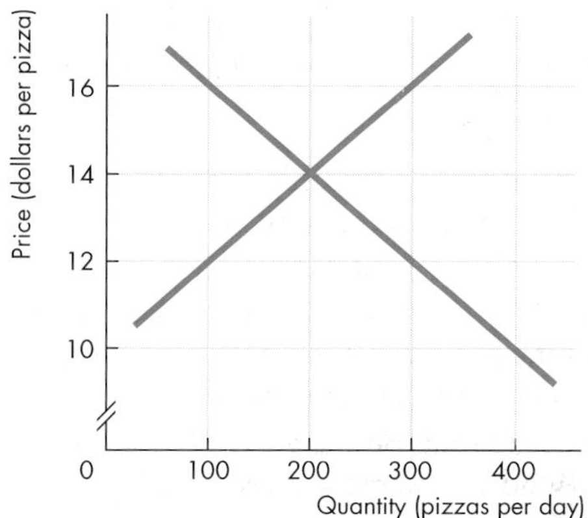

   Label the curves and explain what happens if
   a. The price of a pizza is $16.
   b. The price of a pizza is $12.
7. The table sets out the demand and supply schedules for gum.

Price (cents per pack)	Quantity demanded (millions of packs a week)	Quantity supplied (millions of packs a week)
20	180	60
40	140	100
60	100	140
80	60	180

   a. Draw a graph of the gum market, label the axes and the curves, and mark in the equilibrium price and quantity.
   b. Suppose that the price of gum is 70¢ a pack. Describe the situation in the gum market and explain how the price adjusts.
   c. Suppose that the price of gum is 30¢ a pack. Describe the situation in the gum market and explain how the price adjusts.
   d. If a fire destroys some factories producing gum and the the quantity of gum supplied decreases by 40 million packs a week at each price, explain what happens in the market for gum and illustrate the changes in your graph of the gum market.

e. If an increase in the teenage population increases the quantity of gum demand by 40 million packs a week at each price at the same time as the fire occurs, what are the new equilibrium price and quantity of gum? Illustrate these changes in your graph.

8. The table sets out the demand and supply schedules for potato chips.

Price (cents per bag)	Quantity demanded	Quantity supplied
	(millions of bags per week)	
50	160	130
60	150	140
70	140	150
80	130	160
90	120	170
100	110	180

a. Draw a graph of the potato chip market and mark in the equilibrium price and quantity.
b. Describe the situation in the market for chips and explain how the price adjusts if chips are 60¢ a bag.
c. If a new dip increases the quantity of potato chips demanded by 30 million bags per week at each price, how does the price and quantity of chips change?
d. If a virus destroys potato crops and the quantity of potato chips supplied decreases by 40 million bags a week at each price at the same time as the dip comes onto the market, how does the price and quantity of chips change?

CRITICAL THINKING

1. After you have studied *Reading Between the Lines* on pp. 76–77, answer the following questions:
   a. How does the news article confuse the concepts of "a change in demand" and "a change in the quantity demanded"?
   b. Which of the eight reasons for a rise in the price of gasoline would increase the demand for gasoline and why?
   c. Which of the eight reasons for a rise in the price of gasoline would decrease the supply of gasoline and why?
   d. How do we know that the demand for gasoline increased by more than the supply of gasoline decreased in the summer of 2006?

2. **Eurostar boosted by Da Vinci Code**
   Eurostar, the train service linking London to Paris. . . , said on Wednesday first-half sales rose 6 per cent, boosted by devotees of the blockbuster Da Vinci movie.

   CNN, July 26, 2006

   a. Explain how Da Vinci Code fans helped to raise Eurostar's sales.
   b. CNN commented on the "fierce competition from budget airlines." Explain the effect of this competition on Eurostar's sales.
   c. What markets in Paris do you think these fans influenced? Explain the influence on three markets.

3. **Of gambling, grannies and good sense**
   Nevada has the fastest growing elderly population of any state. . . . Las Vegas has . . . plenty of jobs for the over 50s.

   The Economist, July 26, 2006

   Explain how grannies have influenced the
   a. Demand side of some Las Vegas markets.
   b. Supply side of other Las Vegas markets.

WEB ACTIVITIES

myeconlab **Links to Web sites**

1. Obtain data on the prices and quantities of bananas in 1985 and 2002.
   a. Make a graph to illustrate the market for bananas in 1985 and 2002.
   b. On the graph, show the changes in demand and supply and the changes in the quantity demanded and the quantity supplied that are consistent with the price and quantity data.
   c. Why do you think demand and supply changed?
2. Obtain data on the price of oil since 2000.
   a. Describe how the price of oil changed.
   b. Use a demand-supply graph to explain what happens to the price when supply increases or decreases and demand is unchanged.
   c. What do you predict would happen to the price of oil if a new drilling technology permitted deeper ocean sources to be used?
   d. What do you predict would happen to the price of oil if a clean and safe nuclear technology were developed?

CHAPTER 4

Elasticity

When Prices Tumble, Does Revenue Grow?

The personal computer industry is operating in fiercely competitive conditions. The prices of notebooks tumbled to average less than $1,000 in 2006. Desktop computer prices also tumbled in 2006 to average less than $500. As the prices of personal computers fell, the quantity of computers bought increased. But did the revenues of Acer, Apple, Gateway, Dell, Hewlett-Packard, and the other computer makers grow?

When computer prices fall, the total revenue of computer producers might still grow. But for revenue to grow, the percentage increase in the quantity of computers sold must exceed the percentage fall in the price. Does this happen? And what determines the effect of a change in the price on the quantity sold and revenue? Find the answer in this chapter.

In this chapter, you will learn about a tool that helps us to answer many questions about the changes in prices and quantities traded in markets. You will learn about the elasticities of demand and supply. At the end of the chapter, we'll return to the market for personal computers and see whether lower-priced computers lower or raise the revenues of computer producers.

After studying this chapter, you will be able to

- Define, calculate, and explain the factors that influence the price elasticity of demand
- Define, calculate, and explain the factors that influence the cross elasticity of demand and the income elasticity of demand
- Define, calculate, and explain the factors that influence the elasticity of supply

Price Elasticity of Demand

You know that when supply increases, the equilibrium price falls and the equilibrium quantity increases. But does the price fall by a large amount and the quantity increase by a little? Or does the price barely fall and the quantity increase by a large amount?

The answer depends on the responsiveness of the quantity demanded to a change in price. You can see why by studying Fig. 4.1, which shows two possible scenarios in a local pizza market. Figure 4.1(a) shows one scenario, and Fig. 4.1(b) shows the other.

In both cases, supply is initially S_0. In part (a), the demand for pizza is shown by the demand curve D_A. In part (b), the demand for pizza is shown by the demand curve D_B. Initially, in both cases, the price is \$20 a pizza and the quantity of pizza produced and consumed is 10 pizzas an hour.

Now a large pizza franchise opens up, and the supply of pizza increases. The supply curve shifts rightward to S_1. In case (a), the price falls by an enormous \$15 to \$5 a pizza, and the quantity increases by only 3 to 13 pizzas an hour. In contrast, in case (b), the price falls by only \$5 to \$15 a pizza and the quantity increases by 7 to 17 pizzas an hour.

The different outcomes arise from differing degrees of responsiveness of the quantity demanded to a change in price. But what do we mean by responsiveness? One possible answer is slope. The slope of demand curve D_A is steeper than the slope of demand curve D_B.

In this example, we can compare the slopes of the two demand curves. But we can't always do so. The reason is that the slope of a demand curve depends on the units in which we measure the price and quantity. And we often must compare the demand curves for different goods and services that are measured in unrelated units. For example, a pizza producer might want to compare the demand for pizza with the demand for soft drinks. Which quantity demanded is more responsive to a price change? This question can't be answered by comparing the slopes of two demand curves. The units of measurement of pizza and soft drinks are unrelated. The question can be answered with a measure of responsiveness that is independent of units of measurement. Elasticity is such a measure.

The **price elasticity of demand** is a units-free measure of the responsiveness of the quantity demanded of a good to a change in its price when all other influences on buyers' plans remain the same.

FIGURE 4.1 How a Change in Supply Changes Price and Quantity

myeconlab

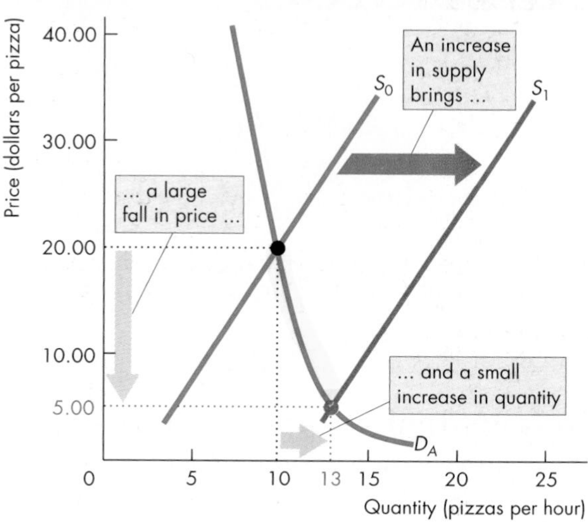

(a) Large price change and small quantity change

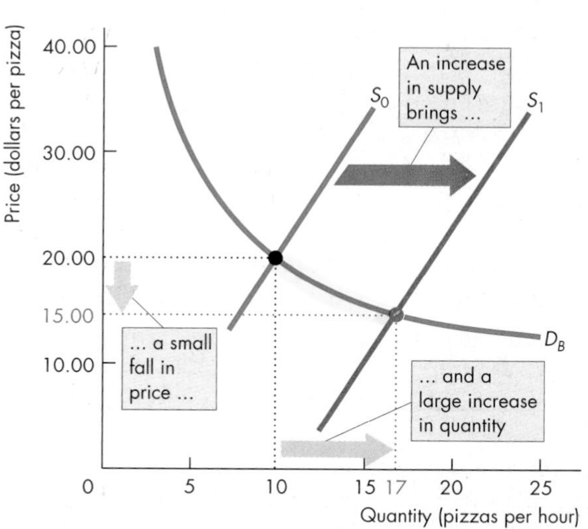

(b) Small price change and large quantity change

Initially the price is \$20 a pizza and the quantity sold is 10 pizzas an hour. Then supply increases from S_0 to S_1. In part (a), the price falls by \$15 to \$5 a pizza, and the quantity increases by 3 to 13 pizzas an hour. In part (b), the price falls by only \$5 to \$15 a pizza, and the quantity increases by 7 to 17 pizzas an hour. The price change is smaller and the quantity change is larger in case (b) than in case (a). The quantity demanded is more responsive to price in case (b) than in case (a).

Calculating Price Elasticity of Demand

We calculate the *price elasticity of demand* by using the formula:

$$\text{Price elasticity of demand} = \frac{\text{Percentage change in quantity demanded}}{\text{Percentage change in price}}.$$

To use this formula, we need to know the quantities demanded at different prices when all other influences on buyers' plans remain the same. Suppose we have the data on prices and quantities demanded of pizza and we calculate the price elasticity of demand for pizza.

Figure 4.2 zooms in on the demand curve for pizza and shows how the quantity demanded responds to a small change in price. Initially, the price is $20.50 a pizza and 9 pizzas an hour are sold—the original point in the figure. The price then falls to $19.50 a pizza, and the quantity demanded increases to 11 pizzas an hour—the new point in the figure. When the price falls by $1 a pizza, the quantity demanded increases by 2 pizzas an hour.

To calculate the price elasticity of demand, we express the changes in price and quantity demanded as percentages of the *average price* and the *average quantity*. By using the average price and average quantity, we calculate the elasticity at a point on the demand curve midway between the original point and the new point. The original price is $20.50 and the new price is $19.50, so the average price is $20. The $1 price decrease is 5 percent of the average price. That is,

$$\Delta P/P_{ave} = (\$1/\$20) \times 100 = 5\%.$$

The original quantity demanded is 9 pizzas and the new quantity demanded is 11 pizzas, so the average quantity demanded is 10 pizzas. The 2 pizza increase in the quantity demanded is 20 percent of the average quantity. That is,

$$\Delta Q/Q_{ave} = (2/10) \times 100 = 20\%.$$

So the price elasticity of demand, which is the percentage change in the quantity demanded (20 percent) divided by the percentage change in price (5 percent) is 4. That is,

$$\text{Price elasticity of demand} = \frac{\%\Delta Q}{\%\Delta P} = \frac{20\%}{5\%} = 4.$$

FIGURE 4.2 Calculating the Elasticity of Demand

myeconlab

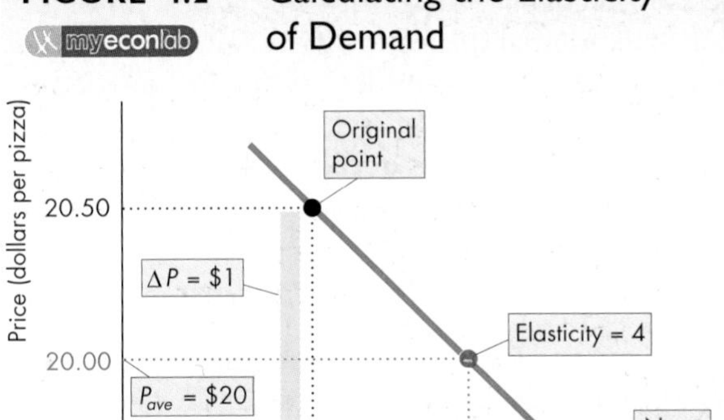

The elasticity of demand is calculated by using the formula:*

$$\text{Price elasticity of demand} = \frac{\text{Percentage change in quantity demanded}}{\text{Percentage change in price}}$$

$$= \frac{\%\Delta Q}{\%\Delta P}$$

$$= \frac{\Delta Q/Q_{ave}}{\Delta P/P_{ave}}$$

$$= \frac{2/10}{1/20}$$

$$= 4.$$

This calculation measures the elasticity at an average price of $20 a pizza and an average quantity of 10 pizzas an hour.

* In the formula, the Greek letter delta (Δ) stands for "change in" and %Δ stands for "percentage change in."

Average Price and Quantity Notice that we use the *average* price and *average* quantity. We do this because it gives the most precise measurement of elasticity—at the midpoint between the original price and the new price. If the price falls from $20.50 to $19.50, the $1 price change is 4.9 percent of $20.50. The 2 pizza change in quantity is 22.2 percent of 9 pizzas, the original quantity. So if we use these numbers, the price elasticity of demand is 22.2 divided by 4.9, which equals 4.5. If the price rises from $19.50 to

\$20.50, the \$1 price change is 5.1 percent of \$19.50. The 2 pizza change in quantity is 18.2 percent of 11 pizzas, the original quantity. So if we use these numbers, the price elasticity of demand is 18.2 divided by 5.1, which equals 3.6.

By using percentages of the *average* price and *average* quantity, we get the same value for the elasticity regardless of whether the price falls from \$20.50 to \$19.50 or rises from \$19.50 to \$20.50.

Percentages and Proportions Elasticity is the ratio of two percentage changes. So when we divide one percentage change by another, the 100s cancel. A percentage change is a *proportionate* change multiplied by 100. The proportionate change in price is $\Delta P/P_{ave}$, and the proportionate change in quantity demanded is $\Delta Q/Q_{ave}$. So if we divide $\Delta Q/Q_{ave}$ by $\Delta P/P_{ave}$ we get the same answer as we get by using percentage changes.

A Units-Free Measure Now that you've calculated a price elasticity of demand, you can see why it is a *units-free measure*. Elasticity is a units-free measure because the percentage change in each variable is independent of the units in which the variable is measured. And the ratio of the two percentages is a number without units.

Minus Sign and Elasticity When the price of a good *rises*, the quantity demanded *decreases* along the demand curve. Because a *positive* change in price brings a *negative* change in the quantity demanded, the price elasticity of demand is a negative number. But it is the magnitude, or *absolute value*, of the price elasticity of demand that tells us how responsive—how elastic—demand is. To compare price elasticities of demand, we use the magnitude of the elasticity and ignore the minus sign.

Inelastic and Elastic Demand

Figure 4.3 shows three demand curves that cover the entire range of possible elasticities of demand. In Fig. 4.3(a), the quantity demanded is constant regardless of the price. If the quantity demanded remains constant when the price changes, then the price elasticity of demand is zero and the good is said to have a **perfectly inelastic demand**. One good that has a very low price elasticity of demand (perhaps zero over some price range) is insulin. Insulin is of such importance to some diabetics that if the price rises or falls, they do not change the quantity they buy.

If the percentage change in the quantity demanded equals the percentage change in price, then the price elasticity equals 1 and the good is said to have a **unit elastic demand**. The demand in Fig. 4.3(b) is an example of unit elastic demand.

Between the cases shown in Fig. 4.3(a) and Fig. 4.3(b) is the general case in which the percentage change in the quantity demanded is less than the percentage change in price. In this case, the price elasticity of demand is between zero and 1 and the good is said to have an **inelastic demand**. Food and

FIGURE 4.3 Inelastic and Elastic Demand

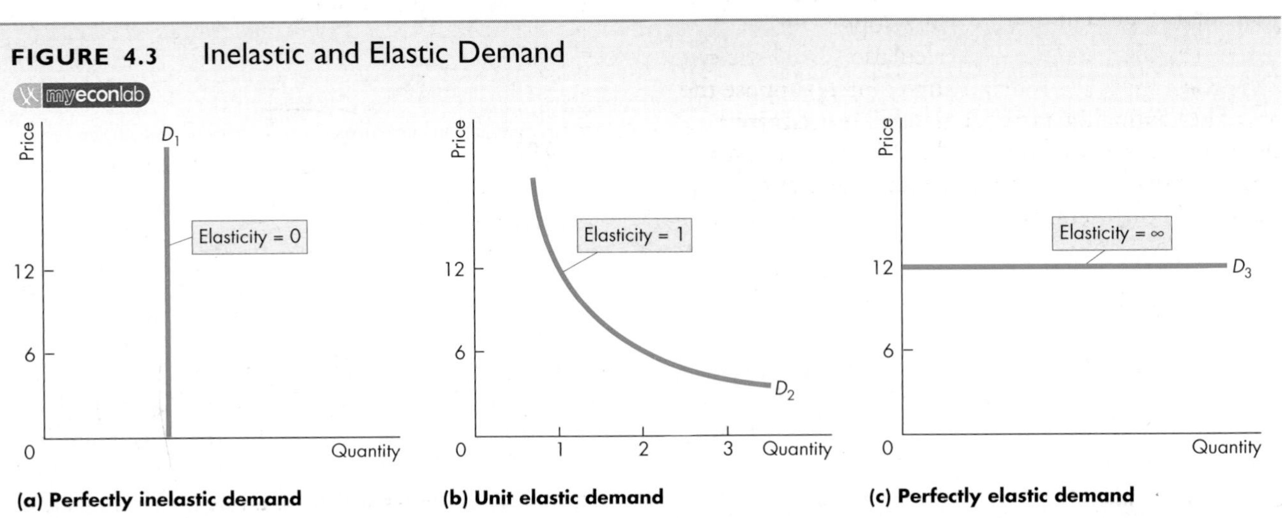

Each demand illustrated here has a constant elasticity. The demand curve in part (a) illustrates the demand for a good that has a zero elasticity of demand. The demand curve in part (b) illustrates the demand for a good with a unit elasticity of demand. And the demand curve in part (c) illustrates the demand for a good with an infinite elasticity of demand.

housing are examples of goods with inelastic demand.

If the quantity demanded changes by an infinitely large percentage in response to a tiny price change, then the price elasticity of demand is infinity and the good is said to have a **perfectly elastic demand.** Figure 4.3(c) shows a perfectly elastic demand. An example of a good that has a very high elasticity of demand (almost infinite) is a soft drink from two campus machines located side by side. If the two machines offer the same soft drinks for the same price, some people buy from one machine and some from the other. But if one machine's price is higher than the other's, by even a small amount, no one will buy from the machine with the higher price. Soft drinks from the two machines are perfect substitutes.

Between the cases in Fig. 4.3(b) and Fig. 4.3(c) is the general case in which the percentage change in the quantity demanded exceeds the percentage change in price. In this case, the price elasticity of demand is greater than 1 and the good is said to have an **elastic demand.** Automobiles and furniture are examples of goods that have elastic demand.

Elasticity Along a Straight-Line Demand Curve

Elasticity and slope are not the same, but they are related. To understand how they are related, let's look at elasticity along a straight-line demand curve—a demand curve that has a constant slope.

Figure 4.4 illustrates the calculation of elasticity along a straight-line demand curve. First, suppose the price falls from \$25 to \$15 a pizza. The quantity demanded increases from zero to 20 pizzas an hour. The average price is \$20 a pizza, and the average quantity is 10 pizzas. So

$$\text{Price elasticity of demand} = \frac{\Delta Q/Q_{ave}}{\Delta P/P_{ave}} = \frac{20/10}{10/20} = 4.$$

That is, the price elasticity of demand at an average price of \$20 a pizza is 4.

Next, suppose that the price falls from \$15 to \$10 a pizza. The quantity demanded increases from 20 to 30 pizzas an hour. The average price is now \$12.50 a pizza, and the average quantity is 25 pizzas an hour. So

$$\text{Price elasticity of demand} = \frac{10/25}{5/12.50} = 1.$$

That is, the price elasticity of demand at an average price of \$12.50 a pizza is 1.

Finally, suppose that the price falls from \$10 to zero. The quantity demanded increases from 30 to 50 pizzas an hour. The average price is now \$5 and the average quantity is 40 pizzas an hour. So

$$\text{Price elasticity of demand} = \frac{20/40}{10/5} = 1/4.$$

That is, the price elasticity of demand at an average price of \$5 a pizza is 1/4.

You've now seen how elasticity changes along a straight-line demand curve. At the mid-point of the curve, demand is unit elastic. Above the mid-point, demand is elastic. Below the mid-point, demand is inelastic.

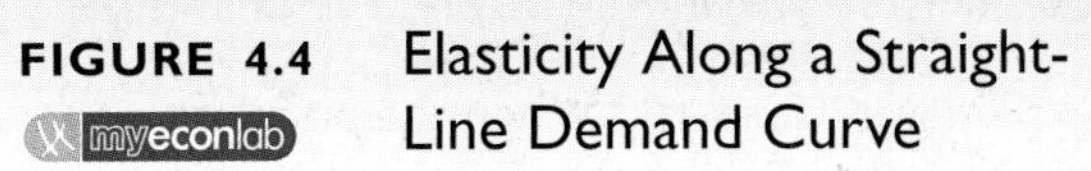

FIGURE 4.4 Elasticity Along a Straight-Line Demand Curve

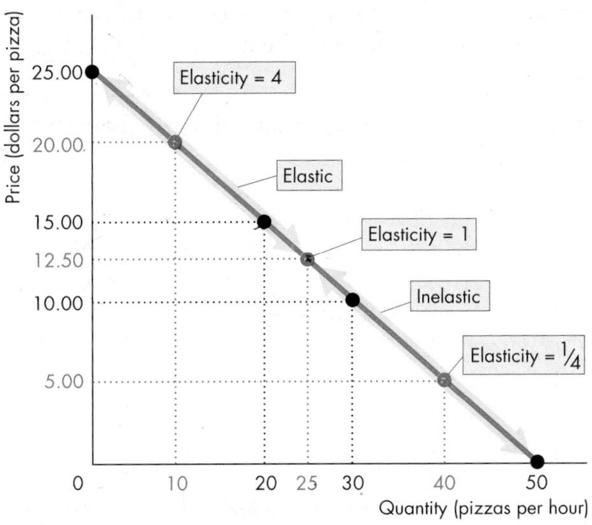

On a straight-line demand curve, elasticity decreases as the price falls and the quantity demanded increases. Demand is unit elastic at the midpoint of the demand curve (elasticity is 1). Above the midpoint, demand is elastic; below the midpoint, demand is inelastic.

Total Revenue and Elasticity

The **total revenue** from the sale of a good equals the price of the good multiplied by the quantity sold. When a price changes, total revenue also changes. But a rise in price does not always increase total revenue. The change in total revenue depends on the elasticity of demand in the following way:

- If demand is elastic, a 1 percent price cut increases the quantity sold by more than 1 percent and total revenue increases.
- If demand is inelastic, a 1 percent price cut increases the quantity sold by less than 1 percent and total revenue decreases.
- If demand is unit elastic, a 1 percent price cut increases the quantity sold by 1 percent and so total revenue does not change.

Figure 4.5 shows how we can use this relationship between elasticity and total revenue to estimate elasticity using the total revenue test. The **total revenue test** is a method of estimating the price elasticity of demand by observing the change in total revenue that results from a change in the price, when all other influences on the quantity sold remain the same.

- If a price cut increases total revenue, demand is elastic.
- If a price cut decreases total revenue, demand is inelastic.
- If a price cut leaves total revenue unchanged, demand is unit elastic.

In Fig. 4.5(a), over the price range from \$25 to \$12.50, demand is elastic. Over the price range from \$12.50 to zero, demand is inelastic. At a price of \$12.50, demand is unit elastic.

Figure 4.5(b) shows total revenue. At a price of \$25, the quantity sold is zero, so total revenue is zero. At a price of zero, the quantity demanded is 50 pizzas an hour and total revenue is again zero. A price cut in the elastic range brings an increase in total revenue—the percentage increase in the quantity demanded is greater than the percentage decrease in price. A price cut in the inelastic range brings a decrease in total revenue—the percentage increase in the quantity demanded is less than the percentage decrease in price. At unit elasticity, total revenue is at a maximum.

FIGURE 4.5 Elasticity and Total Revenue

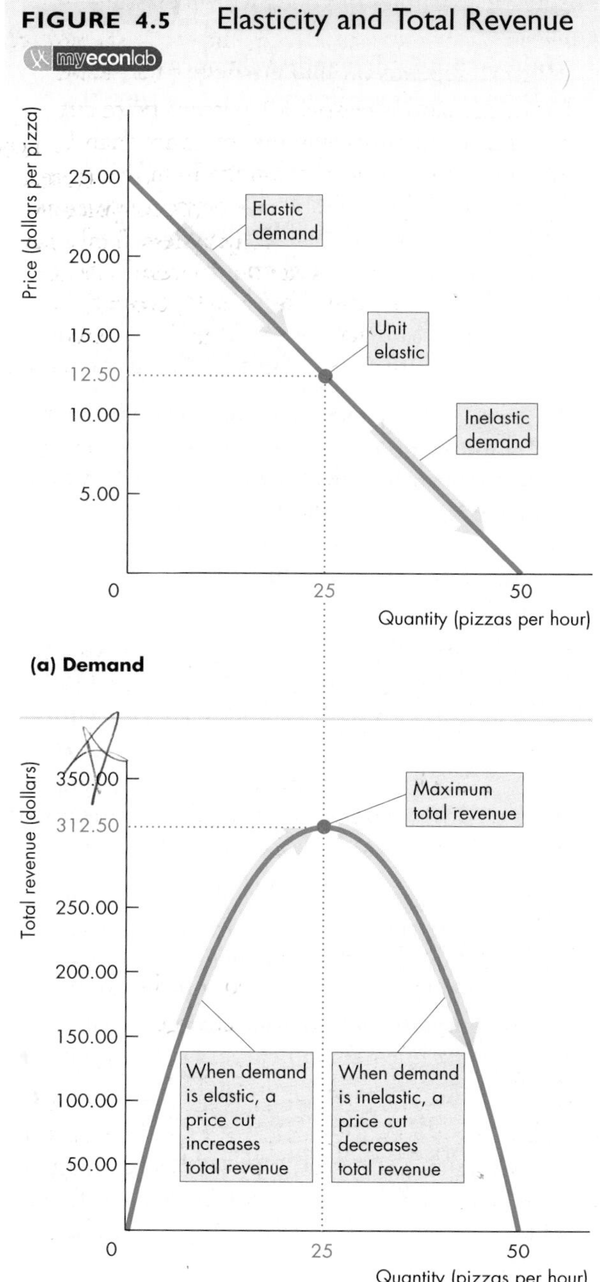

When demand is elastic, in the price range from \$25 to \$12.50, a decrease in price (part a) brings an increase in total revenue (part b). When demand is inelastic, in the price range from \$12.50 to zero, a decrease in price (part a) brings a decrease in total revenue (part b). When demand is unit elastic, at a price of \$12.50 (part a), total revenue is at a maximum (part b).

Your Expenditure and Your Elasticity

When a price changes, the change in your expenditure on the good depends on *your* elasticity of demand.

- If your demand is elastic, a 1 percent price cut increases the quantity you buy by more than 1 percent and your expenditure on the item increases.
- If your demand is inelastic, a 1 percent price cut increases the quantity you buy by less than 1 percent and your expenditure on the item decreases.
- If your demand is unit elastic, a 1 percent price cut increases the quantity you buy by 1 percent and your expenditure on the item does not change.

So if you spend more on an item when its price falls, your demand for that item is elastic; if you spend the same amount, your demand is unit elastic; and if you spend less, your demand is inelastic.

The Factors That Influence the Elasticity of Demand

Table 4.1 lists some estimates of actual elasticities in the real world. You can see that these real-world elasticities of demand range from 1.52 for metals, the item with the most elastic demand in the table, to 0.05 for oil, the item with the most inelastic demand in the table. What makes the demand for some goods elastic and the demand for others inelastic?

The magnitude of the elasticity of demand depends on

- The closeness of substitutes
- The proportion of income spent on the good
- The time elapsed since a price change

Closeness of Substitutes The closer the substitutes for a good or service, the more elastic is the demand for it. For example, oil from which we make gasoline has substitutes but none that are currently very close (imagine a steam-driven, coal-fueled car). So the demand for oil is inelastic. Plastics are close substitutes for metals, so the demand for metals is elastic.

The degree of substitutability between two goods also depends on how narrowly (or broadly) we define them. For example, a personal computer has no really close substitutes, but a Dell PC is a close substitute for a Hewlett Packard PC. So the elasticity of demand for personal computers is lower than the elasticity of demand for a Dell or a Hewlett Packard.

In everyday language we call some goods, such as food and housing, *necessities* and other goods, such as exotic vacations, *luxuries*. A necessity is a good that has poor substitutes and that is crucial for our well-being. So generally, a necessity has an inelastic demand. In Table 4.1, food and oil might be classified as necessities.

A luxury is a good that usually has many substitutes, one of which is not buying it. So a luxury generally has an elastic demand. In Table 4.1, furniture and motor vehicles might be classified as luxuries.

TABLE 4.1 Some Real-World Price Elasticities of Demand

Good or Service	Elasticity
Elastic Demand	
Metals	1.52
Electrical engineering products	1.39
Mechanical engineering products	1.30
Furniture	1.26
Motor vehicles	1.14
Instrument engineering products	1.10
Professional services	1.09
Transportation services	1.03
Inelastic Demand	
Gas, electricity, and water	0.92
Chemicals	0.89
Drinks (all types)	0.78
Clothing	0.64
Tobacco	0.61
Banking and insurance services	0.56
Housing services	0.55
Agricultural and fish products	0.42
Books, magazines, and newspapers	0.34
Food	0.12
Oil	0.05

Sources of data: Ahsan Mansur and John Whalley, "Numerical Specification of Applied General Equilibrium Models: Estimation, Calibration, and Data," in *Applied General Equilibrium Analysis*, eds. Herbert E. Scarf and John B. Shoven (New York: Cambridge University Press, 1984), 109, and Henri Theil, Ching-Fan Chung, and James L. Seale, Jr., *Advances in Econometrics, Supplement I, 1989, International Evidence on Consumption Patterns* (Greenwich, Conn.: JAI Press Inc., 1989), and Geoffrey Heal, Columbia University, Web site.

Proportion of Income Spent on the Good Other things remaining the same, the greater the proportion of income spent on a good, the more elastic is the demand for it.

Think about your own elasticity of demand for chewing gum and housing. If the price of chewing gum doubles, you consume almost as much gum as before. Your demand for gum is inelastic. If apartment rents double, you shriek and look for more students to share accommodation with you. Your demand for housing is more elastic than your demand for gum. Why the difference? Housing takes a large proportion of your budget, and gum takes only a tiny proportion. You don't like either price increase, but you hardly notice the higher price of gum, while the higher rent puts your budget under severe strain.

Figure 4.6 shows the price elasticity of demand for food and the proportion of income spent on food in 10 countries. This figure confirms the general tendency we have just described. The larger the proportion of income spent on food, the larger is the price elasticity of demand for food. For example, in Tanzania, a nation where average incomes are 3.3 percent of incomes in the United States and where 62 percent of income is spent on food, the price elasticity of demand for food is 0.77. In contrast, in the United States, where 12 percent of income is spent on food, the price elasticity of demand for food is 0.12.

Time Elapsed Since Price Change The longer the time that has elapsed since a price change, the more elastic is demand. When the price of oil increased by 400 percent during the 1970s, people barely changed the quantity of oil and gasoline they consumed. But gradually, as more efficient auto and airplane engines were developed, the quantity consumed decreased. The demand for oil has become more elastic as more time has elapsed since the huge price hike. Similarly, when the price of a PC fell, the quantity of PCs demanded increased only slightly at first. But as more people have become better informed about the variety of ways of using a PC, the quantity of PCs bought has increased sharply. The demand for PCs has become more elastic.

FIGURE 4.6 Price Elasticities in 10 Countries

myeconlab

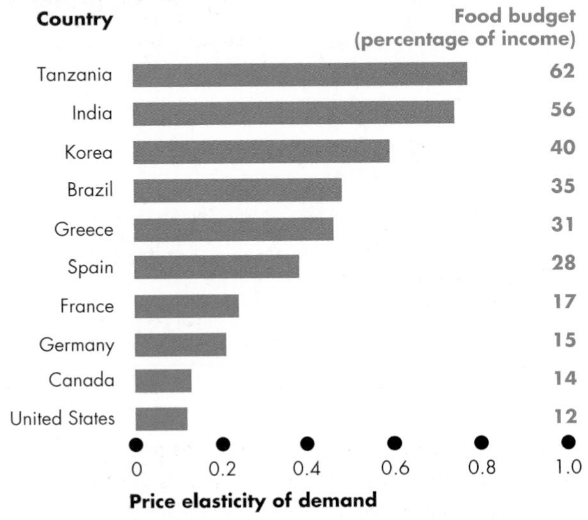

Country	Food budget (percentage of income)
Tanzania	62
India	56
Korea	40
Brazil	35
Greece	31
Spain	28
France	17
Germany	15
Canada	14
United States	12

Price elasticity of demand: 0, 0.2, 0.4, 0.6, 0.8, 1.0

As income increases and the proportion of income spent on food decreases, the demand for food becomes less elastic.

Source of data: Henri Theil, Ching-Fan Chung, and James L. Seale, Jr., *Advances in Econometrics, Supplement 1, 1989, International Evidence on Consumption Patterns* (Greenwich, Conn.: JAI Press, Inc., 1989).

REVIEW QUIZ

1. Why do we need a units-free measure of the responsiveness of the quantity demanded of a good or service to a change in its price?
2. Can you define and calculate the price elasticity of demand?
3. Why, when we calculate the price elasticity of demand, do we express the change in price as a percentage of the *average* price and the change in quantity as a percentage of the *average* quantity?
4. What is the total revenue test and why does it work?
5. What are the main influences on the elasticity of demand that make the demand for some goods elastic and the demand for other goods inelastic?
6. Why is the demand for a luxury generally more elastic than the demand for a necessity?

myeconlab **Study Plan 4.1**

You've now completed your study of the *price* elasticity of demand. Two other elasticity concepts tell us about the effects of other influences on demand. Let's look at these other elasticities of demand.

More Elasticities of Demand

Back at the pizzeria, you are trying to work out how a price rise by the burger shop next door will affect the demand for your pizza. You know that pizzas and burgers are substitutes. And you know that when the price of a substitute for pizza rises, the demand for pizza increases. But by how much?

You also know that pizza and soft drinks are complements. And you know that if the price of a complement of pizza rises, the demand for pizza decreases. So you wonder by how much will a rise in the price of a soft drink decrease the demand for your pizza?

To answer these questions, you need to calculate the cross elasticity of demand. Let's examine this elasticity measure.

Cross Elasticity of Demand

We measure the influence of a change in the price of a substitute or complement by using the concept of the cross elasticity of demand. The **cross elasticity of demand** is a measure of the responsiveness of the demand for a good to a change in the price of a substitute or complement, other things remaining the same. We calculate the *cross elasticity of demand* by using the formula:

$$\text{Cross elasticity of demand} = \frac{\text{Percentage change in quantity demanded}}{\text{Percentage change in price of a substitute or complement}}.$$

The cross elasticity of demand can be positive or negative. It is *positive* for a *substitute* and *negative* for a *complement.*

Substitutes Suppose that the price of pizza is constant and 9 pizzas an hour are sold. Then the price of a burger rises from \$1.50 to \$2.50. No other influence on buying plans changes and the quantity of pizzas sold increases to 11 an hour.

The change in the quantity demanded is +2 pizzas—the new quantity, 11 pizzas, minus the original quantity, 9 pizzas. The average quantity is 10 pizzas. So the quantity of pizzas demanded increases by 20 percent (+20). That is,

$$\Delta Q/Q_{ave} = (+2/10) \times 100 = +20\%.$$

The change in the price of a burger, a substitute for pizza, is +\$1—the new price, \$2.50, minus the original price, \$1.50. The average price is \$2 a burger. So the price of a burger rises by 50 percent (+50). That is,

$$\Delta P/P_{ave} = (+1/2) \times 100 = +50\%.$$

So the cross elasticity of demand for pizza with respect to the price of a burger is

$$\frac{+20\%}{+50\%} = 0.4.$$

Figure 4.7 illustrates the cross elasticity of demand. Pizza and burgers are substitutes. Because they are substitutes, when the price of a burger rises, the demand for pizza increases. The demand curve for pizza shifts rightward from D_0 to D_1. Because a *rise* in the price of a burger brings an *increase* in the demand for pizza, the cross elasticity of demand for pizza with respect to the price of a burger is *positive.* Both the price and the quantity change in the same direction.

FIGURE 4.7 Cross Elasticity of Demand

myeconlab

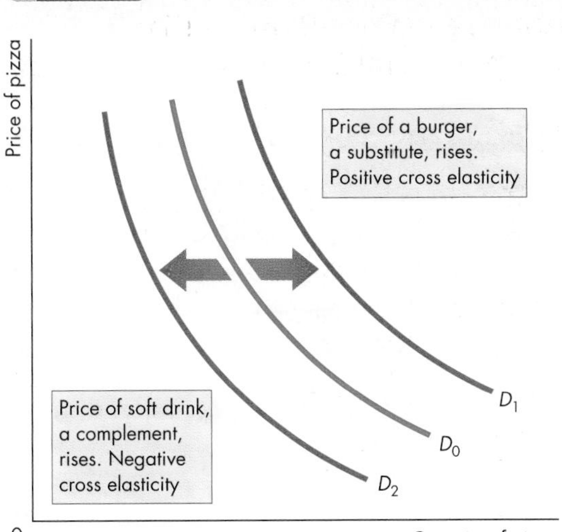

A burger is a *substitute* for pizza. When the price of a burger rises, the demand for pizza increases and the demand curve for pizza shifts rightward from D_0 to D_1. The cross elasticity of the demand is *positive.*

Soft drinks are a *complement* of pizza. When the price of a soft drink rises, the demand for pizza decreases and the demand curve for pizza shifts leftward from D_0 to D_2. The cross elasticity of the demand is *negative.*

Complements Now suppose that the price of pizza is constant and 11 pizzas an hour are sold. Then the price of a soft drink rises from \$1.50 to \$2.50. No other influence on buying plans changes and the quantity of pizzas sold falls to 9 an hour.

The change in the quantity demanded is the opposite of what we've just calculated: The quantity of pizzas demanded decreases by 20 percent (–20).

The change in the price of a soft drink, a complement of pizza, is the same as the percentage change in the price of a burger that we've just calculated: The price rises by 50 percent (+50). So the cross elasticity of demand for pizza with respect to the price of a soft drink is

$$\frac{-20\%}{+50\%} = -0.4.$$

Because pizza and soft drinks are complements, when the price of a soft drink rises, the demand for pizza decreases. The demand curve for pizza shifts leftward from D_0 to D_2. Because a *rise* in the price of a soft drink brings a *decrease* in the demand for pizza, the cross elasticity of demand for pizza with respect to the price of a soft drink is *negative*. The price and quantity change in *opposite* directions.

The magnitude of the cross elasticity of demand determines how far the demand curve shifts. The larger the cross elasticity (absolute value), the greater is the change in demand and the larger is the shift in the demand curve.

If two items are close substitutes, such as two brands of spring water, the cross elasticity is large. If two items are close complements, such as movies and popcorn, the cross elasticity is large.

If two items are somewhat unrelated to each other, such as newspapers and orange juice, the cross elasticity is small—perhaps even zero.

Income Elasticity of Demand

Suppose the economy is expanding and people are enjoying rising incomes. This prosperity is bringing an increase in the demand for most types of goods and services. But by how much will the demand for pizza increase? The answer depends on the **income elasticity of demand**, which is a measure of the responsiveness of the demand for a good or service to a change in income, other things remaining the same.

The income elasticity of demand is calculated by using the formula:

$$\text{Income elasticity of demand} = \frac{\text{Percentage change in quantity demanded}}{\text{Percentage change in income}}.$$

Income elasticities of demand can be positive or negative and fall into three interesting ranges:

- Greater than 1 (*normal* good, income elastic)
- Positive and less than 1 (*normal* good, income inelastic)
- Negative (*inferior* good)

Income Elastic Demand Suppose that the price of pizza is constant and 9 pizzas an hour are sold. Then incomes rise from \$975 to \$1,025 a week. No other influence on buying plans changes and the quantity of pizzas sold increases to 11 an hour.

The change in the quantity demanded is +2 pizzas. The average quantity is 10 pizzas, so the quantity demanded increases by 20 percent. The change in income is +\$50 and the average income is \$1,000, so incomes increase by 5 percent. The income elasticity of demand for pizza is

$$\frac{20\%}{5\%} = 4.$$

The demand for pizza is income elastic. The percentage increase in the quantity of pizza demanded exceeds the percentage increase in income. *When the demand for a good is income elastic, as income increases, the percentage of income spent on that good increases.*

Income Inelastic Demand If the income elasticity of demand is positive but less than 1, demand is income inelastic. The percentage increase in the quantity demanded is positive but less than the percentage increase in income. *When the demand for a good is income inelastic, as income increases, the percentage of income spent on that good decreases.*

Inferior Goods If the income elasticity of demand is negative, the good is an *inferior* good. The quantity demanded of an inferior good and the amount spent on it *decreases* when income increases. Goods in this category include small motorcycles, potatoes, and rice. Low-income consumers buy most of these goods!

Real-World Income Elasticities of Demand

Table 4.2 shows estimates of some real-world income elasticities of demand. The demand for a necessity such as food or clothing is income inelastic, while the demand for a luxury such as transportation, which includes airline and foreign travel, is income elastic.

But what is a necessity and what is a luxury depends on the level of income. For people with a low income, food and clothing can be luxuries. So the *level* of income has a big effect on income elasticities of demand. Figure 4.8 shows this effect on the income elasticity of demand for food in 10 countries. In countries with low incomes, such as Tanzania and India, the income elasticity of demand for food is high. In countries with high incomes, such as the United States, the income elasticity of demand for food is low.

TABLE 4.2 Some Real-World Income Elasticities of Demand

Elastic Demand	
Airline travel	5.82
Movies	3.41
Foreign travel	3.08
Electricity	1.94
Restaurant meals	1.61
Local buses and trains	1.38
Haircuts	1.36
Automobiles	1.07
Inelastic Demand	
Tobacco	0.86
Alcoholic drinks	0.62
Furniture	0.53
Clothing	0.51
Newspapers and magazines	0.38
Telephone	0.32
Food	0.14

Sources of data: H.S. Houthakker and Lester D. Taylor, *Consumer Demand in the United States* (Cambridge, Mass.: Harvard University Press, 1970), and Henri Theil, Ching-Fan Chung, and James L. Seale, Jr., *Advances in Econometrics, Supplement 1, 1989, International Evidence on Consumption Patterns* (Greenwich, Conn.: JAI Press, Inc., 1989).

FIGURE 4.8 Income Elasticities in 10 Countries

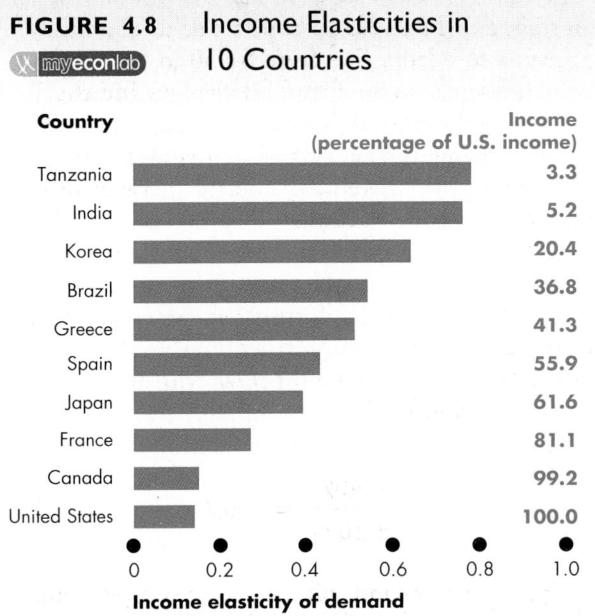

As income increases, the income elasticity of demand for food decreases. Low-income consumers spend a larger percentage of any increase in income on food than do high-income consumers.

Source of data: Henri Theil, Ching-Fan Chung, and James L. Seale, Jr., *Advances in Econometrics, Supplement 1, 1989, International Evidence on Consumption Patterns* (Greenwich, Conn.: JAI Press, Inc., 1989).

REVIEW QUIZ

1. What does the cross elasticity of demand measure?
2. What does the sign (positive versus negative) of the cross elasticity of demand tell us about the relationship between two goods?
3. What does the income elasticity of demand measure?
4. What does the sign (positive versus negative) of the income elasticity of demand tell us about a good?
5. Why does the level of income influence the magnitude of the income elasticity of demand?

myeconlab **Study Plan 4.2**

You've now completed your study of the *cross elasticity* of demand and the *income elasticity* of demand. Let's look at the other side of the market and examine the elasticity of supply.

Elasticity of Supply

You know that when demand increases, the price rises and the quantity increases. But does the price rise by a large amount and the quantity increase by a little? Or does the price barely rise and the quantity increase by a large amount?

The answer depends on the responsiveness of the quantity supplied to a change in price. You can see why by studying Fig. 4.9, which shows two possible scenarios in a local pizza market. Figure 4.9(a) shows one scenario, and Fig. 4.9(b) shows the other.

In both cases, demand is initially D_0. In part (a), the supply of pizza is shown by the supply curve S_A. In part (b), the supply of pizza is shown by the supply curve S_B. Initially, in both cases, the price is $20 a pizza and the quantity produced and consumed is 10 pizzas an hour.

Now increases in incomes and population increase the demand for pizza. The demand curve shifts rightward to D_1. In case (a), the price rises by $10 to $30 a pizza, and the quantity increases by only 3 to 13 pizzas an hour. In contrast, in case (b), the price rises by only $1 to $21 a pizza, and the quantity increases by 10 to 20 pizzas an hour.

The different outcomes arise from differing degrees of responsiveness of the quantity supplied to a change in price. We measure the degree of responsiveness by using the concept of the elasticity of supply.

Calculating the Elasticity of Supply

The **elasticity of supply** measures the responsiveness of the quantity supplied to a change in the price of a good when all other influences on selling plans remain the same. It is calculated by using the formula:

$$\text{Elasticity of supply} = \frac{\text{Percentage change in quantity supplied}}{\text{Percentage change in price}}.$$

We use the same method that you learned when you studied the elasticity of demand. (Refer back to p. 85 to check this method.) Let's calculate the elasticity of supply along the supply curves in Fig. 4.9.

In Fig. 4.9(a), when the price rises from $20 to $30, the price rise is $10 and the average price is $25, so the price rises by 40 percent of the average price. The quantity increases from 10 to 13 pizzas an hour,

FIGURE 4.9 How a Change in Demand Changes Price and Quantity

myeconlab

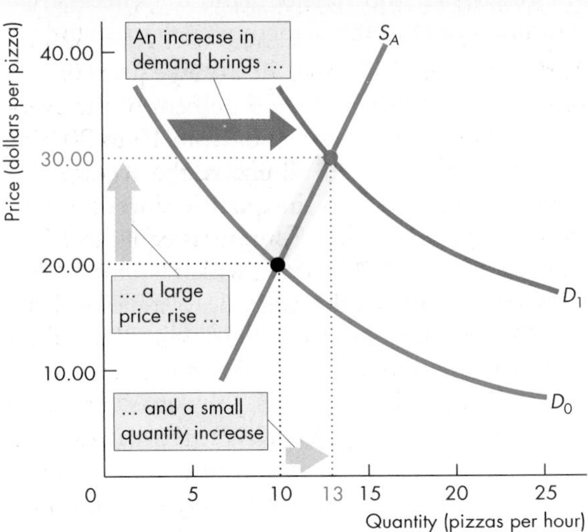

(a) Large price change and small quantity change

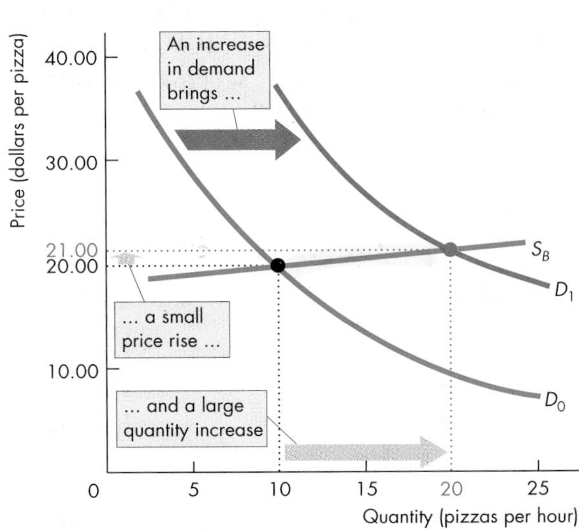

(b) Small price change and large quantity change

Initially, the price is $20 a pizza, and the quantity sold is 10 pizzas an hour. Then increases in incomes and population increase the demand for pizza. The demand curve shifts rightward to D_1. In part (a) the price rises by $10 to $30 a pizza, and the quantity increases by 3 to 13 pizzas an hour. In part (b), the price rises by only $1 to $21 a pizza, and the quantity increases by 10 to 20 pizzas an hour. The price change is smaller and the quantity change is larger in case (b) than in case (a). The quantity supplied is more responsive to price in case (b) than in case (a).

so the increase is 3 pizzas, the average quantity is 11.5 pizzas an hour, and the quantity increases by 26 percent. The elasticity of supply is equal to 26 percent divided by 40 percent, which equals 0.65.

In Fig. 4.9(b), when the price rises from $20 to $21, the price rise is $1 and the average price is $20.50, so the price rises by 4.9 percent of the average price. The quantity increases from 10 to 20 pizzas an hour, so the increase is 10 pizzas, the average quantity is 15 pizzas, and the quantity increases by 67 percent. The elasticity of supply is equal to 67 percent divided by 4.9 percent, which equals 13.67.

Figure 4.10 shows the range of elasticities of supply. If the quantity supplied is fixed regardless of the price, the supply curve is vertical and the elasticity of supply is zero. Supply is perfectly inelastic. This case is shown in Fig. 4.10(a). A special intermediate case is when the percentage change in price equals the percentage change in quantity. Supply is then unit elastic. This case is shown in Fig. 4.10(b). No matter how steep the supply curve is, if it is linear and passes through the origin, supply is unit elastic. If there is a price at which sellers are willing to offer any quantity for sale, the supply curve is horizontal and the elasticity of supply is infinite. Supply is perfectly elastic. This case is shown in Fig. 4.10(c).

The Factors That Influence the Elasticity of Supply

The magnitude of the elasticity of supply depends on

- Resource substitution possibilities
- Time frame for the supply decision

Resource Substitution Possibilities Some goods and services can be produced only by using unique or rare productive resources. These items have a low, even perhaps a zero, elasticity of supply. Other goods and services can be produced by using commonly available resources that could be allocated to a wide variety of alternative tasks. Such items have a high elasticity of supply.

A Van Gogh painting is an example of a good with a vertical supply curve and a zero elasticity of supply. At the other extreme, wheat can be grown on land that is almost equally good for growing corn. So it is just as easy to grow wheat as corn, and the opportunity cost of wheat in terms of forgone corn is almost constant. As a result, the supply curve of wheat is almost horizontal and its elasticity of supply is very large. Similarly, when a good is produced in many different countries (for example, sugar and beef), the supply of the good is highly elastic.

FIGURE 4.10 Inelastic and Elastic Supply

myeconlab

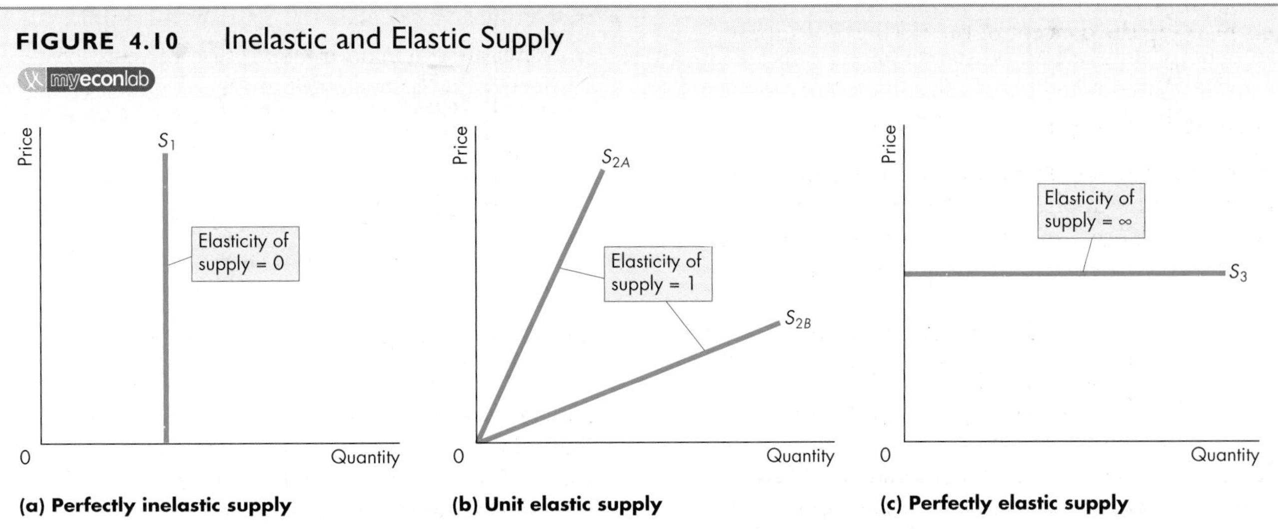

Each supply illustrated here has a constant elasticity. The supply curve in part (a) illustrates the supply of a good that has a zero elasticity of supply. The supply curve in part (b) illustrates the supply of a good with a unit elasticity of supply. All linear supply curves that pass through the origin illustrate supplies that are unit elastic. The supply curve in part (c) illustrates the supply of a good with an infinite elasticity of supply.

The supply of most goods and services lies between these two extremes. The quantity produced can be increased but only by incurring a higher cost. If a higher price is offered, the quantity supplied increases. Such goods and services have an elasticity of supply between zero and infinity.

Time Frame for the Supply Decision To study the influence of the length of time elapsed since a price change, we distinguish three time frames of supply:

1. Momentary supply
2. Long-run supply
3. Short-run supply

When the price of a good rises or falls, the *momentary supply curve* shows the response of the quantity supplied immediately following a price change.

Some goods, such as fruits and vegetables, have a perfectly inelastic momentary supply—a vertical supply curve. The quantities supplied depend on crop-planting decisions made earlier. In the case of oranges, for example, planting decisions have to be made many years in advance of the crop being available. The momentary supply curve is vertical because, on a given day, no matter what the price of oranges, producers cannot change their output. They have picked, packed, and shipped their crop to market, and the quantity available for that day is fixed.

In contrast, some goods have a perfectly elastic momentary supply. Long-distance phone calls are an example. When many people simultaneously make a call, there is a big surge in the demand for telephone cables, computer switching, and satellite time, and the quantity bought increases. But the price remains constant. Long-distance carriers monitor fluctuations in demand and reroute calls to ensure that the quantity supplied equals the quantity demanded without changing the price.

The *long-run supply curve* shows the response of the quantity supplied to a change in price after all the technologically possible ways of adjusting supply have been exploited. In the case of oranges, the long run is the time it takes new plantings to grow to full maturity—about 15 years. In some cases, the long-run adjustment occurs only after a completely new production plant has been built and workers have been trained to operate it—typically a process that might take several years.

The *short-run supply curve* shows how the quantity supplied responds to a price change when only *some* of the technologically possible adjustments to production have been made. The short-run response to a price change is a sequence of adjustments. The first adjustment that is usually made is in the amount of labor employed. To increase output in the short run, firms work their labor force overtime and perhaps hire additional workers. To decrease their output in the short run, firms either lay off workers or reduce their hours of work. With the passage of time, firms can make additional adjustments, perhaps training additional workers or buying additional tools and other equipment.

The short-run supply curve slopes upward because producers can take actions quite quickly to change the quantity supplied in response to a price change. For example, if the price of oranges falls, growers can stop picking and leave oranges to rot on the trees. Or if the price rises, they can use more fertilizer and improved irrigation to increase the yields of their existing trees. In the long run, they can plant more trees and increase the quantity supplied even more in response to a given price rise.

REVIEW QUIZ

1. Why do we need to measure the responsiveness of the quantity supplied of a good or service to a change in its price?
2. Define and calculate the elasticity of supply.
3. What are the main influences on the elasticity of supply that make the supply of some goods elastic and the supply of other goods inelastic?
4. Provide examples of goods or services whose elasticities of supply are (a) zero, (b) greater than zero but less than infinity, and (c) infinity.
5. How does the time frame over which a supply decision is made influence the elasticity of supply? Explain your answer.

myeconlab **Study Plan 4.3**

You have now learned about the elasticities of demand and supply. Table 4.3 summarizes all the elasticities that you've met in this chapter. In the next chapter, we study the efficiency of competitive markets. But first study *Reading Between the Lines* on pp. 98–99, which puts the elasticity of demand to work and looks at the market for personal computers that we described at the beginning of this chapter.

TABLE 4.3 A Compact Glossary of Elasticities

Price Elasticities of Demand

A relationship is described as	When its magnitude is	Which means that
Perfectly elastic	Infinity	The smallest possible increase in price causes an infinitely large decrease in the quantity demanded*
Elastic	Less than infinity but greater than 1	The percentage decrease in the quantity demanded exceeds the percentage increase in price
Unit elastic	1	The percentage decrease in the quantity demanded equals the percentage increase in price
Inelastic	Greater than zero but less than 1	The percentage decrease in the quantity demanded is less than the percentage increase in price
Perfectly inelastic	Zero	The quantity demanded is the same at all prices

Cross Elasticities of Demand

A relationship is described as	When its value is	Which means that
Close substitutes	Large	The smallest possible increase in the price of one good causes an infinitely large increase in the quantity demanded of the other good
Substitutes	Positive	If the price of one good increases, the quantity demanded of the other good also increases
Unrelated goods	Zero	If the price of one good increases, the quantity demanded of the other good remains the same
Complements	Negative	If the price of one good increases, the quantity demanded of the other good decreases

Income Elasticities of Demand

A relationship is described as	When its value is	Which means that
Income elastic (normal good)	Greater than 1	The percentage increase in the quantity demanded is greater than the percentage increase in income
Income inelastic (normal good)	Less than 1 but greater than zero	The percentage increase in the quantity demanded is less than the percentage increase in income
Negative income elastic (inferior good)	Less than zero	When income increases, quantity demanded decreases

Elasticities of Supply

A relationship is described as	When its magnitude is	Which means that
Perfectly elastic	Infinity	The smallest possible increase in price causes an infinitely large increase in the quantity supplied
Elastic	Less than infinity but greater than 1	The percentage increase in the quantity supplied exceeds the percentage increase in the price
Inelastic	Greater than zero but less than 1	The percentage increase in the quantity supplied is less than the percentage increase in the price
Perfectly inelastic	Zero	The quantity supplied is the same at all prices

*In each description, the directions of change may be reversed. For example, in this case, the smallest possible *decrease* in price causes an infinitely large *increase* in the quantity demanded.

READING BETWEEN THE LINES

The Elasticities of Demand for Notebook and Desktop Computers

http://www.nytimes.com

Timing the Electronics Market for the Best Deal on a New PC

May 27, 2006

Lower prices are part of the natural order in the world of electronics. Sometimes, though, the slow but relentless drop in price turns into a torrent. That's happening now in personal computers. . . .

The lower-priced notebooks are pushing desktop prices down, too. "I would expect even more intense price competition," said Charles Smulders, an analyst with Gartner, another market research firm. . . .

When an electronic device breaks through the $1,000 psychological barrier, sales take off. Samir Bhavnani, director for research at Current Analysis, said 37 percent more notebooks have been sold so far this year. About 60 percent of all notebook computers sold last month were priced below $1,000. He credits Dell, saying, "They love getting down in the mud." . . .

Another statistic will tell you just how good consumers have it. While the number of notebooks sold is up 37 percent, revenue growth in the period is up only 15.5 percent, Mr. Bhavnani said. Companies are making less money on each notebook. Desktop computers are literally being given away. Retailers sold 14.8 percent more of them in the first five months of the year, but revenue declined 4 percent, Mr. Bhavnani said. Half of the computers sold for less than $500. . . .

Essence of the Story

- About 60 percent of notebook computers are priced at less than $1,000.
- The lower price of a notebook has pushed down the price of a desktop and half of the desktops are priced at less than $500.
- When an electronic device breaks through the $1,000 psychological barrier, sales take off.
- The quantity of notebooks sold increased by 37 percent in 2006, and the total revenue from the sale of notebooks increased by 15.5 percent.
- The quantity of desktop computers sold increased by 14.8 percent in 2006, and the total revenue from desktops decreased by 4 percent.

- This news article provides information about the changes in quantities and total revenue in the markets for notebook and desktop computers.
- Other things remaining the same, the information about the change in the quantity and total revenue is sufficient to calculate the price elasticity of demand.
- If the price falls and total revenue increases (as in the market for notebooks), demand is elastic.
- And if the price falls and total revenue *decreases* (as in the market for desktops), demand is inelastic.
- But other things did not remain the same in the markets for notebooks and desktops.
- Notebook and desktop computers are *substitutes*. If the price of a notebook falls, the demand for desktops decreases. And if the price of a desktop falls, the demand for notebooks decreases.
- Figure 1 illustrates the market for notebook computers *assuming* that the price elasticity of demand is 4 and given the information in the news article.
- When the price of a desktop is $600, the demand for notebooks is D_0, and when the price of a desktop is $500, the demand for notebooks decreases to D_1.
- In 2006, the price of a notebook decreased from almost $1,200 to about $1,000 (on the average) and the quantity bought increased by 37 percent.
- If we assumed that there was no change in the demand for notebooks, the demand curve would be the light blue curve and the price elasticity of demand would be estimated to be 1.83.
- Figure 2 illustrates the market for desktop computers *assuming* that the price elasticity of demand is 4 and given the information in the news article.
- When the price of a notebook is $1,186, the demand for desktops is D_0, and when the price of a notebook is $1,000, the demand for desktops decreases to D_1.
- In 2006, the price of a desktop decreased from about $600 to about $500 (on the average) and the quantity bought increased by almost 15 percent.
- If we assumed that there was no change in the demand for desktops, the demand curve would be the light blue curve and the price elasticity of demand would be estimated to be 0.77.
- Because other things do not remain the same, there is insufficient information in this news article to calculate the price elasticities of demand for personal computers.
- But other information suggests that the demand for computers is elastic. And the news article says that demand becomes highly elastic at prices below $1,000—what is called the "psychological barrier" below which "sales take off."

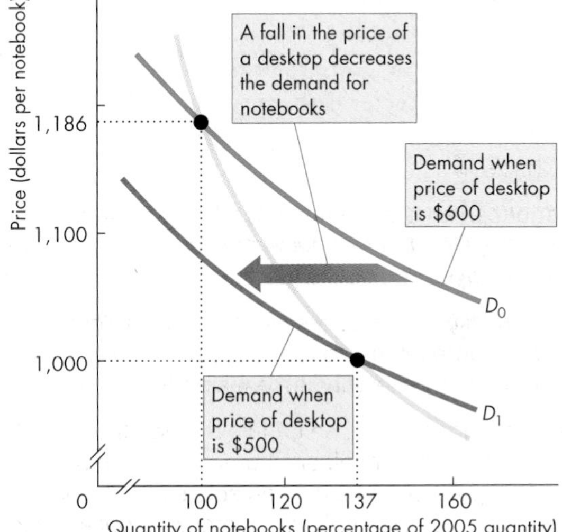

Figure 1 The market for notebook computers

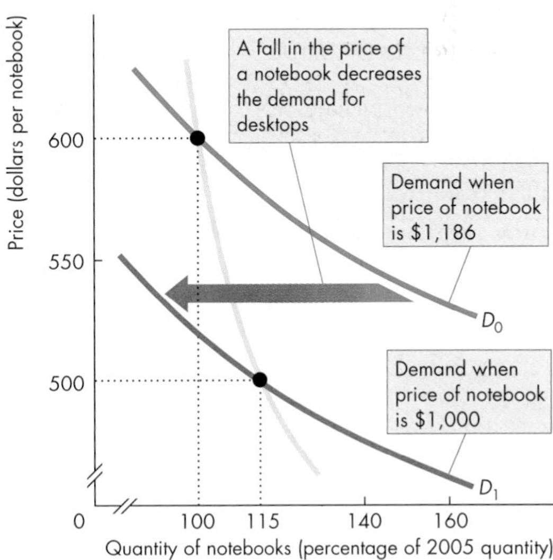

Figure 2 The market for desktop computers

SUMMARY

Key Points

Price Elasticity of Demand (pp. 84–90)

- Elasticity is a measure of the responsiveness of the quantity demanded of a good to a change in its price, other things remaining the same.
- Price elasticity of demand equals the percentage change in the quantity demanded divided by the percentage change in price.
- The larger the magnitude of the price elasticity of demand, the greater is the responsiveness of the quantity demanded to a given change in price.
- Price elasticity of demand depends on how easily one good serves as a substitute for another, the proportion of income spent on the good, and the length of time elapsed since the price change.
- If demand is elastic, a decrease in price leads to an increase in total revenue. If demand is unit elastic, a decrease in price leaves total revenue unchanged. And if demand is inelastic, a decrease in price leads to a decrease in total revenue.

More Elasticities of Demand (pp. 91–93)

- Cross elasticity of demand measures the responsiveness of demand for one good to a change in the price of a substitute or a complement, other things remaining the same.
- The cross elasticity of demand with respect to the price of a substitute is positive. The cross elasticity of demand with respect to the price of a complement is negative.
- Income elasticity of demand measures the responsiveness of demand to a change in income, other things remaining the same. For a normal good, the income elasticity of demand is positive. For an inferior good, the income elasticity of demand is negative.
- When the income elasticity of demand is greater than 1 (income elastic), the percentage of income spent on the good increases as income increases.
- When the income elasticity of demand is less than 1 (income inelastic and inferior), the percentage of income spent on the good decreases as income increases.

Elasticity of Supply (pp. 94–96)

- Elasticity of supply measures the responsiveness of the quantity supplied of a good to a change in its price.
- The elasticity of supply is usually positive and ranges between zero (vertical supply curve) and infinity (horizontal supply curve).
- Supply decisions have three time frames: momentary, long run, and short run.
- Momentary supply refers to the response of sellers to a price change at the instant that the price changes.
- Long-run supply refers to the response of sellers to a price change when all the technologically feasible adjustments in production have been made.
- Short-run supply refers to the response of sellers to a price change after some of the technologically feasible adjustments in production have been made.

Key Figures and Table

Key Terms

PROBLEMS

myeconlab Tests, Study Plan, Solutions*

1. Rain spoils the strawberry crop. As a result, the price rises from $4 to $6 a box and the quantity demanded decreases from 1,000 to 600 boxes a week. Over this price range,
   a. What is the price elasticity of demand?
   b. Describe the demand for strawberries.
2. The figure shows the demand for DVD rentals.

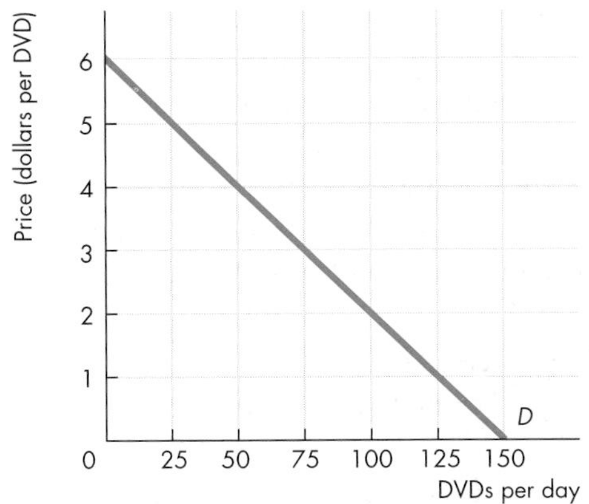

   a. Calculate the elasticity of demand when the price rises from $3 to $5 a DVD.
   b. At what price is the elasticity of demand equal to 1?
3. If the quantity of dental services demanded increases by 10 percent when the price of dental services falls by 10 percent, is the demand for dental services inelastic, elastic, or unit elastic?
4. The demand schedule for computer chips is

Price (dollars per chip)	Quantity demanded (millions of chips per year)
200	50
250	45
300	40
350	35
400	30

   a. What happens to total revenue if the price falls from $400 to $350 a chip?
   b. What happens to total revenue if the price falls from $350 to $300 a chip?
   c. At what price is total revenue at a maximum?
   d. At an average price of $350, is the demand for chips elastic or inelastic?
5. In problem 4, at $250 a chip, is the demand for chips elastic or inelastic? Use the total revenue test to answer this question.
6. Your price elasticity of demand for bananas is 4. If the price of bananas rises by 5 percent, what is the percentage change in
   a. Your expenditure on bananas?
   b. The quantity of bananas you buy?
7. If a 12 percent rise in the price of orange juice decreases the quantity of orange juice demanded by 22 percent and increases the quantity of apple juice demanded by 14 percent, calculate the
   a. Price elasticity of demand for orange juice.
   b. Cross elasticity of demand between orange juice and apple juice.
8. When Alex's income increased from $3,000 to $5,000, he increased his consumption of bagels from 4 to 8 a month and decreased his consumption of doughnuts from 12 to 6 a month. Calculate Alex's income elasticity of demand for
   a. Bagels.
   b. Doughnuts.
9. In 2003, when music downloading first took off, Universal Music slashed the prices of CDs from an average of $21 to an average of $15. The company said that it expected the price cut to boost the quantity of CDs sold by 30 percent.
   a. What was Universal Music's estimate of the price elasticity of demand for CDs?
   b. Given your answer to part (a), if you were making the pricing decision at Universal Music, would you cut the price, raise the price, or leave the price unchanged? Explain your decision.
10. The table gives the supply schedule of long-distance phone calls.

Price (cents per minute)	Quantity supplied (millions of minutes per day)
10	200
20	400
30	600
40	800

    Calculate the elasticity of supply when
    a. The price falls from 40 cents to 30 cents a minute.
    b. The average price is 20 cents a minute.

*Solutions to odd-numbered problems are provided.

CRITICAL THINKING

1. Study *Reading Between the Lines* on pp. 98–99 and then answer the following questions.
   a. Do you think that the demand for notebook computers is 1.83 as implied by the numbers in the news article? Explain why or why not.
   b. Do you think that the demand for desktop computers is 0.77 as implied by the numbers in the news article? Explain why or why not.
   c. What elasticity information would you need to predict the change in the demand for personal computers over the next five years?
2. The demand for illegal drugs is inelastic. Much of the expenditure on illegal drugs comes from crime. Assuming these statements to be correct,
   a. How will a successful campaign that decreases the supply of drugs influence the price of drugs and the amount spent on them?
   b. What will happen to the amount of crime?
   c. What is the most effective way of decreasing the quantity of drugs consumed and decreasing the amount of drug-related crime?
3. **Why the Tepid Response to Higher Gasoline Prices?**

   Most studies find that in the short run—over a year, say— . . . a 10 percent increase in gas prices . . . is associated with a 1 to 2 percent drop in the quantity of gasoline purchased . . .

   From September 2004 to September 2005, the average retail gasoline price jumped to $2.90 a gallon from $1.87 . . . yet gasoline consumption dropped only 3.5 percent . . .

   The New York Times, October 13, 2005

   a. What is the price elasticity of demand for gasoline implied by what most studies have found?
   b. If other things remained the same, what would the data for the year to September 2005 imply about the price elasticity of demand for gasoline?
   c. How does your answer to part (a) compare with your answer to part (b) and what do you think might account for the difference?
4. Estimates of the long-run response to past movements in [gasoline] prices imply that a 10 percent price rise causes 5 to 10 percent less consumption, other things being equal. . . . The nationwide average price of gasoline surged 53 percent from 1998 to 2004, after adjusting for inflation. Yet consumption was up 10 percent in this period.

   Of course, many other things changed in this period. Perhaps most important, [incomes] grew by 19 percent. . . . This would ordinarily be expected to push gasoline sales up about 20 percent. . .

   The New York Times, October 13, 2005

   a. What does the above information about estimates of the long-run response to price movements imply about the long-run price elasticity of demand for gasoline?
   b. What is the income elasticity of demand for gasoline implied by the above information?
   c. If other things remained the same except for the increase in income and the rise in price, what would the data for 1998 to 2004 imply about the price elasticity of demand for gasoline?
   d. List all the factors you can think of that might bias the estimate of the price elasticity of demand for gasoline, using just the data for 1998 to 2004.

WEB ACTIVITIES

myeconlab **Links to Web sites**

1. a. Find the gasoline price in the summer of 2006.
   b. Use the concepts of demand, supply, and elasticity to explain recent changes in the price of gasoline.
   c. Find the price of crude oil.
   d. Use the concepts of demand, supply, and elasticity to explain recent changes in the price of crude oil.
2. a. Find the number of gallons in a barrel and the cost of crude oil in a gallon of gasoline.
   b. What are the other costs that make up the total cost of a gallon of gasoline?
   c. If the price of crude oil falls by 10 percent, by what percentage would you expect the price of gasoline to change, other things remaining the same?
   d. Which demand do you think is more elastic: that for crude oil or gasoline? Why?

CHAPTER 5

Efficiency and Equity

Self-Interest and the Social Interest

Every time you buy a pair of sports shoes or a text-book, fill your gas tank, download some MP3 files, burn a CD, order a pizza, check in at the airport, or even just take a shower, you express your view about how scarce resources should be used. You try to spend your income and your time in ways that get the most out of *your* scarce resources—you make choices that further your *self-interest*. And markets coordinate your decisions along with those of everyone else. But do markets do a good job? Do they enable us to allocate resources between shoes, books, gasoline, music, CD-Rs, pizza, airline services, water, and all the other things we buy in the *social interest*? Could we as a society be better off if we spent more on some things and less on others?

The market economy generates huge incomes for some people and miserable pickings for others. For example, software sales by Microsoft have generated enough profit over the past ten years to rocket Bill Gates, one of its founders, into the position of being one of the richest people in the world. Is it *fair* that Bill Gates is so incredibly rich while others live in miserable poverty?

The social interest has the two dimensions that we've just discussed: efficiency and fairness (or equity). So our central question in this chapter is: Does the market achieve an efficient and fair use of resources?

At the end of the chapter, in *Reading Between the Lines*, we return to the issue that we first raised in Chapter 1 about the use of the world's water resources. Do we use markets and other arrangements that allocate the world's scarce water efficiently?

After studying this chapter, you will be able to

- Describe the alternative methods of allocating scarce resources
- Explain the connection between demand and marginal benefit and define consumer surplus
- Explain the connection between supply and marginal cost and define producer surplus
- Explain the conditions under which markets move resources to their highest-valued uses and the sources of inefficiency in our economy
- Explain the main ideas about fairness and evaluate claims that markets result in unfair outcomes

Resource Allocation Methods

The goal of this chapter is to evaluate the ability of markets to allocate resources efficiently and fairly. But to see whether the market does a good job, we must compare it with its alternatives. Resources are scarce, so they must be allocated somehow. And trading in markets is just one of several alternative methods.

Resources might be allocated by

- Market price
- Command
- Majority rule
- Contest
- First-come, first-served
- Lottery
- Personal characteristics
- Force

Let's briefly examine each method.

Market Price

When a market price allocates a scarce resource, the people who are willing and able to pay that price get the resource. Two kinds of people decide not to pay the market price: those who can afford to pay but choose not to buy and those who are too poor and simply can't afford to buy.

For many goods and services, distinguishing between those who choose not to buy and those who can't afford to buy doesn't matter. But for a few items, it does matter. For example, poor people can't afford to pay school fees and doctors' fees. Because poor people can't afford items that most people consider to be essential, these items are usually allocated by one of the other methods.

Command

A **command system** allocates resources by the order (command) of someone in authority. In the U.S. economy, the command system is used extensively inside firms and government departments. For example, if you have a job, most likely someone tells you what to do. Your labor is allocated to specific tasks by a command.

A command system works well in organizations in which the lines of authority and responsibility are clear and it is easy to monitor the activities being performed. But a command system works badly when the range of activities to be monitored is large and when it is easy for people to fool those in authority. The system works so badly in North Korea, where it is used extensively in place of markets, that it fails even to deliver an adequate supply of food.

Majority Rule

Majority rule allocates resources in the way that a majority of voters choose. Societies use majority rule to elect representative governments that make some of the biggest decisions. For example, majority rule decides the tax rates that end up allocating scarce resources between private use and public use. And majority rule decides how tax dollars are allocated among competing uses such as education and health care.

Majority rule works well when the decisions being made affect large numbers of people and self-interest must be suppressed to use resources most effectively.

Contest

A contest allocates resources to a winner (or a group of winners). Sporting events use this method. Tiger Woods competes with other golfers, and the winner gets the biggest payoff. But contests are more general than those in a sports arena, though we don't normally call them contests. For example, Bill Gates won a contest to provide the world's personal computer operating system.

Contests do a good job when the efforts of the "players" are hard to monitor and reward directly. When a manager offers everyone in the company the opportunity to win a big prize, people are motivated to work hard and try to become the winner. Only a few people end up with a big prize, but many people work harder in the process of trying to win. So total output produced by the workers is much greater than it would be without the contest.

First-Come, First-Served

A first-come, first-served method allocates resources to those who are first in line. Many casual restaurants won't accept reservations. They use first-come, first-served to allocate their scarce tables. Highway space is allocated in this way too: the first to arrive at the on-ramp gets the road space. If too many vehicles enter the highway, the speed slows and people wait in line for some space to become available.

First-come, first-served works best when, as in the above examples, a scarce resource can serve just one user at a time in a sequence. By serving the user who arrives first, this method minimizes the time spent waiting for the resource to become free.

Lottery

Lotteries allocate resources to those who pick the winning number, draw the lucky cards, or come up lucky on some other gaming system. State lotteries and casinos reallocate millions of dollars worth of goods and services every year.

But lotteries are more widespread than jackpots and roulette wheels in casinos. They are used to allocate landing slots to airlines at some airports and have been used to allocate fishing rights and the electromagnetic spectrum used by cell phones.

Lotteries work best when there is no effective way to distinguish among potential users of a scarce resource.

Personal Characteristics

When resources are allocated on the basis of personal characteristics, people with the "right" characteristics get the resources. Some of the resources that matter most to you are allocated in this way. For example, you will choose a marriage partner on the basis of personal characteristics. But this method is also used in unacceptable ways. Allocating the best jobs to white, Anglo-Saxon males and discriminating against visible minorities and women is an example.

Force

Force plays a crucial role, for both good and ill, in allocating scarce resources. Let's start with the ill.

War, the use of military force by one nation against another, has played an enormous role historically in allocating resources. The economic supremacy of European settlers in the Americas and Australia owes much to the use of this method.

Theft, the taking of the property of others without their consent, also plays a large role. Both large-scale organized crime and small-scale petty crime collectively allocate billions of dollars worth of resources annually.

But force plays a crucial positive role in allocating resources. It provides the state with an effective method of transferring wealth from the rich to the poor, and it provides the legal framework in which voluntary exchange in markets takes place.

A legal system is the foundation on which our market economy functions. Without courts to enforce contracts, it would not be possible to do business. But the courts could not enforce contracts without the ability to apply force if necessary. The state provides the ultimate force that enables the courts to do their work.

More broadly, the force of the state is essential to uphold the principle of the rule of law. This principle is the bedrock of civilized economic (and social and political) life. With the rule of law upheld, people can go about their daily economic lives with the assurance that their property will be protected—that they can sue for violations against their property (and be sued if they violate the property of others).

Free from the burden of protecting their property and confident in the knowledge that those with whom they trade will honor their agreements, people can get on with focusing on the activity at which they have a comparative advantage and trading for mutual gain.

REVIEW QUIZ

1. Why do we need methods of allocating scarce resources?
2. Describe the alternative methods of allocating scarce resources.
3. Provide an example of each allocation method that illustrates when it works well.
4. Provide an example of each allocation method that illustrates when it works badly.

myeconlab **Study Plan 5.1**

In the next sections, we're going to see how a market can achieve an efficient use of resources, examine the obstacles to efficiency, and see how sometimes an alternative method might improve on the market. After looking at efficiency, we'll turn our attention to the more difficult issue of fairness.

Demand and Marginal Benefit

Resources are allocated efficiently when they are used in the ways that people value most highly. This outcome occurs when marginal benefit equals marginal cost (Chapter 2, pp. 37–39). So to determine whether a competitive market is efficient, we need to see whether, at the market equilibrium quantity, marginal benefit equals marginal cost. We begin by seeing how market demand reflects marginal benefit.

Demand, Willingness to Pay, and Value

In everyday life, we talk about "getting value for money." When we use this expression, we are distinguishing between *value* and *price*. Value is what we get, and the price is what we pay.

The value of one more unit of a good or service is its marginal benefit. And we measure marginal benefit by the maximum price that is willingly paid for another unit of the good or service. But willingness to pay determines demand. *A demand curve is a marginal benefit curve.*

In Fig. 5.1(a), Lisa is willing to pay $1 for the 30th slice of pizza and $1 is her marginal benefit from that slice. In Fig. 5.1(b), Nick is willing to pay $1 for the 10th slice of pizza and $1 is his marginal benefit from that slice. But for what quantity is the economy willing to pay $1? The answer is provided by the market demand curve.

Individual Demand and Market Demand

The relationship between the price of a good and the quantity demanded by one person is called *individual demand*. And the relationship between the price of a good and the quantity demanded by all buyers is called *market demand*.

The market demand curve is the horizontal sum of the individual demand curves and is formed by adding the quantities demanded by all the individuals at each price.

Figure 5.1(c) illustrates the market demand for pizza if Lisa and Nick are the only people. Lisa's demand curve (part a) and Nick's demand curve (part b) sum horizontally to the market demand curve in part (c).

FIGURE 5.1 Individual Demand, Market Demand, and Marginal Social Benefit

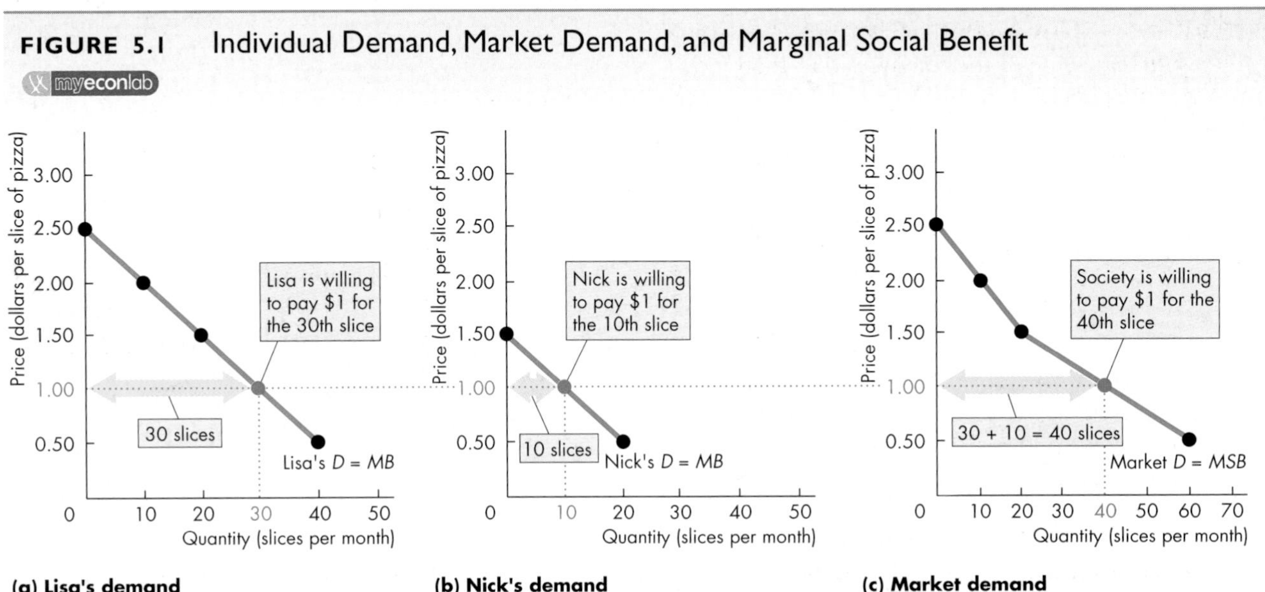

At a price of $1 a slice, the quantity demanded by Lisa is 30 slices and the quantity demanded by Nick is 10 slices, so the quantity demanded by the market is 40 slices. Lisa's demand curve in part (a) and Nick's demand curve in part (b) sum horizontally to the market demand curve in part (c). The market demand curve is the marginal social benefit (*MSB*) curve.

At a price of $1, Lisa demands 30 slices and Nick demands 10 slices, so the quantity demanded by the market at $1 a slice is 40 slices.

So from the market demand curve, we see that the economy (or society) is willing to pay $1 for 40 slices a month. *The market demand curve is the economy's marginal social benefit (MSB) curve.*

Although we're measuring the price in dollars, think of the price as telling us the number of *dollars' worth of other goods and services willingly forgone* to obtain one more slice of pizza.

Consumer Surplus

We don't always have to pay what we are willing to pay—we get a bargain. When people buy something for less than it is worth to them, they receive a consumer surplus. A **consumer surplus** is the value (or marginal benefit) of a good minus the price paid for it, summed over the quantity bought.

Figure 5.2(a) shows Lisa's consumer surplus from pizza when the price is $1 a slice. At this price, she buys 30 slices a month because the 30th slice is worth only $1 to her. But Lisa is willing to pay $2 for the 10th slice, so her marginal benefit from this slice is $1 more than she pays for it—she receives a *consumer surplus* of $1 on the 10th slice.

Lisa's consumer surplus is the sum of the surpluses on *all of the slices she buys*. This sum is the area of the green triangle—the area below the demand curve and above the market price line. The area of this triangle is equal to its base (30 slices) multiplied by its height ($1.50) divided by 2, which is $22.50. The area of the blue rectangle in Fig. 5.2(a) shows what Lisa pays for 30 slices of pizza.

Figure 5.2(b) shows Nick's consumer surplus, and part (c) shows the consumer surplus for the economy. The consumer surplus for the economy is the sum of the consumer surpluses of Lisa and Nick.

All goods and services, like pizza, have decreasing marginal benefit. So people receive more benefit from their consumption than the amount they pay.

REVIEW QUIZ

1 How do we measure the value or marginal benefit of a good or service?
2 What is consumer surplus? How is it measured?

myeconlab **Study Plan 5.2**

FIGURE 5.2 Demand and Consumer Surplus

myeconlab

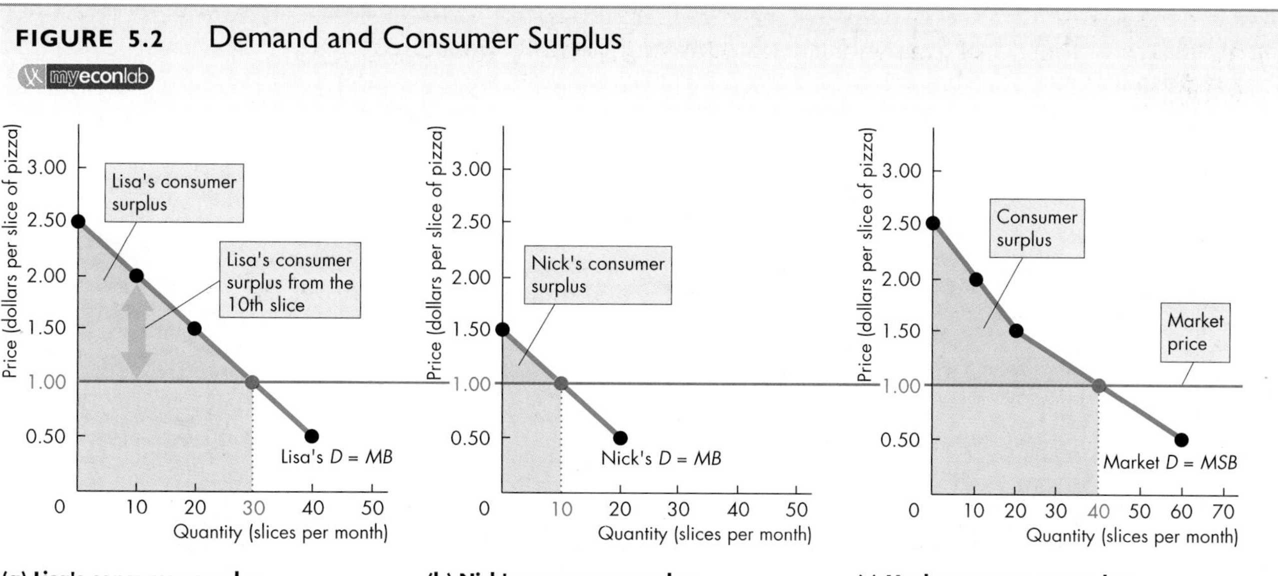

(a) Lisa's consumer surplus

(b) Nick's consumer surplus

(c) Market consumer surplus

Lisa is willing to pay $2.00 for her 10th slice of pizza (part a). At a market price of $1 a slice, Lisa receives a consumer surplus of $1 on the 10th slice. The green triangle shows her consumer surplus on the 30 slices she buys at $1 a slice. The green triangle in part (b) shows Nick's consumer surplus on the 10 slices that he buys at $1 a slice. The green area in part (c) shows the consumer surplus for the economy. The blue rectangles show the amounts spent on pizza.

Supply and Marginal Cost

We are now going to see how market supply reflects marginal cost. This section closely parallels the related ideas about market demand and marginal benefit that you've just studied. Firms are in business to make a profit. To do so, they must sell their output for a price that exceeds the cost of production. Let's investigate the relationship between cost and price.

Supply, Cost, and Minimum Supply-Price

Making a profit means receiving more from the sale of a good or service than the cost of producing it. Just as consumers distinguish between value and price, so producers distinguish between cost and price. Cost is what a producer gives up, and the price is what a producer receives.

The cost of producing one more unit of a good or service is its marginal cost. And marginal cost is the minimum price that producers must receive to induce them to offer to sell another unit of the good or service. But the minimum supply-price determines supply. *A supply curve is a marginal cost curve.*

In Fig. 5.3(a), Max is willing to produce the 100th pizza for $15, his marginal cost of that pizza. In Fig. 5.3(b), Mario is willing to produce the 50th pizza for $15, his marginal cost of that pizza. But what quantity is the economy willing to produce for $15 a pizza? The answer is provided by the *market supply curve.*

Individual Supply and Market Supply

The relationship between the price of a good and the quantity supplied by one producer is called *individual supply*. And the relationship between the price of a good and the quantity supplied by all producers is called *market supply*.

The market supply curve is the horizontal sum of the individual supply curves and is formed by adding the quantities supplied by all the producers at each price.

Figure 5.3(c) illustrates the market supply if Max and Mario are the only producers. Max's supply curve (part a) and Mario's supply curve (part b) sum horizontally to the market supply curve in part (c).

FIGURE 5.3 Individual Supply, Market Supply, and Marginal Social Cost

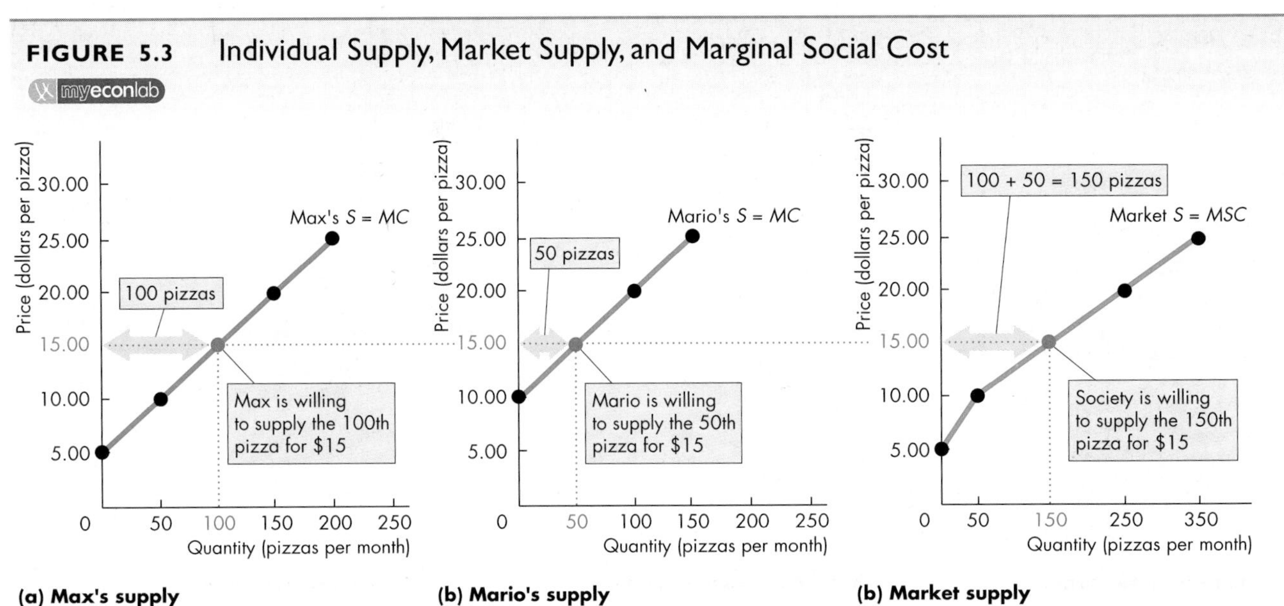

At a price of $15 a pizza, the quantity supplied by Max is 100 pizzas and the quantity supplied by Mario is 50 pizzas, so the quantity supplied by the market is 150 pizzas. Max's supply curve in part (a) and Mario's supply curve in part (b) sum horizontally to the market supply curve in part (c). The market supply curve is the marginal social cost (*MSC*) curve.

At a price of $15 a pizza, Max supplies 100 pizzas and Mario supplies 50 pizzas, so the quantity supplied by the market at $15 a pizza is 150 pizzas.

So from the market supply curve, we see that the economy (or society) is willing to produce 150 pizzas a month for $15 each. *The market supply curve is the economy's marginal social cost (MSC) curve.*

Again, although we're measuring price in dollars, think of the price as telling us the number of *dollars' worth of other goods and services that must be forgone* to obtain one more pizza.

Producer Surplus

When price exceeds marginal cost, the firm receives a producer surplus. A **producer surplus** is the price received for a good minus its minimum supply-price (or marginal cost), summed over the quantity sold.

Figure 5.4(a) shows Max's producer surplus from pizza when the price is $15 a pizza. At this price, he sells 100 pizzas a month because the 100th pizza costs him $15 to produce. But Max is willing to produce the 50th pizza for his marginal cost, which is $10. So he receives a *producer surplus* of $5 on this pizza.

Max's producer surplus is the sum of the surpluses on each pizza he sells. This sum is the area of the blue triangle—the area below the market price and above the supply curve. The area of this triangle is equal to its base (100) multiplied by its height ($10) divided by 2, which is $500. The red area in Fig. 5.4(a) below the supply curve shows what it costs Max to produce 100 pizzas.

Figure 5.4(b) shows Mario's producer surplus and part (c) shows the producer surplus for the economy. The producer surplus for the economy is the sum of the producer surpluses of Max and Mario.

REVIEW QUIZ

1 What is the relationship between the marginal cost, minimum supply-price, and supply?
2 What is producer surplus? How is it measured?

myeconlab **Study Plan 5.3**

Consumer surplus and producer surplus can be used to measure the efficiency of a market. Let's see how we can use these concepts to study the efficiency of a competitive market.

FIGURE 5.4 Supply and Producer Surplus

myeconlab

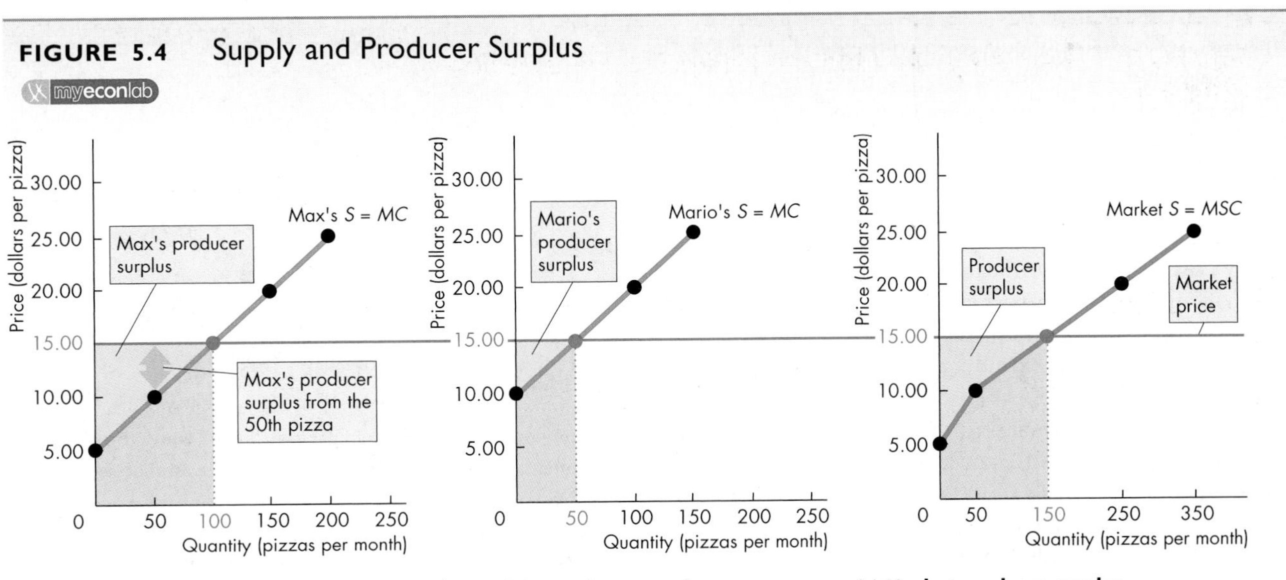

(a) Max's producer surplus **(b) Mario's producer surplus** **(c) Market producer surplus**

Max is willing to produce the 50th pizza for $10 (part a). At a market price of $15 a pizza, Max gets a producer surplus of $5 on the 50th pizza. The blue triangle shows his producer surplus on the 100 pizzas he sells at $15 each. The blue triangle in part (b) shows Mario's producer surplus on the 50 pizzas that he sells at $15 each. The blue area in part (c) shows producer surplus for the economy. The red areas show the cost of producing the pizzas sold.

Is the Competitive Market Efficient?

Figure 5.5(a) shows the market for pizza. The market forces that you studied in Chapter 3 (pp. 70–71) pull the pizza market to its equilibrium price of $15 a pizza and equilibrium quantity of 10,000 pizzas a day. Buyers enjoy a consumer surplus (green area), sellers enjoy a producer surplus (blue area), but is this competitive equilibrium efficient?

Efficiency of Competitive Equilibrium

You've seen that the demand curve tells us the marginal benefit from pizza. If the only people who benefit from pizza are the people who buy it, then the demand curve for pizza measures the marginal benefit to the entire society from pizza. We call the marginal benefit to the entire society, marginal *social* benefit, *MSB*. In this case, the demand curve is also the *MSB* curve.

You've also seen that the supply curve tells us the marginal cost of pizza. If the only people who bear the cost of pizza are the people who produce it, then the supply curve of pizza measures the marginal cost to the entire society of pizza. We call the marginal cost to the entire society, marginal *social* cost, *MSC*. In this case, the supply curve is also the *MSC* curve.

So where the demand curve and the supply curve intersect in part (a), marginal social benefit equals marginal social cost in part (b). This condition delivers an efficient use of resources for the entire society.

If production is less than 10,000 pizzas a day, the marginal pizza is valued more highly than its opportunity cost. If production exceeds 10,000 pizzas a day, the marginal pizza costs more to produce than the value that consumers place on it. Only when 10,000 pizzas a day are produced is the marginal pizza worth exactly what it costs.

The competitive market pushes the quantity of pizza produced to its efficient level of 10,000 a day. If production is less than 10,000 pizzas a day, a shortage raises the price, which increases production. If production exceeds 10,000 pizzas a day, a surplus lowers the price, which decreases production. So a competitive pizza market is efficient.

When the efficient quantity is produced, *total surplus* (the sum of consumer surplus and producer surplus) is maximized. Buyers and sellers acting in their self-interest end up promoting the social interest.

FIGURE 5.5 An Efficient Market for Pizza

myeconlab

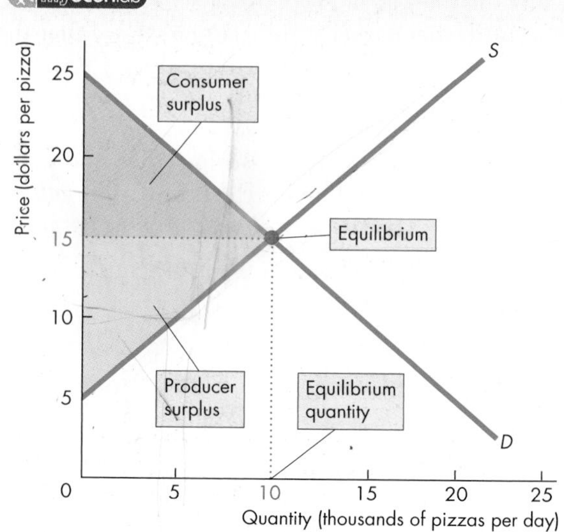

(a) Equilibrium and surpluses

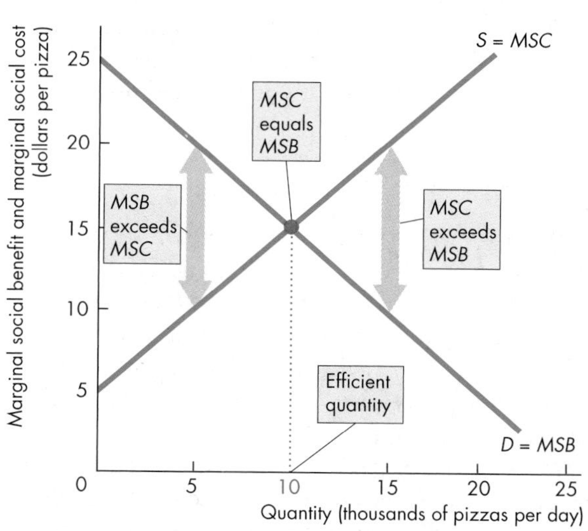

(b) Efficiency

Competitive equilibrium in part (a) occurs when the quantity demanded equals the quantity supplied. Consumer surplus is the area under the demand curve and above the price—the green triangle. Producer surplus is the area above the supply curve and below the price—the blue triangle.

Resources are used efficiently in part (b) when marginal social benefit, *MSB*, equals marginal social cost, *MSC*.

The efficient quantity in part (b) is the same as the equilibrium quantity in part (a). The competitive pizza market produces the efficient quantity of pizza.

The Invisible Hand

Writing in his *Wealth of Nations* in 1776, Adam Smith was the first to suggest that competitive markets send resources to the uses in which they have the highest value (see pp. 54–55). Smith believed that each participant in a competitive market is "led by an invisible hand to promote an end [the efficient use of resources] which was no part of his intention."

You can see the invisible hand at work in the cartoon. The cold drinks vendor has both cold drinks and shade. He has an opportunity cost of each and a minimum supply-price of each. The reader on the park bench has a marginal benefit from a cold drink and from shade. You can see that marginal benefit from shade exceeds the price but the price of a cold drink exceeds its marginal benefit. The transaction that occurs creates a producer surplus and a consumer surplus. The vendor obtains a producer surplus from selling the shade for more than its opportunity cost, and the reader obtains a consumer surplus from buying the shade for less than its marginal benefit. In the third frame of the cartoon, both the consumer and the producer are better off than they were in the first frame. The umbrella has moved to its highest-valued use.

The Invisible Hand at Work Today

The market economy relentlessly performs the activity illustrated in the cartoon and in Fig. 5.5 to achieve an efficient allocation of resources. And rarely has the market been working as hard as it is today. Think about a few of the changes taking place in our economy that the market is guiding toward an efficient use of resources.

New technologies have cut the cost of producing computers. As these advances have occurred, supply has increased and the price has fallen. Lower prices have encouraged an increase in the quantity demanded of this now less costly tool. The marginal social benefit from computers is brought to equality with their marginal social cost.

A Florida frost cuts the supply of oranges. With fewer oranges available, the marginal social benefit increases. A shortage of oranges raises their price, so the market allocates the smaller quantity available to the people who value them most highly.

Market forces persistently bring marginal cost and marginal benefit to equality and maximize total surplus (consumer surplus plus producer surplus).

Underproduction and Overproduction

Inefficiency can occur because either too little of an item is produced—underproduction—or too much is produced—overproduction.

Underproduction In Fig. 5.6(a), the quantity of pizza produced is 5,000 a day. At this quantity, consumers are willing to pay $20 for a pizza that costs only $10 to produce. The quantity produced is inefficient—there is underproduction.

The scale of the inefficiency is measured by **deadweight loss**, which is the decrease in total surplus that results from an inefficient level of production. The gray triangle in Fig. 5.6(a) shows the deadweight loss.

FIGURE 5.6 Underproduction and Overproduction

myeconlab

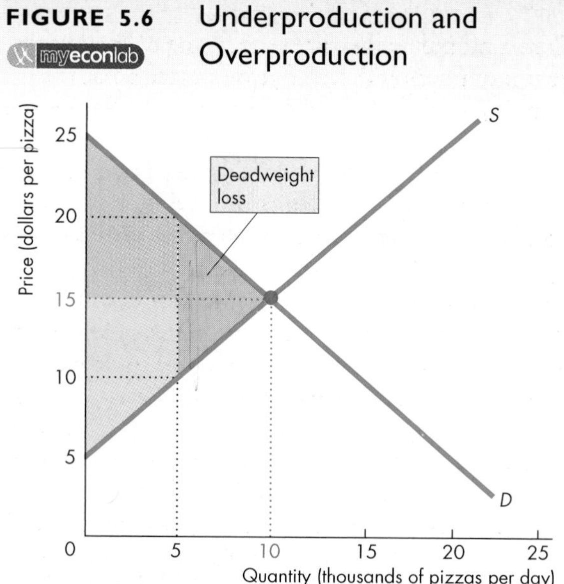

(a) Underproduction

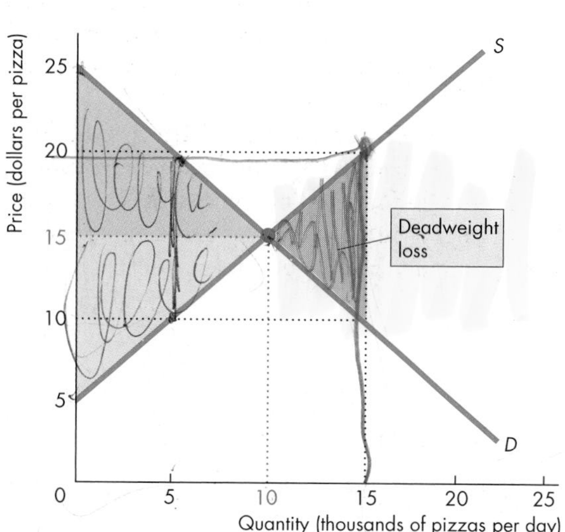

(b) Overproduction

If pizza production is cut to only 5,000 a day, a deadweight loss (the gray triangle) arises (part a). Total surplus (the green and blue areas) is reduced. At 5,000 pizzas, the benefit from one more pizza exceeds its cost. The same is true for all levels of production up to 10,000 pizzas a day.

If production increases to 15,000, a deadweight loss arises (part b). At 15,000 pizzas a day, the cost of the 15,000th pizza exceeds its benefit. The cost of each pizza above 10,000 exceeds its benefit. Total surplus equals the sum of the green and blue areas minus the deadweight loss.

Overproduction In Fig. 5.6(b), the quantity of pizza produced is 15,000 a day. At this quantity, consumers are willing to pay only $10 for a pizza that costs $20 to produce. By producing the 15,000th pizza, $10 of resources are wasted. Again, the gray triangle shows the deadweight loss. The total surplus (the sum of consumer surplus and producer surplus) is smaller than its maximum by the amount of the deadweight loss. The deadweight loss is borne by the entire society. It is not a loss for the consumers and a gain for the producer. It is a *social* loss.

Obstacles to Efficiency

The obstacles to efficiency that bring underproduction or overproduction are

- Price and quantity regulations
- Taxes and subsidies
- Externalities
- Public goods and common resources
- Monopoly
- High transactions costs

Price and Quantity Regulations *Price regulations* that put a cap on the rent a landlord is permitted to charge and laws that require employers to pay a minimum wage sometimes block the price adjustments that balance the quantity demanded and the quantity supplied and lead to underproduction. *Quantity regulations* that limit the amount that a farm is permitted to produce also lead to underproduction.

Taxes and Subsidies *Taxes* increase the prices paid by buyers and lower the prices received by sellers. So taxes decrease the quantity produced and lead to underproduction. *Subsidies*, which are payments by the government to producers, decrease the prices paid by buyers and increase the prices received by sellers. So subsidies increase the quantity produced and lead to overproduction.

Externalities An *externality* is a cost or a benefit that affects someone other than the seller or the buyer of a good. An electric utility creates an external cost by burning coal that brings acid rain and crop damage. The utility doesn't consider the cost of pollution when it decides how much power to produce. The result is overproduction. An apartment owner would provide an *external benefit* if she installed a smoke detector. But she doesn't consider her neighbor's marginal benefit when she is deciding whether to install a smoke detector. There is underproduction.

Public Goods and Common Resources A *public good* is a good or service that is consumed simultaneously by everyone even if they don't pay for it. Examples are national defense and law enforcement. Competitive markets would underproduce a public good because of a *free-rider problem*: It is in each person's interest to free ride on everyone else and avoid paying for her or his share of a public good.

A *common resource* is owned by no one but used by everyone. Atlantic salmon is an example. It is in everyone's self-interest to ignore the costs of their own use of a common resource that fall on others (called the *tragedy of the commons*), which leads to overproduction.

Monopoly A *monopoly* is a firm that is the sole provider of a good or service. Local water supply and cable television are supplied by firms that are monopolies. The self-interest of a monopoly is to maximize its profit. And because the monopoly has no competitors, it can set the price to achieve its self-interested goal. To achieve its goal, a monopoly produces too little and charges too high a price. It leads to underproduction.

High Transactions Costs Stroll around a shopping mall and observe the retail markets in which you participate. You'll see that these markets employ enormous quantities of scarce labor and capital resources. It is costly to operate any market. Economists call the opportunity costs of making trades in a market **transactions costs.**

To use market price as the allocator of scarce resources, it must be worth bearing the opportunity cost of establishing a market. Some markets are just too costly to operate. For example, when you want to play tennis on your local "free" court, you don't pay a market price for your slot on the court. You hang around until the court becomes vacant, and you "pay" with your waiting time. When transactions costs are high, the market might underproduce.

You now know the conditions under which resource allocation is efficient. You've seen how a competitive market can be efficient, and you've seen some impediments to efficiency. But can alternative allocation methods improve on the market?

Alternatives to the Market

When a market is inefficient, can one of the alternative nonmarket methods that we described at the beginning of this chapter do a better job? Sometimes it can.

Often, majority rule might be used in a number of ways in an attempt to improve the allocation of resources. But majority rule has its own shortcomings. A group that pursues the self-interest of its members can become the majority. For example, a price or quantity regulation that creates a deadweight loss is almost always the result of a self-interested group becoming the majority and imposing costs on the minority. Also, with majority rule, votes must be translated into actions by bureaucrats who have their own agendas based on their self-interest.

Managers in firms issue commands and avoid the transactions costs that they would incur if they went to a market every time they needed a job done. First-come, first-served saves a lot of hassle in waiting lines. These lines could have markets in which people trade their place in the line—but someone would have to enforce the agreements. Can you imagine the hassle at a busy ATM if you had to buy your spot at the head of the line?

There is no one efficient mechanism for allocating resources efficiently. But markets, when supplemented by majority rule, by command systems inside firms, and by occasionally using first-come, first-served, do an amazingly good job.

REVIEW QUIZ

1. Do competitive markets use resources efficiently? Explain why or why not.
2. What is deadweight loss and under what conditions does it occur?
3. What are the obstacles to achieving an efficient allocation of resources in the market economy?

myeconlab **Study Plan 5.4**

Is an efficient allocation of resources also a fair allocation? Does the competitive market provide people with fair incomes for their work? Do people always pay a fair price for the things they buy? Don't we need the government to step into some competitive markets to prevent the price from rising too high or falling too low? Let's now study these questions.

Is the Competitive Market Fair?

When a natural disaster strikes, such as a severe winter storm or a hurricane, the prices of many essential items jump. The reason the prices jump is that some people have a greater demand and greater willingness to pay when the items are in limited supply. So the higher prices achieve an efficient allocation of scarce resources. News reports of these price hikes almost never talk about efficiency. Instead, they talk about equity or fairness. The claim that is often made is that it is unfair for profit-seeking dealers to cheat the victims of natural disaster.

Similarly, when low-skilled people work for a wage that is below what most would regard as a "living wage," the media and politicians talk of employers taking unfair advantage of their workers.

How do we decide whether something is fair or unfair? You know when you *think* something is unfair. But how do you *know?* What are the *principles* of fairness?

Philosophers have tried for centuries to answer this question. Economists have offered their answers too. But before we look at the proposed answers, you should know that there is no universally agreed upon answer.

Economists agree about efficiency. That is, they agree that it makes sense to make the economic pie as large as possible and to bake it at the lowest possible cost. But they do not agree about equity. That is, they do not agree about what are fair shares of the economic pie for all the people who make it. The reason is that ideas about fairness are not exclusively economic ideas. They touch on politics, ethics, and religion. Nevertheless, economists have thought about these issues and have a contribution to make. So let's examine the views of economists on this topic.

To think about fairness, think of economic life as a game—a serious game. All ideas about fairness can be divided into two broad groups. They are

- It's not fair if the *result* isn't fair.
- It's not fair if the *rules* aren't fair.

It's Not Fair If the *Result* Isn't Fair

The earliest efforts to establish a principle of fairness were based on the view that the result is what matters. And the general idea was that it is unfair if people's incomes are too unequal. It is unfair that bank presidents earn millions of dollars a year while bank tellers earn only thousands of dollars a year. It is unfair that a store owner enjoys a larger profit and her customers pay higher prices in the aftermath of a winter storm.

There was a lot of excitement during the nineteenth century when economists thought they had made the incredible discovery that efficiency requires equality of incomes. To make the economic pie as large as possible, it must be cut into equal pieces, one for each person. This idea turns out to be wrong, but there is a lesson in the reason that it is wrong. So this nineteenth century idea is worth a closer look.

Utilitarianism The nineteenth century idea that only equality brings efficiency is called *utilitarianism.* **Utilitarianism** is a principle that states that we should strive to achieve "the greatest happiness for the greatest number." The people who developed this idea were known as utilitarians. They included the most eminent thinkers, such as Jeremy Bentham and John Stuart Mill.

Utilitarians argued that to achieve "the greatest happiness for the greatest number," income must be transferred from the rich to the poor up to the point of complete equality—to the point at which there are no rich and no poor.

They reasoned in the following way: First, everyone has the same basic wants and a similar capacity to enjoy life. Second, the greater a person's income, the smaller is the marginal benefit of a dollar. The millionth dollar spent by a rich person brings a smaller marginal benefit to that person than the marginal benefit that the thousandth dollar spent brings to a poorer person. So by transferring a dollar from the millionaire to the poorer person, more is gained than is lost. The two people added together are better off.

Figure 5.7 illustrates this utilitarian idea. Tom and Jerry have the same marginal benefit curve, *MB.* (Marginal benefit is measured on the same scale of 1 to 3 for both Tom and Jerry.) Tom is at point *A.* He earns $5,000 a year, and his marginal benefit of a dollar of income is 3. Jerry is at point *B.* He earns $45,000 a year, and his marginal benefit of a dollar of income is 1. If a dollar is transferred from Jerry to Tom, Jerry loses 1 unit of marginal benefit and Tom gains 3 units. So together, Tom and Jerry are better off. They are sharing the economic pie more efficiently. If a second dollar is transferred, the same thing happens: Tom gains more than Jerry loses. And the same is true for every dollar transferred until they both reach point *C.* At point *C,* Tom and Jerry have

FIGURE 5.7 Utilitarian Fairness

myeconlab

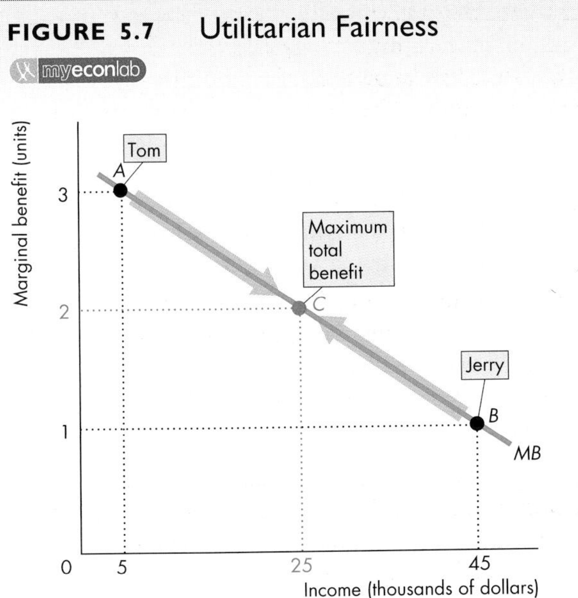

Tom earns $5,000 and has 3 units of marginal benefit at point *A*. Jerry earns $45,000 and has 1 unit of marginal benefit at point *B*. If income is transferred from Jerry to Tom, Jerry's loss is less than Tom's gain. Only when each of them has $25,000 and 2 units of marginal benefit (at point *C*) can the sum of their total benefit increase no further.

$25,000 each, and each has a marginal benefit of 2 units. Now they are sharing the economic pie in the most efficient way. It is bringing the greatest attainable happiness to Tom and Jerry.

The Big Tradeoff One big problem with the utilitarian ideal of complete equality is that it ignores the costs of making income transfers. Recognizing the costs of making income transfers leads to what is called the **big tradeoff**, which is a tradeoff between efficiency and fairness.

The big tradeoff is based on the following facts. Income can be transferred from people with high incomes to people with low incomes only by taxing the high incomes. Taxing people's income from employment makes them work less. It results in the quantity of labor being less than the efficient quantity. Taxing people's income from capital makes them save less. It results in the quantity of capital being less than the efficient quantity. With smaller quantities of both labor and capital, the quantity of goods and services produced is less than the efficient quantity. The economic pie shrinks.

The tradeoff is between the size of the economic pie and the degree of equality with which it is shared. The greater the amount of income redistribution through income taxes, the greater is the inefficiency—the smaller is the economic pie.

There is a second source of inefficiency. A dollar taken from a rich person does not end up as a dollar in the hands of a poorer person. Some of it is spent on administration of the tax and transfer system. The cost of tax-collecting agencies, such as the IRS, and welfare-administering agencies, such as the Health Care Financing Administration, which administers Medicaid and Medicare, must be paid with some of the taxes collected. Also, taxpayers hire accountants, auditors, and lawyers to help them ensure that they pay the correct amount of taxes. These activities use skilled labor and capital resources that could otherwise be used to produce goods and services that people value.

You can see that when all these costs are taken into account, taking a dollar from a rich person does not give a dollar to a poor person. It is even possible that with high taxes, people with low incomes end up being worse off. Suppose, for example, that highly taxed entrepreneurs decide to work less hard and shut down some of their businesses. Low-income workers get fired and must seek other, perhaps even lower-paid work.

Because of the big tradeoff, those who say that fairness is equality propose a modified version of utilitarianism.

Make the Poorest as Well Off as Possible The philosopher, John Rawls, proposed a modified version of utilitarianism in a classic book entitled *A Theory of Justice*, published in 1971. Rawls says that, taking all the costs of income transfers into account, the fair distribution of the economic pie is the one that makes the poorest person as well off as possible. The incomes of rich people should be taxed, and after paying the costs of administering the tax and transfer system, what is left should be transferred to the poor. But the taxes must not be so high that they make the economic pie shrink to the point at which the poorest person ends up with a smaller piece. A bigger share of a smaller pie can be less than a smaller share of a bigger pie. The goal is to make the piece enjoyed by the poorest person as big as possible. Most likely, this piece will not be an equal share.

The "fair results" idea requires a change in the results after the game is over. Some economists say that these changes are themselves unfair and propose a different way of thinking about fairness.

It's Not Fair If the *Rules* Aren't Fair

The idea that it's not fair if the rules aren't fair is based on a fundamental principle that seems to be hardwired into the human brain: the symmetry principle. The **symmetry principle** is the requirement that people in similar situations be treated similarly. It is the moral principle that lies at the center of all the big religions and that says, in some form or other, "Behave toward other people in the way you expect them to behave toward you."

In economic life, this principle translates into *equality of opportunity*. But equality of opportunity to do what? This question is answered by the philosopher Robert Nozick in a book entitled *Anarchy, State, and Utopia*, published in 1974.

Nozick argues that the idea of fairness as an outcome or result cannot work and that fairness must be based on the fairness of the rules. He suggests that fairness obeys two rules:

1. The state must enforce laws that establish and protect private property.
2. Private property may be transferred from one person to another only by voluntary exchange.

The first rule says that everything that is valuable must be owned by individuals and that the state must ensure that theft is prevented. The second rule says that the only legitimate way a person can acquire property is to buy it in exchange for something else that the person owns. If these rules, which are the only fair rules, are followed, then the result is fair. It doesn't matter how unequally the economic pie is shared, provided that the pie is baked by people, each one of whom voluntarily provides services in exchange for the share of the pie offered in compensation.

These rules satisfy the symmetry principle. And if these rules are not followed, the symmetry principle is broken. You can see these facts by imagining a world in which the laws are not followed.

First, suppose that some resources or goods are not owned. They are common property. Then everyone is free to participate in a grab to use these resources or goods. The strongest will prevail. But when the strongest prevails, the strongest effectively *owns* the resources or goods in question and prevents others from enjoying them.

Second, suppose that we do not insist on voluntary exchange for transferring ownership of resources from one person to another. The alternative is *involuntary* transfer. In simple language, the alternative is theft.

Both of these situations violate the symmetry principle. Only the strong acquire what they want. The weak end up with only the resources and goods that the strong don't want.

In a majority rule political system, the strong are those in the majority or those with enough resources to influence opinion and achieve a majority.

In contrast, if the two rules of fairness are followed, everyone, strong and weak, is treated in a similar way. Everyone is free to use their resources and human skills to create things that are valued by themselves and others and to exchange the fruits of their efforts with each other. This set of arrangements is the only one that obeys the symmetry principle.

Fairness and Efficiency If private property rights are enforced and if voluntary exchange takes place in a competitive market, resources will be allocated efficiently if there are no

1. Price and quantity regulations
2. Taxes and subsidies
3. Externalities
4. Public goods and common resources
5. Monopolies
6. High transactions costs

And according to the Nozick rules, the resulting distribution of income and wealth will be fair. Let's study a concrete example to examine the claim that if resources are allocated efficiently, they are also allocated fairly.

Case Study: A Water Shortage in a Natural Disaster

An earthquake has broken the pipes that deliver drinking water to a city. Bottled water is available, but there is no tap water. What is the fair way to allocate the bottled water?

Market Price Suppose that if the water is allocated by market price, the price jumps to $8 a bottle—five times its normal price. At this price, the people who own water can make a large profit by selling it. People who are willing and able to pay $8 a bottle get the water. And because most people can't afford the $8 price, they end up either without water or consuming just a few drops a day.

You can see that the water is being used efficiently. There is a fixed amount available, some people are willing to pay $8 to get a bottle, and the water goes to those people. The people who own and sell water receive a large producer surplus and total surplus (the sum of consumer surplus and producer surplus) is maximized.

In the rules view, the outcome is also fair. No one is denied the water they are willing to pay for. In the results view, the outcome would most likely be regarded as unfair. The lucky owners of water make a killing, and the poorest end up the thirstiest.

Nonmarket Methods Suppose that by a majority vote, the citizens decide that the government will buy all the water, pay for it with a tax, and use one of the nonmarket methods to allocate the water to the citizens. The possibilities now are

Command Someone decides who is the most deserving and needy. Perhaps everyone is given an equal share. Or perhaps government officials and their families end up with most of the water.

Contest Bottles of water are prizes that go to those who are best at a particular contest.

First-come, first-served Water goes to the first off the mark or to those who place the lowest value on their time and can afford to wait in line.

Lottery Water goes to those in luck.

Personal characteristics Water goes to those with the "right" characteristics. Perhaps the old, the young, or pregnant mothers get the water.

Except by chance, none of these methods delivers an allocation of water that is either fair or efficient. It is unfair in the rules view because the tax involves involuntary transfers of resources among citizens. And it is unfair in the results view because the poorest don't end up being made as well off as possible.

The allocation is inefficient for two reasons. First, resources have been used to operate the allocation scheme. Second, some people are willing to pay for more water than they have been allocated and others have been allocated more water than they are willing to pay for.

The second source of inefficiency can be overcome if, after the nonmarket allocation, people are permitted to trade water at its market price. Those who value the water they have at less than the market price sell, and people who are willing to pay the market price to obtain more water buy. Those who value the water most highly are the ones who consume it.

Market Price with Taxes Another approach is to allocate the scarce water using the market price but after the redistribution of buying power by taxing the sellers of water and providing benefits to the poor.

Suppose water owners are taxed on each bottle sold and the revenue from these taxes is given to the poorest people. People are then free, starting from this new distribution of buying power, to trade water at the market price.

Because the owners of water are taxed on what they sell, they have a weaker incentive to offer water for sale and the supply decreases. The equilibrium price rises to more than $8 a bottle. There is now a deadweight loss in the market for water—similar to the loss that arises from underproduction on p. 111. (We study the effects of a tax and show its inefficiency in Chapter 6 on pp. 132–136.)

So the tax is inefficient. In the rules view, the tax is also unfair because it forces the owners of water to make a transfer to others. In the results view, the outcome might be regarded as being fair.

This brief case study illustrates the complexity of ideas about fairness. Economists have a clear criterion of efficiency but no comparably clear criterion of fairness. Most economists regard Nozick as being too extreme and want a fair tax in the rules. But there is no consensus about what would be a fair tax.

REVIEW QUIZ

1. What are the two big approaches to thinking about fairness?
2. What is the utilitarian idea of fairness and what is wrong with it?
3. Explain the big tradeoff. What idea of fairness has been developed to deal with it?
4. What is the main idea of fairness based on fair rules?

myeconlab **Study Plan 5.5**

You've now studied the two biggest issues that run through the whole of economics: efficiency and equity, or fairness. In the next chapter, we study some sources of inefficiency and unfairness. At many points throughout this book—and in your life—you will return to and use the ideas about efficiency and fairness that you've learned in this chapter. *Reading Between the Lines* on pp. 118–119 looks at an example of an inefficiency in our economy today.

READING BETWEEN THE LINES

Inefficiency in Water Use

http://www.nytimes.com

India Digs Deeper, but Wells Are Drying Up, and a Farming Crisis Looms

September 30, 2006

. . . Across India, where most people still live off the land, the chief source of irrigation is groundwater, at least for those who can afford to pump it.

Indian law has virtually no restrictions on who can pump groundwater, how much and for what purpose. Anyone, it seems, can—and does—extract water as long as it is under his or her patch of land. That could apply to homeowner, farmer or industry. . . .

"We forgot that water is a costly item," lamented K. P. Singh, regional director of the Central Groundwater Board, in his office in the city of Jaipur. "Our feeling about proper, judicious use of water vanished."

. . . On a parched, hot morning . . . a train pulled into the railway station at a village called Peeplee Ka Bas. Here, the wells have run dry and the water table fallen so low that it is too salty even to irrigate the fields.

The train came bearing precious cargo: 15 tankers loaded with nearly 120,000 gallons of clean, sweet drinking water.

The water regularly travels more than 150 miles, taking nearly two days, by pipeline and then by rail, so that the residents of a small neighboring town can fill their buckets with water for 15 minutes every 48 hours.

It is a logistically complicated, absurdly expensive proposition. Bringing the water here costs the state about a penny a gallon; the state charges the consumer a monthly flat rate of 58 cents for about 5,300 gallons, absorbing the loss . . .

Essence of the Story

- In India, groundwater is the chief source of irrigation.
- Indian law has few restrictions on who can pump groundwater.
- A regional director of the Central Groundwater Board laments that Indians are behaving as if water were a free resource.
- Where the wells have run dry, water is delivered by pipeline and then by train.
- Water is rationed by permitting residents to fill their buckets with water for 15 minutes every 48 hours.
- Transporting water costs 1 cent per gallon, but consumers pay about 11 cents per 1,000 gallons.

Economic Analysis

- Water is one of the world's most vital resources, and it is used inefficiently.
- Markets in water are not competitive. They are controlled by governments or private producers, and they do not work like the competitive markets that deliver an efficient use of resources.
- The major problem in achieving an efficient use of water is to get it from the places where it is most abundant to the places in which it has the most valuable uses.
- Some places have too little water, and some have too much.
- The news article tells us that the owners of land that has groundwater under it pump the water and sell it and pay little attention to the fact that they will pump the well dry.
- Figure 1 illustrates this situation. The curve *D* shows the demand for water and its marginal social benefit *MSB*. The curve *S* shows the supply of water and its marginal social cost *MSC*.
- Ignoring the high marginal social cost, land owners produce W_A gallons a day, which is greater than the efficient quantity. Farmers are willing to pay *B*, which is less than the marginal social cost *C* but enough to earn the land owner a profit.
- A deadweight loss arises from overproduction.
- Figure 2 shows the situation in places where the wells have run dry.
- A limited quantity of water, W_B, is transported in, and each consumer is restricted to the quantity that can be put into a bucket in 15 minutes every 48 hours.
- Consumers are willing to pay *B* per gallon, which is much more than the marginal social cost *C*.
- The green area shows the consumer surplus, and the red rectangle shows the cost of the water, which is paid by the government and borne by the taxpayers.
- A deadweight loss arises from underproduction.
- The situation in India is replicated in thousands of places around the world.

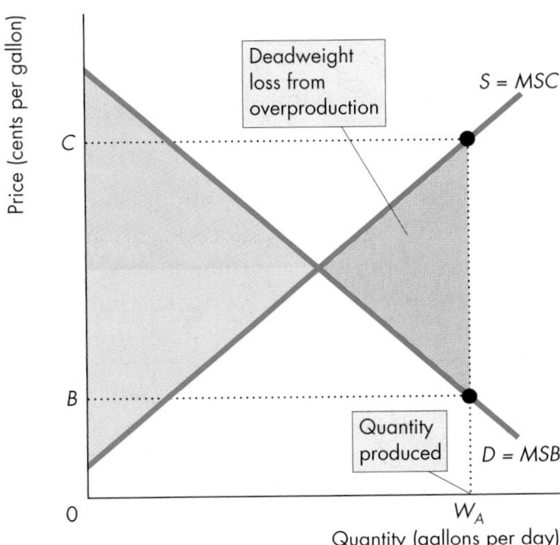

Figure 1 Overproduction where wells are not dry

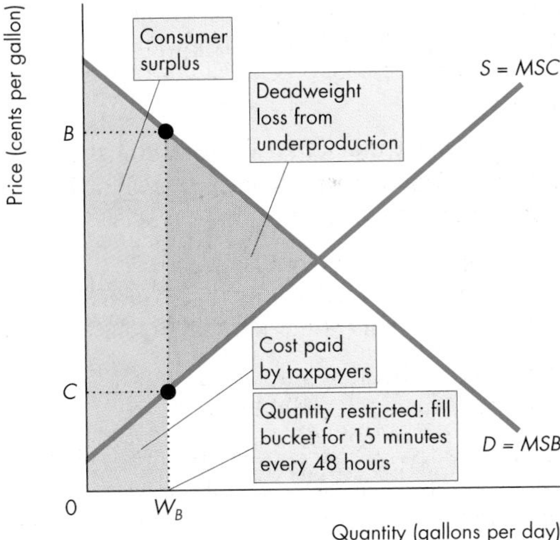

Figure 2 Underproduction where wells run dry

You're the Voter

- Do you think that water is too important to be left to the market to allocate?
- Do you think that water should be shipped from Washington, Alaska, and Canada to California?

SUMMARY

Key Points

Resource Allocation Methods (pp. 104–105)

- Because resources are scarce, some mechanism must allocate them.
- The alternative allocation methods are market price; command; majority rule; contest; first-come, first-served; lottery; personal characteristics; and force.

Demand and Marginal Benefit (pp. 106–107)

- Marginal benefit determines demand, and a demand curve is a marginal benefit curve.
- The market demand curve is the horizontal sum of the individual demand curves and is the marginal social benefit curve.
- Value is what people are *willing to* pay; price is what people *must* pay.
- Consumer surplus equals value minus price, summed over the quantity bought.

Supply and Marginal Cost (pp. 108–109)

- The minimum supply-price determines supply, and the supply curve is the marginal cost curve.
- The market supply curve is the horizontal sum of the individual supply curves and is the marginal social cost curve.
- Opportunity cost is what producers pay; price is what producers receive.
- Producer surplus equals price minus opportunity cost, summed over the quantity sold.

Is the Competitive Market Efficient? (pp. 110–113)

- In a competitive equilibrium, marginal social benefit equals marginal social cost and resource allocation is efficient.
- Buyers and sellers acting in their self-interest end up promoting the social interest.
- The sum of consumer surplus and producer surplus is maximized.
- Producing less than or more than the efficient quantity creates deadweight loss.
- Price and quantity regulations; taxes and subsidies; externalities; public goods and common resources; monopoly; and high transactions costs can create inefficiency and deadweight loss.

Is the Competitive Market Fair? (pp. 114–117)

- Ideas about fairness can be divided into two groups: fair *results* and fair *rules*.
- Fair-results ideas require income transfers from the rich to the poor.
- Fair-rules ideas require property rights and voluntary exchange.

Key Figures

Key Terms

PROBLEMS

myeconlab Tests, Study Plan, Solutions*

1. The table gives the demand schedules for train travel for Ben, Beth, and Bo.

Price (dollars per mile)	Quantity demanded (miles)		
	Ben	Beth	Bo
3	30	25	30
4	25	20	20
5	20	15	10
6	15	10	0
7	10	5	0
8	5	0	0
9	0	0	0

a. Construct the market demand schedule if Ben, Beth, and Bo are the only people in the market.
b. What is marginal social benefit when the quantity is 50 miles? Why?
c. What is each traveler's consumer surplus when the price is $4 a mile?
d. What is the economy consumer surplus when the price is $4 a mile?

2. The table gives the supply schedules for jetski rides by three owners: Ann, Arthur, and Abby.

Price (dollars per ride)	Quantity supplied (rides per day)		
	Ann	Arthur	Abby
10.00	0	0	0
12.50	5	0	0
15.00	10	5	0
17.50	15	10	5
20.00	20	15	10

a. What is each owner's minimum supply-price of 10 rides a day?
b. Which owner has the largest producer surplus when the price of a ride is $17.50? Explain why.
c. What is the marginal social cost of producing 45 rides a day?
d. Construct the market supply schedule if Ann, Arthur, and Abby are the only suppliers of jet-ski rides.

*Solutions to odd-numbered problems are provided.

3. The figure illustrates the market for CDs.

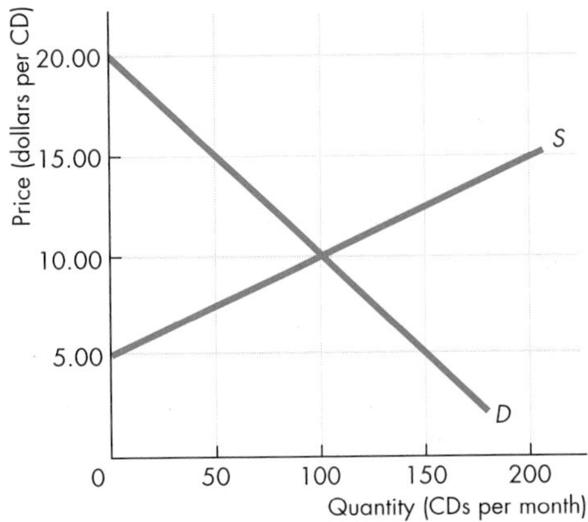

a. What are the equilibrium price and equilibrium quantity of CDs?
b. Shade in the consumer surplus (and label it) and the producer surplus (and label it).
c. Shade in the cost of producing the CDs sold.
d. Calculate total surplus.
e. What is the efficient quantity of CDs?

4. The table gives the demand and supply schedules for sandwiches.

Price (dollars per sandwich)	Quantity demanded (sandwiches per hour)	Quantity supplied (sandwiches per hour)
0	300	0
1	250	50
2	200	100
3	150	150
4	100	200
5	50	250
6	0	300

a. What is the maximum price that consumers are willing to pay for the 200th sandwich?
b. What is the minimum price that producers are willing to accept for the 200th sandwich?
c. Are 200 sandwiches a day less than or greater than the efficient quantity?
d. If the sandwich market is efficient, what is the consumer surplus?
e. If the sandwich market is efficient, what is the producer surplus?
f. If sandwich makers produce 200 a day, what is the deadweight loss?
g. If the demand for sandwiches increases and the sandwich makers continue to produce 200 a day, describe the change in consumer

surplus, producer surplus, total surplus, and the deadweight loss.

5. The table gives the demand and supply schedules for sunscreen. Closure of some factories decreases the quantity of sunscreen produced to 300 bottles a day.

Price (dollars per bottle)	Quantity demanded (bottles per day)	Quantity supplied (bottles per day)
0	800	0
5	700	100
10	600	200
15	500	300
20	400	400
25	300	500
30	200	600

   a. What is the maximum price that consumers are willing to pay for the 300th bottle?
   b. What is the minimum price that producers are willing to accept for the 300th bottle?
   c. Describe the situation in the sunscreen market.
   d. How can the 300 bottles be allocated to beach goers? Which possible methods would be fair and which would be unfair?

CRITICAL THINKING

1. After you have studied *Reading Between the Lines* on pp. 118–119, answer the following questions:
   a. What is the major problem in achieving an efficient use of the world's water?
   b. If there were a global market in water, like there is in oil, how do you think the market would work?
   c. Would a free world market in water achieve an efficient use of the world's water resources? Explain why or why not.
   d. Would a free world market in water achieve a fair use of the world's water resources? Explain why or why not and be clear about the concept of fairness that you are using.
2. **Fight over water rates; Escondido farmers say increase would put them out of business**
   The city is considering significant increases in water rates for agriculture, which historically has paid less than residential and business users. . . . (S)ince 1993, water rates have gone up more than 90 percent for residential customers while agricultural users. . .have seen increases of only about 50 percent, . . .
   The San Diego Union-Tribune, June 14, 2006
   a. Do you think that the allocation of water among San Diego agricultural and residential users is likely to be efficient? Explain your answer.
   b. If agricultural users pay a higher rate for water, will the allocation of resources become more efficient?
   c. If agricultural users pay a higher rate for water, what will happen to the consumer surplus and the producer surplus?
   d. Is the difference in price paid by agricultural and residential users fair?

WEB ACTIVITIES

myeconlab Links to Web sites

1. Visit the Web site of Health Action International and read the article by Catrin Schulte-Hillen entitled "Study concerning the availability and price of AZT." Then answer the following questions and explain your answers using the concepts of marginal benefit, marginal cost, price, consumer surplus, and producer surplus.
   a. What is the range of retail prices of AZT across the countries covered by the study?
   b. How do you think the range of prices influences the efficiency of the market for AZT?
   c. What, if anything, do you think could be done to increase the quantity of AZT and decrease its price?
   d. Canadian online pharmacies sell AZT to Americans for a price below the U.S. price. Does this practice increase or decrease consumer surplus in the United States? Does it increase or decrease producer surplus (i) in the United States and (ii) in Canada?
   e. What do you think must be done to make the market for AZT efficient?

CHAPTER 6

Markets in Action

Turbulent Times

Apartment rents are skyrocketing in Washington, and people are screaming for help. Can the government limit rent increases to help renters live in affordable housing?

Almost every day, a new machine is invented that replaces some workers and increases productivity. Take a look at the machines in McDonald's that have replaced some low-skilled workers. Can we protect low-skilled workers with minimum wage laws that enable people to earn a living wage?

Almost everything we buy is taxed. Beer is one of the most heavily taxed items. How much of the beer tax is paid by the buyer and how much by the seller? Do taxes help or hinder the market in its attempt to move resources to where they are valued most highly?

In 2003, ideal conditions brought record yields and global grain production increased. But in 2000 and 2001, yields were low and global grain production decreased. How do farm prices and revenues react to such output fluctuations and how do subsidies and production quotas affect farmers?

Trading drugs and sharing downloaded music files are illegal activities. How do laws that make trading in a good or service illegal affect its price and the quantity bought and sold?

In this chapter, we use the theory of demand and supply (Chapter 3) and the concepts of elasticity (Chapter 4) and efficiency (Chapter 5) to answer questions like those that we've just posed. In *Reading Between the Lines* at the end of the chapter, we explore the challenge of limiting the illegal downloading and sharing of music files.

After studying this chapter, you will be able to

- Explain how housing markets work and how price ceilings create housing shortages and inefficiency
- Explain how labor markets work and how minimum wage laws create unemployment and inefficiency
- Explain the effects of a tax
- Explain why farm prices and revenues fluctuate and how production subsidies and quotas influence farm production, costs, and prices
- Explain how markets for illegal goods work

Housing Markets and Rent Ceilings

To see how a housing market works, let's transport ourselves to San Francisco in April 1906, as the city is suffering from a massive earthquake and fire. You can sense the enormity of San Francisco's problems by reading a headline from the April 19, 1906, *New York Times* about the first days of the crisis:

> Over 500 Dead, \$200,000,000 Lost in San Francisco Earthquake
>
> Nearly Half the City Is in Ruins and 50,000 Are Homeless

The commander of federal troops in charge of the emergency described the magnitude of the problem:

> Not a hotel of note or importance was left standing. The great apartment houses had vanished . . . two hundred-and-twenty-five thousand people were . . . homeless.[1]

Almost overnight, more than half the people in a city of 400,000 had lost their homes. Temporary shelters and camps alleviated some of the problem, but it was also necessary to utilize the apartment buildings and houses left standing. As a consequence, they had to accommodate 40 percent more people than they had before the earthquake.

The *San Francisco Chronicle* was not published for more than a month after the earthquake. When the newspaper reappeared on May 24, 1906, the city's housing shortage—what would seem to be a major news item that would still be of grave importance—was not mentioned. Milton Friedman and George Stigler describe the situation:

> *There is not a single mention of a housing shortage!* The classified advertisements listed sixty-four offers of flats and houses for rent, and nineteen of houses for sale, against five advertisements of flats or houses wanted. Then and thereafter a considerable number of all types of accommodation except hotel rooms were offered for rent.[2]

How did San Francisco cope with such a devastating reduction in the supply of housing?

The Market Before and After the Earthquake

Figure 6.1 shows the market for housing in San Francisco. The demand curve for housing is D. There is a short-run supply curve, labeled SS, and a long-run supply curve, labeled LS.

Short-Run Supply The short-run supply curve shows the change in the quantity of housing supplied as the rent changes while the number of houses and apartment buildings remains constant. The short-run supply response arises from changes in the intensity with which existing buildings are used. The higher the rent, the greater is the incentive for families to rent out some of the rooms that they previously used themselves.

Long-Run Supply The long-run supply curve shows how the quantity of housing supplied responds to a change in price after enough time has elapsed for new apartment buildings and houses to be erected or for existing ones to be destroyed. In Fig. 6.1, the long-run supply curve is *perfectly elastic*. The marginal cost of building is the same regardless of the number of houses and apartments in existence. And so long as the rent exceeds the marginal cost of building, developers have an incentive to keep on building. So long-run supply is perfectly elastic at a rent equal to marginal cost.

Equilibrium The equilibrium rent and quantity are determined by demand and *short-run* supply. Before the earthquake, the equilibrium rent is \$16 a month and the quantity is 100,000 units of housing.

Figure 6.1(a) shows the situation immediately after the earthquake. Few people died in the earthquake, so demand remains at D. But the devastation decreases supply and shifts the short-run supply curve SS leftward to SS_A. If the rent remains at \$16 a month, only 44,000 units of housing are available. But with only 44,000 units of housing available, the maximum rent that someone is willing to pay for the last available apartment is \$24 a month. So rents rise. In Fig. 6.1(a), the rent rises to \$20 a month.

As the rent rises, the quantity of housing demanded decreases and the quantity supplied increases to 72,000 units. These changes occur because people economize on their use of space and make spare rooms, attics, and basements available to others. The higher rent allocates the scarce housing to the people who value it most highly and are willing to pay the most for it.

But the higher rent has other, long-run effects. Let's look at these long-run effects.

[1] Reported in Milton Friedman and George J. Stigler, "Roofs or Ceilings? The Current Housing Problem," in *Popular Essays on Current Problems*, vol. 1, no. 2 (New York: Foundation for Economic Education, 1946), pp. 3–159.

[2] *Ibid.*, p. 3.

FIGURE 6.1 The San Francisco Housing Market in 1906

myeconlab

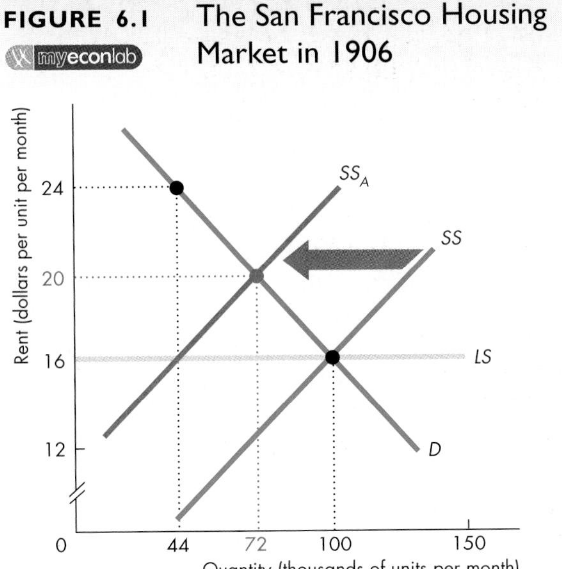

(a) After earthquake

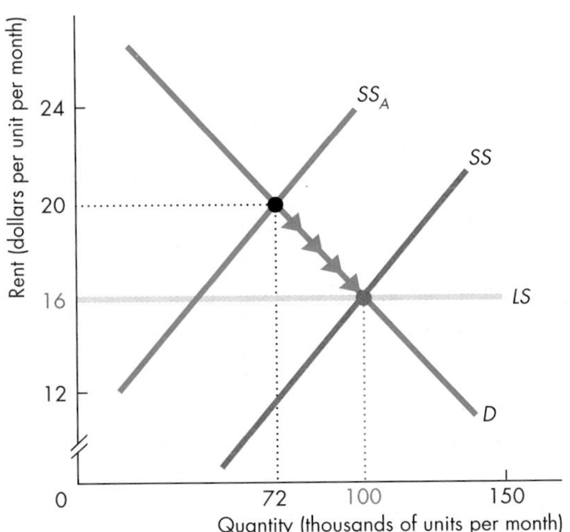

(b) Long-run adjustment

Part (a) shows that before the earthquake, 100,000 housing units were rented at $16 a month. After the earthquake, the short-run supply curve shifts from *SS* to SS_A. The rent rises to $20 a month, and the quantity of housing decreases to 72,000 units.

With rent at $20 a month, there is profit in building new apartments and houses. As the building proceeds, the short-run supply curve shifts rightward (part b). The rent gradually falls to $16 a month, and the quantity of housing increases to 100,000 units—as the arrowed line shows.

Long-Run Adjustments

With sufficient time for new apartments and houses to be constructed, supply increases. The long-run supply curve tells us that in the long run, housing is supplied at a rent of $16 a month. Because the rent of $20 a month exceeds the long-run supply price of $16 a month, there is a building boom. More apartments and houses are built, and the short-run supply curve shifts gradually rightward.

Figure 6.1(b) shows the long-run adjustment. As more housing is built, the short-run supply curve shifts gradually rightward and intersects the demand curve at lower rents and larger quantities. The market equilibrium follows the arrows down the demand curve. The building boom comes to an end when there is no further profit in building new apartments and houses. The process ends when the rent is back at $16 a month, and 100,000 units of housing are available.

We've just seen how a housing market responds to a decrease in supply. And we've seen that a key part of the adjustment process is a rise in the rent. Suppose the government passes a law to stop the rent from rising. What happens then?

A Regulated Housing Market

We're now going to study the effects of a price ceiling in the housing market. A **price ceiling** is a regulation that makes it illegal to charge a price higher than a specified level. When a price ceiling is applied to housing markets, it is called a **rent ceiling**. How does a rent ceiling affect the housing market?

The effect of a price (rent) ceiling depends on whether it is imposed at a level that is above or below the equilibrium price (rent). A price ceiling set above the equilibrium price has no effect. The reason is that the price ceiling does not constrain the market forces. The force of the law and the market forces are not in conflict. But a price ceiling below the equilibrium price has powerful effects on a market. The reason is that the price ceiling attempts to prevent the price from regulating the quantities demanded and supplied. The force of the law and the market forces are in conflict, and one (or both) of these forces must yield to some degree. Let's study the effects of a price ceiling that is set below the equilibrium price by returning to San Francisco. What would have happened in San Francisco if a rent ceiling of $16 a month—the rent before the earthquake—had been imposed?

FIGURE 6.2 A Rent Ceiling

myeconlab

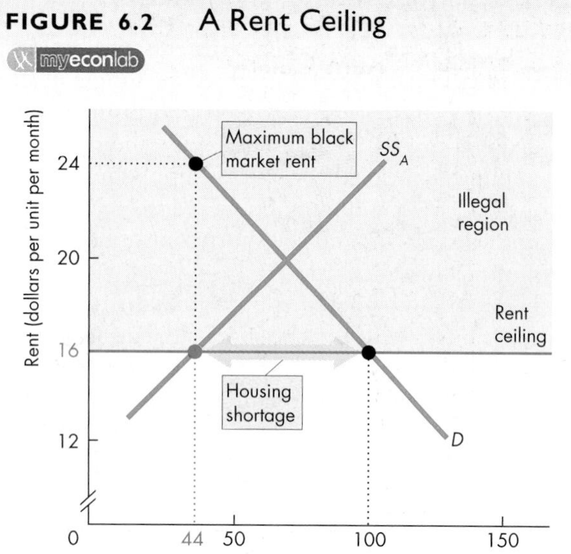

A rent above $16 a month is illegal (in the gray-shaded illegal region). At a rent of $16 a month, the quantity of housing supplied after the earthquake is 44,000 units. Someone is willing to pay $24 a month for the 44,000th unit. Frustrated renters spend time searching for housing and they make deals with landlords in a black market.

Figure 6.2 enables us to answer this question. A rent that exceeds $16 a month is in the gray-shaded illegal region in the figure. At a rent of $16 a month, the quantity of housing supplied is 44,000 units and the quantity demanded is 100,000 units. So there is a shortage of 56,000 units of housing.

But the story does not end here. Somehow, the 44,000 units of available housing must be allocated among people who demand 100,000 units. How is this allocation achieved? When a rent ceiling creates a housing shortage, two developments occur. They are

- Search activity
- Black markets

Search Activity

The time spent looking for someone with whom to do business is called **search activity**. We spend some time in search activity almost every time we buy something. You want the latest hot CD, and you know four stores that stock it. But which store has the best deal? You need to spend a few minutes on the telephone finding out. In some markets, we spend a lot of time searching. An example is the housing market in which we spend a lot of time checking the alternatives available before making a choice.

But when a price is regulated and there is a shortage, search activity increases. In the case of a rent-controlled housing market, frustrated would-be renters scan the newspapers, not only for housing ads but also for death notices! Any information about newly available housing is useful. And they race to be first on the scene when news of a possible supplier breaks.

The *opportunity cost* of a good is equal not only to its price but also to the value of the search time spent finding the good. So the opportunity cost of housing is equal to the rent (a regulated price) plus the time and other resources spent searching for the restricted quantity available. Search activity is costly. It uses time and other resources, such as telephones, cars, and gasoline that could have been used in other productive ways. A rent ceiling controls the rent portion of the cost of housing, but it does not control the opportunity cost, which might even be *higher* than the rent would be if the market were unregulated.

Black Markets

A **black market** is an illegal market in which the price exceeds the legally imposed price ceiling. Black markets occur in rent-controlled housing, and scalpers run black markets in tickets for big sporting events and rock concerts.

When rent ceilings are in force, frustrated renters and landlords constantly seek ways of increasing rents. One common way is for a new tenant to pay a high price for worthless fittings, such as charging $2,000 for threadbare drapes. Another is for the tenant to pay an exorbitant price for new locks and keys—called "key money."

The level of a black market rent depends on how tightly the rent ceiling is enforced. With loose enforcement, the black market rent is close to the unregulated rent. But with strict enforcement, the black market rent is equal to the maximum price that renters are willing to pay.

With strict enforcement of the rent ceiling in the San Francisco example shown in Fig. 6.2, the quantity of housing available remains at 44,000 units. A small number of people offer housing for rent at $24 a month—the highest rent that someone is willing to pay—and the government detects and punishes some of these black market traders.

Inefficiency of Rent Ceilings

In an unregulated market, the market determines the rent at which the quantity demanded equals the quantity supplied. In this situation, scarce resources are allocated efficiently. *Marginal social benefit* equals *marginal social cost* (see Chapter 5, p. 110).

Figure 6.3 shows the inefficiency of a rent ceiling. If the rent is fixed at $16 per month, 44,000 units are supplied. Marginal benefit is $24 a month. The blue triangle above the supply curve and below the rent ceiling line shows producer surplus. Because the quantity of housing is less than the competitive quantity, there is a deadweight loss, shown by the gray triangle. This loss is borne by the consumers who can't find housing and by producers who can't supply housing at the new lower price. Consumers who do find housing at the controlled rent gain. If no one incurs search costs, consumer surplus is shown by the sum of the green triangle and the red rectangle. But search costs might eat up part of the consumer surplus, possibly as much as the amount shown by the red rectangle.

FIGURE 6.3 The Inefficiency of a Rent Ceiling

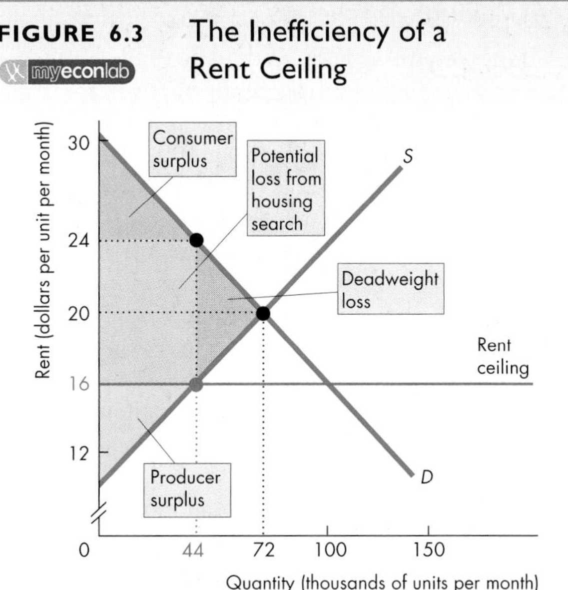

A rent ceiling of $16 a month decreases the quantity of housing supplied to 44,000 units. Producer surplus shrinks, and a deadweight loss arises. If people use no resources in search activity, consumer surplus is the green triangle plus the red rectangle. But if people use resources in search activity equal to the amount shown by the red rectangle, the consumer surplus shrinks to the green triangle.

Are Rent Ceilings Fair?

Do rent ceilings achieve a fairer allocation of scarce housing? Chapter 5 (pp. 114–117) explores the complex ideas about fairness. According to the *fair rules* view, anything that blocks voluntary exchange is unfair, so rent ceilings are unfair. But according to the *fair result* view, a fair outcome is one that benefits the less well off. So according to this view, the fairest outcome is the one that allocates scarce housing to the poorest. To see whether rent ceilings help to achieve a fairer outcome in this sense, we need to consider how the market allocates scarce housing resources in the face of a rent ceiling.

Blocking rent adjustments doesn't eliminate scarcity. Rather, because it decreases the quantity of housing available, it creates an even bigger challenge for the housing market. So somehow, the market must ration a smaller quantity of housing and allocate that housing among the people who demand it.

When the rent is not permitted to allocate scarce housing, what other mechanisms are available? Some possibilities are

- A lottery
- A queue
- Discrimination

Are these mechanisms fair?

A lottery allocates housing to those who are lucky, not to those who are poor. A queue (a method used to allocate housing in England after World War II) allocates housing to those who have the greatest foresight and who get their names on a list first, not to the poorest. Discrimination allocates scarce housing based on the views and self-interest of the owner of the housing. In the case of public housing, it is the self-interest of the bureaucracy that administers the allocation that counts.

In principle, self-interested owners and bureaucrats could allocate housing to satisfy some criterion of fairness. But they are not likely to do so. Discrimination based on friendship, family ties, and criteria such as race, ethnicity, or sex is more likely to enter the equation. We might make such discrimination illegal, but we would not be able to prevent it from occurring.

It is hard, then, to make a case for rent ceilings on the basis of fairness. When rent adjustments are blocked, other methods of allocating scarce housing resources operate that do not produce a fair outcome.

Rent Ceilings in Practice

London, New York, Paris, and San Francisco, four of the world's great cities, have rent ceilings in some part of their housing markets. Boston had rent ceilings for many years but abolished them in 1997. Many other U.S. cities do not have, and never have had, rent ceilings. Among them are Atlanta, Baltimore, Chicago, Dallas, Philadelphia, Phoenix, and Seattle.

We can test for the effects of rent ceilings by comparing the housing markets in cities with and without ceilings. We learn two main lessons from such a comparison.

First, rent ceilings definitely create a housing shortage. Second, they do lower the rents for some but raise them for others. A survey* conducted in 1997 showed that the rents of housing units *actually available for rent* were 2.5 times the average of all rents in New York but equal to the average rent in Philadelphia. The winners from rent ceilings are the families that have lived in a city for a long time. In New York, these families include some rich and famous ones. And it is the voting power of the winners that keeps the rent ceilings in place. The losers are the mobile newcomers.

The bottom line is that in principle and in practice, rent ceilings are inefficient and unfair. They prevent the housing market from operating in the social interest.

REVIEW QUIZ

1. How does a decrease in the supply of housing change the equilibrium rent in the short run?
2. How does the market allocate the scarce housing when the supply of housing decreases?
3. What are the long-run effects of higher rents following a decrease in the supply of housing?
4. What is a rent ceiling and what are its effects if it is set above the equilibrium rent?
5. What are the effects of a rent ceiling that is set below the equilibrium rent?
6. How are scarce housing resources allocated when a rent ceiling is in place?

myeconlab **Study Plan 6.1**

You now know how a price ceiling (rent ceiling) works. Next, we'll learn about the effects of a price floor by studying minimum wages in the labor market.

* William Tucker, "How Rent Control Drives Out Affordable Housing."

The Labor Market and the Minimum Wage

For each one of us, the labor market is the market that influences the jobs we get and the wages we earn. Firms decide how much labor to demand, and the lower the wage rate, the greater is the quantity of labor demanded. Households decide how much labor to supply, and the higher the wage rate, the greater is the quantity of labor supplied. The wage rate adjusts to make the quantity of labor demanded equal to the quantity supplied.

Equilibrium wage rates give some people high incomes but leave many more people with low incomes. And the labor market is constantly hit by shocks that often hit the lowest paid the hardest. The most pervasive of these shocks is the arrival of new labor-saving technologies that decrease the demand for low-skilled workers and lower their wage rates. During the 1980s and 1990s, for example, the demand for telephone operators and television repair technicians decreased. Throughout the past 200 years, the demand for low-skilled farm laborers has steadily decreased.

How does the labor market cope with this continuous decrease in the demand for low-skilled labor? Doesn't it mean that the wage rate of low-skilled workers is constantly falling?

To answer these questions, we must study the market for low-skilled labor in both the short run and the long run.

In the short run, there are a given number of people who have a given skill, training, and experience. The short-run supply of labor describes how the number of hours of labor supplied by this given number of people changes as the wage rate changes. To get them to work more hours, they must be offered a higher wage rate.

In the long run, people can acquire new skills and find new types of jobs. The number of people in the low-skilled labor market depends on the wage rate in this market compared with other opportunities. If the wage rate of low-skilled labor is high enough, people will enter this market. If the wage rate is too low, people will leave it. Some will seek training to enter higher-skilled labor markets, and others will stop working.

The long-run supply of labor is the relationship between the quantity of labor supplied and the wage rate after enough time has passed for people to enter or leave the low-skilled labor market. If people can freely enter and leave the low-skilled labor market, the long-run supply of labor is *perfectly elastic.*

Figure 6.4 shows the market for low-skilled labor. Other things remaining the same, the lower the wage rate, the greater is the quantity of labor demanded by firms. The demand curve for labor, D in part (a), shows this relationship between the wage rate and the quantity of labor demanded. Other things remaining the same, the higher the wage rate, the greater is the quantity of labor supplied by households. But the longer the period of adjustment, the greater is the *elasticity of supply* of labor. The short-run supply curve is SS, and the long-run supply curve is LS. In the figure, long-run supply is assumed to be perfectly elastic (the LS curve is horizontal). This market is in equilibrium at a wage rate of $5 an hour and 22 million hours of labor employed.

What happens if a labor-saving invention decreases the demand for low-skilled labor? Figure 6.4(a) shows the short-run effects of such a change. Before the new technology is introduced, the demand curve is the curve labeled D. After the introduction of the new technology, the demand curve shifts leftward to D_A. The wage rate falls to $4 an hour, and the quantity of labor employed decreases to 21 million hours. But this short-run effect on the wage rate and employment is not the end of the story.

People who are now earning only $4 an hour look around for other opportunities. They see many other jobs (in markets for other types of skills) that pay more than $4 an hour. One by one, workers decide to go back to school or take jobs that pay less but offer on-the-job training. As a result, the short-run supply curve begins to shift leftward.

Figure 6.4(b) shows the long-run adjustment. As the short-run supply curve shifts leftward, it intersects the demand curve D_A at higher wage rates and fewer hours employed. The process ends when workers have no incentive to leave the low-skilled labor market and the short-run supply curve has shifted to SS_A. At this point, the wage rate has returned to $5 an hour and employment has decreased to 20 million hours a year.

Concerned about the incomes of low-paid workers, Congress has enacted a Federal minimum wage law. And many cities and states have introduced living wage regulations that require employers to pay higher wages than those determined by market forces.

Let's look at the effects of minimum wage and living wage regulations.

FIGURE 6.4 A Market for Low-Skilled Labor

myeconlab

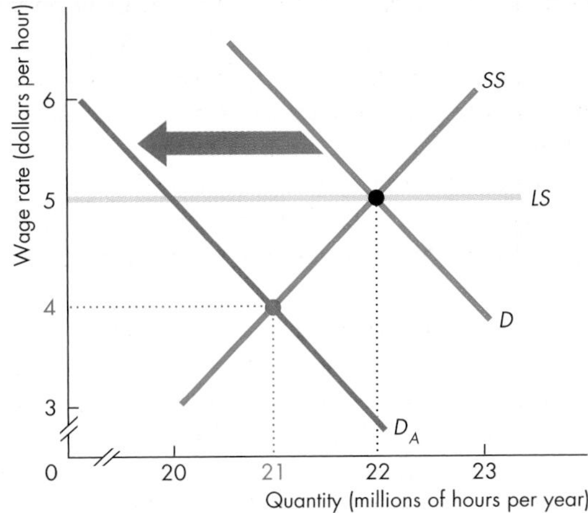

(a) After invention

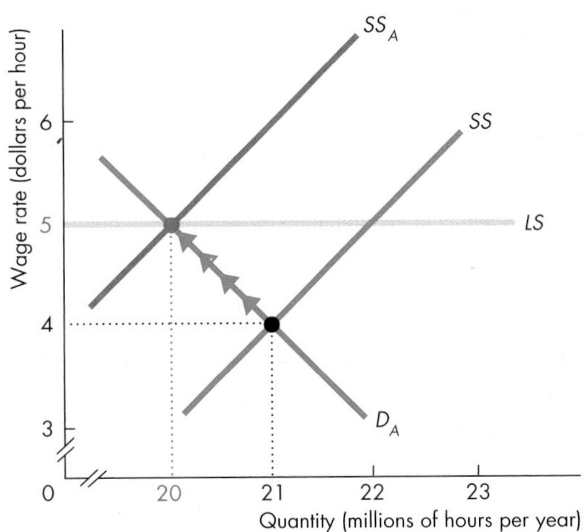

(b) Long-run adjustment

Part (a) shows the immediate effect of a labor-saving invention on the market for low-skilled labor. Initially, the wage rate is $5 an hour and 22 million hours are employed. A labor-saving invention shifts the demand curve from D to D_A. The wage rate falls to $4 an hour, and employment decreases to 21 million hours a year. With the lower wage rate, some workers leave this market, and the short-run supply curve starts to shift gradually leftward to SS_A (part b). The wage rate gradually increases, and the employment level decreases. In the long run, the wage rate returns to $5 an hour and employment decreases to 20 million hours a year.

A Minimum Wage

A **price floor** is a regulation that makes it illegal to trade at a price lower than a specified level. When a price floor is applied to labor markets, it is called a **minimum wage.** If a minimum wage is set *below* the equilibrium wage, the minimum wage has no effect. The minimum wage and market forces are not in conflict. If a minimum wage is set *above* the equilibrium wage, the minimum wage is in conflict with market forces and does have some effects on the labor market. Let's study these effects by returning to the market for low-skilled labor.

Suppose that with an equilibrium wage of $4 an hour (Fig. 6.4a), the government sets a minimum wage at $5 an hour. Figure 6.5 shows the minimum wage as the horizontal red line labeled "Minimum wage." A wage below this level is illegal, in the gray-shaded illegal region. At the minimum wage rate, 20 million hours of labor are demanded (point *A*) and 22 million hours of labor are supplied (point *B*), so 2 million hours of available labor are unemployed.

With only 20 million hours demanded, some workers are willing to supply that 20 millionth hour for $3. Frustrated unemployed workers spend time and other resources searching for hard-to-find jobs.

Inefficiency of a Minimum Wage

In an unregulated labor market, everyone who is willing to work for the going wage rate gets a job. And the market allocates the economy's scarce labor resources to the jobs in which they are valued most highly. The minimum wage frustrates the market mechanism and results in unemployment—wasted labor resources—and an inefficient amount of job search.

Figure 6.6 illustrates the inefficiency of the minimum wage. There is a deadweight loss because at the quantity of labor employed—20 million hours—the value to the firm of the marginal worker exceeds that wage rate for which that person is willing to work.

At this level of employment, unemployed people have a big incentive to spend time and effort looking for work. The red rectangle shows the potential loss from this extra job search. This loss arises because someone who finds a job earns $5 an hour (read off from the demand curve) but would have been willing to work for $3 an hour (read off from the supply curve). So everyone who is unemployed has an incentive to search hard and use resources that are worth the $2-an-hour surplus to find a job.

FIGURE 6.5 Minimum Wage and Unemployment

myeconlab

A wage below $5 an hour is illegal (in the gray-shaded illegal region). At the minimum wage of $5 an hour, 20 million hours are hired but 22 million hours are available. Unemployment—*AB*—of 2 million hours a year is created.

FIGURE 6.6 The Inefficiency of a Minimum Wage

myeconlab

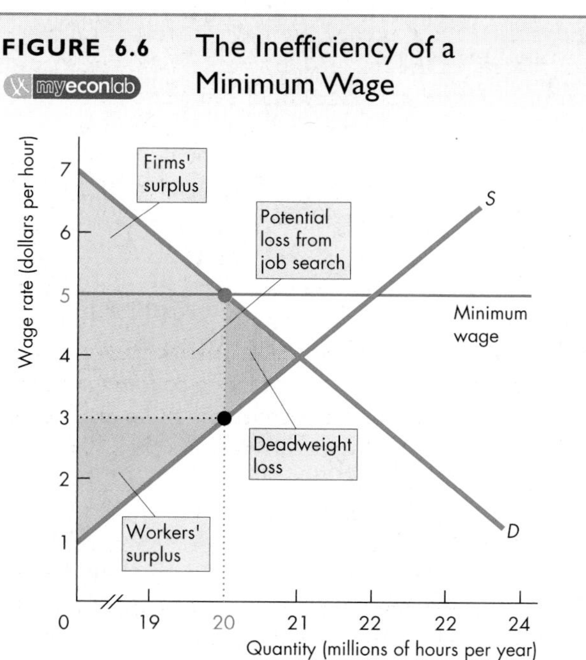

A minimum wage shrinks the firms' surplus (blue area) and workers' surplus (green area) and creates a deadweight loss (gray area). If people use extra resources in job search, the red area shows the potential loss from job search.

The Federal Minimum Wage and Its Effects

A minimum wage in the United States is set by the federal government's Fair Labor Standards Act. In 2007, the federal minimum wage was $5.15 an hour. Some state governments have passed state minimum wage laws that exceed the federal minimum wage. The minimum wage has increased from time to time and has fluctuated between 35 percent and more than 50 percent of the average wage of production workers.

You saw in Fig. 6.5 that the minimum wage brings unemployment. But how much unemployment does it bring? Economists do not agree on the answer to this question. Until recently, most economists believed that the minimum wage was a big contributor to high unemployment among low-skilled young workers. But this view has recently been challenged and the challenge rebutted.

David Card of the University of California at Berkeley (see Talking with . . . on pp. 458–460) and Alan Krueger of Princeton University say that increases in the minimum wage have not decreased employment and created unemployment. From their study of minimum wages in California, New Jersey, and Texas, Card and Krueger say that the employment rate of low-income workers increased following an increase in the minimum wage. They suggest three reasons why higher wages might increase employment. First, workers become more conscientious and productive. Second, workers are less likely to quit, so labor turnover, which is costly, is reduced. Third, managers make a firm's operations more efficient.

Most economists are skeptical about Card and Krueger's suggestions. They ask two questions. First, if higher wages make workers more productive and reduce labor turnover, why don't firms freely pay wage rates above the equilibrium wage to encourage more productive work habits? Second, are there other explanations for the employment responses that Card and Krueger have found?

Card and Krueger got the timing wrong according to Daniel Hamermesh of the University of Texas at Austin. He says that firms cut employment *before* the minimum wage is increased in anticipation of the increase. If he is correct, looking for the effects of an increase *after* it has occurred misses its main effects. Finis Welch of Texas A&M University and Kevin Murphy of the University of Chicago say the employment effects that Card and Krueger found are caused by regional differences in economic growth, not by changes in the minimum wage.

One effect of the minimum wage, according to Fig. 6.5, is an increase in the quantity of labor supplied. If this effect occurs, it might show up as an increase in the number of people who quit school before completing high school to look for work. Some economists say that this response does occur.

A Living Wage

You've seen that the federal minimum wage probably causes unemployment and creates a deadweight loss. Despite these effects of a price floor in the labor market, a popular movement is seeking to create a more pervasive and much higher floor at a living wage. A **living wage** has been defined as an hourly wage rate that enables a person who works a 40-hour work week to rent adequate housing for not more than 30 percent of the amount earned. For example, if the going market rent for a one-bedroom apartment is $180 a week, the living wage is $15 an hour. (Check: 40 hours at $15 an hour is $600, and $180 is 30 percent of $600.)

Living wage laws already operate in St. Louis, St. Paul, Minneapolis, Boston, Oakland, Denver, Chicago, New Orleans, and New York City, and campaigns to expand the living wage are being mounted in many cities and states. The effects of the living wage can be expected to be similar to those of the minimum wage.

REVIEW QUIZ

1. How does a decrease in the demand for low-skilled labor change the wage rate of low-skilled labor in the short run?
2. What are the long-run effects of a fall in the wage rate of low-skilled labor?
3. What is a minimum wage and what are its effects if it is set below the equilibrium wage?
4. What are the effects of a minimum wage or a living wage that is set above the equilibrium wage?

myeconlab **Study Plan 6.2**

Next we're going to study a more widespread government action in markets: taxes. We'll see how taxes change prices and quantities. You will discover the surprising fact that while the government can impose a tax, it can't decide who will pay the tax! And you will see that a tax creates a deadweight loss.

Taxes

Everything you earn and almost everything you buy is taxed. Income taxes and Social Security taxes are deducted from your earnings and sales taxes are added to the bill when you buy something. Employers also pay a Social Security tax for their workers, and producers of tobacco products, alcoholic drinks, and gasoline pay a tax every time they sell something.

Who *really* pays these taxes? Because the income tax and Social Security tax are deducted from your pay, and the sales tax is added to the prices that you pay, isn't it obvious that *you* pay these taxes? And isn't it equally obvious that your employer pays the employer's contribution to the Social Security tax and that tobacco producers pay the tax on cigarettes?

You're going to discover that it isn't obvious who *really* pays a tax and that lawmakers don't make that decision. We begin with a definition of tax incidence.

Tax Incidence

Tax incidence is the division of the burden of a tax between the buyer and the seller. When the government imposes a tax on the sale of a good*, the price paid by the buyer might rise by the full amount of the tax, by a lesser amount, or not at all. If the price paid by the buyer rises by the full amount of the tax, then the burden of the tax falls entirely on the buyer—the buyer pays the tax. If the price paid by the buyer rises by a lesser amount than the tax, then the burden of the tax falls partly on the buyer and partly on the seller. And if the price paid by the buyer doesn't change at all, then the burden of the tax falls entirely on the seller.

Tax incidence does not depend on the tax law. The law might impose a tax on sellers or on buyers, but the outcome is the same in either case. To see why, let's look at the tax on cigarettes in New York City.

A Tax on Sellers

On July 1, 2002, Mayor Bloomberg of New York City raised the tax on the sale of cigarettes from almost nothing to $1.50 a pack. To work out the effects of this tax on the sellers of cigarettes, we begin by examining the effects on demand and supply in the market for cigarettes.

In Fig. 6.7, the demand curve is *D*, and the supply curve is *S*. With no tax, the equilibrium price is $3 per pack and 350 million packs a year are bought and sold.

A tax on sellers is like an increase in cost, so it decreases supply. To determine the position of the new supply curve, we add the tax to the minimum price that sellers are willing to accept for each quantity sold. You can see that without the tax, sellers are willing to offer 350 million packs a year for $3 a pack. So with a $1.50 tax, they will offer 350 million packs a year only if the price is $4.50 a pack. The supply curve shifts to the red curve labeled *S* + *tax on sellers*.

Equilibrium occurs where the new supply curve intersects the demand curve at 325 million packs a year. The price paid by buyers rises by $1 to $4 a pack. And the price received by sellers falls by 50¢ to $2.50 a pack. So buyers pay $1 of the tax and sellers pay the other 50¢.

FIGURE 6.7 A Tax on Sellers

myeconlab

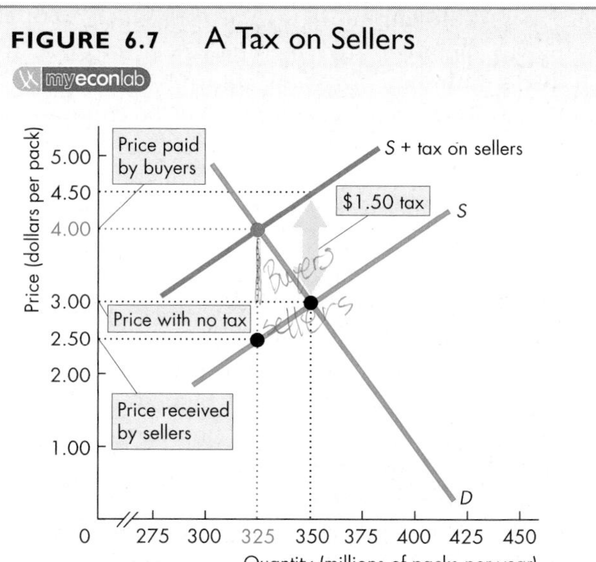

With no tax, 350 million packs a year are bought and sold at $3 a pack. A tax on sellers of $1.50 a pack shifts the supply curve leftward to *S* + *tax on sellers*. The equilibrium quantity decreases to 325 million packs a year, the price paid by buyers rises to $4 a pack, and the price received by sellers falls to $2.50 a pack. The tax raises the price paid by buyers by less than the tax and lowers the price received by sellers, so buyers and sellers share the burden of the tax.

* These propositions also apply to services and factors of production (land, labor, capital).

A Tax on Buyers

Suppose that instead of taxing sellers, New York City taxes cigarette buyers $1.50 a pack.

A tax on buyers lowers the amount they are willing to pay the seller, so it decreases demand and shifts the demand curve leftward. To determine the position of this new demand curve, we subtract the tax from the maximum price that buyers are willing to pay for each quantity bought. You can see, in Fig. 6.8, that without the tax, buyers are willing to buy 350 million packs a year for $3 a pack. So with a $1.50 tax, they are willing to buy 350 million packs a year only if the price including the tax is $3 a pack, which means that they're willing to pay the seller only $1.50 a pack. The demand curve shifts to become the red curve labeled *D – tax on buyers*.

Equilibrium occurs where the new demand curve intersects the supply curve at a quantity of 325 million packs a year. The price received by sellers is $2.50 a pack, and the price paid by buyers is $4.

FIGURE 6.8 A Tax on Buyers

myeconlab

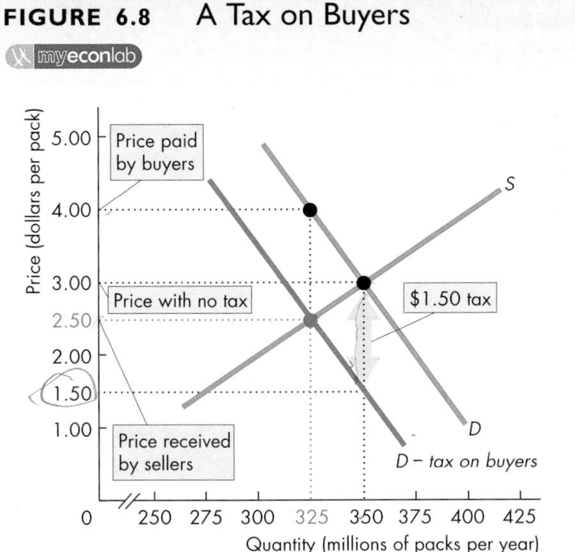

With no tax, 350 million packs a year are bought and sold at $3 a pack. A tax on buyers of $1.50 a pack shifts the demand curve leftward to *D – tax on buyers*. The equilibrium quantity decreases to 325 million packs a year, the price paid by buyers rises to $4 a pack, and the price received by sellers falls to $2.50 a pack. The tax raises the price paid by buyers by less than the tax and lowers the price received by sellers, so buyers and sellers share the burden of the tax.

Equivalence of Tax on Buyers and Sellers

You can see that the tax on buyers in Fig. 6.8 has the same effects as the tax on sellers in Fig. 6.7. In both cases, the equilibrium quantity decreases to 325 million packs a year, the price paid by buyers rises to $4 a pack, and the price received by sellers falls to $2.50 a pack. Buyers pay $1 of the $1.50 tax, and sellers pay the other 50¢ of the tax.

Can We Share the Burden Equally? Suppose that Mayor Bloomberg wants the burden of the cigarette tax to fall equally on buyers and sellers and declares that a 75¢ tax be imposed on each. Is the burden of the tax then shared equally?

You can see that it is not. The tax is still $1.50 a pack. And you've seen that the tax has the same effect regardless of whether it is imposed on sellers or buyers. So imposing half the tax on one and half on the other is like an average of the two cases you've examined. (Draw the demand-supply graph and work out what happens in this case. The demand curve shifts downward by 75¢ and the supply curve shifts upward by 75¢. The new equilibrium quantity is still 325 million packs a year. Buyers pay $4 a pack, of which 75¢ is tax. Sellers receive from buyers $3.25, but must pay a 75¢ tax, so they net $2.50 a pack.)

The key point is that when a transaction is taxed, there are two prices: the price paid by buyers, which includes the tax; and the price received by sellers, which excludes the tax. Buyers respond only to the price that includes the tax, because that is the price they pay. Sellers respond only to the price that excludes the tax, because that is the price they receive.

A tax is like a wedge between the buying price and the selling price. It is the size of the wedge, not the side of the market on which the tax is imposed by the government, that determines the effects of the tax.

The Social Security Tax The Social Security tax is an example of a tax that Congress imposes equally on both buyers and sellers. But the principles you've just learned apply to this tax too. The market for labor, not Congress, decides how the burden of the Social Security tax is divided by firms and workers.

In the New York City cigarette tax examples, the buyers bear twice the burden of the tax borne by sellers. In special cases, either buyers or sellers bear the entire burden. The division of the burden of a tax between buyers and sellers depends on the elasticities of demand and supply, as you will now see.

Tax Division and Elasticity of Demand

The division of the tax between buyers and sellers depends in part on the elasticity of demand. There are two extreme cases:

- Perfectly inelastic demand—buyers pay.
- Perfectly elastic demand—sellers pay.

Perfectly Inelastic Demand Figure 6.9(a) shows the market for insulin, a vital daily medication of diabetics. Demand is perfectly inelastic at 100,000 doses a day, regardless of the price, as shown by the vertical curve *D*. That is, a diabetic would sacrifice all other goods and services rather than not consume the insulin dose that provides good health. The supply curve of insulin is *S*. With no tax, the price is $2 a dose and the quantity is 100,000 doses a day.

If insulin is taxed at 20¢ a dose, we must add the tax to the minimum price at which drug companies are willing to sell insulin. The result is the new supply curve *S* + *tax*. The price rises to $2.20 a dose, but the quantity does not change. Buyers pay the entire sales tax of 20¢ a dose.

Perfectly Elastic Demand Figure 6.9(b) shows the market for pink marker pens. Demand is perfectly elastic at $1 a pen, as shown by the horizontal curve *D*. If pink pens are less expensive than the others, everyone uses pink. If pink pens are more expensive than the others, no one uses pink. The supply curve is *S*. With no tax, the price of a pink marker is $1, and the quantity is 4,000 pens a week.

If a tax of 10¢ a pen is imposed on pink marker pens but not on other colors, we add the tax to the minimum price at which sellers are willing to offer pink pens for sale, and the new supply curve is *S* + *tax*. The price remains at $1 a pen, and the quantity decreases to 1,000 a week. The 10¢ tax leaves the price paid by buyers unchanged but lowers the amount received by sellers by the full amount of the tax. Sellers pay the entire tax of 10¢ a pink pen.

We've seen that when demand is perfectly inelastic, buyers pay the entire tax and when demand is perfectly elastic, sellers pay the entire tax. In the usual case, demand is neither perfectly inelastic nor perfectly elastic and the tax is split between buyers and sellers. But the division depends on the elasticity of demand. The more inelastic the demand, the larger is the amount of the tax paid by buyers.

FIGURE 6.9 Tax and the Elasticity of Demand

myeconlab

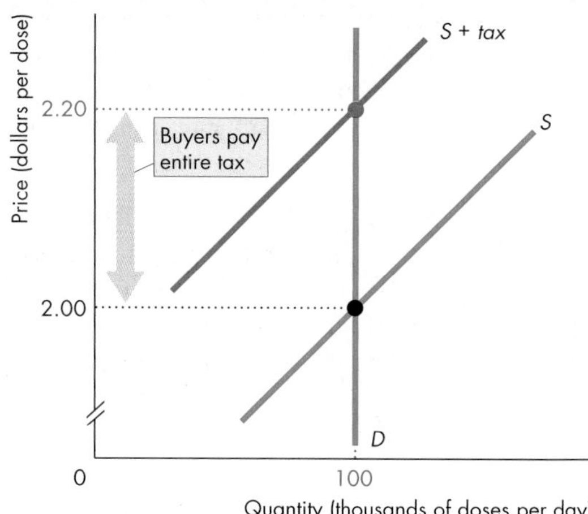

(a) Perfectly inelastic demand

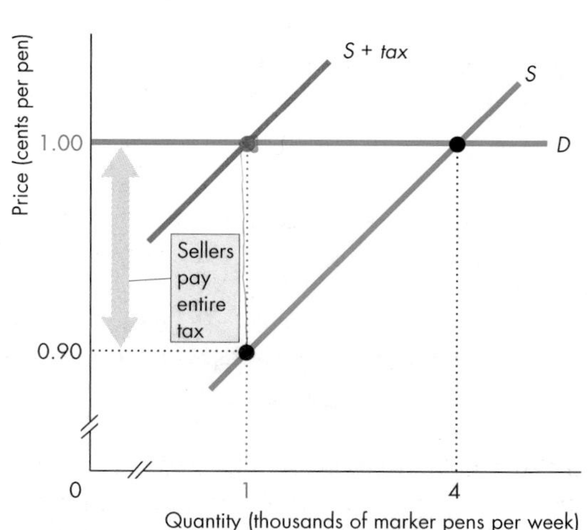

(b) Perfectly elastic demand

Part (a) shows the market for insulin, where demand is perfectly inelastic. With no tax, the price is $2 a dose and the quantity is 100,000 doses a day. A tax of 20¢ a dose shifts the supply curve to *S* + *tax*. The price rises to $2.20 a dose, but the quantity bought does not change. Buyers pay the entire tax.

Part (b) shows the market for pink pens, in which demand is perfectly elastic. With no tax, the price of a pen is $1 and the quantity is 4,000 pens a week. A tax of 10¢ a pink pen shifts the supply curve to *S* + *tax*. The price remains at $1 a pen, and the quantity of pink pens sold decreases to 1,000 a week. Sellers pay the entire tax.

Tax Division and Elasticity of Supply

The division of the tax between buyers and sellers also depends, in part, on the elasticity of supply. Again, there are two extreme cases:

- Perfectly inelastic supply—sellers pay.
- Perfectly elastic supply—buyers pay.

Perfectly Inelastic Supply Figure 6.10(a) shows the market for water from a mineral spring that flows at a constant rate that can't be controlled. Supply is perfectly inelastic at 100,000 bottles a week, as shown by the supply curve *S*. The demand curve for the water from this spring is *D*. With no tax, the price is 50¢ a bottle and the 100,000 bottles that flow from the spring are bought.

Suppose this spring water is taxed at 5¢ a bottle. The supply curve does not change because the spring owners still produce 100,000 bottles a week even though the price they receive falls. But buyers are willing to buy the 100,000 bottles only if the price is 50¢ a bottle. So the price remains at 50¢ a bottle. The tax reduces the price received by sellers to 45¢ a bottle, and sellers pay the entire tax.

Perfectly Elastic Supply Figure 6.10(b) shows the market for sand from which computer-chip makers extract silicon. Supply of this sand is perfectly elastic at a price of 10¢ a pound, as shown by the supply curve *S*. The demand curve for sand is *D*. With no tax, the price is 10¢ a pound and 5,000 pounds a week are bought.

If this sand is taxed at 1¢ a pound, we must add the tax to the minimum supply-price. Sellers are now willing to offer any quantity at 11¢ a pound along the curve *S* + *tax*. A new equilibrium is determined where the new supply curve intersects the demand curve: at a price of 11¢ a pound and a quantity of 3,000 pounds a week. The tax has increased the price buyers pay by the full amount of the tax—1¢ a pound—and has decreased the quantity sold. Buyers pay the entire tax.

We've seen that when supply is perfectly inelastic, sellers pay the entire tax and when supply is perfectly elastic, buyers pay the entire tax. In the usual case, supply is neither perfectly inelastic nor perfectly elastic and the tax is split between buyers and sellers. But how the tax is split depends on the elasticity of supply. The more elastic the supply, the larger is the amount of the tax paid by buyers.

FIGURE 6.10 Tax and the Elasticity of Supply

myeconlab

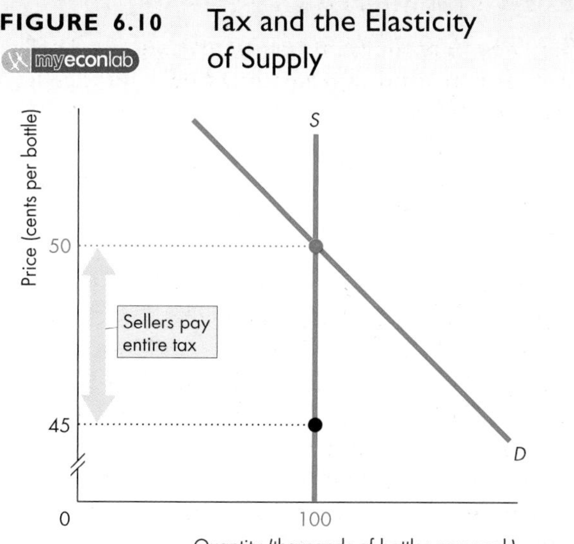

(a) Perfectly inelastic supply

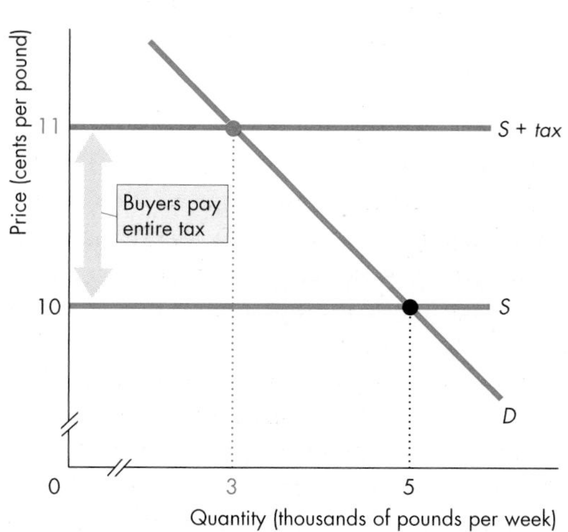

(b) Perfectly elastic supply

Part (a) shows the market for water from a mineral spring. Supply is perfectly inelastic. With no tax, the price is 50¢ a bottle. With a tax of 5¢ a bottle, the price remains at 50¢ a bottle. The number of bottles bought remains the same, but the price received by sellers decreases to 45¢ a bottle. Sellers pay the entire tax.

Part (b) shows the market for sand. Supply is perfectly elastic. With no tax, the price is 10¢ a pound. A tax of 1¢ a pound increases the minimum supply-price to 11¢ a pound. The supply curve shifts to S + *tax*. The price increases to 11¢ a pound. Buyers pay the entire tax.

Taxes in Practice

Supply and demand are rarely perfectly elastic or perfectly inelastic. But some items tend toward one of the extremes. For example, alcohol, tobacco, and gasoline have low elasticities of demand and high elasticities of supply. So the burden of these taxes falls more heavily on buyers than on sellers. Labor has a low elasticity of supply and a high elasticity of demand. So despite Congress's desire to split the Social Security tax equally between workers and employers, the burden of this tax falls mainly on workers.

The most heavily taxed items are those that have either a low elasticity of demand or a low elasticity of supply. For these items, the equilibrium quantity doesn't decrease much when a tax is imposed. So the government collects a large tax revenue and the deadweight loss from the tax is small.

It is unusual to tax an item heavily if neither its demand nor its supply is inelastic. With an elastic supply *and* demand, a tax brings a large decrease in the equilibrium quantity, and a small tax revenue.

FIGURE 6.11 Taxes and Efficiency

myeconlab

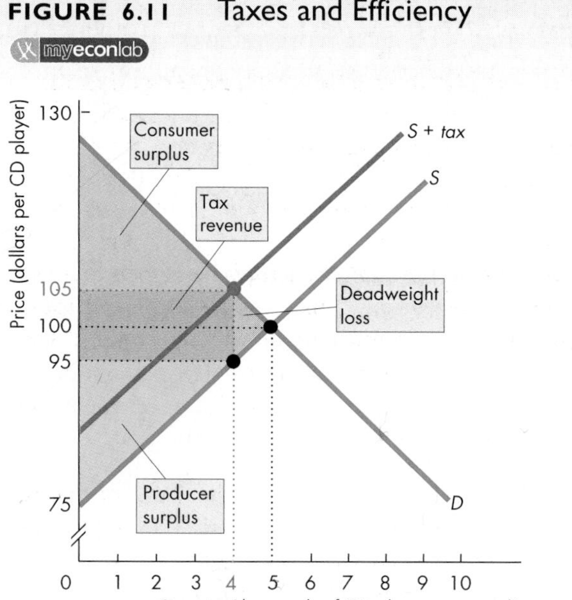

With no tax on CD players, 5,000 a week are bought and sold at $100 each. With a tax of $10 a CD player, the buyers' price rises to $105 a player, the sellers' price falls to $95 a player, and the quantity decreases to 4,000 CD players a week. Consumer surplus shrinks to the green area, and the producer surplus shrinks to the blue area. Part of the loss of total surplus (the sum of consumer surplus and producer surplus) goes to the government as tax revenue, the purple area, and a deadweight loss arises, the gray area.

Taxes and Efficiency

You've seen that a tax places a wedge between the price buyers pay and the price sellers receive. The price buyers pay is also the buyers' willingness to pay, which measures marginal benefit. And the price sellers receive is also the sellers' minimum supply-price, which equals marginal cost.

So because a tax places a wedge between the buyers' price and the sellers' price, it also puts a wedge between marginal benefit and marginal cost and creates inefficiency. With a higher buyers' price and a lower sellers' price, the tax decreases the quantity produced and consumed and a deadweight loss arises. Figure 6.11 shows the inefficiency of a tax on CD players. With a tax, both consumer surplus and producer surplus shrink. Part of each surplus goes to the government in tax revenue—the purple area. And part becomes a deadweight loss—the gray area.

In the extreme cases of perfectly inelastic demand and perfectly inelastic supply, a tax does not change the quantity bought and sold and there is no deadweight loss. The more inelastic is either demand or supply, the smaller is the decrease in quantity and the smaller is the deadweight loss. When demand or supply is perfectly inelastic, the quantity remains constant and no deadweight loss arises.

REVIEW QUIZ

1. How does the elasticity of demand influence the effect of a tax on the price paid by buyers, the price received by sellers, the quantity, the tax revenue, and the deadweight loss?
2. How does the elasticity of supply influence the effect of a tax on the price paid by buyers, the price received by sellers, the quantity, the tax revenue, and the deadweight loss?
3. Why does a tax create a deadweight loss?

myeconlab **Study Plan 6.3**

Your next task is to study intervention in the markets for farm products. These markets have special problems and provide examples of two additional ways of changing market outcomes: subsidies and quotas.

Subsidies and Quotas

An early or late frost, a hot dry summer, and a wet autumn present just a few of the challenges that fill the lives of farmers with uncertainty and sometimes with economic hardship. Fluctuations in the weather bring big fluctuations in farm output. How do changes in farm output affect farm prices and farm revenues? And how might farmers be helped by government intervention in the markets for farm products? Let's look at some agricultural markets and see how they're affected.

Harvest Fluctuations

Figure 6.12 shows the market for wheat. In both parts, the demand curve for wheat is *D*. Once farmers have harvested their crop, they have no control over the quantity supplied and supply is inelastic along a *momentary supply curve*. With a normal harvest, the quantity produced is 20 billion bushels and the momentary supply curve is MS_0. The price is $4 a bushel, and farm revenue (price multiplied by quantity) is $80 billion.

Poor Harvest In Fig. 6.12(a), a poor harvest decreases the quantity supplied to 15 billion bushels. The momentary supply curve shifts leftward to MS_1, the price rises to $6 a bushel, and farm revenue increases to $90 billion. A *decrease* in supply brings a rise in price and an *increase* in farm revenue.

Bumper Harvest In Fig. 6.12(b), a bumper harvest increases the quantity supplied to 25 billion bushels. The momentary supply curve shifts rightward to MS_2, the price falls to $2 a bushel, and farm revenue decreases to $50 billion. An *increase* in supply brings a fall in price and a *decrease* in farm revenue.

Elasticity of Demand Farm revenue and the quantity produced fluctuate in opposite directions because the demand for wheat is *inelastic*. The percentage change in the quantity demanded is less than the percentage change in price. In Fig. 6.12(a), the increase in revenue from the higher price ($30 billion—light blue area) exceeds the decrease in revenue from the smaller quantity ($20 billion—the red area). In Fig. 6.12(b), the decrease in revenue from the lower price ($40 billion—the red area) exceeds the increase in revenue from the larger quantity.

FIGURE 6.12 Harvests, Farm Prices, and Farm Revenue

myeconlab

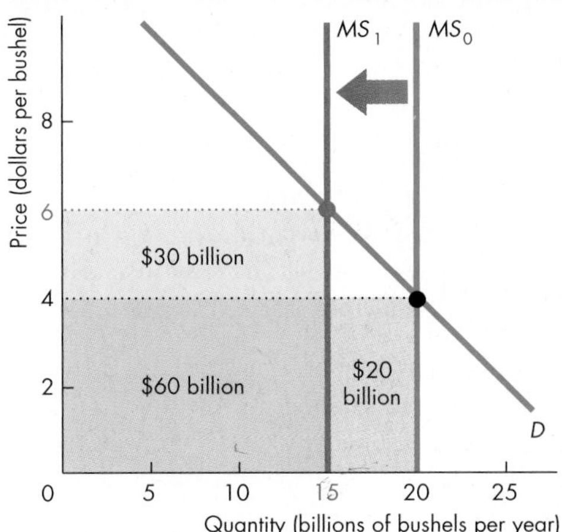

(a) Poor harvest: revenue increases

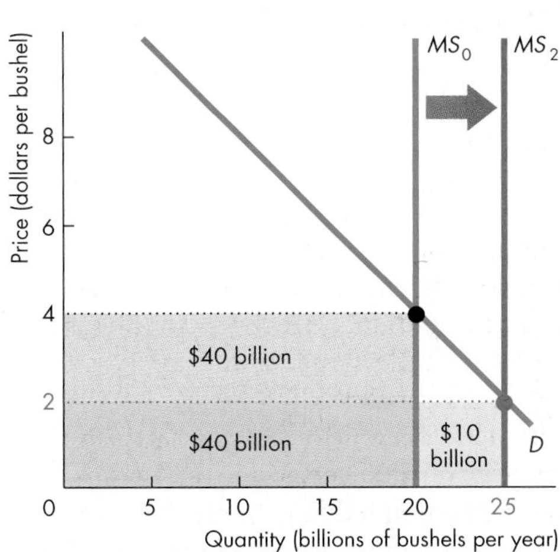

(b) Bumper harvest: revenue decreases

The demand curve is *D*. In normal times, the supply curve is MS_0 and 20 billion bushels are sold for $4 a bushel.

A poor harvest decreases the quantity supplied. The supply curve shifts to MS_1 (part a). The price rises to $6 a bushel, and farm revenue increases by $10 billion—the $30 billion increase from the higher price (light blue area) minus the $20 billion decrease from the smaller quantity (red area).

A bumper harvest increases the quantity supplied. The supply curve shifts to MS_2 (part b). The price falls to $2 a bushel, and farm revenue falls by $30 billion—the $10 billion increase from the larger quantity (light blue area) minus the the $40 billion decrease from the lower price (red area).

If demand is *elastic*, farm revenue and the quantity produced fluctuate in the same direction. Bumper harvests increase revenue, and poor harvests decrease it. But the demand for most agricultural products is inelastic, so the case we've studied is the relevant one.

Avoiding a Fallacy of Composition Although *total* farm revenue increases when there is a poor harvest, the revenue of those *individual* farmers whose entire crop is wiped out decreases. Those whose crop is unaffected gain. So a poor harvest is not good news for all farmers.

Because the markets for farm products often confront farmers with low incomes, government intervention occurs in these markets. Price floors that work a bit like the minimum wage that we've already studied might be used. You've already seen that this type of intervention creates a surplus and is inefficient. These same conclusions apply to markets for farm products.

Two other methods of intervention are often used in markets for farm products. They are

- Subsidies
- Production quotas

Subsidies

The producers of peanuts, sugarbeets, milk, wheat, and many other farm products receive subsidies. A **subsidy** is a payment made by the government to a producer. To discover the effects of a subsidy, we'll look at a market for peanuts. Figure 6.13 shows this market. The demand for peanuts is *D* and the supply of peanuts is *S*. With no subsidy, the price is $40 a ton and the quantity is 40 million tons a year.

Suppose that the government introduces a subsidy to peanut growers of $20 a ton. A subsidy is like a negative tax. You've seen that a tax is equivalent to an increase in cost. So a subsidy is equivalent to a decrease in cost. The subsidy brings an increase in supply.

To determine the position of the new supply curve, we subtract the subsidy from the farmers' minimum supply-price. Without a subsidy, farmers are willing to offer 40 million tons a year for $40 a ton. So with a subsidy of $20 a ton, they will offer 40 million tons a year if the price is as low as $20 a ton. The supply curve shifts to the red curve labeled *S – subsidy*.

FIGURE 6.13 A Subsidy Increases Production

myeconlab

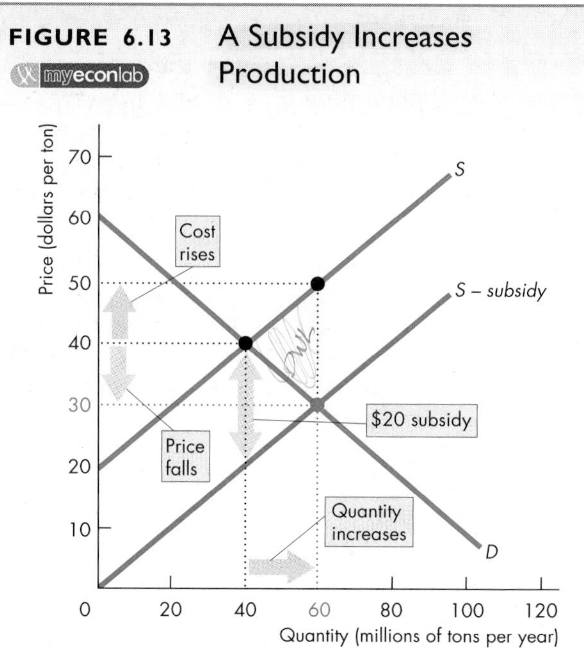

With no subsidy, 40 million tons a year are produced at $40 a ton. A subsidy of $20 a ton shifts the supply curve rightward to *S – subsidy*. The equilibrium quantity increases to 60 million tons a year, the price falls to $30 a ton, and the price plus subsidy received by farmers rises to $50 a ton. In the new equilibrium, marginal cost (on the supply curve) exceeds marginal benefit (on the demand curve) and a deadweight loss arises from overproduction.

Equilibrium occurs where the new supply curve intersects the demand curve at 60 million tons a year. The price falls by $10 to $30 a ton. But the price plus subsidy received by farmers rises by $10 to $50 a ton.

Because the supply curve is the marginal cost curve, and the demand curve is the marginal benefit curve, a subsidy raises marginal cost above marginal benefit and creates a deadweight loss from overproduction.

Subsidies spill over to the rest of the world. Because they lower the price, subsidized farmers offer some of their output for sale on the world market, which lowers the price in the rest of the world. Faced with lower prices, farmers in other countries decrease production and receive smaller revenues.

Farm subsidies are a major obstacle to achieving an efficient use of resources in the global markets for farm products and are a source of tension between the United States, Europe, and poorer developing nations.

Production Quotas

The markets for sugarbeets, tobacco leaf, and cotton, (among others) have, from time to time, been regulated with production quotas. A **production quota** is an upper limit to the quantity of a good that may be produced in a specified period. To discover the effects of quotas, we'll look at a market for sugarbeets in Fig. 6.14. With no quota, the price is $30 a ton and 60 million tons of sugarbeets per year are produced.

Suppose that the sugarbeets growers want to limit total production to get a higher price. They persuade the government to introduce a production quota of 40 million tons of sugarbeets a year.

The effect of a production quota depends on whether it is set below or above the equilibrium quantity. If the government introduced a quota above 60 million tons a year, the equilibrium quantity in Fig. 6.14, nothing would change because sugarbeets growers are already producing less than the quota. But a quota of 40 million is less than the equilibrium quantity. Figure 6.14 shows the effects of this quota.

To implement the quota, each grower is assigned a production limit and the total of the production limits equals 40 million tons. Production that in total exceeds 40 million tons is illegal, so we've shaded the illegal region above the quota. Growers are no longer permitted to produce the equilibrium quantity because it is in the illegal region. As in the case of price ceilings and price floors, market forces and political forces are in conflict.

When the government sets a production quota, it does not regulate the price. Market forces determine it. In the example in Fig. 6.14, with production limited to 40 million tons a year, the market price rises to $50.

The quota not only raises the price, but also *lowers* the marginal cost of producing the quota because the sugarbeets growers slide down their supply (and marginal cost) curves.

A production quota is inefficient because it results in underproduction. At the quota quantity, marginal benefit is equal to the market price and marginal cost is less than the market price, so marginal benefit exceeds marginal cost.

Because of these effects of a quota, such arrangements are often popular with producers and in some cases, producers, not governments, attempt to implement them. But it is hard for quotas to work when they are voluntary. The reason is that each producer has an incentive to cheat and produce a little bit more than the allotted quota. You can see why by comparing the market price and marginal cost. If one producer could get away with a tiny increase in production, her or his profit would increase. But if all producers cheat by producing above the quota, the market moves back toward the unregulated equilibrium and the gain for producers disappears.

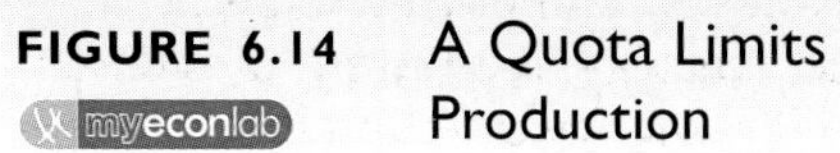

FIGURE 6.14 A Quota Limits Production

myeconlab

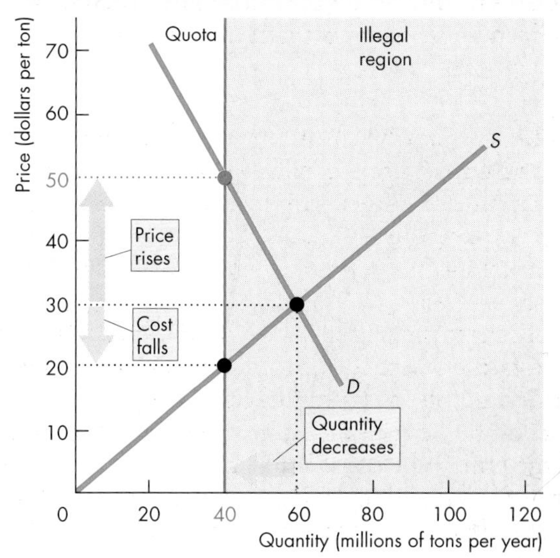

With no quota, 60 million tons a year are produced at $30 a ton. A quota of 40 million tons a year restricts total production to that amount. The equilibrium quantity decreases to 40 million tons a year, the price rises to $50 a ton, and the farmers' marginal cost falls to $20 a ton. In the new equilibrium, marginal cost (on the supply curve) is less than marginal benefit (on the demand curve) and a deadweight loss arises from underproduction.

REVIEW QUIZ

1. How do poor harvests and bumper harvests influence farm prices and farm revenues?
2. Explain how a subsidy influences farm prices and output. How does a subsidy affect farm revenues?
3. Explain how a production quota influences farm prices and output. How does a production quota affect farm revenues?

myeconlab **Study Plan 6.4**

Governments intervene in some markets by making it illegal to trade in a good. Let's now see how these markets work.

Markets for Illegal Goods

The markets for many goods and services are regulated, and buying and selling some goods is illegal. The best-known examples of such goods are drugs, such as marijuana, cocaine, ecstasy, and heroin.

Despite the fact that these drugs are illegal, trade in them is a multibillion-dollar business. This trade can be understood by using the same economic model and principles that explain trade in legal goods. To study the market for illegal goods, we're first going to examine the prices and quantities that would prevail if these goods were not illegal. Next, we'll see how prohibition works. Then we'll see how a tax might be used to limit the consumption of these goods.

A Free Market for a Drug

Figure 6.15 shows the market for a drug. The demand curve, *D*, shows that, other things remaining the same, the lower the price of the drug, the larger is the quantity of the drug demanded. The supply curve, *S*, shows that, other things remaining the same, the lower the price of the drug, the smaller is the quantity supplied. If the drug were not illegal, the quantity bought and sold would be Q_C and the price would be P_C.

FIGURE 6.15 A Market for an Illegal Good

myeconlab

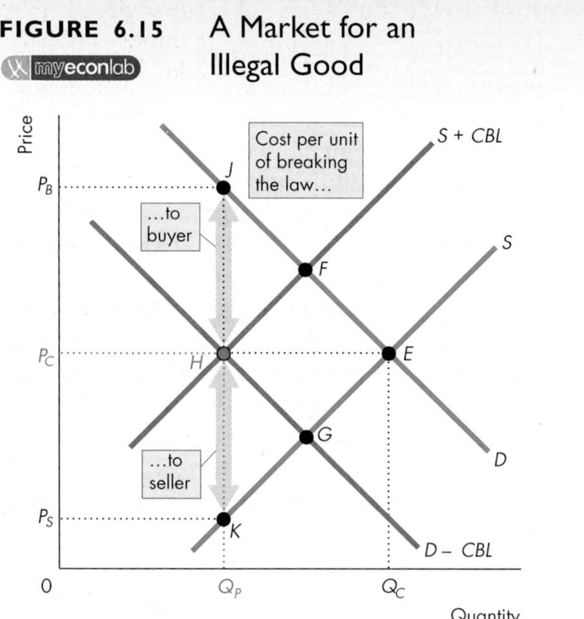

The demand curve for drugs is *D*, and the supply curve is *S*. If drugs are not illegal, the quantity bought and sold is Q_C at a price of P_C—point *E*. If selling drugs is illegal, the cost of breaking the law by selling drugs (*CBL*) is added to the minimum supply-price and supply decreases to *S* + *CBL*. The market moves to point *F*. If buying drugs is illegal, the cost of breaking the law is subtracted from the maximum price that buyers are willing to pay, and demand decreases to *D* – *CBL*. The market moves to point *G*. With both buying and selling illegal, the supply curve and the demand curve shift and the market moves to point *H*. The market price remains at P_C, but the market price plus the penalty for buying rises—point *J*—and the market price minus the penalty for selling falls—point *K*.

A Market for an Illegal Drug

When a good is illegal, the cost of trading in the good increases. By how much the cost increases and who incurs the cost depend on the penalties for violating the law and the effectiveness with which the law is enforced. The larger the penalties and the more effective the policing, the higher are the costs. Penalties might be imposed on sellers, buyers, or both.

Penalties on Sellers Drug dealers in the United States face large penalties if their activities are detected. For example, a marijuana dealer could pay a $200,000 fine and serve a 15-year prison term. A heroin dealer could pay a $500,000 fine and serve a 20-year prison term. These penalties are part of the cost of supplying illegal drugs, and they bring a decrease in supply—a leftward shift in the supply curve. To determine the new supply curve, we add the cost of breaking the law to the minimum price that drug dealers are willing to accept. In Fig. 6.15, the cost of breaking the law by selling drugs (*CBL*) is added to the minimum price that dealers will accept and the supply curve shifts leftward to *S* + *CBL*. If penalties were imposed only on sellers, the market equilibrium would move from point *E* to point *F*.

Penalties on Buyers In the United States, it is illegal to *possess* drugs such as marijuana, cocaine, ecstasy, and heroin. For example, possession of marijuana can bring a prison term of 1 year, and possession of heroin can bring a prison term of 2 years. Penalties fall on buyers, and the cost of breaking the law must be subtracted from the value of the good to determine the maximum price buyers are willing to pay for the drugs. Demand decreases, and the demand curve shifts leftward. In Fig. 6.15, the demand curve shifts to $D - CBL$. If penalties were imposed only on buyers, the market equilibrium would move from point E to point G.

Penalties on Both Sellers and Buyers If penalties are imposed on both sellers *and* buyers, both supply and demand decrease and both the supply curve and the demand curve shift. In Fig. 6.15 the costs of breaking the law are the same for both buyers and sellers, so both curves shift leftward by the same amount. The market equilibrium moves to point H. The market price remains at the competitive market price P_C, but the quantity bought decreases to Q_P. The buyer pays P_C plus the cost of breaking the law, which equals P_B. And the seller receives P_C minus the cost of breaking the law, which equals P_S.

The larger the penalties and the greater the degree of law enforcement, the larger is the decrease in demand and/or supply. If the penalties are heavier on sellers, the supply curve shifts farther than the demand curve and the market price rises above P_C. If the penalties are heavier on buyers, the demand curve shifts farther than the supply curve and the market price falls below P_C. In the United States, the penalties on sellers are larger than those on buyers, so the quantity of drugs traded decreases and the market price increases compared with a free market.

With high enough penalties and effective law enforcement, it is possible to decrease demand and/or supply to the point at which the quantity bought is zero. But in reality, such an outcome is unusual. It does not happen in the United States in the case of illegal drugs. The key reason is the high cost of law enforcement and insufficient resources for the police to achieve effective enforcement. Because of this situation, some people suggest that drugs (and other illegal goods) should be legalized and sold openly but should also be taxed at a high rate in the same way that legal drugs such as alcohol are taxed. How would such an arrangement work?

Legalizing and Taxing Drugs

From your study of the effects of taxes, it is easy to see that the quantity of a drug bought could be decreased if the drug was legalized and taxed. A sufficiently high tax could be imposed to decrease supply, raise the price, and achieve the same decrease in the quantity bought as with a prohibition on drugs. The government would collect a large tax revenue.

Illegal Trading to Evade the Tax It is likely that an extremely high tax rate would be needed to cut the quantity of drugs bought to the level prevailing with a prohibition. It is also likely that many drug dealers and consumers would try to cover up their activities to evade the tax. If they did act in this way, they would face the cost of breaking the law—the tax law. If the penalty for tax law violation is as severe and as effectively policed as drug-dealing laws, the analysis we've already conducted applies also to this case. The quantity of drugs bought would depend on the penalties for law breaking and on the way in which the penalties are assigned to buyers and sellers.

Taxes Versus Prohibition: Some Pros and Cons Which is more effective: prohibition or taxes? In favor of taxes and against prohibition is the fact that the tax revenue can be used to make law enforcement more effective. It can also be used to run a more effective education campaign against illegal drug use. In favor of prohibition and against taxes is the fact that prohibition sends a signal that might influence preferences, decreasing the demand for illegal drugs. Also, some people intensely dislike the idea of the government profiting from trade in harmful substances.

REVIEW QUIZ

1. How does the imposition of a penalty for selling an illegal drug influence demand, supply, price, and the quantity of the drug consumed?
2. How does the imposition of a penalty for possessing an illegal drug influence demand, supply, price, and the quantity of the drug consumed?
3. How does the imposition of a penalty for selling *or* possessing an illegal drug influence demand, supply, price, and the quantity of the drug consumed?
4. Is there any case for legalizing drugs?

myeconlab **Study Plan 6.5**

You now know how to use the demand and supply model to predict prices, to study government actions in markets, and to study the sources and costs of inefficiency. Before you leave this topic, take a look at *Reading Between the Lines* on pp. 142–143 about the market for illegal music downloads.

READING BETWEEN THE LINES

The Market for Illegal Downloads

http://www.nytimes.com

Music Publishers Sue Owner of Web File-Sharing Program

August 5, 2006

A coalition of record companies sued the operators of the file-sharing program LimeWire for copyright infringement on Friday, claiming the company encouraged users to trade music without permission.

The Recording Industry Association of America said in a statement that it had sued the Lime Group, the corporation's executives, and the subsidiaries that designed and distributed LimeWire. The suit was filed in Federal District Court in Manhattan.

The case is the first piracy lawsuit brought against a distributor of file-sharing software since the Supreme Court ruled last year that technology companies could be sued for copyright infringement on the grounds that they encouraged customers to steal music and movies over the Internet.

The record companies—Sony BMG Music Entertainment, Vivendi's Universal Music Group, Time Warner's Warner Music Group and EMI Music—are seeking compensatory and punitive damages, including at least $150,000 for each instance in which a copyrighted song was distributed without permission.

In the complaint, the record companies contend that LimeWire's operators are "actively facilitating, encouraging and enticing" computer users to steal music by failing to block access to copyrighted works and building a business model that allows them to profit directly from piracy.

Like similar programs, LimeWire allows computer users to make files on their PCs available to a multitude of other people all connected to each other, a method known as peer-to-peer file-sharing.

The original Napster software first popularized such swapping of files online before it was forced to shut down in 2001 after record companies sued. . . .

Essence of the Story

- Napster, the software that popularized online music file swapping, was shut down in 2001 after being sued by record companies.
- Five years later, record companies claimed that LimeWire was earning a profit on software that enabled computer users to engage in peer-to-peer file sharing and to steal copyrighted music.
- The record companies sued LimeWire and sought damages, including at least $150,000 for each instance in which a copyrighted song was distributed without permission.

Economic Analysis

- Downloaded music is easily accessible to people with file-sharing programs.
- File-sharing programs are available on the Internet.
- The marginal cost of a downloaded file is zero.
- In Fig. 1, the supply curve *S*, which is also the marginal cost curve, is horizontal along the *x*-axis.
- The demand curve for downloaded music is the downward-sloping curve *D*.
- The equilibrium quantity occurs at an equilibrium price of zero, where the demand curve *D* touches the *x*-axis.
- If the record companies file lawsuits against downloaders, the downloaders are faced with the cost of breaking the law.
- The cost of breaking the law is subtracted from the value of the downloaded music to determine the maximum price that a person is willing to pay for a download.
- In Fig. 1, the demand curve shifts leftward from *D* to *D* − *CBL* and the vertical distance between the two curves is equal to the cost of breaking the law.
- The quantity of downloaded files decreases, but because the supply curve does not shift, the equilibrium price remains at zero.
- But if the record companies sue the creators of the file-sharing programs, as in the news article, the cost of breaking the law falls on the supply side of the market.
- In Fig. 2, the supply curve shifts upward from *S* to *S* + *CBL* when the creator of the file-sharing program is charged an amount *P* for each file that is illegally downloaded.
- If downloaders continue to face the cost of breaking the law, the demand curve *D* − *CBL* is the same as the curve in Fig. 1.
- When both creators of file-sharing programs and downloaders face the cost of breaking the law, the equilibrium quantity of downloaded files falls farther. The price of a download rises to equal the program creators' cost of breaking the law.

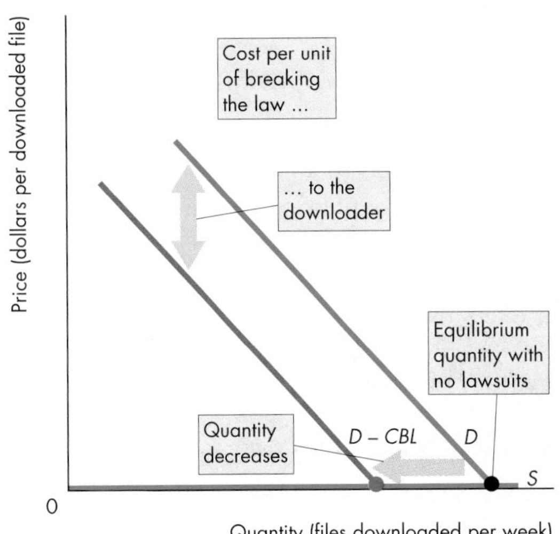

Figure 1 Downloaders face cost of breaking law

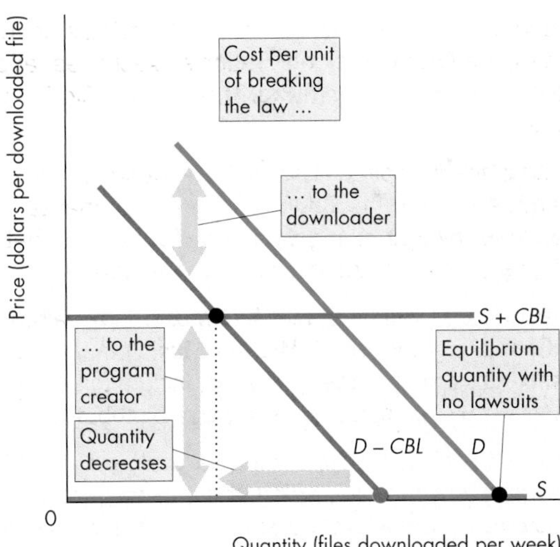

Figure 2 Downloaders and program creators face cost of breaking law

You're the Voter

- Why are record companies suing the creators of file-sharing programs rather than suing the downloaders and file sharers?
- Which do you think would be more effective: filing lawsuits against the creators of file-sharing software or against downloaders and file sharers?
- Would you support a change in the law that made file sharing legal? Explain why or why not.

SUMMARY

Key Points

Housing Markets and Rent Ceilings (pp. 124–128)

- A decrease in the supply of housing raises rents.
- Higher rents stimulate building, and in the long run, the quantity of housing increases and rents fall.
- A rent ceiling that is set below the equilibrium rent creates a housing shortage, wasteful search, and a black market.

The Labor Market and the Minimum Wage (pp. 128–131)

- A decrease in the demand for low-skilled labor lowers the wage rate and reduces employment.
- The lower wage rate encourages people with low skills to acquire more skill, which decreases the supply of low-skilled labor and, in the long run, raises the wage rate of low-skilled labor.
- A minimum wage set above the equilibrium wage rate creates unemployment and increases the amount of time people spend searching for a job.
- A minimum wage hits low-skilled young people hardest.

Taxes (pp. 132–136)

- A tax raises price but usually by less than the tax.
- The shares of a tax paid by buyers and by sellers depend on the elasticity of demand and the elasticity of supply.
- The less elastic the demand or the more elastic the supply, the larger is the share of the tax paid by buyers.
- If demand is perfectly elastic or supply is perfectly inelastic, sellers pay the entire tax. And if demand is perfectly inelastic or supply is perfectly elastic, buyers pay the entire tax.

Subsidies and Quotas (pp. 137–139)

- Farm revenues fluctuate because supply fluctuates. Because the demand for most farm products is inelastic, a decrease in supply increases farm revenue, while an increase in supply decreases farm revenue.
- A subsidy is like a negative tax. It lowers the price and leads to inefficient overproduction.
- A quota leads to inefficient underproduction, which raises the price.

Markets for Illegal Goods (pp. 140–141)

- Penalties on sellers of an illegal good increase the cost of selling the good and decrease its supply. Penalties on buyers of an illegal good decrease their willingness to pay and decrease the demand for the good.
- The higher the penalties and the more effective the law enforcement, the smaller is the quantity bought.
- A tax that is set at a sufficiently high rate will decrease the quantity of a drug bought, but there will be a tendency for the tax to be evaded.

Key Figures

Key Terms

PROBLEMS

myeconlab Tests, Study Plan, Solutions*

1. The figure shows the demand for and supply of rental housing in Townsville.

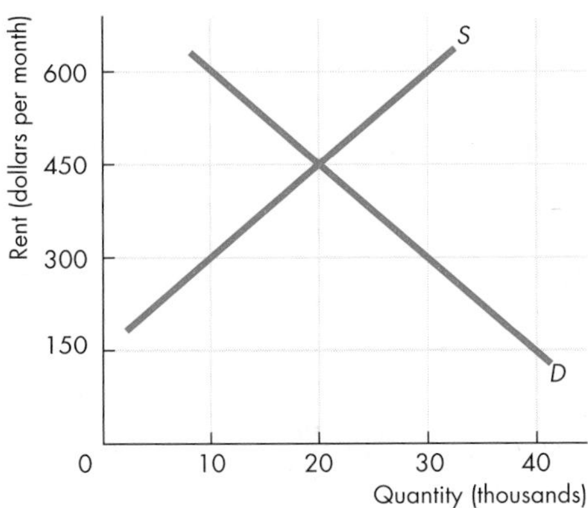

a. What are the equilibrium rent and equilibrium quantity of rental housing?

If a rent ceiling is set at $300 a month, what is

b. The quantity of housing rented?
c. The shortage of housing?
d. The maximum price that someone is willing to pay for the last unit available?

If a rent ceiling is set at $600 a month, what is

e. The quantity of housing rented?
f. The shortage of housing?
g. The maximum price that someone is willing to pay for the last unit of housing available?

2. The table gives the demand for and supply of teenage labor.

Wage rate (dollars per hour)	Quantity demanded (hours per month)	Quantity supplied
4	3,000	1,000
5	2,500	1,500
6	2,000	2,000
7	1,500	2,500
8	1,000	3,000

a. What are the equilibrium wage rate and level of employment?
b. What is the quantity of unemployment?
c. If a minimum wage of $5 an hour is set for teenagers, how many hours do they work?
d. If a minimum wage of $5 an hour is set for teenagers, how many hours are unemployed?
e. If a minimum wage is set at $7 an hour for teenagers, what are the quantities of employment and unemployment?
f. If a minimum wage is set at $7 an hour and demand increases by 500 hours a month, what is the wage rate paid to teenagers and how many hours of their labor are unemployed?

3. The table gives the demand and supply schedules for chocolate brownies.

Price (cents per brownie)	Quantity demanded (millions per day)	Quantity supplied
50	5	3
60	4	4
70	3	5
80	2	6
90	1	7

a. If brownies are not taxed, what is the price of a brownie and how many are bought?
b. If sellers are taxed 20¢ a brownie, what are the price and quantity bought? Who pays the tax?
c. If buyers are taxed 20¢ a brownie, what are the price and quantity bought? Who pays the tax?

4. The demand and supply schedules for roses are

Price (dollars per bunch)	Quantity demanded (bunches per week)	Quantity supplied
10	100	40
12	90	60
14	80	80
16	70	100
18	60	120

a. If roses are not taxed, what is the price and how many bunches are bought?
b. If roses are taxed $6 a bunch, what are the price and quantity bought? Who pays the tax?

5. The demand and supply schedules for rice are

Price (dollars per box)	Quantity demanded (boxes per week)	Quantity supplied
1.00	3,500	500
1.10	3,250	1,000
1.20	3,000	1,500
1.30	2,750	2,000
1.40	2,500	2,500
1.50	2,250	3,000
1.60	2,000	3,500

*Solutions to odd-numbered problems are provided.

What are the price, the marginal cost of producing rice, and the quantity produced if the government

a. Introduces a subsidy of $0.30 a box on rice?
b. Sets a quota of 2,000 boxes a week instead of a subsidy?

6. The figure illustrates the market for a banned substance. What are the equilibrium price and quantity if there is a penalty of $20 a unit on

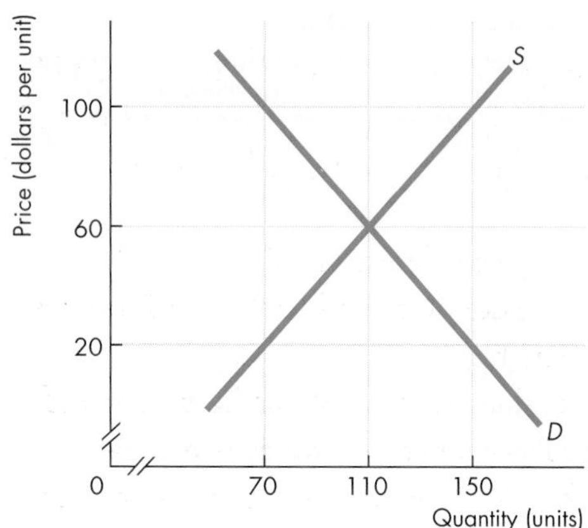

a. Sellers only?
b. Buyers only?
c. Both sellers and buyers?

CRITICAL THINKING

1. Study *Reading Between the Lines* (pp. 142–143) about the market for music downloads.
   a. If a tax per download could be imposed, what factors would need to be considered to use the tax to make the market efficient?
   b. If a new technology were invented that destroyed a music file if it was downloaded illegally, what do you think would happen to the market for downloads and at what price would it operate relative to the price of a CD?
   c. Who would benefit and who would bear the cost, if any, of the new technology in part (b)?
   d. Would the new technology in part (b) make the download market efficient?
2. On December 31, 1776, Rhode Island established wage controls to limit wages to 70¢ a day for carpenters and 42¢ a day for tailors.
   a. Are these wage controls a price ceiling or a price floor? Why might they have been introduced?
   b. If these wage controls are effective, would you expect to see a surplus or a shortage of carpenters and tailors?
3. **Despite Protests, Rent Board Sets 7.25% Increase**

   Rents for New York City's one million rent-stabilized apartments can increase by as much as 7.25 percent over the next two years, the city's Rent Guidelines Board voted last night . . . According to a report . . . costs for the owners of rent-stabilized buildings rose by 7.8 percent in the last year. . . The rent-increase vote comes at a time of growing concern about the ability of the middle class to afford to live in New York City.

   The New York Times, June 28, 2006

   a. If rents for rent-stabilized apartments do not increase, how do you think the market for rental units in New York will develop?
   b. Are rent ceilings in New York helpful to the middle class? Why or why not?
   c. What effect will the increase in the rent ceiling have on the quantity of rent-stabilized apartments?

WEB ACTIVITIES

myeconlab **Links to Web sites**

1. Find information about living wage campaigns and the Harvard Living Wage Campaign.
   a. What is the campaign for a living wage?
   b. How would you distinguish the minimum wage from a living wage?
   c. If the Living Wage Campaign succeeds in raising wages above their equilibrium levels, how would the living wage affect (i) the quantity of labor demanded, (ii) the quantity of labor supplied and, (iii) the amount of unemployment?
   d. Would a living wage above the equilibrium wage be efficient?
   e. Who would gain and who would lose from a living wage above the equilibrium wage?
   f. Would a living wage above the equilibrium wage be fair?
2. Find information about sugar quotas in Europe. Why do you think the European nations assign production quotas for sugar? If the European sugar quotas are less than the equilibrium quantities, who benefits from and who pays for the quotas?

The Amazing Market

The four chapters that you've just studied explain how markets work. The market is an amazing instrument. It enables people who have never met and who know nothing about each other to interact and do business. It also enables us to allocate our scarce resources to the uses that we value most highly. Markets can be very simple or highly organized.

A simple market is one that the American historian Daniel J. Boorstin describes in *The Discoverers* (p. 161). In the late fourteenth century,

> *The Muslim caravans that went southward from Morocco across the Atlas Mountains arrived after twenty days at the shores of the Senegal River. There the Moroccan traders laid out separate piles of salt, of beads from Ceutan coral, and cheap manufactured goods. Then they retreated out of sight. The local tribesmen, who lived in the strip mines where they dug their gold, came to the shore and put a heap of gold beside each pile of Moroccan goods. Then they, in turn, went out of view, leaving the Moroccan traders either to take the gold offered for a particular pile or to reduce the pile of their merchandise to suit the offered price in gold. Once again the Moroccan traders withdrew, and the process went on. By this system of commercial etiquette, the Moroccans collected their gold.*

An organized market is the New York Stock Exchange, which trades many millions of stocks each day. Another is an auction at which the U.S. government sells rights to broadcasters and cellular telephone companies for the use of the airwaves.

All of these markets determine the prices at which exchanges take place and enable both buyers and sellers to benefit.

Everything and anything that can be exchanged is traded in markets. There are markets for goods and services; for resources such as labor, capital, and raw materials; for dollars, pounds, and yen; for goods to be delivered now and for goods to be delivered in the future. Only the imagination places limits on what can be traded in markets.

You began your study of markets in Chapter 3 by learning about the laws of demand and supply. There, you discovered the forces that make prices adjust to coordinate buying plans and selling plans.

The laws of demand and supply that you've learned and used in this chapter were discovered during the nineteenth century by some remarkable economists. We conclude our study of demand and supply and markets by looking at the lives and times of some of these economists and by talking to one of today's most influential economists who studies markets using experimental methods.

PROBING THE IDEAS

Discovering the Laws of Demand and Supply

"The forces to be dealt with are . . . so numerous, that it is best to take a few at a time. . . . Thus we begin by isolating the primary relations of supply, demand, and price."

ALFRED MARSHALL
The Principles of Economics

The Economist

Alfred Marshall *(1842–1924) grew up in an England that was being transformed by the railroad and by the expansion of manufacturing. Mary Paley was one of Marshall's students at Cambridge, and when Alfred and Mary married, in 1877, celibacy rules barred Alfred from continuing to teach at Cambridge. By 1884, with more liberal rules, the Marshalls returned to Cambridge, where Alfred became Professor of Political Economy.*

Many others had a hand in refining the theory of demand and supply, but the first thorough and complete statement of the theory as we know it today was set out by Alfred Marshall, with the acknowledged help of Mary Paley Marshall. Published in 1890, this monumental treatise, The Principles of Economics, *became the textbook on economics on both sides of the Atlantic for almost half a century. Marshall was an outstanding mathematician, but he kept mathematics and even diagrams in the background. His supply and demand diagram appears only in a footnote.*

The Issues

The laws of demand and supply that you studied in Chapter 3 were discovered during the 1830s by Antoine-Augustin Cournot (1801–1877), a professor of mathematics at the University of Lyon, France. Although Cournot was the first to use demand and supply, it was the development and expansion of the railroads during the 1850s that gave the newly emerging theory its first practical applications. Railroads then were at the cutting edge of technology just as airlines are today. And as in the airline industry today, competition among the railroads was fierce.

Dionysius Lardner (1793–1859), an Irish professor of philosophy at the University of London, used demand and supply to show railroad companies how they could increase their profits by cutting rates on long-distance business on which competition was fiercest and by raising rates on short-haul business on which they had less to fear from other transportation suppliers. Today, economists use the principles that Lardner worked out during the 1850s to calculate the freight rates and passenger fares that will give airlines the largest possible profit. And the rates calculated have a lot in common with the railroad rates of the nineteenth century. On local routes on which there is little competition, fares per mile are highest, and on long-distance routes on which the airlines compete fiercely, fares per mile are lowest.

Known satirically among scientists of the day as "Dionysius Diddler," Lardner worked on an amazing range of problems from astronomy to railway engineering to economics. A colorful character, he would have been a regular guest of David Letterman if late-night talk shows had been around in the 1850s. Lardner visited the École des Ponts et Chaussées (School of Bridges and Roads) in Paris and must have learned a great deal from Jules Dupuit.

In France, Jules Dupuit (1804–1866), a French engineer/economist, used demand to calculate the benefits from building a bridge and, once the bridge was built, for calculating the toll to charge for its use. His work was the forerunner of what is today called *cost-benefit analysis.* Working with the principles invented by Dupuit, economists today calculate the costs and benefits of highways, airports, dams, and power stations.

Then

Dupuit used the law of demand to determine whether a bridge or canal would be valued enough by its users to justify the cost of building it. Lardner first worked out the relationship between the cost of production and supply and used demand and supply theory to explain the costs, prices, and profits of railroad operations. He also used the theory to discover ways of increasing revenue by raising rates on short-haul business and lowering them on long-distance freight.

Now

Today, using the same principles that Dupuit devised, economists calculate whether the benefits of expanding airports and air-traffic control facilities are sufficient to cover their costs. Airline companies use the principles developed by Lardner to set their prices and to decide when to offer "seat sales." Like the railroads before them, the airlines charge a high price per mile on short flights, for which they face little competition, and a low price per mile on long flights, for which competition is fierce.

Markets do an amazing job. And the laws of demand and supply help us to understand how markets work. But in some situations, a market must be designed and institutions must be created to enable the market to operate. In recent years, economists have begun to use experiments to design and create markets. One of the chief architects of experimental methods in economics is Charles Holt, whom you can meet on the following pages.

TALKING WITH

Charles A. Holt

Charles A. Holt is the A. Willis Robertson Professor of Political Economy and Director of the Thomas Jefferson Center for Political Economy at the University of Virginia.

Born in 1948 in Richmond, he was an undergraduate at Washington and Lee University and a graduate student at Carnegie-Mellon University. Professor Holt became interested in laboratory experiments as part of his work on auctions and discovered that the data generated by experiments often rejected standard theories. These discoveries sent him on the path of developing new theories that are consistent with experimental data in areas that include rent seeking, auctions, bargaining, and public goods. His research has produced more than a hundred articles and several books.

Professor Holt is also a committed teacher. He has written a series of interactive games and experimental markets for teaching on his Veconlab Web site.

Michael Parkin talked with Charles Holt about his career and the promise held by using experimental methods for research and teaching in economics.

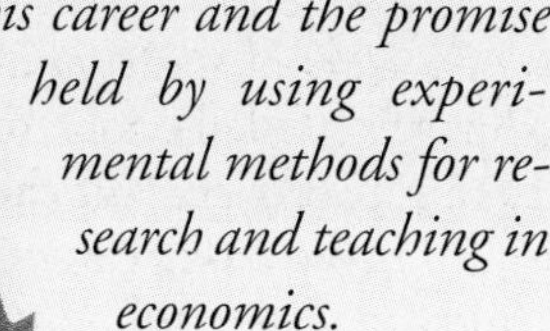

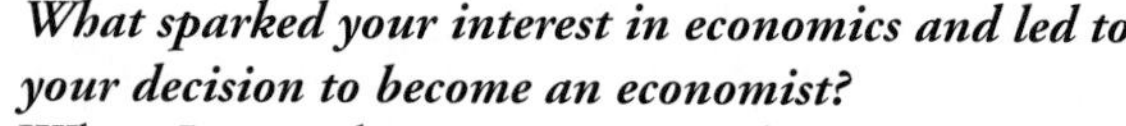

What sparked your interest in economics and led to your decision to become an economist?

When I was taking a summer school history class, the high school coach who was teaching the class remarked, "I don't understand why one baseball team would trade a player with another, don't they see that one person always gets the short end of a deal?" This comment caused me think about how voluntary trade can benefit both parties. For example, a team with two good first basemen could trade one for a pitcher from a team with a full bullpen but nobody at first, and both teams might end up winning more games that season. In the same manner, each trade between willing partners in an economy can make both better off, and lots of trades can create lots of wealth. I later enjoyed reading the ideas of economists like Adam Smith, Milton Friedman, and John Maynard Keynes, who were able to transform a jumble of everyday economic events into a large picture with a coherent organization and purpose.

Based on the wide experience you have with experimental markets, how does the demand and supply model of Alfred Marshall stand up today?

When I first took economics in college, we had to memorize a list of assumptions underlying the model of perfect competition that is represented by the supply and demand graph. These assumptions included "large numbers of buyers and sellers" and "perfect information." The professor would invariably end up by admitting that few actual markets fit this model exactly, but that some markets, for example wheat, might come close.

Vernon Smith's early market experiments, run in his class, showed that prices track the supply-and-demand predictions surprisingly well, even with as few as 3 or 4 traders on each side of the market, and with nobody having any direct information about others' values and costs for the commodity being traded. I ran some experiments of my own to try to stress the model, by giving "power" to one side of the market, but the outcomes were surprisingly competitive. This experience in the laboratory added confidence and enthusiasm to my teaching.

What can we learn about how competitive markets work in classroom experiments?

My coauthor Doug Davis and I ran some experiments in which we let sellers discuss prices while buyers were out of the room, and they invariably tried to fix prices at high levels. When prices were publicly posted for all to see, these conspiracies would raise sellers' earnings and harm buyers, but attempts at collusion generally failed when sellers were able to offer secret discounts to buyers that could not be seen by other sellers. In this case, rampant discounting would drive discounted prices down to near-competitive levels. I remember one group that ended up "fixing" a price, but unknown to them, the price that they fixed was at about the level of the supply and demand intersection. In the experiments, as in actual markets, consumers benefit from lower prices, and the combined benefit of buyers and earnings of sellers rise as prices approach competitive levels.

Can we learn even more by doing web-based experiments? What in particular are the gains from running web-based experiments like those that you've created?

You only have to look at the computer screens of traders in many markets to see that they have large amounts of information available, and yet that they have to rely on arms-length negotiations. Web-based experiments can add this kind of realistic complexity to classroom markets.

For example, the programs can keep track of your cash, interest earnings, dividends, and stock shares while you buy and sell quickly. Often "insiders" have sources of private information, and the web-based experiments can generate and preserve the privacy of this information, as students use it to guide their trading decisions. In particular, I could only dream of doing realistic macroeconomics experiments before I began writing web-based programs, and now these programs allow "workers" and "firms" to interact in markets that are connected by the "circular flow" of money, goods, and labor. In this setting, one can see how a contraction in the money supply may stifle transactions and lead to a "general glut" in which unsold labor and goods results in low levels of consumption and production. It is an exhilarating experience to see how an increase in the money supply in such cases may have "real effects" that pull it out of a slump.

Another example involves the work that I've been doing for the Federal Communications Commission (the FCC) on auction design. Their auctions involve hundreds or thousands of broadcast licenses, and these auctions are run in a series of "rounds" as prices continue to rise. These auctions involve bidders around the country, and naturally, they are controlled by computer software, just as our auction experiments are run in the lab, with bidding screens that have the same "look and feel" as that used in the actual auctions.

You might be wondering why would anyone be concerned about a laboratory setting with students like yourself (earning fairly large amounts of cash) when a real auction occurs every 6 months or so? Think of it this way, an auction may involve billions of dollars of trade, and some auctions have failed badly, with prices that barely get "off the ground." You wouldn't want to try a new auction design without extensive laboratory testing, any more than you would want to launch a multi-billion dollar space shuttle without lots of tests here on earth.

You wouldn't want to try a new auction design without extensive laboratory testing, any more than you would want to launch a multi-billion dollar space shuttle without lots of tests here on earth.

I remember wearing a "NASA Mission Acquisition" nametag at a meeting at Caltech, where results of laboratory experiments were discussed. I later got a chance to talk candidly with some of the NASA officials on the "red-eye" flight back to the East Coast. In particular, I got to ask them what they really hoped to learn from small-scale simulations of the procurement process. Their response was that the amounts of money involved were so large, and the budgeting/procurement process was so complex, that they had a fear of "losing control," and any insights gleaned from controlled laboratory experiments could be extremely valuable.

Many students have been introduced to game theory watching Russell Crowe as mathematics professor John Nash in* A Beautiful Mind. *What have we learned about games from experiments?

Game theory is an elegant apparatus that can yield strikingly accurate predictions of human behavior, especially where the "players" are driven by the profit motive to make careful decisions and to acquire extensive information about what their competitors are doing. One criticism of game theory, however, is that it is all too often based on an assumption that the players are "perfectly rational" and perfectly selfish, not caring much about others' economic well-being.

We all think of ourselves as being rational, but most of us have doubts about the rationality of others. In "Ten Little Treasures of Game Theory, and Ten Intuitive Contradictions," (*American Economic Review*, 2001) Professor Jacob Goeree (Caltech) and I use experiments to show that game theoretic "Nash equilibrium" predictions tend to work well in some games (the "treasures") and badly in others. The intuition here is that games are interactions of thinking humans, so reactions to uncertainty about others may cause "feedback effects" that take behavior away from theoretical predictions based on perfect knowledge and rationality.

Some people are skeptical about experiments. What are some of the easily disposed of criticisms? Are there any compelling criticisms of the experimental approach? How do you respond to them?

Experiments with real people can be used to inject realistic elements into the study of economic behavior. Many economic movements (depressions) are like the movements of planets that cannot be undone or repeated exactly, but controlled experiments allow us the opportunity to obtain repeated observations under controlled conditions. For example, the work for the FCC on auction design involved over 900 student "subjects" who participated in hundreds of auctions, which permitted us to see the major patterns that emerge from random variations due to individual differences and interactions. Some of what we learned seems obvious after the fact, but the experiments gave us the confidence to argue strongly for and against particular changes in auction procedures. Much of the alternative analysis considered by the FCC officials involved computer simulations, which are necessarily based on somewhat mechanical assumptions. Computer simulations can also be quite useful, especially when laboratory experiments are used to refine the assumed behavior rules.

One critique of laboratory experiments is that the subject population is narrowly selected. Hence some economists and political scientists have used "field experiments" in which the participants are in their native environment. This involves some loss of control, but the added realism can be justified when "social context" is important. For example, the effects of appeals to vote on voter turnout are probably best studied in field experiments, where random samples of households are exposed to different "appeal" treatments—a phone call or a knock on the door.

What is your advice to a student who is just setting out to become an economist? Is economics a good subject in which to major? What other subjects work well with economics?

I enjoyed both politics and economics courses in college, but I chose to study economics because I felt that the theories I was learning would still be largely intact in 20 years, which has turned out to be true. Economics offers a nice combination of a firm scientific basis that can be applied to important social problems. These problems are fascinating because of the forward-looking, strategic nature of humans, which are inherently less mechanical than what you might be studying in physical sciences. And the tools that you learn in economics, a mix of theory, intuition, data analysis, and experiments, can be profitably transported to the study of a wide range of social issues. The experimental side of economics has a close tie to psychology, and many of the most interesting policy applications occur in settings where a deep understanding of political processes is helpful.

Utility and Demand

Water, Water, Everywhere

Water is one of our most vital resources. Without water, we would die. It is literally a life and death resource. Contrast water with diamonds. According to the song, they are "a girl's best friend." And both women and men enjoy wearing diamonds. But while diamonds are attractive and bring enjoyment, they are not in the league of water. We could manage perfectly well without them.

If the benefits of water far outweigh the benefits of diamonds, why does water cost practically nothing while diamonds are expensive?

Water and diamonds are not the only pair of items that have prices that seem to bear no relationship to values. A National Football League player, on the average, earns more than 45 times the amount that a child-care worker earns. Do we place less value on the people who take care of our children than on those who provide us with entertaining football games?

After studying this chapter, you will be able to

- Explain what limits a household's consumption choices
- Describe preferences using the concept of utility and distinguish between total utility and marginal utility
- Explain the marginal utility theory of consumer choice
- Use marginal utility theory to predict the effects of changing prices and incomes
- Explain the paradox of value

This chapter presents a theory of consumer choice. The main purpose of this theory is to explain the law of demand—the tendency for the quantity demanded of a good to increase when its price falls. The theory also explains the effects on demand of changes in incomes and the prices of other goods.

The theory of choice that you study in this chapter also explains the paradox that the prices of water and diamonds are so out of proportion to their benefits. And *Reading Between the Lines* at the end of the chapter uses the theory to explain the paradox that a football player seems to be more valuable than a child-care worker.

The Household's Budget

A household's budget places a limit on its consumption choices. And a household's preferences determine which of all its possible choices a household makes. We begin by studying the factors that determine the household's budget and its consumption possibilities.[1]

Consumption Possibilities

A household's consumption choices are constrained by the household's income and by the prices of the goods and services it buys. The household has a given amount of income to spend and cannot influence the prices of the goods and services it buys.

A household's **budget line** describes the limits to its consumption choices. Let's consider Lisa's household. Lisa has an income of $30 a month, and she plans to buy only two goods: movies and soda. The price of a movie is $6; the price of soda is $3 a six-pack. If Lisa spends all her income, she will reach the limits to her consumption of movies and soda.

Figure 7.1 illustrates Lisa's possible consumption of movies and soda. Rows *A* through *F* in the table show six possible ways of allocating $30 to these two goods. For example, Lisa can see 2 movies for $12 and buy 6 six-packs of soda for $18 (row *C*). Points *A* through *F* on the graph illustrate the possibilities presented in the table. The line passing through these points is Lisa's budget line.

Lisa's budget line is a constraint on her choices. It marks the boundary between what she can afford and what she cannot afford. She can afford all the points on the line and those inside it. She cannot afford the points outside the line. Lisa's consumption possibilities depend on the price of a movie, the price of soda, and her income. Her consumption possibilities change when the price of a movie, the price of a six-pack of soda, or her income changes.

The budget line can be described by the relative price of the two goods and the consumer's real income.

FIGURE 7.1 Consumption Possibilities

myeconlab

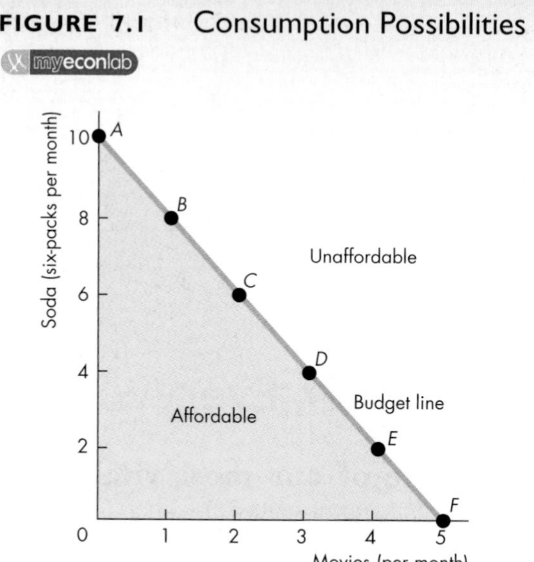

Possibility	Movies: Quantity	Movies: Expenditure (dollars)	Soda: Six-packs	Soda: Expenditure (dollars)
A	0	0	10	30
B	1	6	8	24
C	2	12	6	18
D	3	18	4	12
E	4	24	2	6
F	5	30	0	0

Rows *A* through *F* in the table show six possible ways in which Lisa can allocate $30 to movies and soda. For example, Lisa can buy 2 movies and 6 six-packs of soda (row *C*). The combination in each row costs $30. These possibilities are points *A* through *F* on the graph. The line through those points is a boundary between what Lisa can afford and what she cannot afford. Her choices must lie along the line *AF* or inside the orange area.

Relative Price

A **relative price** is the price of one good divided by the price of another good. The price of a movie is $6 and the price of soda is $3 a six-pack, so the relative price of a movie in terms of soda is $6 per movie divided by $3 per six-pack, which equals 2 six-packs per movie. That is, to see one more movie, Lisa must

[1] This chapter and Chapter 8 deal with the same topic but explain two different methods of representing a household's preferences. The chapters are written on the assumption that you will most likely study only one of them. If you do study both chapters, you will find that the first sections of each, which discuss the household budget constraint, are very similar.

FIGURE 7.2 Changes in Price and Income

myeconlab

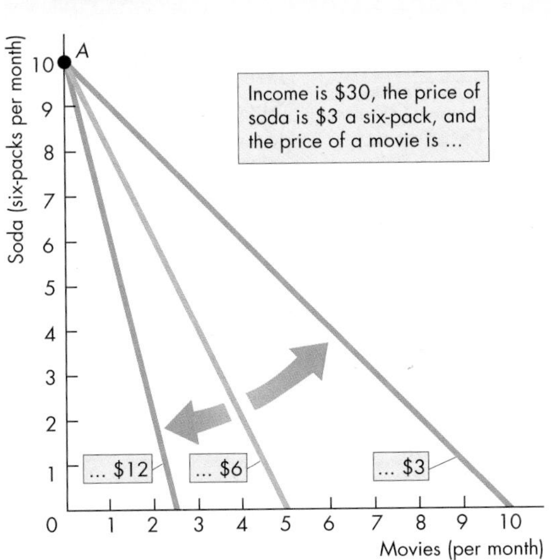

(a) A change in price

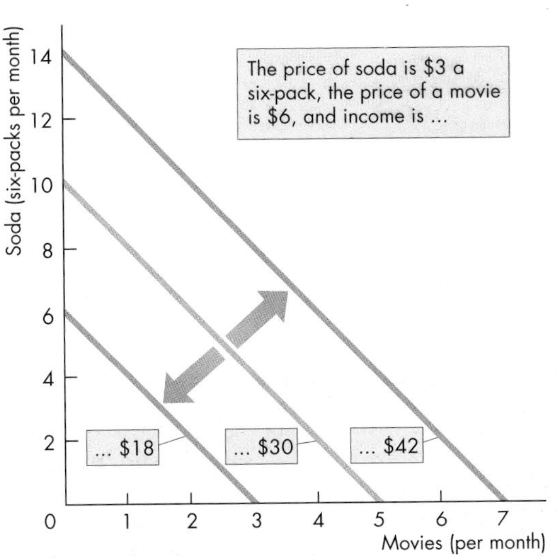

(b) A change in income

In part (a), the price of a movie changes. A fall in the price from $6 to $3 rotates the budget line outward and makes it flatter. A rise in the price from $6 to $12 rotates the budget line inward and makes it steeper.

In part (b), income changes. A rise in income shifts the budget line outward, and a fall in income shifts the budget line inward. But the slope of the budget line does not change when income changes.

give up 2 six-packs. The opportunity cost of a movie is 2 six-packs.

A Price Change The relative price of the good measured on the *x*-axis is the magnitude of the slope of the budget line. And when a price changes, the relative price changes, and the slope of the budget line changes. Figure 7.2(a) illustrates two changes. If the price of a movie falls from $6 to $3, Lisa's budget line rotates outward and she can afford to consume more of both goods. If the price of a movie rises from $6 to $12, Lisa's budget line rotates inward and she cannot afford as much of either good.

Real Income

A household's **real income** is the household's income expressed as the quantity of goods that the household can afford to buy. Expressed in terms of soda, Lisa's real income is 10 six-packs. This quantity is the maximum number of six-packs that she can buy. It is equal to her money income, $30, divided by the price of soda, $3 a six-pack.

A Change in Income Real income in terms of soda is the point at which the budget line intersects the *y*-axis. And when money income changes, real income changes and the budget line shifts. But the slope of the budget line doesn't change. Figure 7.2(b) illustrates two changes in money income. When Lisa's money income rises from $30 to $42, her budget line shifts outward and she can afford to consume more of both goods. When Lisa's money income falls to $18, her budget line shifts inward and she cannot afford as much of either good.

REVIEW QUIZ

1. What does a household's budget line show?
2. How do real income and the relative price influence the budget line?
3. If the price of one good changes, what happens to the relative price and to the slope of the household's budget line?
4. If a household's money income changes and prices do not change, what happens to the household's real income and budget line?

myeconlab **Study Plan 7.1**

Preferences and Utility

How does Lisa divide her available budget between movies and soda? The answer depends on her likes and dislikes—her *preferences*. Economists use the concept of utility to describe preferences. The benefit or satisfaction that a person gets from the consumption of a good or service is called **utility**. Let's now see how we can use the concept of utility to describe preferences.

Total Utility

Total utility is the total benefit that a person gets from the consumption of goods and services. Total utility depends on the level of consumption—more consumption generally gives more total utility. The units of utility are arbitrary. Suppose we tell Lisa that we want to measure her utility. We're going to call the utility from no consumption zero. And we are going to call the utility she gets from 1 movie a month 50 units. We then ask her to tell us, on the same scale, how much she would like 2, 3, and more movies up to 14 a month. We also ask her to tell us, on the same scale, how much she would like 1 six-pack of soda a month, 2 six-packs, and more up to 14 six-packs a month. Table 7.1 shows Lisa's answers.

TABLE 7.1 Lisa's Total Utility from Movies and Soda

Movies		Soda	
Quantity per month	Total utility	Six-packs per month	Total utility
0	0	0	0
1	50	1	75
2	88	2	117
3	121	3	153
4	150	4	181
5	175	5	206
6	196	6	225
7	214	7	243
8	229	8	260
9	241	9	276
10	250	10	291
11	256	11	305
12	259	12	318
13	261	13	330
14	262	14	341

Marginal Utility

Marginal utility is the change in total utility that results from a one-unit increase in the quantity of a good consumed. When the number of six-packs Lisa buys increases from 4 to 5 a month, her total utility from soda increases from 181 units to 206 units. So for Lisa, the marginal utility from consuming a fifth six-pack each month is 25 units. The table in Fig. 7.3 shows Lisa's marginal utility from soda. Notice that marginal utility appears midway between the quantities of soda. It does so because it is the change in consumption from 4 to 5 six-packs that produces the marginal utility of 25 units. The table displays calculations of marginal utility for each number of six-packs that Lisa buys from 1 to 5.

Figure 7.3(a) illustrates Lisa's total utility from soda. The more soda Lisa drinks in a month, the more total utility she gets. Figure 7.3(b) illustrates her marginal utility. This graph tells us that as Lisa drinks more soda, her marginal utility from soda decreases. For example, her marginal utility decreases from 75 units from the first six-pack to 42 units from the second six-pack and to 36 units from the third.

Diminishing Marginal Utility

We call the decrease in marginal utility as the quantity of the good consumed increases the principle of **diminishing marginal utility**.

Marginal utility is positive but diminishes as consumption of a good increases. Why does marginal utility have these two features? In Lisa's case, she likes soda, and the more she drinks the better. That's why marginal utility is positive. The benefit that Lisa gets from the last six-pack consumed is its marginal utility. To see why marginal utility diminishes, think about the following two situations: In one, you've just been studying all through the day and evening and you've been too busy finishing an assignment to go shopping. A friend drops by with a six-pack of soda. The utility you get from that soda is the marginal utility

FIGURE 7.3 Total Utility and Marginal Utility

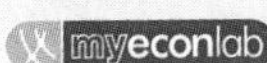

Quantity	Total utility	Marginal utility
0	0	
1	75	75
2	117	42
3	153	36
4	181	28
5	206	25

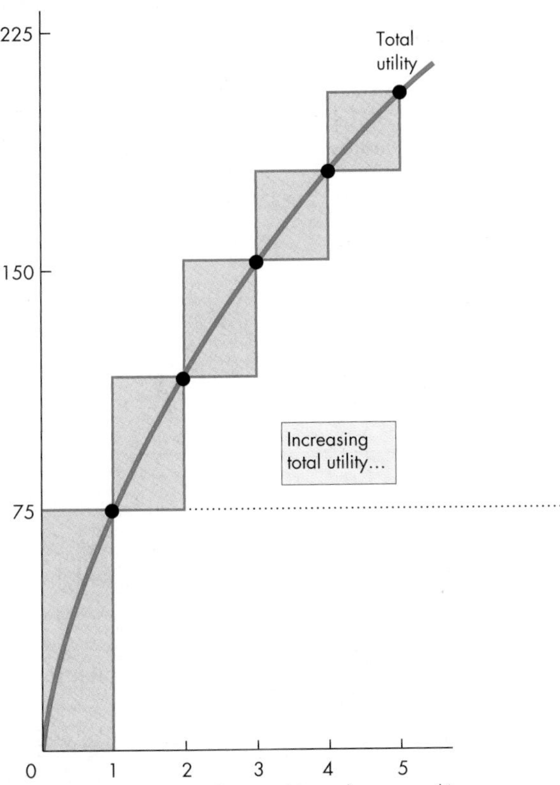

(a) Total utility

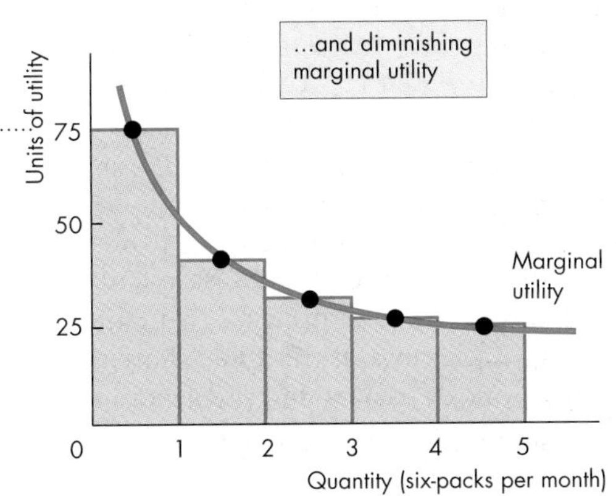

(b) Marginal utility

The table shows that as Lisa consumes more soda, her total utility from soda increases. The table also shows her marginal utility—the change in total utility resulting from the last six-pack she consumes. Marginal utility declines as consumption increases. The figure graphs Lisa's total utility and marginal utility from soda. Part (a) shows her total utility. It also shows as a bar the extra total utility she gains from each additional six-pack—her marginal utility. Part (b) shows how Lisa's marginal utility from soda diminishes by placing the bars shown in part (a) side by side as a series of declining steps.

from one six-pack. In the second situation, you've been on a soda binge. You've been working on an assignment all day but you've guzzled three six-packs while doing so. You are up to your eyeballs in soda. You are happy enough to have one more can. But the thrill that you get from it is not very large. It is the marginal utility of the nineteenth can in a day.

We've now described Lisa's budget and preferences. Our next task is to combine these two elements and see how she chooses what to consume.

REVIEW QUIZ

1. What is utility and how do we use the concept of utility to describe a consumer's preferences?
2. What is the distinction between total utility and marginal utility?
3. What is the key assumption about marginal utility?

myeconlab **Study Plan 7.2**

Maximizing Utility

A household's income and the prices that it faces limit the household's consumption choices, and the household's preferences determine the utility that it can obtain from each consumption possibility. The key assumption of marginal utility theory is that the household chooses the consumption possibility that maximizes its total utility. This assumption of utility maximization is a way of expressing the fundamental economic problem: scarcity. People's wants exceed the resources available to satisfy those wants, so they must make hard choices. In making choices, they try to get the maximum attainable benefit—that is, to maximize total utility.

Let's see how Lisa allocates $30 a month between movies and soda to maximize her total utility. We'll continue to assume that movies cost $6 each and soda costs $3 a six-pack.

The Utility-Maximizing Choice

The most direct way of calculating how Lisa spends her income to maximize her total utility is by making a table like Table 7.2. The rows of this table show the affordable combinations of movies and soda that lie along Lisa's budget line in Fig. 7.1. The table records three things: first, the number of movies seen and the total utility derived from them (the left side of the table); second, the number of six-packs consumed and the total utility derived from them (the right side of the table); and third, the total utility derived from both movies and soda (the center column).

The first row of Table 7.2 records the situation when Lisa watches no movies and buys 10 six-packs. In this case, Lisa gets no utility from movies and 291 units of total utility from soda. Her total utility from movies and soda (the center column) is 291 units. The rest of the table is constructed in the same way.

The consumption of movies and soda that maximizes Lisa's total utility is highlighted in the table. When Lisa sees 2 movies and buys 6 six-packs of soda, she gets 313 units of total utility. This is the best Lisa can do, given that she has only $30 to spend and given the prices of movies and six-packs. If she buys 8 six-packs of soda, she can see only 1 movie. She gets 310 units of total utility, 3 less than the maximum attainable. If she sees 3 movies, she can drink only 4 six-packs. She gets 302 units of total utility, 11 less than the maximum attainable.

TABLE 7.2 Lisa's Utility-Maximizing Combinations

	Movies		Total utility from movies and soda	Soda	
	Quantity per month	Total utility		Total utility	Six-packs per month
A	0	0	291	291	10
B	1	50	310	260	8
C	2	88	313	225	6
D	3	121	302	181	4
E	4	150	267	117	2
F	5	175	175	0	0

We've just described Lisa's consumer equilibrium. A **consumer equilibrium** is a situation in which a consumer has allocated all his or her available income in the way that, given the prices of goods and services, maximizes his or her total utility. Lisa's consumer equilibrium is 2 movies and 6 six-packs.

In finding Lisa's consumer equilibrium, we measured her *total* utility from all the affordable combinations of movies and soda. But there is a better way of determining her consumer equilibrium. It uses the idea that choices are made at the margin—an idea that you first met in Chapter 1. Let's look at this alternative.

Equalizing Marginal Utility per Dollar

A consumer's total utility is maximized by following the rule

> Spend all the available income and equalize the marginal utility per dollar for all goods.

The **marginal utility per dollar** is the marginal utility from a good divided by its price. For example, Lisa's marginal utility from seeing 1 movie a month, MU_M, is 50 units of utility. The price of a movie, P_M, is $6, which means that the marginal utility per dollar from 1 movie a month, MU_M/P_M, is 50 units divided by $6, or 8.33 units of utility per dollar.

You can see why following this rule maximizes total utility by thinking about a situation in which

Lisa has spent all her income but the marginal utilities per dollar are not equal. Suppose that Lisa's marginal utility per dollar for soda, MU_S/P_S, exceeds that for movies. By spending a dollar more on soda and a dollar less on movies, her total utility from soda rises and her total utility from movies falls. But her utility gain from soda exceeds her utility loss from movies, so her total utility increases. Because she's consuming more soda, her marginal utility from soda has fallen. And because she sees fewer movies, her marginal utility from movies has risen. Lisa keeps increasing her consumption of soda and decreasing her consumption of movies until the two marginal utilities per dollar are equal, or when

$$\frac{MU_M}{P_M} = \frac{MU_S}{P_S}.$$

Table 7.3 calculates Lisa's marginal utility per dollar for each good. Each row exhausts Lisa's income of \$30. In row *B*, Lisa's marginal utility from movies is 50 units (use Table 7.1 to calculate the marginal utilities). Because the price of a movie is \$6, Lisa's marginal utility per dollar for movies is 50 units divided by \$6, which is 8.33. Marginal utility per dollar for each good, like marginal utility, decreases as more of the good is consumed.

Lisa maximizes her total utility when the marginal utility per dollar for movies is equal to the marginal utility per dollar for soda—possibility *C*. Lisa consumes 2 movies and 6 six-packs.

TABLE 7.3 Equalizing Marginal Utilities per Dollar

	Movies ($6 each)			Soda ($3 per six-pack)		
	Quantity	Marginal utility	Marginal utility per dollar	Six-packs	Marginal utility	Marginal utility per dollar
A	0	0		10	15	5.00
B	1	50	8.33	8	17	5.67
C	2	38	6.33	6	19	6.33
D	3	33	5.50	4	28	9.33
E	4	29	4.83	2	42	14.00
F	5	25	4.17	0	0	

Figure 7.4 shows why the rule "equalize marginal utility per dollar for all goods" works. Suppose that instead of consuming 2 movies and 6 six-packs (possibility *C*), Lisa consumes 1 movie and 8 six-packs (possibility *B*). She then gets 8.33 units of utility per dollar from movies and 5.67 units per dollar from soda. Lisa can increase her total utility by buying less soda and seeing more movies. If she sees one additional movie and spends less on soda, her total utility from movies increases by 8.33 units per dollar and her total utility from soda decreases by 5.67 units per dollar. Her total utility increases by 2.66 units per dollar, as shown by the blue area.

Or suppose that Lisa consumes 3 movies and 4 six-packs (possibility *D*). In this situation, her

FIGURE 7.4 Equalizing Marginal Utilities per Dollar

myeconlab

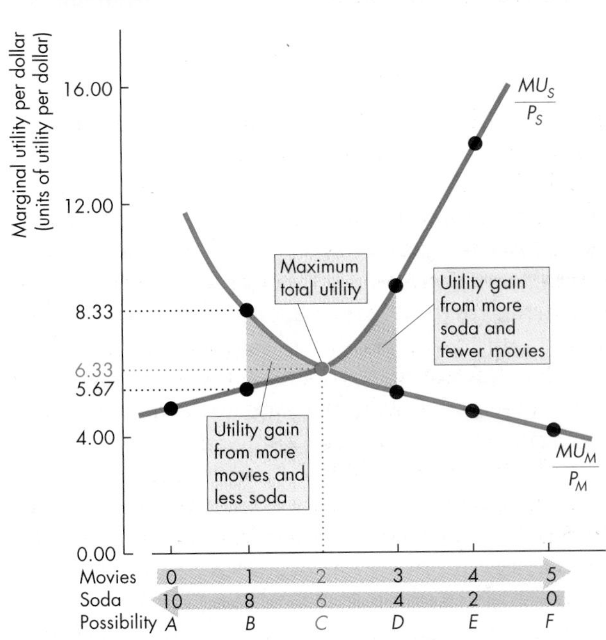

If Lisa sees 1 movie and drinks 8 six-packs (possibility *B*), her marginal utility per dollar for movies exceeds her marginal utility per dollar for soda. She can get more total utility by seeing one more movie and drinking less soda. If she drinks 4 six-packs and sees 3 movies (possibility *D*), her marginal utility per dollar for soda exceeds her marginal utility per dollar for movies. She can increase her total utility by seeing one fewer movie and drinking more soda. When Lisa's marginal utility per dollar for both goods is equal, her total utility is maximized.

marginal utility per dollar for movies (5.50) is less than her marginal utility per dollar for soda (9.33). Lisa can now increase her total utility by seeing one less movie and spending more on soda, as the green area shows.

The Power of Marginal Analysis The method we've just used to find Lisa's utility-maximizing choice of movies and soda is an example of the power of marginal analysis. By comparing the marginal gain from having more of one good with the marginal loss from having less of another good, Lisa is able to ensure that she gets the maximum attainable utility.

The rule to follow is simple: If the marginal utility per dollar for movies exceeds the marginal utility per dollar for soda, see more movies and buy less soda; if the marginal utility per dollar for soda exceeds the marginal utility per dollar for movies, buy more soda and see fewer movies.

More generally, if the marginal gain from an action exceeds the marginal loss, take the action. You will meet this principle time and again in your study of economics. And you will find yourself using it when you make your own economic choices, especially when you must make a big decision.

Units of Utility In maximizing total utility by making the marginal utility per dollar equal for both goods, the units in which utility is measured do not matter. Any arbitrary units will work. It is in this respect that utility is like temperature. Predictions about the freezing point of water don't depend on the temperature scale; and predictions about a household's consumption choice don't depend on the units of utility.

REVIEW QUIZ

1. What is Lisa's goal when she chooses the quantities of movies and soda to consume?
2. What are the two conditions that are met if a consumer is maximizing utility?
3. Explain why equalizing the marginal utility of each good does *not* maximize utility.
4. Explain why equalizing the marginal utility per dollar for each good *does* maximize utility.

myeconlab **Study Plan 7.3**

Predictions of Marginal Utility Theory

We're now going to use marginal utility theory to make some predictions. You will see that marginal utility theory predicts the law of demand. The theory also predicts that a fall in the price of a substitute decreases demand and that for a normal good, a rise in income increases demand. All these effects, which in Chapter 3 we simply assumed, are predictions of marginal utility theory.

A Fall in the Price of a Movie

A fall in the price of a movie, other things remaining the same, changes the quantity of movies demanded and brings a movement along the demand curve for movies. We've already found one point on Lisa's demand curve for movies: When the price of a movie is $6, Lisa sees 2 movies a month. Figure 7.5 shows this point on Lisa's demand curve for movies.

To find another point on her demand curve for movies, we need to work out what Lisa buys when the price of a movie changes. Suppose that the price of a movie falls from $6 to $3 and nothing else changes.

To work out the effect of this change in the price of a movie on Lisa's buying plans, we must first determine the combinations of movies and soda that she can afford at the new prices. Then we calculate the new marginal utilities per dollar. Finally, we determine the combination that makes the marginal utilities per dollar for movies and soda equal.

The rows of Table 7.4 show the combinations of movies and soda that exhaust Lisa's $30 of income when the price of a movie is $3 and the price of a six-pack is $3. Lisa's preferences do not change when prices change, so her marginal utility schedule remains the same as that in Table 7.3. Divide her marginal utility from movies by $3 to get the marginal utility per dollar for movies.

When the price of a movie falls to $3, Lisa sees 5 movies and drinks 5 six-packs. She substitutes movies for soda. Figure 7.5 shows both of these effects. In part (a), we've found another point on Lisa's demand curve for movies. And we've discovered that her demand curve obeys the law of demand. In part (b), we see that a fall in the price of a movie decreases the demand for soda. The demand curve for soda shifts leftward. For Lisa, soda and movies are substitutes.

FIGURE 7.5 A Fall in the Price of a Movie

myeconlab

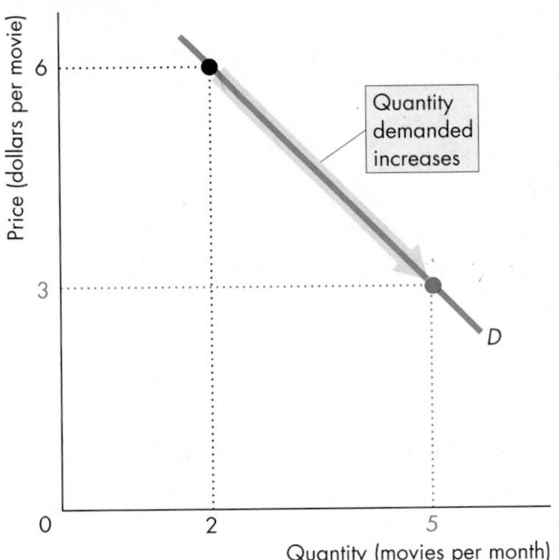

(a) Demand for movies

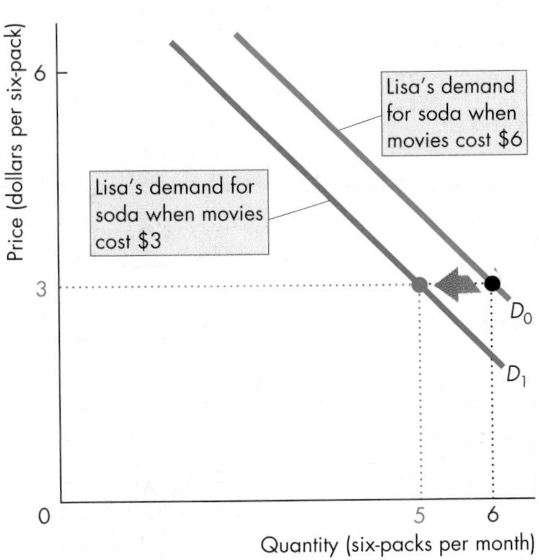

(b) Demand for soda

When the price of a movie falls and the price of soda remains the same, the quantity of movies demanded by Lisa increases, and in part (a), Lisa moves along her demand curve for movies. Also, when the price of a movie falls, Lisa's demand for soda decreases, and in part (b), her demand curve for soda shifts leftward. For Lisa, soda and movies are substitutes.

TABLE 7.4 How a Change in Price of Movies Affects Lisa's Choices

Movies ($3 each)		Soda ($3 per six-pack)	
Quantity	**Marginal utility per dollar**	**Six-packs**	**Marginal utility per dollar**
0		10	5.00
1	16.67	9	5.33
2	**12.67**	8	5.67
3	11.00	7	6.00
4	9.67	**6**	**6.33**
5	8.33	5	8.33
6	7.00	4	9.33
7	6.00	3	12.00
8	5.00	2	14.00
9	4.00	1	25.00
10	3.00	0	

A Rise in the Price of Soda

In Fig. 7.5(b), we know only one point on Lisa's demand curve for soda when the price of a movie is $3. To find Lisa's demand curve for soda, we must see how she responds to a change in the price of soda. Suppose that the price of soda rises from $3 to $6 a six-pack. The rows of Table 7.5 show the combinations of movies and soda that exhaust Lisa's $30 of income when the price of a movie is $3 and the price of a six-pack is $6. Again, Lisa's preferences don't change when the price changes. Divide Lisa's marginal utility from soda by $6 to get her marginal utility per dollar for soda.

Lisa now drinks 2 six-packs a month and sees 6 movies a month. Lisa *substitutes* movies for soda. Figure 7.6 shows both of these effects. In part (a), we've found another point on Lisa's demand curve for soda. And we've confirmed that this demand curve obeys the law of demand. In part (b), we see that a rise in the price of soda increases the demand for movies. The demand curve for movies shifts rightward. This change again tells us that for Lisa, soda and movies are substitutes.

TABLE 7.5 How a Change in Price of Soda Affects Lisa's Choices

Movies ($3 each)		Soda ($6 per six-pack)	
Quantity	Marginal utility per dollar	Six-packs	Marginal utility per dollar
0		5	4.17
2	12.67	4	4.67
4	9.67	3	6.00
6	7.00	2	7.00
8	5.00	1	12.50
10	3.00	0	

Marginal utility theory predicts these two results:

1. When the price of a good rises, the quantity demanded of that good decreases.
2. If the price of one good rises, the demand for another good that can serve as a substitute increases.

These predictions of marginal utility theory sound familiar because they correspond to the assumptions that we made about demand in Chapter 3. There, we assumed that the demand curve for a good slopes downward and that a rise in the price of a substitute increases demand.

We have now seen that marginal utility theory predicts how the quantities of goods and services that people demand respond to price changes. The theory enables us to derive the consumer's demand curve and predict how the demand curve for one good shifts when the price of another good changes.

Marginal utility theory also helps us to predict how demand changes when income changes. Let's study the effects of a change in income on demand.

FIGURE 7.6 A Rise in the Price of Soda

myeconlab

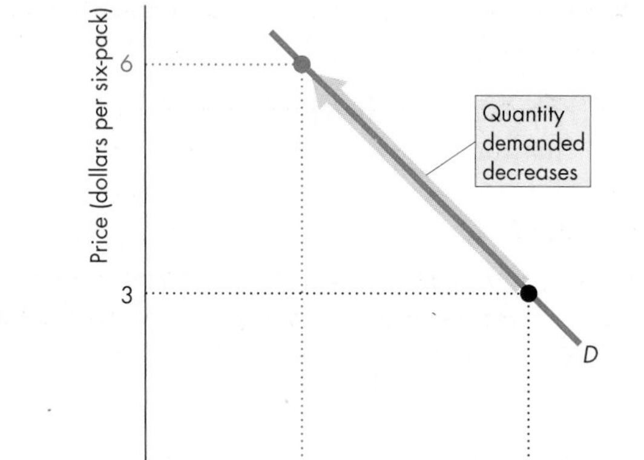

(a) Demand for soda

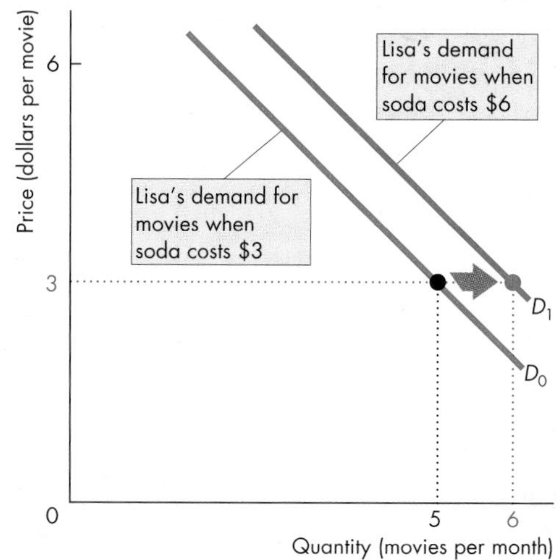

(b) Demand for movies

When the price of soda rises and the price of a movie remains the same, the quantity of soda demanded by Lisa decreases, and in part (a), Lisa moves along her demand curve for soda. Also, when the price of soda rises, Lisa's demand for movies increases, and in part (b), her demand curve for movies shifts rightward.

A Rise in Income

Let's suppose that Lisa's income increases to $42 a month and that the price of a movie is $3 and the price of a six-pack is $3. We saw in Table 7.4 that with these prices and with an income of $30 a month, Lisa sees 5 movies and drinks 5 six-packs of soda a month. We want to compare this choice of movies and soda with Lisa's choice when her income is $42. Table 7.6 shows the calculations needed to make the comparison. With $42, Lisa can see 14 movies a month and buy no soda or buy 14 six-packs a month and see no movies or choose any combination of the two goods in the rows of the table. We calculate the marginal utility per dollar in exactly the same way as we did before and find the quantities at which the marginal utility per dollar for movies and the marginal utility per dollar for soda are equal.

When Lisa's income is $42, the marginal utility per dollar for each good is equal when she sees 7 movies and drinks 7 six-packs of soda a month.

By comparing this situation with that in Table 7.4, we see that with an additional $12 a month, Lisa buys 2 more six-packs of soda and sees 2 more movies a month. Lisa's response arises from her preferences, as described by her marginal utilities. Different preferences would produce different quantitative responses. With a larger income, the consumer always buys more of a *normal* good and less of an *inferior* good. For Lisa, soda and movies are normal goods. When her income increases, Lisa buys more of both goods.

You have now completed your study of the marginal utility theory of a household's consumption choices. Table 7.7 summarizes the key assumptions, implications, and predictions of the theory.

TABLE 7.6 Lisa's Choices with an Income of $42 a Month

Movies ($3 each)		Soda ($3 per six-pack)	
Quantity	**Marginal utility per dollar**	**Six-packs**	**Marginal utility per dollar**
0		14	3.67
1	16.67	13	4.00
2	12.67	12	4.33
3	11.00	11	4.67
4	9.67	10	5.00
5	**8.33**	9	5.33
6	7.00	8	5.67
7	6.00	7	6.00
8	5.00	6	6.33
9	4.00	**5**	**8.33**
10	3.00	4	9.33
11	2.00	3	12.00
12	1.00	2	14.00
13	0.67	1	25.00
14	0.33	0	

TABLE 7.7 Marginal Utility Theory

Assumptions

- A consumer derives utility from the goods consumed.
- Each additional unit of consumption yields additional total utility—marginal utility is positive.
- As the quantity of a good consumed increases, marginal utility decreases.
- A consumer's aim is to maximize total utility.

Implication

Total utility is maximized when all the available income is spent and when the marginal utility per dollar is equal for all goods.

Predictions

- Other things remaining the same, the higher the price of a good, the smaller is the quantity bought (the law of demand).
- The higher the price of a good, the greater is the quantity bought of substitutes for that good.
- The larger the consumer's income, the greater is the quantity demanded of normal goods.

Temperature: An Analogy

Utility is similar to temperature. Both are abstract concepts, and both have units of measurement that are arbitrary. You can't *observe* temperature. You can observe water turning to steam if it is hot enough or turning to ice if it is cold enough. And you can construct an instrument—a thermometer—that can help you to predict when such changes will occur. We call the scale on the thermometer *temperature* and we call the units of temperature *degrees*. But these degree units are arbitrary. We can use Celsius units or Fahrenheit units or some other units.

The concept of utility helps us to make predictions about consumption choices in much the same way that the concept of temperature helps us to make predictions about physical phenomena.

Admittedly, marginal utility theory does not enable us to predict how buying plans change with the same precision that a thermometer enables us to predict when water will turn to ice or steam. But the theory provides important insights into buying plans and has some powerful implications. It helps us to understand why people buy more of a good or service when its price falls and why people buy more of most goods when their incomes increase. It also resolves the paradox of value, as you are about to see.

REVIEW QUIZ

1. When the price of a good falls and the prices of other goods and a consumer's income remain the same, what happens to the consumption of the good whose price has fallen and to the consumption of other goods?
2. Elaborate on your answer to the previous question by using demand curves. For which good is there a change in demand and for which is there a change in the quantity demanded?
3. If a consumer's income increases and if all goods are normal goods, how does the quantity bought of each good change?

myeconlab Study Plan 7.4

We're going to end this chapter by returning to a recurring theme throughout your study of economics: the concept of efficiency and the distinction between price and value.

Efficiency, Price, and Value

Marginal utility theory deepens our understanding of efficiency and clarifies the distinction between value and price. Let's find out how.

Consumer Efficiency

When Lisa allocates her limited budget to maximize utility, she is using her resources efficiently. Any other allocation of her budget wastes some resources.

But when Lisa has allocated her limited budget to maximize utility, she is *on* her demand curve for each good. A demand curve is a description of the quantity demanded at each price when utility is maximized. When we studied efficiency in Chapter 5, we learned that value equals marginal benefit and that a demand curve is also a willingness-to-pay curve. It tells us a consumer's *marginal benefit*—the benefit from consuming an additional unit of a good. You can now give the idea of marginal benefit a deeper meaning:

> Marginal benefit is the maximum price a consumer is willing to pay for an extra unit of a good or service when utility is maximized.

The Paradox of Value

For centuries, philosophers have been puzzled by a paradox that we raised at the start of this chapter. Water, which is essential to life itself, costs little, but diamonds, which are useless in comparison to water, are expensive. Why? Adam Smith tried to solve this paradox. But not until the theory of marginal utility had been developed could anyone give a satisfactory answer.

You can solve this puzzle by distinguishing between *total* utility and *marginal* utility. The total utility that we get from water is enormous. But remember, the more we consume of something, the smaller is its marginal utility. We use so much water that its marginal utility—the benefit we get from one more glass of water—diminishes to a small value. Diamonds, on the other hand, have a small total utility relative to water, but because we buy few diamonds, they have a high marginal utility. When a household has maximized its total utility, it has allocated its budget in the way that makes the marginal utility per dollar equal for all goods. That is, the marginal utility from a good divided by the price of the good is equal for all goods.

FIGURE 7.7 The Paradox of Value

myeconlab

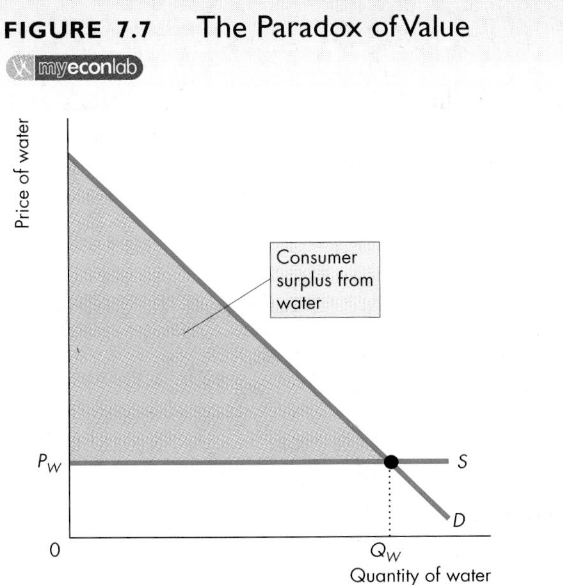

(a) Water

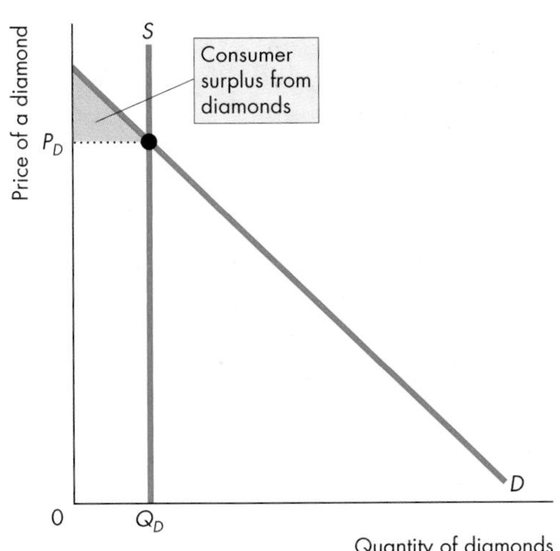

(b) Diamonds

Part (a) shows the demand for and supply of water. Supply is perfectly elastic at the price P_W. At this price, the quantity of water consumed is Q_W and consumer surplus is the large green triangle. Part (b) shows the demand for and supply of diamonds. Supply is perfectly inelastic at the quantity Q_D. At this quantity, the price of a diamond is P_D and consumer surplus is the small green triangle. Water is valuable—has a large consumer surplus—but cheap. Diamonds are less valuable than water—have a smaller consumer surplus—but are expensive.

This equality of marginal utilities per dollar holds true for diamonds and water: Diamonds have a high price and a high marginal utility. Water has a low price and a low marginal utility. When the high marginal utility of diamonds is divided by the high price of a diamond, the result is a number that equals the low marginal utility of water divided by the low price of water. The marginal utility per dollar is the same for diamonds as for water.

Value and Consumer Surplus

Another way to think about the paradox of value uses *consumer surplus*. Figure 7.7 explains the paradox of value by using this idea. The supply of water (part a) is perfectly elastic at price P_W, so the quantity of water consumed is Q_W and the consumer surplus from water is the large green area. The supply of diamonds (part b) is perfectly inelastic at the quantity Q_D, so the price of diamonds is P_D and the consumer surplus from diamonds is the small green area. Water is cheap but brings a large consumer surplus, while diamonds are expensive but bring a small consumer surplus.

REVIEW QUIZ

1. Can you explain why, along a demand curve, a consumer's choices are efficient?
2. Can you explain the paradox of value?
3. Is the marginal utility from water or from diamonds greater? Is the total utility from water or from diamonds greater? Is the consumer surplus from water or from diamonds greater?

myeconlab **Study Plan 7.5**

You have now completed your study of the marginal utility theory. And you've seen how the theory can be used to explain consumption choices. You can see the theory in action once again in *Reading Between the Lines* on pp. 166–167, where it is used to explain why child-care workers earn so much less than football players.

The next chapter presents an alternative theory of household behavior. To help you see the connection between the two theories, we use the same example. We'll meet Lisa again and discover another way of understanding how she gets the most out of her $30 a month.

READING BETWEEN THE LINES

A Paradox of Value in the Labor Market

http://www.nytimes.com

Long Days, Challenging Clients, Potty-Training Experience Useful

September 24, 2006

Like the character played by Eddie Murphy in "Daddy Day Care," Todd Cole needed the push of a layoff to join the small number of men who work as child care providers. . . .

Mr. Cole became a registered family day care provider in February, and the state of New York now allows him to watch six children over the age of 2, as well as two school-age children. . . .

Men make up only about 4 percent of those who provide either care or early childhood education to children 5 and younger, and that number has stayed about the same since the 1980s, said Bryan G. Nelson, founder of MenTeach, a Minneapolis nonprofit group that supports men who teach. . . .

In May 2005, the Bureau of Labor Statistics estimated that child care workers in the state of New York had an annual average wage of $21,850.

http://www.nytimes.com

Vick Signs 10-Year Deal to Remain With the Falcons

December 24, 2005

. . . Michael Vick, 24, became the highest-paid player in the N.F.L. yesterday, when he agreed to a 10-year contract through 2013 that could be worth as much as $130 million, according to an executive with an N.F.L. team who had knowledge of the deal. It includes a $37 million bonus, outstripping the $34.5 million that Indianapolis Colts quarterback Peyton Manning received with his seven-year, $98 million deal last spring. . . .

Essence of the Stories

- In New York, child-care workers earn an average wage of $21,850 per year.
- Todd Cole is allowed to care for 8 children.
- Michael Vick has a 10-year contract with the Atlanta Falcons that will earn him up to $130 million.

Economic Analysis

- If resources are used efficiently, the marginal utility per dollar for the services of a child-care worker equals the marginal utility per dollar for the services of a football player.

- That is,

$$\frac{MU_C}{P_C} = \frac{MU_F}{P_F}$$

where MU_C is the marginal utility and P_C is the price of the services of a child-care worker, and MU_F is the marginal utility and P_F is the price of the services of a football player.

- You've seen in the news articles that a child-care worker earns $21,850 a year (on the average) and that football player Michael Vick will earn $130 million over 10 years, or $13 million a year.

- If we put these numbers into the above formula, we get

$$\frac{MU_C}{\$21{,}850} = \frac{MU_F}{\$13{,}000{,}000}.$$

Equivalently,

$$\frac{MU_F}{MU_C} = 595.$$

- Is the marginal utility from the services of Michael Vick really 595 times that from the services of a child-care worker such as Todd Cole in the news article?

- Think for a minute and you will realize that a child-care worker serves about 8 consumers at a time while a football player, especially one as good as Michael Vick, serves, both live and through television, millions of consumers at a time.

- Assume that Michael Vick serves just 1 million consumers and that Todd Cole serves 8.

- Then the price of Todd Cole's services per customer served is

$$\frac{\$21{,}850}{8} = \$2{,}731.25,$$

and the price of Michael Vick's services per customer served is $13.

- Using these prices of the services per customer served, Todd Cole is worth 210 times as much as Michael Vick.

- Figure 1 shows the market for child-care workers. The equilibrium quantity is 1 million workers, and the wage rate is $21,850 a year.

- Figure 2 shows the market for professional football players. The equilibrium quantity is 1,500 players and the average wage rate is $1,000,000 a year. (Michael Vick earns much more than the average player.)

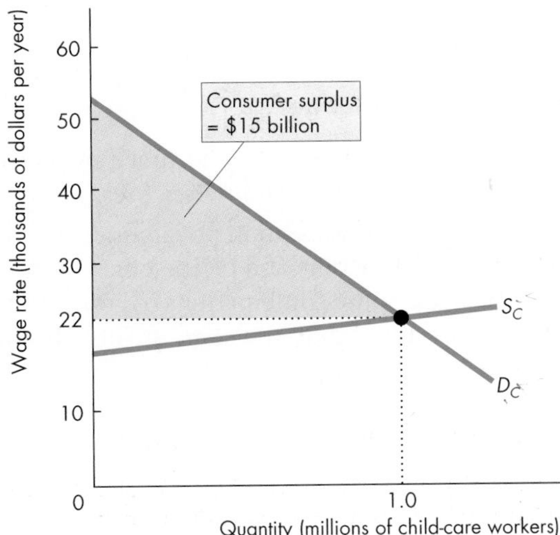

Figure 1 The value of child-care workers

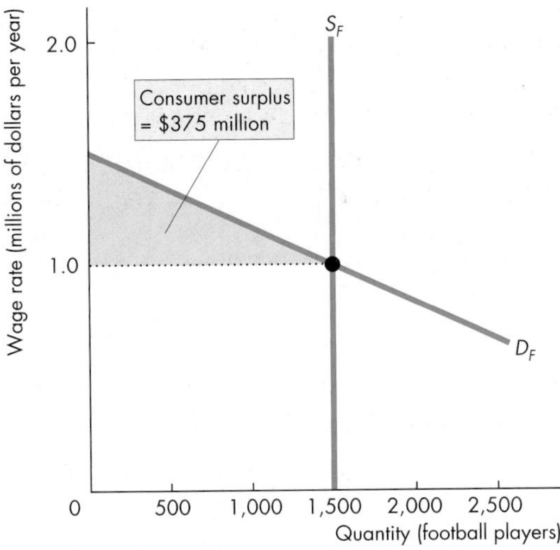

Figure 2 The value of football players

- On the basis of our assumptions, the consumer surplus from child-care workers is much greater than that from football players.

- Although child-care workers earn a smaller wage rate than professional football players, the value placed on child-care workers is far greater than the value placed on football players, by both the individual who consumes their services and society.

SUMMARY

Key Points

The Household's Budget (pp. 154–155)

- A household's choices are determined by its consumption possibilities and preferences.
- A household's consumption possibilities are constrained by its income and by the prices of goods and services. Some combinations of goods and services are affordable, and some are not affordable.

Preferences and Utility (pp. 156–157)

- A household's preferences can be described by marginal utility.
- The key assumption of marginal utility theory is that the marginal utility of a good or service decreases as consumption of the good or service increases.
- Marginal utility theory assumes that people buy the affordable combination of goods and services that maximizes their total utility.

Maximizing Utility (pp. 158–160)

- Total utility is maximized when all the available income is spent and when the marginal utility per dollar for each good is equal.
- If the marginal utility per dollar for good *A* exceeds that for good *B*, total utility increases if the quantity purchased of good *A* increases and the quantity purchased of good *B* decreases.

Predictions of Marginal Utility Theory (pp. 160–164)

- Marginal utility theory predicts the law of demand. That is, other things remaining the same, the higher the price of a good, the smaller is the quantity demanded of that good.
- Marginal utility theory also predicts that, other things remaining the same, the larger the consumer's income, the larger is the quantity demanded of a normal good.

Efficiency, Price, and Value (pp. 164–165)

- When a consumer maximizes utility, he or she is using resources efficiently.
- Marginal utility theory resolves the paradox of value.
- When we talk loosely about value, we are thinking of *total* utility or consumer surplus. But price is related to *marginal* utility.
- Water, which we consume in large amounts, has a high total utility and a large consumer surplus, but the price of water is low and the marginal utility from water is low.
- Diamonds, which we consume in small amounts, have a low total utility and a small consumer surplus, but the price of a diamond is high and the marginal utility from diamonds is high.

Key Figures and Table

Key Terms

PROBLEMS

myeconlab **Tests, Study Plan, Solutions***

1. Jason enjoys DVDs and spy novels and spends $60 a month on them. The price of a DVD is $20 and the price of a spy novel is $10.
   a. Draw Jason's budget line. Label the combinations of DVDs and spy novels that Jason cannot afford and the combinations that Jason can afford.
   b. What is Jason's real income in terms of spy novels?
   c. What is the relative price of a DVD?
2. Jason in problem 1 receives an additional $30 a month to spend on DVDs and spy novels, so that he now has a total of $90 a month to spend on these pursuits. The prices haven't changed.
   a. Draw Jason's new budget line.
   b. What is Jason's real income in terms of spy novels?
   c. What is the relative price of a DVD?
3. Jason in problem 2 continues to receive an additional $30 a month to spend on DVDs and spy novels, so that he still has a total of $90 a month to spend on these pursuits. At the same time, the price of a DVD falls to $15.
   a. Draw Jason's new budget line.
   b. What is Jason's real income in terms of DVDs?
   c. What is Jason's real income in terms of spy novels?
   d. What is the relative price of a DVD?
4. The table shows the utility that Jason gets from DVDs and spy novels.

Quantity per month	Utility from DVDs	Utility from spy novels
1	60	35
2	110	60
3	150	75
4	180	85
5	200	90
6	206	92

   a. Draw graphs showing Jason's total utility from DVDs and from spy novels.
   b. Compare the two utility graphs. What can you say about Jason's preferences?
   c. Draw graphs that show Jason's marginal utility from DVDs and from spy novels.
   d. What do the two marginal utility graphs tell you about Jason's preferences?
   e. If the price of a DVD is $20 and the price of a spy novel is $10, and Jason has $60 to spend on these two goods, how many of each does he buy?
5. Max enjoys windsurfing and snorkeling. The table shows the marginal utility he gets from each activity.

Hours per day	Marginal utility from windsurfing	Marginal utility from snorkeling
1	120	40
2	100	36
3	80	30
4	60	22
5	40	12
6	12	10
7	10	8

   Max has $35 to spend, and he can spend as much time as he likes on his leisure pursuits. Windsurfing equipment rents for $10 an hour, and snorkeling equipment rents for $5 an hour.
   How long does Max spend windsurfing and how long does he spend snorkeling?
6. Max's sister gives him an extra $20 a month to spend on his leisure pursuits, so he now has $55 a month. Everything else remains as in problem 5.
   a. Draw a graph that shows Max's consumption possibilities.
   b. How many hours does Max now choose to windsurf and how many hours does he choose to snorkel?
7. Max in problem 5 is offered a special deal on windsurfing equipment: a rental rate of $5 an hour. How many hours does Max now windsurf and how many hours does he snorkel?
8. Max in problem 5 takes a Club Med vacation, the cost of which includes unlimited sports activities. There is no extra charge for equipment. If Max windsurfs and snorkels for 6 hours a day, how many hours does he windsurf and how many hours does he snorkel?
9. Max's utility schedules are those shown in problem 5, and he has $55 a month to spend on windsurfing and snorkeling. Snorkeling equipment rents

*Solutions to odd-numbered problems are provided.

for $5 an hour.

a. Find two points on Max's demand curve for renting windsurfing equipment.
b. Draw Max's demand curve for renting windsurfing equipment.
c. Is Max's demand for renting windsurfing equipment elastic or inelastic?

10. Max's utility schedules are those shown in problem 5, and he has $55 a month to spend on windsurfing and snorkeling. Snorkeling equipment rents for $5 an hour. The price of renting windsurfing equipment falls from $10 an hour to $5 an hour.
    a. What happens to Max's demand for snorkeling equipment?
    b. Draw Max's demand curve for snorkeling equipment.
    c. What is Max's cross elasticity of demand for snorkeling equipment with respect to the price of windsurfing equipment?
    d. Are snorkeling equipment and windsurfing equipment substitutes or complements for Max?
11. Max's utility schedules are those shown in problem 5. Show the effect on
    a. Max's demand curve for windsurfing equipment when his budget increases from $35 to $55, windsurfing equipment rents for $10 an hour, and snorkeling equipment rents for $5 an hour.
    b. Max's demand curve for snorkeling equipment when his budget increases from $35 to $55, windsurfing equipment rents for $10 an hour, and snorkeling equipment rents for $5 an hour.
    c. Is windsurfing equipment rental a normal good or an inferior good for Max?
    d. Is snorkeling equipment rental a normal good or an inferior good for Max?
12. Ben spends $50 a year on 2 bunches of flowers and $50 a year on 10,000 gallons of tap water. Ben is maximizing utility and his marginal utility from water is 0.5 unit per gallon.
    a. Are flowers or water more valuable to Ben?
    b. Explain how Ben's expenditure on flowers and water illustrates the paradox of value.

CRITICAL THINKING

1. Study *Reading Between the Lines* (pp. 166–167) about the incomes of child-care workers and football players. Suppose that a new technology enables a person to effectively care for 100 children at a time and that an ad-blocking technology makes it impossible for operators of television stations to collect advertising revenue. What will happen to
   a. The marginal utility of a teacher?
   b. The wage rate of a child-care worker?
   c. The number of child-care workers?
   d. The marginal utility of a football player?
   e. The wage rate of a football player?
   f. The number of football players?
2. Smoking is banned on most airline flights. Use marginal utility theory to explain
   a. The effect of the ban on the utility of smokers.
   b. How the ban influences the decisions of smokers.
   c. The effects of the ban on the utility of nonsmokers.
   d. How the ban influences the decisions of nonsmokers.

WEB ACTIVITIES

myeconlab Links to Web sites

1. Read what Henry Schimberg, former CEO of Coca-Cola, said about the market for bottled water. Use marginal utility theory to explain and interpret his remarks.
2. Obtain information about the prices on the Maryland Transit Administration system.
   a. Show the effects of the different ticket options on the consumer's budget line.
   b. How would a person decide whether to pay for each trip, to buy a day pass, or to buy a pass for a longer period? Use marginal utility theory to answer this question.
   c. How do you think the number of riders would change if the price of a single trip fell and the price of a day pass increased?

CHAPTER 8

Possibilities, Preferences, and Choices

Subterranean Movements

Like the continents floating on the earth's mantle, our spending patterns change steadily over time. On such subterranean movements, business empires rise and fall. We now can choose whether to buy our music on a CD or download it and play it on an iPod or burn our own CD. As the prices of a music download, an iPod, and a CD burner have tumbled, people are increasingly buying downloads, and the sales of music CDs have taken a hit.

The prices of electronic textbooks—e-books—have also fallen, and those books are now cheaper than printed textbooks. Yet most students continue to buy printed textbooks. Why, when e-books are cheaper than printed books, have e-books not caught on and replaced printed books in the same way that the new music technologies have replaced CDs?

Subterranean movements also govern the way we spend our time. The average workweek has fallen steadily from 70 hours a week in the nineteenth century to 35 hours a week today. While the average workweek is now much shorter than it once was, far more people now have jobs. Why has the average workweek declined?

In this chapter, we're going to study a model of choice that predicts the effects of changes in prices and incomes on what people buy and the effects of changes in wage rates on how people allocate their time between leisure and work. At the end of the chapter, in *Reading Between the Lines*, we use the model to explain why music downloads are killing CDs but e-books are not replacing printed textbooks.

After studying this chapter, you will be able to

- Describe a household's budget line and show how it changes when prices or income change
- Make a map of preferences by using indifference curves and explain the principle of diminishing marginal rate of substitution
- Predict the effects of changes in prices and income on consumption choices
- Predict the effects of changes in wage rates on work-leisure choices

Consumption Possibilities

Consumption choices are limited by income and by prices. A household has a given amount of income to spend and cannot influence the prices of the goods and services it buys. A household's **budget line** describes the limits to its consumption choices.

Let's look at Lisa's budget line.[1] Lisa has an income of $30 a month to spend. She buys two goods: movies and soda. The price of a movie is $6, and the price of soda is $3 a six-pack. Figure 8.1 shows alternative affordable ways for Lisa to consume movies and soda. Row *A* says that she can buy 10 six-packs of soda and see no movies, a combination of movies and soda that exhausts her monthly income of $30. Row *F* says that Lisa can watch 5 movies and drink no soda—another combination that exhausts the $30 available. Each of the other rows in the table also exhausts Lisa's income. (Check that each of the other rows costs exactly $30.) The numbers in the table define Lisa's consumption possibilities. We can graph Lisa's consumption possibilities as points *A* through *F* in Fig. 8.1.

Divisible and Indivisible Goods Some goods—called divisible goods—can be bought in any quantity desired. Examples are gasoline and electricity. We can best understand household choice if we suppose that all goods and services are divisible. For example, Lisa can consume a half a movie a month on the average by seeing one movie every two months. When we think of goods as being divisible, the consumption possibilities are not just the points *A* through *F* shown in Fig. 8.1, but those points plus all the intermediate points that form the line running from *A* to *F*. Such a line is a budget line.

Lisa's budget line is a constraint on her choices. It marks the boundary between what is affordable and what is unaffordable. She can afford any point on the line and inside it. She cannot afford any point outside the line. The constraint on her consumption depends on prices and her income, and the constraint changes when the price of a good or her income changes. Let's see how by studying the budget equation.

[1] If you have studied Chapter 7 on marginal utility theory, you have already met Lisa. This tale of her thirst for soda and zeal for movies will sound familiar to you—up to a point. But in this chapter, we're going to use a different method for representing preferences—one that does not require us to resort to the idea of utility.

FIGURE 8.1 The Budget Line

myeconlab

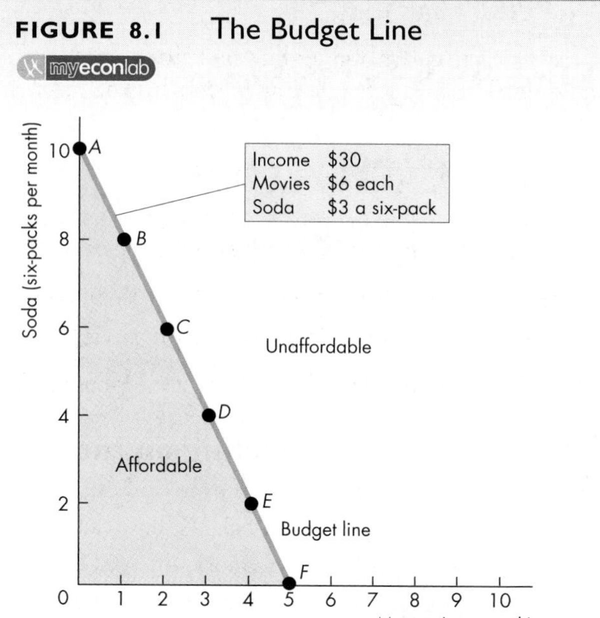

Consumption possibility	Movies (per month)	Soda (six-packs per month)
A	0	10
B	1	8
C	2	6
D	3	4
E	4	2
F	5	0

Lisa's budget line shows the boundary between what she can and cannot afford. The rows of the table list Lisa's affordable combinations of movies and soda when her income is $30, the price of soda is $3 a six-pack, and the price of a movie is $6. For example, row *A* tells us that Lisa spends all of her $30 income when she buys 10 six-packs and sees no movies. The figure graphs Lisa's budget line. Points *A* through *F* on the graph represent the rows of the table. For divisible goods, the budget line is the continuous line *AF*. To calculate the equation for Lisa's budget line, start with expenditure equal to income:

$$\$3Q_S + \$6Q_M = \$30.$$

Divide by $3 to obtain

$$Q_S + 2Q_M = 10.$$

Subtract $2Q_M$ from both sides to obtain

$$Q_S = 10 - 2Q_M.$$

The Budget Equation

We can describe the budget line by using a *budget equation.* The budget equation starts with the fact that

$$\text{Expenditure} = \text{Income}.$$

Expenditure is equal to the sum of the price of each good multiplied by the quantity bought. For Lisa,

$$\text{Expenditure} = (\text{Price of soda} \times \text{Quantity of soda}) + (\text{Price of movie} \times \text{Quantity of movies}).$$

Call the price of soda P_S, the quantity of soda Q_S, the price of a movie P_M, the quantity of movies Q_M, and income Y. We can now write Lisa's budget equation as

$$P_SQ_S + P_MQ_M = Y.$$

Or, using the prices Lisa faces, \$3 for a six-pack and \$6 for a movie, and Lisa's income, \$30, we get

$$\$3Q_S + \$6Q_M = \$30.$$

Lisa can choose any quantities of soda (Q_S) and movies (Q_M) that satisfy this equation. To find the relationship between these quantities, divide both sides of the equation by the price of soda (P_S) to get

$$Q_S + \frac{P_M}{P_S} \times Q_M = \frac{Y}{P_S}.$$

Now subtract the term $P_M/P_S \times Q_M$ from both sides of this equation to get

$$Q_S = \frac{Y}{P_S} - \frac{P_M}{P_S} \times Q_M.$$

For Lisa, income (Y) is \$30, the price of a movie (P_M) is \$6, and the price of soda (P_S) is \$3 a six-pack. So Lisa must choose the quantities of movies and soda to satisfy the equation

$$Q_S = \frac{\$30}{\$3} - \frac{\$6}{\$3} \times Q_M,$$

or

$$Q_S = 10 - 2Q_M.$$

To interpret the equation, look at the budget line in Fig. 8.1 and check that the equation delivers that budget line. First, set Q_M equal to zero. The budget equation tells us that Q_S, the quantity of soda, is Y/P_S, which is 10 six-packs. This combination of Q_M and Q_S is the one shown in row *A* of the table in Fig. 8.1. Next set Q_M equal to 5. Q_S now equals zero (row *F* of the table). Check that you can derive the other rows.

The budget equation contains two variables chosen by the household (Q_M and Q_S) and two variables (Y/P_S and P_M/P_S) that the household takes as given. Let's look more closely at these variables.

Real Income A household's **real income** is the household's income expressed as a quantity of goods the household can afford to buy. Expressed in terms of soda, Lisa's real income is Y/P_S. This quantity is the maximum number of six-packs that she can buy. It is equal to her money income divided by the price of soda. Lisa's income is \$30 and the price of soda is \$3 a six-pack, so her real income in terms of soda is 10 six-packs, which is shown in Fig. 8.1 as the point at which the budget line intersects the *y*-axis.

Relative Price A **relative price** is the price of one good divided by the price of another good. In Lisa's budget equation, the variable P_M/P_S is the relative price of a movie in terms of soda. For Lisa, P_M is \$6 a movie and P_S is \$3 a six-pack, so P_M/P_S is equal to 2 six-packs per movie. That is, to see one more movie, Lisa must give up 2 six-packs.

You've just calculated Lisa's opportunity cost of a movie. Recall that the opportunity cost of an action is the best alternative forgone. For Lisa to see 1 more movie a month, she must forgo 2 six-packs. You've also calculated Lisa's opportunity cost of soda. For Lisa to consume 2 more six-packs a month, she must forgo seeing 1 movie. So her opportunity cost of 2 six-packs is 1 movie.

The relative price of a movie in terms of soda is the magnitude of the slope of Lisa's budget line. To calculate the slope of the budget line, recall the formula for slope (see the Chapter 1 Appendix): Slope equals the change in the variable measured on the *y*-axis divided by the change in the variable measured on the *x*-axis as we move along the line. In Lisa's case (Fig. 8.1), the variable measured on the *y*-axis is the quantity of soda and the variable measured on the *x*-axis is the quantity of movies. Along Lisa's budget line, as soda decreases from 10 to 0 six-packs, movies increase from 0 to 5. So the magnitude of the slope of the budget line is 10 six-packs divided by 5 movies, or 2 six-packs per movie. The magnitude of this slope is exactly the same as the relative price we've just calculated. It is also the opportunity cost of a movie.

A Change in Prices When prices change, so does the budget line. The lower the price of the good measured on the horizontal axis, other things remaining the same, the flatter is the budget line. For example, if the price of a movie falls from \$6 to \$3, real income

FIGURE 8.2 Changes in Prices and Income

myeconlab

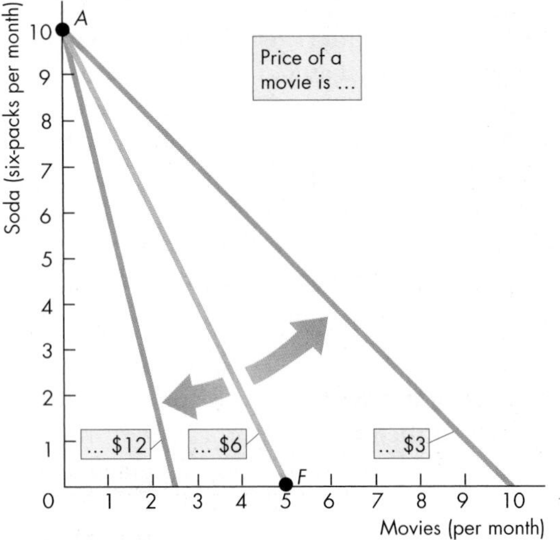

(a) A change in price

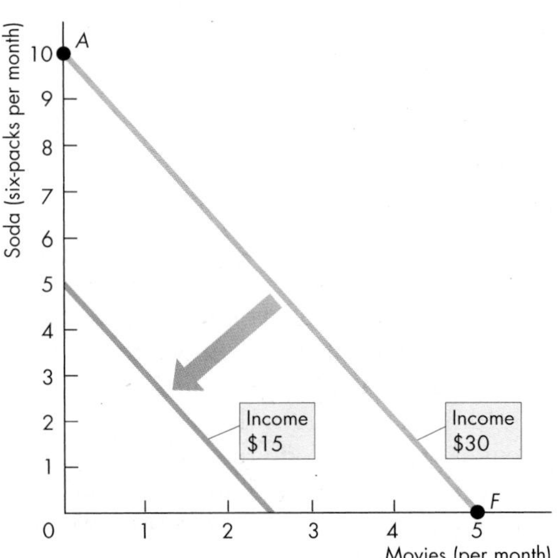

(b) A change in income

In part (a), the price of a movie changes. A fall in the price from $6 to $3 rotates the budget line outward and makes it flatter. A rise in the price from $6 to $12 rotates the budget line inward and makes it steeper.

In part (b), income falls from $30 to $15 while the prices of movies and soda remain constant. The budget line shifts leftward, but its slope does not change.

in terms of soda does not change but the relative price of a movie falls. The budget line rotates outward and becomes flatter, as Fig. 8.2(a) illustrates. The higher the price of the good measured on the horizontal axis, other things remaining the same, the steeper is the budget line. For example, if the price of a movie rises from $6 to $12, the relative price of a movie increases. The budget line rotates inward and becomes steeper, as Fig. 8.2(a) illustrates.

A Change in Income A change in money income changes real income but does not change the relative price. The budget line shifts, but its slope does not change. The bigger a household's money income, the bigger is real income and the farther to the right is the budget line. The smaller a household's money income, the smaller is real income and the farther to the left is the budget line. Figure 8.2(b) shows the effect of a change in money income on Lisa's budget line. The initial budget line when Lisa's income is $30 is the same one that we began with in Fig. 8.1. The new budget line shows how much Lisa can consume if her income falls to $15 a month. The two budget lines have the same slope because the relative price is the same. The new budget line is closer to the origin because Lisa's real income has decreased.

REVIEW QUIZ

1. What does a household's budget line show?
2. How does the relative price and a household's real income influence its budget line?
3. If a household has an income of $40 and buys only bus rides at $4 each and magazines at $2 each, what is the equation of the household's budget line?
4. If the price of one good changes, what happens to the relative price and to the slope of the household's budget line?
5. If a household's money income changes and prices do not change, what happens to the household's real income and budget line?

myeconlab **Study Plan 8.1**

We've studied the limits to what a household can consume. Let's now learn how we can describe preferences and make a map that contains a lot of information about a household's preferences.

Preferences and Indifference Curves

You are going to discover a very neat idea: that of drawing a map of a person's preferences. A preference map is based on the intuitively appealing idea that people can sort all the possible combinations of goods into three groups: preferred, not preferred, and indifferent. To make this idea more concrete, let's ask Lisa to tell us how she ranks various combinations of movies and soda.

Figure 8.3 shows part of Lisa's answer. She tells us that she currently consumes 2 movies and 6 six-packs a month at point *C*. She then lists all the combinations of movies and soda that she says are just as acceptable to her as her current consumption. When we plot these combinations of movies and soda, we get the green curve in Fig. 8.3(a). This curve is the key element in a map of preferences and is called an indifference curve.

An **indifference curve** is a line that shows combinations of goods among which a consumer is *indifferent*. The indifference curve in Fig. 8.3(a) tells us that Lisa is just as happy to consume 2 movies and 6 six-packs a month at point *C* as she is to consume the combination of movies and soda at point *G* or at any other point along the curve.

Lisa also says that she prefers all the combinations of movies and soda above the indifference curve in Fig. 8.3(a)—the yellow area—to those on the indifference curve. And she prefers any combination on the indifference curve to any combination in the gray area below the indifference curve.

The indifference curve in Fig. 8.3(a) is just one of a whole family of such curves. This indifference curve appears again in Fig. 8.3(b) labeled I_1. The curves labeled I_0 and I_2 are two other indifference curves. Lisa prefers any point on indifference curve I_2 to any point on indifference curve I_1, and she prefers any point on I_1 to any point on I_0. We refer to I_2 as being a higher indifference curve than I_1 and I_1 as being higher than I_0.

A preference map is a series of indifference curves that resemble the contour lines on a map. By looking at the shape of the contour lines on a map, we can draw conclusions about the terrain. Similarly, by looking at the shape of indifference curves, we can draw conclusions about a person's preferences.

Let's learn how to "read" a preference map.

FIGURE 8.3 A Preference Map

myeconlab

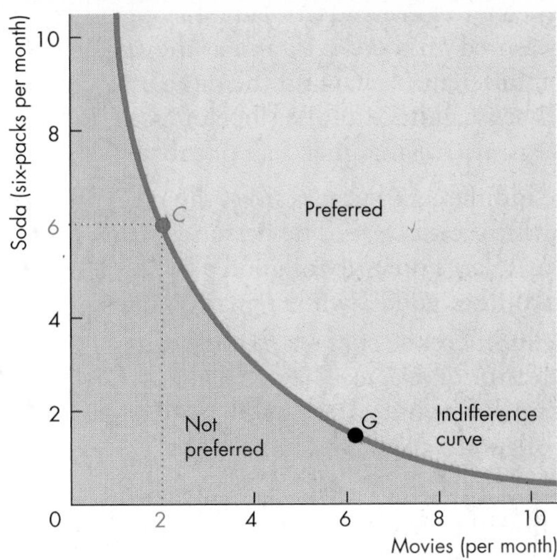

(a) An indifference curve

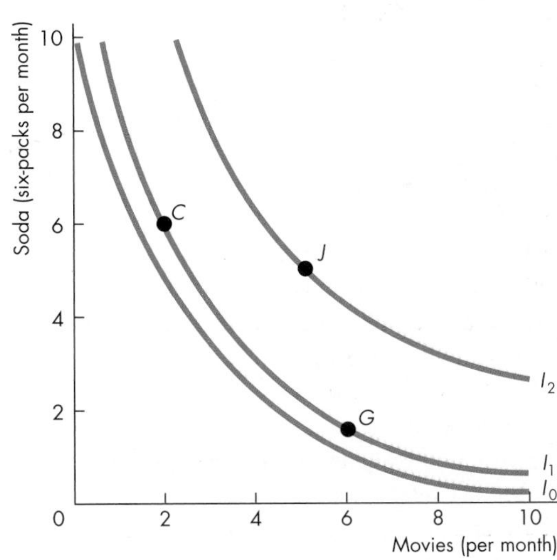

(b) Lisa's preference map

In part (a), Lisa consumes 6 six-packs of soda and 2 movies a month at point *C*. She is indifferent between all the points on the green indifference curve such as *C* and *G*. She prefers any point above the indifference curve (the yellow area) to any point on it, and she prefers any point on the indifference curve to any point below it (the gray area). Part (b) shows three indifference curves—I_0, I_1, and I_2—that are part of Lisa's preference map. She prefers point *J* to point *C* or *G*. So Lisa prefers any point on I_2 to any point on I_1.

Marginal Rate of Substitution

The **marginal rate of substitution** (*MRS*) is the rate at which a person will give up good *y* (the good measured on the *y*-axis) to get an additional unit of good *x* (the good measured on the *x*-axis) and at the same time remain indifferent (remain on the same indifference curve). The magnitude of the slope of an indifference curve measures the marginal rate of substitution.

- If the indifference curve is *steep*, the marginal rate of substitution is *high*. The person is willing to give up a large quantity of good *y* to get an additional unit of good *x* while remaining indifferent.
- If the indifference curve is *flat*, the marginal rate of substitution is *low*. The person is willing to give up a small amount of good *y* to get an additional unit of good *x* to remain indifferent.

Figure 8.4 shows you how to calculate the marginal rate of substitution. Suppose that Lisa drinks 6 six-packs and sees 2 movies at point *C* on indifference curve I_1. To calculate her marginal rate of substitution we measure the magnitude of the slope of the indifference curve at point *C*. To measure this magnitude, place a straight line against, or tangent to, the indifference curve at point *C*. Along that line, as the quantity of soda decreases by 10 six-packs, the number of movies increases by 5—an average of 2 six-packs per movie. So at point *C*, Lisa is willing to give up soda for movies at the rate of 2 six-packs per movie—a marginal rate of substitution of 2.

Now suppose that Lisa drinks 1.5 six-packs and sees 6 movies at point *G* in Fig. 8.4. Her marginal rate of substitution is now measured by the slope of the indifference curve at point *G*. That slope is the same as the slope of the tangent to the indifference curve at point *G*. Here, as the quantity of soda decreases by 4.5 six-packs, the number of movies increases by 9—an average of 1/2 six-pack per movie. So at point *G*, Lisa is willing to give up soda for movies at the rate of 1/2 six-pack per movie—a marginal rate of substitution of 1/2.

As Lisa sees more movies and drinks less soda, her marginal rate of substitution diminishes. Diminishing marginal rate of substitution is the key assumption of consumer theory. A **diminishing marginal rate of substitution** is a general tendency for a person to be willing to give up less of good *y* to get one more unit of good *x*, and at the same time remain indifferent as the quantity of *x* increases. In Lisa's case, she is less willing to give up soda to see one more movie as the number of movies she sees increases.

FIGURE 8.4 The Marginal Rate of Substitution

myeconlab

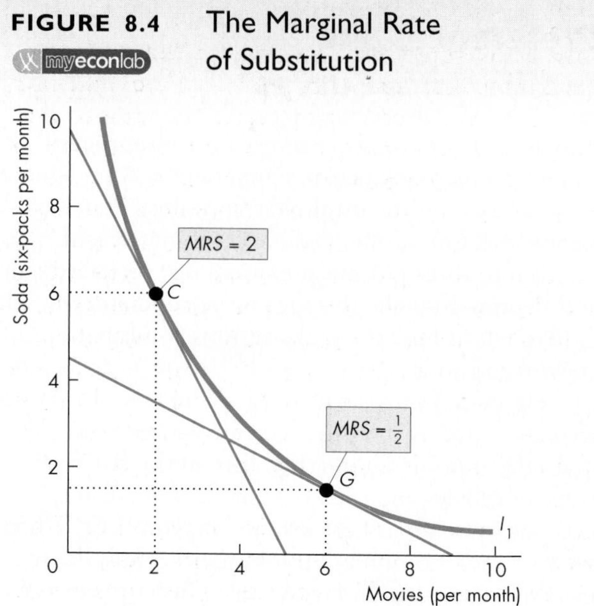

The magnitude of the slope of an indifference curve is called the marginal rate of substitution (*MRS*). The red line at point *C* tells us that Lisa is willing to give up 10 six-packs to see 5 movies. Her marginal rate of substitution at point *C* is 10 divided by 5, which equals 2. The red line at point *G* tells us that Lisa is willing to give up 4.5 six-packs to see 9 movies. Her marginal rate of substitution at point *G* is 4.5 divided by 9, which equals 1/2.

Your Own Diminishing Marginal Rate of Substitution

Think about your own diminishing marginal rate of substitution. Imagine that in a week, you drink 10 six-packs of soda and see no movies. Most likely, you are willing to give up a lot of soda so that you can see just 1 movie. But now imagine that in a week, you drink 1 six-pack and see 6 movies. Most likely, you will now not be willing to give up much soda to see a seventh movie. As a general rule, the greater the number of movies you see, the smaller is the quantity of soda you are willing to give up to see one additional movie.

The shape of a person's indifference curves incorporates the principle of the diminishing marginal rate of substitution because the curves are bowed toward the origin. The tightness of the bend of an indifference curve tells us how willing a person is to substitute one good for another while remaining indifferent. Let's look at some examples that make this point clear.

Degree of Substitutability

Most of us would not regard movies and soda as being close substitutes. We probably have some fairly clear ideas about how many movies we want to see each month and how many cans of soda we want to drink. But to some degree, we are willing to substitute between these two goods. No matter how big a soda freak you are, there is surely some increase in the number of movies you can see that will compensate you for being deprived of a can of soda. Similarly, no matter how addicted you are to the movies, surely some number of cans of soda will compensate you for being deprived of seeing one movie. A person's indifference curves for movies and soda might look something like those shown in Fig. 8.5(a).

Close Substitutes Some goods substitute so easily for each other that most of us do not even notice which we are consuming. The different brands of personal computers are an example. As long as it has an "Intel inside" and runs Windows, most of us don't care whether our PC is a Dell, a Compaq, a Sony, or any of a dozen other brands. The same holds true for marker pens. Most of us don't care whether we use a marker pen from the campus bookstore or one from the local supermarket. When two goods are perfect substitutes, their indifference curves are straight lines that slope downward, as Fig. 8.5(b) illustrates. The marginal rate of substitution is constant.

Complements Some goods cannot substitute for each other at all. Instead, they are complements. The complements in Fig. 8.5(c) are left and right running shoes. Indifference curves of perfect complements are L-shaped. One left running shoe and one right running shoe are as good as one left shoe and two right ones. Having two of each is preferred to having one of each, but having two of one and one of the other is no better than having one of each.

The extreme cases of perfect substitutes and perfect complements shown here don't often happen in reality. But they do illustrate that the shape of the indifference curve shows the degree of substitutability between two goods. The more perfectly substitutable the two goods, the closer are their indifference curves to straight lines and the less quickly does the

FIGURE 8.5 The Degree of Substitutability

myeconlab

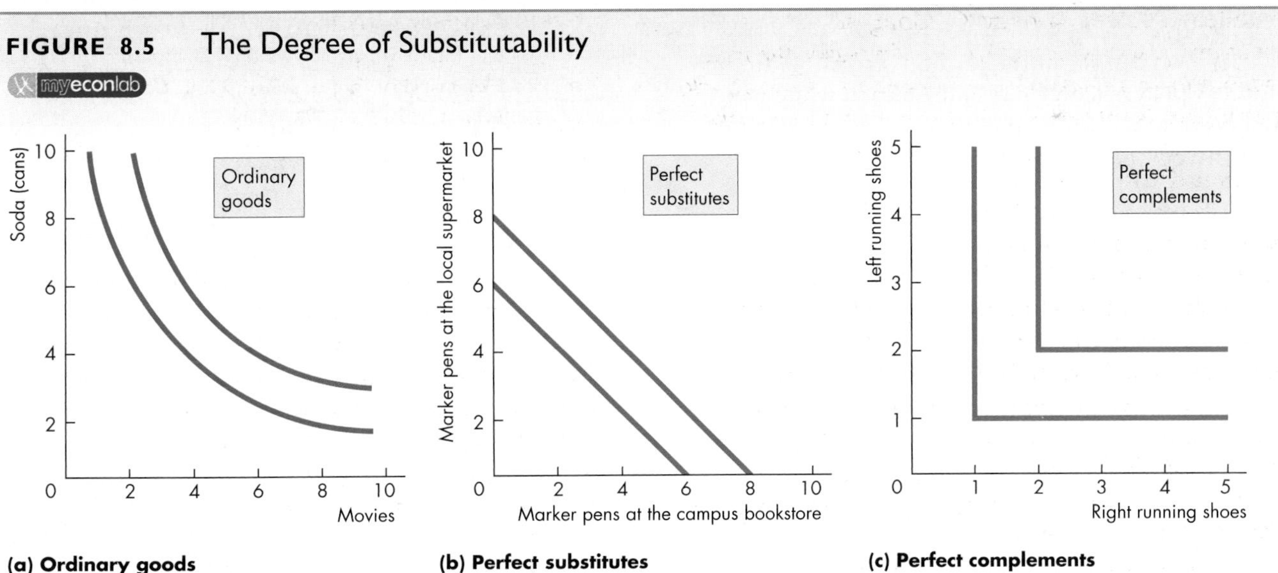

(a) Ordinary goods **(b) Perfect substitutes** **(c) Perfect complements**

The shape of the indifference curves reveals the degree of substitutability between two goods. Part (a) shows the indifference curves for two ordinary goods: movies and soda. To drink less soda and remain indifferent, one must see more movies. The number of movies that compensates for a reduction in soda increases as less soda is consumed. Part (b) shows the indifference curves for two perfect substitutes. For the consumer to remain indifferent, one fewer marker pen from the local supermarket must be replaced by one extra marker pen from the campus bookstore. Part (c) shows two perfect complements—goods that cannot be substituted for each other at all. Having two left running shoes with one right running shoe is no better than having one of each. But having two of each is preferred to having one of each.

"With the pork I'd recommend an Alsatian white or a Coke."

marginal rate of substitution diminish. Poor substitutes for each other have tightly curved indifference curves, approaching the shape of those shown in Fig. 8.5(c).

As you can see in the cartoon, according to the waiter's preferences, Coke and Alsatian white wine are perfect substitutes and each is a complement of pork. We hope the customers agree with him.

REVIEW QUIZ

1. What is an indifference curve and how does a preference map show preferences?
2. Why does an indifference curve slope downward and why is it bowed toward the origin?
3. What do we call the magnitude of the slope of an indifference curve?
4. What is the key assumption about a consumer's marginal rate of substitution?

myeconlab **Study Plan 8.2**

The two components of the model of household choice are now in place: the budget line and the preference map. We will now use these components to work out the household's choice and to predict how choices change when prices and income change.

Predicting Consumer Behavior

We are now going to predict the quantities of movies and soda that Lisa chooses to buy. Figure 8.6 shows Lisa's budget line from Fig. 8.1 and her indifference curves from Fig. 8.3(b). We assume that Lisa consumes at her best affordable point, which is 2 movies and 6 six-packs—at point *C*. Here, Lisa

- Is on her budget line.
- Is on her highest attainable indifference curve.
- Has a marginal rate of substitution between movies and soda equal to the relative price of movies and soda.

For every point inside the budget line, such as point *I*, there are points *on* the budget line that Lisa prefers. For example, she prefers all the points on the budget line between *F* and *H* to point *I*. So she chooses a point on the budget line.

FIGURE 8.6 The Best Affordable Point

myeconlab

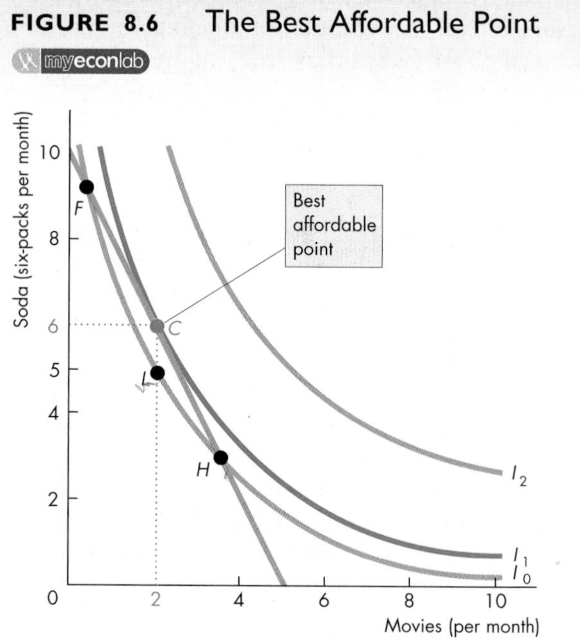

Lisa's best affordable point is *C*. At that point, she is on her budget line and also on the highest attainable indifference curve. At a point such as *H*, Lisa is willing to give up more movies in exchange for soda than she has to. She can move to point *I*, which is just as good as point *H*, and have some unspent income. She can spend that income and move to *C*, a point that she prefers to point *I*.

Every point on the budget line lies on an indifference curve. For example, point H lies on the indifference curve I_0. At point H, Lisa's marginal rate of substitution is less than the relative price. Lisa is willing to give up more movies in exchange for soda than the budget line says she must. So she moves along her budget line from H toward C. As she does so, she passes through a number of indifference curves (not shown in the figure) located between indifference curves I_0 and I_1. All of these indifference curves are higher than I_0, and therefore Lisa prefers any point on them to point H.

But when Lisa gets to point C, she is on the highest attainable indifference curve. If she keeps moving along the budget line, she starts to encounter indifference curves that are lower than I_1. So Lisa chooses point C, her best affordable point.

At the chosen point, the marginal rate of substitution (the magnitude of the slope of the indifference curve) equals the relative price (the magnitude of the slope of the budget line).

Let's use this model of household choice to predict the effects on consumption of changes in prices and income. We'll begin by studying the effect of a change in price.

A Change in Price

The effect of a change in the price on the quantity of a good consumed is called the **price effect**. We will use Fig. 8.7(a) to work out the price effect of a fall in the price of a movie. We start with the price of a movie at $6, the price of soda at $3 a six-pack, and Lisa's income at $30 a month. In this situation, she drinks 6 six-packs and sees 2 movies a month at point C.

Now suppose that the price of a movie falls to $3. With a lower price of a movie, the budget line rotates outward and becomes flatter. (Check back to Fig. 8.2(a) for a refresher on how a price change affects the budget line.) The new budget line is the dark orange one in Fig. 8.7(a).

Lisa's best affordable point is now point J, where she sees 5 movies and drinks 5 six-packs of soda. Lisa drinks less soda and watches more movies now that movies are cheaper. She cuts her soda consumption from 6 to 5 six-packs and increases the number of movies she sees from 2 to 5 a month. Lisa substitutes movies for soda when the price of a movie falls and the price of soda and her income remain constant.

FIGURE 8.7 Price Effect and Demand Curve

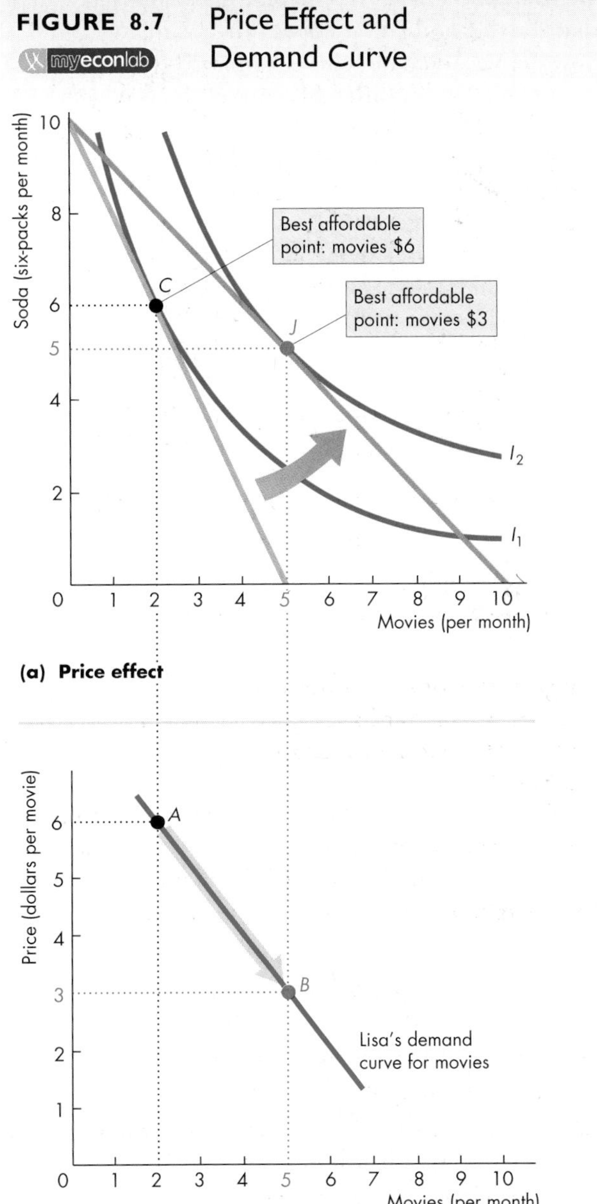

(a) Price effect

(b) Demand curve

Initially, Lisa consumes at point C (part a). If the price of a movie falls from $6 to $3, Lisa consumes at point J. The move from C to J is the price effect.

At a price of $6 a movie, Lisa sees 2 movies a month, at point A in part (b). At a price of $3 a movie, she sees 5 movies a month, at point B. Lisa's demand curve traces out her best affordable quantity of movies as the price of a movie varies.

The Demand Curve In Chapter 3, we asserted that the demand curve slopes downward. We can now derive a demand curve from a consumer's budget line and indifference curves. By doing so, we can see that the law of demand and the downward-sloping demand curve are consequences of the consumer's choosing his or her best affordable combination of goods.

To derive Lisa's demand curve for movies, lower the price of a movie and find her best affordable point at different prices. We've just done this for two movie prices in Fig. 8.7(a). Figure 8.7(b) highlights these two prices and two points that lie on Lisa's demand curve for movies. When the price of a movie is $6, Lisa sees 2 movies a month at point *A*. When the price falls to $3, she increases the number of movies she sees to 5 a month at point *B*. The demand curve is made up of these two points plus all the other points that tell us Lisa's best affordable consumption of movies at each movie price, given the price of soda and Lisa's income. As you can see, Lisa's demand curve for movies slopes downward—the lower the price of a movie, the more movies she watches each month. This is the law of demand.

Next, let's see how Lisa changes her consumption of movies and soda when her income changes.

A Change in Income

The effect of a change in income on consumption is called the **income effect**. Let's work out the income effect by examining how consumption changes when income changes and prices remain constant. Figure 8.8 shows the income effect when Lisa's income falls. With an income of $30 and with the price of a movie at $3 and the price of soda at $3 a six-pack, she consumes at point *J*—5 movies and 5 six-packs. If her income falls to $21, she consumes at point *K*—she sees 4 movies and drinks 3 six-packs. When Lisa's income falls, she consumes less of both goods. Movies and soda are normal goods.

The Demand Curve and the Income Effect A change in income leads to a shift in the demand curve, as shown in Fig. 8.8(b). With an income of $30, Lisa's demand curve is D_0, the same as in Fig. 8.7(b). But when her income falls to $21, she plans to see fewer movies at each price, so her demand curve shifts leftward to D_1.

FIGURE 8.8 Income Effect and Change in Demand

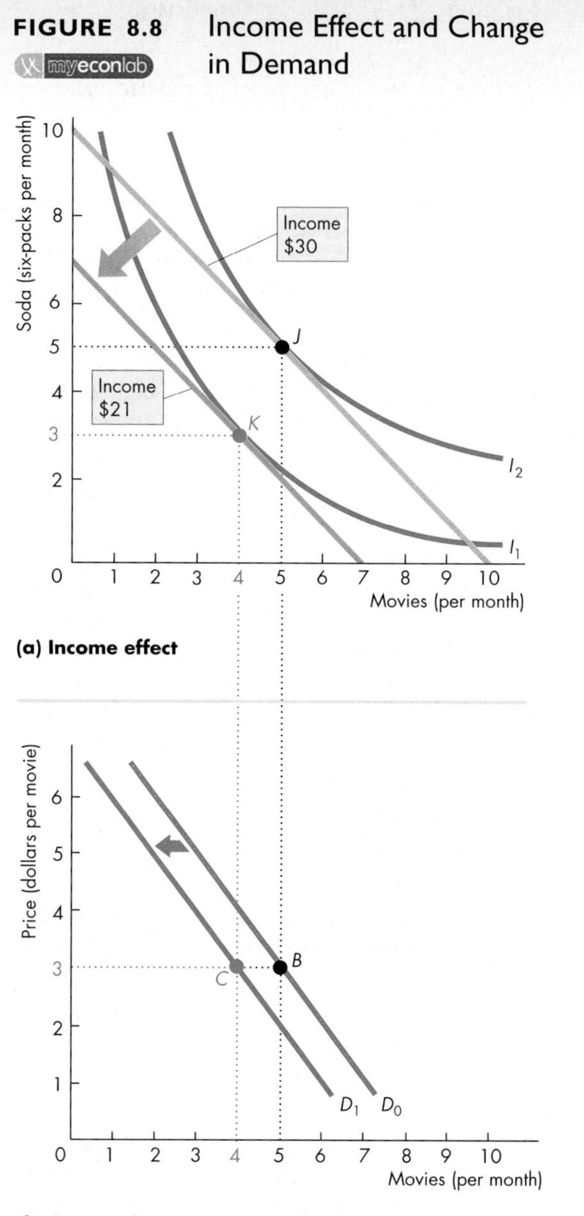

A change in income shifts the budget line, changes the best affordable point, and changes consumption.

In part (a), when Lisa's income decreases from $30 to $21, she consumes less of both movies and soda.

In part (b), Lisa's demand curve for movies when her income is $30 is D_0. When Lisa's income decreases to $21, her demand curve for movies shifts leftward to D_1. Lisa's demand for movies decreases because she now sees fewer movies at each price.

Substitution Effect and Income Effect

For a normal good, a fall in price *always* increases the quantity bought. We can prove this assertion by dividing the price effect into two parts:

- Substitution effect
- Income effect

Figure 8.9(a) shows the price effect, and in Fig. 8.9(b) we separate the price effect into its two parts.

Substitution Effect The **substitution effect** is the effect of a change in price on the quantity bought when the consumer (hypothetically) remains indifferent between the original situation and the new one. To work out Lisa's substitution effect, when the price of a movie falls, we cut her income by enough to leave her on the same indifference curve as before.

When the price of a movie falls from \$6 to \$3, suppose (hypothetically) that we cut Lisa's income to \$21. What's special about \$21? It is the income that is just enough, at the new price of a movie, to keep Lisa's best affordable point on the same indifference curve as her original consumption point *C*. Lisa's budget line is now the light orange line in Fig. 8.9(b). With the lower price of a movie and a smaller income, Lisa's best affordable point is *K* on indifference curve I_1. The move from *C* to *K* is the substitution effect of the price change. The substitution effect of the fall in the price of a movie is an increase in the consumption of movies from 2 to 4. The direction of the substitution effect never varies: When the relative price of a good falls, the consumer substitutes more of that good for the other good.

Income Effect To calculate the substitution effect, we gave Lisa a \$9 pay cut. To calculate the income effect, we give Lisa her \$9 back. The \$9 increase in income shifts Lisa's budget line outward, as shown in Fig. 8.9(b). The slope of the budget line does not change because both prices remain constant. This change in Lisa's budget line is similar to the one illustrated in Fig. 8.8. As Lisa's budget line shifts outward, her consumption possibilities expand and her best affordable point becomes *J* on indifference curve I_2. The move from *K* to *J* is the income effect of the price change. In this example, as Lisa's income increases, she increases her consumption of movies. For Lisa, a movie is a normal good. For a normal good, the income effect reinforces the substitution effect.

FIGURE 8.9 Substitution Effect and Income Effect

myeconlab

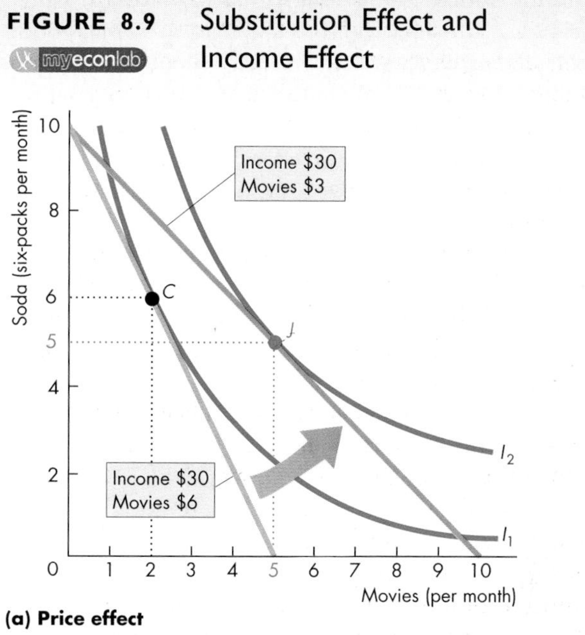

(a) Price effect

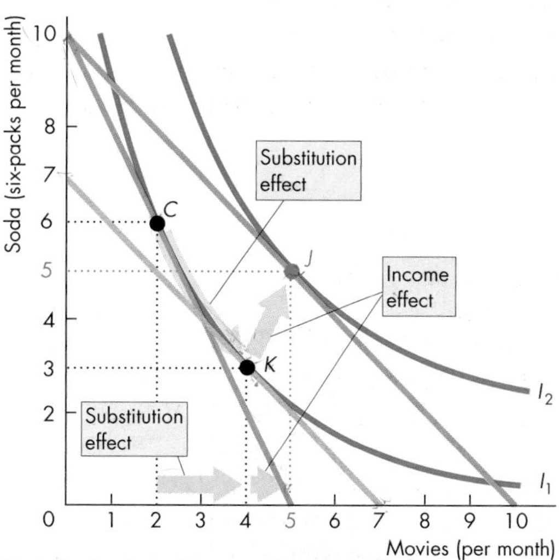

(b) Substitution effect and income effect

The price effect in part (a) can be separated into a substitution effect and an income effect in part (b).

To isolate the substitution effect, we confront Lisa with the new price but keep her on her original indifference curve, I_1. The substitution effect is the move from *C* to *K*.

To isolate the income effect, we confront Lisa with the new price of movies but increase her income so that she can move from the original indifference curve, I_1, to the new one, I_2. The income effect is the move from *K* to *J*.

Inferior Goods The example that we have just studied is that of a change in the price of a normal good. The effect of a change in the price of an inferior good is different. Recall that an inferior good is one whose consumption decreases as income increases. For an inferior good, the income effect is negative. Thus for an inferior good, a lower price does not always lead to an increase in the quantity demanded. The lower price has a substitution effect that increases the quantity demanded. But the lower price also has a negative income effect that reduces the demand for the inferior good. Thus the income effect offsets the substitution effect to some degree. If the negative income effect exceeded the positive substitution effect, the demand curve would slope upward. This case does not appear to occur in the real world.

Back to the Facts

We started this chapter by observing how consumer spending has changed over the years. The indifference curve model explains those changes. The best affordable choices determine spending patterns. Changes in prices and incomes change the best affordable choice and change consumption patterns.

REVIEW QUIZ

1. When a consumer chooses the combination of goods and services to buy, what is she or he trying to achieve?
2. Can you explain the conditions that are met when a consumer has found the best affordable combination of goods to buy? (Use the terms budget line, marginal rate of substitution, and relative price in your explanation.)
3. If the price of a normal good falls, what happens to the quantity demanded of that good?
4. Into what two effects can we divide the effect of a price change?
5. For a normal good, does the income effect reinforce the substitution effect or does it partly offset the substitution effect?

myeconlab **Study Plan 8.3**

The model of household choice can explain many other household choices. Let's look at one of them.

Work-Leisure Choices

Households make many choices other than those about how to spend their income on the various goods and services available. We can use the model of consumer choice to understand many other household choices. Some of these choices are discussed in the part-closer on pp. 192–196. Here we'll study a key choice: how much labor to supply.

Labor Supply

Every week, we allocate our 168 hours between working—called *labor*—and all other activities—called *leisure.* How do we decide how to allocate our time between labor and leisure? We can answer this question by using the theory of household choice.

The more hours we spend on *leisure,* the smaller is our income. The relationship between leisure and income is described by an *income-time budget line.* Figure 8.10(a) shows Lisa's income-time budget line. If Lisa devotes the entire week to leisure—168 hours—she has no income and is at point *Z*. By supplying labor in exchange for a wage, she can convert hours into income along the income-time budget line. The slope of that line is determined by the hourly wage rate. If the wage rate is $5 an hour, Lisa faces the flattest budget line. If the wage rate is $10 an hour, she faces the middle budget line. And if the wage rate is $15 an hour, she faces the steepest budget line.

Lisa buys leisure by not supplying labor and by forgoing income. The opportunity cost of an hour of leisure is the hourly wage rate forgone.

Figure 8.10(a) also shows Lisa's indifference curves for income and leisure. Lisa chooses her best attainable point. This choice of income and time allocation is just like her choice of movies and soda. She gets onto the highest possible indifference curve by making her marginal rate of substitution between income and leisure equal to her wage rate.

Lisa's choice depends on the wage rate she can earn. At a wage rate of $5 an hour, Lisa chooses point *A* and works 20 hours a week (168 minus 148) for an income of $100 a week. At a wage rate of $10 an hour, she chooses point *B* and works 35 hours a week (168 minus 133) for an income of $350 a week. And at a wage rate of $15 an hour, she chooses point *C* and works 30 hours a week (168 minus 138) for an income of $450 a week.

FIGURE 8.10 The Supply of Labor

myeconlab

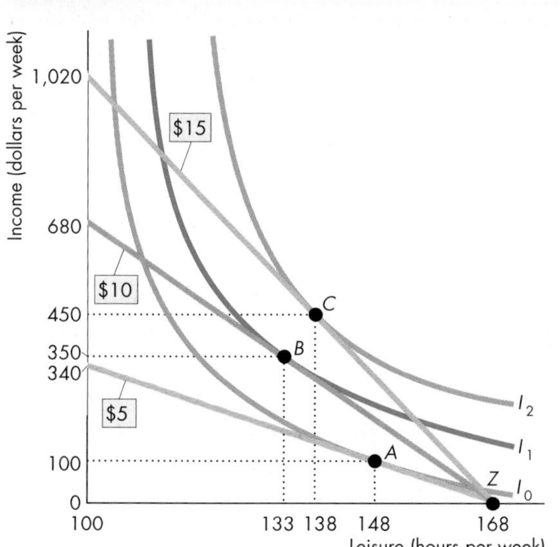

(a) Time allocation decision

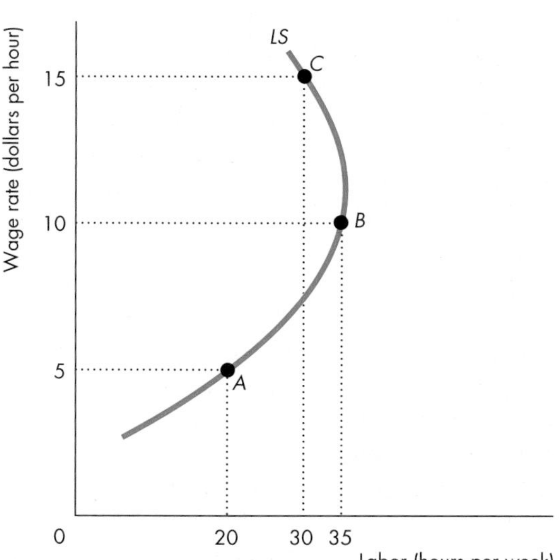

(b) Labor supply curve

In part (a), at a wage rate of $5 an hour, Lisa takes 148 hours of leisure and works 20 hours a week at point *A*. If the wage rate increases from $5 to $10 an hour, she decreases her leisure to 133 hours and increases her work to 35 hours a week at point *B*. But if the wage rate increases from $10 to $15 an hour, Lisa *increases* her leisure to 138 hours and *decreases* her work to 30 hours a week at point *C*. Part (b) shows Lisa's labor supply curve. Points *A*, *B*, and *C* on the supply curve correspond to Lisa's choices in part (a).

The Labor Supply Curve

Figure 8.10(b) shows Lisa's labor supply curve. This curve shows that as the wage rate increases from $5 an hour to $10 an hour, Lisa increases the quantity of labor supplied from 20 hours a week to 35 hours a week. But when the wage rate increases to $15 an hour, she decreases her quantity of labor supplied to 30 hours a week.

Lisa's supply of labor is similar to that described for the economy as a whole at the beginning of this chapter. As wage rates have increased, work hours have decreased. At first, this pattern seems puzzling. We've seen that the hourly wage rate is the opportunity cost of leisure. So a higher wage rate means a higher opportunity cost of leisure. This fact on its own leads to a decrease in leisure and an increase in work hours. But instead, we've cut our work hours. Why? Because our incomes have increased. As the wage rate increases, incomes increase, so people demand more of all normal goods. Leisure is a normal good, so as incomes increase, people demand more leisure.

The higher wage rate has both a *substitution effect* and an *income effect*. The higher wage rate increases the opportunity cost of leisure and so leads to a substitution effect away from leisure. And the higher wage rate increases income and so leads to an income effect toward more leisure. This outcome of rational household choice explains why the average workweek has fallen steadily as wage rates have increased. With higher wage rates, people have decided to use their higher incomes in part to consume more leisure.

REVIEW QUIZ

1. What is the opportunity cost of leisure?
2. Why might a rise in the wage rate lead to an increase in leisure and a decrease in work hours?

myeconlab **Study Plan 8.4**

Reading Between the Lines on pp. 184–185 shows you how the theory of household choice explains why, when e-books are cheaper than print books and CDs are cheaper than downloaded music, people are downloading music and not buying e-books.

In the chapters that follow, we study firms' choices. We'll see how, in the pursuit of profit, firms make choices that determine the supply of goods and services and the demand for productive resources.

READING BETWEEN THE LINES

The Marginal Rate of Substitution Between Discs and Downloads

http://www.nytimes.com

When All the 'Greatest Hits' Are Too Many to Download

February 2, 2006

More than 20 years after the rock band Survivor scored a hit with "Eye of the Tiger," the song is rising up the charts again, notching brisk sales as a single online. Since the song became available on services like iTunes about a year and a half ago, it has sold more than 275,000 copies. . . .

Album sales have dropped for four of the last five years, and while sales of digital singles are booming, that has not yet been enough to offset the drop. Music companies sold more than 350 million singles last year, a jump of 150 percent over the previous year's total. Sales of full digital albums increased even more, rising more than 190 percent to 16.2 million. . . .

http://www.nytimes.com

Trying Again to Make Books Obsolete

October 12, 2006

"The market for downloadable books will grow by 400 percent in each of the next two years, to over $25 billion by 2008," predicted the keynote speaker at the 2001 Women's National Book Association meeting. "Within a few years after the end of this decade, e-books will be the preponderant delivery format for book content."

Whoops.

The great e-book fantasy burst shortly after that speech, along with the rest of the dot-com bubble. In 2003, Barnes & Noble shut its e-book store, Palm sold its e-book business to a Web site and most people left the whole idea for dead.

Not everybody, however. Some die-hards at Sony still believe that, properly designed, the e-book has a future. Their solution is the Sony Reader, a small, sleek, portable screen that will be introduced this month in some malls, at Borders bookstores and at sonystyle.com for $350. . .

Essence of the Stories

- Downloading of music files from the Internet is booming.
- Album sales have decreased during the past five years.
- Electronic books (e-books) are also available for purchase on the Internet.
- But in contrast to music, e-books are not replacing print books.
- A new but costly technology is being launched to make e-books more popular.

Economic Analysis

- Music delivered on a CD and music delivered as a download are substitutes.
- But for two reasons, downloaded music files are more convenient than music on a CD: They can be played on a more convenient portable player, and they can be selected a tune at a time rather than already collected as an album.
- Figure 1 shows Andy's indifference curves for CD music and downloaded music.
- Let's assume that a CD provides Andy with 60 minutes of music a month, and a download provides only 4 minutes of music a month.
- With a monthly music budget of $30 and the price of a CD at $10, Andy can afford to buy 3 CDs a month (180 minutes of music).
- If the price of a downloaded tune is $2.00, Andy buys 2 CDs (120 minutes of music) and 5 tunes (20 minutes of music) a month.
- But if the price of a downloaded tune is $1.00, Andy buys only 1 CD (60 minutes of music) and 20 tunes (80 minutes of music) a month.
- For most people, e-books are poor substitutes for print books. A print book is more convenient for most people.
- When two goods are poor substitutes, the indifference curves that describe preferences are curved and almost horizontal.
- Figure 2 shows Beth's indifference curves for print books and e-books.
- Beth likes regular printed books and doesn't like e-books. She is willing to give up almost no quantity of print books to get an e-book.
- If print books and e-books have the same price and if Beth can afford to buy 4 of either type of book, her budget line is the pale orange line in Fig. 2.
- Beth's best affordable point is C on curve I_1. She buys 4 print books and no e-books.
- Even with the price of an e-book at half the price of a print book (the dark orange budget line in Figure 2), Beth still buys only print books.
- e-books would have to be almost free to induce Beth to switch from print books to e-books.

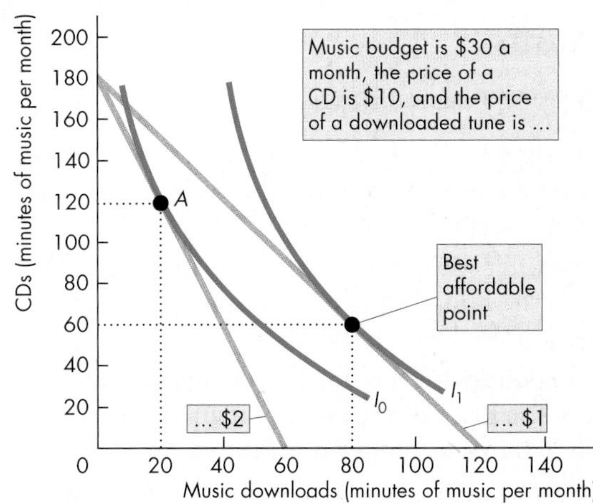

Figure 1 CDs and downloaded tunes

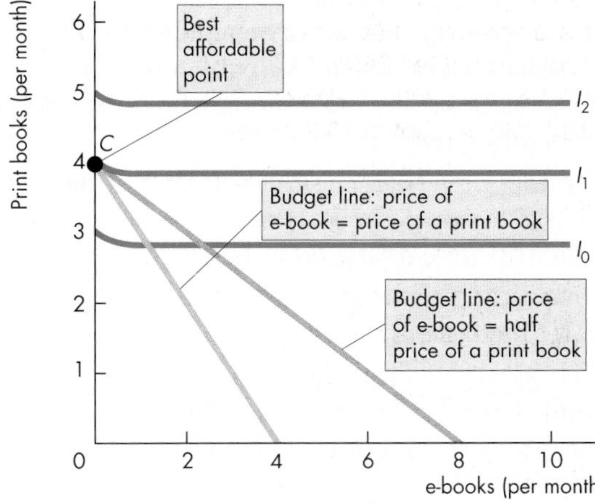

Figure 2 Print books and e-books

SUMMARY

Key Points

Consumption Possibilities (pp. 172–174)

- The budget line is the boundary between what the household can and cannot afford given its income and the prices of goods.
- The point at which the budget line intersects the *y*-axis is the household's real income in terms of the good measured on that axis.
- The magnitude of the slope of the budget line is the relative price of the good measured on the *x*-axis in terms of the good measured on the *y*-axis.
- A change in price changes the slope of the budget line. A change in income shifts the budget line but does not change its slope.

Preferences and Indifference Curves (pp. 175–178)

- A consumer's preferences can be represented by indifference curves. An indifference curve joins all the combinations of goods among which the consumer is indifferent.
- A consumer prefers any point above an indifference curve to any point on it and any point on an indifference curve to any point below it.
- The magnitude of the slope of an indifference curve is called the marginal rate of substitution.
- The marginal rate of substitution diminishes as consumption of the good measured on the *y*-axis decreases and consumption of the good measured on the *x*-axis increases.

Predicting Consumer Behavior (pp. 178–182)

- A household consumes at its best affordable point. This point is on the budget line and on the highest attainable indifference curve and has a marginal rate of substitution equal to relative price.
- The effect of a price change (the price effect) can be divided into a substitution effect and an income effect.
- The substitution effect is the effect of a change in price on the quantity bought when the consumer (hypothetically) remains indifferent between the original situation and the new situation.
- The substitution effect always results in an increase in consumption of the good whose relative price has fallen.
- The income effect is the effect of a change in income on consumption.
- For a normal good, the income effect reinforces the substitution effect. For an inferior good, the income effect works in the opposite direction to the substitution effect.

Work-Leisure Choices (pp. 182–183)

- The indifference curve model of household choice enables us to understand how a household allocates its time between work and leisure.
- Work hours have decreased and leisure hours have increased because the income effect on the demand for leisure has been greater than the substitution effect.

Key Figures

Key Terms

PROBLEMS

myeconlab Tests, Study Plan, Solutions*

1. Sara's income is $12 a week. The price of popcorn is $3 a bag, and the price of cola is $3 a can.
   a. What is Sara's real income in terms of cola?
   b. What is her real income in terms of popcorn?
   c. What is the relative price of cola in terms of popcorn?
   d. What is the opportunity cost of a can of cola?
   e. Calculate the equation for Sara's budget line (placing bags of popcorn on the left side of the equation).
   f. Draw a graph of Sara's budget line with cola on the x-axis.
   g. In part (f), what is the slope of Sara's budget line? What determines its value?
2. Sara's income falls from $12 a week to $9 a week. The price of popcorn remains at $3 a bag, and the price of cola remains at $3 a can.
   a. What is the effect of the fall in Sara's income on her real income in terms of cola?
   b. What is the effect of the decrease in Sara's income on her real income in terms of popcorn?
   c. What is the effect of the decrease in Sara's income on the relative price of cola in terms of popcorn?
   d. What is the slope of Sara's new budget line if it is drawn with cola on the x-axis?
3. Sara's income is $12 a week. The price of popcorn rises from $3 to $6 a bag, and the price of cola remains at $3 a can.
   a. What is the effect of the rise in the price of popcorn on Sara's real income in terms of cola?
   b. What is the effect of the rise in the price of popcorn on Sara's real income in terms of popcorn?
   c. What is the effect of the rise in the price of popcorn on the relative price of cola in terms of popcorn?
   d. What is the slope of Sara's new budget line if it is drawn with cola on the x-axis?
4. Rashid consumes only books and CDs and the figure shows his preferences.

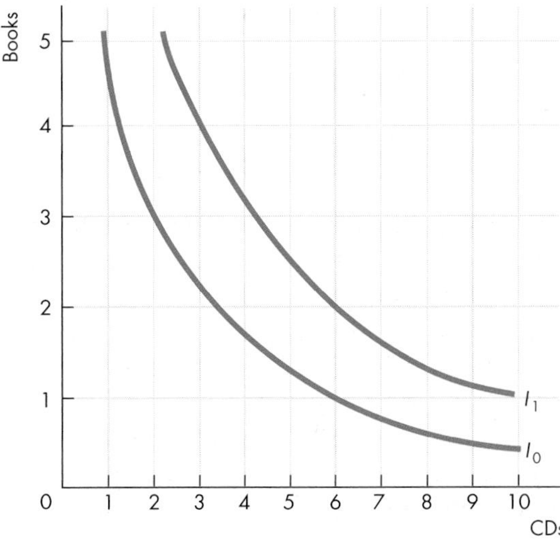

   a. When Rashid chooses the consumption point of 3 books and 2 CDs, what is his marginal rate of substitution?
   b. When Rashid chooses the consumption point of 2 books and 6 CDs, what is his marginal rate of substitution?
   c. Do Rashid's indifference curves display a diminishing marginal rate of substitution? Explain why or why not.
5. Draw figures that show your indifference curves for the following pairs of goods. For each pair, explain whether the goods are perfect substitutes, perfect complements, or neither. If the goods are neither, discuss the shape of the indifference curve you have drawn and explain how your marginal rate of substitution changes as the quantities of the two goods change.
   The pairs of goods are
   a. Right gloves and left gloves
   b. Coca-Cola and Pepsi
   c. Baseball balls and bats
   d. Tylenol and acetaminophen (the generic form of Tylenol)
   e. Eye glasses and contact lenses
   f. Desktop computers and laptop computers
   g. Skis and ski poles
6. Sara's income is $12 a week. The price of popcorn is $3 a bag, and the price of cola is $3 a can. The figure (on the next page) illustrates Sara's preferences for popcorn and cola.

*Solutions to odd-numbered problems are provided.

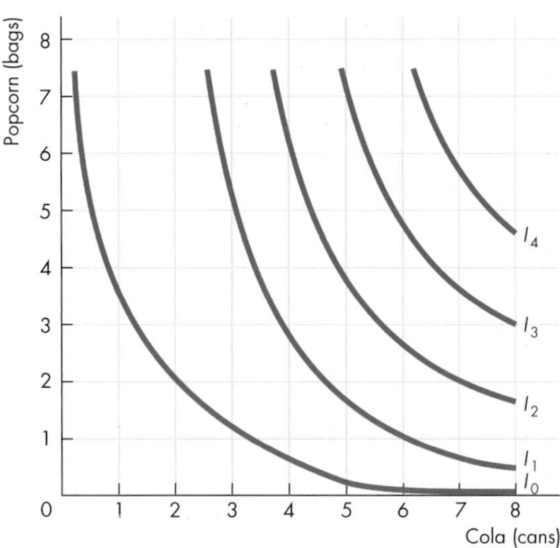

a. What quantities of popcorn and cola does Sara buy?
b. What is Sara's marginal rate of substitution at the point at which she consumes?

7. Now suppose that in problem 6, the price of cola falls to $1.50 a can and the price of popcorn and Sara's income remain the same.
   a. What quantities of cola and popcorn does Sara now buy?
   b. Find two points on Sara's demand curve for cola. Draw Sara's demand curve.
   c. Find the substitution effect of the price change.
   d. Find the income effect of the price change.
   e. Is cola a normal good or an inferior good?
8. Pam has chosen her best affordable combination of cookies and comic books. She spends all of her income on 30 cookies at $1 each and 5 comic books at $2 each. The price of a cookie falls to 50¢ and the price of a comic book rises to $5.
   a. Will Pam be able and want to buy 30 cookies and 5 comic books next month?
   b. Which situation does Pam prefer: cookies at $1 and comic books at $2 or cookies at 50¢ and comic books at $5?
   c. If Pam changes the quantities that she buys, which good will she buy more of and which will she buy less of?
   d. When the prices change next month, will there be an income effect and a substitution effect at work or just one of them?

CRITICAL THINKING

1. Study *Reading Between the Lines* about music and e-book downloads on pp. 184–185, and then answer the following questions.
   a. How do you buy music?
   b. Sketch your budget constraint for music and other items.
   c. Sketch your indifference curves for music and other goods.
   d. What do you predict would happen to the way that you buy music if the price of a CD increased and the price of a music download decreased, leaving you able to buy exactly the same quantity of music as you buy now?
2. The sales tax is a tax on goods. Some people say that a consumption tax, a tax that is paid on both goods and services, would be better. If we replaced the sales tax with a consumption tax,
   a. What would happen to the relative price of CD-Rs and haircuts?
   b. What would happen to the budget line showing the quantities of CD-Rs and haircuts you can afford to buy?
   c. How would you change your purchases of CD-Rs and haircuts?
   d. Which type of tax is better for the consumer and why?

   Use a graph to illustrate your answers and to show the substitution effect and the income effect of the price change.

WEB ACTIVITIES

myeconlab Links to Web sites

1. Obtain information about the prices of cell phone service and first-class mail.
   a. Sketch the budget constraint for a consumer who spent $50 a month on these two goods in 2000 and 2006.
   b. Can you say whether the consumer was better off or worse off in 2006 than in 2000?
   c. Sketch some indifference curves for cell phone calls and first-class letters mailed and show the income effect and the substitution effect of the changes in prices that occurred between 2000 and 2006.

APPENDIX

Marginal Utility and Indifference Curves

After studying Chapters 7 and 8 and this appendix, you will be able to

- Explain the connection between utility and indifference curves
- Explain why maximizing utility is the same as choosing the best affordable point
- Explain why utility exists

Two Ways of Describing Preferences

The marginal utility model describes preferences by using the concept of utility. An increase in the quantity consumed of a good brings an increase in the total utility derived from that good and a decrease in its marginal utility (see Table 7.1, p. 156, and Figure 7.3, p. 157.)

The indifference curve model describes preferences by using the concepts of preference and indifference to define a map of indifference curves. A higher indifference curve is preferred to a lower one. The marginal rate of substitution diminishes down along an indifference curve (see Figure 8.3, p. 175, and Figure 8.4, p. 176).

The indifference curve model doesn't need the concept of utility. In fact, it was developed precisely because economists wanted a more objective way of describing preferences. But we can interpret the indifference curve model by using the concept of utility.

Because a consumer is indifferent among the combinations of goods at all the points on an indifference curve, these combinations provide the same amount of total utility. An indifference curve is a constant utility curve.

You can see the connection between utility and an indifference map by looking at Figure A8.1. Part (a) provides information about the total utility from movies and soda. It is based on Table 7.1, (p. 156), but instead of listing the quantities of the two goods and the total utility arising from each quantity consumed, the numbers are arranged with movies across the bottom and soda down the side. With no soda, the

FIGURE A8.1 Total Utility and the Indifference Map

myeconlab

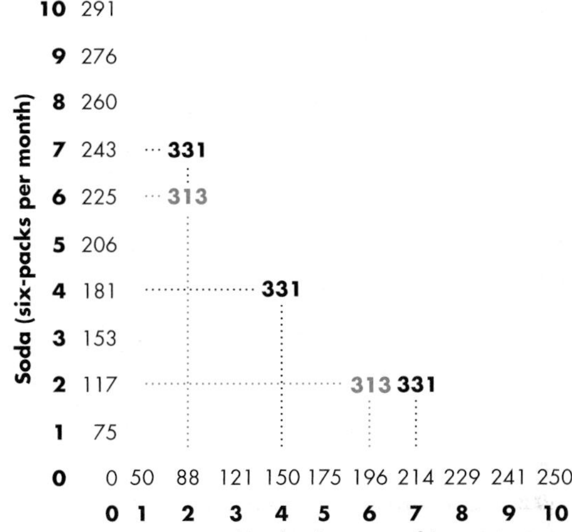

(a) Total utility

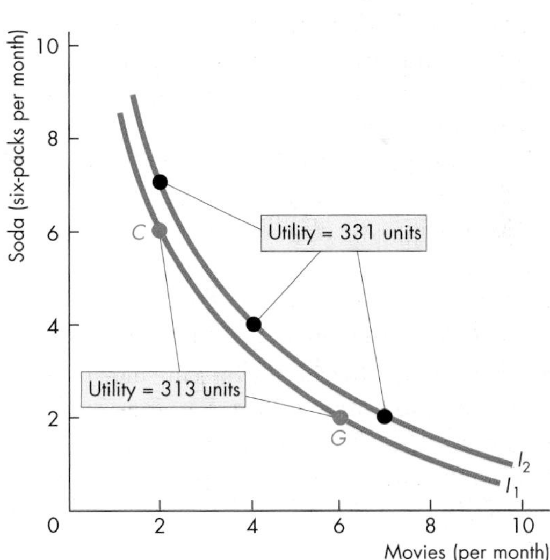

(b) Indifference curves

We can represent preferences by using the concept of utility or indifference curves. In the table, Lisa's total utility depends on the quantities of movies and soda that she consumes. Different combinations can yield the same total utility. These combinations lie on the same indifference curve. The figure shows two indifference curves: one for 313 units of utility and one for 331 units of utility.

total utility from 6 movies is 196 units. And with no movies, the total utility from 2 six-packs is 117 units.

Figure A8.1(a) also shows the total utility from some other combinations of movies and soda. For example the total utility from 6 movies and 2 six-packs is 313 units (196 plus 117). Part (a) shows another combination that delivers 313 units and three combinations that deliver 331 units of utility.

The figure shows the indifference curves associated with these two levels of total utility.

Maximizing Utility Is Choosing the Best Affordable Point

In the marginal utility model, Lisa maximizes total utility by spending her income on the combination of movies and soda that makes the marginal utility per dollar spent on movies equal to the marginal utility per dollar spent on soda. That is,

$$MU_M/P_M = MU_S/P_S, \qquad (1)$$

where MU_M is the marginal utility of a movie, P_M is the price of a movie, MU_S is the marginal utility of soda, and P_S is the price of soda.

In the indifference curve model, Lisa chooses the best affordable point by spending her income on the combination of movies and soda that makes the marginal rate of substitution (*MRS*) equal to the relative price of the two goods. That is,

$$MRS = P_M/P_S. \qquad (2)$$

Maximizing total utility and choosing the best affordable point are the same. To see why, first multiply both sides of equation (1) above by P_M and divide both sides by MU_S to obtain

$$MU_M/MU_S = P_M/P_S. \qquad (3)$$

This equation states that the ratio of the marginal utilities of the two goods is equal to the relative price of the two goods.

Inspect equations (2) and (3) and you can see that if the two ways of describing a consumer's choice are the same, then the marginal rate of substitution must equal the ratio of the marginal utilities of the two goods. That is,

$$MRS = MU_M/MU_S. \qquad (4)$$

To establish that this proposition is true, note that total utility changes when the quantities consumed change in the following way:

$$\Delta U = MU_M \times \Delta Q_M + MU_S \times \Delta Q_S, \qquad (5)$$

where Δ means "change in," Q_M is the quantity of movies consumed, and Q_S is the quantity of soda consumed.

Recall that along an indifference curve, total utility is constant so the change in total utility is zero. Then, along an indifference curve, it must be the case that

$$0 = MU_M \times \Delta Q_M + MU_S \times \Delta Q_S, \qquad (6)$$

or

$$MU_M \times \Delta Q_M = -MU_S \times \Delta Q_S. \qquad (7)$$

Divide both sides of equation (7) by MU_S and by ΔQ_M to obtain

$$MU_M/MU_S = -\Delta Q_S/\Delta Q_M. \qquad (8)$$

This equation tells us that along an indifference curve, the change in the quantity of soda consumed divided by the change in the quantity of movies consumed equals the ratio of the marginal utilities of movies and soda.

But $-\Delta Q_S/\Delta Q_M$ (rise over run) is the slope of the indifference curve. And, removing the minus sign, $\Delta Q_S/\Delta Q_M$ is the marginal rate of substitution of movies for soda. So,

$$MRS = \Delta Q_S/\Delta Q_M = MU_M/MU_S. \qquad (9)$$

You've now seen that the two models of consumer choice make identical predictions about the quantities that a consumer chooses. Spending the available budget with the marginal utility per dollar spent the same for both goods is the same as spending the available budget with the marginal rate of substitution between the two goods equal to their relative price.

Utility Exists!

The indifference curve model is powerful because its only assumptions are that people can rank alternative combinations of goods as preferred or indifferent and that the marginal rate of substitution diminishes. From these assumptions, we can derive the downward-sloping demand curve. We can also easily visualize the effects of changes in prices and income on a consumer's choice.

The indifference curve model is also powerful because its assumptions imply the existence of utility and of (generally) diminishing marginal utility.

By observing the prices of goods and the quantities consumed, we can infer a consumer's marginal utilities at each quantity.

Making the Most of Life

The powerful forces of demand and supply shape the fortunes of families, businesses, nations, and empires in the same unrelenting way that the tides and winds shape rocks and coastlines. You saw in Chapters 3 through 6 how these forces raise and lower prices, increase and decrease quantities bought and sold, cause revenues to fluctuate, and send resources to their most valuable uses.

These powerful forces begin quietly and privately with the choices that each one of us makes.

Chapters 7 and 8 probe these individual choices. Chapter 7 explores the marginal utility theory of human decisions. This theory explains people's consumption plans. It also explains people's consumption of leisure time and its flip side, the supply of work time. Marginal utility theory can even be used to explain "non-economic" choices, such as whether to marry and how many children to have. In a sense, there are no non-economic choices. If there is scarcity, there must be choice. And economics studies all such choices.

Chapter 8 describes a tool that enables us to make a map of people's likes and dislikes, a tool called an *indifference curve*. Indifference curves are considered an advanced topic, so this chapter is *strictly optional*. But the presentation of indifference curves in Chapter 8 is the clearest and most straightforward available, so if you want to learn about this tool, this chapter is the place to do so.

The earliest economists (Adam Smith and his contemporaries) did not have a very deep understanding of households' choices. It was not until the nineteenth century that progress was made in this area. On the following pages, you can spend some time with Jeremy Bentham, the person who pioneered the use of the concept of utility to the study of human choices, and with Steven Levitt of the University of Chicago, who is one of today's most influential students of human behavior.

PROBING THE IDEAS

People as Rational Decision Makers

"... It is the greatest happiness of the greatest number that is the measure of right and wrong."

JEREMY BENTHAM
Fragment on Government

The Economist

Jeremy Bentham *(1748–1832), who lived in London, was the son and grandson of a lawyer and was himself trained as a barrister. But he rejected the opportunity to maintain the family tradition and, instead, spent his life as a writer, activist, and Member of Parliament in the pursuit of rational laws that would bring the greatest happiness to the greatest number of people.*

Bentham, whose embalmed body is preserved to this day in a glass cabinet in the University of London, was the first person to use the concept of utility to explain human choices. But in Bentham's day, the distinction between explaining and prescribing was not a sharp one, and Bentham was ready to use his ideas to tell people how they ought to behave. He was one of the first to propose pensions for the retired, guaranteed employment, minimum wages, and social benefits such as free education and free medical care.

The Issues

The economic analysis of human behavior in the family, the workplace, the markets for goods and services, the markets for labor services, and financial markets is based on the idea that our behavior can be understood as a response to scarcity. Everything we do can be understood as a choice that maximizes total benefit subject to the constraints imposed by our limited resources and technology. If people's preferences are stable in the face of changing constraints, then we have a chance of predicting how they will respond to an evolving environment.

The economic approach explains the incredible change that has occurred during the past 100 years in the way women allocate their time as the consequence of changing constraints, not of changing attitudes. Technological advances have equipped the nation's farms and factories with machines that have increased the productivity of both women and men, thereby raising the wages they can earn. The increasingly technological world has increased the return to education for both women and men and has led to a large increase in high school and college graduates of both sexes. And equipped with an ever-widening array of gadgets and appliances that cut the time taken to do household jobs, an increasing proportion of women have joined the labor force.

The economic explanation might not be correct, but it is a powerful one. And if it is correct, the changing attitudes are a consequence, not a cause, of the economic advancement of women.

Then

Economists explain people's actions as the consequences of choices that maximize total utility subject to constraints. In the 1890s, fewer than 20 percent of women chose market employment, and most of those who did had low-paying and unattractive jobs. The other 80 percent of women chose nonmarket work in the home. What constraints led to these choices?

Now

By 2002, more than 60 percent of women were in the labor force, and although many had low-paying jobs, women were increasingly found in the professions and in executive positions. What brought about this dramatic change compared with 100 years earlier? Was it a change in preferences or a change in the constraints that women face?

Steven Levitt, whom you can meet on the following pages, shows us how economic reasoning combined with the data generated by natural experiments deepens our understanding of an astonishing range of human choices.

TALKING WITH

Steven D. Levitt

Steven D. Levitt is Alvin H. Baum Professor of Economics at the University of Chicago. Born in Minneapolis, he was an undergraduate at Harvard and a graduate student at MIT. Among his many honors, he was recently awarded the John Bates Clark Medal given to the best economist under 40.

Professor Levitt has studied an astonishingly wide range of human choices and their outcomes. He has examined the effects of policing on crime, shown that realtors get a higher price when they sell their own homes than when they sell other people's, devised a test to detect cheating teachers, and studied the choices of drug dealers and gang members. Much of this research has been popularized in Freakonomics *(Steven D. Levitt and Stephen J. Dubner, HarperCollins in 2005). What unifies this apparently diverse body of research is the use of natural experiments. Professor Levitt has an incredible ability to find just the right set of events and the data the events have generated to enable him to isolate the effect he's looking for.*

Michael Parkin talked with Steven Levitt about his career and the progress that economists have made in understanding how people respond to incentives in all aspects of life.

Why did you become an economist?

As a freshman in college, I took introductory economics. All the ideas made perfect sense to me—it was the way I naturally thought. My friends were befuddled. I thought, "This is the field for me!"

The idea of rational choice made at the margin lies at the heart of economics. Would you say that your work generally supports that idea or challenges it? Can you provide some examples?

I don't like the word "rational" in this context. I think economists model agents as being rational just for convenience. What really matters is whether people respond to incentives. My work very much supports the idea that humans in all types of circumstances respond strongly to incentives. I've seen it with drug dealers, auto thieves, sumo wrestlers, real estate agents, and elementary school teachers, just to name a few examples.

Can you elaborate? What are the incentives to which drug dealers respond? And does an understanding of these responses tell us anything about how public policy might influence drug use?

The incentives people face differ depending on their particular circumstances. Drug dealers, for instance, want to make money, but they also want to avoid being arrested or even killed. In the data we have on drug sellers, we see that when the drug trade is more lucrative, dealers are willing to take greater risks of arrest to carve out a share of the market. On the other hand, they also do their best to minimize their risks. For example, crack sellers used to carry the crack with them. When laws were passed imposing stiff penalties on anyone caught with anything more than a minimal amount of crack, drug dealers responded by storing the crack somewhere else, and retrieving only the amount being sold to the current client. Sumo wrestlers, on the other hand, care mostly about their official ranking. Sometimes matches occur where one wrestler has more to lose or gain than the other wrestler. We find that sumo wrestlers make corrupt deals to make sure the wrestler who needs the win is the one who actually wins.

Why is an economist interested in crime and cheating?
I think of economics as being primarily about a way of looking at the world and a set of tools for thinking clearly. The topics you apply these tools to are unlimited. That is why I think economics has been so powerful. If you understand economics and use the tools wisely, you will be a better business person, doctor, public servant, parent.

I think of economics as being primarily about a way of looking at the world and a set of tools for thinking clearly.

What is the economic model of crime, and how does it help to design better ways of dealing with criminal activity? Can you illustrate by talking a bit about your work on the behavior of auto thieves?
The economic model of crime argues that people have a choice of either working for a wage in the legal sector or earning money from illegal activity. The model carefully lays out the set of costs associated with being a criminal (e.g., forgone wages and being punished) and benefits (e.g., the loot) associated with crime and analyzes how a maximizing individual will choose whether to commit crimes and how much crime to commit. One reason the model is useful is because it lays out the various ways in which public policy might influence crime rates. For instance, we can increase the probability of a criminal getting caught or make the prison sentence longer for those who are caught. The government might also try to intervene in the labor market to make legal work more attractive—for instance, with a minimum wage.

What is the problem in figuring out whether more police leads to less crime? How did you find the answer?
We think that when you add more police, crime will fall because the cost of being a criminal goes up because of increased detection. From a public policy perspective, understanding how much crime falls in response to police is an important question. In practice, it is hard to answer this question because we don't randomly hire police. Rather, where crime is bad, there is greater demand for police and thus more police. If you just look at different cities, the places with the most police also have the most crime, but it is not because police cause crime, it is because crime causes police to be hired.

To figure out a causal impact of police on crime, you would like to do a randomized experiment where you added a lot of police at random to some cities and took them away in other cities. That is something you cannot really do in real life. So instead, the economist has to look for "natural experiments" to answer the question.

I used the timing of mayoral elections. It turns out that mayors hire a lot of police before elections to "look tough on crime." If elections do not otherwise affect crime, then the election is kind of like a randomizing device that puts more police in some cities every once in a while. Indeed, I found that crime goes down in the year following elections once the police hired are up and running. It is indirect evidence, but it is an example of how economists use their toolbox to handle difficult questions.

If you just look at different cities, the places with the most police also have the most crime, but it is not because police cause crime, it is because crime causes police to be hired.

Your work shows that legalized abortion leads to less crime. Can you explain how you reach that conclusion? Can you also explain its implications for the pro-life, pro-choice debate?
The theory is simple: Unwanted children have hard lives (including being much more likely to be criminals); after legalized abortion, there are fewer unwanted children. Therefore, there should be less crime (with a 15–20 year lag while the babies grow up and reach high-crime ages).

We looked at what happened to crime 15–20 years after *Roe* v. *Wade*, in states with high and low abortion rates and in states that legalized abortion a few years earlier than the rest of the country. We could even look at people born immediately before or after abortion became legal.

All the evidence pointed the same way: Crime fell a lot because abortion was legalized.

Our results, however, don't have large implications for the abortion debate. If abortion is murder, as pro-life advocates argue, then the changes in crime we see are trivial in comparison. If a woman simply has the right to control her body, as pro-choice advocates argue, then our estimates about crime are likewise irrelevant.

Our results have more to say about unwantedness: There are big benefits to making sure that children who are brought into the world are wanted and well cared for, through either birth control, adoption, abortion, or parental education.

. . . every time I observed anything in the world I asked myself, "Is that a natural experiment?"

Terrorism is on everyone's minds these days. And presumably, terrorists respond to incentives. Have you thought about how we might be able to use the insights of economics to better understand and perhaps even combat terrorism?

Terrorism is an unusually difficult question to tackle through incentives. The religious terrorists we are most worried about are willing to give up their lives to carry out terrorist acts. So the only punishment we can really offer is preventing them from committing the act by catching them beforehand or maybe minimizing the damage they can do. Unlike typical criminals, the threat of punishing them after the fact will not help deter the crime. Luckily, even among extremists, there are not many people willing to give their lives for a cause.

Can a student learn how to use natural experiments or do you have a gift that is hard to teach?

I don't think I have such a gift. Most people who are good at something are good because they have worked hard and practiced. That is certainly true with me.

For a while, I just walked around and every time I observed anything in the world I asked myself, "Is that a natural experiment?" Every once in a while I stumbled onto one because I was on the lookout.

What else can a student who wants to become a natural experimenting economist or broader social scientist do to better prepare for that career?

I would say that the best thing students can do is to try to really apply what they are learning to their lives, rather than just memorizing for an exam and quickly forgetting. If you are passionate about economics (or anything else for that matter), you are way ahead of others who are just trying to get by.

CHAPTER 9

Organizing Production

Spinning a Web

In the fall of 1990, a British scientist named Tim Berners-Lee invented the World Wide Web. This remarkable idea paved the way for the creation and growth of thousands of profitable businesses. One of these businesses is Google, Inc. Built on the idea of two Stanford University graduate students, Larry Page and Sergey Brin, Google, Inc. opened its door for business—a garage door!—in 1998. In just a few years, Google became the world's most used, most efficient, and most profitable search engine.

How do Google and the other 20 million firms that operate in the United States make their business decisions? How do they operate efficiently?

One way in which firms seek to operate efficiently is by establishing incentives for their top executives, managers, and workers. What are the incentive schemes that firms use and how do they work?

Most of the firms that you know the names of don't make things. They buy and sell things. For example, most of the components of a Dell personal computer are made by other firms. Intel makes its processor chip, other firms make the hard drive, modem, the CD drive, sound card, and so on. Why doesn't Dell make its own computer components? How do firms decide what to make themselves and what to buy in the marketplace from other firms?

In this chapter, we are going to learn about firms and the choices they make to cope with scarcity. In *Reading Between the Lines* at the end of the chapter, we'll look at competition in the search engine business between Google and Yahoo!. But we begin by studying the economic problems and choices that are common to all firms.

After studying this chapter, you will be able to

- Explain what a firm is and describe the economic problem that *all* firms face
- Distinguish between technological efficiency and economic efficiency
- Define and explain the principal-agent problem and describe how different types of business organizations cope with this problem
- Describe and distinguish between different types of markets in which firms operate
- Explain why markets coordinate some economic activities and firms coordinate others

The Firm and Its Economic Problem

The 20 million firms in the United States differ in size and in the scope of what they do. But they all perform the same basic economic functions. Each **firm** is an institution that hires factors of production and organizes those factors to produce and sell goods and services. Our goal is to predict firms' behavior. To do so, we need to know a firm's goals and the constraints it faces. We begin with the goals.

The Firm's Goal

If you asked a group of entrepreneurs what they are trying to achieve, you would get many different answers. Some would talk about making a high-quality product, others about business growth, others about market share, and others about the job satisfaction of their work force. All of these goals might be pursued, but they are not the fundamental goal. They are means to a deeper goal.

A firm's goal is to maximize profit. A firm that does not seek to maximize profit is either eliminated or bought by firms that do seek to maximize profit.What exactly is the profit that a firm seeks to maximize? To answer this question, let's look at Sidney's Sweaters.

Measuring a Firm's Profit

Sidney runs a successful business that makes sweaters. Sidney's Sweaters receives $400,000 a year for the sweaters it sells. Its expenses are $80,000 a year for wool, $20,000 for utilities, $120,000 for wages, $5,000 for lease of a computer from Dell, Inc., and $5,000 in interest on a bank loan. With receipts of $400,000 and expenses of $230,000, Sidney's Sweaters' annual surplus is $170,000.

Sidney's accountant lowers this number by $20,000, which he says is the depreciation (fall in value) of the firm's buildings and knitting machines during the year. (Accountants use Internal Revenue Service rules based on standards established by the Financial Accounting Standards Board to calculate the depreciation.) So the accountant reports that the profit of Sidney's Sweaters is $150,000 a year.

The accountant measures cost and profit to ensure that the firm pays the correct amount of income tax and to show the bank how its loan has been used. But we want to predict the decisions that a firm makes. These decisions respond to *opportunity cost* and *economic profit.*

Opportunity Cost

The *opportunity cost* of any action is the highest-valued alternative forgone. The action that you choose not to take—the highest-valued alternative forgone—is the cost of the action that you choose to take. For a firm, the opportunity cost of production is the value of the firm's best alternative use of its resources.

Opportunity cost is a real alternative forgone. But so that we can compare the cost of one action with that of another action, we express opportunity cost in money units. A firm's opportunity cost includes both

- Explicit costs
- Implicit costs

Explicit Costs Explicit costs are paid in money. The amount paid for a resource could have been spent on something else, so it is the opportunity cost of using the resource. For Sidney's Sweaters, its expenditure on wool, utilities, wages, and interest are explicit costs.

Firms often lease capital—computers, photocopiers, earth-moving equipment, and so on. Sidney's Sweaters leases a computer and the payment it makes to Dell is also an explicit cost.

Implicit Costs A firm incurs implicit costs when it forgoes an alternative action but does not make a payment. A firm incurs implicit costs when it

1. Uses its own capital.
2. Uses its owner's time or financial resources.

The cost of using capital owned by the firm is an implicit cost—and an opportunity cost—because the firm could have rented the capital to another firm. The rental income forgone is the firm's opportunity cost of using the capital it owns. This opportunity cost is called the **implicit rental rate** of capital.

If a firm uses the capital it owns, it incurs an implicit cost, which is made up of

1. Economic depreciation
2. Interest forgone

Economic depreciation is the change in the *market* value of capital over a given period. It is calculated as the market price of the capital at the beginning of the period minus its market price at the end of the period. For example, suppose that Sidney's Sweaters could have sold its buildings and knitting machines on December 31, 2005, for $400,000. If it can sell the same capital on December 31, 2006, for $375,000, its economic depreciation during 2006 is $25,000—the fall in the market value of the buildings and machines. This $25,000 is an implicit cost of using the capital during 2006.

The funds used to buy capital could have been used for some other purpose. And in their next best use, they would have earned an interest income. This forgone interest is part of the opportunity cost of using the capital. For example, Sidney's Sweaters could have bought bonds instead of a knitting factory. The interest forgone on the bonds is an implicit cost of operating the knitting factory.

Cost of Owner's Resources A firm's owner often supplies entrepreneurial ability—the factor of production that organizes the business, makes business decisions, innovates, and bears the risk of running the business. The return to entrepreneurship is profit, and the return that an entrepreneur can expect to receive on the average is called **normal profit**.

The entrepreneur's normal profit is part of a firm's opportunity cost, because it is the cost of a forgone alternative—running another firm. If normal profit in the textile business is $50,000 a year, this amount is Sidney's normal profit and it is part of Sidney's Sweaters' opportunity costs.

As well as being the entrepreneur, the owner of a firm can supply labor, which earns a wage. The opportunity cost of the owner's labor is the wage income that the owner forgoes by not taking the best alternative job. Suppose that, in addition to being the entrepreneur, Sidney could supply labor to another firm and earn $40,000 a year. By working for his own business, Sidney forgoes $40,000 a year and this amount is part of Sidney's Sweaters' opportunity cost.

Economic Profit

What is the bottom line—the profit or loss of the firm? A firm's **economic profit** is equal to its total revenue minus its total cost. The firm's total cost is the sum of its explicit costs and implicit costs. And the implicit costs, remember, include *normal profit*. The return to entrepreneurial ability is greater than normal in a firm that makes a positive economic profit. And the return to entrepreneurial ability is less than normal in a firm that makes a negative economic profit—a firm that incurs an economic loss.

Economic Accounting: A Summary

Table 9.1 summarizes the economic accounting. Sidney's Sweaters' total revenue is $400,000. Its opportunity cost (explicit costs plus implicit costs) is $365,000. And its economic profit is $35,000.

To achieve the objective of maximum profit—maximum economic profit—a firm must make five basic decisions:

1. What goods and services to produce and in what quantities
2. How to produce—the techniques of production to use
3. How to organize and compensate its managers and workers
4. How to market and price its products
5. What to produce itself and what to buy from other firms

In all these decisions, a firm's actions are limited by the constraints that it faces. Our next task is to learn about these constraints.

TABLE 9.1 Economic Accounting

Item		Amount
Total Revenue		**$400,000**
Costs		
Wool	$80,000	
Utilities	20,000	
Wages paid	120,000	
Dell lease paid	5,000	
Bank interest paid	5,000	
Total Explicit Costs		$230,000
Sidney's wages forgone	40,000	
Sidney's interest forgone	20,000	
Economic depreciation	$25,000	
Sidney's normal profit	$50,000	
Total Implicit Costs		$135,000
Total Cost		**$365,000**
Economic Profit		**$35,000**

The Firm's Constraints

Three features of its environment limit the maximum profit a firm can make. They are

- Technology
- Information
- Market

Technology Constraints Economists define technology broadly. A **technology** is any method of producing a good or service. Technology includes the detailed designs of machines. It also includes the layout of the workplace. And it includes the organization of the firm. For example, the shopping mall is a technology for producing retail services. It is a different technology from the catalog store, which in turn is different from the downtown store.

It might seem surprising that a firm's profits are limited by technology because it seems that technological advances are constantly increasing profit opportunities. Almost every day, we learn about some new technological advance that amazes us. With computers that speak and recognize our own speech and cars that can find the address we need in a city we've never visited, we can accomplish more than ever.

Technology advances over time. But at each point in time, to produce more output and gain more revenue, a firm must hire more resources and incur greater costs. The increase in profit that the firm can achieve is limited by the technology available. For example, by using its current plant and work force, Ford can produce some maximum number of cars per day. To produce more cars per day, Ford must hire more resources, which increases its costs and limits the increase in profit that it can make by selling the additional cars.

Information Constraints We never possess all the information we would like to have to make decisions. We lack information about both the future and the present. For example, suppose you plan to buy a new computer. When should you buy it? The answer depends on how the price is going to change in the future. Where should you buy it? The answer depends on the prices at hundreds of different computer shops. To get the best deal, you must compare the quality and prices in every shop. But the opportunity cost of this comparison exceeds the cost of the computer!

Similarly, a firm is constrained by limited information about the quality and effort of its work force, the current and future buying plans of its customers, and the plans of its competitors. Workers might slacken off when the manager believes they are working hard. Customers might switch to competing suppliers. Firms might have to compete against competition from a new firm.

Firms try to create incentive systems for workers to ensure that they work hard even when no one is monitoring their efforts. And firms spend millions of dollars on market research. But none of these efforts and expenditures eliminate the problems of incomplete information and uncertainty. And the cost of coping with limited information itself limits profit.

Market Constraints What each firm can sell and the price it can obtain are constrained by its customers' willingness to pay and by the prices and marketing efforts of other firms. Similarly, the resources that a firm can buy and the prices it must pay for them are limited by the willingness of people to work for and invest in the firm. Firms spend billions of dollars a year marketing and selling their products. Some of the most creative minds strive to find the right message that will produce a knockout television advertisement. Market constraints and the expenditures firms make to overcome them limit the profit a firm can make.

REVIEW QUIZ

1. Why do firms seek to maximize profit? What happens to firms that don't pursue this goal?
2. Why do accountants and economists calculate a firm's cost and profit in different ways?
3. What are the items that make opportunity cost differ from the accountant's cost measure?
4. Why is normal profit an opportunity cost?
5. What are the constraints that a firm faces? How does each constraint limit the firm's profit?

myeconlab **Study Plan 9.1**

In the rest of this chapter and in Chapters 10 through 13, we study the decisions that firms make. We're going to learn how we can predict a firm's behavior as the response to both the constraints that it faces and to changes in those constraints. We begin by taking a closer look at the technology constraints that firms face.

Technological and Economic Efficiency

Microsoft employs a large work force, and most Microsoft workers possess a large amount of human capital. But the firm uses a small amount of physical capital. In contrast, a coal-mining company employs a huge amount of mining equipment (physical capital) and almost no labor. Why? The answer lies in the concept of efficiency. There are two concepts of production efficiency: technological efficiency and economic efficiency. **Technological efficiency** occurs when the firm produces a given output by using the least amount of inputs. **Economic efficiency** occurs when the firm produces a given output at the least cost. Let's explore the two concepts of efficiency by studying an example.

Suppose that there are four alternative techniques for making TV sets:

A. *Robot production.* One person monitors the entire computer-driven process.
B. *Production line.* Workers specialize in a small part of the job as the emerging TV set passes them on a production line.
C. *Bench production.* Workers specialize in a small part of the job but walk from bench to bench to perform their tasks.
D. *Hand-tool production.* A single worker uses a few hand tools to make a TV set.

Table 9.2 sets out the amounts of labor and capital required by each of these four methods to make 10 TV sets a day.

Which of these alternative methods are technologically efficient?

Technological Efficiency

Recall that technological efficiency occurs when the firm produces a given output by using the least amount of inputs. Inspect the numbers in the table and notice that method *A* uses the most capital but the least labor. Method *D* uses the most labor but the least capital. Method *B* and method *C* lie between the two extremes. They use less capital but more labor than method *A* and less labor but more capital than method *D*. Compare methods *B* and *C*. Method *C* requires 100 workers and 10 units of capital to produce 10 TV sets. Those same 10 TV sets can be produced by method *B* with 10 workers and the same 10 units of capital. Because method *C* uses the same amount of capital and more labor than method *B*, method *C* is not technologically efficient.

Are any of the other methods not technologically efficient? The answer is no. Each of the other three methods is technologically efficient. Method *A* uses more capital but less labor than method *B*, and method *D* uses more labor but less capital than method *B*.

Which of the alternative methods are economically efficient?

Economic Efficiency

Recall that economic efficiency occurs when the firm produces a given output at the least cost. Suppose that labor costs $75 per person-day and that capital costs $250 per machine-day. Table 9.3(a) calculates the costs of using the different methods. By inspecting the table, you can see that method *B* has the lowest cost. Although method *A* uses less labor, it uses too much expensive capital. And although method *D* uses less capital, it uses too much expensive labor.

Method *C*, which is technologically inefficient, is also economically inefficient. It uses the same amount of capital as method *B* but 10 times as much labor. So it costs more. A technologically inefficient method is never economically efficient.

Although *B* is the economically efficient method in this example, method *A* or *D* could be economically efficient with different input prices.

Suppose that labor costs $150 a person-day and capital costs only $1 a machine-day. Table 9.3(b) now shows the costs of making a TV set. In this case, method *A* is economically efficient. Capital is now so

TABLE 9.2 Four Ways of Making 10 TV Sets a Day

	Method	Quantities of inputs: Labor	Capital
A	Robot production	1	1,000
B	Production line	10	10
C	Bench production	100	10
D	Hand-tool production	1,000	1

TABLE 9.3 The Costs of Different Ways of Making 10 TV Sets a Day

(a) Four ways of making TVs

Method	Labor cost ($75 per day)		Capital cost ($250 per day)		Total cost	Cost per TV set
A	$75	+	$250,000	=	$250,075	$25,007.50
B	750	+	2,500	=	3,250	325.00
C	7,500	+	2,500	=	10,000	1,000.00
D	75,000	+	250	=	75,250	7,525.00

(b) Three ways of making TVs: High labor costs

Method	Labor cost ($150 per day)		Capital cost ($1 per day)		Total cost	Cost per TV set
A	$150	+	$1,000	=	$1,150	$115.00
B	1,500	+	10	=	1,510	151.00
D	150,000	+	1	=	150,001	15,000.10

(c) Three ways of making TVs: High capital costs

Method	Labor cost ($1 per day)		Capital cost ($1,000 per day)		Total cost	Cost per TV set
A	$1	+	$1,000,000	=	$1,000,001	$100,000.10
B	10	+	10,000	=	10,010	1,001.00
D	1,000	+	1,000	=	2,000	200.00

cheap relative to labor that the method that uses the most capital is the economically efficient method.

Next, suppose that labor costs only $1 a person-day while capital costs $1,000 a machine-day. Table 9.3(c) shows the costs in this case. Method *D*, which uses a lot of labor and little capital, is now the least-cost method and the economically efficient method.

From these examples, you can see that while technological efficiency depends only on what is feasible, economic efficiency depends on the relative costs of resources. The economically efficient method is the one that uses a smaller amount of a more expensive resource and a larger amount of a less expensive resource.

A firm that is not economically efficient does not maximize profit. Natural selection favors efficient firms and opposes inefficient firms. Inefficient firms go out of business or are taken over by firms with lower costs.

REVIEW QUIZ

1. Is a firm technologically efficient if it uses the latest technology? Why or why not?
2. Is a firm economically inefficient if it can cut costs by producing less? Why or why not?
3. Explain the key distinction between technological efficiency and economic efficiency.
4. Why do some firms use large amounts of capital and small amounts of labor while others use small amounts of capital and large amounts of labor?

myeconlab **Study Plan 9.2**

Next we study information constraints that firms face and the diversity of organization structures they generate.

Information and Organization

Each firm organizes the production of goods and services by combining and coordinating the productive resources it hires. But there is variety across firms in how they organize production. Firms use a mixture of two systems:

- Command systems
- Incentive systems

Command Systems

A **command system** is a method of organizing production that uses a managerial hierarchy. Commands pass downward through the hierarchy, and information passes upward. Managers spend most of their time collecting and processing information about the performance of the people under their control and making decisions about what commands to issue and how best to get those commands implemented.

The military uses the purest form of command system. A commander-in-chief (in the United States, the President) makes the big decisions about strategic objectives. Beneath this highest level, generals organize their military resources. Beneath the generals, successively lower ranks organize smaller and smaller units but pay attention to ever-increasing degrees of detail. At the bottom of the managerial hierarchy are the people who operate weapons systems.

Command systems in firms are not as rigid as those in the military, but they share some similar features. A chief executive officer (CEO) sits at the top of a firm's command system. Senior executives who report to and receive commands from the CEO specialize in managing production, marketing, finance, personnel, and perhaps other aspects of the firm's operations. Beneath these senior managers might be several tiers of middle management ranks that stretch downward to the managers who supervise the day-to-day operations of the business. Beneath these managers are the people who operate the firm's machines and who make and sell the firm's goods and services.

Small firms have one or two layers of managers, while large firms have several layers. As production processes have become ever more complex, management ranks have swollen. Today, more people have management jobs than ever before. But the information revolution of the 1990s slowed the growth of management, and in some industries, it reduced the number of layers of managers and brought a shakeout of middle managers.

Managers make enormous efforts to be well informed. And they try hard to make good decisions and issue commands that end up using resources efficiently. But managers always have incomplete information about what is happening in the divisions of the firm for which they are responsible. It is for this reason that firms use incentive systems as well as command systems to organize production.

Incentive Systems

An **incentive system** is a method of organizing production that uses a market-like mechanism inside the firm. Instead of issuing commands, senior managers create compensation schemes that will induce workers to perform in ways that maximize the firm's profit.

Selling organizations use incentive systems most extensively. Sales representatives who spend most of their working time alone and unsupervised are induced to work hard by being paid a small salary and a large performance-related bonus.

But incentive systems operate at all levels in a firm. CEOs' compensation plans include a share in the firm's profit, and factory floor workers sometimes receive compensation based on the quantity they produce.

Mixing the Systems

Firms use a mixture of commands and incentives. And they choose the mixture that maximizes profit. They use commands when it is easy to monitor performance or when a small deviation from an ideal performance is very costly. They use incentives when monitoring performance is either not possible or too costly to be worth doing.

For example, it is easy to monitor the performance of workers on a production line. And if one person works too slowly, the entire line slows. So a production line is organized with a command system.

In contrast, it is costly to monitor a CEO. For example, what did Ken Lay (former CEO of Enron) contribute to the initial success and subsequent failure of Enron? This question can't be answered with certainty, yet Enron's stockholders had to put someone in charge of the business and provide that person with an incentive to maximize their returns. The performance of Enron illustrates the nature of this problem, known as the principal-agent problem.

The Principal-Agent Problem

The **principal-agent problem** is the problem of devising compensation rules that induce an *agent* to act in the best interest of a *principal.* For example, the stockholders of Enron are *principals,* and the firm's managers are *agents.* The stockholders (the principals) must induce the managers (agents) to act in the stockholders' best interest. Similarly, Bill Gates (a principal) must induce the programmers who are working on the next generation of Windows (agents) to work efficiently.

Agents, whether they are managers or workers, pursue their own goals and often impose costs on a principal. For example, the goal of stockholders of Citicorp (principals) is to maximize the firm's profit—its true profit, not some fictitious paper profit. But the firm's profit depends on the actions of its managers (agents), and they have their own goals. Perhaps a manager takes a customer to a ball game on the pretense that she is building customer loyalty, when in fact she is simply enjoying on-the-job leisure. This same manager is also a principal, and her tellers are agents. The manager wants the tellers to work hard and attract new customers so that she can meet her operating targets. But the workers enjoy conversations with each other and take on-the-job leisure. Nonetheless, the firm constantly strives to find ways of improving performance and increasing profits.

Coping with the Principal-Agent Problem

Issuing commands does not address the principal-agent problem. In most firms, the shareholders can't monitor the managers and often the managers can't monitor the workers. Each principal must create incentives that induce each agent to work in the interests of the principal. Three ways of attempting to cope with the principal-agent problem are

- Ownership
- Incentive pay
- Long-term contracts

Ownership By assigning ownership (or part-ownership) of a business to a manager or worker, it is sometimes possible to induce a job performance that increases a firm's profits. Part-ownership schemes for senior managers are quite common, but they are less common for workers. When United Airlines was running into problems a few years ago, it made most of its employees owners of the company.

Incentive Pay Incentive pay schemes—pay related to performance—are very common. They are based on a variety of performance criteria such as profits, production, or sales targets. Promoting an employee for good performance is another example of an incentive pay scheme.

Long-Term Contracts Long-term contracts tie the long-term fortunes of managers and workers (agents) to the success of the principal(s)—the owner(s) of the firm. For example, a multiyear employment contract for a CEO encourages that person to take a long-term view and devise strategies that achieve maximum profit over a sustained period.

These three ways of coping with the principal-agent problem give rise to different types of business organization. Each type of business organization is a different response to the principal-agent problem. Each type uses ownership, incentives, and long-term contracts in different ways. Let's look at the main types of business organization.

Types of Business Organization

The three main types of business organization are

- Proprietorship
- Partnership
- Corporation

Proprietorship A *proprietorship* is a firm with a single owner—a proprietor—who has unlimited liability. *Unlimited liability* is the legal responsibility for all the debts of a firm up to an amount equal to the entire wealth of the owner. If a proprietorship cannot pay its debts, those to whom the firm owes money can claim the personal property of the owner. Some farmers, computer programmers, and artists are examples of proprietorships.

The proprietor makes management decisions, receives the firm's profits, and is responsible for its losses. Profits from a proprietorship are taxed at the same rate as other sources of the proprietor's personal income.

Partnership A *partnership* is a firm with two or more owners who have unlimited liability. Partners must agree on an appropriate management structure and on how to divide the firm's profits among themselves. The profits of a partnership are taxed as the personal income of the owners. But each partner is legally liable for all the debts of the partnership (limited only by the wealth of that individual partner). Liability for the full debts of the partnership is called *joint unlimited liability*. Most law firms are partnerships.

Corporation A *corporation* is a firm owned by one or more limited liability stockholders. *Limited liability* means that the owners have legal liability only for the value of their initial investment. This limitation of liability means that if the corporation becomes bankrupt, its owners are not required to use their personal wealth to pay the corporation's debts.

Corporations' profits are taxed independently of stockholders' incomes. Stockholders pay a capital gains tax on the profit they earn when they sell a stock for a higher price than they paid for it. Corporate stocks generate capital gains when a corporation retains some of its profit and reinvests it in profitable activities. So retained earnings are taxed twice because the capital gains they generate are taxed. Until recently, dividend payments were also taxed twice but this anomaly has now been corrected.

Pros and Cons of Different Types of Firms

The different types of business organization arise as different ways of trying to cope with the principal-agent problem. Each has advantages in particular situations. And because of its special advantages, each type continues to exist. Each type also has its disadvantages, which explains why it has not driven out the other two.

Table 9.4 summarizes these and other pros and cons of the different types of firms.

TABLE 9.4 The Pros and Cons of Different Types of Firms

Type of Firm	Pros	Cons
Proprietorship	■ Easy to set up ■ Simple decision making ■ Profits taxed only once as owner's income	■ Bad decisions not checked by need for consensus ■ Owner's entire wealth at risk ■ Firm dies with owner ■ Cost of capital and labor is high relative to that of a corporation
Partnership	■ Easy to set up ■ Diversified decision making ■ Can survive withdrawal of partner ■ Profits taxed only once as owners' incomes	■ Achieving consensus may be slow and expensive ■ Owners' entire wealth at risk ■ Withdrawal of partner may create capital shortage ■ Cost of capital and labor is high relative to that of a corporation
Corporation	■ Owners have limited liability ■ Large-scale, low-cost capital available ■ Professional management not restricted by ability of owners ■ Perpetual life ■ Long-term labor contracts cut labor costs	■ Complex management structure can make decisions slow and expensive ■ Retained profits taxed twice: as company profit and as stockholders' capital gains

FIGURE 9.1 The Proportions of the Three Types of Firms

myeconlab

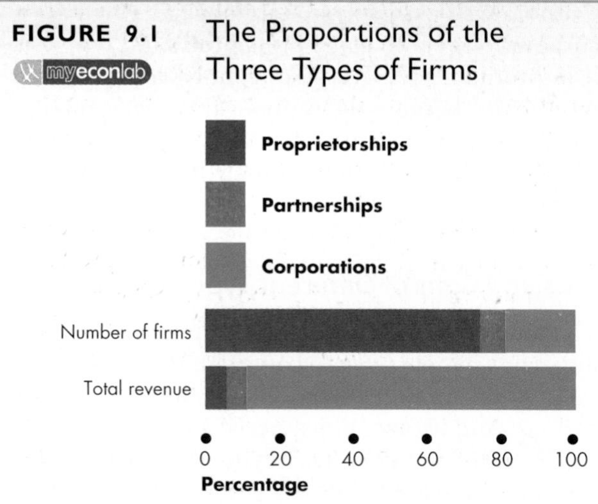

(a) Number of firms and total revenue

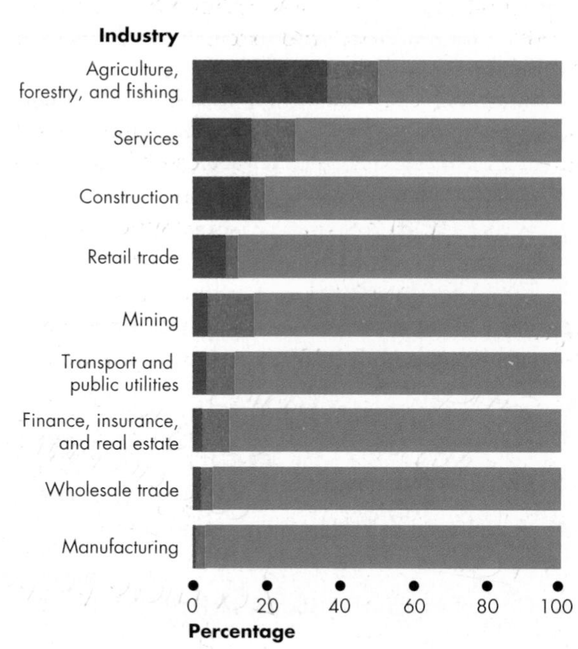

(b) Total revenue in various industries

Three quarters of all firms are proprietorships, almost one fifth are corporations, and only a twentieth are partnerships. Corporations account for 86 percent of total revenue (part a). But proprietorships and partnerships account for a significant percentage of total revenue in some industries (part b).

Source of data: U.S. Bureau of the Census, *Statistical Abstract of the United States: 2001*.

The Proportions of Different Types of Firms

Figure 9.1(a) shows the proportions of the three main types of firms in the U.S. economy. The figure also shows that the revenue of corporations is much larger than that of the other types of firms. Although only 18 percent of all firms are corporations, they generate 86 percent of total revenue.

Figure 9.1(b) shows the percentage of total revenue generated by the different types of firms in various industries. Proprietorships in agriculture, forestry, and fishing generate about 40 percent of the total revenue in those sectors. Proprietorships in the service sector, construction, and retail trades also generate a large percentage of total revenue. Partnerships in agriculture, forestry, and fishing generate about 15 percent of total revenue. Partnerships are more prominent in services; mining; and finance, insurance, and real estate than in other sectors. Corporations dominate all sectors and have the manufacturing field almost to themselves.

Why do corporations dominate the business scene? Why do the other types of business survive? And why are proprietorships and partnerships more prominent in some sectors? The answers to these questions lie in the pros and cons of the different types of business organization that are summarized in Table 9.4. Corporations dominate where a large amount of capital is used. But proprietorships dominate where flexibility in decision making is critical.

REVIEW QUIZ

1. Explain the distinction between a command system and an incentive system.
2. What is the principal-agent problem? What are three ways in which firms try to cope with it?
3. What are the three types of firms? Explain the major advantages and disadvantages of each.
4. Why do all three types of firms survive and in which sectors is each type most prominent?

myeconlab **Study Plan 9.3**

You've now seen how technology constraints and information constraints influence firms. We'll now look at market constraints and see how they influence the environment in which firms compete for business.

Markets and the Competitive Environment

The markets in which firms operate vary a great deal. Some are highly competitive, and profits in these markets are hard to come by. Some appear to be almost free from competition, and firms in these markets earn large profits. Some markets are dominated by fierce advertising campaigns in which each firm seeks to persuade buyers that it has the best products. And some markets display a warlike character.

Economists identify four market types:

1. Perfect competition
2. Monopolistic competition
3. Oligopoly
4. Monopoly

Perfect competition arises when there are many firms, each selling an identical product, many buyers, and no restrictions on the entry of new firms into the industry. The many firms and buyers are all well informed about the prices of the products of each firm in the industry. The worldwide markets for corn, rice, and other grain crops are examples of perfect competition.

Monopolistic competition is a market structure in which a large number of firms compete by making similar but slightly different products. Making a product slightly different from the product of a competing firm is called **product differentiation**. Product differentiation gives the firm in monopolistic competition an element of market power. The firm is the sole producer of the particular version of the good in question. For example, in the market for frozen foods, hundreds of firms make their own version of the perfect dish. Each of these firms is the sole producer of a particular brand. Differentiated products are not necessarily different products. What matters is that consumers perceive them to be different. For example, different brands of aspirin are chemically identical (acetylsalicylic acid) and differ only in their packaging.

Oligopoly is a market structure in which a small number of firms compete. Computer software, airplane manufacture, and international air transportation are examples of oligopolistic industries. Oligopolies might produce almost identical products, such as the colas produced by Coke and Pepsi. Or they might produce differentiated products such as Chevrolet's Lumina and Ford's Taurus.

Monopoly arises when there is one firm, which produces a good or service that has no close substitutes and in which the firm is protected by a barrier preventing the entry of new firms. In some places, the phone, gas, electricity, and water suppliers are local monopolies—monopolies restricted to a given location. Microsoft Corporation, the software developer that created Windows, the operating system used by PCs, is an example of a global monopoly.

Perfect competition is the most extreme form of competition. Monopoly is the most extreme absence of competition. The other two market types fall between these extremes.

Many factors must be taken into account to determine which market structure describes a particular real-world market. One of these factors is the extent to which the market is dominated by a small number of firms. To measure this feature of markets, economists use indexes called measures of concentration. Let's look at these measures.

Measures of Concentration

Economists use two measures of concentration:

- The four-firm concentration ratio
- The Herfindahl-Hirschman Index

The Four-Firm Concentration Ratio The **four-firm concentration ratio** is the percentage of the value of sales accounted for by the four largest firms in an industry. The range of the concentration ratio is from almost zero for perfect competition to 100 percent for monopoly. This ratio is the main measure used to assess market structure.

Table 9.5 shows two calculations of the four-firm concentration ratio: one for tire makers and one for printers. In this example, 14 firms produce tires. The largest four have 80 percent of the sales, so the four-firm concentration ratio is 80 percent. In the printing industry, with 1,004 firms, the largest four firms have only 0.5 percent of the sales, so the four-firm concentration ratio is 0.5 percent.

A low concentration ratio indicates a high degree of competition, and a high concentration ratio indicates an absence of competition. A monopoly has a concentration ratio of 100 percent—the largest (and only) firm has 100 percent of the sales. A four-firm concentration ratio that exceeds 60 percent is regarded as an indication of a market that is highly concentrated and dominated by a few firms in an oligopoly. A ratio of less than 60 percent is regarded as an indication of a competitive market.

The Herfindahl-Hirschman Index The **Herfindahl-Hirschman Index**—also called the HHI—is the square of the percentage market share of each firm summed over the largest 50 firms (or summed over all the firms if there are fewer than 50) in a market. For example, if there are four firms in a market and the market shares of the firms are 50 percent, 25 percent, 15 percent, and 10 percent, the Herfindahl-Hirschman Index is

$$\text{HHI} = 50^2 + 25^2 + 15^2 + 10^2 = 3{,}450.$$

TABLE 9.5 Concentration Ratio Calculations

Tire makers		Printers	
Firm	**Sales (millions of dollars)**	**Firm**	**Sales (millions of dollars)**
Top, Inc.	200	Fran's	2.5
ABC, Inc.	250	Ned's	2.0
Big, Inc.	150	Tom's	1.8
XYZ, Inc.	100	Jill's	1.7
Largest 4 firms	700	Largest 4 firms	8.0
Other 10 firms	175	Other 1,000 firms	1,592.0
Industry	875	Industry	1,600.0

Four-firm concentration ratios:

Tire makers: $\frac{700}{875} \times 100 = 80$ percent

Printers: $\frac{8}{1{,}600} \times 100 = 0.5$ percent

In perfect competition, the HHI is small. For example, if each of the largest 50 firms in an industry has a market share of 0.1 percent, then the HHI is $0.1^2 \times 50 = 0.5$. In a monopoly, the HHI is 10,000. The firm has 100 percent of the market: $100^2 = 10{,}000$.

The HHI became a popular measure of the degree of competition during the 1980s, when the Justice Department used it to classify markets. A market in which the HHI is less than 1,000 is regarded as being competitive. A market in which the HHI lies between 1,000 and 1,800 is regarded as being moderately competitive. But a market in which the HHI exceeds 1,800 is regarded as being uncompetitive. The Justice Department scrutinizes any merger of firms in a market in which the HHI exceeds 1,000 and is likely to challenge a merger if the HHI exceeds 1,800.

Concentration Measures for the U.S. Economy

Figure 9.2 shows a selection of concentration ratios and HHIs for the United States calculated by the U.S. Department of Commerce.

Industries that produce chewing gum, household laundry equipment, light bulbs, breakfast cereal, and motor vehicles have a high degree of concentration and are oligopolies. The ice cream, milk, clothing, concrete blocks and bricks, and commercial printing industries have low concentration measures and are highly competitive. The pet food and cookies and crackers industries are moderately concentrated. They are examples of monopolistic competition.

Concentration measures are a useful indicator of the degree of competition in a market. But they must be supplemented by other information to determine a market's structure. Table 9.6 summarizes the range of other information, along with the measures of concentration that determine which market structure describes a particular real-world market.

FIGURE 9.2 Concentration Measures in the United States

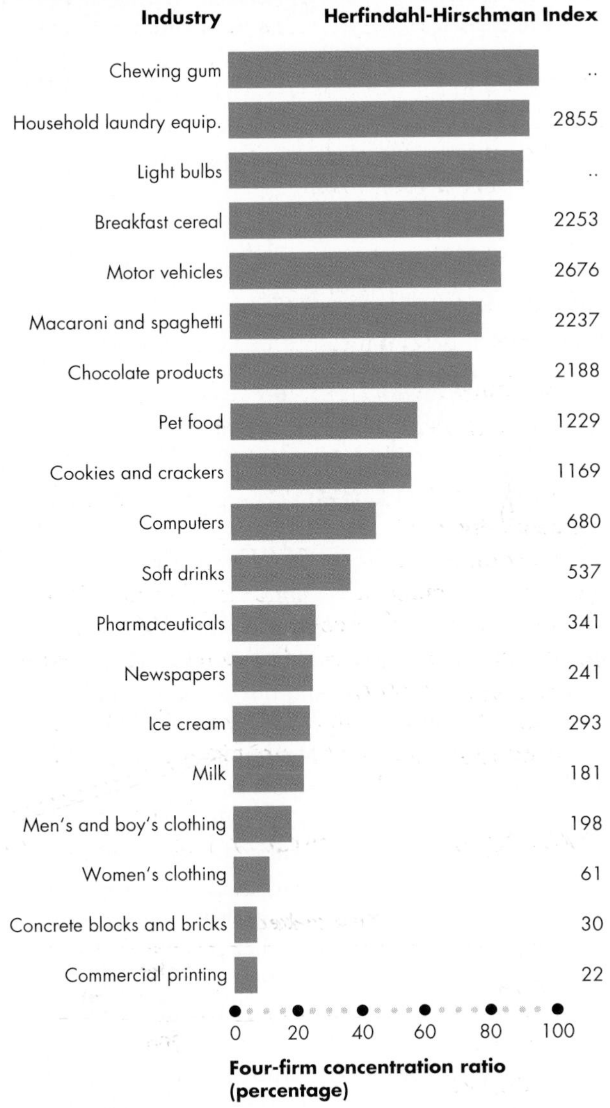

The industries that produce chewing gum, household laundry equipment, light bulbs, breakfast cereal, and motor vehicles are highly concentrated, while those that produce ice cream, milk, clothing, concrete blocks and bricks, and commercial printing are highly competitive. The industries that produce pet foods and cookies and crackers have an intermediate degree of concentration.

Source of data: Concentration Ratios in Manufacturing, (Washington, D.C.: U.S. Department of Commerce, 1996).

Limitations of Concentration Measures

The three main limitations of using only concentration measures as determinants of market structure are their failure to take proper account of

- The geographical scope of the market
- Barriers to entry and firm turnover
- The correspondence between a market and an industry

TABLE 9.6 Market Structure

Characteristics	Perfect competition	Monopolistic competition	Oligopoly	Monopoly
Number of firms in industry	Many	Many	Few	One
Product	Identical	Differentiated	Either identical or differentiated	No close substitutes
Barriers to entry	None	None	Moderate	High
Firm's control over price	None	Some	Considerable	Considerable or regulated
Concentration ratio	0	Low	High	100
HHI (approx. ranges)	Less than 100	101 to 999	More than 1,000	10,000
Examples	Wheat, corn	Food, clothing	Automobiles, cereals	Local water supply

Geographical Scope of Market Concentration measures take a national view of the market. Many goods are sold in a *national* market, but some are sold in a *regional* market and some in a *global* one. The newspaper industry consists of local markets. The concentration measures for newspapers are low, but there is a high degree of concentration in the newspaper industry in most cities. The auto industry has a global market. The biggest three U.S. car producers account for 92 percent of cars sold by U.S. producers, but they account for a smaller percentage of the total U.S. car market (including imports) and a smaller percentage of the global market for cars.

Barriers to Entry and Firm Turnover Concentration measures don't measure barriers to entry. Some industries are highly concentrated but have easy entry and an enormous amount of turnover of firms. For example, many small towns have few restaurants, but there are no restrictions on opening a restaurant and many firms attempt to do so.

Also, an industry might be competitive because of *potential entry*—because a few firms in a market face competition from many firms that can easily enter the market and will do so if economic profits are available.

Market and Industry Correspondence To calculate concentration ratios, the Department of Commerce classifies each firm as being in a particular industry. But markets do not always correspond closely to industries for three reasons.

First, markets are often narrower than industries. For example, the pharmaceutical industry, which has a low concentration ratio, operates in many separate markets for individual products—for example, measles vaccine and AIDS-fighting drugs. These drugs do not compete with each other, so this industry, which looks competitive, includes firms that are monopolies (or near monopolies) in markets for individual drugs.

Second, most firms make several products. For example, Westinghouse makes electrical equipment and, among other things, gas-fired incinerators and plywood. So this one firm operates in at least three separate markets. But the Department of Commerce classifies Westinghouse as being in the electrical goods and equipment industry. The fact that Westinghouse competes with other producers of plywood does not show up in the concentration numbers for the plywood market.

Third, firms switch from one market to another depending on profit opportunities. For example,

Motorola, which today produces cellular telephones and other communications products, has diversified from being a TV and computer chip maker. Motorola no longer produces TVs. Publishers of newspapers, magazines, and textbooks are today rapidly diversifying into Internet and multimedia products. These switches among industries show that there is much scope for entering and exiting an industry, and so measures of concentration have limited usefulness.

Despite their limitations, concentration measures do provide a basis for determining the degree of competition in an industry when they are combined with information about the geographical scope of the market, barriers to entry, and the extent to which large, multiproduct firms straddle a variety of markets.

FIGURE 9.3 The Market Structure of the U.S. Economy

myeconlab

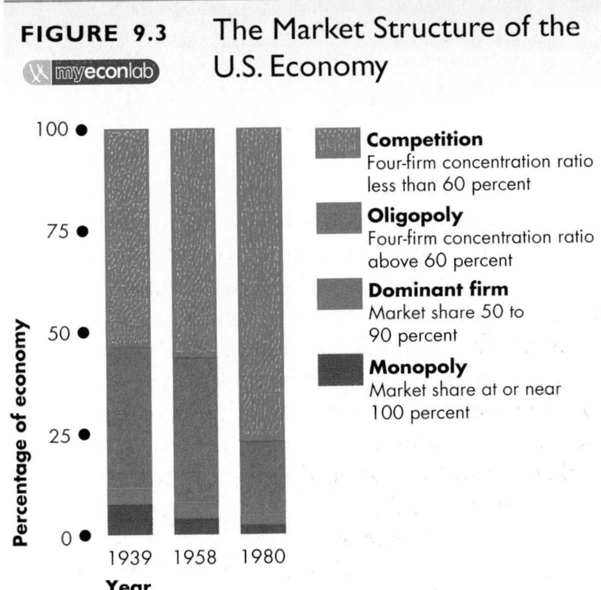

Three quarters of the U.S. economy is effectively competitive (perfect competition or monopolistic competition), one fifth is oligopoly, and the rest is monopoly. The economy became more competitive between 1939 and 1980. (Professor Shepherd, whose 1982 study remains the latest word on this topic, suspects that although some industries have become more concentrated, others have become less concentrated, so the net picture has probably not changed much since 1980.)

Source of data: William G. Shepherd, "Causes of Increased Competition in the U.S. Economy, 1939–1980," *Review of Economics and Statistics*, November 1982, pp. 613–626. © MIT Press Journals. Reprinted by permission.

Market Structures in the U.S. Economy

How competitive are the markets of the United States? Do most U.S. firms operate in competitive markets or in non-competitive markets?

Figure 9.3 provides part of the answer to these questions. It shows the market structure of the U.S. economy and the trends in market structure between 1939 and 1980. (Unfortunately, comparable data for the 1980s and 1990s are not available.)

In 1980, three quarters of the value of goods and services bought and sold in the United States was traded in markets that are essentially competitive—markets that have almost perfect competition or monopolistic competition. Monopoly and the dominance of a single firm accounted for about 5 percent of sales. Oligopoly, which is found mainly in manufacturing, accounted for about 18 percent of sales.

Over the period covered by the data in Fig. 9.3, the U.S. economy became increasingly competitive. You can see that the competitive markets have expanded most (the blue areas) and the oligopoly markets have shrunk most (the red areas).

But also during the past decades, the U.S. economy has become much more exposed to competition from the rest of the world. Figure 9.3 does not capture this international competition.

REVIEW QUIZ

1. What are the four market types? Explain the distinguishing characteristics of each.
2. What are the two measures of concentration? Explain how each measure is calculated.
3. Under what conditions do the measures of concentration give a good indication of the degree of competition in a market?
4. Is our economy competitive? Is it becoming more competitive or less competitive?

myeconlab **Study Plan 9.4**

You now know the variety of market types and the way we classify firms and industries into the different market types. Our final question in this chapter is: What determines the things that firms decide to buy from other firms rather than produce for themselves?

Markets and Firms

A firm is an institution that hires factors of production and organizes them to produce and sell goods and services. To organize production, firms coordinate the economic decisions and activities of many individuals. But firms are not the only coordinators of economic decisions. You learned in Chapter 3 that markets also coordinate decisions. They do so by adjusting prices and making the decisions of buyers and sellers consistent—making the quantity demanded equal to the quantity supplied for each good and service.

Market Coordination

Markets can coordinate production. For example, markets might coordinate the production of a rock concert. A promoter hires a stadium, some stage equipment, audio and video recording engineers and technicians, some rock groups, a superstar, a publicity agent, and a ticket agent—all market transactions—and sells tickets to thousands of rock fans, audio rights to a recording company, and video and broadcasting rights to a television network—another set of market transactions. Alternatively, if rock concerts were produced like cornflakes, the firm producing them would own all the capital used (stadiums, stage, sound and video equipment) and would employ all the labor needed (singers, engineers, and salespeople).

Outsourcing, buying parts or products from other firms, is another example of market coordination. Dell uses outsourcing for all the components of the computers it produces. The major automakers use outsourcing for windshields and windows, gearboxes, tires, and many other car parts.

What determines whether a firm or markets coordinate a particular set of activities? How do firms decide whether to buy from another firm or manufacture an item themselves? The answer is cost. Taking account of the opportunity cost of time as well as the costs of the other inputs, firms use the method that costs least. In other words, they use the economically efficient method.

Firms coordinate economic activity when they can perform a task more efficiently than markets can. In such a situation, it is profitable to set up a firm. If markets can perform a task more efficiently than a firm can, firms will use markets, and any attempt to set up a firm to replace such market coordination will be doomed to failure.

Why Firms?

Firms are often more efficient than markets as coordinators of economic activity because they can achieve

- Lower transactions costs
- Economies of scale
- Economies of scope
- Economies of team production

Transactions Costs The idea that firms exist because there are activities in which firms are more efficient than markets was first suggested by University of Chicago economist and Nobel Laureate Ronald Coase. Coase focused on the firm's ability to reduce or eliminate transactions costs. **Transactions costs** are the costs that arise from finding someone with whom to do business, of reaching an agreement about the price and other aspects of the exchange, and of ensuring that the terms of the agreement are fulfilled. Market transactions require buyers and sellers to get together and to negotiate the terms and conditions of their trading. Sometimes, lawyers have to be hired to draw up contracts. A broken contract leads to still more expenses. A firm can lower such transactions costs by reducing the number of individual transactions undertaken.

Consider, for example, two ways of getting your rattling car fixed.

> *Firm coordination*: You take the car to the garage. The garage owner coordinates parts and tools as well as the mechanic's time, and your car gets fixed. You pay one bill for the entire job.
>
> *Market coordination*: You hire a mechanic, who diagnoses the problems and makes a list of the parts and tools needed to fix them. You buy the parts from the local wrecker's yard and rent the tools from ABC Rentals. You hire the mechanic again to fix the problems. You return the tools and pay your bills—wages to the mechanic, rental to ABC, and the cost of the parts used to the wrecker.

What determines the method that you use? The answer is cost. Taking account of the opportunity cost of your own time as well as the costs of the other inputs that you would have to buy, you will use the method that costs least. In other words, you will use the economically efficient method.

The first method requires that you undertake only one transaction with one firm. It's true that the firm has to undertake several transactions—hiring the labor and buying the parts and tools required to do the job. But the firm doesn't have to undertake those transactions simply to fix your car. One set of such transactions enables the firm to fix hundreds of cars. Thus there is an enormous reduction in the number of individual transactions that take place if people get their cars fixed at the garage rather than going through an elaborate sequence of market transactions.

Economies of Scale When the cost of producing a unit of a good falls as its output rate increases, **economies of scale** exist. Automakers, for example, experience economies of scale because as the scale of production increases, the firm can use cost-saving equipment and highly specialized labor. An automaker that produces only a few cars a year must use hand-tool methods that are costly. Economies of scale arise from specialization and the division of labor that can be reaped more effectively by firm coordination rather than market coordination.

Economies of Scope A firm experiences **economies of scope** when it uses specialized (and often expensive) resources to produce a *range of goods and services.* For example, Microsoft hires specialist programmers, designers, and marketing experts and uses their skills across a range of software products. As a result, Microsoft coordinates the resources that produce software at a lower cost than an individual can who buys all these services in markets.

Economies of Team Production A production process in which the individuals in a group specialize in mutually supportive tasks is team production. Sport provides the best example of team activity. In baseball, some team members specialize in pitching and some in batting. In basketball, some team members specialize in defense and some in offense. The production of goods and services offers many examples of team activity. For example, production lines in automobile and TV manufacturing plants work most efficiently when individual activity is organized in teams, each specializing in a small task. You can also think of an entire firm as being a team. The team has buyers of raw material and other inputs, production workers, and salespeople. Each individual member of the team specializes, but the value of the output of the team and the profit that it earns depend on the coordinated activities of all the team's members. The idea that firms arise as a consequence of the economies of team production was first suggested by Armen Alchian and Harold Demsetz of the University of California at Los Angeles.

Because firms can economize on transactions costs, reap economies of scale and economies of scope, and organize efficient team production, it is firms rather than markets that coordinate most of our economic activity. But there are limits to the economic efficiency of firms. If a firm becomes too big or too diversified in the things that it seeks to do, the cost of management and monitoring per unit of output begins to rise, and at some point, the market becomes more efficient at coordinating the use of resources. IBM is an example of a firm that became too big to be efficient. In an attempt to restore efficient operations, IBM split up its large organization into a number of "Baby Blues," each of which specializes in a segment of the computer market.

Sometimes firms enter into long-term relationships with each other that make it difficult to see where one firm ends and another begins. For example, GM has long-term relationships with suppliers of windows, tires, and other parts. Wal-Mart has long-term relationships with suppliers of the goods it sells. Such relationships make transactions costs lower than they would be if GM or Wal-Mart went shopping on the open market each time it wanted new supplies.

REVIEW QUIZ

1. What are the two ways in which economic activity can be coordinated?
2. What determines whether a firm or markets coordinate production?
3. What are the main reasons why firms can often coordinate production at a lower cost than markets can?

myeconlab **Study Plan 9.5**

Reading Between the Lines on pp. 214–215 explores the Internet search business. We continue to study firms and their decisions in the next four chapters. In Chapter 10, we learn about the relationships between cost and output at different output levels. These cost-output relationships are common to all types of firms in all types of markets. We then turn to problems that are specific to firms in different types of markets.

READING BETWEEN THE LINES

Battling for Markets in Internet Search

http://money.cnn.com

Yawns for Yahoo, Ga-Ga for Google

Earnings from the two search leaders are coming and guess what? Google's eating Yahoo's lunch.

October 13, 2006

. . . Yahoo stunned Wall Street last month when chief financial officer Sue Decker somewhat casually said at a Goldman Sachs conference in New York that sales for the quarter would be at the low end of the company's forecast due to softness in auto and financial services advertising. . . .

Google, on the other hand, keeps wowing the Street. It bested sales and profit forecasts for the second quarter back in July.

And on Monday, Google unveiled a deal to buy YouTube, the popular online video sharing site, for $1.6 billion, a marriage uniting the top search engine and No. 1 video site. Analysts were raving about Google's chances to get a big piece of the potentially lucrative online video advertising market. . . .

Yahoo is playing catch-up with Google in the hot market for paid search, ads tied to specific keyword queries. According to the most recent numbers from Web tracking firm comScore Networks, Google widened its lead in search over Yahoo in August. . . .

And looking ahead to next year, Yahoo could face a much tougher challenge from Google in so-called display advertising, sales of video ads, banners and other ads not tied to search results, thanks to Google's pending deal for YouTube.

Yahoo has so far maintained an edge over Google in display advertising, which tends to be more attractive to big brand-name companies than search ads. But it is a big market opportunity for Google.

Essence of the Story

- Yahoo! lags behind Google in the market for advertising tied to keyword queries—known as paid search.
- Yahoo! leads Google in sales of video ads, banners, and other ads not tied to search results—known as display advertising.
- By buying YouTube (for $1.6 billion), Google has created a marriage of the top search engine and the top video sharing site.
- Google is expected to gain a large share of the profitable online video advertising market, which big brand-name companies use.

Economic Analysis

▶ Like all firms, Yahoo! and Google aim to maximize profit.

▶ Also, like all firms, Yahoo! and Google face constraints imposed by technology and the market.

▶ These firms provide search engines to access information on the Internet.

▶ People who use a search engine demand information, and Yahoo! and Google (and other firms) supply information.

▶ The equilibrium price of search engine services to their users is zero!

▶ To generate revenue and profit, search engine providers offer advertising services.

▶ Two types of advertising are offered: paid search and display.

▶ Google's focus is on paid search—see Figs. 1 and 2. Yahoo!'s focus is on display—see Fig. 3.

▶ To attract either type of advertising, a firm must be able to offer the advertiser access to a large potential customer base.

▶ To maximize the use of their search engines, Google and Yahoo! offer a variety of enticements to users.

▶ One enticement is the quality of the search engine itself. Most people think that Google has the better search technology. But Yahoo! is working on improved search.

▶ Another enticement is a variety of related attractions. Yahoo!'s photo-sharing service is an example.

▶ Search engines can also generate more revenue by enabling advertisers to more precisely target their potential customers. Again, the quality of the search technology is the key ingredient. And again, Google is reckoned by many to have the edge.

▶ Google hopes to attract even more users and to increase its ability to use video and other display technologies through its acquisition of YouTube.

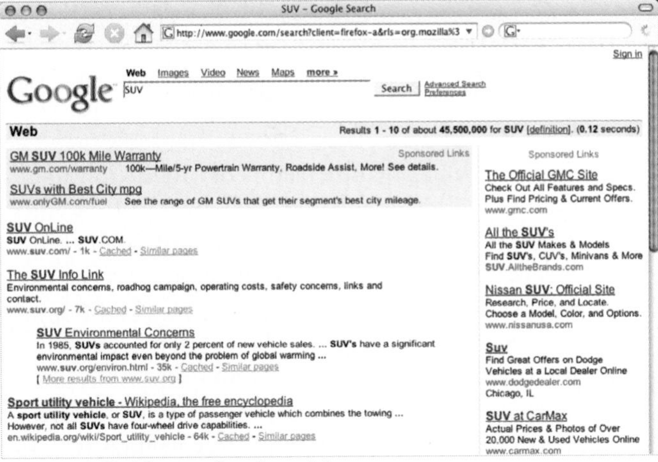

Figure 1 Paid search advertising

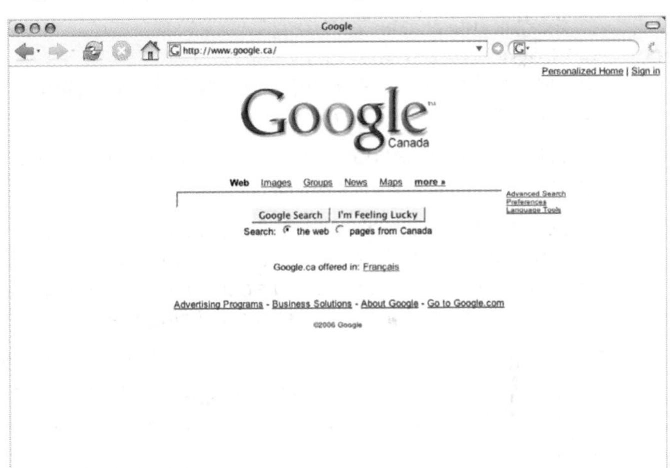

Figure 2 Google's focus is search

Figure 3 Yahoo! features display advertising

SUMMARY

Key Points

The Firm and Its Economic Problem (pp. 198–200)

- Firms hire and organize factors of production to produce and sell goods and services.
- Firms seek to maximize economic profit, which is total revenue minus opportunity cost.
- A firm's opportunity cost of production is the sum of explicit costs and the implicit costs of using the firm's capital and the owner's resources.
- Normal profit is the opportunity cost of entrepreneurship and is part of the firm's explicit costs.
- Technology, information, and markets limit a firm's profit.

Technological and Economic Efficiency (pp. 201–202)

- A method of production is technologically efficient when a firm produces a given output by using the least amount of inputs.
- A method of production is economically efficient when the cost of producing a given output is as low as possible.

Information and Organization (pp. 203–206)

- Firms use a combination of command systems and incentive systems to organize production.
- Faced with incomplete information and uncertainty, firms induce managers and workers to perform in ways that are consistent with the firm's goals.
- Proprietorships, partnerships, and corporations use ownership, incentive pay, and long-term contracts to cope with the principal-agent problem.

Markets and the Competitive Environment (pp. 207–211)

- In perfect competition, many sellers offer an identical product to many buyers and entry is free.
- In monopolistic competition, many sellers offer slightly different products to many buyers and entry is free.
- In oligopoly, a small number of sellers compete.
- In monopoly, one firm produces an item that has no close substitutes and the firm is protected by a barrier to entry that prevents the entry of competitors.

Markets and Firms (pp. 212–213)

- Firms coordinate economic activities when they can perform a task more efficiently—at lower cost—than markets can.
- Firms economize on transactions costs and achieve the benefits of economies of scale, economies of scope, and economies of team production.

Key Figures and Tables

Key Terms

PROBLEMS

myeconlab **Tests, Study Plan, Solutions***

1. One year ago, Jack and Jill set up a vinegar-bottling firm (called JJVB). Use the following information to calculate JJVB's explicit costs and implicit costs during its first year of operation:
   a. Jack and Jill put $50,000 of their own money into the firm.
   b. They bought equipment for $30,000.
   c. They hired one employee to help them for an annual wage of $20,000.
   d. Jack gave up his previous job, at which he earned $30,000, and spent all his time working for JJVB.
   e. Jill kept her old job, which paid $30 an hour, but gave up 10 hours of leisure each week (for 50 weeks) to work for JJVB.
   f. JJVB bought $10,000 of goods and services from other firms.
   g. The market value of the equipment at the end of the year was $28,000.
   h. Jack and Jill have a $100,000 home loan on which they pay an interest rate of 6 percent a year.
2. Four methods of completing a tax return and the time taken by each method are: with a PC, one hour; with a pocket calculator, 12 hours; with a pocket calculator and paper and pencil, 12 hours; and with a pencil and paper, 16 hours. The PC and its software cost $1,000, the pocket calculator costs $10, and the pencil and paper cost $1.
   a. Which, if any, of the methods is technologically efficient?
   b. Which method is economically efficient if the wage rate is
      (i) $5 an hour?
      (ii) $50 an hour?
      (iii) $500 an hour?
3. Alternative ways of laundering 100 shirts are

Method	Labor (hours)	Capital (machines)
A	1	10
B	5	8
C	20	4
D	50	1

   a. Which methods are technologically efficient?
   b. Which method is economically efficient if the hourly wage rate and implicit rental rate of capital are
      (i) Wage rate $1, rental rate $100?
      (ii) Wage rate $5, rental rate $50?
      (iii) Wage rate $50, rental rate $5?
4. Wal-Mart has more than 3,700 stores, more than one million employees, and total revenues of close to a quarter of a trillion dollars in the United States alone. Sarah Frey-Talley runs the family-owned Frey Farms in Illinois and supplies Wal-Mart with pumpkins and other fresh produce.
   a. How do you think Wal-Mart coordinates its activities? Is it likely to use mainly a command system or also to use incentive systems? Why or why not?
   b. How do you think Sarah Frey-Talley coordinates the activities of Frey Farms? Is she likely to use mainly a command system or also to use incentive systems? Why?
   c. Describe, compare, and contrast the principal-agent problems faced by Wal-Mart and Frey Farms. How might these firms cope with their principal-agent problems?
5. Sales of the firms in the tattoo industry are

Firm	Sales (dollars per year)
Bright Spots	450
Freckles	325
Love Galore	250
Native Birds	200
Other 15 firms	800

   a. Calculate the four-firm concentration ratio.
   b. What is the structure of the tattoo industry?
6. Market shares of chocolate makers are

Firm	Market share (percent)
Mayfair, Inc.	15
Bond, Inc.	10
Magic, Inc.	20
All Natural, Inc.	15
Truffles, Inc.	25
Gold, Inc.	15

   a. Calculate the Herfindahl-Hirschman Index.
   b. What is the structure of the chocolate industry?

*Solutions to odd-numbered problems are provided.

7. In 2003 and 2004, Lego, the Danish toymaker that produces colored plastic bricks, incurred economic losses. The firm faced competition from low-cost copies of its products and faced a fall in the number of 5- to 9-year-old boys (its main customers) in many rich countries. In 2004, Lego launched a plan to restore profits. It fired 3,500 of its 8,000 workers; closed factories in Switzerland and the United States; opened factories in Eastern Europe and Mexico; and introduced performance-based pay for its managers. Lego reported a return to profit in 2005. (Based on **Picking up the pieces**, *The Economist*, October 28, 2006.)
   a. Describe the problems that Lego faced in 2003 and 2004 using the concepts of the three types of constraint that all firms face.
   b. Which of the actions that Lego took to restore profits addressed an inefficiency? How did Lego seek to achieve economic efficiency?
   c. Which of the actions that Lego took to restore profits addressed an information and organization problem? How did Lego change the way in which it coped with the principal-agent problem?
   d. In what type of market does Lego operate?
8. Two leading design firms, Astro Studios of San Francisco and Hers Experimental Design Laboratory, Inc. of Osaka, Japan, worked with Microsoft to design the Xbox 360 video game console. IBM, ATI, and SiS designed the Xbox 360's hardware. Two firms, Flextronics & Wistron, and Celestica, manufacture the Xbox 360 at their plants in China.
   a. Describe the roles of market coordination and coordination by firms in the design, manufacture, and marketing of the Xbox 360.
   b. Why do you think Microsoft works with a large number of other firms rather than performing all the tasks required to bring the Xbox to market at its headquarters in Seattle?
   c. What are the roles of transactions costs, economies of scale, economies of scope, and economies of team production in the design, manufacture, and marketing of the Xbox?
   d. Why do you think the Xbox is designed in America and Japan but built in China?

CRITICAL THINKING

1. Study *Reading Between the Lines* about Google and Yahoo! on pp. 214–215, and then answer the following questions:
   a. What are the products that Google and Yahoo! sell?
   b. How do Internet search engine providers generate revenue and earn a profit?
   c. What is the distinction between paid search advertising and display advertising? What types of firms use the latter?
   d. Why do you think Google has bought YouTube? How will this purchase enable Google to increase its revenue and profit?
   e. What technological changes might increase the profitability of Internet search?
2. Federal Express enters into contracts with independent truck operators who offer FedEx service and who are rewarded by the volume (cubic meters) of packages they carry.
   a. Why do you think FedEx operates in this way rather than hiring more of its own drivers and rewarding them with a wage?
   b. What incentive problems might arise from the arrangement that FedEx uses?
3. Why do you think that Dell Computers buys computer components from other firms?

WEB ACTIVITIES

myeconlab **Links to Web sites**

1. Read James D. Miller's views on providing airport security services.
   a. What is Mr. Miller's argument concerning the best way to organize airport security?
   b. Explain Mr. Miller's views using the principal-agent analysis. Who is the principal and who is the agent?
   c. What exactly is the principal-agent problem in providing airport security services?
   d. Why might a private provider offer better security than a public provider?
   e. Do you think that a private provider would operate at a lower cost than a public provider? Why or why not?

CHAPTER 10

Output and Costs

Survival of the Fittest

Size does not guarantee survival in business. Even large firms disappear or get eaten up by other firms. But remaining small does not guarantee survival either. Every year, millions of small businesses close down. Call a random selection of restaurants and fashion boutiques from the 1995 yellow pages and see how many have vanished. What does a firm have to do to be a survivor?

Firms differ in lots of ways—from mom-and-pop convenience stores to multinational giants producing high-tech goods. But regardless of their size or what they produce, all firms must decide how much to produce and how to produce it. How do firms make these decisions?

Most automakers in the United States could produce more cars than they can sell. Why do automakers have expensive equipment lying around that isn't fully used? Many electric utilities in the United States don't have enough production equipment on hand to meet demand on the coldest and hottest days and must buy power from other producers. Why don't these firms install more equipment so that they can supply the market themselves?

We are going to answer these questions in this chapter. To do so, we are going to study the economic decisions of a small, imaginary firm: Cindy's Sweaters, Inc., a producer of knitted sweaters. By studying the way Cindy copes with her firm's economic problems, we will be able to get a clear view of the problems that face all firms—small ones like a mom-and-pop convenience store as well as big firms such as automakers and electric utilities. We're going to begin by describing the time frames in which firm's make decisions. At the end of the chapter, in *Reading Between the Lines*, we'll look at the reasons why a speculated merger between Ford and GM didn't happen and would not have been a good idea.

After studying this chapter, you will be able to

- Distinguish between the short run and the long run
- Explain the relationship between a firm's output and labor employed in the short run
- Explain the relationship between a firm's output and costs in the short run and derive a firm's short-run cost curves
- Explain the relationship between a firm's output and costs in the long run and derive a firm's long-run average cost curve

Decision Time Frames

People who operate firms make many decisions. And all of the decisions are aimed at one overriding objective: maximum attainable profit. But the decisions are not all equally critical. Some of the decisions are big ones. Once made, they are costly (or impossible) to reverse. If such a decision turns out to be incorrect, it might lead to the failure of the firm. Some of the decisions are small ones. They are easily changed. If one of these decisions turns out to be incorrect, the firm can change its actions and survive.

The biggest decision that any firm makes is what industry to enter. For most entrepreneurs, their background knowledge and interests drive this decision. But the decision also depends on profit prospects—on the expectation that total revenue will exceed total cost.

The firm that we study has already chosen the industry in which to operate. It has also chosen its most effective method of organization. But it has not decided the quantity to produce, the quantities of factors of production to hire, or the price at which to sell its output.

Decisions about the quantity to produce and the price to charge depend on the type of market in which the firm operates. Perfect competition, monopolistic competition, oligopoly, and monopoly all confront the firm with their own special problems.

But decisions about *how* to produce a given output do not depend on the type of market in which the firm operates. These decisions are similar for *all* types of firms in *all* types of markets.

The actions that a firm can take to influence the relationship between output and cost depend on how soon the firm wants to act. A firm that plans to change its output rate tomorrow has fewer options than one that plans to change its output rate six months or six years from now.

To study the relationship between a firm's output decision and its costs, we distinguish between two decision time frames:

- The short run
- The long run

The Short Run

The **short run** is a time frame in which the quantity of at least one factor of production is fixed. For most firms, capital, land, and entrepreneurship are fixed factors of production and labor is the variable factor of production. We call the fixed factors of production the firm's *plant*: In the short run, a firm's plant is fixed.

For Cindy's Sweaters, the fixed plant is its factory building and its knitting machines. For an electric power utility, the fixed plant is its buildings, generators, computers, and control systems.

To increase output in the short run, a firm must increase the quantity of a variable factor of production, which is usually labor. So to produce more output, Cindy's Sweaters must hire more labor and operate its knitting machines for more hours per day. Similarly, an electric power utility must hire more labor and operate its generators for more hours per day.

Short-run decisions are easily reversed. The firm can increase or decrease its output in the short run by increasing or decreasing the amount of labor it hires.

The Long Run

The **long run** is a time frame in which the quantities of *all* factors of production can be varied. That is, the long run is a period in which the firm can change its *plant*.

To increase output in the long run, a firm is able to choose whether to change its plant as well as the quantity of labor it hires. Cindy's Sweaters can decide whether to install more knitting machines, use a new type of machine, reorganize its management, or hire more labor. Long-run decisions are *not* easily reversed. Once a plant decision is made, the firm usually must live with it for some time. To emphasize this fact, we call the past expenditure on a plant that has no resale value a **sunk cost**. A sunk cost is irrelevant to the firm's current decisions. The only costs that influence its current decisions are the short-run cost of changing its labor inputs and the long-run cost of changing its plant.

REVIEW QUIZ

1. Distinguish between the short run and the long run.
2. Why is a sunk cost irrelevant?

myeconlab Study Plan 10.1

We're going to study costs in the short run and the long run. We begin with the short run and describe the technology constraint the firm faces.

Short-Run Technology Constraint

To increase output in the short run, a firm must increase the quantity of labor employed. We describe the relationship between output and the quantity of labor employed by using three related concepts:

1. Total product
2. Marginal product
3. Average product

These product concepts can be illustrated either by product schedules or by product curves. Let's look first at the product schedules.

Product Schedules

Table 10.1 shows some data that describe Cindy's Sweaters' total product, marginal product, and average product. The numbers tell us how Cindy's Sweaters' production increases as more workers are employed. They also tell us about the productivity of Cindy's Sweaters' labor force.

Focus first on the columns headed "Labor" and "Total product." **Total product** is the maximum output that a given quantity of labor can produce. You can see from the numbers in these columns that as Cindy's employs more labor, total product increases. For example, when Cindy's employs 1 worker, total product is 4 sweaters a day, and when Cindy's employs 2 workers, total product is 10 sweaters a day. Each increase in employment increases total product.

The **marginal product** of labor is the increase in total product that results from a one-unit increase in the quantity of labor employed with all other inputs remaining the same. For example, in Table 10.1, when Cindy's increases employment from 2 to 3 workers and does not change its capital, the marginal product of the third worker is 3 sweaters—total product increases from 10 to 13 sweaters.

Average product tells how productive workers are on the average. The **average product** of labor is equal to total product divided by the quantity of labor employed. For example, in Table 10.1, the average product of 3 workers is 4.33 sweaters per worker—13 sweaters a day divided by 3 workers.

If you look closely at the numbers in Table 10.1, you can see some patterns. As Cindy's hires more labor, marginal product at first increases and then begins to decrease. For example, marginal product increases from 4 sweaters a day for the first worker to 6 sweaters a day for the second worker and then decreases to 3 sweaters a day for the third worker. Also average product at first increases and then decreases. You can see the relationships between the quantity of labor hired and the three product concepts more clearly by looking at the product curves.

TABLE 10.1 Total Product, Marginal Product, and Average Product

	Labor (workers per day)	Total product (sweaters per day)	Marginal product (sweaters per additional worker)	Average product (sweaters per worker)
A	0	0		
			4	
B	1	4		4.00
			6	
C	2	10		5.00
			3	
D	3	13		4.33
			2	
E	4	15		3.75
			1	
F	5	16		3.20

Total product is the total amount produced. Marginal product is the change in total product that results from a one-unit increase in labor. For example, when labor increases from 2 to 3 workers a day (row *C* to row *D*), total product increases from 10 to 13 sweaters a day. The marginal product of going from 2 to 3 workers is 3 sweaters. Average product is total product divided by the quantity of labor employed. For example, the average product of 3 workers is 4.33 sweaters per worker (13 sweaters a day divided by 3 workers).

Product Curves

The product curves are graphs of the relationships between employment and the three product concepts you've just studied. They show how total product, marginal product, and average product change as employment changes. They also show the relationships among the three concepts. Let's look at the product curves.

Total Product Curve

Figure 10.1 shows Cindy's Sweaters' total product curve, *TP*. As employment increases, so does the number of sweaters knitted. Points *A* through *F* in the figure correspond to the same rows in Table 10.1. Points *A* through *F* in the figure correspond to the same rows in Table 10.1. These points show total product as the quantity of labor changes by one day of labor. But labor is divisible into hours and even minutes. By varying the amount of labor in the smallest units possible, we can draw the total product curve shown in Fig. 10.1.

Notice the shape of the total product curve. As employment increases from zero to 1 worker a day, the curve becomes steeper. Then, as employment increases to 3, 4, and 5 workers a day, the curve becomes less steep.

The total product curve is similar to the *production possibilities frontier* (explained in Chapter 2). It separates the attainable output levels from those that are unattainable. All the points that lie above the curve are unattainable. Points that lie below the curve, in the orange area, are attainable. But they are inefficient—they use more labor than is necessary to produce a given output. Only the points *on* the total product curve are technologically efficient.

FIGURE 10.1 Total Product Curve

myeconlab

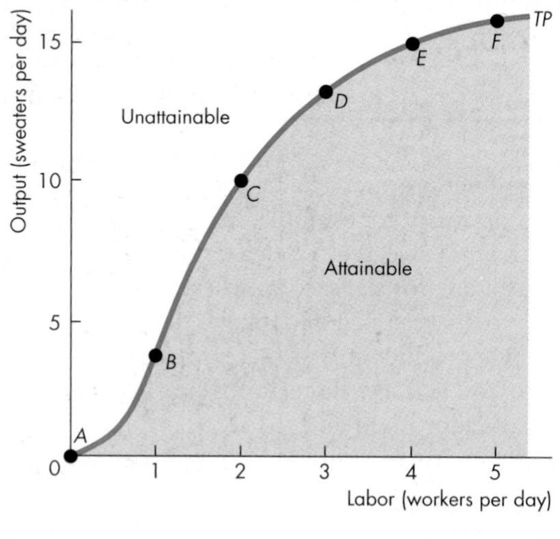

The total product curve, *TP*, is based on the data in Table 10.1. The total product curve shows how the quantity of sweaters changes as the quantity of labor employed changes. For example, 2 workers can produce 10 sweaters a day (point *C*). Points *A* through *F* on the curve correspond to the rows of Table 10.1. The total product curve separates attainable outputs from unattainable outputs. Points below the *TP* curve are inefficient.

Marginal Product Curve

Figure 10.2 shows Cindy's Sweaters' marginal product of labor. Part (a) reproduces the total product curve from Fig. 10.1. Part (b) shows the marginal product curve, *MP*.

In part (a), the orange bars illustrate the marginal product of labor. The height of each bar measures marginal product. Marginal product is also measured by the slope of the total product curve. Recall that the slope of a curve is the change in the value of the variable measured on the *y*-axis—output—divided by the change in the variable measured on the *x*-axis—labor—as we move along the curve. A one-unit increase in labor, from 2 to 3 workers, increases output from 10 to 13 sweaters, so the slope from point *C* to point *D* is 3 sweaters per worker, the same as the marginal product that we've just calculated.

Again varying the amount of labor in the smallest units possible, we can draw the marginal product curve shown in Fig. 10.2(b). The *height* of this curve measures the *slope* of the total product curve at a point. Part (a) shows that an increase in employment from 2 to 3 workers increases output from 10 to 13 sweaters (an increase of 3). The increase in output of 3 sweaters appears on the vertical axis of part (b) as the marginal product of going from 2 to 3 workers. We plot that marginal product at the midpoint between 2 and 3 workers. Notice that marginal product shown in Fig. 10.2(b) reaches a peak at 1.5 workers, and at that point, marginal product is 6 sweaters per worker. The peak occurs at 1.5 workers because the total product curve is steepest when employment increases from 1 worker to 2 workers.

The total product and marginal product curves differ across firms and types of goods. Ford Motor Company's product curves are different from those of Jim's Burger Stand, which in turn are different from those of Cindy's Sweaters. But the shapes of the product curves are similar because almost every production process has two features:

- Increasing marginal returns initially
- Diminishing marginal returns eventually

Increasing Marginal Returns Increasing marginal returns occur when the marginal product of an additional worker exceeds the marginal product of the

FIGURE 10.2 Total Product and Marginal Product

myeconlab

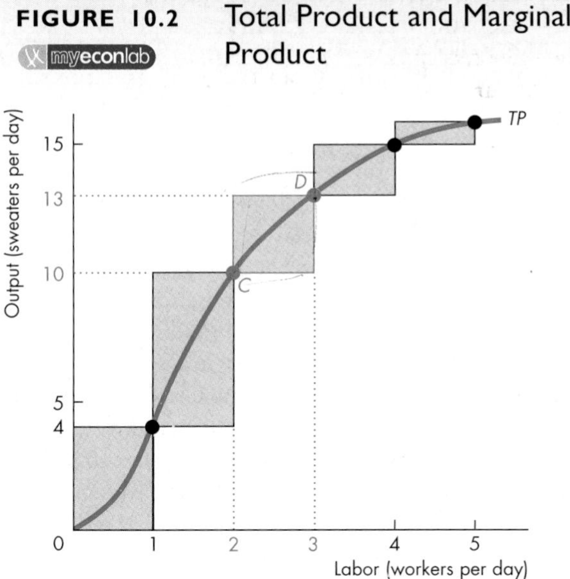

(a) Total product

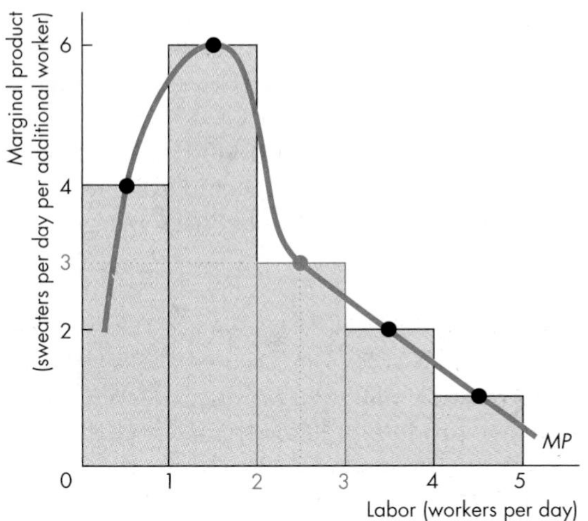

(b) Marginal product

Marginal product is illustrated by the orange bars. For example, when labor increases from 2 to 3 workers a day, marginal product is the orange bar whose height is 3 sweaters. (Marginal product is shown midway between the quantities of labor to emphasize that it is the result of *changing* the quantity of labor.) The steeper the slope of the total product curve (*TP*) in part (a), the larger is marginal product (*MP*) in part (b). Marginal product increases to a maximum (in this example when the second worker is employed) and then declines—diminishing marginal product.

previous worker. Increasing marginal returns arise from increased specialization and division of labor in the production process.

For example, if Cindy's employs just one worker, that person must learn all the aspects of sweater production: running the knitting machines, fixing breakdowns, packaging and mailing sweaters, buying and checking the type and color of the wool. All these tasks must be performed by that one person.

If Cindy's hires a second person, the two workers can specialize in different parts of the production process. As a result, two workers produce more than twice as much as one. The marginal product of the second worker is greater than the marginal product of the first worker. Marginal returns are increasing.

Diminishing Marginal Returns Most production processes experience increasing marginal returns initially. But all production processes eventually reach a point of *diminishing* marginal returns. **Diminishing marginal returns** occur when the marginal product of an additional worker is less than the marginal product of the previous worker.

Diminishing marginal returns arise from the fact that more and more workers are using the same capital and working in the same space. As more workers are added, there is less and less for the additional workers to do that is productive. For example, if Cindy's hires a third worker, output increases but not by as much as it did when it hired the second worker. In this case, after two workers are hired, all the gains from specialization and the division of labor have been exhausted. By hiring a third worker, the factory produces more sweaters, but the equipment is being operated closer to its limits. There are even times when the third worker has nothing to do because the machines are running without the need for further attention. Hiring more and more workers continues to increase output but by successively smaller amounts. Marginal returns are diminishing. This phenomenon is such a pervasive one that it is called a "law"—the law of diminishing returns. The **law of diminishing returns** states that

> As a firm uses more of a variable factor of production, with a given quantity of the fixed factor of production, the marginal product of the variable factor eventually diminishes.

You are going to return to the law of diminishing returns when we study a firm's costs. But before we do that, let's look at the average product of labor and the average product curve.

Average Product Curve

Figure 10.3 illustrates Cindy's Sweaters' average product of labor and shows the relationship between average product and marginal product. Points *B* through *F* on the average product curve *AP* correspond to those same rows in Table 10.1. Average product increases from 1 to 2 workers (its maximum value at point *C*) but then decreases as yet more workers are employed. Notice also that average product is largest when average product and marginal product are equal. That is, the marginal product curve cuts the average product curve at the point of maximum average product. For the number of workers at which marginal product exceeds average product, average product is increasing. For the number of workers at which marginal product is less than average product, average product is decreasing.

The relationship between the average and marginal product curves is a general feature of the relationship between the average and marginal values of any variable. Let's look at a familiar example.

FIGURE 10.3 Average Product

myeconlab

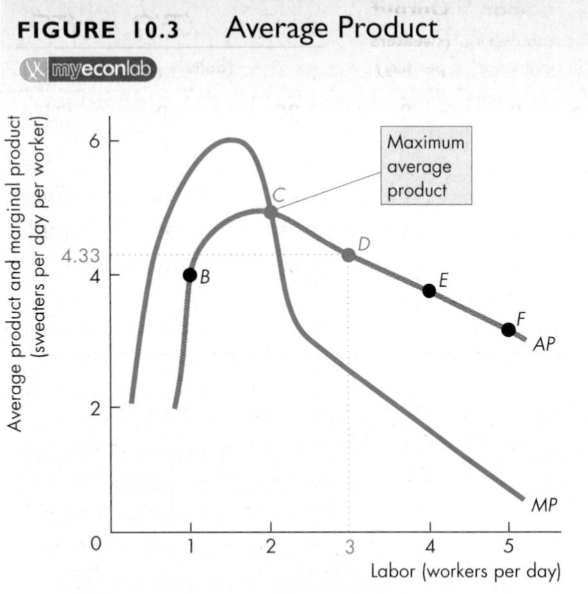

The figure shows the average product of labor and the connection between the average product and marginal product. With 1 worker per day, marginal product exceeds average product, so average product is increasing. With 2 workers per day, marginal product equals average product, so average product is at its maximum. With more than 2 workers per day, marginal product is less than average product, so average product is decreasing.

Marginal Grade and Grade Point Average

To see the relationship between average product and marginal product, think about the similar relationship between Cindy's marginal grade and average grade over five semesters. (Suppose Cindy is a part-time student who takes just one course each semester.) In the first semester, Cindy takes calculus and her grade is a C (2.0). This grade is her marginal grade. It is also her average grade—her GPA. In the next semester, Cindy takes French and gets a B (3.0). French is Cindy's marginal course, and her marginal grade is 3.0. Her GPA rises to 2.5. Because her marginal grade exceeds her average grade, it pulls her average up. In the third semester, Cindy takes economics and gets an A (4.0)—her new marginal grade. Because her marginal grade exceeds her GPA, it again pulls her average up. Cindy's GPA is now 3.0, the average of 2.0, 3.0, and 4.0. The fourth semester, she takes history and gets a B (3.0). Because her marginal grade is equal to her average, her GPA does not change. In the fifth semester, Cindy takes English and gets a D (1.0). Because her marginal grade, a 1.0, is below her GPA of 3.0, her GPA falls.

Cindy's GPA increases when her marginal grade exceeds her GPA. Her GPA falls when her marginal grade is below her GPA. And her GPA is constant when her marginal grade equals her GPA. The relationship between Cindy's marginal and average grades is exactly the same as that between marginal product and average product.

REVIEW QUIZ

1. Explain how the marginal product of labor and the average product of labor change as the quantity of labor employed increases (a) initially and (b) eventually.
2. What is the law of diminishing returns? Why does marginal product eventually diminish?
3. Explain the relationship between marginal product and average product. How does average product change when marginal product exceeds average product? How does average product change when average product exceeds marginal product? Why?

myeconlab **Study Plan 10.2**

Cindy's cares about its product curves because they influence its costs. Let's look at Cindy's costs.

Short-Run Cost

To produce more output in the short run, a firm must employ more labor, which means that it must increase its costs. We describe the relationship between output and cost by using three cost concepts:

- Total cost
- Marginal cost
- Average cost

Total Cost

A firm's **total cost** (TC) is the cost of *all* the factors of production it uses. We separate total cost into total *fixed* cost and total *variable* cost.

Total fixed cost (TFC) is the cost of the firm's fixed factors. For Cindy's Sweaters, total fixed cost includes the cost of renting knitting machines and *normal profit*, which is the opportunity cost of Cindy's entrepreneurship (see Chapter 9, p. 199). The quantities of fixed factors don't change as output changes, so total fixed cost is the same at all outputs.

Total variable cost (TVC) is the cost of the firm's variable factors. For Cindy's, labor is the variable factor, so this component of cost is its wage bill. Total variable cost changes as total product changes.

Total cost is the sum of total fixed cost and total variable cost. That is,

$$TC = TFC + TVC.$$

The table in Fig. 10.4 shows Cindy's total costs. With one knitting machine that Cindy's rents for \$25 a day, TFC is \$25. To produce sweaters, Cindy's hires labor, which costs \$25 a day. TVC is the number of workers multiplied by \$25. For example, to produce 13 sweaters a day, Cindy's hires 3 workers and TVC is \$75. TC is the sum of TFC and TVC, so to produce 13 sweaters a day, Cindy's total cost, TC, is \$100. Check the calculation in each row of the table.

Figure 10.4 shows Cindy's total cost curves, which graph total cost against output. The green total fixed cost curve (TFC) is horizontal because total fixed cost is a constant at \$25. It does not change when output changes. The purple total variable cost curve (TVC) and the blue total cost curve (TC) both slope upward because total variable cost increases as output increases. The arrows highlight total fixed cost as the vertical distance between the TVC and TC curves.

Let's now look at Cindy's marginal cost.

FIGURE 10.4 Total Cost Curves

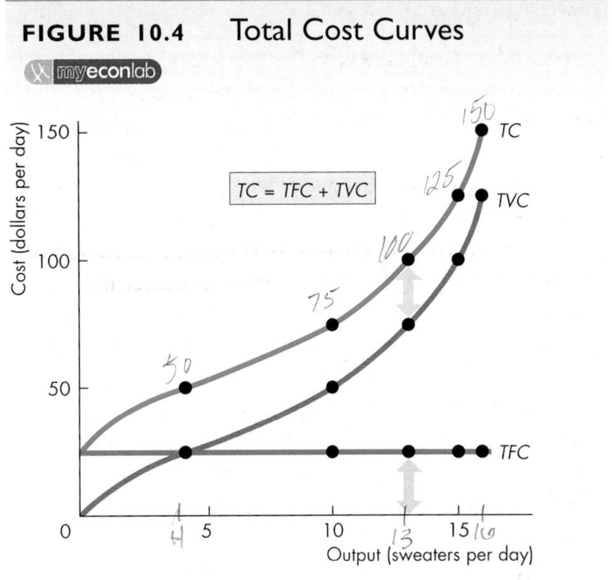

	Labor (workers per day)	Output (sweaters per day)	Total fixed cost (*TFC*)	Total variable cost (*TVC*)	Total cost (*TC*)
			(dollars per day)		
A	0	0	25	0	25
B	1	4	25	25	50
C	2	10	25	50	75
D	3	13	25	75	100
E	4	15	25	100	125
F	5	16	25	125	150

Cindy's rents a knitting machine for \$25 a day. This amount is Cindy's total fixed cost. Cindy's hires workers at a wage rate of \$25 a day, and this cost is Cindy's total variable cost. For example, if Cindy's employs 3 workers, total variable cost is 3 × \$25, which equals \$75. Total cost is the sum of total fixed cost and total variable cost. For example, when Cindy's employs 3 workers, total cost is \$100—total fixed cost of \$25 plus total variable cost of \$75. The graph shows Cindy's Sweaters' total cost curves. Total fixed cost (TFC) is constant—it graphs as a horizontal line—and total variable cost (TVC) increases as output increases. Total cost (TC) increases as output increases. The vertical distance between the total cost curve and the total variable cost curve is total fixed cost, as illustrated by the two arrows.

Marginal Cost

In Fig. 10.4, total variable cost and total cost increase at a decreasing rate at small levels of output and then begin to increase at an increasing rate as output increases. To understand this pattern in the change in total cost as output increases, we need to use the concept of *marginal cost.*

A firm's **marginal cost** is the increase in total cost that results from a one-unit increase in output. We calculate marginal cost as the increase in total cost divided by the increase in output. The table in Fig. 10.5 shows this calculation. When, for example, output increases from 10 sweaters to 13 sweaters, total cost increases from \$75 to \$100. The change in output is 3 sweaters, and the change in total cost is \$25. The marginal cost of one of those 3 sweaters is (\$25 ÷ 3), which equals \$8.33.

Figure 10.5 graphs the marginal cost data in the table as the red marginal cost curve, *MC*. This curve is U-shaped because when Cindy's Sweaters hires a second worker, marginal cost decreases, but when it hires a third, a fourth, and a fifth worker, marginal cost successively increases.

Marginal cost decreases at low outputs because of economies from greater specialization. It eventually increases because of the *law of diminishing returns.* The law of diminishing returns means that each additional worker produces a successively smaller addition to output. So to get an additional unit of output, ever more workers are required. Because more workers are required to produce one additional unit of output, the cost of the additional unit of output—marginal cost—must eventually increase.

Marginal cost tells us how total cost changes as output changes. The final cost concept tells us what it costs, on the average, to produce a unit of output. Let's now look at Cindy's Sweaters' average costs.

Average Cost

There are three average costs:

1. Average fixed cost
2. Average variable cost
3. Average total cost

Average fixed cost (*AFC*) is total fixed cost per unit of output. **Average variable cost** (*AVC*) is total variable cost per unit of output. **Average total cost** (*ATC*) is total cost per unit of output. The average cost concepts are calculated from the total cost concepts as follows:

$$TC = TFC + TVC.$$

Divide each total cost term by the quantity produced, *Q*, to get

$$\frac{TC}{Q} = \frac{TFC}{Q} + \frac{TVC}{Q},$$

or

$$ATC = AFC + AVC.$$

The table in Fig. 10.5 shows the calculation of average total cost. For example, in row *C* output is 10 sweaters. Average fixed cost is (\$25 ÷ 10), which equals \$2.50, average variable cost is (\$50 ÷ 10), which equals \$5.00, and average total cost is (\$75 ÷ 10), which equals \$7.50. Note that average total cost is equal to average fixed cost (\$2.50) plus average variable cost (\$5.00).

Figure 10.5 shows the average cost curves. The green average fixed cost curve (*AFC*) slopes downward. As output increases, the same constant total fixed cost is spread over a larger output. The blue average total cost curve (*ATC*) and the purple average variable cost curve (*AVC*) are U-shaped. The vertical distance between the average total cost and average variable cost curves is equal to average fixed cost—as indicated by the two arrows. That distance shrinks as output increases because average fixed cost declines with increasing output.

The marginal cost curve (*MC*) intersects the average variable cost curve and the average total cost curve at their minimum points. That is, when marginal cost is less than average cost, average cost is decreasing, and when marginal cost exceeds average cost, average cost is increasing. This relationship holds for both the *ATC* curve and the *AVC* curve and is another example of the relationship you saw in Fig. 10.3 for average product and marginal product and in Cindy's course grades.

Why the Average Total Cost Curve Is U-Shaped

Average total cost, *ATC,* is the sum of average fixed cost, *AFC,* and average variable cost, *AVC.* So the shape of the *ATC* curve combines the shapes of the *AFC* and *AVC* curves. The U shape of the average

FIGURE 10.5 Marginal Cost and Average Costs

myeconlab

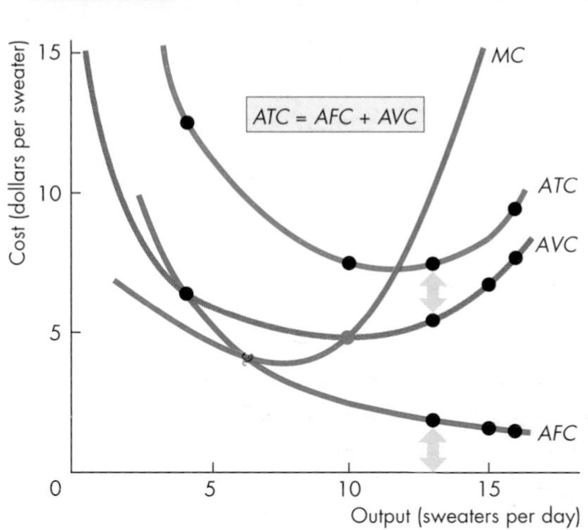

Marginal cost is calculated as the change in total cost divided by the change in output. When output increases from 4 to 10 sweaters, an increase of 6 sweaters, total cost increases by \$25 and marginal cost is \$25 ÷ 6, which equals \$4.17. Each average cost concept is calculated by dividing the related total cost by output. When 10 sweaters are produced, *AFC* is \$2.50 (\$25 ÷ 10), *AVC* is \$5 (\$50 ÷ 10), and *ATC* is \$7.50 (\$75 ÷ 10).

The graph shows that the marginal cost curve (*MC*) is U-shaped and intersects the average variable cost curve and the average total cost curve at their minimum points. Average fixed cost (*AFC*) decreases as output increases. The average total cost curve (*ATC*) and average variable cost curve (*AVC*) are U-shaped. The vertical distance between these two curves is equal to average fixed cost, as illustrated by the two arrows.

	Labor (workers per day)	Output (sweaters per day)	Total fixed cost (*TFC*)	Total variable cost (*TVC*)	Total cost (*TC*)	Marginal cost (*MC*) (dollars per additional sweater)	Average fixed cost (*AFC*)	Average variable cost (*AVC*)	Average total cost (*ATC*)
			(dollars per day)				(dollars per sweater)		
A	0	0	25	0	25		—	—	—
						6.25			
B	1	4	25	25	50		6.25	6.25	12.50
						4.17			
C	2	10	25	50	75		2.50	5.00	7.50
						8.33			
D	3	13	25	75	100		1.92	5.77	7.69
						12.50			
E	4	15	25	100	125		1.67	6.67	8.33
						25.00			
F	5	16	25	125	150		1.56	7.81	9.38

total cost curve arises from the influence of two opposing forces:

1. Spreading total fixed cost over a larger output
2. Eventually diminishing returns

When output increases, the firm spreads its total fixed cost over a larger output and so its average fixed cost decreases—its average fixed cost curve slopes downward.

Diminishing returns means that as output increases, ever-larger amounts of labor are needed to produce an additional unit of output. So average variable cost eventually increases, and the *AVC* curve eventually slopes upward.

The shape of the average total cost curve combines these two effects. Initially, as output increases, both average fixed cost and average variable cost decrease, so average total cost decreases and the *ATC* curve slopes downward. But as output increases further and diminishing returns set in, average variable cost begins to increase. Eventually, average variable cost increases more quickly than average fixed cost decreases, so average total cost increases and the *ATC* curve slopes upward.

Cost Curves and Product Curves

The technology that a firm uses determines its costs. Figure 10.6 shows the links between the firm's technology constraint (its product curves) and its cost curves. The upper part of the figure shows the average product curve and the marginal product curve—like those in Fig. 10.3. The lower part of the figure shows the average variable cost curve and the marginal cost curve—like those in Fig. 10.5.

The figure highlights the links between technology and costs. As labor increases initially, marginal product and average product rise and marginal cost and average variable cost fall. Then, at the point of maximum marginal product, marginal cost is a minimum. As labor increases further, marginal product diminishes and marginal cost increases. But average product continues to rise, and average variable cost continues to fall. Then, at the point of maximum average product, average variable cost is a minimum. As labor increases further, average product diminishes and average variable cost increases.

Shifts in the Cost Curves

The position of a firm's short-run cost curves depends on two factors:

- Technology
- Prices of factors of production

Technology A technological change that increases productivity shifts the total product curve upward. It also shifts the marginal product curve and the average product curve upward. With a better technology, the same factors of production can produce more output, so technological change lowers costs and shifts the cost curves downward.

For example, advances in robot production techniques have increased productivity in the automobile industry. As a result, the product curves of Chrysler, Ford, and GM have shifted upward, and their cost curves have shifted downward. But the relationships between their product curves and cost curves have not changed. The curves are still linked in the way shown in Fig. 10.6.

Often, a technological advance results in a firm using more capital, a fixed factor, and less labor, a variable factor. For example, today the telephone companies use computers to provide directory assistance in

FIGURE 10.6 Product Curves and Cost Curves

myeconlab

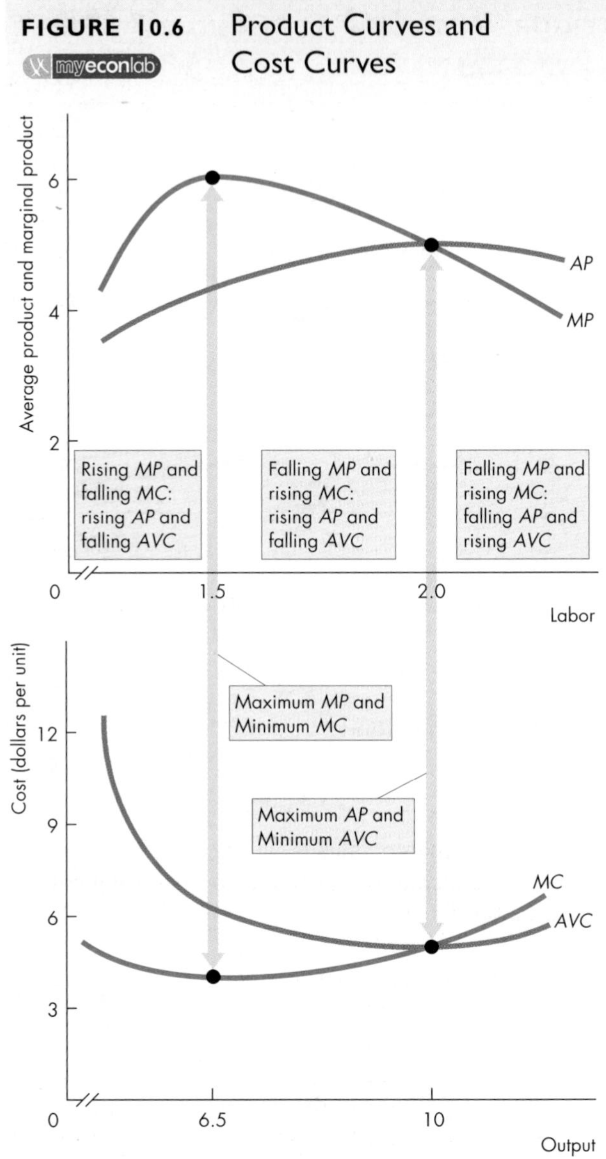

A firm's marginal product curve is linked to its marginal cost curve. If as the firm hires more labor its marginal product rises, its marginal cost falls. If marginal product is a maximum, marginal cost is a minimum. If as the firm hires more labor its marginal product diminishes, its marginal cost rises.

A firm's average product curve is linked to its average variable cost curve. If as the firm hires more labor its average product rises, its average variable cost falls. If average product is a maximum, average variable cost is a minimum. If as the firm hires more labor its average product diminishes, its average variable cost rises.

TABLE 10.2 A Compact Glossary of Costs

Term	Symbol	Definition	Equation
Fixed cost		Cost that is independent of the output level; cost of a fixed input	
Variable cost		Cost that varies with the output level; cost of a variable input	
Total fixed cost	*TFC*	Cost of the fixed inputs	
Total variable cost	*TVC*	Cost of the variable inputs	
Total cost	*TC*	Cost of all inputs	$TC = TFC + TVC$
Output (total product)	*TP*	Total quantity produced (output *Q*)	
Marginal cost	*MC*	Change in total cost resulting from a one-unit increase in total product	$MC = \Delta TC \div \Delta Q$
Average fixed cost	*AFC*	Total fixed cost per unit of output	$AFC = TFC \div Q$
Average variable cost	*AVC*	Total variable cost per unit of output	$AVC = TVC \div Q$
Average total cost	*ATC*	Total cost per unit of output	$ATC = AFC + AVC$

place of the human operators they used in the 1980s. When such a technological change occurs, total cost decreases, but fixed costs increase and variable costs decrease. This change in the mix of fixed cost and variable cost means that at low output levels, average total cost might increase, while at high output levels, average total cost decreases.

Prices of Factors of Production An increase in the price of a factor of production increases costs and shifts the cost curves. But how the curves shift depends on which factor price changes. An increase in rent or some other component of *fixed* cost shifts the fixed cost curves (*TFC* and *AFC*) upward and shifts the total cost curve (*TC*) upward but leaves the variable cost curves (*AVC* and *TVC*) and the marginal cost curve (*MC*) unchanged. An increase in wages or another component of *variable* cost shifts the variable cost curves (*TVC* and *AVC*) upward and shifts the marginal cost curve (*MC*) upward but leaves the fixed cost curves (*AFC* and *TFC*) unchanged. So, for example, if truck drivers' wages increase, the variable cost and marginal cost of transportation services increase. If the interest expense paid by a trucking company increases, the fixed cost of transportation services increases.

You've now completed your study of short-run costs. All the concepts that you've met are summarized in a compact glossary in Table 10.2.

REVIEW QUIZ

1 What relationships do a firm's short-run cost curves show?
2 How does marginal cost change as output increases (a) initially and (b) eventually?
3 What does the law of diminishing returns imply for the shape of the marginal cost curve?
4 What is the shape of the average fixed cost curve and why?
5 What are the shapes of the average variable cost curve and the average total cost curve and why?

myeconlab **Study Plan 10.3**

Long-Run Cost

In the short run, a firm can vary the quantity of labor but the quantity of capital is fixed. So the firm has variable costs of labor and fixed costs of capital. In the long run, a firm can vary both the quantity of labor and the quantity of capital. So in the long run, all the firm's costs are variable. We are now going to study the firm's costs in the long run, when *all* costs are variable costs and when the quantities of labor and capital vary.

The behavior of long-run cost depends on the firm's *production function*, which is the relationship between the maximum output attainable and the quantities of both labor and capital.

The Production Function

Table 10.3 shows Cindy's Sweaters' production function. The table lists total product schedules for four different quantities of capital. We identify the quantity of capital by the plant size. The numbers for Plant 1 are for a factory with 1 knitting machine—the case we've just studied. The other three plants have 2, 3, and 4 machines. If Cindy's Sweaters doubles its capital from 1 to 2 knitting machines, the various amounts of labor can produce the outputs shown in the second column of the table. The other two columns show the outputs of yet larger quantities of capital. Each column of the table could be graphed as a total product curve for each plant.

TABLE 10.3 The Production Function

Labor (workers per day)	Output (sweaters per day)			
	Plant 1	Plant 2	Plant 3	Plant 4
1	4	10	13	15
2	10	15	18	20
3	13	18	22	24
4	15	20	24	26
5	16	21	25	27
Knitting machines (number)	1	2	3	4

The table shows the total product data for four quantities of capital. The greater the plant size, the larger is the total product for any given quantity of labor. But for a given plant size, the marginal product of labor diminishes. And for a given quantity of labor, the marginal product of capital diminishes.

Diminishing Returns Diminishing returns occur at all four quantities of capital as the quantity of labor increases. You can check that fact by calculating the marginal product of labor in plants with 2, 3, and 4 machines. At each plant size, as the quantity of labor increases, the marginal product of labor (eventually) diminishes.

Diminishing Marginal Product of Capital
Diminishing returns also occur as the quantity of capital increases. You can check that fact by calculating the marginal product of capital at a given quantity of labor. The *marginal product of capital* is the change in total product divided by the change in capital when the quantity of labor is constant—equivalently, the change in output resulting from a one-unit increase in the quantity of capital. For example, if Cindy's has 3 workers and increases its capital from 1 machine to 2 machines, output increases from 13 to 18 sweaters a day. The marginal product of capital is 5 sweaters per day. If Cindy increases the number of machines from 2 to 3, output increases from 18 to 22 sweaters per day. The marginal product of the third machine is 4 sweaters per day, down from 5 sweaters per day for the second machine.

Let's now see what the production function implies for long-run costs.

Short-Run Cost and Long-Run Cost

Continue to assume that Cindy can hire workers for \$25 per day and rent knitting machines for \$25 per machine per day. Using these factor prices and the data in Table 10.3, we can calculate and graph the average total cost curves for factories with 1, 2, 3, and 4 knitting machines. We've already studied the costs of a factory with 1 machine in Figs. 10.4 and 10.5. In Fig. 10.7, the average total cost curve for that case is ATC_1. Figure 10.7 also shows the average total cost curve for a factory with 2 machines, ATC_2, with 3 machines, ATC_3, and with 4 machines, ATC_4.

FIGURE 10.7 Short-Run Costs of Four Different Plants

myeconlab

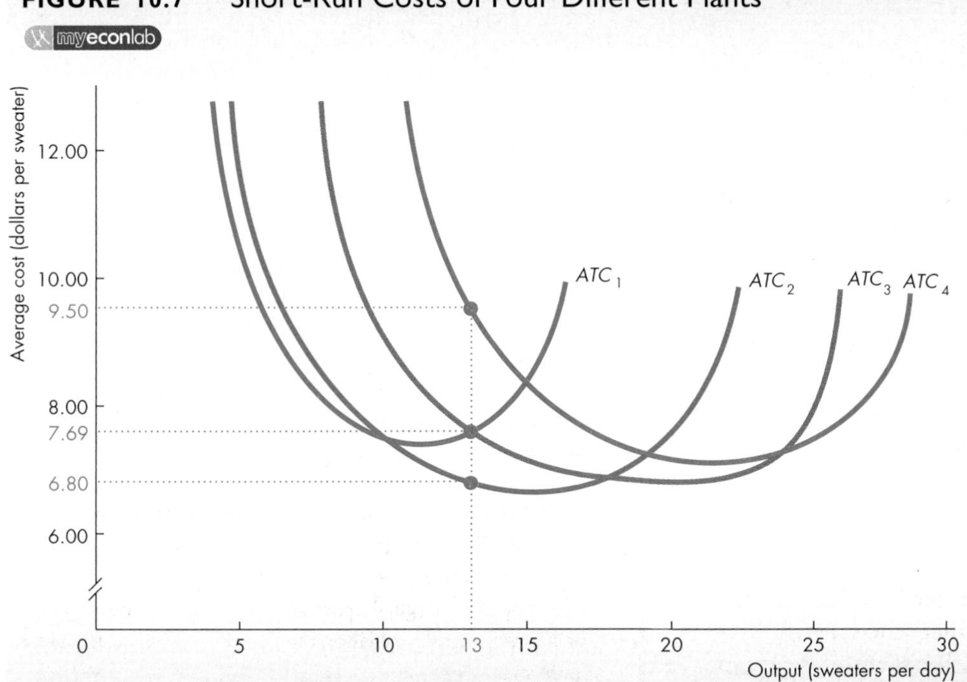

The figure shows short-run average total cost curves for four different quantities of capital. Cindy's can produce 13 sweaters a day with 1 knitting machine on ATC_1 or with 3 knitting machines on ATC_3 for an average cost of \$7.69 per sweater. Cindy's can produce the same number of sweaters by using 2 machines on ATC_2 for \$6.80 per sweater or by using 4 machines on ATC_4 for \$9.50 per sweater. If Cindy's produces 13 sweaters a day, the least-cost method of production—the long-run method—is with 2 machines on ATC_2.

You can see, in Fig. 10.7, that plant size has a big effect on the firm's average total cost. Two things stand out:

1. Each short-run *ATC* curve is U-shaped.
2. For each short-run *ATC* curve, the larger the plant, the greater is the output at which average total cost is a minimum.

Each short-run average total cost curve is U-shaped because, as the quantity of labor increases, its marginal product at first increases and then diminishes. And this pattern in the marginal product of labor, which we examined in some detail for the plant with 1 knitting machine on pp. 222–223, occurs at all plant sizes.

The minimum average total cost for a larger plant occurs at a greater output than it does for a smaller plant because the larger plant has a higher total fixed cost and therefore, for any given output, a higher average fixed cost.

Which short-run average cost curve Cindy's operates on depends on its plant size. But in the long run, Cindy's chooses its plant size. And which plant size it chooses depends on the output it plans to produce. The reason is that the average total cost of producing a given output depends on the plant size.

To see why, suppose that Cindy plans to produce 13 sweaters a day. With 1 machine, the average total cost curve is ATC_1 (in Fig. 10.7) and the average total cost of 13 sweaters a day is \$7.69 per sweater. With 2 machines, on ATC_2, average total cost is \$6.80 per sweater. With 3 machines, on ATC_3, average total cost is \$7.69 per sweater, the same as with 1 machine. Finally, with 4 machines, on ATC_4, average total cost is \$9.50 per sweater.

The economically efficient plant size for producing a given output is the one that has the lowest average total cost. For Cindy's, the economically efficient plant to use to produce 13 sweaters a day is the one with 2 machines.

In the long run, Cindy's chooses the plant size that minimizes average total cost. When a firm is producing a given output at the least possible cost, it is operating on its *long-run average cost curve.*

The **long-run average cost curve** is the relationship between the lowest attainable average total cost and output when both the plant size and labor are varied.

The long-run average cost curve is a planning curve. It tells the firm the plant size and the quantity of labor to use at each output to minimize cost. Once the plant size is chosen, the firm operates on the short-run cost curves that apply to that plant size.

The Long-Run Average Cost Curve

Figure 10.8 shows Cindy's Sweaters' long-run average cost curve, *LRAC*. This long-run average cost curve is derived from the short-run average total cost curves in Fig. 10.7. For output rates up to 10 sweaters a day, average total cost is the lowest on ATC_1. For output rates between 10 and 18 sweaters a day, average total cost is the lowest on ATC_2. For output rates between 18 and 24 sweaters a day, average total cost is the lowest on ATC_3. And for output rates in excess of 24 sweaters a day, average total cost is the lowest on ATC_4. The segment of each average total cost curve with the lowest average total cost is highlighted in dark blue in Fig. 10.8. This dark blue scallop-shaped curve made up of the four segments of average total cost curves is the *LRAC* curve.

Economies and Diseconomies of Scale

Economies of scale are features of a firm's technology that lead to falling long-run average cost as output increases. When economies of scale are present, the *LRAC* curve slopes downward. The *LRAC* curve in Fig. 10.8 shows that Cindy's Sweaters experiences economies of scale for outputs up to 15 sweaters a day.

With given factor prices, economies of scale occur if the percentage increase in output exceeds the percentage increase in all factors of production. For example, if output increases by more than 10 percent when a firm increases its labor and capital by 10 percent, its average total cost falls. Economies of scale are present.

The main source of economies of scale is greater specialization of both labor and capital. For example, if GM produces 100 cars a week, each worker must perform many different tasks and the capital must be general-purpose machines and tools. But if GM produces 10,000 cars a week, each worker specializes and becomes highly proficient in a small number of tasks.

Diseconomies of scale are features of a firm's technology that lead to rising long-run average cost as output increases. When diseconomies of scale are present, the *LRAC* curve slopes upward. In Fig. 10.8, Cindy's Sweaters experiences diseconomies of scale at outputs greater than 15 sweaters a day.

With given factor prices, diseconomies of scale occur if the percentage increase in output is less than the percentage increase in all factors of production. For example, if output increases by less than 10 percent when a firm increases its labor and capital by

FIGURE 10.8 Long-Run Average Cost Curve

myeconlab

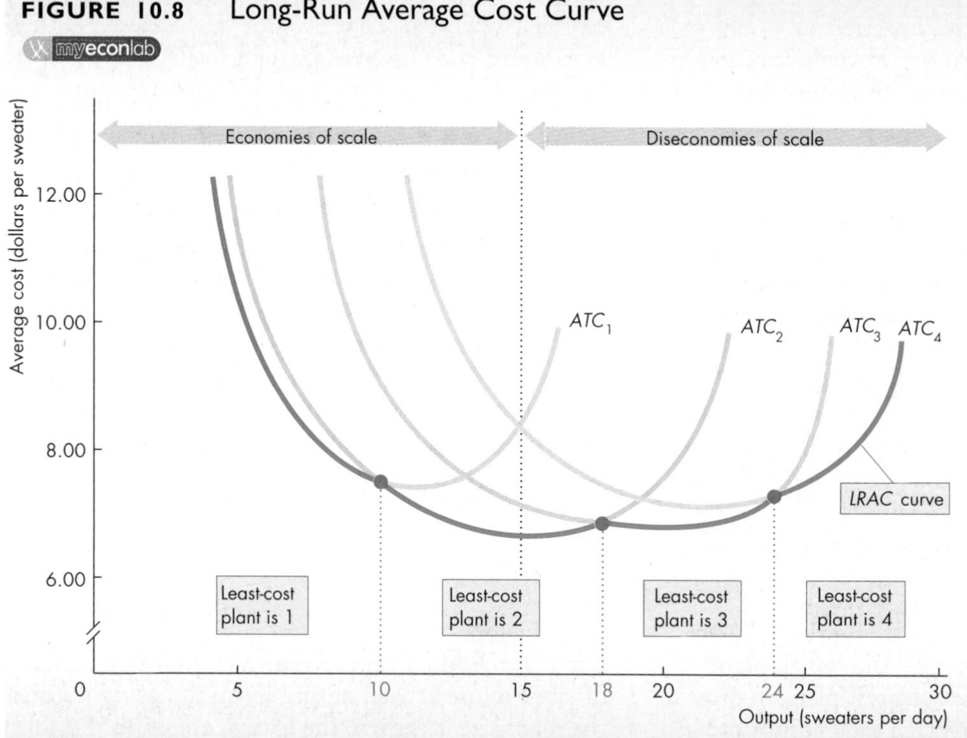

In the long run, Cindy's Sweaters can vary both its capital and labor. The long-run average cost curve traces the lowest attainable average total cost of production. Cindy's Sweaters produces on its long-run average cost curve if it uses 1 machine to produce up to 10 sweaters a day, 2 machines to produce between 10 and 18 sweaters a day, 3 machines to produce between 18 and 24 sweaters a day, and 4 machines to produce more than 24 sweaters a day. Within these ranges, Cindy's Sweaters varies its output by varying its labor.

10 percent, its average total cost rises. Diseconomies of scale are present.

The main source of diseconomies of scale is the difficulty of managing a very large enterprise. The larger the firm, the greater is the challenge of organizing it and the greater is the cost of communicating both up and down the management hierarchy and among managers. Eventually, management complexity brings rising average cost.

Diseconomies of scale occur in all production processes but perhaps only at a very large output rate.

Constant returns to scale are features of a firm's technology that lead to constant long-run average cost as output increases. When constant returns to scale are present, the *LRAC* curve is horizontal.

Constant returns to scale occur if the percentage increase in output equals the percentage increase in all factors of production. For example, if output increases by exactly 10 percent when a firm increases its labor and capital by 10 percent, then constant returns to scale are present.

For example, Ford can double its output of ZX2s by doubling its production facility. It can build an identical production line and hire an identical number of workers. With two identical production facilities, Ford produces exactly twice as many cars.

Minimum Efficient Scale A firm experiences economies of scale up to some output level. Beyond that level, it moves into constant returns to scale or diseconomies of scale. A firm's **minimum efficient scale** is the smallest quantity of output at which long-run average cost reaches its lowest level.

The minimum efficient scale plays a role in determining market structure, as you will learn in the next three chapters. The minimum efficient scale also helps to answer some questions about real businesses.

Economies of Scale at Cindy's Sweaters The technology that Cindy's Sweaters uses, shown in Table 10.3, illustrates economies of scale and diseconomies of scale. If Cindy's increases its factors of production from 1 machine and 1 worker to 2 of each, a 100 percent increase, output increases by more than 100 percent from 4 to 15 sweaters a day. Cindy's experiences economies of scale, and its long-run average cost decreases. But if Cindy's increases its factor of production to 3 machines and 3 workers, a 50 percent increase, output increases by less than 50 percent, from 15 to 22 sweaters a day. Now Cindy's experiences diseconomies of scale, and its long-run average cost increases. Its minimum efficient scale is at 15 sweaters a day.

Producing Cars and Generating Electric Power Why do automakers have expensive equipment lying around that isn't fully used? You can now answer this question. An automaker uses the plant that minimizes the average total cost of producing the output that it can sell. But it operates below the minimum efficient scale. Its short-run average total cost curve looks like ATC_1. If it could sell more cars, it would produce more cars and its average total cost would fall.

Why do many electric utilities have too little production equipment to meet demand on the coldest and hottest days and so have to buy power from other producers? You can now see why this happens and why an electric utility doesn't build more generating capacity. A power producer uses the plant size that minimizes the average total cost of producing the output that it can sell on a normal day. But it produces above the minimum efficient scale and experiences diseconomies of scale. Its short-run average total cost curve looks like ATC_3. With a larger plant size, its average total costs of producing its normal output would be higher.

REVIEW QUIZ

1. What does a firm's production function show and how is it related to a total product curve?
2. Does the law of diminishing returns apply to capital as well as labor? Explain why or why not.
3. What does a firm's long-run average cost curve show? How is it related to the firm's short-run average cost curves?
4. What are economies of scale and diseconomies of scale? How do they arise? What do they imply for the shape of the long-run average cost curve?
5. What is a firm's minimum efficient scale?

myeconlab **Study Plan 10.4**

Reading Between the Lines on pp. 234–235 applies what you've learned about a firm's short-run and long-run cost curves. It looks at the cost curves of Ford and GM and explains why a merger of these two firms wouldn't be a smart move.

READING BETWEEN THE LINES

Mergers and Costs

http://www.nytimes.com

G.M. Talked With Ford About Merger, Report Says

September 19, 2006

As Detroit waits to learn whether General Motors will pursue a tricontinental alliance with Nissan and Renault, word has emerged that the company briefly pondered a linkup with an archrival in its own backyard.

Executives at G.M. and Ford Motor, according to a report on Monday in Automotive News, a trade journal, held discussions about a partnership or merger this year. But industry analysts quickly dismissed the notion of the two struggling automakers possibly joining forces.

"While no longer quite as unthinkable as it once was," Efraim Levy, a Standard & Poor's automotive analyst, wrote in a note to clients, "we consider it highly doubtful that a merger would take place and do not see the benefits for either company as they attempt to restructure." . . .

News that the two automakers would even consider a broad partnership comes as Detroit is reeling from both companies' plans to cut thousands of jobs and close dozens of plants as part of their turnaround efforts. Profits have been elusive for Detroit's automakers, most recently because high gasoline prices have cut into sales of their lucrative sport utility vehicles and pickup trucks. . . .

Essence of the Story

- It has been reported that General Motors, Nissan, and Renault might consider trying to form an alliance.
- Another report says that General Motors and Ford Motor Company might seek a merger.
- An auto analyst, Efraim Levy, says that it is hard to see any benefits for either company from a merger.
- Both companies plan to cut thousands of jobs and close dozens of plants.

Economic Analysis

▶ The big three U.S. automakers are having a hard time competing with Japanese and European automakers.

▶ It has been speculated that two of the big three, Ford and GM, might attempt a merger.

▶ Mergers occur when two firms can eliminate duplicate production facilities while maintaining or increasing total product.

▶ The big U.S. automakers are unusual in that most of their costs are fixed.

▶ Even much of the cost of labor is fixed because unions have negotiated retirement and redundancy packages that pay workers after they leave the firms.

▶ Both companies are trying to lower their costs by closing plants and laying off thousands of workers.

▶ A merger between these two firms is unlikely to achieve any cost saving for either firm beyond what they can accomplish separately. The figures illustrate why.

▶ Figure 1 shows how an automaker might lower its average variable cost by increasing total product.

▶ In this example, if the firm produces 8 million vehicles a year (a rough average of what Ford and GM produce), the average total cost is $25,000 per vehicle (again, a rough average of Ford's and GM's average total cost).

▶ If the firm could increase production, average total cost would fall along the *ATC* curve.

▶ Figure 2 illustrates the likely effects of a merger.

▶ Separately, each firm has an average total cost curve ATC_0.

▶ If the firms merged, there would be no major cost saving. So the new firm would have fixed costs roughly equal to double those of one of the firms.

▶ The average total cost curve of the new bigger firm would be ATC_1.

▶ Total product of the new firm would be (roughly) double that of each firm before the merger, and the average total cost would be unchanged.

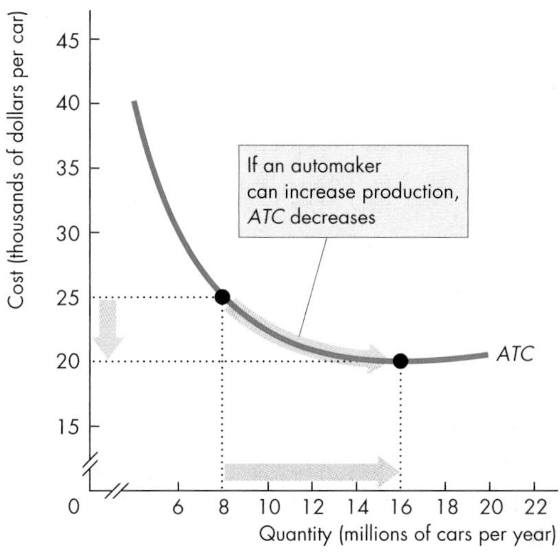

Figure 1 An automaker like GM or Ford

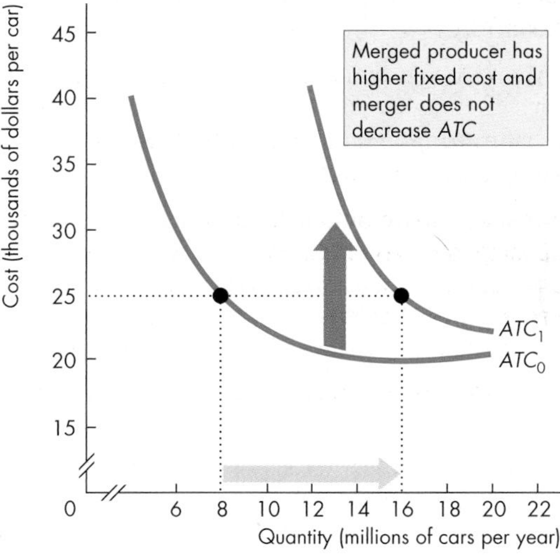

Figure 2 An automaker like a merged GM and Ford

SUMMARY

Key Points

Decision Time Frames (p. 220)

- In the short run, the quantity of at least one factor of production is fixed and the quantities of the other factors of production can be varied.
- In the long run, the quantities of all factors of production can be varied.

Short-Run Technology Constraint (pp. 221–224)

- A total product curve shows the quantity a firm can produce with a given quantity of capital and different quantities of labor.
- Initially, the marginal product of labor increases as the quantity of labor increases, but eventually, marginal product diminishes—the law of diminishing returns.
- Average product increases initially and eventually diminishes.

Short-Run Cost (pp. 225–229)

- As output increases, total fixed cost is constant, and total variable cost and total cost increase.
- As output increases, average fixed cost decreases and average variable cost, average total cost, and marginal cost decrease at low outputs and increase at high outputs. These cost curves are U-shaped.

Long-Run Cost (pp. 230–233)

- There is a set of short-run cost curves for each different plant size. There is one least-cost plant size for each output. The larger the output, the larger is the plant size that will minimize average total cost.
- The long-run average cost curve traces out the lowest attainable average total cost at each output when both capital and labor inputs can be varied.
- With economies of scale, the long-run average cost curve slopes downward. With diseconomies of scale, the long-run average cost curve slopes upward.

Key Figures and Table

Key Terms

PROBLEMS

myeconlab **Tests, Study Plan, Solutions***

1. Sue's Surfboards' total product schedule is

Labor (workers per week)	**Output** (surfboards per week)
1	30
2	70
3	120
4	160
5	190
6	210
7	220

   a. Draw the total product curve.
   b. Calculate the average product of labor and draw the average product curve.
   c. Calculate the marginal product of labor and draw the marginal product curve.
   d. Over what output range does the firm enjoy the benefits of increased specialization and division of labor?
   e. Over what output range does the firm experience diminishing marginal product of labor?
   f. Over what range of output does this firm experience an increasing average product of labor but a diminishing marginal product of labor?
   g. Explain how it is possible for a firm to experience simultaneously an increasing *average* product of labor but a diminishing *marginal* product of labor.
2. Sue's Surfboards has the total product schedule shown in problem 1. Each worker is paid $500 a week and the firm's total fixed cost is $1,000 a week.
   a. Calculate total cost, total variable cost, and total fixed cost for each output and draw the short-run total cost curves.
   b. Calculate average total cost, average fixed cost, average variable cost, and marginal cost at each output and draw the short-run average and marginal cost curves.
   c. Draw the *AP*, *MP*, *AVC*, and *MC* curves like those in Figure 10.6.
3. The owner of the building that Sue's Surfboards rents increases the rent by $200 a week. Everything else remains as described in problems 1 and 2. Explain what changes occur in Sue's Surfboards' short-run average cost curve and marginal cost curve.
4. The labor union that represents the workers at Sue's Surfboards negotiates a pay increase of $100 a week for each worker. Everything else remains as described in problems 1 and 2. Explain how Sue's Surfboards' short-run average cost curve and marginal cost curve change.
5. Bill's Bakery has a fire and Bill loses some of his cost data. The bits of paper that he recovers after the fire provide the information in the following table (all the cost numbers are dollars).

TP	*AFC*	*AVC*	*ATC*	*MC*
10	120	100	220	
				80
20	***A***	***B***	150	
				90
30	40	90	130	
				130
40	30	***C***	***D***	
				E
50	24	108	132	

   Bill asks you to come to his rescue and provide the missing data in the five spaces identified as ***A***, ***B***, ***C***, ***D***, and ***E***.
6. Sue's Surfboards, described in problems 1 and 2, buys a second plant and the total product of each quantity of labor increases by 50 percent. The total fixed cost of operating each plant is $1,000 a week. Each worker is paid $500 a week.
   a. Set out the average total cost curve when Sue's Surfboards operates two plants.
   b. Draw the long-run average cost curve.
   c. Over what output ranges is it efficient to operate one plant and two plants?
7. The table shows the production function of Bonnie's Balloon Rides.

Labor (workers per day)	**Output** (rides per day)			
	Plant 1	**Plant 2**	**Plant 3**	**Plant 4**
10	4	10	13	15
20	10	15	18	20
30	13	18	22	24
40	15	20	24	26
50	16	21	25	27
Balloons (number)	1	2	3	4

*Solutions to odd-numbered problems are provided.

Bonnie's pays $500 a day for each balloon it rents and $25 a day for each balloon operator it hires.

a. Find and graph the average total cost curve for each plant size.
b. Draw Bonnie's long-run average cost curve.
c. What is Bonnie's minimum efficient scale?
d. Explain how Bonnie's uses its long-run average cost curve to decide how many balloons to rent.

8. A firm is producing at minimum average total cost with its current plant. Explain, using the concepts of economies of scale and diseconomies of scale, the circumstances in which the firm
   a. Can lower its average total cost by increasing its plant size.
   b. Can lower its average total cost by decreasing its plant size.
   c. Cannot lower its average total cost.

   Sketch the firm's short-run average total cost curve and long-run average cost curve for each of the three cases.
9. The cost of producing electricity using hydro power is about one third of the cost of using coal, oil, or nuclear power plants and is less than one quarter the cost of using gas turbine plants. Most of the cost differences comes from differences in fuel costs. But part of the cost difference comes from differences in plant costs. It costs less to build a hydroelectric plant than a coal, oil, or nuclear plant. Gas turbine plants cost the least to build but are the most expensive to operate.

   (Based on *Projected Costs of Generating Electricity,* International Energy Agency, 2005)
   a. Use the above information to sketch the average cost curves for electricity production (*AFC, AVC,* and *ATC*) using three technologies: (i) hydro, (ii) coal, oil, or nuclear, and (iii) gas turbine.
   b. Use the above information to sketch the marginal cost curves for electricity production using three technologies: (i) hydro, (ii) coal, oil, or nuclear, and (iii) gas turbine.
   c. Given the cost differences among the different methods of generating electricity, why do we use more than one method? If we could use one method, which would it be?

CRITICAL THINKING

1. Study *Reading Between the Lines* on pp. 234–235 and then answer the following questions:
   a. What are the main ways in which Ford and GM can decrease average total cost?
   b. Why are most of the costs of Ford and GM fixed costs?
   c. Do Ford and GM experience economies of scale, constant returns to scale, or diseconomies of scale?
   d. How would Ford's and GM's average total cost change if the firms closed some plants?
   e. How would Ford's and GM's average total cost change if the firms could increase total product?
   f. How would Ford's and GM's average total cost change if the firms decreased total product?
   g. Why would a merger of Ford and GM be unlikely to lower the merged firm's average total cost?

WEB ACTIVITIES

myeconlab Links to Web sites

1. Obtain information about the cost of producing pumpkins.
   a. List all the costs referred to on the Web page.
   b. For each item, say whether it is a fixed cost or a variable cost.
   c. Make some assumptions and sketch the average cost curves and the marginal cost curve for producing pumpkins.
2. Obtain information about the cost of producing vegetables. For one of the vegetables (your choice):
   a. List all the costs referred to on the Web page.
   b. For each item, say whether it is a fixed cost or a variable cost.
   c. Sketch the average cost curves and the marginal cost curve for producing the vegetable you've chosen.
   d. Do you think this vegetable is produced with economies of scale, constant returns to scale, or diseconomies of scale? Provide reasons.

CHAPTER 11

Perfect Competition

The Busy Bee

The next time you eat a nut or a piece of fruit, think about the busy bee that pollinated the tree on which it grew and the beekeepers who rented their hives to the farmers. Across the United States, from Vermont to California, beekeepers are struggling under the strain of a parasite that is killing their bees. But the prices that those who still have bees can get for renting out hives to pollinate fruit and nut trees has more than doubled.

How does competition in beekeeping and other industries affect prices and profits? What causes some firms to enter an industry and others to leave it? What are the effects on profits and prices of new firms entering and old firms leaving an industry?

In October 2006, more than 3 million people were unemployed because they had been laid off by the firms that previously employed them. Why do firms lay off workers? Why do firms temporarily shut down?

Over the past few years, the prices of personal computers have fallen sharply. For example, a slow computer cost almost $4,000 a few years ago, and a fast one costs only $500 today. What goes on in an industry when the price of its output falls sharply? What happens to the profits of the firms producing such goods? The pollination services of bees, computers, and most other goods are produced by more than one firm, and these firms compete for sales.

To study competitive markets, we are going to build a model of a market in which competition is as fierce and extreme as possible—more extreme than in the examples we've just considered. We call this situation "perfect competition." In *Reading Between the Lines* at the end of the chapter, we'll return to the market for pollination services and see how it copes with a drastic decrease in the quantity of bees.

After studying this chapter, you will be able to

- Define perfect competition
- Explain how firms make their supply decisions and why they sometimes shut down temporarily and lay off workers
- Explain how price and output in an industry are determined and why firms enter and leave the industry
- Predict the effects of a change in demand and of a technological advance
- Explain why perfect competition is efficient

What Is Perfect Competition?

The firms that you study in this chapter face the force of raw competition. We call this extreme form of competition perfect competition. **Perfect competition** is an industry in which

- Many firms sell identical products to many buyers.
- There are no restrictions on entry into the industry.
- Established firms have no advantage over new ones.
- Sellers and buyers are well informed about prices.

Farming, fishing, wood pulping and paper milling, the manufacture of paper cups and plastic shopping bags, grocery retailing, photo finishing, lawn service, plumbing, painting, dry cleaning, and the provision of laundry services are all examples of highly competitive industries.

How Perfect Competition Arises

Perfect competition arises if the minimum efficient scale of a single producer is small relative to the demand for the good or service. A firm's *minimum efficient scale* is the smallest quantity of output at which long-run average cost reaches its lowest level. (See Chapter 10, p. 233.) Where the minimum efficient scale of a firm is small relative to market demand, there is room for many firms in an industry.

Second, perfect competition arises if each firm is perceived to produce a good or service that has no unique characteristics so that consumers don't care which firm they buy from.

Price Takers

Firms in perfect competition are price takers. A **price taker** is a firm that cannot influence the market price and that sets its own price at the market price.

The key reason why a perfectly competitive firm is a price taker is that it produces a tiny proportion of the total output of a particular good and buyers are well informed about the prices of other firms.

Imagine that you are a wheat farmer in Kansas. You have a thousand acres under cultivation—which sounds like a lot. But compared to the millions of acres in Colorado, Oklahoma, Texas, Nebraska, and the Dakotas, as well as the millions more in Canada, Argentina, Australia, and Ukraine, your thousand acres is a drop in the ocean. Nothing makes your wheat any better than any other farmer's, and all the buyers of wheat know the price at which they can do business.

If the market price of wheat is $4 a bushel and you ask for $4.10, no one will buy from you. People can go to the next farmer and the next and the one after that and buy all they need for $4 a bushel. If you set your price at $3.90, you'll have lots of buyers. But you can sell all your output for $4 a bushel, so you're just giving away 10¢ a bushel. You can do no better than sell for the market price—you are a *price taker*.

Economic Profit and Revenue

A firm's goal is to maximize *economic profit*, which is equal to total revenue minus total cost. Total cost is the *opportunity cost* of production, which includes *normal profit*, the return that the entrepreneur can expect to receive on the average in an alternative business. (See Chapter 9, p. 199.)

A firm's **total revenue** equals the price of its output multiplied by the number of units of output sold (price × quantity). **Marginal revenue** is the change in total revenue that results from a one-unit increase in the quantity sold. Marginal revenue is calculated by dividing the change in total revenue by the change in the quantity sold.

Figure 11.1 illustrates these revenue concepts. In part (a), the market demand curve, *D*, and market supply curve, *S*, determine the market price. The market price remains at $25 a sweater regardless of the quantity of sweaters that Cindy's produces. The best Cindy's can do is to sell its sweaters at this price.

Total Revenue Total revenue is equal to the price multiplied by the quantity sold. In the table in Fig. 11.1, if Cindy's sells 9 sweaters, the firm's total revenue is 9 × $25, which equals $225.

Figure 11.1(b) shows the firm's total revenue curve (*TR*), which graphs the relationship between total revenue and the quantity sold. At point *A* on the *TR* curve, Cindy's sells 9 sweaters and has a total revenue of $225. Because each additional sweater sold brings in a constant amount—$25—the total revenue curve is an upward-sloping straight line.

Marginal Revenue Marginal revenue is the change in total revenue that results from a one-unit increase in quantity. In the table in Fig. 11.1, when the quantity sold increases from 8 to 9 sweaters, total revenue increases from $200 to $225. Marginal revenue is

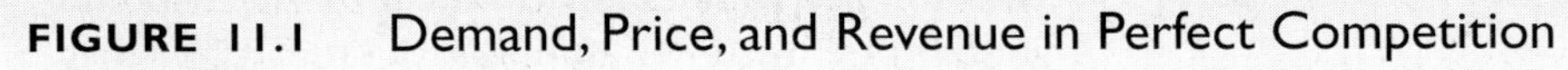

FIGURE 11.1 Demand, Price, and Revenue in Perfect Competition

myeconlab

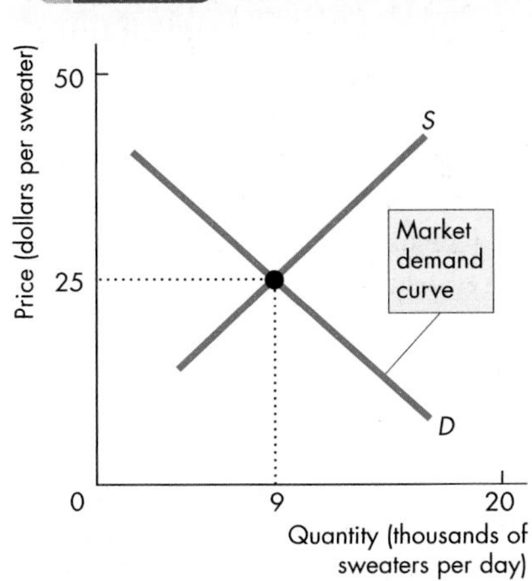

(a) Sweater market

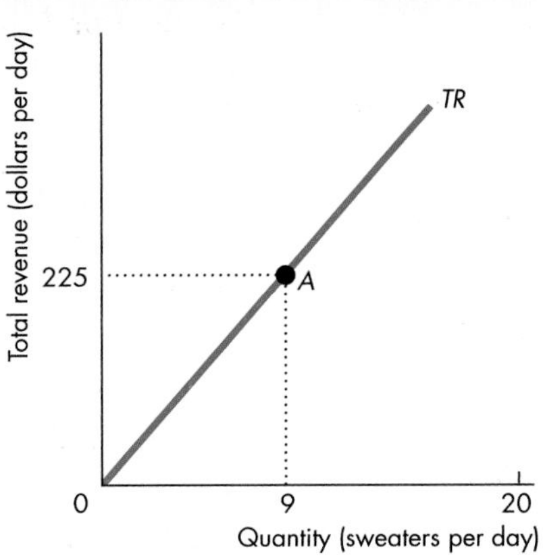

(b) Cindy's total revenue

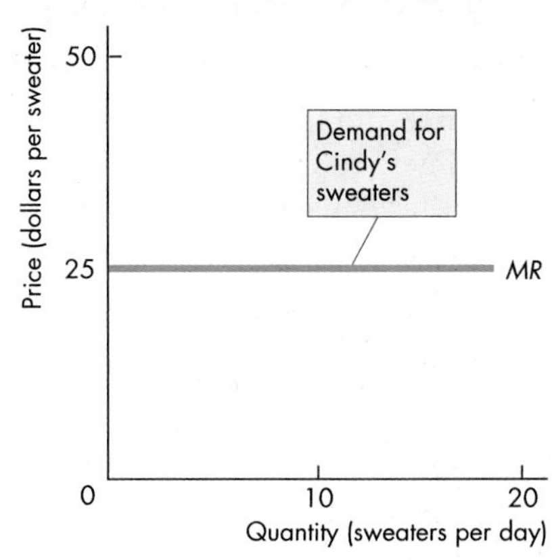

(c) Cindy's marginal revenue

Quantity sold (Q) (sweaters per day)	Price (P) (dollars per sweater)	Total revenue ($TR = P \times Q$) (dollars)	Marginal revenue ($MR = \Delta TR/\Delta Q$) (dollars per additional sweater)
8	25	200	
			25
9	25	225	
			25
10	25	250	

In part (a), market demand and market supply determine the market price (and quantity). Part (b) shows Cindy's total revenue curve (TR). Point A corresponds to the second row of the table—Cindy's sells 9 sweaters at $25 a sweater, so total revenue is $225. Part (c) shows Cindy's marginal revenue curve (MR). This curve is also the demand curve for Cindy's sweaters. Cindy's Sweaters faces a perfectly elastic demand for its sweaters at the market price of $25 a sweater.

$25 a sweater. Because the price remains constant when the quantity sold changes, the change in total revenue that results from a one-unit increase in the quantity sold equals price—in perfect competition, marginal revenue equals price.

Figure 11.1(c) shows Cindy's marginal revenue curve (MR) which is a horizontal line at the going market price.

The firm can sell any quantity it chooses at the market price. So the demand curve for the firm's product is a horizontal line at the market price, the same as the firm's marginal revenue curve.

Demand for Firm's Product and Market Demand A horizontal demand curve is perfectly elastic. So the firm faces a perfectly elastic demand for its output. One of Cindy's sweaters is a *perfect substitute* for sweaters from the factory next door or from any other factory. Notice, though, that the *market* demand for sweaters in Fig. 11.1(a) is not perfectly elastic. The market demand curve is downward-sloping, and its elasticity depends on the substitutability of sweaters for other goods and services.

REVIEW QUIZ

1 Why is a firm in perfect competition a price taker?
2 In perfect competition, what is the relationship between the demand for the firm's output and the market demand?
3 In perfect competition, why is a firm's marginal revenue curve also the demand curve for the firm's output?

myeconlab **Study Plan 11.1**

The Firm's Decisions in Perfect Competition

Firms in a perfectly competitive industry face a given market price and have the revenue curves that you've studied. These revenue curves summarize the market constraint faced by a perfectly competitive firm.

Firms also face a technology constraint, which is described by the product curves (total product, average product, and marginal product) that you studied in Chapter 10. The technology available to the firm determines its costs, which are described by the cost curves (total cost, average cost, and marginal cost) that you also studied in Chapter 10.

The goal of the competitive firm is to make the maximum economic profit possible, given the constraints it faces. To achieve this objective, a firm must make four key decisions: two in the short run and two in the long run.

Short-Run Decisions The short run is a time frame in which each firm has a given plant and the number of firms in the industry is fixed. But many things can change in the short run, and the firm must react to these changes. For example, the price for which the firm can sell its output might fluctuate with the season or general business conditions. The firm must react to such short-run price fluctuations and decide

1. Whether to produce or to shut down temporarily
2. If the decision is to produce, what quantity to produce

Long-Run Decisions The long run is a time frame in which each firm can change the size of its plant and decide whether to leave the industry. Other firms can decide whether to enter the industry. So in the long run, both the plant size of each firm and the number of firms in the industry can change. Also in the long run, the constraints that firms face can change. For example, the demand for the good can permanently fall, or a technological advance can change the industry's costs. The firm must react to such long-run changes and decide

1. Whether to increase or decrease its plant size
2. Whether to stay in an industry or leave it

The Firm and the Industry in the Short Run and the Long Run To study a competitive industry, we begin by looking at an individual firm's short-run decisions. We then see how the short-run decisions of all firms in a competitive industry combine to determine the industry price, output, and economic profit. We then turn to the long run and study the effects of long-run decisions on the industry price, output, and economic profit. All the decisions we study are driven by the pursuit of a single objective: maximization of economic profit.

Profit-Maximizing Output

A perfectly competitive firm maximizes economic profit by choosing its output level. One way of finding the profit-maximizing output is to study a firm's total revenue and total cost curves and find the output level at which total revenue exceeds total cost by the largest amount. Figure 11.2 shows how to do this for Cindy's Sweaters. The table lists Cindy's total revenue and total cost at different outputs, and part (a) of the figure shows Cindy's total revenue and total cost curves. These curves are graphs of the numbers shown in the first three columns of the table. The total revenue curve (*TR*) is the same as that in Fig. 11.1(b). The total cost curve (*TC*) is similar to the one that you met in Chapter 10: As output increases, so does total cost.

Economic profit equals total revenue minus total cost. The fourth column of the table in Fig. 11.2 shows Cindy's economic profit, and part (b) of the figure illustrates these numbers as Cindy's profit curve *EP.* This curve shows that Cindy's makes an economic profit at outputs between 4 and 12 sweaters a day. At outputs less than 4 sweaters a day, Cindy's incurs an economic loss. It also incurs an economic loss if output exceeds 12 sweaters a day. At outputs of 4 sweaters and 12 sweaters a day, total cost equals total revenue and Cindy's economic profit is zero. An output at which total cost equals total revenue is called a *break-even point.* The firm's economic profit is zero. Normal profit is part of the firm's costs, so at the break-even point, the entrepreneur makes normal profit.

Notice the relationship between the total revenue, total cost, and profit curves. Economic profit is measured by the vertical distance between the total revenue and total cost curves. When the total revenue curve in Fig. 11.2(a) is above the total cost curve,

FIGURE 11.2 Total Revenue, Total Cost, and Economic Profit

myeconlab

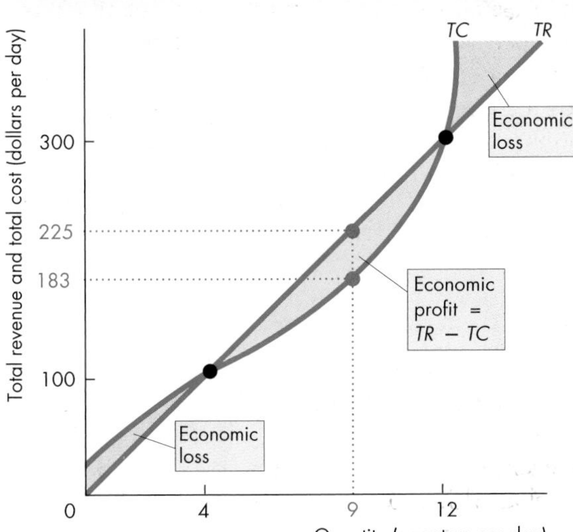

(a) Revenue and cost

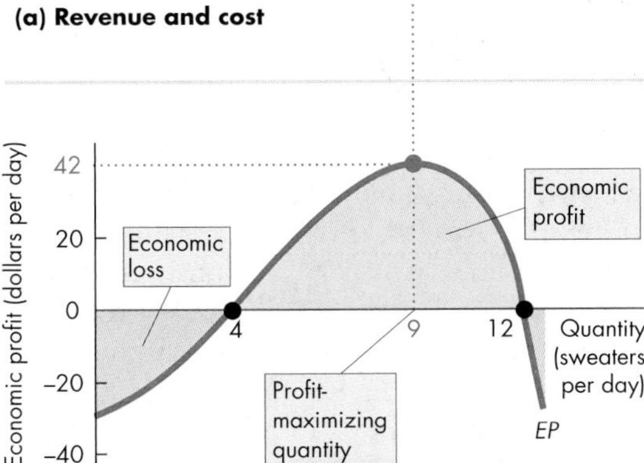

(b) Economic profit and loss

Quantity (Q) (sweaters per day)	Total revenue (TR) (dollars)	Total cost (TC) (dollars)	Economic profit (TR – TC) (dollars)
0	0	22	–22
1	25	45	–20
2	50	66	–16
3	75	85	–10
4	100	100	0
5	125	114	11
6	150	126	24
7	175	141	34
8	200	160	40
9	225	183	42
10	250	210	40
11	275	245	30
12	300	300	0
13	325	360	–35

The table lists Cindy's total revenue, total cost, and economic profit. Part (a) graphs the total revenue and total cost curves. Economic profit, in part (a), is the height of the blue area between the total cost and total revenue curves. Cindy's makes maximum economic profit, \$42 a day (\$225 – \$183), when it produces 9 sweaters—the output at which the vertical distance between the total revenue and total cost curves is at its largest. At outputs of 4 sweaters a day and 12 sweaters a day, Cindy's makes zero economic profit—these are break-even points. At outputs less than 4 and greater than 12 sweaters a day, Cindy's incurs an economic loss. Part (b) of the figure shows Cindy's profit curve. The profit curve is at its highest when economic profit is at a maximum and cuts the horizontal axis at the break-even points.

between 4 and 12 sweaters, the firm is making an economic profit and the profit curve in Fig. 11.2(b) is above the horizontal axis. At the break-even point, where the total cost and total revenue curves intersect, the profit curve intersects the horizontal axis. The profit curve is at its highest when the distance between *TR* and *TC* is greatest. In this example, profit maximization occurs at an output of 9 sweaters a day. At this output, Cindy's Sweaters makes an economic profit of \$42 a day.

Marginal Analysis

Another way of finding the profit-maximizing output is to use *marginal analysis* and compare marginal revenue, *MR*, with marginal cost, *MC*. As output increases, marginal revenue remains constant but marginal cost changes. At low output levels, marginal cost decreases, but it eventually increases. So where the marginal cost curve intersects the marginal revenue curve, marginal cost is rising.

If marginal revenue exceeds marginal cost (if $MR > MC$), then the extra revenue from selling one more unit exceeds the extra cost incurred to produce it. The firm makes an economic profit on the marginal unit, so its economic profit increases if output *increases*.

If marginal revenue is less than marginal cost (if $MR < MC$), then the extra revenue from selling one more unit is less than the extra cost incurred to produce it. The firm incurs an economic loss on the marginal unit, so its economic profit decreases if output increases and its economic profit increases if output *decreases*.

If marginal revenue equals marginal cost (if $MR = MC$), economic profit is maximized. The rule $MR = MC$ is an example of marginal analysis. Let's check that this rule for finding the profit-maximizing output works by returning to Cindy's Sweaters.

Look at Fig. 11.3. The table records Cindy's marginal revenue and marginal cost. Marginal revenue is a constant $25 a sweater. Over the range of outputs shown in the table, marginal cost increases from $19 a sweater to $35 a sweater.

Focus on the highlighted rows of the table. If Cindy increases output from 8 sweaters to 9 sweaters, marginal revenue is $25 and marginal cost is $23. Because marginal revenue exceeds marginal cost, economic profit increases. The last column of the table shows that economic profit increases from $40 to $42, an increase of $2. This economic profit from the ninth sweater is shown as the blue area in the figure.

If Cindy increases output from 9 sweaters to 10 sweaters, marginal revenue is still $25 but marginal cost is $27. Because marginal revenue is less than marginal cost, economic profit decreases. The last column of the table shows that economic profit decreases from $42 to $40. This loss from the tenth sweater is shown as the red area in the figure.

Cindy maximizes economic profit by producing 9 sweaters a day, the quantity at which marginal revenue equals marginal cost.

FIGURE 11.3 Profit-Maximizing Output

myeconlab

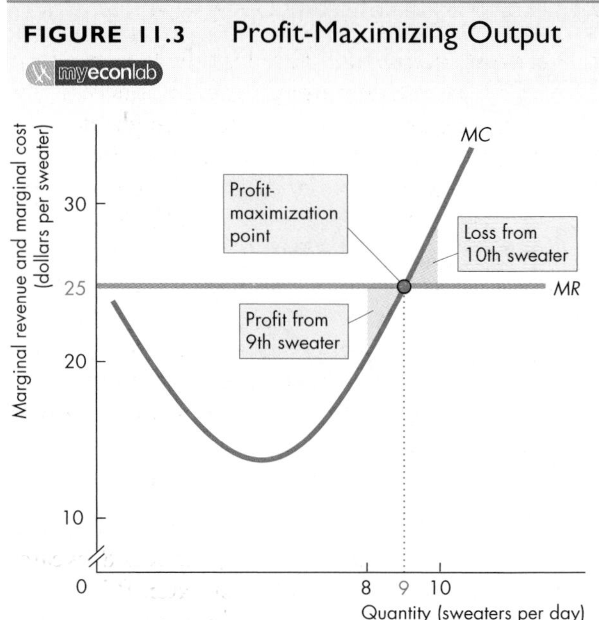

Quantity (Q) (sweaters per day)	Total revenue (TR) (dollars)	Marginal revenue (MR) (dollars per additional sweater)	Total cost (TC) (dollars)	Marginal cost (MC) (dollars per additional sweater)	Economic profit (TR – TC) (dollars)
7	175		141		34
		25		19	
8	200		160		40
		25		23	
9	225		183		42
		25		27	
10	250		210		40
		25		35	
11	275		245		30

Another way of finding the profit-maximizing output is to determine the output at which marginal revenue equals marginal cost. The table shows that if output increases from 8 to 9 sweaters, marginal cost is $23, which is less than the marginal revenue of $25. If output increases from 9 to 10 sweaters, marginal cost is $27, which exceeds the marginal revenue of $25. The figure shows that marginal cost and marginal revenue are equal when Cindy's produces 9 sweaters a day. If marginal revenue exceeds marginal cost, an increase in output increases economic profit. If marginal revenue is less than marginal cost, an increase in output decreases economic profit. If marginal revenue equals marginal cost, economic profit is maximized.

Profits and Losses in the Short Run

In short-run equilibrium, although the firm produces the profit-maximizing output, it does not necessarily end up making an economic profit. It might do so, but it might alternatively break even or incur an economic loss. Economic profit (or loss) per sweater is price, P, minus average total cost, ATC. So economic profit (or loss) is $(P - ATC) \times Q$. If price equals average total cost, a firm breaks even—the entrepreneur makes normal profit. If price exceeds average total cost, a firm makes an economic profit. If price is less than average total cost, a firm incurs an economic loss. Figure 11.4 shows these three possible short-run profit outcomes.

Three Possible Profit Outcomes In Fig. 11.4(a), the price of a sweater is $20. Cindy's produces 8 sweaters a day. Average total cost is $20 a sweater. Price equals average total cost (*ATC*), so Cindy's Sweaters breaks even (zero economic profit) and Cindy makes normal profit.

In Fig. 11.4(b), the price of a sweater is $25. Profit is maximized when output is 9 sweaters a day. Here, price exceeds average total cost, so Cindy's makes an economic profit. This economic profit is $42 a day. It is made up of $4.67 per sweater ($25.00 − $20.33) multiplied by the number of sweaters ($4.67 × 9 = $42). The blue rectangle shows this economic profit. The height of that rectangle is profit per sweater, $4.67, and the length is the quantity of sweaters produced, 9 a day, so the area of the rectangle is Cindy's economic profit of $42 a day.

In Fig. 11.4(c), the price of a sweater is $17. Here, price is less than average total cost and Cindy's incurs an economic loss. Price and marginal revenue are $17 a sweater, and the profit-maximizing (in this case, loss-minimizing) output is 7 sweaters a day. Cindy's total revenue is $119 a day (7 × $17). Average total cost is $20.14 a sweater, so the economic loss is $3.14 per sweater ($20.14 − $17.00). This loss per sweater multiplied by the number of sweaters is $22 ($3.14 × 7 = $22). The red rectangle shows this economic loss. The height of that rectangle is economic loss per sweater, $3.14, and the length is the quantity of sweaters produced, 7 a day, so the area of the rectangle is Cindy's economic loss of $22 a day.

FIGURE 11.4 Three Possible Profit Outcomes in the Short Run

myeconlab

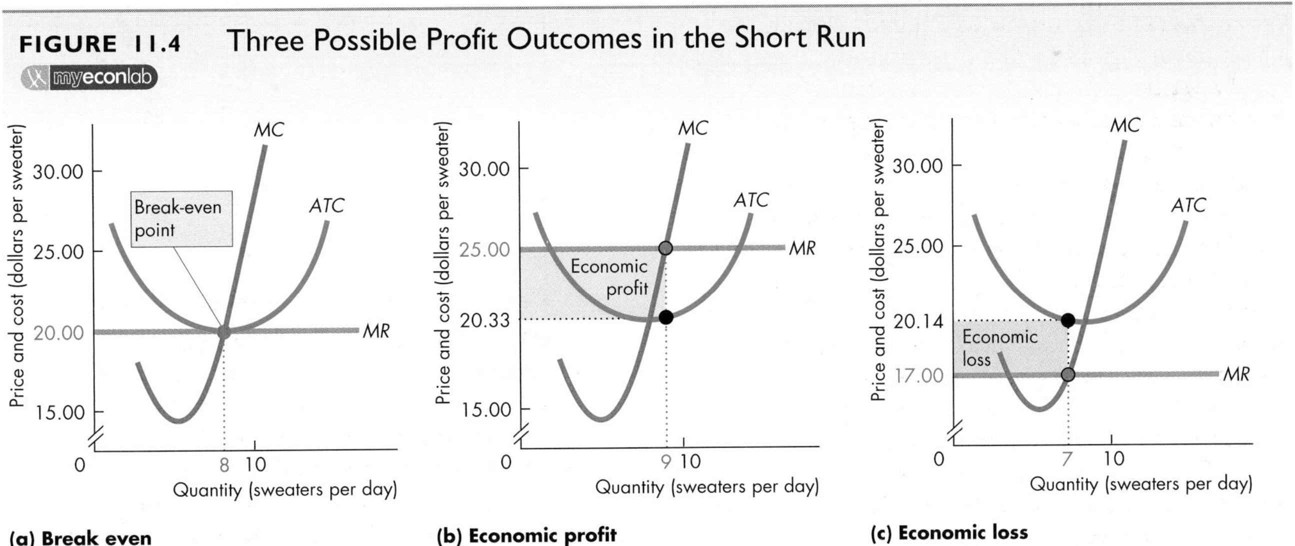

In the short run, the firm might break even (make zero economic profit), make an economic profit, or incur an economic loss. If the price equals minimum average total cost, the firm breaks even and makes zero economic profit (part a). If the price exceeds the average total cost of producing the profit-maximizing output, the firm makes an economic profit equal to the area of the blue rectangle in part (b). If the price is below minimum average total cost, the firm incurs an economic loss equal to the area of the red rectangle in part (c).

The Firm's Short-Run Supply Curve

A perfectly competitive firm's short-run supply curve shows how the firm's profit-maximizing output varies as the market price varies, other things remaining the same. Figure 11.5 shows how to derive Cindy's supply curve. Part (a) shows Cindy's marginal cost and average variable cost curves, and part (b) shows its supply curve. There is a direct link between the marginal cost and average variable cost curves and the supply curve. Let's see what that link is.

Temporary Plant Shutdown In the short run, a firm cannot avoid incurring its fixed cost. But the firm can avoid variable costs by temporarily laying off its workers and shutting down. If a firm shuts down, it produces no output and it incurs a loss equal to total fixed cost. This loss is the largest that a firm need incur. A firm shuts down if price falls below the minimum of average variable cost. The **shutdown point** is the output and price at which the firm just covers its total variable cost—point *T* in Fig. 11.5(a). If the price is \$17, the marginal revenue curve is MR_0 and the profit-maximizing output is 7 sweaters a day at point *T*. But both price and average variable cost equal \$17, so Cindy's total revenue equals total variable cost. Cindy's incurs an economic loss equal to total fixed cost. At a price below \$17, no matter what quantity Cindy produces, average *variable* cost exceeds price and the firm's loss exceeds total fixed cost. At a price below \$17, the firm shuts down temporarily.

The Short-Run Supply Curve If the price is above minimum average variable cost, Cindy maximizes profit by producing the output at which marginal cost equals price. At a price of \$25, the marginal revenue curve is MR_1 and Cindy maximizes profit by producing 9 sweaters. At a price of \$31, the marginal revenue curve is MR_2 and Cindy produces 10 sweaters.

Cindy's short-run supply curve, shown in Fig. 11.5(b), has two separate parts: First, at prices that exceed minimum average variable cost, the supply curve is the same as the marginal cost curve above the shutdown point (*T*). Second, at prices below minimum average variable cost, Cindy shuts down and produces nothing. The supply curve runs along the *y*-axis. At a price of \$17, Cindy is indifferent between shutting down and producing 7 sweaters a day. Either way, Cindy's incurs an economic loss equal to total fixed cost.

FIGURE 11.5 A Firm's Supply Curve

myeconlab

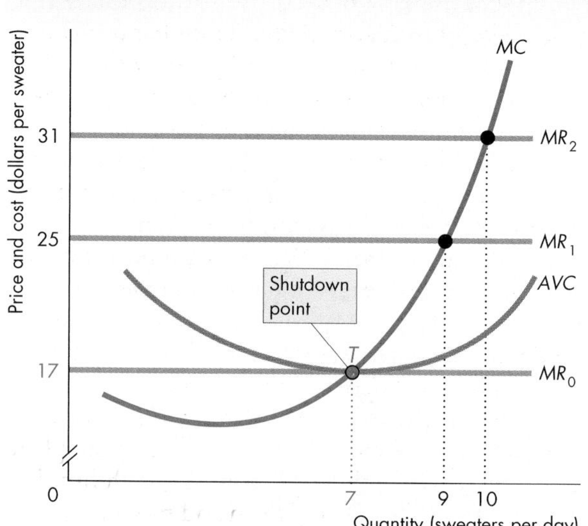

(a) Marginal cost and average variable cost

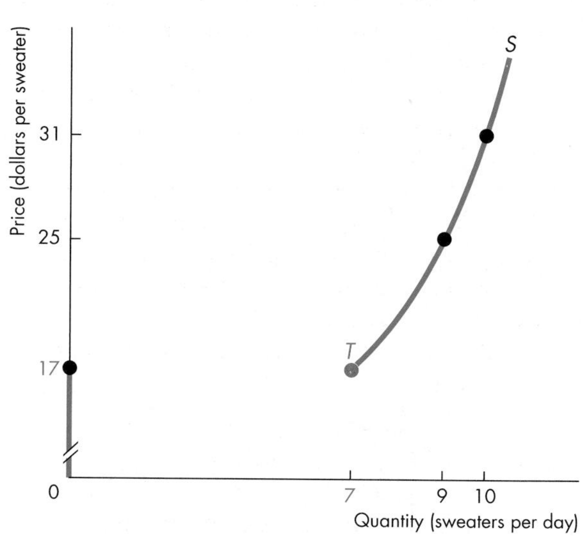

(b) Cindy's short-run supply curve

Part (a) shows Cindy's profit-maximizing output at various market prices. At \$25 a sweater, Cindy produces 9 sweaters. At \$17 a sweater, Cindy produces 7 sweaters. At any price below \$17 a sweater, Cindy produces nothing. Cindy's shutdown point is *T*. Part (b) shows Cindy's supply curve—the number of sweaters Cindy will produce at each price. It is made up of the marginal cost curve (part a) at all points above minimum average variable cost and the vertical axis at all prices below minimum average variable cost.

Short-Run Industry Supply Curve

The **short-run industry supply curve** shows the quantity supplied by the industry at each price when the plant size of each firm and the number of firms remain constant. The quantity supplied by the industry at a given price is the sum of the quantities supplied by all firms in the industry at that price.

Figure 11.6 shows the supply curve for the competitive sweater industry. In this example, the industry consists of 1,000 firms exactly like Cindy's Sweaters. At each price, the quantity supplied by the industry is 1,000 times the quantity supplied by a single firm.

The table in Fig. 11.6 shows the firm's and the industry's supply schedule and how the industry supply curve is constructed. At prices below $17, every firm in the industry shuts down; the quantity supplied by the industry is zero. At a price of $17, each firm is indifferent between shutting down and producing nothing or operating and producing 7 sweaters a day. Some firms will shut down, and others will supply 7 sweaters a day. The quantity supplied by each firm is *either* 0 or 7 sweaters, but the quantity supplied by the industry is *between* 0 (all firms shut down) and 7,000 (all firms produce 7 sweaters a day each).

To construct the industry supply curve, we sum the quantities supplied by the individual firms. Each of the 1,000 firms in the industry has a supply schedule like Cindy's. At prices below $17, the industry supply curve runs along the *y*-axis. At a price of $17, the industry supply curve is horizontal—supply is perfectly elastic. As the price rises above $17, each firm increases its quantity supplied and the quantity supplied by the industry increases by 1,000 times that of one firm.

REVIEW QUIZ

1 Why does a firm in perfect competition produce the quantity at which marginal cost equals price?
2 What is the lowest price at which a firm produces an output? Explain why.
3 What is the relationship between a firm's supply curve, its marginal cost curve, and its average variable cost curve?
4 How do we derive an industry supply curve?

myeconlab Study Plan 11.2

FIGURE 11.6 Industry Supply Curve

myeconlab

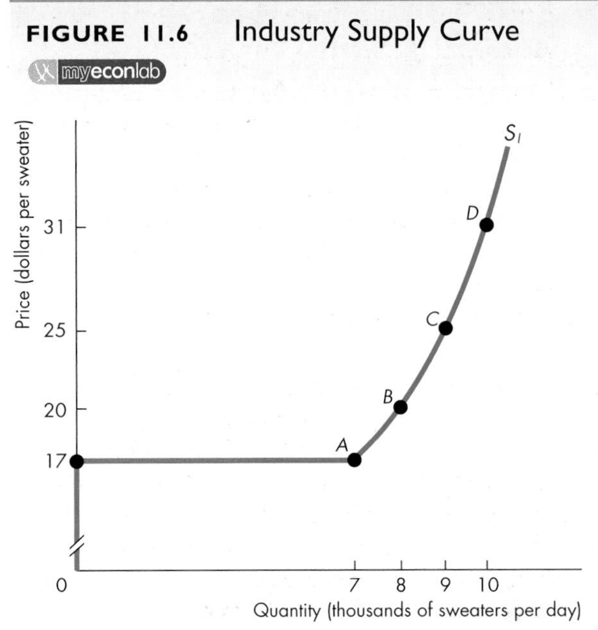

	Price (dollars per sweater)	Quantity supplied by Cindy's Sweaters (sweaters per day)	Quantity supplied by industry (sweaters per day)
A	17	0 or 7	0 to 7,000
B	20	8	8,000
C	25	9	9,000
D	31	10	10,000

The industry supply schedule is the sum of the supply schedules of all individual firms. An industry that consists of 1,000 identical firms has a supply schedule similar to that of the individual firm, but the quantity supplied by the industry is 1,000 times as large as that of the individual firm (see the table). The industry supply curve is S_I. Points *A*, *B*, *C*, and *D* correspond to the rows of the table. At the shutdown price of $17, each firm produces either 0 or 7 sweaters per day. The industry supply is perfectly elastic at the shutdown price.

So far, we have studied a single firm in isolation. We have seen that the firm's profit-maximizing actions depend on the market price, which the firm takes as given. But how is the market price determined? Let's find out.

Output, Price, and Profit in Perfect Competition

To determine the market price and the quantity bought and sold in a perfectly competitive market, we need to study how market demand and market supply interact. We begin this process by studying a perfectly competitive market in the short run when the number of firms is fixed and each firm has a given plant size.

Short-Run Equilibrium

Market demand and market supply determine the market price and industry output. Figure 11.7 shows a short-run equilibrium. The supply curve *S* is the same as S_I in Fig. 11.6. If the market demand is shown by the demand curve D_1, the equilibrium price is $20 a sweater. Each firm takes this price as given and produces its profit-maximizing output, which is 8 sweaters a day. Because the industry has 1,000 firms, industry output is 8,000 sweaters a day.

A Change in Demand

Changes in demand bring changes to short-run industry equilibrium. Figure 11.7 shows these changes.

If demand increases, the demand curve shifts rightward to D_2. The price rises to $25. At this price, each firm maximizes profit by increasing output. The new output is 9 sweaters a day for each firm and 9,000 sweaters a day for the industry.

If demand decreases, the demand curve shifts leftward to D_3. The price now falls to $17. At this price, each firm maximizes profit by decreasing its output. The new output is 7 sweaters a day for each firm and 7,000 sweaters a day for the industry.

If the demand curve shifts farther leftward than D_3, the price remains constant at $17 because the industry supply curve is horizontal at that price. Some firms continue to produce 7 sweaters a day, and others temporarily shut down. Firms are indifferent between these two activities, and whichever they choose, they incur an economic loss equal to total fixed cost. The number of firms continuing to produce is just enough to satisfy the market demand at a price of $17 a sweater.

FIGURE 11.7 Short-Run Equilibrium

myeconlab

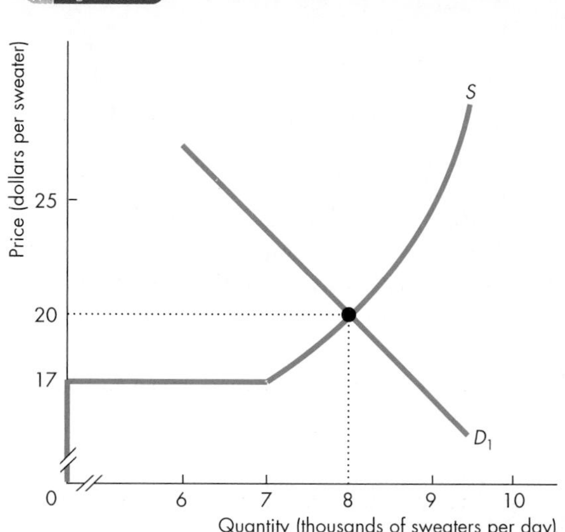

(a) Equilibrium

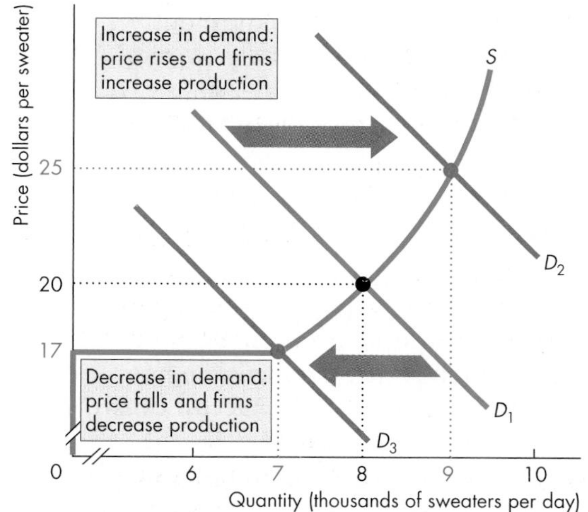

(b) Change in equilibrium

In part (a), the industry supply curve is S. Demand is D_1, and the price is $20. At this price, each firm produces 8 sweaters a day and the industry produces 8,000 sweaters a day. In part (b), when demand increases to D_2, the price rises to $25 and each firm increases its output to 9 sweaters a day. Industry output is 9,000 sweaters a day. When demand decreases to D_3, the price falls to $17 and each firm decreases its output to 7 sweaters a day. Industry output is 7,000 sweaters a day.

Long-Run Adjustments

In short-run equilibrium, a firm might make an economic profit, incur an economic loss, or break even. Although each of these three situations is a short-run equilibrium, only one of them is a long-run equilibrium. To see why, we need to examine the forces at work in a competitive industry in the long run.

In the long run, an industry adjusts in two ways:

- Entry and exit
- Changes in plant size

Let's look first at entry and exit.

Entry and Exit

In the long run, firms respond to economic profit and economic loss by either entering or exiting an industry. Firms enter an industry in which firms are making an economic profit, and firms exit an industry in which firms are incurring an economic loss. Temporary economic profit and temporary economic loss do not trigger entry and exit. But the prospect of persistent economic profit or loss does.

Entry and exit influence price, the quantity produced, and economic profit. The immediate effect of these decisions is to shift the industry supply curve. If more firms enter an industry, supply increases and the industry supply curve shifts rightward. If firms exit an industry, supply decreases and the industry supply curve shifts leftward.

Let's see what happens when new firms enter an industry.

The Effects of Entry Figure 11.8 shows the effects of entry. Suppose that all the firms in this industry have cost curves like those in Fig. 11.4. At any price greater than $20 a sweater, firms make an economic profit. At any price less than $20 a sweater, firms incur an economic loss. And at a price of $20 a sweater, firms make zero economic profit. Also suppose that the demand curve for sweaters is *D*. If the industry supply curve is S_1, sweaters sell for $23, and 7,000 sweaters a day are produced. Firms in the industry make an economic profit.

This economic profit is a signal for new firms to enter the industry. As these events unfold, supply increases and the industry supply curve shifts rightward to S0. With the greater supply and unchanged demand, the market price falls from $23 to $20 a sweater and the quantity produced by the industry increases from 7,000 to 8,000 sweaters a day.

Industry output increases, but Cindy's Sweaters, like each other firm in the industry, *decreases* output! Because the price falls, each firm moves down its supply curve and produces less. But because the number of firms in the industry increases, the industry as a whole produces more.

Because price falls, each firm's economic profit decreases. When the price falls to $20 a sweater, economic profit disappears and each firm makes a zero economic profit.

You have just discovered a key proposition:

As new firms enter an industry, the price falls and the economic profit of each existing firm decreases.

An example of this process occurred during the 1980s in the personal computer industry. When IBM introduced its first PC, there was little competition

FIGURE 11.8 Entry and Exit

myeconlab

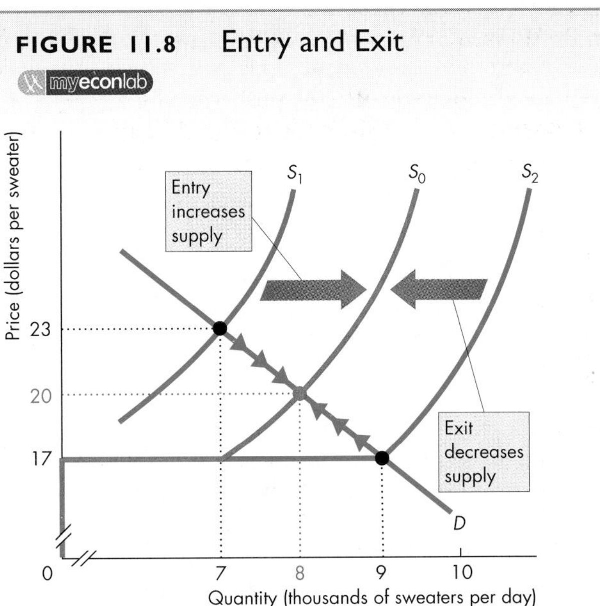

When new firms enter the sweater industry, the industry supply curve shifts rightward, from S_1 to S_0. The equilibrium price falls from $23 to $20, and the quantity produced increases from 7,000 to 8,000 sweaters.

When firms exit the sweater industry, the industry supply curve shifts leftward, from S_2 to S_0. The equilibrium price rises from $17 to $20, and the quantity produced decreases from 9,000 to 8,000 sweaters.

and the price of a PC gave IBM a big profit. But new firms such as Compaq, NEC, Dell, and a host of others entered the industry with machines that were technologically identical to IBM's. In fact, they were so similar that they came to be called "clones." The massive wave of entry into the personal computer industry shifted the industry supply curve rightward and lowered the price and the economic profit.

Let's now look at the effects of exit.

The Effects of Exit Figure 11.8 also shows the effects of exit. Suppose that firms' costs and the market demand are the same as before. But now suppose the supply curve is S_2. The market price is \$17, and 9,000 sweaters a day are produced. Firms in the industry now incur an economic loss. This economic loss is a signal for some firms to exit the industry. As firms exit, the industry supply curve shifts leftward to S_0. With the decrease in supply, industry output decreases from 9,000 to 8,000 sweaters and the price rises from \$17 to \$20 a sweater.

As the price rises, Cindy's Sweaters, like each other firm in the industry, moves up along its supply curve and increases output. That is, for each firm that remains in the industry, the profit-maximizing output increases. Because the price rises and each firm sells more, economic loss decreases. When the price rises to \$20, each firm makes a zero economic profit.

You've now discovered a second key proposition:

As firms leave an industry, the price rises and the economic loss of each remaining firm decreases.

The same PC industry that saw a large amount of entry during the 1980s and 1990s has seen some exit. For example, in 2001, IBM, the firm that first launched the PC, announced that it would no longer produce PCs. The intense competition from Compaq, NEC, Dell, and others that entered the industry following IBM's lead has lowered the price and eliminated the economic profit. So IBM now concentrates on servers and other parts of the computer market.

IBM exited the PC market because it was incurring economic losses. Its exit decreased supply and made it possible for the remaining firms in the industry to make zero economic profit.

You've now seen how economic profits induce entry, which in turn lowers profits. And you've seen how economic losses induce exit, which in turn eliminates losses. Let's now look at changes in plant size.

Changes in Plant Size

A firm changes its plant size if, by doing so, it can lower its costs and increase its economic profit. You can probably think of lots of examples of firms that have changed their plant size.

One example that has almost certainly happened near your campus in recent years is a change in the plant size of Kinko's or similar copy shops. Another is the number of FedEx vans that you see on the streets and highways. And another is the number of square feet of retail space devoted to selling computers and video games. These are examples of firms increasing their plant size to seek larger profits.

There are also many examples of firms that have decreased their plant size to avoid economic losses. One of these is Schwinn, the Chicago-based maker of bicycles. As competition from Asian bicycle makers became tougher, Schwinn cut back. Many firms have scaled back their operations—a process called *downsizing*—in recent years.

Figure 11.9 shows a situation in which Cindy's Sweaters has an incentive to increase its plant size. Suppose with its current plant, Cindy's marginal cost curve is MC_0, and its short-run average total cost curve is $SRAC_0$. The market price is \$25 a sweater, so Cindy's marginal revenue curve is MR_0. Cindy's maximizes profit by producing 6 sweaters a day.

Cindy's Sweaters' long-run average cost curve is *LRAC*. By increasing its plant size—installing more knitting machines—Cindy's Sweaters can move along its long-run average cost curve. As Cindy's Sweaters increases its plant size, its short-run marginal cost curve shifts rightward.

Recall that a firm's short-run supply curve is linked to its marginal cost curve. As Cindy's marginal cost curve shifts rightward, so does its supply curve. If Cindy's Sweaters and the other firms in the industry increase their plants, the short-run industry supply curve shifts rightward and the market price falls. The fall in the market price limits the extent to which Cindy's can profit from increasing its plant size.

Figure 11.9 also shows Cindy's Sweaters in a long-run competitive equilibrium. This situation arises when the market price has fallen to \$20 a sweater. Marginal revenue is MR_1, and Cindy's maximizes profit by producing 8 sweaters a day. In this situation, Cindy's cannot increase profit by changing the plant size. Cindy's is producing at minimum long-run average cost (point *M* on *LRAC*).

FIGURE 11.9 Plant Size and Long-Run Equilibrium

myeconlab

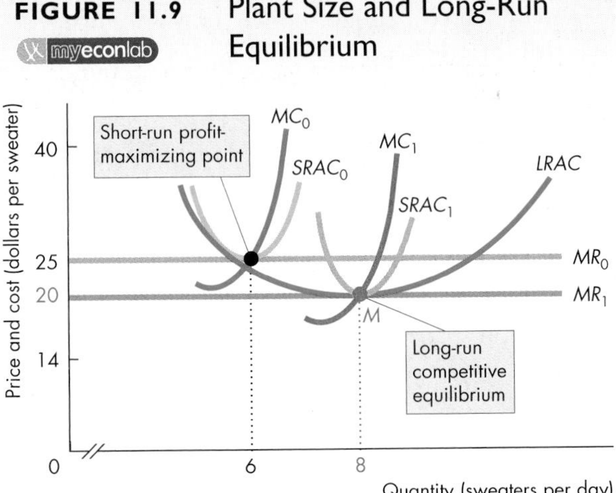

Initially, Cindy's plant has marginal cost curve MC_0 and short-run average total cost curve $SRAC_0$. The market price is $25 a sweater, and Cindy's marginal revenue is MR_0. The short-run profit-maximizing quantity is 6 sweaters a day. Cindy's Sweaters can increase profit by increasing the plant size. If all firms in the sweater industry increase their plant sizes, the short-run industry supply increases and the market price falls. In long-run equilibrium, a firm operates with the plant size that minimizes its average total cost. Here, Cindy's Sweaters operates the plant with short-run marginal cost MC_1 and short-run average cost $SRAC_1$. Cindy's Sweaters is also on its long-run average cost curve *LRAC* and produces at point *M*. Its output is 8 sweaters a day, and its average total cost equals the price of a sweater: $20.

Because Cindy's Sweaters is producing at minimum long-run average cost, it has no incentive to change its plant size. A bigger plant or a smaller plant has a higher long-run average cost. If Fig. 11.9 describes the situation of all firms in the sweater industry, the industry is in long-run equilibrium. No firm has an incentive to change its plant size. Also, because each firm is making zero economic profit, no firm has an incentive to enter or to leave the industry.

Long-Run Equilibrium

Long-run equilibrium occurs in a competitive industry when economic profit is zero (when firms earn normal profit). If the firms in a competitive industry are making an economic profit, new firms enter the industry. If firms can lower their costs by increasing their plant size, they expand. Each of these actions increases industry supply, shifts the industry supply curve rightward, lowers the price, and decreases economic profit.

Firms continue to enter the industry and profit decreases as long as firms in the industry are earning positive economic profits. When economic profit has been eliminated, firms stop entering the industry. And when firms are operating with the least-cost plant size, they stop expanding.

If the firms in a competitive industry are incurring an economic loss, some firms exit the industry. If firms can lower their costs by decreasing their plant size, they downsize. Each of these actions decreases industry supply, shifts the industry supply curve leftward, raises the price, and decreases economic loss.

Firms continue to exit and economic loss continues to decrease as long as firms in the industry are incurring economic losses. When economic loss has been eliminated, firms stop exiting the industry. And when firms are operating with the least-cost plant size, they stop downsizing. So in long-run equilibrium in a competitive industry, firms neither enter nor exit the industry and old firms neither expand nor downsize. Each firm makes zero economic profit.

REVIEW QUIZ

1. In perfect competition, when market demand decreases, explain how the price of the good and the output of each firm changes in the short run.
2. If the firms in a competitive industry earn an economic profit, what happens to supply, price, output, and economic profit in the long run?
3. If the firms in a competitive industry incur an economic loss, what happens to supply, price, output, and economic profit in the long run?

myeconlab **Study Plan 11.3**

You've seen how a competitive industry adjusts toward its long-run equilibrium. But a competitive industry is rarely *in* a state of long-run equilibrium. A competitive industry is constantly and restlessly evolving toward such an equilibrium. But the constraints that firms in the industry face are constantly changing. The two most persistent sources of change are in tastes and technology. Let's see how a competitive industry reacts to such changes.

Changing Tastes and Advancing Technology

Increased awareness of the health hazards of smoking has caused a decrease in the demand for tobacco and cigarettes. The development of inexpensive car and air transportation has caused a huge decrease in the demand for long-distance trains and buses. Solid-state electronics have caused a large decrease in the demand for TV and radio repair. The development of good-quality inexpensive clothing has decreased the demand for sewing machines. What happens in a competitive industry when there is a permanent decrease in the demand for its product?

The development of the microwave oven has produced an enormous increase in demand for paper, glass, and plastic cooking utensils and for plastic wrap. The widespread use of the personal computer has brought a huge increase in the demand for CD-Rs. What happens in a competitive industry when the demand for its output increases?

Advances in technology are constantly lowering the costs of production. New biotechnologies have dramatically lowered the costs of producing many food and pharmaceutical products. New electronic technologies have lowered the cost of producing just about every good and service. What happens in a competitive industry when technological change lowers its production costs?

Let's use the theory of perfect competition to answer these questions.

A Permanent Change in Demand

Figure 11.10(a) shows a competitive industry that initially is in long-run equilibrium. The demand curve is D_0, the supply curve is S_0, the market price is P_0, and industry output is Q_0. Figure 11.10(b) shows a single firm in this initial long-run equilibrium. The firm produces q_0 and makes zero economic profit.

Now suppose that demand decreases and the demand curve shifts leftward to D_1, as shown in Fig. 11.10(a). The price falls to P_1, and the quantity supplied by the industry decreases from Q_0 to Q_1 as the industry slides down its short-run supply curve S_0. Figure 11.10(b) shows the situation facing a firm. Price is now below the firm's minimum average total cost, so the firm incurs an economic loss. But to keep its loss to a minimum, the firm adjusts its output to keep marginal cost equal to price. At a price of P_1, each firm produces an output of q_1.

The industry is now in short-run equilibrium but not long-run equilibrium. It is in short-run equilibrium because each firm is maximizing profit. But it is not in long-run equilibrium because each firm is incurring an economic loss—its average total cost exceeds the price.

The economic loss is a signal for some firms to leave the industry. As they do so, short-run industry supply decreases and the supply curve gradually shifts leftward. As industry supply decreases, the price rises. At each higher price, a firm's profit-maximizing output is greater, so the firms remaining in the industry increase their output as the price rises. Each firm slides up its marginal cost or supply curve in Fig. 11.10(b). That is, as firms exit the industry, industry output decreases but the output of the firms that remain in the industry increases.

Eventually, enough firms leave the industry for the industry supply curve to have shifted to S_1 in Fig. 11.10(a). At this time, the price has returned to its original level, P_0. At this price, the firms remaining in the industry produce q_0, the same quantity that they produced before the decrease in demand. Because firms are now making zero economic profit, no firm wants to enter or exit the industry. The industry supply curve remains at S_1, and industry output is Q_2. The industry is again in long-run equilibrium.

The difference between the initial long-run equilibrium and the final long-run equilibrium is the number of firms in the industry. A permanent decrease in demand has decreased the number of firms. Each remaining firm produces the same output in the new long-run equilibrium as it did initially and earns zero economic profit. In the process of moving from the initial equilibrium to the new one, firms incur economic losses.

We've just worked out how a competitive industry responds to a permanent *decrease* in demand. A permanent increase in demand triggers a similar response, except in the opposite direction. The increase in demand brings a higher price, economic profit, and entry. Entry increases industry supply and eventually lowers the price to its original level and economic profit to zero.

The demand for Internet service increased permanently during the 1990s and huge profit opportunities arose in this industry. The result was a massive

FIGURE 11.10 A Decrease in Demand

myeconlab

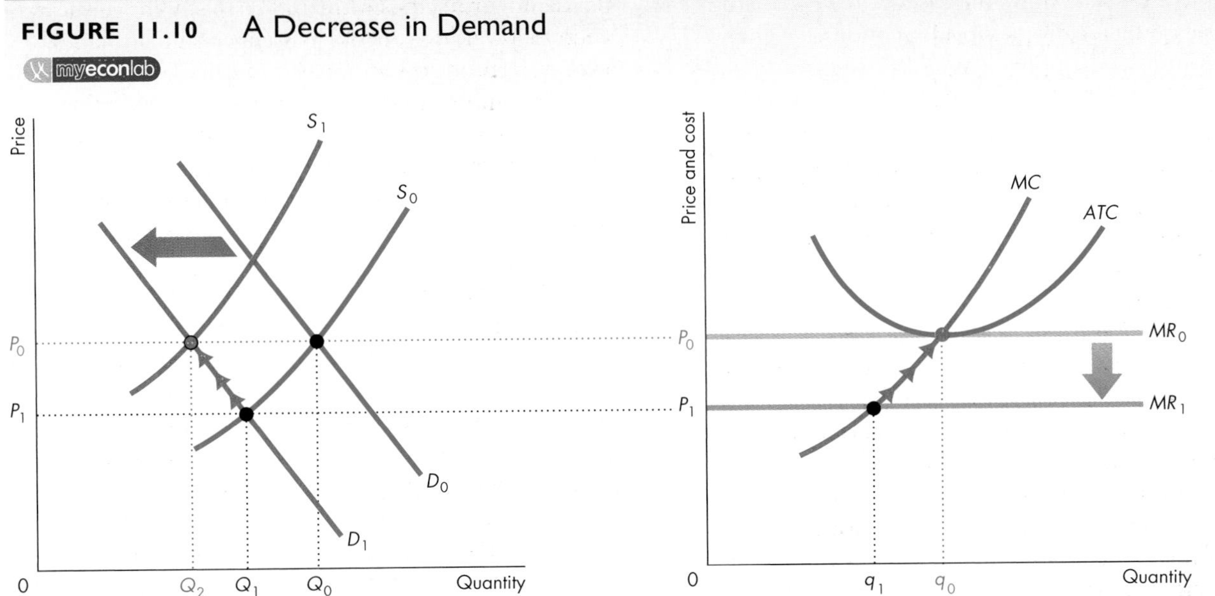

(a) Industry

(b) Firm

An industry starts out in long-run competitive equilibrium. Part (a) shows the industry demand curve D_0, the industry supply curve S_0, the equilibrium quantity Q_0, and the market price P_0. Each firm sells its output at price P_0, so its marginal revenue curve is MR_0 in part (b). Each firm produces q_0 and makes zero economic profit.

Demand decreases permanently from D_0 to D_1 (part a). The market price falls to P_1, each firm decreases its output to q_1 (part b), and industry output decreases to Q_1 (part a).

In this new situation, firms incur economic losses and some firms leave the industry. As they do so, the industry supply curve gradually shifts leftward, from S_0 to S_1. This shift gradually raises the market price from P_1 back to P_0. While the price is below P_0, firms incur economic losses and some firms leave the industry. Once the price has returned to P_0, each firm makes zero economic profit. Firms have no further incentive to leave the industry. Each firm produces q_0, and industry output is Q_2.

rate of entry of Internet service providers. The process of competition and change in the Internet service industry is similar to what we have just studied but with an increase in demand rather than a decrease in demand.

We've now studied the effects of a permanent change in demand for a good. In doing so, we began and ended in a long-run equilibrium and examined the process that takes a market from one equilibrium to another. It is this process, not the equilibrium points, that describes the real world.

One feature of the predictions that we have just generated seems odd: In the long run, regardless of whether demand increases or decreases, the market price returns to its original level. Is this outcome inevitable? In fact, it is not. It is possible for the equilibrium market price in the long run to remain the same, rise, or fall.

External Economies and Diseconomies

The change in the long-run equilibrium price depends on external economies and external diseconomies. **External economies** are factors beyond the control of an individual firm that lower the firm's costs as the *industry* output increases. **External diseconomies** are factors outside the control of a firm that raise the firm's costs as the *industry* output increases. With no external economies or external diseconomies, a firm's costs remain constant as the industry output changes.

Figure 11.11 illustrates these three cases and introduces a new supply concept: the long-run industry supply curve.

A **long-run industry supply curve** shows how the quantity supplied by an industry varies as the market price varies after all the possible adjustments have been made, including changes in plant size and the number of firms in the industry.

Figure 11.11(a) shows the case we have just studied—no external economies or diseconomies. The long-run industry supply curve (LS_A) is perfectly elastic. In this case, a permanent increase in demand from D_0 to D_1 has no effect on the price in the long run. The increase in demand brings a temporary increase in price to P_S and a short-run quantity increase from Q_0 to Q_S. Entry increases short-run supply from S_0 to S_1, which lowers the price from P_S back to P_0, and increases the quantity to Q_1.

Figure 11.11(b) shows the case of external diseconomies. The long-run industry supply curve (LS_B) slopes upward. A permanent increase in demand from D_0 to D_1 increases the price in both the short run and the long run. The increase in demand brings a temporary increase in price to P_S and a short-run quantity increase from Q_0 to Q_S. Entry increases short-run supply from S_0 to S_2, which lowers the price from P_S to P_2 and increases the quantity to Q_2.

One source of external diseconomies is congestion. The airline industry provides a good example. With bigger airline industry output, congestion at airports and airspace increase and results in longer delays and extra waiting time for passengers and airplanes. These external diseconomies mean that as the output of air transportation services increases (in the absence of technological advances), average cost increases. As a result, the long-run industry supply curve is upward sloping. So a permanent increase in demand brings an increase in quantity and a rise in the price. (Industries with external diseconomies might nonetheless have a falling price because technological advances shift the long-run supply curve downward.)

Figure 11.11(c) shows the case of external economies. In this case, the long-run industry supply curve (LS_C) slopes downward. A permanent increase in demand from D_0 to D_1 increases the price in the short run and lowers it in the long run. Again, the increase in demand brings a temporary increase in price to P_S, and a short-run quantity increase from Q_0 to Q_S. Entry increases short-run supply from S_0 to S_3, which lowers the price to P_3 and increases the quantity to Q_3.

An example of external economies is the growth of specialist support services for an industry as it

FIGURE 11.11 Long-Run Changes in Price and Quantity

myeconlab

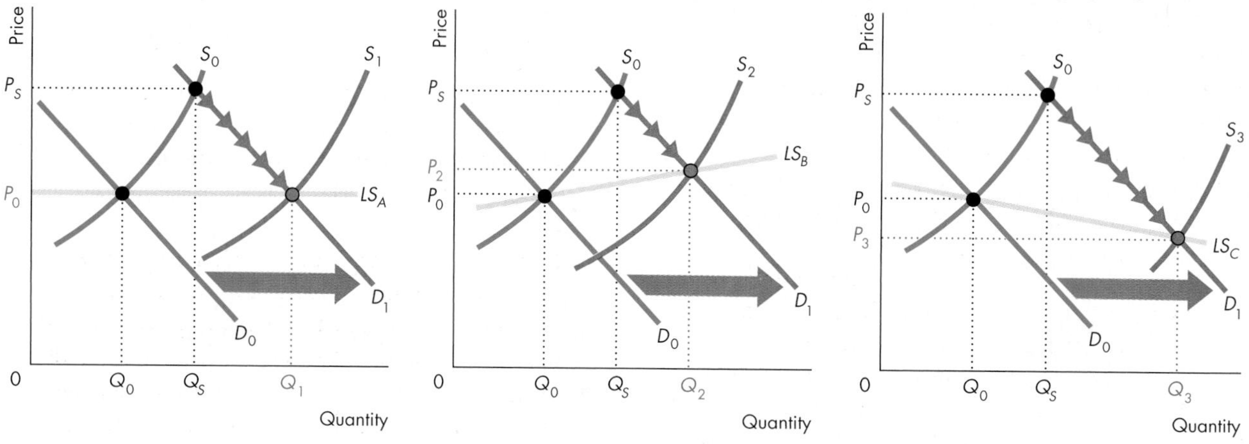

(a) Constant-cost industry

(b) Increasing-cost industry

(c) Decreasing-cost industry

Three possible changes in price and quantity occur in the long run. When demand increases from D_0 to D_1, entry occurs and the industry supply curve shifts rightward from S_0 to S_1. In part (a), the long-run industry supply curve, LS_A, is horizontal. The quantity increases from Q_0 to Q_1, and the price remains constant at P_0.

In part (b), the long-run industry supply curve is LS_B; the price rises to P_2, and the quantity increases to Q_2. This case occurs in industries with external diseconomies. In part (c), the long-run industry supply curve is LS_C; the price falls to P_3, and the quantity increases to Q_3. This case occurs in an industry with external economies.

expands. As farm output increased in the nineteenth and early twentieth centuries, the services available to farmers expanded. New firms specialized in the development and marketing of farm machinery and fertilizers. As a result, average farm costs decreased. Farms enjoyed the benefits of external economies. As a consequence, as the demand for farm products increased, the output increased but the price fell.

Over the long term, the prices of many goods and services have fallen, not because of external economies but because of technological change. Let's now study this influence on a competitive market.

Technological Change

Industries are constantly discovering lower-cost techniques of production. Most cost-saving production techniques cannot be implemented, however, without investing in new plant and equipment. As a consequence, it takes time for a technological advance to spread through an industry. Some firms whose plants are on the verge of being replaced will be quick to adopt the new technology, while other firms whose plants have recently been replaced will continue to operate with an old technology until they can no longer cover their average variable cost. Once average variable cost cannot be covered, a firm will scrap even a relatively new plant (embodying an old technology) in favor of a plant with a new technology.

New technology allows firms to produce at a lower cost. As a result, as firms adopt a new technology, their cost curves shift downward. With lower costs, firms are willing to supply a given quantity at a lower price or, equivalently, they are willing to supply a larger quantity at a given price. In other words, industry supply increases, and the industry supply curve shifts rightward. With a given demand, the quantity produced increases and the price falls.

Two forces are at work in an industry undergoing technological change. Firms that adopt the new technology make an economic profit. So there is entry by new-technology firms. Firms that stick with the old technology incur economic losses. They either exit the industry or switch to the new technology.

As old-technology firms disappear and new-technology firms enter, the price falls and the quantity produced increases. Eventually, the industry arrives at a long-run equilibrium in which all the firms use the new technology and make a zero economic profit. Because in the long run competition eliminates economic profit, technological change brings only temporary gains to producers. But the lower prices and better products that technological advances bring are permanent gains for consumers.

The process that we've just described is one in which some firms experience economic profits and others experience economic losses. It is a period of dynamic change for an industry. Some firms do well, and others do badly. Often, the process has a geographical dimension—the expanding new technology firms bring prosperity to what was once the boondocks, and traditional industrial regions decline. Sometimes, the new-technology firms are in a foreign country, while the old-technology firms are in the domestic economy. The information revolution of the 1990s produced many examples of changes like these. Commercial banking, which was traditionally concentrated in New York, San Francisco, and other large cities now flourishes in Charlotte, North Carolina, which has become the nation's number three commercial banking city. Television shows and movies, traditionally made in Los Angeles and New York, are now made in large numbers in Orlando.

Technological advances are not confined to the information and entertainment industries. Even food production is undergoing a major technological change because of genetic engineering.

REVIEW QUIZ

1 Describe the course of events in a competitive industry following a permanent decrease in demand. What happens to output, price, and economic profit in the short run and in the long run?
2 Describe the course of events in a competitive industry following a permanent increase in demand. What happens to output, price, and economic profit in the short run and in the long run?
3 Describe the course of events in a competitive industry following the adoption of a new technology. What happens to output, price, and economic profit in the short run and in the long run?

myeconlab **Study Plan 11.4**

We've seen how a competitive industry operates in the short run and the long run. But is a competitive industry efficient?

Competition and Efficiency

A competitive industry can achieve an efficient use of resources. You first studied efficiency in Chapter 2. Then in Chapter 5, using only the concepts of demand, supply, consumer surplus, and producer surplus, you saw how a competitive market achieves efficiency. Now that you have learned what lies behind the demand and supply curves of a competitive market, you can gain a deeper understanding of the efficiency of a competitive market.

Efficient Use of Resources

Recall that resource use is efficient when we produce the goods and services that people value most highly (see Chapter 2, p. 39 and Chapter 5, p. 110). If someone can become better off without anyone else becoming worse off, resources are *not* being used efficiently. For example, suppose we produce a computer that no one wants and no one will ever use and, at the same time, some people are clamoring for more video games. If we produce one less computer and reallocate the unused resources to produce more video games, some people will become better off and no one will be worse off. So the initial resource allocation was inefficient.

In the more technical language that you have learned, resource use is efficient when marginal social benefit equals marginal social cost. In the computer and video games example, the marginal social benefit of a video game exceeds its marginal social cost. And the marginal social cost of a computer exceeds its marginal social benefit. So by producing fewer computers and more video games, we move resources toward a higher-valued use.

Choices, Equilibrium, and Efficiency

We can use what you have learned about the decisions made by consumers and competitive firms and market equilibrium to describe an efficient use of resources.

Choices Consumers allocate their budgets to get the most value possible out of them. And we derive a consumer's demand curve by finding how the best budget allocation changes as the price of a good changes. So consumers get the most value out of their resources at all points along their demand curves. If the people who consume a good or service are the only ones who benefit from it, there are no external benefits and the market demand curve is the marginal social benefit curve.

Competitive firms produce the quantity that maximizes profit. And we derive the firm's supply curve by finding the profit-maximizing quantity at each price. So firms get the most value out of their resources at all points along their supply curves. If the firms that produce a good or service bear all the costs of producing it, there are no external costs and the market supply curve is the marginal social cost curve.

Equilibrium and Efficiency Resources are used efficiently when marginal social benefit equals marginal social cost. And competitive equilibrium achieves this efficient outcome because for consumers, price equals marginal social benefit and for producers, price equals marginal social cost.

The gains from trade are the consumer surplus plus the producer surplus. The gains from trade for consumers are measured by *consumer surplus,* which is the area below the demand curve and above the price paid. (See Chapter 5, p. 107.) The gains from trade for producers are measured by *producer surplus,* which is the area above the supply curve and below the price received. (See Chapter 5, p. 109.) The total gains from trade are the sum of consumer surplus and producer surplus. When the market for a good or service is in equilibrium, the gains from trade are maximized.

Illustrating an Efficient Allocation Figure 11.12 illustrates an efficient allocation in perfect competition in long-run equilibrium. Part (a) shows the situation of an individual firm, and part (b) shows the market. The equilibrium market price is P^*. At that price, each firm makes zero economic profit. Each firm has a plant size that enables it to produce at the lowest possible average total cost. In this situation, consumers are as well off as possible because the good cannot be produced at a lower cost and the price equals that least possible cost.

In part (b), consumers are efficient at all points on the market demand curve, $D = MSB$. Producers are efficient at all points on the market supply curve, $S = MSC$. Resources are used efficiently at the quantity Q^* and price P^*. At this point, marginal social benefit equals marginal social cost, and the sum of producer surplus (blue area) and consumer surplus (green area) is maximized.

FIGURE 11.12 Efficiency of Perfect Competition

myeconlab

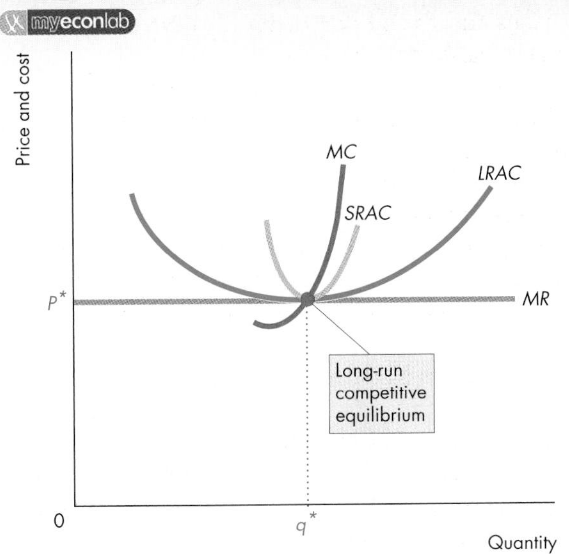

(a) A single firm

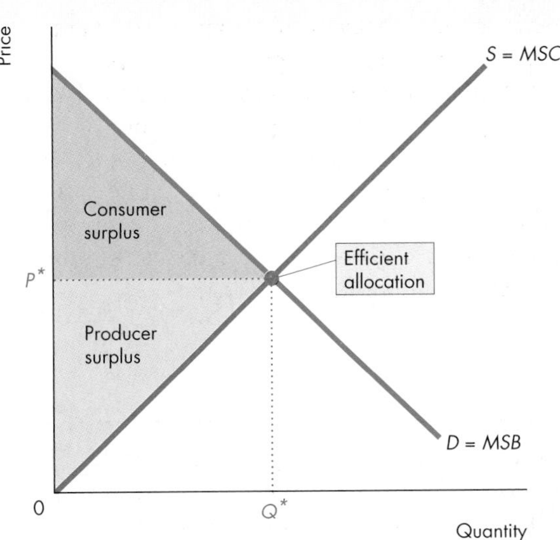

(b) A market

In part (a), a firm in perfect competition produces at the lowest possible long-run average total cost at q^*. In part (b), consumers have made the best available choices and are on the market demand curve and firms are producing at least cost and are on the market supply curve. With no external benefits or external costs, resources are used efficiently at the quantity Q^* and the price P^*. Perfect competition achieves an efficient use of resources.

When firms in perfect competition are away from long-run equilibrium, either entry or exit is taking place and the market is moving toward the situation depicted in Figure 11.12. But the market is still efficient. As long as marginal social benefit (on the market demand curve) equals marginal social cost (on the market supply curve), the market is efficient. But it is only in long-run equilibrium that consumers pay the lowest possible price.

REVIEW QUIZ

1. State the conditions that must be met for resources to be allocated efficiently.
2. Describe the choices that consumers make and explain why consumers are efficient on the market demand curve.
3. Describe the choices that producers make and explain why producers are efficient on the market supply curve.
4. Explain why resources are used efficiently in a competitive market.

myeconlab **Study Plan 11.5**

You've now completed your study of perfect competition. And *Reading Between the Lines* on pp. 258–259 gives you an opportunity to use what you have learned to understand recent events in the competitive market for the pollination services of bees.

Although many markets approximate the model of perfect competition, many do not. In Chapter 12, we study markets at the opposite extreme of market power: monopoly. Then, in Chapter 13, we'll study markets that lie between perfect competition and monopoly: monopolistic competition (competition with monopoly elements) and oligopoly (competition among a few producers). When you have completed this study, you'll have a tool kit that will enable you to understand the variety of real-world markets.

READING BETWEEN THE LINES

Competition in the Orchard

http://nytimes.com

A Parasite Devastates Bees, And Farmers Are Worried

May 2, 2005

"Do you want to see a ghost town?" Joe Linelho asked. He pulled the lid off one of his beehives and worked one of the honey frames loose with a small blade. Not a bee responded to the intrusion. The hundreds of little hexagonal cells, where young bees should be incubating, were empty, and at the center hung a cluster of bees, all dead. . . .

"This is a national problem," said Kevin Hackett, national program leader for bees and pollination at the Agriculture Department's Research Service. "We've lost at least half of our hives, and 70 percent in some areas. With a couple of million hives in the U.S., and you reduce that population by half, that's very serious."

The problem is not just about honey. Bees are needed to pollinate $15 billion worth of agricultural products a year. Growers report increasing competition, and rising prices, for the hives that are moved around the country in the spring, from the almonds in California in February to the apples, blueberries and other fruits elsewhere later in the season. . . .

. . . most of the losses are being attributed to the Varroa mite, which came into the country in the early 1980s, Mr. Raybold said, and began by devastating the country's wild honeybee population. . . .

Fruit growers usually pay $30 to $40 to have a hive placed among their plants in the spring, with the hive's owner keeping the honey. But Chris Heintz, director of research for the Almond Board of California, said she had heard reports of growers paying more than $100 per hive. . . .

Essence of the Story

- The Varroa mite, which has been in the United States since the early 1980s, has devastated the honeybee population.
- The number of active beehives has decreased by 50 percent and in some areas by 70 percent.
- Both honey production and pollination have decreased.
- Fruit growers usually pay $30 to $40 per hive with the hive's owner keeping the honey in return for pollination services.
- The price per hive has increased to more than $100.

Economic Analysis

- Beekeepers produce two goods: honey and pollination services.
- Here, we focus on the competitive market for pollination services.
- Orchard farmers rent hives of bees from beekeepers and pay a fee for the service.
- Figure 1 shows the market for pollination services.
- The demand curve D is the demand by orchard farmers.
- The supply curve S_0 is the supply by beekeepers before the Varroa mite devastated the honeybee population.
- The market was in equilibrium at a price of \$40 per hive and a quantity Q_0.
- Figure 2 shows the cost and revenue curves for an individual beekeeper.
- Before the mite attack, the marginal revenue curve is MR_0, the marginal cost curve is MC, and the average total cost curve is ATC.
- The beekeeper maximizes profit by producing q_0 and the firm is assumed to be in long-run equilibrium.
- As the Varroa mite attacks, many beekeepers lose their honeybees and go out of business.
- Supply decreases, and in Fig. 1, the supply curve shifts leftward to S_1.
- The price for renting a hive rises to \$100 and the equilibrium quantity decreases to Q_1.
- Figure 2 shows what happens to a beekeeper who remains in business and escapes the Varroa mite.
- The rise in price shifts the marginal revenue curve upward to MR_1.
- To maximize profit, the beekeeper increases the number of hives rented to orchard farmers to q_1.
- The firm now makes an economic profit shown by the blue rectangle.
- The situation shown in Fig. 1 and 2 is a short-run equilibrium. Because firms are making a positive economic profit, entry will occur in the long run as people breed more bees and try to overcome the Varroa mite.
- If it is costly to overcome the Varroa mite, beekeeping costs will increase and economic profit will decrease.
- Eventually, either because more bees are bred or because the cost of beekeeping rises, a new long-run equilibrium will emerge in which economic profit is again zero and beekeepers earn normal profit.

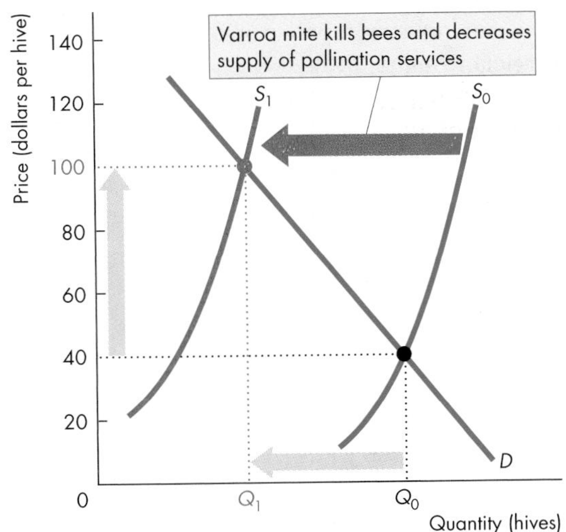

Figure 1 The market for pollination services

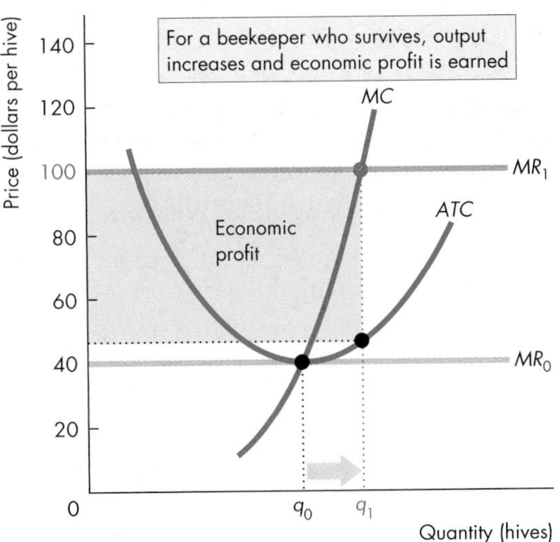

Figure 2 One beekeeper

SUMMARY

Key Points

What Is Perfect Competition? (pp. 240–241)

- A perfectly competitive firm is a price taker.

The Firm's Decisions in Perfect Competition (pp. 242–247)

- The firm produces the output at which marginal revenue (price) equals marginal cost.
- In short-run equilibrium, a firm can make an economic profit, incur an economic loss, or break even.
- If price is less than minimum average variable cost, the firm temporarily shuts down.
- A firm's supply curve is the upward-sloping part of its marginal cost curve above minimum average variable cost.
- An industry supply curve shows the sum of the quantities supplied by each firm at each price.

Output, Price, and Profit in Perfect Competition (pp. 248–251)

- Market demand and market supply determine price.
- Persistent economic profit induces entry. Persistent economic loss induces exit.
- Entry and plant expansion increase supply and lower price and profit. Exit and downsizing decrease supply and raise price and profit.
- In long-run equilibrium, economic profit is zero (the entrepreneur makes normal profit). There is no entry, exit, plant expansion, or downsizing.

Changing Tastes and Advancing Technology (pp. 252–255)

- A permanent decrease in demand leads to a smaller industry output and a smaller number of firms.
- A permanent increase in demand leads to a larger industry output and a larger number of firms.
- The long-run effect of a change in demand on price depends on whether there are external economies (the price falls) or external diseconomies (the price rises) or neither (the price remains constant).
- New technologies increase supply and in the long run lower the price and increase the quantity.

Competition and Efficiency (pp. 256–257)

- Resources are used efficiently when we produce goods and services in the quantities that people value most highly.
- When there are no external benefits and external costs, perfect competition achieves an efficient allocation. In long-run equilibrium, consumers pay the lowest possible price, marginal social benefit equals marginal social cost, and the sum of consumer surplus and producer surplus is maximized.

Key Figures

Key Terms

PROBLEMS

myeconlab Tests, Study Plan, Solutions*

1. Lin's fortune cookies are identical to those of dozens of other firms and there is free entry in the fortune cookie market. Buyers and sellers are well informed about prices.
   a. Based on the above information, in what type of market does Lin's fortune cookies operate?
   b. What determines the price of fortune cookies?
   c. What determines Lin's marginal revenue of fortune cookies?
   d. If fortune cookies sell for $10 a box and Lin offers his cookies for sale at $10.50 a box, how many boxes does he sell?
   e. If fortune cookies sell for $10 a box and Lin offers his cookies for sale at $9.50 a box, how many boxes does he sell?
   f. What is the elasticity of demand for Lin's fortune cookies and how does it differ from the elasticity of the market demand for fortune cookies?
2. Quick Copy is one of the many copy shops near the campus. The figure shows Quick Copy's cost curves. The market price of copying one page is 10 cents.

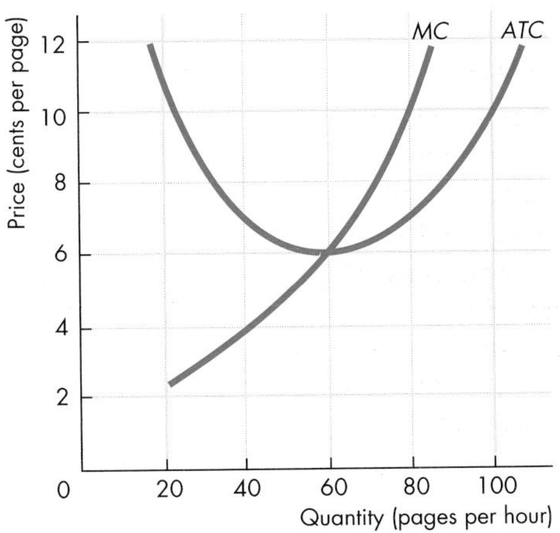

   a. What is Quick Copy's marginal revenue?
   b. What is Quick Copy's profit-maximizing output?
   c. What is Quick Copy's economic profit?

*Solutions to odd-numbered problems are provided.

3. Pat's Pizza Kitchen is a price taker. Its costs are

Output (pizzas per hour)	Total cost (dollars per hour)
0	10
1	21
2	30
3	41
4	54
5	69

   a. What is Pat's profit-maximizing output and how much economic profit does Pat make if the market price is (i) $14, (ii) $12, and (iii) $10?
   b. What is Pat's shutdown point?
   c. Derive Pat's supply curve.
   d. At what price will firms with costs the same as Pat's exit the pizza industry in the long run?
   e. At what price will firms with costs the same as Pat's enter the pizza industry in the long run?
4. The market demand schedule for paper is

Price (dollars per box)	Quantity demanded (thousands of boxes per week)
3.65	500
5.20	450
6.80	400
8.40	350
10.00	300
11.60	250
13.20	200

   The market is perfectly competitive, and each firm has the following costs when it uses its least-cost plant size:

Output (boxes per week)	Marginal cost (dollars per additional box)	Average variable cost (dollars per box)	Average total cost (dollars per box)
200	6.40	7.80	12.80
250	7.00	7.00	11.00
300	7.65	7.10	10.43
350	8.40	7.20	10.06
400	10.00	7.50	10.00
450	12.40	8.00	10.22
500	20.70	9.00	11.00

   There are 1,000 firms in the industry.
   a. What is the market price?

b. What is the industry's output?
c. What is the output produced by each firm?
d. What is the economic profit earned or economic loss incurred by each firm?
e. Do firms enter or exit the industry in the long run?
f. What is the number of firms in the long run?
g. What is the market price in the long run?
h. What is the equilibrium quantity in the long run?

5. As the quality of computer monitors improves, more and more people stop printing documents and instead read them on the screen. In the market for paper, demand permanently decreases and the demand schedule becomes

Price (dollars per box)	Quantity demanded (thousands of boxes per week)
2.95	500
4.13	450
5.30	400
6.48	350
7.65	300
8.83	250
10.00	200
11.18	150

The costs remain the same as in the table on the previous page.

a. What now are the market price, industry output, and economic profit or loss of each firm?
b. What now is the long-run equilibrium price, industry output, and economic profit or loss of each firm?
c. Does this industry experience external economics, external diseconomies, or constant cost? Illustrate by drawing the long-run supply curve.

6. A perfectly competitive industry is in long-run equilibrium. Answer the following questions and give explanations.

a. Can consumer surplus be increased?
b. Can producer surplus be increased?
c. Can a consumer become better off by making a substitution away from this industry?
d. Can the good be produced for a lower average total cost?

CRITICAL THINKING

1. Study *Reading Between the Lines* about the market for pollination services on pp. 258–259, and then answer the following questions.
   a. What are the features of the market for pollination services that make it an example of perfect competition?
   b. If a beekeeper's minimum average variable cost exceeds the price of renting a hive, what will the beekeeper do and why?
   c. What are the forces that move the market for pollination services to long-run equilibrium and what are the profits in the market in the long run?
   d. If it was discovered that American-made honey has previously unknown nutritional properties that prolong life, how would the markets for honey and pollination services be affected in the short run and in the long run?
2. Why have the prices of pocket calculators and DVD players fallen? What do you think has happened to the costs and economic profits of the firms that make these products?
3. What has been the effect of an increase in world population on the wheat market and the individual wheat farmer?
4. How has the diaper service industry been affected by the decrease in the U.S. birth rate and the development of disposable diapers?

WEB ACTIVITIES

myeconlab Links to Web sites

1. Study the report about quotas in imports of textiles from China.
   a. Why is the United States limiting textile imports?
   b. Draw a demand and supply graph and a graph to illustrate the cost and revenue curves of an individual U.S. textile producer. Use these graphs to illustrate the effects on price, quantity, economic profit, and consumer surplus of the quota.
   c. Do you think the quota is good for Americans? Explain why or why not.

CHAPTER 12

Monopoly

Dominating the Internet

eBay and Google are dominant players in the markets they serve. Because most buyers use eBay, most sellers do too. And because most sellers use eBay, so do most buyers. This phenomenon, called a network externality, makes it hard for any other firm to break into the Internet auction business. Because Google is such a good search engine, most people use it to find what they're seeking on the Internet. And because most people use it, most Web site operators who want hits advertise with Google.

eBay and Google are obviously not like firms in perfect competition. They don't face a market-determined price. They can choose their own prices. How do firms like these choose the quantity to produce and the price at which to sell it? How does their behavior compare with that of firms in perfectly competitive industries? Do they charge prices that are too high and that damage the interests of consumers? What benefits do they bring?

As a student, you get lots of discounts: when you get your hair cut, go to a museum, or go to a movie. When you take a trip by air, you almost never pay the full fare. Instead, you buy a discounted ticket. Are the people who operate barbershops, museums, movie theaters, and airlines simply generous folks who don't maximize profit? Aren't they throwing profit away by offering discounts?

In this chapter, we study markets in which the firm can influence the price. We also compare the performance of the firm in such a market with that in a competitive market and examine whether monopoly is as efficient as competition. In *Reading Between the Lines* at the end of the chapter, we'll take a look at what's been happening to airfares as low-cost airlines have put a squeeze on the traditional airlines.

After studying this chapter, you will be able to

- Explain how monopoly arises and distinguish between single-price monopoly and price-discriminating monopoly
- Explain how a single-price monopoly determines its output and price
- Compare the performance and efficiency of single-price monopoly and competition
- Explain how price discrimination increases profit
- Explain how monopoly regulation influences output, price, economic profit, and efficiency

Market Power

Market power and competition are the two forces that operate in most markets. **Market power** is the ability to influence the market, and in particular the market price, by influencing the total quantity offered for sale.

The firms in perfect competition that you studied in Chapter 11 have no market power. They face the force of raw competition and are price takers. The firms that we study in this chapter operate at the opposite extreme. They face no competition and exercise raw market power. We call this extreme monopoly. A **monopoly** is a firm that produces a good or service for which no close substitute exists and that is protected by a barrier that prevents other firms from selling that good or service. In monopoly, the firm is the industry.

Examples of monopoly include the firms that operate the pipelines and cables that bring gas, water, and electricity to your home. Microsoft Corporation, the software firm that created the Windows operating system, is close to being a monopoly.

How Monopoly Arises

Monopoly has two key features:

- No close substitutes
- Barriers to entry

No Close Substitutes If a good has a close substitute, even though only one firm produces it, that firm effectively faces competition from the producers of substitutes. Water supplied by a local public utility is an example of a good that does not have close substitutes. While it does have a close substitute for drinking—bottled spring water—it has no effective substitutes for showering or washing a car.

Monopolies are constantly under attack from new products and ideas that substitute for products produced by monopolies. For example, FedEx, UPS, the fax machine, and e-mail have weakened the monopoly of the U.S. Postal Service. Similarly, the satellite dish has weakened the monopoly of cable television companies.

But new products also are constantly creating monopolies. An example is Microsoft's monopoly in the DOS operating system during the 1980s and in the Windows operating system today.

Barriers to Entry Legal or natural constraints that protect a firm from potential competitors are called **barriers to entry**. A firm can sometimes create its own barrier to entry by acquiring a significant portion of a key resource. For example, De Beers controls more than 80 percent of the world's supply of natural diamonds. But most monopolies arise from two other types of barrier: legal barriers and natural barriers.

Legal Barriers to Entry Legal barriers to entry create legal monopoly. A **legal monopoly** is a market in which competition and entry are restricted by the granting of a public franchise, government license, patent, or copyright.

A *public franchise* is an exclusive right granted to a firm to supply a good or service. Examples are the U.S. Postal Service, which has the exclusive right to carry first-class mail. A *government license* controls entry into particular occupations, professions, and industries. Examples of this type of barrier to entry occur in medicine, law, dentistry, schoolteaching, architecture, and many other professional services. Licensing does not always create a monopoly, but it does restrict competition.

A *patent* is an exclusive right granted to the inventor of a product or service. A *copyright* is an exclusive right granted to the author or composer of a literary, musical, dramatic, or artistic work. Patents and copyrights are valid for a limited time period that varies from country to country. In the United States, a patent is valid for 20 years. Patents encourage the *invention* of new products and production methods. They also stimulate *innovation*—the use of new inventions—by encouraging inventors to publicize their discoveries and offer them for use under license. Patents have stimulated innovations in areas as diverse as soybean seeds, pharmaceuticals, memory chips, and video games.

Natural Barriers to Entry Natural barriers to entry create a **natural monopoly**: an industry in which economies of scale enable one firm to supply the entire market at the lowest possible cost.

Figure 12.1 shows a natural monopoly in the distribution of electric power. Here, the market demand curve for electric power is *D*, and the long-run average cost curve is *LRAC*. Because long-run average cost decreases as output increases, economies of scale prevail over the entire length of the *LRAC* curve. One firm can produce 4 million kilowatt-hours at 5 cents a kilowatt-hour. At this price, the quantity demanded is 4 million kilowatt-hours. So if the price was 5 cents, one firm could supply the entire market. If two firms shared the market equally, it would cost each of them 10 cents a kilowatt-hour to produce a total of 4 million kilowatt-hours. If four firms shared the market equally, it would cost each of them 15 cents a kilowatt-hour to produce a total of 4 million kilowatt-hours. So in conditions like those shown in Fig. 12.1, one firm can supply the entire market at a lower cost than two or more firms can. The distribution of electric power is an example of natural monopoly.

Most monopolies are regulated in some way by government agencies. We will study such regulation at the end of this chapter. But for two reasons, we'll begin by studying unregulated monopoly. First, we can better understand why governments regulate monopolies and the effects of regulation if we also know how an unregulated monopoly behaves. Second, even in industries with more than one producer, firms often have a degree of monopoly power,

FIGURE 12.1 Natural Monopoly

myeconlab

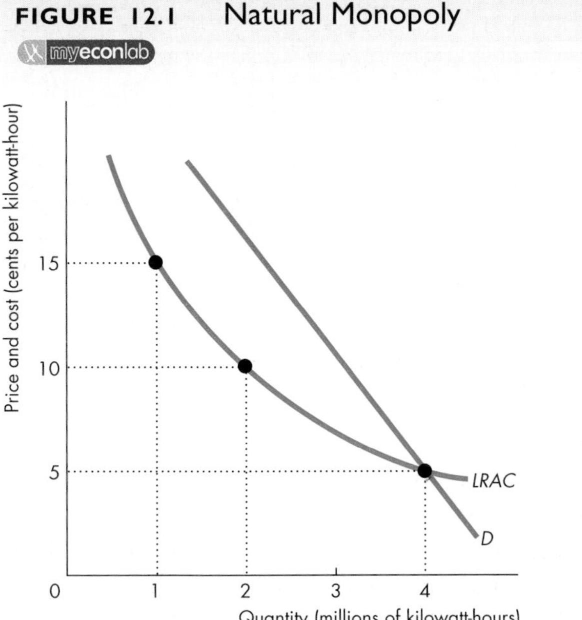

The market demand curve for electric power is *D*, and the long-run average cost curve is *LRAC*. Economies of scale exist over the entire *LRAC* curve. One firm can distribute 4 million kilowatt-hours at a cost of 5 cents a kilowatt-hour. This same total output costs 10 cents a kilowatt-hour with two firms and 15 cents a kilowatt-hour with four firms. So one firm can meet the market demand at a lower cost than two or more firms can, and the market is a natural monopoly.

and the theory of monopoly sheds light on the behavior of such firms and industries.

A major difference between monopoly and competition is that a monopoly sets its own price. But in doing so, it faces a market constraint. Let's see how the market limits a monopoly's pricing choices.

Monopoly Price-Setting Strategies

All monopolies face a tradeoff between price and the quantity sold. To sell a larger quantity, the monopoly must charge a lower price. But there are two broad monopoly situations that create different tradeoffs. They are

- Single price
- Price discrimination

Single Price De Beers sells diamonds (of a given size and quality) for the same price to all its customers. If it tried to sell at a low price to some customers and at a higher price to others, only the low-price customers would buy from De Beers. Others would buy from De Beers' low-price customers. De Beers is a *single-price* monopoly. A **single-price monopoly** is a firm that must sell each unit of its output for the same price to all its customers.

Price Discrimination Airlines offer a dizzying array of different prices for the same trip. Pizza producers charge one price for a single pizza and almost give away a second pizza. These are examples of *price discrimination.* **Price discrimination** is the practice of selling different units of a good or service for different prices.

When a firm price discriminates, it looks as though it is doing its customers a favor. In fact, it is charging the highest possible price for each unit sold and making the largest possible profit.

REVIEW QUIZ

1. How does monopoly arise?
2. How does a natural monopoly differ from a legal monopoly?
3. Distinguish between a price-discriminating monopoly and a single-price monopoly.

myeconlab **Study Plan 12.1**

A Single-Price Monopoly's Output and Price Decision

To understand how a single-price monopoly makes its output and price decision, we must first study the link between price and marginal revenue.

Price and Marginal Revenue

Because in a monopoly there is only one firm, the demand curve facing the firm is the market demand curve. Let's look at Bobbie's Barbershop, the sole supplier of haircuts in Cairo, Nebraska. The table in Fig. 12.2 shows the market demand schedule. At a price of \$20, she sells no haircuts. The lower the price, the more haircuts per hour Bobbie can sell. For example, at \$12, consumers demand 4 haircuts per hour (row *E*).

Total revenue (*TR*) is the price (*P*) multiplied by the quantity sold (*Q*). For example, in row *D*, Bobbie sells 3 haircuts at \$14 each, so total revenue is \$42. *Marginal revenue* (*MR*) is the change in total revenue (ΔTR) resulting from a one-unit increase in the quantity sold. For example, if the price falls from \$16 (row *C*) to \$14 (row *D*), the quantity sold increases from 2 to 3 haircuts. Total revenue rises from \$32 to \$42, so the change in total revenue is \$10. Because the quantity sold increases by 1 haircut, marginal revenue equals the change in total revenue and is \$10. Marginal revenue is placed between the two rows to emphasize that marginal revenue relates to the *change* in the quantity sold.

Figure 12.2 shows the market demand curve and marginal revenue curve (*MR*) and also illustrates the calculation we've just made. Notice that at each level of output, marginal revenue is less than price—the marginal revenue curve lies below the demand curve. Why is marginal revenue *less* than price? It is because when the price is lowered to sell one more unit, two opposing forces affect total revenue. The lower price results in a revenue loss, and the increased quantity sold results in a revenue gain. For example, at a price of \$16, Bobbie sells 2 haircuts (point *C*). If she lowers the price to \$14, she sells 3 haircuts and has a revenue gain of \$14 on the third haircut. But she now receives only \$14 on the first two—\$2 less than before. As a result, she loses \$4 of revenue on the first 2 haircuts. To calculate marginal revenue, she must deduct this amount from the revenue gain of \$14. So her marginal revenue is \$10, which is less than the price.

FIGURE 12.2 Demand and Marginal Revenue

myeconlab

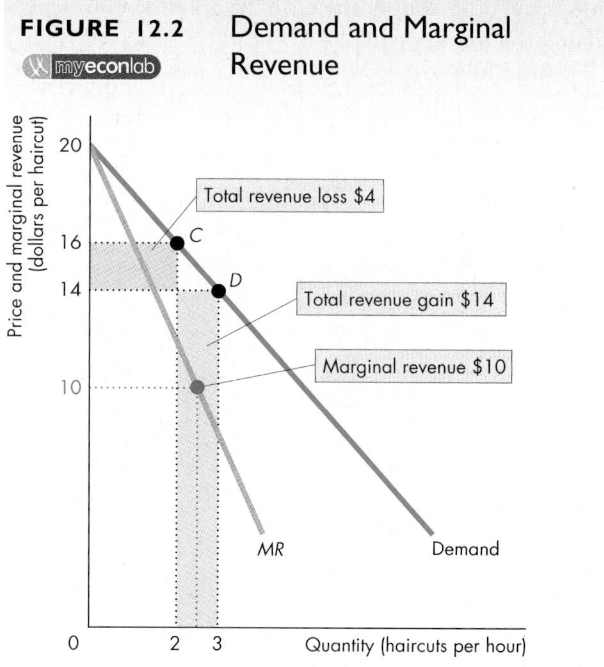

	Price (*P*) (dollars per haircut)	Quantity demanded (*Q*) (haircuts per hour)	Total revenue ($TR = P \times Q$) (dollars)	Marginal revenue ($MR = \Delta TR/\Delta Q$) (dollars per haircut)
A	20	0	0	
				18
B	18	1	18	
				14
C	**16**	**2**	**32**	
				10
D	**14**	**3**	**42**	
				6
E	12	4	48	
				2
F	10	5	50	

The table shows the demand schedule. Total revenue (*TR*) is price multiplied by quantity sold. For example, in row *C*, the price is \$16 a haircut, Bobbie sells 2 haircuts, and total revenue is \$32. Marginal revenue (*MR*) is the change in total revenue that results from a one-unit increase in the quantity sold. For example, when the price falls from \$16 to \$14 a haircut, the quantity sold increases by 1 haircut and total revenue increases by \$10. Marginal revenue is \$10. The demand curve and the marginal revenue curve, *MR*, are based on the numbers in the table and illustrate the calculation of marginal revenue when the price falls from \$16 to \$14 a haircut.

Marginal Revenue and Elasticity

A single-price monopoly's marginal revenue is related to the *elasticity of demand* for its good. The demand for a good can be *elastic* (the elasticity of demand is greater than 1), *inelastic* (the elasticity of demand is less than 1), or *unit elastic* (the elasticity of demand is equal to 1). Demand is *elastic* if a 1 percent fall in price brings a greater than 1 percent increase in the quantity demanded. Demand is *inelastic* if a 1 percent fall in price brings a less than 1 percent increase in the quantity demanded. And demand is *unit elastic* if a 1 percent fall in price brings a 1 percent increase in the quantity demanded. (See Chapter 4, pp. 86–87.)

If demand is elastic, a fall in price brings an increase in total revenue—the revenue gain from the increase in quantity sold outweighs the revenue loss from the lower price—and marginal revenue is *positive*. If demand is inelastic, a fall in price brings a decrease in total revenue—the revenue gain from the increase in quantity sold is outweighed by the revenue loss from the lower price—and marginal revenue is *negative*. If demand is unit elastic, total revenue does not change—the revenue gain from the increase in quantity sold offsets the revenue loss from the lower price—and marginal revenue is *zero*. (The relationship between total revenue and elasticity is explained in Chapter 4, p. 86.)

Figure 12.3 illustrates the relationship between marginal revenue, total revenue, and elasticity. As the price of a haircut gradually falls from \$20 to \$10, the quantity of haircuts demanded increases from 0 to 5 an hour. Over this output range, marginal revenue is positive (part a), total revenue increases (part b), and the demand for haircuts is elastic. As the price falls from \$10 to \$0 a haircut, the quantity of haircuts demanded increases from 5 to 10 an hour. Over this output range, marginal revenue is negative (part a), total revenue decreases (part b), and the demand for haircuts is inelastic. When the price is \$10 a haircut, marginal revenue is zero (part a), total revenue is a maximum (part b), and the demand for haircuts is unit elastic.

In Monopoly, Demand Is Always Elastic The relationship between marginal revenue and elasticity of demand that you've just discovered implies that a profit-maximizing monopoly never produces an output in the inelastic range of the market demand curve. If it did so, it could charge a higher price, produce a smaller quantity, and increase its profit. Let's now look at a monopoly's price and output decision.

FIGURE 12.3 Marginal Revenue and Elasticity

myeconlab

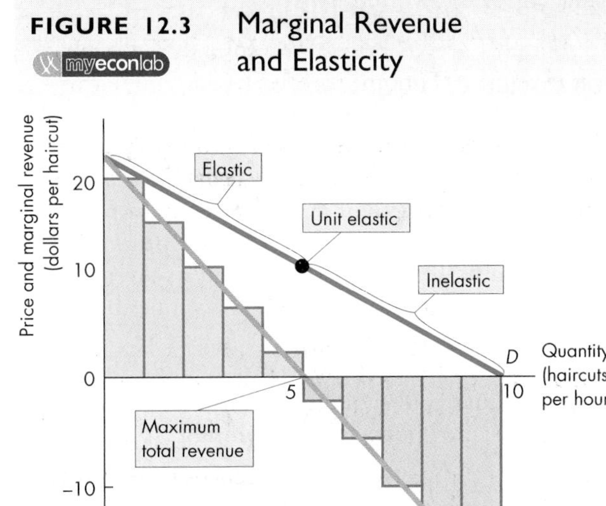

(a) Demand and marginal revenue curves

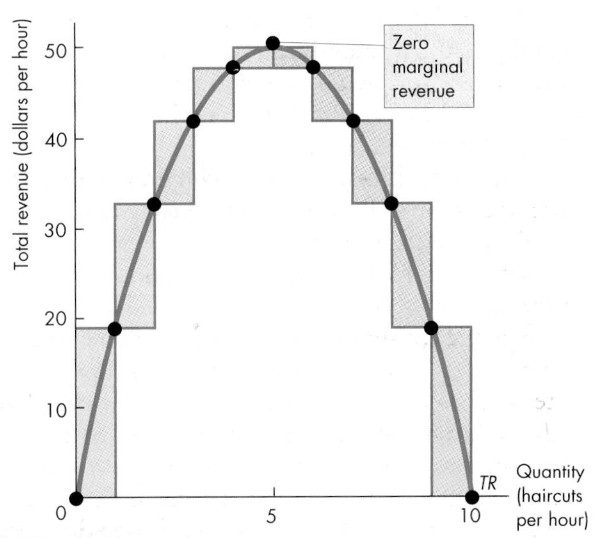

(b) Total revenue curve

In part (a), the demand curve is *D* and the marginal revenue curve is *MR*. In part (b), the total revenue curve is *TR*. Over the range from 0 to 5 haircuts an hour, a price cut increases total revenue, so marginal revenue is positive—as shown by the blue bars. Demand is elastic. Over the range from 5 to 10 haircuts an hour, a price cut decreases total revenue, so marginal revenue is negative—as shown by the red bars. Demand is inelastic. At 5 haircuts an hour, total revenue is maximized and marginal revenue is zero. Demand is unit elastic.

Price and Output Decision

A monopoly sets its price and output at the levels that maximize economic profit. To determine this price and output level, we need to study the behavior of both cost and revenue as output varies. A monopoly faces the same types of technology and cost constraints as a competitive firm. So its costs (total cost, average cost, and marginal cost) behave just like those of a firm in perfect competition. And its revenues (total revenue, price, and marginal revenue) behave in the way we've just described.

Table 12.1 provides information about Bobbie's costs, revenues, and economic profit and Figure 12.4 shows the same information graphically.

Maximizing Economic Profit You can see in Table 12.1 and Fig. 12.4(a) that total cost (*TC*) and total revenue (*TR*) both rise as output increases, but *TC* rises at an increasing rate and *TR* rises at a decreasing rate. Economic profit, which equals *TR* minus *TC*, increases at small output levels, reaches a maximum, and then decreases. The maximum profit ($12) occurs when Bobbie sells 3 haircuts for $14 each. If she sells 2 haircuts for $16 each or 4 haircuts for $12 each, her economic profit will be only $8.

Marginal Revenue Equals Marginal Cost You can see in Table 12.1 and Fig. 12.4(b) Bobbie's marginal revenue (*MR*) and marginal cost (*MC*).

When Bobbie increases output from 2 to 3 haircuts, *MR* is $10 and *MC* is $6. *MR* exceeds *MC* by $4 and Bobbie's profit increases by that amount. If Bobbie increases output yet further, from 3 to 4 haircuts, *MR* is $6 and *MC* is $10. In this case, *MC* exceeds *MR* by $4, so profit decreases by that amount. When *MR* exceeds *MC*, profit increases if output increases. When *MC* exceeds *MR*, profit increases if output *decreases*. When *MC* equals *MR*, profit is maximized.

Figure 12.4(b) shows the maximum profit as price (on the demand curve *D*) minus average total cost (on the *ATC* curve) multiplied by the quantity produced—the blue rectangle.

Maximum Price the Market Will Bear Unlike a firm in perfect competition, a monopoly influences the price of what it sells. But a monopoly doesn't set the price at the maximum *possible* price. At the maximum possible price, the firm would be able to sell only one unit of output, which in general is less than the profit-maximizing quantity. Rather, a monopoly produces the profit-maximizing quantity and sells that quantity for the highest price it can get.

TABLE 12.1 A Monopoly's Output and Price Decision

Price (*P*) (dollars per haircut)	Quantity demanded (*Q*) (haircuts per hour)	Total revenue ($TR = P \times Q$) (dollars)	Marginal revenue ($MR = \Delta TR/\Delta Q$) (dollars per haircut)	Total cost (*TC*) (dollars)	Marginal cost ($MC = \Delta TC/\Delta Q$) (dollars per haircut)	Profit ($TR - TC$) (dollars)
20	0	0		20		−20
			18		1	
18	1	18		21		−3
			14		3	
16	2	32		24		+8
			10		6	
14	3	42		30		+12
			6		10	
12	4	48		40		+8
			2		15	
10	5	50		55		−5

This table gives the information needed to find the profit-maximizing output and price. Total revenue (*TR*) equals price multiplied by the quantity sold. Profit equals total revenue minus total cost (*TC*). Profit is maximized when 3 haircuts are sold at a price of $14 each. Total revenue is $42, total cost is $30, and economic profit is $12 ($42 − $30).

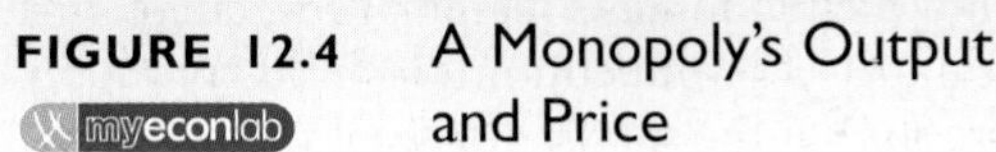

FIGURE 12.4 A Monopoly's Output and Price

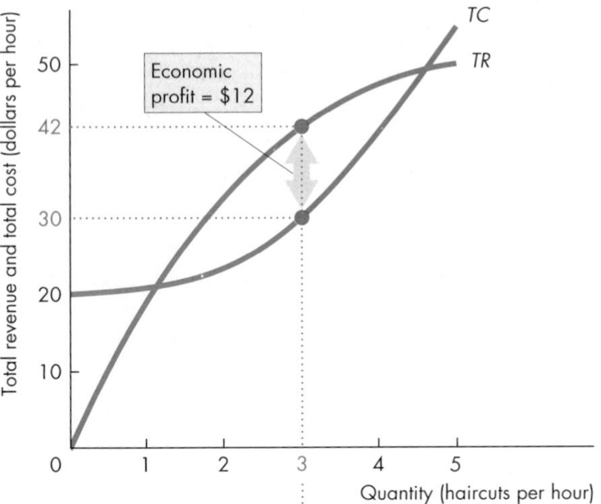

(a) Total revenue and total cost curves

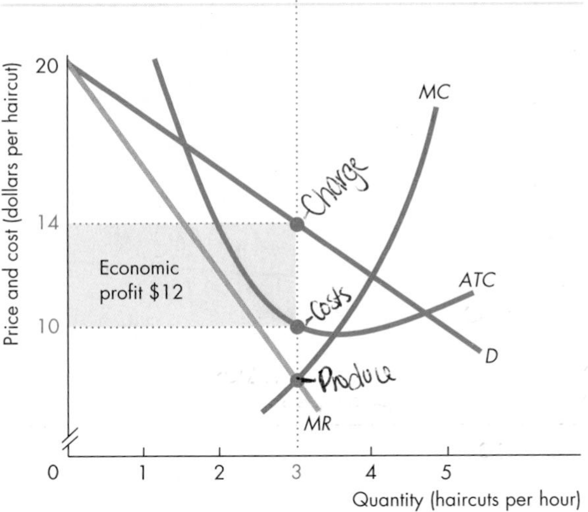

(b) Demand and marginal revenue and cost curves

In part (a), economic profit is the vertical distance equal to total revenue (*TR*) minus total cost (*TC*) and it is maximized at 3 haircuts an hour. In part (b), economic profit is maximized when marginal cost (*MC*) equals marginal revenue (*MR*). The profit-maximizing output is 3 haircuts an hour. The price is determined by the demand curve (*D*) and is $14 a haircut. The average total cost of a haircut is $10, so economic profit, the blue rectangle, is $12—the profit per haircut ($4) multiplied by 3 haircuts.

All firms maximize profit by producing the output at which marginal revenue equals marginal cost. For a competitive firm, price equals marginal revenue, so price also equals marginal cost. For a monopoly, price exceeds marginal revenue, so price also exceeds marginal cost.

A monopoly charges a price that exceeds marginal cost, but does it always make an economic profit? In Fig. 12.4(b), Bobbie produces 3 haircuts an hour. Her average total cost is $10 (on the *ATC* curve) and her price is $14 (on the *D* curve), so her profit per haircut is $4 ($14 minus $10). Bobbie's economic profit is shown by the blue rectangle, which equals the profit per haircut ($4) multiplied by the number of haircuts (3), for a total of $12.

If firms in a perfectly competitive industry make a positive economic profit, new firms enter. That does *not* happen in monopoly. Barriers to entry prevent new firms from entering an industry which is a monopoly. So a monopoly can make a positive economic profit and might continue to do so indefinitely. Sometimes that profit is large, as in the international diamond business.

Bobbie makes a positive economic profit. But suppose that the owner of the shop that Bobbie rents increases Bobbie's rent. If Bobbie pays an additional $12 an hour for rent, her fixed cost increases by $12 an hour. Her marginal cost and marginal revenue don't change, so her profit-maximizing output remains at 3 haircuts an hour. Her profit decreases by $12 an hour to zero. If Bobbie pays more than an additional $12 an hour for her shop rent, she incurs an economic loss. If this situation were permanent, Bobbie would go out of business.

REVIEW QUIZ

1. What is the relationship between marginal cost and marginal revenue when a single-price monopoly maximizes profit?
2. How does a single-price monopoly determine the price it will charge its customers?
3. What is the relationship between price, marginal revenue, and marginal cost when a single-price monopoly is maximizing profit?
4. Why can a monopoly make a positive economic profit even in the long run?

myeconlab **Study Plan 12.2**

Single-Price Monopoly and Competition Compared

Imagine an industry that is made up of many small firms operating in perfect competition. Then imagine that a single firm buys out all these small firms and creates a monopoly.

What will happen in this industry? Will the price rise or fall? Will the quantity produced increase or decrease? Will economic profit increase or decrease? Will either the original competitive situation or the new monopoly situation be efficient?

These are the questions we're now going to answer. First, we look at the effects of monopoly on the price and quantity produced. Then we turn to the questions about efficiency.

Comparing Price and Output

Figure 12.5 shows the market we'll study. The market demand curve is D. The demand curve is the same regardless of how the industry is organized. But the supply side and the equilibrium are different in monopoly and competition. First, let's look at the case of perfect competition.

Perfect Competition Initially, with many small perfectly competitive firms in the market, the market supply curve is S. This supply curve is obtained by summing the supply curves of all the individual firms in the market.

In perfect competition, equilibrium occurs where the supply curve and the demand curve intersect. The price is P_C, and the quantity produced by the industry is Q_C. Each firm takes the price P_C and maximizes its profit by producing the output at which its own marginal cost equals the price. Because each firm is a small part of the total industry, there is no incentive for any firm to try to manipulate the price by varying its output.

Monopoly Now suppose that this industry is taken over by a single firm. Consumers do not change, so the market demand curve remains the same as in the case of perfect competition. But now the monopoly recognizes this demand curve as a constraint on the price at which it can sell its output. The monopoly's marginal revenue curve is MR.

The monopoly maximizes profit by producing the quantity at which marginal revenue equals marginal cost. To find the monopoly's marginal cost curve, first recall that in perfect competition, the industry supply curve is the sum of the supply curves of the firms in the industry. Also recall that each firm's supply curve is its marginal cost curve (see Chapter 11, pp. 246–247). So when the industry is taken over by a single firm, the competitive industry's supply curve becomes the monopoly's marginal cost curve. To remind you of this fact, the supply curve is also labeled MC.

The output at which marginal revenue equals marginal cost is Q_M. This output is smaller than the competitive output Q_C. And the monopoly charges the price P_M, which is higher than P_C. We have established that

Compared to a perfectly competitive industry, a single-price monopoly produces a smaller output and charges a higher price.

We've seen how the output and price of a monopoly compare with those in a competitive industry. Let's now compare the efficiency of the two types of market.

FIGURE 12.5 Monopoly's Smaller Output and Higher Price

myeconlab

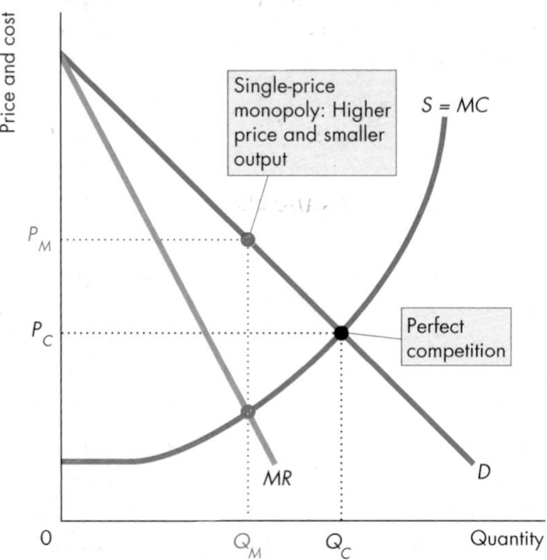

A competitive industry produces the quantity Q_C at price P_C. A single-price monopoly produces the quantity Q_M at which marginal revenue equals marginal cost and sells that quantity for the price P_M. Compared to perfect competition, a single-price monopoly produces a smaller output and charges a higher price.

Efficiency Comparison

You saw in Chapter 11 (pp. 256–257) that perfect competition (with no external costs and benefits) is efficient. Figure 12.6(a) illustrates the efficiency of perfect competition and serves as a benchmark against which to measure the inefficiency of monopoly.

Along the demand curve and marginal social benefit curve ($D = MSB$), consumers are efficient. Along the supply curve and marginal social cost curve ($S = MSC$), producers are efficient. In competitive equilibrium, the price is P_C, the quantity is Q_C, and marginal social benefit equals marginal social cost.

Consumer surplus is the green triangle under the demand curve and above the equilibrium price (see Chapter 5, p. 107). *Producer surplus* is the blue area above the supply curve and below the equilibrium price (see Chapter 5, p. 109). The sum of the consumer surplus and producer surplus is maximized.

Also, in long-run competitive equilibrium, entry and exit ensure that each firm produces its output at the minimum possible long-run average cost.

To summarize: At the competitive equilibrium, marginal social benefit equals marginal social cost; the sum of consumer surplus and producer surplus is maximized; firms produce at the lowest possible long-run average cost; and resource use is efficient.

Figure 12.6(b) illustrates the inefficiency of monopoly and the sources of that inefficiency. A monopoly produces Q_M and sells its output for P_M. The smaller output and higher price drive a wedge between marginal social benefit and marginal social cost and create a *deadweight loss*. The gray triangle shows the deadweight loss and its magnitude is a measure of the inefficiency of monopoly.

Consumer surplus shrinks for two reasons. First, consumers lose by having to pay more for the good. This loss to consumers is a gain for the producer and increases the producer surplus. Second, consumers lose by getting less of the good, and this loss is part of the deadweight loss.

Although the monopoly gains from a higher price, it loses some of the original producer surplus because of the smaller monopoly output. That loss is another part of the deadweight loss.

Because a monopoly restricts output below the level in perfect competition and faces no competitive threat, it does not produce at the minimum possible long-run average cost. As a result, monopoly damages the consumer interest in three ways: It produces less, it increases the cost of production, and it increases the price to above the increased cost of production.

FIGURE 12.6 Inefficiency of Monopoly

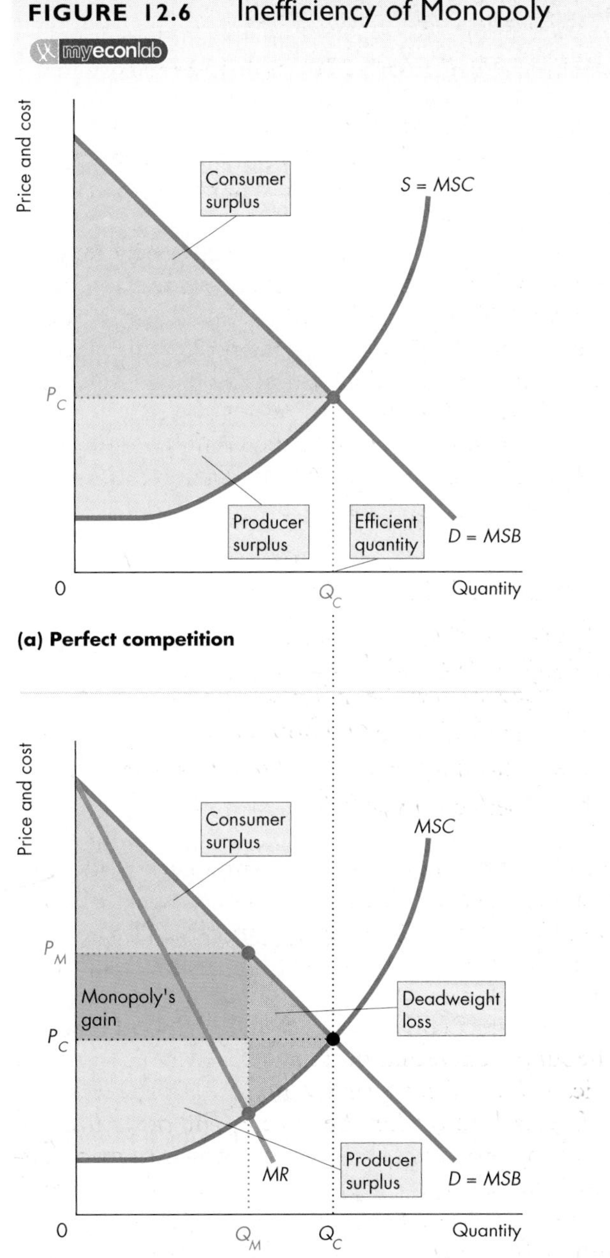

In perfect competition (part a), output is Q_C and the price is P_C. Marginal social benefit (MSB) equals marginal social cost (MSC); consumer surplus (the green triangle) plus producer surplus (the blue area) is maximized; and in the long-run, firms produce at the lowest possible average cost. Monopoly (part b) restricts output to Q_M and raises the price to P_M. Consumer surplus shrinks, the monopoly gains, and a deadweight loss (the gray triangle) arises.

Redistribution of Surpluses

You've seen that monopoly is inefficient because marginal social benefit exceeds marginal social cost and there is deadweight loss—a social loss. But monopoly also brings a *redistribution* of surpluses.

Some of the lost consumer surplus goes to the monopoly. In Fig. 12.6, the monopoly takes the difference between the higher price, P_M, and the competitive price, P_C, on the quantity sold, Q_M. So the monopoly takes the part of the consumer surplus shown by the darker blue rectangle. This portion of the loss of consumer surplus is not a loss to society. It is redistribution from consumers to the monopoly producer.

Rent Seeking

You've seen that monopoly creates a deadweight loss and is inefficient. But the social cost of monopoly can exceed the deadweight loss because of an activity called rent seeking. Any surplus—consumer surplus, producer surplus, or economic profit—is called **economic rent**. And **rent seeking** is the pursuit of wealth by capturing economic rent.

You've seen that a monopoly makes its economic profit by diverting part of consumer surplus to itself—by converting consumer surplus into economic profit. So the pursuit of economic profit by a monopoly is rent seeking. It is the attempt to capture consumer surplus.

Rent seekers pursue their goals in two main ways. They might

- Buy a monopoly
- Create a monopoly

Buy a Monopoly To rent seek by buying a monopoly, a person searches for a monopoly that is for sale at a lower price than the monopoly's economic profit. Trading of taxicab licenses is an example of this type of rent seeking. In some cities, taxicabs are regulated. The city restricts both the fares and the number of taxis that can operate so that operating a taxi results in economic profit. A person who wants to operate a taxi must buy a license from someone who already has one. People rationally devote time and effort to seeking out profitable monopoly businesses to buy. In the process, they use up scarce resources that could otherwise have been used to produce goods and services. The value of this lost production is part of the social cost of monopoly. The amount paid for a monopoly is not a social cost because the payment is just a transfer of an existing producer surplus from the buyer to the seller.

Create a Monopoly Rent seeking by creating monopoly is mainly a political activity. It takes the form of lobbying and trying to influence the political process. Such influence might be sought by making campaign contributions in exchange for legislative support or by indirectly seeking to influence political outcomes through publicity in the media or more direct contacts with politicians and bureaucrats. An example of a monopoly created in this way is the government-imposed restrictions on the quantities of textiles that may be imported into the United States. Another is a regulation that limits the number of oranges that may be sold in the United States. These are regulations that restrict output and increase price.

This type of rent seeking is a costly activity that uses up scarce resources. Taken together, firms spend billions of dollars lobbying Congress, state legislators, and local officials in the pursuit of licenses and laws that create barriers to entry and establish a monopoly. Everyone has an incentive to rent seek, and because there are no barriers to entry into rent seeking, there is a great deal of competition in this activity. The winners of the competition become monopolists.

Rent-Seeking Equilibrium

Barriers to entry create monopoly. But there is no barrier to entry into rent seeking. Rent seeking is like perfect competition. If an economic profit is available, a new rent seeker will try to get some of it. And competition among rent seekers pushes up the price that must be paid for a monopoly to the point at which the rent seeker makes zero economic profit by operating the monopoly. For example, competition for the right to operate a taxi in New York City leads to a price of more than $100,000 for a taxi license, which is sufficiently high to eliminate the economic profit made by taxi operators.

Figure 12.7 shows a rent-seeking equilibrium. The cost of rent seeking is a fixed cost that must be added to a monopoly's other costs. Rent seeking and rent-seeking costs increase to the point at which no economic profit is made. The average total cost curve, which includes the fixed cost of rent seeking, shifts upward until it just touches the demand curve. Economic profit is zero. It has been lost in rent seeking. Consumer surplus is unaffected. But the deadweight

FIGURE 12.7 Rent-Seeking Equilibrium

myeconlab

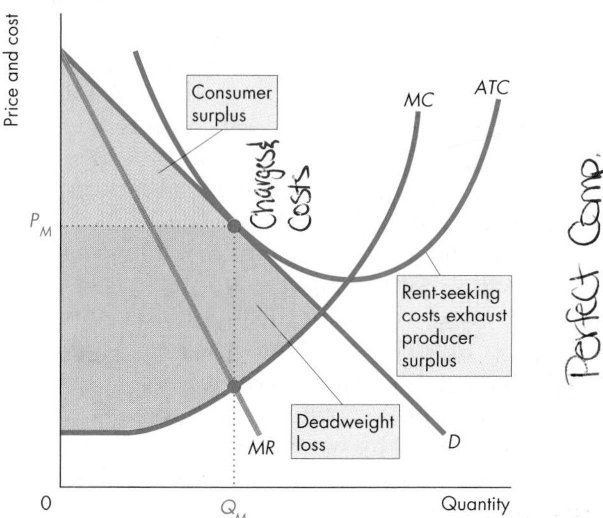

With competitive rent seeking, a monopoly uses all its economic profit to maintain its monopoly. The firm's rent-seeking costs are fixed costs. They add to total fixed cost and to average total cost. The *ATC* curve shifts upward until, at the profit-maximizing price, the firm breaks even.

loss of monopoly now includes the original deadweight loss triangle plus the lost producer surplus, shown by the enlarged gray area in the figure.

REVIEW QUIZ

1. Why does a single-price monopoly produce a smaller output and charge a higher price than what would prevail if the industry were perfectly competitive?
2. How does a monopoly transfer consumer surplus to itself?
3. Why is a single-price monopoly inefficient?
4. What is rent seeking and how does it influence the inefficiency of monopoly?

myeconlab **Study Plan 12.3**

So far, we've considered only a single-price monopoly. But many monopolies do not operate with a single price. Instead, they price discriminate. Let's now see how price-discriminating monopoly works.

Price Discrimination

Price discrimination—selling a good or service at a number of different prices—is widespread. You encounter it when you travel, go to the movies, get your hair cut, buy pizza, or visit an art museum. Most price discriminators are not monopolies, but monopolies price discriminate when they can do so.

To be able to price discriminate, a monopoly must

1. Identify and separate different buyer types.
2. Sell a product that cannot be resold.

Price discrimination is charging different prices for a single good or service because of differences in buyers' willingness to pay and not because of differences in production costs. So not all price *differences* are price *discrimination*. Some goods that are similar but not identical have different prices because they have different production costs. For example, the cost of producing electricity depends on time of day. If an electric power company charges a higher price during the peak consumption periods from 7:00 to 9:00 in the morning and from 4:00 to 7:00 in the evening than it does at other times of the day, the electric power company is not price discriminating.

At first sight, it appears that price discrimination contradicts the assumption of profit maximization. Why would a movie theater allow children to see movies at half price? Why would a hairdresser charge students and senior citizens less? Aren't these firms losing profit by being nice to their customers?

Deeper investigation shows that far from losing profit, firms that price discriminate make bigger profits than they would otherwise. So a monopoly has an incentive to find ways of discriminating and charging each buyer the highest possible price. Some people pay less with price discrimination, but others pay more.

Price Discrimination and Consumer Surplus

The key idea behind price discrimination is to convert consumer surplus into economic profit. Demand curves slope downward because the value that people place on any good decreases as the quantity of that good increases. When all the units of the good are sold for a single price, consumers benefit. The benefit is the value the consumers get from each unit of the good minus the price actually paid for it. This benefit is *consumer surplus.* Price discrimination is an attempt by a monopoly to capture as much of the consumer surplus as possible for itself.

To extract every dollar of consumer surplus from every buyer, the monopoly would have to offer each individual customer a separate price schedule based on that customer's own willingness to pay. Clearly, such price discrimination cannot be carried out in practice because a firm does not have enough information about each consumer's demand curve.

But firms try to extract as much consumer surplus as possible, and to do so, they discriminate in two broad ways:

- Among units of a good
- Among groups of buyers

Discriminating Among Units of a Good One method of price discrimination charges each buyer a different price on each unit of a good bought. A discount for bulk buying is an example of this type of discrimination. The larger the quantity bought, the larger is the discount—and the lower is the price. (Note that some discounts for bulk arise from lower costs of production for greater bulk. In these cases, such discounts are not price discrimination.)

Discriminating Among Groups of Buyers Price discrimination often takes the form of discriminating among different groups of consumers on the basis of age, employment status, or some other easily distinguished characteristic. This type of price discrimination works when each group has a different average willingness to pay for the good or service.

For example, a face-to-face sales meeting with a customer might bring a large and profitable order. For salespeople and other business travelers, the marginal benefit from a trip is large and the price that such a traveler will pay for a trip is high. In contrast, for a vacation traveler, any of several different trips and even no vacation trip are options. So for vacation travelers, the marginal benefit of a trip is small and the price that such a traveler will pay for a trip is low. Because business travelers are willing to pay more than vacation travelers are, it is possible for an airline to profit by price discriminating between these two groups. Similarly, because students have a lower willingness to pay for a haircut than do working people, it is possible for a hairdresser to profit by price discriminating between these two groups.

Let's see how an airline exploits the differences in demand by business and vacation travelers and increases its profit by price discriminating.

Profiting by Price Discriminating

Global Airlines has a monopoly on an exotic route. Figure 12.8 shows the market demand curve (D) for travel on this route. It also shows Global Airline's marginal revenue curve (MR), marginal cost curve (MC), and average total cost curve (ATC).

Initially, Global is a single-price monopoly and maximizes its profit by producing 8,000 trips a year (the quantity at which MR equals MC). The price is \$1,200 per trip. The average total cost of producing a trip is \$600, so economic profit is \$600 a trip. On 8,000 trips, Global's economic profit is \$4.8 million a year, shown by the blue rectangle. Global's customers enjoy a consumer surplus shown by the green triangle.

FIGURE 12.8 A Single Price of Air Travel

myeconlab

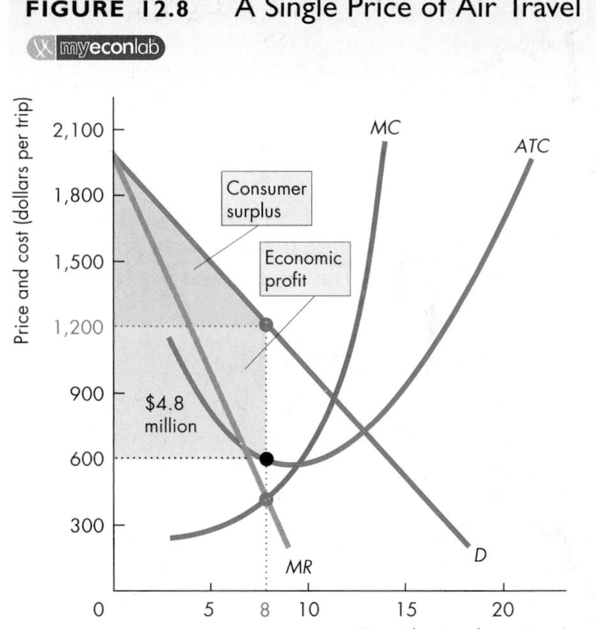

Global Airlines has a monopoly on an air route. The market demand curve is D. Global Airline's marginal revenue curve is MR, marginal cost curve is MC, and its average total cost curve is ATC. As a single-price monopoly, Global maximizes profit by selling 8,000 trips a year at \$1,200 a trip. Its profit is \$4.8 million a year—the blue rectangle. Global's customers enjoy a consumer surplus—the green triangle.

Global is struck by the fact that many of its customers are business travelers, and it suspects they are willing to pay more than $1,200 a trip. So Global does some market research, which reveals that some business travelers are willing to pay as much as $1,800 a trip. Also, these customers frequently change their travel plans at the last moment. Another group of business travelers is willing to pay $1,600. These customers know a week ahead when they will travel, and they never want to stay over a weekend. Yet another group would pay up to $1,400. These travelers know two weeks ahead when they will travel and also don't want to stay away over a weekend.

So Global announces a new fare schedule. No restrictions, $1,800; 7-day advance purchase, nonrefundable, $1,600; 14-day advance purchase, nonrefundable, $1,400; 14-day advance purchase, must stay over a weekend, $1,200.

Figure 12.9 shows the outcome with this new fare structure and also shows why Global is pleased

FIGURE 12.9 Price Discrimination

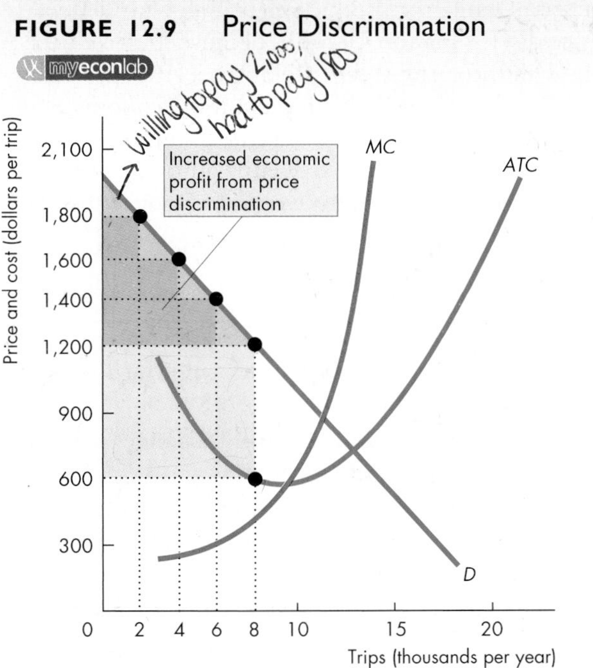

Global revises its fare structure: no restrictions at $1,800, 7-day advance purchase at $1,600, 14-day advance purchase at $1,400, and must stay over a weekend at $1,200. Global sells 2,000 trips at each of its four new fares. Its economic profit increases by $2.4 million a year to $7.2 million a year, which is shown by the original blue rectangle plus the dark blue steps. Global's customers' consumer surplus shrinks.

with its new fares. It sells 2,000 seats at each of its four prices. Global's economic profit increases by the dark blue steps. Its economic profit is now its original $4.8 million a year plus an additional $2.4 million from its new higher fares. Consumer surplus has shrunk to the sum of the smaller green area.

Perfect Price Discrimination

Perfect price discrimination occurs if a firm is able to sell each unit of output for the highest price anyone is willing to pay for it. In such a case, the entire consumer surplus is eliminated and captured by the producer. To practice perfect price discrimination, a firm must be creative and come up with a host of prices and special conditions each one of which appeals to a tiny segment of the market.

With perfect price discrimination, something special happens to marginal revenue. For the perfect price discriminator, the market demand curve becomes the marginal revenue curve. The reason is that when the price is cut to sell a larger quantity, the firm sells only the marginal unit at the lower price. All the other units continue to be sold for the highest price that each buyer is willing to pay. So for the perfect price discriminator, marginal revenue *equals* price and the demand curve becomes the marginal revenue curve.

With marginal revenue equal to price, Global can obtain even greater profit by increasing output up to the point at which price (and marginal revenue) is equal to marginal cost.

So Global now seeks additional travelers who will not pay as much as $1,200 a trip but who will pay more than marginal cost. Global gets more creative and comes up with vacation specials and other fares that have combinations of advance reservation, minimum stay, and other restrictions that make these fares unattractive to its existing customers but attractive to a different group of travelers. With all these fares and specials, Global increases sales, extracts the entire consumer surplus, and maximizes economic profit.

Figure 12.10 shows the outcome with perfect price discrimination. The dozens of fares paid by the original travelers who are willing to pay between $1,200 and $2,000 have extracted the entire consumer surplus from this group and converted it into economic profit for Global.

The new fares between $900 and $1,200 have attracted 3,000 additional travelers but taken their entire consumer surplus also. Global now makes an economic profit of more than $9 million.

FIGURE 12.10 Perfect Price Discrimination

myeconlab

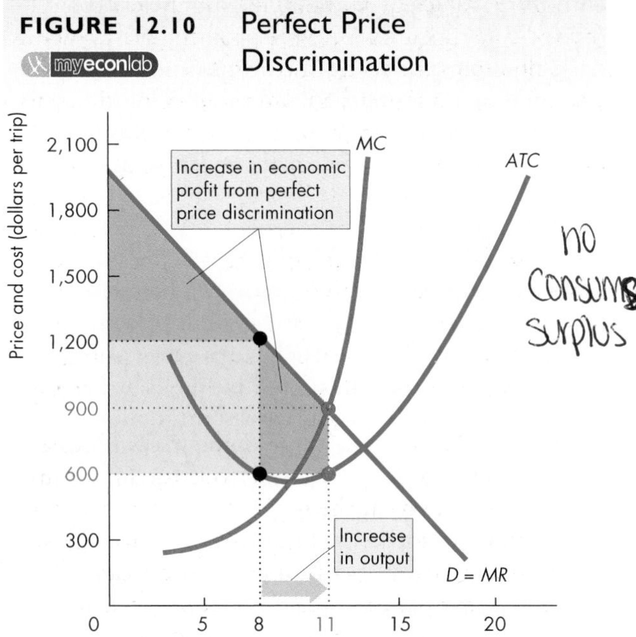

Dozens of fares discriminate among many different types of business traveler, and many new low fares with restrictions appeal to vacation travelers. With perfect price discrimination, the market demand curve becomes Global's marginal revenue curve. Economic profit is maximized when the lowest price equals marginal cost. Global sells 11,000 trips and makes an economic profit of $9.35 million a year.

Real-world airlines are just as creative as Global, as you can see in the cartoon!

Would it bother you to hear how little I paid for this flight?

From William Hamilton, "Voodoo Economics," © 1992 by The Chronicle Publishing Company, p.3. Reprinted with permission of Chronicle Books.

Efficiency and Rent Seeking with Price Discrimination

With perfect price discrimination, output increases to the point at which price equals marginal cost—where the marginal cost curve intersects the demand curve. This output is identical to that of perfect competition. Perfect price discrimination pushes consumer surplus to zero but increases the monopoly's producer surplus to equal the sum of consumer surplus and producer surplus in perfect competition. Deadweight loss with perfect price discrimination is zero. So perfect price discrimination achieves efficiency.

The more perfectly the monopoly can price discriminate, the closer its output is to the competitive output and the more efficient is the outcome.

But there are two differences between perfect competition and perfect price discrimination. First, the distribution of the total surplus is different. It is shared by consumers and producers in perfect competition, while the producer gets it all with perfect price discrimination. Second, because the producer grabs all the surplus, rent seeking becomes profitable.

People use resources in pursuit of economic rent, and the bigger the rents, the more resources get used in pursuing them. With free entry into rent seeking, the long-run equilibrium outcome is that rent seekers use up the entire producer surplus.

REVIEW QUIZ

1. What is price discrimination and how is it used to increase a monopoly's profit?
2. Explain how consumer surplus changes when a monopoly price discriminates.
3. Explain how consumer surplus, economic profit, and output change when a monopoly perfectly price discriminates.
4. What are some of the ways that real-world airlines use to price discriminate?

myeconlab **Study Plan 12.4**

You've seen that monopoly is profitable for the monopoly but costly for consumers. It results in inefficiency. Because of these features of monopoly, it is subject to policy debate and regulation. We'll now study the key monopoly policy issues.

Monopoly Policy Issues

Monopoly looks bad when we compare it with competition. Monopoly is inefficient, and it captures consumer surplus and converts it into producer surplus or pure waste in the form of rent-seeking costs. If monopoly is so bad, why do we put up with it? Why don't we have laws that crack down on monopoly so hard that it never rears its head? We do indeed have laws that limit monopoly power and regulate the prices that monopolies are permitted to charge. But monopoly also brings some benefits. We begin this review of monopoly policy issues by looking at the benefits of monopoly. We then look at monopoly regulation.

Gains from Monopoly

The main reason why monopoly exists is that it has potential advantages over a competitive alternative. These advantages arise from

- Incentives to innovation
- Economies of scale and economies of scope

Incentives to Innovation Invention leads to a wave of innovation as new knowledge is applied to the production process. Innovation may take the form of developing a new product or a lower-cost way of making an existing product. Controversy has raged over whether large firms with market power or small competitive firms lacking such market power are the most innovative. It is clear that some temporary market power arises from innovation. A firm that develops a new product or process and patents it obtains an exclusive right to that product or process for the term of the patent.

But does the granting of a monopoly, even a temporary one, to an innovator increase the pace of innovation? One line of reasoning suggests that it does. Without protection, an innovator is not able to enjoy the profits from innovation for very long. Thus the incentive to innovate is weakened. A contrary argument is that a monopoly can afford to be lazy while competitive firms cannot. Competitive firms must strive to innovate and cut costs even though they know that they cannot hang on to the benefits of their innovation for long. But that knowledge spurs them on to greater and faster innovation.

The evidence on whether monopoly leads to greater innovation than competition is mixed. Large firms do more research and development than do small firms. But research and development are inputs into the process of innovation. What matters is not input but output. Two measures of the output of research and development are the number of patents and the rate of productivity growth. On these measures, it is not clear that bigger is better. But as a new process or product spreads through an industry, the large firms adopt the new process or product more quickly than do small firms. So large firms help to speed the process of diffusion of technological change.

Economies of Scale and Scope Economies of scale and economies of scope can lead to natural monopoly. And as you saw at the beginning of this chapter, in a natural monopoly, a single firm can produce at a lower average cost than a number of firms can.

A firm experiences *economies of scale* when an increase in its output of a good or service brings a decrease in the average total cost of producing it (see Chapter 10, p. 232). A firm experiences *economies of scope* when an increase in the *range of goods produced* brings a decrease in average total cost (see Chapter 9, p. 213). Economies of scope occur when different goods can share specialized (and usually costly) capital resources. For example, McDonald's can produce both hamburgers and french fries at a lower average total cost than can two separate firms—a burger firm and a french fries firm—because at McDonald's, hamburgers and french fries share the use of specialized food storage and preparation facilities. A firm that produces a wide range of products can hire specialist computer programmers, designers, and marketing experts whose skills can be used across the product range, thereby spreading their costs and lowering the average total cost of production of each of the goods.

There are many examples in which a combination of economies of scale and economies of scope arise, but not all of them lead to monopoly. Some examples are the brewing of beer, the manufacture of refrigerators and other household appliances, the manufacture of pharmaceuticals, and the refining of petroleum.

Examples of industries in which economies of scale are so significant that they lead to a natural monopoly are becoming rare. Public utilities such as gas, electric power, local telephone service, and garbage collection once were natural monopolies. But technological advances now enable us to separate the *production* of electric power or natural gas from its *distribution*. The provision of water, though, remains a natural monopoly.

A large-scale firm that has control over supply and can influence price—and therefore behaves like the monopoly firm that you've studied in this chapter—can reap these economies of scale and scope. Small, competitive firms cannot. Consequently, there are situations in which the comparison of monopoly and competition that we made earlier in this chapter is not valid. Recall that we imagined the takeover of a large number of competitive firms by a monopoly firm. But we also assumed that the monopoly would use exactly the same technology as the small firms and have the same costs. If one large firm can reap economies of scale and scope, its marginal cost curve will lie below the supply curve of a competitive industry made up of many small firms. It is possible for such economies of scale and scope to be so large as to result in a larger output and lower price under monopoly than a competitive industry would achieve.

Where significant economies of scale and scope exist, it is usually worth putting up with monopoly and regulating its price.

Regulating Natural Monopoly

Where demand and cost conditions create a natural monopoly, a federal, state, or local government agency usually steps in to regulate the price of the monopoly. By regulating a monopoly, some of the worst aspects of monopoly can be avoided or at least moderated. Let's look at monopoly price regulation.

Figure 12.11 shows the demand curve *D*, the marginal revenue curve *MR*, the long-run average cost curve *LRAC*, and the marginal cost curve *MC* for a natural gas distribution company that is a natural monopoly.

The firm's marginal cost is constant at 10 cents per cubic foot. But average cost decreases as output increases. The reason is that the natural gas company has a large investment in pipelines and has economies of scale. At low output levels, average cost is extremely high. The long-run average cost curve slopes downward because as the number of cubic feet sold increases, the high cost of the distribution system is spread over a larger number of units.

This one firm can supply the entire market at the lowest possible cost because long-run average cost is falling even when the entire market is supplied. (Refer back to p. 264–265 if you need a quick refresher on natural monopoly.)

Profit Maximization First, suppose the natural gas company is not regulated and instead maximizes profit. Figure 12.11 shows the outcome. The company produces 2 million cubic feet a day, the quantity at which marginal cost equals marginal revenue. It prices the gas at 20 cents a cubic foot and makes an economic profit of 2 cents a cubic foot, or $40,000 a day.

This outcome is fine for the gas company, but it is inefficient. The price of gas is 20 cents a cubic foot when its marginal cost is only 10 cents a cubic foot. Also, the gas company is making a big profit. What can regulation do to improve this outcome?

The Efficient Regulation If the monopoly regulator wants to achieve an efficient use of resources, it must require the gas monopoly to produce the quantity of gas that brings marginal social benefit into equality with marginal social cost. With no external benefits, marginal social benefit is what the consumer is willing to pay and is shown by the demand curve. With no external costs, marginal social cost is shown by the firm's marginal cost curve. You can see in Fig. 12.11 that this outcome occurs if the price is regulated at 10 cents per cubic foot and if 4 million cubic feet per day are produced.

The regulation that produces this outcome is called a marginal cost pricing rule. A **marginal cost pricing rule** sets price equal to marginal cost. It maximizes total surplus in the regulated industry. In this example, that surplus is all consumer surplus and it equals the area of the triangle beneath the demand curve and above the marginal cost curve.

The marginal cost pricing rule is efficient. But it leaves the natural monopoly incurring an economic loss. Because average cost is falling as output increases, marginal cost is below average cost. And because price equals marginal cost, price is below average cost. Average cost minus price is the loss per unit produced. It's obvious that a natural gas company that is required to use a marginal cost pricing rule will not stay in business for long. How can a company cover its costs and, at the same time, obey a marginal cost pricing rule?

One possibility is price discrimination. The company might charge a higher price to some customers but marginal cost to the customers who pay least. Another possibility is to use a two-part price (called a two-part tariff). For example, the gas company might charge a monthly fixed fee that covers its fixed cost and then charge for gas consumed at marginal cost.

FIGURE 12.11 Regulating a Natural Monopoly

myeconlab

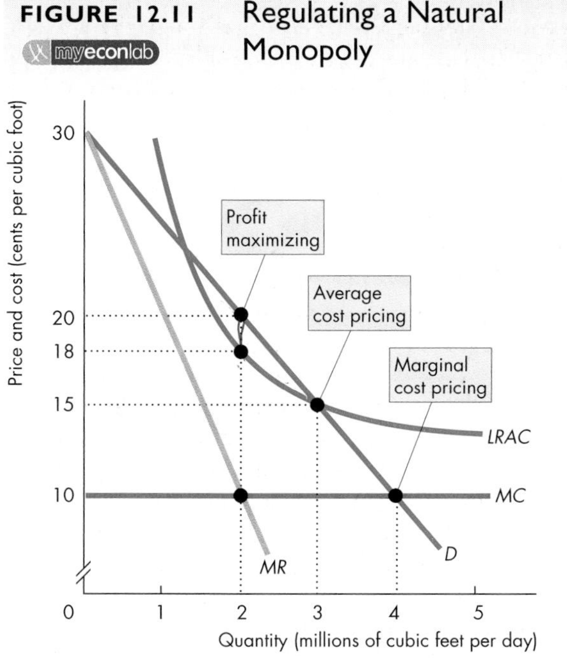

A natural monopoly is an industry in which average cost is falling even when the entire market demand is satisfied. A natural gas producer faces the demand curve *D*. The firm's marginal cost is constant at 10 cents per cubic foot, as shown by the curve labeled *MC*. The long-run average cost curve is *LRAC*.

A profit-maximizing monopoly produces 2 million cubic feet a day and charges a price of 20 cents per cubic foot. An average cost pricing rule sets the price at 15 cents per cubic foot. The monopoly produces 3 million cubic feet per day and makes zero economic profit. A marginal cost pricing rule sets the price at 10 cents per cubic foot. The monopoly produces 4 million cubic feet per day and incurs an economic loss.

But a natural monopoly cannot always cover its costs in these ways. If a natural monopoly cannot cover its total cost from its customers, and if the government wants it to follow a marginal cost pricing rule, the government must give the firm a subsidy. In such a case, the government raises the revenue for the subsidy by taxing some other activity. But as we saw in Chapter 6, taxes themselves generate deadweight loss. Thus the deadweight loss resulting from additional taxes must be subtracted from the efficiency gained by forcing the natural monopoly to adopt a marginal cost pricing rule.

Average Cost Pricing Regulators almost never impose efficient pricing because of its consequences for the firm's economic profit. Instead, they compromise by permitting the firm to cover its costs and to break even (make zero economic profit). So pricing to cover total cost means setting price equal to average cost—called an **average cost pricing rule.**

Figure 12.11 shows the average cost pricing outcome. The natural gas company charges 15 cents a cubic foot and sells 3 million cubic feet per day. This outcome is better for consumers than the unregulated profit-maximizing outcome. The price is 5 cents a cubic foot lower, and the quantity consumed is 1 million cubic feet per day more. And the outcome is better for the producer than the marginal cost pricing rule outcome. The firm breaks even (makes zero economic profit). The outcome is inefficient but less so than the unregulated profit-maximizing outcome.

REVIEW QUIZ

1. What are the two main reasons why monopoly is worth tolerating?
2. Provide some examples of economies of scale and economies of scope?
3. Why might the incentive to innovate be greater for a monopoly than for a small competitive firm?
4. What is the price that achieves an efficient outcome for a regulated monopoly? And what is the problem with this price?
5. Compare the consumer surplus, producer surplus, and deadweight loss that arise from average cost pricing with those that arise from profit-maximization pricing and marginal cost pricing.

myeconlab **Study Plan 12.5**

You've now studied perfect competition and monopoly. *Reading Between the Lines* on pp. 280–281 looks at airfares in the United States as low-cost airlines have cut the market power of traditional airlines. In the next chapter, we study markets that lie between the extremes of perfect competition and monopoly and that blend elements of the two.

READING BETWEEN THE LINES

Airline Monopolies Fade

http://www.nytimes.com

Commercial Travelers Feel Less Gouged . . .

January 14, 2006

Clients of his educational software firm, the Critical Skills Group, reimburse him for his travel costs, but Charles C. Jett said it still offended him to be charged $1,900 to fly round trip to Los Angeles. "I wouldn't charge anyone that," Mr. Jett said.

Increasingly, neither would airlines, which are becoming less inclined to try to charge very high fares, a trend that has pleased Mr. Jett. He paid just $400 recently to fly to and from San Francisco. "The price was a lot lower than I thought it was going to be."

Business travelers have long been irritated to know that the casually dressed person in the next seat—a vacationer or a student headed back to college—paid a lot less to be on the same flight.

A substantial gap still remains between business and leisure fares. But . . . the ratio of domestic business fares to leisure fares, tracked by Harrell Associates, an airline consulting firm in New York, has fallen to about four to one today from about six to one as recently as a year ago. Average one-way business fares fell to $400 from $600 and leisure fares held steady at about $100.

The expansion of low-cost carriers like Southwest Airlines into more markets has forced traditional carriers, including American Airlines and United Airlines, to reduce fares, including those of business travelers. The Internet, which allows travelers to comparison shop far more effectively than in the past, helps, too. . . .

Essence of the Story

- Business travelers pay higher airfares than leisure travelers do, on the average.
- A New York airline consulting firm reports that the ratio of domestic business fares to leisure fares fell from about six to one in 2005 to about four to one in 2006.
- The average one-way business fare fell from $600 to $400, and the average leisure fare remained at about $100.
- The entry of low-cost carriers into more markets has forced traditional carriers to cut all their fares.
- The Internet has made it easy to compare fares and get the best deal.

Economic Analysis

- To study monopoly in the market for air travel, we must consider each route as a market.

- If only one airline has the right to fly a given route, that airline acts as a monopoly on that route.

- Before the expansion of the role of low-cost budget airlines, the traditional airlines such as American Airlines and United Airlines had a monopoly on some routes.

- On most of these routes, the airlines carry both business travelers and leisure travelers.

- The two types of traveler have different demand curves. The business traveler is willing to pay a higher price, if necessary, and has a less elastic demand than does the leisure traveler.

- Figure 1 shows the demand for business travel on a route for which a traditional airline has a monopoly.

- The airline maximizes profit by carrying the number of business travelers at which marginal revenue equals marginal cost and charging the highest price that travelers will pay for that quantity.

- The profit-maximizing outcome in Fig. 1 is a quantity of 1,000 trips per month at a price of $600 per trip.

- Because marginal cost, in this example, is constant at $100 a trip, the monopoly would maximize profit by offering trips to leisure travelers for $100 a trip.

- Because the low-cost airlines are now flying routes that were previously flown only by the traditional airlines, business travelers have a choice. And some choose the low-price, no-frills option.

- This competition from low-price airlines decreases the demand for business travel and willingness to pay by business travelers.

- Figure 2 shows these effects on the traditional airline.

- Demand becomes more elastic, and the demand curve shifts from D_0 to D_1.

- This example has been set up to leave the profit-maximizing quantity unchanged at 1,000 trips per month, but the price falls to $400 per trip.

- Because marginal cost is constant at $100 per trip, the price for leisure travel remains at $100 per trip.

You're the Voter

- Do you think the airlines are efficient?

- Do you think that the suppliers of air travel services operate in a competitive market or a monopoly market?

- What changes in the regulation or deregulation of airlines would you vote for to make the industry more efficient?

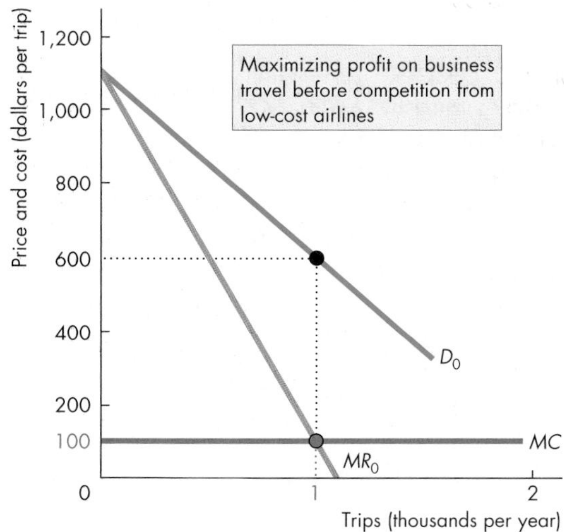

Figure 1 United and American Airlines before entry

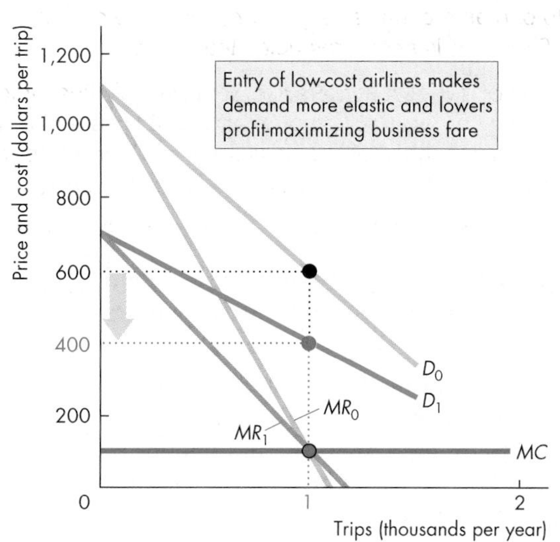

Figure 2 The effect of entry of low-cost airlines

SUMMARY

Key Points

Market Power (pp. 264–265)

- A monopoly is an industry with a single supplier of a good or service that has no close substitutes and in which barriers to entry prevent competition.
- Barriers to entry may be legal (public franchise, license, patent, copyright, firm owns control of a resource) or natural (created by economies of scale).
- A monopoly might be able to price discriminate when there is no resale possibility.
- Where resale is possible, a firm charges one price.

A Single-Price Monopoly's Output and Price Decision (pp. 266–269)

- A monopoly's demand curve is the market demand curve and a single-price monopoly's marginal revenue is less than price.
- A monopoly maximizes profit by producing the output at which marginal revenue equals marginal cost and by charging the maximum price that consumers are willing to pay for that output.

Single-Price Monopoly and Competition Compared (pp. 270–273)

- A single-price monopoly charges a higher price and produces a smaller quantity than a perfectly competitive industry.
- A single-price monopoly restricts output and creates a deadweight loss.
- The total loss that arises from monopoly equals the deadweight loss plus the cost of the resources devoted to rent seeking.

Price Discrimination (pp. 273–276)

- Price discrimination is an attempt by the monopoly to convert consumer surplus into economic profit.
- Perfect price discrimination extracts the entire consumer surplus. Such a monopoly charges a different price for each unit sold and obtains the maximum price that each consumer is willing to pay for each unit bought.
- With perfect price discrimination, the monopoly produces the same output as would a perfectly competitive industry.
- Rent seeking with perfect price discrimination might eliminate the entire consumer surplus and producer surplus.

Monopoly Policy Issues (pp. 277–279)

- A monopoly with large economies of scale and economies of scope can produce a larger quantity at a lower price than a competitive industry can achieve, and monopoly might be more innovative than small competitive firms.
- Efficient regulation requires a monopoly to charge a price equal to marginal cost, but for a natural monopoly, such a price is less than average cost.
- Average cost pricing is a compromise pricing rule that covers a firm's costs and allows the firm to break even but it is not efficient.

Key Figures and Table

Key Terms

PROBLEMS

myeconlab **Tests, Study Plan, Solutions***

1. The United States Postal Service has a monopoly on non-urgent First Class Mail and the exclusive right to put mail in private mailboxes. Pfizer Inc. makes LIPITOR, a prescription drug that lowers cholesterol. Cox Communications is the sole provider of cable television service in some parts of San Diego.
   a. What are the substitutes, if any, for the goods and services described above?
   b. What are the barriers to entry, if any, that protect these three firms from competition?
   c. Which of these three firms, if any, is a natural monopoly? Explain your answer and illustrate it by drawing an appropriate figure.
   d. Which of these three firms, if any, is a legal monopoly? Explain your answer.
   e. Which of these three firms are most likely to be able to profit from price discrimination and which are most likely to sell their good or service for a single price?
2. Minnie's Mineral Springs, a single-price monopoly, faces the market demand schedule:

Price (dollars per bottle)	Quantity demanded (bottles per hour)
10	0
8	1
6	2
4	3
2	4
0	5

   a. Calculate Minnie's total revenue schedule.
   b. Calculate its marginal revenue schedule.
   c. Draw a graph of market demand curve and Minnie's marginal revenue curve.
   d. Why is Minnie's marginal revenue less than the price?
   e. At what price is Minnie's total revenue maximized?
   f. Over what range of prices is the demand for water from Minnie's Mineral Springs elastic?
   g. Why will Minnie not produce a quantity at which the market demand for water is inelastic?

*Solutions to odd-numbered problems are provided.

3. Minnie's Mineral Springs faces the demand schedule in problem 2 and has the following total cost schedule:

Quantity produced (bottles per hour)	Total cost (dollars)
0	1
1	3
2	7
3	13
4	21
5	31

   a. Calculate the marginal cost of producing each output listed in the table.
   b. Calculate Minnie's profit-maximizing output and price.
   c. Calculate the economic profit.
4. The figure illustrates the situation facing the publisher of the only newspaper containing local news in an isolated community.

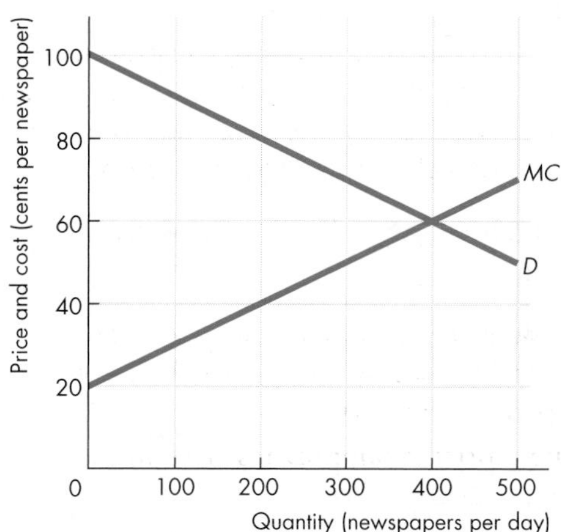

   a. On the graph, mark the profit-maximizing quantity and price.
   b. What is the publisher's daily total revenue?
   c. At the price charged, is the demand for this newspaper elastic or inelastic? Why?
   d. What are consumer surplus and deadweight loss? Mark each on your graph.
   e. Explain why this market might encourage rent seeking.
   f. If this market were perfectly competitive, what would be the quantity, price, consumer surplus, and producer surplus? Mark each on your graph.

5. La Bella Pizza can produce a pizza for a marginal cost of $2. Its standard price is $14.99 per pizza. It offers a second pizza for $4.99. It also distributes coupons that give a $5 rebate on a standard-price pizza.
   a. How can La Bella Pizza make a larger economic profit with this range of prices than it could if it sold every pizza for $14.99?
   b. Draw a figure that illustrates your answer to part (a).
   c. Can you think of a way of increasing La Bella Pizza's economic profit even more?
   d. Is La Bella Pizza more efficient than it would be if it charged just one price?
6. The figure shows a situation similar to that facing Calypso U.S. Pipeline, a firm that operates a natural gas distribution system in the United States. Calypso is a natural monopoly that cannot price discriminate.

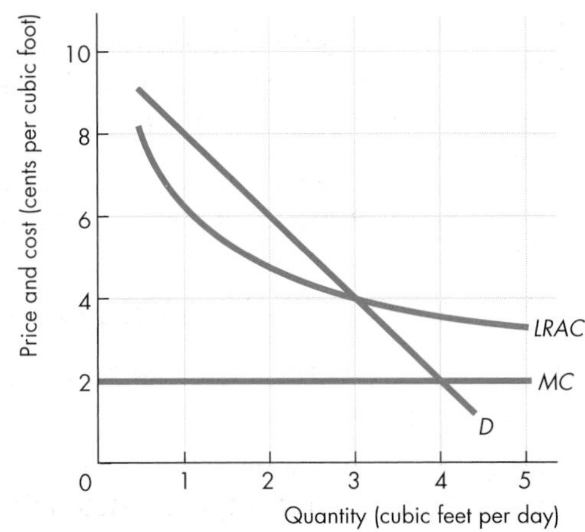

   What quantity will Calypso produce and at what price if Calypso is
   a. An unregulated profit-maximizing firm?
   b. Regulated to make zero economic profit?
   c. Regulated to be efficient?
7. Given the information provided in the figure in problem 6, what is the producer surplus, consumer surplus, and deadweight loss if the firm is
   a. An unregulated profit-maximizing firm?
   b. Regulated to make zero economic profit?
   c. Regulated to be efficient?

CRITICAL THINKING

1. Study *Reading Between the Lines* on pp. 280– 281 and then answer the following questions:
   a. Why might an airline operate as a monopoly even though there are many airlines?
   b. What are the changes in the airline industry reported in the news article that have lowered the price of business air travel?
   c. If the Internet did not exist, how would the demand for business travel be different?
   d. How can you explain the large gap between the price of a business ticket and the price of a leisure ticket on the same route and even on the same airplane?
   e. Should airlines be regulated to lower the price of business travel? Why or why not?

WEB ACTIVITIES

myeconlab Links to Web sites

1. Find the statement by Ralph Nader about Microsoft.
   a. What are Ralph Nader's main claims about Microsoft?
   b. Do you agree with Ralph Nader? Why or why not?
   c. If some other operating systems are better than Windows, why don't they take off?
   d. Does Ralph Nader identify the main costs to the consumer of Microsoft's practices? Explain why or why not.
2. Study the market for computer chips.
   a. Is it correct to call Intel a monopoly? Why or why not?
   b. How does Intel try to raise barriers to entry in this market?
3. Study the story about Heartland Towing of Omaha, Nebraska.
   a. Is Heartland Towing a monopoly? Why or why not?
   b. What economic phenomenon does this news article illustrate?
   c. Do you think Heartland Towing ends up earning an economic profit? Why or why not?

CHAPTER 13

Monopolistic Competition and Oligopoly

PC War Games

The PC price war has been raging for some time. But during 2006, the war became very hot. The age of the $1,000 laptop and $500 desktop had arrived. Dell was one of the most aggressive price cutters. But despite slashing its prices by up to $700 per machine, Dell lost its position as market leader to Hewlett-Packard. These two firms, along with Lenovo, Acer, and Toshiba, accounted for one half of the global market of 60 billion PCs in 2006.

In the market for PCs, the two big firms, Dell and Hewlett-Packard, must pay close attention to what the other firm is doing. But these two firms also compete with the other firms in the market.

In some markets, there are only two firms. Computer chips are an example. The chips that drive most PCs are made by Intel and Advanced Micro Devices. How does competition between just two chip makers work?

When a small number of firms compete in a market, do they operate in the social interest, like firms in perfect competition? Or do they restrict output to increase profit, like a monopoly?

The theories of perfect competition and monopoly don't predict the behavior of the firms we've just described. To understand how markets work when only a handful of firms compete, we need the richer models that are explained in this chapter. In *Reading Between the Lines* at the end of this chapter, we'll return to the market for personal computers and see how Dell and Hewlett-Packard slugged it out for dominance in 2006.

After studying this chapter, you will be able to

- Define and identify monopolistic competition
- Explain how price and output are determined in a monopolistically competitive industry
- Explain why advertising costs are high in a monopolistically competitive industry
- Define and identify oligopoly
- Explain two traditional oligopoly models
- Use game theory to explain how price and output are determined in oligopoly
- Use game theory to explain other strategic decisions

What Is Monopolistic Competition?

You have studied perfect competition, in which a large number of firms produce at the lowest possible cost, make zero economic profit, and are efficient. And you've studied monopoly, in which a single firm restricts output, produces at a higher cost and price than in perfect competition, and is inefficient.

Most real-world markets are competitive but not perfectly competitive because firms in these markets possess some power to set their prices as monopolies do. We call this type of market *monopolistic competition.*

Monopolistic competition is a market structure in which

- A large number of firms compete.
- Each firm produces a differentiated product.
- Firms compete on product quality, price, and marketing.
- Firms are free to enter and exit.

Large Number of Firms

In monopolistic competition, as in perfect competition, the industry consists of a large number of firms. The presence of a large number of firms has three implications for the firms in the industry.

Small Market Share In monopolistic competition, each firm supplies a small part of the total industry output. Consequently, each firm has only limited power to influence the price of its product. Each firm's price can deviate from the average price of other firms by a relatively small amount.

Ignore Other Firms A firm in monopolistic competition must be sensitive to the average market price of the product. But the firm does not pay attention to any one individual competitor. Because all the firms are relatively small, no one firm can dictate market conditions, and so no one firm's actions directly affect the actions of the other firms.

Collusion Impossible Firms in monopolistic competition would like to be able to conspire to fix a higher price—called *collusion.* But because there are many firms, collusion is not possible.

Product Differentiation

A firm practices **product differentiation** if it makes a product that is slightly different from the products of competing firms. A differentiated product is one that is a close substitute but not a perfect substitute for the products of the other firms. Some people will pay more for one variety of the product, so when its price rises, the quantity demanded falls, but it does not (necessarily) fall to zero. For example, Adidas, Asics, Diadora, Etonic, Fila, New Balance, Nike, Puma, and Reebok all make differentiated running shoes. Other things remaining the same, if the price of Adidas running shoes rises and the prices of the other shoes remain constant, Adidas sells fewer shoes and the other producers sell more. But Adidas shoes don't disappear unless the price rises by a large enough amount.

Competing on Quality, Price, and Marketing

Product differentiation enables a firm to compete with other firms in three areas: product quality, price, and marketing.

Quality The quality of a product is the physical attributes that make it different from the products of other firms. Quality includes design, reliability, the service provided to the buyer, and the buyer's ease of access to the product. Quality lies on a spectrum that runs from high to low. Some firms—such as Dell Computer Corp.—offer high-quality products. They are well designed and reliable, and the customer receives quick and efficient service. Other firms offer a lower-quality product that is less well designed, that might not work perfectly, and that the buyer must travel some distance to obtain.

Price Because of product differentiation, a firm in monopolistic competition faces a downward-sloping demand curve. So, like a monopoly, the firm can set both its price and its output. But there is a tradeoff between the product's quality and price. A firm that makes a high-quality product can charge a higher price than a firm that makes a low-quality product can.

Marketing Because of product differentiation, a firm in monopolistic competition must market its product. Marketing takes two main forms: advertising and packaging. A firm that produces a high-quality product wants to sell it for a suitably high price. To be able to do so, it must advertise and package its product in a way that convinces buyers that they are getting the higher quality for which they are paying a higher price. For example, pharmaceutical companies advertise and package their brand-name drugs to persuade buyers that these items are superior to the lower-priced generic alternatives. Similarly, a low-quality producer uses advertising and packaging to persuade buyers that although the quality is low, the low price more than compensates for this fact.

Entry and Exit

In monopolistic competition, firms can enter and exit. Consequently, a firm cannot make an economic profit in the long run. When firms make an economic profit, new firms enter the industry. This entry lowers prices and eventually eliminates economic profit. When firms incur economic losses, some firms leave the industry. This exit increases prices and profits and eventually eliminates the economic loss. In long-run equilibrium, firms neither enter nor leave the industry and the firms in the industry make zero economic profit.

Examples of Monopolistic Competition

Figure 13.1 shows 10 industries that are good examples of monopolistic competition. These industries have a large number of firms (shown in parentheses after the name of the industry). In the most concentrated of these industries, audio and video equipment, the largest 4 firms produce only 30 percent of the industry's total sales and the largest 20 firms produce 75 percent of total sales. The number on the right is the Herfindahl-Hirschman Index. Producers of clothing, jewelry, computers, and sporting goods operate in monopolistic competition.

REVIEW QUIZ

1. What are the distinguishing characteristics of monopolistic competition?
2. How do firms in monopolistic competition compete?
3. In addition to the examples in Fig. 13.1, provide some examples of industries near your school that operate in monopolistic competition.

myeconlab **Study Plan 13.1**

FIGURE 13.1 Examples of Monopolistic Competition

myeconlab

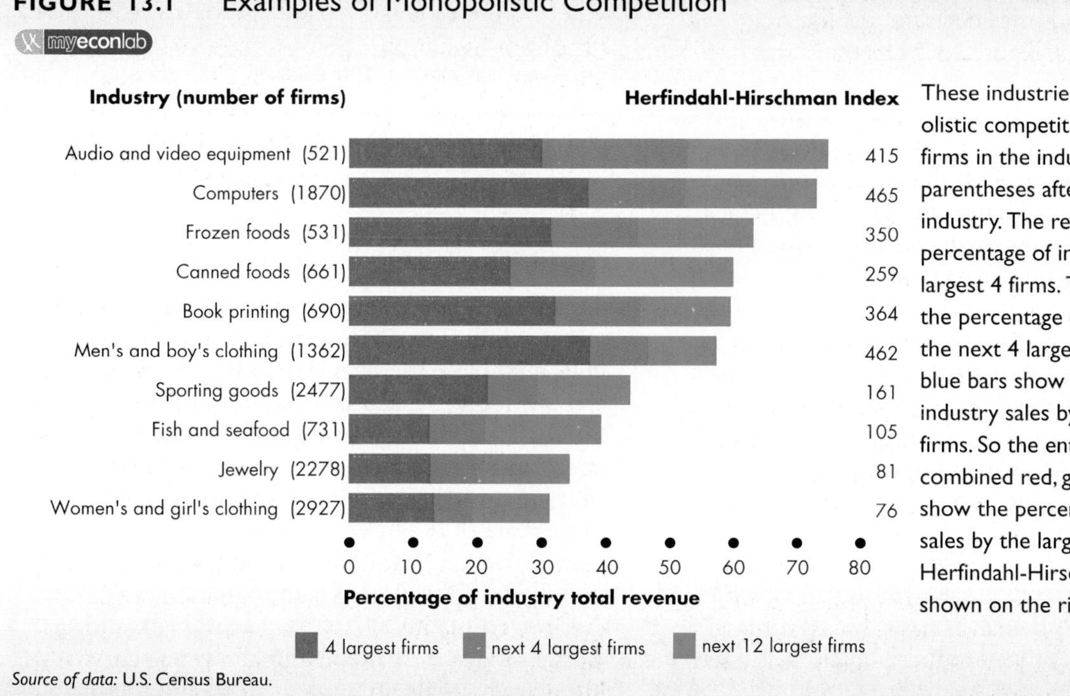

These industries operate in monopolistic competition. The number of firms in the industry is shown in parentheses after the name of the industry. The red bars show the percentage of industry sales by the largest 4 firms. The green bars show the percentage of industry sales by the next 4 largest firms, and the blue bars show the percentage of industry sales by the next 12 largest firms. So the entire length of the combined red, green, and blue bars show the percentage of industry sales by the largest 20 firms. The Herfindahl-Hirschman Index is shown on the right.

Source of data: U.S. Census Bureau.

Price and Output in Monopolistic Competition

Suppose you've been hired by VF Corporation, the firm that owns Nautica Clothing Corporation, to manage the production and marketing of Nautica jackets. Think about the decisions that you must make at Nautica. First, you must decide on the design and quality of jackets and on your marketing program. Second, you must decide on the quantity of jackets to produce and the price at which to sell them.

We'll suppose that Nautica has already made its decisions about design, quality, and marketing and now we'll concentrate on the output and pricing decision. We'll study quality and marketing decisions in the next section.

For a given quality of jackets and marketing activity, Nautica faces given costs and market conditions. How, given its costs and the demand for its jackets, does Nautica decide the quantity of jackets to produce and the price at which to sell them?

The Firm's Short-Run Output and Price Decision

In the short run, a firm in monopolistic competition makes its output and price decision just like a monopoly firm does. Figure 13.2 illustrates this decision for Nautica jackets.

The demand curve for Nautica jackets is *D*. This demand curve tells us the quantity of Nautica jackets demanded at each price, given the prices of other jackets. It is not the demand curve for jackets in general.

The *MR* curve shows the marginal revenue curve associated with the demand curve for Nautica jackets. It is derived just like the marginal revenue curve of a single-price monopoly that you studied in Chapter 12.

The *ATC* curve and the *MC* curve show the average total cost and the marginal cost of producing Nautica jackets.

Nautica's goal is to maximize its economic profit. To do so, it produces the output at which marginal revenue equals marginal cost. In Fig. 13.2, this output is 125 jackets a day. Nautica charges the price that buyers are willing to pay for this quantity, which is determined by the demand curve. This price is $75 per jacket. When Nautica produces 125 jackets a day, its average total cost is $25 per jacket and it makes an economic profit of $6,250 a day ($50 per jacket multiplied by 125 jackets a day). The blue rectangle shows Nautica's economic profit.

FIGURE 13.2 Economic Profit in the Short Run

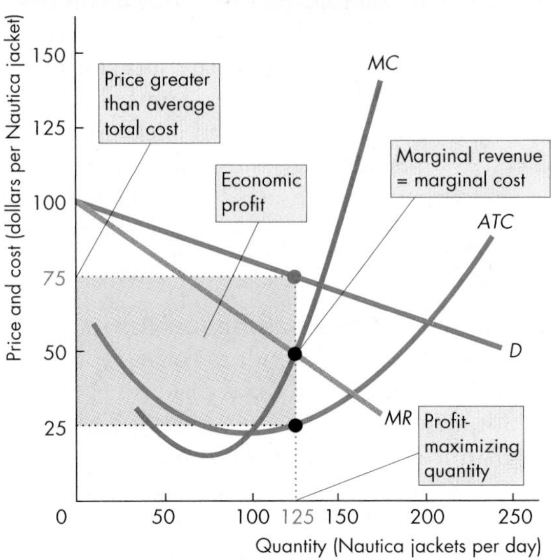

Profit is maximized where marginal revenue equals marginal cost. The profit-maximizing quantity is 125 jackets a day. The price of $75 a jacket exceeds the average total cost of $25 a jacket, so the firm makes an economic profit of $50 a jacket. The blue rectangle illustrates economic profit, which equals $6,250 a day ($50 a jacket multiplied by 125 jackets a day).

Profit Maximizing Might Be Loss Minimizing

Figure 13.2 shows that Nautica is earning a large economic profit. But such an outcome is not inevitable. A firm might face a level of demand for its product that is too low for it to make an economic profit.

Excite@Home was such a firm. Offering high-speed Internet service over the same cable that provides television, Excite@Home hoped to capture a large share of the Internet portal market in competition with AOL, MSN, and a host of other providers.

Figure 13.3 illustrates the situation facing Excite@Home in 2001. The demand curve for its portal service is *D*, the marginal revenue curve is *MR*, the average total cost curve is *ATC*, and the marginal cost curve is *MC*. Excite@Home maximized profit—

FIGURE 13.3 Economic Loss in the Short Run

myeconlab

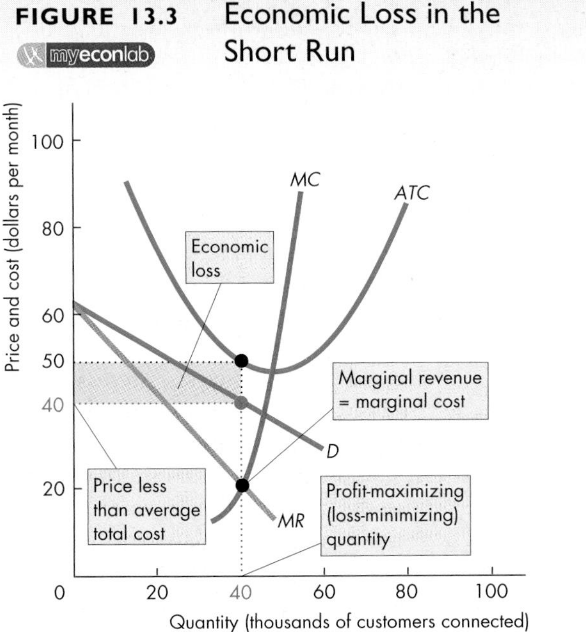

Profit is maximized where marginal revenue equals marginal cost. The loss-minimizing quantity is 40,000 customers. The price of $40 a month is less than the average total cost of $50 a month, so the firm incurs an economic loss of $10 a customer. The red rectangle illustrates economic loss, which equals $400,000 a month ($10 a customer multiplied by 40,000 customers).

equivalently, it minimized its loss—by producing the output at which marginal revenue equals marginal cost. In Fig. 13.3, this output is 40,000 customers. Excite@Home charged the price that buyers were willing to pay for this quantity, which was determined by the demand curve and which was $40 a month. With 40,000 customers, Excite@Home's average total cost was $50 per customer, so it incurred an economic loss of $400,000 a month ($10 a customer multiplied by 40,000 customers). The red rectangle shows Excite@Home's economic loss.

So far, the firm in monopolistic competition looks like a single-price monopoly. It produces the quantity at which marginal revenue equals marginal cost and then charges the price that buyers are willing to pay for that quantity, determined by the demand curve. The key difference between monopoly and monopolistic competition lies in what happens next when firms either make an economic profit or incur an economic loss.

Long Run: Zero Economic Profit

A firm like Excite@Home is not going to incur an economic loss for long. Eventually, it goes out of business. Also, there is no restriction on entry into monopolistic competition, so if firms in an industry are making economic profit, other firms have an incentive to enter that industry.

As the Gap and other firms start to make jackets similar to those made by Nautica, the demand for Nautica jackets decreases. The demand curve for Nautica jackets and the marginal revenue curve shift leftward. And as these curves shift leftward, the profit-maximizing quantity and price fall.

Figure 13.4 shows the long-run equilibrium. The demand curve for Nautica jackets and the marginal revenue curve have shifted leftward. The firm produces 75 jackets a day and sells them for $25 each. At this output level, average total cost is also $25 per jacket.

FIGURE 13.4 Output and Price in the Long Run

myeconlab

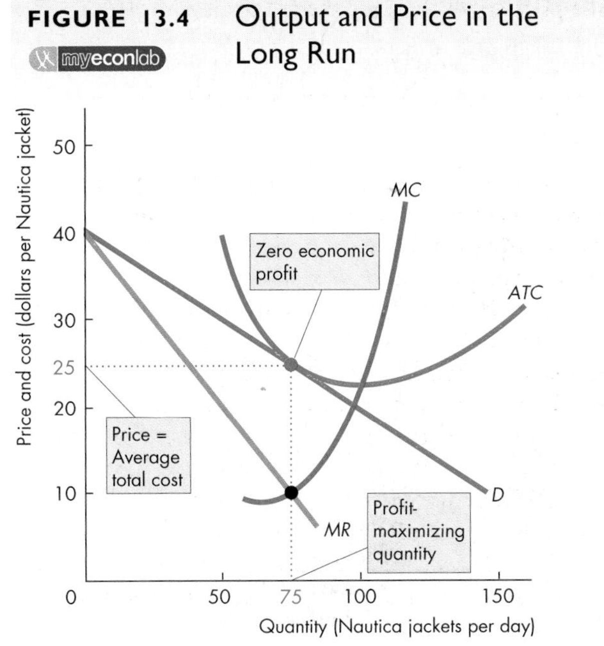

Economic profit encourages entry, which decreases the demand for each firm's product. When the demand curve touches the *ATC* curve at the quantity at which *MR* equals *MC*, the market is in long-run equilibrium. The output that maximizes profit is 75 jackets a day, and the price is $25 per jacket. Average total cost is also $25 per jacket, so economic profit is zero.

So Nautica is making zero economic profit on its jackets. When all the firms in the industry are making zero economic profit, there is no incentive for new firms to enter.

If demand is so low relative to costs that firms incur economic losses, exit will occur. As firms leave an industry, the demand for the products of the remaining firms increases and their demand curves shift rightward. The exit process ends when all the firms in the industry are making zero economic profit.

Monopolistic Competition and Perfect Competition

Figure 13.5 compares monopolistic competition and perfect competition and highlights two key differences between them:

- Excess capacity
- Markup

Excess Capacity A firm has excess capacity if it produces below its efficient scale, which is the quantity at which average total cost is a minimum—the quantity at the bottom of the U-shaped *ATC* curve. In Fig. 13.5, the efficient scale is 100 jackets a day. Nautica (part a) produces 75 Nautica jackets a day and has *excess capacity* of 25 jackets a day. But if all jackets are alike and are produced by firms in perfect competition (part b) each firm produces 100 jackets a day, which is the efficient scale. Average total cost is the lowest possible only in *perfect* competition.

You can see the excess capacity in monopolistic competition all around you. Family restaurants (except for the truly outstanding ones) almost always have some empty tables. You can always get a pizza delivered in less than 30 minutes. It is rare that every pump at a gas station is in use with customers waiting in line. There is always an abundance of realtors ready to help find or sell a home. These industries are examples of monopolistic competition. The firms

FIGURE 13.5 Excess Capacity and Markup

myeconlab

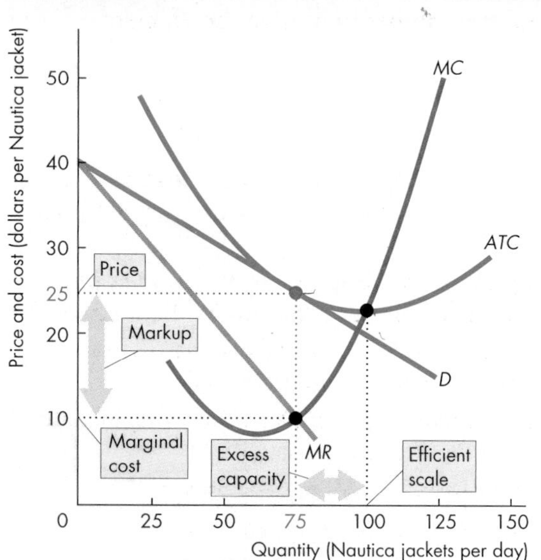

(a) Monopolistic competition

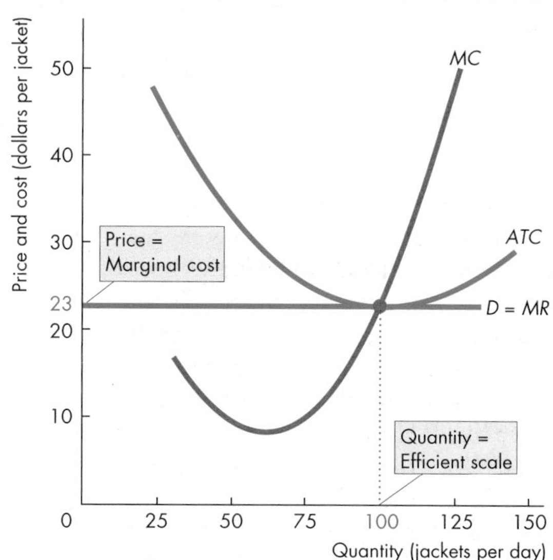

(b) Perfect competition

The efficient scale is 100 jackets a day. In monopolistic competition in the long run, because the firm faces a downward-sloping demand curve for its product, the quantity produced is less than the efficient scale and the firm has excess capacity. Price exceeds marginal cost by the amount of the markup.

In contrast, because in perfect competition the demand for each firm's product is perfectly elastic, the quantity produced equals the efficient scale and price equals marginal cost. The firm produces at the least possible cost and there is no markup.

have excess capacity. They could sell more by cutting their prices, but they would then incur losses.

Markup A firm's markup is the amount by which price exceeds marginal cost. Figure 13.5(a) shows Nautica's markup. In perfect competition, price always equals marginal cost and there is no markup. Figure 13.5(b) shows this case. In monopolistic competition, buyers pay a higher price than in perfect competition and also pay more than marginal cost.

Is Monopolistic Competition Efficient?

Resources are used efficiently when marginal social benefit equals marginal social cost. Price equals marginal social benefit and the firm's marginal cost equals marginal social cost (assuming there are no external benefits or costs). So if the price of a Nautica jacket exceeds the marginal cost of producing it, the quantity of Nautica jackets produced is less than the efficient quantity. And you've just seen that in long-run equilibrium in monopolistic competition, price *does* exceed marginal cost. So is the quantity produced in monopolistic competition less than the efficient quantity?

Making the Relevant Comparison Two economists meet in the street, and one asks the other how her husband is. "Compared to what?" is the quick reply. This bit of economic wit illustrates a key point: Before we can conclude that something needs fixing, we must check out the available alternatives.

The markup that drives a gap between price and marginal cost in monopolistic competition arises from product differentiation. It is because Nautica jackets are not quite the same as jackets from Banana Republic, CK, Diesel, DKNY, Earl Jackets, Gap, Levi, Ralph Lauren, or any of the other dozens of producers of jackets that the demand for Nautica jackets is not perfectly elastic. The only way in which the demand for jackets from Nautica might be perfectly elastic is if there is only one kind of jacket and all firms make it. In this situation, Nautica jackets are indistinguishable from all other jackets. They don't even have identifying labels.

If there was only one kind of jacket, the total benefit of jackets would almost certainly be less than it is with variety. People value variety. And people value variety not only because it enables each person to select what he or she likes best but also because it provides an external benefit. Most of us enjoy seeing variety in the choices of others. Contrast a scene from the China of the 1960s, when everyone wore a Mao tunic, with the China of today, where everyone wears the clothes of their own choosing. Or contrast a scene from the Germany of the 1930s, when almost everyone who could afford a car owned a first-generation Volkswagen Beetle, with the world of today with its enormous variety of styles and types of automobiles.

If people value variety, why don't we see infinite variety? The answer is that variety is costly. Each different variety of any product must be designed, and then customers must be informed about it. These initial costs of design and marketing—called setup costs—mean that some varieties that are too close to others already available are just not worth creating.

The Bottom Line Product variety is both valued and costly. The efficient degree of product variety is the one for which the marginal social benefit of product variety equals its marginal social cost. The loss that arises because the quantity produced is less than the efficient quantity is offset by the gain that arises from having a greater degree of product variety. So compared to the alternative—product uniformity—monopolistic competition might be efficient.

REVIEW QUIZ

1. How does a firm in monopolistic competition decide how much to produce and at what price to offer its product for sale?
2. Why can a firm in monopolistic competition make an economic profit only in the short run?
3. Why do firms in monopolistic competition operate with excess capacity?
4. Why is there a price markup over marginal cost in monopolistic competition?
5. Is monopolistic competition efficient?

myeconlab **Study Plan 13.2**

You've seen how the firm in monopolistic competition determines its output and price in both the short run and the long run when it produces a given product and undertakes a *given* marketing effort. But how does the firm choose its product quality and marketing effort? We'll now study these decisions.

Product Development and Marketing

When we studied Nautica's price and output decision, we assumed that it had already made its product quality and marketing decisions. We're now going to study these decisions and the impact they have on the firm's output, price, and economic profit.

Innovation and Product Development

The prospect of new firms entering the industry keeps firms in monopolistic competition on their toes!

To enjoy economic profits, firms in monopolistic competition must be continually seeking ways of keeping one step ahead of imitators—other firms who imitate the success of the economically profitable firms.

One major way of trying to maintain economic profit is for a firm to seek out new products that will provide it with a competitive edge, even if only temporarily. A firm that introduces a new and differentiated product faces a demand that is less elastic and is able to increase its price and make an economic profit. Eventually, imitators will make close substitutes for the innovative product and compete away the economic profit arising from an initial advantage. So to restore economic profit, the firm must again innovate.

Profit-Maximizing Product Innovation The decision to innovate and develop a new or improved product is based on the same type of profit-maximizing calculation that you've already studied.

Innovation and product development are costly activities, but they also bring in additional revenues. The firm must balance the cost and revenue at the margin. The marginal dollar spent on developing a new or improved product is the marginal cost of product development. The marginal dollar that the new or improved product earns for the firm is the marginal revenue of product development. At a low level of product development, the marginal revenue from a better product exceeds the marginal cost. At a high level of product development, the marginal cost of a better product exceeds the marginal revenue. When the marginal cost and marginal revenue of product development are equal, the firm is undertaking the profit-maximizing amount of product development.

Efficiency and Product Innovation Is the profit-maximizing amount of product innovation also the efficient amount? Efficiency is achieved if the marginal social benefit of a new and improved product equals its marginal social cost.

The marginal social benefit of an innovation is the increase in price that consumers are willing to pay for it. The marginal social cost is the amount that the firm must pay to make the innovation. Profit is maximized when marginal *revenue* equals marginal cost. But in monopolistic competition, marginal revenue is less than price, so product innovation is probably not pushed to its efficient level.

Monopolistic competition brings many product innovations that cost little to implement and are purely cosmetic such as new and improved packaging or a new scent in laundry powder. And even when there is a genuine improved product, it is never as good as what the consumer is willing to pay for. For example, "The Legend of Zelda: Twilight Princess," is regarded as an almost perfect and very cool game, but reviewers complain that it isn't quite perfect. It is a game with features whose marginal revenue equal the marginal cost of creating them.

Advertising

Designing and developing products that are actually different from those of its competitors helps a firm achieve some product differentiation. But firms also attempt to create a consumer perception of product differentiation even when actual differences are small. Advertising and packaging are the principal means firms use to achieve this end. A Canon PowerShot camera is a different product from a Kodak EasyShare. But the actual differences are not the main ones that Canon emphasizes in its marketing. The deeper message is that if you use a Canon, you can be like Maria Sharapova (or some other high-profile successful person).

Advertising Expenditures Firms in monopolistic competition incur huge costs to ensure that buyers appreciate and value the differences between their own products and those of their competitors. So a large proportion of the prices that we pay cover the cost of selling a good. And this proportion is increasing. Advertising in newspapers and magazines and on radio, television, and the Internet is the main selling cost. But it is not the only one. Selling costs include the cost of shopping malls that look like movie sets, glossy catalogs and brochures, and the salaries, airfare, and hotel bills of salespeople.

The total scale of advertising costs is hard to estimate, but some components can be measured. A survey conducted by a commercial agency suggests that for cleaning supplies and toys, around 15 percent of the price of an item is spent on advertising. Figure 13.6 shows estimates for some industries.

For the U.S. economy as a whole, there are some 20,000 advertising agencies, which employ more than 200,000 people and have sales of $45 billion. But these numbers are only part of the total cost of advertising because firms have their own internal advertising departments, the costs of which we can only guess.

Advertising expenditures and other selling costs affect the profits of firms in two ways: They increase costs, and they change demand. Let's look at these effects.

Selling Costs and Total Costs Selling costs such as advertising expenditures increase the costs of a monopolistically competitive firm above those of a perfectly competitive firm or a monopoly. Advertising costs and other selling costs are fixed costs. They do not vary as total output varies. So, just like fixed production costs, advertising costs per unit decrease as production increases.

Figure 13.7 shows how selling costs and advertising expenditures change a firm's average total cost. The blue curve shows the average total cost of production. The red curve shows the firm's average total cost of production plus advertising. The height of the red area between the two curves shows the average fixed cost of advertising. The *total* cost of advertising is fixed. But the *average* cost of advertising decreases as output increases.

Figure 13.7 shows that if advertising increases the quantity sold by a large enough amount, it can lower average total cost. For example, if the quantity sold increases from 25 jackets a day with no advertising to 100 jackets a day with advertising, average total cost falls from $60 to $40 a jacket. The reason is that although the *total* fixed cost has increased, the greater fixed cost is spread over a greater output, so average total cost decreases.

FIGURE 13.6 Advertising Expenditures

myeconlab

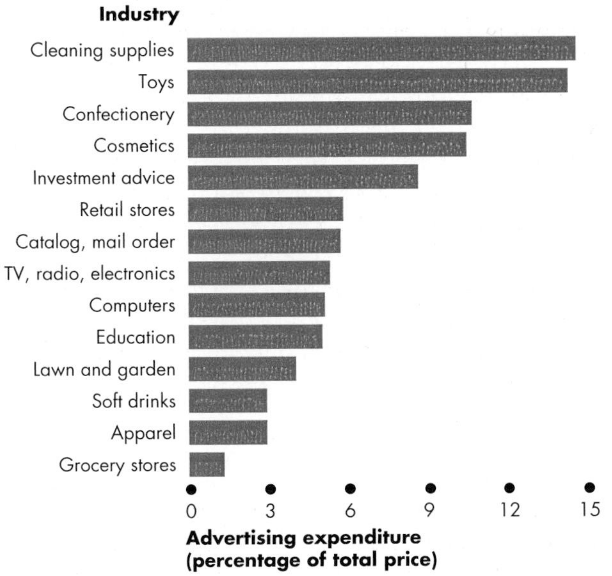

Industry
Cleaning supplies
Toys
Confectionery
Cosmetics
Investment advice
Retail stores
Catalog, mail order
TV, radio, electronics
Computers
Education
Lawn and garden
Soft drinks
Apparel
Grocery stores

0 3 6 9 12 15
Advertising expenditure (percentage of total price)

Advertising expenditures are a large part of total revenue received by producers of cleaning supplies, toys, confectionery, and cosmetics.

Source of data: From Schoenfeld & Associates, Lincolnwood, IL. Reported at www.toolkit.cch.com/text/p03_7006.asp.

FIGURE 13.7 Selling Costs and Total Cost

myeconlab

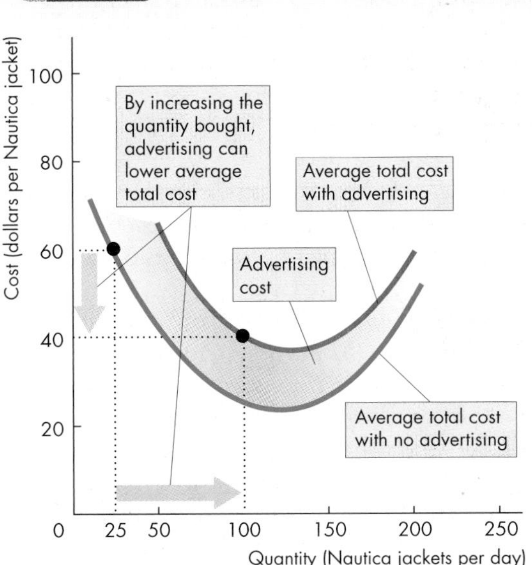

Selling costs such as the cost of advertising are fixed costs. When added to the average total cost of production, selling costs increase average total cost by a greater amount at small outputs than at large outputs. If advertising enables sales to increase from 25 jackets a day to 100 jackets a day, average total cost *falls* from $60 to $40 a jacket.

Selling Costs and Demand Advertising and other selling efforts change the demand for a firm's product. But how? Does demand increase or does it decrease? The most natural answer is that advertising increases demand. By informing people about the quality of its products or by persuading people to switch from the products of other firms, a firm might expect to increase the demand for its own products.

But all firms in monopolistic competition advertise. And all seek to persuade customers that they have the best deal. If advertising enables a firm to survive, the number of firms in the market might increase. And to the extent that the number of firms does increase, advertising *decreases* the demand faced by any one firm. It also makes the demand for any one firm's product more elastic. So advertising can end up not only lowering average total cost but also lowering the markup and the price.

Figure 13.8 illustrates this possible effect of advertising. In part (a), with no advertising, the demand for Nautica jackets is not very elastic. Profit is maximized at 75 jackets per day, and the markup is large. In part (b), advertising, which is a fixed cost, increases average total cost from ATC_0 to ATC_1 but leaves marginal cost unchanged at MC. Demand becomes much more elastic, the profit-maximizing quantity increases, and the markup shrinks.

Using Advertising to Signal Quality

Some advertising, like the Maria Sharapova Canon camera ads on television and in glossy magazines or the huge number of dollars that Coke and Pepsi spend, seems hard to understand. There doesn't seem to be any concrete information about a camera in the glistening smile of a tennis player. And surely everyone knows about Coke and Pepsi. What is the gain from pouring millions of dollars a month into advertising these well-known colas?

One answer is that advertising is a signal to the consumer of a high-quality product. A **signal** is an action taken by an informed person (or firm) to send a

FIGURE 13.8 Advertising and the Markup

myeconlab

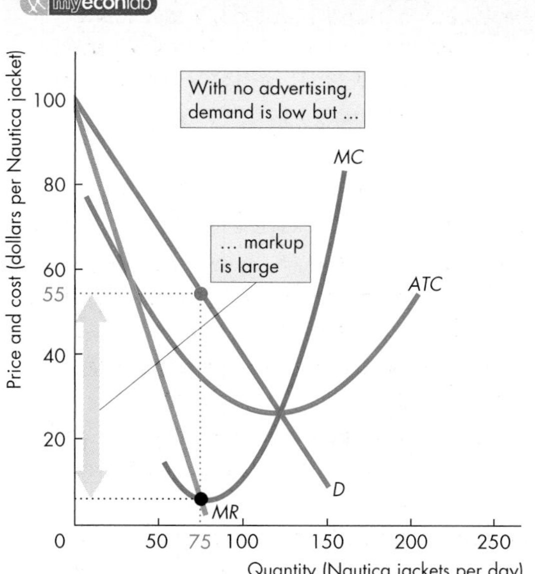

(a) No firms advertise

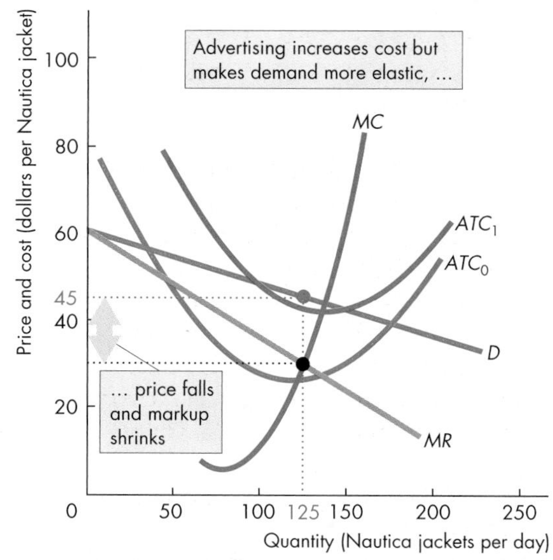

(b) All firms advertise

If no firms advertise, demand for each firm's product is low and not very elastic. The profit-maximizing output is small, the markup is large, and the price is high.

Advertising increases average total cost and shifts the *ATC* curve upward from ATC_0 to ATC_1. If all firms advertise, the demand for each firm's product becomes more elastic. Output increases, the price falls, and the markup shrinks.

message to uninformed people. Think about two colas: Coke and Oke. Oke knows that its cola is not very good and that its taste varies a lot depending on which cheap batch of unsold cola it happens to buy each week. So Oke knows that while it could get a lot of people to try Oke by advertising, they would all quickly discover what a poor product it is and switch back to the cola they bought before. Coke, in contrast, knows that its product has a high-quality consistent taste and that once consumers have tried it, there is a good chance they'll never drink anything else. On the basis of this reasoning, Oke doesn't advertise but Coke does. And Coke spends a lot of money to make a big splash.

Cola drinkers who see Coke's splashy ads know that the firm would not spend so much money advertising if its product were not truly good. So consumers reason that Coke is indeed a really good product. The flashy expensive ad has signaled that Coke is really good without saying anything about Coke.

Notice that if advertising is a signal, it doesn't need any specific product information. It just needs to be expensive and hard to miss. That's what a lot of advertising looks like. So the signaling theory of advertising predicts much of the advertising that we see.

Brand Names

Many firms create and spend a lot of money promoting a brand name. Why? What benefit does a brand name bring to justify the sometimes high cost of establishing it?

The basic answer is that a brand name provides information about the quality of a product to consumers and an incentive to the producer to achieve a high and consistent quality standard.

To see how a brand name helps the consumer, think about how you use brand names to get information about quality. You're on a road trip, and it is time to find a place to spend the night. You see roadside advertisements for Holiday Inn and Embassy Suites and for Joe's Motel and Annie's Driver's Stop. You know about Holiday Inn and Embassy Suites because you've stayed in them before. And you've seen their advertisements. You know what to expect from them. You have no information at all about Joe's and Annie's. They might be better than the lodging you do know about, but without that knowledge, you're not going to chance them. You use the brand name as information and stay at Holiday Inn.

This same story explains why a brand name provides an incentive to achieve high and consistent quality. Because no one would know whether Joe's and Annie's were offering a high standard of service, they have no incentive to do so. But equally, because everyone expects a given standard of service from Holiday Inn, a failure to meet a customer's expectation would almost surely lose that customer to a competitor. So Holiday Inn has a strong incentive to deliver what it promises in the advertising that creates its brand name.

Efficiency of Advertising and Brand Names

To the extent that advertising and brand names provide consumers with information about the precise nature of product differences and about product quality, they benefit the consumer and enable a better product choice to be made. But the opportunity cost of the additional information must be weighed against the gain to the consumer.

The final verdict on the efficiency of monopolistic competition is ambiguous. In some cases, the gains from extra product variety unquestionably offset the selling costs and the extra cost arising from excess capacity. The tremendous varieties of books and magazines, clothing, food, and drinks are examples of such gains. It is less easy to see the gains from being able to buy a brand-name drug that has a chemical composition identical to that of a generic alternative. But many people do willingly pay more for the brand-name alternative.

REVIEW QUIZ

1. What are the two main ways, other than by adjusting price, in which a firm in monopolistic competition competes with other firms?
2. Why might product innovation and development be efficient and why might it be inefficient?
3. How does a firm's advertising expenditure influence its cost curves? Does average total cost increase or decrease?
4. How does a firm's advertising expenditure influence the demand for its product? Does demand increase or decrease?
5. Why is it difficult to determine whether monopolistic competition is efficient or inefficient? What is your opinion about the bottom line and why?

myeconlab **Study Plan 13.3**

What Is Oligopoly?

Oligopoly, like monopolistic competition, lies between perfect competition and monopoly. The firms in oligopoly might produce an identical product and compete only on price, or they might produce a differentiated product and compete on price, product quality, and marketing. **Oligopoly** is a market structure in which

- Natural or legal barriers prevent the entry of new firms.
- A small number of firms compete.

Barriers to Entry

Natural or legal barriers to entry can create oligopoly. You saw in Chapter 12 how economies of scale and demand form a natural barrier to entry that can create a *natural monopoly*. These same factors can create a *natural oligopoly*.

Figure 13.9 illustrates two natural oligopolies. The demand curve, *D* (in both parts of the figure), shows the demand for taxi rides in a town. If the average total cost curve of a taxi company is ATC_1 in part (a), the market is a natural **duopoly**—an oligopoly market with two firms. You can probably see some examples of duopoly where you live. Some cities have only two taxi companies, two car rental firms, two copy centers, or two college bookstores.

The lowest price at which the firm would remain in business is $10 a ride. At that price, the quantity of rides demanded is 60 a day, the quantity that can be provided by just two firms. There is no room in this market for three firms. But if there were only one firm, it would make an economic profit and a second firm would enter to take some of the business and economic profit.

If the average total cost curve of a taxi company is ATC_2 in part (b), the efficient scale of one firm is 20 rides a day. This market is large enough for three firms.

A legal oligopoly arises when a legal barrier to entry protects the small number of firms in a market. A city might license two taxi firms or two bus companies, for example, even though the combination of demand and economies of scale leaves room for more than two firms.

FIGURE 13.9 Natural Oligopoly

myeconlab

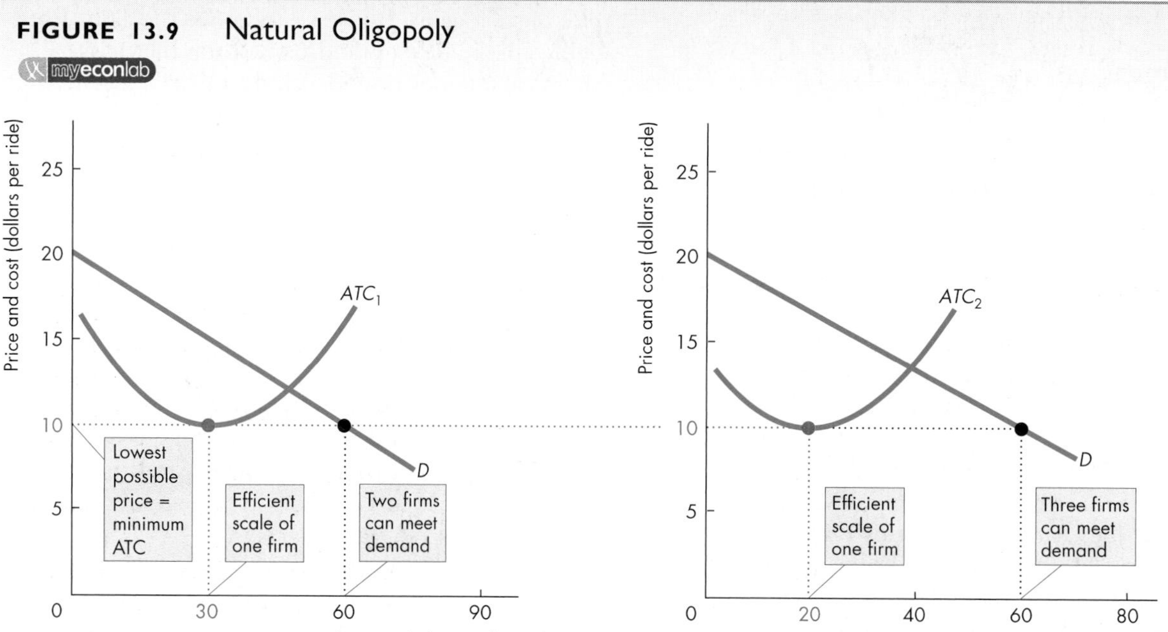

(a) Natural duopoly

(b) Natural oligopoly with three firms

The lowest possible price is $10 a ride, which is the minimum average total cost. When a firm produces 30 rides a day, the efficient scale, two firms can satisfy the market demand. This natural oligopoly has two firms—a natural duopoly.

When the efficient scale of one firm is 20 rides per day, three firms can satisfy the market demand at the lowest possible price. This natural oligopoly has three firms.

Small Number of Firms

Because barriers to entry exist, oligopoly consists of a small number of firms, each of which has a large share of the market. Such firms are interdependent, and they face a temptation to cooperate to increase their joint economic profit.

Interdependence With a small number of firms in a market, each firm's actions influence the profits of all the other firms. When Penny Stafford opened her coffee shop in Bellevue, Washington, a nearby Starbucks coffee shop took a hit. Within days, Starbucks began to attract Penny's customers with enticing offers and lower prices. Starbucks survived but Penny eventually went out of business. Penny Stafford and Starbucks were interdependent.

Temptation to Cooperate When a small number of firms share a market, they can increase their profits by forming a cartel and acting like a monopoly. A **cartel** is a group of firms acting together—colluding—to limit output, raise price, and increase economic profit. Cartels are illegal, but they do operate in some markets. But for reasons that you'll discover in this chapter, cartels tend to break down.

Examples of Oligopoly

Figure 13.10 shows some examples of oligopoly. The dividing line between oligopoly and monopolistic competition is hard to pin down. As a practical matter, we identify oligopoly by looking at concentration ratios, the Herfindahl-Hirschman Index, and information about the geographical scope of the market and barriers to entry. The HHI that divides oligopoly from monopolistic competition is generally taken to be 1,000. An HHI below 1,000 is usually an example of monopolistic competition, and a market in which the HHI exceeds 1,000 is usually an example of oligopoly.

REVIEW QUIZ

1. What are the two distinguishing characteristics of oligopoly?
2. Why are firms in oligopoly interdependent?
3. Why do firms in oligopoly face a temptation to collude?
4. Can you think of some examples of oligopolies that you buy from?

myeconlab **Study Plan 13.4**

FIGURE 13.10 Examples of Oligopoly

Industry (number of firms)	Herfindahl-Hirschman Index
Cigarettes (9)	–
Glass bottles and jars (11)	2,960
Washing machines and dryers (10)	2,870
Batteries (35)	2,883
Light bulbs (54)	2,849
Breakfast cereals (48)	2,446
House slippers (22)	2,053
Automobiles (173)	2,350
Chocolate (152)	2,567
Motorcycles (373)	2,037

Source of data: U.S. Census Bureau.

These industries operate in oligopoly. The number of firms in the industry is shown in parentheses after the name of the industry. The red bars show the percentage of industry sales by the largest 4 firms. The green bars show the percentage of industry sales by the next 4 largest firms, and the blue bars show the percentage of industry sales by the next 12 largest firms. So the entire length of the combined red, green, and blue bars shows the percentage of industry sales by the largest 20 firms. The Herfindahl-Hirschman Index is shown on the right.

Two Traditional Oligopoly Models

Suppose you run one of three gas stations in a small town. You're trying to decide whether to cut your price. To make your decision, you must predict how the other firms will react and calculate the effects of those reactions on your profit. If you cut your price and your competitors don't cut theirs, you sell more and the other two firms sell less. But won't the other firms cut their prices too and make your profits fall. So what will you do?

Several models have been developed to explain the prices and quantities in oligopoly markets. The models fall into two broad groups: traditional models and game theory models. We'll look at examples of both types, starting with two traditional models.

The Kinked Demand Curve Model

The kinked demand curve model of oligopoly is based on the assumption that each firm believes that if it raises its price, others will not follow, but if it cuts its price, other firms will cut theirs.

Figure 13.11 shows the demand curve (D) that a firm believes it faces. The demand curve has a kink at the current price, P, and quantity, Q. At prices above P, a small price rise brings a big decrease in the quantity sold. The other firms hold their current price and the firm has the highest price for the good, so it loses market share. At prices below P, even a large price cut brings only a small increase in the quantity sold. In this case, other firms match the price cut, so the firm gets no price advantage over its competitors.

FIGURE 13.11 The Kinked Demand Curve Model

myeconlab

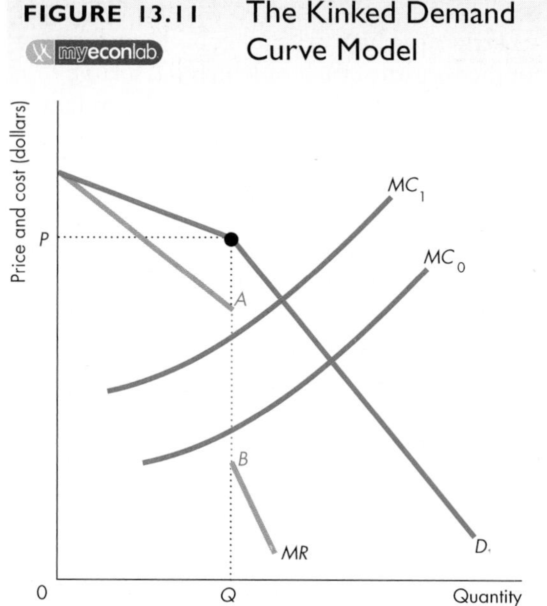

The price in an oligopoly market is P. Each firm believes it faces the demand curve D. At prices above P, a small price rise brings a big decrease in the quantity sold because other firms do not raise their prices. At prices below P, even a big price cut brings only a small increase in the quantity sold because other firms also cut their prices. Because the demand curve is kinked, the marginal revenue curve, MR, has a break AB. Profit is maximized by producing Q. The marginal cost curve passes through the break in the marginal revenue curve. Marginal cost changes inside the range AB leave the price and quantity unchanged.

The kink in the demand curve creates a break in the marginal revenue curve (MR). To maximize profit, the firm produces the quantity at which marginal cost equals marginal revenue. That quantity, Q, is where the marginal cost curve passes through the gap AB in the marginal revenue curve. If marginal cost fluctuates between A and B, like the marginal cost curves MC_0 and MC_1, the firm does not change its price or its output. Only if marginal cost fluctuates outside the range AB does the firm change its price and output. So the kinked demand curve model predicts that price and quantity are insensitive to small cost changes.

But this model has a problem. If marginal cost increases by enough to cause the firm to increase its price and if all firms experience the same increase in marginal cost, they all increase their prices together. The firm's belief that others will not join it in a price rise is incorrect. A firm that bases its actions on beliefs that are wrong does not maximize profit and might even end up incurring an economic loss.

Dominant Firm Oligopoly

A second traditional model explains a dominant firm oligopoly, which arises when one firm—the dominant firm—has a big cost advantage over the other firms and produces a large part of the industry output. The dominant firm sets the market price and the other firms are price takers. Examples of dominant firm oligopoly are a large gasoline retailer or a big video rental store that dominates its local market.

FIGURE 13.12 A Dominant Firm Oligopoly

myeconlab

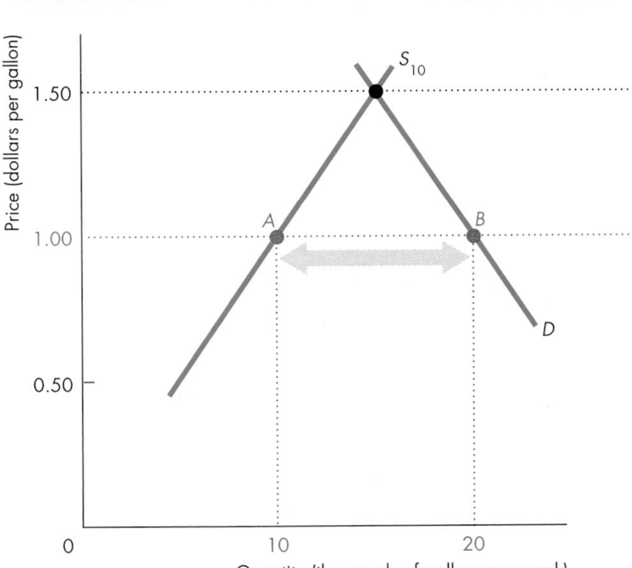

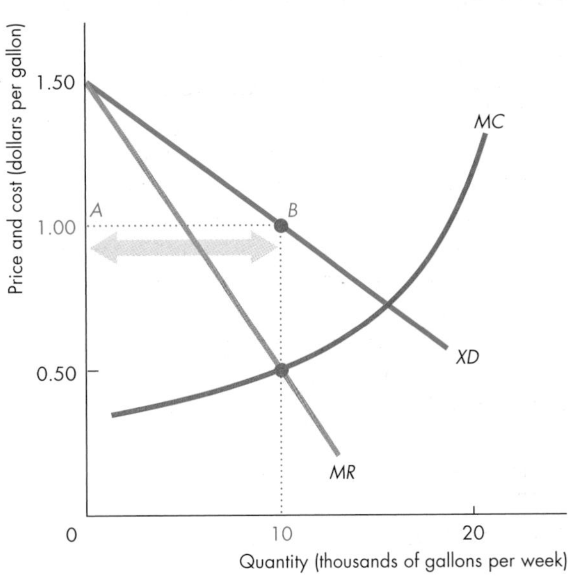

(a) Ten small firms and market demand

The demand curve for gas in a city is D in part (a). There are 10 small competitive firms that together have a supply curve of S_{10}. In addition, there is 1 large firm, Big-G, shown in part (b). Big-G faces the demand curve XD, determined as the market demand D minus the supply of the 10 small firms S_{10}—the demand that is not satisfied by the small firms.

(b) Big-G's price and output decision

Big-G's marginal revenue curve is MR, and marginal cost curve is MC. Big-G sets its output to maximize profit by equating marginal cost and marginal revenue. This output is 10,000 gallons per week. The price at which Big-G can sell this quantity is $1 a gallon. The 10 small firms take this price, and each firm sells 1,000 gallons per week, point A in part (a).

To see how a dominant firm oligopoly works, suppose that 11 firms operate gas stations in a city. Big-G is the dominant firm. Figure 13.12 shows the market for gas in this city. In part (a), the demand curve D tells us the total quantity of gas demanded in the city at each price. The supply curve S_{10} is the supply curve of the 10 small firms. Part (b) shows the situation facing Big-G. Its marginal cost curve is MC. Big-G faces the demand curve XD, and its marginal revenue curve is MR. The demand curve XD shows the excess demand not met by the 10 small firms. For example, at a price of $1 a gallon, the quantity demanded is 20,000 gallons, the quantity supplied by the 10 small firms is 10,000 gallons, and the excess quantity demanded is 10,000 gallons, measured by the distance AB in both parts of the figure.

To maximize profit, Big-G operates like a monopoly. It sells 10,000 gallons a week, where its marginal revenue equals its marginal cost, for a price of $1 a gallon. The 10 small firms take the price of $1 a gallon. They behave just like firms in perfect competition. The quantity of gas demanded in the entire city at $1 a gallon is 20,000 gallons, as shown in part (a). Of this amount, Big-G sells 10,000 gallons and the 10 small firms each sell 1,000 gallons.

REVIEW QUIZ

1. What does the kinked demand curve model predict and why must it sometimes make a prediction that contradicts its basic assumption?
2. Do you think a market with a dominant firm is in long-run equilibrium? Explain why or why not.

myeconlab **Study Plan 13.5**

The traditional models don't enable us to understand all oligopoly markets and we're now going to study some newer models based on game theory.

Oligopoly Games

Economists think about oligopoly as a game, and to study oligopoly markets they use a set of tools called game theory. **Game theory** is a tool for studying *strategic behavior*—behavior that takes into account the expected behavior of others and the recognition of mutual interdependence. Game theory was invented by John von Neumann in 1937 and extended by von Neumann and Oskar Morgenstern in 1944 (pp. 318–319). Today, it is one of the major research fields in economics.

Game theory seeks to understand oligopoly as well as other forms of economic, political, social, and even biological rivalries by using a method of analysis specifically designed to understand games of all types, including the familiar games of everyday life (see Talking with Drew Fudenberg on pp. 320–322). We will begin our study of game theory and its application to the behavior of firms by thinking about familiar games.

What Is a Game?

What is a game? At first thought, the question seems silly. After all, there are many different games. There are ball games and parlor games, games of chance and games of skill. But what is it about all these different activities that make them games? What do all these games have in common? We're going to answer these questions by looking at a game called "the prisoners' dilemma." This game captures the essential features of many games, including oligopoly, and it gives a good illustration of how game theory works and how it generates predictions.

The Prisoners' Dilemma

Art and Bob have been caught red-handed, stealing a car. Facing airtight cases, they will receive a sentence of two years each for their crime. During his interviews with the two prisoners, the district attorney begins to suspect that he has stumbled on the two people who were responsible for a multimillion-dollar bank robbery some months earlier. But this is just a suspicion. He has no evidence on which he can convict them of the greater crime unless he can get them to confess. But how can he extract a confession? The answer is by making the prisoners play a game. So the district attorney makes the prisoners play the game that we will now describe.

All games share four common features:

- Rules
- Strategies
- Payoffs
- Outcome

Rules Each prisoner (player) is placed in a separate room and cannot communicate with the other prisoner. Each is told that he is suspected of having carried out the bank robbery and that

> If both of them confess to the larger crime, each will receive a sentence of 3 years for both crimes.
>
> If he alone confesses and his accomplice does not, he will receive only a 1-year sentence while his accomplice will receive a 10-year sentence.

Strategies In game theory, **strategies** are all the possible actions of each player. Art and Bob each have two possible actions:

1. Confess to the bank robbery.
2. Deny having committed the bank robbery.

Because there are two players, each with two strategies, there are four possible outcomes:

1. Both confess.
2. Both deny.
3. Art confesses and Bob denies.
4. Bob confesses and Art denies.

Payoffs Each prisoner can work out his *payoff* in each of these situations, and we can tabulate the four possible payoffs for each of the prisoners in what is called a payoff matrix for the game. A **payoff matrix** is a table that shows the payoffs for every possible action by each player for every possible action by each other player.

Table 13.1 shows a payoff matrix for Art and Bob. The squares show the payoffs for each prisoner—the red triangle in each square shows Art's and the blue triangle shows Bob's. If both prisoners confess (top left), each gets a prison term of 3 years. If Bob confesses but Art denies (top right), Art gets a 10-year sentence and Bob gets a 1-year sentence. If Art confesses and Bob denies (bottom left), Art gets a 1-year sentence and Bob gets a 10-year sentence. Finally, if both of them deny (bottom right), neither can be convicted of the bank robbery charge but both are sentenced for the car theft—a 2-year sentence.

Outcome The choices of both players determine the outcome of the game. To predict that outcome, we use an equilibrium idea proposed by John Nash of Princeton University (who received the Nobel Prize for Economic Science in 1994 and was the subject of the 2001 movie *A Beautiful Mind*). In **Nash equilibrium**, player *A* takes the best possible action given the action of player *B* and player *B* takes the best possible action given the action of player *A*.

In the case of the prisoners' dilemma, the Nash equilibrium occurs when Art makes his best choice given Bob's choice and when Bob makes his best choice given Art's choice.

To find the Nash equilibrium, we compare all the possible outcomes associated with each choice and eliminate those that are dominated—that are not as good as some other choice. Let's find the Nash equilibrium for the prisoners' dilemma game.

TABLE 13.1 Prisoners' Dilemma Payoff Matrix

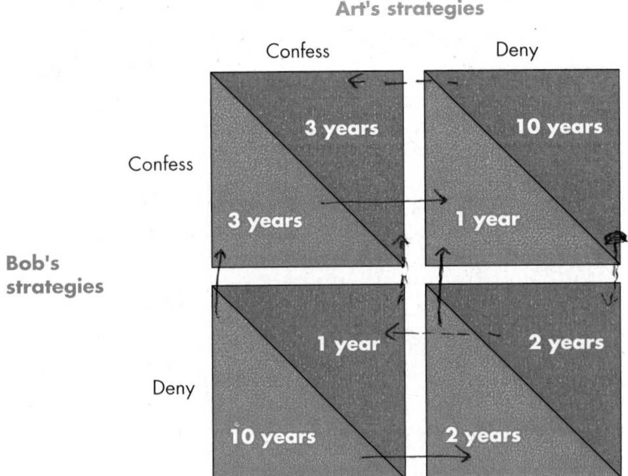

Each square shows the payoffs for the two players, Art and Bob, for each possible pair of actions. In each square, the red triangle shows Art's payoff and the blue triangle shows Bob's. For example, if both confess, the payoffs are in the top left square. The equilibrium of the game is for both players to confess and each gets a 3-year sentence.

Finding the Nash Equilibrium Look at the situation from Art's point of view. If Bob confesses (top row), Art's best action is to confess because in that case, he is sentenced to 3 years rather than 10 years. If Bob denies (bottom row), Art's best action is still to confess because in that case he receives 1 year rather than 2 years. So Art's best action is to confess.

Now look at the situation from Bob's point of view. If Art confesses (left column), Bob's best action is to confess because in that case, he is sentenced to 3 years rather than 10 years. If Art denies (right column), Bob's best action is still to confess because in that case, he receives 1 year rather than 2 years. So Bob's best action is to confess.

Because each player's best action is to confess, each does confess, each goes to jail for 3 years, and the district attorney has solved the bank robbery. This is the Nash equilibrium of the game.

The Dilemma Now that you have found the outcome to the prisoners' dilemma, you can better see the dilemma. The dilemma arises as each prisoner contemplates the consequences of denying. Each prisoner knows that if both of them deny, they will receive only a 2-year sentence for stealing the car. But neither has any way of knowing that his accomplice will deny. Each poses the following questions: Should I deny and rely on my accomplice to deny so that we will both get only 2 years? Or should I confess in the hope of getting just 1 year (provided that my accomplice denies) knowing that if my accomplice does confess, we will both get 3 years in prison? The dilemma leads to the equilibrium of the game.

A Bad Outcome For the prisoners, the equilibrium of the game, with each confessing, is not the best outcome. If neither of them confesses, each gets only 2 years for the lesser crime. Isn't there some way in which this better outcome can be achieved? It seems that there is not, because the players cannot communicate with each other. Each player can put himself in the other player's place, and so each player can figure out that there is a best strategy for each of them. The prisoners are indeed in a dilemma. Each knows that he can serve 2 years only if he can trust the other to deny. But each prisoner also knows that it is not in the best interest of the other to deny. So each prisoner knows that he must confess, thereby delivering a bad outcome for both.

The firms in an oligopoly are in a similar situation to Art and Bob in the prisoners' dilemma game. Let's see how we can use this game to understand oligopoly.

An Oligopoly Price-Fixing Game

We can use game theory and a game like the prisoners' dilemma to understand price fixing, price wars, and other aspects of the behavior of firms in oligopoly. We'll begin with a price-fixing game.

To understand price fixing, we're going to study the special case of duopoly—an oligopoly with two firms. Duopoly is easier to study than oligopoly with three or more firms, and it captures the essence of all oligopoly situations. Somehow, the two firms must share the market. And how they share it depends on the actions of each. We're going to describe the costs of the two firms and the market demand for the item they produce. We're then going to see how game theory helps us to predict the prices charged and the quantities produced by the two firms in a duopoly.

Cost and Demand Conditions Two firms, Trick and Gear, produce switchgears. They have identical costs. Figure 13.13(a) shows their average total cost curve (*ATC*) and marginal cost curve (*MC*). Figure 13.13(b) shows the market demand curve for switchgears (*D*). The two firms produce identical switchgears, so one firm's switchgear is a perfect substitute for the other's. So the market price of each firm's product is identical. The quantity demanded depends on that price—the higher the price, the smaller is the quantity demanded.

This industry is a natural duopoly. Two firms can produce this good at a lower cost than either one firm or three firms can. For each firm, average total cost is at its minimum when production is 3,000 units a week. And when price equals minimum average total cost, the total quantity demanded is 6,000 units a week. So two firms can just produce that quantity.

Collusion We'll suppose that Trick and Gear enter into a collusive agreement. A **collusive agreement** is an agreement between two (or more) producers to form a cartel to restrict output, raise the price, and increase profits. Such an agreement is illegal in the United States and is undertaken in secret.The strategies that firms in a cartel can pursue are to

- Comply
- Cheat

A firm that complies carries out the agreement. A firm that cheats breaks the agreement to its own benefit and to the cost of the other firm.

Because each firm has two strategies, there are four possible combinations of actions for the firms:

1. Both firms comply.
2. Both firms cheat.
3. Trick complies and Gear cheats.
4. Gear complies and Trick cheats.

FIGURE 13.13 Costs and Demand

myeconlab

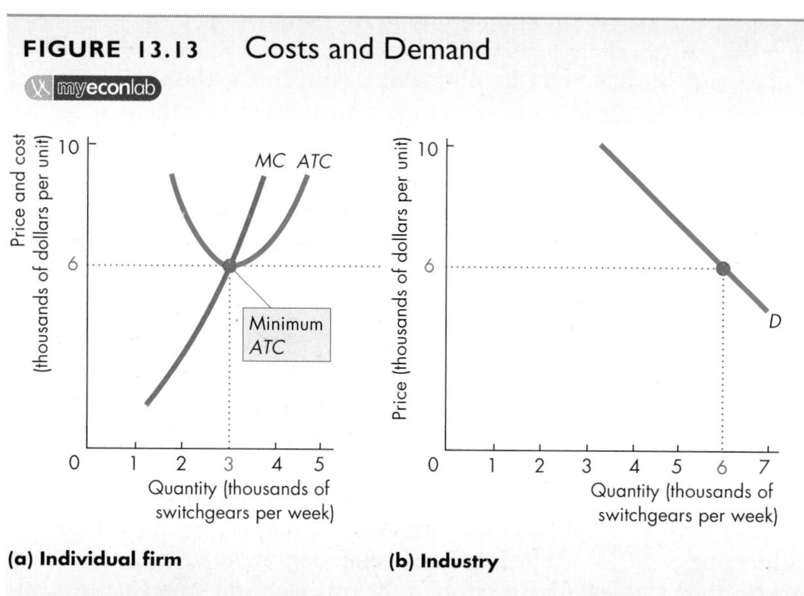

The average total cost curve for each firm is *ATC*, and the marginal cost curve is *MC* (part a). Minimum average total cost is $6,000 a unit, and it occurs at a production of 3,000 units a week.

Part (b) shows the market demand curve. At a price of $6,000, the quantity demanded is 6,000 units per week. The two firms can produce this output at the lowest possible average cost. If the market had one firm, it would be profitable for another to enter. If the market had three firms, one would exit. There is room for only two firms in this industry. It is a natural duopoly.

Colluding to Maximize Profits Let's work out the payoffs to the two firms if they collude to make the maximum profit for the cartel by acting like a monopoly. The calculations that the two firms perform are the same calculations that a monopoly performs. (You can refresh your memory of these calculations by looking at Chapter 12, pp. 268–269.) The only thing that the firms in duopoly must do beyond what a monopoly does is to agree on how much of the total output each of them will produce.

Figure 13.14 shows the price and quantity that maximize industry profit for the duopoly. Part (a) shows the situation for each firm, and part (b) shows the situation for the industry as a whole. The curve labeled *MR* is the industry marginal revenue curve. This marginal revenue curve is like that of a single-price monopoly (Chapter 12, p. 266). The curve labeled MC_I is the industry marginal cost curve if each firm produces the same quantity of output. That curve is constructed by adding together the outputs of the two firms at each level of marginal cost. That is, at each level of marginal cost, industry output is twice the output of each individual firm. So the curve MC_I in part (b) is twice as far to the right as the curve *MC* in part (a).

To maximize industry profit, the firms in the duopoly agree to restrict output to the rate that makes the industry marginal cost and marginal revenue equal. That output rate, as shown in part (b), is 4,000 units a week. The demand curve shows that the highest price for which the 4,000 switchgears can be sold is $9,000 each. Trick and Gear agree to charge this price.

To hold the price at $9,000 a unit, production must be 4,000 units a week. So Trick and Gear must agree on output rates for each of them that total 4,000 units a week. Let's suppose that they agree to split the market equally so that each firm produces 2,000 switchgears a week. Because the firms are identical, this division is the most likely.

The average total cost (*ATC*) of producing 2,000 switchgears a week is $8,000, so the profit per unit is $1,000 and economic profit is $2 million (2,000 units × $1,000 per unit). The economic profit of each firm is represented by the blue rectangle in Fig. 13.14(a).

We have just described one possible outcome for a duopoly game: The two firms collude to produce the monopoly profit-maximizing output and divide that output equally between themselves. From the industry point of view, this solution is identical to a monopoly. A duopoly that operates in this way is indistinguishable from a monopoly. The economic profit that is made by a monopoly is the maximum total profit that can be made by the duopoly when the firms collude.

But with price greater than marginal cost, either firm might think of trying to increase profit by cheating on the agreement and producing more than the agreed amount. Let's see what happens if one of the firms does cheat in this way.

FIGURE 13.14 Colluding to Make Monopoly Profits

myeconlab

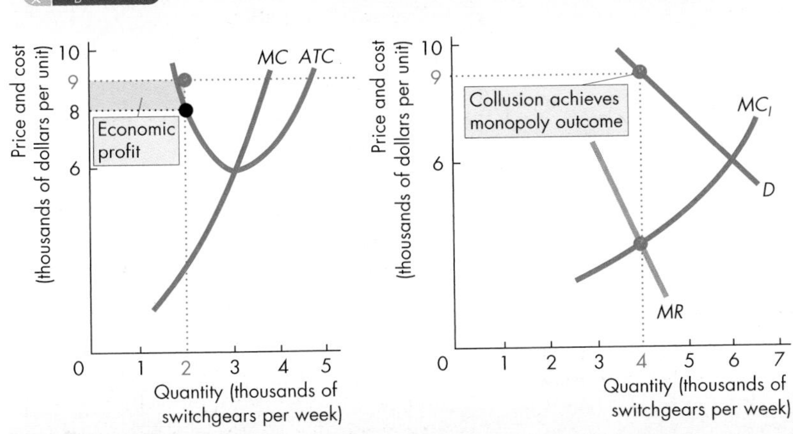

The industry marginal cost curve, MC_I in part (b), is the horizontal sum of the two firms' marginal cost curves, *MC* in part (a). The industry marginal revenue curve is *MR*. To maximize profit, the firms produce 4,000 units a week (the quantity at which marginal revenue equals marginal cost). They sell that output for $9,000 a unit. Each firm produces 2,000 units a week. Average total cost is $8,000 a unit, so each firm makes an economic profit of $2 million (blue rectangle)—2,000 units multiplied by $1,000 profit a unit.

One Firm Cheats on a Collusive Agreement To set the stage for cheating on their agreement, Trick convinces Gear that demand has decreased and that it cannot sell 2,000 units a week. Trick tells Gear that it plans to cut its price so that it can sell the agreed 2,000 units each week. Because the two firms produce an identical product, Gear matches Trick's price cut but still produces only 2,000 units a week.

In fact, there has been no decrease in demand. Trick plans to increase output, which it knows will lower the price, and Trick wants to ensure that Gear's output remains at the agreed level.

Figure 13.15 illustrates the consequences of Trick's cheating. Part (a) shows Gear (the complier); part (b) shows Trick (the cheat); and part (c) shows the industry as a whole. Suppose that Trick increases output to 3,000 units a week. If Gear sticks to the agreement to produce only 2,000 units a week, total output is 5,000 a week, and given demand in part (c), the price falls to $7,500 a unit.

Gear continues to produce 2,000 units a week at a cost of $8,000 a unit and incurs a loss of $500 a unit, or $1 million a week. This economic loss is shown by the red rectangle in part (a). Trick produces 3,000 units a week at an average total cost of $6,000 each. With a price of $7,500, Trick makes a profit of $1,500 a unit and therefore an economic profit of $4.5 million. This economic profit is the blue rectangle in part (b).

We've now described a second possible outcome for the duopoly game: One of the firms cheats on the collusive agreement. In this case, the industry output is larger than the monopoly output and the industry price is lower than the monopoly price. The total economic profit made by the industry is also smaller than the monopoly's economic profit. Trick (the cheat) makes an economic profit of $4.5 million, and Gear (the complier) incurs an economic loss of $1 million. The industry makes an economic profit of $3.5 million. This industry profit is $0.5 million less than the economic profit that a monopoly would make. But the profit is distributed unevenly. Trick makes a bigger economic profit than it would under the collusive agreement, while Gear incurs an economic loss.

A similar outcome would arise if Gear cheated and Trick complied with the agreement. The industry profit and price would be the same, but in this case, Gear (the cheat) would make an economic profit of $4.5 million and Trick (the complier) would incur an economic loss of $1 million.

Let's next see what happens if both firms cheat.

FIGURE 13.15 One Firm Cheats

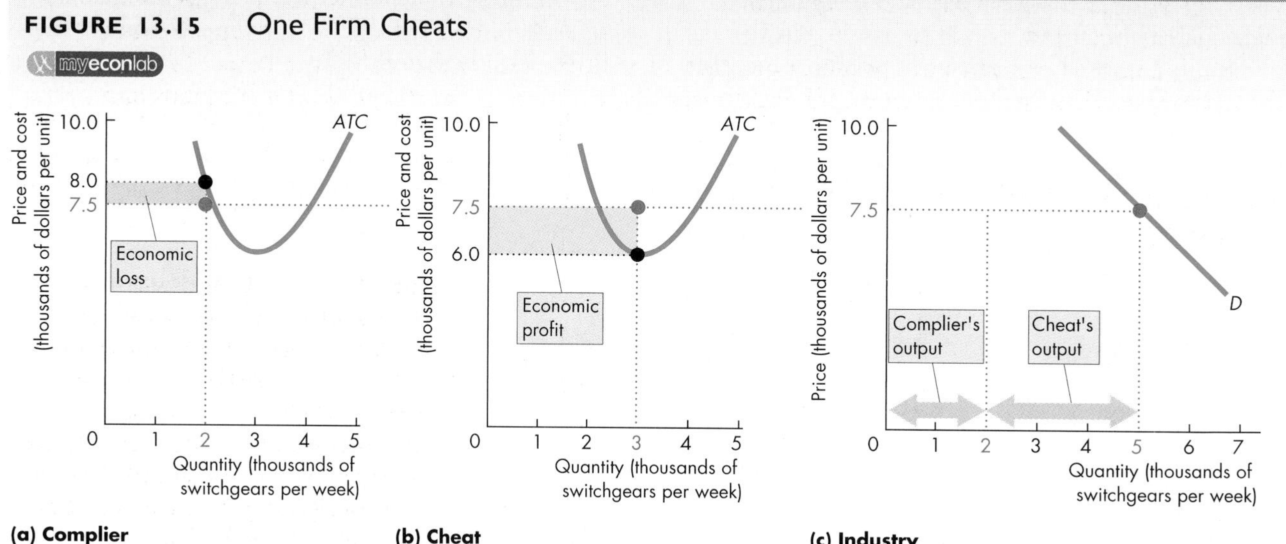

One firm, shown in part (a), complies with the agreement and produces 2,000 units. The other firm, shown in part (b), cheats on the agreement and increases its output to 3,000 units a week. Given the market demand curve, shown in part (c), and with a total production of 5,000 units a week, the price falls to $7,500 a unit. At this price, the complier in part (a) incurs an economic loss of $1 million ($500 per unit × 2,000 units), shown by the red rectangle. In part (b), the cheat makes an economic profit of $4.5 million ($1,500 per unit × 3,000 units), shown by the blue rectangle.

Both Firms Cheat Suppose that both firms cheat and that each firm behaves like the cheating firm that we have just analyzed. Each tells the other that it is unable to sell its output at the going price and that it plans to cut its price. But because both firms cheat, each will propose a successively lower price. As long as price exceeds marginal cost, each firm has an incentive to increase its production—to cheat. Only when price equals marginal cost is there no further incentive to cheat. This situation arises when the price has reached $6,000. At this price, marginal cost equals price. Also, price equals minimum average total cost. At a price less than $6,000, each firm incurs an economic loss. At a price of $6,000, each firm covers all its costs and makes zero economic profit. Also, at a price of $6,000, each firm wants to produce 3,000 units a week, so the industry output is 6,000 units a week. Given the demand conditions, 6,000 units can be sold at a price of $6,000 each.

Figure 13.16 illustrates the situation just described. Each firm, in part (a), produces 3,000 units a week, and its average total cost is a minimum ($6,000 per unit). The market as a whole, in part (b), operates at the point at which the market demand curve (*D*) intersects the industry marginal cost curve (MC_I). Each firm has lowered its price and increased its output to try to gain an advantage over the other firm. Each has pushed this process as far as it can without incurring an economic loss.

We have now described a third possible outcome of this duopoly game: Both firms cheat. If both firms cheat on the collusive agreement, the output of each firm is 3,000 units a week and the price is $6,000 a unit. Each firm makes zero economic profit.

The Payoff Matrix Now that we have described the strategies and payoffs in the duopoly game, we can summarize the strategies and the payoffs in the form of the game's payoff matrix. Then we can find the Nash equilibrium.

Table 13.2 sets out the payoff matrix for this game. It is constructed in the same way as the payoff matrix for the prisoners' dilemma in Table 13.1. The squares show the payoffs for the two firms—Gear and Trick. In this case, the payoffs are profits. (For the prisoners' dilemma, the payoffs were losses.)

The table shows that if both firms cheat (top left), they achieve the perfectly competitive outcome—each firm makes zero economic profit. If both firms comply (bottom right), the industry makes the monopoly profit and each firm makes an economic profit of $2 million. The top right and bottom left squares show the payoff if one firm cheats while the other complies. The firm that cheats makes an economic profit of $4.5 million, and the one that complies incurs a loss of $1 million.

Nash Equilibrium in the Duopolists' Dilemma The duopolists have a dilemma like the prisoners' dilemma. Do they comply or cheat? To answer this question, we must find the Nash equilibrium.

FIGURE 13.16 Both Firms Cheat

myeconlab

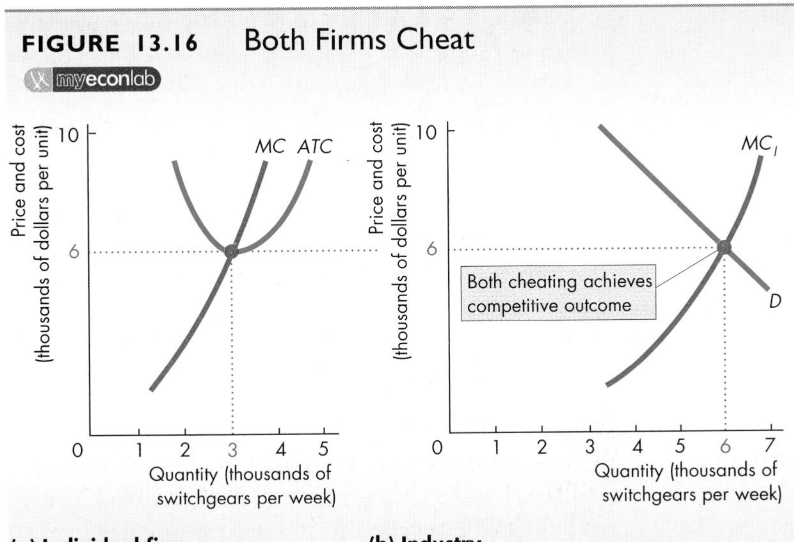

If both firms cheat by increasing production, the collusive agreement collapses. The limit to the collapse is the competitive equilibrium. Neither firm will cut price below $6,000 (minimum average total cost) because to do so will result in losses. In part (a), each firm produces 3,000 units a week at an average total cost of $6,000. In part (b), with a total production of 6,000 units, the price falls to $6,000. Each firm now makes zero economic profit. This output and price are the ones that would prevail in a competitive industry.

TABLE 13.2 Duopoly Payoff Matrix

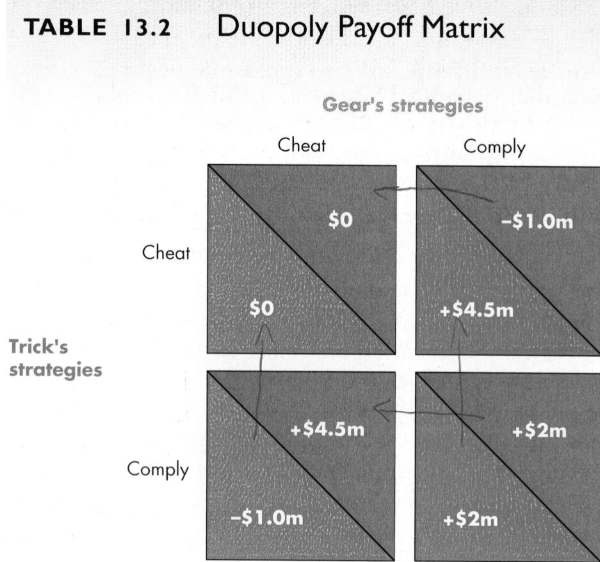

Each square shows the payoffs from a pair of actions. For example, if both firms comply with the collusive agreement, the payoffs are recorded in the bottom right square. The red triangle shows Gear's payoff, and the blue triangle shows Trick's. In Nash equilibrium, both firms cheat.

Look at things from Gear's point of view. Gear reasons as follows: Suppose that Trick cheats. If I comply, I will incur an economic loss of $1 million. If I also cheat, I will make zero economic profit. Zero is better than *minus* $1 million, so I'm better off if I cheat. Now suppose Trick complies. If I cheat, I will make an economic profit of $4.5 million, and if I comply, I will make an economic profit of $2 million. A $4.5 million profit is better than a $2 million profit, so I'm better off if I cheat. So regardless of whether Trick cheats or complies, it pays Gear to cheat. Cheating is Gear's best strategy.

Trick comes to the same conclusion as Gear because the two firms face an identical situation. So both firms cheat. The Nash equilibrium of the duopoly game is that both firms cheat. And although the industry has only two firms, they charge the same price and produce the same quantity as those in a competitive industry. Also, as in perfect competition, each firm makes zero economic profit.

This conclusion is not general and will not always arise. We'll see why not first by looking at some other games that are like the prisoners' dilemma. Then we'll broaden the types of games we consider.

Other Oligopoly Games

Firms in oligopoly must decide whether to mount expensive advertising campaigns; whether to modify their product; whether to make their product more reliable and more durable; whether to price discriminate and, if so, among which groups of customers and to what degree; whether to undertake a large research and development (R&D) effort aimed at lowering production costs; and whether to enter or leave an industry.

All of these choices can be analyzed as games that are similar to the one that we've just studied. Let's look at one example: an R&D game.

An R&D Game

Disposable diapers were first marketed in 1966. The two market leaders from the start of this industry have been Procter & Gamble (the maker of Pampers) and Kimberly-Clark (the maker of Huggies). Procter & Gamble has about 40 percent of the total market, and Kimberly-Clark has about 33 percent. When the disposable diaper was first introduced, it had to be cost-effective in competition with reusable, laundered diapers. A costly research and development effort resulted in the development of machines that could make disposable diapers at a low enough cost to achieve that initial competitive edge. But new firms tried to get into the business and take market share away from the two industry leaders, and the industry leaders themselves battled each other to maintain or increase their own market share.

During the early 1990s, Kimberly-Clark was the first to introduce Velcro closures. And in 1996, Procter & Gamble was the first to introduce "breathable" diapers into the U.S. market.

The key to success in this industry (as in any other) is to design a product that people value highly relative to the cost of producing them. The firm that creates the most highly valued product and also develops the least-cost technology for producing it gains a competitive edge, undercutting the rest of the market, increasing its market share, and increasing its profit. But the R&D that must be undertaken to achieve product improvements and cost reductions is costly. So the cost of R&D must be deducted from the profit resulting from the increased market share that lower costs achieve. If no firm does R&D, every firm can be better off, but if one firm initiates the R&D activity, all must follow.

Table 13.3 illustrates the dilemma (with hypothetical numbers) for the R&D game that Kimberly-Clark and Procter & Gamble play. Each firm has two strategies: Spend $25 million a year on R&D or spend nothing on R&D. If neither firm spends on R&D, they make a joint profit of $100 million: $30 million for Kimberly-Clark and $70 million for Procter & Gamble (bottom right of the payoff matrix). If each firm conducts R&D, market shares are maintained but each firm's profit is lower by the amount spent on R&D (top left square of the payoff matrix). If Kimberly-Clark pays for R&D but Procter & Gamble does not, Kimberly-Clark gains a large part of Procter & Gamble's market. Kimberly-Clark profits, and Procter & Gamble loses (top right square of the payoff matrix). Finally, if Procter & Gamble conducts R&D and Kimberly-Clark does not, Procter & Gamble gains market share from Kimberly-Clark, increasing its profit, while Kimberly-Clark incurs a loss (bottom left square).

TABLE 13.3 Pampers Versus Huggies: An R&D Game

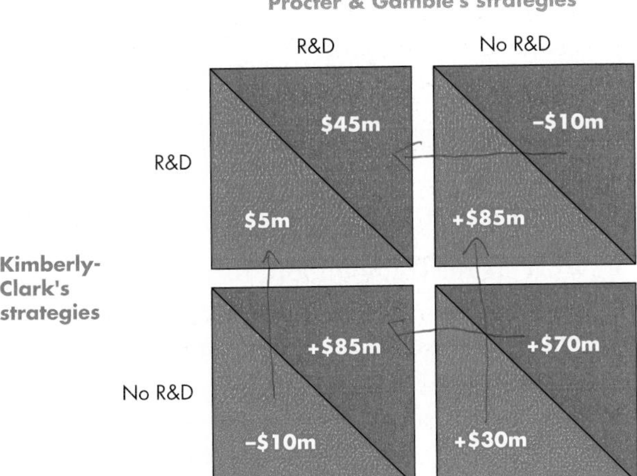

If both firms undertake R&D, their payoffs are those shown in the top left square. If neither firm undertakes R&D, their payoffs are in the bottom right square. When one firm undertakes R&D and the other one does not, their payoffs are in the top right and bottom left squares. The red triangle shows Procter & Gamble's payoff, and the blue triangle shows Kimberly-Clark's. The Nash equilibrium for this game is for both firms to undertake R&D. The structure of this game is the same as that of the prisoners' dilemma.

Confronted with the payoff matrix in Table 13.3, the two firms calculate their best strategies. Kimberly-Clark reasons as follows: If Procter & Gamble does not undertake R&D, we will make $85 million if we do and $30 million if we do not; so it pays us to conduct R&D. If Procter & Gamble conducts R&D, we will lose $10 million if we don't and make $5 million if we do. Again, R&D pays off. So conducting R&D is the best strategy for Kimberly-Clark. It pays, regardless of Procter & Gamble's decision.

Procter & Gamble reasons similarly: If Kimberly-Clark does not undertake R&D, we will make $70 million if we follow suit and $85 million if we conduct R&D. It therefore pays to conduct R&D. If Kimberly-Clark does undertake R&D, we will make $45 million by doing the same and lose $10 million by not doing R&D. Again, it pays us to conduct R&D. So for Procter & Gamble, R&D is also the best strategy.

Because R&D is the best strategy for both players, it is the Nash equilibrium. The outcome of this game is that both firms conduct R&D. They make less profit than they would if they could collude to achieve the cooperative outcome of no R&D.

The real-world situation has more players than Kimberly-Clark and Procter & Gamble. A large number of other firms share a small portion of the market, all of them ready to eat into the market share of Procter & Gamble and Kimberly-Clark. So the R&D effort by these two firms not only serves the purpose of maintaining shares in their own battle, but also helps to keep barriers to entry high enough to preserve their joint market share.

The Disappearing Invisible Hand

All the games that we've studied are versions of the prisoners' dilemma. The essence of that game lies in the structure of its payoffs. The worst possible outcome for each player arises from cooperating when the other player cheats. The best possible outcome, for each player to cooperate, is not a Nash equilibrium because it is in neither player's *self-interest* to cooperate if the other one cooperates. It is this failure to achieve the best outcome for both players—the best social outcome if the two players are the entire economy—that led John Nash to claim (as he was portrayed as doing in the movie *A Beautiful Mind*) that he had challenged Adam Smith's idea that we are always guided, as if by an invisible hand, to promote the social interest when we are pursuing our self-interest.

A Game of Chicken

The Nash equilibrium for the prisoners' dilemma is called a **dominant strategy equilibrium**, which is an equilibrium in which the best strategy of each player is to cheat (deny) *regardless of the strategy of the other player*. Not all games have such an equilibrium, and one that doesn't is a game called "chicken."

In a graphic, if disturbing, version of this game, two cars race toward each other. The first driver to swerve and avoid a crash is "chicken." The payoffs are a big loss for both if no one "chickens," zero for the chicken, and a gain for the player who hangs tough.

If player 1 chickens, player 2's best strategy is to hang tough. And if player 1 hangs tough, player 2's best strategy is to chicken.

For an economic form of this game, suppose the R&D that creates a new diaper technology results in information that cannot be kept secret or patented, so both firms benefit from the R&D of either firm. The chicken in this case is the firm that does the R&D.

Table 13.4 illustrates a payoff matrix for an R&D game of chicken between Kimberly-Clark and Procter & Gamble. Each firm has two strategies: Do the R&D (and "chicken") or do not do the R&D (and hang tough).

If neither "chickens," there is no R&D and each firm makes zero additional profit. If each firm conducts R&D—each "chickens"—each firm makes $5 million (the profit from the new technology minus the cost of the research). If one of the firms does the R&D, the payoffs are $1 million for the chicken and $10 million for the one who hangs tough.

Confronted with the payoff matrix in Table 13.4, the two firms calculate their best strategies. Kimberly-Clark is better off doing R&D if Procter & Gamble does not undertake it. Procter & Gamble is better off doing R&D if Kimberly-Clark doesn't do it. There are two equilibrium outcomes: One firm does the R&D, but we can't predict which firm it will be.

You can see that it isn't a Nash equilibrium if no firm does the R&D because one firm would then be better off doing it. And you can see that it isn't a Nash equilibrium if both firms do the R&D because then one firm would be better off not doing it.

The firms could toss a coin or use some other random device to make a decision in this game. In some circumstances, such a strategy—called a mixed strategy—is actually better for both firms than choosing any of the strategies we've considered.

TABLE 13.4 An R&D Game of Chicken

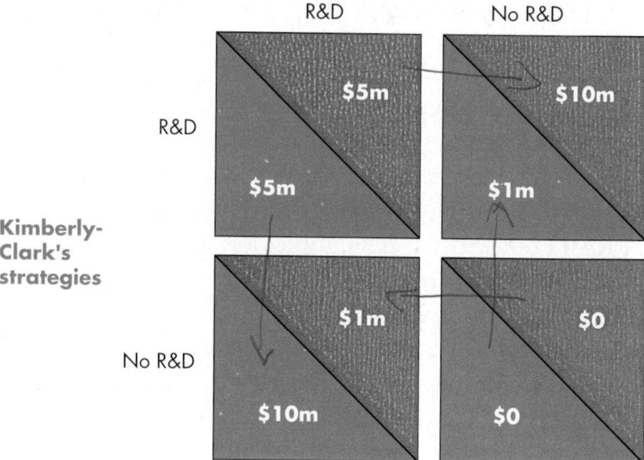

If both firms undertake R&D, their payoffs are those shown in the top left square. If neither firm undertakes R&D, their payoffs are in the bottom right square. When one firm undertakes R&D and the other one does not, their payoffs are in the top right and bottom left squares. The red triangle shows Procter & Gamble's payoff, and the blue triangle shows Kimberly-Clark's. The equilibrium for this R&D game of chicken is for only one firm to undertake R&D. We cannot tell which firm will do the R&D and which will not.

REVIEW QUIZ

1. What are the common features of all games?
2. Describe the prisoners' dilemma game and explain why the Nash equilibrium delivers a bad outcome for both players.
3. Why does a collusive agreement to restrict output and raise price create a game like the prisoners' dilemma?
4. What creates an incentive for firms in a collusive agreement to cheat and increase production?
5. What is the equilibrium strategy for each firm in a duopolists' dilemma and why do the firms not succeed in colluding to raise the price and profits?
6. Describe two structures of payoffs for an R&D game and contrast the prisoners' dilemma and chicken game.

myeconlab Study Plan 13.6

Repeated Games and Sequential Games

The games that we've studied are played just once. In contrast, many real-world games are played repeatedly. This feature of games turns out to enable real-world duopolists to cooperate, collude, and make a monopoly profit.

Another feature of the games that we've studied is that the players move simultaneously. But in many real-world situations, one player moves first and then the other moves—the play is sequential rather than simultaneous. This feature of real-world games creates a large number of possible outcomes.

We're now going to examine these two aspects of strategic decision-making.

A Repeated Duopoly Game

If two firms play a game repeatedly, one firm has the opportunity to penalize the other for previous "bad" behavior. If Gear cheats this week, perhaps Trick will cheat next week. Before Gear cheats this week, won't it consider the possibility that Trick will cheat next week? What is the equilibrium of this game?

Actually, there is more than one possibility. One is the Nash equilibrium that we have just analyzed. Both players cheat, and each makes zero economic profit forever. In such a situation, it will never pay one of the players to start complying unilaterally because to do so would result in a loss for that player and a profit for the other. But a **cooperative equilibrium** in which the players make and share the monopoly profit is possible.

A cooperative equilibrium might occur if cheating is punished. There are two extremes of punishment. The smallest penalty is called "tit for tat." A *tit-for-tat strategy* is one in which a player cooperates in the current period if the other player cooperated in the previous period but cheats in the current period if the other player cheated in the previous period. The most severe form of punishment is called a trigger strategy. A *trigger strategy* is one in which a player cooperates if the other player cooperates but plays the Nash equilibrium strategy forever thereafter if the other player cheats.

In the duopoly game between Gear and Trick, a tit-for-tat strategy keeps both players cooperating and making monopoly profits. Let's see why with an example.

Table 13.5 shows the economic profit that Trick and Gear will make over a number of periods under two alternative sequences of events: colluding and cheating with a tit-for-tat response by the other firm.

If both firms stick to the collusive agreement in period 1, each makes an economic profit of $2 million. Suppose that Trick contemplates cheating in period 1. The cheating produces a quick $4.5 million economic profit and inflicts a $1 million economic loss on Gear. But a cheat in period 1 produces a response from Gear in period 2. If Trick wants to get back into a profit-making situation, it must return to the agreement in period 2 even though it knows that Gear will punish it for cheating in period 1. So in period 2, Gear punishes Trick and Trick cooperates. Gear now makes an economic profit of $4.5 million, and Trick incurs an economic loss of $1 million. Adding up the profits over two periods of play, Trick would have made more profit by cooperating—$4 million compared with $3.5 million.

What is true for Trick is also true for Gear. Because each firm makes a larger profit by sticking with the collusive agreement, both firms do so and the monopoly price, quantity, and profit prevail.

In reality, whether a cartel works like a one-play game or a repeated game depends primarily on the

TABLE 13.5 Cheating with Punishment

	Collude		Cheat with tit-for-tat	
Period of play	Trick's profit (millions of dollars)	Gear's profit (millions of dollars)	Trick's profit (millions of dollars)	Gear's profit (millions of dollars)
1	2	2	4.5	−1.0
2	2	2	−1.0	4.5
3	2	2	2.0	2.0
4	.	.	.	.

If duopolists repeatedly collude, each makes a profit of $2 million per period of play. If one player cheats in period 1, the other player plays a tit-for-tat strategy and cheats in period 2. The profit from cheating can be made for only one period and must be paid for in the next period by incurring a loss. Over two periods of play, the best that a duopolist can achieve by cheating is a profit of $3.5 million, compared to an economic profit of $4 million by colluding.

number of players and the ease of detecting and punishing cheating. The larger the number of players, the harder it is to maintain a cartel.

Games and Price Wars A repeated duopoly game can help us understand real-world behavior and, in particular, price wars. Some price wars can be interpreted as the implementation of a tit-for-tat strategy. But the game is a bit more complicated than the one we've looked at because the players are uncertain about the demand for the product.

Playing a tit-for-tat strategy, firms have an incentive to stick to the monopoly price. But fluctuations in demand lead to fluctuations in the monopoly price, and sometimes, when the price changes, it might seem to one of the firms that the price has fallen because the other has cheated. In this case, a price war will break out. The price war will end only when each firm is satisfied that the other is ready to cooperate again. There will be cycles of price wars and the restoration of collusive agreements. Fluctuations in the world price of oil might be interpreted in this way.

Some price wars arise from the entry of a small number of firms into an industry that had previously been a monopoly. Although the industry has a small number of firms, the firms are in a prisoners' dilemma and they cannot impose effective penalties for price cutting. The behavior of prices and outputs in the computer chip industry during 1995 and 1996 can be explained in this way. Until 1995, the market for Pentium chips for IBM-compatible computers was dominated by one firm, Intel Corporation, which was able to make maximum economic profit by producing the quantity of chips at which marginal cost equaled marginal revenue. The price of Intel's chips was set to ensure that the quantity demanded equaled the quantity produced. Then in 1995 and 1996, with the entry of a small number of new firms, the industry became an oligopoly. If the firms had maintained Intel's price and shared the market, together they could have made economic profits equal to Intel's profit. But the firms were in a prisoners' dilemma. So prices fell toward the competitive level.

Let's now study a sequential game. There are many such games, and the one we'll examine is among the simplest. It has an interesting implication and it will give you the flavor of this type of game. The sequential game that we'll study is an entry game in a contestable market.

A Sequential Entry Game in a Contestable Market

If two firms play a sequential game, one firm makes a decision at the first stage of the game and the other makes a decision at the second stage.

We're going to study a sequential game in a **contestable market**—a market in which firms can enter and leave so easily that firms in the market face competition from *potential* entrants. Examples of contestable markets are routes served by airlines and by barge companies that operate on the major waterways. These markets are contestable because firms could enter if an opportunity for economic profit arose and could exit with no penalty if the opportunity for economic profit disappeared.

If the Herfindahl-Hirschman Index (p. 208) is used to determine the degree of competition, a contestable market appears to be uncompetitive. But a contestable market can behave as if it were perfectly competitive. To see why, let's look at an entry game for a contestable air route.

A Contestable Air Route Agile Air is the only firm operating on a particular route. Demand and cost conditions are such that there is room for only one airline to operate. Wanabe, Inc., is another airline that could offer services on the route.

We describe the structure of a sequential game by using a *game tree* like that in Fig. 13.17. At the first stage, Agile Air must set a price. Once the price is set and advertised, Agile can't change it. That is, once set, Agile's price is fixed and Agile can't react to Wanabe's entry decision. Agile can set its price at either the monopoly level or the competitive level.

At the second stage, Wanabe must decide whether to enter or to stay out. Customers have no loyalty (there are no frequent flyer programs) and they buy from the lowest-price firm. So if Wanabe enters, it sets a price just below Agile's and takes all the business.

Figure 13.17 shows the payoffs from the various decisions (Agile's in the red triangles and Wanabe's in the blue triangles).

To decide on its price, Agile's CEO reasons as follows: Suppose that Agile sets the monopoly price. If Wanabe enters, it earns 90 (think of all payoff numbers as thousands of dollars). If Wanabe stays out, it earns nothing. So Wanabe will enter. In this case Agile will lose 50.

FIGURE 13.17 Agile Versus Wanabe: A Sequential Entry Game in a Contestable Market

myeconlab

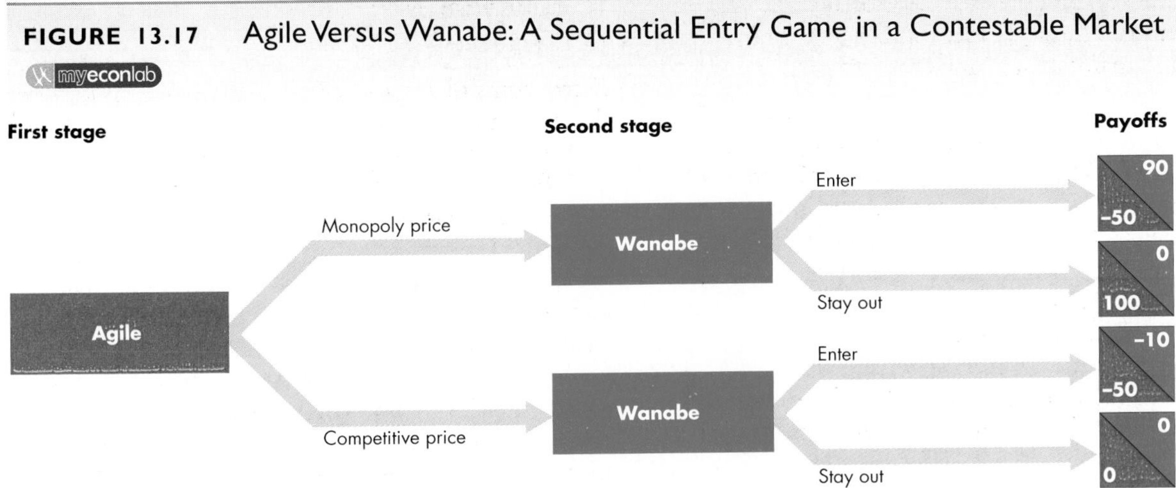

If Agile sets the monopoly price, Wanabe makes 90 (thousand dollars) by entering and earns nothing by staying out. So if Agile sets the monopoly price, Wanabe enters.

If Agile sets the competitive price, Wanabe earns nothing if it stays out and incurs a loss if it enters. So if Agile sets the competitive price, Wanabe stays out.

Now suppose that Agile sets the competitive price. If Wanabe stays out, it earns nothing and if it enters, it loses 10, so Wanabe will stay out. In this case, Agile will make zero economic profit.

Agile's best strategy is to set its price at the competitive level and make zero economic profit. The option of earning 100 by setting the monopoly price with Wanabe staying out is not available to Agile. If Agile sets the monopoly price, Wanabe enters, undercuts Agile, and takes all the business.

In this example, Agile sets its price at the competitive level and makes zero economic profit. A less costly strategy, called **limit pricing**, sets the price at the highest level that inflicts a loss on the entrant. Any loss is big enough to deter entry, so it is not always necessary to set the price as low as the competitive price. In the example of Agile and Wanabe, at the competitive price, Wanabe incurs a loss of 10 if it enters. A smaller loss would still keep Wanabe out.

This game is interesting because it points to the possibility of a monopoly behaving like a competitive industry and serving the social interest without regulation. But the result is not general and depends on one crucial feature of the setup of the game: At the second stage, Agile is locked into the price set at the first stage.

If Agile could change its price in the second stage, it would want to set the monopoly price if Wanabe stayed out—100 with the monopoly price beats zero with the competitive price. But Wanabe can figure out what Agile would do, so the price set at the first stage has no effect on Wanabe. Agile sets the monopoly price and Wanabe might either stay out or enter.

We've looked at two of the many possible repeated and sequential games, and you've seen how these types of game can provide insights into the complex forces that determine prices and profits.

REVIEW QUIZ

1. If a prisoners' dilemma game is played repeatedly, what punishment strategies might the players employ and how does playing the game repeatedly change the equilibrium?
2. If a market is contestable, how does the equilibrium differ from that of a monopoly?

myeconlab **Study Plan 13.7**

Monopolistic competition and oligopoly are the most common market structures that you encounter in your daily life. *Reading Between the Lines* on pp. 312–313 looks at a game played by Dell and HP in the market for personal computers.

So far, except for a brief look at monopoly policy issues at the end of Chapter 12, we've studied unregulated market power. Your task in the next chapter is to see how regulation and U.S. antitrust law influence market power.

READING BETWEEN THE LINES

Dell and HP in a Market Share Game

http://www.nytimes.com

The Old Price-War Tactic May Not Faze Rivals Now

May 13, 2006

Dell is sharply reducing prices on its computers.

The tactic is classic, straight out of the playbook that made the company the world's largest computer maker. As overall demand for personal computers slows, lower your prices. Profit margins will take a temporary hit, but the move would hurt competitors worse as you take market share and enjoy revenue growth for years to come.

Dell did it in 2000 and it worked beautifully. But after Dell rolled out the plan last month, knocking as much as $700 off a $1,200 Inspiron and $500 off a $1,079 Dimension desktop, many of the securities analysts who follow the company, based in Round Rock, Tex., said that this time around it could be folly. . . .

What changed? . . . More than anything else, Dell's competitors have changed. In particular, Hewlett-Packard is no longer the bloated and slow-moving company it was six years ago. . . .

The most telling evidence of the new landscape for PCs was seen in statistics on worldwide shipments. While the industry grew 12.9 percent in the first three months of the year, . . . Dell's shipments grew 10.2 percent. It was the first time since analysts began tracking Dell that its shipments grew more slowly than the industry's. Hewlett's shipments, meanwhile, grew 22.2 percent. . . .

Inside Hewlett, however, there is a feeling that it can beat Dell without resorting to price wars. . . . The company has started an ambitious marketing campaign to make that point with ads that proclaim, "the computer is personal again." . . .

The campaign . . . will feature celebrities and how they individualize their computers . . . [HP] has added technology like QuickPlay, which lets a user view a DVD or listen to a CD without waiting for the laptop's operating system to boot up. The ads will say, "Don't boot. Play." . . .

Essence of the Story

- In April 2006, Dell slashed its prices.
- Dell cut its prices in 2000 and increased its market share and revenue in the years that followed.
- But experts say the price cut will not work as well today.
- Hewlett-Packard (HP) is much stronger than it was six years ago.
- Total PC shipments increased by 12.9 percent in the first quarter of 2006: Dell's shipments increased by 10.2 percent, and HP's increased by 22.2 percent.
- HP says that it can beat Dell without a price cut. Instead it will launch a campaign to market PCs with new and improved features that play DVDs and CDs without booting the operating system.

Economic Analysis

- The global PC market has many firms, but two firms dominate the market: Dell and Hewlett-Packard (HP).

- Figure 1 shows the market shares in the global PC market. You can see that Dell and HP are the two biggest players but that almost 50 percent of the market is served by small firms.

- Table 1 shows the payoff matrix (millions of dollars of profit) for the game played by Dell and HP in 2000. (The numbers are hypothetical.)

- This game has a dominant strategy equilibrium similar to that for the duopoly game on p. 306.

- If HP cuts its price, Dell makes a larger profit by cutting its price (+$10m versus –$10m), and if HP holds its price constant, Dell again makes a larger profit by cutting its price (+$40m versus zero).

- So Dell's best strategy is to cut its price.

- If Dell cuts its price, HP makes a larger profit by cutting its price (+$5m versus –$20m), and if Dell holds its price constant, HP again makes a larger profit by cutting its price (+$10m versus zero).

- So HP's best strategy is to cut its price.

- Table 2 shows the payoffs from the game between Dell and HP in 2006.

- This game, too, has a dominant strategy equilibrium.

- If HP cuts its price, Dell makes a larger profit by cutting its price (+$10m versus –$10m), and if HP improves its marketing and design, Dell again makes a larger profit by cutting its price (+$5m versus –$20m).

- So Dell's best strategy is to cut its price.

- If Dell cuts its price, HP makes a larger profit by improving its marketing and design (+$20m versus +$10m), and if Dell holds its price constant, HP again makes a larger profit by improving its marketing and design (+$40m versus +$20m).

- So HP's best strategy is to improve its marketing and design.

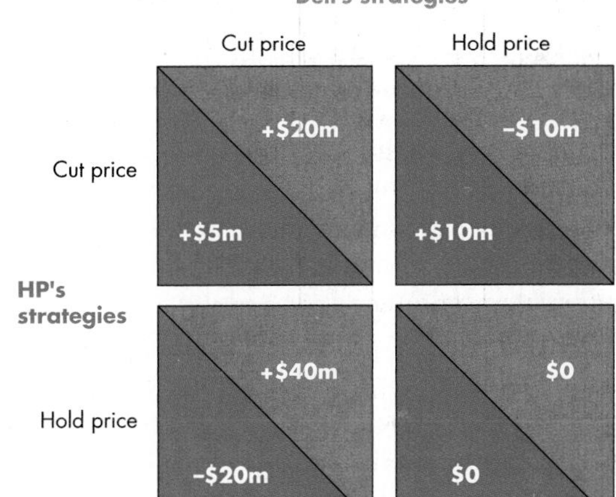

HP's strategies \ Dell's strategies	Cut price	Hold price
Cut price	+$20m / +$5m	–$10m / +$10m
Hold price	+$40m / –$20m	$0 / $0

Table 1 The strategies and equilibrium in 2000

HP's strategies \ Dell's strategies	Cut price	Hold price
Cut price	+$10m / +$10m	–$10m / +$20m
Improve marketing and design	+$5m / +$20m	–$20m / +$40m

Table 2 The strategies and equilibrium in 2006

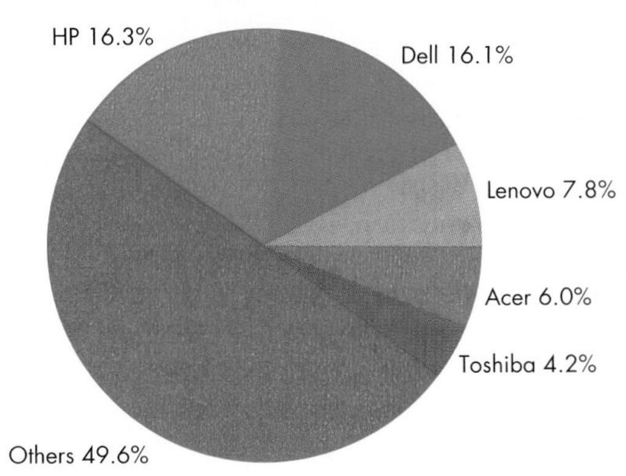

Figure 1 Market shares in the PC market in 2006

SUMMARY

Key Points

What Is Monopolistic Competition? (pp. 286–287)

- Monopolistic competition occurs when a large number of firms compete with each other on product quality, price, and marketing.

Price and Output in Monopolistic Competition (pp. 288–291)

- Each firm in monopolistic competition faces a downward-sloping demand curve and produces the profit-maximizing quantity.
- Entry and exit result in zero economic profit and excess capacity in long-run equilibrium.

Product Development and Marketing (pp. 292–295)

- Firms in monopolistic competition innovate and develop new products.
- Advertising expenditures increase total cost, but average total cost might fall if the quantity sold increases by enough.
- Advertising expenditures might increase demand, but demand might decrease if competition increases.
- Whether monopolistic competition is inefficient depends on the value we place on product variety.

What Is Oligopoly? (pp. 296–297)

- Oligopoly is a market in which a small number of firms compete.

Two Traditional Oligopoly Models (pp. 298–299)

- If rivals match price cuts but do not match price hikes, each firm faces a kinked demand curve.
- If one firm dominates a market, it acts like a monopoly and the small firms act as price takers.

Oligopoly Games (pp. 300–308)

- Oligopoly is studied by using game theory, which is a method of analyzing strategic behavior.
- In a prisoners' dilemma game, two prisoners acting in their own interest harm their joint interest.
- An oligopoly (duopoly) price-fixing game is a prisoners' dilemma in which the firms might collude or cheat.
- In Nash equilibrium, both firms cheat and output and price are the same as in perfect competition.
- Firms' decisions about advertising and R&D can be studied by using game theory.

Repeated Games and Sequential Games (pp. 309–311)

- In a repeated game, a punishment strategy can produce a cooperative equilibrium in which price and output are the same as in a monopoly.
- In a sequential contestable market game, a small number of firms can behave like firms in perfect competition.

Key Figures and Tables

Key Terms

PROBLEMS

myeconlab **Tests, Study Plan, Solutions***

1. The figure shows the situation facing Lite and Kool, Inc., a producer of running shoes.

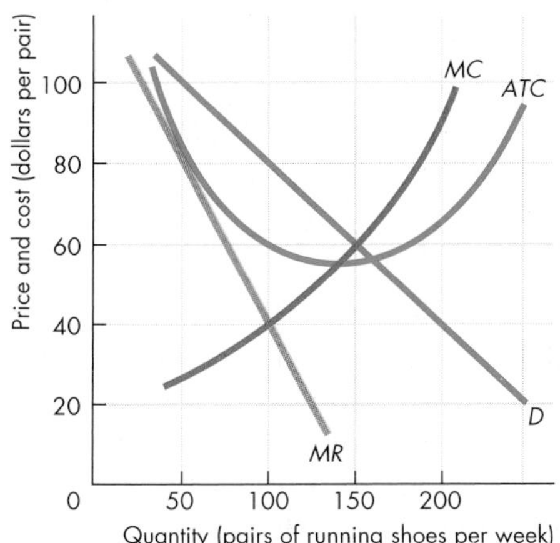

   a. What quantity does Lite and Kool produce?
   b. What is the price of a pair of Lite and Kool shoes?
   c. How much economic profit does Lite and Kool make?
2. In the market for running shoes, all the firms face a similar demand curve and have similar cost curves to those of Lite and Kool in problem 1.
   a. What happens to the price of running shoes in the long run?
   b. What happens to the quantity of running shoes produced by Lite and Kool in the long run?
   c. What happens to the quantity of running shoes in the entire market in the long run?
   d. Does Lite and Kool produce at minimum average total cost in the long run? Explain your answer.
   e. What is the relationship between Lite and Kool's price and marginal cost?
3. Suppose that Tommy Hilfiger's marginal cost of a jacket is $100 and at one of the firm's shops, total fixed cost is $2,000 a day. The profit-maximizing number of jackets sold in this shop is 20 a day. Then the shops nearby start to advertise their jackets. The Tommy Hilfiger shop now spends $2,000 a day advertising its jackets, and its profit-maximizing number of jackets sold jumps to 50 a day.
   a. What is this shop's average total cost of a jacket sold before the advertising begins?
   b. What is this shop's average total cost of a jacket sold after the advertising begins?
   c. Can you say what happens to the price of a Tommy Hilfiger jacket? Why or why not?
   d. Can you say what happens to Tommy's markup? Why or why not?
   e. Can you say what happens to Tommy's economic profit? Why or why not?
4. Two firms make most of the chips that power a PC: Intel and Advanced Micro Devices. What makes the market for PC chips a duopoly? Sketch the market demand curve and cost curves that describe the situation in this market and that prevent other firms from entering.
5. The price at which Wal-Mart can buy flat panel TVs has fallen, and the firm is making a decision about whether to lower its selling price. It believes that if it lowers its price, all its competitors will lower their prices too. Wal-Mart also believes that if it raises its price, none of its competitors would raise theirs.
   a. Draw a figure to illustrate the situation that Wal-Mart believes it faces in the market for flat panel TVs.
   b. Do you predict that Wal-Mart will lower its flat-panel TV prices? Explain and illustrate your answer.
6. Big Joe's Trucking has lower costs than the other 20 small truckers in the market. The market operates like a dominant firm oligopoly and is initially in equilibrium. Then the demand for trucking services increases. Explain the effects of the increase in demand on the price, output, and economic profit of
   a. Big Joe's.
   b. A typical small firm.
7. Consider a game with two players and in which each player is asked a question. The players can answer the question honestly or lie. If both answer honestly, each receives $100. If one answers honestly and the other lies, the liar receives $500 and the honest player gets nothing. If both lie, then each receives $50.
   a. Describe strategies and payoffs of this game.

*Solutions to odd-numbered problems are provided.

b. Construct the payoff matrix.
c. What is the equilibrium of this game?
d. Compare this game to the prisoners' dilemma. Are the two games similar or different? Explain your answer.

8. Soapy, Inc. and Suddies, Inc. are the only producers of soap powder. They collude and agree to share the market equally. If neither firm cheats on the agreement, each makes $1 million profit. If either firm cheats, the cheat makes a profit of $1.5 million, while the complier incurs a loss of $0.5 million. If both cheat, they break even. Neither firm can monitor the other's actions.
   a. What are the strategies in this game?
   b. Construct the payoff matrix for this game.
   c. What is the equilibrium of this game if it is played only once?
   d. Is the equilibrium a dominant strategy equilibrium? Explain.
9. If Soapy, Inc. and Suddies, Inc. repeatedly play the duopoly game that has the payoffs described in problem 8 on each round of play,
   a. What now are the strategies that each firm might adopt?
   b. Does the game now have a cooperative equilibrium?
   c. If the payoffs from one firm cheating changed to a profit of $1.4 million for the cheat and a loss of $0.5 million for the complier, would the game have a cooperative equilibrium?

CRITICAL THINKING

1. Study *Reading Between the Lines* on pp. 312– 313 and then answer the following questions.
   a. What are the strategies of Dell and HP in 2000 and in 2006?
   b. Why, according to the news article, was Dell having a harder time in 2006 than it had in 2000?
   c. Why wouldn't HP launch its new product and marketing campaign *and* cut its price?
   d. What do you think Dell must do to restore its place as market leader?
   e. How would you describe the global market for PCs? Is it an example of oligopoly or monopolistic competition?
2. Suppose that Netscape and Microsoft each develop their own versions of an amazing new Web browser that allows advertisers to target consumers with great precision. Also, the new browser is easier and more fun to use than existing browsers. Each firm is trying to decide whether to sell the browser or to give it away. What are the likely benefits from each action? Which action is likely to occur?
3. Why do Coca-Cola and PepsiCo spend huge amounts on advertising? Do they benefit? Does the consumer benefit? Explain your answer.
4. Microsoft with Xbox 360, Nintendo with Wii, and Sony with PlayStation 3 are slugging it out in the market for the latest generation of video games consoles. Xbox 360 was the first to market; Wii has the lowest price; PS3 uses the most advanced technology and has the highest price.
   a. Describe the competition among these firms in the market for consoles as a game.
   b. What are the strategies in this game concerning design, marketing, and price?
   c. What turned out to be the equilibrium of the game?
   d. Can you think of reasons why the three consoles are so different?

WEB ACTIVITIES

myeconlab Links to Web sites

1. Obtain information about the market for vitamins.
   a. In what type of market are vitamins sold?
   b. What illegal act occurred in the vitamins market during the 1990s?
   c. Describe the actions of BASF and Roche as a game and set out a hypothetical payoff matrix for the game.
   d. Is the game played by BASF and Roche a one-shot game or a repeated game? How do you know which type of game it is?
2. Obtain information about the market for art and antiques.
   a. What illegal act occurred in the art and antiques auction market during the 1990s?
   b. Describe the game played by Sotheby's and Christie's and set out a payoff matrix.

Managing Change

Our economy is constantly changing. Every year, new goods appear and old ones disappear. New firms are born, and old ones die. This process of change is initiated and managed by firms operating in markets. When a new product is invented, just one or two firms sell it initially. For example, when the personal computer first became available, there was an Apple or an IBM. The IBM-PC had just one operating system, DOS, made by Microsoft. One firm, Intel, made the chip that ran the IBM-PC. These are examples of industries in which the producer has market power to determine the price of the product and the quantity produced. The extreme case of a single producer that cannot be challenged by new competitors is *monopoly*, which Chapter 12 explained.

But not all industries with just one producer are monopolies. In many cases, the firm that is first to produce a new good faces severe competition from new rivals. One firm facing potential competition is the case of a *contestable market*. If demand increases and makes space for more than one firm, an industry becomes increasingly competitive. Even with just two rivals, the industry changes its face in a dramatic way. *Duopoly* —the case of just two producers—illustrates this dramatic change. The two firms must pay close attention to each other's production and prices and must predict the effects of their own actions on the actions of the other firm. We call this situation one of *strategic interdependence*. As the number of rivals grows, the industry becomes an *oligopoly*, a market in which a small number of firms devise strategies and pay close attention to the strategies of their competitors.

With the continued arrival of new firms in an industry, the market eventually becomes competitive. Competition might be limited because each firm produces its own special version or brand of a good. This case is called *monopolistic competition* because it has elements of both monopoly and competition. Chapter 13 explored the behavior of firms in all of these types of markets that lie between monopoly at the one extreme and perfect competition at the other.

When competition is extreme—the case that we call *perfect competition*—the market changes again in a dramatic way. Now the firm is unable to influence the price. Chapter 11 explained this case.

Often, an industry that is competitive becomes less so as the bigger and more successful firms in the industry begin to swallow up the smaller firms, either by driving them out of business or by acquiring their assets. Through this process, an industry might return to oligopoly or even monopoly. You can see such a movement in the auto and banking industries today.

By studying firms and markets, we gain a deeper understanding of the forces that allocate scarce resources and begin to see the anatomy of the invisible hand.

Many economists have advanced our understanding of these forces, and we'll now meet two of them. John von Neumann pioneered game theory, and Drew Fudenberg is one of today's leading students of strategic behavior.

PROBING THE IDEAS

Market Power

"Real life consists of bluffing, of little tactics of deception, of asking yourself what is the other man going to think I mean to do."

JOHN VON NEUMANN, told to Jacob Bronowski (in a London taxi) and reported in *The Ascent of Man*

The Economist

John von Neumann *was one of the great minds of the twentieth century. Born in Budapest, Hungary, in 1903, Johnny, as he was known, showed early mathematical brilliance. His first mathematical publication was an article that grew out of a lesson with his tutor, which he wrote at the age of 18! But it was at the age of 25, in 1928, that von Neumann published the article that began a flood of research on game theory—a flood that has still not subsided today. In that article, he proved that in a zero-sum game (such as sharing a pie), there exists a best strategy for each player.*

Von Neumann invented the computer and built the first modern practical computer, and he worked on the Manhattan Project, which developed the atomic bomb at Los Alamos, New Mexico, during World War II.

Von Neumann believed that the social sciences would progress only if they used mathematical tools. But he believed that they needed different tools from those developed from the physical sciences.

The Issues

It is not surprising that firms with market power will charge higher prices than those charged by competitive firms. But how much higher?

This question has puzzled generations of economists. Adam Smith said, "The price of a monopoly is upon every occasion the highest which can be got." But he was wrong. Antoine-Augustin Cournot (see p. 148) first worked out the price a monopoly will charge. It is not the "highest which can be got" but the price that maximizes profit. Cournot's work was not appreciated until almost a century later when Joan Robinson explained how a monopoly sets its price.

Questions about monopoly became urgent and practical during the 1870s, a time when rapid technological change and falling transportation costs enabled huge monopolies to emerge in the United States. Monopolies dominated oil, steel, railroads, tobacco, and even sugar. Industrial empires grew ever larger.

The success of the nineteenth century monopolies led to the creation of our antitrust laws—laws that limit the use of market power. Those laws have been used to prevent monopolies from being set up and to break up existing monopolies. They were used during the 1960s to end a conspiracy between General Electric, Westinghouse, and other firms when they colluded to fix their prices instead of competing with each other. The laws were used during the 1980s to bring greater competition to long-distance telecommunication. But in spite of antitrust laws, near monopolies still exist. Among the most prominent today are those in computer chips and operating systems. Like their forerunners, today's near monopolies make huge profits. But unlike the situation in the nineteenth century, the technological change taking place today is strengthening the forces of competition. Today's information technologies are creating substitutes for services that previously had none. Direct satellite TV is competing with cable, and new phone companies are competing with the traditional phone monopolies.

Then

Ruthless greed, exploitation of both workers and customers—these are the traditional images of monopolies and the effects of their market power. These images appeared to be an accurate description during the 1880s, when monopolies stood at their peak of power and influence. One monopolist, John D. Rockefeller, Sr., built his giant Standard Oil Company, which by 1879 was refining 90 percent of the nation's oil and controlling its entire pipeline capacity.

Now

Despite antitrust laws that regulate monopolies, they still exist. One is the monopoly in cable television. In many cities, one firm decides which channels viewers will receive and the price they will pay. During the 1980s, with the advent of satellite technology and specialist cable program producers such as CNN and HBO, the cable companies expanded their offerings. At the same time, they steadily increased prices and their businesses became very profitable. But the very technologies that made cable television profitable are now challenging its market power. Direct satellite TV services and TV services via the Internet are eroding cable's monopoly and bringing greater competition to this market.

Today, many economists who work on microeconomics use the ideas that John von Neumann pioneered. Game theory is the tool of choice. One economist who has made good use of this tool and done much to refine it is Drew Fudenberg of Harvard University, whom you can meet on the following pages.

TALKING WITH

Drew Fudenberg

Drew Fudenberg is the Frederic E. Abbe Professor of Economics at Harvard University. Born in New York City in 1957, he studied applied mathematics at Harvard and economics at M.I.T., where he was awarded a Ph.D. in 1981. He began his research and teaching career at the University of California, Berkeley, and moved to M.I.T. in 1987 and to Harvard in 1993.

Professor Fudenberg is a leading game theorist and has worked on an incredibly wide range of problems that arise in games when players don't have enough information to play in the way they play the games that we describe in Chapter 13. This work has resulted in more than 60 articles and two major books: with Jean Tirole, Game Theory *(MIT Press, 1991) and with David K. Levine,* The Theory of Learning in Games *(MIT Press, 1998).*

Michael Parkin talked with Drew Fudenberg about his career, the promise held by game theory, and some of the results of his research.

Professor Fudenberg, was math a better undergraduate major than economics for a career in economics?

Math is a good preparation for graduate study in economics, particularly for economic theory, in part because some of the results are useful but mostly because it provides good training in abstract thinking and rigorous arguments.

That said, I didn't major in math but in "applied math," which at Harvard is a fairly flexible program that includes physics, computer science, and an area of application of the student's choice in addition to math and applied math classes. As an undergraduate, I actually took as many economics classes as math and applied math classes combined. Looking back, given how my research interests have developed, I probably should have taken more math and probability classes than I did. But I did leave college with what is probably the most important math skill for an economist: the willingness to pick up a textbook to learn new tools as they are needed.

Why did you become an economist?

I really enjoyed my economics classes in college, and by taking some graduate classes as an undergraduate, I found that I'd be able to hold my own in graduate school. I was lucky to have inspirational teachers such as Ken Arrow, Howard Raiffa, and Michael Spence, and to have an advisor (Steven Shavell) who encouraged me to think about graduate study and to start reading journals as an undergraduate. By senior year, I had narrowed things down to either economics or law, and I chose economics that spring.

Principles of economics texts (including this one) introduce game theory as a tool for understanding the strategic behavior of oligopolies. Can you provide some examples of the wider use of game theory?

Game theory is used in many areas of economics. It helps us to study the credibility of a central bank in its pursuit of anti-inflationary monetary policy, the dilemma faced by a government about whether to tax capital or renege on its debt, the negotiations between labor unions and management, the decisions of developing economies to nationalize foreign-owned assets, pretrial negotiations by lawyers, and lobbying by interest groups.

Game theory is also used outside economics. Political scientists use it to gain insights into arms races and other strategic decisions, and biologists use it to study the dynamics of the evolution and survival of species.

Some economists think that game theory is the only game worth playing. Others think that it has no empirical content. How would you explain the achievements and the promise of game theory to a beginning student?

The current state of game theory is far from perfect, but it does help us understand and make predictions about a very large and important set of situations. Everything in economics can be viewed as a game. There is no real gain from doing so in the case of single-agent decisions (where there are no other agents) or in the case of a perfectly competitive economy (where each agent cares only about the market price and his own decisions). But in all other cases, the only alternative to a game theoretic analysis seems to be no analysis at all.

... the only alternative to a game theoretic analysis seems to be no analysis at all.

Game theory has proved to be a useful way to think about qualitative issues like "how does repeated interaction help support cooperation" and "how might a dominant firm in a market with network externalities exploit its position," and it has long been used to motivate and explain the outcomes of games played in economics laboratory experiments.

It is more difficult to use game theory in econometric studies of field data, but there has been a lot of progress in this area in recent years, in part due to my colleagues Ariel Pakes and Susan Athey.

The germs of truth behind the "no empirical content" criticism are that (a) seemingly small changes in the specification of a game can sometimes lead to large changes in its set of equilibria and (b) even when we are pretty sure we know the game being played, the predictions can be less accurate than we'd like. Of course, these same complaints can be made about many fields, but I have to admit that both academic and real-world life would be simpler if these complaints weren't true.

In the games that you study, players have limited knowledge. How is it possible for economists to study games in which the players don't know the payoffs and can't predict the actions of the other players?

The standard Nash equilibrium solution concept says that each player's strategy is a best response to the strategies being used by the others. The concept itself says nothing about the players' knowledge of the game being played nor about when and how a play might come to resemble an equilibrium. In some games, careful reasoning by sophisticated players will lead them to play the equilibrium the very first time they are in the game.

But in game theory experiments it is more typical for play to start away from the equilibrium and then move toward it as the players acquire more experience with the game. This adjustment can be the result of learning by human subjects who know they are in a game, but that's not necessary: Nash equilibrium can also arise when the players are genetically programmed agents who don't think at all, as in the games played by genes that evolutionary biologists study.

So the fact that the agents don't know the game doesn't make game theory irrelevant. However, these adaptive processes take time, and in many settings, it is not clear whether one should expect observed play to approximate an equilibrium.

It is fairly easy to distinguish equilibrium and nonequilibrium play in the lab, where the experimenter controls the payoff, and more difficult to do so in field data where the payoffs are part of what is being estimated.

The empirical application of game theory has advanced a lot in recent years but has mostly maintained equilibrium as an assumption. Devising empirical tests for equilibrium is one of the leading open problems in applied game theory.

How does someone get a reputation and how does that help to get a better outcome? Does reputation always improve the outcome?

To get a reputation for "doing *x*," you simply have to do *x* every chance you get! This may have some short-run costs, but if you will be playing this game very often and are patient, it can be worth incurring the costs to build the reputation you want.

To get a reputation for "doing *x*," you simply have to do *x* every chance you get!

Conversely, a short-run player or an impatient player isn't willing to invest in a reputation. The simplest case is of a single long-run player facing one short-run player after another in sequence, with the two sides choosing their actions simultaneously each round and the actions being observed by all subsequent players. Here, the opportunity to build a reputation can't hurt the long-run player, and it typically helps. Things get more complicated if there are two or more long-run players each trying to build their own reputation or if the actions played in a round are sequential instead of simultaneous.

For example, it's hard to build the reputation of "doing *x* after your opponent does *y*," if your opponent never plays *y*!

One of your earliest papers has the intriguing title "The Fat-Cat Effect, the Puppy-Dog Ploy, and the Lean and Hungry Look." What did you study in this paper and what did you discover?

Earlier papers by Michael Spence and Avinash Dixit had shown how an incumbent firm might want to "overinvest" in capital to induce a subsequent ("second period") entrant to enter on a smaller scale. The logic of those papers was that by investing more in capital, the firm would lower its second-period cost of production, which would lead it to have higher second-period output, and that in turn would lead the entrant to produce less, which is to the incumbent's advantage.

Jean Tirole and I provided a systematic analysis and taxonomy of the way that an incumbent can alter its investment decisions to influence the behavior of a potential entrant. We identified four possible strategies and then spent several weeks looking for good names for each of them.

Here is the list: The "top dog" strategy is the one studied by Spence and Dixit, namely the incumbent does extra investment to make itself big and tough. With product competition, this strategy both induces the entrant to produce less and makes it more likely to stay out, so it is a good strategy for both entry accommodation and entry deterrence.

The "fat cat" strategy is to do extra investment to make oneself fat and nonaggressive. This strategy is a good way to accommodate if nonaggressive play induces a favorable response from the entrant, but it is never a good way to deter entry.

The "puppy dog ploy" is more or less the reverse: underinvestment to be small and nonthreatening.

Finally, the "lean and hungry look" is staying lean and mean to intimidate rivals. This strategy turns out to apply when the first-period investment is in advertising as opposed to physical capital.

What advice do you have for someone who is just beginning to study economics? What other subjects do you think work well alongside economics? Do you have some reading suggestions?

I read Heilbronner's *The Worldly Philosophers* as part of my first economics class, and I still like it for an overview of the field. I also recommend the economic history of Douglas North, notably his *Structure and Change in Economic History*, and David S. Landes's *The Unbound Prometheus: Technological Change and Industrial Development in Western Europe from 1750 to the Present.*

I advise my students to regularly skim periodicals such as the *Economist*, the *Financial Times*, and the *Wall Street Journal* for interesting articles. As the students become more advanced, they should make an effort to regularly look at economics journals to see what current research looks like and whether any of the topics interest them.

In terms of coursework in other subjects, I advise students who are interested in graduate study in economics to learn math through an introduction to real analysis and to take one class each in probability and statistics. Some familiarity with computer programming is useful; this can be acquired either in or out of class. Beyond that, it comes down to the student's interests.

Regulation and Antitrust Law

Social Interest or Self-Interest?

When you use tap water or the local telephone service, or consume a brand-name drug, you buy from a regulated monopoly. How are these industries regulated, and do the regulations work in the interest of everyone—the social interest—or do they serve the self-interest of the producer?

Some years ago, PepsiCo and 7-Up wanted to merge. Coca-Cola and Dr Pepper also wanted to merge. The government blocked these mergers with its antitrust laws. It used these same laws to permit mergers of big banks and to break up the American Telephone and Telegraph Company (AT&T), an action that brought the competition you see in today's market for long-distance telephone service.

The government also used its antitrust laws to charge Microsoft with monopolizing the markets for computer operating systems and Web browsers.

In *Reading Between the Lines* at the end of the chapter, we look at the market power of pharmaceutical companies protected by patents and see the effects of competition in the markets for drugs.

This chapter surveys the regulation and antitrust law that is designed to limit the power of firms in monopoly and oligopoly markets and to protect the interest of the consumer.

After studying this chapter, you will be able to

- Explain the economic theory of government and how government activity arises from market failure and redistribution
- Define regulation and antitrust law and distinguish between the social interest and capture theories of regulation
- Explain how regulation and deregulation affect prices, outputs, profits, and the distribution of the gains
- Explain how antitrust law has been applied in a number of landmark cases and how it is used today

The Economic Theory of Government

The economic theory of government explains the economic roles of governments, the economic choices that they make, and the consequences of those choices.

Governments exist for two major reasons. First, they establish and maintain property rights and set the rules for the redistribution of income and wealth. Property rights are the foundation on which all market activity takes place. They replace stealing with a rule-based and law-enforced system for redistributing income and wealth.

Second, governments provide mechanisms for allocating scarce resources when the market economy results in inefficiency—a situation called **market failure**. When market failure occurs, too many of some things and too few of some other things are produced. Choices made in the pursuit of self-interest have not served the social interest. By reallocating resources, it is possible to make some people better off while making no one worse off.

In this and following chapters, we're going to study five economic problems that governments and public choices address. They are

- Monopoly and oligopoly regulation
- Externalities
- The provision of public goods
- The use of common resources
- Income redistribution

Monopoly and Oligopoly Regulation

Monopoly and oligopoly can prevent resources from being allocated efficiently. Every business tries to maximize profit, and when monopoly or oligopoly exists, firms try to increase profit by restricting output and keeping the price high. For example, Microsoft has a (near) monopoly in personal computer operating systems, and the price that Microsoft is able to get for a copy of Windows vastly exceeds the marginal cost of producing it. Other practices, such as forcing consumers to buy an operating system and a Web browser in a single package, might be against the social interest, but they also provide Microsoft with a bigger profit.

Governments regulate monopoly and oligopoly and enact antitrust laws that prevent cartels and other restrictions on competition. We study these regulations and laws in the next parts of this chapter.

Externalities

When a chemical factory (legally) dumps its waste into a river and kills the fish, it imposes a cost—called an *external cost*—on the members of a fishing club who fish downstream. When a homeowner fills her garden with spring bulbs, she generates an external benefit for all the passers-by. External costs and external benefits are not usually taken into account by the people whose actions create them. The chemical factory does not take the fishing club's wishes into account when it decides whether to dump waste into the river. The homeowner does not take her neighbors' views into account when she decides to fill her garden with flowers. We study externalities in Chapter 15.

The Provision of Public Goods

Some goods and services are consumed by everyone, and no one can be excluded from the benefits that arise from them. Examples are national defense, law and order, and sewage and waste disposal services. A national defense system can't isolate individuals and refuse to protect them. Airborne diseases from untreated sewage don't favor some people and hit others. A good or service that is consumed by everyone is called a *public good.*

The market economy fails to deliver the efficient quantity of public goods because of a *free-rider problem.* Everyone tries to free ride on everyone else because the good is available to all, whether they pay for it or not.

We'll provide a more thorough description of public goods and the free-rider problem in Chapter 16. We'll also study the factors that influence the scale of provision of public goods in that chapter.

The Use of Common Resources

Some resources are owned by no one and used by everyone. Examples are fish in the ocean, lakes, and national parks. Every week, hundreds of boats scoop up thousands of tons of fish from the Atlantic Ocean. The consequence is that the stocks of some species—Atlantic cod is one of them—are dangerously depleted.

The market economy fails to use common resources efficiently because no one has an incentive to conserve what everyone else is free to use.

We'll describe this problem more thoroughly in Chapter 16, where we'll also review some ideas for coping with the problem.

Income Redistribution

The market economy delivers an unequal distribution of income and wealth, and income support systems and progressive income taxes influence the distribution of the gains from economic activity. You've already seen, in Chapter 6, how taxes affect markets and create deadweight losses. We'll look at the role of taxes in redistributing income in Chapter 18 after learning how factor markets operate.

Before we begin to study these problems from which government activity arises, let's look at the arena in which governments operate: the "political marketplace."

Public Choice and the Political Marketplace

Government is a complex organization made up of millions of individuals, each with his or her own economic objectives. Government policy is the outcome of the choices made by these individuals. To analyze these choices, economists have developed a *public choice theory* of the political marketplace.

The actors in the political marketplace, shown in Fig. 14.1 are

- Voters
- Firms
- Politicians
- Bureaucrats

Voters Voters are consumers in the political marketplace. In the markets for goods and services, people express their preferences by their willingness to pay. In the political marketplace, they express their preferences by their votes, campaign contributions, and lobbying activity. Public choice theory assumes that people support the policies they believe will make them better off and oppose the policies that they believe will make them worse off. It is voters' perceptions rather than reality that guide their choices.

Firms Firms are also consumers in the political marketplace. They don't express their preferences by their votes, but they are the main source of campaign contributions and lobbying activity. Public choice theory assumes that entrepreneurs support the policies that benefit their firms and oppose the policies that damage their interest. Again, it is perceptions rather than reality that guide these choices.

Politicians Politicians are the "entrepreneurs" of the political marketplace. Public choice theory assumes that the objective of a politician is to get elected and to remain in office. Votes to a politician are like economic profit to a firm. To get enough votes, politicians propose policies that they expect will appeal to a majority of voters. But election campaigns are costly operations. So politicians also pay close attention to the demands of the firms that provide the bulk of the funds that get used to run the campaigns.

Bureaucrats Bureaucrats are the hired officials in government departments. They are the producers in the political marketplace. Public choice theory assumes that bureaucrats aim to maximize their own utility and that to achieve this objective, they try to maximize the budgets of their departments.

FIGURE 14.1 The Political Marketplace

myeconlab

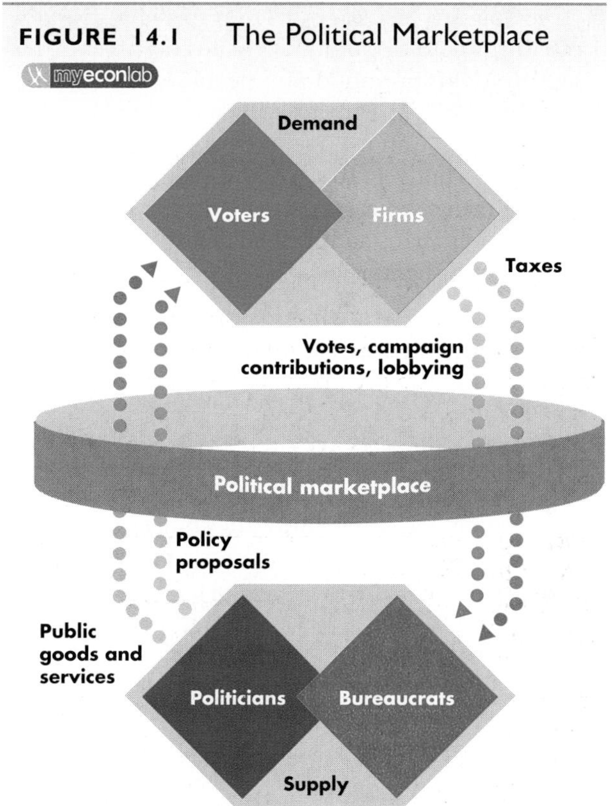

Voters express their demands for policies with their votes, and voters and firms express demands by making campaign contributions and lobbying. Politicians propose policies that appeal to a majority of voters and to firms whose campaign contributions they seek. Bureaucrats try to maximize the budgets of their departments. A political equilibrium is a situation in which no group can improve its position by making a different choice.

The bigger the budget of a department, the greater is the prestige of its chief and the larger is the opportunity for promotion for people farther down the bureaucratic ladder. So all the members of a department have an interest in maximizing the department's budget. To maximize their budgets, bureaucrats devise programs that they expect will appeal to politicians and they help politicians to explain their programs to voters.

Political Equilibrium

Voters, firms, politicians, and bureaucrats make choices that best further their own objectives. But each group is constrained by the preferences of the other groups and by what is technologically feasible. The outcome that results from the choices of voters, firms, politicians, and bureaucrats is a **political equilibrium**, which is a situation in which all their choices are compatible and in which no group can improve its position by making a different choice.

Being in a political equilibrium is not the same thing as everyone being in agreement. Some politicians and their supporters devote resources to trying to change existing laws and regulations to their advantage. Other politicians and their supporters devote resources to opposing change. But no politician, bureaucrat, voter, or firm thinks it worthwhile to change the resources they are devoting to these activities.

REVIEW QUIZ

1. What are the two main reasons why government activity exists?
2. What is market failure and what are the major sources of market failure? Can you think of some examples of market failure on your school campus?
3. Describe the political marketplace. Who are the demanders and who are the suppliers in the political market? How do the demanders "pay" the suppliers?

myeconlab **Study Plan 14.1**

The rest of this chapter looks at the public choices that we make in regulating and controlling monopoly and oligopoly.

Monopoly and Oligopoly Regulation

Government intervenes in monopoly and oligopoly markets to influence prices, quantities produced, and the distribution of the gains from economic activity in two main ways:

- Regulation
- Antitrust law

Regulation consists of rules administered by a government agency to influence economic activity by determining prices, product standards and types, and the conditions under which new firms may enter an industry.

Antitrust law is law that regulates and prohibits certain kinds of market behavior, such as monopoly and monopolistic practices.

Before we describe these methods of influencing the behavior of firms, we're going to study the economic theory of monopoly and oligopoly regulation.

The Economic Theory of Regulation

The economic theory of the regulation of monopoly and oligopoly is part of the broader public choice theory that we've just reviewed. There is a demand for regulation, a supply of regulation, and an equilibrium amount and type of regulation.

The Demand for Regulation People and firms demand the regulation that makes them better off and they express this demand through political activity: voting, lobbying, and making campaign contributions.

Consumers demand regulation that increases consumer surplus and firms demand regulation that increases producer surplus. The greater the number of people or firms that can benefit from a regulation, the greater is the demand for it. But numbers alone do not always translate into an effective political force because it is costly to organize for political action. A more powerful influence on the demand for regulation is the gain per person or per firm that results from it.

The Supply of Regulation Politicians supply the regulations that increase their campaign funds and that get them enough votes to achieve and maintain office.

If a regulation benefits a large number of people and by enough for it to be noticed, that regulation appeals to politicians and is supplied. If a regulation benefits a large number of people but by too small an amount per person to be noticed, that regulation does not appeal to politicians and is not supplied.

If a regulation benefits a *small* number of people but by a large amount per person, that regulation also appeals to politicians because it helps them to get campaign funds from those who gain.

Equilibrium Regulation In political equilibrium, regulation might be in the social interest or in the self-interest of producers. The **social interest theory** of regulation is that politicians supply the regulation that achieves an efficient allocation of resources. According to this view, the political process works well, relentlessly seeks out deadweight loss, and introduces regulations that eliminate it. For example, where monopoly practices exist, the political process introduces price regulations to ensure that outputs increase and prices fall to their competitive levels.

The **capture theory** of regulation is that regulation is in the self-interest of producers. The key idea of capture theory is that the cost of political organization is high and the political process will supply only those regulations that increase the surplus of small, easily identified groups that have low organization costs. Such regulations are supplied even if they impose costs on others, provided that those costs are spread thinly and widely enough that they do not decrease votes.

Political liberals tend to believe that regulation is in the social interest and that when it is not, sufficient goodwill and hard work can ensure that the regulation is changed. Political conservatives tend to believe that most regulation is in the self-interest of producers and that no regulation is better for the social interest than the regulation that we have.

REVIEW QUIZ

1. How do consumers and producers express their demand for regulation?
2. What regulations do politicians supply?
3. Distinguish between the social interest and capture theories of regulation.

myeconlab Study Plan 14.2

We're now going to look at the regulations that exist in our economy today, examine how they work, and see if we can determine whose interests they serve.

Regulation and Deregulation

The past 25 years have seen big changes in the way the U.S. economy is regulated. We're going to examine some of these changes. To begin, we'll look at what is regulated and at the scope of regulation. Then we'll turn to the regulatory process and examine how regulators control prices and other aspects of market behavior. Finally, we'll tackle the more difficult and controversial questions: Why do we regulate some things but not others? Who benefits from the regulations that we have—consumers or producers?

The Scope of Regulation

The first federal regulatory agency, the Interstate Commerce Commission (ICC), was set up in 1887 to control prices, routes, and the quality of service of interstate railroads. Its scope was later extended to trucking lines, bus lines, water carriers, and, in more recent years, oil pipelines. Following the establishment of the ICC, the federal regulatory environment remained static until the years of the Great Depression. Then, in the 1930s, more agencies were established: the Federal Power Commission, the Federal Communications Commission, the Securities and Exchange Commission, the Federal Maritime Commission, the Federal Deposit Insurance Corporation, and, in 1938, the Civil Aeronautical Agency, which was replaced in 1940 by the Civil Aeronautics Board. There was a further lull until the establishment during the 1970s of the Copyright Royalty Tribunal and the Federal Energy Regulatory Commission. In addition to these, there are many state and local regulatory commissions.

In the mid-1970s, almost one quarter of the economy was subject to some form of regulation. Heavily regulated industries—those subject both to price regulation and to regulation of entry of new firms—were electricity, natural gas, telephones, airlines, highway freight services, and railroads.

During the 1980s and 1990s, a deregulation process stimulated competition in broadcasting, telecommunications, banking and finance, and all forms of transportation (both passengers and freight via air, rail, and road).

What exactly do regulatory agencies do? How do they regulate?

The Regulatory Process

Though regulatory agencies vary in size and scope and in the detailed aspects of economic life that they control, all agencies have features in common.

First, the bureaucrats who are the key decision makers in a regulatory agency are appointed by the President or Congress in the case of federal agencies and by state and local governments. In addition, all agencies have a permanent bureaucracy made up of experts in the industry being regulated and often recruited from the regulated firms. Agencies have financial resources, voted by Congress or state or local legislatures, to cover the costs of their operations.

Second, each agency adopts a set of practices or operating rules for controlling prices and other aspects of economic performance. These rules and practices are based on well-defined physical and financial accounting procedures, but they are extremely complicated in practice and hard to administer.

In a regulated industry, individual firms are usually free to determine the technology that they will use. But they are not free to determine the prices at which they will sell their output, the quantities that they will sell, or the markets that they will serve. The regulatory agency grants certification to a company to serve a particular market with a particular line of products, and the agency determines the level and structure of prices that will be charged. In some cases, the agency also determines the scale of output permitted.

To analyze the way in which regulation works, it is convenient to distinguish between the regulation of natural monopoly and the regulation of cartels. Let's begin with the regulation of natural monopoly.

Natural Monopoly

Natural monopoly was defined in Chapter 12 (p. 264) as an industry in which one firm can supply the entire market at a lower price than two or more firms can. Examples of natural monopoly include local distribution of cable television signals, electricity and gas, and urban rail services. For these activities, most of the costs are fixed and the larger the output, the lower is the monopoly's average cost. It is much more expensive to have two or more competing sets of wires, pipes, and train lines serving every neighborhood than it is to have a single set. (What is a natural monopoly changes over time as technology changes. With the introduction of fiber-optic cables, telephone companies and cable TV companies can compete with each other in both markets, so what was once a natural monopoly is becoming a more competitive industry. Direct satellite TV is also beginning to break the cable TV monopoly.)

Let's consider the example of cable TV, which is shown in Fig. 14.2. The demand curve for cable TV is *D*. The cable TV company's marginal cost curve is *MC*. That marginal cost curve is (assumed to be) horizontal at \$10 per household per month—that is, the cost of providing each additional household with a month of cable programming is \$10. But to serve just one customer, the cable company must invest in satellite receiving dishes, cables, and control equipment. These high costs of capital mean that the firm experiences economies of scale. Its long-run average cost curve (*LRAC*) slopes downward because as the

FIGURE 14.2 Natural Monopoly: Marginal Cost Pricing

myeconlab

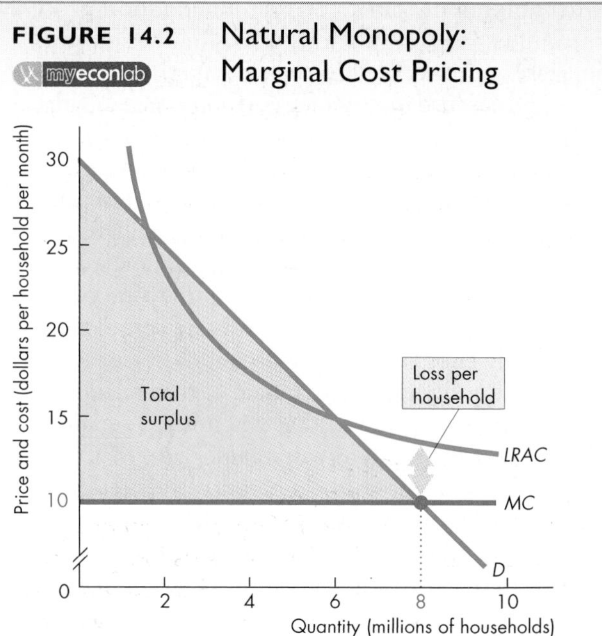

A natural monopoly is a firm with economies of scale that enable it to supply the entire market at the lowest possible cost. A cable TV operator faces the demand curve *D*. The firm's marginal cost is constant at \$10 per household per month, as shown by the curve labeled *MC*. With economies of scale, the long-run average cost curve, *LRAC*, slopes downward. A marginal cost pricing rule sets the price at \$10 a month, with 8 million households being served. The consumer surplus is shown as the green area. The firm incurs a loss on each household, indicated by the red arrow. To remain in business, the firm must price discriminate, use a two-part tariff, or receive a subsidy.

number of households served increases, the capital cost is spread over a larger number of households. (If you need to refresh your memory on long-run cost and economies of scale, take a quick look back at Chapter 10, p. 226.)

Regulation in the Social Interest How will cable TV be regulated according to the social interest theory? In social interest theory, regulation maximizes total surplus (the sum of consumer surplus and producer surplus), which occurs if marginal cost equals price. As you can see in Fig. 14.2, that outcome occurs if the price is regulated at $10 per household per month and if 8 million households are served. Such a regulation is called a marginal cost pricing rule. A **marginal cost pricing rule** sets price equal to marginal cost. It maximizes total surplus in the regulated industry.

A natural monopoly that is regulated to set price equal to marginal cost incurs an economic loss. Because its average cost curve is falling, marginal cost is below average cost. Because price equals marginal cost, price is below average cost. Average cost minus price is the loss per unit produced. It's obvious that a company that is required to use a marginal cost pricing rule will not stay in business for long. How can a company cover its costs and, at the same time, obey a marginal cost pricing rule?

One possibility is price discrimination (see Chapter 12, pp. 273-276). Another possibility is to use a two-part price (called a two-part tariff). For example, local telephone companies can charge consumers a monthly fee for being connected to the telephone system and then charge a price equal to marginal cost for each local call. A cable TV operator can charge a one-time connection fee that covers its loss per unit and then charge a monthly fee equal to marginal cost.

If a natural monopoly cannot cover its total cost from its customers, and if the government wants it to follow a marginal cost pricing rule, the government must give the firm a subsidy. In such a case, the government raises the revenue for the subsidy by taxing some other activity. But as we saw in Chapter 6, taxes themselves generate deadweight loss.

The deadweight loss that results from additional taxes must be subtracted from the efficiency gained by forcing the natural monopoly to adopt a marginal cost pricing rule.

It is possible that deadweight loss will be minimized by permitting the natural monopoly to charge a higher price than marginal cost rather than by taxing some other sector of the economy to subsidize the natural monopoly. Such a pricing arrangement is called an average cost pricing rule. An **average cost pricing rule** sets price equal to average cost. Figure 14.3 shows the average cost pricing solution. The cable TV operator charges $15 a month and serves 6 million households. A deadweight loss arises, which is shown by the gray triangle in the figure.

The marginal cost pricing rule and the average cost pricing rule that we've just examined are easier to state than to implement. The major obstacle to implementing them is that the regulator knows less than the regulated firm about the cost of production.

The regulator does not directly observe the firm's costs and doesn't know how hard the firm is trying to minimize cost. For this reason, regulators use one of two practical rules:

- Rate of return regulation
- Price cap regulation

Let's see whether these rules deliver an outcome that is in the social interest or the self-interest of the producer.

FIGURE 14.3 Natural Monopoly: Average Cost Pricing

myeconlab

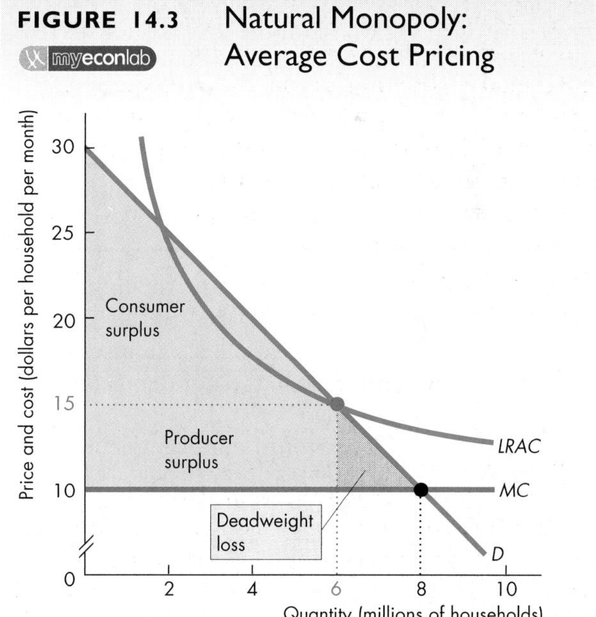

Average cost pricing sets the price equal to average cost. The cable TV operator charges $15 a month and serves 6 million households. In this situation, the firm breaks even—average cost equals price. Deadweight loss, shown by the gray triangle, is generated. Consumer surplus is reduced to the green area.

Rate of Return Regulation Under **rate of return regulation**, a regulated firm must justify its price by showing that the price enables it to earn a specified target percent return on its capital. The target rate of return is determined with reference to what is normal in competitive industries. This rate of return is part of the opportunity cost of the natural monopoly and part of the firm's average cost.

If the regulator could observe the firm's total cost and also know that the firm had minimized total cost, it would accept only a price proposal from the firm that was equivalent to average cost pricing.

The outcome would be like that in Fig. 14.3, where the regulated price is $15 a month and 6 million households are served. In this case, rate of return regulation would result in a price that favors the consumer and prevents the producer from maximizing economic profit. The monopoly will have failed to capture the regulator, and the outcome will be closer to that predicted by the social interest theory of regulation.

But the managers of a regulated firm might not minimize cost. And if the firm is regulated to achieve a target rate of return, the managers have an incentive to inflate costs and raise price. One way to inflate the firm's costs is to spend on inputs that are not strictly required for the production of the good. On-the-job luxury in the form of sumptuous office suites, limousines, free baseball tickets (disguised as public relations expenses), company jets, lavish international travel, and entertainment are all ways in which managers can inflate costs.

Managers also have an incentive to use more capital than the efficient amount because the more capital they use, the larger is the total return they are permitted to earn. Managers also have an incentive to make larger-than-required charges for depreciation and losses from bad debts.

If the cable TV operator in our example manages to persuade the regulator that its true average total cost curve is that shown as *LRAC (inflated)* in Fig. 14.4, then the regulator, applying the normal rate of return principle, will accept the firm's proposed price of $20 a month. In this example, the price and quantity will be the same as those under unregulated monopoly.

Price Cap Regulation For the reason we've just examined, rate of return regulation is increasingly being replaced by price cap regulation. A **price cap regulation** is a price ceiling—a rule that specifies the highest price the firm is permitted to set. This type of regulation gives the firm an incentive to operate efficiently and to keep costs under control. Price cap regulation has become common for the electricity and telecommunications industries and is replacing rate of return regulation.

To see how a price cap works, let's suppose that the cable TV operator in our example is subject to this type of regulation. Figure 14.5 shows what happens.

Without regulation, the firm maximizes profit by serving 4 million households and charging a price of $20 a month. If a price cap is set at $15 a month, the firm is permitted to sell any quantity it chooses at that price or at a lower price. With 4 million households, the firm now incurs an economic loss. It can decrease the loss by *increasing* output to 6 million households. But to serve more than 6 million households, the firm would have to cut its price and incur an economic loss. So the profit-maximizing quantity is 6 million households—the same as with average cost pricing.

FIGURE 14.4 Natural Monopoly: Inflating Cost

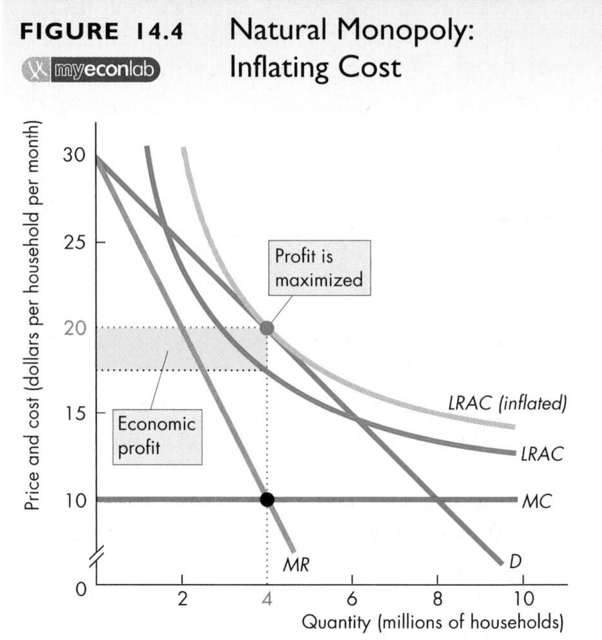

If the cable TV operator is able to inflate its costs to *LRAC (inflated)* and persuade the regulator that these are genuine minimum costs of production, rate of return regulation results in a price of $20 a month—the profit-maximizing price. To the extent that the producer can inflate costs above average cost, the price rises, output decreases, and deadweight loss increases.

FIGURE 14.5 Price Cap Regulation of Natural Monopoly

myeconlab

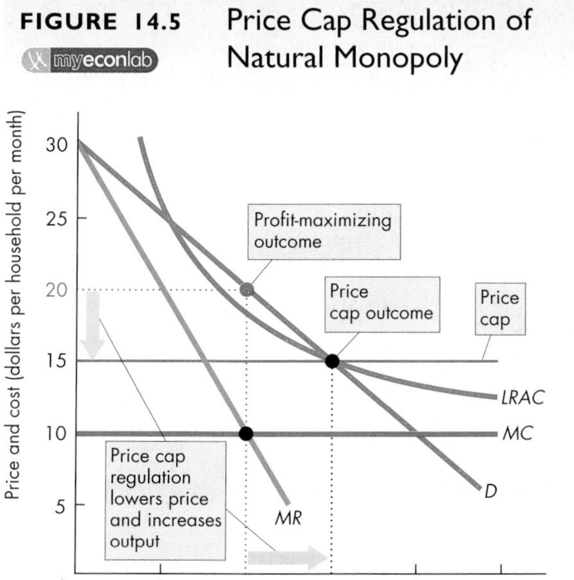

If the cable TV operator is subject to a price cap regulation, the price cap limits the price that may be charged. By serving less than 6 million households, the firm incurs an economic loss. By serving more than 6 million households, the firm also incurs an economic loss. Only at an output of 6 million can the firm break even. The firm has an incentive to keep costs as low as possible and to produce the quantity demanded at the price cap.

Notice that a price cap lowers the price and increases output. This outcome is in sharp contrast to the effect of a price ceiling in a competitive market that you studied in Chapter 6 (pp. 124–127). The reason is that in an unregulated monopoly, the profit-maximizing output is less than the competitive output and the price cap regulation replicates the conditions of a competitive market.

In Fig. 14.5, the price cap delivers average cost pricing. In practice, the regulator might set the cap too high. For this reason, price cap regulation is often combined with **earnings sharing regulation**, under which profits that rise above a target level must be shared with the firm's customers.

The regulator might alternatively set the price too low. If this occurs, there can be a shortage such as that faced by the California power industry in 2001.

Social Interest or Capture in Natural Monopoly Regulation?

It is not clear whether natural monopoly regulation produces prices and quantities that more closely correspond with the predictions of capture theory or with social interest theory. But one thing is clear: Price regulation does not require natural monopolies to use the marginal cost pricing rule. If it did, most natural monopolies would make losses and receive hefty government subsidies to enable them to remain in business.

There is an exception. Many telephone companies use marginal cost pricing. They cover their total cost by charging a flat fee each month for being connected to their system and then permit each call to be made at its marginal cost—zero.

A test of whether natural monopoly regulation is in the social interest or the self-interest of the producer is to examine the rates of return earned by regulated natural monopolies. If those rates of return are significantly higher than those in the rest of the economy, then, to some degree, the regulator might have been captured by the producer. If the rates of return in the regulated monopoly industries are similar to those in the rest of the economy, then we cannot tell for sure if the regulator has been captured because we cannot know the extent to which costs have been inflated by the managers of the regulated firms.

Table 14.1 shows the rates of return in regulated natural monopolies as well as the economy's average rate of return in the 1960s and 1970s. In the 1960s, rates of return in regulated natural monopolies were somewhat below the economy average; in the 1970s, those returns exceeded the economy average. Overall, the rates of return achieved by regulated natural monopolies were not very different from those in the rest of the economy. We can conclude from these data either that natural monopoly regulation does, to some degree, serve the social interest or that natural monopoly managers inflate their costs by amounts sufficiently large to disguise the fact that they have captured the regulator and that the social interest is not being served.

A final test of whether regulation of natural monopoly is in the social interest or the self-interest of producers is to study the changes in consumer surplus and producer surplus following deregulation. Microeconomists have researched this issue, and their conclusions are summarized in Table 14.2. In the case of railroad deregulation, which occurred during the

TABLE 14.1 Rates of Return in Regulated Monopolies

Industry	Rates of return 1962–69	Rates of return 1970–77
Electricity	3.2	6.1
Gas	3.3	8.2
Railroad	5.1	7.2
Average of above	**3.9**	**7.2**
Economy average	**6.6**	**5.1**

Source of data: Paul W. MacAvoy, *The Regulated Industries and the Economy* (New York: W.W. Norton, 1979), pp. 49–60.

1980s, both consumers and producers gained—and by large amounts. The gains from deregulation of telecommunications and cable television were smaller and accrued only to the consumer. These findings suggest that railroad regulation hurts everyone, while regulation of telecommunications and cable television hurts only the consumer.

We've now examined the regulation of natural monopoly. Let's next turn to regulation in oligopoly—the regulation of cartels.

TABLE 14.2 Gains from Deregulating Natural Monopolies

Industry	Consumer surplus increase	Producer surplus increase	Total surplus increase
	(billions of 1990 dollars)		
Railroads	8.5	3.2	11.7
Telecommunications	1.2	0.0	1.2
Cable television	0.8	0.0	0.8
Total	10.5	3.2	13.7

Source of data: Clifford Winston, "Economic Deregulation: Days of Reckoning for Microeconomists," *Journal of Economic Literature*, Vol. 31, September 1993, pp. 1263–1289, and the author's calculations.

Cartel Regulation

A *cartel* is a collusive agreement among a number of firms that is designed to restrict output and achieve a higher profit for the cartel's members. Cartels are illegal in the United States and in most other countries. But international cartels can sometimes operate legally, such as the international cartel of oil producers known as OPEC (the Organization of Petroleum Exporting Countries).

Illegal cartels can arise in oligopoly industries. An oligopoly is a market structure in which a small number of firms compete with each other. We studied oligopoly (and duopoly—two firms competing for a market) in Chapter 13. There, we saw that if firms manage to collude and behave like a monopoly, they can set the same price and sell the same total quantity as a monopoly firm would. But we also discovered that in such a situation, each firm will be tempted to cheat, increasing its own output and profit at the expense of the other firms. The result of such cheating on the collusive agreement is the unraveling of the monopoly equilibrium and the emergence of a competitive outcome with zero economic profit for producers. Such an outcome benefits consumers at the expense of producers.

How is oligopoly regulated? Does regulation prevent monopoly practices or does it encourage those practices? According to the social interest theory, oligopoly is regulated to ensure a competitive outcome. According to the capture theory, oligopoly regulators are captured by the firms and the regulation enables the firms to make an economic profit and operate against the social interest.

Let's look at these two possible outcomes in the oligopoly market for trucking tomatoes from the San Joaquin Valley to Los Angeles, illustrated in Fig. 14.6. The market demand curve for trips is *D*. The industry marginal cost curve—and the competitive supply curve—is *MC*.

If this industry is regulated in the social interest, the price will be set so that marginal social benefit equals marginal cost. The price will be $20 a trip, and there will be 300 trips a week. A price cap regulation at $20 a trip could achieve this outcome.

How would this industry be regulated according to the capture theory? Regulation that is in the producer's self-interest will maximize profit. To find the outcome in this case, we need to determine the price and quantity when marginal cost equals marginal revenue. The marginal revenue curve is *MR*. So marginal cost equals marginal revenue at 200 trips a week. The price of a trip is $30.

One way of achieving this outcome is to place an output limit on each firm in the industry. If there are 10 trucking companies, an output limit of 20 trips per company ensures that the total number of trips in a week is 200. Penalties can be imposed to ensure that no single producer exceeds its output limit.

All the firms in the industry would support this type of regulation because it helps to prevent cheating and to maintain a monopoly outcome. Each firm knows that without effectively enforced production quotas, every firm has an incentive to increase output. (For each firm, price exceeds marginal cost, so a greater output brings a larger profit.) So each firm wants a method of preventing output from rising above the industry profit-maximizing level, and the quotas enforced by regulation achieve this end. With this type of cartel regulation, the regulator enables a cartel to operate legally and in its own best interest.

FIGURE 14.6 Collusive Oligopoly

myeconlab

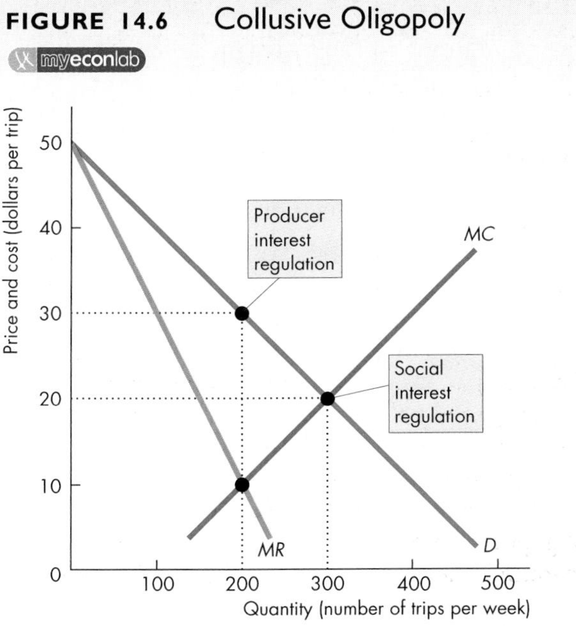

Ten trucking firms transport tomatoes from the San Joaquin Valley to Los Angeles. The demand curve is *D*, and the industry marginal cost curve is *MC*. Under competition, the *MC* curve is the industry supply curve. If the industry is competitive, the price of a trip will be $20 and 300 trips will be made each week. Producers will demand regulation that restricts entry and limits output to 200 trips a week, where industry marginal revenue (*MR*) is equal to industry marginal cost (*MC*). This regulation raises the price to $30 a trip and results in each producer making maximum profit—as if it is a monopoly.

Social Interest or Capture in Cartel Regulation?

What does cartel regulation do in practice? Some regulation has benefited the producer. When the Interstate Commerce Commission regulated trucking, producers persistently made economic profits. Also, by forming a strong labor union, truck drivers captured a large part of the producer surplus.

Some regulation has benefited both the producer and the consumer. When the Civil Aeronautics Board regulated the airlines, they made economic profits. But they competed on quality, which increased costs and eventually eroded profits.

Table 14.3 provides some evidence in support of the conclusion that regulation increased profits in the trucking and airline industries. If regulation ensured a competitive outcome, rates of return in regulated oligopolies would be no higher than those in the economy as a whole. As the numbers in Table 14.3 show, rates of return in airlines and trucking were close to twice the economy average rate of return in the 1960s. In the 1970s, the rate of return in trucking remained higher than the economy average (although by a smaller margin than had prevailed in the 1960s). Airline rates of return in the 1970s fell to below the economy average. The overall picture that emerges from examining data on rates of return is mixed. The regulation of oligopoly does not always result in higher profit, but there are many situations in which it does.

TABLE 14.3 Rates of Return in Regulated Oligopolies

	Rates of return	
Industry	**1962–69**	**1970–77**
Airline	12.8	3.0
Trucking	13.6	8.1
Economy average	**6.6**	**5.1**

Source of data: Paul W. MacAvoy, *The Regulated Industries and the Economy* (New York: W.W. Norton, 1978), pp. 49–60.

Further evidence on cartel and oligopoly regulation can be obtained from the performance of prices and profit following deregulation. If, following deregulation, prices and profit fall, then, to some degree, the regulation must have been serving the self-interest of the producer.

In contrast, if, following deregulation, prices and profits remain constant or increase, then the regulation may be presumed to have been serving the social interest. Because there has been a substantial amount of deregulation in recent years, we can use this test of oligopoly regulation to see which of the two theories better fits the facts.

The evidence is mixed, but in the cases of the airline and trucking industries, the two main oligopolies that have been deregulated, prices fell and there was a large increase in the volume of business. Table 14.4 summarizes the estimated effects of deregulation of airlines and trucking on consumer surplus, producer surplus, and total surplus. Most of the gains were in consumer surplus. In the case of the airlines, there was a gain in producer surplus as well.

But the table shows that in the trucking industry, producer surplus decreased by almost $5 billion a year. This outcome implies that regulation of the trucking industry benefited the producer by restricting competition and enabling prices to be higher than their competitive levels.

Making Predictions

Most industries have a few producers and many consumers. In this situation, public choice theory predicts that regulation protects producer interests and that politicians are rewarded with campaign contributions rather than votes. But there are situations in which the consumer interest has prevailed. There are also cases in which the balance has switched from producer to consumer, as seen in the deregulation process that began in the late 1970s.

Deregulation has occurred for three main reasons. First, economists have become more confident and vocal in predicting the gains from deregulation. Second, a large increase in energy prices in the 1970s increased the cost of regulation borne by consumers. These price hikes made route regulation in the transportation sector extremely costly and changed the balance in the political equilibrium in favor of consumers. Third, technological change ended some natural monopolies. New technologies enabled small producers to offer low-cost long-distance telephone services. These producers wanted a share of the business—and profit—of AT&T. Furthermore, as communication technology improves, the cost of communication falls and the cost of organizing larger groups of consumers also falls.

If this line of reasoning is correct, there will be more social interest regulation and deregulation in the future.

TABLE 14.4 Gains from Deregulating Oligopolies

Industry	Consumer surplus gain	Producer surplus gain	Total surplus gain
	(billions of 1990 dollars)		
Airline	11.8	4.9	16.7
Trucking	15.4	−4.8	10.6
Total	27.2	0.1	27.3

Source of data: Clifford Winston, "Economic Deregulation: Days of Reckoning for Microeconomists," *Journal of Economic Literature*, Vol. 31, September 1993, pp. 1263–1289, and the author's calculations.

REVIEW QUIZ

1. When did regulation begin in the United States, what was regulated, and when did deregulation take hold?
2. Why does natural monopoly need to be regulated?
3. What pricing rule enables a natural monopoly to operate in the social interest and why is that rule difficult to implement?
4. How does rate of return regulation work and what problems does it create?
5. How does price cap regulation work and what problems is it designed to overcome?
6. How might cartels be regulated in the social interest?

myeconlab **Study Plan 14.3**

Let's now leave regulation and turn to the other method of intervention in markets: antitrust law.

Antitrust Law

Antitrust law provides an alternative way in which the government may influence the marketplace. As in the case of regulation, antitrust law can be formulated in the social interest, to maximize total surplus, or in private interests, to maximize the surplus of special interest groups such as producers.

The Antitrust Laws

The first antitrust law, the Sherman Act, was passed in 1890 in an atmosphere of outrage and disgust at the actions and practices of J.P. Morgan, John D. Rockefeller, and W.H. Vanderbilt—the so-called robber barons. Ironically, the most lurid stories of the actions of these great American capitalists are not of their monopolization and exploitation of consumers but of their sharp practices against each other. Nevertheless, monopolies did emerge—for example, the control of the oil industry by John D. Rockefeller.

A wave of mergers at the beginning of the twentieth century produced stronger antitrust laws. The Clayton Act of 1914 supplemented the Sherman Act, and the Federal Trade Commission, an agency charged with enforcing the antitrust laws, was created.

Table 14.5 summarizes the two main provisions of the Sherman Act. Section 1 of the act is precise: Conspiring with others to restrict competition is illegal. But Section 2 is general and imprecise. Just what is an "attempt to monopolize"? The Clayton Act and its two amendments, the Robinson-Patman Act of 1936 and the Celler-Kefauver Act of 1950, which outlaw specific practices, provided greater precision. Table 14.6 describes these practices and summarizes the main provisions of these three acts.

TABLE 14.5 The Sherman Act of 1890

Section 1:

Every contract, combination in the form of trust or otherwise, or conspiracy, in restraint of trade or commerce among the several States, or with foreign nations, is hereby declared to be illegal.

Section 2:

Every person who shall monopolize, or attempt to monopolize, or combine or conspire with any other person or persons, to monopolize any part of the trade or commerce among the several States, or with foreign nations, shall be deemed guilty of a felony.

TABLE 14.6 The Clayton Act and Its Amendments

Clayton Act	**1914**
Robinson-Patman Act	**1936**
Celler-Kefauver Act	**1950**

These acts prohibit the following practices *only if* they substantially lessen competition or create monopoly:

1. Price discrimination
2. Contracts that require other goods to be bought from the same firm (called *tying arrangements*)
3. Contracts that require a firm to buy all its requirements of a particular item from a single firm (called *requirements contracts*)
4. Contracts that prevent a firm from selling competing items (called *exclusive dealing*)
5. Contracts that prevent a buyer from reselling a product outside a specified area (called *territorial confinement*)
6. Acquiring a competitor's shares or assets
7. Becoming a director of a competing firm

Three Antitrust Policy Debates

Price fixing is *always* a violation of the antitrust law. If the Justice Department can prove the existence of price fixing, a defendant can offer no acceptable excuse. But other practices are more controversial and generate debate among antitrust lawyers and economists. We'll examine three of these practices:

- Resale price maintenance
- Tying arrangements
- Predatory pricing

Resale Price Maintenance Most manufacturers sell their products to the final consumer indirectly through a wholesale and retail distribution system. **Resale price maintenance** occurs when a manufacturer agrees with a distributor on the price at which the product will be resold.

Resale price maintenance (also called vertical price fixing) *agreements* are illegal under the Sherman Act. But it isn't illegal for a manufacturer to refuse to supply a retailer who doesn't accept guidance on what the price should be.

Does resale price maintenance create an inefficient or efficient use of resources? Economists can be found on both sides of this question.

Resale price maintenance is inefficient if it enables dealers to operate a cartel and charge the monopoly price. But resale price maintenance might be efficient if it enables a manufacturer to induce dealers to provide the efficient standard of service in selling a product. Suppose, for example, that SilkySkin wants shops to create an inviting space in which to display and demonstrate the use of its new unbelievably effective moisturizing cream. With resale price maintenance, SilkySkin can offer all retailers the same incentive and compensation. Without resale price maintenance, some cut-price stores might offer SilkySkin products at such a low price that shops with the expensive display wouldn't sell any products.

Tying Arrangements A **tying arrangement** is an agreement to sell one product only if the buyer agrees to buy another, different product. With tying, the only way the buyer can get the one product is to also buy the other product. When you bought this textbook, you also bought access to a Web site. If the only way to buy access to the Web site were to buy the textbook, these products would be tied. (You can't buy the book, new, without the Web site. But you can buy the Web site access without the book, so the products are not actually tied.)

Could publishers of textbooks make more money by tying a book and access to a Web site? The answer is sometimes but not always. Suppose that you and other students are willing to pay \$40 for a book and \$10 for access to a Web site. The publisher can sell these items separately for these prices or bundled for \$50. There is no gain to the publisher from bundling.

But now suppose that you and only half of the students are willing to pay \$40 for a book and \$10 for a Web site and the other half of the students are willing to pay \$40 for a Web site and \$10 for a book. Now if the two items are sold separately, the publisher can charge \$40 for the book and \$40 for the Web site. Half the students buy the book but not the Web site, and the other half buy the Web site but not the book. But if the book and Web site are bundled for \$50, everyone buys the bundle and the publisher makes an extra \$10 per student. In this case, bundling has enabled the publisher to price discriminate.

Predatory Pricing **Predatory pricing** is setting a low price to drive competitors out of business with the intention of setting a monopoly price when the competition has gone. John D. Rockefeller's Standard Oil Company was the first to be accused of this practice in the 1890s, and it has been claimed often in antitrust cases since then. It is easy to see that predatory pricing is an idea, not a reality. Economists are skeptical that predatory pricing occurs. They point out that a firm that cuts its price below the profit-maximizing level loses during the low-price period. Even if it succeeds in driving its competitors out of business, new competitors will enter as soon as the price is increased. So any potential gain from a monopoly position is temporary. A high and certain loss is a poor exchange for a temporary and uncertain gain. No case of predatory pricing has been definitively found.

A Recent Antitrust Showcase: The United States Versus Microsoft

In 1998, the U.S. Department of Justice along with a number of states charged Microsoft, the world's largest producer of software for personal computers, with violations of both sections of the Sherman Act. A 78-day trial followed that pitched two prominent MIT economics professors against each other (Franklin Fisher for the government and Richard Schmalensee for Microsoft).

The Case Against Microsoft The claims against Microsoft were that it

- Possessed monopoly power
- Used predatory pricing and tying arrangements
- Used other anticompetitive practices

It was claimed that with 80 percent of the market for PC operating systems, Microsoft had excessive monopoly power. This monopoly power arose from two barriers to entry: economies of scale and network economies. Microsoft's average total cost falls as production increases (economies of scale) because the fixed costs of developing an operating system such as Windows is large while the marginal cost of producing one copy of Windows is small. Further, as the number of Windows users increases, the range of Windows applications expands (network economies), so a potential competitor would need to produce not only a competing operating system but also an entire range of supporting applications as well.

When Microsoft entered the Web browser market with its Internet Explorer (IE), it offered the browser for a zero price. This price was viewed as *predatory pricing*. Microsoft integrated IE with Windows so that anyone who uses this operating system would not need a separate browser such as Netscape Communicator. Microsoft's competitors claimed that this practice was an illegal *tying arrangement*.

Microsoft's Response Microsoft challenged all these claims. It said that Windows was vulnerable to competition from other operating systems such as Linux and Apple's Mac OS and that there was a permanent threat of competition from new entrants.

Microsoft claimed that integrating Internet Explorer with Windows provided a single, unified product of greater consumer value like a refrigerator with a chilled water dispenser or an automobile with a stereo player.

The Outcome The court agreed that Microsoft was in violation of the Sherman Act and ordered that it be broken into two firms: an operating systems producer and an applications producer. Microsoft successfully appealed this order. But in the final judgment, Microsoft was ordered to disclose details about how its operating system works to other software developers so that they could compete effectively against Microsoft. In the summer of 2002, Microsoft began to comply with this order.

We end this chapter by examining the rules that guide merger decisions.

Merger Rules

The Federal Trade Commission (FTC) uses guidelines to determine which mergers it will examine and possibly block. The Herfindahl-Hirschman Index (HHI) is one of these guidelines (see Chapter 9, pp. 208–209). A market in which the HHI is less than 1,000 is regarded as competitive. An index between 1,000 and 1,800 indicates a moderately concentrated market, and a merger in this market that would increase the index by 100 points is challenged by the FTC. An index above 1,800 indicates a concentrated market, and a merger in this market that would increase the index by 50 points is challenged.

The FTC used these guidelines to block proposed mergers in the market for soft drinks. PepsiCo wanted to buy 7-Up and Coca-Cola wanted to buy Dr Pepper. The market for carbonated soft drinks is highly concentrated. Coca-Cola has a 39 percent share, PepsiCo has 28 percent, Dr Pepper is next with 7 percent and 7-Up follows with 6 percent. One other producer, RJR, has a 5 percent market share. So the five largest firms in this market have an 85 percent market share.

The PepsiCo and 7-Up merger would have increased the HHI by more than 300 points, the Coca-Cola and Dr Pepper merger would have increased it by more than 500 points, and both mergers together would have increased the index by almost 800 points. The FTC decided that increases in the HHI of these magnitudes were not in the social interest and blocked the mergers.

Social Interest or Self-Interest?

It is clear from the historical contexts in which antitrust law has evolved that its intent has been to protect and pursue the social interest and restrain the profit-seeking and anticompetitive actions of producers. But it is also clear from the above brief history of antitrust legislation and cases that, from time to time, the interest of the producer has had an influence on the way in which the law has been interpreted and applied. Nevertheless, the overall thrust of antitrust law appears to have been directed toward achieving efficiency and therefore to serving the social interest.

REVIEW QUIZ

1. What are the four acts of Congress that make up our antitrust laws? When were these laws enacted?
2. When is price fixing not a violation of the antitrust laws?
3. What is an attempt to monopolize an industry?
4. Review the issues in the debates about resale price maintenance, tying arrangements, and predatory pricing.
5. Under what circumstances is a merger unlikely to be approved?

myeconlab **Study Plan 14.4**

In *Reading Between the Lines*, on pp. 338–339, you can look at a recent attempt to use the law to limit the market power exercised by the pharmaceutical companies and open them to greater international competition.

READING BETWEEN THE LINES

Market Power of Pharmaceutical Companies

http://www.nytimes.com

Roche Tells Indonesia That It Can Produce Tamiflu Without a License

November 26, 2005

Roche, the Swiss drug maker, said yesterday that Indonesia could make Tamiflu without its license because the medicine, which may treat avian influenza, is not protected by a patent in the Southeast Asian nation.

"We've informed the government they can produce it for local use," said Martina Rupp, a spokeswoman in Switzerland for Roche. "Quality guidelines will have to be assured by the Indonesian government." . . .

Roche said yesterday that it would supply Taiwan with 1.3 million more treatments of Tamiflu next year, for a total of 2.3 million. Taiwan's government had said it would issue a compulsory license to make Tamiflu locally in December, even without a license from Roche, if its orders were not filled on time. Roche has a patent for Tamiflu in Taiwan.

"We are confident that we will be in a position to deliver the quantities of Tamiflu requested by the Taiwanese government in the required timelines," said David Reddy, leader of Roche's pandemics unit.

Countries worldwide are stockpiling Tamiflu on concern the H5N1 virus, which has killed 68 people in Asia, may mutate into a form that can spread among humans. More than 150 third parties are interested in gaining licenses to make Tamiflu, Roche said this month. Roche said Nov. 10 that it was in advanced discussions to allow Vietnam to undertake the final production step locally.

India said last month that it would allow Ranbaxy Laboratories and Cipla, the country's two biggest drug makers, to produce generic versions of Tamiflu. Roche does not have a patent in India for Tamiflu. . . .

Essence of the Story

- Tamiflu is a patented drug made by Roche and used to treat the H5N1 bird flu virus, which has killed 68 people in Asia.
- More than 150 drug producers want to make Tamiflu.
- Roche has a patent for Tamiflu in Taiwan and will supply that country with a total of 2.3 million treatments, under a threat by the government to make Tamiflu in Taiwan without a license.
- Roche does not have a patent in Indonesia or India, and these countries might produce Tamiflu.

Economic Analysis

- The cost of developing a new pharmaceutical drug is high, and a new drug receives a patent, which gives its developer a monopoly in that drug for the duration of the patent.
- The marginal cost of producing a drug is low.
- Figure 1 shows the market for patented Tamiflu.
- The demand curve is *D*, the marginal revenue curve is *MR*, and the marginal cost curve is *MC*. The position and slope of the demand curve are assumed and the marginal cost of $2 is also assumed.
- The profit-maximizing quantity is Q_M, where marginal revenue, *MR*, equals marginal cost, *MC*.
- The profit-maximizing price is $5 a dose (approximately the actual market price of Tamiflu).
- At the profit-maximizing quantity and price, the producer (Roche) makes a producer surplus (some of which goes to cover the cost of developing the drug), and a deadweight loss arises.
- Figure 2 shows the market for the same drug but sold in its generic form of oseltamivir in a competitive market.
- In a competitive market, the marginal cost curve is also the supply curve *S*. The equilibrium quantity is now Q_C and the price, which equals marginal cost, is $2 a dose.
- A pharmaceutical company such as Roche might restrict international trade in its drugs and operate a monopoly in the United States like that in Fig. 1 and permit a competitive market to operate in some other countries, such as Taiwan, Indonesia, India, and Vietnam, like that in Fig. 2.
- But if Internet pharmacies make Asian-produced oseltamivir available in the U.S. market, Roche will not be able to maintain its monopoly price.
- Although the monopoly pricing of a drug brings a deadweight loss, a drug company would have no incentive to bear the development cost of a new drug if the producer surplus were zero.
- So if we weigh the future benefits against the current costs, the market for a patented drug might not be as inefficient as the deadweight loss implies.

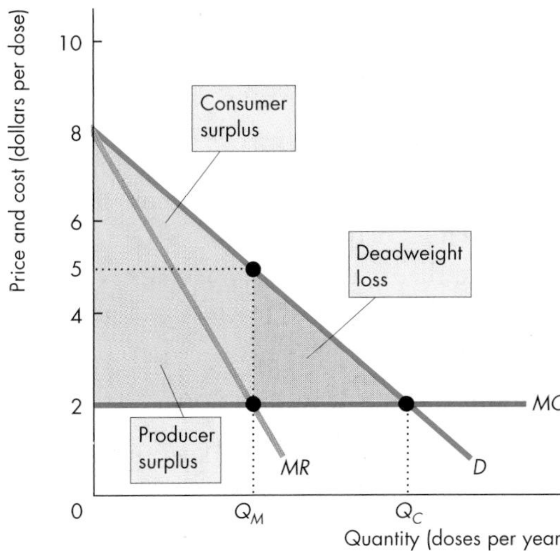

Figure 1 The market for Tamiflu

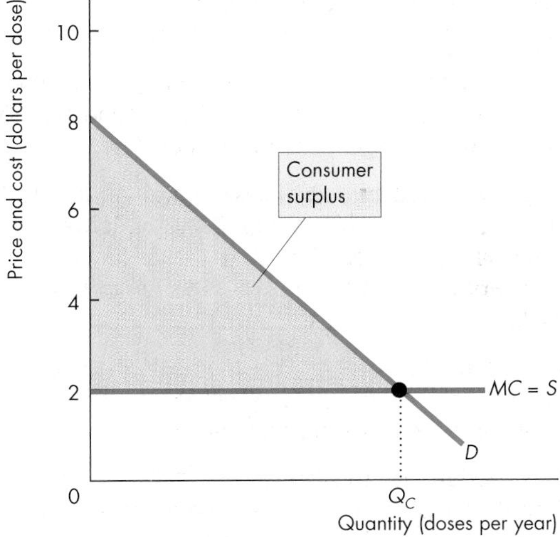

Figure 2 The market for generic oseltamivir

You're the Voter

- Should a drug company be permitted to sell a new drug with patent protection from the competition that a generic drug brings? Why or why not?
- Should international trade in drugs be permitted or blocked? Why?

SUMMARY

Key Points

The Economic Theory of Government (pp. 324–326)

- Government exists to regulate monopoly and oligopoly, cope with externalities, provide public goods, control the use of common resources, and reduce economic inequality.
- Public choice theory explains how voters, firms, politicians, and bureaucrats interact in a political marketplace.

Monopoly and Oligopoly Regulation (pp. 326–327)

- Government uses regulation and antitrust law to intervene in monopoly and oligopoly markets.
- Consumers demand regulation that increases consumer surplus, and firms demand regulation that increases producer surplus.
- Equilibrium regulation might be in the social interest and eliminate deadweight loss or in the self-interest of producers who capture the regulators.

Regulation and Deregulation (pp. 327–334)

- Federal regulation began in 1887 and expanded until the mid-1970s, after which time much deregulation has occurred.
- Politically appointed bureaucrats conduct regulation.
- A natural monopoly or a cartel might be regulated by a marginal cost pricing rule, an average cost pricing rule, a rate of return target, or a price cap.
- Both natural monopoly and cartel regulation have often been in the self-interest of the producer and deregulation has generally been in the social interest.

Antitrust Law (pp. 335–337)

- The first antitrust law, the Sherman Act, was passed in 1890, and the law was strengthened in 1914 when the Clayton Act was passed and the Federal Trade Commission was created.
- All price-fixing agreements are violations of the Sherman Act, and no acceptable excuse exists.
- Resale price maintenance might be efficient if it enables a producer to ensure the efficient level of service by distributors.
- Tying arrangements can enable a monopoly to price discriminate and increase profit, but in many cases, tying would not increase profit.
- Predatory pricing is unlikely to occur because it brings losses and only temporary potential gains.
- The Federal Trade Commission uses guidelines such as the Herfindahl-Hirschman Index to determine which mergers to investigate and possibly block.
- The intent of antitrust law is to protect the social interest. This intent has been served most of the time. But sometimes producer self-interest has influenced the application of the law.

Key Figures and Table

Key Terms

PROBLEMS

myeconlab **Tests, Study Plan, Solutions***

1. Elixir Springs, Inc., is an unregulated natural monopoly that bottles Elixir, a unique health product with no substitutes. The fixed costs incurred by Elixir Springs are $150,000 a year, and its marginal cost is 10¢ a bottle. The figure illustrates the demand for Elixir.

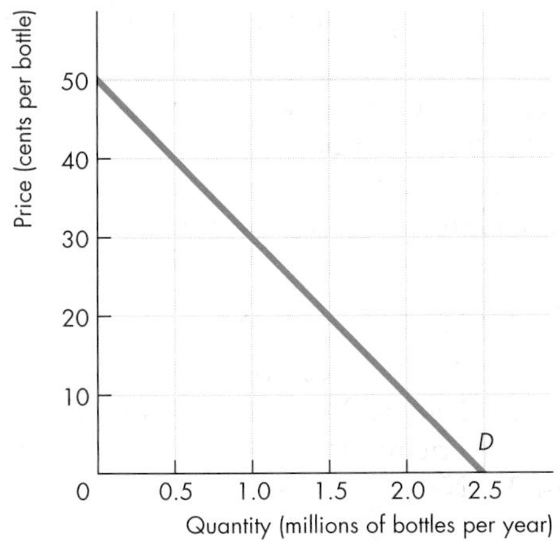

   a. What is the price of a bottle of Elixir?
   b. How many bottles does Elixir Springs sell?
   c. Does Elixir Springs maximize total surplus or producer surplus?

2. The government imposes a marginal cost pricing rule on Elixir Springs in problem 1.
   a. What is the price of a bottle of Elixir?
   b. How many bottles does Elixir Springs sell?
   c. What is Elixir Springs' producer surplus?
   d. What is the consumer surplus?
   e. Is the regulation in the social interest? Explain.

3. The government imposes an average cost pricing rule on Elixir Springs in problem 1.
   a. What is the price of a bottle of Elixir?
   b. How many bottles does Elixir Springs sell?
   c. What is Elixir Springs' producer surplus?
   d. What is the consumer surplus?
   e. Is the regulation in the social interest? Explain.

4. The government imposes rate of return regulation on Elixir Springs in problem 1. If Elixir Springs captures the regulator,
   a. What is the price of a bottle of Elixir?
   b. How many bottles does Elixir Springs sell?
   c. What is the inflated average total cost at the quantity produced?

*Solutions to odd-numbered problems are provided.

5. Two airlines share an international route. The figure shows the demand curve for trips on this route and the marginal cost curve that each firm faces. This air route is regulated.

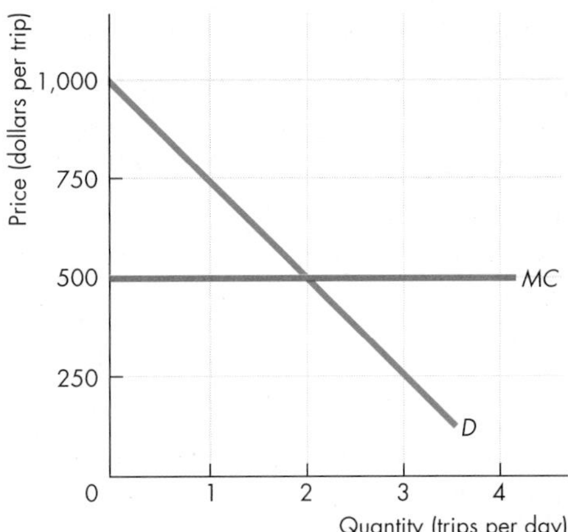

   a. What is the price of a trip and what is the number of trips per day if the regulation is in the social interest?
   b. What is the price of a trip and what is the number of trips per day if the regulation is in the producer's interest?
   c. What is the deadweight loss in part (b)?
   d. What do you need to know to predict whether the regulation will be in the social interest or the producer's interest?

6. Suppose that in problem 5, the air route is unregulated. What is the price of a trip and what is the number of trips per day if the airlines can form an effective cartel?

7. Suppose that in problem 5, the air route is unregulated but the price of a trip has been driven down to the competitive level because the airlines are unable to form an effective cartel. One airline would like to drive the other airline off the route and considers practicing predatory pricing. Could the airline succeed in eliminating competition in the short run and in the long run? Why or why not?

8. What charges, if any, might be brought under the antitrust law in each of the following situations?
   a. The owners of the only two taxi companies in a town are discovered holding secret meetings to fix their prices.
   b. Walgreens proposes to buy Rite Aid and other major pharmacies.

c. A producer of hair care products opens a chain of hair salons.
d. A video rental store requires customers to rent a foreign-produced movie with every Hollywood-produced movie they rent.
e. Access to a cooking website is given only with the subscription to a monthly food magazine.

9. Explain the difference between regulation and antitrust law. To what situations does each apply? Give an example of the use of each.
10. Describe the difference between the ways in which the two parts of the Sherman Act have been applied. Why do you think one part has been interpreted more strictly than the other?
11. Suppose that Burger King, McDonald's, and Wendy's proposed a merger into a single Super Burger Chain.
    a. Would such a merger be in the social interest? Explain.
    b. What would happen to the price of a burger?
    c. What would happen to consumer surplus, producer surplus, and deadweight loss if such a merger occurred?
    d. Would the antitrust authorities block such a merger? Why or why not?

CRITICAL THINKING

1. After you have studied *Reading Between the Lines* on pp. 338–339, answer the following questions:
    a. Does the sale of a patented drug violate U.S. antitrust laws?
    b. Why might a drug company want to price discriminate?
    c. Do you think a drug company can successfully price discriminate?
    c. If Congress made it legal to import pharmaceutical drugs from Southeast Asia what would happen to the price of drugs in the United States? What would happen to producer surplus, consumer surplus, and deadweight loss?
2. **OPEC Cuts Production 4% to Prop Up Prices**
    OPEC producers sought to reassert their grip on falling oil markets on Thursday by backing a production cut of 1.2 million barrels a day, and suggested more reductions could follow this year to prop up sagging prices.

    The New York Times, October 20, 2006

    OPEC is an international cartel that operates outside the scope of the U.S. antitrust laws.
    a. Given the news in this article, and if U.S. antitrust laws could be extended to cover OPEC, would OPEC be in violation of the law? If so, explain which part of the law it would violate. If not, explain why not.
    b. What would happen to the world price of oil and the quantity of oil consumed if OPEC were made to operate under antitrust laws like those of the United States?

WEB ACTIVITIES

myeconlab Links to Web sites

1. Visit the FTC and read the press release on the consent order for the AOL–Time Warner merger.
    a. What conditions did the FTC impose when it approved the merger?
    b. What are the markets in which AOL–Time Warner operates? Which of these markets, if any, are competitive and in which of them, if any, might AOL–Time Warner be a monopoly?
    c. Who benefits from the AOL–Time Warner merger? Draw a diagram that illustrates the directions of the changes in price, output, producer surplus, and consumer surplus that you think resulted from the merger.
2. Visit the FTC and read the press release on the charge that Intel Corporation has abused its monopoly position.
    a. What does the FTC say that Intel did in violation of the antitrust law?
    b. Do you agree with the FTC? Why or why not?
    c. Draw a figure that illustrates how Intel benefited and others lost from its actions.
3. Read the order issued by the court to break up Microsoft.
    a. What exactly did the court order?
    b. How do you think the software industry would have changed if the breakup order had been implemented?

CHAPTER 15

Externalities

Greener and Smarter

We burn huge quantities of fossil fuels—coal, natural gas, and oil—that cause acid rain and global warming. We dump toxic waste into rivers, lakes, and oceans. These environmental issues are simultaneously everybody's problem and nobody's problem. How can we take account of the damage that we cause others every time we turn on our heating or air-conditioning systems?

Almost every day, we hear about a new discovery—in medicine, engineering, chemistry, physics, or even economics. The advance of knowledge seems boundless. And more and more people are learning more and more of what is already known. The stock of knowledge is increasing, apparently without bound. We are getting smarter. But are we getting smarter fast enough? Are we spending enough on research and education? Do enough people remain in school for long enough? And do we work hard enough at school? Would we be better off if we spent more on research and education?

In this chapter, we study the problems that arise because many of our actions create externalities. They affect other people, for ill or good, in ways that we do not usually take into account when we make our own economic choices. We study two big areas—pollution and knowledge—in which externalities are especially important. Externalities are a major source of *market failure.* When market failure occurs, we must either live with the inefficiency it creates or try to achieve greater efficiency by making some *public choices.* This chapter studies these choices. In *Reading Between the Lines* at the end of the chapter, we look at an attempt to deal with air pollution in California.

After studying this chapter, you will be able to

- Explain how externalities arise
- Explain why negative externalities lead to inefficient overproduction and how property rights, emission charges, marketable permits, and taxes can be used to achieve a more efficient outcome
- Explain why positive externalities lead to inefficient underproduction and how public provision, subsidies, vouchers, and patents can increase economic efficiency

Externalities in Our Lives

A cost or benefit that arises from production and falls on someone other than the producer, or a cost or benefit that arises from consumption and falls on someone other than the consumer is called an **externality**. Let's review the range of externalities, classify them, and look at some everyday examples.

An externality can arise from either *production* or *consumption*, and it can be either a **negative externality**, which imposes an external cost, or a **positive externality**, which provides an external benefit. So there are four types of externalities:

- Negative production externalities
- Positive production externalities
- Negative consumption externalities
- Positive consumption externalities

Negative Production Externalities

The Lincoln Tunnel, which connects New Jersey to Manhattan under the Hudson River, is 1.5 miles long. Yet it can take 2 hours to get through the tunnel in the worst traffic. Each rush-hour user of the Lincoln Tunnel imposes a negative production externality on the other users.

When you run your air-conditioning, use hot water, drive a car, or even take a bus or train, your action contributes to pollution of the atmosphere. Pollution is another example of a negative production externality.

Positive Production Externalities

If a honey farmer locates beehives beside an orange grower's orchard, two positive production externalities arise. The honey farmer gets a positive production externality from the orange grower because the bees collect pollen and nectar from orange blossoms. And the orange grower gets a positive production externality because the bees pollinate the blossoms.

Negative Consumption Externalities

Negative consumption externalities are a source of irritation for most of us. Smoking tobacco in a confined space creates fumes that many people find unpleasant and that pose a health risk. Smoking creates a negative consumption externality. To deal with this externality, in many places and in almost all public places, smoking is banned. But banning smoking imposes a negative consumption externality on smokers! The majority imposes a cost on the minority—the smokers who would prefer to consume tobacco while dining or taking a plane trip.

Noisy parties and outdoor rock concerts are other examples of negative consumption externalities. They are also examples of the fact that a simple ban on an activity is not a solution. Banning noisy parties avoids the external cost on sleep-seeking neighbors, but it results in the sleepers imposing an external cost on the fun-seeking partygoers.

Permitting dandelions to grow in lawns, not picking up leaves in the fall, and allowing a dog to bark loudly or to foul a neighbor's lawn are other sources of negative consumption externalities.

Positive Consumption Externalities

When you get a flu vaccination, you lower your risk of getting infected this winter. But if you avoid the flu, your neighbor who didn't get vaccinated has a better chance of avoiding it too. Flu vaccination generates positive consumption externalities.

When the owner of a historic building restores it, everyone who sees the building gets pleasure from it. Similarly, when someone erects a spectacular house—such as those built by Frank Lloyd Wright during the 1920s and 1930s—or another exciting building—such as the Chrysler Building and the Empire State Building in New York or the Wrigley Building in Chicago—an external consumption benefit flows to everyone who has an opportunity to view it. Education, which we examine in this chapter, is another example of this type of externality.

REVIEW QUIZ

1 What are the four types of externality?
2 Try to think of an example of each type of externality, different from the ones described above.
3 How are the externalities that you've described addressed, either by the market or by public policy?

myeconlab Study Plan 15.1

Negative Externalities: Pollution

Pollution is not a new problem and is not restricted to rich industrial countries. Preindustrial towns and cities in Europe had sewage disposal problems that created cholera epidemics and plagues that killed millions. London's air in the Middle Ages was dirtier than that of Los Angeles today. Some of the worst pollution today is found in Russia and China. Nor is the desire to find solutions to pollution new. The development in the fourteenth century of garbage and sewage disposal is an example of early attempts to tackle pollution.

Popular discussions of pollution usually pay little attention to economics. They focus on physical aspects of the problem, not on the costs and benefits. A common assumption is that if people's actions cause *any* pollution, those actions must cease. In contrast, an economic study of pollution emphasizes costs and benefits. An economist talks about the efficient amount of pollution. This emphasis on costs and benefits does not mean that economists, as citizens, do not share the same goals as others and value a healthy environment. Nor does it mean that economists have the right answers and everyone else has the wrong ones (or vice versa). The starting point for an economic analysis of pollution is the demand for a pollution-free environment.

The Demand for a Pollution-Free Environment

The demand for a pollution-free environment is greater today than it has ever been. We express this demand by joining organizations that lobby for antipollution regulations and policies. We vote for politicians who support the policies that we want to see implemented. We buy "green" products, even if we pay a bit more to do so. And we pay higher housing costs and commuting costs to live in pleasant neighborhoods.

The demand for a pollution-free environment has grown for two main reasons. First, as our incomes increase, we demand a larger range of goods and services, and one of these "goods" is a pollution-free environment. We value clean air, unspoiled natural scenery, and wildlife, and we are willing and able to pay for them.

Second, as our knowledge of the effects of pollution grows, we are able to take measures that reduce those effects. For example, now that we know how sulfur dioxide causes acid rain and how clearing rain forests destroys natural stores of carbon dioxide, we are able, in principle, to design measures that limit these problems.

Let's look at the range of pollution problems that have been identified and the actions that create those problems.

The Sources of Pollution

Economic activity pollutes air, water, and land, and these individual areas of pollution interact through the *ecosystem*.

Air Pollution Sixty percent of our air pollution comes from road transportation and industrial processes. Only 16 percent arises from electric power generation.

A common belief is that air pollution is getting worse. In many developing countries, air pollution *is* getting worse. But air pollution in the United States is getting less severe for most substances. Figure 15.1 shows the trends in the concentrations of six air pollutants. Lead has been almost eliminated from our air. Sulfur dioxide, carbon monoxide, and suspended particulates have been reduced to around a half of their 1980 levels. And even the more stubborn ozone and nitrogen dioxide have been reduced to around 70 percent of their 1980 levels.

These reductions in levels of air pollution are even more impressive when they are compared with the level of economic activity. Between 1970 and 2000, total production in the United States increased by 158 percent. During this same period, vehicle miles traveled increased by 143 percent, energy consumption increased by 45 percent, and the population increased by 36 percent. While all this economic activity was on the increase, air pollution from all sources *decreased* by 29 percent.

While the facts about the sources and trends in air pollution are not in doubt, there is disagreement about the *effects* of air pollution. The least controversial is *acid rain* caused by sulfur dioxide and nitrogen oxide emissions from coal- and oil-fired generators of electric utilities. Acid rain begins with air pollution, and it leads to water pollution and damages vegetation.

More controversial are airborne substances (suspended particulates) such as lead from leaded gasoline. Some scientists believe that in sufficiently large concentrations, these substances (189 of which have currently been identified) cause cancer and other life-threatening conditions.

FIGURE 15.1 Trends in Air Pollution

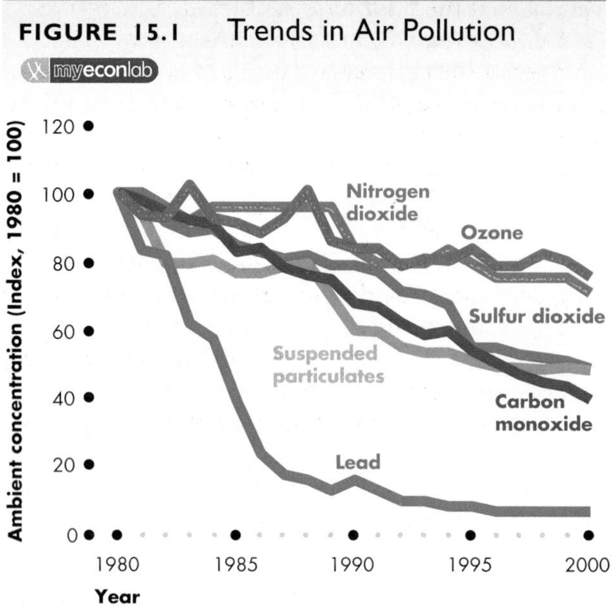

Lead has almost been eliminated from our air; concentrations of carbon monoxide, sulfur dioxide, and suspended particulates have decreased to about 50 percent of their 1980 levels; and nitrogen dioxide and ozone have fallen to about 70 percent of their 1980 levels.

Source of data: U.S. Environmental Protection Agency, *National Air Quality and Emissions Trends Report, 1999 and 2000.*

Even more controversial is *global warming,* which some scientists believe results from the carbon dioxide emissions. The earth's average temperature has increased over the past 100 years, but most of the increase occurred *before* 1940. Determining what causes changes in the earth's temperature and isolating the effect of carbon dioxide from other factors are proving to be difficult.

Equally controversial is the problem of *ozone layer depletion.* There is no doubt that a hole in the ozone layer exists over Antarctica and that the ozone layer protects us from cancer-causing ultraviolet rays from the sun. But how our industrial activity influences the ozone layer is simply not understood at this time.

One air pollution problem has almost been eliminated: lead from gasoline. In part, this happened because the cost of living without leaded gasoline, it turns out, is not high. But sulfur dioxide and the so-called greenhouse gases are a much tougher problem to tackle. Their alternatives are costly or have pollution problems of their own. The major sources of these pollutants are road vehicles and electric utilities. Road vehicles can be made "greener" in a variety of ways. One is with new fuels, and some alternatives being investigated are alcohol, natural gas, propane and butane, and hydrogen. Another way of making cars and trucks "greener" is to change the chemistry of gasoline. Refiners are working on reformulations of gasoline that reduce tailpipe emissions. Similarly, electricity can be generated in cleaner ways by harnessing wind power, solar power, tidal power, or geothermal power. While technically possible, these methods are more costly than conventional carbon-fueled generators. Another alternative is nuclear power. This method is good for air pollution but creates a potential long-term problem for land and water pollution because there is no known entirely safe method of disposing of spent nuclear fuel.

Water Pollution The largest sources of water pollution are the dumping of industrial waste and treated sewage in lakes and rivers and the runoff from fertilizers. A more dramatic source is the accidental spilling of crude oil into the oceans such as the *Exxon Valdez* spill in Alaska in 1989.

There are two main alternatives to polluting the waterways and oceans. One is the chemical processing of waste to render it inert or biodegradable. The other, in wide use for nuclear waste, is to use land sites for storage in secure containers.

Land Pollution Land pollution arises from dumping toxic waste products. Ordinary household garbage does not pose a pollution problem unless contaminants from dumped garbage seep into the water supply. This possibility increases as landfills reach capacity and less suitable landfill sites are used. It is estimated that 80 percent of existing landfills will be full by 2010. Some regions (New York, New Jersey, and other East Coast states) and some countries (Japan and the Netherlands) are seeking less costly alternatives to landfill, such as recycling and incineration. Recycling is an apparently attractive alternative, but it requires an investment in new technologies to be effective. Incineration is a high-cost alternative to landfill, and it produces air pollution. Furthermore, these alternatives are not free, and they become efficient only when the cost of using landfill is high.

We've seen that the demand for a pollution-free environment has grown, and we've described the range of pollution problems. Let's now look at the economics of these problems. The starting point is the distinction between private costs and social costs.

Private Costs and Social Costs

A *private cost* of production is a cost that is borne by the producer of a good or service. *Marginal cost* is the cost of producing an *additional unit* of a good or service. So **marginal private cost** (*MC*) is the cost of producing an additional unit of a good or service that is borne by the producer of that good or service.

You've seen that an *external cost* is a cost of producing a good or service that is *not* borne by the producer but borne by other people. A **marginal external cost** is the cost of producing an additional unit of a good or service that falls on people other than the producer.

Marginal social cost (*MSC*) is the marginal cost incurred by the entire society—by the producer and by everyone else on whom the cost falls—and is the sum of marginal private cost and marginal external cost. That is,

$$MSC = MC + \text{Marginal external cost.}$$

We express costs in dollars. But we must always remember that a cost is an opportunity cost—what we give up to get something. A marginal external cost is what someone other than the producer of a good or service must give up when the producer makes one more unit of the good or service. Something real, such as a clean river or clean air, is given up.

Valuing an External Cost Economists use market prices to put a dollar value on the cost of pollution. For example, suppose that there are two similar rivers, one polluted and the other clean. Five hundred identical homes are built along the side of each river. The homes on the clean river rent for $2,500 a month, and those on the polluted river rent for $1,500 a month. If the pollution is the only detectable difference between the two rivers and the two locations, the rent decrease of $1,000 per month is the cost of the pollution. For the 500 homes on the polluted river, the external cost is $500,000 a month.

External Cost and Output Figure 15.2 shows an example of the relationship between output and cost in a chemical industry that pollutes. The marginal cost curve, *MC*, describes the marginal private cost borne by the firms that produce the chemical. Marginal cost increases as the quantity of chemical produced increases. If the firms dump waste into a river, they impose an external cost that increases with the amount of the chemical produced. The marginal social cost curve, *MSC*, is the sum of marginal private cost and marginal external cost. For example, when output is 4,000 tons of chemical a month, marginal private cost is $100 a ton, marginal external cost is $125 a ton, and marginal social cost is $225 a ton.

In Fig. 15.2, when the quantity of chemical produced increases, the amount of pollution increases and the external cost of pollution increases.

Figure 15.2 shows the relationship between the quantity of chemical produced and the cost of the pollution it creates, but it doesn't tell us how much pollution gets created. That quantity depends on how the market for the chemical operates. First, we'll see what happens when the industry is free to pollute.

FIGURE 15.2 An External Cost

myeconlab

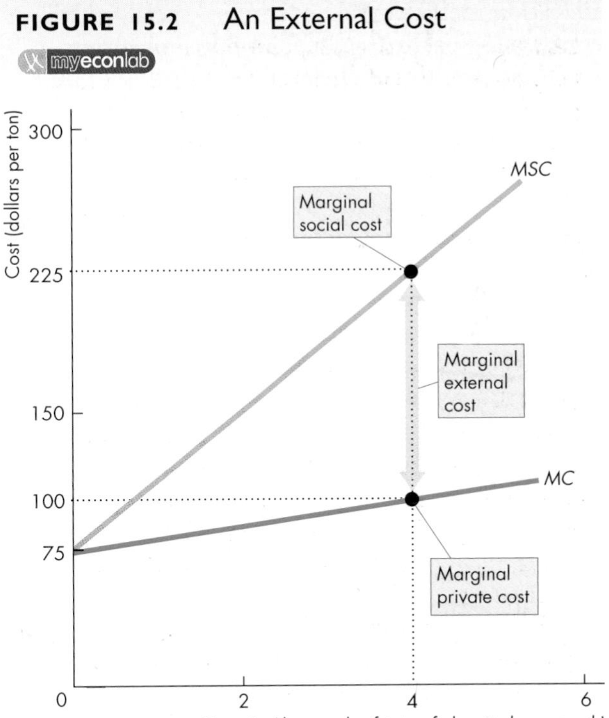

The *MC* curve shows the marginal private cost borne by the factories that produce a chemical. The *MSC* curve shows the sum of marginal private cost and marginal external cost. When output is 4,000 tons of chemical a month, marginal private cost is $100 a ton, marginal external cost is $125 a ton, and marginal social cost is $225 a ton.

Production and Pollution: How Much?

When an industry is unregulated, the amount of pollution it creates depends on the market equilibrium price and quantity of the good produced. In Fig. 15.3, the demand curve for a pollution-creating chemical is *D*. This curve also measures the marginal social benefit, *MSB*, of the chemical. The supply curve is *S*. This curve also measures the producers' marginal private cost, *MC*. The supply curve is the marginal private cost curve because when firms make their production and supply decisions, they consider only the costs that they will bear. Market equilibrium occurs at a price of $100 a ton and 4,000 tons of chemical a month.

This equilibrium is inefficient. You learned in Chapter 5 that the allocation of resources is efficient when marginal social benefit equals marginal social cost. But we must count all the costs—private and external—when we compare marginal social benefit and marginal social cost. So with an external cost, the allocation is efficient when marginal social benefit equals marginal *social* cost. This outcome occurs when the quantity of chemical produced is 2,000 tons a month. The unregulated market overproduces by 2,000 tons of chemical a month and creates a deadweight loss shown by the gray triangle.

How can the people who live by the polluted river get the chemical factories to decrease their output of chemical and create less pollution? If some method can be found to achieve this outcome, everyone—the owners of the chemical factories and the residents of the riverside homes—can gain. Let's explore some solutions.

FIGURE 15.3 Inefficiency with an External Cost

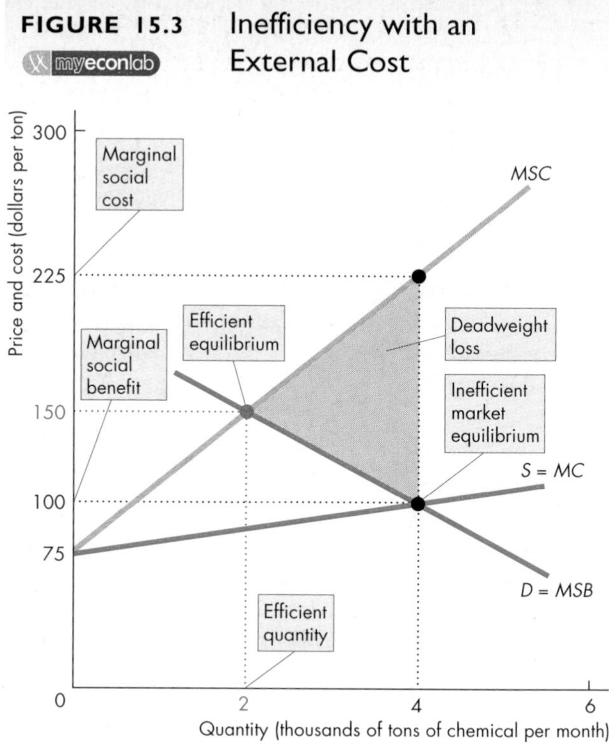

The supply curve is the marginal private cost curve, *S* = *MC*. The demand curve is the marginal social benefit curve, *D* = *MSB*. Market equilibrium at a price of $100 a ton and 4,000 tons a month is inefficient because marginal social cost exceeds marginal social benefit. The efficient quantity is 2,000 tons a month. The gray triangle shows the deadweight loss created by the pollution externality.

Property Rights

Sometimes it is possible to reduce the inefficiency arising from an externality by establishing a property right where one does not currently exist. **Property rights** are legally established titles to the ownership, use, and disposal of factors of production and goods and services that are enforceable in the courts.

Suppose that the chemical factories own the river and the 500 homes alongside it. The rent that people are willing to pay depends on the amount of pollution. Using the earlier example, people are willing to pay $2,500 a month to live alongside a pollution-free river but only $1,500 a month to live with the pollution created by 4,000 tons of chemical a month. If the factories produce this quantity, they lose $1,000 a month for each home and a total of $500,000 a month.

The chemical factories are now confronted with the cost of their pollution—forgone rent from the people who live by the river.

Figure 15.4 illustrates the outcome by using the same example as in Fig. 15.3. With property rights in place, the *MC* curve no longer measures all the costs that the factories face in producing the chemical. It excludes the pollution costs that they must now bear. The *MSC* curve now becomes the marginal private cost curve *MC*. All the costs fall on the factories, so the market supply curve is based on all the marginal costs and is the curve labeled *S* = *MC* = *MSC*.

Market equilibrium now occurs at a price of $150 a ton and 2,000 tons of chemical a month. This outcome is efficient. The factories still produce some pollution, but it is the efficient quantity.

FIGURE 15.4 Property Rights Achieve an Efficient Outcome

myeconlab

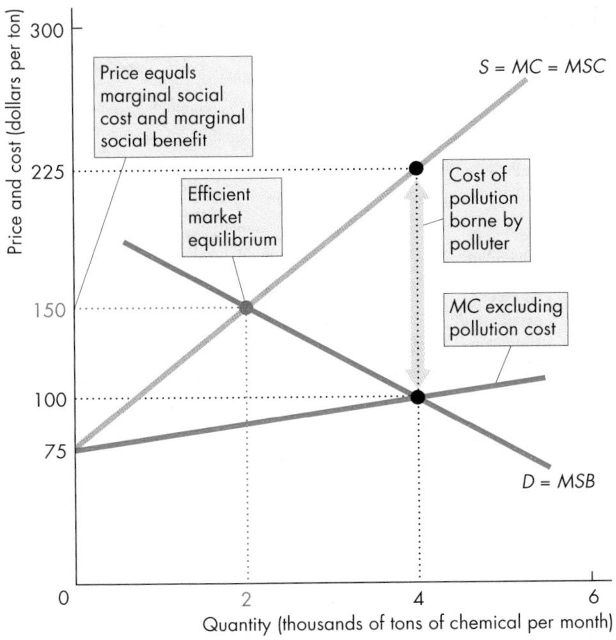

With property rights, the marginal cost curve that excludes pollution costs shows only part of the producers' marginal cost. The marginal private cost curve includes the cost of pollution, so the supply curve is $S = MC = MSC$. Market equilibrium is at a price of \$150 a ton and 2,000 tons of chemical a month and is efficient because marginal social cost equals marginal social benefit. The efficient quantity of pollution is not zero.

The Coase Theorem

Does it matter how property rights are assigned? Does it matter whether the polluter or the victim of the pollution owns the resource that might be polluted? Until 1960, everyone thought that it did matter. But in 1960, Ronald Coase (see p. 380) had a remarkable insight, now called the Coase theorem.

The **Coase theorem** is the proposition that if property rights exist, if only a small number of parties are involved, and if transactions costs are low, then private transactions are efficient. There are no externalities because the transacting parties take all the costs and benefits into account. Furthermore, it doesn't matter who has the property rights.

Application of the Coase Theorem In the example that we've just studied, the factories own the river and the homes. Suppose that instead, the residents own their homes and the river. Now the factories must pay a fee to the homeowners for the right to dump their waste. The greater the quantity of waste dumped into the river, the more the factories must pay. So again, the factories face the opportunity cost of the pollution they create. The quantity of chemical produced and the amount of waste dumped are the same whoever owns the homes and the river. If the factories own them, they bear the cost of pollution because they receive a lower income from home rents. And if the residents own the homes and the river, the factories bear the cost of pollution because they must pay a fee to the homeowners. In both cases, the factories bear the cost of their pollution and dump the efficient amount of waste into the river.

The Coase solution works only when transactions costs are low. **Transactions costs** are the opportunity costs of conducting a transaction. For example, when you buy a house, you incur a series of transactions costs. You might pay a realtor to help you find the best place and a lawyer to run checks that assure you that the seller owns the property and that after you've paid for it, the ownership has been properly transferred to you.

In the example of the homes alongside a river, the transactions costs that are incurred by a small number of chemical factories and a few homeowners might be low enough to enable them to negotiate the deals that produce an efficient outcome. But in many situations, transactions costs are so high that it would be inefficient to incur them. In these situations, the Coase solution is not available.

Suppose, for example, that everyone owns the airspace above their homes up to, say, 10 miles. If someone pollutes your airspace, you can charge a fee. But to collect the fee, you must identify who is polluting your airspace and persuade them to pay you. Imagine the costs of negotiating and enforcing agreements with the 50 million people who live in your part of the United States (and perhaps in Canada or Mexico) and the several thousand factories that emit sulfur dioxide and create acid rain that falls on your property! In this situation, we use public choices to cope with externalities. But the transactions costs that block a market solution are real costs, so attempts by the government to deal with externalities offer no easy solution. Let's look at some of these attempts.

Government Actions in the Face of External Costs

The three main methods that governments use to cope with externalities are

- Taxes
- Emission charges
- Marketable permits

Taxes The government can use taxes as an incentive for producers to cut back on pollution. Taxes used in this way are called **Pigovian taxes,** in honor of Arthur Cecil Pigou, the British economist who first worked out this method of dealing with externalities during the 1920s.

By setting the tax equal to the marginal external cost, firms can be made to behave in the same way as they would if they bore the cost of the externality directly. To see how government actions can change market outcomes in the face of externalities, let's return to the example of the chemical factories and the river.

Assume that the government has assessed the marginal external cost accurately and imposes a tax on the factories that exactly equals this cost. Figure 15.5 illustrates the effects of this tax.

The demand curve and marginal social benefit curve, $D = MSB$, and the firms' marginal cost curve, MC, are the same as in Fig. 15.3. The pollution tax equals the marginal external cost of the pollution. We add this tax to the marginal private cost to find the market supply curve. This curve is the one labeled $S = MC + tax = MSC$. This curve is the market supply curve because it tells us the quantity supplied at each price given the firms' marginal cost and the tax they must pay. This curve is also the marginal social cost curve because the pollution tax has been set equal to the marginal external cost.

Demand and supply now determine the market equilibrium price at $150 a ton and a quantity at 2,000 tons of chemical a month. At this quantity of chemical production, the marginal social cost is $150 and the marginal social benefit is $150, so the outcome is efficient. The firms incur a marginal cost of $88 a ton and pay a tax of $62 a ton. The government collects tax revenue of $124,000 a month.

Emission Charges Emission charges are an alternative to a tax for confronting a polluter with the external cost of pollution. The government sets a price per unit of pollution. The more pollution a firm creates, the more it pays in emission charges. This method of dealing with pollution externalities has been used only modestly in the United States but is common in Europe where, for example, France, Germany, and the Netherlands make water polluters pay a waste disposal charge.

FIGURE 15.5 A Pollution Tax to Achieve an Efficient Outcome

myeconlab

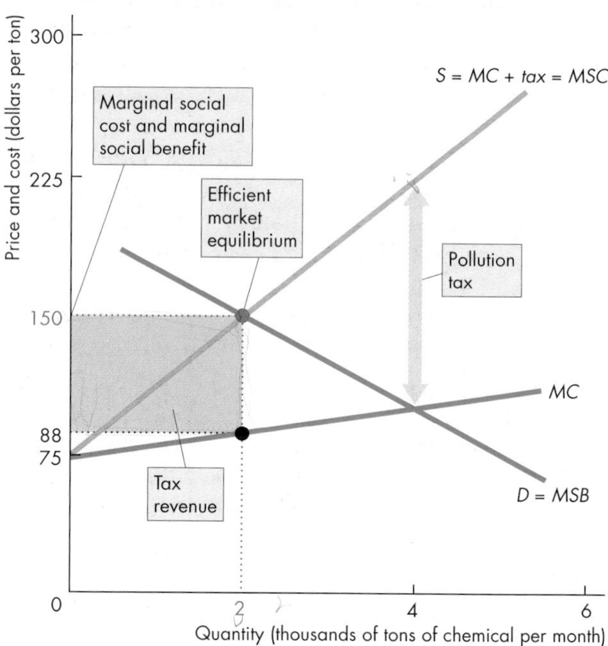

A pollution tax is imposed equal to the marginal external cost of pollution. The supply curve becomes the marginal private cost curve, MC, plus the tax—$S = MC + tax$. Market equilibrium is at a price of $150 a ton and 2,000 tons of chemical a month and is efficient because marginal social cost equals marginal social benefit. The government collects a tax revenue shown by the purple rectangle.

To work out the emission charge that achieves efficiency, the government needs a lot of information about the polluting industry that, in practice, is rarely available.

Marketable Permits Instead of taxing or imposing emission charges on polluters, each potential polluter might be assigned a permitted pollution limit. Each firm knows its own costs and benefits of pollution, and making pollution limits marketable is a clever way of using this private information that is unknown to the government. The government issues each firm a permit to emit a certain amount of pollution, and firms can buy and sell these permits. Firms that have a low marginal cost of reducing pollution sell their permits, and firms that have a high marginal cost of reducing pollution buy permits. The market in permits determines the price at which firms trade permits. Each firm buys or sells permits until its marginal cost of pollution equals the market price of a permit.

This method of dealing with pollution provides an even stronger incentive than do emission charges to find technologies that pollute less because the price of a permit to pollute rises as the demand for permits increases.

The Market for Emission Permits in the United States Trading in lead pollution permits became common during the 1980s, and this marketable permit program has been rated a success. It enabled lead to be virtually eliminated from the atmosphere of the United States (see Fig. 15.1). But this success might not easily translate to other situations because lead pollution has some special features. First, most lead pollution came from a single source: leaded gasoline. Second, lead in gasoline is easily monitored. Third, the objective of the program was clear: to eliminate lead in gasoline.

The Environmental Protection Agency is now considering using marketable permits to promote efficiency in the control of chlorofluorocarbons, the gases that are believed to damage the ozone layer.

REVIEW QUIZ

1. What is the distinction between private cost and social cost?
2. How does a negative externality prevent a competitive market from allocating resources efficiently?
3. How can a negative externality be eliminated by assigning property rights? How does this method of coping with an externality work?
4. How do taxes help us to cope with negative externalities? At what level must a pollution tax be set if it is to induce firms to produce the efficient quantity of pollution?
5. How do emission charges and marketable pollution permits work?

myeconlab **Study Plan 15.2**

Positive Externalities: Knowledge

Knowledge comes from education and research. To study the economics of knowledge, we must distinguish between private benefits and social benefits.

Private Benefits and Social Benefits

A *private benefit* is a benefit that the consumer of a good or service receives. *Marginal benefit* is the benefit from an *additional unit* of a good or service. So a **marginal private benefit** (*MB*) is the benefit from an additional unit of a good or service that the consumer of that good or service receives.

The *external benefit* from a good or service is the benefit that someone other than the consumer receives. A **marginal external benefit** is the benefit from an additional unit of a good or service that people other than the consumer enjoy.

Marginal social benefit (*MSB*) is the marginal benefit enjoyed by society—by the consumer of a good or service (marginal private benefit) plus the marginal benefit enjoyed by others (the marginal external benefit). That is,

$$MSB = MB + \text{Marginal external benefit.}$$

Figure 15.6 shows an example of the relationship between marginal private benefit, marginal external benefit, and marginal social benefit. The marginal benefit curve, *MB*, describes the marginal private benefit—such as expanded job opportunities and higher incomes—enjoyed by college graduates. Marginal private benefit decreases as the quantity of education increases.

But college graduates generate external benefits. On the average, they tend to be better citizens. Their crime rates are lower, and they are more tolerant of the views of others. A society with a large number of college graduates can support activities such as high-quality newspapers and television channels, music, theater, and other organized social activities.

In the example in Fig. 15.6, the marginal external benefit is $15,000 per student per year when 15 million students enroll in college. The marginal social benefit curve, *MSB*, is the sum of marginal private benefit and marginal external benefit. For example, when 15 million students a year enroll in college, the marginal private benefit is $10,000 per student and

FIGURE 15.6 An External Benefit

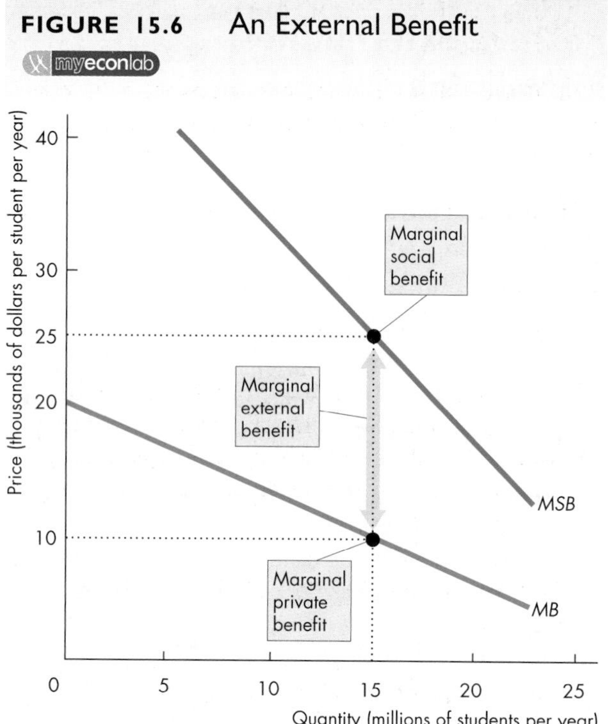

The *MB* curve shows the marginal private benefit enjoyed by the people who receive a college education. The *MSB* curve shows the sum of marginal private benefit and marginal external benefit. When 15 million students attend college, marginal private benefit is $10,000 per student, marginal external benefit is $15,000 per student, and marginal social benefit is $25,000 per student.

FIGURE 15.7 Inefficiency with an External Benefit

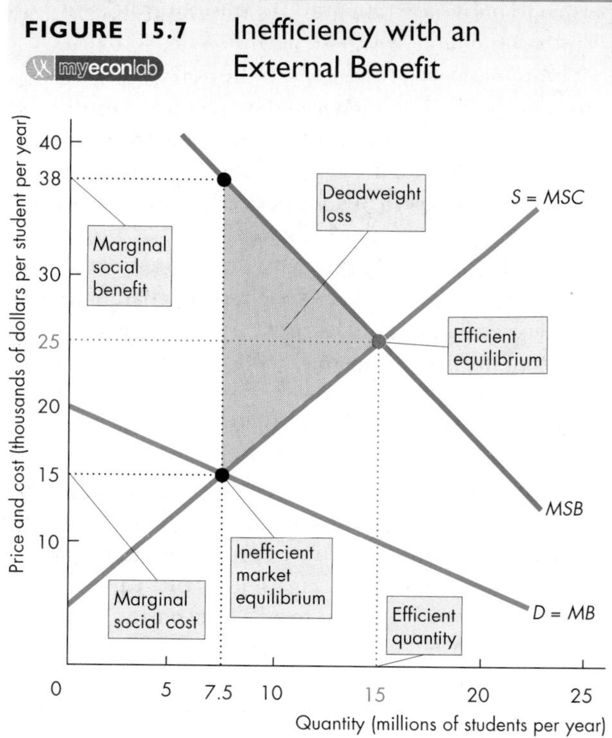

The market demand curve is the marginal private benefit curve, *D* = *MB*. The supply curve is the marginal social cost curve, *S* = *MSC*. Market equilibrium at a tuition of $15,000 a year and 7.5 million students is inefficient because marginal social benefit exceeds marginal social cost. The efficient quantity is 15 million students. A deadweight loss arises (gray triangle) because too few students enroll in college.

the marginal external benefit is $15,000 per student, so the marginal social benefit is $25,000 per student.

When people make schooling decisions, they ignore its external benefits and consider only its private benefits. So if education were provided by private schools that charged full-cost tuition, we would produce too few college graduates.

Figure 15.7 illustrates the underproduction if the government left education to the private market. The supply curve is the marginal social cost curve, *S* = *MSC*. The demand curve is the marginal private benefit curve, *D* = *MB*. Market equilibrium occurs at a tuition of $15,000 per student per year and 7.5 million students per year. At this equilibrium, marginal social benefit is $38,000 per student, which exceeds marginal social cost by $15,000. There are too few students in college. The efficient number is 15 million per year, where marginal social benefit equals marginal social cost. The gray triangle shows the deadweight loss.

Underproduction similar to that in Fig. 15.7 would occur in grade school and high school if an unregulated market produced it. When children learn basic reading, writing, and number skills, they receive the private benefit of increased earning power. But even these basic skills bring the external benefit of developing better citizens.

External benefits also arise from the discovery of new knowledge. When Isaac Newton worked out the formulas for calculating the rate of response of one variable to another—calculus—everyone was free to use his method. When a spreadsheet program called VisiCalc was invented, Lotus Corporation and Microsoft were free to copy the basic idea and create 1-2-3 and Excel. When the first shopping mall was built and found to be a successful way of arranging retailing, everyone was free to copy the idea, and malls spread like mushrooms.

Once someone has discovered a basic idea others can copy it. They do have to work to copy an idea, so they face an opportunity cost. But they do not usually have to pay a fee to use it. When people make decisions, they ignore the external benefits and consider only the private benefits.

When people make decisions about the amount of education or research to undertake, they balance the marginal private cost against the marginal private benefit. They ignore the external benefit. As a result, if we left education and research to unregulated market forces, we would get too little of these activities.

To get closer to producing the efficient quantity of a good or service that generates an external benefit, we make public choices, through governments, to modify the market outcome.

Government Actions in the Face of External Benefits

Four devices that governments can use to achieve a more efficient allocation of resources in the presence of external benefits are

- Public provision
- Private subsidies
- Vouchers
- Patents and copyrights

Public Provision Under **public provision**, a public authority that receives its revenue from the government produces the good or service. The education services produced by the public universities, colleges, and schools are examples of public provision.

Figure 15.8(a) shows how public provision might overcome the underproduction that arises in Fig. 15.7.

FIGURE 15.8 Public Provision or Private Subsidy to Achieve an Efficient Outcome

myeconlab

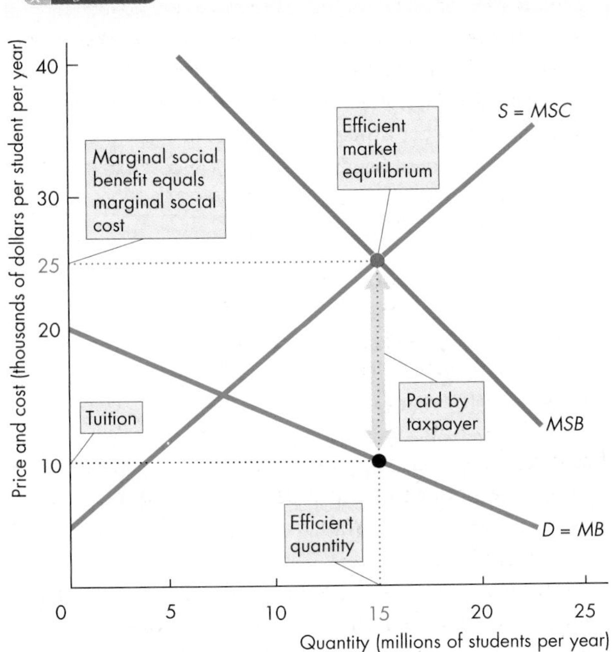

(a) Public provision

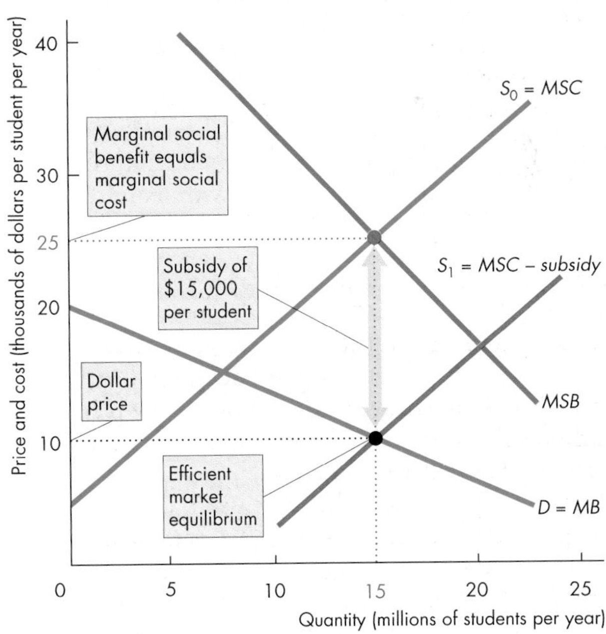

(b) Private subsidy

In part (a), marginal social benefit equals marginal social cost with 15 million students per year, the efficient quantity. Tuition is set at $10,000 per student equal to marginal private benefit. Taxpayers cover the other $15,000 of cost per student.

In part (b), with a subsidy of $15,000 per student, the supply curve is S_1 = *MSC – subsidy*. The equilibrium price is $10,000, and the market equilibrium is efficient with 15 million students per year. Marginal social benefit equals marginal social cost.

Public provision cannot lower the cost of production, so marginal social cost is the same as before. Marginal private benefit and marginal external benefit are also the same as before.

The efficient quantity occurs where marginal social benefit equals marginal social cost. In Fig. 15.8(a), this quantity is 15 million students. Tuition is set to ensure that the efficient number of students enrolls. That is, tuition is set equal to the marginal private benefit at the efficient quantity. In Fig. 15.8(a), tuition is $10,000 a year. The rest of the cost of the public university is borne by the taxpayers and, in this example, is $15,000 per student per year.

Private Subsidies A **subsidy** is a payment that the government makes to private producers. By making the subsidy depend on the level of output, the government can induce private decision makers to consider external benefits when they make their choices.

Figure 15.8(b) shows how a subsidy to private colleges works. In the absence of a subsidy, the market supply curve is $S_0 = MSC$. The demand curve is the marginal private benefit curve, $D = MB$. If the government provides a subsidy to colleges of $15,000 per student per year, we must subtract the subsidy from the college's marginal cost to find the new market supply curve. That curve is $S_1 = MSC - subsidy$. The market equilibrium is tuition of $10,000 a year and 15 million students a year. The marginal social cost of educating 15 million students is $25,000 and the marginal social benefit is $25,000. So with marginal social cost equal to marginal social benefit, the subsidy has achieved an efficient outcome. The tuition and the subsidy just cover the colleges' marginal cost.

Vouchers A **voucher** is a token that the government provides to households, which they can use to buy specified goods or services. Food stamps are examples of vouchers. The vouchers (stamps) can be spent only on food and are designed to improve the diet and health of extremely poor families.

School vouchers have been advocated as a means of improving the quality of education and have been used in Cleveland and Milwaukee.

A school voucher allows parents to choose the school their children will attend and to use the voucher to pay part of the cost. The school cashes the vouchers to pay its bills. A voucher could be provided to a college student in a similar way, and although technically not a voucher, a federal Pell Grant has a similar effect.

FIGURE 15.9 Vouchers Achieve an Efficient Outcome

myeconlab

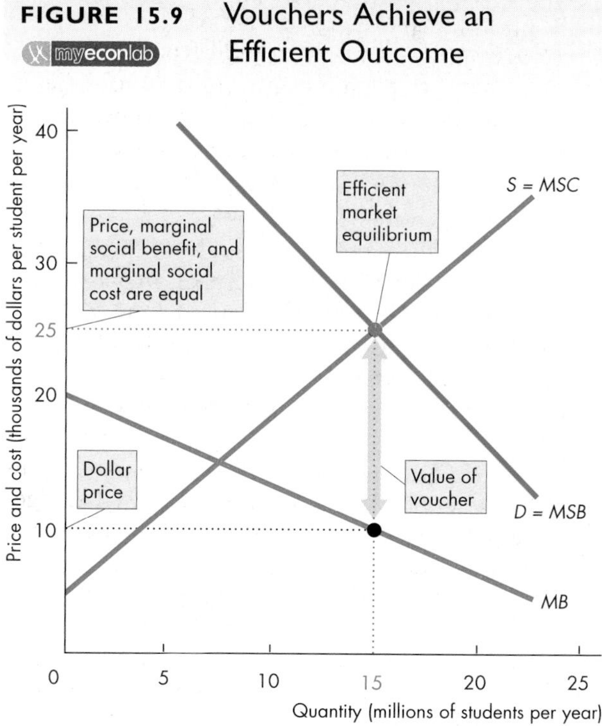

With vouchers, buyers are willing to pay *MB* plus the value of the voucher, so the demand curve becomes the marginal social benefit curve, *D* = *MSB*. Market equilibrium is efficient with 15 million students enrolled in college because price, marginal social benefit, and marginal cost are equal. The tuition consists of the dollar price of $10,000 and a voucher valued at $15,000.

Because vouchers can be spent only on a specified item, they increase the willingness to pay for that item and so increase the demand for it. Figure 15.9 shows how a voucher system works. The government provides a voucher per student equal to the marginal external benefit. Parents (or students) use these vouchers to supplement the dollars they pay for education. The marginal social benefit curve becomes the demand for college education, $D = MSB$. The market equilibrium occurs at a price of $25,000 per student per year, and 15 million students attend college. Each student pays $10,000 tuition, and schools collect an additional $15,000 per student from the voucher.

If the government estimates the value of the external benefit correctly and makes the value of the voucher equal the marginal external benefit, the outcome from the voucher scheme is efficient.

Marginal social cost equals marginal social benefit, and the deadweight loss is eliminated.

Vouchers are similar to subsidies, but their advocates say that they are more efficient than subsidies because the consumer can monitor school performance more effectively than the government can.

Patents and Copyrights Knowledge might be an exception to the principle of diminishing marginal benefit. Additional knowledge (about the right things) makes people more productive. And there seems to be no tendency for the additional productivity from additional knowledge to diminish.

For example, in just 15 years, advances in knowledge about microprocessors have given us a sequence of processor chips that has made our personal computers increasingly powerful. Each advance in knowledge about how to design and manufacture a processor chip has brought apparently ever larger increments in performance and productivity. Similarly, each advance in knowledge about how to design and build an airplane has brought apparently ever larger increments in performance: Orville and Wilbur Wright's 1903 Flyer was a one-seat plane that could hop a farmer's field. The Lockheed Constellation, designed in 1949, was an airplane that could fly 120 passengers from New York to London, but with two refueling stops in Newfoundland and Ireland. The latest version of the Boeing 747 can carry 400 people nonstop from Los Angeles to Sydney, Australia, or New York to Tokyo (flights of 7,500 miles that take 13 hours). Similar examples can be found in agriculture, biogenetics, communications, engineering, entertainment, and medicine.

One reason why the stock of knowledge increases without diminishing returns is the sheer number of different techniques that can in principle be tried. Paul Romer explains this fact. "Suppose that to make a finished good, 20 different parts have to be attached to a frame, one at a time. A worker could proceed in numerical order, attaching part one first, then part two.... Or the worker could proceed in some other order, starting with part 10, then adding part seven.... With 20 parts, ... there are [more] different sequences ... than the total number of seconds that have elapsed since the big bang created the universe, so we can be confident that in all activities, only a very small fraction of the possible sequences have ever been tried."[1]

Think about all the processes, all the products, and all the different bits and pieces that go into each, and you can see that we have only begun to scratch around the edges of what is possible.

Because knowledge is productive and generates external benefits, it is necessary to use public policies to ensure that those who develop new ideas have incentives to encourage an efficient level of effort. The main way of providing the right incentives uses the central idea of the Coase theorem and assigns property rights—called **intellectual property rights**—to creators. The legal device for establishing intellectual property rights is the patent or copyright. A **patent** or **copyright** is a government-sanctioned exclusive right granted to the inventor of a good, service, or productive process to produce, use, and sell the invention for a given number of years. A patent enables the developer of a new idea to prevent others from benefiting freely from an invention for a limited number of years.

Although patents encourage invention and innovation, they do so at an economic cost. While a patent is in place, its holder has a monopoly. And monopoly is another source of inefficiency (which is explained in Chapter 12). But without a patent, the effort to develop new goods, services, or processes is diminished and the flow of new inventions is slowed. So the efficient outcome is a compromise that balances the benefits of more inventions against the cost of temporary monopoly in newly invented activities.

REVIEW QUIZ

1. What is special about knowledge that creates external benefits?
2. How might governments use public provision, private subsidies, and vouchers to achieve an efficient amount of education?
3. How might governments use public provision, private subsidies, vouchers, and patents and copyrights to achieve an efficient amount of research and development?

myeconlab **Study Plan 15.3**

Reading Between the Lines on pp. 356–357 looks at the pollution created by property development in California and a debate about whether to make developers pay a fee.

[1] Paul Romer, "Ideas and Things," in *The Future Surveyed*, supplement to *The Economist*, September 11, 1993, pp. 71–72.

READING BETWEEN THE LINES

Fighting Air Pollution in California

http://www.nytimes.com

California Builders Fight Air Pollution Fee

August 27, 2006

Developers and air quality regulators are locked in a legal battle over new construction fees for the California Central Valley intended to reduce the region's chronic smog problem.

The fees, which went into effect in March in eight counties in this fast-growing valley, are the most far-reaching in the country in their effort to link development and air pollution. A legal campaign to have them thrown out is being watched closely in other parts of the state, including Southern California and the San Francisco Bay Area, where officials say they hope to impose similar fees. . . .

The fees are part of a new regulation by the San Joaquin Valley Air Pollution Control District requiring builders of commercial and residential projects to use energy-saving technology and traffic-reduction features in their projects. The rule requires payment into a fund for pollution control. The idea is to make developers more accountable for the explosion in traffic and emissions that typically accompany building. . . .

"This rule fails miserably," said Tim Coyle, senior vice president and spokesman for the California Building Industry Association, among the groups involved in the lawsuit. "They haven't even established that there is a science to support the notion that new housing contributes to poor air quality."

The lawsuit, filed in Fresno County Superior Court, asserts that the district has exceeded its authority by imposing fees that duplicate regulations already covered by other state agencies. It also argues that the district has failed to demonstrate how the fees would reduce pollution or how the district would spend the money it collects, which could top $100 million a year when the rule is in full effect in 2010. . . .

Essence of the Story

- New construction fees must be paid by property developers in California's Central Valley.
- The fees, which went into effect in March 2006, aim to curb air pollution.
- A new regulation also requires builders to use energy-saving technology and traffic-reduction features in their projects.
- A spokesman for the California Building Industry Association says there is no evidence that new housing contributes to poor air quality.
- A lawsuit asserts that the fees duplicate regulations already in place and will not reduce pollution.

Economic Analysis

- California's Central Valley has a chronic smog problem, and commercial and residential property development is adding to this problem.
- The situation in California is an example of an external cost.
- With no actions to deal with the external cost, too much property development occurs and a deadweight loss arises from the overproduction.
- Figure 1 illustrates the market for property development in California's Central Valley.
- The demand curve, *D*, is also the marginal social benefit curve.
- The curve labeled *MC* shows the marginal cost of property development borne by the developers.
- The curve labeled *MSC* shows the marginal social cost of property development, including the external pollution cost.
- With an unregulated and competitive market, the quantity of development is Q_1.
- The vertical distance between the *MC* curve and the *MSC* curve is the marginal external cost from pollution and the gray triangle is the deadweight loss created.
- The property developers make a producer surplus shown by the blue triangle.
- Figure 2 shows the effects of a regulation that requires developers to use clean technologies that prevent pollution.
- To avoid pollution, developers must use a more costly technology and their marginal cost rises from MC_0 to MC_1, which is also the new marginal social cost curve. (The *assumed* marginal cost of avoiding pollution equals one half of the marginal cost of the pollution itself. This assumption might be optimistic.)
- The equilibrium quantity of development decreases to Q_E. If the regulation succeeds in preventing additional pollution, the deadweight loss is avoided, but the developers' producer surplus shrinks.
- The proposal to charge developers a fee takes some of their producer surplus. But the fee does not change the marginal cost of development, so it has no effect on the quantity of development or the amount of pollution.
- It is important to recognize that a Pigovian tax (see p. 350) must change the producer's marginal cost if it is to influence the quantity produced.

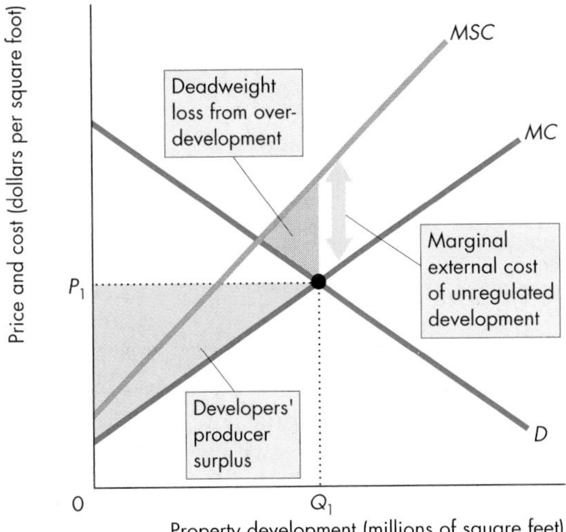

Figure 1 The unregulated California property market

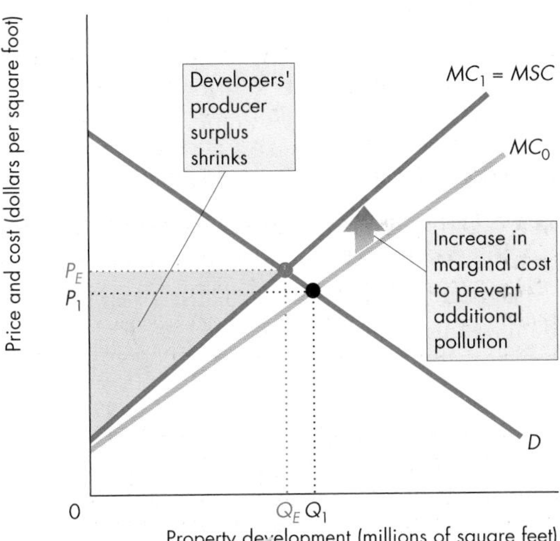

Figure 2 The regulated California property market

You're the Voter

- Would you vote to make developers pay a fee on new property? Why or why not?
- If a development fee is to be paid, how would you vote to spend the revenue raised by the fee?

SUMMARY

Key Points

Externalities in Our Lives (p. 344)

- An externality can arise from either a production activity or a consumption activity.
- A negative externality imposes an external cost.
- A positive externality provides an external benefit.

Negative Externalities: Pollution (pp. 345–351)

- External costs are costs of production that fall on people other than the producer of a good or service. Marginal social cost equals marginal private cost plus marginal external cost.
- Producers take account only of marginal private cost and produce more than the efficient quantity when there is a marginal external cost.
- Sometimes it is possible to overcome a negative externality by assigning a property right.
- When property rights cannot be assigned, governments might overcome externalities by using taxes, emission charges, or marketable permits.

Positive Externalities: Knowledge (pp. 351–355)

- External benefits are benefits that are received by people other than the consumer of a good or service. Marginal social benefit equals marginal private benefit plus marginal external benefit.
- External benefits from education arise because better-educated people tend to be better citizens, commit fewer crimes, and support social activities.
- External benefits from research arise because once someone has worked out a basic idea, others can copy it.
- Vouchers or subsidies to schools or the provision of public education below cost can achieve a more efficient provision of education.
- Patents and copyrights create intellectual property rights and an incentive to innovate. But they do so by creating a temporary monopoly, the cost of which must be balanced against the benefit of more inventive activity.

Key Figures

Key Terms

PROBLEMS

myeconlab Tests, Study Plan, Solutions*

1. Classify each of the following items as creating a negative externality, a positive externality, an externality arising from production, an externality arising from consumption, or not an externality.
   a. Airplanes take off from LaGuardia Airport during the U.S. Open tennis tournament, which is located nearby.
   b. A sunset over the Pacific Ocean
   c. An increase in the number of people who are studying for graduate degrees
   d. A person wears perfume while attending an orchestra concert.
   e. A homeowner plants an attractive garden in front of his house.
   f. A person drives while drunk.
   g. A bakery bakes bread.
2. The table provides information about costs and benefits that arise from the production of pesticide that pollutes a lake used by a trout farmer.

Output of pesticide (tons per week)	Pesticide producer's MC	Marginal external cost	Marginal social benefit of pesticide
	(dollars per ton)		
0	0	0	250
1	5	33	205
2	15	67	165
3	30	100	130
4	50	133	100
5	75	167	75
6	105	200	55
7	140	233	40

   a. If no one owns the lake and if there is no regulation of pollution, what is the quantity of pesticide produced and what is the marginal cost of pollution borne by the trout farmer?
   b. If the trout farm owns the lake, how much pesticide is produced and what does the pesticide producer pay the farmer per ton?
   c. If the pesticide producer owns the lake, and if a pollution-free lake rents for $1,000 a week, how much pesticide is produced and how much rent does the farmer pay the factory for the use of the lake?
   d. Compare the quantities of pesticide produced in parts (b) and (c) and explain the relationship between these quantities.
3. Back at the pesticide plant and trout farm described in problem 2, suppose that no one owns the lake and that the government introduces a pollution tax.
   a. What is the tax per ton of pesticide produced that achieves an efficient outcome?
   b. Explain the connection between your answer to part (a) and the answer to problem 2.
4. Using the information provided in problem 2, suppose that no one owns the lake and that the government issues two marketable pollution permits, one to the farmer and one to the factory. Each permit allows the same amount of pollution of the lake, and the total amount of pollution is the efficient amount.
   a. What is the quantity of pesticide produced?
   b. What is the market price of a pollution permit? Who buys and who sells a permit?
   c. What is the connection between your answer and the answers to problems 2 and 3?
5. Betty and Anna work at the same office in Philadelphia. They both must attend a meeting in Pittsburgh, and they have decided to drive to the meeting together. Betty is a cigarette smoker and her marginal benefit from smoking one package of cigarettes a day is $40. The price of a package of cigarettes is $6. Anna dislikes cigarette smoke, and her marginal benefit from a smoke-free environment is $50 a day. What is the outcome if
   a. Betty drives her car with Anna as a passenger
   b. Anna drives her car with Betty as a passenger
6. Most nurses in the United States receive their education in community colleges. Mainly because of differences in class size, the cost of educating a nurse is about four times that of an average community college student. Community college budgets depend on the number of students and not on the subjects taught.
   a. Explain why this funding arrangement might be expected to lead to an inefficiency in the number of nurses trained.
   b. Suggest a better arrangement and explain how it would work.

*Solutions to odd-numbered problems are provided.

7. The marginal cost of educating a student is $4,000 a year and is constant. The figure shows the marginal private benefit curve.

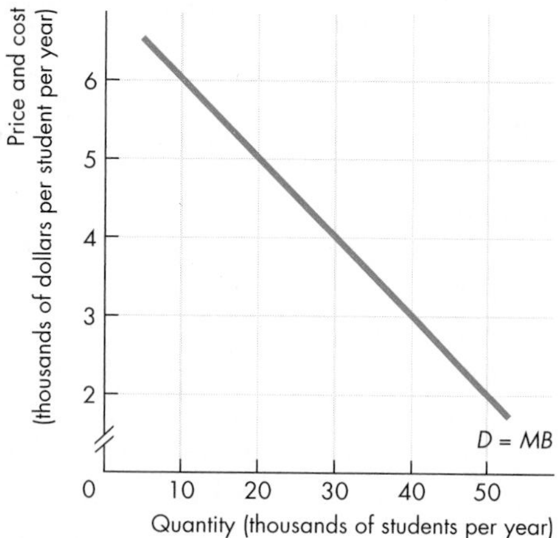

   a. With no government involvement and if the schools are competitive, how many students are enrolled and what is the tuition?
   b. The external benefit from education is $2,000 per student per year and is constant. If the government provides the efficient amount of education, how many school places does it offer and what is the tuition?

CRITICAL THINKING

1. After you have studied *Reading Between the Lines* on pp. 356–357, answer the following questions:
   a. How does property development create pollution in California's Central Valley?
   b. What are the pros and cons of stiffening the regulations that property developers face?
   c. If a technological advance eliminates pollution from automobiles but costs as much to implement as the marginal external pollution cost of existing automobiles, would the adoption of the new technology improve the efficiency of resource allocation? Explain, using figures like those on p. 357.
2. **Merck Loses Protection For Patent On Zocor**

   Today, Merck's cholesterol-lowering drug Zocor loses its United States patent protection, . . . That change will cost Merck billions of dollars a year. . . . Zocor, . . . generated sales last year for Merck of . . . $4.4 billion worldwide. But beginning today, three other drug companies will be legally allowed to sell simvastatin, the active ingredient in Zocor. . . . As a result, the price of a dose of simvastatin will probably drop 30 percent or more in the next few days, and by as much as 90 percent next year

   The New York Times, June 23, 2006

   a. Who wins when a patent expires? Who loses when a patent expires?
   b. Would anyone gain if the length of a patent on a new drug was increased?
   c. Do drug patents generate an external benefit or an external cost?

WEB ACTIVITIES

myeconlab Links to Web sites

1. Obtain two viewpoints on global warming and then answer these questions:
   a. What are the benefits and costs of greenhouse gas emissions?
   b. Do you think environmentalists are correct in the view that greenhouse gas emissions must be cut or do you think the costs of reducing greenhouse gas emissions exceed the benefits?
   c. If greenhouse gas emissions are to be reduced, should firms be assigned production limits or marketable permits?
2. Visit the Cape Cod Times and read the article about wind farms off the New England coast.
   a. What types of externalities arise in the production of electricity using wind technologies?
   b. Comparing the externalities from wind technologies with those from burning coal and oil, which do you think are more widespread and affect more people?
   c. How do you think the external costs of using wind technologies should be dealt with? Compare all the alternative methods suggested by the range of solutions considered in this chapter.
   d. Can you think of reasons why, despite the lower external costs, a campaign against the use of wind technology might be more successful than a campaign against the use of coal or oil?

CHAPTER 16

Public Goods and Common Resources

Free Riding and Overusing the Commons

What's the difference between the Los Angeles Police Department and Brinks Security, between fish in the Pacific Ocean and fish produced by a Seattle fish farm, and between a live Coldplay concert and a show on network television?

Why does government provide some goods and services such as the enforcement of law and order and national defense? Why don't we let private firms produce these items and let people buy the quantities that they demand in the marketplace? Is the scale of provision of these government-provided services correct? Or do governments produce either too much or too little of these items?

More and more people with ever-increasing incomes demand ever greater quantities of most goods and services. One item that we demand more and more of is fish grown wild in the ocean. The fish stocks of the world's oceans are not owned by anyone. They are common resources, and everyone is free to use them. Are our fish stocks being overused? Are we in danger of bringing extinction to some species? Must the price of fish inevitably keep rising? What can be done to conserve the world's fish stocks?

These are the questions that we study in this chapter. We begin by classifying goods and resources. We then explain what determines the scale of government provision of public services. Finally, we study the tragedy of the commons. In *Reading Between the Lines* at the end of the chapter, we look at a pressing tragedy of the commons in the world today: the problem of overuse of the tropical rain forests.

After studying this chapter, you will be able to

- Distinguish among private goods, public goods, and common resources
- Explain how the free-rider problem arises and how the quantity of public goods is determined
- Explain the tragedy of the commons and its possible solutions

Classifying Goods and Resources

Goods, services, and resources differ in the extent to which people can be *excluded* from consuming them and in the extent to which one person's consumption *rivals* the consumption of others.

A good is **excludable** if only the people who pay for it are able to enjoy its benefits. Brinks's security services, East Point Seafood's fish, and a Coldplay concert are examples.

A good is **nonexcludable** if everyone benefits from it regardless of whether they pay for it. The services of the LAPD, fish in the Pacific Ocean, and a concert on network television are examples.

A good is **rival** if one person's use of it decreases the quantity available for someone else. A Brinks's truck can't deliver cash to two banks at the same time. A fish can be consumed only once.

A good is **nonrival** if one person's use of it does not decrease the quantity available for someone else. The services of the LAPD and a concert on network television are nonrival.

A Fourfold Classification

Figure 16.1 classifies goods, services, and resources into four types.

Private Goods A **private good** is both rival and excludable. A can of Coke and a fish on East Point Seafood's farm are examples of private goods.

Public Goods A **public good** is both nonrival and nonexcludable. A public good can be consumed simultaneously by everyone, and no one can be excluded from enjoying its benefits. National defense is the best example of a public good.

Common Resources A **common resource** is rival and nonexcludable. A unit of a common resource can be used only once, but no one can be prevented from using what is available. Ocean fish are a common resource. They are rival because a fish taken by one person isn't available for anyone else, and they are nonexcludable because it is difficult to prevent people from catching them.

Natural Monopolies In a natural monopoly, economies of scale exist over the entire range of output for which there is a demand (see p. 264). A special case of natural monopoly arises when the good or service can be produced at zero marginal cost. Such a good is nonrival. If it is also excludable, it is produced by a natural monopoly. The Internet and cable television are examples.

FIGURE 16.1 Fourfold Classification of Goods

myeconlab

	Excludable	Nonexcludable
	Private goods	**Common resources**
Rival	Food and drink Car House	Fish in ocean Atmosphere National parks
	Natural monopolies	**Public goods**
Nonrival	Internet Cable television Bridge or tunnel	National defense The law Air traffic control

A private good is one for which consumption is rival and from which consumers can be excluded. A public good is one for which consumption is nonrival and from which it is impossible to exclude a consumer. A common resource is one that is rival but nonexcludable. A good that is nonrival but excludable is produced by a natural monopoly.

Two Problems

Public goods create a **free-rider problem**—the absence of an incentive for people to pay for what they consume. *Common resources* create a problem called the **tragedy of the commons**—the absence of incentives to prevent the overuse and depletion of a resource.

The rest of this chapter looks more closely at the free-rider problem and the tragedy of the commons and examines public choice solutions to them.

REVIEW QUIZ

1 Distinguish among public goods, private goods, common resources, and natural monopolies.
2 Provide examples of goods (or services or resources) in each of the four categories that differ from the examples in this section.

myeconlab **Study Plan 16.1**

Public Goods and the Free-Rider Problem

Suppose that for its defense, a country must launch some surveillance satellites. The benefit provided by a satellite is the value of its services. The *value* of a *private* good is the maximum amount that a person is willing to pay for one more unit, which is shown by the person's demand curve. The *value* of a *public* good is the maximum amount that *all* the people are willing to pay for one more unit of it. To calculate the value placed on a public good, we use the concepts of total benefit and marginal benefit.

The Benefit of a Public Good

Total benefit is the dollar value that a person places on a given quantity of a good. The greater the quantity of a good, the larger is a person's total benefit. *Marginal benefit* is the increase in total benefit that results from a one-unit increase in the quantity of a good.

Figures 16.2(a) and 16.2(b) show the marginal benefits that arise from defense satellites for a society with only two people, Lisa and Max, whose marginal benefits are graphed as MB_L and MB_M, respectively. The marginal benefit from a public good (like that from a private good) diminishes as the quantity of the good increases. For Lisa, the marginal benefit from the first satellite is \$80 and that from the second is \$60. By the time five satellites are deployed, Lisa's marginal benefit is zero. For Max, the marginal benefit from the first satellite is \$50 and that from the second is \$40. By the time five satellites are deployed, Max perceives only \$10 worth of marginal benefit.

Part (c) shows the economy's marginal social benefit curve, *MSB*. The marginal social benefit curve for a *public* good is different from the marginal social benefit curve for a *private* good. To obtain the marginal social benefit curve for a private good, we sum the quantities demanded by all individuals at each *price*—we sum the individual marginal benefit curves *horizontally* (see Chapter 5, p. 106). But to find the marginal social benefit curve of a *public* good, we sum the marginal benefits of all individual at each *quantity*—we sum the individual marginal benefit curves *vertically*. So the curve *MSB* in part (c) is the marginal social benefit curve for the economy made up of Lisa and Max. For each satellite, Lisa's marginal benefit

FIGURE 16.2 Benefits of a Public Good

myeconlab

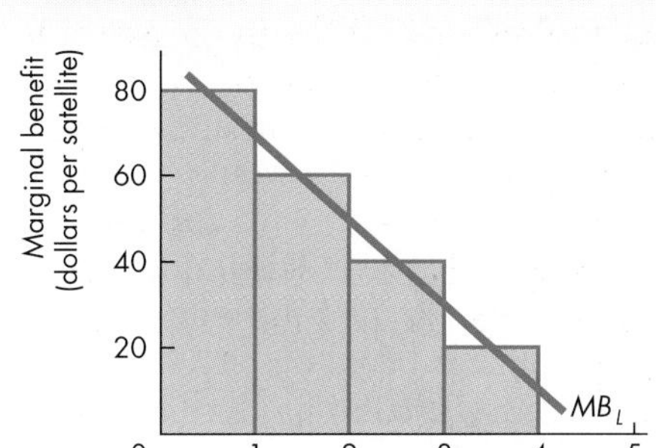

(a) Lisa's marginal benefit

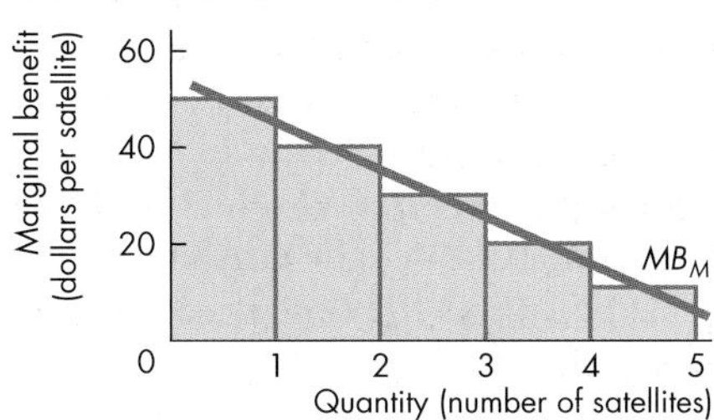

(b) Max's marginal benefit

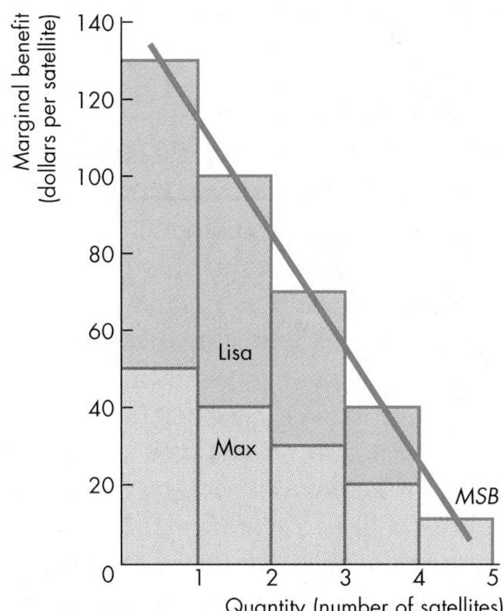

(c) Economy's marginal social benefit

The marginal social benefit at each quantity of the public good is the sum of the marginal benefits of all individuals. The marginal benefit curves are MB_L for Lisa and MB_M for Max. The economy's marginal social benefit curve is *MSB*.

is added to Max's marginal benefit because they *both* consume the services of each satellite.

The Efficient Quantity of a Public Good

An economy with two people would not buy any satellites—because the total benefit would fall far short of the cost. But an economy with 250 million people might. To determine the efficient quantity, we need to take the cost as well as the benefit into account.

The cost of a satellite is based on technology and the prices of the resources used to produce it (just like the cost of producing sweaters, which you studied in Chapter 10).

Figure 16.3 sets out the benefits and costs. The second and third columns of the table show the total and marginal benefits. The next two columns show the total and marginal costs of producing satellites. The final column shows net benefit—total benefit minus total cost.

The total benefit curve, *TB*, and total cost curve, *TC*, are graphed in Fig. 16.3(a). The efficient quantity is the one that maximizes *net benefit* and occurs when two satellites are provided.

The fundamental principles of marginal analysis that you have used to explain how consumers maximize utility and how firms maximize profit can also be used to calculate the efficient scale of provision of a public good. Figure 16.3(b) shows this alternative approach. The marginal social benefit curve is *MSB*, and the marginal social cost curve is *MSC*. When marginal social benefit exceeds marginal social cost, net benefit increases if the quantity produced increases. When marginal social cost exceeds marginal social benefit, net benefit increases if the quantity produced decreases. Marginal social benefit equals marginal social cost with two satellites. So making marginal social cost equal to marginal social benefit maximizes net benefit and uses resources efficiently.

Private Provision

We have now worked out the quantity of satellites that maximizes net benefit. Would a private firm—North Pole Protection, Inc.—deliver that quantity? It would not. To do so, it would have to collect $15 billion to cover its costs—or $60 from each of the 250 million people in the economy. But no one would have an incentive to buy his or her "share" of the satellite system. Everyone would reason as follows: The number of satellites provided by North Pole Protection, Inc., is not affected by my $60. But my own private consumption is greater if I free ride and do not pay my share of the cost of the satellite system. If I do not pay, I enjoy the same level of security and I can buy more private goods. Therefore I will spend my $60 on other goods and free ride on the public good. This is the free-rider problem.

If everyone reasons the same way, North Pole Protection has zero revenue and so provides no satellites. Because two satellites is the efficient level, private provision is inefficient.

Public Provision

Suppose there are two political parties, the Hawks and the Doves, that agree with each other on all issues except for the quantity of satellites. The Hawks would like to provide four satellites at a total cost of $50 billion, with total benefits of $50 billion and a net benefit of zero, as shown in Fig. 16.3(a). The Doves would like to provide one satellite at a cost of $5 billion, a benefit of $20 billion, and a net benefit of $15 billion—see Fig. 16.3(a).

Before deciding on their policy proposals, the two political parties do a "what-if" analysis. Each party reasons as follows: If each party offers the satellite program it wants—Hawks four satellites and Doves one satellite—the voters will see that they will get a net benefit of $15 billion from the Doves and zero net benefit from the Hawks, and the Doves will win the election.

Contemplating this outcome, the Hawks realize that they are too hawkish to get elected. They must scale back their proposal to two satellites at a total cost of $15 billion. Total benefit is $35 billion, and net benefit is $20 billion. So if the Doves stick with one satellite, the Hawks will win the election.

Contemplating this outcome, the Doves realize that they must match the Hawks. They too propose to provide two satellites. If the two parties offer the same number of satellites, the voters are indifferent between the parties. They flip coins to decide their votes, and each party receives around 50 percent of the vote.

The result of the politicians' "what-if" analysis is that each party offers two satellites, so regardless of who wins the election, this is the quantity of satellites installed. And this quantity is efficient. It maximizes the perceived net benefit of the voters. In this example, competition in the political marketplace results in the efficient provision of a public good. But for this outcome to occur, voters must be well informed and evaluate the alternatives. As you will see below, they do not always have an incentive to achieve this outcome.

FIGURE 16.3 The Efficient Quantity of a Public Good

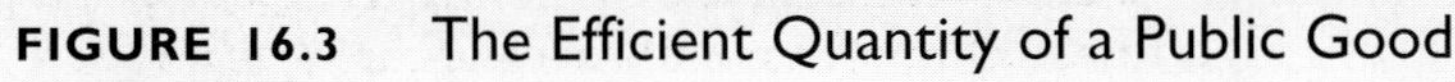

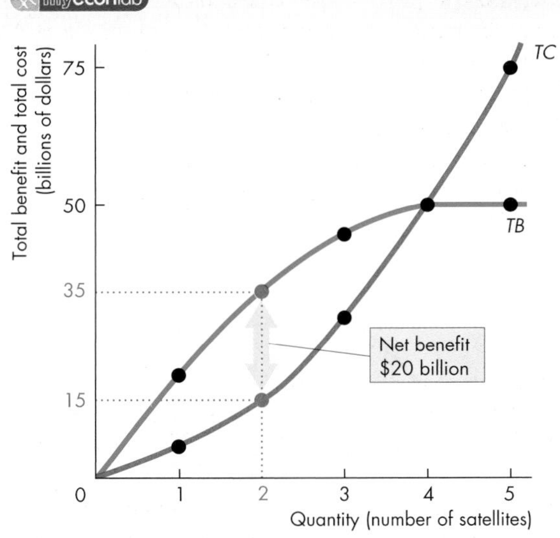

(a) Total benefit and total cost

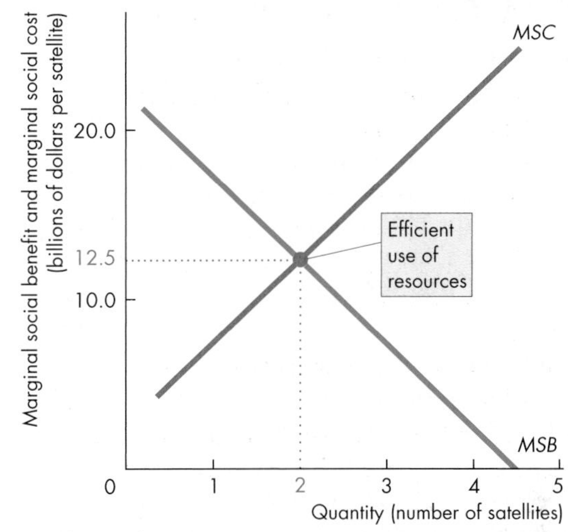

(b) Marginal social benefit and marginal social cost

Quantity (number of satellites)	Total benefit (billions of dollars)	Marginal social benefit (billions of dollars per satellite)	Total cost (billions of dollars)	Marginal social cost (billions of dollars per satellite)	Net benefit (billions of dollars)
0	0		0		0
		20		5	
1	20		5		15
		15		10	
2	35		15		20
		10		15	
3	45		30		15
		5		20	
4	50		50		0
		0		25	
5	50		75		–25

Net benefit—the vertical distance between the total benefit curve, *TB*, and the total cost curve, *TC*—is maximized when two satellites are installed (part a) and where marginal social benefit, *MSB*, equals marginal social cost, *MSC* (part b).

The Doves would like one satellite, and the Hawks would like four. But each party recognizes that its only hope of being elected is to provide two satellites—the quantity that maximizes net benefit.

The Principle of Minimum Differentiation In the example we've just studied, both parties propose identical policies. This tendency toward identical policies is an example of the **principle of minimum differentiation**, which is the tendency for competitors to make themselves similar to appeal to the maximum number of clients or voters. This principle not only describes the behavior of political parties but also explains why fast-food restaurants cluster in the same block and even why new auto models have similar features. If McDonald's opens a restaurant in a new location, it is likely that Burger King will open next door to McDonald's rather than a mile down the road. If Chrysler designs a new van with a sliding door on the driver's side, most likely Ford will too.

The Role of Bureaucrats

We have analyzed the behavior of politicians but not that of the bureaucrats who translate the choices of the politicians into programs and who control the day-to-day activities that deliver public goods. Let's now see how the economic choices of bureaucrats influence the political equilibrium.

To do so, we'll stick with the previous example. We've seen that competition between two political parties delivers the efficient quantity of satellites. But will the Defense Department—the Pentagon—cooperate and accept this outcome?

Suppose the Pentagon's objective is to maximize the defense budget. With two satellites being provided at least cost, the defense budget is $15 billion (see Fig. 16.3). To increase its budget, the Pentagon might do two things. First, it might try to persuade the politicians that two satellites cost more than $15 billion. As Fig. 16.4 shows, if possible, the Pentagon would like to convince Congress that two satellites cost $35 billion—equal to the entire total benefit. Second, and pressing its position even more strongly, the Pentagon might argue for more satellites. It might press for four satellites and a budget of $50 billion. In this situation, total benefit and total cost are equal and net benefit is zero.

The Pentagon wants to maximize its budget, but won't the politicians prevent it from doing so because the Pentagon's preferred outcome will cost votes? They will if voters are well informed and know what is best for them. But voters might be rationally ignorant. In this case, well-informed interest groups might enable the Pentagon to achieve its objective.

FIGURE 16.4 Bureaucratic Overprovision

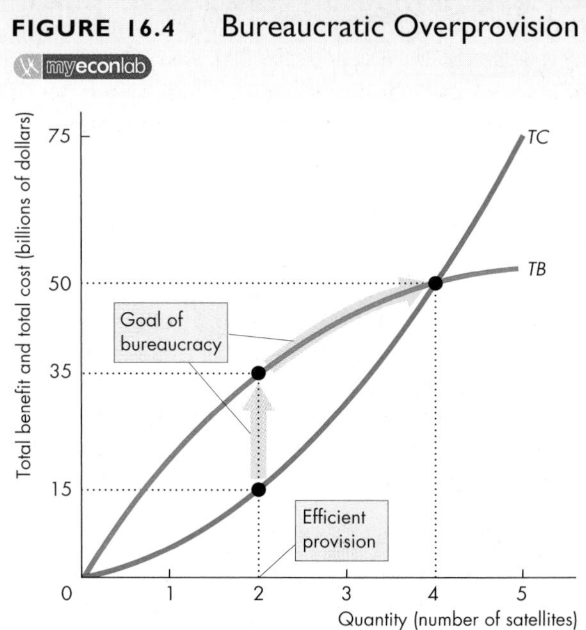

The goal of a bureaucracy is to maximize its budget. A bureaucracy that maximizes its budget will seek to increase its budget until its total cost equals total benefit. Then it will use its budget to expand output and expenditure. Here, the Pentagon tries to get $35 billion to provide two satellites. It would like to increase the quantity of satellites to four with a budget of $50 billion.

Rational Ignorance

A principle of public choice theory is that it is rational for a voter to be ignorant about an issue unless that issue has a perceptible effect on the voter's income. **Rational ignorance** is the decision *not* to acquire information because the cost of doing so exceeds the expected benefit. For example, each voter knows that he or she can make virtually no difference to the defense policy of the U.S. government. Each voter also knows that it would take an enormous amount of time and effort to become even moderately well informed about alternative defense technologies. So voters remain relatively uninformed about the technicalities of defense issues. (Though we are using defense policy as an example, the same applies to all aspects of government economic activity.)

All voters are consumers of national defense. But not all voters are producers of national defense. Only a small number are in this latter category. Voters who own or work for firms that produce satellites have a direct personal interest in defense because it affects their incomes. These voters have an incentive to become well informed about defense issues and to operate a political lobby aimed at furthering their own interests. In collaboration with the defense bureaucracy, these voters exert a larger influence than do the relatively uninformed voters who only consume this public good.

When the rationality of the uninformed voter and special interest groups are taken into account, the political equilibrium provides public goods in excess of the efficient quantity. So in the satellite example, three or four satellites might be installed rather than the efficient quantity, which is two satellites.

Two Types of Political Equilibrium

We've seen that two types of political equilibrium are possible: efficient and inefficient. These two types of political equilibrium correspond to two theories of government:

- Social interest theory
- Public choice theory

Social Interest Theory Social interest theory predicts that governments make choices that achieve efficiency. This outcome occurs in a perfect political system in which voters are fully informed about the effects of policies and refuse to vote for outcomes that can be improved upon.

Public Choice Theory Public choice theory predicts that governments make choices that result in inefficiency. This outcome occurs in political markets in which voters are rationally ignorant and base their votes only on issues that they know affect their own net benefit. Voters pay more attention to their interests as producers than their interests as consumers, and public officials also act in their own best interest. The result is *government failure* that parallels market failure.

Why Government Is Large and Grows

Now that we know how the quantity of public goods is determined, we can explain part of the reason for the growth of government. Government grows in part because the demand for some public goods increases at a faster rate than the demand for private goods. There are two possible reasons for this growth:

- Voter preferences
- Inefficient overprovision

Voter Preferences The growth of government can be explained by voter preferences in the following way. As voters' incomes increase (as they do in most years), the demand for many public goods increases more quickly than income. (Technically, the *income elasticity of demand* for many public goods is greater than 1—see Chapter 4, pp. 92–93.) These goods include public health, education, national defense, highways, airports, and air-traffic control systems. If politicians did not support increases in expenditures on these items, they would not get elected.

Inefficient Overprovision Inefficient overprovision might explain the *size* of government but not its *growth rate*. It (possibly) explains why government is *larger* than its efficient scale, but it does not explain why governments use an increasing proportion of total resources.

Voters Strike Back

If government grows too large relative to the value that voters place on public goods, there might be a voter backlash against government programs and a large bureaucracy. Electoral success during the 1990s at the state and federal levels required politicians of all parties to embrace smaller, leaner, and more efficient government. The September 11 attacks have led to a greater willingness to pay for security but have probably not lessened the desire for lean government.

Another way in which voters—and politicians—can try to counter the tendency of bureaucrats to expand their budgets is to privatize the production of public goods. Government *provision* of a public good does not automatically imply that a government-operated bureau must *produce* the good. Garbage collection (a public good) is often done by a private firm, and experiments are being conducted with private fire departments and even private prisons.

REVIEW QUIZ

1. What is the free-rider problem and why does it make the private provision of a public good inefficient?
2. Under what conditions will competition for votes among politicians result in an efficient quantity of a public good?
3. How do rationally ignorant voters and budget-maximizing bureaucrats prevent competition in the political marketplace from producing the efficient quantity of a public good? Do they result in too much or too little public provision of public goods?

myeconlab **Study Plan 16.2**

You've seen how public goods create a free-rider problem that would result in the underprovision of such goods. We're now going to learn about common resources and see why they result in the opposite problem—the overuse of such resources.

Common Resources

Atlantic Ocean cod stocks have been declining since the 1950s, and some marine biologists fear that this species is in danger of becoming extinct in some regions. The whale population of the South Pacific has been declining also, and some groups are lobbying to establish a whale sanctuary in the waters around Australia and New Zealand to regenerate the population. Since the start of the Industrial Revolution in 1750, the concentration of carbon dioxide in the atmosphere has steadily increased. It is estimated that it is about 30 percent higher today than it was in 1750.

These situations involve common property, and the problem that we have identified is called the tragedy of the commons.

The Tragedy of the Commons

The *tragedy of the commons* is the absence of incentives to prevent the overuse and depletion of a commonly owned resource. If no one owns a resource, no one considers the effects of her or his use of the resource on others.

The Original Tragedy of the Commons The term "tragedy of the commons" comes from fourteenth century England where areas of rough grassland surrounded villages. The commons were open to all and used for grazing cows and sheep owned by the villagers.

Because the commons were open to all, no one had an incentive to ensure that the land was not over grazed. The result was a severe over-grazing situation. Because the commons were over grazed, the quantity of cows and sheep that they could feed kept on falling.

During the sixteenth century, the price of wool increased and England became a wool exporter to the world. Sheep farming became profitable, and sheep owners wanted to gain more effective control of the land they used. So the commons were gradually enclosed and privatized. Overgrazing ended, and land use became more efficient.

A Tragedy of the Commons Today One of today's pressing tragedies of the commons is overfishing. Several fish species have been seriously over fished, and one of them is Atlantic Cod.

To study the tragedy of the commons, we'll use the Atlantic Cod as an example.

Sustainable Production

Sustainable production is the rate of production that can be maintained indefinitely. In the case of ocean fish, the sustainable production is the quantity of fish (of a given species) that can be caught each year into the indefinite future.

This production rate depends on the existing stock of fish and the number of boats that go fishing. For a given stock of fish, sending more boats to sea increases the quantity of fish caught. But sending too many boats to sea depletes the stock.

So as the number of boats increases, the quantity of fish caught increases as long as the stock is maintained. But above some crucial level, as more boats go fishing, the stock of fish decreases and the number of fish caught also decreases.

Table 16.1 provides some numbers that illustrate the relationship between the number of boats that go fishing and the quantity of fish caught. The numbers in this example are hypothetical.

TABLE 16.1 Sustainable Production: Total, Average, and Marginal Catch

	Boats (thousands)	Total catch (thousands of tons per month)	Average catch (tons per boat)	Marginal catch (tons per boat)
A	0	0		
				90
B	1	90	90	
				70
C	2	160	80	
				50
D	3	210	70	
				30
E	4	240	60	
				10
F	5	250	50	
				−10
G	6	240	40	
				−30
H	7	210	30	
				−50
I	8	160	20	
				−70
J	9	90	10	
				−90
K	10	0	0	

As the number of fishing boats increases, the quantity of fish caught increases up to the maximum sustainable catch and then decreases. The average catch and marginal catch decrease as the number of boats increases.

Total Catch The total catch is the sustainable rate of production. The numbers in the first two columns of Table 16.1 show the relationship between the number of fishing boats and the total catch, and Fig. 16.5 illustrates this relationship.

You can see that as the number of boats increases from zero to 5,000, the sustainable catch increases to a maximum of 250,000 tons a month. As the number of boats increases above 5,000, the sustainable catch begins to decrease. By the time 10,000 boats are fishing, the fish stock is depleted to the point at which no fish can be caught.

With more than 5,000 boats, there is overfishing. Overfishing arises if the number of boats increases to the point at which the fish stock begins to fall and the remaining fish are harder to find and catch.

Average Catch The average catch is the catch per boat and equals the total catch divided by the number of boats. The numbers in the third column of Table 16.1 show the average catch.

With 1,000 boats, the total catch is 90,000 tons and the catch per boat is 90 tons. With 2,000 boats, the total catch is 160,000 tons, and the catch per boat is 80 tons. As more boats take to the ocean, the catch per boat decreases. By the time 8,000 boats are fishing, each boat is catching just 20 tons a month.

The decreasing average catch is an example of the principle of diminishing returns.

Marginal Catch The marginal catch is the change in the total catch that occurs when one more boat joins the existing number. It is calculated as the change in the total catch divided by the increase in the number of boats. The numbers in the fourth column of Table 16.1 show the marginal catch.

For example, in rows *C* and *D* of the table, when the number of boats increases by 1,000, the catch increases by 50,000 tons, so the increase in the catch per boat equals 50 tons. In the table, we place this amount midway between the two rows because it is the marginal catch at 2,500 boats, midway between the two levels that we used to calculate it.

Notice that the marginal catch, like the average catch, decreases as the number of boats increases. Also notice that the marginal catch is always less than the average catch.

When the number of boats reaches that at which the sustainable catch is a maximum, the marginal catch is zero. At a larger number of boats, the marginal catch becomes negative—more boats decrease the total catch.

FIGURE 16.5 Sustainable Production of Fish

myeconlab

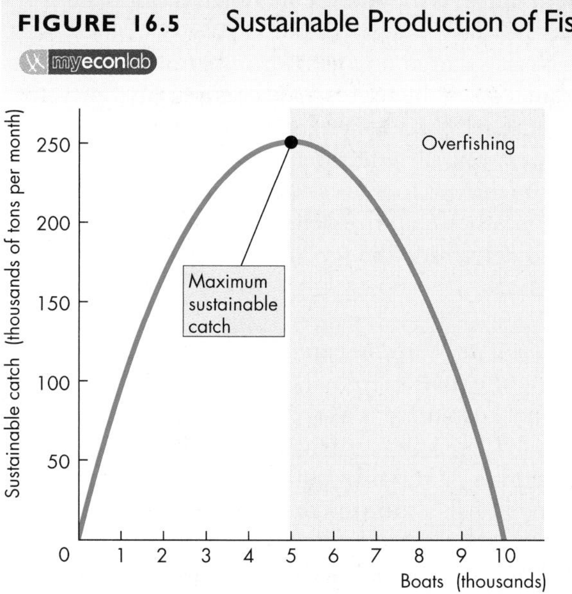

As the number of boats increases, the sustainable catch increases up to a maximum. Beyond that number, more boats will diminish the fish stock and the sustainable catch decreases. Overfishing occurs when the maximum sustainable catch decreases.

An Overfishing Equilibrium

The tragedy of the commons is that common resources are overused. Why might the fish stock be overused? Why might overfishing occur? Why isn't the maximum number of boats that take to the sea the number that maximizes the sustainable catch—5,000 in this example?

To answer this question, we need to look at the marginal cost and marginal private benefit to an individual fisher.

Suppose that the marginal cost of a fishing boat is the equivalent of 20 tons of fish a month. That is, to cover the opportunity cost of maintaining and operating a boat, the boat must catch 20 tons of fish a month. This quantity of fish also provides the boat owner with normal profit (part of the cost of operating the boat), so the boat owner is willing to go fishing.

The marginal private benefit of operating a boat is the quantity of fish the boat can catch. This quantity is the average catch that we've just calculated.

The average catch is the marginal private benefit because that is the quantity of fish that the boat owner gets by taking the boat to sea.

The boat owner will go fishing as long as the average catch (marginal private benefit) exceeds the marginal cost. And the boat owner will maximize profit when marginal private benefit equals marginal cost.

Figure 16.6 shows the marginal cost curve, *MC*, and the marginal private benefit curve, *MB*. The *MB* curve is based on the numbers for the average catch in Table 16.1.

You can see in Fig. 16.6 that with fewer than 8,000 boats, each boat catches more fish than it costs to catch them. Because boat owners can gain from fishing, the number of boats is 8,000 and there is an overfishing equilibrium.

If one boat owner stopped fishing, the overfishing would be less severe. But that boat owner would be giving up an opportunity to earn an economic profit.

The self-interest of the boat owner is to fish, but the social interest is to limit fishing. The quantity of fish caught by each boat decreases as additional boats go fishing. But when individual boat owners are deciding whether to fish, they ignore this decrease. They consider only the marginal *private* benefit. The result is an *inefficient* overuse of the resource.

FIGURE 16.6 Why Overfishing Occurs

myeconlab

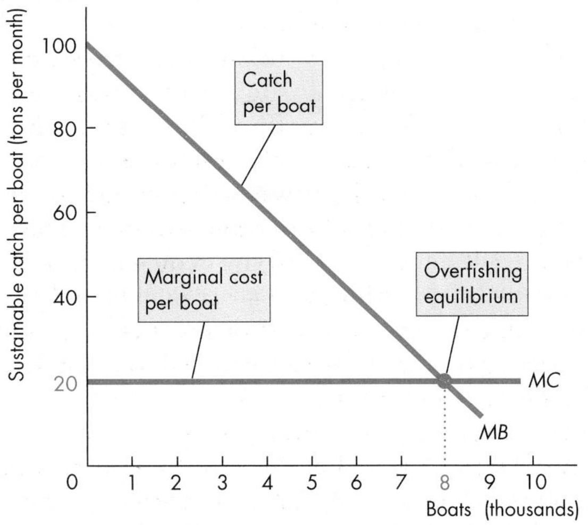

The average catch decreases as the number of boats increases. The average catch per boat is the marginal private benefit, *MB*, of a boat. The marginal cost of a boat is equivalent to 20 tons of fish, shown by the curve *MC*. The equilibrium number of boats is 8,000—an overfishing equilibrium.

The Efficient Use of the Commons

What is the efficient use of a common resource? It is the use of the resource that makes the marginal cost of using the resource equal to the marginal *social* benefit from its use.

Marginal Social Benefit The marginal *social* benefit of a boat is the boat's marginal catch—the increase in the total catch that results from an additional boat. The reason is that when an additional boat puts to sea, it catches the average catch but it decreases the average catch for itself and for every other boat. The *marginal social benefit* is the *increase* in the quantity of fish caught per boat, not the average number of fish caught.

We calculated the marginal catch in Table 16.1 and we repeat part of that table for convenience in Fig. 16.7. The figure also shows the marginal private benefit curve, *MB*, and the marginal social benefit curve, *MSB*.

Notice that at any given number of boats, marginal social benefit is less than marginal private benefit. Each boat benefits privately from the average catch, but the addition of one more boat *decreases* the catch of every boat, and this decrease must be subtracted from the catch of the additional boat to determine the social benefit from the additional boat.

Efficient Use With no external costs, the marginal social cost equals marginal cost. In Fig. 16.7, the marginal cost curve is also the marginal social cost curve, $MC = MSC$. Efficiency is achieved when *MSB* equals *MSC* with 4,000 boats, each catching 60 tons of fish a month. You can see in the table that when the number of boats increases from 3,000 to 4,000 (with 3,500 being the midpoint), marginal social benefit is 30 tons, which exceeds marginal social cost. When the number of boats increases from 4,000 to 5,000 (with 4,500 being the midpoint), marginal social benefit is 10 tons, which is less than marginal social cost. At 4,000 boats, marginal social benefit is 20 tons, which equals marginal social cost.

FIGURE 16.7 Efficient Use of a Common Resource

myeconlab

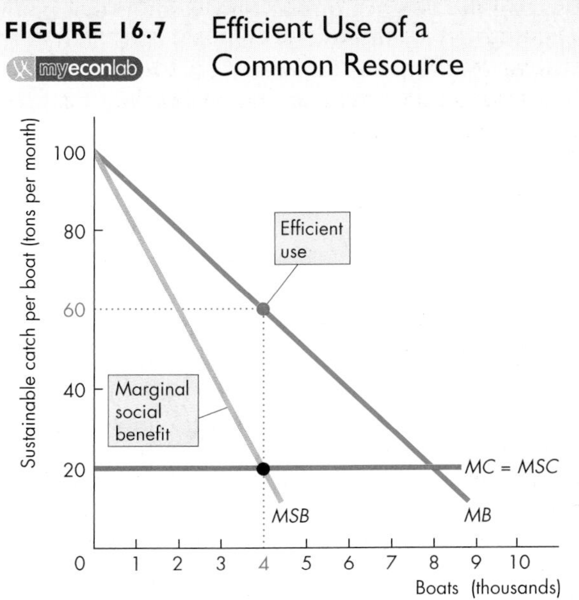

	Boats (thousands)	Total catch (thousands of tons per month)	Marginal private benefit (tons per boat)	Marginal social benefit (tons per boat)
A	0	0		
				90
B	1	90	90	
				70
C	2	160	80	
				50
D	3	210	70	
				30
E	4	240	60	
				10
F	5	250	50	

The marginal social benefit of a fishing boat is the change in total benefit that results from an additional boat. The table shows that when the number of boats increases from 2,000 to 3,000 (from row *C* to row *D*), the total catch increases from 160,000 to 210,000 tons a month and marginal catch and marginal social benefit is 50 tons.

The figure graphs the marginal social benefit curve, *MSB*, and the marginal private benefit curve, *MB*. Marginal social benefit is less than marginal private benefit and decreases as the number of boats increases. The efficient number of boats is that at which marginal social benefit equals marginal social cost of $20 a boat and is 4,000. The common resource is used efficiently.

Achieving an Efficient Outcome

Defining the conditions under which a common resource is used efficiently is easier than bringing those conditions about. To use a common resource efficiently, it is necessary to design an incentive mechanism that confronts the users of the resource with the marginal social consequences of their actions. The same principles apply to common resources as those that you met when you studied externalities in Chapter 15.

Three main methods might be used to achieve the efficient use of a common resource. They are

- Property rights
- Quotas
- Individual transferable quotas (ITQs)

Property Rights A common resource that no one owns and that anyone is free to use contrasts with *private property*, which is a resource that *someone* owns and has an incentive to use in the way that maximizes its value. One way of overcoming the tragedy of the commons is to remove the commons and make the resource private property. By assigning private property rights, each owner faces the same conditions as society faces. The *MSB* curve of Fig. 16.7 becomes the marginal *private* benefit curve, and the use of the resource is efficient.

The private property solution to the tragedy of the commons *is* available in some cases. It was the solution to the original tragedy of the commons in England's Middle Ages. It is also a solution that has been used to prevent the airwaves that we use to carry our cell phone messages from being overused. The right to use this space—called the frequency spectrum—has been auctioned by governments to the highest bidders, and the owner of a particular part of the spectrum is the only one permitted to use it (or to license someone else to use it).

But assigning private property rights is not always feasible. It would be difficult, for example, to assign private property rights to the oceans. It would not be impossible, but the cost of enforcing private property rights over thousands of square miles of ocean would be high. And it would be even more difficult to assign and protect private property rights to the atmosphere.

In some cases, there is an emotional objection to assigning private property rights. When private property rights are too costly to assign and enforce, some form of government intervention is used, and quotas are the simplest.

Quotas You studied the effects of a quota in Chapter 6 (p. 139) and learned that a quota can drive a wedge between marginal social benefit and marginal social cost and create deadweight loss. But in that earlier example, the market was efficient without a quota. In the case of the use of a common resource, the market is inefficient and is overproducing. So a quota that limits production can bring a move toward a more efficient outcome.

Figure 16.8 shows a quota that achieves an efficient use of a common resource. A quota is set for total production at the quantity at which marginal social benefit equals marginal social cost. Here, that quantity is what 4,000 boats can produce. Individual boat owners are assigned their own share of the total permitted catch. If everyone sticks to the assigned quota, the outcome is efficient.

There are two problems in implementing a quota. First, it is in everyone's self-interest to cheat and use more of a common resource than the amount based on the assigned quota. The reason is that marginal private benefit exceeds marginal cost. So by catching more than the allocated quota, each boat owner gets a higher income. If everyone breaks the quota, overproduction returns and the tragedy of the commons remains.

Second, marginal cost is not, in general, the same for every producer. Some producers have a comparative advantage in using a resource.

Efficiency requires that the quotas are allocated to the producers with the lowest marginal cost. But the government department that allocates quotas does not possess information about individual marginal cost. Even if the government tried to get this information, producers would have an incentive to lie about their costs in order to get a bigger quota.

So a quota can work, but only if the activities of every producer can be monitored and all producers have the same marginal cost. Where producers are difficult or very costly to monitor or where marginal costs vary across producers, a quota cannot achieve an efficient outcome.

FIGURE 16.8 Using a Quota to Use a Common Resource Efficiently

myeconlab

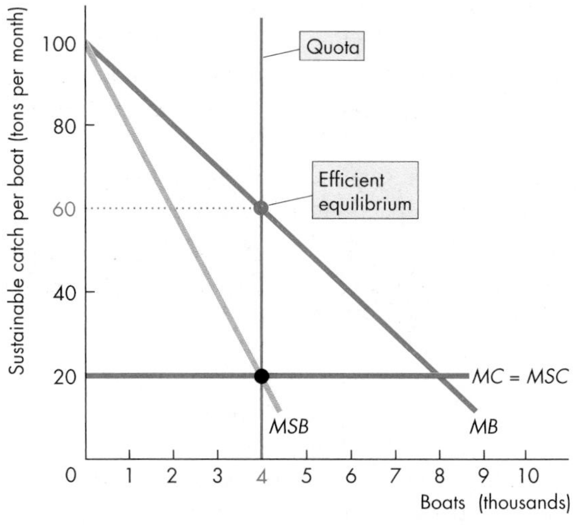

A quota is set at the efficient quantity, which makes the number of boats equal to the quantity at which marginal social benefit, *MSB*, equals marginal cost, *MC*. If the quota is enforced, the outcome is efficient.

Individual Transferable Quotas Where producers are difficult to monitor and where marginal costs differ across producers, a more sophisticated quota system can be used. An **individual transferable quota (ITQ)** is a production limit that is assigned to an individual who is free to transfer the quota to someone else. A market in ITQs emerges, and ITQs are transferred at their market price.

Figure 16.9 shows how ITQs work. In the market for ITQs, the price is the highest price that an ITQ is worth. If the number of ITQs issued equals the efficient production level, that price will equal the amount shown in the figure. This price equals the marginal private benefit at the quota quantity minus the private marginal cost of using a boat. The price rises to this level because people who don't have a quota would be willing to pay this amount to acquire the right to fish. And people who do own a quota could sell it for this price, so not to sell it is to incur an opportunity cost. The result is that the marginal cost, which now includes the cost of the ITQ, rises from MC_0 to MC_1. The equilibrium is efficient.

Individual differences in marginal cost do not prevent an ITQ system from delivering the efficient outcome. Producers that have a low marginal cost are willing and able to pay more for a quota than are producers that have a high marginal cost. The market price of a quota will equal the marginal cost of the

FIGURE 16.9 Individual Transferable Quotas to Use a Common Resource Efficiently

myeconlab

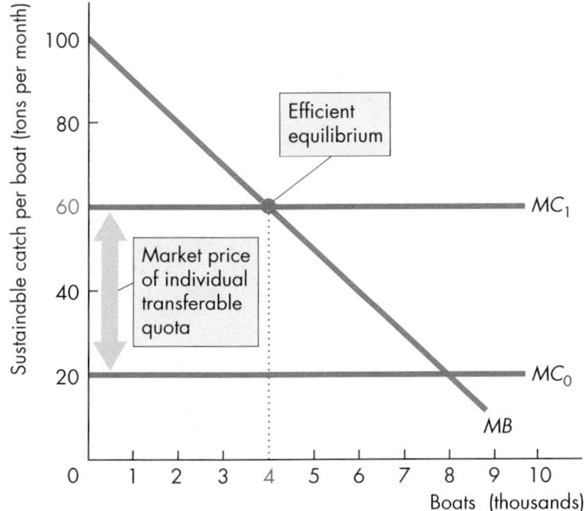

ITQs are issued on a scale that keeps output at the efficient level. The market price of an ITQ equals the marginal private benefit minus marginal cost. Because each user of the common resource faces the opportunity cost of using the resource, self-interest achieves the social interest.

marginal producer at the efficient quantity. Producers with higher marginal costs will not produce.

Public Choice and the Political Equilibrium

You saw in the previous part of this chapter where we studied the provision of public goods that a political equilibrium might be inefficient—that there might be government failure.

This same political outcome might arise in the face of a tragedy of the commons. Defining an efficient allocation of resources and designing an ITQ system to achieve that allocation is not sufficient to ensure that the political process delivers the efficient outcome. In the case of the ocean fish stock, some countries have achieved an efficient political equilibrium, but not all have done so.

There is wide agreement among economists that ITQs offer the most effective tool for dealing with overfishing and achieving an efficient use of the stock of ocean fish. So a political commitment to ITQs is an efficient outcome, and an unwillingness to use ITQs is an inefficient political outcome.

Australia and New Zealand have introduced ITQs to conserve fish stocks in the South Pacific and Southern Oceans. The evidence from these examples suggests that ITQs work well. Fishing boat operators have an incentive to cheat and produce more than the amount for which they have a quota. But such cheating seems to be relatively rare. And producers that have paid for a quota have an incentive to monitor and report on cheating by others who have not paid the market price for a quota.

So ITQs do the job they are designed to do: Help to maintain fish stocks. But they also reduce the size of the fishing industry. This consequence of ITQs puts them against the self-interest of fishers.

In all countries, the fishing industry opposes restrictions on its activities. But in Australia and New Zealand, the opposition is not strong enough to block ITQs. In contrast, in the United States the opposition is so strong that the fishing industry has persuaded Congress to outlaw ITQs. In 1996, Congress passed the Sustainable Fishing Act that puts a moratorium on ITQs. The result of this act is that earlier attempts to introduce ITQs in the Gulf of Mexico and the Northern Pacific were abandoned.

REVIEW QUIZ

1. What is the tragedy of the commons?
2. Provide two examples of the tragedy of the commons, including one from your own neighborhood.
3. Describe the conditions under which a common resource is used efficiently.
4. Review three methods that might achieve the efficient use of a common resource and explain the obstacles to efficiency.

myeconlab **Study Plan 16.3**

Reading Between the Lines on pp. 374–375 looks at the overuse of tropical rain forests.

The next chapter begins a new part of your study of microeconomics and examines the third big question: For whom are goods and services produced? We examine the markets for factors of production and discover how wage rates and other incomes are determined.

READING BETWEEN THE LINES

Rain Forests: A Tragedy of the Commons

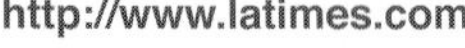

http://www.latimes.com

Puerto Rico Rain Forest on Edge

April 23, 2006

The scent of flowering tropical plants fills the moist air amid a chorus of whistling birds and singing frogs. The only other sound for a mile in any direction is the roar of a 100-foot waterfall.

Despite 28,000 acres of such lovely scenes, the tropical rain forest that Puerto Rico's prehistoric Taino Indians called El Yunque, or "Land of the White Clouds," is in grave danger. Thousands of acres of forests and green lands . . . are being cleared at a torrid pace. . . .

There are consequences to clearing these lands, beyond harm to hundreds of rare plants and wildlife in El Yunque. The rain forest, 25 miles east of metropolitan San Juan, provides one-third of the island's fresh drinking water. . . .

Tropical forests such as El Yunque constitute about 6% of Earth's surface and account for 50% to 80% of the world's plant species. Rain forests once covered 14% of the planet's land surface, but have shrunk due to development and deforestation.

Some of the development has arrived within 30 feet of El Yunque's main entrance.

"I'd like to think we live in harmony with El Yunque," said Martha Herrera, 69, who bought a two-story house next to the rain forest a decade ago.

"Some people say I'm hurting El Yunque. But how am I hurting anything?" she asked as her three dogs and flock of chickens roamed in and out of the park one recent morning.

About a quarter-mile away, construction crews were pouring concrete as they rushed to finish a 20-acre condominium complex.

"People who buy these units want the views of the rain forest," said Hecter Ramirez, 35, a construction worker at the site. "I have a job. That's important to my family and me. People tell me this isn't going to damage anything."

El Yunque is home to 240 native tree species—more than any other national forest. Federally listed endangered plants grow in the forest too, such as the miniature orchid and palo de jazmin. . . .

Essence of the Story

- Puerto Rico's El Yunque tropical rain forest has 240 native tree species—more than any other national forest.
- Tropical forests, which have shrunk from 14 percent to 6 percent of earth's surface, account for 50 to 80 percent of the world's plant species.
- The rain forest near San Juan provides one third of the island's fresh drinking water.
- Puerto Rico's tropical rain forest is being cleared at a torrid pace.
- Condominium construction is taking place close to the rain forest.
- Construction workers and people who buy condominiums say they aren't doing any damage.

Economic Analysis

- The tropical rain forests of Puerto Rico grow on land that some people want to build on.
- These forests are also home to many rare species of tree, a source of drinking water, and a carbon-dioxide sink that helps to maintain the earth's atmosphere.
- The forests are common property.
- The private incentive to exploit these forest resources is strong.
- And because no one owns the forests, there is no incentive to conserve the resources and use them on a sustainable basis.
- The result is overuse, just like the overuse of the commons of England in the Middle Ages.
- The figures illustrate the tragedy of the commons in a tropical rain forest.
- Figure 1 shows the relationship between the sustainable production of wood from a rain forest and the number of lumber producers working the forest.
- Figure 2 shows the marginal private benefit and marginal private cost of a producer and the marginal social benefit and marginal social cost of wood.
- The marginal private cost of felling a tree incurred by a producer is assumed to be zero.
- For a common resource, the marginal private benefit received by a producer is *MB* and *LD* producers acting in their self-interest deplete the resource. Sustainable production decreases to zero.
- For a privately owned resource, the marginal social benefit curve, *MSB*, becomes the marginal private benefit curve. Self-interest results in *LP* producers who maximize the sustainable output of the rain forest.
- If the only benefit from the rain forest were its timber, maximum sustainable timber output would be efficient.
- But external benefits arise from the diversity of the wildlife supported by the forest, so marginal social cost exceeds the zero marginal private cost.
- Production in the social interest—the efficient level of production—is achieved with *LS* producers and is less than the maximum sustainable production.

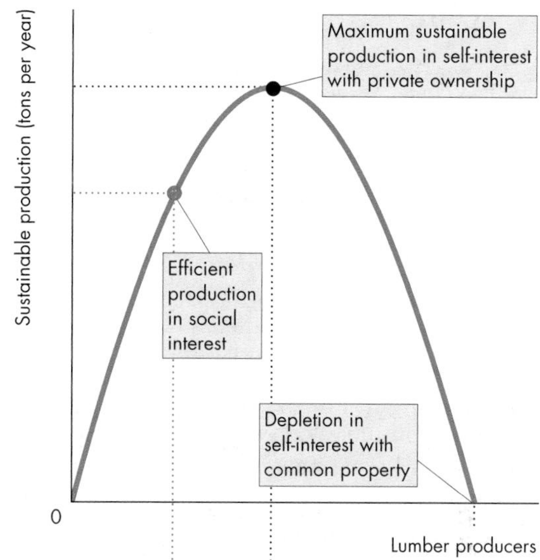

Figure 1 Rain forest timber production

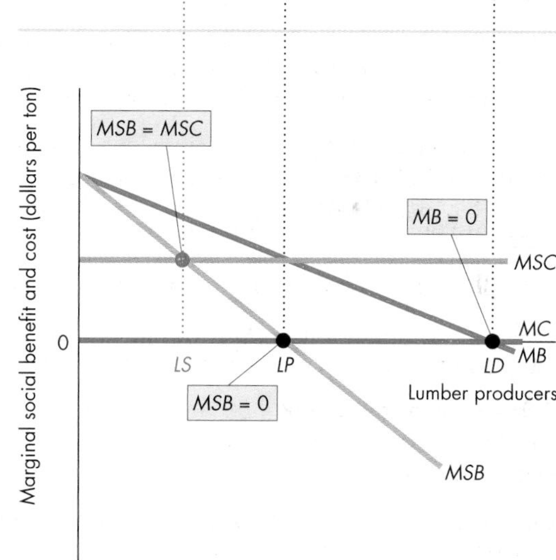

Figure 2 Marginal benefits and marginal costs

You're the Voter

- Would you support a law that banned the importing of products made from tropical rain forests? Provide your reasons.

SUMMARY

Key Points

Classifying Goods and Resources (p. 362)

- A private good is a good or service that is rival and excludable.
- A public good is a good or service that is nonrival and nonexcludable.
- A common resource is a resource that is rival but nonexcludable.

Public Goods and the Free-Rider Problem (pp. 363–367)

- Because a public good is a good or service that is *nonrival* and *nonexcludable*, it creates a *free-rider* problem: No one has an incentive to pay their share of the cost of providing a public good.
- The efficient level of provision of a public good is that at which net benefit is maximized. Equivalently, it is the level at which marginal social benefit equals marginal social cost.
- Competition between political parties, each of which tries to appeal to the maximum number of voters, can lead to the efficient scale of provision of a public good and to both parties proposing the same policies—the principle of minimum differentiation.
- Bureaucrats try to maximize their budgets, and if voters are rationally ignorant, public goods might be provided in quantities that exceed those that maximize net benefit.

Common Resources (pp. 368–373)

- Common resources create a problem that is called the tragedy of the commons—no one has a private incentive to conserve the resources and use them at an efficient rate.
- A common resource is used to the point at which the marginal private benefit equals the marginal cost.
- A common resource might be used efficiently by creating a private property right, setting a quota, or issuing individual transferable quotas.

Key Figures

Key Terms

PROBLEMS

myeconlab Tests, Study Plan, Solutions*

1. Classify each of the following items as excludable, nonexcludable, rival, nonrival, a public good, a private good, or a common resource.
   a. Gettysburg National Military Park
   b. A Big Mac
   c. Brooklyn Bridge
   d. The Grand Canyon
   e. Air
   f. Police protection
   g. Sidewalks
   h. U.S. Postal Service
   i. FedEx
   j. The MyEconLab Web site
2. For each of the following goods, explain whether there is a free-rider problem. If there is no such problem, how is it avoided?
   a. July 4th fireworks display
   b. Interstate 81 in Virginia
   c. Wireless Internet access in hotels
   d. Sharing downloaded music
   e. The public library in your city
3. The figure provides information about a sewage disposal system that a city of 1 million people is considering installing.

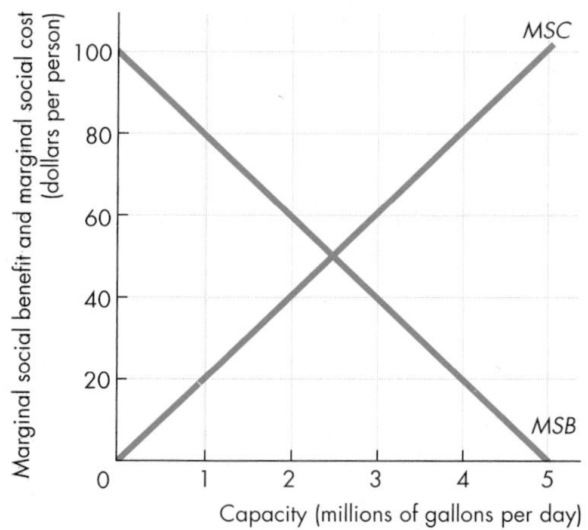

   a. What is the capacity that achieves maximum net benefit?
   b. How much will each person have to pay in taxes to pay for the efficient capacity level?
   c. What is the political equilibrium if voters are well informed?
   d. What is the political equilibrium if voters are rationally ignorant and bureaucrats achieve the highest attainable budget?
4. The table shows the value of cod caught in the North Atlantic Ocean by American and European fishing boats. The marginal cost of operating a boat is $80,000 a month.

Number of boats	Value of cod caught (thousands of dollars per month)
0	0
10	2,000
20	3,400
30	4,200
40	4,400
50	4,000
60	3,000
70	1,400

   a. What is the marginal private benefit of a fishing boat at each quantity of boats shown in the table?
   b. What is the marginal social benefit of a fishing boat at each quantity of boats shown in the table?
   c. With no regulation of cod fishing, what is the equilibrium number of boats and the value of cod caught?
   d. Is the equilibrium in part (c) an overfishing equilibrium?
   e. What is the efficient number of boats?
   f. What is the efficient value of the cod catch?
   g. Do you think that the consumers of fish and the fishing industry will agree about how much cod should be caught?
   h. If the United States, Canada, and the European Union imposed a quota to limit the catch to the efficient quantity, what would be the total value of the catch under the quota?
   i. If the United States, Canada, and the European Union issued ITQs to fishing boats to limit the catch to the efficient quantity, what would be the price of an ITQ?

*Solutions to odd-numbered problems are provided.

CRITICAL THINKING

1. After you have studied *Reading Between the Lines* on pp. 374–375, answer the following questions:
   a. What is happening in Puerto Rico that is causing the depletion of the country's tropical rain forests?
   b. How would the creation of private property rights in Puerto Rico's rain forests change the way in which the forest resources are used?
   c. Would private ownership solve all the problems of resource overuse? If not, why not?
2. Your city council is considering upgrading its system for controlling traffic signals. The council believes that by installing computers, it can improve the speed of the traffic flow. The bigger the computer the council buys, the better job it can do. The mayor and the other elected officials who are working on the proposal want to determine the scale of the system that will win them the most votes. The city bureaucrats want to maximize the budget. Suppose that you are an economist who is observing this public choice. Your job is to calculate the quantity of this public good that uses resources efficiently.
   a. What data would you need to reach your own conclusions?
   b. What does the public choice theory predict will be the quantity chosen?
   c. How could you, as an informed voter, attempt to influence the choice?
3. **Where the Tuna Roam**

   ... to the first settlers, the Great Plains posed the same problem as the oceans today: It was a vast, open area where there seemed to be no way to protect animals against relentless human predators. ... But animals thrived in the West once the settlers divvied up the land and ingeniously devised new ways to protect their livestock. ... Today the ocean is still pretty much an open range, and the fish are suffering the consequences. ... fishermen have a personal incentive to make as much as they can this year, even if they're destroying their own profession in the process. They figure any fish they don't take for themselves will just be taken by someone else. ...

   The New York Times, November 4, 2006

   a. What are the similarities between the problems faced by the earliest settlers in the West and today's fishers?
   b. Can the tragedy of the commons in the oceans be eliminated in the same manner used by the early settlers on the plains?
   c. How can ITQs change the short-term outlook of fishers to a long-term outlook?
4. Benjamin Franklin created a volunteer fire brigade in Philadelphia following a major fire in 1736. The idea of volunteer fire brigades quickly gained popularity, and many companies were formed. Each company paid for its own equipment and located it at strategic locations throughout the city.
   a. Explain the free-rider problem associated with these early fire companies.
   b. How could the early fire companies solve this free-rider problem?
   c. Why is this fire-fighting system not in place in the United States today?

WEB ACTIVITIES

myeconlab **Links to Web sites**

1. Visit Ed Clarke's Public Goods Web site and read his article on demand revealing processes.
   a. What is a demand revealing process and what is its purpose?
   b. Why might using a demand revealing process deliver a more efficient level of public goods than our current political system?
   c. Why might our current political system deliver a more efficient level of public goods than would a demand revealing process?
2. Visit the ITT Industries Web site and read the article on "The Rising Tide of Water Markets."
   a. What is the purpose of a water market?
   b. What do you think are the main advantages of the market mechanism as a means of allocating scarce water resources?
   c. What do you think are the main disadvantages of the market mechanism as a means of allocating scarce water resources?
   d. Why do you think we don't use the market mechanism more widely to allocate scarce water resources?
   e. Write a short executive summary of your view on using the market to allocate scarce water resources.

We, the People, ...

Thomas Jefferson knew that creating a government of the people, by the people, and for the people was a huge enterprise and one that could easily go wrong. Creating a constitution that made despotic and tyrannical rule impossible was relatively easy. The founding fathers did their best to practice sound economics. They designed a sophisticated system of incentives—of carrots and sticks–to make the government responsive to public opinion and to limit the ability of individual self-interests to gain at the expense of the majority. But they were not able to create a constitution that effectively blocks the ability of special interest groups to capture the consumer and producer surpluses that result from specialization and exchange.

We have created a system of government to deal with five economic problems. The market economy enables monopoly to restrict production and charge too high a price. It produces too large a quantity of some goods and services, the production of which creates pollution. It would produce too small a quantity of those public goods and services that we must consume together, such as national defense and air-traffic control. It allows common resources, such as rain forests and ocean fish, to be overused. And it generates a distribution of income and wealth that most people believe is too unequal. So we need a government to help cope with these economic problems. But as the founding fathers knew would happen, when governments get involved in the economy, people try to steer the government's actions in directions that bring personal gains at the expense of the general interest.

The three chapters in this part explained the problems with which the market has a hard time coping. Chapter 14 overviewed the entire range of problems and studied one of them, antitrust law and the regulation of natural monopoly, more deeply. Chapter 15 dealt with externalities. It examined the external costs imposed by pollution and the external benefits that come from education and research. It described some of the ways in which externalities can be dealt with. And it explained that one way of coping with externalities is to strengthen the market and "internalize" the externalities rather than to intervene in the market. And Chapter 16 studied the problems created by public goods and the tragedy of the common resources.

Many economists have thought long and hard about the problems discussed in this part. But none has had as profound an effect on our ideas in this area as Ronald Coase, whom you can meet on the following page. You can also meet Caroline Hoxby of Harvard University, an economist whose work has shed important light on public choice issues, especially in the field of education.

PROBING THE IDEAS

Externalities and Property Rights

"The question to be decided is: is the value of fish lost greater or less than the value of the product which contamination of the stream makes possible?"

RONALD H. COASE
The Problem of Social Cost

The Economist

Ronald Coase *(1910–), was born in England and educated at the London School of Economics, where he was deeply influenced by his teacher, Arnold Plant, and by the issues of his youth: communist central planning versus free markets.*

Professor Coase has lived in the United States since 1951. He first visited America as a 20-year-old on a traveling scholarship during the depths of the Great Depression. It was on this visit, and before he had completed his bachelor's degree, that he conceived the ideas that 60 years later were to earn him the 1991 Nobel Prize for Economic Science.

Ronald Coase discovered and clarified the significance of transactions costs and property rights for the functioning of the economy. He has revolutionized the way we think about property rights and externalities and has opened up the growing field of law and economics.

The Issues

As knowledge accumulates, we are becoming more sensitive to environmental externalities. We are also developing more sensitive methods of dealing with them. But all the methods involve a public choice.

Urban smog, which is both unpleasant and dangerous to breathe, forms when sunlight reacts with emissions from the tailpipes of automobiles. Because of this external cost of auto exhaust, we set emission standards and tax gasoline. Emission standards increase the cost of a car, and gasoline taxes increase the cost of the marginal mile traveled. The higher costs decrease the quantity demanded of road transportation and so decrease the amount of pollution it creates. Is the value of cleaner urban air worth the higher cost of transportation? The public choices of voters, regulators, and lawmakers answer this question.

Acid rain, which imposes a cost on everyone who lives in its path, falls from sulfur-laden clouds produced by electric utility smokestacks. This external cost is being tackled with a market solution. This solution is marketable permits, the price and allocation of which are determined by the forces of supply and demand. Private choices determine the demand for pollution permits, but a public choice determines the supply.

As cars stream onto an urban freeway during the morning rush hour, the highway clogs and becomes an expensive parking lot. Each rush hour traveler imposes external costs on all the others. Today, road users bear private congestion costs but do not face a share of the external congestion costs that they create. But a market solution to this problem is now technologically feasible. It is a solution that charges road users a fee similar to a toll that varies with time of day and degree of congestion. Confronted with the social marginal cost of their actions, each road user makes a choice and the market for highway space is efficient. Here, a public choice to use a market solution leaves the final decision about the degree of congestion to private choices.

Then

Chester Jackson, a Lake Erie fisherman, recalls that when he began fishing on the lake, boats didn't carry drinking water. Fishermen drank from the lake. Speaking after World War II, Jackson observed, "Can't do that today. Those chemicals in there would kill you." Farmers used chemicals, such as the insecticide DDT, that got carried into the lake by runoff. Industrial waste and trash were also dumped in the lake in large quantities. As a result, Lake Erie became badly polluted during the 1940s and became incapable of sustaining a viable fish stock.

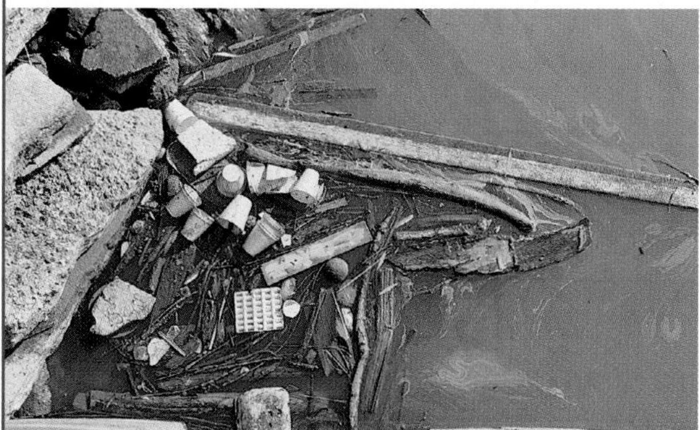

Now

Today, Lake Erie supports a fishing industry, just as it did in the 1930s. No longer treated as a garbage dump for chemicals, the lake is regenerating its ecosystem. Fertilizers and insecticides are now recognized as products that have potential externalities, and their external effects are assessed by the Environmental Protection Agency before new versions are put into widespread use. Dumping industrial waste into rivers and lakes is now subject to much more stringent regulations and penalties. Lake Erie's externalities have been dealt with by one of the methods available: government regulation.

Caroline Hoxby, whom you can meet on the following pages, has done much to improve our understanding of policy choices in education.

TALKING WITH

Caroline M. Hoxby

Caroline M. Hoxby is the Allie S. Freed Professor of Economics at Harvard University. Born in Cleveland, Ohio, she was an undergraduate at Harvard and a graduate student at Oxford and MIT.

Professor Hoxby is a leading student of the economics of education. She has written many articles on this topic and has published books entitled The Economics of School Choice *and* College Choices *(both University of Chicago Press, 2003 and 2004, respectively). She is Program Director of the Economics of Education Program at the National Bureau of Economic Research, serves on several other national boards that study education issues, and has advised or provided testimony to several state legislatures and the United States Congress.*

Michael Parkin talked with Caroline Hoxby about her work and the progress that economists have made in understanding how the financing and provision of education influence the quality of education and the equality of access to it.

Why did you decide to become an economist?

I've wanted to be an economist from about the age of 13. That was when I took my first class in economics (an interesting story in itself) and discovered that all of the thoughts swimming around in my head belonged to a "science" and there was an entire body of people who understood this science—a lot better than I did, anyway. I can still recall reading *The Wealth of Nations* for the first time; it was a revelation.

What drew you to study the economics of education?

We all care about education, perhaps because it is the key means by which opportunity is (or should be) extended to all in the United States. Also, nearly everyone now acknowledges that highly developed countries like the United States rely increasingly on education as the engine of economic growth. Thus, one reason I was drawn to education is its importance. However, what primarily drew me was that education issues were so clearly begging for economic analysis and that there was so little of it. I try hard to understand educational institutions and problems, but I insist on bringing economic logic to bear on educational issues.

Why is education different from fast food? Why don't we just let people buy it from private firms that are regulated to maintain quality standards analogous to the safety standards that the FDA imposes on fast-food producers?

The thing that makes education different from fast food is not that we cannot buy it from private institutions that are regulated to maintain quality standards. We do this all the time—think of private schools and colleges. What makes education different is that it is (a) an investment, not consumption, and (b) the capital markets for financing the investments work poorly when left on their own. Essentially, our country has an interest in every person investing optimally in his or her education. To make investments, however, people need funds that allow them to attend good schools and take time away from work. Children don't have these funds and cannot arrange for loans that they may or may not pay off decades later. Therefore, children depend on their families for funds, and families do not necessarily have the funds to invest optimally or the right incentives to do so. Society has a role in filling the gaps in the capital market; it fills this role by public funding of elementary and secondary education, government guaranteed loans, college savings programs, and so on. There is no particular reason, however, why government needs to actually run schools; it can provide the funding without actually providing schooling.

In one of your papers, you posed the question: Does competition among public schools benefit students or taxpayers? What are the issues, what was your answer, and how did you arrive at it?

We are all familiar with the fact that families choose public schools when they choose where to live. This traditional form is by far the most pervasive form of school choice in the United States, and few parents who exercise it would be willing to give it up. Yet, until quite recently, we did not know whether having such traditional school choice was good for students (high achievement) or taxpayers (more efficient schools). It is important to know because some people in the United States, especially poor people who live in central cities, are unable to exercise this form of school choice. Economists hypothesized that this lack of choice might be a reason why many children from poor, central city families receive such a deficient education, especially considering the dollars spent in their schools (which spend significantly more than the median school).

To investigate this hypothesis, I examined all of the metropolitan areas in the United States. They vary a great deal in the degree of traditional choice available to parents. On one extreme, there is a group of metropolitan areas with hundreds of school districts. On the other extreme, there is a group of metropolitan areas with only one school district. Most are somewhere in between. A family in a metropolitan area with one district may have no easy way of "escaping" a badly run district administration. A family in a metropolitan area with hundreds of districts can choose among several districts that match well with its job location, housing preferences, and so on.

Looking across metropolitan areas with many districts (lots of potential competition from traditional school choice) and few districts (little potential competition), I found that areas with greater competition had substantially higher student achievement for any given level of school spending. This suggests that schools are more efficient producers of achievement when they face competition.

What do we know about the relative productivity of public and private schools?

It is somewhat difficult to say whether achievement is higher at public or private schools in the United States. The best studies use randomly assigned private school scholarships, follow the same children over time, or use "natural experiments" in which some areas accidentally end up with more private schools than others. These studies tend to find that, for the same student, private schools produce achievement that is up to 10 percent higher. However, for understanding which type of school is more productive, we actually do not need private schools to have higher achievement. For the sake of argument, let's "call it a draw" on the achievement question.

In recent studies comparing achievement in public and private schools, the public schools spent an average of $9,662 per student and the private schools spent an average of $2,427 per student. These spending numbers, combined with achievement that we will call equal, suggest that the private schools were 298 percent more productive. I would not claim that this number is precisely correct; we could think of some minor adjustments. But it is difficult not to conclude that the private schools are significantly more productive. They produce equal achievement for a fraction of the cost.

What can economists say about the alternative methods of financing education? Is there a voucher solution that could work?

There is definitely a voucher solution that could work because vouchers are inherently an extremely flexible policy. People often see the word "voucher" and think of, say, a $2000 voucher being given to a small share of children. But this need not be so. Anything that we can do with public school financing we can do better with a voucher because vouchers can be specific to a student, whereas the government can never ensure that funds get to an individual student by giving those funds to his or her district.

Any well-designed voucher system will give schools an incentive to compete. However, when designing vouchers, we can also build in remedies for a variety of educational problems. Vouchers can be used to ensure that disabled children get the funding they need and the program choices they need. Compared to current school finance programs, vouchers can do a better job of ensuring that low-income families have sufficient funds to invest in the child's education. Well-designed vouchers can encourage schools to make their student bodies socioeconomically diverse. Economists should say to policy makers: "Tell me your goals; I'll design you a voucher."

Economists should say to policy makers: "Tell me your goals; I'll design you a voucher."

Is there a conflict between efficiency and equity in the provision of quality education?

To raise the public funds that allow all families to invest optimally in their children's education, we have to have taxes. Taxes always create some deadweight loss, so we always create some inefficiency when we raise the funds we need to provide equitable educational opportunities. However, if the funds are used successfully and actually induce people to make optimal investments in their education, we have eliminated much more inefficiency than the taxes created. Thus, in an ideal world, there need not be a conflict between efficiency and equity.

In the real world, public funds are often raised with taxes (creating deadweight loss) and then are not successfully used. If we spend twice as much on public schools and do not have higher achievement to show for it, then there are no efficiency gains to overwhelm the efficiency losses from taxation. In other words, to avoid a conflict between equity and efficiency, we must learn how to use public funds productively in education. This is what the economics of education is all about.

What advice do you have for a student who is just starting to study economics? Is economics a good subject in which to major? What other subjects go well alongside it? And do you have anything special to say to women who are making a career choice? What must we do to get more women in our subject?

Students who are just starting to study economics should do two things. First, learn the tools even if they seem abstruse. Once you have mastered the tools, you will be able to "see the forest for the trees." As long as you don't master the tools, you will be in the trees and will find it hard to think about economic problems. Second, think about economic problems! The real world is a great moving textbook of economics, once you have the tools to analyze it.

Economics is a great subject in which to major because it trains you for life, for many careers, and for the thinking that you would need in a leadership position. I think that it is the best training for a future career in business, the law, or policy making. Don't forget nonprofits: every year, nonprofit organizations try to hire people with economics skills who are also interested in charitable schemes.

Math and statistics courses are complementary to economics because they make it easier for a student to master the tools quickly. Economics goes well with many studies in the arts and sciences, too. It all depends on what you want to use economics for. If you want to do health policy making, take economics along with premedical courses. If you want to be a policy maker in the performing arts, take economics along with music.

I wish that there were more women in economics. Our field loses far too many talented minds. Also, women who need to understand economics for their careers are sometimes without it. To aspiring women economists, I can only say to hang in there. Mastering economics is empowering. You will never have to worry about your opinion not being taken seriously if you are a good economist.

Markets for Factors of Production

Many Happy Returns

It may not be your birthday, and even if it is, chances are you are spending most of it working. But at the end of the week or month (or, if you're devoting all your time to college, when you graduate), you will receive the *returns* from your labor. Those returns vary a lot. Demetrio Luna, who spends his days in a small container suspended from the top of Houston's high-rise buildings cleaning windows, makes a happy return of $12 an hour. Katie Couric, who anchors the CBS evening news show each weekday, makes a very happy return of $15 million a year. Some differences in earnings might seem surprising. For example, your college football coach might earn much more than your economics professor. Why aren't *all* jobs well paid?

Most of us have little trouble spending our paycheck. But most of us do manage to save some of what we earn. What determines the amount of saving that people do and the returns they make on that saving?

Some people earn their income by supplying natural resources such as oil. What determines the price of a natural resource such as oil? And what determines when we will run out of oil and other nonrenewable resources?

What happens if we tax big incomes? Do the people who earn those incomes just shrug and put up with the tax but continue to supply the same quantity of resources? Or do taxes shrink the quantities of resources supplied?

In this chapter, we study the markets for factors of production—labor, capital, natural resources—and learn how their prices and people's incomes are determined. We'll see that some, but not all, high incomes can be taxed without adverse effect. And we'll see in *Reading Between the Lines* at the end of the chapter why universities often pay their football coaches more than they pay professors.

After studying this chapter, you will be able to

- Explain the link between a factor price and factor income
- Explain what determines demand, supply, the wage rate, and employment in a competitive labor market
- Explain why wage rates can be higher or lower than those in a competitive labor market
- Explain what determines demand, supply, the interest rate, saving, and investment in the capital market
- Explain what determines demand, supply, price, and the rate of use of a nonrenewable resource
- Explain the concept of economic rent and distinguish between economic rent and opportunity cost

Factor Prices and Incomes

Goods and services are produced using the *four factors of production—labor, capital, land,* and *entrepreneurship* (see Chapter 1, pp. 3–4). Incomes are determined by the quantities of the factors used and by factor prices. The factor prices are the *wage* rate earned by labor, the *interest* rate earned by capital, the *rental* rate earned by land, and the *normal profit* rate earned by entrepreneurship. In addition, a residual income, *economic profit* (or *economic loss*), is earned (or borne) by the firm's owners, who might be the entrepreneur or the stockholders.

Factors of production, like goods and services, are traded in markets. Some factor markets are competitive and behave similarly to competitive markets for goods and services. Some labor markets have noncompetitive elements.

Demand and supply is the main tool used to understand a competitive factor market. Firms demand factors of production and households supply them.

The demand for a factor of production is called a **derived demand** because it is *derived* from the demand for the goods and services produced by the factor. The quantity demanded of a factor of production is the quantity that firms plan to hire during a given time period and at a given factor price. The law of demand applies to factors of production just as it does to goods and services. The lower the factor price, other things remaining the same, the greater is the quantity demanded of that factor.

The quantity supplied of a factor of production also depends on its price. With a possible exception that you'll see later in this chapter, the law of supply applies to factors of production. The higher the price of a factor, other things remaining the same, the greater is the quantity supplied of that factor.

Figure 17.1 shows a factor market. The demand curve for the factor is *D*, and the supply curve of the factor is *S*. The equilibrium factor price is *PF*, and the equilibrium quantity is *QF*. The income earned by the factor is its price multiplied by the quantity used. In Fig. 17.1, the factor income equals the area of the blue rectangle.

A change in demand or supply changes the equilibrium price, quantity, and income. An increase in demand shifts the demand curve rightward and increases income. An increase in supply shifts the supply curve rightward and income might increase, decrease, or remain constant depending on the elasticity of demand for the factor. If demand is elastic, income rises; if demand is inelastic, income falls; and if demand is unit elastic, income remains constant (see Chapter 4, p. 88).

FIGURE 17.1 Demand and Supply in a Factor Market

myeconlab

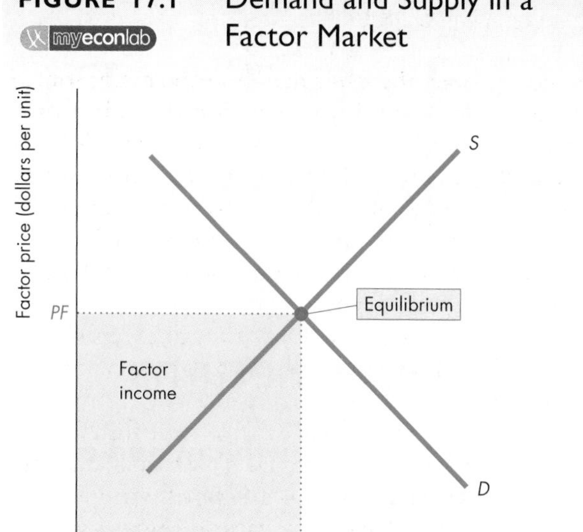

The demand curve for a factor of production, *D*, slopes downward, and the supply curve, *S*, slopes upward. Where the demand and supply curves intersect, the factor price, *PF*, and the quantity of the factor used, *QF*, are determined. The factor income is the product of the factor price and the quantity of the factor, as represented by the blue rectangle.

REVIEW QUIZ

1. Why do we call the demand for a factor of production a derived demand? From what is it derived?
2. Why does an increase in the supply of a factor of production have an ambiguous effect on the factor income?

myeconlab **Study Plan 17.1**

The rest of this chapter explores the influences on the demand for and supply of factors of production. We begin with the market for labor.

Labor Markets

For most people, the labor market is the major source of income. And for many people, it is the only source of income. In 2002, labor income represented 72 percent of total income. And in that year, the average amount earned per hour of work—the economy-wide average hourly wage rate—was close to $25 (of which $21 was paid out as a wage or salary and $4 was paid in supplementary benefits).

The average wage rate hides a lot of diversity across individual wage rates. You can see some of that diversity in Fig. 17.2, which shows a sample of wage rates for twenty jobs. (These numbers are for 2001, which is the most recent year for which this detail of information was available at the time of writing.)

The Bureau of Labor Statistics publishes wage data for 711 job categories, and of these, 78 percent pay below the average and 22 percent pay above the average. This distribution around the average means that a small number of people earn more than the average but their wage rates exceed the average by a large amount.

The range of average hourly wage rates in Fig. 17.2 is from $7 to almost $70. At the low end of the wage distribution are fast-food workers, motion picture projectionists, bank tellers, and retail salespersons. Computer support specialists (such as the people who answer your tech support calls) earn just about the average wage rate. Technical writers (such as the people who write the manuals that tell you how to use all the features on your cell phone) earn a bit more than the average. A sampling of the jobs that pay wage rates that exceed the average includes financial analysts and economists. But economists earn less than air traffic controllers, dentists, and surgeons. (John Maynard Keynes said that he hoped economists would one day become as useful as dentists. Maybe the wage rates are telling us that they are not yet there!)

To understand these wage rates, we must probe the forces that influence the demand for labor and the supply of labor. We'll begin on the demand side of the labor market.

The Demand for Labor

There is a link between the quantity of labor that a firm employs and the quantity of output that it plans to produce. The *total product curve* shows that link (see Chapter 10, p. 222).

FIGURE 17.2 Wage Rates in Twenty Jobs

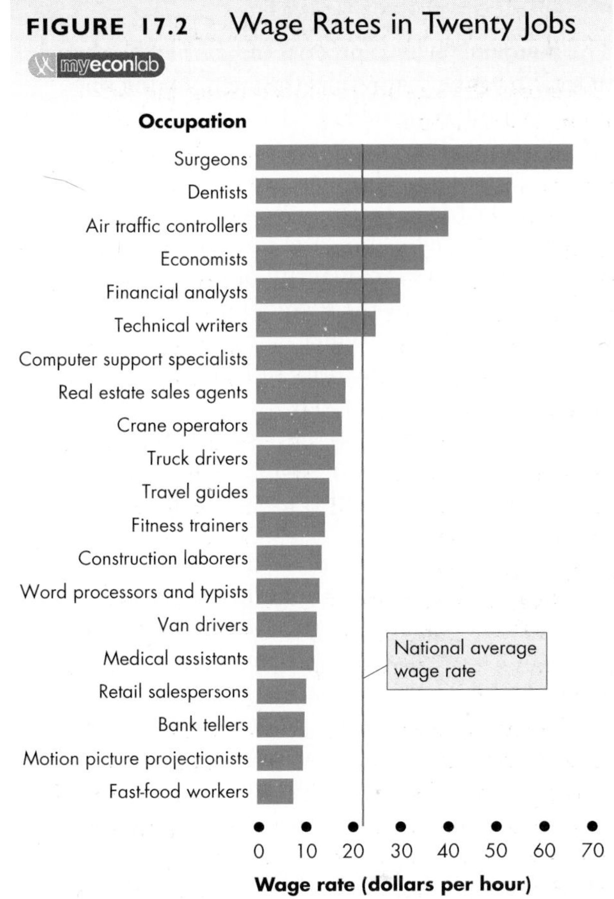

The national (economy-wide) wage rate is $21 an hour. Twenty jobs selected from the 711 jobs for which the BLS reports wage rate data show a sample of the distribution of wage rates around the national average. Most jobs pay wage rates below the national average. And some of the jobs that pay above the average exceed it by a large amount.

Source of data: Bureau of Labor Statistics.

A firm's demand for labor is the flip side of its supply of output. A firm produces the quantity that maximizes profit. And the profit-maximizing quantity is that at which marginal revenue equals marginal cost. To produce the profit-maximizing quantity, a firm hires the profit-maximizing quantity of labor.

What is the profit-maximizing quantity of labor? And how does it change as the wage rate changes? We can answer these questions by comparing the marginal revenue earned by hiring one more worker with the marginal cost of that worker. Let's look first at the marginal revenue side of this comparison.

Marginal Revenue Product

The **marginal revenue product** of labor is the change in total revenue that results from employing one more unit of labor. Table 17.1 shows you how to calculate marginal revenue product.

The first two columns show the total product schedule for Max's Wash 'n' Wax car wash service. The numbers tell us how the number of car washes per hour varies as the quantity of labor varies. The third column shows the *marginal product of labor*—the change in total product that results from a one-unit increase in the quantity of labor employed (see Chapter 10, p. 221 to review this concept.)

The car wash market is perfectly competitive, and Max can sell as many washes as he chooses at $4 a wash, the assumed market price. So Max's *marginal revenue* is $4 a wash.

Given this information, we can calculate *marginal revenue product* (the fourth column). It equals marginal product multiplied by marginal revenue. For example, the marginal product of the second worker is 4 car washes an hour, and because marginal revenue is $4 a wash, the marginal revenue product of the second worker is $16 (4 washes at $4 each).

The last two columns of Table 17.1 show an alternative way of calculating the marginal revenue product of labor. Total revenue is equal to total product multiplied by price. For example, two workers produce 9 washes per hour and generate a total revenue of $36 (9 washes at $4 each). One worker produces 5 washes per hour and generates a total revenue of $20 (5 washes at $4 each). Marginal revenue product, in the sixth column, is the change in total revenue from hiring one more worker. When the second worker is hired, total revenue increases from $20 to $36, an increase of $16. So the marginal revenue product of the second worker is $16, which agrees with our previous calculation.

Diminishing Marginal Revenue Product As the quantity of labor increases, marginal revenue product diminishes. For a firm in perfect competition, marginal revenue product diminishes because marginal product diminishes. For a monopoly (or in monopolistic competition or oligopoly), marginal revenue product diminishes for a second reason. When more labor is hired and total product increases, the firm must cut its price to sell the extra product. So marginal product *and* marginal revenue decrease, both of which bring decreasing marginal revenue product.

TABLE 17.1 Marginal Revenue Product at Max's Wash 'n' Wax

	Quantity of labor (L) (workers)	Total product (TP) (car washes per hour)	Marginal product ($MP = \Delta TP/\Delta L$) (washes per worker)	Marginal revenue product ($MRP = MR \times MP$) (dollars per worker)	Total revenue ($TR = P \times TP$) (dollars)	Marginal revenue product ($MRP = \Delta TR/\Delta L$) (dollars per worker)
A	0	0			0	
			5	20		20
B	1	5			20	
			4	16		16
C	2	9			36	
			3	12		12
D	3	12			48	
			2	8		8
E	4	14			56	
			1	4		4
F	5	15			60	

The car wash market is perfectly competitive and the price is $4 a wash, so marginal revenue is $4 a wash. Marginal revenue product equals marginal product (column 3) multiplied by marginal revenue. For example, the marginal product of the second worker is 4 washes and marginal revenue is $4 a wash, so the marginal revenue product of the second worker (in column 4) is $16. Alternatively, if Max hires 1 worker (row *B*), total product is 5 washes an hour and total revenue is $20 (column 5). If he hires 2 workers (row *C*), total product is 9 washes an hour and total revenue is $36. By hiring the second worker, total revenue rises by $16—the marginal revenue product of the second worker is $16.

The Labor Demand Curve

Figure 17.3 shows how the labor demand curve is derived. The *marginal revenue product curve* graphs the marginal revenue product of labor at each quantity hired. Figure 17.3(a) is Max's marginal revenue product curve. The *x*-axis measures the number of workers that Max hires, and the *y*-axis measures the marginal revenue product of labor. The blue bars show the marginal revenue product of labor as Max employs more workers. These bars correspond to the numbers in Table 17.1. The curve labeled *MRP* is Max's marginal revenue product curve.

A firm's marginal revenue product curve is also its demand for labor curve. Figure 17.3(b) shows Max's demand for labor curve, *D*. The horizontal axis measures the number of workers hired—the same as in part (a). The vertical axis measures the wage rate in dollars per hour. In Fig. 17.3(a), when Max increases the quantity of labor employed from 2 workers an hour to 3 workers an hour, marginal revenue product is $12 an hour. In Fig. 17.3(b), at a wage rate of $12 an hour, Max hires 3 workers.

The marginal revenue product curve is also the demand for labor curve because the firm hires the profit-maximizing quantity of labor. If the wage rate is *less* than marginal revenue product, the firm can increase its profit by employing one more worker. Conversely, if the wage rate is *greater* than marginal revenue product, the firm can increase its profit by employing one fewer worker.

But if the wage rate *equals* marginal revenue product, then the firm cannot increase its profit by changing the number of workers it employs. The firm is making the maximum possible profit. So the quantity of labor demanded by the firm is such that the wage rate equals the marginal revenue product of labor.

Because the marginal revenue product curve is also the demand curve, and because marginal revenue product diminishes as the quantity of labor employed increases, the demand for labor curve slopes downward. The lower the wage rate, other things remaining the same, the more workers a firm hires.

When we studied the firm's output decision, we discovered that a condition for maximum profit is that marginal revenue equals marginal cost. We've now discovered another condition for maximum profit: Marginal revenue product of labor equals the wage rate. Let's study the connection between these two conditions.

FIGURE 17.3 The Demand for Labor at Max's Wash 'n' Wax

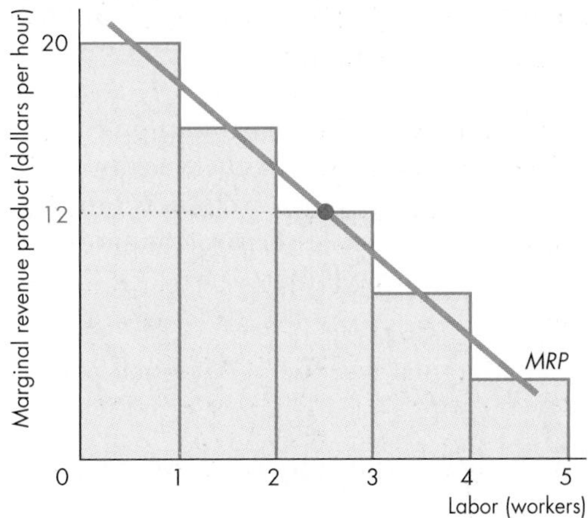

(a) Marginal revenue product

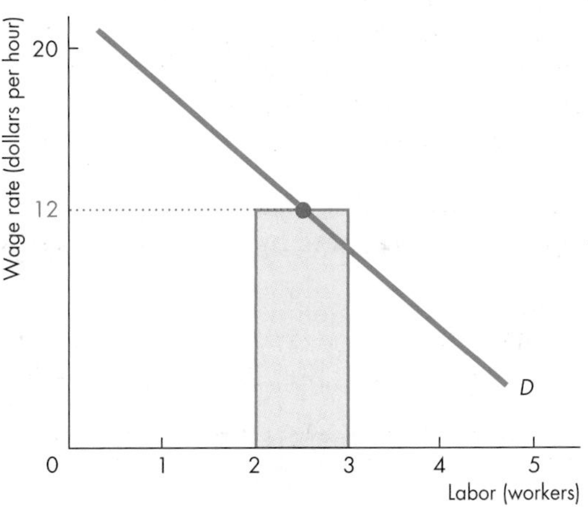

(b) Demand for labor

Max's Wash 'n' Wax operates in a perfectly competitive car wash market and can sell any quantity of washes at $4 a wash. The blue bars in part (a) represent the firm's marginal revenue product of labor. They are based on the numbers in Table 17.1. The orange line is the firm's marginal revenue product of labor curve. Part (b) shows Max's demand for labor curve. This curve is identical to Max's marginal revenue product curve. Max demands the quantity of labor that makes the wage rate equal to the marginal revenue product of labor. The demand for labor curve slopes downward because marginal revenue product diminishes as the quantity of labor employed increases.

Equivalence of Two Conditions for Profit Maximization

Profit is maximized when, at the quantity of labor hired, *marginal revenue product* equals the wage rate and when, at the output produced, *marginal revenue* equals *marginal cost.*

These two conditions for maximum profit are equivalent. The quantity of labor that maximizes profit produces the output that maximizes profit.

To see the equivalence of the two conditions for maximum profit, first recall that

$$\text{Marginal revenue product} = \text{Marginal revenue} \times \text{Marginal product}.$$

If we call marginal revenue product MRP, marginal revenue MR, and marginal product MP, we have

$$MRP = MR \times MP.$$

If we call the wage rate W, the first condition for profit to be maximized is

$$MRP = W.$$

But $MRP = MR \times MP$, so

$$MR \times MP = W.$$

This equation tells us that when profit is maximized, marginal revenue multiplied by marginal product equals the wage rate.

Divide the last equation by MP to obtain

$$MR = W \div MP.$$

This equation states that when profit is maximized, marginal revenue equals the wage rate divided by the marginal product of labor.

The wage rate divided by the marginal product of labor equals marginal cost. It costs the firm W to hire one more hour of labor. But the labor produces MP units of output. So the cost of producing one of those units of output, which is marginal cost, is W divided by MP.

If we call marginal cost MC, then

$$MR = MC,$$

which is the second condition for maximum profit.

Because the first condition for maximum profit implies the second condition, these two conditions are equivalent. Table 17.2 summarizes the calculations you've just done and shows the equivalence of the two conditions for maximum profit.

TABLE 17.2 Two Conditions for Maximum Profit

Symbols

Marginal product	***MP***
Marginal revenue	***MR***
Marginal cost	***MC***
Marginal revenue product	***MRP***
Wage rate	***W***

Two Conditions for Maximum Profit

1. $MR = MC$ 2. $MRP = W$

Equivalence of Conditions

1.	$MRP/MP = \mathbf{MR}$	=	$\mathbf{MC} = W/MP$
	Multiply by MP to give $MRP = MR \times MP$ Flipping the equation over		Multiply by MP to give $MC \times MP = W$ Flipping the equation over
2.	$MR \times MP = \mathbf{MRP}$	=	$\mathbf{W} = MC \times MP$

The two conditions for maximum profit are that marginal revenue (*MR*) equals marginal cost (*MC*) and that marginal revenue product (*MRP*) equals the wage rate (*W*). These two conditions are equivalent because marginal revenue product (*MRP*) equals marginal revenue (*MR*) multiplied by marginal product (*MP*) and the wage rate (*W*) equals marginal cost (*MC*) multiplied by marginal product (*MP*).

Max's Numbers Check the numbers for Max's Wash 'n' Wax and confirm that the conditions you've just examined work. Max's profit-maximizing labor decision is to hire 3 workers if the wage rate is $12 an hour. When Max hires 3 workers, marginal product is 3 washes an hour. Max sells the 3 washes for a marginal revenue of $4 a wash. So marginal revenue product is 3 washes multiplied by $4 a wash, which equals $12 an hour. At a wage rate of $12 an hour, Max is maximizing profit.

Equivalently, Max's marginal cost is $12 an hour divided by 3 washes an hour, which equals $4 a wash. At a marginal revenue of $4 a wash, Max is maximizing profit.

You've discovered that the law of demand applies for labor just as it does for goods and services. Other things remaining the same, the lower the wage rate (the price of labor), the greater is the quantity of labor demanded.

Let's now study the influences that change the demand for labor and shift the demand for labor curve.

Changes in the Demand for Labor

The demand for labor depends on three factors:

1. The price of the firm's output
2. Other factor prices
3. Technology and capital

The Price of the Firm's Output The higher the price of the firm's output, the greater is the firm's demand for labor. The price of output affects the demand for labor through its influence on marginal revenue product. A higher price for the firm's output increases marginal revenue, which, in turn, increases the marginal revenue product of labor. A change in the price of a firm's output leads to a shift in the firm's demand for labor curve. If the price of the firm's output increases, the demand for labor increases and the demand for labor curve shifts rightward.

Other Factor Prices If the price of some other factor of production changes, the demand for labor changes, but only in the *long run* when all factors of production can be varied. The effect of a change in some other factor price depends on whether that factor is a *substitute* for or a *complement* of labor. Computers are substitutes for telephone operators but complements of word processor operators. So if computers become less costly to use, the demand for telephone operators decreases but the demand for word processor operators increases.

Technology and Capital An advance in technology or an increase in capital that changes the marginal product of labor changes the demand for labor. There is a general belief that advances in technology and capital accumulation destroy jobs and therefore decrease the demand for labor. But while new technologies and capital are substitutes for some types of labor and decrease the demand for labor, they are complements of other kinds and increase the demand for labor. For example, the electronic telephone exchange is a substitute for telephone operators, so the arrival of this new technology has decreased the demand for telephone operators. This same new technology is a complement of systems managers, programmers, and electronic engineers. So its arrival has increased the demand for these types of labor.

Again, these effects on the demand for labor are long-run effects that occur when a firm adjusts all its resources and incorporates new technologies into its production process.

Table 17.3 summarizes the influences on a firm's demand for labor.

TABLE 17.3 A Firm's Demand for Labor

The Law of Demand
(Movements along the demand curve for labor)

The quantity of labor demanded by a firm

Decreases if:	*Increases if:*
■ The wage rate increases	■ The wage rate decreases

Changes in Demand
(Shifts in the demand curve for labor)

A firm's demand for labor

Decreases if:	*Increases if:*
■ The price of the firm's output decreases	■ The price of the firm's output increases
■ The price of a substitute for labor falls.	■ The price of a substitute for labor rises.
■ The price of a complement of labor rises.	■ The price of a complement of labor falls.
■ A new technology or new capital decreases the marginal product of labor	■ A new technology or new capital increases the marginal product of labor

Market Demand

So far, we've studied the demand for labor by an individual firm. The market demand for labor is the total demand by all firms. The market demand for labor is derived (similarly to the market demand for any good or service) by adding together the quantities demanded by all firms at each wage rate. Because each firm's demand for labor curve slopes downward, so does the market demand for labor curve.

Elasticity of Demand for Labor

The elasticity of demand for labor measures the responsiveness of the quantity of labor demanded to the wage rate. This elasticity is important because it tells us how labor income changes when the supply of labor changes. An increase in supply (other things remaining the same) lowers the wage rate. If demand is inelastic, an increase in supply also lowers labor income. But if demand is elastic, an increase in supply lowers the wage rate and increases labor income. And if the demand for labor is unit elastic, a change in supply leaves labor income unchanged.

The demand for labor is less elastic in the short run, when only the quantity of labor can be varied, than in the long run, when the quantities of labor and other factors of production can be varied. The elasticity of demand for labor depends on the

- Labor intensity of the production process
- Elasticity of demand for the good produced
- Substitutability of capital for labor

Labor Intensity A labor-intensive production process is one that uses a lot of labor and little capital. Home building is an example. The greater the degree of labor intensity, the more elastic is the demand for labor. To see why, first suppose that wages are 90 percent of total cost. A 10 percent increase in the wage rate increases total cost by 9 percent. Firms will be sensitive to such a large change in total cost, so if the wage rate increases, firms will decrease the quantity of labor demanded by a relatively large amount. But if wages are 10 percent of total cost, a 10 percent increase in the wage rate increases total cost by only 1 percent. Firms will be less sensitive to this increase in total cost, so if the wage rate increases, firms will decrease the quantity of labor demanded by a relatively small amount.

Elasticity of Demand for the Good Produced The greater the elasticity of demand for the good, the larger is the elasticity of demand for the labor used to produce it. An increase in the wage rate increases the marginal cost of producing the good and decreases the supply of it. The decrease in the supply of the good increases the price of the good and decreases the quantity demanded of the good and the quantities of the factors of production used to produce it. The greater the elasticity of demand for the good, the larger is the decrease in the quantity demanded of the good and so the larger is the decrease in the quantities of the factors of production used to produce it.

Substitutability of Capital for Labor The more easily capital can be used instead of labor in production, the more elastic is the long-run demand for labor. For example, it is easy to use robots rather than assembly-line workers in car factories and grape-picking machines rather than labor in vineyards. So the demand for these types of labor is elastic. At the other extreme, it is difficult (though possible) to substitute computers for newspaper reporters, bank loan officers, and teachers. So the demand for these types of labor is inelastic.

Let's now turn from the demand side of the labor market to the supply side and examine the decisions that people make about how to allocate time between working and other activities.

The Supply of Labor

People can allocate their time to two broad activities: labor supply and leisure. (Leisure is a catch-all term. It includes all activities other than supplying labor.) For most people, leisure is more enjoyable than supplying labor. We'll look at the labor supply decision of Jill, who is like most people. She enjoys her leisure time, and she would be pleased if she didn't have to spend her weekends working a supermarket checkout line.

But Jill has chosen to work weekends. The reason is that she is offered a wage rate that exceeds her *reservation wage*. Jill's reservation wage is the lowest wage at which she is willing to supply labor. If the wage rate exceeds her reservation wage, she supplies some labor. But how much labor does she supply? The quantity of labor that Jill supplies depends on the wage rate.

Substitution Effect Other things remaining the same, the higher the wage rate Jill is offered, at least over a range, the greater is the quantity of labor that she supplies. The reason is that Jill's wage rate is her *opportunity cost of leisure.* If she quits work an hour early to catch a movie, the cost of that extra hour of leisure is the wage rate that Jill forgoes. The higher the wage rate, the less willing Jill is to forgo the income and take the extra leisure time. This tendency for a higher wage rate to induce Jill to work longer hours is a *substitution effect.*

But there is also an *income effect* that works in the opposite direction to the substitution effect.

Income Effect The higher Jill's wage rate, the higher is her income. A higher income, other things remaining the same, induces Jill to increase her demand for most goods. Leisure is one of those goods. Because an increase in income creates an increase in the demand for leisure, it also creates a decrease in the quantity of labor supplied.

Backward-Bending Supply of Labor Curve As the wage rate rises, the substitution effect brings an increase in the quantity of labor supplied while the income effect brings a decrease in the quantity of labor supplied. At low wage rates, the substitution effect is larger than the income effect, so as the wage rate rises, people supply more labor. But as the wage rate continues to rise, the income effect eventually becomes larger than the substitution effect and the quantity of labor supplied decreases. The labor supply curve is *backward bending.*

Figure 17.4(a) shows the labor supply curves for Jill, Jack, and Kelly. Each labor supply curve is backward bending, but the three people have different reservation wage rates.

Market Supply The market supply of labor curve is the sum of the individual supply curves. Figure 17.4(b) shows the market supply curve, S_M, derived from the supply curves of Jill, Jack, and Kelly (S_A, S_B, and S_C, respectively) in Fig. 17.4(a). At a wage rate of less than \$1 an hour, no one supplies labor. At a wage rate of \$1 an hour, Jill works but Jack and Kelly don't. As the wage rate increases and reaches \$7 an hour, all three of them are working. The market supply curve S_M eventually bends backward, but it has a long upward-sloping section.

Changes in the Supply of Labor The supply of labor changes when influences other than the wage rate

FIGURE 17.4 The Supply of Labor

myeconlab

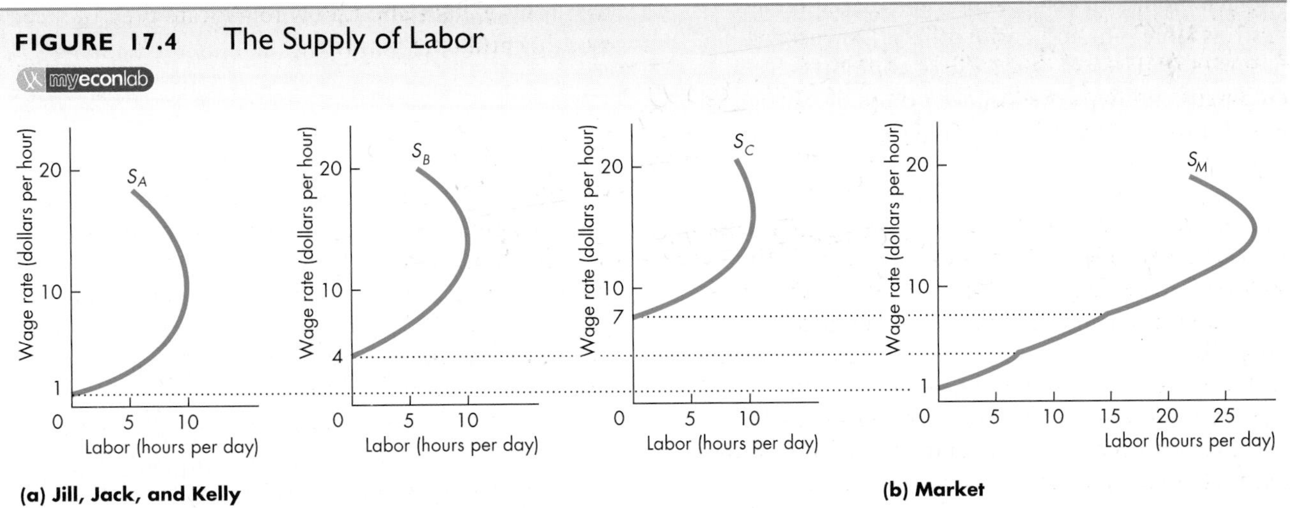

Part (a) shows the labor supply curves of Jill, Jack, and Kelly (S_A, S_B, and S_C, respectively). Each person has a reservation wage below which she or he will supply no labor. As the wage rate rises, the quantity of labor supplied increases to a maximum and then begins to decrease as the wage rate rises further. Each person's supply curve eventually bends backward. Part (b) shows how, by adding the quantities of labor supplied by each person at each wage rate, we derive the market supply curve of labor, S_M. The market supply curve has a long upward-sloping section before it bends backward.

change. The key factors that change the supply of labor and that over the years have increased it are

1. Increases in adult population
2. Technological change and capital accumulation in home production

As the adult population has increased and as technological change and capital accumulation in the home have decreased the time needed to produce meals, laundry services, and cleaning services, the supply of labor has increased.

Let's now build on what we've learned about the demand for labor and the supply of labor and study labor market equilibrium and the trends in wage rates and employment.

Labor Market Equilibrium

Wages and employment are determined by equilibrium in the labor market as you saw in Fig. 17.1. Over the years, the equilibrium wage rate and employment level have both increased. You can now explain why.

Trends in the Demand for Labor The demand for labor has *increased* because of technological change and capital accumulation, and the demand for labor curve has shifted steadily rightward.

Technological change and capital accumulation destroy some jobs and create others. Downsizing has become a catchword as the use of computers has eliminated millions of jobs, even those of managers.

But technological change and capital accumulation create more jobs than they destroy and *on the average*, the new jobs pay more than the old ones did. But to benefit from the advances in technology, people must acquire new skills and change their jobs. For example, during the past 20 years, the demand for typists has fallen almost to zero. But the demand for people who can type (on a computer rather than a typewriter) and do other tasks as well has increased. And the output of these people is worth more than that of a typist. So the demand for people with typing (and other) skills has increased.

Trends in the Supply of Labor The supply of labor has increased because of population growth and technological change as well as capital accumulation in the home. The mechanization of home production of fast-food preparation services (the freezer and the microwave oven) and laundry services (the automatic washer and dryer and wrinkle-free fabrics) has decreased the time spent on activities that once were full-time jobs and have led to a large increase in the supply of labor. As a result, the supply of labor curve has shifted steadily rightward, but at a slower pace than the shift in the demand curve.

Trends in Equilibrium Because technological advances and capital accumulation have increased demand by more than population growth and technological change in home production have increased supply, both wage rates and employment have increased. But not everyone has shared in the increased prosperity that comes from higher wage rates. Some groups have been left behind, and some have even seen their wage rates fall. Why?

Two key reasons can be identified. First, technological change affects the marginal product of different groups in different ways. High-skilled computer-literate workers have benefited from the information revolution while low-skilled workers have suffered. The demand for the services of the first group has increased, and the demand for the services of the second group has decreased. (Draw a supply and demand figure, and you will see that these changes widen the wage difference between the two groups.) Second, international competition has lowered the marginal revenue product of low-skilled workers and so has decreased the demand for their labor. We look further at skill differences and at trends in the distribution of income in Chapter 18.

REVIEW QUIZ

1. What links the quantity that a firm produces and the quantity of labor it employs?
2. What is the distinction between marginal revenue product and marginal revenue? Provide an example that illustrates the distinction.
3. When a firm's marginal revenue product equals the wage rate, marginal revenue also equals marginal cost. Why? Provide a numerical example different from that in the text.
4. What determines the amount of labor that households plan to supply?
5. Describe and explain the trends in wage rates and employment.

myeconlab Study Plan 17.2

Labor Market Power

In some labor markets, workers organized by labor unions possess market power and are able to raise the wage rate above the competitive level. In some other labor markets, a large employer dominates the demand side of the market and can exert market power that lowers the wage rate below its competitive level. But an employer might also decide to pay more than the competitive wage rate to attract the best workers. Let's look at these cases.

Labor Unions

A **labor union** is an organized group of workers that aims to increase wages and influence other job conditions. The two types of unions are craft unions and industrial unions. A *craft union* is a group of workers who have a similar range of skills but work in many different industries. Examples are the carpenters' union (UBC) and the electrical workers union (IBEW). An *industrial union* is a group of workers who have a variety of skills and job types but work in the same industry. The United Auto Workers (UAW) and the Steelworkers Union (USWA) are examples of industrial unions.

Most unions are members of the AFL-CIO, which was created in 1955 when the American Federation of Labor (AFL) and the Congress of Industrial Organizations (CIO) combined.

Unions vary enormously in size. Craft unions are the smallest, and industrial unions are the biggest. Union strength peaked in the 1950s, when 35 percent of the labor force belonged to unions. That percentage has declined steadily and is now 12 percent.

Unions negotiate with employers in a process called *collective bargaining*. A *strike*, a group decision to refuse to work under prevailing conditions, is the main weapon available to the union. A *lockout*, a firm's refusal to operate its plant and employ its workers, is the main weapon available to the employer. Each party uses the threat of a strike or a lockout to try to get an agreement in its own favor. Sometimes, when the two parties in the collective bargaining process cannot agree on the wage rate or other conditions of employment, they agree to submit their disagreement to binding arbitration. *Binding arbitration* is a process in which a third party—an arbitrator—determines wages and other employment conditions on behalf of the negotiating parties.

Unions' Objectives and Constraints A union has three broad objectives: It seeks to

1. Increase compensation
2. Improve working conditions
3. Expand job opportunities

A union's ability to pursue its objectives is restricted by two sets of constraints—one on the supply side of the labor market and the other on the demand side. On the supply side, the union's activities are limited by how well it can restrict nonunion workers from offering their labor in the same market as union labor. The larger the fraction of the work force controlled by the union, the more effective the union can be in this regard. It is difficult for unions to operate in markets where there is an abundant supply of willing nonunion labor. For example, the market for farm labor in southern California is very tough for a union to organize because of the ready flow of nonunion, often illegal, labor from Mexico. At the other extreme, unions in the construction industry can better pursue their goals because they can influence the number of people who can obtain skills as electricians, plasterers, and carpenters. The professional associations of dentists and physicians are best able to restrict the supply of dentists and physicians. These groups control the number of qualified workers by controlling either the examinations that new entrants must pass or entrance into professional degree programs.

On the demand side of the labor market, the union faces a tradeoff that arises from firms' profit-maximizing decisions. Because labor demand curves slope downward, anything a union does that increases the wage rate or other employment costs decreases the quantity of labor demanded.

Let's see how unions operate in an otherwise competitive labor market.

A Union Enters a Competitive Labor Market When a union enters a competitive labor market, it seeks to increase the wage rate and to increase the demand for the labor of its members. That is, the union tries to take actions that shift the demand curve for its members' labor rightward.

Figure 17.5 illustrates a labor market. The demand curve is D_C, and the supply curve is S_C. Before the union enters the market, the wage rate is \$7 an hour and 100 hours of labor are employed.

Now suppose that a union is formed to organize

the workers in this market. The union can attempt to increase the wage rate in this market in two ways. It can try to restrict the supply of labor, or it can try to stimulate the demand for labor. First, look at what happens if the union has sufficient control over the supply of labor to be able to artificially restrict that supply below its competitive level—to S_U. If that is all the union is able to do, employment falls to 85 hours of labor and the wage rate rises to $8 an hour. The union simply picks its preferred position along the demand curve that defines the tradeoff it faces between employment and the wage rate.

You can see that if the union can only restrict the supply of labor, it raises the wage rate but decreases the number of jobs available. Because of this outcome, unions try to increase the demand for labor and shift the demand curve rightward. Let's see what they might do to achieve this outcome.

FIGURE 17.5 A Union Enters a Competitive Labor Market

myeconlab

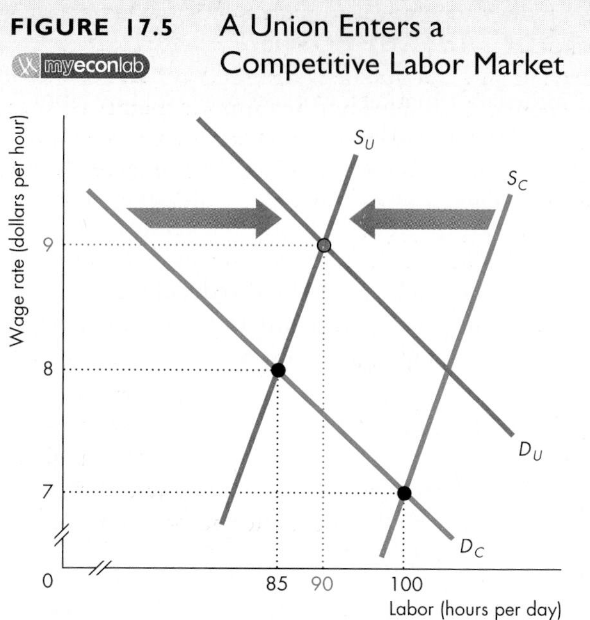

In a competitive labor market, the demand curve is D_C and the supply curve is S_C. Competitive equilibrium occurs at a wage rate of $7 an hour with 100 hours a day employed. By restricting employment below the competitive level, the union shifts the supply of labor to S_U. If the union can do no more than that, the wage rate will increase to $8 an hour but employment will fall to 85 hours a day. If the union can increase the demand for labor (by increasing the demand for the good produced by union members or by raising the price of substitute labor) and shift the demand curve to D_U, then it can increase the wage rate still higher, to $9 an hour, and achieve employment of 90 hours a day.

How Unions Try to Change the Demand for Labor

The union tries to change the demand for labor in two ways. First, it tries to make the demand for union labor less elastic. Second, it tries to increase the demand for union labor. Making the demand for labor less elastic does not eliminate the tradeoff between employment and the wage rate. But it does make the tradeoff less unfavorable. If a union can make the demand for labor less elastic, it can increase the wage rate at a lower cost in terms of lost employment opportunities. But if the union can increase the demand for labor, it might even be able to increase both the wage rate and the employment opportunities of its members. Some of the methods used by the unions to change the demand for the labor of its members are to

- Increase the marginal product of union members
- Encourage import restrictions
- Support minimum wage laws
- Support immigration restrictions
- Increase demand for the good produced

Unions try to increase the marginal product of their members, which in turn increases the demand for their labor, by organizing and sponsoring training schemes, by encouraging apprenticeship and other on-the-job training activities, and by professional certification.

Unions lobby to restrict imports and encourage people to buy goods made by unionized workers in the United States.

Unions support minimum wage laws to increase the cost of employing low-skilled labor. An increase in the wage rate of low-skilled labor leads to a decrease in the quantity demanded of low-skilled labor and to an increase in demand for high-skilled union labor, a substitute for low-skilled labor.

Restrictive immigration laws decrease the supply of foreign workers. As a result, the demand for union labor in the United States increases.

Because the demand for labor is a derived demand, an increase in the demand for the good produced by union labor increases the demand for union labor. The garment workers' union urging us to buy union-made clothes and the UAW asking us to buy only American cars made by union workers are examples of attempts by unions to increase the demand for union labor.

Figure 17.5 illustrates the effects of an increase in the demand for the labor of a union's members. If the union can also take steps that increase the demand for labor to D_U, it can achieve an even bigger increase in the wage rate with a smaller fall in employment. By maintaining the restricted labor supply at S_U, the union increases the wage rate to $9 an hour and achieves an employment level of 90 hours a day.

Because a union restricts the supply of labor in the market in which it operates, the union's actions increase the supply of labor in nonunion markets. Workers who can't get union jobs must look elsewhere for work. This increase in the supply of labor in nonunion markets lowers the wage rate in those markets and further widens the gap between union and nonunion wages.

The Scale of Union-Nonunion Wage Gap How much of a difference to wage rates do unions make? To answer this question, we must look at the wages of unionized and nonunionized workers who do similar work. The evidence suggests that after allowing for skill differences, the union-nonunion wage gap lies between 10 percent and 25 percent. For example, unionized airline pilots earn about 25 percent more than nonunion pilots with the same level of skill.

Let's now look at a labor market in which the employer possesses market power.

Monopsony in the Labor Market

A market in which there is a single buyer is called **monopsony**. In a monopsony labor market, there is one employer and the wage rate is the lowest at which the firm can attract the labor it plans to hire.

With the growth of large-scale production over the last century, large manufacturing plants such as coal mines, steel and textile mills, and car manufacturers became the major employer in some regions, and in some places a single firm employed almost all the labor. Today, in some parts of the country, managed health care organizations are the major employer of health care professionals. In some communities, Wal-Mart is the main employer of sales clerks. These firms have market power.

Let's see how a monopsony uses its power to lower the wage rate below the level paid by firms that must compete for their labor.

Like all firms, a monopsony has a downward-sloping marginal revenue product curve, which is *MRP* in Fig. 17.6. This curve tells us the extra revenue the monopsony receives by selling the output produced by an extra hour of labor. The supply of labor curve is *S*. This curve tells us how many hours are supplied at each wage rate. It also tells us the minimum wage for which a given quantity of labor is willing to work.

A monopsony recognizes that to hire more labor, it must pay a higher wage; equivalently, by hiring less labor, it can pay a lower wage. Because a monopsony controls the wage rate, the marginal cost of labor exceeds the wage rate. The marginal cost of labor is shown by the curve *MCL*. The relationship between the marginal cost of labor curve and the supply curve is similar to the relationship between the marginal cost and average cost curves that you studied in Chapter 10. The supply curve is like the average cost of labor curve. In Fig. 17.6, the firm can hire 49

FIGURE 17.6 A Monopsony Labor Market

myeconlab

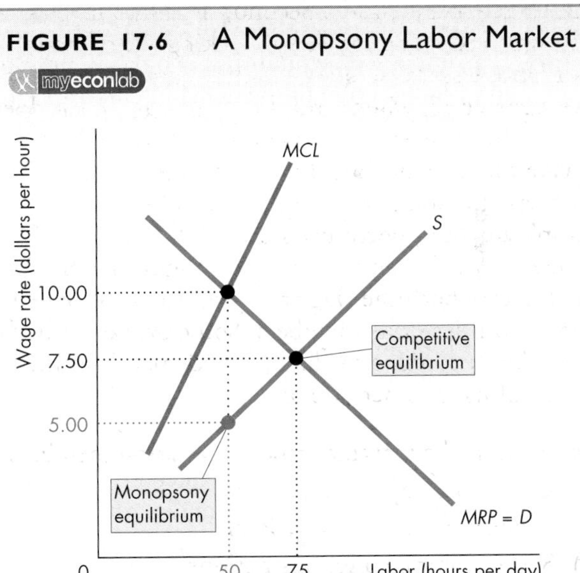

A monopsony is a market structure in which there is a single buyer. A monopsony in the labor market has a marginal revenue product curve *MRP* and faces a labor supply curve *S*. The marginal cost of labor curve is *MCL*. Making the marginal cost of labor equal to marginal revenue product maximizes profit. The monopsony hires 50 hours of labor a day and pays the lowest wage rate for which that quantity of labor will work, which is $5 an hour.

hours of labor for a wage rate of just below $4.90 an hour. The firm's total labor cost is $240. But suppose that the firm hires 50 hours of labor. It can hire the 50th hour of labor for $5 an hour. The total cost of labor is now $250 an hour. So hiring the 50th hour of labor increases the cost of labor from $240 to $250, which is a $10 increase. The marginal cost of labor is $10 an hour. The curve *MCL* shows the $10 marginal cost of hiring the 50th hour of labor.

To calculate the profit-maximizing quantity of labor to hire, the firm sets the marginal cost of labor equal to the marginal revenue product of labor. That is, the firm wants the cost of the last worker hired to equal the extra total revenue brought in. In Fig. 17.6, this outcome occurs when the monopsony employs 50 hours of labor. What is the wage rate that the monopsony pays? To hire 50 hours of labor, the firm must pay $5 an hour, as shown by the supply of labor curve. So each worker is paid $5 an hour. But the marginal revenue product of labor is $10 an hour, which means that the firm makes an economic profit of $5 on the last hour of labor that it hires.

Compare this outcome with that in a competitive labor market. If the labor market shown in Fig. 17.6 were competitive, equilibrium would occur at the point of intersection of the demand curve and the supply curve. The wage rate would be $7.50 an hour, and 75 hours of labor a day would be employed. So compared with a competitive labor market, a monopsony decreases both the wage rate and employment.

The ability of a monopsony to cut the wage rate and employment and make an economic profit depends on the elasticity of labor supply. If the supply of labor is highly elastic, a monopsony has little power to cut the wage rate and employment to boost its profit.

A Union and a Monopsony In Chapter 12, we discovered that in monopoly, the seller determines the market price. We've now seen that in monopsony—a market with a single buyer—the buyer determines the price. Suppose that a union operates in a monopsony labor market. A union is like a monopoly. If the union (monopoly seller) faces a monopsony buyer, the situation is called **bilateral monopoly**. In bilateral monopoly, the wage rate is determined by bargaining.

In Fig. 17.6, if the monopsony is free to determine the wage rate and the level of employment, it hires 50 hours of labor for a wage rate of $5 an hour. But suppose that a union represents the workers. The union agrees to maintain employment at 50 hours but seeks the highest wage rate the employer can be forced to pay. That wage rate is $10 an hour—the wage rate that equals the marginal revenue product of labor. The union might not be able to get the wage rate up to $10 an hour, but it won't accept $5 an hour. The monopsony firm and the union bargain over the wage rate, and the result is an outcome between $10 an hour and $5 an hour.

The outcome of the bargaining depends on the costs that each party can inflict on the other as a result of a failure to agree on the wage rate. The firm can shut down the plant and lock out its workers, and the workers can shut down the plant by striking. Each party knows the other's strength and knows what it will lose if it does not agree to the other's demands.

If the two parties are equally strong and they realize it, they will split the gap between $5 and $10 and agree to a wage rate of $7.50 an hour. If one party is stronger than the other—and both parties know that—the agreed wage will favor the stronger party. Usually, an agreement is reached without a strike or a lockout. The threat is usually enough to bring the bargaining parties to an agreement. When a strike or lockout does occur, it is usually because one party has misjudged the costs each party can inflict on the other.

Minimum wage laws have interesting effects in monopsony labor markets. Let's study these effects.

Monopsony and the Minimum Wage In a competitive labor market, a minimum wage that exceeds the equilibrium wage decreases employment (see Chapter 6, p. 130). In a monopsony labor market, a minimum wage can increase both the wage rate and employment. Let's see how.

Figure 17.7 shows a monopsony labor market in which the wage rate is $5 an hour and 50 hours of labor are employed. A minimum wage law is passed that requires employers to pay at least $7.50 an hour. The monopsony now faces a perfectly elastic supply of labor at $7.50 an hour up to 75 hours. Above 75 hours, a wage above $7.50 an hour must be paid to hire additional hours of labor. Because the wage rate is a fixed $7.50 an hour up to 75 hours, the marginal cost of labor is also constant at $7.50 up to 75 hours. Beyond 75 hours, the marginal cost of labor rises above $7.50 an hour. To maximize profit, the monopsony sets the marginal cost of labor equal to the marginal revenue product of labor. That is, the monopsony hires 75 hours of labor at $7.50 an hour.

FIGURE 17.7 Minimum Wage Law in Monopsony

myeconlab

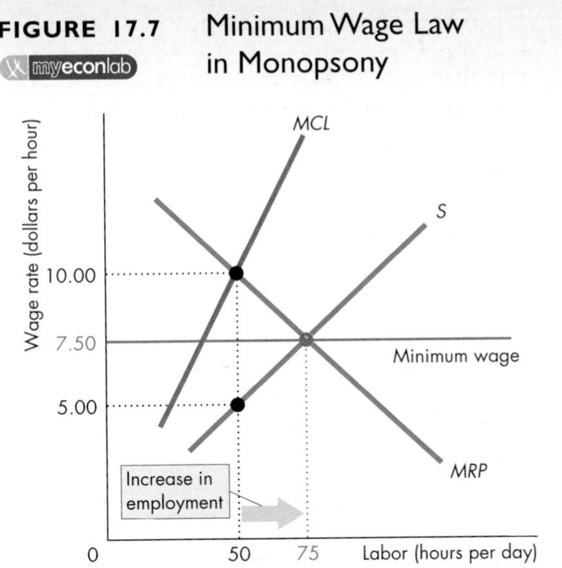

In a monopsony labor market, the wage rate is $5 an hour and 50 hours a day are hired. If a minimum wage law increases the wage rate to $7.50 an hour, employment increases to 75 hours a day.

The minimum wage law has made the supply of labor perfectly elastic and made the marginal cost of labor the same as the wage rate up to 75 hours. The law has not affected the supply of labor or the marginal cost of labor at employment levels above 75 hours. The minimum wage law has succeeded in raising the wage rate by $2.50 an hour and increasing the amount of labor employed by 25 hours.

Efficiency Wages

An **efficiency wage** is a wage rate that a firm pays above the competitive equilibrium wage rate with the aim of attracting the most productive workers.

In a perfectly competitive labor market, firms and workers are well informed. Workers know exactly what they are being hired to do and firms can observe the marginal product of each worker. In this state of complete knowledge of all the relevant factors, a firm would never pay more than the going competitive market wage rate.

In some labor markets, the employer is not able to observe a worker's marginal product. It is costly to monitor all the actions of every worker. For example, if McDonald's employed enough managers to keep a close watch on the activities of all the servers, its costs would be very high. And who would monitor all those managers? Because it is costly to monitor everything that a worker does, workers have some power. They might work hard or shirk.

If every firm pays its workers the going competitive wage rate, some workers will choose to work hard and some will choose to shirk. And threatening to fire a shirker won't help much because the shirker knows another job can be found at the going wage and the firm doesn't know if it will replace one shirker with a hard worker or another shirker.

If a firm pays a wage rate above the competitive level—an efficiency wage—the threat of being fired for shirking has some force. A fired worker can expect to find another job but only at the lower market equilibrium wage rate. So the worker now has an incentive not to shirk. Also, hard workers will be more likely to want to work for the firm, so if a shirking worker is fired, most likely the firm will attract a hard worker as the replacement.

So a firm that pays an efficiency wage attracts more productive workers but at the cost of a higher wage bill. So the firm must decide just how much more than the competitive wage to pay. The firm makes this decision by making the marginal improvement in productivity equal the marginal cost of the higher wage rate. If most firms pay an efficiency wage, the quantity of labor supplied will exceed the quantity demanded and unemployment will arise that strengthens the incentive that workers face and further discourages shirking.

REVIEW QUIZ

1. What are the methods that labor unions use to increase the wage rates of their members above the levels of nonunion wage rates?
2. What is a monopsony and why is a monopsony able to pay a lower wage rate than a firm in a competitive labor market?
3. How is the wage rate determined when a union faces a monopsony?
4. What is the effect of a minimum wage law on the level of employment in a monopsony labor market?
5. What is an efficiency wage and how does it work?

myeconlab **Study Plan 17.3**

Capital Markets

Capital markets are the channels through which firms obtain *financial* resources to buy *physical* capital resources. *Physical capital* is the *stock* of tools, instruments, machines, buildings, and other constructions that firms use to produce goods and services. Physical capital also includes the inventories of raw material and semi-finished and finished goods that firms hold. These capital resources are called *physical capital* to emphasize that they are real physical objects. They are goods that have been produced by some firms and bought by other firms. Physical capital is a *stock*—a quantity of objects that exists at a given time. But each year, that stock changes. It is depleted as old capital wears out and it is replenished and added to as firms buy new items of capital.

The markets in which each item of physical capital is traded are not the capital markets. They are goods markets just like the ones that you've studied in Chapters 11, 12, and 13. For example, the prices and quantities of tower cranes and earth movers are determined in the markets for those items.

A firm buys many different items of capital during a given time period. The dollar value of those capital goods is called the firm's *investment*. But it is the objects themselves that are the capital, not the dollars of value that they represent.

The financial resources used to buy physical capital are called *financial capital*. These resources come from saving. The interest rate is the "price of capital," which adjusts to make the quantity of financial capital supplied equal to the quantity demanded.

For most of us, capital markets are where we make our biggest-ticket transactions. We borrow in a capital market to buy a home. And we lend in capital markets to build up a fund on which to live when we retire.

Do the rates of return in capital markets increase over time as wage rates do? Figure 17.8 answers this question by showing the record from 1960 to 2005. Measuring the interest rate as a *real* interest rate, which means that we subtract the loss in the value of money from inflation, the rate of return to capital has fluctuated. It averaged 2.8 percent a year during the 1960s, became negative during the 1970s, climbed to 9 percent a year during the 1980s, steadied to average 4.6 percent a year during the 1990s and early 2000s, and then fell to 2 percent in 2005.

FIGURE 17.8 The Rate of Return to Capital: 1960–2005

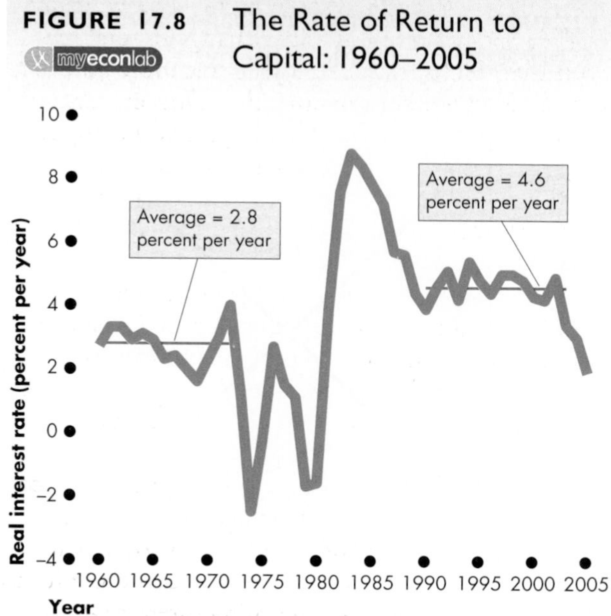

The real interest rate (the interest rate adjusted for inflation) fluctuated between a negative return in 1974 and 1975 and a high of 9 percent in 1984. It was steady at 2.8 percent during the 1960s and at 4.6 percent during the 1990s and early 2000s. It fell to 2 percent in 2005.

Sources of data: Economic Report of the President, 2006.

The ideas you've already met in your study of demand and supply in the labor market apply to the capital market as well. But there is a special feature of capital: People must compare the *present* expenditure on capital with the *future* income it will earn.

Let's look at the demand for capital.

The Demand for Capital

A firm's demand for *financial* capital stems from its demand for *physical* capital, and the amount that a firm plans to borrow in a given time period is determined by its *planned investment*—its planned purchases of new capital. This decision is driven by the firm's attempt to maximize profit.The factors that determine investment and borrowing plans are the

- Marginal revenue product of capital
- Interest rate

Let's see how these factors influence Tina's investment and borrowing decisions.

Marginal Revenue Product of Capital The *marginal revenue product of capital* is the change in total revenue that results from employing one more unit of capital. Suppose, for example, that Tina, an accountant who operates Taxfile, Inc., buys a new computer and software, which increases Taxfile's revenue by $1,150 a year for the next two years. Then the marginal revenue product of this computer is $1,150 a year.

The marginal revenue product of capital diminishes as the quantity of capital increases. Capital is just like labor in this respect. If Tina buys a second computer, Taxfile's total revenue will increase by less than the $1,150 generated by the first computer.

Interest Rate The interest rate is the opportunity cost of the funds borrowed to finance investment. The interest rate is also the opportunity cost of a firm using its own funds because it could lend those funds to another firm and earn the going interest rate on the loan. The higher the interest rate, the smaller is the quantity of planned investment and borrowing in the capital market.

Firms demand the quantity of capital that makes the marginal revenue product of capital equal to the expenditure on capital. But the expenditure on capital is a *present* outlay and the marginal revenue product is a *future* return. The higher the interest rate, the smaller is the *present value* of future returns, and so the smaller is the quantity of planned investment. (The Appendix on pp. 413–416 provides the technical details on comparing present and future values.)

Demand Curve for Capital

A firm's demand curve for capital shows the relationship between the quantity of financial capital demanded by the firm and the interest rate, other things remaining the same. Figure 17.9(a) shows Tina's demand curve for capital. Tina demands no capital at an interest rate of 12 percent a year; but at an interest rate of 8 percent a year, she spends $2,000 on a new computer; and at an interest rate of 4 percent a year, she spends $4,000 on two new computers.

Figure 17.9(b) shows the market demand curve for capital, *KD*, which is the horizontal sum of the demand curves of all firms. In the figure, the quantity of capital demanded in the entire capital market is $1,500 billion when the interest rate is 6 percent a year.

FIGURE 17.9 A Firm's Demand and the Market Demand for Capital

myeconlab

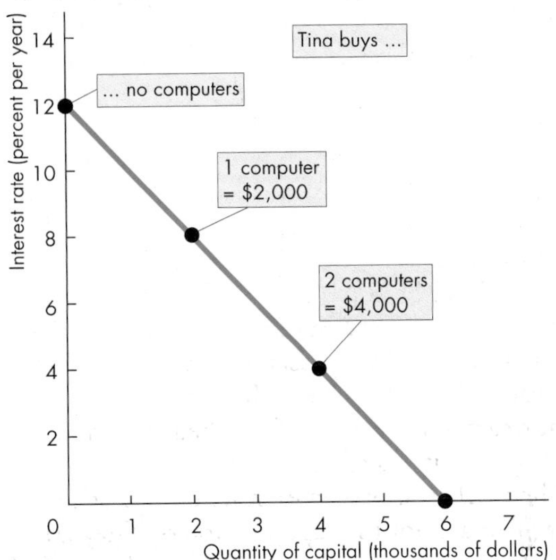

(a) Taxfile's demand curve for capital

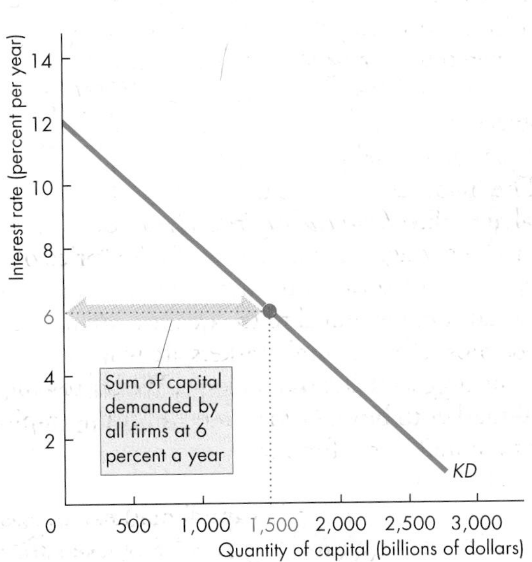

(b) Market demand curve for capital

For each firm, the lower the interest rate, the greater is the quantity of capital demanded. The market demand curve is the (horizontal) sum of the firms' demand curves.

You've seen how the demand for capital is determined. Let's now look at the supply side of the capital market.

The Supply of Capital

The quantity of capital supplied results from people's saving decisions. The main factors that determine saving are

- Income
- Expected future income
- Interest rate

Let's see how these factors influence Aaron's saving decisions.

Income Saving is the act of converting *current* income into *future* consumption. When Aaron's income increases, he plans to consume more both now and in the future. But to increase *future* consumption, Aaron must save today. So, other things remaining the same, the higher Aaron's income, the more he saves.

Expected Future Income If Aaron's current income is high and his expected future income is low, he will have a high level of saving. But if Aaron's current income is low and his expected future income is high, he will have a low (perhaps even negative) level of saving.

Students have low current incomes compared with expected future incomes so they tend to consume more than they earn. In middle age, most people are earning more than they expect to earn when they retire. So they save for their retirement years.

Interest Rate A dollar saved today grows into a dollar plus interest tomorrow. The higher the interest rate, the greater is the amount that a dollar saved today becomes in the future. So the higher the interest rate, the greater is the opportunity cost of current consumption. With a higher opportunity cost of current consumption, Aaron cuts his current consumption and increases his saving.

Supply Curve of Capital

The supply curve of capital shows the relationship between the quantity of capital supplied and the interest rate, other things remaining the same. The curve KS_0 in Fig. 17.10 is a supply curve of capital. An increase in the interest rate brings an increase in the quantity of capital supplied and a movement along the supply curve.

Let's now use what we've learned about the demand for and supply of capital and see how the interest rate is determined.

Capital Market Equilibrium

Saving plans and investment plans are coordinated through capital markets, and the interest rate adjusts to make these plans compatible.

Figure 17.10 shows the capital market. The demand for capital is KD_0, and the supply of capital is KS_0. The equilibrium interest rate is 6 percent a year, and the quantity of capital—the amount of investment by firms and saving by households—is $1,500 billion.

If the interest rate exceeded 6 percent a year, the quantity of capital supplied would exceed the quantity of capital demanded and the interest rate would fall. The interest rate would keep falling until the surplus of capital was eliminated.

If the interest rate were less than 6 percent a year, the quantity of capital demanded would exceed the quantity of capital supplied and the interest rate would rise. The interest rate would keep rising until the shortage of capital was eliminated.

FIGURE 17.10 Capital Market Equilibrium

myeconlab

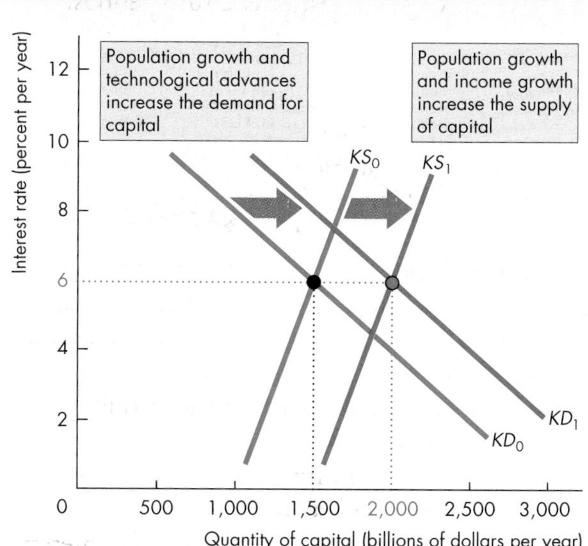

Initially, the demand for capital is KD_0 and the supply of capital is KS_0. The equilibrium interest rate is 6 percent a year, and the quantity of capital is $1,500 billion. Over time, both the demand and supply of capital increase to KD_1 and KS_1. The quantity of capital increases, but the interest rate is constant. The demand and supply of capital are influenced by common and related factors.

Changes in Demand and Supply

Over time, both the demand for capital and the supply of capital increase. The demand curve shifts rightward to KD_1, and the supply curve shifts to KS_1. Both curves shift because the same or related forces influence them. Population growth increases both demand and supply. Technological advances increase demand and bring higher incomes, which in turn increase supply. Because both demand and supply increase over time, the quantity of capital increases but the interest rate remains constant.

In reality, the real interest rate fluctuates, as you can see in Fig. 17.8. The reason is that the demand for capital and the supply of capital do not change in lockstep. Sometimes rapid technological change brings an increase in the demand for capital *before* it brings the higher incomes that increase the supply of capital. When this sequence of events occurs, the real interest rate rises. The first half of the 1980s was such a time, as you can see in Fig. 17.8.

At other times, the demand for capital grows slowly or even decreases temporarily. In this situation, supply outgrows demand and the real interest rate falls. Figure 17.8 shows that the mid-1970s and the period from 1984 through 1991 were two such periods.

REVIEW QUIZ

1. What is the distinction between *physical* capital and *financial* capital and what is the capital market?
2. What is the marginal product of capital?
3. What is special about the comparison of the marginal product of capital and the expenditure on capital?
4. What are the main influences on a firm's demand for capital?
5. Why does the quantity of capital demanded depend on the interest rate?
6. How can we explain the changes in the interest rate in the United States?

myeconlab **Study Plan 17.4**

The lessons that we've just learned about capital markets can be used to understand the prices of nonrenewable natural resources. Let's see how.

Natural Resource Markets

Natural resources, or what economists call *land*, fall into two categories:

- Renewable
- Nonrenewable

Renewable natural resources are resources that are repeatedly replenished by nature. Examples are land (in its everyday sense), rivers, lakes, rain, wind, and sunshine.

Nonrenewable natural resources are resources that nature does not replenish. Once used, they are no longer available. Examples are coal, natural gas, and oil—the so-called hydrocarbon fuels.

The demand for natural resources as inputs into production is based on the same principle of marginal revenue product as the demand for labor (and the demand for capital). But the supply of a natural resource is special. Let's look first at the supply of a renewable natural resource.

The Supply of a Renewable Natural Resource

The quantity of land and other renewable natural resources is fixed. The quantity supplied cannot be changed by individual decisions. People can vary the amount of land they own. But when one person buys some land, another person sells it. The aggregate quantity of land supplied of any particular type and in any particular location is fixed, regardless of the decisions of any individual. This fact means that the supply of each particular piece of land is perfectly inelastic. Figure 17.11 illustrates such a supply. Regardless of the rent, the quantity of land supplied on Chicago's "Magnificent Mile" is a fixed number of square feet.

Because the supply of land is fixed regardless of its rent, rent is determined by demand. The greater the demand for a specific piece of land, the higher is its rent.

Expensive land can be, and is, used more intensively than inexpensive land. For example, high-rise buildings enable land to be used more intensively. However, to use land more intensively, it has to be combined with another factor of production: capital. An increase in the amount of capital per block of land does not change the supply of land itself.

FIGURE 17.11 The Supply of Land

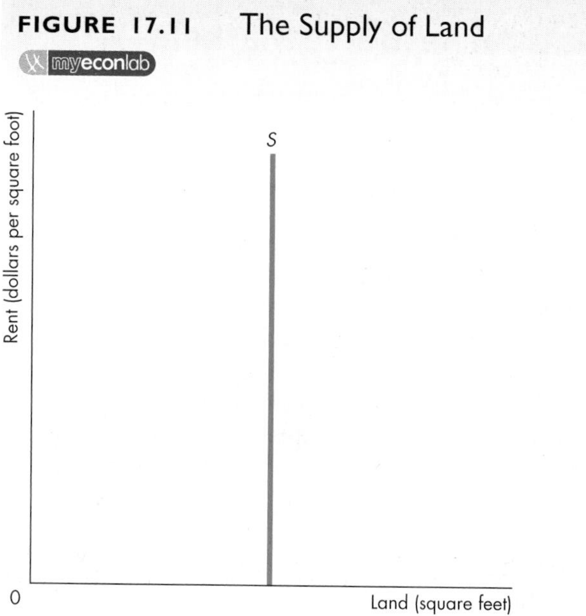

The supply of a given piece of land is perfectly inelastic. No matter what the rent, no more land than the quantity that exists can be supplied.

Although the supply of each type of land is fixed and its supply is perfectly inelastic, each individual firm, operating in competitive land markets, faces an elastic supply of land. For example, Fifth Avenue in New York City has a fixed amount of land, but Doubleday, the bookstore, could rent some space from Saks, the department store. Each firm can rent the quantity of land that it demands at the going rent, as determined in the marketplace. So, provided that land markets are competitive, firms are price takers in these markets, just as they are in the markets for other productive resources.

The Supply of a Nonrenewable Natural Resource

The *stock* of a natural resource is the quantity in existence at a given time. This quantity is fixed and is independent of the price of the resource. The *known* stock of a natural resource is the quantity that has been discovered. This quantity increases over time because advances in technology enable ever less accessible sources to be discovered. Both of these *stock* concepts influence the price of a nonrenewable natural resource. But the influence is indirect. The direct influence on price is the rate at which the resource is supplied for use in production—called the *flow* supply.

The flow supply of a nonrenewable natural resource is *perfectly elastic* at a price that equals the present value of the expected price next period.

To see why, think about the economic choices of Saudi Arabia, a country that possesses a large inventory of oil. Saudi Arabia can sell an additional billion barrels of oil right now and use the income it receives to buy U.S. bonds. Or it can keep the billion barrels in the ground and sell them next year. If it sells the oil and buys bonds, it earns the interest rate on the bonds. If it keeps the oil and sells it next year, it earns the amount of the price increase or loses the amount of the price decrease between now and next year.

If Saudi Arabia expects the price of oil to rise next year by a percentage that *equals* the current interest rate, the price that it expects next year equals $(1 + r)$ multiplied by this year's price. For example, if this year's price is \$60 a barrel and the interest rate is 5 percent a year ($r = 0.5$), then next year's expected price is $1.05 \times \$60$, which equals \$63 a barrel.

With the price expected to rise to \$63 next year, Saudi Arabia is indifferent between selling now for \$60 and not selling now but waiting until next year and selling for \$63. Saudi Arabia expects to make the same return either way. So at \$60 a barrel, Saudi Arabia will sell whatever quantity is demanded.

But if Saudi Arabia expects the price to rise next year by a percentage that *exceeds* the current interest rate, then Saudi Arabia expects to make a bigger return by hanging on to the oil than by selling the oil and buying bonds. So it keeps the oil and sells none. And if Saudi Arabia expects the price to rise next year by a percentage that is *less than* the current interest rate, the bond gives a bigger return than the oil, so Saudi Arabia sells as much oil as it can this year.

The minimum price at which Saudi Arabia is willing to sell oil is the present value of the expected future price. At this price, it will sell as much oil as buyers demand. So its supply is perfectly elastic.

Price and the Hotelling Principle

Figure 17.12 shows the equilibrium in a nonrenewable natural resource market. Because flow supply is perfectly elastic at the present value of next period's expected price, the actual price of the natural resource equals the present value of next period's expected price. Also, because the current price equals the present value of the expected future price, the

FIGURE 17.12 A Nonrenewable Natural Resource Market

myeconlab

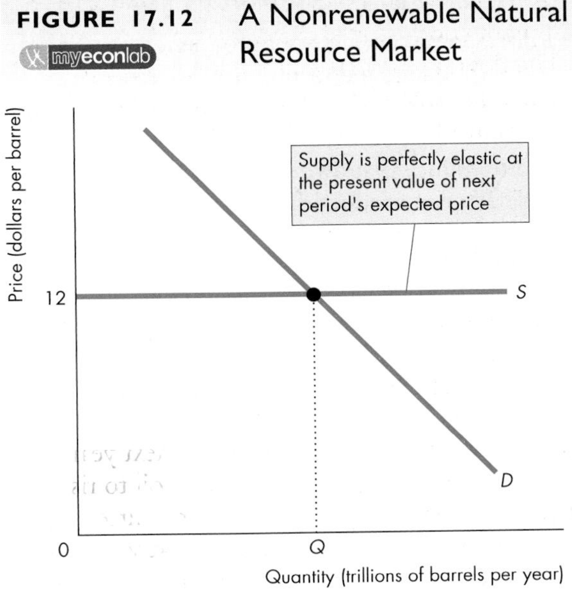

The flow supply of a nonrenewable natural resource is perfectly elastic at the *present value* of next period's expected price. The demand for a nonrenewable natural resource is determined by its marginal revenue product. The price is determined by supply and equals the *present value* of next period's expected price.

price of the resource is expected to rise at a rate equal to the interest rate.

The proposition that the price of a resource is expected to rise at a rate equal to the interest rate is called the *Hotelling Principle*. It was first realized by Harold Hotelling, a mathematician and economist at Columbia University. But as Fig. 17.13 shows, *actual* prices do not follow the path *predicted* by the Hotelling Principle. Why do the prices of nonrenewable natural resources sometimes fall rather than follow their expected path and increase over time?

The key reason is that the future is unpredictable. Expected technological change is reflected in the price of a natural resource. But a previously unexpected new technology that leads to the discovery or the more efficient use of a nonrenewable natural resource causes its price to fall. Over the years, as technology has advanced, we have become more efficient in our use of nonrenewable natural resources. And we haven't just become more efficient. We've become more efficient than we expected to.

FIGURE 17.13 Falling Resource Prices

myeconlab

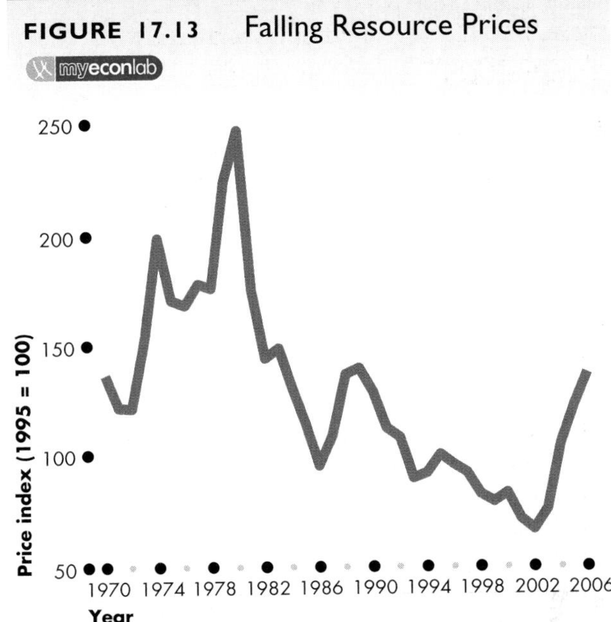

The prices of metals (here a price index that measures the average of the prices of aluminum, copper, iron ore, lead, manganese, nickel, silver, tin, and zinc) have tended to fall over time, not rise as predicted by the Hotelling Principle. The reason is that unanticipated advances in technology have decreased the cost of extracting resources and greatly increased the exploitable known reserves.

Source of data: International Financial Statistics (various issues), Washington, DC: International Monetary Fund.

REVIEW QUIZ

1. Why is the supply of a *renewable* natural resource such as land perfectly inelastic?
2. At what price is the flow supply of a nonrenewable natural resource perfectly elastic and why?
3. Why is the price of a nonrenewable natural resource expected to rise at a rate equal to the interest rate?
4. Why do the prices of nonrenewable resources not follow the path predicted by the Hotelling Principle?

myeconlab **Study Plan 17.5**

People supply factors of production to earn an income. But some people earn enormous incomes. Are such incomes necessary to induce people to work and supply other factors? Let's answer this question.

Economic Rent, Opportunity Cost, and Taxes

You've now seen how demand and supply in factor markets determine factor prices and quantities. And you've seen that the demand for a factor of production is determined by its marginal revenue product and the supply of a factor of production is determined by the resources available and by people's choices about their use.

People who supply a factor of production that has a large marginal revenue product or that has a small supply receive a high factor price. And the people who supply a factor of production that has a small marginal revenue product or that has a large supply receive a low factor price.

The elasticity of supply of a factor of production determines the extent to which its income represents the opportunity cost of using that factor. And this same elasticity determines how the burden of a tax in a factor market is shared between the supplier and the user of the factor. We're now going to explore these issues beginning with the distinction between economic rent and opportunity cost.

Economic Rent and Opportunity Cost

The total income of a factor of production is made up of its economic rent and its opportunity cost. **Economic rent** is the income received by the owner of a factor of production over and above the amount required to induce that owner to offer the factor for use. Any factor of production can receive an economic rent. The income required to induce the supply of a factor of production is the opportunity cost of using the factor—the value of the factor in its next best use.

Figure 17.14(a) illustrates the way in which a factor income has an economic rent and opportunity cost component. The figure shows the market for a factor of production. It could be *any* factor of production—labor, capital, or land—but we'll suppose that it is labor. The demand curve is *D*, and the supply curve is *S*. The wage rate is *W*, and the quantity employed is *C*. The income earned is the sum of the red and green areas. The red area below the supply curve measures opportunity cost, and the green area above the supply curve but below the factor price measures economic rent.

To see why the area below the supply curve measures opportunity cost, recall that a supply curve can be interpreted in two different ways. It shows the

FIGURE 17.14 Economic Rent and Opportunity Cost

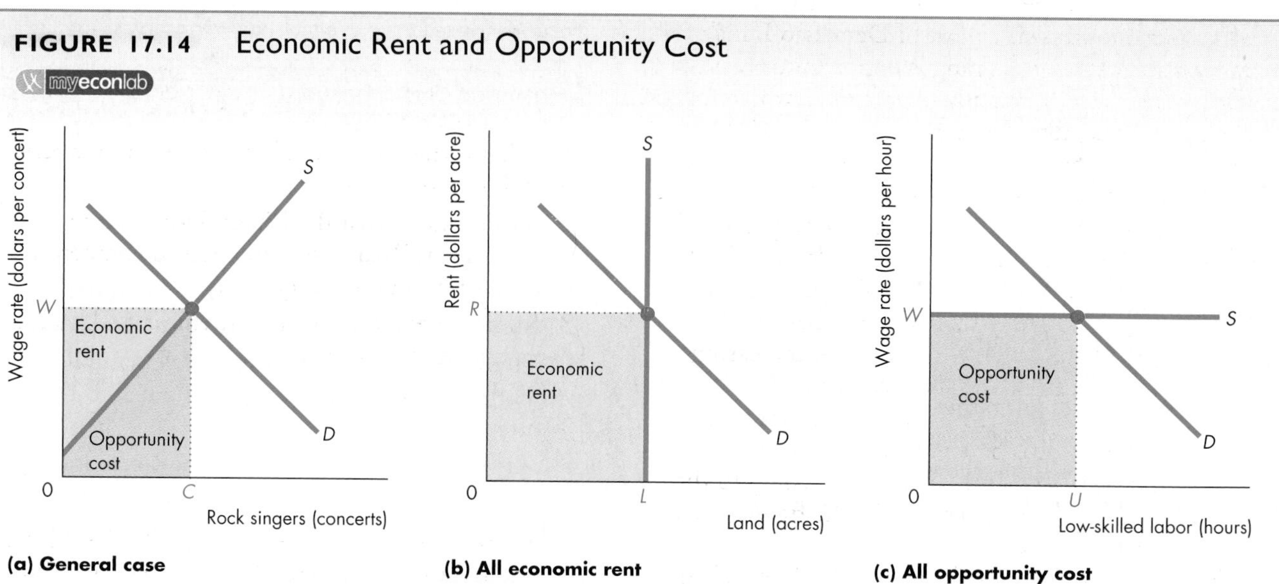

When the supply curve of a factor slopes upward—the general case—as in part (a), part of the factor income is economic rent (the green area) and part is opportunity cost (the red area). When the supply of a factor is perfectly inelastic (the supply curve is vertical), as in part (b), the entire factor income is economic rent. When the supply of the factor is perfectly elastic, as in part (c), the factor's entire income is opportunity cost.

quantity supplied at a given price, and it shows the minimum price at which a given quantity is willingly supplied. If suppliers receive only the minimum amount required to induce them to supply each unit of the factor, they will be paid a different price for each unit. The prices will trace the supply curve, and the income received will be entirely opportunity cost—the red area in Fig. 17.14(a).

The concept of economic rent is similar to that of producer surplus (see Chapter 5, p. 109). Economic rent is the price a person receives for the use of a factor minus the minimum price at which a given quantity of the factor is willingly supplied.

Economic rent is *not* the same thing as the "rent" that a farmer pays for the use of some land or the "rent" that you pay for your apartment. Everyday "rent" is a price paid for the services of land or a building. *Economic rent* is a component of the income received by any factor of production.

The portion of the factor income that consists of economic rent depends on the elasticity of the supply of the factor. When the supply of a factor is perfectly inelastic, its entire income is economic rent. Most of the income received by Garth Brooks and Pearl Jam is economic rent. Also, a large part of Katie Couric's income is economic rent. When the supply of a factor of production is perfectly elastic, none of its income is economic rent. Most of Demetrio Luna's income from window cleaning is opportunity cost. In general, when supply is neither perfectly elastic nor perfectly inelastic, like that illustrated in Fig. 17.14(a), some part of the factor income is economic rent and the other part is opportunity cost.

Figure 17.14(b) shows the market for a parcel of land in New York City. The quantity of land is fixed in size at L acres. Therefore the supply curve of the land is vertical—perfectly inelastic. No matter what the rent on the land is, there is no way of increasing the quantity that can be supplied. Suppose that the demand curve in Fig. 17.14(b) shows the marginal revenue product of this block of land. Then it commands a rent of R. The entire income accruing to the owner of the land is the green area in the figure. This income is *economic rent.*

Figure 17.14(c) shows the market for low-skilled labor in a poor country such as India or China. A large quantity of labor is available for work at the going wage rate (in this case, W). The supply of labor is perfectly elastic. The entire income earned by these workers is opportunity cost. They receive no economic rent.

Implications of Economic Rent for Taxes

The share of the burden of a tax and the inefficiency created by a tax depend on the elasticity of supply. If supply is perfectly inelastic, the burden of a tax is borne entirely by the supplier (see Chapter 6, p. 135). So if a tax is imposed on the income of a factor of production with a perfectly inelastic supply, the supplier bears the entire tax. Also, if supply is perfectly inelastic, the tax has no effect on the quantity supplied and no effect on efficiency. The only effect of the tax is to transfer buying power from the factor owner to the government.

But notice that the situation in which a tax has no effect on efficiency is when the entire factor income is economic rent. Taxing economic rent is efficient.

If the supply of a factor of production is not perfectly inelastic, a tax on that factor's income is borne at least partly by the buyer. Also, because the buyer faces a higher factor price, the quantity demanded decreases and an inefficiency arises.

But now notice that this situation in which a tax brings inefficiency is when some of the factor income is an opportunity cost. In the extreme case in which the buyer pays the entire tax, the entire factor income is opportunity cost and none is economic rent.

REVIEW QUIZ

1. What is the distinction between economic rent and opportunity cost?
2. Is the income that the Miami Heat pays to Shaquille O'Neal economic rent or compensation for his opportunity cost?
3. Is a tax on economic rent more efficient than a tax on opportunity cost?

myeconlab **Study Plan 17.6**

Reading Between the Lines on pp. 408–409 looks at the market for college football coaches and compares it with the market for professors.

The next chapter looks at how the market economy distributes income and explains the trends in the distribution of income. The chapter also looks at the efforts by governments to redistribute income and modify the market outcome.

READING BETWEEN THE LINES

Labor Markets in Action

http://www.nytimes.com

An Awkward Coexistence On Campus

November 9, 2005

It is worth a take-home exam to discover how the brains behind higher education have lost their minds in the pursuit of football superiority.

Were they hypnotized by the numbing metronome of hook 'em Horns hand signals or snake-charmed by the Super Bowl rings on the fingers of Charlie Weis? Were they paid off by boosters who buy their socks and yachts only in team colors or simply sucked into a devious three-legged race to be one of two teams in the B.C.S. title game?

All of the above has conspired to lead university caretakers into establishing the $3 million club for college coaches. After Notre Dame handed a 10-year extension to Weis last week reportedly worth $30 to $40 million, the N.C.A.A. reached a new level in fiscal lunacy.

Where is intelligent life on campus? At the University of Texas, there is a cosmic star, but he is not named Mack Brown. He is called Big Steve by Texas students and ponders the energy of empty space, but he doesn't dash through gaping holes opened by the offensive line.

Steven Weinberg is a Texas physics professor who grew up in the Bronx, taught at Harvard and won the Nobel Prize in 1979 before being wooed to Texas three years later in one of the university's most famous hires this side of Darrell Royal. . . .

Somehow, Mack Brown's $2.1 million salary still gets paid. As The Austin-American Statesman has reported, Weinberg is the university's highest-paid faculty member, at around $400,000 by most accounts. Upon his arrival, he was rumored to have had his salary contractually linked to that of the head football coach. If only, he says. . . .

Essence of the Story

- Charlie Weis, head football coach at the University of Notre Dame, has a 10-year contract that is reported to be worth between $30 to $40 million—more than $3 million a year.
- Steven Weinberg, a physics professor at the University of Texas who won the Nobel Prize in 1979, is reported to be the university's highest-paid faculty member, with a salary of about $400,000 a year.

Economic Analysis

- The market for college football coaches is competitive.
- The market for professors is also competitive.
- The demand for both coaches and professors is determined by the marginal revenue product of each group.
- The marginal revenue product of a coach depends on the coach's ability to win games and the additional revenue that the college or university can raise from its alumni and other contributors when its football team is successful.
- The marginal revenue product of a professor depends on the professor's ability to attract students and research funding.
- For any given quantity of coaches and professors, the marginal revenue product of a professor almost certainly exceeds that of a coach.
- But the equilibrium wage rate of a coach and that of a professor depend on the marginal revenue product of each group and on the supply of each.
- The supply of coaches is small and probably inelastic.
- The supply of professors is large and most likely elastic.
- The supply of coaches is inelastic because few people have the talent demanded by this specialized activity.
- The supply of professors is elastic because they are generally well-educated people who can do many alternative jobs.
- Equilibrium in the market for coaches occurs at a higher wage rate and a much smaller quantity than does the equilibrium in the market for professors.
- Figure 1 shows the two markets. Notice that there is a break in the *x*-axis because the quantity of professors is much greater than that of coaches.
- The demand curve for coaches is D_C, and the demand curve for professors is D_P. The supply curve of coaches is S_C, and the supply curve of professors is S_P.

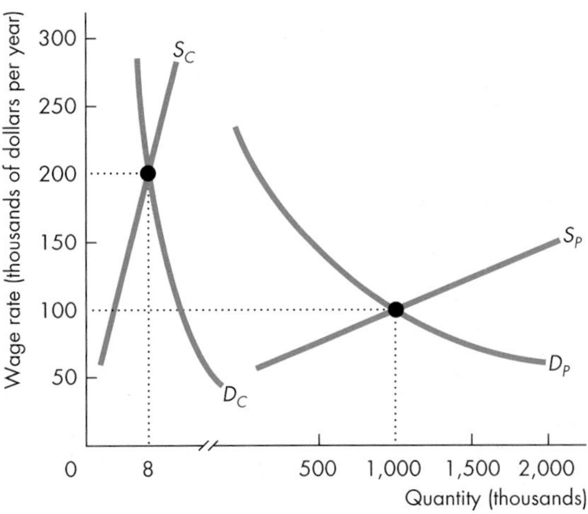

Figure 1 The markets for coaches and professors

- The equilibrium quantity of coaches is 8,000, and the equilibrium quantity of professors is 1 million.
- The equilibrium wage rate of a coach is $200,000 a year, and the equilibrium wage rate of a professor is $100,000 a year.
- Because the supply of coaches is inelastic, a large part of their income is economic rent.
- But colleges and universities can't lower the wage rate of a coach because each school faces a perfectly elastic supply of coaches at the going market-determined equilibrium wage rate.
- Some coaches, such as Charlie Weis, and some professors, such as Steven Weinberg, earn much more than the average coach and the average professor in the figure because these individuals are exceptional and the supply of truly outstanding coaches and professors is smaller than the supply of average coaches and average professors.

SUMMARY

Key Points

Factor Prices and Incomes (p. 386)

- The demand for and supply of a factor of production determines the equilibrium factor price and factor income.
- Factor income changes in the same direction as a change in the demand for the factor. The effect of a change in the supply of a factor on factor income depends on the elasticity of demand.

Labor Markets (pp. 387–394)

- The marginal revenue product of labor determines the demand for labor.
- The quantity of labor supplied increases as the wage rate increases, but at high wage rates, the supply curve eventually bends backward.
- Wage rates increase because demand increases by more than supply.

Labor Market Power (pp. 395–399)

- A labor union can raise the wage rate by restricting the supply or increasing the demand for labor.
- A monopsony can lower the wage rate below the competitive level.
- A minimum wage in monopsony can increase employment and raise the wage rate

Capital Markets (pp. 400–403)

- The capital market determines the interest rate on the financial resources that are used to buy physical capital.
- To make an investment decision, a firm compares the *present value* of the marginal revenue product of capital with the expenditure on capital.
- The higher the interest rate, the greater is the amount of saving and the quantity of capital supplied.
- Capital market equilibrium determines the real interest rate.

Natural Resource Markets (pp. 403–405)

- The demand for natural resources is determined by marginal revenue product.
- The supply of land is inelastic.
- The flow supply of nonrenewable natural resources is perfectly elastic at a price equal to the present value of the expected future price.
- The price of nonrenewable natural resources is expected to rise at a rate equal to the interest rate but fluctuates and sometimes falls.

Economic Rent, Opportunity Cost, and Taxes (pp. 406–407)

- Economic rent is the income above opportunity cost earned by the owner of a factor of production.
- When the supply of a factor is perfectly inelastic, its entire income is made up of economic rent, and when supply is perfectly elastic, the entire income is made up of opportunity cost.
- A tax on economic rent is an efficient tax.

Key Figures and Tables

Key Terms

PROBLEMS

myeconlab **Tests, Study Plan, Solutions***

1. The figure illustrates the market for blueberry pickers.

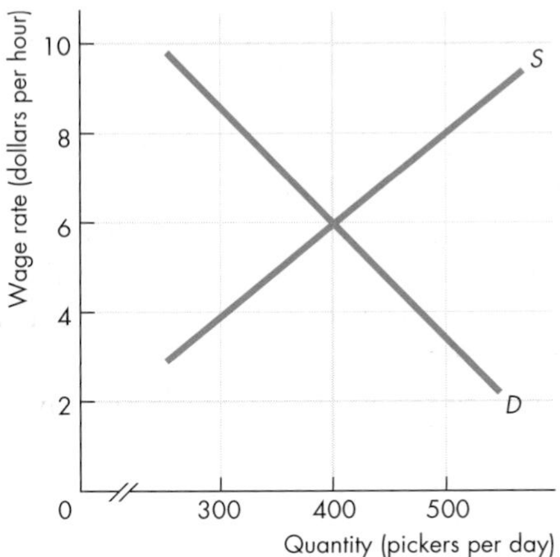

   a. What is the wage rate in this market?
   b. How many blueberry pickers get hired?
   c. What is the total income received by blueberry pickers?

   If the demand for blueberry pickers decreases by 100 pickers a day,

   d. What is the new wage rate?
   e. How many pickers are laid off?
   f. What is the total income paid to pickers?

2. Wanda owns a fish shop. She employs students to sort and pack the fish. Students can pack the following amounts of fish in an hour:

Number of students	Quantity of fish (pounds)
1	20
2	50
3	90
4	120
5	145
6	165
7	180
8	190

   Wanda can sell her fish for 50¢ a pound, and the wage rate of packers is $7.50 an hour.

   a. Calculate the marginal product of the students and draw the marginal product curve.
   b. Calculate the marginal revenue product of the students and draw the marginal revenue product curve.
   c. Find Wanda's demand for labor curve.
   d. How many students does Wanda employ?

3. Back at Wanda's fish shop described in problem 2, the price of fish falls to 33.33¢ a pound but fish packers' wages remain at $7.50 an hour.
   a. What happens to the students' marginal product?
   b. What happens to Wanda's marginal revenue product?
   c. What happens to her demand for labor curve?
   d. What happens to the number of students that she employs?

4. Back at Wanda's fish shop described in problem 2, packers' wages increase to $10 an hour but the price of fish remains at 50¢ a pound.
   a. What happens to marginal revenue product?
   b. What happens to Wanda's demand for labor curve?
   c. How many students does Wanda employ?

5. Using the information provided in problem 2, calculate Wanda's marginal revenue, marginal cost, and marginal revenue product. Show that when Wanda is making maximum profit, marginal cost equals marginal revenue and marginal revenue product equals the wage rate.

6. **In Modern Rarity, Workers Form Union at Small Chain**

   Among the thousands of stores in New York's low-income neighborhoods, labor unions have virtually no presence, except in a few supermarkets. But in a remarkable culmination to a yearlong struggle, 95 workers at a chain of 10 sneaker stores have formed a union. . . . On Jan. 18, after three months of negotiations, the two sides signed a contract. The three-year accord sets wages at $7.25 an hour, rising to $7.50 on July 1.

   The New York Times, February 5, 2006

   a. What type of labor union has been formed at sneaker stores?
   b. Why are labor unions scarce in New York's low-income neighborhoods?
   c. Who wins from this new union contract? Who loses?
   d. How can this union try to change the demand for labor?

*Solutions to odd-numbered problems are provided.

7. Which of the following items are nonrenewable natural resources, which are renewable natural resources, and which are not natural resources? Explain your answers.
   a. Trump Tower
   b. Lake Michigan
   c. Coal in a West Virginia coal mine
   d. The Internet
   e. Yosemite National Park
   f. Power generated by wind turbines
8. **Trump Group Selling Parcel For $1.8 Billion**
   A consortium of Hong Kong investors and Donald J. Trump are selling a stretch of riverfront land and three buildings on the Upper West Side for about $1.8 billion in the largest residential sale in city history, . . . If it is completed, . . .the deal should be a windfall for the investors and Mr. Trump, who acquired the land for less than $100 million a decade ago during a real estate recession. . . .

   The New York Times, June 1, 2005
   a. Why has the price of land on the Upper West Side of New York City increased over the last decade? Include in your answer a discussion of the demand for land and the supply of land.
   b. Is the Trump Group earning economic rent or opportunity cost?
   c. Is the supply of land on the Upper West Side perfectly inelastic?

*9. Keshia operates a bookkeeping service. She is considering buying four new laptop computers, which will each have a life of three years and after that will be worthless. The price of each laptop is $1,600. The marginal revenue product of the first laptop in each year is $700. The marginal revenue product of the second laptop in each year is $625. The marginal revenue product of the third laptop in each year is $575. And the marginal revenue product of the fourth laptop in each year is $500. How many laptops will Keshia buy if the interest rate is
   a. 2 percent a year
   b. 4 percent a year
   c. 6 percent a year

*To answer this question, you need to study the Appendix on pp. 413–416.

CRITICAL THINKING

1. Study *Reading Between the Lines* on pp. 408–409 and answer the following questions:
   a. What determines the marginal revenue product of a college football coach?
   b. Do you think the marginal revenue product of a head coach is higher than that of an assistant coach? Why or why not?
   c. What determines the marginal revenue product of a professor?
   d. Do you think the marginal revenue product of a professor of economics is higher than that of a professor of English? Why or why not?
   e. Why does a coach earn a higher wage rate than a professor earns, on the average?
   f. Explain what would happen to a university that decided to pay coaches and professors the same wage rate.
2. "We are running out of natural resources and must take urgent action to conserve our precious reserves." "There is no shortage of resources that the market cannot cope with." Debate these two views. List the pros and cons for each.
3. Why do we keep finding new reserves of oil? Why don't we do a once-and-for-all big survey that catalogs the earth's entire inventory of natural resources?

WEB ACTIVITIES

myeconlab **Links to Web sites**

1. Read the article on "Trends in Hours of Work Since the Mid-1970s."
   a. What are the trends in hours of work since the mid-1970s?
   b. Are the trends for men the same as those for women? What are the similarities and differences?
   c. Do you think the trends arise from changes on the demand side of the labor market or from changes on the supply side?
   d. What additional information would you need to be sure about your answer to part (c)?

Present Value and Discounting

After studying this appendix, you will be able to

- Explain how to calculate the present value of a future amount of money
- Explain how a firm uses a present value calculation to make an investment decision
- Explain the relationship between present value and the interest rate

Comparing Current and Future Dollars

To decide how much capital to buy, a firm must compare the present expenditure on capital, with the future marginal revenue product of capital. To compare a present expenditure on capital with its future return, we convert the future return to a "present value."

The **present value** of a future amount of money is the amount that, if invested today, will grow to be as large as that future amount when the interest that it will earn is taken into account.

So the present value of a future amount of money is smaller than the future amount. The calculation that we use to convert a future amount of money to a present value is called **discounting**.

The easiest way to understand discounting and present value is to consider how a present value grows to a future amount of money because of *compound interest*.

Compound Interest

Compound interest is the interest on an initial investment plus the interest on the interest that the investment has previously earned. Because of compound interest, a present amount of money (a present value) grows into a larger future amount. The future amount is equal to the present amount (present value) plus the interest it will earn in the future. That is,

$$\text{Future amount} = \text{Present value} + \text{Interest income.}$$

The interest in the first year is equal to the present value multiplied by the interest rate, r, so

$$\text{Amount after 1 year} = \text{Present value} + (r \times \text{Present value})$$

or

$$\text{Amount after 1 year} = \text{Present value} \times (1 + r).$$

If you invest $100 today and the interest rate is 10 percent a year ($r = 0.1$), one year from today you will have $110—the original $100 plus $10 interest. Check that the above formula delivers that answer: $\$100 \times 1.1 = \$110$.

If you leave this $110 invested to earn 10 percent during a second year, at the end of that year, you will have

$$\text{Amount after 2 years} = \text{Present value} \times (1 + r)^2.$$

With the numbers of the previous example, you invest $100 today at an interest rate of 10 percent a year ($r = 0.1$). After one year you have $110—the original $100 plus $10 interest. And after the second year, you have $121. In the second year, you earned $10 on your initial $100 plus $1 on the $10 interest that you earned in the first year. Check that the above formula delivers that answer: $\$100 \times (1.1)^2 = \$100 \times 1.21 = \$121$.

If you leave your $100 invested for n years, it will grow to

$$\text{Amount after } n \text{ years} = \text{Present value} \times (1 + r)^n.$$

With an interest rate of 10 percent a year, your $100 will be $195 after 7 years ($n = 7$)—almost double the present value of $100.

Discounting a Future Amount

We have just calculated future amounts one year, two years, and n years in the future from the present value and an interest rate. To calculate the present value of these future amounts, we just work backward.

To find the present value of an amount one year in the future, we divide the future amount by $(1 + r)$.

That is,

$$\text{Present value} = \frac{\text{Amount of money one year in the future}}{(1 + r)}.$$

Let's check that we can use the present value formula by calculating the present value of $110 one year from now when the interest rate is 10 percent a year. You'll be able to guess that the answer is $100 because we just calculated that $100 invested today at 10 percent a year becomes $110 in one year. So the present value of $110 one year from the present is $100. But let's use the formula. Putting the numbers into the above formula, we have

$$\text{Present value} = \frac{\$110}{(1 + 0.1)}$$
$$= \frac{\$110}{1.1} = \$100.$$

To calculate the present value of an amount of money two years in the future, we use the formula:

$$\text{Present value} = \frac{\text{Amount of money two years in future}}{(1 + r)^2}.$$

Use this formula to calculate the present value of $121 two years from now at an interest rate of 10 percent a year. With these numbers, the formula gives

$$\text{Present value} = \frac{\$121}{(1 + 0.1)^2}$$
$$= \frac{\$121}{(1.1)^2}$$
$$= \frac{\$121}{1.21}$$
$$= \$100.$$

We can calculate the present value of an amount of money n years in the future by using the general formula

$$\text{Present value} = \frac{\text{Amount of money } n \text{ years in future}}{(1 + r)^n}.$$

For example, if the interest rate is 10 percent a year, $100 to be received 10 years from now has a present value of $38.55. That is, if $38.55 is invested today at 10 percent a year it accumulates to $100 in 10 years.

Present Value of a Sequence of Future Amounts

You've seen how to calculate the present value of an amount of money one year in the future, two years in the future, and n years in the future. Most practical applications of present value calculate the present value of a sequence of future amounts of money that spread over several years. To calculate the present value of a sequence of amounts over several years, we use the formula you have learned and apply it to each year. We then sum the present values for all the years to find the present value of the sequence of amounts.

For example, suppose that a firm expects to receive $100 a year for each of the next five years. And suppose that the interest rate is 10 percent a year (0.1 a year). The present value (PV) of these five payments of $100 each is calculated by using the following formula

$$PV = \frac{\$100}{1.1} + \frac{\$100}{1.1^2} + \frac{\$100}{1.1^3} + \frac{\$100}{1.1^4} + \frac{\$100}{1.1^5},$$

which equals

$$PV = \$90.91 + \$82.64 + \$75.13 + \$68.30 + \$62.09$$
$$= \$379.07.$$

You can see that the firm receives $500 over five years. But because the money arrives in the future, it is not worth $500 today. Its present value is only $379.07. And the farther in the future the money arrives, the smaller is its present value. The $100 received one year in the future is worth $90.91 today. But the $100 received five years in the future is worth only $62.09 today.

Many personal and business decisions turn on calculations like the one we've just made. Decisions to buy or rent an apartment; to pay off a student loan or let it run another year; to invest in new capital. We'll now see how a firm uses the concept of present value to make an investment decision.

Present Value and Investment Decision

Tina runs Taxfile, Inc., a firm that sells advice to taxpayers. Tina is considering buying a new computer that costs $2,000 and has a life of two years. If Tina buys the computer, she will pay $2,000 now and she expects new business to bring in an additional $1,150 at the end of each of the next two years.

To calculate the present value, *PV*, of the marginal revenue product of a new computer, Tina calculates

$$PV = \frac{MRP_1}{(1 + r)} + \frac{MRP_2}{(1 + r)^2}.$$

Here, MRP_1 is the marginal revenue product received by Tina at the end of the first year. It is converted to a present value by dividing it by $(1 + r)$, where r is the interest rate (expressed as a proportion). The term MRP_2 is the marginal revenue product received at the end of the second year. It is converted to a present value by dividing it by $(1 + r)^2$..

If Tina can borrow or lend at an interest rate of 4 percent a year, the present value of her marginal revenue product is given by

$$PV = \frac{\$1{,}150}{(1 + 0.04)} + \frac{\$1{,}150}{(1 + 0.04)^2}$$

$$PV = \$1{,}106 + \$1{,}063$$

$$PV = \$2{,}169.$$

The present value of $1,150 one year in the future is $1,150 divided by 1.04 (4 percent as a proportion is 0.04). The present value of $1,150 two years in the future is $1,150 divided by $(1.04)^2$. Tina works out those two present values and then adds them to get the present value of the future flow of marginal revenue product, which is $2,169.

Parts (a) and (b) of Table A17.1 summarize the data and the calculations we've just made. Review these calculations and make sure you understand them.

The Decision to Buy

Tina decides whether to buy the computer by comparing the present value of its future flow of marginal revenue product with its purchase price. She makes this comparison by calculating the net present value (*NPV*) of the computer. **Net present value** is the present value of the future flow of marginal revenue product generated by the capital minus the price of the capital. If the net present value is positive, the firm buys additional capital. If the net present value is negative, the firm does not buy additional capital. Table A17.1(c) shows the calculation of Tina's net present value of a computer. The net present value is $169—greater than zero—so Tina buys the computer.

Like all other factors of production, capital is subject to diminishing marginal returns. The greater the amount of capital employed, the smaller is its marginal revenue product. So if Tina buys a second or a third computer, she gets successively smaller marginal revenue products from the additional machines.

Table A17.2(a) sets out Tina's marginal revenue products for one, two, and three computers. The

TABLE A17.1 Net Present Value of an Investment—Taxfile, Inc.

(a) Data

Price of computer	$2,000
Life of computer	2 years
Marginal revenue product	$1,150 at end of each year
Interest rate	4% a year

(b) Present value of the flow of marginal revenue product

$$PV = \frac{MRP_1}{(1 + r)} + \frac{MRP_2}{(1 + r)^2}$$

$$= \frac{\$1{,}150}{1.04} + \frac{\$1{,}150}{(1.04)^2}$$

$$= \$1{,}106 + \$1{,}063$$

$$= \$2{,}169$$

(c) Net present value of investment

NPV = *PV* of marginal revenue product – Price of computer

= $2,169 – $2,000

= $169

TABLE A17.2 Taxfile's Investment Decision

(a) Data

Price of computer	$2,000
Life of computer	2 years
Marginal revenue product:	
Using 1 computer	$1,150 a year
Using 2 computers	$1,100 a year
Using 3 computers	$1,050 a year

(b) Present value of the flow of marginal revenue product

If r = 0.04 (4% a year):

Using 1 computer: $PV = \frac{\$1,150}{1.04} + \frac{\$1,150}{(1.04)^2} = \$2,169$

Using 2 computers: $PV = \frac{\$1,100}{1.04} + \frac{\$1,100}{(1.04)^2} = \$2,075$

Using 3 computers: $PV = \frac{\$1,050}{1.04} + \frac{\$1,050}{(1.04)^2} = \$1,980$

If r = 0.08 (8% a year):

Using 1 computer: $PV = \frac{\$1,150}{1.08} + \frac{\$1,150}{(1.08)^2} = \$2,051$

Using 2 computers: $PV = \frac{\$1,100}{1.08} + \frac{\$1,100}{(1.08)^2} = \$1,962$

If r = 0.12 (12% a year):

Using 1 computer: $PV = \frac{\$1,150}{1.12} + \frac{\$1,150}{(1.12)^2} = \$1,944$

marginal revenue product of one computer (the case just reviewed) is $1,150 a year. The marginal revenue product of a second computer is $1,100 a year, and the marginal revenue product of a third computer is $1,050 a year. Table A17.2(b) shows the calculations of the present values of the marginal revenue products of the first, second, and third computers.

You've seen that with an interest rate of 4 percent a year, the net present value of one computer is positive. The table shows that the net present value of a second computer is also positive, so Tina buys a second computer. But the net present value of a third computer is negative, so Tina does not buy a third computer.

Present Value and the Interest Rate

The higher the interest rate, the smaller is the present value of a given future amount of money. The numbers in Table A17.2(b) illustrate this fact. When the interest rate rises to 8 percent a year, the present value of the first computer falls to $2,051 and when the interest rate rises to 12 percent a year, the present value of the first computer falls to $1,944.

Because a firm invests only if the net present value is positive, other things remaining the same, as the interest rate rises, the quantity of capital demanded decreases. The calculations in Table A17.2 generate Taxfile's demand curve for capital in Fig. A17.1, which shows the value of the computers demanded at each interest rate. The higher the interest rate, the smaller is the quantity of *physical* capital demanded. But to finance the purchase of *physical* capital, firms demand *financial* capital. So the higher the interest rate, the smaller is the quantity of *financial* capital demanded.

FIGURE A17.1 Taxfile's Demand for Capital

myeconlab

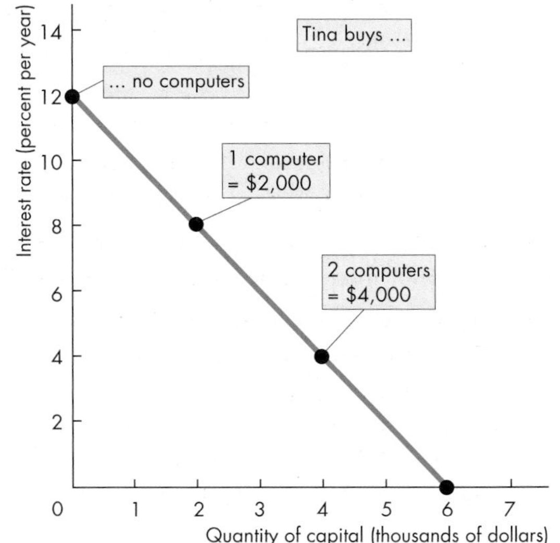

The higher the interest rate, the smaller is the present value of a future amount of money and the smaller is the quantity of capital demanded.

CHAPTER 18

Economic Inequality

Rags and Riches

Six percent of adults in Los Angeles County, some 375,000 people, experienced homelessness during the past five years. In this same part of the nation is Beverly Hills, with its mansions that are home to some fabulously wealthy movie stars. Los Angeles is not unusual. In New York City, where Donald Trump has built a luxury apartment tower with a penthouse priced at $13 million, more than 20,000 people, 9,000 of whom are children, seek a bed in a shelter for the homeless every night. Extreme poverty and extreme wealth exist side by side in every major city in the United States and in most parts of the world.

How many rich and poor people are there in the United States? How are income and wealth distributed? And are the rich getting richer and the poor getting poorer?

What causes inequality in the distribution of economic well-being?

How much redistribution does the government do to limit extreme poverty?

In this chapter, we study economic inequality—its extent, its sources, and the things governments do to make it less extreme. We begin by looking at some facts about economic inequality in the United States. We end, in *Reading Between the Lines*, by looking at the changing gap between the highest and lowest incomes over the past twenty years.

After studying this chapter, you will be able to

- Describe the inequality in income and wealth in the United States in 2005 and the trends in inequality
- Explain the features of the labor market that contribute to economic inequality
- Describe the scale of income redistribution by governments

Measuring Economic Inequality

The most commonly used measure of economic inequality is the distribution of annual income. The Census Bureau defines income as **money income**, which equals *market income* plus cash payments to households by government. **Market income** equals wages, interest, rent, and profit earned in factor markets, before paying income taxes.

The Distribution of Income

Figure 18.1 shows the distribution of annual income across the 113 million households in the United States in 2005. Note that the *x*-axis measures household income and the *y*-axis is percentage of households.

The most common household income, called the *mode* income, was received by the 6.4 percent of the households whose incomes fell between \$10,000 and \$15,000. The value of \$13,000 marked on the figure is an estimate.

The middle level of household income in 2005, called the *median* income, was \$46,326. Fifty percent of households have an income that exceeds the median and fifty percent have an income below the median.

The average household money income in 2005, called the *mean* income, was \$63,344. This number equals total household income, about \$7.16 trillion, divided by the 113 million households.

You can see in Fig. 18.1 that the mode income is less than the median income and the median income is less than the mean income. This feature of the distribution of income tells us that there are more households with low incomes than with high incomes. And some of the high incomes are very high.

The income distribution in Fig. 18.1 is called a *positively skewed* distribution, which means that it has a long tail of high values. This distribution shape contrasts with a *bell-shaped* distribution such as the distribution of people's heights. In a bell-shaped distribution, the mean, median, and mode are all equal.

Another way of looking at the distribution of income is to measure the percentage of total income received by each given percentage of households. Data are reported for five groups—called *quintiles* or fifth shares—each consisting of 20 percent of households.

FIGURE 18.1 The Distribution of Income in the United States in 2005

myeconlab

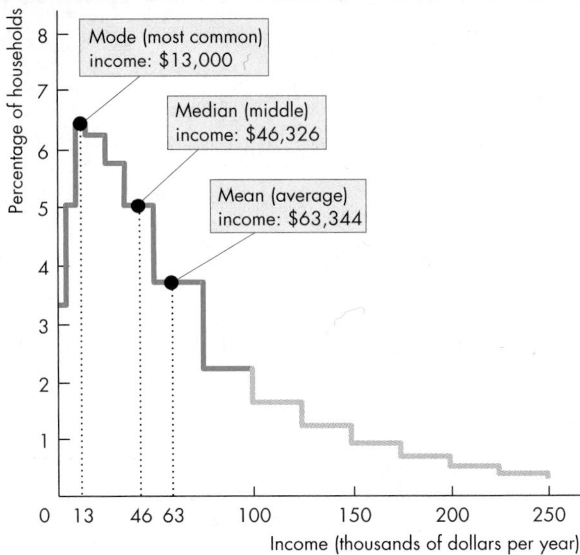

The distribution of income is positively skewed. The mode (most common) income is less than the median (middle) income, which in turn is less than the mean (average) income. The shape of the distribution above \$100,000 is an indication rather than a precise measure, and the distribution goes up to several million dollars a year.

Source of data: U.S. Bureau of the Census, "Income, Poverty, and Health Insurance Coverage in the United States: 2005," *Current Population Reports*, P-60-231 (Washington, DC: U.S. Government Printing Office, 2006).

Figure 18.2 shows the distribution based on these shares in 2005. The poorest 20 percent of households received 3.4 percent of total income; the second poorest 20 percent received 8.6 percent of total income; the middle 20 percent received 14.6 percent of total income; the next highest 20 percent received 23.0 percent of total income; and the highest 20 percent received 50.4 percent of total income.

The distribution of income in Fig. 18.1 and the quintile shares in Fig. 18.2 tell us that income is distributed unequally. But we need a way of comparing the distribution of income in different periods and using different measures. A neat graphical tool called the *Lorenz curve* enables us to make such comparisons.

FIGURE 18.2 U.S. Quintile Shares in 2005

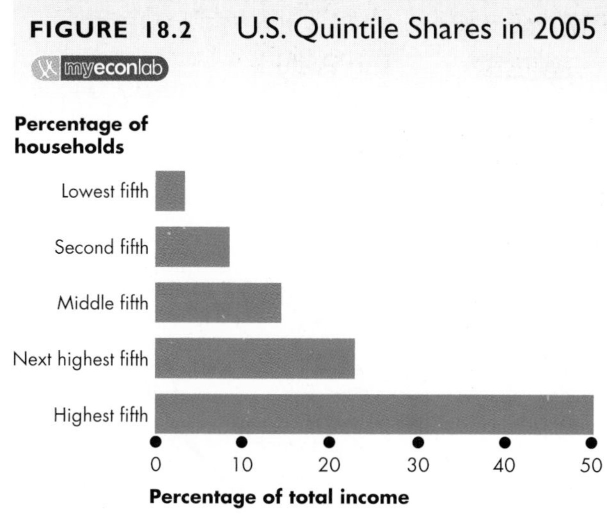

Households (percentage)	Income (percentage of total income)
Lowest 20	3.4
Second 20	8.6
Middle 20	14.6
Next highest 20	23.0
Highest 20	50.4

In 2005, the poorest 20 percent of households received 3.4 percent of total income; the second poorest 20 percent received 8.6 percent; the middle 20 percent received 14.6 percent; the next highest 20 percent received 23.0 percent; and the highest 20 percent received 50.4 percent.

Source of data: U.S. Bureau of the Census, "Income, Poverty, and Health Insurance Coverage in the United States: 2005," *Current Population Reports*, P-60-231 (Washington, DC: U.S. Government Printing Office, 2006).

FIGURE 18.3 The Income Lorenz Curve in 2005

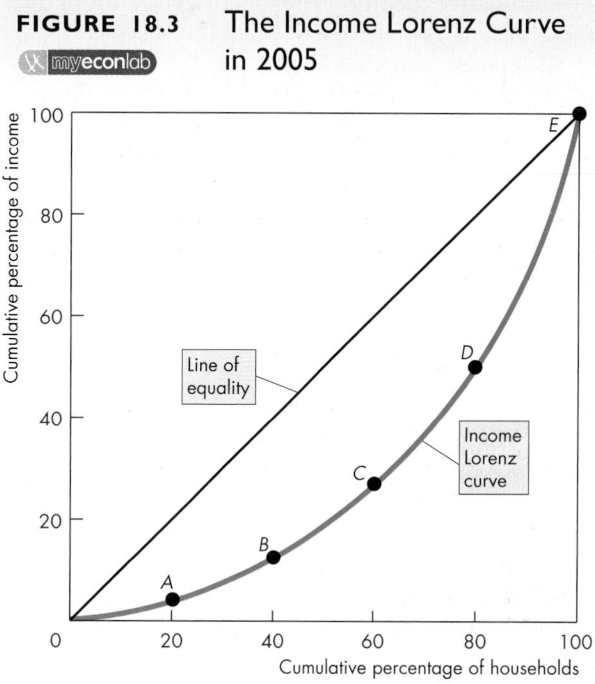

	Households		Income	
	Percentage	Cumulative percentage	Percentage	Cumulative percentage
A	Lowest 20	20	3.4	3.4
B	Second 20	40	8.6	12.0
C	Middle 20	60	14.6	26.6
D	Next highest 20	80	23.0	49.6
E	Highest 20	100	50.4	100.0

The cumulative percentage of income is graphed against the cumulative percentage of households. Points *A* through *E* on the Lorenz curve correspond to the rows of the table. If incomes were distributed equally, each 20 percent of households would receive 20 percent of total income and the Lorenz curve would fall along the line of equality. The Lorenz curve shows that income is unequally distributed.

Source of data: U.S. Bureau of the Census, "Income, Poverty, and Health Insurance Coverage in the United States: 2005," *Current Population Reports*, P-60-231 (Washington, DC: U.S. Government Printing Office, 2006).

The Income Lorenz Curve

The income **Lorenz curve** graphs the cumulative percentage of income against the cumulative percentage of households. Figure 18.3 shows the income Lorenz curve using the quintile shares from Fig. 18.2. The table shows the percentage of income of each quintile group. For example, row *A* tells us that the lowest quintile of households receives 3.4 percent of total income. The table also shows the *cumulative* percentages of households and income. For example, row *B* tells us that the lowest two quintiles (lowest 40 percent) of households receive 12.0 percent of total income (3.4 percent for the lowest quintile and 8.6 percent for the next lowest). The Lorenz curve graphs the cumulative income shares against the cumulative household percentages.

If income were distributed equally across all the households, each quintile would receive 20 percent of total income and the cumulative percentages of income received by the cumulative percentages of households would fall along the straight line labeled "Line of equality." The actual distribution of income is shown by the curve labeled "Income Lorenz curve." The closer the Lorenz curve is to the line of equality, the more equal is the distribution of income.

The Distribution of Wealth

The distribution of wealth provides another way of measuring economic inequality. A household's **wealth** is the value of the things that it owns at a *point in time*. In contrast, income is the amount that the household receives over a given *period of time*.

Figure 18.4 shows the Lorenz curve for wealth in the United States in 1998 (the most recent year for which we have wealth distribution data). The median household wealth in 1998 was $60,700. Wealth is extremely unequally distributed, and for this reason, the data are grouped by seven unequal groups of households. The poorest 40 percent of households own only 0.2 percent of total wealth (row *A'* in the table in Fig. 18.4). The richest 20 percent of households own 83.4 percent of total wealth. Because this group owns almost all the wealth, we need to break the group into smaller bits. That is what rows *D'* through *G'* do. You can see that the richest 1 percent of households own 38.1 percent of total wealth.

Figure 18.4 shows the income Lorenz curve (from Fig. 18.3) alongside the wealth Lorenz curve. You can see that the Lorenz curve for wealth is much farther away from the line of equality than the Lorenz curve for income is, which means that the distribution of wealth is much more unequal than the distribution of income.

Wealth Versus Income

We've seen that wealth is much more unequally distributed than is income. Which distribution provides the better description of the degree of inequality? To answer this question, we need to think about the connection between wealth and income.

Wealth is a stock of assets, and income is the flow of earnings that results from the stock of wealth. Suppose that a person owns assets worth

FIGURE 18.4 Lorenz Curves for Income and Wealth

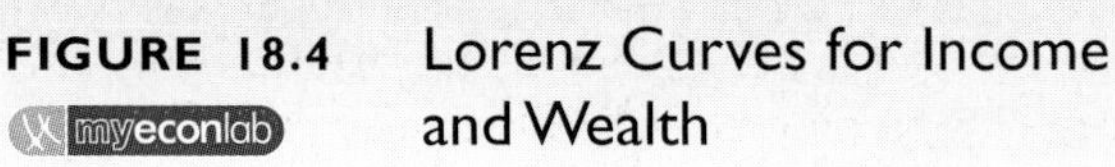

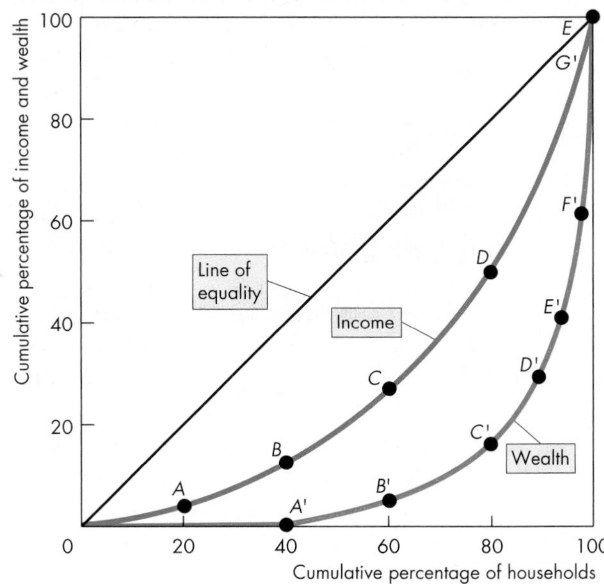

	Households		Wealth	
	Percentage	Cumulative percentage	Percentage	Cumulative percentage
A'	Lowest 40	40	0.2	0.2
B'	Next 20	60	4.5	4.7
C'	Next 20	80	11.9	16.6
D'	Next 10	90	12.5	29.1
E'	Next 5	95	11.5	40.6
F'	Next 4	99	21.3	61.9
G'	Highest 1	100	38.1	100.0

The cumulative percentage of wealth is graphed against the cumulative percentage of households. Points *A'* through *G'* on the Lorenz curve for wealth correspond to the rows of the table. By comparing the Lorenz curves for income and wealth, we can see that wealth is distributed much more unequally than is income.

Sources of data: U.S. Bureau of the Census, "Income, Poverty, and Health Insurance Coverage in the United States: 2005," *Current Population Reports*, P-60-231 (Washington, DC: U.S. Government Printing Office, 2006); and Edward N. Wolff, "Recent Trends in Wealth Ownership, 1938–1998," Jerome Levy Economics Institute Working Paper No. 300, April 2000.

$1 million—has a wealth of $1 million. If the rate of return on assets is 5 percent a year, then this person receives an income of $50,000 a year from those assets. We can describe this person's economic condition by using either the wealth of $1 million or the income of $50,000. When the rate of return is 5 percent a year, $1 million of wealth equals $50,000 of income in perpetuity. Wealth and income are just different ways of looking at the same thing.

But in Fig. 18.4, the distribution of wealth is more unequal than the distribution of income. Why? It is because the wealth data do not include the value of human capital, while the income data measure income from all wealth, including human capital.

Table 18.1 illustrates the consequence of omitting human capital from the wealth data. Lee has twice the wealth and twice the income of Peter. But Lee's human capital is less than Peter's—$200,000 compared with $499,000. And Lee's income from human capital of $10,000 is less than Peter's income from human capital of $24,950. Lee's nonhuman capital is larger than Peter's—$800,000 compared with $1,000. And Lee's income from nonhuman capital of $40,000 is larger than Peter's income from nonhuman capital of $50.

When Lee and Peter are surveyed by the Census Bureau in a national wealth and income survey, their incomes are recorded as $50,000 and $25,000, respectively, which implies that Lee is twice as well off as Peter. And their tangible assets are recorded as $800,000 and $1,000, respectively, which implies that Lee is 800 times as wealthy as Peter.

Because the national survey of wealth excludes human capital, the income distribution is a more accurate measure of economic inequality than the wealth distribution.

Annual or Lifetime Income and Wealth?

A typical household's income changes over time. It starts out low, grows to a peak when the household's workers reach retirement age, and then falls after retirement. Also, a typical household's wealth changes over time. Like income, it starts out low, grows to a peak at the point of retirement, and falls after retirement.

Suppose we look at three households that have identical lifetime incomes. One household is young, one is middle-aged, and one is retired. The middle-aged household has the highest income and wealth, the retired household has the lowest, and the young household falls in the middle. The distributions of annual income and wealth in a given year are unequal, but the distributions of lifetime income and wealth are equal. So some of the inequality in annual income arises because different households are at different stages in the life cycle. But we can see *trends* in the income distribution using annual income data.

TABLE 18.1 Capital, Wealth, and Income

	Lee		Peter	
	Wealth	**Income**	**Wealth**	**Income**
Human capital	200,000	10,000	499,000	24,950
Other capital	800,000	40,000	1,000	50
Total	$1,000,000	$50,000	$500,000	$25,000

When wealth is measured to include the value of human capital as well as other forms of capital, the distribution of income and the distribution of wealth display the same degree of inequality.

Trends in Inequality

To see trends in the income distribution, we need a measure that enables us to rank distributions on the scale of more equal and less equal. No perfect scale exists, but one that is much used is called the Gini ratio. The **Gini ratio** is based on the Lorenz curve and equals the ratio of the area between the line of equality and the Lorenz curve to the entire area beneath the line of equality. If income is equally distributed, the Lorenz curve is the same as the line of equality, so the Gini ratio is zero. If one person has all the income and everyone else has none, the Gini ratio is 1.

Figure 18.5 shows the U.S. Gini ratio from 1970 to 2005. The figure shows breaks in the data in 1992 and 2000 because in those years, the Census Bureau changed its method of collecting the data and definitions, so the numbers before and after the breaks can't be compared. Despite the breaks in the series, the Gini ratio has clearly increased, which means that on this measure, incomes have become less equal.

The major change is that the share of income received by the richest 20 percent of households has increased. No one knows for sure why this trend has occurred, but a possibility that we'll explore in the next section is that technological change has increased the marginal product of high-skilled workers and decreased the marginal product of low-skilled workers.

FIGURE 18.5 The U.S. Gini Ratio: 1970–2005

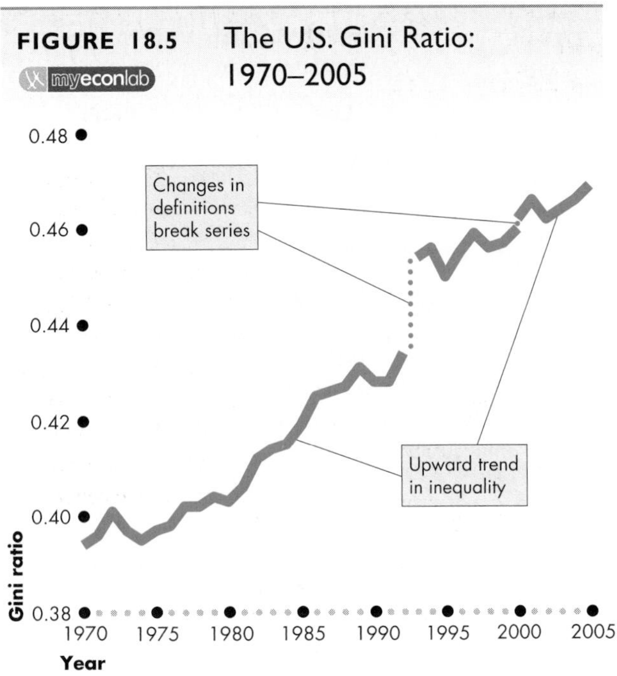

Measured by the Gini ratio, the distribution of income in the United States became more unequal between 1970 and 2005. The percentage of income earned by the richest 20 percent of households increased through these years. Changes in definitions make the numbers before and after 1992 and before and after 2000 not comparable. Despite the breaks in the data, the trends are still visible.

Source of data: U.S. Bureau of the Census, "Income, Poverty, and Health Insurance Coverage in the United States: 2005," *Current Population Reports*, P-60-231 (Washington, DC: U.S. Government Printing Office, 2006).

Who Are the Rich and the Poor?

The highest incomes in the United States are earned by high-profile movie stars, sports stars, and television personalities and by less well known but very highly paid chief executives of large corporations. The lowest incomes are earned by people who scratch out a living doing seasonal work on farms. But aside from these extremes, what are the characteristics of people who earn high incomes and people who earn low incomes?

Four characteristics stand out:

- Education
- Type of household
- Age of householder
- Race and ethnicity

Education The median household income in the United States in 2005 was $46,326. Education brought the largest spread around this median. A person who had not completed grade 9 lived in a household in which the average income was $20,000 in 2005. At the other extreme, and again on the average, a person with a professional degree (such as a medical or law degree) lived in a household in which the average income was more than $100,000. Just completing high school raises average household income by more than $10,000 per year. And getting a bachelor's degree adds another $34,000 a year to a household's income, on the average.

Type of Household The Census Bureau divides households into *family households* and *non-family households*. Most non-family households are single people who live alone. Men who live alone received about $34,000 on the average in 2005. Women who live alone received $23,000 on the average. Married couples received about $66,000 on the average in 2005. In contrast, men with children and no wife present received $46,000 while women with children and no husband present received only $31,000.

Age of Householder Households with the oldest and youngest householders have lower incomes than do those with middle-aged householders. In 2005, when the householder was aged between 45 and 54, household income averaged $62,000. And when the householder was aged between 35 and 45, household income averaged $58,000. When the householder was aged between 15 and 24, average household income was close to $29,000. And for householders over 65, the average household income was only $26,000.

Race and Ethnicity White households had an average income in 2005 of $51,000, while black households had an average income of $31,000. Households of Hispanic origin were a bit better off, with an average income of $36,000. Best off of all were Asian households, in which the average income was $61,000.

Figure 18.6 provides a quick visual summary of the numbers that we've just described. The figure also shows the small effect that region of residence has on income per person. Incomes were highest in the Northeast and West and lowest in the South, with the Midwest falling between these extremes.

FIGURE 18.6 The Distribution of Income per Person by Selected Household Characteristics in 2005

myeconlab

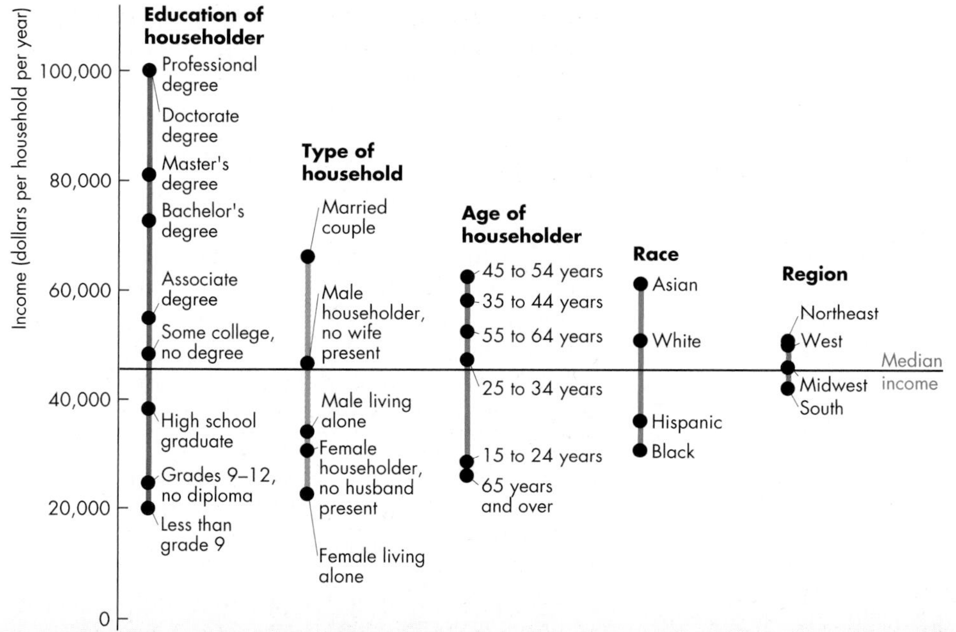

The median household income in 2005 was $46,326. Education is the single biggest factor affecting income distribution, but type of household, householder's age, and race play roles. Region of residence is not a very important source of inequality.

Source of data: U.S. Bureau of the Census, "Income, Poverty, and Health Insurance Coverage in the United States: 2005," *Current Population Reports*, P-60-231 (Washington, DC: U.S. Government Printing Office, 2006).

Poverty

Households at the low end of the income distribution are so poor that they are considered to be living in poverty. **Poverty** is a situation in which a household's income is too low to be able to buy the quantities of food, shelter, and clothing that are deemed necessary. Poverty is a relative concept. Millions of people living in Africa and Asia survive on incomes of less than $400 a year. In the United States, the poverty level is calculated each year by the Social Security Administration. In 2005, the poverty level for a four-person household was an income of $19,971. In that year, 37 million Americans—12.6 percent of the population—lived in households that had incomes below the poverty level. Many of these households benefited from Medicare and Medicaid, two government programs that aid the poorest households and lift some of them above the poverty level.

The distribution of poverty by race is unequal: 8.5 percent of white Americans live in poor households compared to 22 percent of Hispanic-origin Americans and 25 percent of African Americans.

Poverty is also influenced by household status. More than 31 percent of households in which the householder is a female with no husband present had incomes below the poverty level.

Despite the widening of the income distribution, poverty rates are falling.

REVIEW QUIZ

1. Which is distributed more unequally, income or wealth? Why? Which is the better measure?
2. Has the distribution of income become more equal or more unequal? Which quintile share has changed most?
3. What are the main characteristics of people who earn large incomes and who earn small incomes?
4. What is poverty and how does its incidence vary across the races?

myeconlab **Study Plan 18.1**

The Sources of Economic Inequality

We've described economic inequality in the United States. Our task now is to explain it. We began this task in Chapter 17 by learning about the forces that influence demand and supply in the markets for labor, capital, and land. We're now going to deepen our understanding of these forces.

Inequality arises from unequal labor market outcomes and from unequal ownership of capital. We'll begin by looking at labor markets and two features of them that contribute to differences in income:

- Human capital
- Discrimination

Human Capital

A clerk in a law firm earns less than a tenth of the amount earned by the attorney he assists. An operating room assistant earns less than a tenth of the amount earned by the surgeon she works with. A bank teller earns less than a tenth of the amount earned by the bank's CEO. These differences in earnings arise from differences in human capital.

Suppose there are just two levels of human capital, which we'll call high-skilled labor and low-skilled labor. The low-skilled labor might represent the law clerk, the operating room assistant, or the bank teller, and the high-skilled labor might represent the attorney, the surgeon, or the bank's CEO. We'll first look at the market demand for these two types of labor.

The Demand for High-Skilled and Low-Skilled Labor

High-skilled workers can perform tasks that low-skilled labor would perform badly or perhaps cannot perform at all. Imagine an untrained person doing open-heart surgery. High-skilled labor has a higher marginal revenue product than does low-skilled labor. As we learned in Chapter 17, a firm's demand for labor curve is the same as the marginal revenue product of labor curve.

Figure 18.7(a) shows the demand curves for high-skilled and low-skilled labor. The demand curve for high-skilled labor is D_H, and that for low-skilled labor is D_L. At any given level of employment, firms are willing to pay a higher wage rate to a high-skilled worker than to a low-skilled worker. The gap between the two wage rates measures the marginal revenue product of skill; for example, at an employment level of 2,000 hours, firms are willing to pay $12.50 an hour for a high-skilled worker and only $5 an hour for a low-skilled worker, a difference of $7.50 an hour. So the marginal revenue product of skill is $7.50 an hour.

The Supply of High-Skilled and Low-Skilled Labor

High-skilled labor contains more human capital than does low-skilled labor, and human capital is costly to acquire. The opportunity cost of acquiring human capital includes expenditures on tuition and textbooks and also forgone or reduced earnings while the skill is being acquired. When a person goes to school full time, that cost is the total earnings forgone. But some people acquire skills on the job—on-the-job training. Usually, a worker undergoing on-the-job training is paid a lower wage than one doing a comparable job but not undergoing training. In such a case, the cost of acquiring the skill is the difference between the wage paid to a person not being trained and that paid to a person being trained.

The position of the supply curve of high-skilled labor reflects the cost of acquiring human capital. Figure 18.7(b) shows two supply curves: one for high-skilled labor and the other for low-skilled labor. The supply curve for high-skilled labor is S_H, and that for low-skilled labor is S_L.

The high-skilled labor supply curve lies above the low-skilled labor supply curve. The vertical distance between the two supply curves is the compensation that high-skilled labor requires for the cost of acquiring the skill. For example, suppose that the quantity of low-skilled labor supplied is 2,000 hours at a wage rate of $5 an hour. This wage rate compensates the low-skilled workers mainly for their time on the job. To induce high-skilled workers to supply 2,000 hours of labor, firms must pay a wage rate of $8.50 an hour.

Wage Rates of High-Skilled and Low-Skilled Labor

The demand for and supply of high-skilled and low-skilled labor determine the two wage rates. Figure 18.7(c) brings the demand curves and the supply curves for high-skilled and low-skilled labor together. Equilibrium occurs in the market for low-skilled labor (on the blue supply and demand curves) at a wage rate of $5 an hour, and a quantity of low-skilled labor of 2,000 hours. Equilibrium occurs in the market for high-skilled labor (on the green supply and

FIGURE 18.7 Skill Differentials

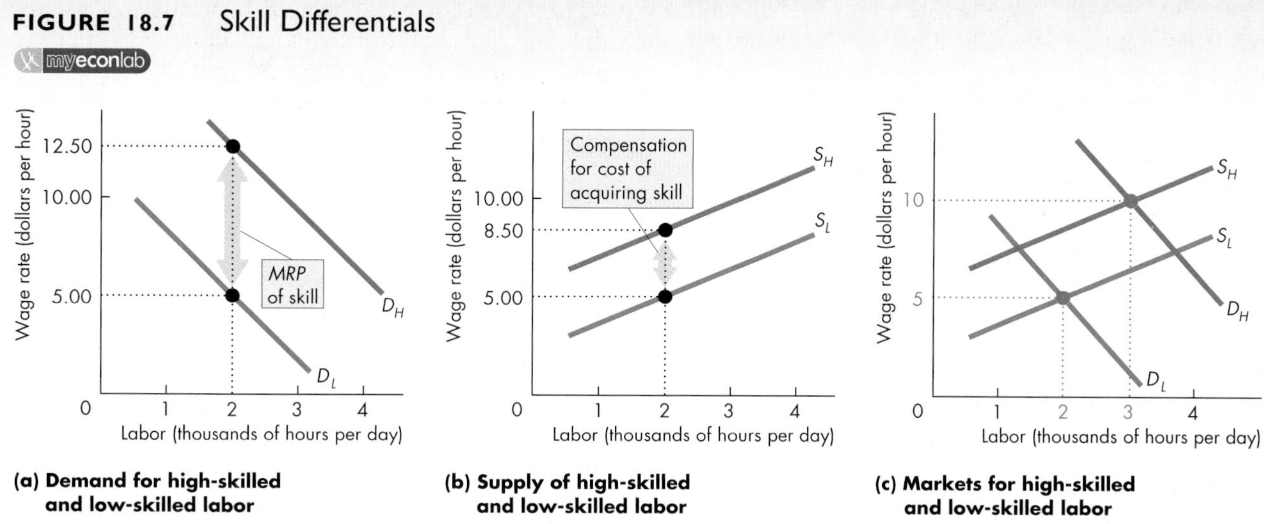

Part (a) illustrates the marginal revenue product of skill. Low-skilled labor has a marginal revenue product that gives rise to the demand curve marked D_L. High-skilled labor has a higher marginal revenue product than does low-skilled labor, so the demand curve for high-skilled labor, D_H, lies to the right of D_L. The vertical distance between these two curves is the marginal revenue product of the skill.

Part (b) illustrates the cost of acquiring skill. The supply curve for low-skilled labor is S_L. The supply curve for high-skilled labor is S_H. The vertical distance between these two curves is the required compensation for the cost of acquiring a skill.

Part (c) shows the equilibrium employment and the wage differential. Low-skilled workers provide 2,000 hours of labor at a wage rate of $5 an hour. High-skilled workers provide 3,000 hours of labor at a wage rate of $10 an hour.

demand curves) at a wage rate of $10 an hour, and a quantity of high-skilled labor of 3,000 hours.

The equilibrium wage rate of high-skilled labor is higher than that of low-skilled labor for two reasons: First, high-skilled labor has a higher marginal revenue product than low-skilled labor, so at a given wage rate, the quantity of high-skilled labor demanded exceeds that of low-skilled labor. Second, skills are costly to acquire, so at a given wage rate, the quantity of high-skilled labor supplied is less than that of low-skilled labor. The wage differential (in this case, $5 an hour) depends on both the marginal revenue product of the skill and the cost of acquiring it. The higher the marginal revenue product of a skill or the more costly it is to acquire a skill, the larger is the wage differential between high-skilled and low-skilled labor.

Do Education and Training Pay? Rates of return on high school and college education have been estimated to be in the range of 5 percent to 10 percent a year after allowing for inflation, which suggest that a college degree is a better investment than almost any other that a person can undertake.

Inequality Explained by Human Capital Differences
Human capital differences help to explain some of the inequality that we observe.

High-income households tend to be better educated, middle-aged, Asian or white, and married couples (see Fig. 18.6). Human capital differences are correlated with these household characteristics. Education contributes directly to human capital. Age contributes indirectly to human capital because older workers have more experience than younger workers. Human capital differences can also explain a small part of the inequality associated with sex and race. A larger proportion of men (25 percent) than women (20 percent) have completed four years of college, and a larger proportion of whites (24 percent) than blacks (13 percent) have completed a bachelor's degree or higher. These differences in education levels among the sexes and the races are becoming smaller, but they have not been eliminated.

Career interruptions can decrease human capital. A person (most often a woman) who interrupts a career to rear young children usually returns to the labor force with a lower earning capacity than a similar person who has kept working. Likewise, a person who has suffered a spell of unemployment often finds a new job at a lower wage rate than that of a similar person who has not been unemployed.

Trends in Inequality Explained by Technological Change and Globalization You've seen that high-income households have earned an increasing share of total income while low-income households have earned a decreasing share: The distribution of income in the United States has become more unequal. Technological change and globalization are two possible sources of this increased inequality.

Technological Change Information technologies such as computers and laser scanners are *substitutes* for low-skilled labor: They perform tasks that previously were performed by low-skilled labor. The introduction of these technologies has lowered the marginal product and the demand for low-skilled labor. These same technologies require high-skilled labor to design, program, and run them. High-skilled labor and the information technologies are *complements*. So the introduction of these technologies has increased the marginal product and demand for high-skilled labor.

Figure 18.8 illustrates the effects on wages and employment. The supply of low-skilled labor (part a) and that of high-skilled labor (part b) are S, and initially, the demand in each market is D_0. The low-skill wage rate is \$5 an hour, and the high-skill wage rate is \$10 an hour. The demand for low-skilled labor decreases to D_1 in part (a) and the demand for high-skilled labor increases to D_1 in part (b). The low-skill wage rate falls to \$4 an hour and the high-skill wage rate rises to \$15 an hour.

Globalization The entry of China and other developing countries into the global economy has lowered the prices of many manufactures. Lower prices for what a firm sells lower the marginal revenue product of the firm's workers and decrease the demand for their labor. A situation like that in Fig. 18.8(a) occurs, the wage rate falls, and employment shrinks.

At the same time, the growing global economy increases the demand for services that employ high-skilled workers, and the marginal revenue product of and demand for high-skilled labor increases. A situation like that in Fig. 18.8(b) occurs, the wage rate rises, and employment opportunities for high-skilled workers expand.

FIGURE 18.8 Explaining the Trend in Income Distribution

myeconlab

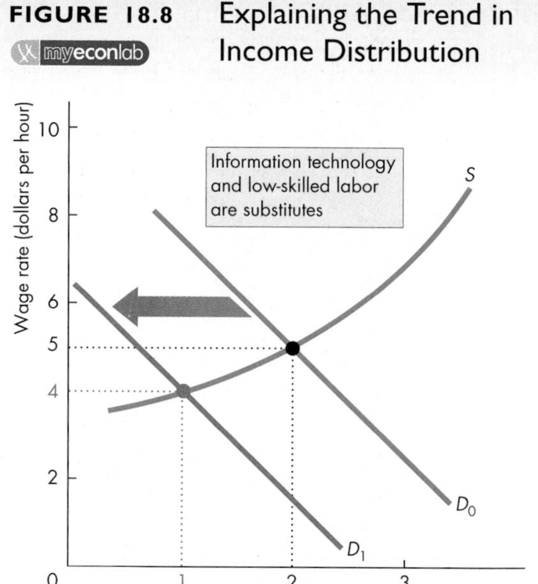

(a) A decrease in demand for low-skilled labor

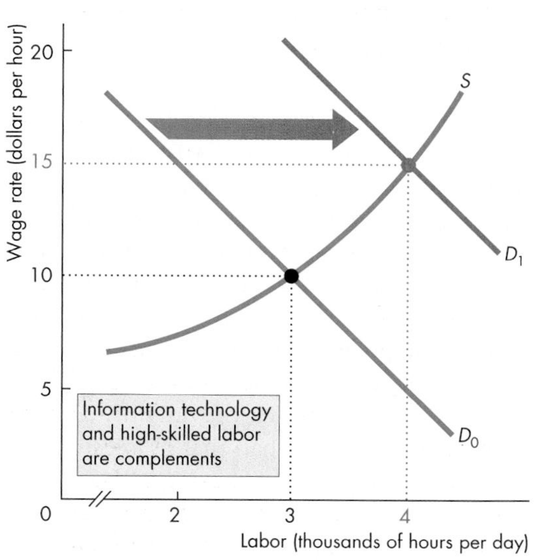

(b) An increase in demand for high-skilled labor

Low-skilled labor in part (a) and information technologies are substitutes. Advances in information technology decrease the demand for low-skilled labor and lower its wage rate. High-skilled labor in part (b) and information technologies are complements. Advances in information technology increase the demand for high-skilled labor and raise its wage rate.

Discrimination

Human capital differences can explain some of the economic inequality that we observe. Discrimination is another possible source of inequality.

Suppose that black females and white males have identical abilities as investment advisors. Figure 18.9 shows the supply curves of black females, S_{BF} (in part a), and of white males, S_{WM} (in part b). The marginal revenue product of investment advisors shown by the two curves labeled *MRP* in parts (a) and (b) is the same for both groups.

If everyone is free of race and sex prejudice, the market determines a wage rate of $40,000 a year for investment advisors. But if the customers are prejudiced against women and minorities, this prejudice is reflected in the wage rate and employment.

Suppose that the perceived marginal revenue product of the black females, when discriminated against, is MRP_{DA}. Suppose that the perceived marginal revenue product for white males, the group discriminated in favor of, is MRP_{DF}. With these *MRP* curves, black females earn $20,000 a year and only 1,000 black females work as investment advisors. White males earn $60,000 a year, and 3,000 of them work as investment advisors.

Counteracting Forces Economists disagree about whether prejudice actually causes wage differentials, and one line of reasoning implies that it does not. In the above example, customers who buy from white men pay a higher service charge for investment advice than do the customers who buy from black women. This price difference acts as an incentive to encourage people who are prejudiced to buy from the people against whom they are prejudiced. This force could be strong enough to eliminate the effects of discrimination altogether. Suppose, as is true in manufacturing, that a firm's customers never meet its workers. If such a firm discriminates against women or minorities, it can't compete with firms who hire these groups because its costs are higher than those of the nonprejudiced firms. Only firms that do not discriminate survive in a competitive industry.

Whether because of discrimination or from some other source, women and visible minorities do earn lower incomes than white males. Another possible source of lower wage rates of women arises from differences in the relative degree of specialization of women and men.

FIGURE 18.9 Discrimination

myeconlab

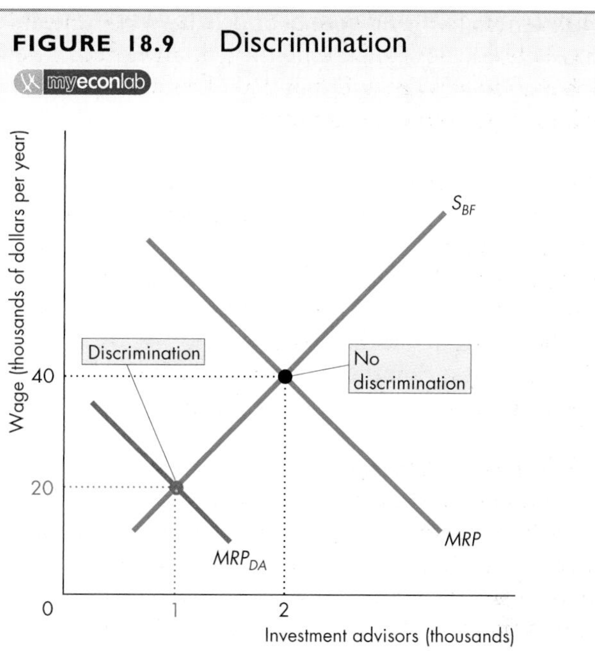

(a) Black females

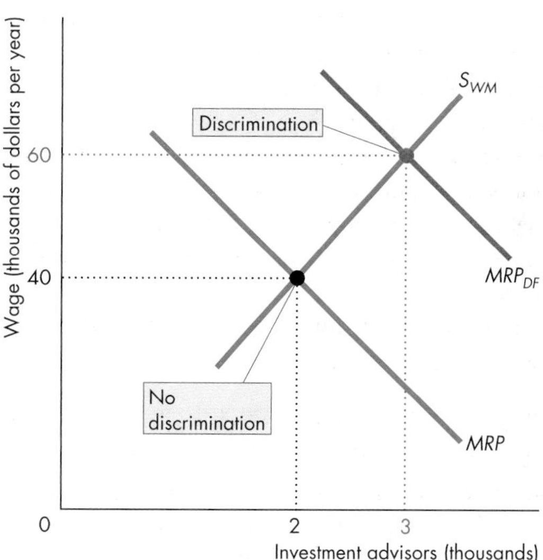

(b) White males

With no discrimination, the wage rate is $40,000 a year and 2,000 of each group are hired. With discrimination against blacks and women, the marginal revenue product curve in part (a) is MRP_{DA} and that in part (b) is MRP_{DF}. The wage rate for black women falls to $20,000 a year, and only 1,000 are employed. The wage rate for white men rises to $60,000 a year, and 3,000 are employed.

Differences in the Degree of Specialization Couples must choose how to allocate their time between working for a wage and doing jobs in the home, such as cooking, cleaning, shopping, organizing vacations, and, most important, bearing and rearing children. Let's look at the choices of Bob and Sue.

Bob might specialize in earning an income and Sue in taking care of the home. Or Sue might specialize in earning an income and Bob in taking care of the home. Or both of them might earn an income and share home production jobs.

The allocation they choose depends on their preferences and on the earning potential of each of them. The choice of an increasing number of households is for each person to diversify between earning an income and doing some home chores. But in most households, Bob will specialize in earning an income and Sue will both earn an income and bear a larger share of the task of running the home. With this allocation, Bob will probably earn more than Sue. If Sue devotes time and effort to ensuring Bob's mental and physical well-being, the quality of Bob's market labor will be higher than it would be if he were diversified. If the roles were reversed, Sue would be able to supply market labor that earns more than Bob.

To test whether the degree of specialization accounts for earnings differences between the sexes, economists have compared the incomes of never-married men and women. They have found that, on the average, with equal amounts of human capital, the wages of these two groups are the same.

We've examined some sources of inequality in the labor market. Let's now look at the way inequality arises from unequal ownership of capital.

Unequal Wealth

You've seen that inequality in wealth (excluding human capital) is much greater than inequality in income. This inequality arises from saving and transfers of wealth from one generation to the next.

The higher a household's income, the more that household tends to save and pass on to the next generation. Saving is not always a source of increased inequality. If a household saves to redistribute an uneven income over its life cycle and enable consumption to fluctuate less than income, saving decreases inequality. If a lucky generation that has a high income saves a large part of that income and leaves capital to a succeeding generation that is unlucky, this act of saving also decreases the degree of inequality. But two features of intergenerational transfers of wealth lead to increased inequality: People can't inherit debts, and marriage tends to concentrate wealth.

Can't Inherit Debt Although a person may die in debt—with negative wealth—a debt can't be forced onto the next generation of a family. So inheritance only adds to a future generation's wealth; it cannot decrease it.

Most people inherit nothing or a very small amount. A few people inherit an enormous fortune. As a result, intergenerational transfers make the distribution of income persistently more unequal than the distribution of ability and job skills. A household that is poor in one generation is more likely to be poor in the next. A household that is wealthy in one generation is more likely to be wealthy in the next. And marriage reinforces this tendency.

Marriage and Wealth Concentration People tend to marry within their own socioeconomic class—a phenomenon called *assortative mating*. In everyday language, "like attracts like." Although there is a good deal of folklore that "opposites attract," perhaps such Cinderella tales appeal to us because they are so rare in reality. Wealthy people seek wealthy partners.

Because of assortative mating, wealth becomes more concentrated in a small number of families and the distribution of wealth becomes more unequal.

REVIEW QUIZ

1. What role does human capital play in accounting for income inequality?
2. What role might discrimination play in accounting for income inequality?
3. What are the possible reasons for income inequality by sex and race?
4. How might technological change and globalization influence the distribution of income?
5. Does inherited wealth make the distribution of income less equal or more equal?
6. Why does wealth inequality persist across generations?

myeconlab **Study Plan 18.2**

Next, we're going to see how taxes and government programs redistribute income and decrease the degree of economic inequality.

Income Redistribution

The three main ways in which governments in the United States redistribute income are

- Income taxes
- Income maintenance programs
- Subsidized services

Income Taxes

Income taxes may be progressive, regressive, or proportional. A **progressive income tax** is one that taxes income at an average rate that increases with income. A **regressive income tax** is one that taxes income at an average rate that decreases with income. A **proportional income tax** (also called a *flat-rate income tax*) is one that taxes income at a constant average rate, regardless of the level of income.

The tax rates that apply in the United States are composed of two parts: federal and state taxes. Some cities, such as New York City, also have an income tax. There is variety in the detailed tax arrangements in the individual states, but the tax system, at both the federal and state levels, is progressive. The poorest working households receive money from the government through an earned income tax credit. Successively higher-income households pay 10 percent, 15 percent, 25 percent, 28 percent, 33 percent, and 35 percent of each additional dollar earned.

Income Maintenance Programs

Three main types of programs redistribute income by making direct payments (in cash, services, or vouchers) to people in the lower part of the income distribution. They are

- Social security programs
- Unemployment compensation
- Welfare programs

Social Security Programs The main social security program is OASDHI—Old Age, Survivors, Disability, and Health Insurance. Monthly cash payments to retired or disabled workers or their surviving spouses and children are paid for by compulsory payroll taxes on both employers and employees. In 2005, total social security expenditure was budgeted at $550 billion, and the standard monthly social security check for a married couple was a bit more than $1,000.

The other component of social security is Medicare, which provides hospital and health insurance for the elderly and disabled.

Unemployment Compensation To provide an income to unemployed workers, every state has established an unemployment compensation program. Under these programs, a tax is paid that is based on the income of each covered worker and such a worker receives a benefit when he or she becomes unemployed. The details of the benefits vary from state to state.

Welfare Programs The purpose of welfare is to provide incomes for people who do not qualify for social security or unemployment compensation. They are

1. Supplementary Security Income (SSI) program, designed to help the neediest elderly, disabled, and blind people
2. Temporary Assistance for Needy Households (TANF) program, designed to help households that have inadequate financial resources
3. Food Stamp program, designed to help the poorest households obtain a basic diet
4. Medicaid, designed to cover the costs of medical care for households receiving help under the SSI and TANF programs

Subsidized Services

A great deal of redistribution takes place in the United States through the provision of subsidized services—services provided by the government at prices below the cost of production. The taxpayers who consume these goods and services receive a transfer in kind from the taxpayers who do not consume them. The two most important areas in which this form of redistribution takes place are health care and education—both kindergarten through grade 12 and college and university.

In 2005–2006, students enrolled in the University of California system paid annual tuition fees of $6,780. The cost of providing a year's education at the University of California was probably about $20,000. So households with a member enrolled in one of these institutions received a benefit from the government of more than $13,000 a year.

Government provision of health-care services has grown to the scale of private provision. Programs such as Medicaid and Medicare bring high-quality and high-cost health care to millions of people who earn too little to buy such services themselves.

The Scale of Income Redistribution

A household's *market income* tells us what a household earns in the absence of government redistribution. You've seen that market income is *not* the official basis for measuring the distribution of income that we used in Figs. 18.1 through 18.6. The Census Bureau's measure is *money income* (market income plus cash transfers from the government). But market income is the correct starting point for measuring the scale of income redistribution.

We begin with market income and then subtract taxes and add the amounts received in benefits. The result is the distribution of income after taxes and benefits. The data available on benefits exclude the value of subsidized services such as college, so the resulting distribution might understate the total amount of redistribution from the rich to the poor.

Figure 18.10 shows the scale of redistribution in 2001, the most recent year for which the Census Bureau has provided these data. In part (a), the blue Lorenz curve describes the market distribution of income and the green Lorenz curve shows the distribution of income after all taxes and benefits, including Medicaid and Medicare benefits. (The Lorenz curve based on money income in Fig. 18.3 lies between the two curves in Fig. 18.10.)

The distribution after taxes and benefits is less unequal than is the market distribution. The lowest 20 percent of households received only 0.9 percent of market income but 4.6 percent of income after taxes and benefits. The highest 20 percent of households received 55.6 percent of market income, but only 46.7 percent of income after taxes and benefits.

Figure 18.10(b) highlights the percentage of total income redistributed among the five groups. The share of total income received by the lowest 60 percent of households increased. The share received by the fourth quintile barely changed. And the share received by the highest quintile fell by 8.9 percent.

FIGURE 18.10 Income Redistribution

myeconlab

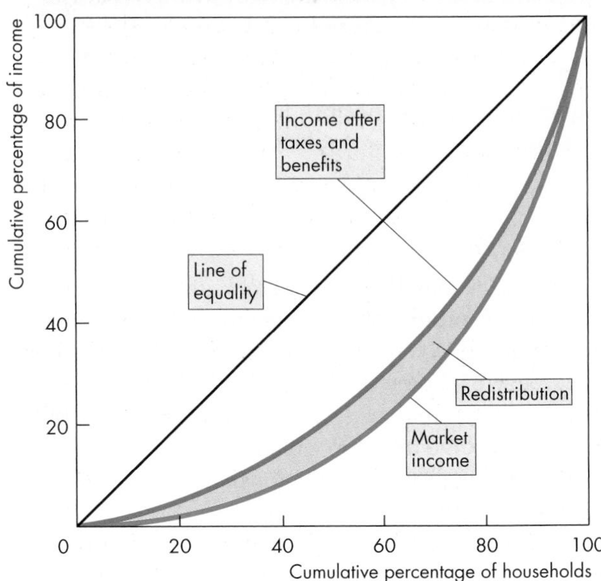

(a) Income distribution before and after redistribution

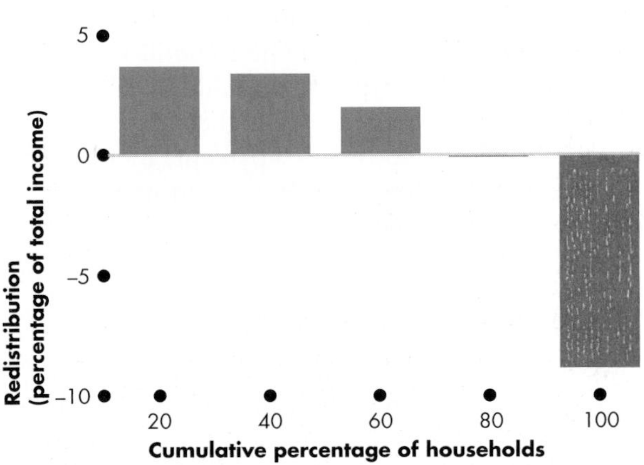

(b) The scale of redistribution

In 2001, the 20 percent of households with the lowest incomes received net benefits that increased their share of total income from 0.9 percent of market income to 4.6 percent after taxes and benefits. The 20 percent of households with the highest incomes paid taxes that decreased their share from 55.6 percent of market income to 46.7 percent of income after taxes and benefits.

Source of data: U.S. Bureau of the Census, "Money Income in the United States: 2001," *Current Population Reports*, P-60-200 (Washington, DC: U.S. Government Printing Office, 2003).

The Big Tradeoff

The redistribution of income creates what has been called the **big tradeoff**, a tradeoff between equity and efficiency. The big tradeoff arises because redistribution uses scarce resources and weakens incentives.

A dollar collected from a rich person does not translate into a dollar received by a poor person. Some of it gets used up in the process of redistribution. Tax-collecting agencies such as the Internal Revenue Service and welfare-administering agencies (as well as tax accountants and lawyers) use skilled labor, computers, and other scarce resources to do their work. The bigger the scale of redistribution, the greater is the opportunity cost of administering it.

But the cost of collecting taxes and making welfare payments is a small part of the total cost of redistribution. A bigger cost arises from the inefficiency (deadweight loss) of taxes and benefits. Greater equality can be achieved only by taxing productive activities such as work and saving. Taxing people's income from their work and saving lowers the after-tax income they receive. This lower after-tax income makes them work and save less, which in turn results in smaller output and less consumption not only for the rich who pay the taxes but also for the poor who receive the benefits.

It is not only taxpayers who face weaker incentives to work. Benefit recipients also face weaker incentives. In fact, under the welfare arrangements that prevailed before the 1996 reforms, the weakest incentives to work were those faced by households that benefited from welfare. When a welfare recipient got a job, benefits were withdrawn and eligibility for programs such as Medicaid ended, so the household in effect paid a tax of more than 100 percent on its earnings. This arrangement locked poor households in a welfare trap.

So the agencies that determine the scale and methods of income redistribution must pay close attention to the incentive effects of taxes and benefits. Let's close this chapter by looking at one way in which lawmakers are tackling the big tradeoff today.

A Major Welfare Challenge Young women who have not completed high school, have a child (or children), live without a partner, and more likely are black or Hispanic than white are among the poorest people in the United States today. They and their children present a major welfare challenge.

First, their numbers are large. In 2005, there were 14 million single-mother families. This number is 12 percent of families. In 1997 (the most recent year with census data), single mothers were owed $26 billion in child support. Of this amount, $10 billion was not paid and 30 percent of the women received no support from their children's fathers.

The long-term solution to the problem of these people is education and job training—acquiring human capital. The short-term solutions are enforcing child support payments by absent fathers and former spouses and providing welfare.

Welfare must be designed to minimize the disincentive to pursue the long-term goal of becoming self-supporting. The current welfare program in the United States tries to walk this fine line.

Passed in 1996, the Personal Responsibility and Work Opportunities Reconciliation Act strengthened the Office of Child Support Enforcement and increased the penalties for nonpayment of support. The act also created the Temporary Assistance for Needy Households (TANF) program. TANF is a block grant paid to the states, which administer payments to individuals. It is not an open-ended entitlement program. An adult member of a household that is receiving assistance must either work or perform community service, and there is a five-year limit for assistance.

REVIEW QUIZ

1 How do governments in the United States redistribute income?
2 Describe the scale of redistribution in the United States.
3 What is one of the major welfare challenges today and how is it being tackled in the United States?

myeconlab **Study Plan 18.3**

We've examined economic inequality in the United States, and we've seen how inequality arises. And we've seen that inequality has been increasing. *Reading Between the Lines* on pp. 432–433 looks at the increasing inequality during the 1980s and 1990s.

The next chapter studies some problems for the market economy that arise from uncertainty and incomplete information. But unlike the cases we studied in Chapters 15 and 16, the market does a good job of coping with the problems, as you're about to discover.

READING BETWEEN THE LINES

Trends in Inequality

http://www.nytimes.com

Income Gap in New York Is Called Nation's Highest

January 27, 2006

New York continues to have the highest income disparity between rich and poor of any state, according to a new study by two national economic policy groups.

The average income of the richest fifth of New York State families is 8.1 times the average income of the poorest fifth, according to the study, which drew from census data compiled by the Economic Policy Institute and the Center on Budget and Policy Priorities, two liberal research groups based in Washington.

Nationwide, families in the top fifth made 7.3 times more than those in the bottom fifth. While New York has been at the top of the income gap list for several years, it ranked 11th in the early 1980s, when the difference between the average income of the top and bottom fifths was 5.6 times. . . .

The average income of families in the top 20 percent in New York State was $130,431, compared with $16,076 for the bottom fifth, according to data in the report.

From 1980–1982 to 2001–2003, the periods examined in the study, average incomes grew by 18.9 percent nationwide, or $2,664, for the poorest families and 58.5 percent, or $45,101, for families among the top fifth of income earners.

"The biggest thing is the decline in wages for the low and moderate income people," said Elizabeth McNichol, an author of the report. "Part of it is large periods of higher than average unemployment, globalization—jobs going overseas—the shift from manufacturing jobs to lower paying service sector jobs, immigration, the weakening of unions, and the fact that the federal minimum wage has been declining relative to inflation." . . .

Essence of the Story

- In 2001–2003, the average income of families in the top 20 percent in New York State was 8.1 times the average income of the bottom 20 percent.
- In 1980–1982, the average income of families in the top 20 percent in New York State was 5.6 times the average income of the bottom 20 percent.
- In 2001–2003, the average income of families in the top 20 percent in the United States was 7.3 times the average income of the bottom 20 percent.
- From 1980–1982 to 2001–2003, average incomes grew by 58.5 percent for families in the top 20 percent and by 18.9 percent for families in the bottom 20 percent.
- Several factors contributed to the increased inequality.

Economic Analysis

- Between 1980–1982 and 2001–2003, according to the study reported in the article, the income share of the highest 20 percent of New York families increased from 5.6 times to 8.1 times that of the lowest 20 percent.
- Elizabeth McNichol lists some factors that she says caused these changes.
- But these factors have a deeper cause that we can understand as a consequence of changes in demand and supply in the markets for low-skilled and high-skilled labor during the 1980s and 1990s.
- In Fig. 1, the demand curve for low-skilled labor in 1979 is D_{79} and the supply curve of low-skilled labor is S_{79}. By 2000, demand increased to D_{00} and supply increased to S_{00}.
- Because supply increased by more than demand, the quantity of low-skilled labor increased but the wage rate fell.
- The supply of low-skilled labor increased partly because of immigration. The demand for low-skilled labor increased but by less than supply for the reason that we identify in the chapter: New technologies are a substitute for low-skilled labor.
- In Fig. 2, the demand curve for high-skilled labor in 1979 is D_{79} and the supply curve of high-skilled labor is S_{79}. By 2000, demand increased to D_{00} and supply increased to S_{00}.
- Because demand increased by more than supply, the quantity of high-skilled labor increased and the wage rate rose.
- The supply of high-skilled labor increased slowly because the new technologies require a higher level of education to complement them.
- The demand for high-skilled labor increased by a large amount because the new technologies that changed the structure of the economy increased the marginal revenue product of highly educated workers.

You're the Voter

- Do you think the government needs to take any special actions to deal with the widening income gap?
- Describe the actions you recommend and explain their likely effects or explain why you think no actions are needed and what you think will happen to the wage gap over the next ten years.

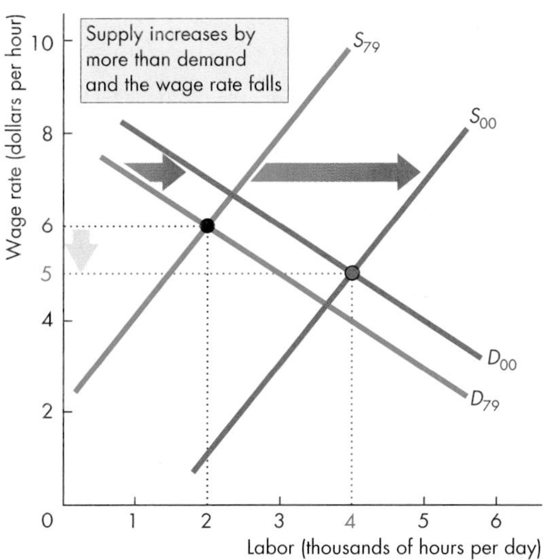

Figure 1 A market for low-skilled labor

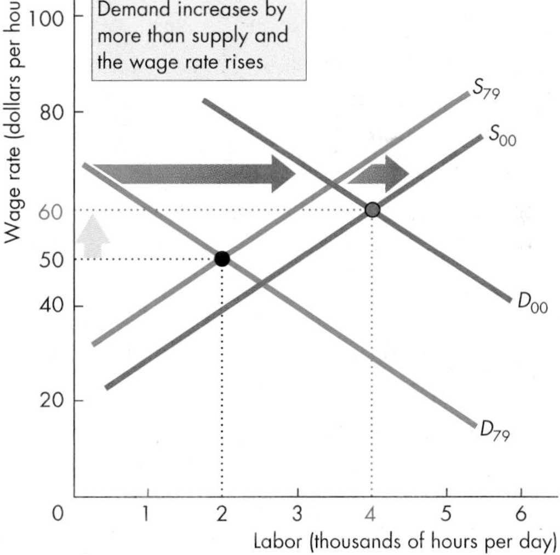

Figure 2 A market for high-skilled labor

SUMMARY

Key Points

Measuring Economic Inequality (pp. 418–423)

- In 2005, the mode money income was $13,000 a year, the median money income was $46,326, and the mean money income was $63,344.
- The income distribution is positively skewed.
- In 2005, the poorest 20 percent of households received 3.4 percent of total income and the wealthiest 20 percent received 50.4 percent of total income.
- Wealth is distributed more unequally than income because the wealth data exclude the value of human capital.
- Since 1970, the distribution of income has become more unequal.
- Education, type of household, age of householder, and race all influence household income.

The Sources of Economic Inequality (pp. 424–428)

- Inequality arises from differences in human capital.
- Trends in the distribution of human capital that arise from technological change and globalization can explain some of the trend in increased inequality.
- Inequality might arise from discrimination.
- Inequality between men and women might arise from differences in the degree of specialization.
- Intergenerational transfers of wealth lead to increased inequality because people can't inherit debts and assortative mating tends to concentrate wealth.

Income Redistribution (pp. 429–431)

- Governments redistribute income through progressive income taxes, income maintenance programs, and subsidized services.
- Redistribution increases the share of total income received by the lowest 60 percent of households and decreases the share of total income received by the highest quintile. The share of the fourth quintile barely changes.
- Because the redistribution of income weakens incentives, it creates a tradeoff between equity and efficiency.
- Effective redistribution seeks to support the long-term solution to low income, which is education and job training—acquiring human capital.

Key Figures

Key Terms

Big tradeoff, 430
Gini ratio, 421
Lorenz curve, 419
Market income, 418
Money income, 418
Poverty, 423
Progressive income tax, 429
Proportional income tax, 429
Regressive income tax, 429
Wealth, 420

PROBLEMS

myeconlab Tests, Study Plan, Solutions*

1. The table shows money income shares in the United States in 1967.

Households	Money income (percent of total)
Lowest 20%	4.0
Second 20%	10.8
Third 20%	17.3
Fourth 20%	24.2
Highest 20%	43.7

   a. What is money income?
   b. Draw a Lorenz curve for the United States in 1967 and compare it with the Lorenz curve in 2005 shown in Fig. 18.3.
   c. Was U.S. money income distributed more equally or less equally in 2005 than it was in 1967?
   d. Can you think of some reasons for the differences in the distribution of money income in the United States in 1967 and 2005?

2. The following figure shows the demand for and supply of low-skilled labor.

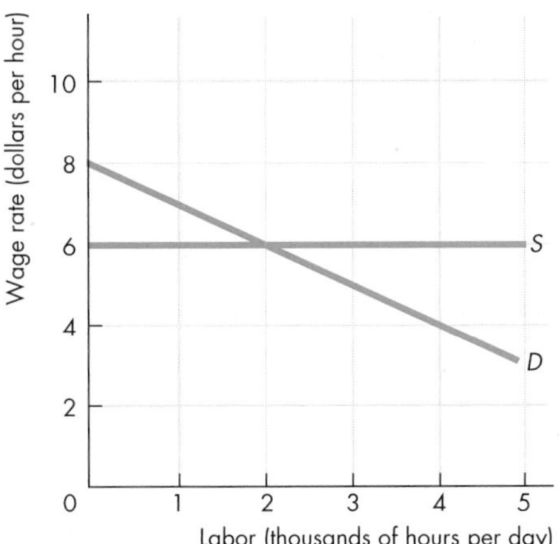

The marginal revenue product of a high-skilled worker is $8 an hour greater than that of a low-skilled worker. (The marginal revenue product at each employment level is $8 greater than that of a low-skilled worker.) The cost of acquiring the skill adds $6 an hour to the wage that must be offered to attract high-skilled labor.

   a. What is the wage rate of low-skilled labor?
   b. What is the quantity of low-skilled labor employed?
   c. What is the wage rate of high-skilled labor?
   d. What is the quantity of high-skilled labor employed?
   e. Why does the wage rate of a high-skilled worker exceed that of a low-skilled worker by exactly the cost of acquiring the skill?

3. The following figure shows the demand for and supply of workers who are discriminated against. Suppose that there is a group of workers in the same industry who are not discriminated against, and their marginal revenue product is perceived to be twice the marginal revenue product of the workers who are discriminated against. Suppose also that the supply of workers who do not face discrimination is 2,000 hours per day less at each wage rate.

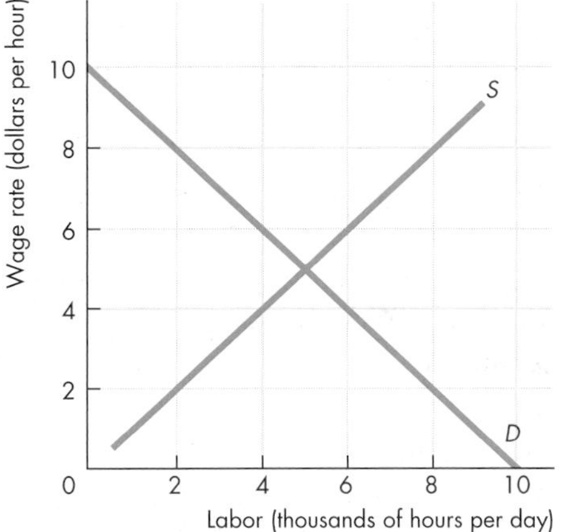

   a. What is the wage rate of a worker who is discriminated against?
   b. What is the wage rate of a worker who does not face discrimination?
   c. What is the quantity of workers employed who are discriminated against?
   d. What is the quantity of workers employed who do not face discrimination?

4. The table shows three tax payments schemes.

Before-tax income (dollars)	Plan A tax (dollars)	Plan B tax (dollars)	Plan C tax (dollars)
10,000	1,000	1,000	2,000
20,000	2,000	4,000	2,000
30,000	3,000	9,000	2,000

*Solutions to odd-numbered problems are provided.

Which tax payment plan

a. Is proportional?
b. Is regressive?
c. Is progressive?
d. Increases inequality?
e. Lessens inequality?
f. Has no effect on inequality?

5. The table shows the distribution of market income in the United States in 2005.

Households	Market income (percent of total)
Lowest 20%	1.1
Second 20%	7.1
Third 20%	13.9
Fourth 20%	22.8
Highest 20%	55.1

a. What is the definition of market income?
b. Draw the Lorenz curve for the distribution of market income.
c. Compare the distribution of market income with the distribution of money income shown in Fig. 18.3. Which distribution is more unequal and why?

6. Use the information provided in problem 5 and in Fig. 18.3.
a. What is the percentage of total income that is redistributed from the highest income group?
b. What are the percentages of total income that are redistributed to the lower income groups?
c. Describe the effects of increasing the amount of income redistribution in the United States to the point at which the lowest income group receives 15 percent of total income and the highest income group receives 30 percent of total income.

7. Incomes in China and India are a small fraction of incomes in the United States. But incomes in China and India are growing at more than twice the rate of those in the United States. Given this information, what can you say about
a. Changes in inequality between people in China and India and people in the United States?
b. The world Lorenz curve and Gini ratio?

CRITICAL THINKING

1. After you have studied *Reading Between the Lines* on pp. 432–433, answer the following questions.
a. What are the broad facts reported in the news article about the gap in the incomes of the highest and lowest 20 percent?
b. List the factors that contributed to the rising income gap according to Elizabeth McNichol. Of these factors, which do you think made the biggest contribution?
c. Of the factors that contributed to the rising income gap according to Elizabeth McNichol, which do you think account for the national trend and which account for the more extreme changes in New York State?
d. What policy issues are raised by the information reported in the news article?
e. How, if at all, do you think the tax system, the welfare system, or the education system should be changed to influence the distribution of income?

WEB ACTIVITIES

myeconlab **Links to Web sites**

1. Obtain data on income distribution and poverty for your own state. Then
a. Describe the main facts about the income distribution and poverty in your state.
b. Compare the situation in your state with that in the rest of the country.
c. Why do you think your state is performing better or worse (as the case may be) than the nation as a whole?

2. Download the World Bank's Deininger and Squire Data Set on income distribution in a large number of countries.
a. Which country in the data set has the most unequal distribution?
b. Which country in the data set has the most equal distribution?
c. Can you think of reasons that might explain the differences in income distribution in the two countries you've identified?

CHAPTER 19

Uncertainty and Information

Lotteries and Lemons

Life is like a lottery. You work hard in school, but what will the payoff be? Will you get an interesting, high-paying job or a miserable, low-paying one? You set up a summer business and work hard at it. But will you make enough income to keep you in school next year or will you get wiped out? How do people make a decision when they don't know what its consequences will be?

As you drive across an intersection on a green light, you see a car on your left that's still moving. Will it stop or will it run the red light? You buy insurance against such a risk, and insurance companies gain from your business. Why are we willing to buy insurance at prices that leave insurance companies with a gain?

Buying a new car—or a used car—is fun, but it's also scary. You could get stuck with a lemon. Just about every complicated product you buy could be defective. How do car dealers and retailers induce us to buy goods that might turn out to be lemons?

Most people with funds to invest hold a diversity of assets rather than the one asset they think will have the highest return. Why does it pay to diversify?

Although markets do a good job in helping people to use scarce resources efficiently, there are impediments to efficiency. Can markets lead to an efficient outcome when there is uncertainty and incomplete information?

In this chapter, we answer questions such as these. And in *Reading Between the Lines* at the end of the chapter, we look at one way in which markets help you to get the right job and the problem that arises if grades in high schools, colleges, and universities are inflated.

After studying this chapter, you will be able to

- Explain how people make decisions when they are uncertain about the consequences
- Explain why people buy insurance and how insurance companies make a profit
- Explain why buyers search
- Explain how markets cope with private information
- Explain how people use financial markets to lower risk
- Explain how the presence of uncertainty and incomplete information influence the ability of markets to achieve an efficient allocation of resources

Uncertainty and Risk

Although we live in an uncertain world, we rarely ask what uncertainty is. Yet to explain how we make decisions and do business with each other in an uncertain world, we need to think more deeply about uncertainty. What exactly is uncertainty? We also live in a risky world. Is risk the same as uncertainty? Let's begin by defining uncertainty and risk and distinguishing between them.

Uncertainty is a situation in which more than one event may occur but we don't know which one. For example, when farmers plant their crops, they are uncertain about the weather during the growing season.

In ordinary speech, risk is the probability of incurring a loss (or some other misfortune). In economics, **risk** is a situation in which more than one outcome may occur and the *probability* of each possible outcome can be estimated. A *probability* is a number between 0 and 1 that measures the chance of some possible event occurring. A 0 probability means that the event will not happen. A probability of 1 means that the event will occur for sure—with certainty. A probability of 0.5 means that the event is just as likely to occur as not. An example is the probability of a tossed coin falling heads. In a large number of tosses, about half of them will be heads and the other half tails.

Sometimes, probabilities can be measured. For example, the probability that a tossed coin will come down heads is based on the fact that in a large number of tosses, half are heads and half are tails; the probability that an automobile in Chicago in 2008 will be involved in an accident can be estimated by using police and insurance records of previous accidents; the probability that you will win a lottery can be estimated by dividing the number of tickets you have bought by the total number of tickets bought.

Some situations cannot be described by using probabilities based on past observed events. These situations might be unique events, such as the introduction of a new product. How much will sell and at what price? Because the product is new, there is no previous experience on which to base a probability. But the questions can be answered by looking at past experience with *similar* new products, supported by some judgments. Such judgments are called *subjective probabilities.*

Regardless of whether the probability of some event occurring is based on actual data or judgments—or even guesses—we can use probability to study the way in which people make decisions in the face of uncertainty. The first step in doing this is to describe how people assess the cost of risk.

Measuring the Cost of Risk

Some people are more willing to bear risk than others, but almost everyone prefers less risk to more, other things remaining the same. We measure people's attitudes toward risk by using their utility of wealth schedules and curves. The **utility of wealth** is the amount of utility a person attaches to a given amount of wealth. The greater a person's wealth, other things remaining the same, the higher is the person's total utility. Greater wealth brings higher total utility, but as wealth increases, each additional unit of wealth increases total utility by a smaller amount. That is, the *marginal utility of wealth diminishes.*

Figure 19.1 sets out Tania's utility of wealth schedule and curve. Each point *A* through *E* on Tania's utility of wealth curve corresponds to the row of the table identified by the same letter. You can see that as her wealth increases, so does her total utility of wealth. You can also see that her marginal utility of wealth diminishes. When wealth increases from $3,000 to $6,000, total utility increases by 20 units, but when wealth increases by a further $3,000 to $9,000, total utility increases by only 10 units.

We can use Tania's utility of wealth to measure her cost of risk. Let's see how Tania evaluates two summer jobs that involve different amounts of risk.

One job, working as a painter, pays enough for her to save $5,000 by the end of the summer. There is no uncertainty about the income from this job and hence no risk. If Tania takes this job, by the end of the summer her wealth will be $5,000. The other job, working as a telemarketer selling subscriptions to a magazine, is risky. If she takes this job, her wealth at the end of the summer depends entirely on her success at selling. She might be a good salesperson or a poor one. A good salesperson makes $9,000 in a summer, and a poor one makes $3,000. Tania has never tried telemarketing, so she doesn't know how successful she'll be. She assumes that she has an equal chance—a probability of 0.5—of making either $3,000 or $9,000. Which outcome does Tania prefer: $5,000 for sure from the painting job or a 50

FIGURE 19.1 The Utility of Wealth

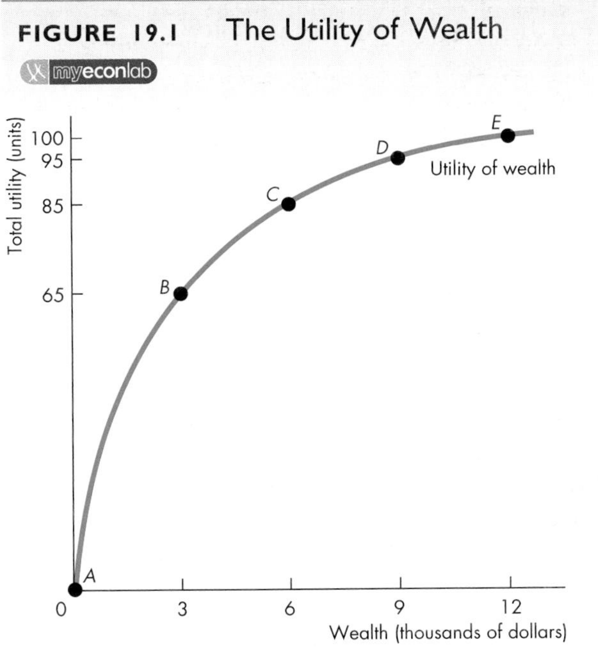

	Wealth (thousands of dollars)	Total utility (units)	Marginal utility (units)
A	0	0	
			65
B	3	65	
			20
C	6	85	
			10
D	9	95	
			5
E	12	100	

The table shows Tania's utility of wealth schedule, and the figure shows her utility of wealth curve. Utility increases as wealth increases, but the marginal utility of wealth diminishes.

percent chance of either $3,000 or $9,000 from the telemarketing job?

When there is uncertainty, people do not know the *actual* utility they will get from taking a particular action. But it is possible to calculate the utility they *expect* to get. **Expected utility** is the average utility arising from all possible outcomes. So, to choose her summer job, Tania calculates the expected utility from each job. Figure 19.2 shows how she does this.

If Tania takes the painting job, she has $5,000 of wealth and 80 units of utility. There is no uncertainty, so her expected utility equals her actual utility—80 units. But suppose she takes the telemarketing job.

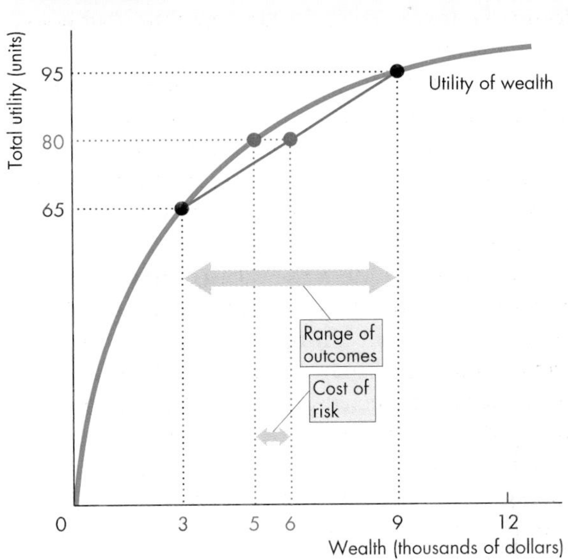

If Tania's wealth is $5,000 and she bears no risk, her utility is 80 units. If she bears an equal probability of having $9,000 with a utility of 95 or $3,000 with a utility of 65, her expected wealth is $6,000. But her expected utility is 80 units—the same as with $5,000 and no uncertainty. Tania is indifferent between these two alternatives. Tania's extra $1,000 of expected wealth is just enough to offset her extra risk.

If she makes $9,000, her utility is 95 units, and if she makes $3,000, her utility is 65 units. Tania's *expected income* is the average of these two outcomes and is $6,000—($9,000 × 0.5) + ($3,000 × 0.5). This average is called a *weighted average*, the weights being the probabilities of each outcome (both 0.5 in this case). Tania's *expected utility* is the average of these two possible total utilities and is 80 units—(95 × 0.5) + (65 × 0.5).

Tania chooses the job that maximizes her expected utility. In this case, the two alternatives give the same expected utility—80 units—so she is indifferent between them. She is equally likely to take either job. The difference between Tania's expected wealth of $6,000 from the risky job and $5,000 from the no-risk job—$1,000—is just large enough to offset the additional risk that Tania bears.

The calculations that we've just done enable us to measure Tania's cost of risk. The cost of risk is the amount by which expected wealth must be increased to give the same expected utility as a no-risk situation. In Tania's case, the cost of the risk arising from an uncertain income of $3,000 or $9,000 is $1,000.

If the amount Tania can make from painting remains at $5,000 and the expected income from telemarketing also remains constant while its range of uncertainty increases, Tania will take the painting job. To see this conclusion, suppose that good telemarketers make $12,000 and poor ones make nothing. The average income from telemarketing is unchanged at $6,000, but the range of uncertainty has increased. The table in Fig. 19.1 shows that Tania gets 100 units of utility from a wealth of $12,000 and zero units of utility from a wealth of zero. So in this case, Tania's expected utility from telemarketing is 50 units—(100 × 0.5) + (0 × 0.5). Because the expected utility from telemarketing is now less than that from painting, she chooses painting.

Risk Aversion and Risk Neutrality

There is a huge difference between Mike Holmgren, head coach of the Seattle Seahawks, who favors a cautious running game, and Peyton Manning, quarterback of the Indianapolis Colts, who favors a risky passing game. They have different attitudes toward risk. Mike is more *risk averse* than is Peyton. Tania is also *risk averse*. The shape of the utility of wealth curve tells us about the attitude toward risk—about the person's degree of *risk aversion*. The more rapidly a person's marginal utility of wealth diminishes, the more risk averse that person is. You can see this fact best by considering the case of *risk neutrality*. A risk-neutral person cares only about *expected wealth* and doesn't mind how much uncertainty there is.

Figure 19.3 shows the utility of wealth curve of a risk-neutral person. It is a straight line, and the marginal utility of wealth is constant. If this person has an expected wealth of $6,000, expected utility is 50 units regardless of the range of uncertainty around that average. An equal probability of having $3,000 or $9,000 gives the same expected utility as a certain $6,000. When Tania's risk increased to this range, she needed an extra $1,000. This person does not. Even if the range of risk becomes $0 to $12,000, the risk-neutral person still gets the same expected utility as a certain $6,000 gives. Most real people are risk averse, and their utility of wealth curves look like Tania's. But the case of risk neutrality illustrates the importance and the consequences of the shape of the utility of wealth curve for a person's degree of risk aversion.

FIGURE 19.3 Risk Neutrality

myeconlab

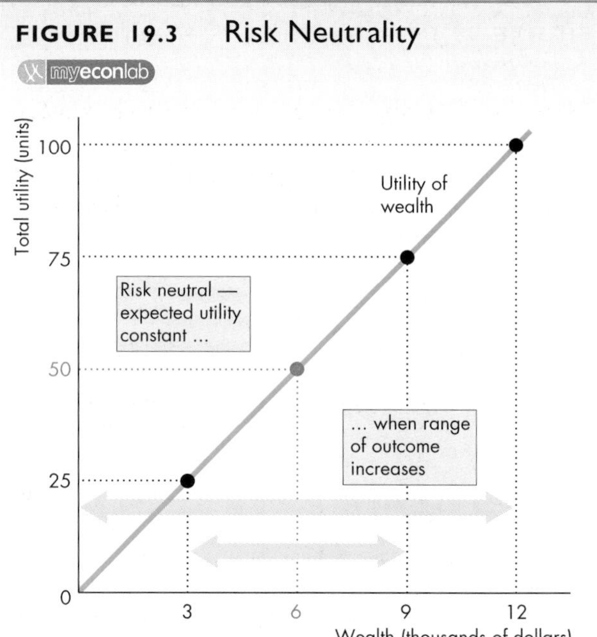

People's dislike of risk implies a diminishing marginal utility of wealth. A (hypothetical) risk-neutral person has a linear utility of wealth curve and a constant marginal utility of wealth. For a risk-neutral person, expected utility does not depend on the range of uncertainty, and the cost of risk is zero.

REVIEW QUIZ

1. How do people make decisions when they are faced with uncertain outcomes? What do they try to achieve?
2. How can we measure the cost of risk?
3. What determines the amount that someone would be willing to pay to avoid risk? Is the cost of risk the same for everyone?
4. What is a risk-neutral person and how much would such a person pay to avoid risk?

myeconlab **Study Plan 19.1**

Most people are risk averse. Let's now see how insurance enables them to reduce the risk they bear.

Insurance

One way of reducing the risk we bear is to buy insurance. How does insurance reduce risk? Why do people buy insurance? And what determines the amount we spend on insurance? Before we answer these questions, let's look at the insurance industry in the United States today.

Insurance Industry in the United States

We spend close to 15 percent of our income, on the average, on private insurance. That's as much as we spend on housing and more than we spend on cars and food. In addition, we buy insurance through our taxes in the form of social security and unemployment insurance. When we buy private insurance, we enter into an agreement with an insurance company to pay an agreed price—called a *premium*—in exchange for benefits to be paid to us if some specified event occurs.

The four main types of insurance we buy are

- Health
- Life
- Property and casualty
- Auto

Health Health insurance reduces the risk of financial loss in the event of illness. It can provide funds to cover both lost earnings and the cost of medical care. Figure 19.4 shows that health insurance premiums were around $660 billion in 2004.

Life Life insurance reduces the risk of financial loss in the event of death. Almost 80 percent of households in the United States have life insurance, and the average amount of coverage is $150,000. Figure 19.4 shows that total life insurance premiums paid in 2004 were more than $630 billion.

Property and Casualty Property and casualty insurance reduces the risk of financial loss in the event of an accident involving damage to persons or property. It includes workers' compensation; fire, earthquake, and professional malpractice insurance; and a host of smaller items. Figure 19.4 shows that we spent $210 billion on these types of insurance in 2004.

FIGURE 19.4 The Insurance Industry

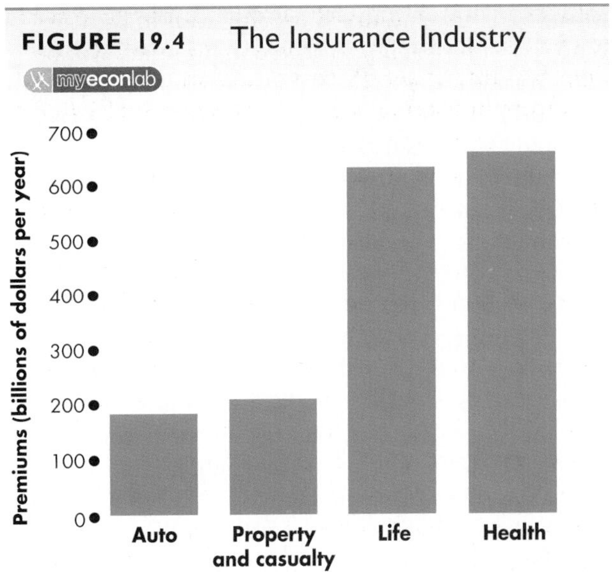

Total expenditure on private insurance was $1.7 trillion in 2004. Most is spent on life insurance and health insurance.

Source of data: U.S. Bureau of the Census, *Statistical Abstract of the United States 2007*, Tables 121, 1206, and 1207.

Auto Auto insurance reduces the risk of financial loss in the event of an auto accident or theft. Figure 19.4 shows that we spent $180 billion on auto insurance in 2004.

How Insurance Works

Insurance works by pooling risks. It is possible and profitable because people are risk averse. The probability of any one person having a serious auto accident is small, but the cost of an accident to the person involved is enormous. For a large population, the probability of one person having an accident is the proportion of the population that does have an accident. Because this probability can be estimated, the total cost of accidents can be predicted. An insurance company can pool the risks of a large population and share the costs. It does so by collecting premiums from everyone and paying out benefits to those who suffer a loss. If the insurance company does its calculations correctly, it collects at least as much in premiums as it pays out in benefits and operating costs.

To see why people buy insurance and why it is profitable, let's consider an example. Dan has the utility of wealth curve shown in Fig. 19.5. He owns a car worth $10,000, and that is his only wealth. If there is no risk of his having an accident, his utility will be 100 units. But there is a 10 percent chance (a probability of 0.1) that he will have an accident within a year. Suppose Dan does not buy insurance. If he does have an accident, his car is worthless, and with no insurance, he has no wealth and no utility. Because the probability of an accident is 0.1, the probability of *not* having an accident is 0.9. Dan's expected wealth, therefore, is $9,000 ($10,000 × 0.9 + $0 × 0.1), and his expected utility is 90 units (100 × 0.9 + 0 × 0.1).

In Fig. 19.5, Dan also gets 90 units of utility if he faces no uncertainty and his wealth is $7,000. For Dan, having $7,000 with no risk is just as good as having $10,000 with a 10 percent chance of losing everything. But Dan would have $7,000 of wealth and bear no risk if he bought $10,000 of auto insurance for $3,000. He would have 90 units of utility and be just as well off insuring against the risk as bearing it. If Dan bought auto insurance for less than $3,000, his total utility would rise. So Dan has a demand for auto insurance at premiums less than $3,000 per $10,000 of coverage.

If there are lots of people like Dan, an insurance company can share their risks. Sharing risks is called *risk pooling*. To pool the risks of Dan and everyone like him, an insurance company agrees to pay each person who has an accident $10,000. The company pays out $10,000 to one tenth of the people insured, or an average of $1,000 per insured person. This amount is the insurance company's minimum premium for such insurance. It is less than the value of insurance to Dan because Dan is risk averse. He is willing to pay something to reduce the risk he bears.

If the insurance company's operating expenses are a further $1,000 and it offers insurance for $2,000, the company covers all its costs—the amounts paid out to policyholders for their losses plus the company's operating expenses. Dan and all the other people like him maximize utility by buying insurance.

FIGURE 19.5 The Gains from Insurance

myeconlab

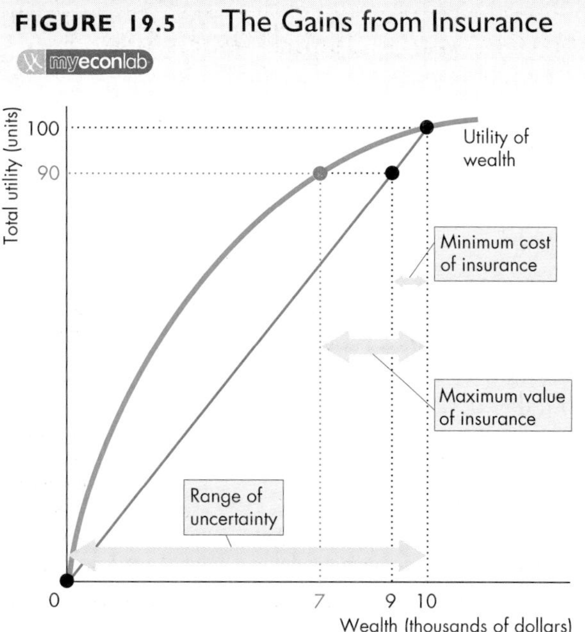

Dan has a car valued at $10,000 that gives him a utility of 100 units, but there is a 0.1 probability that he will have an accident, making his car worthless (wealth and utility equal to zero). With no insurance, his expected wealth is $9,000 and his expected utility is 90 units. His guaranteed wealth is $7,000. Dan will pay up to $3,000 for insurance. If an insurance company can offer Dan insurance for $1,000, there is a potential gain from insurance for both Dan and the insurance company.

REVIEW QUIZ

1. What types of insurance do we buy and how large a percentage of our incomes do we spend on insurance (on the average)?
2. How does insurance work? How can people avoid unwanted outcomes by insuring against them?
3. How can an insurance company offer people a deal worth taking? Why don't the amounts paid in by insurers only just cover the amounts paid out by insurance companies to claimants?

myeconlab **Study Plan 19.2**

Much of the uncertainty that we face arises from ignorance. We just don't know all the things we could benefit from knowing. But knowledge or information is not free. And government intervention is of little use in dealing with this problem. Governments usually are even less well informed than buyers and sellers. Faced with incomplete information, we must make decisions about how much information to acquire. Let's now study the choices we make about obtaining information and how markets cope with incomplete information.

Information

We spend a huge quantity of our scarce resources on economic information. **Economic information** includes data on the prices, quantities, and qualities of goods and services and factors of production.

In the models of perfect competition, monopoly, and monopolistic competition, information is free. Everyone has all the information he or she needs. Households are completely informed about the prices of the goods and services they buy and the factors of production they sell. Similarly, firms are completely informed about consumers' preferences and about the prices and products of other firms.

In contrast, information is scarce in the real world. If it were not, we wouldn't need *The Wall Street Journal* and CNN. And we wouldn't need to shop around for bargains or spend time looking for a job. The opportunity cost of economic information—the cost of acquiring information on prices, quantities, and qualities of goods and services and factors of production—is called **information cost.**

The fact that many economic models ignore information costs does not make these models useless. They give us insights into the forces generating trends in prices and quantities over periods long enough for information limits not to be important. But information is the essence of some markets and to understand them, we must take information problems into account. Let's look at some of the consequences of information cost.

Searching for Price Information

When many firms sell the same good or service, there is a range of prices and buyers want to find the lowest price. But searching takes time and is costly. So buyers must balance the expected gain from further search against the cost of further search. To perform this balancing act, buyers use a decision rule called the *optimal-search rule*—or *optimal-stopping rule.* The optimal-search rule is

- Search for a lower price until the expected marginal benefit of additional search equals the marginal cost of search.
- When the expected marginal benefit from additional search is less than or equal to the marginal cost of search, stop searching and buy.

To implement the optimal-search rule, each buyer chooses her or his own reservation price. The buyer's **reservation price** is the highest price that the buyer is willing to pay for a good. The buyer will continue to search for a lower price if the lowest price so far found exceeds the reservation price but will stop searching and buy if the lowest price found is less than or equal to the reservation price. At the buyer's reservation price, the expected marginal benefit of search equals the marginal cost of search.

Figure 19.6 illustrates the optimal-search rule. Suppose you've decided to buy a used Mazda Miata. Your marginal cost of search is $\$C$ per dealer visited and is shown by the horizontal red line in the figure. This cost includes the value of your time, which is the amount that you could have earned by working instead of cruising around used car lots, and the amount spent on transportation and advice. Your expected marginal benefit from visiting one more

FIGURE 19.6 Optimal-Search Rule

myeconlab

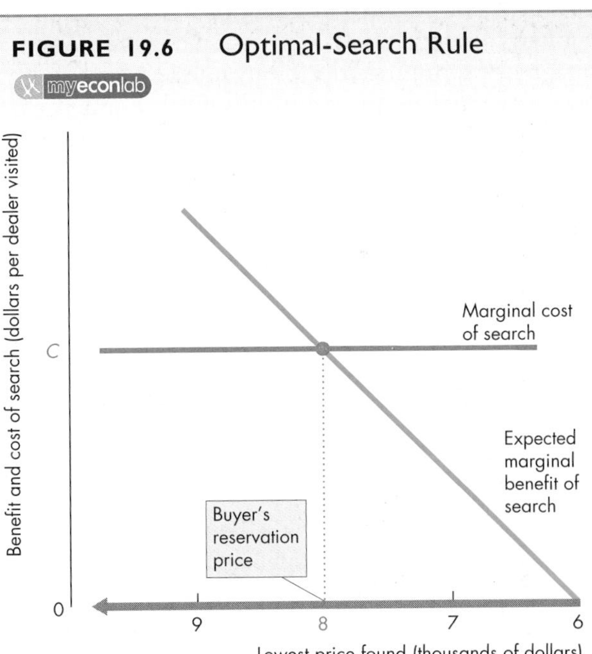

The marginal cost of search is constant at $C. As the lowest price found (measured from right to left on the horizontal axis) declines, the expected marginal benefit of further search diminishes. The lowest price found at which the marginal cost equals the expected marginal benefit is the reservation price. The optimal-search rule is to search until the reservation price is found and then buy at that lowest found price.

dealer depends on the lowest price that you've found. The lower the price you've already found, the smaller is your expected marginal benefit from visiting one more dealer, as shown by the blue curve in the figure.

The price at which expected marginal benefit equals marginal cost is your reservation price—$8,000 in Fig. 19.4. If you find a price equal to or below your reservation price, you stop searching and buy. If you find a price above your reservation price, you continue to search for a lower price. Individual shoppers differ in their marginal cost of search and so have different reservation prices. As a result, identical items can be found selling for a range of prices.

A Real Car Shopping Trip Real car shoppers are confronted with a much bigger problem than the one we've just studied. There are many more dimensions of the car they are looking for than its price. They could spend almost forever gathering information about the alternatives. But at some point in their search, they decide they've done enough looking and make a decision to buy. Your imaginary shopping trip to buy a used Mazda Miata rationalizes their decision. Real shoppers think, "The benefit I expect from further search is insufficient to make it worth going on with the process." They don't do the calculations we've just done—at least, not explicitly—but their actions can be explained by those calculations.

REVIEW QUIZ

1. What types of economic information do people find useful?
2. Why is economic information scarce and how do people economize on its use?
3. What is the buyer's reservation price?
4. What determines the opportunity cost of economic information?
5. How do you decide to keep searching for an item, rather than stop searching?
6. How do you decide when to stop searching for a lower-priced item to buy?

myeconlab **Study Plan 19.3**

Sometimes, information is simply not available to either a buyer or a seller. The next section examines three examples of this type of situation.

Private Information

So far we have looked at situations in which, with the expenditure of enough effort, information is available to everyone. But not all situations are like this. For example, someone might have private information. **Private information** is information that is available to one person but is too costly for anyone else to obtain.

Private information affects many economic transactions. One is your knowledge about your driving. You know much more than your auto insurance company does about how carefully and defensively you drive. Another is your knowledge about your work effort. You know far more than your employer about how hard you work. Yet another is your knowledge about the quality of your car. You know whether it's a lemon. But the person to whom you are about to sell it does not and can't find out until after he or she has purchased it from you.

Private information creates two problems:

1. Moral hazard
2. Adverse selection

Moral hazard exists when one of the parties to an agreement has an incentive *after the agreement is made* to act in a manner that brings additional benefits to himself or herself at the expense of the other party. Moral hazard arises because it is too costly for the injured party to monitor the actions of the advantaged party. For example, Jackie hires Mitch as a salesperson and pays him a fixed wage regardless of his sales. Mitch faces a moral hazard. He has an incentive to put in the least possible effort, benefiting himself and lowering Jackie's profits. For this reason, salespeople are usually paid by a formula that makes their income higher, the greater is the volume (or value) of their sales.

Adverse selection is the tendency for people to enter into agreements in which they can use their private information to their own advantage and to the disadvantage of the less informed party. For example, if Jackie offers salespeople a fixed wage, she will attract lazy salespeople. Hardworking salespeople will prefer *not* to work for Jackie because they can earn more by working for someone who pays by results. The fixed-wage contract adversely selects those with private information (knowledge about their work habits) who can use that knowledge to their own advantage and to the disadvantage of the other party.

A variety of devices have evolved that enable markets to function in the face of moral hazard and adverse selection. We've just seen one, the use of incentive payments for salespeople. Let's look at some more and also see how moral hazard and adverse selection influence three real-world markets:

- The market for used cars
- The market for loans
- The market for insurance

The Market for Used Cars

When a person buys a car, it might turn out to be a lemon. If the car is a lemon, it is worth less to the buyer and to everyone else than if it has no defects. Does the used car market have two prices reflecting these two values—a low price for lemons and a higher price for cars without defects? It does not. To see why, let's look at a used car market, first with no dealer warranties and second with warranties.

Used Cars Without Warranties To make the points as clearly as possible, we'll make some extreme assumptions. There are just two kinds of cars: lemons and those without defects. A lemon is worth $1,000 to both its current owner and anyone who buys it. A car without defects is worth $5,000 to both its current owner and potential future owners. Whether a car is a lemon is private information that is available only to the current owner. Buyers of used cars can't tell whether they are buying a lemon until *after* they have bought the car and learned as much about it as its current owner knows. There are no dealer warranties.

Because buyers can't tell the difference between a lemon and a good car, they are willing to pay only one price for a used car. What is that price? Are they willing to pay $5,000, the value of a good car? They are not, because there is at least some probability that they are buying a lemon worth only $1,000. If buyers are not willing to pay $5,000 for a used car, are the owners of good cars willing to sell? They are not, because a good car is worth $5,000 to them, so they hang onto their cars. Only the owners of lemons are willing to sell—as long as the price is $1,000 or higher. But, reason the buyers, if only the owners of lemons are selling, all the used cars available are lemons, so the maximum price worth paying is $1,000. So the market for used cars is a market for lemons, and the price is $1,000.

Moral hazard exists in the car market because sellers have an incentive to claim that lemons are good cars. But, given the assumptions in the above description of the car market, no one believes such claims. *Adverse selection* exists, resulting in only lemons actually being traded. The market for used cars is not working well. Good used cars just don't get bought and sold, but people want to be able to buy and sell good used cars. How can they do so? The answer is by introducing warranties into the market.

Used Cars with Warranties Buyers of used cars can't tell a lemon from a good car, but car dealers sometimes can. For example, they might have regularly serviced the car. They know, therefore, whether they are buying a lemon or a good car and can offer $1,000 for lemons and $5,000 for good cars.[1] But how can they convince buyers that it is worth paying $5,000 for what might be a lemon? The answer is by giving a guarantee in the form of a warranty. The dealer *signals* which cars are good ones and which are lemons. A **signal** is an action taken outside a market that conveys information that can be used by that market. There are many examples of signals, one of which is students' grades. Your grades act as a *signal* to potential employers.

In the case of the used cars, dealers take actions in the market for car repairs that can be used by the market for cars. For each good car sold, the dealer gives a warranty. The dealer agrees to pay the costs of repairing the car if it turns out to have a defect. Cars with a warranty are good; cars without a warranty are lemons.

Why do buyers believe the signal? It is because the cost of sending a false signal is high. A dealer who gives a warranty on a lemon ends up paying the high cost of repairs—and risks gaining a bad reputation. A dealer who gives a warranty only on good cars has no repair costs and a reputation that gets better and better. It pays to send an accurate signal. It is rational, therefore, for buyers to believe the signal. Warranties break the lemon problem and enable the used car market to function with two prices: one for lemons and one for good cars.

[1]In this example, to keep the numbers simple, we'll ignore dealers' profit margins and other costs of doing business and suppose that dealers buy cars for the same price as they sell them. The principles are the same with dealers' profit margins.

The Market for Loans

The market for bank loans is one in which private information plays a crucial role. Let's see how.

The quantity of loans demanded by borrowers depends on the interest rate. The lower the interest rate, the greater is the quantity of loans demanded—the demand curve for loans is downward-sloping. The supply of loans by banks and other lenders depends on the cost of lending. This cost has two parts. One is interest, and this interest cost is determined in the market for bank deposits—the market in which the banks borrow the funds that they lend. The other part of the cost of lending is the cost of bad loans—loans that are not repaid—called the default cost. The interest cost of a loan is the same for all borrowers. The default cost of a loan depends on the quality of the borrower.

Suppose that borrowers fall into two classes: low-risk and high-risk. Low-risk borrowers seldom default on their debts and then only for reasons beyond their control. For example, a firm might borrow to finance a project that fails and be unable to repay the bank. High-risk borrowers take high risks with the money they borrow and frequently default on their loans. For example, a firm might borrow to speculate in high-risk mineral prospecting that has a very small chance of paying off.

If banks can separate borrowers into risk categories, they supply loans to low-risk borrowers at one interest rate and to high-risk borrowers at another, higher interest rate. Real banks do this as much as possible. But they cannot always separate their borrowers. They have no sure way of knowing whether they are lending to a low-risk or a high-risk borrower.

So the banks charge the same interest rate to both low-risk and high-risk borrowers. If they offered loans to everyone at the low-risk interest rate, borrowers would face *moral hazard* and the banks would attract a lot of high-risk borrowers—*adverse selection*. Most borrowers would default, and the banks would incur economic losses. If the banks offered loans to everyone at the high-risk interest rate, most low-risk borrowers, with whom the banks would like to do profitable business, would be unwilling to borrow.

Faced with moral hazard and adverse selection, banks use *signals* to discriminate between borrowers, and they *ration* or limit loans to amounts below the amounts demanded. To restrict the amounts they are willing to lend to borrowers, banks use signals such as length of time in a job, ownership of a home, marital status, age, and business record.

Figure 19.7 shows how the market for loans works in the face of moral hazard and adverse selection. The demand curve for loans is D, and the supply curve is S. The supply curve is horizontal—perfectly elastic supply—because it is assumed that banks have access to a large quantity of funds that have a constant marginal cost of r. With no loan limits, the interest rate is r and the quantity of loans is Q. Because of moral hazard and adverse selection, the banks set loan limits based on signals and restrict the total loans to L. At the interest rate r, there is an excess demand for loans. A bank cannot increase its profit by making more loans because it can't identify the type of borrower taking the loans. Because the signals used mean that more high-risk borrowers are unsatisfied than low-risk borrowers, it is likely that additional loans will be biased toward high-risk borrowers.

FIGURE 19.7 The Market for Loans

myeconlab

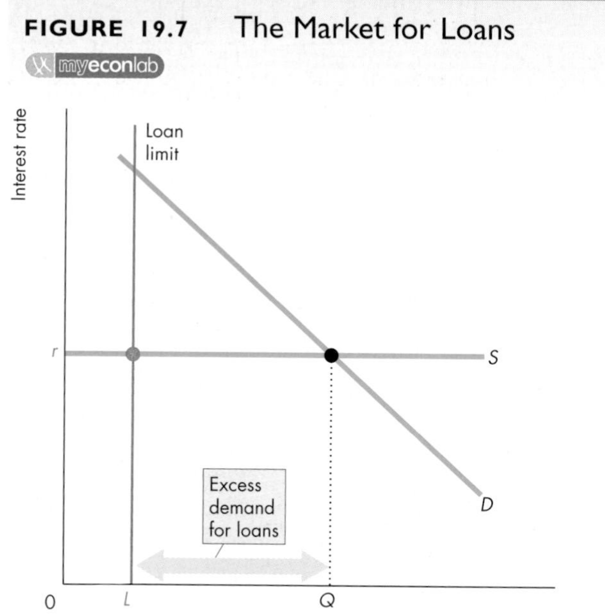

If a bank supplied loans on demand at the going interest rate r, the quantity of loans would be Q, but most of the loans would be taken by high-risk borrowers. Banks use signals to distinguish between low-risk and high-risk borrowers, and they limit the total loans to L and ration them. Banks have no incentive to increase interest rates and increase the quantity of loans because the additional loans would be to high-risk borrowers.

The Market for Insurance

People who buy insurance face moral hazard, and insurance companies face adverse selection. *Moral hazard* arises because a person with insurance against a loss has less incentive than an uninsured person to avoid the loss. For example, a business with fire insurance has less incentive to install a fire alarm or sprinkler system than a business with no fire insurance does. *Adverse selection* arises because people who create greater risks are more likely to buy insurance. For example, a person with a family history of serious illness is more likely to buy health insurance than is a person with a family history of good health.

Insurance companies have an incentive to find ways around the moral hazard and adverse selection problems. By doing so, they can lower premiums for low-risk people and raise premiums for high-risk people. Let's see how insurance companies use signaling to get around these private information problems in the market for auto insurance.

One device used is the "no-claim" bonus. A driver accumulates a no-claim bonus by driving safely and avoiding accidents. The greater the bonus, the greater is the incentive to drive carefully.

Another device used is a deductible. A deductible is the amount of a loss that the insured person agrees to bear. The premium is smaller the greater is the deductible, and the decrease in the premium is more than proportionate to the increase in the deductible. By offering insurance with full coverage—no deductible—on terms that are attractive only to the highest-risk people and by offering coverage with a deductible on more favorable terms that are attractive to other people, insurance companies can do profitable business with everyone. High-risk people choose policies with low deductibles and high premiums; low-risk people choose policies with high deductibles and low premiums.

REVIEW QUIZ

1 How does private information create moral hazard and adverse selection?
2 How do markets for cars use warranties to cope with private information?
3 How do markets for insurance use no-claim bonuses to cope with private information?

myeconlab **Study Plan 19.4**

Managing Risk in Financial Markets

Risk is a dominant feature of markets for stocks and bonds—indeed for any asset whose price fluctuates. One thing people do to cope with risky asset prices is diversify their asset holdings.

Diversification to Lower Risk

The idea that diversification lowers risk is very natural. It is just an application of not putting all one's eggs into the same basket. How exactly does diversification reduce risk? Let's consider an example.

Suppose there are two risky projects that you can undertake. Each involves investing $100,000. The two projects are independent of each other, but they both promise the same degree of risk and return.

On each project, you will either make $50,000 or lose $25,000, and the chance that either of these will happen is 50 percent. The expected return on each project is ($50,000 × 0.5) + (−$25,000 × 0.5), which is $12,500. But because the two projects are completely independent, the outcome of one project in no way influences the outcome of the other.

Undiversified Suppose you risk everything, investing the $100,000 in either Project 1 or Project 2. You will either make $50,000 or lose $25,000. Because the probability of each of these outcomes is 50 percent, your expected return is the average of these two outcomes—an expected return of $12,500. But in this case only one project is chosen, so there is no chance that you will actually make a return of $12,500.

Diversified Now suppose that you put 50 percent of your money into Project 1 and 50 percent into Project 2. (Someone else puts up the other money in these two projects.) Because the two projects are independent, you now have *four* possible returns:

1. Lose $12,500 on each project, and your return is −$25,000.
2. Make $25,000 on Project 1 and lose $12,500 on Project 2, and your return is $12,500.
3. Lose $12,500 on Project 1 and make $25,000 on Project 2, and your return is $12,500.
4. Make $25,000 on each project, and your return is $50,000.

Each of these four possible outcomes is equally probable—each has a 25 percent chance of occurring. So your expected return is $12,500. You have lowered the chance that you will earn $50,000, but you have also lowered the chance that you will lose $25,000. And you have increased the chance that you will actually make your expected return of $12,500. By diversifying your portfolio of assets, you have reduced its riskiness while maintaining an expected return of $12,500.

If you are risk averse—if your utility of wealth curve looks like Tania's, which you studied earlier in this chapter—you'll prefer the diversified portfolio to the one that is not diversified. That is, your *expected utility* with a diversified set of assets is greater.

A common way to diversify is to buy stocks in different corporations. Let's look at the market in which these stocks are traded.

The Stock Market

The prices of the stocks are determined by demand and supply. But demand and supply in the stock market is dominated by one thing: the expected future price. If the price of a stock today is higher than the expected price tomorrow, people will sell the stock today. If the price of a stock today is less than its expected price tomorrow, people will buy the stock today. As a result of such trading, today's price equals tomorrow's expected price, and so today's price embodies all the relevant information that is available about the stock. A market in which the actual price embodies all currently available relevant information is called an **efficient market.**

In an efficient market, it is impossible to forecast changes in price. Why? If your forecast is that the price is going to rise tomorrow, you will buy now. Your action of buying today is an increase in demand today and increases *today's* price. It's true that your action—the action of a single trader—is not going to make much difference to a huge market like the New York Stock Exchange. But if traders in general expect a higher price tomorrow and they all act today on the basis of that expectation, then today's price will rise. It will keep on rising until it reaches the expected future price, because only at that price do traders see no profit in buying more stock today.

There is an apparent paradox about efficient markets. Markets are efficient because people try to make a profit. They seek a profit by buying at a low price and selling at a high price. But the very act of buying and selling to make a profit means that the market price moves to equal its expected future value. When it has done that, no one, not even those who are seeking to profit, can *predictably* make a profit. Every profit opportunity seen by traders leads to an action that produces a price change that removes the profit opportunity for others. The stockbroker in the cartoon is being refreshingly honest with his client in the advice he's offering.

"We're expecting stocks to rally but we don't know which ones and when."

So an efficient market has two features:

1. Its price equals the expected future price and embodies all the available information.
2. No *forecastable* profit opportunities are available.

The key thing to understand about an efficient market such as the stock market is that if something can be anticipated, it will be, and the anticipation of a future event will affect the *current* price of a stock.

REVIEW QUIZ

1. How does diversification lower risk and how does it affect the expected rate of return?
2. What does it mean to say that the stock market is efficient? Is the term "efficient" being used in the normal way?

myeconlab **Study Plan 19.5**

Uncertainty, Information, and the Invisible Hand

A recurring theme throughout microeconomics is the big question: When do choices made in the pursuit of *self-interest* also promote the *social interest?* When does the invisible hand work well and when does it fail us? You've learned about the concept of efficiency, a major component of what we mean by the social interest. And you've seen that while competitive markets generally do a good job in helping to achieve efficiency, impediments such as monopoly and the absence of well-defined property rights can prevent the attainment of an efficient use of resources.

How do uncertainty and incomplete information affect the ability of self-interested choices to lead to a social interest outcome? Are these features of economic life another reason why markets fail and why some type of government intervention is required to achieve efficiency?

These are hard questions, and there are no definitive answers. But there are some useful things that we can say about the effects of uncertainty and a lack of complete information on the efficiency of resource use. We'll begin our brief review of this issue by thinking about information as just another good.

Information as a Good

More information is generally useful. And less uncertainty about the future is generally useful. Think about information as one of the goods that we want more of.

The most basic lesson about efficiency that you learned in Chapter 2 can be applied to information. Along our production possibilities frontier, we face a tradeoff between information and all other goods and services. Information, like everything else, can be produced at an increasing opportunity cost—an increasing marginal cost. For example, we could get more accurate weather forecasts, but only at increasing marginal cost, as we increased the amount of information that we gather from the atmosphere and the amount of money that we spend on supercomputers to process the data.

The principle of decreasing marginal benefit also applies to information. More information is valuable, but the more you know, the less you value another increment of information. For example, knowing that it will rain tomorrow is valuable information. Knowing the amount of rain to within an inch is even more useful. But knowing the amount of rain to within a millimeter probably isn't worth much more.

Because the marginal cost of information is increasing and the marginal benefit is decreasing, there is an efficient amount of information. It would be inefficient to be overinformed.

In principle, competitive markets in information might deliver this efficient quantity. Whether they actually do so is hard to determine.

Monopoly in Markets that Cope with Uncertainty

There are probably large economies of scale in providing services that cope with uncertainty and incomplete information. The insurance industry, for example, is highly concentrated. Where monopoly elements exist, exactly the same inefficiency issues arise as occur in markets where uncertainty and incomplete information are not big issues. So it is likely that in some information markets, including insurance markets, there is underproduction arising from the attempt to maximize monopoly profit.

REVIEW QUIZ

1 Thinking about information as a good, what information would you be willing to pay for?
2 Of the information you are willing to pay for, what can you buy in an information market and what can't you buy?
3 Why are some of the markets that provide information likely to be dominated by monopolies?

myeconlab Study Plan 19.6

We've seen how people cope with uncertainty and how markets work when there are information problems. *Reading Between the Lines* on pages 450–451 looks at the way grades work as signals in the labor market and sort students by ability so that employers can hire the type of labor they seek. You'll discover that grade inflation is inefficient.

The next chapter studies international trade. It builds on what you learned in Chapter 2 about production possibilities and opportunity cost and shows how comparative advantage enables international trade to bring gains to all countries.

READING BETWEEN THE LINES

Grades as Signals

http://www.nytimes.com

Can Tough Grades Be Fair Grades?

June 7, 2006

Over the span of his college career, Andrew Lipovsky has taken summer courses at Pace and Columbia in New York, spent three semesters at Northeastern here, and then transferred across town to Boston University last year. While he has majored in business, he has incidentally performed a kind of science experiment, in which he has been the control and those four universities the variables.

He earned grade-point averages of 3.2 at Columbia, 3.5 at Northeastern and 3.8 at Pace, a range solidly in the A's and B's. Then, in his two years at Boston University, he compiled only a 2.4, the borderline between B minus and C plus. When he had to repeat some of the same business courses at Boston that he already had taken at Northeastern, part of the transfer process, his marks dropped by as much as two full grade points.

The conclusion Mr. Lipovsky drew, an extremely common one among Boston University students, is that he was the victim of "grade deflation." By that euphemism, the students mean that, bending to unofficial but pervasive pressure from the university administration, professors force marks to conform to a curve.

"They want to make it harder," said Mr. Lipovsky, a 20-year-old from Manhattan. "They want a B.U. grade to mean something. But here's the problem. When I apply to grad school, the admissions officers don't know of this policy. It's not written down. The administration denies there is grade deflation." . . .

Essence of the Story

- Andrew Lipovsky has taken summer courses and compared his grades across four universities.
- His grade-point averages were 3.2 at Columbia, 3.5 at Northeastern, 3.8 at Pace, and 2.4 at Boston University.
- Mr. Lipovsky says that Boston University students are victims of "grade deflation" achieved by making grades conform to a curve.

- Accurate grades provide valuable information to students and potential employers about a student's ability.

- Boston University wants to provide accurate information and avoid grade inflation—awarding a high grade to most students—because this practice fails to provide information about a student's ability.

- The labor market for new college graduates works badly with grade inflation and works well with accurate grading.

- Figure 1 shows a labor market for new college graduates when there is grade inflation.

- Students with high ability are not distinguished from other students, and the supply curve represents the supply of students of all ability levels.

- The demand curve shows the employers' willingness to hire new workers without knowledge of their true ability.

- Students get hired for a low wage rate. Eventually, they get sorted by ability as employers discover the true ability of their workers from on-the-job performance.

- Figures 2 and 3 show the outcome with accurate grading.

- In Fig. 2, students with high grades get high-wage jobs.

- In Fig. 3, students with low grades get low-wage jobs.

- The outcomes in Figs. 2 and 3 that arise immediately with accurate grading occur eventually with grade inflation as information about ability accumulates.

- But the cost to the student and the employer of discovering true ability is greater with grade inflation than with accurate grading.

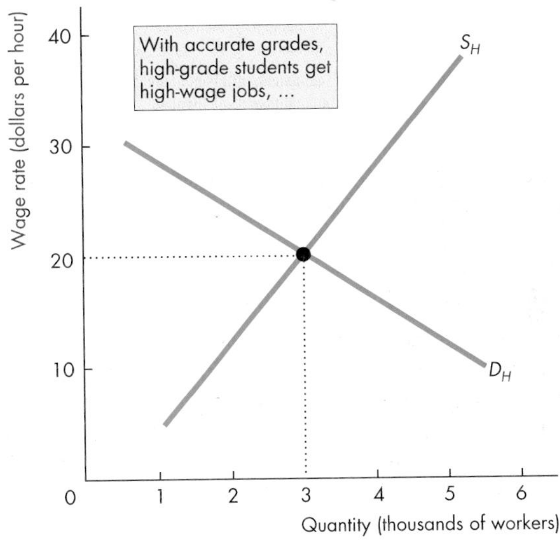

Figure 2 The market for A students

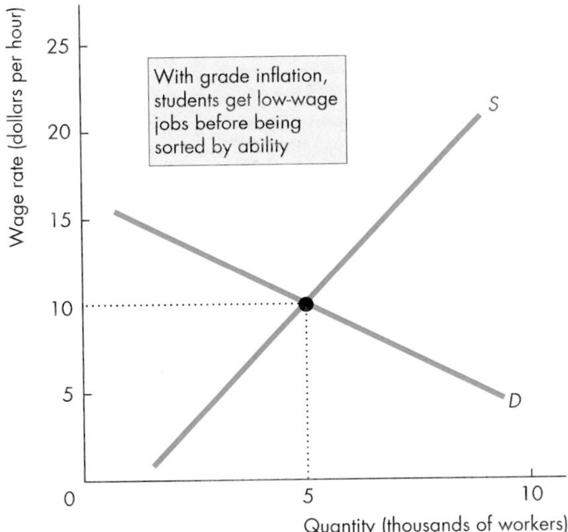

Figure 1 Market with grade inflation

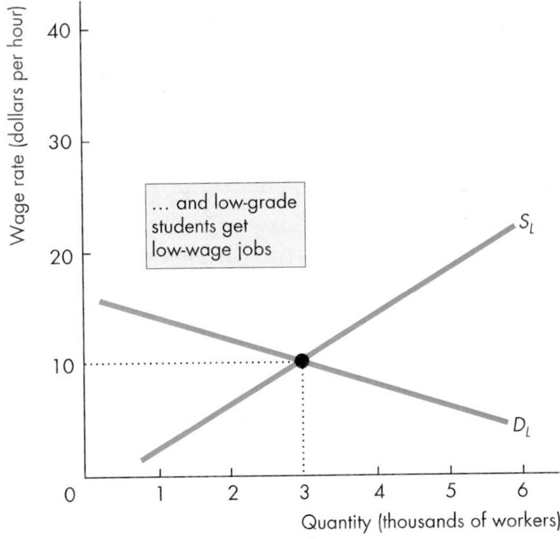

Figure 3 The market for D students

SUMMARY

Key Points

Uncertainty and Risk (pp. 438–440)

- Uncertainty is a situation in which more than one event may occur but we don't know which one.
- Risk is uncertainty with the probability attached to each possible outcome.
- A person's attitude toward risk, called the degree of risk aversion, is described by a utility of wealth schedule and curve.
- Faced with uncertainty, people choose the action that maximizes expected utility.

Insurance (pp. 441–442)

- We spend 15 percent of our income on insurance to reduce the risk we bear.
- The four main types of insurance are health, life, property and casualty, and auto.
- By pooling risks, insurance companies can reduce the risks people face (from insured activities) at a lower cost than the value placed on the lower risk.

Information (pp. 443–444)

- Buyers search for the least-cost source of supply and stop when the expected marginal benefit of search equals the marginal cost of search.
- The price at which the search stops is less than or equal to the buyer's reservation price.

Private Information (pp. 444–447)

- Private information is one person's knowledge that is too costly for anyone else to discover.
- Private information creates the problems of moral hazard (the use of private information to the advantage of the informed and the disadvantage of the uninformed after an agreement is made) and adverse selection (the tendency for people to enter into agreements in which they can use their private information to their own advantage and to the disadvantage of the less informed party).
- Devices that enable markets to function in the face of moral hazard and adverse selection are incentive payments, guarantees such as warranties, rationing, and signals.

Managing Risk in Financial Markets (pp. 447–448)

- Risk can be reduced by diversifying asset holdings, which combines the returns on projects that are independent of each other.
- A common way to diversify is to buy stocks in different corporations. Stock prices are determined by the expected future price of the stock.
- Expectations about future stock prices are based on all the information that is available and regarded as relevant.
- A market in which the price equals the expected future price is an efficient market.

Uncertainty, Information, and the Invisible Hand (p. 449)

- Less uncertainty and more information can be viewed as a good that has increasing marginal cost and decreasing marginal benefit.
- Competitive information markets might be efficient, but economies of scale might bring inefficient underproduction of information and insurance.

Key Figures

Key Terms

PROBLEMS

myeconlab Tests, Study Plan, and Solutions*

1. The figure shows Lee's utility of wealth curve.

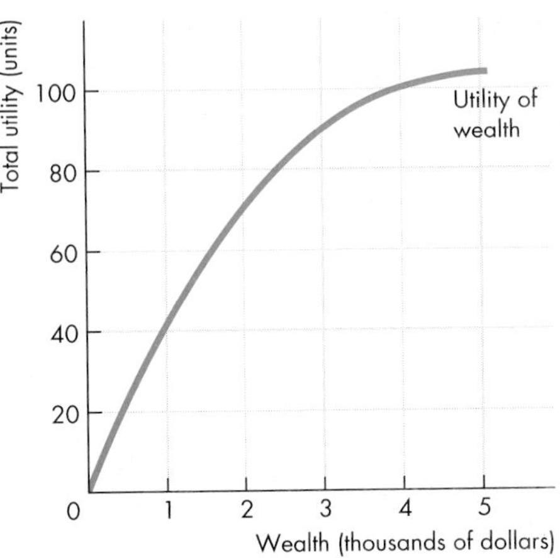

Lee is offered a job as a salesperson in which there is a 50 percent chance that she will make $4,000 a month and a 50 percent chance that she will make nothing.

   a. What is Lee's expected income from taking this job?
   b. What is Lee's expected utility from taking this job?
   c. How much would another firm have to offer Lee with certainty to persuade her not to take the risky sales job?
   d. What is Lee's cost of risk?

2. Jimmy and Zenda have the following utility of wealth schedules:

Wealth	Jimmy's utility	Zenda's utility
0	0	0
100	200	512
200	300	640
300	350	672
400	375	678
500	387	681
600	393	683
700	396	684

   a. What are Jimmy's and Zenda's expected utilities from a bet that gives them a 50 percent change of having a wealth of $600 and a 50 percent chance of having nothing?
   b. Calculate Jimmy's and Zenda's marginal utility of wealth schedules.
   c. Who is more risk averse, Jimmy or Zenda? How do you know?
   d. Who is more likely to buy insurance, Jimmy or Zenda?

3. Suppose that Jimmy and Zenda in problem 2 have $400 each and that each sees a business project that involves committing the entire $400 to the project. They reckon that the project could return $600 (a profit of $200) with a probability of 0.85 or $200 (a loss of $200) with a probability of 0.15. Who goes for the project and who hangs onto the initial $400?

4. Lee in problem 1 has built a small weekend shack on a steep, unstable hillside. She spent all her wealth, which is $5,000, on this project. There is a 75 percent chance that the house will be washed down the hill and be worthless. How much is Lee willing to pay for an insurance policy that pays her $5,000 if the house is washed away?

5. Lee in problem 1 is shopping for a new car. She plans to borrow the money to pay for the car from the bank. Describe in detail the search problems that Lee faces. What information does she find useful? How does she obtain it? How does she make her decisions?

6. Zaneb is a high-school teacher and is well known in her community for her honesty and integrity. She is shopping for a new car and plans to borrow the money to pay for it from her local bank.

   a. Does Zaneb create any moral hazard or adverse selection problems either for the bank or the car dealer? Explain your answer.
   b. Do the bank or the car dealer create any moral hazard or adverse selection problems for Zaneb? Explain your answer.
   c. What arrangements is Zaneb likely to encounter that are designed to help cope with the moral hazard and adverse selection problems she encounters in her car buying and bank loan transactions?

7. Suppose that there are three national football leagues: The Time League, The Goal Difference League, and The Bonus for Win League. The

*Solutions to odd-numbered problems are provided.

leagues are of equal quality, but the players in each league are paid differently. In The Time League, they are paid by the hour for time spent practicing and time spent playing. In The Goal Difference league, they are paid an amount that depends on the number of points that the team scores minus the number of points scored against it. In The Bonus for Win League, the players are paid one wage for a loss, a higher wage for a tie, and the highest wage of all for a win.
   a. Briefly describe the predicted differences in the quality of the games played by each of these leagues.
   b. Which league will be the most attractive to players?
   c. Which league will generate the largest profits?
8. **Phillies hamstrung by Burrell's no-trade clause**
   Phillies general manager Pat Gillick, . . .who previously built winners in Toronto, Baltimore and Seattle, is no fan of blanket no-trade clauses. Gillick is so averse to giving out complete no-trade provisions that he says it could be a "deal breaker" when the Phillies negotiate with big free agents this winter.
   ESPN.com, November 8, 2006
   a. Provide an example of private information that a baseball player who wants a no-trade clause possesses.
   b. Does a baseball player with a no-trade clause present a moral hazard to his baseball team?
   c. Does a baseball player with a no-trade clause present adverse selection problems to his baseball team?
9. At 11:10 a.m. on November 21, 2006, one share of Google traded for $504.07. Viewed from that time and date, if the market for Google shares is efficient
   a. What would you expect the price of one share of Google to be on November 22, 2006?
   b. What profit would you expect to earn by selling one share of Google today or by holding that share for another week and then selling it?
10. Explain why you would increase your expected utility by spreading your wealth across the stocks of Google, General Motors, eBay, and Microsoft instead of putting all your wealth into the stocks of just one of these companies. Would you also increase your expected wealth? Explain why or why not.

CRITICAL THINKING

1. After you have studied *Reading Between the Lines* on pp. 450–451, answer the following questions:
   a. What information do accurate grades provide that grade inflation hides?
   b. If grade inflation became widespread in high schools, colleges, and universities, what new arrangements do you predict would emerge to provide better information about student ability?
   c. Do you think grade inflation is in anyone's self-interest? Explain who benefits and how they benefit from grade inflation.
   d. How do you think grade inflation might be controlled?
2. Why do you think it is not possible to buy insurance against having to put up with a low-paying, miserable job? Explain why a market in insurance of this type would not work.
3. Although you can't buy insurance against the risk of being sold a lemon, the market does give you some protection. How? What are the main ways in which markets overcome the lemon problem?
4. Merck discovers a new drug that is expected to bring big profits. What happens to the price of Merck's stock? Why wouldn't people put all their wealth into Merck's stock?

WEB ACTIVITIES

myeconlab **Links to Web sites**

1. Obtain information on the prices of three stocks that interest you.
   a. Describe the change in the prices of these stocks over the past month.
   b. If you had bought $1,000 of each of these stocks (a total of $3,000) one month ago, how much would your stock be worth today?
   c. If you had $3,000, would you use some of it to buy these stocks? How much would you put in each stock? How much would you keep in cash?
   d. Form a group with other students and compare your answers to part (c). Which of you is the most risk averse? Which of you is the least risk averse? Explain your answer.

For Whom?

During the past 35 years, the rich have been getting richer and the poor poorer. This trend is new. From the end of World War II until 1965, the poor got richer at a faster pace than the rich and the gap between rich and poor narrowed a bit. What are the forces that generate these trends? The answer to this question is the forces of demand and supply in factor markets. These forces determine wages, interest rates, rents, and the prices of natural resources. These forces also determine people's incomes.

The three categories of resources are human, capital, and natural. Human resources include labor, human capital, and entrepreneurship. The income of labor and human capital depends on wage rates and employment levels, which are determined in labor markets. The income from capital depends on interest rates and the quantity of capital, which are determined in capital markets. The income from natural resources depends on prices and quantities that are determined in natural resource markets. Only the return to entrepreneurship is not determined directly in a market. That return is normal profit plus economic profit, and it depends on how successful each entrepreneur is in the business that he or she runs.

The first two chapters in this part study the forces at play in factor markets and explain how those forces have led to changes in the distribution of income.

The overview of all the factor markets in Chapter 17 explained how the demand for factors of production results from the profit-maximizing decisions of firms. You studied these decisions from a different angle in Chapters 9–13, where you learned how firms choose their profit-maximizing output and price. Chapter 17 explained how a firm's profit-maximizing decisions determine its demand for factors of production. It also explained how factor supply decisions are made and how equilibrium in factor markets determines factor prices and the incomes of owners of factors of production. Some of the biggest incomes earned by superstars are a surplus that we call *economic rent.*

Chapter 17 used labor resources and the labor market as its main example. But it also looked at some special features of capital markets and natural resource markets.

Chapter 18 studied the distribution of income. This chapter took you back to the fundamentals of economics and answered one of the big economic questions: Who consumes the goods and services produced?

Chapter 19 is different from the other two. It looked at the problems of uncertainty and private information and showed how the market handles these problems.

Many outstanding economists have advanced our understanding of factor markets and the role they play in helping to resolve the conflict between the demands of humans and the resources available. One of them is Thomas Robert Malthus, whom you can meet on the following page. You can also enjoy the insights of David Card, a professor of economics at the University of California, Berkeley, and a prominent contemporary labor economist.

PROBING THE IDEAS

Running Out of Resources

"The passion between the sexes has appeared in every age to be so nearly the same, that it may always be considered, in algebraic language, as a given quantity."

THOMAS ROBERT MALTHUS
An Essay on the Principle of Population

The Economist

Thomas Robert Malthus *(1766–1834), an English clergyman and economist, was an extremely influential social scientist. In his best-selling* Essay on the Principle of Population, *published in 1798, he predicted that population growth would outstrip food production and said that wars, famine, and disease were inevitable unless population growth was held in check by what he called "moral restraint." By "moral restraint," he meant marrying at a late age and living a celibate life. He married at the age of 38 a wife of 27, marriage ages that he recommended for others.*

Malthus's ideas were regarded as too radical in their day. And they led Thomas Carlyle, a contemporary thinker, to dub economics the "dismal science." But the ideas of Malthus had a profound influence on Charles Darwin, who got the key idea that led him to the theory of natural selection from reading the Essay on the Principle of Population. *And David Ricardo and the classical economists were strongly influenced by Malthus's ideas.*

The Issues

Is there a limit to economic growth, or can we expand production and population without effective limit? Thomas Malthus gave one of the most influential answers to these questions in 1798. He reasoned that population, unchecked, would grow at a geometric rate—1, 2, 4, 8, 16 ...—while the food supply would grow at an arithmetic rate—1, 2, 3, 4, 5 ... . To prevent the population from outstripping the available food supply, there would be periodic wars, famines, and plagues. In Malthus's view, only what he called moral restraint could prevent such periodic disasters.

As industrialization proceeded through the nineteenth century, Malthus's idea came to be applied to all natural resources, especially those that are exhaustible.

Modern-day Malthusians believe that his basic idea is correct and that it applies not only to food but also to every natural resource. In time, these prophets of doom believe, we will be reduced to the subsistence level that Malthus predicted. He was a few centuries out in his predictions but not dead wrong.

One modern-day Malthusian is ecologist Paul Ehrlich, who believes that we are sitting on a "population bomb." Governments must, says Ehrlich, limit both population growth and the resources that may be used each year.

In 1931, Harold Hotelling developed a theory of natural resources with different predictions from those of Malthus. The Hotelling Principle is that the relative price of an exhaustible natural resource will steadily rise, bringing a decline in the quantity used and an increase in the use of substitute resources.

Julian Simon (who died in 1998) challenged both the Malthusian gloom and the Hotelling Principle. He believed that people are the "ultimate resource" and predicted that a rising population lessens the pressure on natural resources. A bigger population provides a larger number of resourceful people who can work out more efficient ways of using scarce resources. As these solutions are found, the prices of exhaustible resources actually fall. To demonstrate his point, in 1980, Simon bet Ehrlich that the prices of five metals—copper, chrome, nickel, tin, and tungsten—would fall during the 1980s. Simon won the bet!

Then

No matter whether it is agricultural land, an exhaustible natural resource, or the space in the center of Chicago, and no matter whether it is 2007 or, as shown here, 1892, there is a limit to what is available, and we persistently push against that limit. Economists see urban congestion as a consequence of the value of doing business in the city center relative to the cost. They see the price mechanism, bringing ever-higher rents and prices of raw materials, as the means of allocating and rationing scarce natural resources. Malthusians, in contrast, explain congestion as the consequence of population pressure, and they see population control as the solution.

Now

In Tokyo, the pressure on space is so great that in some residential neighborhoods, a parking space costs \$1,700 a month. To economize on this expensive space—and to lower the cost of car ownership and hence boost the sale of new cars—Honda, Nissan, and Toyota, three of Japan's big car producers, developed a parking machine that enables two cars to occupy the space of one. The most basic of these machines costs a mere \$10,000—less than 6 months' parking fees.

Malthus developed his ideas about population growth in a world in which incentives played a limited role. For example, he didn't consider the opportunity cost of women's time a factor that would influence population growth. But today, the opportunity cost of women's time is a crucial factor because women play an expanded role in the labor force. One economist who has made significant contributions to our knowledge of labor markets is David Card of the University of California, Berkeley. You can meet Professor Card on the following pages.

TALKING WITH

David Card

David Card is Class of 1950 Professor of Economics and Director of the Center for Labor Economics at the University of California, Berkeley, and Faculty Research Associate at the National Bureau of Economic Research.

Born in Canada, Professor Card obtained his B.A. at Queens University, Kingston, Ontario, in 1977 and his Ph.D. at Princeton University in 1983. He has received many honors, the most notable of which is the American Economic Association's John Bates Clark Prize, awarded to the best economist under 40.

Professor Card's research on labor markets and the effects of public policies on earnings, jobs, and the distribution of income has produced around 150 articles in several books. His most recent book (co-edited with Alan Auerbach and John Quigley) is Poverty, the Distribution of Income, and Public Policy *(New York: Russell Sage Foundation, 2006). An earlier book (co-authored with Alan B. Krueger),* Myth and Measurement: The New Economics of the Minimum Wage *(Princeton, NJ: Princeton University Press, 1995), made a big splash and upset one of the most fundamental beliefs about the effects of minimum wages.*

Michael Parkin talked with David Card about his work and the progress that economists have made in understanding how public policies can influence the distribution of income and economic well-being.

Professor Card, what attracted you to economics?
When I went to university I had no intention of studying economics: I was planning to be a physics major. I was helping a friend with her problem set and started reading the supply and demand section of the textbook. I was impressed with how well the model seemed to describe the paradox that a bumper crop can be bad for farmers. I read most of the book over the next few days. The next year, I signed up as an economics major.

Almost all your work is grounded in data. You are an empirical economist. How do you go about your work, where do your data come from, and how do you use data?
The data I use come from many different sources. I have collected my own data from surveys; transcribed data from historical sources and government publications; and used computerized data files based on records from Censuses and surveys in the United States, Canada, Britain, and other countries.

An economist can do three things with data. The first is to develop simple statistics on basic questions such as "What fraction of families live in poverty?" For this, one needs to understand how the data were collected and processed and how the questions were asked. For example, the poverty rate depends on how you define a "family." If a single mother and her child live with the mother's parents, the income of the mother and the grandparents is counted as "family income."

The second thing economists do with data is develop descriptive comparisons. For example, I have compared the wage differences between male and female workers. Again, the details are important.

For example, the male-female wage differential is much bigger if you look at annual earnings than at earnings per hour, because women work fewer hours per year.

Once you've established some simple facts, you start to get ideas for possible explanations. You can also rule out a lot of other ideas.

The most difficult thing that empirical economists try to do is infer a causal relationship.

The third and most difficult thing that empirical economists try to do is infer a causal relationship. In rare instances, we have a true experiment in which a random subgroup of volunteers is enrolled in a "treatment group" and the remainder become the "control group." The Self Sufficiency Program (SSP)—an experimental welfare reform demonstration in Canada—was conducted this way. Because of random assignment, we know that the treatment and control groups would have looked very similar in the absence of the treatment. Thus when we see a difference in behavior, such as the higher level of work activity by single parents in the treatment group of SSP, we can infer that the financial incentives of SSP caused people to work more.

Most often, we don't have an experiment. We see a group of people who are subject to some "treatment" (such as a higher minimum wage) and we try to construct a comparison group by finding some other group similar to the treatment group who tell us what the treatment group would have looked like in the absence of treatment. If we can't find a compelling comparison group, we have to be cautious.

In your book on the minimum wage with Alan Krueger, you reported that an increase in the minimum wage increased employment—the opposite of the conventional wisdom. How did you reach that conclusion?

We studied several instances where minimum wages were raised in one place but not in another. For example, when we found out that the New Jersey legislature had recently voted to raise the minimum wage, we set up a survey of fast-food restaurants in New Jersey and in nearby parts of Pennsylvania. We surveyed the stores a few months before the New Jersey minimum went up and then again one year later, after the minimum had been raised. The first-round survey found that conditions were very similar in the two states. In the second round, we found that although wages were now higher in New Jersey, employment was also slightly higher. It was very important to have the first-round survey to benchmark any differences that existed prior to the rise in the minimum. Thus, we argued that any differential changes in New Jersey relative to Pennsylvania from the first round to the second round were most plausibly due to the minimum wage.

How did you explain what you found?

We argued that many employers in New Jersey before the rise in the minimum were operating with vacancies and would have liked to hire more workers but could not do so without raising their wages. In this situation, an increase in the minimum wage can cause some employers to hire more and others to hire less. On average, the net effect on employment can be small. What we saw was a rise in wages and a reduction in vacancies in New Jersey, coupled with a small gain in employment.

You've examined just about every labor market policy. Let's talk about welfare payments to single mothers: How do they influence labor market decisions?

The Self Sufficiency Program welfare demonstration in Canada tested an earnings subsidy as an alternative to conventional welfare payments. The problem with conventional welfare is that recipients have no incentive to work: If they earn \$1, their payments are reduced by \$1. That led Milton Friedman in the early 1950s to advocate an alternative "negative income tax" program, such as SSP, in which recipients who earn more only lose a fraction of their benefits (in the case of SSP, 50 cents per dollar earned). The results showed that this alternative system encourages single parents to work more.

Immigration has been big news in recent years. Can you describe your work on this issue and your findings?

My research has tried to understand whether the

arrival of low-skilled immigrants hurts the labor market opportunities for less-skilled natives. One of my papers studies the effect of the Mariel Boatlift, which occurred in 1980 following a political uprising that led Fidel Castro to declare that people who wanted to leave Cuba were free to exit from the port of Mariel. Within days, a flotilla of small boats from the United States began transporting people to Miami, and 150,000 people eventually left. Over one half stayed in Miami, creating a huge "shock" to the supply of low-skilled labor. I studied the effect by looking at wages and unemployment rates for various groups in Miami and in a set of comparison cities that had very similar wage and employment trends in the previous decade. I found that the influx of the boatlift had no discernible effect on wages or unemployment of other workers in Miami. My later work has confirmed that the Miami story seems to hold in most other cities. Cities can absorb big inflows of low-skilled immigrants with remarkably little negative impact on natives.

The distribution of income has become increasingly unequal. Do we know why?

There are many sources. Family incomes have become more unequal in part because of a rise in families with two very high-wage earners. These families have pulled away from the rest, creating a widening distribution. The very richest families, whose incomes are above the 95th or 99th percentile of the income distribution, earn an increasingly large share of national income. The trends in income for this group account for most of the rise in inequality we have seen in the last 10 years.

... find out what life is like for other people. ... The best economists are observant and thoughtful social scientist.

Unfortunately, it is very hard to study this group because they represent such a small fraction of families, and they are often under-reported on surveys. The best available data, from tax returns, don't tell us much about the sources of this group's success, though it seems to be due to labor market earnings rather than to previous investments or family wealth.

There is a large literature on wage inequality among the larger "middle" of the population: people who earn up to $150,000 per year, for example. Wage inequality for men in this group rose very sharply in the early 1980s in the United States, rose a little more between 1985 and 1990, and was fairly stable (or even decreasing) in the 1990s. Some of the rise in the 1980s was due to decreases in unionization, and some was due to the changing effects of the minimum wage, which fell in real terms in the early 1980s, and then gained in the early to mid-1990s.

Some researchers ascribe the rest of the trend in wage inequality to the spread of computers and increasing demands for highly skilled workers. Others blame international trade and, most recently, immigration. Those explanations are hard to evaluate because we don't really see the forces of new technology or trade that affect any particular worker. One thing we do know is that wage inequality trends were quite different in many other countries. Canada, for instance, had relatively modest rises in inequality in the 1980s.

What advice do you have for someone who is just beginning to study economics? What other subjects do you think work well alongside economics? Do you have some reading suggestions?

The part of economics that most interests me is the behavior of people in their everyday life. People constantly have to answer questions such as: Should I get more education? How much should I save? Should I send my children to the local public school? It's extremely important to see how these questions are answered by different people: people from poorer families or other countries or who had to make very different choices. Take any opportunity to find out what life is like for other people. You can learn a lot from reading novels, spending a year abroad, or taking classes in sociology or history. The best economists are observant and thoughtful social scientists. My other piece of advice is study mathematics. The more mathematics training you have, the more easily you can understand what economists are doing. Newton invented calculus to study the motion of planets, but economics benefits from the same tools.

CHAPTER 20

Trading with the World

Silk Routes and Sucking Sounds

Since ancient times, people have expanded their trading as far as technology allowed. Marco Polo opened up the silk route between Europe and China in the thirteenth century. Today, container ships laden with cars and electronics and Boeing 747s stuffed with farm-fresh foods ply sea and air routes, carrying billions of dollars worth of goods. Why do people go to such great lengths to trade with those in other nations?

In 1994, the United States entered into a free trade agreement with Canada and Mexico—the North American Free Trade Agreement, or NAFTA. Some people predicted a "giant sucking sound" as jobs were transferred from high-wage Michigan to low-wage Mexico. Can we compete with a country that pays its workers a fraction of U.S. wages?

Workers in China earn even less than those in Mexico, and today, just about every manufactured object that we buy seems to be made in China. How can we compete with low-wage China and the other low-wage Asian nations? Are there any industries, besides perhaps making Hollywood movies and building large passenger jets, in which we have an advantage?

Would it be a good idea to limit imports from China and other countries by putting a tariff or a quota on those imports?

In this chapter, we're going to learn about international trade and discover how all nations can gain from trading with other nations. You will discover that all nations can compete, no matter how high their wages. But you will also learn why, despite the fact that international trade brings benefits to all, governments restrict trade. In *Reading Between the Lines* at the end of the chapter, we'll look at the growing trade with China and see why we all benefit from it.

After studying this chapter, you will be able to

- Describe the trends and patterns in international trade
- Explain comparative advantage and explain why all countries can gain from international trade
- Explain why international trade restrictions reduce the volume of imports and exports and reduce our consumption possibilities
- Explain the arguments that are used to justify international trade restrictions and show how they are flawed
- Explain why we have international trade restrictions

Patterns and Trends in International Trade

The goods and services that we buy from people in other countries are called **imports**. The goods and services that we sell to people in other countries are called **exports**. What are the most important things that we import and export? Most people would probably guess that a rich nation such as the United States imports raw materials and exports manufactured goods. Although that is one feature of U.S. international trade, it is not its most important feature. The bulk of our exports *and* imports is manufactured goods. We sell foreigners earth-moving equipment, airplanes, supercomputers, and scientific equipment, and we buy televisions, DVD players, blue jeans, and T-shirts from them. Also, we are a major exporter of agricultural products and raw materials. And we import and export a huge volume of services.

Trade in Goods

Manufactured goods account for 55 percent of our exports and 68 percent of our imports. Industrial materials (raw materials and semimanufactured items) account for 14 percent of our exports and 15 percent of our imports, and agricultural products account for only 8 percent of our exports and 4 percent of our imports. Our largest individual export and import items are capital goods and automobiles. But goods account for only 70 percent of our exports and 84 percent of our imports. The rest of our international trade is in services.

Trade in Services

You may be wondering how a country can "export" and "import" services. Here are some examples.

If you take a vacation in France and travel there on an Air France flight from New York, you import transportation services from France. The money you spend in France on hotel bills and restaurant meals is also classified as the import of services. Similarly, the money spent by a French student on vacation in the United States is a U.S. export of services to France.

When we import TV sets from South Korea, the owner of the ship that transports them might be Greek and the company that insures them might be British. The payments that we make for transportation and insurance are imports of services. Similarly, when an American shipping company transports California wine to Tokyo, the transportation cost is a U.S. export of a service to Japan. Our international trade in these types of services is large and growing.

Geographical Patterns of International Trade

The United States has trading links with every part of the world, but Canada is our biggest trading partner. In 2006, 20 percent of our exports went to Canada and 17 percent of our imports came from Canada. Japan is our second biggest trading partner, accounting for 8 percent of exports and 9 percent of imports in 2006. The regions in which our trade is largest are the European Union—with 24 percent of our exports and 23 percent of our imports in 2006—and Latin America—with 20 percent of our exports and 18 percent of our imports in 2006.

Trends in the Volume of Trade

In 1960, we exported 3.5 percent of total output and imported 4 percent of the goods and services that we bought. In 2006, we exported 10 percent of total output and imported 15 percent of the goods and services that we bought.

On the export side, capital goods, automobiles, food, and raw materials have remained large items and held a roughly constant share of total exports. But the composition of imports has changed. Food and raw material imports have fallen steadily. Imports of fuel increased dramatically during the 1970s but fell during the 1980s. Imports of machinery have grown and today approach 50 percent of total imports.

Net Exports and International Borrowing

The value of exports minus the value of imports is called **net exports.** In 2006, U.S. net exports were a negative $780 billion. Our imports were $780 billion more than our exports. When we import more than we export, as we did in 2006, we borrow from foreigners or sell some of our assets to them. When we export more than we import, we make loans to foreigners or buy some of their assets.

myeconlab Study Plan 20.1

The Gains from International Trade

The fundamental force that generates international trade is *comparative advantage*. And the basis of comparative advantage is divergent *opportunity costs*. You met these ideas in Chapter 2 (pp. 42–45), when we learned about the gains from specialization and exchange between Joe and Liz.

Joe and Liz each specialize in producing just one good and then trade with each other. Most nations do not go to the extreme of specializing in a single good and importing everything else. But nations can increase the consumption of all goods if they redirect their scarce resources toward the production of those goods and services in which they have a comparative advantage.

To see how this outcome occurs, we'll apply the same basic ideas that we learned in the case of Joe and Liz to trade among nations. We'll begin by recalling how we can use the production possibilities frontier to measure opportunity cost. Then we'll see how divergent opportunity costs bring comparative advantage and gains from trade for countries as well as for individuals even though no country completely specializes in the production of just one good.

Opportunity Cost in Farmland

Farmland (a fictitious country) can produce grain and cars at any point inside or along its production possibilities frontier, *PPF*, shown in Fig. 20.1. (We're holding constant the output of all the other goods that Farmland produces.) The Farmers (the people of Farmland) are consuming all the grain and cars that they produce, and they are operating at point *A* in the figure. That is, Farmland is producing and consuming 15 billion bushels of grain and 8 million cars each year. What is the opportunity cost of a car in Farmland?

We can answer that question by calculating the slope of the production possibilities frontier at point *A*. The magnitude of the slope of the frontier measures the opportunity cost of one good in terms of the other. To measure the slope of the frontier at point *A*, place a straight line tangential to the frontier at point *A* and calculate the slope of that straight line. Recall that the formula for the slope of a line is the change in the value of the variable measured on the y-axis divided by the change in the value of the variable measured on the x-axis as we move along the line. Here, the variable measured on the y-axis is billions of bushels of grain, and the variable measured on the x-axis is millions of cars. So the slope is the change in the number of bushels of grain divided by the change in the number of cars.

As you can see from the red triangle at point *A* in Fig. 20.1, if the number of cars produced increases by 2 million, grain production decreases by 18 billion bushels. Therefore the magnitude of the slope is 18 billion divided by 2 million, which equals 9,000. To get one more car, the people of Farmland must give up 9,000 bushels of grain. So the opportunity cost of 1 car is 9,000 bushels of grain. Equivalently, 9,000 bushels of grain cost 1 car. For the people of Farmland, these opportunity costs are the prices they face. The price of a car is 9,000 bushels of grain, and the price of 9,000 bushels of grain is 1 car.

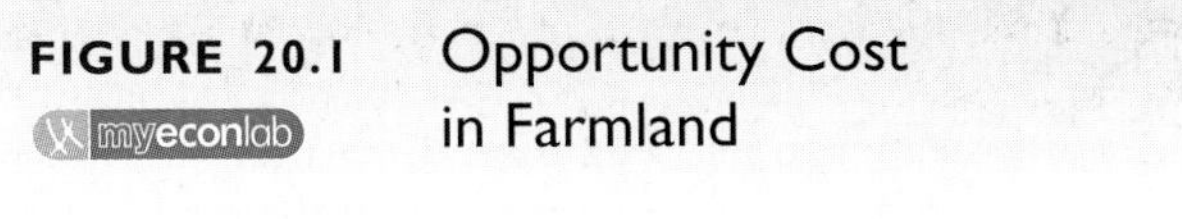

FIGURE 20.1 Opportunity Cost in Farmland

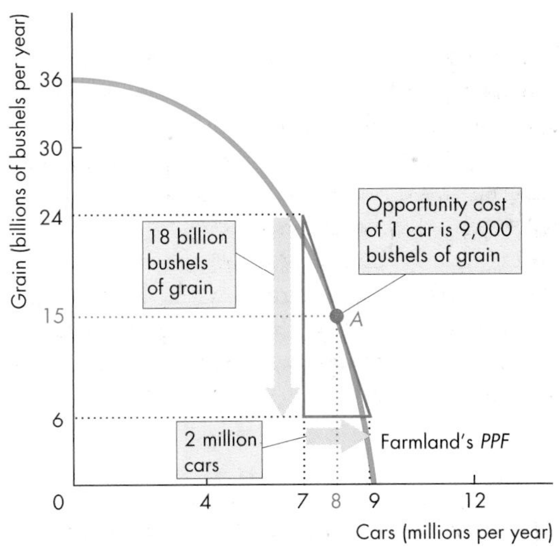

Farmland produces and consumes 15 billion bushels of grain and 8 million cars a year. That is, it produces and consumes at point *A* on its production possibilities frontier. Opportunity cost is equal to the magnitude of the slope of the *PPF*. The red triangle tells us that at point *A*, 18 billion bushels of grain must be forgone to get 2 million cars. That is, at point *A*, 2 million cars cost 18 billion bushels of grain. Equivalently, 1 car costs 9,000 bushels of grain or 9,000 bushels of grain cost 1 car.

Opportunity Cost in Mobilia

Figure 20.2 shows the production possibilities frontier of Mobilia (another fictitious country). Like the Farmers, the Mobilians consume all the grain and cars that they produce. Mobilia consumes 18 billion bushels of grain a year and 4 million cars, at point *A*'.

Let's calculate the opportunity costs in Mobilia. At point *A*', the opportunity cost of a car is equal to the magnitude of the slope of the red line tangential to Mobilia's *PPF*. You can see from the red triangle that the magnitude of the slope of Mobilia's *PPF* is 6 billion bushels of grain divided by 6 million cars, which equals 1,000 bushels of grain per car. To get one more car, the Mobilians must give up 1,000 bushels of grain. So the opportunity cost of 1 car is 1,000 bushels of grain, or equivalently, the opportunity cost of 1,000 bushels of grain is 1 car. These are the prices faced in Mobilia.

Comparative Advantage

Cars are cheaper in Mobilia than in Farmland. One car costs 9,000 bushels of grain in Farmland but only 1,000 bushels of grain in Mobilia. But grain is cheaper in Farmland than in Mobilia—9,000 bushels of grain cost only 1 car in Farmland, while that same amount of grain costs 9 cars in Mobilia.

Mobilia has a comparative advantage in car production. Farmland has a comparative advantage in grain production. A country has a **comparative advantage** in producing a good if it can produce that good at a lower opportunity cost than any other country. Let's see how opportunity cost differences and comparative advantage generate gains from international trade.

FIGURE 20.2 Opportunity Cost in Mobilia

myeconlab

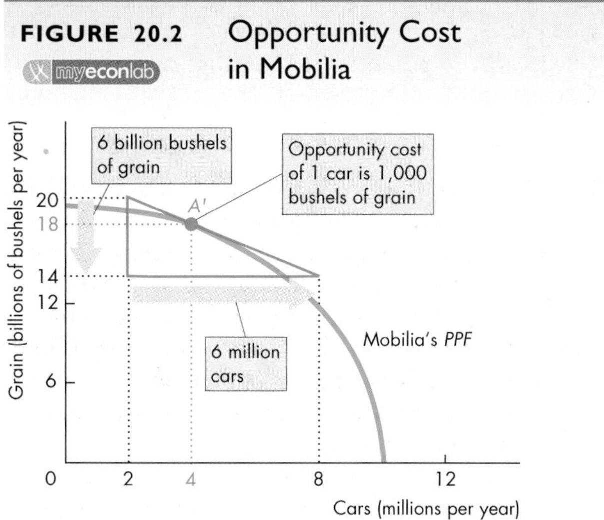

Mobilia produces and consumes 18 billion bushels of grain and 4 million cars a year at point A' on its production possibilities frontier. Opportunity cost is equal to the magnitude of the slope of the *PPF* The red triangle tells us that at point A', 6 billion bushels of grain must be forgone to get 6 million cars. That is, at point A', 6 million cars cost 6 billion bushels of grain. Equivalently, 1 car costs 1,000 bushels of grain or 1,000 bushels of grain cost 1 car.

The Gains from Trade: Cheaper to Buy Than to Produce

If Mobilia bought grain for what it costs Farmland to produce it, then Mobilia could buy 9,000 bushels of grain for 1 car. That is much lower than the cost of growing grain in Mobilia, where it costs 9 cars to produce 9,000 bushels of grain. If the Mobilians can buy grain at the low Farmland price, they will reap some gains.

If the Farmers can buy cars for what it costs Mobilia to produce them, they will be able to obtain a car for 1,000 bushels of grain. Because it costs 9,000 bushels of grain to produce a car in Farmland, the Farmers would gain from such an opportunity.

In this situation, it makes sense for Mobilians to buy their grain from Farmers and for Farmers to buy their cars from Mobilians. But at what price will Farmland and Mobilia engage in mutually beneficial international trade?

The Terms of Trade

The quantity of grain that Farmland must pay Mobilia for a car is Farmland's **terms of trade** with Mobilia. Because the United States exports and imports many different goods and services, we measure the terms of trade in the real world as an index number that averages the terms of trade over all the items we trade.

The forces of international supply and demand determine the terms of trade. Figure 20.3 illustrates these forces in the Farmland–Mobilia international car market. The quantity of cars *traded internationally* is measured on the *x*-axis. On the *y*-axis, we measure the price of a car. This price is expressed as the *terms of trade*: bushels of grain per car. If no international trade takes place, the price of a car in Farmland is 9,000

FIGURE 20.3 International Trade in Cars

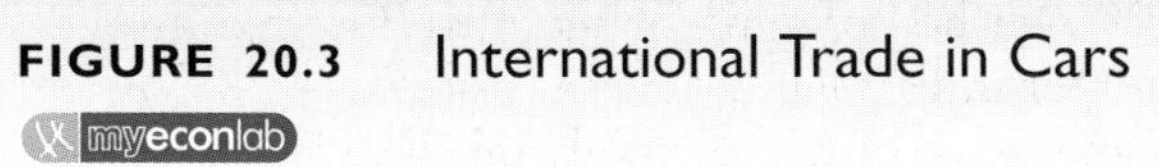

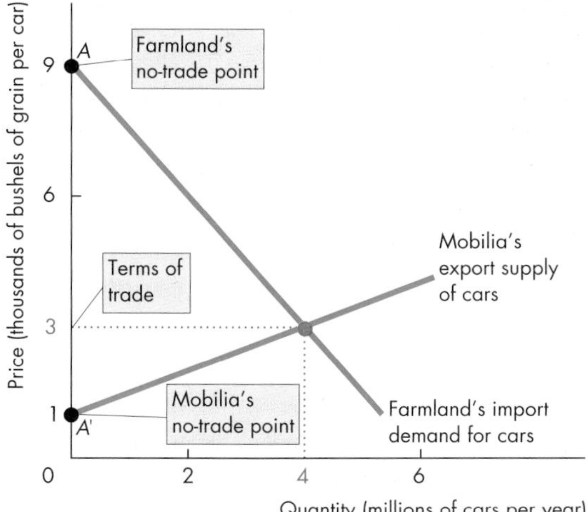

Farmland's import demand curve for cars is downward sloping, and Mobilia's export supply curve of cars is upward sloping. With no international trade, the price of a car is 9,000 bushels of grain in Farmland (point *A*) and 1,000 bushels of grain in Mobilia (point *A'*).

With free international trade, the price (terms of trade) is determined where the export supply curve intersects the import demand curve: 3,000 bushels of grain per car. At that price, 4 million cars a year are imported by Farmland and exported by Mobilia. The value of grain exported by Farmland and imported by Mobilia is 12 billion bushels a year, the quantity required to pay for the cars imported.

bushels of grain, its opportunity cost, indicated by point *A*. The no-trade point *A* in Fig. 20.3 corresponds to point *A* in Fig. 20.1. The lower the price of a car in the international market (terms of trade), the greater is the quantity of cars that the Farmers are willing to import from the Mobilians. This fact is illustrated by the downward-sloping curve, which shows Farmland's import demand for cars.

Again, if no trade takes place, the price of a car in Mobilia is 1,000 bushels of grain, its opportunity cost, indicated by point *A'*. The no-trade point *A'* in Fig. 20.3 corresponds to point *A'* in Fig. 20.2. The higher the price of a car in the international market, the greater is the quantity of cars that Mobilians are willing to export to Farmers. This fact is illustrated by Mobilia's export supply of cars—the upward-sloping line in Fig. 20.3.

The international market in cars determines the equilibrium terms of trade (price) and quantity traded. This equilibrium occurs where the import demand curve intersects the export supply curve. In this case, the equilibrium terms of trade are 3,000 bushels of grain per car. Mobilia exports and Farmland imports 4 million cars a year. Notice that the terms of trade are lower than the no-trade price in Farmland but higher than the no-trade price in Mobilia.

Balanced Trade

The number of cars exported by Mobilia—4 million a year—is exactly equal to the number of cars imported by Farmland. How does Farmland pay for the cars it imports? The answer is by exporting grain. How much grain does Farmland export? You can find the answer by noticing that for 1 car, Farmland must pay 3,000 bushels of grain. So for 4 million cars, Farmland pays 12 billion bushels of grain. Farmland's exports of grain are 12 billion bushels a year, and Mobilia imports this same quantity of grain.

Mobilia exchanges 4 million cars for 12 billion bushels of grain each year, and Farmland exchanges 12 billion bushels of grain for 4 million cars. Trade is balanced. For each country, the value received from exports equals the value paid out for imports.

Changes in Production and Consumption

We've seen that international trade makes it possible for Farmers to buy cars at a lower price than what it costs them to produce a car and to sell their grain for a higher price. International trade also enables Mobilians to sell their cars for a higher price and buy grain for a lower price than it costs them to produce grain. Both countries gain. How is it possible for *both* countries to gain? What are the changes in production and consumption that accompany these gains?

An economy that does not trade with other economies has identical production and consumption possibilities. Without trade, the economy can consume only what it produces. But with international trade, an economy can consume different quantities of goods from those that it produces. The production possibilities frontier describes the limits of what a country can produce, but it does not describe the limits to what it can consume. Figure 20.4 will help you to see the distinction between production possibilities and consumption possibilities when a country trades with other countries.

FIGURE 20.4 Expanding Consumption Possibilities

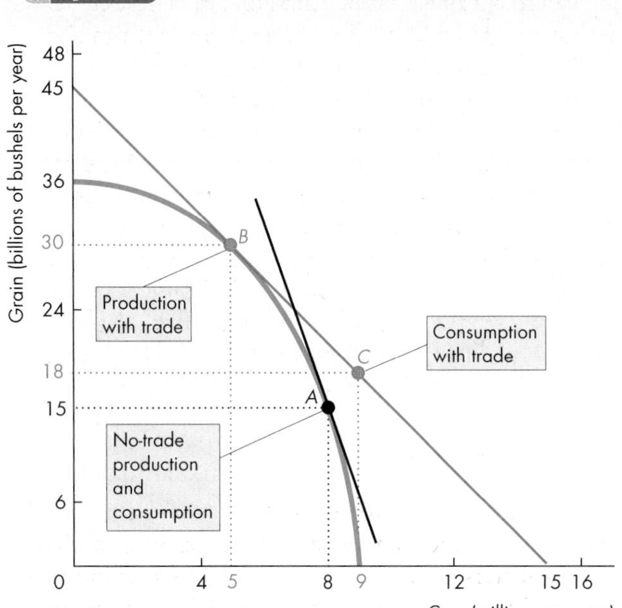

(a) Farmland

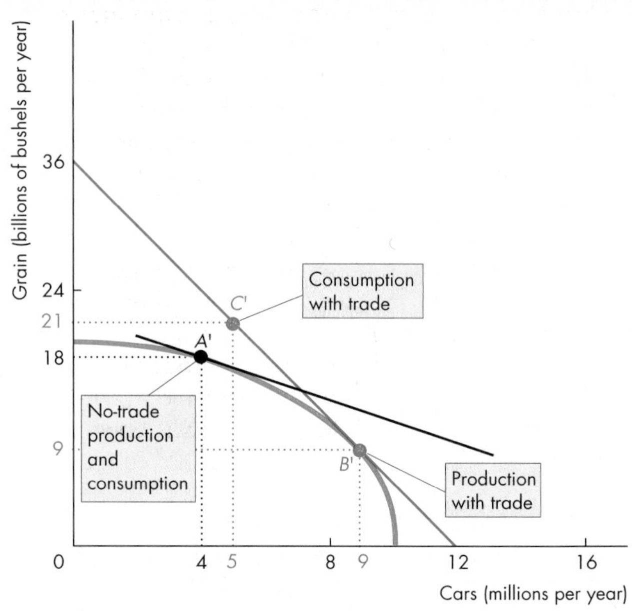

(b) Mobilia

With no international trade, the Farmers produce and consume at point *A* and the opportunity cost of a car is 9,000 bushels of grain (the slope of the black line in part a). Also, with no international trade, the Mobilians produce and consume at point *A*' and the opportunity cost of 1,000 bushels of grain is 1 car (the slope of the black line in part b).

Goods can be exchanged internationally at a price of 3,000 bushels of grain for 1 car along the red line in each part of the figure. In part (a), Farmland decreases its production of cars and increases its production of grain, moving from *A* to *B*. Farmland exports grain and imports cars, and it consumes at point *C*. The Farmers have more of both cars and grain than they would if they produced all their own consumption goods—at point *A*.

In part (b), Mobilia increases car production and decreases grain production, moving from *A*' to *B*'. Mobilia exports cars and imports grain, and it consumes at point *C*'. The Mobilians have more of both cars and grain than they would if they produced all their own consumption goods—at point *A*'.

First, notice that Fig. 20.4 has two parts: part (a) for Farmland and part (b) for Mobilia. The production possibilities frontiers that you saw in Figs. 20.1 and 20.2 are reproduced here. The slopes of the two black lines represent the opportunity costs in the two countries when there is no international trade. Farmland produces and consumes at point *A*, and Mobilia produces and consumes at *A*'. The opportunity cost of a car is 9,000 bushels of grain in Farmland and 1,000 bushels of grain in Mobilia.

Consumption Possibilities The red line in each part of Fig. 20.4 shows the country's consumption possibilities with international trade. These two red lines have the same slope, and the magnitude of that slope is the opportunity cost of a car in terms of grain on the world market: 3,000 bushels per car. The *slope* of the consumption possibilities line is common to both countries because its magnitude equals the *world* price. But the position of a country's consumption possibilities line depends on the country's production possibilities. A country cannot produce outside its production possibilities curve, so its consumption possibilities curve touches its production possibilities curve. So Farmland could choose to consume at point *B* with no international trade or, with international trade, at any point on its red consumption possibilities line.

Free Trade Equilibrium With international trade, the producers of cars in Mobilia can sell their cars for a higher price. As a result, they increase the quantity of cars they produce. At the same time, grain producers in Mobilia receive a lower price for their grain, and so they reduce the quantity of grain produced. Producers in Mobilia adjust their output by moving along their *PPF* until the opportunity cost in Mobilia equals the world price (the opportunity cost in the world market). This situation arises when Mobilia is producing at point *B*' in Fig. 20.4(b).

But the Mobilians do not consume at point *B*'. That is, they do not increase their consumption of cars and decrease their consumption of grain. Instead, they sell some of the cars they produce to Farmland in exchange for some of Farmland's grain. They trade internationally. But to see how that works out, we first need to check in with Farmland to see what's happening there.

In Farmland, producers of cars now receive a lower price and producers of grain can sell their grain for a higher price. As a consequence, producers in Farmland decrease car production and increase grain production. They adjust their outputs by moving along the *PPF* until the opportunity cost of a car in terms of grain equals the world price (the opportunity cost on the world market). They move to point *B* in part (a). But the Farmers do not consume at point *B*. Instead, they trade some of their additional grain production for the now cheaper cars from Mobilia.

The figure shows us the quantities consumed in the two countries. We saw in Fig. 20.3 that Mobilia exports 4 million cars a year and Farmland imports those cars. We also saw that Farmland exports 12 billion bushels of grain a year and Mobilia imports that grain. So Farmland's consumption of grain is 12 billion bushels a year less than it produces, and its consumption of cars is 4 million a year more than it produces. Farmland consumes at point *C* in Fig. 20.4(a).

Similarly, we know that Mobilia consumes 12 billion bushels of grain more than it produces and 4 million cars fewer than it produces. Mobilia consumes at point *C*' in Fig. 20.4(b).

Calculating the Gains from Trade

You can now literally see the gains from trade in Fig. 20.4. Without trade, Farmers produce and consume at *A* (part a)—a point on Farmland's production possibilities frontier. With international trade, Farmers consume at point *C* in part (a)—a point *outside* the production possibilities frontier. At point *C*, Farmers are consuming 3 billion bushels of grain a year and 1 million cars a year more than before. These increases in consumption of both cars and grain, beyond the limits of the production possibilities frontier, are the Farmers' gains from international trade.

Mobilians also gain. Without trade, they consume at point *A*' in part (b)—a point on Mobilia's production possibilities frontier. With international trade, they consume at point *C*'—a point *outside* their production possibilities frontier. With international trade, Mobilia consumes 3 billion bushels of grain a year and 1 million cars a year more than they would without trade. These are the gains from international trade for Mobilia.

Gains for Both Countries

Trade between the Farmers and the Mobilians does not create winners and losers. Both countries are winners. Farmers selling grain and Mobilians selling cars face an increased demand for their products because the demand by foreigners is added to domestic demand. With an increase in demand, the price rises.

Farmers buying cars and Mobilians buying grain face an increased supply of these products because the foreign supply is added to domestic supply. With an increase in supply, the price falls.

Gains from Trade in Reality

The gains from trade between Farmland and Mobilia that we have just studied occur in a model economy—in a world economy that we have imagined. But these same phenomena occur every day in the real global economy.

Comparative Advantage in the Global Economy We buy TVs and DVD players from Korea, machinery from Europe, and fashion goods from Hong Kong. In exchange, we sell machinery, grain and lumber, airplanes, computers, and financial services. All this international trade is generated by comparative advantage, just like the international trade between Farmland and Mobilia in our model economy. All international trade arises from comparative advantage, even when trade is in similar goods such as tools and machines. At first thought, it seems puzzling that countries exchange manufactured goods. Why doesn't each developed country produce all the manufactured goods its citizens want to buy?

Trade in Similar Goods Why does the United States produce automobiles for export and at the same time import large quantities of automobiles from Canada, Japan, Korea, and Western Europe? Wouldn't it make more sense to produce all the cars that we buy here in the United States? After all, we have access to the best technology available for producing cars. Autoworkers in the United States are surely as productive as their fellow workers in Canada, Western Europe, and Asia. So why does the United States have a comparative advantage in some types of cars and Asia and Europe in others?

Diversity of Taste and Economies of Scale The first part of the answer is that people have a tremendous diversity of taste. Let's stick with the example of cars. Some people prefer a sports car, some prefer a limousine, some prefer a regular, full-size car, some prefer a sport utility vehicle, and some prefer a minivan. In addition to size and type of car, there are many other dimensions in which cars vary. Some have low fuel consumption, some have high performance, some are spacious and comfortable, some have a large trunk, some have four-wheel drive, some have front-wheel drive, some have a radiator grill that looks like a Greek temple, others resemble a wedge. People's preferences across these many dimensions vary. The tremendous diversity in tastes for cars means that people value variety and are willing to pay for it in the marketplace.

The second part of the answer to the puzzle is *economies of scale*—the tendency for the average cost to be lower, the larger the scale of production. In such situations, larger and larger production runs lead to ever lower average costs. Production of many goods, including cars, involves economies of scale. For example, if a car producer makes only a few hundred (or perhaps a few thousand) cars of a particular type and design, the producer must use production techniques that are much more labor-intensive and much less automated than those employed to make hundreds of thousands of cars in a particular model. With short production runs and labor-intensive production techniques, costs are high. With very large production runs and automated assembly lines, production costs are much lower. But to obtain lower costs, the automated assembly lines have to produce a large number of cars.

It is the combination of diversity of taste and economies of scale that determines opportunity cost, produces comparative advantages, and generates such a large amount of international trade in similar commodities. With international trade, each car manufacturer has the whole world market to serve. Each producer can specialize in a limited range of products and then sell its output to the entire world market. This arrangement enables large production runs on the most popular cars and feasible production runs even on the most customized cars demanded by only a handful of people in each country.

The situation in the market for cars is also present in many other industries, especially those producing specialized equipment and parts. For example, the United States exports computer central processor chips but imports memory chips, exports mainframe computers but imports PCs, and exports specialized video equipment but imports DVD players. International trade in similar but slightly different manufactured products is profitable.

REVIEW QUIZ

1. What is the fundamental source of the gains from international trade?
2. In what circumstances can countries gain from international trade?
3. What determines the goods and services that a country will export?
4. What determines the goods and services that a country will import?
5. What is comparative advantage and what role does it play in determining the amount and type of international trade that occurs?
6. How can it be that all countries gain from international trade and that there are no losers?
7. Provide some examples of comparative advantage in today's world.
8. Why does the United States both export and import automobiles?

myeconlab **Study Plan 20.2**

You've now seen how free international trade brings gains for all countries. But international trade is not free in our world. We'll now take a brief look at the history and the effects of international trade restrictions. We'll see that free trade brings the greatest possible benefits and that international trade restrictions are costly.

International Trade Restrictions

Governments restrict international trade to protect domestic industries from foreign competition by using two main tools:

1. Tariffs
2. Nontariff barriers

A **tariff** is a tax that is imposed by the importing country when an imported good crosses its international boundary. A **nontariff barrier** is any action other than a tariff that restricts international trade. Examples of nontariff barriers are quantitative restrictions and licensing regulations limiting imports. First, let's look at tariffs.

The History of Tariffs

U.S. tariffs today are modest in comparison with their historical levels. Figure 20.5 shows the average tariff rate—total tariffs as a percentage of total imports. You can see in this figure that this average reached a peak of 20 percent in 1933. In that year, three years after the passage of the Smoot-Hawley Act, one third of our imports was subject to a tariff and on those imports the tariff rate was 60 percent. The average tariff in Fig. 20.5 for 1933 is 60 percent multiplied by 1/3, which equals 20 percent. Today, the average tariff rate is less than 2 percent.

In 1947, the United States and 22 other countries signed the **General Agreement on Tariffs and Trade** (GATT). From its formation, GATT organized a series of "rounds" of negotiations that resulted in a steady process of tariff reduction. The final round, the Uruguay Round, started in 1986 and completed in 1994, led to the creation of the **World Trade Organization** (WTO).

In 2001, the WTO embarked on an ambitious program known as the *Doha Development Agenda*, which seeks to create free world trade in all goods and services, including agriculture. The major challenge of this program is to open markets for developing countries in the developed world. Limited progress has been made in this program in conferences held in Cancún in 2003, Geneva in 2004, and Hong Kong in 2005, and this program is ongoing.

FIGURE 20.5 U.S. Tariffs: 1930–2006

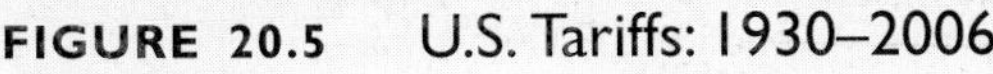

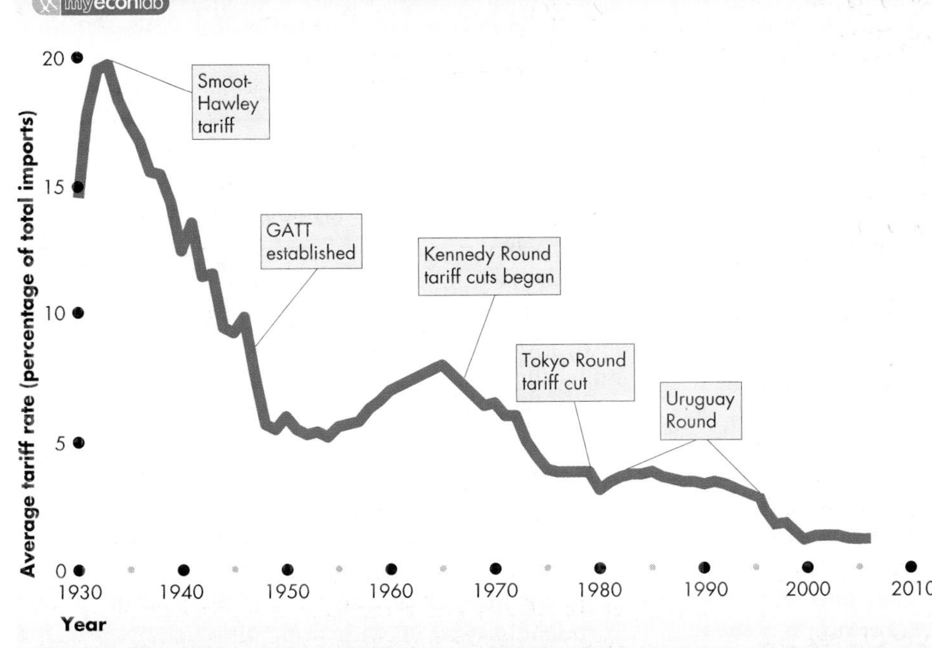

The Smoot-Hawley Act, which was passed in 1930, took U.S. tariffs to a peak average rate of 20 percent in 1933. (One third of imports was subject to a tariff rate of 60 percent.) Since the establishment of GATT in 1947, tariffs have steadily declined in a series of negotiating rounds, the most significant of which are identified in the figure. Tariffs are now as low as they have ever been.

Sources of data: U.S. Bureau of the Census, *Historical Statistics of the United States, Colonial Times to 1970*, Bicentennial Edition, Part I (Washington, D.C., 1975); Series U-212: updated from *Statistical Abstract of the United States:* various editions.

In addition to the agreements under the GATT and the WTO, the United States is a party to the **North American Free Trade Agreement** (NAFTA), which became effective on January 1, 1994, and under which barriers to international trade between the United States, Canada, and Mexico will be virtually eliminated after a 15-year phasing-in period.

In other parts of the world, trade barriers have virtually been eliminated among the member countries of the European Union, which has created the largest unified tariff-free market in the world. In 1994, discussions among the Asia-Pacific Economic Cooperation (APEC) led to an agreement in principle to work toward a free-trade area that embraces China, all the economies of East Asia and the South Pacific, Chile, Peru, Mexico, and the United States and Canada. These countries include the fastest-growing economies and hold the promise of heralding a global free-trade area.

The effort to achieve freer trade underlines the fact that trade in some goods is still subject to a high tariff. Textiles and footwear are among the goods that face the highest tariffs, and rates on these items average more than 10 percent. Some individual items face a tariff much higher than the average. For example, when you buy a pair of blue jeans for $30, you pay about $7 more than you would if there were no tariffs on textiles. Other goods that are protected by tariffs are agricultural products, energy and chemicals, minerals, and metals. The meat, cheese, and sugar that you consume cost significantly more because of protection than they would with free international trade.

The temptation for governments to impose tariffs is a strong one. First, tariffs provide revenue to the government. Second, they enable the government to satisfy special interest groups in import-competing industries. But, as we'll see, free international trade brings enormous benefits that are reduced when tariffs are imposed. Let's see how.

How Tariffs Work

To see how tariffs work, let's return to the example of trade between Farmland and Mobilia. Figure 20.6 shows the international market for cars in which these two countries are the only traders. The volume of trade and the price of a car are determined at the point of intersection of Mobilia's export supply curve of cars and Farmland's import demand curve for cars.

FIGURE 20.6 The Effects of a Tariff

myeconlab

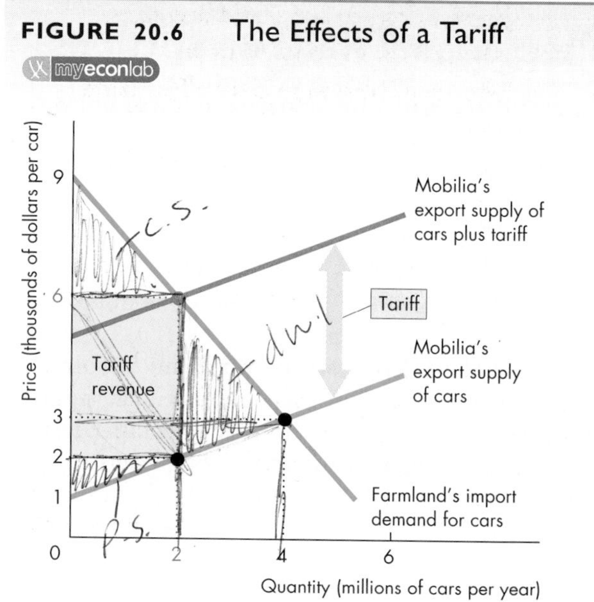

Farmland imposes a tariff on car imports from Mobilia. The tariff increases the price that Farmers have to pay for a car and shifts the supply curve of cars in Farmland leftward. The vertical distance between the original supply curve and the new one is the amount of the tariff, $4,000 per car. The price of a car in Farmland increases, and the quantity of cars imported decreases. The government of Farmland collects a tariff revenue of $4,000 per car—a total of $8 billion on the 2 million cars imported. Farmland's exports of grain decrease because Mobilia now has a lower income from its exports of cars.

In Fig. 20.6, these two countries trade cars and grain in exactly the same way that we saw in Fig. 20.3: Mobilia exports cars, and Farmland exports grain. The volume of car imports into Farmland is 4 million a year, and the world market price of a car is 3,000 bushels of grain. Figure 20.6 expresses prices in dollars rather than in units of grain and is based on a money price of grain of $1 a bushel. With grain costing $1 a bushel, the money price of a car is $3,000.

Now suppose that the government of Farmland, perhaps under pressure from car producers, decides to impose a tariff on imported cars. In particular, suppose that a tariff of $4,000 per car is imposed. (This is a huge tariff, but the car producers of Farmland are fed up with competition from Mobilia.) What happens?

- The supply of cars in Farmland decreases.
- The price of a car in Farmland rises.
- The quantity of cars imported by Farmland decreases.
- The government of Farmland collects the tariff revenue.
- Resource use is inefficient.
- The *value* of exports changes by the same amount as the *value* of imports, and trade remains balanced.

Change in the Supply of Cars Farmland cannot import cars at Mobilia's export supply price. It must pay that price plus the $4,000 tariff. So the supply curve in Farmland shifts leftward. The new supply curve is labeled "Mobilia's export supply of cars plus tariff." The vertical distance between Mobilia's original export supply curve and the new supply curve is the tariff of $4,000 a car.

Rise in Price of a Car A new equilibrium occurs where the new supply curve intersects Farmland's import demand curve for cars. That equilibrium is at a price of $6,000 a car, up from $3,000 with free trade.

Fall in Imports Car imports fall from 4 million to 2 million cars a year. At the higher price of $6,000 a car, domestic car producers increase their production. Domestic grain production decreases as resources are moved into the expanding car industry.

Tariff Revenue Total expenditure on imported cars by the Farmers is $6,000 a car multiplied by the 2 million cars imported ($12 billion). But not all of that money goes to the Mobilians. They receive $2,000 a car, or $4 billion for the 2 million cars. The difference—$4,000 a car, or a total of $8 billion for the 2 million cars—is collected by the government of Farmland as tariff revenue.

Inefficiency The people of Farmland are willing to pay $6,000 for the marginal car imported. But the opportunity cost of that car is $2,000. So there is a gain from trading an extra car. In fact, there are gains—willingness to pay exceeds opportunity cost—all the way up to 4 million cars a year. Only when 4 million cars are being traded is the maximum price that a Farmer is willing to pay equal to the minimum price that is acceptable to a Mobilian. Restricting trade reduces the gains from trade.

Trade Remains Balanced With free trade, Farmland was paying $3,000 a car and buying 4 million cars a year from Mobilia. Farmland was paying Mobilia $12 billion a year for imported cars. With a tariff of $4,000 a car, Farmland's imports have decreased to 2 million cars a year and the price paid to Mobilia has fallen to $2,000 a car. The total amount Farmland has paid to Mobilia for imports has fallen to $4 billion a year. Doesn't this fact mean that Farmland now has a balance of trade surplus? It does not.

The price of a car in Mobilia has fallen but the price of grain remains at $1 a bushel. So the relative price of a car has fallen, and the relative price of grain has increased. With free trade, the Mobilians could buy 3,000 bushels of grain for one car. Now they can buy only 2,000 bushels for a car.

With a higher relative price of grain, the quantity demanded by the Mobilians decreases and Mobilia imports less grain. But because Mobilia imports less grain, Farmland exports less grain. In fact, Farmland's grain industry suffers from two sources. First, there is a decrease in the quantity of grain sold to Mobilia. Second, there is increased competition for resources from the now-expanded car industry. The tariff leads to a contraction in the scale of the grain industry in Farmland.

It seems paradoxical at first that a country imposing a tariff on cars hurts its own export industry, lowering its exports of grain. It might help to think of it this way: Mobilians buy grain with the money they make from exporting cars to Farmland. If they export fewer cars, they cannot afford to buy as much grain. In fact, in the absence of any international borrowing and lending, Mobilia must cut its imports of grain by exactly the same amount as the loss in revenue from its export of cars. Grain imports into Mobilia are cut back to a value of $4 billion, the amount that can be paid for by the new lower revenue from Mobilia's car exports. Trade is still balanced. The tariff cuts the value of imports and exports by the same amount. The tariff has no effect on the *balance* of trade, but it reduces the *volume* of trade.

The result that we have just derived is perhaps one of the most misunderstood aspects of international economics. On countless occasions, politicians and others call for tariffs to remove a balance of trade deficit or argue that lowering tariffs would produce a balance of trade deficit. They reach this conclusion by failing to work out all the implications of a tariff.

Let's now look at nontariff barriers.

Nontariff Barriers

The two main forms of nontariff barriers are

1. Quotas
2. Voluntary export restraints

A **quota** is a quantitative restriction on the import of a particular good, which specifies the maximum amount of the good that may be imported in a given period of time. A **voluntary export restraint** (VER) is an agreement between two governments in which the government of the exporting country agrees to restrain the volume of its own exports.

Quotas are especially prominent in textiles and agriculture. VERs have been used in U.S. trade with Japan in a wide range of products, and more recently in textile trade with China (see *Reading Between the Lines* on pp. 478–479).

How Quotas Work

Suppose that Farmland puts a quota on car imports of 2 million a year. Figure 20.7 shows the effects of this action. The quota is shown by the vertical red line at 2 million cars a year. Farmland car importers buy that quantity from Mobilia and pay $2,000 a car. But because the quantity of cars imported is restricted to 2 million cars a year, people in Farmland are willing to pay $6,000 per car. This is the price of a car in Farmland.

The value of imports falls to $4 billion (the same as in the case of the tariff). With lower incomes from car exports and with a higher relative price of grain, Mobilians cut back on their imports of grain in exactly the same way that they did under a tariff.

The key difference between a quota and a tariff lies in who collects the gap between the exporter's supply price and the domestic price. In the case of a tariff, the government of the importing country receives the gap. In the case of a quota, it goes to the importer.

How VERs Work

A VER is like a quota allocated to each exporter. The effects of a VER are similar to those of a quota but differ from them in that the gap between the domestic price and the export price is captured not by domestic importers but by the foreign exporter. The government of the exporting country has to establish procedures for allocating the restricted volume of exports among its producers.

FIGURE 20.7 The Effects of a Quota

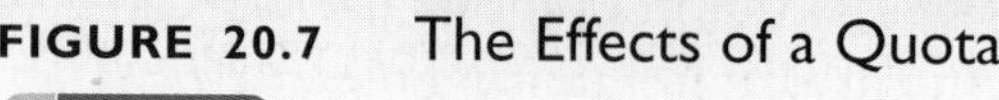

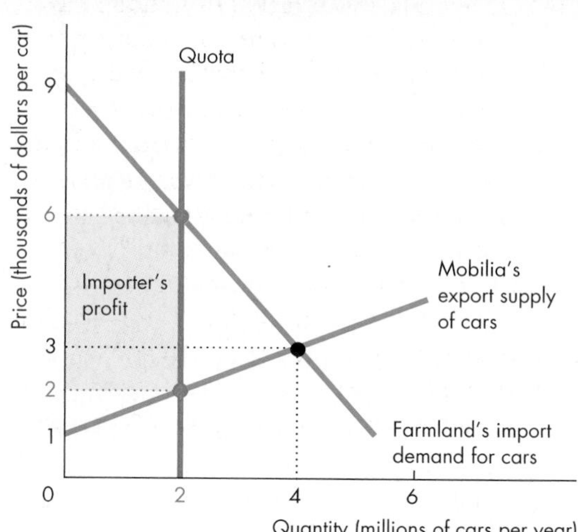

Farmland imposes a quota of 2 million cars a year on car imports from Mobilia. That quantity appears as the vertical line labeled "Quota." Because the quantity of cars imported by Farmland is restricted to 2 million, the price of a car in Farmland increases to $6,000. Importing cars is profitable because Mobilia is willing to supply cars at $2,000 each. There is competition for import quotas.

REVIEW QUIZ

1. What are the tools that a country can use to restrict international trade?
2. What do international trade restrictions do to the gains from international trade?
3. Which is best for a country: restricted trade, no trade, or free trade? Why?
4. What does a tariff on imports do to the volume of imports and the volume of exports?
5. In the absence of international borrowing and lending, how do tariffs and other international trade restrictions influence the total value of imports and exports and the balance of trade?

myeconlab **Study Plan 20.3**

We're now going to look at some commonly heard arguments for restricting international trade and see why they are almost never correct.

The Case Against Protection

For as long as nations and international trade have existed, people have debated whether a country is better off with free international trade or with protection from foreign competition. The debate continues, but for most economists, a verdict has been delivered and is the one you have just seen. Free trade promotes prosperity for all countries; protection is inefficient. We've seen the most powerful case for free trade in the example of how Farmland and Mobilia both benefit from their comparative advantage. But there is a broader range of issues in the free trade versus protection debate. Let's review these issues.

Three arguments for restricting international trade are

- The national security argument
- The infant-industry argument
- The dumping argument

The National Security Argument

The national security argument for protection is that a country must protect the industries that produce defense equipment and armaments and those on which the defense industries rely for their raw materials and other intermediate inputs. This argument for protection does not withstand close scrutiny.

First, it is an argument for international isolation, for in a time of war, there is no industry that does not contribute to national defense.

Second, if the case is made for boosting the output of a strategic industry, it is more efficient to achieve this outcome with a subsidy to the firms in the industry, with the subsidy financed out of taxes. Such a subsidy would keep the industry operating at the scale judged appropriate, and free international trade would keep the prices faced by consumers at their world market levels.

The Infant-Industry Argument

The so-called **infant-industry argument** for protection is that it is necessary to protect a new industry to enable it to grow into a mature industry that can compete in world markets. The argument is based on the idea of *dynamic comparative advantage*, which can arise from *learning-by-doing* (see Chapter 2).

Learning-by-doing is a powerful engine of productivity growth, and comparative advantage does evolve and change because of on-the-job experience. But these facts do not justify protection.

First, the infant-industry argument is valid only if the benefits of learning-by-doing *not only* accrue to the owners and workers of the firms in the infant industry but also *spill over* to other industries and parts of the economy. For example, there are huge productivity gains from learning-by-doing in the manufacture of aircraft. But almost all of these gains benefit the stockholders and workers of Boeing and other aircraft producers. Because the people making the decisions, bearing the risk, and doing the work are the ones who benefit, they take the dynamic gains into account when they decide on the scale of their activities. In this case, almost no benefits spill over to other parts of the economy, so there is no need for government assistance to achieve an efficient outcome.

Second, even if the case is made for protecting an infant industry, it is more efficient to do so by a subsidy to the firms in the industry, with the subsidy financed out of taxes. Such a subsidy would encourage the industry to mature and to compete with efficient world producers and keep the prices faced by consumers at their world market levels.

The Dumping Argument

Dumping occurs when a foreign firm sells its exports at a lower price than its cost of production. Dumping might be used by a firm that wants to gain a global monopoly. In this case, the foreign firm sells its output at a price below its cost to drive domestic firms out of business. When the domestic firms have gone, the foreign firm takes advantage of its monopoly position and charges a higher price for its product. Dumping is usually regarded as a justification for temporary tariffs, which are called *countervailing duties*.

But there are powerful reasons to resist the dumping argument for protection. First, it is virtually impossible to detect dumping because it is hard to determine a firm's costs. As a result, the test for dumping is whether a firm's export price is below its domestic price. But this test is a weak one because it can be rational for a firm to charge a low price in markets in which the quantity demanded is highly sensitive to price and a higher price in a market in which demand is less price-sensitive.

Second, it is hard to think of a good that is produced by a natural *global* monopoly. So even if all the domestic firms in some industry were driven out of business, it would always be possible to find many alternative foreign sources of supply and to buy the good at prices determined in competitive markets.

Third, if a good or service were a truly global natural monopoly, the best way of dealing with it would be by regulation—just as in the case of domestic monopolies. Such regulation would require international cooperation.

The three arguments for protection that we've just examined have an element of credibility. The counterarguments are in general stronger, however, so these arguments do not make the case for protection. But they are not the only arguments that you might encounter. There are many other new arguments against globalization and for protection. The most common of them are that protection

- Saves jobs
- Allows us to compete with cheap foreign labor
- Brings diversity and stability
- Penalizes lax environmental standards
- Protects national culture
- Prevents rich countries from exploiting developing countries

Saves Jobs

The argument is that when we buy shoes from Brazil or shirts from Taiwan, U.S. workers in these industries lose their jobs. With no earnings and poor prospects, these workers become a drain on welfare and spend less, causing a ripple effect of further job losses. The proposed solution is to ban imports of cheap foreign goods and protect U.S. jobs. This argument does not withstand scrutiny for three reasons.

First, free trade does cost some jobs, but it also creates other jobs. It brings about a global rationalization of labor and allocates labor resources to their highest-valued activities. International trade in textiles has cost tens of thousands of jobs in the United States as textile mills and other factories closed. But tens of thousands of jobs have been created in other countries as textile mills opened. And tens of thousands of U.S. workers got better-paying jobs than textile workers because U.S. export industries expanded and created new jobs. More jobs were created than destroyed.

Second, imports create jobs. They create jobs for retailers that sell imported goods and firms that service those goods. They also create jobs by creating incomes in the rest of the world, some of which are spent on imports of U.S.-made goods and services.

Although protection does save particular jobs, it does so at a high cost. For example, until 2005, textile jobs in the United States were protected by an international agreement called the Multifiber Arrangement. The U.S. International Trade Commission (ITC) has estimated that because of quotas, 72,000 jobs existed in textiles that would otherwise have disappeared and that the annual clothing expenditure in the United States was \$15.9 billion, or \$160 per family, higher than it will be with free trade. Equivalently, the ITC estimated that each textile job saved cost \$221,000 a year.

Allows Us to Compete with Cheap Foreign Labor

With the removal of tariffs in U.S. trade with Mexico, people said we would hear a "giant sucking sound" as jobs rushed to Mexico (shown in the cartoon). Let's see what's wrong with this view.

The labor cost of a unit of output equals the wage rate divided by labor productivity. For example, if a U.S. autoworker earns \$30 an hour and produces

"I don't know what the hell happened—one minute I'm at work in Flint, Michigan, then there's a giant sucking sound and suddenly here I am in Mexico."

15 units of output an hour, the average labor cost of a unit of output is \$2. If a Mexican auto assembly worker earns \$3 an hour and produces 1 unit of output an hour, the average labor cost of a unit of output is \$3. Other things remaining the same, the higher a worker's productivity, the higher is the worker's wage rate. High-wage workers have high productivity. Low-wage workers have low productivity.

Although high-wage U.S. workers are more productive, on the average, than low-wage Mexican workers, there are differences across industries. U.S. labor is relatively more productive in some activities than in others. For example, the productivity of U.S. workers in producing movies, financial services, and customized computer chips is relatively higher than their productivity in the production of metals and some standardized machine parts. The activities in which U.S. workers are relatively more productive than their Mexican counterparts are those in which the United States has a *comparative advantage*. By engaging in free trade, increasing our production and exports of the goods and services in which we have a comparative advantage and decreasing our production and increasing our imports of the goods and services in which our trading partners have a comparative advantage, we can make ourselves and the citizens of other countries better off.

Brings Diversity and Stability

A diversified investment portfolio is less risky than one that has all the eggs in one basket. The same is true for an economy's production. A diversified economy fluctuates less than does an economy that produces only one or two goods.

But big, rich, diversified economies such as those of the United States, Japan, and Europe do not have this type of stability problem. Even a country such as Saudi Arabia that produces only one good (in this case, oil) can benefit from specializing in the activity at which it has a comparative advantage and then investing in a wide range of other countries to bring greater stability to its income and consumption.

Penalizes Lax Environmental Standards

Another argument for protection is that many poorer countries, such as Mexico, do not have the same environmental policies that we have and, because they are willing to pollute and we are not, we cannot compete with them without tariffs. So if they want free trade with the richer and "greener" countries, they must clean up their environments to our standards.

This argument for international trade restrictions is weak. First, not all poorer countries have significantly lower environmental standards than the United States has. Many poor countries and the former communist countries of Eastern Europe do have bad environmental records. But some countries enforce strict laws. Second, a poor country cannot afford to be as concerned about its environment as a rich country can. The best hope for a better environment in Mexico and in other developing countries is rapid income growth through free trade. As their incomes grow, developing countries will have the *means* to match their desires to improve their environment. Third, poor countries have a comparative advantage at doing "dirty" work, which helps rich countries to achieve higher environmental standards than they otherwise could.

Protects National Culture

The national culture argument for protection is not heard much in the United States, but it is a commonly heard argument in Canada and Europe.

The expressed fear is that free trade in books, magazines, movies, and television programs means U.S. domination and the end of local culture. So, the reasoning continues, it is necessary to protect domestic "culture" industries from free international trade to ensure the survival of a national cultural identity.

Protection of these industries is common and takes the form of nontariff barriers. For example, local content regulations on radio and television broadcasting and in magazines is often required.

The cultural identity argument for protection has no merit. Writers, publishers, and broadcasters want to limit foreign competition so that they can earn larger economic profits. There is no actual danger to national culture. In fact, many of the creators of so-called American cultural products are not Americans but the talented citizens of other countries, ensuring the survival of their national cultural identities in Hollywood! Also, if national culture is in danger, there is no surer way of helping it on its way out than by impoverishing the nation whose culture it is. And protection is an effective way of doing just that.

Prevents Rich Countries from Exploiting Developing Countries

Another argument for protection is that international trade must be restricted to prevent the people of the rich industrial world from exploiting the poorer people of the developing countries, forcing them to work for slave wages.

Child labor and near-slave labor is a serious problem that is rightly condemned. But by trading with poor countries, we increase the demand for the goods that these countries produce and, more significantly, we increase the demand for their labor. When the demand for labor in developing countries increases, the wage rate also increases. So, rather than exploiting people in developing countries, trade can improve their opportunities and increase their incomes.

We have reviewed the arguments that are commonly heard in favor of protection and the counterarguments against them. There is one counterargument to protection that is general and quite overwhelming. Protection invites retaliation and can trigger a trade war. The best example of a trade war occurred during the Great Depression of the 1930s when the Smoot-Hawley tariff was introduced in the United States. Country after country retaliated with its own tariff, and in a short period, world trade had almost disappeared. The costs to all countries were large and led to a renewed international resolve to avoid such self-defeating moves in the future. They also led to the creation of GATT and are the impetus behind NAFTA, APEC, and the European Union.

REVIEW QUIZ

1 Can we achieve national security goals, stimulate the growth of new industries, or restrain foreign monopoly by restricting international trade? If so, explain how.
2 Can we save jobs, compensate for low foreign wages, make the economy more diversified, compensate for costly environmental policies, protect national culture, or protect developing countries from being exploited by restricting international trade? If so, explain how.
3 What is the main argument against international trade restrictions?

myeconlab Study Plan 20.4

Why Is International Trade Restricted?

Why, despite all the arguments against protection, is trade restricted? There are two key reasons:

- Tariff revenue
- Rent seeking

Tariff Revenue

Government revenue is costly to collect. In the developed countries such as the United States, a well-organized tax collection system is in place that can generate billions of dollars of income tax and sales tax revenues. This tax collection system is made possible by the fact that most economic transactions are done by firms that must keep properly audited financial records. Without such records, the revenue collection agencies (the Internal Revenue Service in the United States) would be severely hampered in the work. Even with audited financial accounts, some proportion of potential tax revenue is lost. Nonetheless, for the industrialized countries, the income tax and sales taxes are the major sources of revenue and the tariff plays a very small role.

But governments in developing countries have a difficult time collecting taxes from their citizens. Much economic activity takes place in an informal economy with few financial records, so only a small amount of revenue is collected from income taxes and sales taxes. The one area in which economic transactions are well recorded and audited is in international trade. So this activity is an attractive base for tax collection in these countries and is used much more extensively than it is in the developed countries.

Rent Seeking

Rent seeking is the major reason why international trade is restricted. **Rent seeking** is lobbying and other political activity that seek to capture the gains from trade. Free trade increases consumption possibilities *on the average*, but not everyone shares in the gain and some people even lose. Free trade brings benefits to some and imposes costs on others, with total benefits exceeding total costs. It is the uneven distribution of costs and benefits that is the principal source of impediment to achieving more liberal international trade.

Returning to our example of trade in cars and grain between Farmland and Mobilia, the benefits to Farmland from free trade accrue to all the producers of grain and to those producers of cars who do not bear the costs of adjusting to a smaller car industry. These costs are transition costs, not permanent costs. The costs of Farmland's move to free trade are borne by the car producers and their employees who have to become grain producers. In Mobilia, the benefits from free trade accrue to car producers and those grain producers who do not bear the transition costs to a small grain industry. The losers are the grain producers and their employees who have to produce cars.

The number of people who gain, in general, is large compared with the number who lose. So the gain per person is small but the loss per person to those who bear the loss is large. Because the loss that falls on those who bear it is large, it will pay those people to incur considerable expense to lobby against free trade. On the other hand, it will not pay those who gain to organize to achieve free trade. The gain from trade for any one person is too small for that person to spend much time or money on a political organization to achieve free trade. The loss from free trade will be seen as being so great by those bearing that loss that they *will* find it profitable to join a political organization to prevent free trade. Each group is optimizing—weighing benefits against costs and choosing the best action for themselves. The anti-free-trade group will, however, undertake a larger quantity of political lobbying than the pro-free-trade group.

Compensating Losers

If, in total, the gains from free international trade exceed the losses, why don't those who gain compensate those who lose so that everyone is in favor of free trade? To some degree, such compensation does take place. When Congress approved the NAFTA deal with Canada and Mexico, it set up a $56 million fund to support and retrain workers who lost their jobs as a result of the new trade agreement. During the first six months of the operation of NAFTA, only 5,000 workers applied for benefits under this scheme.

The losers from freer international trade are also compensated indirectly through the normal unemployment compensation arrangements. But only limited attempts are made to compensate those who lose. The main reason why full compensation is not attempted is that the costs of identifying all the losers and estimating the value of their losses would be enormous. Also, it would never be clear whether a person who has fallen on hard times is suffering because of free trade or for other reasons that might be largely under his or her control. Furthermore, some people who look like losers at one point in time might, in fact, end up gaining. The young autoworker who loses his job in Michigan and becomes a computer assembly worker in Minneapolis resents the loss of work and the need to move. But a year or two later, looking back on events, he counts himself fortunate. He has made a move that has increased his income and given him greater job security.

It is because we do not, in general, compensate the losers from free international trade that protectionism is such a popular and permanent feature of our national economic and political life.

REVIEW QUIZ

1. What are the two main reasons for imposing tariffs on imports?
2. What type of country benefits most from the revenue from tariffs? Provide some examples of such countries.
3. Does the United States need to use tariffs to raise revenue for the government? Explain why or why not.
4. If international trade restrictions are costly, why do we use them? Why don't the people who gain from trade organize a political force that is strong enough to ensure that their interests are protected?

myeconlab **Study Plan 20.5**

You've seen why all nations gain from specialization and trade. By producing goods in which we have a comparative advantage and trading some of our production for that of others, we expand our consumption possibilities. Placing restriction on that trade reduces our gains from international trade. By opening our country up to free trade, the market for the things that we sell expands and their relative price rises. The market for the things that we buy also expands, and their relative price falls.

Reading Between the Lines on pp. 478–479 looks at the globalization of production and the gains to Americans and Asians as production in China and trade between China and the United States expand.

READING BETWEEN THE LINES

The Gains from Globalization

http://www.nytimes.com

China and U.S. Expected to Reach Deal on Textiles

November 7, 2005

An agreement to limit for three years the surging growth of Chinese textile imports to the United States is expected to be completed as early as this week, Bush administration officials said yesterday.

. . . Worries that trade frictions could disrupt textile shipments from China have made some American retailers reluctant to place large orders. The deal is reportedly similar to an agreement reached last summer to limit Chinese clothing exports to the European Union, which followed disruption of supplies to retailers.

. . . China bought $278 million of American textile products in 2004, while selling 52 times that much, or $14.6 billion, to the United States, according to the United States trade representative's office. In 2002, the United States had 651,000 jobs in textile mills and apparel-making, less than half the number in 1990, data from the Census Bureau show.

. . . Overall Chinese textile exports to the United States surged 54 percent in the first eight months of this year, to $17.7 billion, the Chinese government reported last month. American officials put the figure at 46 percent.

. . . North Carolina had 350,000 textile jobs in 1972, but more than 90 percent of them will be gone by the end of this decade, Mark Vitner, a senior economist at Wachovia Bank in Charlotte, said yesterday. He said production had not declined as sharply because Chinese imports encouraged the state's companies to make investments in automated machinery, which cut payrolls.

China sold 700 million pairs of socks to the United States in the first eight months of this year, up from fewer than 12 million four years ago, and sales of jeans, underwear and other labor-intensive items are up as much as tenfold this year compared with 2004.

Essence of the Story

- China is expected to agree to limit textile exports to the United States.
- In 2004, for every $1 that China spent on U.S.-produced textiles, the United States spent $52 on textiles produced in China.
- Employment in textiles production in the United States has fallen, and it has done so especially strongly in North Carolina.
- Chinese textile exports to the United States grew by 54 percent in the first eight months of 2005.
- China sold 700 million pairs of socks to the United States in the first eight months of 2005, up from fewer than 12 million four years earlier.
- Sales of jeans and underwear were up tenfold in 2005 over 2004.

- With free trade, goods are produced where their opportunity cost of production is lowest.
- Clothing can be produced at a lower opportunity cost in China than in the United States.
- By specializing in items at which we have a comparative advantage and buying our clothes from China, we gain and China gains.
- We gain because our clothes cost less; China gains because it can sell clothing to us for a higher price than its cost of production.
- We also gain because we sell China items such as large passenger jets for more than our cost of production, and China gains because it can buy items like passenger jets for a lower price that its cost of producing them.
- Table 1 contains some illustrative numbers, and Fig. 1 shows these numbers graphically.
- The United States can produce Nike outfits or other goods and services. The opportunity cost in the United States of 1 unit of Nike outfits is 1 unit of other goods and services.
- China can also produce Nike outfits or other goods and services. The opportunity cost in China of 1 unit of Nike outfits is 0.5 unit of other goods and services.
- But if China produces Nike outfits and the United States produces other goods and services, the two countries can expand their consumption possibilities.
- In Fig. 2, China produces 40 units of Nike outfits and the United States produces 100 units of other goods and services.
- If the two countries trade 1 unit of Nike outfits for 0.75 unit of other goods and services, the United States gets Nike outfits for less than its opportunity cost of producing them and China sells the outfits for more than its opportunity cost of producing them.
- Table 1 shows the trading possibilities, and each country can trade along its trade line in Fig. 2.
- The United States buys goods from China, but China also buys goods from the United States.

You're the Voter

- Do you think that U.S. trade with China and other low-income Asian countries should be free?
- Would you vote for measures to keep the jobs that produce clothing in the United States? Explain why or why not.

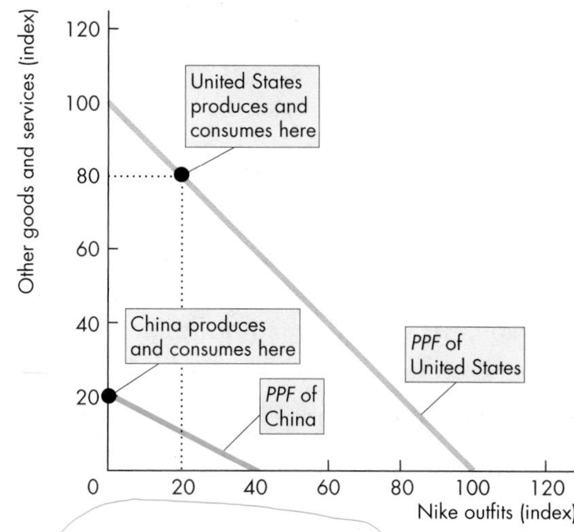

Figure 1 No trade

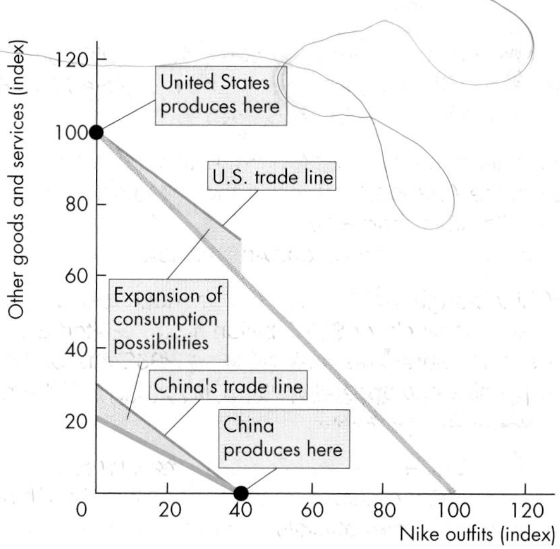

Figure 2 Free trade

	Other goods and services			
	Production possibilities		Trading possibilities	
Nike outfits	United States	China	United States	China
0	100	20	100	30
20	80	10	85	15
40	60	0	70	0
100	0			

Table 1 Production possibilities and trading possibilities for China and the United States

SUMMARY

Key Points

Patterns and Trends in International Trade (p. 462)

- Large flows of trade take place between countries, most of which is in manufactured goods exchanged among rich industrialized countries.
- Since 1960, the U.S. international trade has almost tripled.

The Gains from International Trade (pp. 463–468)

- Comparative advantage is the fundamental source of the gains from trade.
- Comparative advantage exists when opportunity costs between countries diverge.
- By increasing its production of goods and services in which it has a comparative advantage and then trading some of the increased output, a country can consume at points outside its production possibilities frontier.
- In the absence of international borrowing and lending, trade is balanced as prices adjust to reflect the international supply of and demand for goods and services.
- The world price balances the production and consumption plans of the trading parties. At the equilibrium price, trade is balanced.
- Comparative advantage explains the international trade that takes place in the world.
- But trade in similar goods arises from economies of scale in the face of diversified tastes.

International Trade Restrictions (pp. 469–472)

- Countries restrict international trade by imposing tariffs, quotas, and voluntary export restraints.
- International trade restrictions raise the domestic price of imported goods, lower the volume of imports, and reduce the total value of imports.
- International trade restrictions also reduce the total value of exports by the same amount as the reduction in the value of imports.

The Case Against Protection (pp. 473–476)

- Arguments that protection is necessary for national security, to protect infant industries, and to prevent dumping are weak.
- Arguments that protection saves jobs, allows us to compete with cheap foreign labor, makes the economy diversified and stable, penalizes lax environmental standards, protects national culture, and prevents rich countries from exploiting developing countries are fatally flawed.

Why Is International Trade Restricted? (pp. 476–477)

- Trade is restricted because tariffs raise government revenue and because protection brings a small loss to a large number of people and a large gain per person to a small number of people.

Key Figures

Key Terms

PROBLEMS

myeconlab Tests, Study Plan, Solutions*

1. The table provides information about Virtual Reality's production possibilities.

TV sets (per day)		Computers (per day)
0	and	36
10	and	35
20	and	33
30	and	30
40	and	26
50	and	21
60	and	15
70	and	8
80	and	0

   a. Calculate Virtual Reality's opportunity cost of a TV set when it produces 10 sets a day.
   b. Calculate Virtual Reality's opportunity cost of a TV set when it produces 40 sets a day.
   c. Calculate Virtual Reality's opportunity cost of a TV set when it produces 70 sets a day.
   d. Using the answers to parts (a), (b), and (c), sketch the relationship between the opportunity cost of a TV set and the quantity of TV sets produced in Virtual Reality.

2. The table provides information about Vital Sign's production possibilities.

TV sets (per day)		Computers (per day)
0	and	18.0
10	and	17.5
20	and	16.5
30	and	15.0
40	and	13.0
50	and	10.5
60	and	7.5
70	and	4.0
80	and	0

   a. Calculate Vital Sign's opportunity cost of a TV set when it produces 10 sets a day.
   b. Calculate Vital Sign's opportunity cost of a TV set when it produces 40 sets a day.
   c. Calculate Vital Sign's opportunity cost of a TV set when it produces 70 sets a day.
   d. Using the answers to parts (a), (b), and (c), sketch the relationship between the opportunity cost of a TV set and the quantity of TV sets produced in Vital Sign.

3. Suppose that with no international trade, Virtual Reality in problem 1 produces and consumes 10 TV sets a day and Vital Signs in problem 2 produces and consumes 60 TV sets a day. Now suppose that the two countries begin to trade.
   a. Which country exports TV sets?
   b. What adjustments are made to the amount of each good produced by each country?
   c. What adjustments are made to the amount of each good consumed by each country?
   d. What can you say about the terms of trade (the price of a TV set expressed as computers per TV set) under free trade?

4. Suppose that with no international trade, Virtual Reality in problem 1 produces and consumes 50 TV sets a day and Vital Sign in problem 2 produces and consumes 20 TV sets a day. Now suppose that the two countries begin to trade.
   a. Which country exports TV sets?
   b. What adjustments are made to the amount of each good produced by each country?
   c. What adjustments are made to the amount of each good consumed by each country?
   d. What can you say about the terms of trade (the price of a TV set expressed as computers per TV set) under free trade?

5. Compare the total quantities of each good produced in problems 1 and 2 with the total quantities of each good produced in problems 3 and 4.
   a. Does free trade increase or decrease the total quantities of TV sets and computers produced in both cases? Why?
   b. What happens to the price of a TV set in Virtual Reality in the two cases? Why does it rise in one case and fall in the other?
   c. What happens to the price of a computer in Vital Sign in the two cases? Why does it rise in one case and fall in the other?

6. Compare the international trade in problem 3 with that in problem 4.
   a. Why does Virtual Reality export TV sets in one of the cases and import them in the other case?
   b. Do the TV producers or the computer producers gain in each case?
   c. Do consumers gain in each case?

*Solutions to odd-numbered problems are provided.

7. The figure depicts the world market for soybeans.

   a. With no trade, what are the prices of soybeans in the two countries?
   b. With free trade, what is the price of soybeans?
   c. What quantity of soybeans is traded?
8. If the importer of soybeans in problem 7 imposes
   a. A tariff of $2 per bushel, what is the price of soybeans in the importing country and the tariff revenue?
   b. A quota of 300 million bushels, who gains from the quota?

CRITICAL THINKING

1. Study *Reading Between the Lines* on pp. 478–479 and then answer the following questions.
   a. What changes are occurring in the global market for clothing?
   b. Why is China going to become the biggest producer of clothing?
   c. Do you think that Americans should be concerned about who makes their clothes?
   d. Will the United States run out of activities at which it has a comparative advantage? Explain your answer.
2. **Trading Up**

   . . . the cost of protecting jobs in uncompetitive sectors through tariffs is foolishly high, . . . The Federal Reserve Bank of Dallas reported in 2002 that saving a job in the sugar industry cost American consumers $826,000 in higher prices a year, saving a dairy industry job cost $685,000 per year and saving a job in the manufacturing of women's handbags cost $263,000.

   The New York Times, June 26, 2006

   a. What are the arguments for saving the jobs mentioned in this news article?
   b. Explain why these arguments are faulty.
   c. Is there any merit to saving these jobs?
3. **Vows of New Aid to the Poor Leave the Poor Unimpressed**

   . . . the United States, the European Union and Japan [plan] to eliminate duties and quotas on almost all goods from up to 50 of the world's poor nations, . . . The proposal for duty-free, quota-free treatment is so divisive among developing countries that even some negotiators . . . are saying that the plan must be broadened. . . .

   The New York Times, December 15, 2005

   a. Why do the United States, the European Union, and Japan want to eliminate trade barriers on imports from only the poorest countries?
   b. Who will win from the elimination of these trade barriers? Who will lose?
   c. Why is the plan divisive among developing countries?

WEB ACTIVITIES

myeconlab **Links to Web sites**

1. Study the *Reading Between the Lines* on steel dumping, then answer the following questions:
   a. What is the argument for limiting steel imports?
   b. Evaluate the argument. Is it correct or incorrect in your opinion? Why?
   c. Would you vote to eliminate steel imports? Why or why not?
   d. Would you vote differently if you lived in another steel-producing country? Why or why not?
2. Visit the Public Citizen Global Trade Watch, the Department of Commerce, and the government of Canada. Review the three assessments of NAFTA and then answer the following questions:
   a. What is the assessment of the Public Citizen Global Trade Watch?
   b. What are the assessments of the Department of Commerce and the government of Canada?
   c. Which view do you think is correct? Why?
   d. Would you vote to maintain NAFTA? Why or why not?

It's a Small World

The scale of international trade, borrowing, and lending, both in absolute dollar terms and as a percentage of total world production, expands every year. One country, Singapore, imports and exports goods and services in a volume that exceeds its own production. The world's largest nation, China, returned to the international economic stage during the 1980s and is now a major producer of manufactured goods.

International economic activity is large because today's economic world is small and because communication is so incredibly fast. But today's world is not a new world. From the beginning of recorded history, people have traded over large and steadily increasing distances. The great Western civilizations of Greece and Rome traded not only around the Mediterranean but also into the Gulf of Arabia. The great Eastern civilizations traded around the Indian Ocean. By the Middle Ages, the East and the West were routinely trading overland on routes pioneered by Venetian traders and explorers such as Marco Polo. When, in 1497, Vasco da Gama opened a sea route between the Atlantic and Indian Oceans around Africa, a new trade between East and West began, which brought tumbling prices of Eastern goods in Western markets.

The European discovery of the Americas and the subsequent opening up of Atlantic trade continued the process of steady globalization. So the developments of the 1990s, amazing though many of them are, represent a continuation of an ongoing expansion of human horizons.

Chapter 20 described and explained international trade in goods and services. In this chapter, you came face to face with one of the biggest policy issues of all ages: free trade versus protection and the globalization debate. The chapter explained how all nations can benefit from free international trade.

You saw how protection from competition brings big benefits to a few and small losses to the many. The total gains from protection are dwarfed by the total losses, but because the losses are spread thinly and the gains thickly, protectionism always has its supporters and political backers.

Chapter 20 does not explain international deficits and surpluses. You will meet this topic if you take a course in *macroeconomics*. In such a course, you will learn that our international deficit depends not on how efficient we are, but on how much we spend and save. Nations with high saving rates, everything else the same, have international surpluses.

The global economy is big news these days. And it has always attracted attention. On the next page, you can meet the economist who first understood comparative advantage: David Ricardo. And you can meet one of today's leading international economists: Jagdish Bhagwati of Columbia University.

PROBING THE IDEAS

Gains from International Trade

"Under a system of perfectly free commerce, each country naturally devotes its capital and labor to such employments as are most beneficial to each."

DAVID RICARDO
The Principles of Political Economy and Taxation, 1817

The Economist

David Ricardo *(1772–1832) was a highly successful 27-year-old stockbroker when he stumbled on a copy of Adam Smith's* Wealth of Nations *(see p. 54) on a weekend visit to the country. He was immediately hooked and went on to become the most celebrated economist of his age and one of the all-time great economists. One of his many contributions was to develop the principle of comparative advantage, the foundation on which the modern theory of international trade is built. The example he used to illustrate this principle was the trade between England and Portugal in cloth and wine.*

The General Agreement on Tariffs and Trade was established as a reaction against the devastation wrought by beggar-my-neighbor tariffs imposed during the 1930s. But it is also a triumph for the logic first worked out by Smith and Ricardo.

The Issues

Until the mid-eighteenth century, it was generally believed that the purpose of international trade was to keep exports greater than imports and pile up gold. If gold was accumulated, it was believed, the nation would prosper; if gold was lost through an international deficit, the nation would be drained of money and impoverished. These beliefs are called *mercantilism*, and the *mercantilists* were pamphleteers who advocated with missionary fervor the pursuit of an international surplus. If exports did not exceed imports, the mercantilists wanted imports restricted.

In the 1740s, David Hume explained that as the quantity of money (gold) changes, so also does the price level, and the nation's *real* wealth is unaffected. In the 1770s, Adam Smith argued that import restrictions would lower the gains from specialization and make a nation poorer. Thirty years later, David Ricardo proved the law of comparative advantage and demonstrated the superiority of free trade. Mercantilism was intellectually bankrupt but remained politically powerful.

Gradually, through the nineteenth century, the mercantilist influence waned and North America and Western Europe prospered in an environment of increasingly free international trade. But despite remarkable advances in economic understanding, mercantilism never quite died. It had a brief and devastating revival in the 1920s and 1930s when tariff hikes brought about the collapse of international trade and accentuated the Great Depression. It subsided again after World War II with the establishment of the General Agreement on Tariffs and Trade (GATT).

But mercantilism lingers on. The often expressed view that the United States should restrict Chinese imports and reduce its deficit with China and fears that NAFTA will bring economic ruin to the United States are modern manifestations of mercantilism. It would be interesting to have David Hume, Adam Smith, and David Ricardo commenting on these views. But we know what they would say: the same things that they said to the eighteenth century mercantilists. And they would still be right today.

Then

In the eighteenth century, when mercantilists and economists were debating the pros and cons of free international exchange, the transportation technology that was available limited the gains from international trade. Sailing ships with tiny cargo holds took close to a month to cross the Atlantic Ocean. But the potential gains were large, and so was the incentive to cut shipping costs. By the 1850s, the clipper ship had been developed, cutting the journey from Boston to Liverpool to only 12 1⁄4 days. Half a century later, 10,000-ton steamships were sailing between America and England in just 4 days. As sailing times and costs declined, the gains from international trade increased and the volume of trade expanded.

Now

The container ship has revolutionized international trade and contributed to its continued expansion. Today, most goods cross the oceans in containers—metal boxes—packed into and piled on top of ships like this one. Container technology has cut the cost of ocean shipping by economizing on handling and by making cargoes harder to steal, lowering insurance costs. It is unlikely that there would be much international trade in goods such as television sets and VCRs without this technology. High-value and perishable cargoes such as flowers and fresh foods, as well as urgent courier packages, travel by air. Every day, dozens of cargo-laden 747s fly between every major U.S. city and to destinations across the Atlantic and Pacific Oceans.

Jagdish Bhagwati, whom you can meet on the following pages, is one of the most distinguished international economists. He has contributed to our understanding of the effects of international trade and trade policy on economic growth and development and has played a significant role in helping to shape today's global trading arrangements.

Jagdish Bhagwati

Jagdish Bhagwati is University Professor at Columbia University. Born in India in 1934, he studied at Cambridge University in England, MIT, and Oxford University before returning to India. He returned to teach at MIT in 1968 and moved to Columbia in 1980. A prolific scholar, Professor Bhagwati also writes in leading newspapers and magazines throughout the world. He has been much honored for both his scientific work and his impact on public policy. His greatest contributions are in international trade but extend also to developmental problems and the study of political economy.

Michael Parkin talked with Jagdish Bhagwati about his work and the progress that economists have made in understanding the benefits of international economic integration since the pioneering work of Ricardo.

Professor Bhagwati, what attracted you to economics?
When you come from India, where poverty hits the eye, it is easy to be attracted to economics, which can be used to bring prosperity and create jobs to pull up the poor into gainful employment.

I learned later that there are two broad types of economist: those who treat the subject as an arid mathematical toy and those who see it as a serious social science.

If Cambridge, where I went as an undergraduate, had been interested in esoteric mathematical economics, I would have opted for something else. But the Cambridge economists from whom I learned—many among the greatest figures in the discipline—saw economics as a social science. I therefore saw the power of economics as a tool to address India's poverty and was immediately hooked.

Who had the greatest impact on you at Cambridge?
Most of all, it was Harry Johnson, a young Canadian of immense energy and profound analytical gifts. Quite unlike the shy and reserved British dons, Johnson was friendly, effusive, and supportive of students who flocked around him. He would later move to Chicago, where he became one of the most influential members of the market-oriented Chicago school. Another was Joan Robinson, arguably the world's most impressive female economist.

When I left Cambridge for MIT, going from one Cambridge to the other, I was lucky to transition from one phenomenal set of economists to another. At MIT, I learned much from future Nobel laureates Paul Samuelson and Robert Solow. Both would later become great friends and colleagues when I joined the MIT faculty in 1968.

After Cambridge and MIT, you went to Oxford and then back to India. What did you do in India?
I joined the Planning Commission in New Delhi, where my first big job was to find ways of raising the bottom 30 percent of India's population out of poverty to a "minimum income" level.

And what did you prescribe?

My main prescription was to "grow the pie." My research suggested that the share of the bottom 30 percent of the pie did not seem to vary dramatically with differences in economic and political systems. So growth in the pie seemed to be the principal (but not the only) component of an antipoverty strategy. To supplement growth's good effects on the poor, the Indian planners were also dedicated to education, health, social reforms, and land reforms. Also, the access of the lowest-income and socially disadvantaged groups to the growth process and its benefits was to be improved in many ways, such as extension of credit without collateral.

My main prescription was to "grow the pie" ... Today, this strategy has no rivals. Much empirical work shows that where growth has occurred, poverty has lessened.

Today, this strategy has no rivals. Much empirical work shows that where growth has occurred, poverty has lessened. It is nice to know that one's basic take on an issue of such central importance to humanity's well-being has been borne out by experience!

You left India in 1968 to come to the United States and an academic job at MIT. Why?

While the decision to emigrate often reflects personal factors—and they were present in my case—the offer of a professorship from MIT certainly helped me make up my mind. At the time, it was easily the world's most celebrated department. Serendipitously, the highest-ranked departments at MIT were not in engineering and the sciences but in linguistics (which had Noam Chomsky) and economics (which had Paul Samuelson). Joining the MIT faculty was a dramatic breakthrough: I felt stimulated each year by several fantastic students and by several of the world's most creative economists.

We hear a lot in the popular press about fair trade and level playing fields. What's the distinction between free trade and fair trade? How can the playing field be unlevel?

Free trade simply means allowing no trade barriers such as tariffs, subsidies, and quotas. Trade barriers make domestic prices different from world prices for traded goods. When this happens, resources are not being used efficiently. Basic economics from the time of Ricardo tells us why free trade is good for us and why barriers to trade harm us, though our understanding of this doctrine today is far more nuanced and profound than it was at its creation.

Fair trade, on the other hand, is almost always a sneaky way of objecting to free trade. If your rivals are hard to compete with, you are not likely to get protection simply by saying that you cannot hack it. But if you say that your rival is an "unfair" trader, that is an easier sell! As international competition has grown fiercer, cries of "unfair trade" have therefore multiplied. The lesser rogues among the protectionists ask for "free and fair trade," whereas the worst ones ask for "fair, not free, trade."

Fair trade ... is almost always a sneaky way of objecting to free trade.

At the end of World War II, the General Agreement of Tariffs and Trade (GATT) was established and there followed several rounds of multilateral trade negotiations and reductions in barriers to trade. How do you assess the contribution of GATT and its successor, the World Trade Organization (WTO)?

The GATT has made a huge contribution by overseeing massive trade liberalization in industrial goods among the developed countries. GATT rules, which "bind" tariffs to negotiated ceilings, prevent the raising of tariffs and have prevented tariff wars like those of the 1930s in which mutual and retaliatory tariff barriers were raised, to the detriment of everyone.

The GATT was folded into the WTO at the end of the Uruguay Round of trade negotiations, and the WTO is institutionally stronger. For instance, it has a binding dispute settlement mechanism, whereas the GATT had no such teeth. It is also more ambitious in its scope, extending to new areas such as the environment, intellectual property protection, and investment rules.

Running alongside the pursuit of multilateral free trade has been the emergence of bilateral trade agreements such as NAFTA and the European Union (EU). How do you view the bilateral free trade areas in today's world?

Unfortunately, there has been an explosion of bilateral free trade areas today. By some estimates, the ones in place and others being plotted approach 400! Each bilateral agreement gives preferential treatment to its trading partner over others. Because there are now so many bilateral agreements, such as those between the United States and Israel and between the United States and Jordan, the result is a chaotic pattern of different tariffs depending on where a product comes from. Also, "rules of origin" must be agreed upon to determine whether a product is, say, Jordanian or Taiwanese if Jordan qualifies for a preferential tariff but Taiwan does not and Taiwanese inputs enter the Jordanian manufacture of the product.

I have called the resulting crisscrossing of preferences and rules of origin the "spaghetti bowl" problem. The world trading system is choking under these proliferating bilateral deals. Contrast this complexity with the simplicity of a multilateral system with common tariffs for all WTO members.

We now have a world of uncoordinated and inefficient trade policies.

We now have a world of uncoordinated and inefficient trade policies. The EU makes bilateral free trade agreements with different non-EU countries, so the United States follows with its own bilateral agreements; and with Europe and the United States doing it, the Asian countries, long wedded to multilateralism, have now succumbed to the mania.

Instead, if the United States had provided leadership by rewriting rules to make the signing of such bilateral agreements extremely difficult, this plague on the trading system today might well have been averted.

Despite the benefits that economics points to from multilateral free trade, the main organization that pursues this goal, the WTO, is having a very hard time with the anti-globalization movement. What can we say about globalization that puts the WTO and its work in proper perspective?

The anti-globalization movement contains a diverse set of activists. Essentially, they all claim to be stakeholders in the globalization phenomenon. But there are those who want to drive a stake through the system, as in Dracula films, and there are those who want to exercise their stake in the system. The former want to be heard; the latter, to be listened to. For a while, the two disparate sets of critics were milling around together, seeking targets of opportunity at international conferences such as WTO's November 2000 meeting in Seattle, where the riots broke out. Now things have settled down, and the groups that want to work systematically and seriously at improving the global economy's functioning are much more in play.

But the WTO is also seen, inaccurately for the most part, as imposing trade sanctions that override concerns such as environmental protection. For example, U.S. legislation bans the importing of shrimp that is harvested without the use of turtle-excluding devices. India and others complained, but the WTO upheld the U.S. legislation. Ignorant of the facts, demonstrators took to the streets dressed as turtles protesting the WTO decision!

What advice do you have for a student who is just starting to study economics? Is economics a good subject in which to major?

I would say: enormously so. In particular, we economists bring three unique insights to good policy making.

First, economists look for second- and subsequent-round effects of actions.

Second, we correctly emphasize that a policy cannot be judged without using a counterfactual. It is a witticism that an economist, when asked how her husband was, said, "compared to what?"

Third, we uniquely and systematically bring the principle of social cost and social benefit to our policy analysis.

Absolute advantage A person has an absolute advantage if that person is more productive than another person. (p. 42)

Adverse selection The tendency for people to enter into agreements in which that can use their private information to their own advantage and to the disadvantage of the less-informed party. (p. 444)

Allocative efficiency A situation in which we cannot produce more of any good without giving up some of another good that we *value more highly.* (p. 39)

Antitrust law A law that regulates and prohibits certain kinds of market behavior, such as monopoly and monopolistic practices. (p. 326)

Average cost pricing rule A rule that sets price to cover cost including normal profit, which means setting the price equal to average total cost. (pp. 279, 329)

Average fixed cost Total fixed cost per unit of output. (p. 226)

Average product The average product of a factor of production. It equals total product divided by the quantity of the factor employed. (p. 221)

Average total cost Total cost per unit of output. (p. 226)

Average variable cost Total variable cost per unit of output. (p. 226)

Barriers to entry Legal or natural constraints that protect a firm from potential competitors. (p. 264)

Big tradeoff The conflict between equality and efficiency. (pp. 10, 115, 430)

Bilateral monopoly A situation in which a single seller (a monopoly) faces a single buyer (a monopsony). (p. 398)

Black market An illegal market in which the price exceeds the legally imposed price ceiling. (p. 126)

Budget line The limits to a household's consumption choices. (pp. 154, 172)

Capital The tools, equipment, buildings, and other constructions that businesses use to produce goods and services. (p. 4)

Capital accumulation The growth of capital resources, including human capital. (p. 40)

Capture theory A theory of regulation that states that regulation is in the self-interest of producers. (p. 327)

Cartel A group of firms that has entered into a collusive agreement to restrict output and increase prices and profits. (p. 297)

Ceteris paribus Other things being equal—all other relevant things remaining the same. (p. 13)

Change in demand A change in buyers' plans that occurs when some influence on those plans other than the price of the good changes. It is illustrated by a shift of the demand curve. (p. 62)

Change in supply A change in sellers' plans that occurs when some influence on those plans other than the price of the good changes. It is illustrated by a shift of the supply curve. (p. 67)

Change in the quantity demanded A change in buyers' plans that occurs when the price of a good changes but all other influences on buyers' plans remain unchanged. It is illustrated by a movement along the demand curve. (p. 65)

Change in the quantity supplied A change in sellers' plans that occurs when the price of a good changes but all other influences on sellers' plans remain unchanged. It is illustrated by a movement along the supply curve. (p. 68)

Coase theorem The proposition that if property rights exist, if only a small number of parties are involved, and transactions costs are low, then private transactions are efficient. (p. 349)

Collusive agreement An agreement between two (or more) producers to restrict output, raise the price, and increase profits. (p. 302)

Command system A method of allocating resources by the order (command) of someone in authority. In a firm a managerial hierarchy organizes production. (pp. 104, 203)

Common resource A resource that is rival and nonexcludable. (p. 362)

Comparative advantage A person or country has a comparative advantage in an activity if that person or country can perform the activity at a lower opportunity cost than anyone else or any other country. (pp. 42, 464)

Competitive market A market that has many buyers and many sellers, so no single buyer or seller can influence the price. (p. 60)

Complement A good that is used in conjunction with another good. (p. 63)

Constant returns to scale Features of a firm's technology that lead to constant long-run average cost as output increases. When constant returns to scale are present, the *LRAC* curve is horizontal. (p. 233)

Consumer equilibrium A situation in which a consumer has allocated all his or her available income in the way that, given the prices of goods and services, maximizes his or her total utility. (p. 158)

Consumer surplus The value (or marginal benefit) of a good minus the price paid for it, summed over the quantity bought. (p. 107)

Contestable market A market in which firms can enter and leave so easily that firms in the market face competition from potential entrants. (p. 310)

Cooperative equilibrium The outcome of a game in which the players make and share the monopoly profit. (p. 309)

Copyright A government-sanctioned exclusive right granted to the inventor of a good, service, or productive process to produce, use, and sell the invention for a given number of years. (p. 355)

Cross elasticity of demand The responsiveness of the demand for a good to a change in the price of a substitute or complement, other things remaining the same. It is calculated as the percentage change in the quantity demanded of the good divided by the percentage change in the price of the substitute or complement. (p. 91)

Cross-section graph A graph that shows the values of an economic variable for different groups or categories at a point in time. (p. 18)

Deadweight loss A measure of inefficiency. It is equal to the decrease in total surplus that results from an inefficient level of production. (p. 111)

Demand The entire relationship between the price of the good and the quantity demanded of it when all other influences on buyers' plans remain the same. It is illustrated by a demand curve and described by a demand schedule. (p. 61)

Demand curve A curve that shows the relationship between the quantity demanded of a good and its price when all other influences on consumers' planned purchases remain the same. (p. 62)

Derived demand Demand for a factor of production, which is derived from the demand for the goods and services produced by that factor. (p. 386)

Diminishing marginal rate of substitution The general tendency for a person to be willing to give up less of good y to get one more unit of good x, and at the same time remain indifferent, as the quantity of good x increases. (p. 176)

Diminishing marginal returns The tendency for the marginal product of an additional unit of a factor of production to be less than the marginal product of the previous unit of the factor. (p. 223)

Diminishing marginal utility The decrease in marginal utility as the quantity consumed increases. (p. 156)

Direct relationship A relationship between two variables that move in the same direction. (p. 20)

Discounting The conversion of a future amount of money to its present value. (p. 413)

Diseconomies of scale Features of a firm's technology that lead to rising long-run average cost as output increases. (p. 232)

Dominant strategy equilibrium A Nash equilibrium in which the best strategy for each player is to cheat (deny) regardless of the strategy of the other player. (p. 308)

Dumping The sale by a foreign firm of exports at a lower price than the cost of production. (p. 473)

Duopoly A market structure in which two producers of a good or service compete. (p. 296)

Dynamic comparative advantage A comparative advantage that a person or country possesses as a result of having specialized in a particular activity and then, as a result of learning-by-doing, having become the producer with the lowest opportunity cost. (p. 45)

Earnings sharing regulation A regulation that if a firm's profits rise above a target level, they must be shared with the firm's customers. (p. 331)

Economic depreciation The change in the market value of capital over a given period. (p. 198)

Economic efficiency A situation that occurs when the firm produces a given output at the least cost. (p. 201)

Economic growth The expansion of production possibilities that results from capital accumulation and technological change. (p. 40)

Economic information Data on price, quantities, and qualities of goods and services and factors of production. (p. 443)

Economic model A description of some aspect of the economic world that includes only those features of the world that are needed for the purpose at hand. (p. 12)

Economic profit A firm's total revenue minus its total cost. (p. 199)

Economic rent Any surplus—consumer surplus, producer surplus or economic profit. The income received by the owner of a factor of production over and above the amount required to induce that owner to offer the factor for use. (pp. 272, 406)

Economics The social science that studies the choices that we make as we cope with *scarcity* and the *incentives* that influence and reconcile those choices. (p. 2)

Economic theory A generalization that summarizes what we think we understand about the economic choices that people make and the performance of industries and entire economies. (p. 12)

Economies of scale Features of a firm's technology that lead to a falling long-run average cost as output increases. (pp. 213, 232)

Economies of scope Decreases in average total cost that occur when a firm uses specialized resources to produce a range of goods and services. (p. 213)

Efficiency wage A real wage rate that is set above the equilibrium wage rate and that balances the costs and benefits of this higher wage rate to maximize the firm's profit. (p. 399)

Efficient market A market in which the actual price embodies all currently available relevant information. Resources are sent to their highest-values use. (p. 448)

Elastic demand Demand with a price elasticity greater than 1; other things remaining the same, the percentage change in the quantity demanded exceeds the percentage change in price. (p. 87)

Elasticity of demand The responsiveness of the quantity demanded of a good to a change in its price, other things remaining the same. (p. 84)

Elasticity of supply The responsiveness of the quantity supplied of a good to a change in its price, other things remaining the same. (p. 94)

Entrepreneurship The human resource that organizes the other three factors of production: labor, land, and capital. (p. 4)

Equilibrium price The price at which the quantity demanded equals the quantity supplied. (p. 70)

Equilibrium quantity The quantity bought and sold at the equilibrium price. (p. 70)

Excludable A good or service or a resource is excludable if it is possible to prevent someone from enjoying the benefit of it. (p. 362)

Expected utility The average utility arising from all possible outcomes. (p. 439)

Exports The goods and services that we sell to people in other countries. (p. 462)

External diseconomies Factors outside the control of a firm that raise the firm's costs as the industry produces a larger output. (p. 253)

External economies Factors beyond the control of a firm that lower the firm's costs as the industry produces a larger output. (p. 253)

Externality A cost or a benefit that arises from production and falls on someone other than the producer, or a cost or a benefit that arises from consumption and falls on someone other than the consumer. (p. 344)

Factors of production The resources used to produce goods and services. (p. 3)

Firm An economic unit that hires factors of production and organizes those factors to produce and sell goods and services. (pp. 45, 198)

Four-firm concentration ratio A measure of market power that is calculated as the percentage of the value of sales accounted for by the four largest firms in an industry. (p. 208)

Free-rider problem The absence of an incentive for people to pay for what they consume. (p. 362)

Game theory A tool that economists use to analyze strategic behavior—behavior that takes into account the expected behavior of others and the recognition of mutual interdependence. (p. 300)

General Agreement on Tariffs and Trade An international agreement signed in 1947 to reduce tariffs on international trade. (p. 469)

Gini ratio The ratio of the area between the line of equality and the Lorenz curve to the entire area beneath the line of equality. (p. 421)

Goods and services All the objects that people value and produce to satisfy human wants. (p. 3)

Herfindahl–Hirschman Index A measure of market power that is calculated as the square of the market share of each firm (as a percentage) summed over the largest 50 firms (or over all firms if there are fewer than 50) in a market. (p. 208)

Human capital The knowledge and skill that people obtain from education, on-the-job training, and work experience. (p. 3)

Implicit rental rate The firm's opportunity cost of using its own capital. (p. 198)

Imports The goods and services that we buy from people in other countries. (p. 462)

Incentive A reward that encourages or a penalty that discourages an action. (p. 2)

Incentive system A method of organizing production that uses a market-like mechanism inside the firm. (p. 203)

Income effect The effect of a change in income on consumption, other things remaining the same. (p. 180)

Income elasticity of demand The responsiveness of demand to a change in income, other things remaining the same. It is calculated as the percentage change in the quantity demanded divided by the percentage change in income. (p. 92)

Indifference curve A line that shows combinations of goods among which a consumer is indifferent. (p. 175)

Individual transferable quota (ITQ) A production limit that is assigned to an individual who is free to transfer the quota to someone else. (p. 372)

Inelastic demand A demand with a price elasticity between 0 and 1; the percentage change in the quantity demanded is less than the percentage change in price. (p. 86)

Infant-industry argument The argument that it is necessary to protect a new industry to enable it to grow into a mature industry that can compete in world markets. (p. 473)

Inferior good A good for which demand decreases as income increases. (p. 64)

Information cost The opportunity cost of economic information—the cost of acquiring information on prices, quantities, and qualities of goods and services and resources. (p. 443)

Intellectual property rights Property rights for discoveries owned by the creators of knowledge. (p. 355)

Interest The income that capital earns. (p. 4)

Inverse relationship A relationship between variables that move in opposite directions. (p. 21)

Labor The work time and work effort that people devote to producing goods and services. (p. 3)

Labor union An organized group of workers whose purpose is to increase wages and to influence other job conditions. (p. 395)

Land All the gifts of nature that we use to produce goods and services. (p. 3)

Law of demand Other things remaining the same, the higher the price of a good, the smaller is the quantity demanded of it; the lower the price of a good, the larger is the quantity demanded of it. (p. 61)

Law of diminishing returns As a firm uses more of a variable input, with a given quantity of other inputs (fixed inputs), the marginal product of the variable input eventually diminishes. (p. 223)

Law of supply Other things remaining the same, the higher the price of a good, the greater is the quantity supplied of it. (p. 66)

Learning-by-doing People become more productive in an activity (learn) just by repeatedly producing a particular good or service (doing). (p. 45)

Legal monopoly A market structure in which there is one firm and entry is restricted by the granting of a public franchise, government license, patent, or copyright. (p. 264)

Limit pricing The practice of setting the price at the highest level that inflicts a loss on an entrant. (p. 311)

Linear relationship A relationship between two variables that is illustrated by a straight line. (p. 20)

Living wage An hourly wage rate that enables a person who works a 40 -hour work week to rent adequate housing for not more than 30 percent of the amount earned. (p. 131)

Long run A period of time in which the quantities of all resources can be varied. (p. 220)

Long-run average cost curve The relationship between the lowest attainable average total cost and output when both plant size and labor are varied. (p. 231)

Long-run industry supply curve A curve that shows how the quantity supplied by an industry varies as the market price varies after all the possible adjustments have been made, including changes in plant size and the number of firms in the industry. (p. 253)

Lorenz curve A curve that graphs the cumulative percentage of income or wealth against the cumulative percentage of households. (p. 419)

Macroeconomics The study of the performance of the national economy and the global economy. (p. 2)

Margin When a choice is changed by a small amount or by a little at a time, the choice is made at the margin. (p. 11)

Marginal benefit The benefit that a person receives from consuming one more unit of a good or service. It is measured as the maximum amount that a person is willing to pay for one more unit of the good or service. (pp. 11, 38)

Marginal benefit curve A curve that shows the relationship between the marginal benefit of a good and the quantity of that good consumed. (p. 38)

Marginal cost The opportunity cost of producing one more unit of a good or service. It is the best alternative forgone. It is calculated as the increase in total cost divided by the increase in output. (pp. 11, 37, 226)

Marginal cost pricing rule A rule that sets the price of a good or service equal to the marginal cost of producing it. (pp. 278, 329)

Marginal external benefit The benefit from an additional unit of a good or service that people other than the consumer enjoy. (p. 351)

Marginal external cost The cost of producing an additional unit of a good or service that falls on people other than the producer. (p. 347)

Marginal private benefit The benefit from an additional unit of a good or service that the consumer of that good or service receives. (p. 351)

Marginal private cost The cost of producing an additional unit of a good or service that is borne by the producer of that good or service. (p. 347)

Marginal product The increase in total product that results from a one-unit increase in the variable input, with all other inputs remaining the same. It is calculated as the increase in total product divided by the increase in the variable input employed, when the quantities of all other inputs are constant. (p. 221)

Marginal rate of substitution The rate at which a person will give up good *y* (the good measured on the *y*-axis) to get an additional unit of good *x* (the good measured on the *x*-axis) and at the same time remain indifferent (remain on the same indifference curve). (p. 176)

Marginal revenue The change in total revenue that results from a one-unit increase in the quantity sold. It is calculated as the change in total revenue divided by the change in quantity sold. (p. 240)

Marginal revenue product The change in total revenue that results from employing one more unit of a factor of production (labor) while the quantity of all other factors remains the same. It is calculated as the increase in total revenue divided by the increase in the quantity of the factor (labor). (p. 388)

Marginal social benefit The marginal benefit enjoyed by society—by the consumer of a good or service (marginal private benefit) plus the marginal benefit enjoyed by others (marginal external benefit). (p. 351)

Marginal social cost The marginal cost incurred by the entire society—by the producer and by everyone else on whom the cost falls—and is the sum of marginal private cost and marginal external cost. (p. 347)

Marginal utility The change in total utility resulting from a one-unit increase in the quantity of a good consumed. (p. 156)

Marginal utility per dollar The marginal utility from a good divided by its price. (p. 158)

Market Any arrangement that enables buyers and sellers to get information and to do business with each other. (p. 46)

Market failure A state in which the market does not allocate resources efficiently. (p. 324)

Market income The wages, interest, rent, and profit earned in factor markets and before paying income taxes. (p. 418)

Market power The ability to influence the market, and in particular the market price, by influencing the total quantity offered for sale. (p. 264)

Microeconomics The study of the choices that individuals and businesses make, the way these choices interact in markets, and the influence of governments. (p. 2)

Minimum efficient scale The smallest quantity of output at which the long-run average cost curve reaches its lowest level. (p. 233)

Minimum wage A regulation that makes the hiring of labor below a specified wage rate illegal. The lowest wage at which a firm may legally hire labor. (p. 130)

Money Any commodity or token that is generally acceptable as the means of payment. (p. 46)

Money income Market income plus cash payments to households by the government. (p. 418)

Money price The number of dollars that must be given up in exchange for a good or service. (p. 60)

Monopolistic competition A market structure in which a large number of firms compete by making similar but slightly different products. (pp. 207, 286)

Monopoly A market structure in which there is one firm, which produces a good or service that has no close substitutes and in which the firm is protected from competition by a barrier preventing the entry of new firms. (pp. 207, 264)

Monopsony A market in which there is a single buyer. (p. 397)

Moral hazard A situation in which one of the parties to an agreement has an incentive after the agreement is made to act in a manner that brings additional benefits to himself or herself at the expense of the other party. (p. 444)

Nash equilibrium The outcome of a game that occurs when player A takes the best possible action given the action of player B and player B takes the best possible action given the action of player A. (p. 301)

Natural monopoly A monopoly that occurs when one firm can supply the entire market at a lower price than two or more firms can. (p. 264)

Negative externality An externality that arises from either production or consumption and that imposes an external cost. (p. 344)

Negative relationship A relationship between variables that move in opposite directions. (p. 21)

Net exports The value of exports of goods and services minus the value of imports of goods and services. (p. 462)

Net present value The present value of the future flow of marginal revenue product generated by capital minus the cost of the capital. (p. 415)

Nonexcludable A good or service or a resource is nonexcludable if it is impossible (or extremely costly) to prevent someone from benefiting from it. (p. 362)

Nonrenewable natural resources Natural resources that can be used only once and that cannot be replaced once they have been used. (p. 403)

Nonrival A good or service or a resource is nonrival if its use by one person does not decrease the quantity available for someone else. (p. 362)

Nontariff barrier Any action other than a tariff that restricts international trade. (p. 469)

Normal good A good for which demand increases as income increases. (p. 64)

Normal profit The return that an entrepreneur can expect to receive on the average. (p. 199)

North American Free Trade Agreement An agreement, which became effective on January 1, 1994, to eliminate all barriers to international trade between the United States, Canada, and Mexico after a 15-year phasing-in period. (p. 470)

Oligopoly A market structure in which a small number of firms compete. (pp. 207, 296)

Opportunity cost The highest-valued alternative that we give up to get something. (p. 10)

Patent A government-sanctioned exclusive right granted to the inventor of a good, service, or productive process to produce, use, and sell the invention for a given number of years. (p. 355)

Payoff matrix A table that shows the payoffs for every possible action by each player for every possible action by each other player. (p. 300)

Perfect competition A market in which there are many firms each selling an identical product; there are many buyers; there are no restrictions on entry into the industry; firms in the industry have no advantage over potential new entrants; and firms and buyers are well informed about the price of each firm's product. (pp. 207, 240)

Perfectly elastic demand Demand with an infinite price elasticity; the quantity demanded changes by an infinitely large percentage in response to a tiny price change. (p. 87)

Perfectly inelastic demand Demand with a price elasticity of zero; the quantity demanded remains constant when the price changes. (p. 86)

Perfect price discrimination Price discrimination that extracts the entire consumer surplus. (p. 275)

Pigovian taxes Taxes that are used as an incentive for producers to cut back on an activity that creates an external cost. (p. 350)

Political equilibrium The outcome that results from the choices of voters, firms, politicians, and bureaucrats. (p. 326)

Positive externality An externality that arises from either production or consumption and that provides an external benefit. (p. 344)

Positive relationship A relationship between two variables that move in the same direction. (p. 20)

Poverty A state in which a household's income is too low to be able to buy the quantities of food, shelter, and clothing that are deemed necessary. (p. 423)

Predatory pricing Setting a low price to drive competitors out of business with the intention of setting the monopoly price when the competition has gone. (p. 336)

Preferences A description of a person's likes and dislikes. (p. 38)

Present value The amount of money that, if invested today, will grow to be as large as a given future amount when the interest that it will earn is taken into account. (p. 413)

Price cap regulation A regulation that specifies the highest price that the firm is permitted to set. (p. 330)

Price ceiling A regulation that makes it illegal to charge a price higher than a specified level. (p. 125)

Price discrimination The practice of selling different units of a good or service for different prices or of charging one customer different prices for different quantities bought. (p. 265)

Price effect The effect of a change in the price on the quantity of a good consumed, other things remaining the same. (p. 179)

Price elasticity of demand A units-free measure of the responsiveness of the quantity demanded of a good to a change in its price, when all other influences on buyers' plans remain the same. (p. 84)

Price floor A regulation that makes it illegal to trade at a price lower than a specified level. (p. 130)

Price taker A firm that cannot influence the price of the good or service it produces. (p. 240)

Principal–agent problem The problem of devising compensation rules that induce an *agent* to act in the best interest of a *principal.* (p. 204)

Principle of minimum differentiation The tendency for competitors to make themselves identical as they try to appeal to the maximum number of clients or voters. (p. 365)

Private good A good or service that is both rival and excludable. (p. 362)

Private information Information that is available to one person but is too costly for anyone else to obtain. (p. 444)

Producer surplus The price of a good minus its minimum supply-price, summed over the quantity sold. (p. 109)

Product differentiation Making a product slightly different from the product of a competing firm. (pp. 207, 286)

Production efficiency A situation in which the economy cannot produce more of one good without producing less of some other good. (p. 35)

Production possibilities frontier The boundary between the combinations of goods and services that can be produced and the combinations that cannot. (p. 34)

Production quota An upper limit to the quantity of a good that may be produced in a specified period. (p. 139)

Profit The income earned by entrepreneurship. (p. 4)

Progressive income tax A tax on income at an average rate that increases with the level of income. (p. 429)

Property rights Social arrangements that govern the ownership, use, and disposal of anything that people value that are enforceable in the courts. (pp. 46, 348)

Proportional income tax A tax on income at a constant average rate, regardless of the level of income. (p. 429)

Public good A good or service that is both nonrival and nonexcludable—it can be consumed simultaneously by everyone and from which no one can be excluded. (p. 362)

Public provision The production of a good or service by a public authority that receives its revenue from the government. (p. 353)

Quantity demanded The amount of a good or service that consumers plan to buy during a given time period at a particular price. (p. 61)

Quantity supplied The amount of a good or service that producers plan to sell during a given time period at a particular price. (p. 66)

Quota A quantitative restriction on the import of a particular good, which specifies the maximum amount that can be imported in a given time period. (p. 472)

Rate of return regulation A regulation that requires the firm to justify its price by showing that the price enables it to earn a specified target percent return on its capital. (p. 330)

Rational ignorance The decision not to acquire information because the cost of doing so exceeds the expected benefit. (p. 366)

Real income A household's income expressed as a quantity of goods that the household can afford to buy. (pp. 155, 173)

Regressive income tax A tax on income at an average rate that decreases with the level of income. (p. 429)

Regulation Rules administered by a government agency to influence economic activity by determining price, product standards and types, and conditions under which a new firm may enter an industry. (p. 326)

Relative price The ratio of the price of one good or service to the price of another good or service. A relative price is an opportunity cost. (pp. 60, 154, 173)

Renewable natural resources Natural resources that can be used repeatedly without depleting what is available for future use. (p. 403)

Rent The income that land earns. (p. 4)

Rent ceiling A regulation that makes it illegal to charge a rent higher than a specified level. (p. 125)

Rent seeking The pursuit of wealth by capturing economic rent—consumer surplus, producer surplus, or economic profit. (pp. 272, 476)

Resale price maintenance Agreement between a manufacturer and a distributor on the price at which the product will be sold. (p. 335)

Reservation price The highest price that a buyer is willing to pay for a good. (p. 443)

Risk A situation in which more than one outcome might occur and the probability attached to each possible outcome can be estimated. (p. 438)

Rival A good or service or a resource is rival if its use by one person decreases the quantity available for someone else. (p. 362)

Scarcity Our inability to satisfy all our wants. (p. 2)

Scatter diagram A diagram that plots the value of one variable against the value of another. (p. 19)

Search activity The time spent looking for someone with whom to do business. (p. 126)

Self-interest The choices that you think are best for you. (p. 5)

Short run The period of time in which the quantity of at least one factor of production is fixed and the quantities of the other factors can be varied. The fixed factor is usually capital—that is, the firm has a given plant size. (p. 220)

Short-run industry supply curve A curve that shows the quantity supplied by the industry at each price when the plant size of each firm and the number of firms in the industry remain the same. (p. 247)

Shutdown point The output and price at which the firm just covers its total variable cost. In the short run, the firm is indifferent between producing the profit-maximizing output and shutting down temporarily. (p. 246)

Signal An action taken by an informed person (or firm) to send a message to uninformed people or an action taken outside a market that conveys information that can be used by the market. (pp. 294, 445)

Single-price monopoly A monopoly that must sell each unit of its output for the same price to all its customers. (p. 265)

Slope The change in the value of the variable measured on the *y*-axis divided by the change in the value of the variable measured on the *x*-axis. (p. 24)

Social interest Choices that are the best for society as a whole. (p. 5)

Social interest theory A theory that politicians supply the regulation that achieves an efficient allocation of resources. (p. 327)

Strategies All the possible actions of each player in a game. (p. 300)

Subsidy A payment made by the government to a producer. (pp. 138, 354)

Substitute A good that can be used in place of another good. (p. 63)

Substitution effect The effect of a change in price of a good or service on the quantity bought when the consumer (hypothetically) remains indifferent between the original and the new consumption situations—that is, the consumer remains on the same indifference curve. (p. 181)

Sunk cost The past cost of buying a plant that has no resale value. (p. 220)

Supply The entire relationship between the price of a good and the quantity supplied of it when all other influences on producers' planned sales remain the same. It is described by a supply schedule and illustrated by a supply curve. (p. 66)

Supply curve A curve that shows the relationship between the quantity supplied of a good and its price when all other influences on producers' planned sales remain the same. (p. 66)

Symmetry principle A requirement that people in similar situations be treated similarly. (p. 116)

Tariff A tax that is imposed by the importing country when an imported good crosses its international boundary. (p. 469)

Tax incidence The division of the burden of the tax between the buyer and the seller. (p. 132)

Technological change The development of new goods and of better ways of producing goods and services. (p. 40)

Technological efficiency A situation that occurs when the firm produces a given output by using the least amount of inputs. (p. 201)

Technology Any method of producing a good or service. (p. 200)

Terms of trade The quantity of goods and services that a country exports to pay for its imports of goods and services. (p. 464)

Time-series graph A graph that measures time (for example, months or years) on the *x*-axis and the variable or variables in which we are interested on the *y*-axis. (p. 18)

Total cost The cost of all the productive resources that a firm uses. (p. 225)

Total fixed cost The cost of the firm's fixed inputs. (p. 225)

Total product The total output produced by a firm in a given period of time. (p. 221)

Total revenue The value of a firm's sales. It is calculated as the price of the good multiplied by the quantity sold. (pp. 88, 240)

Total revenue test A method of estimating the price elasticity of demand by observing the change in total revenue that results from a change in the price, when all other influences on the quantity sold remain the same. (p. 88)

Total utility The total benefit that a person gets from the consumption of goods and services. (p. 156)

Total variable cost The cost of all the firm's variable inputs. (p. 225)

Tradeoff A constraint that involves giving up one thing to get something else. (p. 9)

Tragedy of the commons The absence of incentives to prevent the overuse and depletion of a resource. (p. 362)

Transactions costs The opportunity costs of making trades in a market. The costs that arise from finding someone with whom to do business, of reaching an agreement about the price and other aspects of the exchange, and of ensuring that the terms of the agreement are fulfilled. (pp. 113, 212, 349)

Trend The general tendency for a variable to move in one direction. (p. 18)

Tying arrangement An agreement to sell one product only if the buyer agrees to buy another, different product. (p. 336)

Uncertainty A situation in which more than one event might occur but it is not know which one. (p. 438)

Unit elastic demand Demand with a price elasticity of 1; the percentage change in the quantity demanded equals the percentage change in price. (p. 86)

Utilitarianism A principle that states that we should strive to achieve "the greatest happiness for the greatest number of people." (p. 114)

Utility The benefit or satisfaction that a person gets from the consumption of a good or service. (p. 156)

Utility of wealth The amount of utility that a person attaches to a given amount of wealth. (p. 438)

Voluntary export restraint An agreement between two governments in which the government of the exporting country agrees to restrain the volume of its own exports. (p. 472)

Voucher A token that the government provides to households, which they can use to buy specified goods and services. (p. 354)

Wages The income that labor earns. (p. 4)

Wealth The value of all the things people own at a point in time—the market value of their assets. (p. 420)

World Trade Organization An international organization that places greater obligations on its member countries to observe the GATT rules. (p. 469)

INDEX

Key terms and pages on which they are defined appear in **boldface.**

PHOTO CREDITS

Adam Smith (p. 54) Corbis-Bettmann.

Pin factory (p. 55) Culver Pictures.

Silicon wafer (p. 55) Bruce Ando/Tony Stone Images.

Alfred Marshall (p. 148) Stock Montage.

Railroad bridge (p. 149) National Archives.

Airport (p. 149) PhotoDisc, Inc.

Charlie Holt (p. 150) University of Virginia/ Rebecca Arrington

Jeremy Bentham (p. 192) Corbis-Bettmann.

Women factory workers (p. 193) Keystone-Mast Collection (V22542) UCR/California Museum of Photography, University of California, Riverside.

Man and woman in office (p. 193) PhotoDisc, Inc.

Wheat field (p. 207) PhotoDisc, Inc.

Grocery store aisle (p. 207) Courtesy of Beth Anderson.

Vending machines (p. 207) Dick Morton.

Windows 2000 (p. 207) Corbis.

Google screen capture (p. 215) © 2006 Google

Yahoo! screen capture (p. 215) Copyright © 2007 Yahoo! Inc. All rights reserved.

John von Neumann (p. 318) Stock Montage.

Cartoon of the power of monopoly (p. 319) Culver Pictures.

Cable worker (p. 319) Don Wilson/Weststock.

Ronald Coase (p. 380) David Joel/David Joel Photography.

Great Lakes pollution (p. 381) Jim Baron/The Image Finders.

Fishing boat on Lake Erie (p. 381) Patrick Mullen.

Caroline M. Hoxby (p. 382) E. S. Lee.

Thomas Robert Malthus (p. 456) Corbis-Bettmann.

Tremont Street, Boston traffic, 1870 (p. 457) Courtesy of The Bostonian Society/Old State House.

Parking machine (p. 457) Mark E. Gibson.

David Card (p. 458) Photo courtesy of Stuart Schwartz.

David Ricardo (p. 484) Corbis-Bettmann.

Clipper ship (p. 485) North Wind Picture Archives.

Container ship (p. 485) © M. Timothy O'Keefe/Weststock.

The Addison-Wesley Series in Economics

Abel/Bernanke/Croushore
Macroeconomics

Bade/Parkin
Foundations of Economics

Bierman/Fernandez
Game Theory with Economic Applications

Binger/Hoffman
Microeconomics with Calculus

Boyer
Principles of Transportation Economics

Branson
Macroeconomic Theory and Policy

Bruce
Public Finance and the American Economy

Byrns/Stone
Economics

Carlton/Perloff
Modern Industrial Organization

Caves/Frankel/Jones
World Trade and Payments: An Introduction

Chapman
Environmental Economics: Theory, Application, and Policy

Cooter/Ulen
Law and Economics

Downs
An Economic Theory of Democracy

Ehrenberg/Smith
Modern Labor Economics

Ekelund/Tollison
Economics

Fusfeld
The Age of the Economist

Gerber
International Economics

Ghiara
Learning Economics

Gordon
Macroeconomics

Gregory
Essentials of Economics

Gregory/Stuart
Russian and Soviet Economic Performance and Structure

Hartwick/Olewiler
The Economics of Natural Resource Use

Hoffman/Averett
Women and the Economy: Family, Work, and Pay

Holt
Markets, Games, and Strategic Behavior

Hubbard
Money, the Financial System, and the Economy

Hughes/Cain
American Economic History

Husted/Melvin
International Economics

Jehle/Reny
Advanced Microeconomic Theory

Johnson-Lans
A Health Economics Primer

Klein
Mathematical Methods for Economics

Krugman/Obstfeld
International Economics

Laidler
The Demand for Money

Leeds/von Allmen/Schiming
Economics

Leeds/von Allmen
The Economics of Sports

Lipsey/Courant/Ragan
Economics

Melvin
International Money and Finance

Miller
Economics Today

Miller
Understanding Modern Economics

Miller/Benjamin
The Economics of Macro Issues

Miller/Benjamin/North
The Economics of Public Issues

Mills/Hamilton
Urban Economics

Mishkin
The Economics of Money, Banking, and Financial Markets

Mishkin
The Economics of Money, Banking, and Financial Markets, Alternate Edition

Murray
Econometrics: A Modern Introduction

Parkin
Economics

Perloff
Microeconomics

Perman/Common/McGilvray/Ma
Natural Resources and Environmental Economics

Phelps
Health Economics

Riddell/Shackelford/Stamos/Schneider
Economics: A Tool for Critically Understanding Society

Ritter/Silber/Udell
Principles of Money, Banking, and Financial Markets

Rohlf
Introduction to Economic Reasoning

Ruffin/Gregory
Principles of Economics

Sargent
Rational Expectations and Inflation

Scherer
Industry Structure, Strategy, and Public Policy

Stock/Watson
Introduction to Econometrics

Stock/Watson
Introduction to Econometrics, Brief Edition

Studenmund
Using Econometrics

Tietenberg
Environmental and Natural Resource Economics

Tietenberg
Environmental Economics and Policy

Todaro/Smith
Economic Development

Waldman
Microeconomics

Waldman/Jensen
Industrial Organization: Theory and Practice

Weil
Economic Growth

Williamson
Macroeconomics

The Addison-Wesley Series in Economics

Abel/Bernanke/Croushore
Macroeconomics

Bade/Parkin
Foundations of Economics

Bierman/Fernandez
Game Theory with Economic Applications

Binger/Hoffman
Microeconomics with Calculus

Boyer
Principles of Transportation Economics

Branson
Macroeconomic Theory and Policy

Bruce
Public Finance and the American Economy

Byrns/Stone
Economics

Carlton/Perloff
Modern Industrial Organization

Caves/Frankel/Jones
World Trade and Payments: An Introduction

Chapman
Environmental Economics: Theory, Application, and Policy

Cooter/Ulen
Law and Economics

Downs
An Economic Theory of Democracy

Ehrenberg/Smith
Modern Labor Economics

Ekelund/Tollison
Economics

Fusfeld
The Age of the Economist

Gerber
International Economics

Ghiara
Learning Economics

Gordon
Macroeconomics

Gregory
Essentials of Economics

Gregory/Stuart
Russian and Soviet Economic Performance and Structure

Hartwick/Olewiler
The Economics of Natural Resource Use

Hoffman/Averett
Women and the Economy: Family, Work, and Pay

Holt
Markets, Games, and Strategic Behavior

Hubbard
Money, the Financial System, and the Economy

Hughes/Cain
American Economic History

Husted/Melvin
International Economics

Jehle/Reny
Advanced Microeconomic Theory

Johnson-Lans
A Health Economics Primer

Klein
Mathematical Methods for Economics

Krugman/Obstfeld
International Economics

Laidler
The Demand for Money

Leeds/von Allmen/Schiming
Economics

Leeds/von Allmen
The Economics of Sports

Lipsey/Courant/Ragan
Economics

Melvin
International Money and Finance

Miller
Economics Today

Miller
Understanding Modern Economics

Miller/Benjamin
The Economics of Macro Issues

Miller/Benjamin/North
The Economics of Public Issues

Mills/Hamilton
Urban Economics

Mishkin
The Economics of Money, Banking, and Financial Markets

Mishkin
The Economics of Money, Banking, and Financial Markets, Alternate Edition

Murray
Econometrics: A Modern Introduction

Parkin
Economics

Perloff
Microeconomics

Perman/Common/McGilvray/Ma
Natural Resources and Environmental Economics

Phelps
Health Economics

Riddell/Shackelford/Stamos/Schneider
Economics: A Tool for Critically Understanding Society

Ritter/Silber/Udell
Principles of Money, Banking, and Financial Markets

Rohlf
Introduction to Economic Reasoning

Ruffin/Gregory
Principles of Economics

Sargent
Rational Expectations and Inflation

Scherer
Industry Structure, Strategy, and Public Policy

Stock/Watson
Introduction to Econometrics

Stock/Watson
Introduction to Econometrics, Brief Edition

Studenmund
Using Econometrics

Tietenberg
Environmental and Natural Resource Economics

Tietenberg
Environmental Economics and Policy

Todaro/Smith
Economic Development

Waldman
Microeconomics

Waldman/Jensen
Industrial Organization: Theory and Practice

Weil
Economic Growth

Williamson
Macroeconomics

Microeconomic Data

These microeconomic data series show some of the trends in what, how, and for whom goods and services are produced — the central questions of microeconomics. You will find these data in a spreadsheet that you can download from your MyEconLab Web site.

		1980	1981	1982	1983	1984	1985	1986	1987	1988	1989	1990
WHAT WE PRODUCE												
Percentage of gross domestic product												
1	Agriculture, forestry, fishing, and hunting	1.8	2.0	1.8	1.3	1.6	1.5	1.4	1.7	1.6	1.7	1.7
2	Mining	2.4	2.9	2.5	1.9	1.8	1.5	1.0	1.5	1.4	1.4	1.5
3	Construction	4.4	3.9	3.7	3.7	3.9	4.1	4.4	4.6	4.6	4.5	4.3
4	Durable goods	11.3	11.0	10.0	9.8	10.3	9.8	9.5	10.2	10.2	9.9	9.4
5	Nondurable goods	8.5	8.5	8.2	7.8	7.4	7.2	6.6	6.9	7.0	7.0	7.0
6	Utilities	4.0	4.1	4.5	4.4	4.3	4.2	4.1	2.6	2.4	2.5	2.5
7	Wholesale trade	6.5	6.4	6.3	6.1	6.3	6.2	6.1	6.0	6.2	6.2	6.0
8	Retail trade	8.3	8.2	8.3	8.5	8.6	8.7	8.7	7.4	7.2	7.1	6.9
9	Transportation and warehousing	3.1	2.9	2.7	2.7	2.8	2.7	2.7	3.2	3.2	3.0	2.9
10	Finance, insurance, real estate, rental, and leasing	12.3	12.5	13.1	13.4	13.4	13.6	14.0	17.7	17.8	17.8	18.0
11	Professional and business services	—	—	—	—	—	—	—	8.7	9.1	9.4	9.8
12	Information	—	—	—	—	—	—	—	3.9	3.8	3.8	3.9
13	Educational services, health care, and social assistance	—	—	—	—	—	—	—	6.0	6.1	6.3	6.7
14	Arts, entertainment, recreation, accommodation, and food services	—	—	—	—	—	—	—	3.2	3.3	3.3	3.4
15	Other services, except government	—	—	—	—	—	—	—	2.4	2.4	2.4	2.5
HOW WE PRODUCE												
16	Average weekly hours	35.2	35.2	34.7	34.9	35.1	34.9	34.7	34.7	34.6	34.5	34.3
	Employment (percentage of total)											
17	Agriculture	3.7	3.6	3.5	3.3	3.1	2.9	2.7	2.6	2.6	2.4	2.4
18	Mining	1.0	1.1	1.1	0.9	0.9	0.8	0.7	0.6	0.6	0.6	0.6
19	Construction	4.5	4.3	4.0	4.0	4.3	4.5	4.5	4.5	4.6	4.5	4.4
20	Manufacturing	18.9	18.6	17.4	16.9	17.1	16.6	16.0	15.7	15.6	15.3	14.9
21	Services	66.7	66.9	67.4	67.6	67.7	69.0	69.5	69.9	70.8	71.6	72.2
22	Other	5.2	5.6	6.5	7.2	7.0	6.2	6.7	6.7	5.9	5.6	5.5
	FOR WHOM WE PRODUCE											
23	Wage rate (dollars per hour)	6.84	7.43	7.86	8.19	8.48	8.73	8.92	9.13	9.43	9.80	10.19
24	Real wage rate (2000 dollars per hour)	12.66	12.57	12.53	12.56	12.53	12.52	12.52	12.47	12.46	12.48	12.49
25	Stock price index (Dow Jones)	891	933	884	1,190	1,178	1,328	1,793	2,276	2,061	2,509	2,679
26	Real stock price index (2000 dollars)	1,649	1,578	1,410	1,825	1,742	1,905	2,516	3,109	2,723	3,194	3,283
27	Interest rate Aaa (percent per year)	11.9	14.2	13.8	12.0	12.7	11.4	9.0	9.4	9.7	9.3	9.3
28	Real interest rate (percent per year)	2.9	4.8	7.7	8.1	9.0	8.3	6.8	6.6	6.3	5.5	5.5
	GOVERNMENT IN THE ECONOMY											
29	Government receipts (billions of dollars)	807	927	949	1,008	1,121	1,222	1,299	1,414	1,513	1,639	1,724
30	Government expenditures (billions of dollars)	879	996	1,106	1,206	1,308	1,434	1,534	1,617	1,695	1,816	1,970
31	Government surplus(+)/deficit(–) (billions of dollars)	–73	–70	–158	–198	–187	–212	–234	–203	–182	–177	–246
32	Government debt (billions of dollars)	712	789	925	1,137	1,307	1,507	1,741	1,890	2,052	2,191	2,412